Broker-Dealer Regulation

Broker-Dealer Regulation

Cases and Analysis

Cheryl Nichols
HOWARD UNIVERSITY SCHOOL OF LAW

CAROLINA ACADEMIC PRESS
Durham, North Carolina

ISBN 978-0-76989-197-2
e-ISBN 978-0-76989-350-1
LCCN 2016959315

Carolina Academic Press, LLC
700 Kent Street
Durham, North Carolina 27701
Telephone (919) 489-7486
Fax (919) 493-5668
www.cap-press.com

Printed in the United States of America

To Mark McGibbon

Contents

Illustrations and Tables

Tables

Table of Cases

Preface

This book is designed for a stand-alone course on the regulatory framework of broker-dealers and does not require any prerequisite courses. All materials in the book are presented from the perspective of the broker-dealer and encourage active learning by allowing students to grapple with real-world, context-based problem solving through the use of hypotheticals. Each chapter contains hypotheticals designed to contextualize the various regulatory issues pertinent to broker-dealers in many instances simulating the attorney-client relationship. Each chapter also includes notes that cover topics not found in the cases. Part I of the textbook is designed to provide an overview of the regulatory framework for the broker-dealer industry along with the various business models used by broker-dealers to conduct their securities businesses. Students should gain an understanding of the various business models and the basic functional organization (front, middle, and back offices) of a typical broker-dealer. In addition, Chapter 2 contains a glossary of frequently used terms in the broker-dealer industry and is designed to serve as a reference tool in understanding the materials in the chapters that follow. Part II focuses on broker-dealer self-regulation with an emphasis on registration and supervisory responsibilities. Part III analyzes the regulatory framework governing broker-dealer participation in public offerings of securities. Part IV considers the rules and regulations designed to ensure broker-dealer financial responsibility. Part V examines broker-dealer fraud prosecuted under § 10(b) and Rule 10b-5 of the Securities Exchange Act of 1934 and identifies specific types of broker-dealer fraud typically alleged in disputes between broker-dealers and their customers. Part VI includes an analysis of the use of securities arbitration in resolving disputes among broker-dealers and between broker-dealers and their customers. Finally, Part VII explores the regulatory framework of the market structure of the U.S. securities markets including trading venues.

The book is not only appropriate for law school courses but the author has used similar materials to teach law students and graduate business students (M.B.A. with a finance concentration) in the same classroom. In fact, many of the topics covered coincide with regulatory topics tested in the Series 7 Examination, which is the basic examination required to enter the securities industry. In addition, the book is ideally suited for securities arbitration clinics representing individual investors in disputes with their broker-dealers. In particular, the book covers many of the legal and business skills required to resolve small investor claims. Chapter 11 focuses specifically on the types of fraudulent broker-dealer conduct perpetrated against individual investors that can only be resolved through securities arbitration.

The book also embodies a multi-disciplinary approach to learning through its Master Project—the Broker-Dealer Mock Registration Project available on the book's website. The Master Project requires students to act as consultants to a broker-dealer seeking to register with the Securities and Exchange Commission and to become a member of FINRA. This is a real-world project in which students must use legal and business-related knowledge to complete successfully. For example, in the context of providing legal advice to a broker-dealer seeking to register with the Securities and Exchange Commission, the attorney must identify and analyze applicable federal securities laws and evaluate the broker-dealer's business plan for compliance with applicable FINRA rules. Specifically, the Master Project aids students' understanding of the economic incentives of the business of being a broker-dealer and the effects of the broker-dealer regulatory framework on profitability.

The book's website contains additional materials, including a user-friendly teacher's manual designed for both professors experienced and new to the laws governing broker-dealers. The website also contains a library of materials (some of which did not make it into the book) organized by chapter and topic along with PowerPoint slides for many of the chapters. Please regularly check the website for updated materials.

Finally, it is my intention to include two additional topics in the broker-dealer regulatory framework—advertising regulation and anti-money laundering. I would greatly appreciate any suggestions for incorporation in future editions.

Editorial Note and Acknowledgments

As with other casebooks, my editing of the cases has omitted most footnotes and case and statute citations without indication. Footnote numbers in cases are as in the original with no renumbering to account for omitted footnotes.

I have many people to thank for helping with this book at various stages. I am particularly grateful to my research assistants Bria Adams, Nnaemeka K. Anyanwu, Jimmie Covington, Brandon J. Smith, Manonh Soumahoro, and Brittany Williams for their invaluable research and editorial assistance. I would also like to thank Barry Summer, Bruce Sanders, W. Sherman Rogers, Kurt L. Schmoke, Neal A. Seiden, and Rochelle McAllister for their editorial assistance and support. Two of my very dear friends deserve special recognition for contributions above and beyond the call of duty—Ronald L. Crawford and Raquel Russell.

Broker-Dealer Regulation

Chapter 1

Overview of the Broker-Dealer Industry

I. Introduction

The broker-dealer industry is quite complex and highly regulated because broker-dealers are key participants in U.S. securities markets, which are vital to our economic progress. In its role as intermediary between buyers and sellers in the U.S. securities markets, the broker-dealer must adapt its business model to meet the needs of a securities industry that is constantly changing to meet the capital needs of businesses and to provide investment products for investors. The broker-dealer, as an intermediary, performs many diverse activities in the U.S. securities markets. For individual and institutional customers, broker-dealers may provide such services as investment advice, financial planning, and exotic products and trading strategies to preserve and grow their assets. It also may provide investment banking services such as underwriting and placing securities of companies with investors as well as advice about mergers and acquisitions. Some broker-dealers also provide merchant banking services, which involve buying, restructuring, and then selling companies. Broker-dealers may also act a market-makers, i.e., holding themselves out to the public as willing to buy and sell securities at specified prices and amounts. Finally, they may also engage in proprietary trading, i.e., buying and selling securities using their own money for their own benefit instead of on behalf of their customers. In essence, broker-dealers as intermediaries are critical to the market infrastructure of the U.S. securities markets. Chapter 2 explores the various types of broker-dealer business models and functions of broker-dealers.

The operational complexity of the broker-dealer industry has resulted in an extensive regulatory framework designed to ensure broker-dealer solvency and to prevent investor abuse. At its core is the registration requirement with the Securities and Exchange Commission ("SEC") and the membership requirement with the Financial Industry Regulatory Authority ("FINRA") contained in § 15 of the Securities Exchange Act of 1934 ("the Exchange Act"). With few exceptions, broker-dealers are required to register with the SEC and to become a member of FINRA in order to effect transactions in securities in the U.S. securities markets. These registration requirements subject the broker-dealer to a myriad of SEC rules and regulations along with rules adopted by regulatory entities such as FINRA, the New York Stock Exchange ("NYSE"), and the NASDAQ Stock Market ("NASDAQ").[1] For example, broker-dealers must have sufficient capital to support their business activities, must establish and maintain books and records prescribed under the federal securities laws and SEC and FINRA rules, must submit to periodic inspections and examinations of their operations and sales practices by the SEC and FINRA, and must supervise their employees with a view toward preventing and detecting violations of the federal securities laws and FINRA rules.

This textbook is designed as an introduction to the many rules and regulations governing the operations and sales practices of broker-dealers in the U.S. securities markets. First, Chapter 1 examines significant events that shaped both the broker-dealer business model and its regulatory framework. It then provides an overview of the current regulatory framework for the broker-dealer industry and its primary regulators, before in-depth coverage in subsequent chapters.

A. Development of the Broker-Dealer Industry

The ever-expanding offering of services and products by broker-dealers, market forces, the financial crisis of 2008, and technology has led to consolidation and increased complexity in the broker-dealer industry. The 1967 Paperwork Crisis ("Paperwork Crisis") was one significant event that spurred consolidation and increased complexity, resulting in the failure of many broker-dealers due to operational and financial difficulties. Essentially, the broker-dealer industry was not prepared for the massive increase in trading volume that occurred during the Paperwork Crisis. In 1967, 15-million-share trading days were not uncommon and even 20- and 30-million-share trading days were experienced. For example, the total 1967 trading volume on the NYSE reached 2.53 billion shares, an increase of 33 1/3 percent over the previous year. This unexpected increase in trading volume resulted in chaos in the back offices of many broker-dealers who were unable to maintain accurate books and records and to ensure accurate and timely clearing and settlement of transactions; moreover, one broker-dealer's difficulties resulted in contagion at other broker-dealers. A study conducted by the SEC found that:

> Apart from the inability of broker-dealers to keep their records current, the number of errors in the handling and recording of transactions multiplied. The back offices of many a broker-dealer resembled a trackless forest. Since the broker-dealer industry is a highly interdependent community, the problems of the less efficient firms had a rippling effect on the entire broker-dealer community; and inter-dealer clearing systems, as well as the transfer facilities of banks, were similarly taxed beyond their capacities. The entire machinery for the delivery and transfer of securities and the concomitant remittance of funds became clogged. Even those broker-dealers who attempted belatedly

---

1. Broker-dealers also must register with state securities authorities; however, broker-dealer operations and market participant activities are not subject to state securities laws. State securities regulators do have authority to prosecute broker-dealer fraud under applicable state securities laws. See Chapter 3.

to stem the tide by computerizing their operations or augmenting their back office personnel could not keep pace with the volume; in fact, they were caught on a worse treadmill in that, by the time they were able to research their errors ... they were confronted with a greater number of errors to contend with. The expensive computerized hardware which was thrown in the breach malfunctioned; and since parallel manual records were often not maintained during a reasonable trial period, the use of the computer increased the already existing confusion. Moreover, the employment of newly recruited and untrained or inadequately trained individuals who were put to work in the back offices resulted in a further increase in the number of errors. The combination of all of these factors culminated in such a critical predicament for some firms that they not only lost control of their records, but experienced a new phenomenon—the loss of control over the securities which were or were supposed to be in their possession for delivery, custody or safekeeping. The efforts by the Commission and the self regulatory organizations to build a dike against this torrent proved of little avail. Study, pp. 13–14.

The downturn in the U.S. securities markets in 1968–1970, which included a bear market from 1969–1970, only exacerbated existing operational problems in the broker-dealer industry. Both stock prices and volume began a gradual, sustained decline that created new difficulties for broker-dealers. During this period a number of broker-dealers had just expanded their branch office and transaction processing facilities to meet the massive demand in 1967, resulting in a substantial increase in overhead expenses. The bear market also resulted in significant decreases in commission income and underwriting fees for broker-dealers. Concurrently, broker-dealers were still forced to spend money to resolve back office errors discovered during the Paperwork Crisis. The combination of the bear market, high overhead expenses, and the sharp drop in revenue from commissions and underwriting fees resulted in the failure of many broker-dealers during this time. Only the large, highly-capitalized, and well-managed broker-dealers were able to withstand this onslaught. These events also led to the enactment of the Securities Investor Protection Act in 1970 ("SIPA").

SIPA established the Securities Investor Protection Corporation (SIPC), a non-profit membership corporation, to return customer funds and securities within specified limits upon the failure of their broker-dealer. All broker-dealers must be members of SIPC, with a few exceptions.[2] When a broker-dealer is liquidated, bankrupt, or in financial trouble and customer funds and securities are missing, SIPC returns customer assets for each customer up to $500,000 including a $250,000 limit for cash only.

---

2. The following broker-dealers are excluded: (1) those whose principal business, in the determination of SIPC, taking into account business of affiliated entities, is conducted outside the U.S. and its territories and possessions; (2) those whose business consists exclusively of (a) the distribution of shares of registered open end investment companies or unit investment trusts, (b) the sale of variable annuities, (c) the business of insurance, or (d) the business of rendering investment advisory services to one or more registered investment companies or insurance company separate accounts; and (3) those registered with respect to transactions in security futures products.

SIPC is funded by assessments from member broker-dealers (based on a percentage of their revenues) and interest on U.S. Government securities bought by SIPC ("SIPC"). It also has a $2.5 billion line of credit with the U.S. Treasury. When the SIPC fund falls below its current target level of $2.5 billion, SIPC assesses its members. SIPC also manages the liquidation and sale of broker-dealers experiencing financial difficulties. Generally, the liquidation begins with a court-appointed trustee for the broker-dealer that operates under SIPC oversight.

The amendments to the federal securities laws in 1975 ("1975 Amendments")[3] also fueled consolidation in the broker-dealer industry. This consolidation began with the elimination of fixed commission rates, initially the primary source of revenue for broker-dealers. Prior to 1975, the NYSE required its members to charge fixed commission rates for any transactions executed on its facilities. In fact, this practice of fixed commission rates on stock exchanges was long-standing and could be traced back to 1792. The SEC eliminated this practice in 1975 after many years of study and several hearings with the adoption of Rule 19b-3 of the Exchange Act ("Exchange Act Rule 19b-3"), which required competitive commission rates. The justification for the elimination of fixed commission rates was that the securities markets had changed because of significant participation by the general public, and therefore, stock exchanges could no longer be regarded as private clubs. In the adopting release for Exchange Act Rule 19b-3, the SEC noted that "[b]etween World War II and the early 1970s, the public flocked into the securities markets, and financial institutions increasingly participated in those markets.... The fixed minimum stock exchange commission on large orders ... led to the growth of complex reciprocal relationships between, on the one hand, institutions (particularly mutual fund managers and banks) and, on the other, broker-dealers. This ... had the effect of making commission rates for institutions negotiable but limiting the extent to which the ultimate investor ... [h]as benefited from such negotiation."[4] Without fixed commission rates, broker-dealers could no longer rely primarily on commissions as their primary source of revenue and were forced to generate revenue from other sources that required more capital, such as principal transactions (e.g., proprietary trading). This need for more capital, again, produced consolidation through either liquidation or acquisition of smaller broker-dealers by larger, better capitalized broker-dealers.

The passage of the Gramm-Leach Bliley Act in 1999 ("Gramm-Leach Bliley")[5] provided another significant boost to consolidation in the broker-dealer industry. Gramm-Leach Bliley eliminated the barriers between commercial banking, investment banking, and insurance. Gramm-Leach Bliley authorized the creation of financial holding companies that were allowed to engage in several types of financial services including commercial and investment banking, securities, and insurance. Functional regulation was imposed, which meant that the financial holding companies' commercial banking activities would continue to be regulated by bank regulators, securities activities would

---

3. Public Law 94-29, 89 Stat. 97 (Jun. 4, 1975).
4. 40 F.R. 35 or 7394.
5. Pub. L. 106-102, 113 Stat. 1338, enacted November 12, 1999)

be regulated by the SEC and state securities regulators, and insurance activities would be regulated by state insurance regulators. The elimination of such barriers facilitated the formation of large, complex financial services conglomerates such as Bank of America, Citibank, and J.P. Morgan, which provide a wide array of financial services through multiple operating subsidiaries, including broker-dealers.

The financial crisis of 2008 led to more consolidation in the broker-dealer industry and witnessed the end of the independent investment bank. It adversely affected financial conglomerates with broker-dealer operating subsidiaries and resulted in the failure of two of the largest investment banks — Lehman Brothers and Bear Stearns. Lehman Brothers, to the consternation of Wall Street, was allowed to fail and filed bankruptcy; Bear Stearns was sold to J.P. Morgan for a song. Although the 2008 financial crisis in the U.S. was reflected in, among other things, mortgages to subprime borrowers and financial engineering in the form of collateralized debt obligations and credit default swaps, the financial crisis adversely affected broker-dealers. Broker-dealers were unable to act as effective intermediaries in the U.S. securities markets because they were unable to fund their business activities. During this time, even the largest broker-dealers experienced funding difficulties, resulting in Merrill Lynch eventually being acquired by Bank of America and Goldman Sachs and Morgan Stanley becoming bank holding companies and later converting to financial holding companies. The funding problems of broker-dealers were caused primarily by the broker-dealer industry's reliance on wholesale funding to finance their business activities.

The wholesale funding model relies on unstable, short-term funding to meet the funding needs of broker-dealers. However, the assets of broker-dealers may be of long duration and are potentially risky. The broker-dealer primarily uses repurchase agreements or "repos," a type of short-term collateralized loan, as a major source of funding for all of its assets. Repos are used by broker-dealers because their structure allows access to relatively low-cost financing. Repos as utilized by broker-dealers are functionally overnight loans to broker-dealers that are fully collateralized by highly liquid securities, such as U.S. government securities, owned by the broker-dealer. Specifically, a repo is the sale of a security with a simultaneous commitment by the seller to repurchase the security from the buyer at a future date at a predetermined price, including interest. The security is held as collateral and protects the buyer from the risk that the seller might not be able to repurchase the security as agreed. In return, the broker-dealer has the relatively low-cost financing required to operate its business. Many of the repos executed by broker-dealers were with money market funds as counterparties. As is well known, money market funds also experienced financial difficulties during the financial crisis of 2008. Consequently, the primary source of funding for the broker-dealer industry evaporated and the Federal Reserve was forced to intervene in order to provide temporary funding facilities to support the money market industry and the broker-dealer industry, among others.

Since the financial crisis of 2008, much regulation has focused on planning and managing liquidity risk in the event of future funding crises, which has further consolidated the broker-dealer industry. Regulators have emphasized the implementation of best practices to manage liquidity risk and are conducting stress tests similar to those used in the banking industry. The cost of managing liquidity risk, while manageable for large broker-dealers, may be unaffordable to smaller broker-dealers. Legal fees, technology investment, compliance implementation, and other costs running into millions of dollars for a single broker-dealer have resulted in smaller firms consolidating.

1. *Technology and the Broker-Dealer Industry*

Technology has changed the very structure of the broker-dealer industry and its interactions with its customers, again fueling consolidation. Technology began to be used for a myriad of broker-dealer activities, such as supplying information for trading decisions, ordering and routing of securities transactions, and providing direct market access to broker-dealer customers, something that more and more institutional customers began demanding. Technology also was used to assist in the management of relationships with broker-dealer customers and to meet regulatory and compliance requirements, e.g., recordkeeping requirements. However, building the necessary technology infrastructure involves time and generally millions of dollars. Many broker-dealers or their financial holding companies have turned to the capital markets for the funds needed to invest in the necessary hardware and software. This access to capital markets and consolidation is especially evident in the independent broker-dealer space, which is dominated by a few major players. The independent broker-dealer model is discussed in Chapter 2. The impact of technology on the securities industry as a whole is discussed in Chapter 14 (Market Regulation).

Technology has also facilitated the establishment of dark pools by broker-dealers. Dark pools are electronic trading facilities (i.e., alternative trading systems ("ATSs")) that do not display broker-dealer quotations to the public and are generally used by institutional investors. The broker-dealer quotations disseminated in dark pools are only available to subscribers, a subset of market participants, that pay a fee to the dark pool operator. As noted by the SEC, if dark pools share information about trading interests with other dark pools, they may function like private networks that exclude public investors. FINRA and the SEC, however, have imposed certain reporting requirements on ATSs (including dark pools) to minimize the possibility of a two-tiered U.S. securities market — one for retail public investors and another for institutional investors with better pricing and lower execution costs. Dark pools are discussed in detail in Chapter 14.

The most recent manifestation of the impact of technology on the broker-dealer industry is high-frequency trading ("HFT"). The hallmark of HFT is that it allows broker-dealers to execute securities transactions in microseconds and even nanoseconds. Although a precise definition of HFT does not exist, it is generally described as autonomous computerized trading (using algorithms) that seeks quick profits using high-speed connections to national exchanges. The problem is unfair competition between the broker-dealers that have the capital to invest in the technological infrastructure required to engage in high-frequency trading and those that do not.

In essence, HFT broker-dealers must engage in co-location, i.e., trading centers (such as the NYSE) rent rack space to HFT broker-dealers to enable them to place their servers in close physical proximity to the matching engines of trading centers. HFT broker-dealers must engage in co-location in order to minimize latency, i.e., "the overall time it takes to receive signals from a trading venue, make trading decisions, and transmit the resulting order messages back to the trading venue. Most HFT broker-dealers rely on this direct data feed from trading centers instead of the consolidated data feed disseminated through securities information processors.[6] Co-location is required by HFT broker-dealers because light and electrical signals travel at a finite speed of 186,000 miles per second in a vacuum and are even slower through fiber-optic cables and other media. Consequently, locating the computers of HFT broker-dealers next to the servers of trading centers is needed to provide the fastest delivery of market data and transaction execution.

Finally, the increasing use of technology has required the SEC to adopt a regulation focused directly on computer system integrity—Regulation Systems Compliance and Integrity ("Reg SCI"). Although technology has enhanced speed, capacity, efficiency, and sophistication of the trading functions that are available to broker-dealers and other market participants, it has also resulted in operational problems with such automated systems, such as the flash crash of May 6, 2010—the day on which the prices of many U.S.-based equity products experienced an extraordinarily rapid decline and recovery spurred by the algorithmic trading of a trader for a large mutual fund. As the SEC noted in its adopting release of Reg SCI, "[g]iven the speed and interconnected nature of the U.S. securities markets, a seemingly minor systems problem at a single entity can quickly create losses and liability for market participants, and spread rapidly across the national market system, potentially creating widespread damage and harm to market participants, including investors."[7] Although the flash crash of May 6, 2010, is discussed in detail in Chapter 14, Reg SCI is beyond the scope of this textbook.

B. National Securities Exchanges and other Trading Facilities in U.S. Securities Markets

National Securities Exchanges ("exchanges") provide a marketplace or trading facilities for bringing together purchasers and sellers of securities and are self-regulatory organizations (SROs) registered with the SEC under § 6 of the Exchange Act. Section 5 of the Exchange Acts requires exchanges effecting transactions in securities to register with the SEC unless exempted by the SEC. Registration with the SEC as an SRO under §§ 6 and 19 of the Exchange Act means that an exchange must, among other things,

---

6. Distribution of the consolidated data feed requires an extra step when compared to direct data feeds obtained through co-location. The SROs must transmit market data to plan processors (SIPs) and the SIPs must consolidate the information and distribute it to the public. Consequently, individual data feeds from SROs and to electronic communications networks (ECNs) that include consolidated data feed information are distributed faster than the same market data in the consolidated data feeds.

7. Exchange Act Rel. No. 73639 (Nov. 19, 2014).

ensure that its members who are broker-dealers comply with the federal securities laws and meet certain ethical, professional, and operational standards. National securities exchanges must also provide their broker-dealer members with fair representation in the governance of the exchange and allocate reasonable dues, fees, and other charges among their members. Broker-dealers must be registered first with the SEC pursuant to § 15 of the Exchange Act in order to become members of a national securities exchange. (See Chapter 3 for a detailed discussion of broker-dealer registration requirements). Specifically, § 6(a) of the Exchange Act requires exchanges to adopt and enforce rules designed to ensure compliance with the federal securities laws for their member broker-dealers and to maintain a fair, orderly, and efficient market. The SEC must approve all SRO rules before they take effect; it also examines SRO practices and, when appropriate, conducts disciplinary actions and imposes sanctions for an SRO's failure to enforce its rules against member broker-dealers.

National Securities Exchanges are also responsible for adopting and enforcing listing criteria for securities permitted to trade on their exchanges. Section 12(a) of the Exchange Act prohibits member broker-dealers from effecting transactions in any security on a national securities exchange unless the security is registered on the exchange. The security must be registered with the exchange by complying with the procedures contained in § 12(b) of the Exchange Act before it is permitted to be listed on the exchange for trading by its member broker-dealers. Registration requirements for securities under § 12(b) include the submission of an application by the issuer to the exchange containing, among other things, information about its organization, financial structure, nature of its business, and the rights and privileges embodied in the issuer's securities. Exchange listing requirements are discussed below.

Currently there are 18 national securities exchanges registered with the SEC under § 6 of the Exchange Act. The NYSE and NASDAQ are the most recognized in the U.S. securities markets.

1. The New York Stock Exchange

The New York Stock Exchange remains a leading market for equities trading and listings. The NYSE was founded in 1792 when 24 stockbrokers signed the Buttonwood Agreement on Wall Street in New York City. Under the Buttonwood Agreement, a centralized exchange in the form of an auction market was formed for trading in the U.S. securities markets. Under the Buttonwood Agreement, the stock brokers agreed to deal only with each other and to operate by charging commissions of one-quarter percent. This centralized exchange formally became the NYSE 25 years later in March 1817, by adopting a body of officers and setting rules of conduct. The auction market system of trading adopted by the NYSE occurred manually on a trading floor by "open outcry" by exchange members. This manual system of trading used member firms designated as specialists to provide liquidity by making bids and offers, when necessary to supplement investors' bids and offers; specifically each specialist was required to make a continuous market in securities assigned to it by the NYSE by matching buyers with sellers, keeping investors informed, committing capital when needed, and being accountable for maintaining a fair and orderly market in its assigned securities. The introduction of telegraphic communications fueled the NYSE's rise as the major auction market in the U.S. securities markets. After the Civil War, the NYSE grew rapidly because of the capital needed to fund the tremendous expansion of the U.S. economy, such as the building of railroads and the development of mass production. The development of the electric stock ticker in 1867 and the introduction of the installation of telephones in 1878 also fueled the growth of the NYSE. The resulting increase in activity caused the NYSE to cap membership at 1,060 seats, which was later increased to 1,100. By the time of the Stock Market Crash of 1929, trading and speculation in the stock market had become engrained in the American culture. After the Crash of 1929 and the resulting Great Depression, the value of securities traded on the NYSE was virtually extinguished and led the way to the enactment of the federal securities laws, discussed below, which subjected the NYSE to extensive government regulation for the first time in its history. The NYSE was now required to register with the SEC as an SRO, subjecting it to the oversight of the SEC.

The widespread availability of technology in the form of automation and electronic communication systems led to the demutualization of the NYSE and its conversion to a for-profit stock corporation trading on itself. The ever-increasing importance of technology required to compete effectively in the U.S. securities markets required access to more capital than could be obtained in a member-owned organization. Beginning in approximately 2000, the NYSE converted from a member-owned association to a for-profit corporation and offered its shares to the public. Although this conversion raised concerns about conflicts between the shareholder profit motive and proper self-regulation, the SEC has nevertheless permitted this transition. Trading on the NYSE is now conducted through highly automated trading systems with high-speed order responses and executions. The old system of manual trading using specialists to provide liquidity by making bids and offers, when necessary to supplement investors' bids and offers, no longer exists. The NYSE now uses designated market makers instead of specialists to provide liquidity and to maintain fair and orderly markets in assigned securities. See Chapter 2 for more information about the types of broker-dealers trading on the NYSE.

NYSE has quantitative and qualitative listing standards that issuers must meet in order for their securities to be permitted to trade on the NYSE. Quantitative standards include financial and distribution requirements. For example, an issuer must have an aggregate adjusted pre-tax income for the last three fiscal years of at least $10 million, at least 400 shareholders, publicly held shares of 1.1 million with a market value of $100 million, a minimum share price of $4.00, and average monthly trading volume of 1 million. Qualitative listing standards include corporate governance requirements. For example, issuers must have a majority of independent directors, a nominating/corporate governance committee composed entirely of independent directors, a compensation committee composed entirely of independent directors, an audit committee composed entirely of independent directors with financial management expertise (e.g., accounting), shareholder approval of equity compensation plans, corporate governance guidelines such as director qualification standards and responsibilities, and a code of business conduct and ethics for directors, officers, and employees.

2. *The NASDAQ Stock Market*

The NASDAQ Stock Market ("NASDAQ") is also a national securities exchange registered with the SEC under §§ 6 and 19 of the Exchange Act, but this was not always the case. NASDAQ began as an electronic quotation system in 1971 for securities traded in the over-the-counter or OTC market. At this time, it was a wholly owned subsidiary of the only national securities association registered with the SEC, the National Association of Securities Dealers, Inc. ("NASD") now known as Financial Industry Regulatory Authority ("FINRA"). Initially, NASDAQ was only used by broker-dealers in the OTC market who would publish their bid and ask quotations to other broker-dealers participating in the OTC market. Using NASDAQ, OTC broker-dealers could obtain real-time prices and better order execution. NASDAQ also encouraged institutional investors to participate in the OTC market. Prior to NASDAQ, quotes in the OTC market were disseminated using paper copy, newspapers, and a number of private electronic systems. Essentially, NASDAQ was a telecommunications network that linked thousands of geographically dispersed broker-dealers; it did not have a central trading floor like the NYSE. NASDAQ continued, with advances in technology, to improve its trading systems over the years and fundamentally changed the nature of the U.S. securities markets. For example, it introduced screen-based order routing and execution systems, and the ability to use generic desktop computers running the appropriate software as NASDAQ workstations. This enabled OTC broker-dealers to have real-time responses to quote updates, trade reports, and order routing. In 1984, NASDAQ introduced its Small Order Execution System "(SOES")". SOES permitted broker-dealers registered with NASDAQ to execute small orders automatically against the quotation of a market maker at the best bid or best offer. In 1988, NASDAQ introduced SelectNet, a system that allowed broker-dealers registered with NASDAQ to route orders to a particular NASDAQ registered participant.[8] However, all of NASDAQ's trading systems, including SOES and SelectNet, were not integrated; this created the possibility that a broker-dealer could have a double liability exposure for the same quote, i.e., the broker-dealer could receive a SelectNet order that it would be obligated to execute and a SOES execution against the same quote. NASDAQ resolved this problem with the introduction of its SuperMontage system in 2002. Essentially, SuperMontage combined and improved NASDAQ's many trading systems into a single platform capable of trading securities listed on NASDAQ, as well as securities listed on other markets such as the NYSE.

Continuing advances in technology allowed NASDAQ to become a fully operational exchange and resulted in the NASD's divestiture of NASDAQ. In 2000, the NASD began a series of transactions to end its ownership of NASDAQ. Restricted shares of

---

8. By this time, NASDAQ participants included electronic communication networks or ECNs as well as broker-dealers. ECNs are discussed in detail in Chapter 14.

NASDAQ were sold by the NASD in 2000 through a private placement offering to a combination of Wall Street firms—NASDAQ-listed companies and institutional investors. Trading restrictions expired in 2002 and NASDAQ shares began trading on the OTC Bulletin Board (now the OTC Markets Group) under the ticker symbol NDAQ. On February 9, 2005, NASDAQ listed its shares on itself following an offering of secondary shares priced at $9 per share.

In January 2006, the SEC approved NASDAQ's application to become a fully operational registered national exchange. As a registered SRO, NASDAQ, like the NYSE, was now responsible for regulating its broker-dealer members and establishing listing requirements for its listed securities. In August 2006, NASDAQ began operating independently from the NASD as a national securities exchange registered with the SEC. In December 2006, NASDAQ ceased to be a subsidiary of NASD.

3. Alternative Trading Systems

Alternative trading systems ("ATS") are private trading systems that facilitate electronic trading by bringing together buyers and sellers of securities and include Electronic Communication Networks ("ECNs") and so-called Dark Pools. However, they are distinct from exchanges because they do not engage in self-regulatory conduct, make markets, or provide a listing service for securities. As such, ATSs have subscribers, not members, who are generally institutional investors and other broker-dealers willing to buy or sell securities by submitting bid or offer quotations, market orders, limit orders, or other priced orders. ECNs, a type of ATS, are computerized trading facilities that match customer buy and sell orders directly through a computer. ECNs accept orders directly from their own subscribers in addition to customer orders routed from other broker-dealers. ECNs post orders on their systems for subscribers to view and then automatically match such orders for execution. The first ECN, Instinet, was created in 1969 and obtained widespread use in the broker-dealer industry in the 1980s. The adoption of the SEC's order-handling rules in 1996 facilitated the development of ECNs and broadened their subscriber base to include retail investors. The adoption of Regulation ATS further integrated alternative trading systems into the national market system for U.S. securities markets by requiring an ATS to be registered as either a broker-dealer or a national securities exchange. Regulation ATS is discussed in detail in Chapter 14.

Dark pools are private computerized trading facilities that accept, match, and execute orders to buy and sell securities received from its subscribers. Subscribers include asset managers, broker-dealers, and institutional investors. Because dark pools originally were established, in part, to meet the demand from institutional investors seeking to buy or sell big blocks of shares without causing large price movements, the quotations of their subscribers are not displayed to the public—they are only communicated among the dark pool's subscribers and perhaps other dark pools. This inequity has been addressed by the SEC and FINRA by requiring dark pools to report certain trade information to FINRA. These reporting requirements are discussed in detail in Chapter 14.

C. Overview of the Broker-Dealer Regulatory Framework

The regulatory framework for the broker-dealer industry is based on self-regulation with oversight by the SEC. This means that SROs are responsible for most of the day-to-day responsibilities for broker-dealer and market oversight. Even before the enactment of federal laws regulating broker-dealers, the industry had established some form of self-regulation. Broker-dealers trading exchange-listed securities were required to comply with the rules of the exchange of which they were a member. As noted previously, the NYSE engaged in self-regulation beginning with the Buttonwood Agreement, which required its members to conform to formal trading rules. The NYSE later adopted a constitution and subsequently adopted rules governing its member broker-dealers, including financial responsibility rules. It also adopted rules governing its listed issuers, which included registration and financial reporting rules. The NYSE's self-regulatory status became legally mandated with the enactment of the Securities Exchange Act of 1934 pursuant to §§ 5 and 6. Broker-dealers trading in the OTC market also engaged in self-regulation before the imposition of federal regulation in 1938 made membership mandatory. In 1933, dealers in the OTC market formed the Investment Bankers Code Committee ("IBCC"), which adopted industry best practices. The Investment Bankers Conference Code replaced the IBCC. However, both the IBCC and the Investment Bankers Conference Code were voluntary organizations—broker-dealers trading in the OTC market were not required to join. Unlike the NYSE, neither of these organizations garnered sufficient membership to engage in meaningful self-regulation of the much larger number of OTC broker-dealers. Congress passed The Maloney Act in 1938 to remedy this problem. The Maloney Act amended the Exchange Act to establish an additional type of SRO—registered national securities associations. The National Association of Securities Dealers, Inc., registered as an SRO with the SEC in 1939. In the summer of 2007, NASD and NYSE member regulation combined to become FINRA. FINRA is the largest of the only two national securities associations registered with the SEC under § 15A of the Exchange Act.

The current regulatory framework for the broker-dealer industry is dominated by a single SRO—FINRA—overseen by the SEC. The foundation of the broker-dealer regulatory framework is registration with the SEC, which requires the broker-dealer to become a member of FINRA. FINRA administers the process of registration with the SEC and becoming a member of FINRA. Specifically, the regulatory framework hierarchy is as follows: (1) The federal securities laws; (2) administration and implementation of the federal securities laws by the SEC with significant delegated authority to SROs (primarily FINRA); and (3) state regulation, excluding financial responsibility and operations, by the state securities administrators.

1. The Securities and Exchange Commission

The SEC was established in 1934 pursuant to § 4 of the Exchange Act as an independent federal agency to protect investors, maintain fair, orderly, and efficient markets, and facilitate capital formation subsequent to the stock market crash in October 1929. It is composed of five presidentially appointed commissioners, with staggered five-year terms, who must be confirmed by the Senate. No more than three commissioners may belong to the same political party. The President appoints one of these commissioners as the chair of the SEC. The chair serves as the SEC's chief executive officer and, therefore, is solely responsible for overseeing agency operations, including the hiring and firing of SEC staff. All SEC commissioners are responsible for reviewing and approving enforcement cases and formal orders of investigation, along with the development, consideration, and execution of policies and rules. The first chair of the SEC was Joseph P. Kennedy, the father of President John F. Kennedy. Generally, the chairs have been men, but under President Obama, two women were appointed to serve as chair—Mary Schapiro and Mary Jo White. The SEC has enormous responsibilities in addition to regulating broker-dealers and SROs; its responsibilities also include interpreting and enforcing the federal securities laws, issuing new rules and amending existing rules when required, overseeing the inspection of investment advisers, fostering capital formation, promoting fair and orderly markets, and coordinating U.S. securities regulation with federal, state, and foreign authorities.

Headquartered in Washington, DC, the SEC has 11 regional offices throughout the United States. Although the regional offices are responsible for investigating and litigating potential violations of the federal securities laws, each regional office has its own examination staff responsible for, among other duties, performing examinations of broker-dealers. The SEC's functional responsibilities are organized into five divisions and 23 offices, each headquartered in Washington, DC. The five divisions are Enforcement, Corporation Finance, Trading and Markets, Investment Management, and Economic and Risk Analysis. Each of these divisions is responsible for developing, monitoring, and maintaining the regulatory framework for broker-dealers, except Investment Management, which oversees investment advisers and investment companies. Of the 23 offices, one of the offices—the Office of Compliance Inspections and Examinations—is directly involved in monitoring broker-dealer compliance with the federal securities laws. The major divisions and offices specifically addressing the activities in the broker-dealer industry include: (a) Corporation Finance; (b) Enforcement; (c) Economic and Risk Analysis; (d) Trading and Markets; and (e) Office of Compliance Inspections and Examinations.

a. Corporation Finance

The Division of Corporation Finance ("CorpFin") oversees corporate disclosure in the U.S. securities markets. Essentially, CorpFin seeks to ensure that investors receive material information about companies whose securities are publicly traded in order to assist investors in making informed investment decisions. It does this by, among other things, reviewing disclosure documents of publicly held companies required to be filed with the SEC under the Securities Act and the Exchange Act. These required documents include registration statements for securities not previously offered for sale to the public, and annual and quarterly filings that disclose information about the companies' financial condition and business practices. CorpFin also provides guidance about disclosure requirements through administrative interpretations of the Securities

Act and the Exchange Act and recommends new regulations or the amendment of existing regulations, to implement these statutes to the SEC. Where appropriate, CorpFin refers matters to the Division of Enforcement for investigation and possible prosecution for violations of the federal securities laws. Broker-dealer activities are regulated by this division both in underwriting securities in the primary market and in company reporting and disclosure requirements in the secondary market.

b. Enforcement

The Division of Enforcement ("Enforcement") is the law enforcement arm of the SEC and it prosecutes cases on behalf of the SEC. Enforcement staff investigate possible violations of the federal securities laws and, if violations are discovered, recommend that the SEC bring civil actions in federal court or administrative proceedings before independent administrative law judges. Investigations commenced by Enforcement staff on behalf of the SEC are conducted privately. Following an investigation, Enforcement staff present their findings to the SEC for its review. Based on this review, the SEC can authorize the Enforcement staff to file a case in federal court or to bring an administrative action or both. If the action is brought in federal court, the Enforcement staff files a complaint with a U.S. District Court and requests a sanction or a remedy; available sanctions and remedies include injunctions, disgorgement (return of illegal profits), and civil monetary penalties. The court may also bar or suspend an individual from serving as a corporate officer or director. The decision of the U.S. District Court may be appealed to the appropriate U.S. Court of Appeals. If the SEC authorizes the Enforcement staff to bring an action as an administrative proceeding, an order is filed with the secretary of the SEC to commence the action, which is presided over by an administrative law judge ("ALJ"). The ALJ conducts a hearing and issues an initial decision, which contains findings of fact and legal conclusions, along with sanctions. Sanctions may include cease-and-desist orders, suspension or revocation of broker-dealer registrations, censures, bars from association with the securities industry, civil monetary penalties, and disgorgement. Initial decisions issued by the ALJ may be appealed to the five commissioners of the SEC sitting as a body and the decision may be affirmed, reversed, modified, or remanded for additional hearings. The final decision of the five commissioners may be appealed to the appropriate U.S. Court of Appeals.

c. Economic and Risk Analysis

The Division of Economic and Risk Analysis ("DERA") was established to integrate economic analysis and data analytics into the SEC's policymaking, rulemaking, enforcement, and examinations. DERA works with other SEC divisions and offices to assist in the determination of the need for regulatory action, to analyze the potential economic effects of SEC rules, and to develop data-driven analyses of market activity. It also provides quantitative and qualitative research and support with respect to risk assessment in order to assist the SEC in anticipating, identifying, and managing risks—focused on, among other things, the early identification of potential fraud. DERA also assists Enforcement in its proceedings and settlement negotiations by providing economic and quantitative analysis.

d. Trading and Markets

The Division of Trading and Markets ("Trading and Markets") performs day-to-day oversight, on behalf of the SEC, of the major market participants, including SROs (e.g., FINRA), broker-dealers, clearing agencies, transfer agents, securities information processors, SIPC, and credit rating agencies. The SEC's financial integrity program for broker-dealers is conducted by Trading and Markets. The financial integrity program is embodied in the SEC's net capital, customer protection, related books and records, and notification rules examined in Chapters 7 and 9. Other responsibilities include reviewing proposed new rules and the modification of existing rules filed with the SEC by SROS. Trading and Markets staff also assist the SEC in establishing rules and issuing interpretations with respect to the operation and surveillance of the U.S. securities markets.

e. Office of Compliance Inspections and Examinations

The Office of Compliance Inspections and Examinations ("OCIE") conducts the SEC's National Examination Program ("NEP"). Under the NEP, OCIE conducts examinations and inspections of the SEC's registered entities, including broker-dealers, transfer agents, SROs such as FINRA, transfer agents, and clearing agencies. In performing its functions, OCIE has implemented specialized working groups ("SWGs") in several key areas as a resource to examiners in providing subject matter expertise, including equity market structure and trading practices, marketing and sales practices, microcap fraud, and transfer agents. Data tools and analysis are increasingly playing a significant role in enforcing the federal securities laws. Accordingly, OCIE has established several specialized units to assist the SEC in utilizing data-driven examination and analysis in its NEP. OCIE's Risk Analysis and Surveillance Group ("RAS") aggregates and analyzes data collected from SEC registrant filings and from external sources, regarding broker-dealer business activities and marketing-related efforts to identify activity that may warrant examination. OCIE's Quantitative Analytics Unit (QAU), comprised of highly skilled technologists, develops analytic tools to support the NEP such as the National Exam Analytics Tool ("NEAT"), which enables examiners to access and systematically analyze years' worth of a broker-dealer's trading in minutes. The Quantitative Analysis Unit has also developed tools to enable examiners to detect suspicious activity in areas such as high-frequency trading. OCIE's Risk Analysis Examination Team ("RAE") uses technology and specialized skills to conduct examinations of some of the largest broker-dealers; it analyzes transactions cleared by broker-dealers over several years in order to identify problematic behavior across multiple firms, including unsuitable recommendations, misrepresentations, deficient supervision, and churning.

2. The Federal Securities Laws

The SEC is charged with enforcing and implementing the federal securities laws through rulemaking. The federal securities laws and their corresponding rules and regulations, at their core, are based on disclosure of information required to allow investors to make informed investment decisions. However, with respect to broker-dealers, the SEC is also responsible for maintaining fair dealing and protecting against fraud. The laws that govern the U.S. securities industry are the: Securities Act of 1933; Securities Exchange Act of 1934; Trust Indenture Act of 1939; Investment Company Act of 1940; Investment Advisers Act of 1940; Sarbanes-Oxley Act of 2002; Dodd-Frank Wall Street Reform and Consumer Protection Act of 2010; and Jumpstart Our Business Startups (JOBS) Act of 2012. The Securities Act of 1993 ("Securities Act") governs the activities conducted in the primary securities market, i.e., the distribution of an issuer's securities for the first time and new issues of issuer securities already trading in the secondary market. Its core purposes are to provide investors with the material information required to make an informed investment decision and to protect them from fraud in the distribution of securities in U.S. securities markets. These core purposes are accomplished by requiring issuers, with the assistance of market participants such as broker-dealers, to register their securities with the SEC unless there is an available exemption to the registration requirement under § 5 of the Securities Act. Registration of the issuer's securities is designed to provide accurate disclosure to investors; it does not guarantee that the security is a good investment. This information is available to all prospective investors on the SEC's Electronic Data Gathering and Retrieval database or EDGAR. The registration requirements of the Securities Act and their relationship to broker-dealers is discussed in detail in Chapters 5 and 6.

The Securities Exchange Act of 1934 ("Exchange Act") established the SEC and gave it wide-ranging authority over the securities industry, including broker-dealers. The SEC has the power to register, regulate, and oversee broker-dealers and other market intermediaries and participants—including transfer agents, clearing agencies, and SROs such as FINRA, the primary regulator of broker-dealers in the U.S. securities markets. The SEC is also authorized to require periodic reporting and to sanction broker-dealers, along with issuers, for conduct prohibited under the federal securities laws. Issuers whose securities are publicly traded are required to report specified information to the SEC periodically and to provide shareholders with information (proxy materials) to enable participation in the management of public companies through the election of directors and approval of other corporate action. The Exchange Act also governs tender offers and prohibits insider trading and other fraudulent conduct. Broker-dealer fraud prohibited under the Exchange Act is discussed in detail in Chapter 12. However, because the Exchange Act and rules promulgated thereunder regulate the conduct and activities of broker-dealers, relevant sections of the Exchange Act are examined throughout this textbook. Moreover, the core of the broker-dealer regulatory framework, registration with the SEC, is contained in § 15 of the Exchange Act. Broker-dealer registration is the topic of Chapter 3.

The Trust Indenture Act of 1939 ("Indenture Act") governs the offer and sale of debt securities to the public. Among other things, the Indenture Act governs the standards of the terms embodied in the formal agreement between the issuer of debt securities and the debtholder, i.e., the debt indenture. Currently, the SEC rarely brings cases under the Indenture Act. The Indenture Act was adopted after the Great Depression to require issuers of debt securities to provide for a trustee to protect and enforce the rights of investors or bondholders. Among other requirements, the Indenture Act requires issuers to provide specified information to trustees, including certificates of officers of the company and opinions of counsel regarding compliance with the indenture. An examination of the Indenture Act is beyond the scope of this textbook.

The Investment Company Act of 1940 governs the organization and regulation of companies that engage primarily in investing, reinvesting, and trading in securities, and that offer their own securities to the public. A familiar type of investment company is a mutual fund. The ICA requires these companies to register with the SEC unless there is an available exemption. In addition, the ICA requires disclosure of conflicts of interest and the financial condition and investment policies of investment companies to investors on a regular basis. Registered investment companies must also disclose information about their investment objects and their organizational structure and operations. The examination of the regulatory framework governing investment companies is beyond the scope of this textbook.

The Investment Advisers Act of 1940 governs the regulation and oversight of investment advisers. Investment advisers engage in the business of providing investment advice to the public for the least compensation. Like the ICA, the IA is designed, among other things, to protect investors from conflicts of interest and fraudulent conduct. Again, registration with the SEC is required for investment advisers who make investment decisions for investors' assets or assets under management. Generally, only investment advisers with assets under management exceeding $100 million, or who advise registered investment companies, must register with the SEC. All other investment advisers are generally required to register with the appropriate state securities regulator. The examination of the regulatory framework governing investment advisers is beyond the scope of this textbook.

The Sarbanes-Oxley Act of 2002 ("SOX") was the first substantial amendment of the federal securities laws since the 1975 Amendments and was a result of the accounting frauds in the early 2000s such as Worldcom and Enron. Accordingly, its amendments focused on reforms to enhance corporate governance, financial disclosures and, of course, to combat corporate and accounting fraud. The Enron scandal, revealed in October 2001, led to the bankruptcy of Enron and the dissolution of Arthur Andersen, formerly one of the largest accounting firms in the United States. Enron's fraud was conducted through complex accounting that misrepresented its earnings and financial condition and was supported by Arthur Andersen, its accountant. Arthur Andersen was sued criminally, resulting in its demise, despite the fact that it was subsequently acquitted. The Worldcom scandal, which occurred one year after Enron, was an $11 billion accounting fraud (accounting misstatements hid its poor financial condition) resulting in the demise of the company and a 25-year prison sentence for its CEO. A significant result of these frauds was the establishment of the Public Company Accounting Oversight Board ("PCAOB") to oversee the activities of accounting firms that conduct audits of issuers whose shares are publicly traded.

The Dodd-Frank Wall Street Reform and Consumer Protection Act of 2010 (Dodd-Frank) was enacted in connection with the financial crisis of 2008. It was enacted to reshaped the regulatory framework of the U.S. financial services industry, including the U.S. securities markets. Dodd-Frank resulted in changes in many areas, including consumer protection, trading restrictions, credit ratings, financial products, corporate governance, and disclosure. Among other requirements directly affecting broker-dealers, Dodd-Frank required auditors of registered broker-dealers to register with the PCAOB, thus subjecting such auditors to the oversight of the PCAOB. Specifically, registered broker-dealers are now required to have their annual financial statements certified by a PCAOB-registered accounting firm. This also means that certain broker-dealers, like issuers, must pay a support fee to PCAOB to support PCAOB's budget. Broker-dealers with more than $5 million in average, quarterly tentative net capital must pay an appropriate portion of the PCAOB's accounting support fee. PCAOB is also required to evaluate supplemental information submitted with the broker-dealer's FOCUS report, which is the monthly report that broker-dealers must submit under Exchange Act Rule 17a-5 detailing their financial and business operations. Broker-dealers registered with SIPC must also file annual reports detailing their financial and business operations with SIPC. In addition, broker-dealers must file with FINRA a report concerning their custody arrangements for customer funds and securities. The broker-dealer's financial responsibility and custody of customer assets requirements are discussed in Chapter 7.

The Jumpstart Our Business Startups Act of 2012 ("JOBS Act") was enacted to increase American job creation and economic growth by improving access to the public capital markets for emerging growth companies. An emerging growth company ("EGC") is defined under the JOBS Act as an issuer whose total annual gross revenues are less than $1 billion during its most recently completed fiscal year. The JOBS Act modified the way in which a broker-dealer could act as an underwriter and distribute research on behalf of an EGC. The JOBS Act permits, among other things, the underwriter to engage in oral or written communications with potential investors that are qualified institutional buyers or institutions that are accredited investors either prior to or following the date of filing a registration statement with the SEC, as long as such communications are accompanied or preceded by a prospectus that complies with § 10(a) of the Securities Act. It also permits analysts to participate in EGC management presentations with broker-dealer sales force personnel. Under the JOBS Act, broker-dealers are allowed to publish or distribute research and to make a public appearance with respect to the securities of an EGC at any time after the EGC's IPO date or before the expiration of lock-up agreements between the underwriter and the EGC or its stockholders. The public offering process is discussed in detail in Chapter 5. The JOBS Act also created a new exemption for offerings of crowdfunded securities, i.e., it exempts issuers from the registration requirements of § 5 of the Securities Act for offerings that do not exceed $1 million. These crowdfunded offerings must be conducted through registered broker-dealers or a funding portal (a new type of securities market intermediary) registered with the SEC. Funding portals are exempt from the registration requirements of broker-dealers enumerated in § 15 of the Exchange Act, but are required to register as a funding portal with the SEC and to become a member of FINRA. Persons operating a platform or mechanism that offers and sells securities under Rule 506 of Regulation D are exempt from the broker-dealer registration requirements of § 15(a)(1) of the Exchange Act. However, this exemption is not available to any person who receives compensation in connection with the purchase or sale of such securities.

3. *The Financial Industry Regulatory Authority, Inc.*

FINRA is the largest SRO regulating broker-dealers in the U.S. securities markets. Section 15(b)(1)(B) of the Exchange Act requires membership in FINRA or with an Exchange in order to register with the SEC. FINRA is not part of the government, but is organized as a not-for-profit member corporation under the laws of the State of Delaware. FINRA is managed by a Board of Governors elected by its members. The Board of Governors has 23 members and must consist of the CEO and representatives from the public (non-securities industry), a floor broker-dealer member of a national securities exchange, an independent dealer/insurance affiliate broker-dealer, an investment company affiliate broker-dealer, three small broker-dealers, one mid-size broker-dealer, and three large broker-dealers; in addition, the number of public governors must exceed the number of industry governors. All governors, excluding the CEO, serve for a term of three years and no governor can serve more than two consecutive terms. All member broker-dealers are entitled to vote to amend FINRA's bylaws and to adopt its rules.

FINRA has two wholly owned significant subsidiaries: FINRA Investor Education Foundation ("the Foundation") and FINRA Regulation, Inc. ("FINRA REG"). The Foundation was established to provide underserved Americans with investment knowledge, skills, and tools. The Foundation conducts its activities by awarding grants, establishing financial education programs, and funding research designed to develop financial education materials and tools for investors, educators, librarians, and grantees. In 2009 the Foundation launched its investor Advocacy Clinic Program, which provides start-up funding and assistance to law schools to establish investor advocacy clinics. These clinics provide attorney representation for investors when they have disputes with a broker-dealer for relatively modest dollar amounts in securities arbitration proceedings. FINRA REG has its own board of directors but is subject to the authority of, and oversight by, FINRA under the Plan of Allocation and Delegation of Functions by FINRA to FINRA Regulation, Inc. ("Delegation Plan"). Its board is elected by FINRA and FINRA is its sole stockholder. FINRA REG's responsibilities include: (1) establishing and interpreting rules and regulations governing its broker-dealer members and their associated persons; (2) the administration, interpretation, and enforcement of FINRA Rules; (3) developing and adopting necessary or appropriate rule changes relating to business and sales practices of its member broker-dealers, including financial responsibility, qualifications for FINRA membership and association with FINRA member broker-dealers, advertising practices, and clearance and settlement of securities transactions; (4) assuring compliance with FINRA rules and federal securities laws through examination, surveillance (broker-dealer trading activities), investigation, enforcement, and disciplinary actions; (5) operating the Central Registration Depository ("CRD")[9]; (6) developing and adopting rule changes applicable to the collection, processing, and dissemination of quotation and transaction information for securities traded in the OTC market along with corresponding trading practices; (7) maintaining and enhancing the integrity, fairness, efficiency, and competitiveness of the OTC securities market; and (8) developing and adopting rule changes relating to arbitration, mediation, or other resolution of disputes among and between FINRA broker-dealer members, their associated persons, and customers. In addition, FINRA REG provides regulatory services under contract with other registered national securities exchanges, including the NYSE and NASDAQ. These regulatory services include market and financial surveillance reviews, investigations, examinations, and the disciplinary process.

FINRA REG is also responsible for establishing and maintaining the National Adjudicatory Council ("NAC"). The NAC is authorized to act for FINRA with respect to an appeal or review of a disciplinary proceeding, a statutory disqualification proceeding, or a membership proceeding as well as to review offers of settlement and letters of acceptance, waiver, and consent ("AWC"). The NAC also must consider and make recommendations to the FINRA Board on policy and rule changes relating to the business and sales practices of FINRA member broker-dealers and their associated persons—along with enforcement policies, including the imposition of fines and other sanctions. The NAC consists of 14 members equally divided between non-securities industry and securities industry members, and all members are appointed by the FINRA Board for a term of three years. The NAC must appoint a Review Subcommittee of two to four members composed of non-securities industry and securities industry members to determine whether decisions rendered in disciplinary and membership proceedings should be called for review by the NAC.

FINRA REG also operates through District Committees established to assist in administering its affairs in a manner consistent with applicable law. The District Committees are also organized into regions to promote efficiency and administration. See Table 1.1 for a list of FINRA REG's current District Committees and Regions. Each District Committee must consist of at least five but no more than 20 members elected with terms restricted to the later of three years or until a successor is elected and qualified. Qualifications for serving on a District Committee include being a principal of a member broker-dealer and election by member broker-dealers within the territory

---

9. The CRD (Web CRD) is the central licensing and registration system for the U.S. securities industry and its regulators. It contains the registration records of registered broker-dealers and the qualification, employment, and disclosure histories (including disciplinary actions) of registered representatives associated with such broker-dealers.

of the District Committee. Among other responsibilities, District Committee members must serve as panelists in disciplinary proceedings, consider and recommend policies and rule changes to the FINRA REG Board, and undertake to educate FINRA members and other broker-dealers in their respective districts.

Table 1.1. FINRA Districts and Regions

District Number/Region	States/ Counties
1	Hawaii; in the State of California, the Counties of Monterey, San Benito, Fresno, and Inyo, and the remainder of the State North or West of such Counties; and in the State of Nevada, the Counties of Esmeralda and Nye, and the remainder of the State North or West of such Counties.
2	In the State of California, that part of the State South or East of the Counties of Monterey, San Benito, Fresno, and Inyo; and in the State of Nevada, that part of the State South or East of the Counties of Esmeralda and Nye, and all Pacific possessions and territories of the U.S.
3	States of Alaska, Arizona, Colorado, Idaho, Montana, New Mexico, Oregon, Utah, Washington, and Wyoming.
4	States of Iowa, Kansas, Minnesota, Missouri, Nebraska, North Dakota, and South Dakota.
5	States of Alabama, Arkansas, Louisiana, Mississippi, Oklahoma, and Tennessee.
6	State of Texas.
7	States of Florida, Georgia, North Carolina, and South Carolina; Territories of Puerto Rico and the Virgin Islands.
8	States of Illinois, Indiana, Kentucky, Michigan, Ohio, and Wisconsin.
9	The District of Columbia and the States of Delaware, Maryland, New Jersey, Pennsylvania, Virginia, West Virginia, and New York (except for the five Boroughs of New York City and the Counties of Nassau and Suffolk).
10	In the State of New York, the five Boroughs of New York City and the Counties of Nassau and Suffolk.
11	States of Connecticut, Maine, Massachusetts, New Hampshire, Rhode Island, and Vermont.
Midwest Region	Districts 4 and 8.
New York Region	District 10.
North Region	Districts 9 and 11.
South Region	Districts 5, 6, and 7.
West Region	Districts 1, 2, and 3.

FINRA REG also regulates the OTC markets for listed and unlisted equities, corporate bonds, asset-backed instruments, certain government agency instruments, municipal securities, and other fixed-income instruments. The regulatory framework for the OTC markets is discussed in Chapter 14. The following is a discussion of significant FINRA REG departments.

a. FINRA REG Departments

1. Office of Dispute Resolution

The Office of Dispute Resolution ("ODR") operates the largest alternative dispute resolution forum for securities disputes between and among investors, broker-dealers, and their associated persons. With respect to investors, ODR's market share is based on account opening documentation, used by FINRA member broker-dealers, that requires the resolution of disputes with their customers using ODR's forum. ODR provides two methods of dispute resolution: Arbitration and Mediation. Both arbitration and mediation are conducted under FINRA's codes of arbitration and mediation. Arbitration administered by ODR is a formal dispute resolution process in which the parties select arbitrators (neutral third parties) who listen to the arguments and evidence presented by the parties and then render a final and binding decision. Mediation is also conducted by a neutral third party but, unlike arbitration, agreements reached between the disputing parties are not binding until the parties sign a settlement agreement. ODR maintains and administers the roster of neutrals used in its dispute resolution forum. The roster contains both securities industry and public neutrals who are not employees of FINRA. Alternative dispute resolution is discussed in detail in Chapter 12.

2. Department of Market Regulation

The Department of Market Regulation ("DMR") monitors and regulates OTC trading of exchange-listed and non-exchange-listed securities for compliance with FINRA rules and federal securities laws. It is comprised of two units: Surveillance and Examination. The surveillance unit reviews trading activity for broker-dealer compliance with regulatory requirements. It performs its surveillance responsibilities by collecting and integrating trading data across exchanges and alternative trading systems to detect abusive patterns of trading, such as algorithm gaming and front-running. The examination unit conducts on-site reviews of broker-dealers' financial and operational condition for compliance with FINRA rules and federal securities laws. The examination unit performs its responsibilities by, among other activities, reviewing the broker-dealer's order execution quality along with its compliance with trading rules and reporting obligations. DMR also has a legal section that prosecutes cases resulting from the activities of its surveillance and examination units.

3. Department of Member Regulation

The Department of Member Regulation is responsible for conducting on-site examinations for compliance by the broker-dealer with FINRA and SEC rules and for administering the Membership Application Program ("MAP"). The department conducts both routine and cause examinations of broker-dealers. Routine examinations focus on core aspects of a broker-dealer's business, along with those that present heightened regulatory risk. If exceptions to applicable FINRA rules or federal securities laws, rules and regulations are found during a routine examination of the broker-dealer, the broker-dealer must submit a formal written response to FINRA identifying corrective action that will be taken by the broker-dealer. Cause examinations are conducted as a result of customer allegations of harm and are typically directed toward individual registered representatives and supervisors. MAP is responsible for reviewing and approving or denying new applications for FINRA membership along with approval or denial of significant changes to the business operations of existing members. The membership process and the corresponding rules and requirements are discussed in detail in Chapter 3.

4. Office of Fraud Detection and Market Intelligence

The Office of Fraud Detection and Market Intelligence ("OFDMI") acts as FINRA's central point of contact for fraud-related issues, including insider trading. It collects and evaluates information to identify fraud from various sources, including broker-dealer regulatory filings, tips, and investor complaints. OFDMI conducts its responsibilities through four units: (1) The insider trading Surveillance Group, (2) The Fraud Surveillance Group, (3) The Central Review Group, and (3) The Office of the Whistleblower. OFDMI regularly makes referrals to the SEC and other law enforcement agencies for further investigation and prosecution.

5. Department of Enforcement

The Department of Enforcement is responsible for investigating potential violations of the federal securities laws and FINRA rules and bringing formal disciplinary actions against member broker-dealers and their associated persons. In performing its responsibilities, Enforcement works closely with Market Regulation and Member Regulation. It also may receive referrals for disciplinary actions from other FINRA departments and offices. Disciplinary actions are brought administratively and are initially heard and decided by hearing officers in FINRA's Office of Hearing Officers. Hearing officers are not involved in the investigative process and are independent of, and physically separated from, other FINRA departments. Procedures for disciplinary actions brought by Enforcement are either a settlement or a formal complaint. Settlements are memorialized in an Acceptance, Waiver, and Consent ("AWC") signed by the broker-dealer. Formal complaints are heard and decided by a panel composed of one hearing officer and two securities industry panelists. A variety of sanctions may be imposed, including suspension or expulsion of a broker-dealer from FINRA membership and barring individuals from association with any member broker-dealer. Hearing decisions may be appealed to the NAC and are reviewed de novo. NAC decisions represent final FINRA action — unless FINRA's Board of Governors decides to review the NAC's decision — and may be appealed to the SEC.

b. FINRA's Rulemaking Process

All FINRA rules must be approved by the SEC before they become final. The process is described in detail in the webcast series "What to Expect,"[10] set forth below.

The "What to Expect" Webcast Series: Rulemaking Process

Overview

The rulemaking process follows some standard procedures with opportunities for firm [broker-dealer member] involvement.

Generally, unless a legal exception exists, there is a public comment period after the SEC publishes a rule proposal in the *Federal Register*. There may also be subsequent comment periods if there are material amendments in response to comments which would need to be republished.

FINRA's general process is to publish a proposed rule for comment in a *Regulatory Notice* before filing it with the SEC. Sometimes, however, FINRA does not do this first round of publication. This is because a proposed rule change may be technical or not material, or because FINRA determines that time is of the essence for the proposed rule change.

FINRA is responsible for developing rules that govern the conduct of the US securities industry in areas as diverse as sales practices, advertising, transactions with customers, marketplace rules and corporate finance.

The process for rule development is a participatory one with broad input from [securities] industry members, trade associations, other regulators and the public. This happens through the comment process, other informal consultations and through FINRA's standing industry committees.

The Rulemaking Process

New rule proposals come from a number of sources. Some are ideas that member firms, investors and other interested parties suggest. Others are FINRA-initiated rule proposals based on proactive analysis of data and trends. Rule proposals may also be based on recommendations from the SEC or other regulators. They can also come from FINRA advisory and standing committees, which are comprised of industry representatives. These include our Advisory Council, the Small Firm Advisory Board, subject-matter expert committees like the Independent Dealer/Insurance Affiliate Committee and the Variable Insurance Product Committee, and geographically-based district committees. FINRA maintains these committees to provide feedback in a variety of areas including rulemaking.

Once an idea for a possible rule proposal is identified, the FINRA subject-matter experts research and develop it. A working draft or overview is then presented to

---

10. © 2017 FINRA. All rights reserved. FINRA is a registered trademark of the Financial Industry Regulatory Authority, Inc. Reprinted with permission from FINRA.

FINRA management for review. The proposal is then typically presented at FINRA's standing and District committee meetings that are conducted while a proposal is being considered. Following review by various FINRA committees, all rule proposals are presented to the Small Firm Advisory Board. That group exists to ensure that issues of particular interest and concern to small firms are effectively communicated to and considered by the FINRA Board of Governors.

Once this review is complete, FINRA staff considers any comments and prepares a presentation to the FINRA Board of Governors. That document describes the rule proposal along with its purpose and background, as well as the views of the Small Firm Advisory Board and the standing committees that considered the matter....

Depending on the details of the rule proposal, the Board of Governors may authorize the publication of a *Regulatory Notice* to solicit comment on the proposal from firms and the public. The Board may also authorize direct filing of the proposal with the SEC.

If comments are requested, FINRA will notify firms through FINRA's Weekly Update email and on finra.org. FINRA often asks firms to comment to help shape rules with greater precision and to ensure consideration of the operational impact of implementing the proposal.

When FINRA issues a *Regulatory Notice* soliciting comment on a rule proposal, the comment period typically is open for one to two months. FINRA accepts comments by hard copy or electronically. All comments become part of the rule proposal's "official record" and are posted on FINRA's Web site.

Depending on the comments, and whether any significant changes are being made, FINRA staff will either return to the Board with a revised proposal or file the proposal with the SEC. In certain cases, the comment process has persuaded FINRA to conclude that the proposed rule was not the best course of action and decide not to pursue the proposal.

When FINRA pursues a rule proposal, it is filed with the SEC and posted on FINRA's Web site within two business days after filing. Once filed, SEC staff reviews the rule proposal to determine whether it is consistent with the requirements of the Securities Exchange Act of 1934. During this process, SEC staff will often confer with FINRA. As a result, FINRA staff may determine to make subsequent modifications to the rule proposal.

After the SEC receives the rule proposal, the next step in the rule process is to publish the proposal for comment in the *Federal Register*. Generally, the comment period is open for 21 days following the publication date. In certain limited instances, the SEC may grant accelerated approval to a proposal. Also, in some limited situations specified in the Exchange Act, FINRA may file the rule for immediate effectiveness. The SEC has 60 days to consider whether a rule change filed for immediate effectiveness should be canceled or allowed to remain in effect.

Depending on the types of comments received, SEC staff typically requests a FINRA response. As a result, FINRA may decide to propose amendments to the rule proposal.

Depending on the changes, the SEC may also choose to republish the revised rule proposal for comment in the *Federal Register*. If the SEC approves the final rule, it places an official announcement in the *Federal Register*. After that, FINRA issues a *Regulatory Notice* announcing SEC approval of the rule, which also summarizes the new rule or rule amendments, includes the rule text and announces the effective date. In many cases, the effective date will be a set number of days following publication of the *Notice*.

FINRA monitors the implementation of significant new rules to determine if they are working as anticipated. This rule review is a proactive way of determining if the research and industry collaboration on a rule's development is producing the desired results. If it is not, then FINRA revisits the rule. If it is producing the desired results, it will stay in effect until a regulatory need arises to change or rescind it.

Figure 1.1

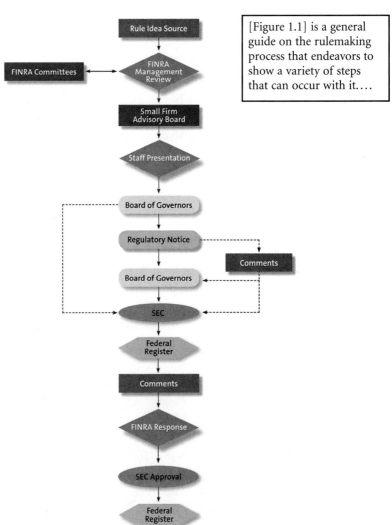

[Figure 1.1] is a general guide on the rulemaking process that endeavors to show a variety of steps that can occur with it....

Hypothetical One

Carlota Durham, the Director of Human Resources at Success First, has decided to hire a new registered representative and has asked for your assistance. The prospective employee's name is Jane J. Wolfenbarger [CRD# 2734169], and she is currently working at PFS Investments, Inc. [CRD# 10111]. Although Carlota has heard wonderful things about Jane, she has not heard very many good things about PFS Investments, Inc. Carlota has asked you to review the backgrounds of both Jane and PFS Investments, Inc. She also wants you to confirm Jane's qualifications. You are quite familiar with FINRA's Web CRD and decide to use BrokerCheck to quickly ascertain whether Jane or PFS Investments, Inc. have a disciplinary history that might adversely affect Success First's stellar reputation. You are also eager to provide all information available about both Jane and PFS Investments, Inc. What types of information will you obtain from BrokerCheck about Jane and PFS Investments, Inc. for your report to Carlota?

Chapter 2

An Introduction to the Business of Broker-Dealers

Regulatory Authority

Securities Exchange Act of 1934 Sections 3(a)(4) and (5); 3(a)(67); 3(a)(68); 15(a),(b) and (c); 15B; 17(a)

Exchange Act Rules 3a67-1; 15c3-1; 15c3-3; 17a-3; 17a-4; 17h-1T; 17h-2T; 19b-3

Investment Advisers Act of 1940 Sections 203 and 206

Investment Advisers Act Rule 206(4)-7

FINRA Rules 4311(b)(3) and (b)(4)

Commodity Exchange Act Section 1(a)(47)

Commodity Exchange Act Rule 1.3

A basic understanding of broker-dealer business models is essential to understanding the regulatory framework for broker-dealers and to advise broker-dealer clients effectively. The purpose of this chapter is to establish a foundation on which to build an understanding of the subsequent discussion of issues in the laws and regulations governing broker-dealers and to serve as a reference tool throughout the course. Accordingly, this chapter does not contain cases and only has minimal direct reference to applicable rules and regulations. In addition, a glossary containing many of the terms used in this chapter and subsequent chapters is included to minimize the learning curve regarding the nomenclature used in the broker-dealer regulatory framework.

Motivating Hypothetical

Carmen Alvarez, the CEO of Success First (a broker-dealer registered with the SEC and a member of FINRA) has decided that it's time for Success First to give back to the local minority community by establishing an externship program. She has decided to partner with a local university that serves a primarily minority student population. After an extensive application and interview process, she has selected two students with outstanding academic records and who are finance majors. To ensure that the students obtain the skills and knowledge essential to working in the broker-dealer industry, she has established a training program that includes a classroom component. Each week, the students are required to attend a two-hour class about selected topics in the broker-dealer industry. Examinations similar in format to the Series 7 examination and group activities are used to assess student understanding of the broker-dealer industry. Carmen has also provided study materials that correspond to the information contained in this chapter.

I. Introduction

Broker-dealers are engaged in the business of effecting transactions in securities. In fact, the term broker-dealer is not one term—it describes two separate entities; the terms *broker* and *dealer* are defined separately in Section 3(a) of the Exchange Act. A broker, defined in Section 3(a)(4) of the Exchange Act, is any person engaged in the business of effecting transactions in securities for the account of others. A dealer, defined in Section 3(a)(5) of the Exchange Act, is any person engaged in the business of effecting transactions in securities for its own account. The terms *broker* and *dealer* are used together because most financial entities engaged in the business of effecting transactions in securities act as both brokers and dealers. In addition, the organizational structure of broker-dealers is quite complex and many are units of large financial conglomerates.

II. Broker-Dealer Business Models

Broker-dealer business models are varied and complex. Therefore, this chapter provides an overview of two basic broker-dealer business models—wire houses and independent broker-dealers. The wire house business model is the original or traditional business model and was predominant. In the wire house business model, registered representatives are generally employees and offer proprietary products to customers. Use of the independent broker-dealer business model is growing, in part, because it allows registered representatives to serve their customers with non-proprietary products; it also supports their entrepreneurial aspirations because most are also self-employed business owners. Proponents of the independent business model contend that it provides financial services to middle America, while wire houses primarily focus on wealthy individuals and institutional customers. Moreover, the Financial Services Institute, a non-profit association representing independent broker-dealers, asserts that 64 percent of all practicing registered representatives operate in the independent broker-dealer channel and that this trend is growing.

Competition, changes in the law, and the 2008 financial crisis have led to institutional integration in the broker-dealer industry. As a result, a single financial holding company may have affiliates and/or subsidiaries that utilize several business models. Although this trend toward institutional integration is not new to the wire house business model, now it has entered the independent broker-dealer channel and is expected to continue as margins on financial products shrink and compliance costs rise, due in part to increased regulation resulting from the Dodd-Frank Act.

A. Traditional or Wire House Broker-Dealers

Traditional, or "wire house" broker-dealers are generally large, old-line firms with national, and even global, branch system networks that provide their customers with a broad array of services and products. The term *wire house* refers to the fact that at the turn of the twentieth century, such firms had become established institutions on Wall Street and had telegraph connections with their branch offices or correspondent firms in various parts of the country.[1] The wire house business model was originally heavily weighted toward transaction-based compensation, i.e., employees effected transactions in securities for a commission. In short, broker-dealers using the wire house business model are full service broker-dealers with a national network of employees or individual investment professionals, some employing tens of thousands. Key characteristics of wire houses or traditional broker-dealers include: individual investment professionals are hired as employees; a wide range of products and services, many of which are proprietary products, are offered; large offices are located in major cities; and clients are institutional customers and high-net-worth individuals (e.g., $1 million or more, excluding the primary residence). Wire house firms provide their customers with a full range of broker-dealer functions, including clearance, settlement, and advisory services; they also offer financial planning, investment banking, and a variety of investment alternatives, including traditional debt and equity securities along with proprietary products such as mutual funds, synthetic securities (e.g., index baskets[2] and equity swaps[3]), partnership interests, and trading strategies to protect their customers from market risk (hedging) and market mispricing (arbitrage).

Generally, wire houses maintain a permanent labor force, which they monitor and train. Employees are trained to comply with the firm's specific goals and philosophy and, most important, to use the firm's own methods in the sale of the firm's proprietary products. Employees are paid bonuses for successfully selling such products. In fact, employees may be pressured to market the firm's proprietary products over non-firm products.

There has been a consolidation in the broker-dealer industry, including wire house broker-dealers, over the years due to market forces and the 2008 financial crisis. This consolidation began with the elimination of fixed commission rates, which was

---

1. Most wire houses had a "customer" room for customers to observe the price quotation blackboards or stock tickers. *Id.* Complaints were made that some brokers' offices were "luxuriously furnished and sometimes equipped with lunch rooms, and liquor in order to increase the lure of the ticker." Report of the Governor's Committee on Speculation in Securities and Commodities (June 7, 1909), reprinted in WILLIAM C. VAN ANTWERP, THE STOCK EXCHANGE FROM WITHIN 415, 426 (1913).

2. An index basket is a portfolio of securities constructed to match or track components of a market index such as the Standard & Poor's 500 Index (S&P 500).

3. An equity swap is a contract between two parties who agree to exchange a future set of cash flows for a specified period. One set of cash flows is pegged to a floating rate and the other set is pegged to the performance of a stock or stock market index. Equity swaps are used, among other reasons, to avoid rules governing the particular type of investment that an institution can hold.

the primary source of income for broker-dealers. Due to reduced commission income, broker-dealers turned to other sources to create income streams to replace the significant decrease in commission revenue. As a result, many broker-dealers began to engage in more principal transactions, including proprietary trading, risk arbitrage, and merchant banking; these type of activities required more capital and led to consolidation from mergers of wire house broker-dealers to compete not only in the United States but also globally. Although wire houses represented approximately four percent of the total broker-dealer industry, they generated the majority of the industry's revenue (approximately 58%) and accounted for approximately 87 percent of all assets in the securities industry in 2014.[4] Currently, only five remain: Morgan Stanley Smith Barney, Bank of America's Merrill Lynch, UBS, Goldman Sachs, and Wells Fargo.

B. Independent Broker-Dealers

The defining characteristic of the independent broker-dealer business model ("IBD") is the independent contractor relationship between the IBD and the investment professional. The investment professional establishes her own financial services firm[5] and associates with the IBD to meet the financial services needs of her customers, which may include providing investment advice as well as insurance products. This means that the investment professional is not an employee of the IBD but is associated with the IBD through a formal contract describing the terms of the independent contractor relationship between the IBD and the investment professional. Such contracts typically contain boilerplate language that states that the investment professional is free from IBD control in operating her financial services business except for supervisory responsibilities imposed under the federal securities laws. For example:

> The Company has no right to control or direct the Contractor in the rules of Securities [compliance with applicable securities laws], not only as to the result to be accomplished by the work but also as to the details and means by which the result is to be accomplished excepting that the Company shall have responsibility and right to perform such supervisory overview required by the Securities and Exchange Commission, Securities Regulatory Associations and Exchanges, and the state and political subdivision.... Except for the aforementioned, the Contractor is completely free from the will and control of the Company not only as to what shall be done but how it shall be done.[6]

The independent contractor relationship benefits both the investment professional and the IBD. The IBD's cost structure is reduced because the investment professional is not an employee of the IBD. Accordingly, the IBD is not required to withhold taxes

---

4. SIFMA 2015 Fact Book, available at: http://www.sifma.org/factbook/.

5. The investment professional's business may be established using any business form, including a limited liability company or a corporation.

6. Brief of Plaintiff Appellants at 35, *Hollinger v. Titan Capital Corp.*, 914 F.2d 1564 (9th Cir. 1990) (No. 3837).

under the Federal Insurance Contributions Act (FICA),[7] is not subject to minimum wage and overtime provisions of the Fair Labor Standards Act,[8] and is not subject to the National Labor Relations Act,[9] which, among other things, protects the rights of employees to bargain collectively, and imposes fair labor practices on employers. The investment professional also receives tax benefits because her income is subject to taxation as self-employment income, but not to FICA or the Federal Unemployment Tax Act.[10] But probably most important to the investment professional is the control derived from owning her own business and the avoidance of high start-up costs associated with establishing a new broker-dealer. Broker-dealer start-up costs can be significant because compliance with the broker-dealer regulatory framework requires, among other things, a substantial investment in staff and technology to meet record-keeping and reporting mandates under the federal securities laws and SRO rules. Under the IBD model, the investment professional's overhead is appreciably reduced because she is only responsible for traditional overhead costs associated with operating a business. For example, the investment professional pays for office space, staff compensation, utilities, telephone service, etc.; however, she does not have to pay to set up the IT department needed to execute and report trades as required under the federal securities laws. In addition, the IBD industry asserts that the independent contractor relationship benefits the investing public because it facilitates the provision of financial services for middle-class clients, not just high-net-worth individuals.[11] However, the independent contractor relationship may adversely impact effective supervision because it results in many offices with few employees dispersed over a large geographic area.[12]

Unlike wire house employees, the independent contractor relationship allows the investment professional to retain more of the commissions and fees generated from sales and services provided to customers, i.e., the payout ratio for investment professionals is higher. For example, if the investment professional provides services to her customers that generate advisory fees of $1, she retains $1. The IBD is compensated through fixed fees for services required by the investment professional to operate her financial services business. The payout ratio under the IBD model may be as low as 85 percent and as high as 100 percent depending on the terms of the contract between

---

7. FICA, 42 U.S.C. §§ 210-1397 (2012), imposes taxes on both employees and employers to finance the payment of old-age, survivor, and disability insurance benefits payable under Title II of the Social Security Act and the costs of hospital and post-hospital Medicare services of Social Security beneficiaries.

8. *See* Fair Labor Standards Act of 1938, 29 U.S.C. §§ 201–219 (2012).

9. *See* 29 U.S.C. §§ 157–159 (2013). NLRA established the right of employees to self-organize, the procedure for elections to determine preference for a union, and exclusive union bargaining rights. Only employees are eligible to participate in this process.

10. Federal Unemployment Tax Act, 23 U.S.C. Ch. 23 (2015) imposes a federal employer tax used to help fund state workforce agencies.

11. Interview with David Bellaire, General Council, Financial Services Institute, on September 24, 2013.

12. *See* Chapter 4, Section II.B. for examples of supervisory difficulties in the IBD industry.

the IBD and the investment professional. Comparatively, the payout ratio for wire house employees may be as low as 25 percent and as high as 50 percent. Both the IBD and the investment professional benefit from set fees charged for services and products provided by the IBD to assist the investment professional in operating her financial services business. In essence, the investment professional only pays for services that she needs to operate her business. Box 2.1 provides an example of the payout ratio for services provided by Securities Service Network, an Iowa-based IBD.

Box 2.1
Securities Services Network (SSN)

98% payout on Brokerage Business. Clearing through both National Financial and Pershing, we offer our advisors a 98% payout on commission and advisory business.

94% payout on Direct Business. We have one of the highest payouts in the industry for mutual funds, variable annuities, variable universal life and third-party money managers.

Low-Cost Advisory Programs. Our fee-based advisory programs can save you money. SSN offers fee-based brokerage accounts with low or no platform fees with no ticket charges.

IBDs share a number of similar business characteristics. Generally they are not self-clearing[13] and provide traditional broker-dealer services, such as processing transactions, paying commissions, acting as custodians of assets for registered investment advisers, and monitoring compliance. Many also own or affiliate with an entity registered with the SEC as an investment adviser ("Corporate RIA") to support the advisory business of investment professionals.[14] In addition, most IBDs are not owned by large financial holding companies. In fact, many are privately owned businesses. Products offered are mainly non-proprietary products and usually include mutual funds and variable insurance. Unlike wire houses, there is no pressure for the investment professional to sell certain products because they are proprietary products of the broker-dealer and therefore generate higher profits. In essence, IBDs provide front-, middle-, and back-office support for investment professionals using technology in the form of proprietary investment platforms, not proprietary investment products. However, despite this comprehensive support, the investment professional has the primary relationship with the customer, not the IBD.

---

13. Clearing firms are the primary source of technology used to monitor compliance by IBDs. The most commonly used clearing firms are Pershing, LLC and National Financial. However, some of the largest IBDs are self-clearing.

14. The IBD may establish its Corporate RIA as an affiliated company (e.g., the IBD and Corporate RIA are separate entities but have common ownership) or the IBD and Corporate RIA are the same entity (i.e., the same entity is registered with the SEC as both a broker-dealer and an investment adviser).

Competition among IBDs, especially among the top four, has led to a significant expansion of services and products offered to the investment professional. Expanded services include customer acquisition and retention, business consulting, technology training, independent research, portfolio management and reporting, clearing and compliance, and investment advisory services. Expanded product offerings include alternative investments, cash and banking services, estate planning, exchange-traded funds or ETFs, asset management programs, and 529 plans.[15] Expanded services may be offered internally or through a third party. For example, a smaller IBD might offer asset management programs or clearing and settlement services through a third party, while the larger IBDs have these capabilities in-house.

Several practice models are supported by IBDs for investment professionals: (1) commission only; (2) dually registered; (3) hybrid; and (4) asset custody. Generally, all practice models are supported through the independent contractor relationship except for asset custody.

1. The Commission-Only Practice Model

Figure 2.1. Commission-Only Practice Model

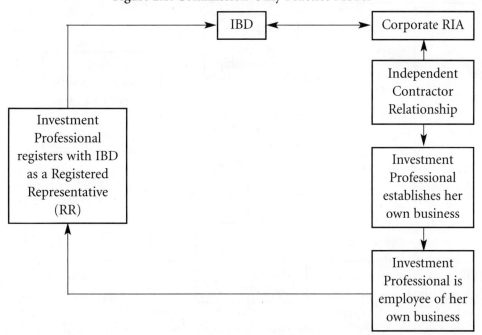

In the commission-only practice model, the IBD provides support only for the investment professional's broker-dealer business.[16] The investment professional establishes her own financial services business, of which she is an employee and registers

---

15. 529 plans or qualified tuition plans, authorized under §529 of the Internal Revenue Code, are tax-advantaged savings plans that encourage saving for the future costs of a college education.

16. In this chapter, *broker-dealer business* is defined as business conducted by a registered representative of a broker-dealer to provide broker-dealer services, for which the registered representative

with the broker-dealer as a registered representative as required under federal securities laws. The investment professional must be associated with the IBD as a registered representative because Sections 15(a) and (b) of the Exchange Act prohibit effecting transactions in securities unless registered with the SEC.[17]

2. The Dually-Registered Practice Model

Figure 2.2. Dually Registered Practice Model

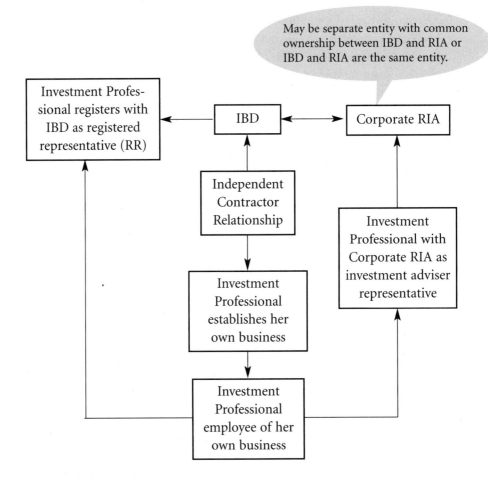

---

typically charges a commission, and incidental investment advice within the broker-dealer exemption from the Investment Advisers Act of 1940.

17. It shall be unlawful for any broker or dealer which is either a person other than a natural person or a natural person not associated with a broker or dealer which is a person other than a natural person (other than such a broker or dealer whose business is exclusively intrastate and who does not make use of any facility of a national securities exchange) to … effect any transactions in, … any security (other than an exempted security or commercial paper, bankers' acceptances, or commercial bills) unless such broker or dealer is registered in accordance with subsection (b) of this section. 15 U.S.C. § 78o(a). A broker or dealer may be registered by filing with the Commission an application for registration … 15 U.S.C. § 78o(b)(1). See Chapter 3 for more information about broker-dealer registration requirements.

In the dually registration practice model, the IBD provides support services and products for the investment professional's broker-dealer business and her advisory business.[18] This practice model requires the IBD to monitor compliance with applicable securities laws under two regulatory structures. The advisory business is regulated under the Investment Advisers Act. Section 203 of the Investment Advisers Act requires entities engaged in the investment advisory business to register with the SEC or applicable state regulatory authorities;[19] investment professionals providing investment advice to customers must also register with the SEC, or applicable state regulatory authorities, as investment adviser representatives. The broker-dealer business is regulated under the Exchange Act. Section 15 of the Exchange Act requires broker-dealers to register with the SEC and applicable state authorities and to become members of FINRA; investment professionals engaged in the broker-dealer business must be associated with a registered broker-dealer by registering as registered representatives with FINRA and applicable state regulatory authorities. In reality, this means that investment adviser firms and investment adviser representatives are primarily regulated by the SEC or state regulatory authorities, while broker-dealers and registered representatives are primarily regulated by the SEC and FINRA. Of course, the SEC has regulatory authority over both investment advisers and broker-dealers under the federal securities laws.

Supervision is a critical component of the compliance services provided by IBDs to their investment professionals. The IBD must monitor compliance with applicable securities laws by investment professionals associated with them as registered representatives and investment adviser representatives. This means that there must be at least one appropriately licensed and registered principal responsible for supervising the advisory[20] and broker-dealer businesses of the investment professional. With respect to the broker-dealer business, this requirement is met by an employee of the IBD or an appropriately licensed and registered investment professional.[21] However, the investment professional may only supervise other RRs or IARs registered with the IBD; she is prohibited from supervising her own business.[22]

---

18. In this chapter, *advisory business* is defined as business for which an investment professional, acting in the capacity of an investment adviser representative of an entity registered with the SEC as an investment adviser, typically charges a fee as a percentage of assets under management for providing investment advice.

19. *See* North American Securities Administrators Association, http://www.nasaa.org/industry-resources/investment-advisers/ia-switch-resources/state-investment-adviser-registration-information/.

20. Compliance requirements for RIAs are established under Section 206 and Rule 206(4)-7 of the Investment Advisers Act, and include the appointment of a properly licensed and registered person to monitor compliance with applicable securities laws. However, a full discussion of these requirements is beyond the scope of this text.

21. Investment professionals acting as supervisors are compensated for this service by receiving an override, i.e., they receive a portion of the revenue generated by the branches that they supervise.

22. *See* Chapter 4 for more information about the supervisory requirements of the broker-dealer regulatory framework.

3. The Hybrid Practice Model

Figure 2.3. The Hybrid Practice Model

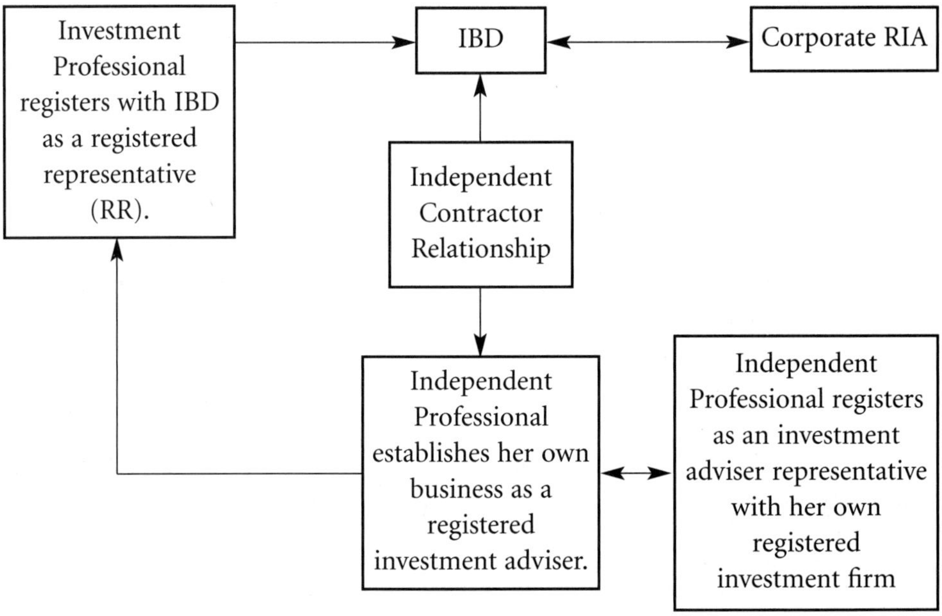

The hybrid practice model[23] also allows the investment professional to conduct both broker-dealer and advisory businesses. However, it is distinguished from the dually registered practice platform by the ownership of the registered investment adviser and regulatory responsibilities. The investment professional establishes a business entity that registers with the SEC or applicable state regulatory authority as an investment adviser (RIA). The investment professional then registers as an investment adviser representative with her own RIA firm, not the Corporate RIA of the IBD. However, the investment professional registers as a registered representative with the IBD in order to conduct her broker-dealer business. This also means that the regulatory structure is different from the dually registered practice platform. Supervision of the advisory business is the responsibility of the investment adviser's RIA firm, not the IBD. The IBD is responsible for supervising the broker-dealer business of the investment professional.

4. The Asset Custody Practice Model

The asset custody practice model requires the IBD to act as a custodian of the investment professional's assets. Specifically, the IBD holds the securities and cash of the customers of the investment professional for safekeeping. Among other require-

---

23. The author realizes that the terms *dually registered* and *hybrid* are sometimes used interchangeably. However, we have determined to define these terms in accordance with definitions used by the Financial Services Institute.

ments, federal securities laws require independent RIAs to hold their customers' securities and cash with a qualified custodian. Broker-dealers subject to the registration requirements in Section 15(b)(1) of the Exchange Act are qualified custodians.[24] The independent custodian may be a broker-dealer and, among other things, is required to provide periodic account statements (at least quarterly) to the investment adviser's customers about their securities and cash.[25] The IBD has no supervisory responsibilities because the investment professional does not register with the IBD as a registered representative nor does she register as an investment adviser representative with the IBD's Corporate RIA. This means that the IBD has no supervisory responsibilities under federal or state securities laws. Supervision, among other things, is the responsibility of the RIA firm owned by the investment professional. Under this type of independent contractor relationship, the investment professional receives 100 percent payout on all revenues generated from providing products and services to her customers.

Notes and Questions

1. How do the broker-dealer business models and categories relate to one another, if at all?

2. Who are the predominant users of prime brokers and why?

3. The debate between wire house versus independent business model continues and may lead to the creation of sub-business models within wire houses in order to compete for talent. In a January 2012 article in THINKADVISOR titled *Wirehouses Seen Making Big Push into Independent BD Space* by Gil Weinreich, the debate and possible responses were framed as follows:[26]

   An industry analyst predicts that several of the wirehouse brokerage firms will soon be entering the independent broker-dealer market—a bold forecast given the wirehouses' longtime messaging that brokers lose valuable support and branding by breaking away from their firms. The report by broker-dealer market research firm Tiburon Strategic Advisors says that establishing a semi-independent model is one way—indeed a likely way—that wirehouses, like Bank of America and Morgan Stanley, can respond to the flight of brokers to independent broker-dealers. A just-released report from Cerulli Associates projects that wirehouse assets under management will fall to 35% in 2013 from 43% in 2010, though Cerulli research director Bing Waldert told AdvisorOne that the wirehouse firms themselves planned much of the attrition as

---

24. *See* Rule 206(4)-2 of the Investment Advisers Act of 1940, 17 C.F.R. § 275.206(4)-2 (2015).

25. The account statements must identify the amount of cash and each security in the account at the end of the period and set forth all transactions in the account during that period.

26. ThinkAdvisor, available at: http://www.thinkadvisor.com/2012/01/19/wirehouses-seen-making-big-push-into-independent-b.

a means of focusing their businesses on profitability. The Tiburon report, ... argues that wirehouses will deploy various means, including higher retention bonuses and more aggressive recruiting, to stem the tide of departing brokers[i.e., investment professionals]. It adds that 12% of wirehouse and regional BDs leave their firms for other firms or to start their own firms each year, but that most of them (two-thirds) are really just going in circles, switching from one wirehouse firm to another in order to capture the recruiting firm's signing bonuses. Nevertheless, the independent broker-dealer market—once looked down on as the resting place of failed wirehouse brokers—is gaining ground, with well-regarded firms such as Raymond James garnering most of their recruits from wirehouses. A semi-independent space within wirehouses would mean that advisors would receive a higher payout but would pay their own rent, and for their own staffing and technology. "We think we will continue to see a steady move of advisors into the 'indie' channels, including independent BDs, RIAs and dual-registered, of a couple percent for the next several years, but [the trend] will be inversely impacted by the number and attractiveness of advisor retention packages that may be issued by the four wires," Sorrentino said. But the Fiserv executive also sees room for more accommodating wirehouse platforms, noting that Wells Fargo and Merrill Lynch already offer contractor-advisor business models where the [financial advisor] pays for services themselves in exchange for a higher payout. "I think more will adopt a Raymond James model that allows for four different models of practice ownership: the more of a contractor model the more the [financial advisor] has to pay for his own services," Sorrentino said.

Hypothetical One

Carmen wants to ensure that the interns understand the complexity of the broker-dealer industry. She has developed an assignment that requires the interns to prepare an organizational chart of a broker-dealer, its holding company, subsidiaries, and affiliates. The organizational chart must include a short title describing each entity's business, e.g., independent broker-dealer, bank, etc. Carmen has selected the financial holding company Raymond James for the interns to use in completing the assignment. The interns are required to use Raymond James' most recent Form 10-K to identify its holding company, subsidiaries, and affiliates.

III. Categories of Broker-Dealers

This overview of the categories of broker-dealers is neither exhaustive nor definitive in light of the complexity of the broker-dealer industry. Some operate solely as broker-dealers and others operate within financial conglomerates of various sizes. Others concentrate on different aspects of the securities markets. Accordingly, this section is organized using four major categories: (1) Full service and discount, (2) Market focus, (3) Functional focus, and (4) Insurance-affiliated.

A. Full Service and Discount Broker-Dealers

Since 1997, the securities markets have changed significantly due in large part to the increasing use of technology and the Order Handling Rules.[27] This shift in market structure has led to a blurring of the lines between full service and discount broker-dealers. Moreover, technology is now a critical, competitive factor, because online or electronic trading has become the predominant method of trading in the U.S. and the world. As a result, both full-service and discount broker-dealers offer online trading to their customers. However, some differences remain between full service and discount broker-dealers, with respect to the types of services and products offered and fees charged, that follow the original distinctions between the two business models.

The full service broker-dealer was the principal business model before technology became a critical competitive factor in the markets. Full service broker-dealers provide investment advice[28] and a comprehensive range of services and products, including trade execution, margin loans, clearing and settlement, and related services. Full service broker-dealers often have trading discretion over their customers' accounts, and provide research reports from in-house analysts working in their research departments. They also engage in investment banking activities, such as underwriting securities, debt financing, advising on mergers and acquisitions, structuring derivatives and similar transactions, and merchant banking. The cost of the many services provided by the full service broker-dealer is bundled into the overall commissions charged to customers, which were fixed prior to 1975.

The discount broker-dealer business model developed from the deregulation of trading commissions in 1975. Prior to 1975, broker-dealers imposed a fixed schedule of fees for trade execution services. On May 1, 1975, the SEC prohibited the use of fixed commission rates with the adoption of Rule 19b-3 of the Exchange Act. The SEC determined that there was no economic reason for fixed commission rates and that competition would provide a level and structure of commission rates that would better serve the investing public. Former rule 19b-3, among other things,

---

27. *See* U.S. Equity Mkt. Structure Study, Exchange Act Release No. 34-30920, [1991-1992 Transfer Binder] Fed. Sec. L. Rep. (CCH) ¶ 82,906 (July 14, 1992). In this release, the SEC emphasized the importance of price improvement opportunities in determining best execution. The broker-dealer's duty of best execution imposes a duty to exercise reasonable care to obtain the most advantageous terms for a customer. *See* Order Execution Obligations, Exchange Act Release No. 37619A, 1996 WL 506154 (Sept. 6, 1996) (providing a full discussion of the SEC's Order Handling Rules). See Chapter 14 for more information about a broker-dealer's duty of best execution.

28. Broker-dealers commonly give a certain amount of advice to their customers in the course of their regular business. This does not require registration under the Investment Advisers Act of 1940 because such advice is incidental to their regular business. Opinion of General Counsel Relating to Section 202(a)(11)(C) of the Investment Advisers Act of 1940. Investment Advisers Act Release No. 1 (Oct. 28, 1940), 11 FR 10996 (Oct 28, 1940).

... essentially prohibit[ed] any exchange from adopting or retaining any rule that require[ed] ... its members to charge fixed rates of commission for transactions executed on or by the use of the facilities of such exchange....[29]

The adoption of Exchange Act Rule 19b-3 allowed broker-dealers to negotiate commission rates for trade execution. This deregulation resulted in a significant reduction in commissions and paved the way for increased participation of small or retail investors. Today, the U.S. has one of the largest retail investor classes in the world.

Initially, discount broker-dealers only offered trade execution for very low commissions. This meant that customers of discount broker-dealers could trade securities, at very low commission rates, without the expense of paying for, among other services, advice and in-house research, i.e., services offered by full-service broker-dealers that they might not require.

Today, technology has allowed discount broker-dealers to offer online trading and many of the services offered by full service broker-dealers.[30] In fact, discount broker-dealers pioneered the broker-dealer industry's move to online trading and pushed full service broker-dealers to offer online trading to their customers in order to compete effectively. Full-service broker-dealers have unbundled their broker-dealer services allowing customers, for example, the option of purchasing discount broker-dealer services, including electronic or on-line trading at reduced commissions. This unbundling allows full service broker-dealer customers who do not want or need additional services, such as investment advice or the ability to trade securities at a lower cost. For example, Merrill Lynch & Co., Inc. ("Merrill Lynch"), an old-line full-service broker-dealer, offers trade execution at reduced or discounted commissions through its discount broker-dealer Merrill Edge to compete with large discount broker-dealers such as E*Trade Financial Corporation ("E*Trade"). Merrill Edge offers the same products and services as E*Trade at competitive pricing. However, Merrill Lynch still offers bundled services for its more well-heeled clients through Merrill Lynch Wealth Management. Merrill Lynch Wealth Management customers receive, among other services, fee-based advisory services and in-house research reports.

Technology continues to increase competition and to converge the business models of full-service and discount broker-dealers. Both offer many of the same products and services at competitive pricing. Both personalize web content to create content relevant to each customer striving to create customer loyalty, lower administrative costs, increased

---

29. 17 C.F.R. § 249.19b-3 (1987). Rule 19b-3, along with several other rules, was deemed to be obsolete by the SEC in 1988. *See* Rescission of Rules Under the Sec. Exch. Act of 1934, 53 FR 41205 (Oct. 20, 1988).

30. Discount brokers achieve cost savings in part due to new market linkages provided by technological innovation. Discount brokers then pass these savings on to customers in the form of reduced commissions. The advent of online trading permits the further reduction of brokerage commissions. Because of the low cost involved, brokers reduce commissions. E*Trade Group, Inc. offers trades for as low as $14.95 per trade. Datek Securities Corp. launched on-line trading of securities for $9.99 per trade. And Lombard cut its per trade commission base from $34 to $14.95. Bruce Rule, *Commission-cutting Grows for On-line Trading; Investors Demand Discounts, but Volume Increases*, Inv. Dealer's Digest, Sept. 23, 1996, at 10.

revenues, and cross-sell products and services. For example, both E*Trade and Merrill Edge offer fee-based investment advice and research reports. Also, like full service broker-dealers, many large discount broker-dealers now own, or are affiliated with, banks in order to offer their customers checking and savings accounts, loans, and mortgages.

B. Market Focus

1. Exchange Member Firms

Exchanges provide a market place or facilities for bringing together purchasers and sellers of securities. The two largest exchanges in the US are the New York Stock Exchange ("NYSE") and the NASDAQ Stock Market ("NASDAQ"). Both exchanges are self-regulatory organizations (SROs) registered with the SEC. Registration with the SEC as an SRO means that an exchange must, among other things, ensure that its members comply with applicable securities laws and its own rules. The SEC must approve all SRO rules before they take effect; it also examines SRO practices and, when appropriate, conducts disciplinary actions and imposes sanctions for an SRO's failure to enforce its rules against member broker-dealers.

In order to trade on an exchange, the broker-dealer must be a member of the exchange. Membership requires broker-dealers to agree to follow all rules adopted by the exchange for governing its members.

a. NYSE Member firms

i. Designated Market Makers (formerly specialists)

Designated Market Makers (DMMs), formerly specialists, are member broker-dealers of the NYSE. NYSE member broker-dealers were specialists before the NYSE transitioned from a floor-based, member-owned market, to a primarily electronic, publicly traded exchange. A specialist was an exchange member that held itself out as being willing to buy and sell a particular security for its own account on a regular or continuous basis, i.e., the broker-dealer was a market maker in that particular security. Specialists were assigned specific securities (each security listed on the NYSE was assigned to a single specialist) and remained at a particular location on the exchange floor (a post) during trading hours. This meant that the specialist had extensive

---

NYSE Designated Market Maker Firms

1. Barclays Capital Inc.
2. Brendan E. Cryan and Company, LLC
3. Goldman, Sachs & Company
4. J. Streicher & Co., LLC
5. KCG
6. Virtu Financial Capital Markets, LLC

knowledge about the depth of the market and the effect of market events on its assigned stocks—a considerable advantage. Essentially, a specialist performed three functions: (1) maintaining fair and orderly markets in its assigned securities; (2) conducting market-making activities; and (3) executing orders.

Now, DMMs are responsible for maintaining fair and orderly markets in their assigned NYSE listed securities.[31] DMMs manage a physical auction (just like their specialist predecessors) combined with an automated auction, which includes algorithmic quotes from other DMMs and market participants. Specifically, a DMM must make continuous markets in its assigned securities by matching buyers with sellers, keeping investors informed, committing capital when needed, being accountable for the market in its assigned securities, and ensuring that all customer orders have an equal opportunity to interact and receive the best possible execution. The DMM must, throughout the trading day, make firm and continuous two-sided quotes (bid and ask) that accurately reflect market conditions; generally, the DMM's quotes are disseminated electronically through market-data systems to the public and interact with other quotes and orders, including those on the trading floor. If there is an imbalance between buy and sell orders, the DMM may buy or sell the security for its own account, committing its own capital. The goal is to offset imbalances between supply and demand.

ii. Floor Brokers

Floor brokers are members positioned on the floor of the NYSE at the point of sale during openings, closings, and unique intra-day occurrences to execute trades. Floor brokers do not work exclusively for any DMM and receive orders directly from various sources, including broker-dealers, hedge funds, mutual funds, pension funds, day traders, and even some high-net-worth individuals. Essentially, floor brokers execute agency orders[32] and act as a market information-gathering and delivery service for their customers.

iii. Supplemental Liquidity Providers

Supplemental Liquidity Providers (SLPs) are upstairs (off the exchange floor) NYSE members who provide liquidity[33] in assigned NYSE-listed securities. This category of membership was established to provide additional liquidity and add competition to the NYSE's existing group of liquidity providers, e.g., DMMs and a proprietary trading[34] unit of a member broker-dealer. SLP members electronically enter proprietary orders or quotes from off the exchange floor at the National Best Bid ("NBB")[35] or

---

31. The issuer may select the DMM or may delegate this authority to the NYSE.

32. Orders to buy or sell securities that a broker-dealer executes on behalf of a customer with another broker-dealer or investor.

33. Liquidity refers to how easy it is to buy and sell securities in the stock market, in this case the NYSE.

34. Orders to buy or sell securities that the broker-dealer executes for its own account, not his customer.

35. National best bid means the highest price at which a broker-dealer is willing to purchase a particular security from a customer. See Chapter 14 discussing best execution.

the National Best Offer ("NBO")[36] in each of their assigned securities in round lots averaging at least 10 percent of the trading day;[37] they must add liquidity in their assigned securities by providing average daily volume of more than 10 million shares on a monthly basis. The NYSE pays SLPs a financial rebate when they post liquidity in an assigned security that executes against incoming orders. "The NYSE believes that by requiring an SLP to quote at the NBB or the NBO a percentage of the regular trading day in their [sic] assigned securities, and by paying an SLP a rebate when its posted interest results in an execution, [it] is rewarding aggressive liquidity providers in the market …"[38]

Unlike DMMs, more than one SLP may be assigned to the same security. While all NYSE-listed securities must be assigned to a DMM, not all such securities are required to be assigned to an SLP. In addition, an NYSE member that acts as an SLP is not permitted to act as a DMM on the floor of the NYSE in the same security. However, SLPs have access to the same market data published by the NYSE and all other automated trading centers, as well as trading information published on the Consolidated Tape[39] and on the NYSE Open Book.[40]

An SLP may be a proprietary trading unit (SLP-Prop) or a registered market maker (SLMM).[41] A single NYSE member may elect to be both. However, a single NYSE member may not act as an SLP-Prop and an SLMM in the same security unless it has more than one business unit and employs appropriate information barriers to preclude any coordinated trading between the two units. To qualify as an SLP-Prop, a member firm must have adequate technology to support electronic trading through the NYSE's systems and facilities; use mnemonics that identify its trading activities in its assigned securities to the NYSE; have adequate trading infrastructure to support its trading activity, including support and administrative staff; have quoting and volume performance that demonstrates its ability to meet the 10 percent average quoting requirement and the average daily volume requirement of more than 10 million shares on a monthly basis in each of its assigned securities; have a disciplinary history that is consistent with just and equitable business practices; and have adequate information

---

36. National best offer means the lowest price at which a broker-dealer is willing to sell a security to a customer. See Chapter 14 discussing best execution.

37. Non-displayed liquidity will not be counted as credit toward the 10 percent quoting requirement.

38. Self-Regulatory Orgs., Exchange Act Release No. 34-58877, 94 SEC Docket 1407 (Oct. 29, 2008).

39. The "consolidated tape" is a high-speed, electronic system that reports the latest price and volume data on sales of exchange-listed stocks. The data reflected on the consolidated tape are generated by various market centers, including all securities exchanges, electronic communications networks (ECNs), and third-market broker-dealers.

40. The NYSE Open Book, refreshed every five seconds, is provided by NYSE to vendors and customers and displays the depth of the market in real time. It also discloses limit order interest at the best bid and offer as well as prices below the best bid and above the best offer.

41. Qualifications for SLP-Props are contained in NYSE Rule 107B(c) and qualifications for SLMMs are contained in NYSE Rule 107B(d).

barriers between the SLP-Prop unit and the NYSE member's customer, research, and investment banking business.

SLMMs' qualifications encompass SLP-Prop requirements, as well as additional qualifications and increased regulatory obligations. SLMM qualifications include maintaining a continuous two-sided quotation in its assigned securities that is virtually identical to the DMM two-sided quotation (bid and ask). As market makers, SLMMs are required to assist in the maintenance of fair and orderly markets in their assigned securities insofar as reasonably practicable. Also, SLMMs must maintain a minimum amount of net capital and use specific mnemonics to allow the NYSE to track their market-making activities.

Figure 2.4

SLP-Prop Supplemental Liquidity Firms
1. HRT Financial LLC
2. Latour Trading, LLC
3. Tradebot Systems, Inc.
4. Virtu Financial BD LLC

SLMM Supplemental Liquidity Firms
5. KCG Americas LLC
6. Goldman, Sachs & Company
7. Citadel Securities LLC
8. IMC Chicago LLC

---

iv. Retail Liquidity Providers

Retail Liquidity Providers (RLPs) are NYSE members that place market or limit orders,[42] offering improved prices to orders coming in from retail investors.[43] The NYSE's retail liquidity program is designed to combat the matching of retail and institutional orders directly inside the broker-dealer's internal pools of orders rather than on the NYSE. The goal of the NYSE's retail liquidity program is to bring order flow back to the NYSE and to increase liquidity. Similar to trading conducted in a broker-dealer's own internal pool of capital, RLP trading is conducted on a special platform offering improved prices that are not displayed to the public. Specifically, RLPs must provide prices that match or improve upon levels in the public markets and are allowed to use sub-penny pricing. For example, if a lawyer trading stocks

---

42. A limit order is an order to buy or sell a stock at a specific price or better. A buy limit order can only be executed at the limit price or lower. A sell limit order may only be executed at the limit price or higher.

43. A retail order is an agency order that originated from a natural person and not a trading algorithm or any other computerized methodology. Self-Regulatory Orgs., Exchange Act Release No. 34-67347, 104 SEC Docket 116 (July 3, 2012).

from her home office wanted to sell shares of Twitter, Inc., at the bid price of $ 25.00 a share, a tenth-of-a-cent improvement on the NYSE would see her order filled for $25.10, instead of $25.00. RLPs must be approved as DMMs or SLPs and must have mnemonics or the ability to accommodate an NYSE-supplied designation that identifies their trading activity in their assigned securities. Finally, RLPs are permitted to enter retail price improvement orders only in their assigned securities and must maintain retail price improvement orders that are better than the NYSE's best bid or offer at least five percent of the trading day in each of their assigned securities.

Also, RLPs may elect to be Retail Member Organizations (RMO). An RMO conducts a retail business or handles retail orders on behalf of non-NYSE member broker-dealers. RMOs must be DMMs or SLPs and attest to the NYSE that all order flow qualifies as retail orders. An RMO must include in its application an attestation that the order flow qualifies as retail orders.

b. NASDAQ Member Firms

i. NASDAQ Market Makers

NASDAQ Market Makers ("NMM")[44] are broker-dealers who are members of the NASDAQ Stock Market ("NASDAQ") that buy and sell securities at prices that they display in NASDAQ for their own account (principal trades) and for customer accounts (agency trades).[45] NMMs actively compete for investor orders by displaying quotations (bid and ask) and customer limit orders in securities they quote in NASDAQ. NMM trading activities include entering, retrieving, monitoring, and adjusting quotations in response to changing market conditions (all quotations must be firm and automatically executable for their displayed and non-displayed size in NASDAQ);[46] entering and executing orders in NASDAQ; comparing and clearing trades through automated services; and registering the number of securities approved by the broker-dealer's local FINRA District Office.[47] Requirements to become, and obligations of, NMMs include:

> [F]or each security ... be willing to buy and sell the security for its own account on a continuous basis during regular market hours and ... enter and maintain a two-sided trading interest (Two-Sided Obligation) that is identified to NAS-DAQ as the interest meeting the obligation and is displayed in NASDAQ's quotation montage at all times. Interest eligible to be considered as part of a[n NNM'S] Two-Sided Obligation shall have a displayed quotation size of at least one normal unit of trading ... a "normal unit of trading" shall be 100 shares. After an execution against its Two-Sided Obligation, a[n NMM] must

---

44. NASDAQ Market Participant qualification requirements are contained in NASDAQ Rule 4611.

45. NASDAQ Electronic Communication Network (ECNs) and order entry firms may also act as market makers. NASDAQ Rule 4613(b)(1).

46. NASDAQ Rule 4613(b).

47. *See How to Become a Market Maker*, NASDAQ, http://www.nasdaqtrader.com/Trader.aspx?id =MarketMakerProcess.

ensure that additional trading interest exists in NASDAQ to satisfy its Two-Sided Obligation either by immediately entering new interest to comply with this obligation to maintain continuous two-sided quotations or by identifying existing interest on the NASDAQ book that will satisfy this obligation.[48]

Although NMMs conduct activities similar to market makers on the NYSE, there are several important distinctions. NMMs, unlike market makers on the NYSE, choose the securities in which they will make a market. Also, NMMs are not located at a post on an exchange floor; they can be anywhere in the world as long as they have a computer and an Internet connection. Most important, NMMs are not charged with the responsibility of maintaining fair and orderly markets in the securities in which they choose to make a market. NASDAQ Rule 4613 simply requires them to engage in a course of dealings for their own account to assist in the maintenance, insofar as reasonably practicable, of fair and orderly markets.

ii. NASDAQ Order Entry Firm

Another type of NASDAQ member broker-dealer is the NASDAQ Order Entry Firm (NOE). The primary difference between NOEs and NNMs is that NNMs commit capital, while NOEs do not. Specifically, NOEs enter customer orders into NASDAQ for execution against displayed orders and quotations. NOEs increase liquidity by bringing additional orders into the NASDAQ System.

iii. Market Quality Program Market Maker (MQP MM)

Market Quality Program Market Makers (MQP MMs) are participants in NASDAQ's Market Quality Program (MQP), a proprietary market structure initiated by NASDAQ in a pilot program that began in the second quarter of 2013. MQP is an optional listing program that allows certain exchange traded fund (ETF)[49] issuers to contribute funds to NASDAQ that may be used to pay market makers that improve the liquidity and quality of the markets in such ETFs. According to NASDAQ, the program is needed because

> ... one of the unintended consequences of market fragmentation in the current U.S. Securities markets has been a lack of liquidity and price discovery in listed securities outside of the top 100 traded names, and a disturbing absence of market attention paid to small growth companies by market participants. [NASDAQ] believes that the MQP proposal offers a practical and positive solution.[50]

---

48. Self-Regulatory Orgs., Exchange Act Release No. 34-69195, 2013 WL 1154358 (Mar. 20, 2013).

49. ETFs are a type of exchange-traded investment fund that must register with the SEC. Like mutual funds, ETFs allow investors to pool their money in a fund that invests in stocks, bonds, or other assets and to receive an interest in the pool. Unlike mutual funds, ETFs are traded on a national stock exchange at market prices that may not be the same as the net asset value of its shares, i.e., the value of the ETF's assets minus its liabilities divided by the number of shares outstanding.

50. *How Roadblocks in Public Markets Prevent Job Creation on Main Street: Hearing Before the Subcomm. on TARP, Fin. Servs. & Bailouts of Pub. & Private Programs of the H. Comm. on Oversight & Gov't Reform*, 112th Cong. 8 (2011) (statement of Eric Noll, Exec. Vice President, NASDAQ OMX Group). *See also* NASDAQ Rule 5950.

In MQP, an ETF issuer/sponsor pays NASDAQ an annual MQP fee of $50,000 to $100,000 per ETF, in addition to the NASDAQ standard listing fees, and chooses which funds will be in the MQP. On a quarterly basis, NASDAQ will make MQP payments only to those MQP MMs that meet liquidity and market quality standards. In addition to MQP eligibility standards shown in figure B, All MQP MMs must be registered first as NMMs.

Figure 2.5. MQP Mechanics

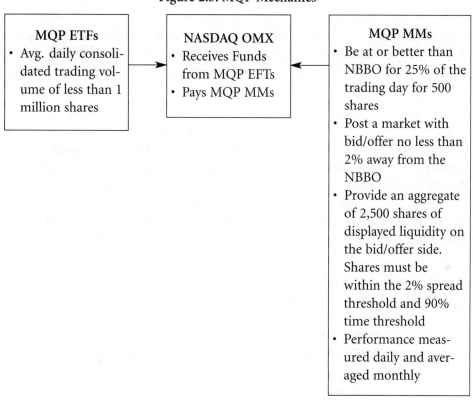

MQP ETFs
- Avg. daily consolidated trading volume of less than 1 million shares

NASDAQ OMX
- Receives Funds from MQP EFTs
- Pays MQP MMs

MQP MMs
- Be at or better than NBBO for 25% of the trading day for 500 shares
- Post a market with bid/offer no less than 2% away from the NBBO
- Provide an aggregate of 2,500 shares of displayed liquidity on the bid/offer side. Shares must be within the 2% spread threshold and 90% time threshold
- Performance measured daily and averaged monthly

2. Security-Based Swap Dealer and Major Security-Based Swap Participants

Security-based swap dealers and major security-based swap participants are categories of securities dealers, created by The Dodd-Frank Act, that are required to register with the SEC.[51] A security-based swap dealer is any person that: (1) holds themselves out as a dealer in security-based swaps, (2) makes a market in security-based swaps, and (3) regularly enters into security-based swaps with others as an or-

---

51. The Dodd-Frank Act also established swap dealers and major swap participants that are subject to CFTC regulation under the Commodity Exchange Act (CEA). The CFTC and its authority under the CEA, along with the registration requirements and regulatory framework for security-based swap dealers and security-based major swap participants are beyond the scope of this textbook.

dinary course of business for their own account, or (4) is commonly known in the trade as a dealer or market maker in security-based swaps.[52]

A major security-based swap participant includes any person who satisfies one of three tests enumerated in Rule 3a67-1 of the Exchange Act.[53] A major security-based swap participant is any person who is not a security-based swap dealer and (1) maintains a substantial position[54] in any of the major categories of security-based swaps, (2) whose outstanding security-based swaps create substantial counterparty exposure that could have serious adverse effects on the financial stability of the U.S. banking system or financial markets, or (3) is a financial entity that: (i) is highly leveraged relative to the amount of capital such entity holds and that is not subject to capital requirements established by an appropriate federal banking agency; and (ii) maintains a substantial position in outstanding security-based swaps in any major category.

A security-based swap is defined in Section 761(a) of the Dodd-Frank Act, which added new Section 3(a)(68) to the Exchange Act. A security-based swap is any agreement, contract, or transaction that is a swap[55] and that is based on a narrow-based security index, or a single security or loan, or any interest therein or on the value thereof, or the occurrence or non-occurrence of an event relating to a single issuer of a security or the issuers of securities in a narrow-based security index, provided that such event directly affects the financial statements, financial condition, or financial obligations of the issuer.[56]

3. *Municipal Securities Broker-Dealers*

Municipal securities broker-dealers are engaged in the business of effecting transactions in municipal securities. Municipal securities dealers are engaged in the business of buying and selling municipal securities for their own account. Municipal securities brokers engage in the business of effecting transactions in municipal securities for

---

52. 15 U.S.C. § 78c(a)(71) (2015).

53. Exchange Act Rule 3a67-1, 17 C.F.R. § 240.3a67-1 (2015).

54. The term *substantial position* is defined in Exchange Act Rule 3a67-3, 17 C.F.R. § 240.3a67-3 (2015).

55. The term *swap* is defined in Section 1(a)(47) of the Commodity Exchange Act (CEA) and is quite detailed and comprehensive, though certain agreements, contracts, and transactions are excluded from the definition. It includes, for example, interest rate swaps, commodity swaps, currency swaps, equity swaps, and credit default swaps. Congress directed both the Commission and the Securities and Exchange Commission to further define the term *swap* (and *security-based swap*) jointly. The SEC and the CFTC in 2012 adopted rules and interpretations to clarify that a few types of transactions in particular are swaps. These include foreign currency options, commodity options, non-deliverable forwards in foreign exchange, cross-currency swaps, forward rate agreements, contracts for differences, options to enter into swaps, and forward swaps. *See* 7 U.S.C. § 1a(47)(2015) and 17 C.F.R. § 1.3 (2016).

56. A discussion of the mechanics of security-based swaps is beyond the scope of this textbook. However, a thorough discussion of the types of instruments that qualify as security-based swaps is contained in SEC Exchange Act Release No. 34-67453, *Further Definition of "Swap," "Security-Based Swap," and "Security-Based Swap Agreement"; Mixed Swaps; Security-Based Swap Agreement Recordkeeping*, Exchange Act Release No. 34-67453, 104 SEC Docket 430 (July 18, 2012).

the account of others. Both are regulated by the SEC and the Municipal Securities Rulemaking Board (MSRB), a self-regulatory organization registered with the SEC. The MSRB's mission is to promote a fair and efficient municipal securities market by adopting rules for municipal dealers and municipal advisors and by collecting and disseminating market information about municipal securities; as an SRO, all MSRB activities, including rulemaking, are subject to approval by the SEC.[57]

A municipal security is a security that is the direct obligation of, or is guaranteed by, a state or any political subdivision or instrumentality of a state. Generally, municipal bonds are used to finance capital projects and maturity dates typically range from one to 30 years. Interest rates may be fixed or variable. Types of municipal securities include general obligation and revenue bonds. General obligation bonds are payable from the general funds of the state or local government, typically, taxes or appropriations made by the state legislature. Revenue bonds are payable from a specific source of revenue; the issuer of revenue bonds is not permitted to pay principal and interest on its bonds from any source other than the source specifically pledged to the bond.[58]

C. Functional Focus

Broker-dealers may be described by the various functions they perform. This section provides a general overview of some of the more common functions performed by broker-dealers, but by no means is exhaustive.

1. Clearing Broker-Dealers[59]

Despite its name, a clearing broker-dealer performs clearing and settlement functions for other broker-dealers. The clearing function requires a comparison of trade order details of the seller with those of the buyer to make sure that there is a common understanding of the terms of the trade. The resulting compared trade is cleared by essentially advising the seller and the buyer of their delivery and payment obligations. Settlement occurs with the actual delivery of securities to the buyer and the payment of money to the seller. The increasing use of technology in the securities industry has led to clearing and settlement being essentially bookkeeping entries rather than the physical movement of money and securities certificates.

Clearing broker-dealers are necessary because of the volume of trades and the high-cost of clearing and settling trades. Without the ability to outsource the clearing and settling functions (a back-office activity)[60] to clearing broker-dealers, many smaller

---

57. For more information about the MSRB, see *Creation of the MSRB*, MSRB, http://www.msrb.org/About-MSRB/About-the-MSRB/Creation-of-the-MSRB.aspx.

58. Generally, the interest on municipal securities is exempt from federal income tax and may also be exempt from state and local taxes in the state where the municipal security was issued.

59. See Chapter 14 for a discussion of the regulatory framework governing the national clearing and settlement system for equity securities in U.S. securities markets.

60. See Section IV.C. of this chapter for more information about the clearing and settlement functions.

broker-dealers could not afford to enter the securities business. Only a few broker-dealers in the United States clear and settle for themselves or clear and settle for other broker-dealers. Broker-dealers using the services of another broker-dealer to clear and settle have entered into a correspondent relationship. The parties to this relationship are identified by various names. For example, the clearing broker-dealer is sometimes called a correspondent clearer, while the other side of this relationship may be called a correspondent firm. Despite the nomenclature, the correspondent relationship between two broker-dealers means that one broker-dealer clears and settles trades entered into by another broker-dealer on behalf of itself or its clients. The duties of clearing broker-dealers vary greatly and are determined solely by contract within regulatory constraints.[61] Some broker-dealers may decide to use a clearing broker-dealer for all of their back office needs. Others may maintain some activities in-house, such as trade execution and use the clearing broker-dealer for all other back office functions.

Clearing broker-dealers are generally members of a clearing agency, which are SROs registered with the SEC. The National Securities Clearing Corporation is the largest U.S. clearing agency.[62] Among other services, it provides clearing and settlement and a guarantee of completion for all trades involving equities, corporate and municipal debt, money market instruments, ADRs,[63] ETFs, unit investment trusts, mutual funds, insurance products, and other securities. The NYSE and NASDAQ require members to clear and settle through a clearing agency registered with the SEC; however, members may determine not to use a registered clearing agency if both parties to the transaction agree.[64]

2. Prime Brokers

Prime broker arrangements were designed to speed settlement of securities trades for large retail and institutional customers who trade actively by providing financing and clearing for the customer's securities transactions wherever they are executed.

---

61. The SEC and SROs have specific rules regarding clearing and settlement activities. Indeed, the SEC has brought several enforcement cases against clearing firms for failure to meet their clearing obligations, including timeliness.

62. NSCC is a subsidiary of the Depository Trust & Clearing Corporation ("DTCC"), which is the largest entity in the world providing clearing, settlement, and depository services to global capital markets, including the United States. *See National Securities Clearing Corporation (NSCC)*, DTCC, http://www.dtcc.com/about/businesses-and-subsidiaries/nscc.aspx.

63. ADRs or American Depository Receipts are used to trade the stocks of most foreign companies that trade in the U.S. markets. U.S. depositary banks issue these ADRs. Each ADR represents one or more shares of foreign stock or a fraction of a share. An ADR gives the investor the right to obtain the foreign stock it represents, but U.S. investors usually find it more convenient to own the ADR. The price of an ADR corresponds to the price of the foreign stock in its home market, adjusted to the ratio of the ADRs to foreign company shares.

64. *See* NYSE Rule 132 and NASDAQ Rule 4618.

Generally, the prime brokerage arrangement consists of three parties: (1) the prime broker, (2) the executing broker, and (3) the customer. The prime broker is a registered broker-dealer that clears and finances customer trades executed by one or more other registered broker-dealers on behalf of the customer. The executing broker is a registered broker-dealer that executes customer trades (in the name of the prime broker) and forwards such customer-originated trades to the prime broker for clearance and settlement. Each of the customer's executing broker-dealers receives a letter from the prime broker agreeing to clear and carry each trade placed by the customer with the executing broker where the customer directs delivery of money or securities to be made to, or by, the prime broker. The customer, an actively trading institutional investor, maintains its account with the prime broker; orders placed with the executing broker at the behest of the customer are executed through an account with the executing broker in the name of the prime broker for the benefit of the customer.

The prime broker arrangement is advantageous to the customer because the prime broker serves as a clearing facility and accountant for all the customer's trades, wherever executed, and acts as a central custodian for all the customer's securities and funds. For example, the customer receives one account statement detailing its trading activity instead of several account statements from each executing broker-dealer. Additional services provided by prime brokerage arrangements may include capital introductions, securities lending, leveraged trade execution, cash management, margin arrangements, batch reporting, data feeds, phones, and even office space.

Prime brokerage arrangements grew significantly alongside the growth of hedge funds. Hedge funds and prime brokerage arrangements are inextricably related because trading strategies used by hedge funds require the services provided by prime brokerage arrangements. For example, hedge funds typically use more than one broker-dealer to execute trades and trading strategies. Prime brokerage arrangements allow all trades executed by different broker-dealers to be cleared and settled in one account. In addition, hedge funds typically engage in margin trading, which requires lending arrangements for securities and cash.

Contracts govern the relationship between the parties in prime brokerage arrangements, i.e., the relationship between the prime broker, the executing broker, and the customer. There is a contract between the prime broker and the executing broker enumerating their respective obligations and responsibilities. There are also contracts between the customer and the prime broker, and the customer and the executing broker, in which the customer confirms the different responsibilities undertaken by the prime broker and the executing broker. Figure 2.6 summarizes the prime brokerage arrangement.

Figure 2.6

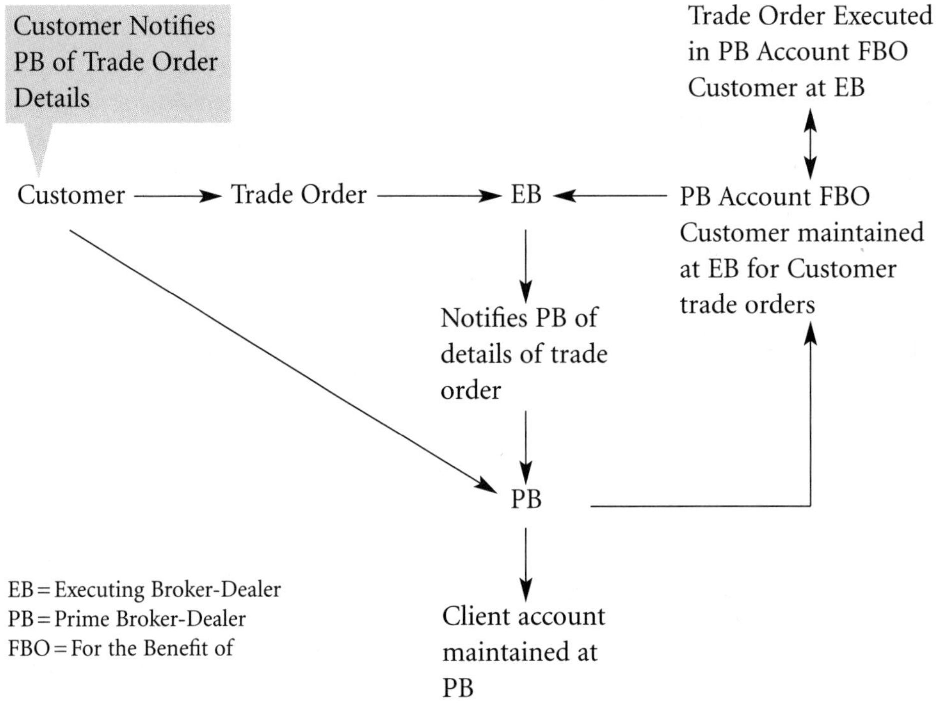

Customer Notifies
PB of Trade Order
Details

Trade Order Executed
in PB Account FBO
Customer at EB

Customer ——→ Trade Order ——→ EB ←—— PB Account FBO
Customer maintained
at EB for Customer
trade orders

Notifies PB of
details of trade
order

PB

Client account
maintained at
PB

EB = Executing Broker-Dealer
PB = Prime Broker-Dealer
FBO = For the Benefit of

3. Primary Dealers

Primary dealers are broker-dealers that trade in the U.S. government securities market.[65] The U.S. government securities market consists of securities issued or guaranteed by the U.S. government, including bonds, bills (T-bills) and notes (T-notes). The primary dealer system was established by the Federal Reserve Bank of New York (NY Fed) in 1960, and currently consists of 21 primary dealers.[66] Primary dealers trade in U.S. government securities directly with the NY Fed. The NY Fed, in turn, trades on behalf of the Federal Reserve System in order to implement U.S. monetary policy, i.e., the buying and selling of U.S. government securities in the secondary

---

65. U.S. chartered banks (commercial banks, thrifts, National banks, or state banks) that are subject to official supervision by bank supervisors may also act as primary dealers. In addition to primary dealers, there are secondary dealers in government securities that market new issues and act as market makers in government securities. As with primary dealers, some secondary dealers may be commercial banks and broker-dealers. SECURITIES PRIMARY LAW SOURCEBOOK, Volume A, Section C, Matthew Bender & Company, Inc. (2015).

66. Broker-dealers acting as primary dealers include BMO Capital Markets Corp.; BNP Paribas Securities Corp.; Barclays Capital Inc.; Cantor Fitzgerald & Co.; Citigroup Global Markets Inc.; Credit Suisse Securities (USA) LLC; Daiwa Capital Markets America Inc.; Deutsche Bank Securities Inc.; Goldman, Sachs & Co.; HSBC Securities (USA) Inc.; Jefferies LLC; J.P. Morgan Securities LLC; Merrill Lynch, Pierce, Fenner & Smith Incorporated; Mizuho Securities USA Inc.; Morgan Stanley & Co. LLC; Normura Securities International, Inc.; RBC Capital Markets, LLC; RBS Securities Inc.; Societe Generale, New York Branch; TD Securities (USA) LLC, and UBS Securities LLC.

market to influence money and credit conditions in the economy. Essentially, primary dealers serve as trading counterparties of the NY Fed and are the core group of underwriters for U.S. government securities. Specifically, primary dealer obligations include: (1) participating consistently in open market operations in accordance with the direction of the Federal Open Market Committee (FOMC);[67] (2) providing market information and analysis to the NY Fed's trading desk to assist in the formulation and implementation of monetary policy; (3) participating in all auctions of U.S. government securities; and (4) making reasonable markets for the NY Fed when it transacts on behalf of its foreign official account-holders.

Foreign-owned broker-dealers may not be newly designated, or continue, as primary dealers if the NY Fed and the Board of Governors concludes that the country in which a foreign parent is domiciled does not provide the same competitive opportunities to U.S. companies as it does to domestic firms in the underwriting and distribution of government debt. Currently, only foreign-owned broker-dealers in France, Germany, Japan, the Netherlands, Switzerland, the United Kingdom, Canada, and Israel may be primary dealers.[68]

4. Introducing Broker-Dealers

An introducing broker-dealer is a firm that has determined to enter into a business relationship with another broker-dealer (generally much larger than the introducing broker-dealer) to perform certain functions in connection with trading for itself and its customers. This business relationship is memorialized in a contract generally identified as a clearing agreement. The two parties to such clearing agreements are identified as the introducing broker-dealer and the carrying or clearing broker-dealer. There are two major categories of clearing agreements: (1) fully disclosed and (2) omnibus clearing agreements. In fully disclosed carrying agreements, the introducing broker-dealer discloses to the carrying broker-dealer the names, addresses, securities positions, and other relevant data about its customers. In an omnibus clearing agreement, the introducing broker-dealer maintains a single account in its own name with the carrying broker-dealer and does not disclose identifying information about its individual customers. However, under the omnibus clearing agreement, the introducing broker-dealer must provide the carrying broker-dealer with notice that all securities transactions executed in the omnibus account will be for its customers' accounts only.[69] Under both types of clearing agreements, the cus-

---

67. The FOMC sets monetary policy for the Federal Reserve System and decides whether the Federal Reserve will join the Treasury Department in foreign exchange (FX) intervention. There are 12 voting members of the FOMC: the seven members of the Board of Governors and the presidents of five of the 12 Federal Reserve Banks. The president of the NY Fed is a permanent voting member in light of its unique activities in implementing monetary policy. The presidents of the other Federal Reserve Banks rotate, serving one-year terms. By tradition, the chairman of the Board of Governors serves as chairman of the FOMC.

68. *See* Primary Dealers Act of 1988, 22 U.S.C. §§ 5341-5342 (2012).

69. Customers that might be partners of the introducing broker-dealer are excluded.

tomers' trades are cleared through the carrying broker-dealer and the customers of the introducing broker-dealer deal only with the introducing broker-dealer, not the clearing broker-dealer.

The business relationship represented by the clearing agreement is beneficial for both parties. The carrying broker-dealer receives an income stream from the introducing broker-dealer based on the services provided. These services vary but allow the introducing broker-dealer to avoid substantial start-up and maintenance costs associated with middle- and back-office operations. For example, the introducing broker-dealer may only take its customers' orders and then submit them to the carrying broker-dealer for execution, who then completes other required activities (e.g., reporting, clearing, and settlement). In addition, by entering into a clearing agreement with the carrying broker-dealer, the introducing broker-dealer avoids significant technology costs required to generate confirmations, stock records, back-office records, as well as the personnel to perform other back-office activities. Also, such agreements are beneficial to the introducing broker-dealer because it reduces the minimum net capital required under SEC rules; generally, the greater the middle and back-office activities performed by a broker-dealer, the greater the level of net capital required.[70]

Even though clearing agreements memorialize business relationships, the allocation of regulatory responsibilities within clearing agreements is regulated by SROs, of which both the introducing broker-dealer and the carrying broker-dealer must be members. FINRA Rule 4311 governs carrying agreements between its member broker-dealers to ensure compliance with financial responsibility and customer protection rules and regulations of FINRA and the SEC.[71] FINRA Rule 4311 prohibits carrying agreements between its member broker-dealers and non-member broker-dealers, unless specifically approved by FINRA.[72] It also requires an introducing broker-dealer acting as an intermediary broker-dealer for another introducing broker-dealer (a so-called piggyback or intermediary clearing arrangement) to notify the carrying broker-dealer of the existence of intermediary broker-dealer arrangements and to disclose the identity of the broker-dealer for whom it is performing this service. Essentially, the carrying agreement must identify and bind every direct and indirect recipient of clearing services as a party to the clearing agreement.[73] FINRA must pre-approve any clearing agreement used by member broker-dealers, as well as any material change in an existing clearing agreement. Also, the clearing broker-dealer must notify FINRA of any clearing agreement 10 business days prior to performing any activities under

---

70. *See* Exchange Act Rule 15c3-1(a)(2)(i), 17 C.F.R. § 240.15c3-1(a)(2)(i) (2014). See also Chapter 9 for more information about the net capital rule.

71. FINRA Rule 4311(c) allocates specific regulatory activities that must be performed by the clearing broker-dealer.

72. Unless otherwise permitted by FINRA under FINRA Rule 4311(a)(1). For non-U.S. registered broker-dealers, see FINRA Rule 4311(a)(2).

73. *See Regulatory Notice 11-26: SEC Approves Consolidated Financial Responsibility and Related Operational Rules*, FINRA 3-6 (Aug. 1, 2011), https://www.finra.org/web/groups/industry/ip/reg/notice/documents/notices/p123733.pdf.

the clearing agreement.[74] The clearing broker-dealer must conduct appropriate due diligence before entering into a clearing agreement with any new introducing broker-dealer; effective due diligence must include an assessment of the financial, operational, credit, and reputational risk of the clearing agreement on the clearing broker-dealer.[75]

D. Insurance-Affiliated Broker-Dealers

Insurance-affiliated broker-dealers are unique in their structure, operation, products, and services. Securities activities of such broker-dealers are a component of a life insurance business; therefore, most employees of such entities are both insurance agents and registered representatives. Moreover, many of the registered representatives operate principally as insurance agents. As a result, many registered representatives of insurance-affiliated broker-dealers are often present in numerous small, geographically dispersed offices, which is significantly different from broker-dealers engaged in a full-scale securities business. This means that securities activities in which such employees engage are often conducted through the vehicle of an insurance distribution system.

Securities products offered by insurance-affiliated broker-dealers are generally focused on the distribution of mutual funds and variable insurance contracts (e.g., annuities). Sales of individual stocks and bonds by such broker-dealers frequently constitute an incidental amount of business relative to the sale of insurance products. Mutual funds can only be sold by insurance agents who are also registered representatives of broker-dealers and the mutual funds sold by such registered representatives are generally non-proprietary; once the customer makes her initial purchase of mutual fund shares from the registered representative, the primary relationship is between the customer and the mutual fund, not the insurance-affiliated broker-dealer; it is the mutual fund, not the broker-dealer, that knows the customer and sends account statements directly to the customer.

A variable annuity is a type of insurance contract that is deemed to be a security under the federal securities laws. Variable annuities are contracts in which premiums paid by an annuitant to an issuer are invested primarily in common stock and other equities; however, the periodic benefit payments guaranteed by the issuer to the annuitant when the annuitant reaches a certain age are based primarily on the success or failure of the issuer's investment policy. The annuitant may receive a lot, a little, or nothing at all; thus there is no guarantee of benefits to the annuitant.[76] Such characteristics are the same as the risk incurred by investors purchasing individual stocks and bonds. As a result, variable annuities must be registered under the Securities Act and can only be sold by registered representatives of broker-dealers.

---

74. FINRA Rule 4311(b)(3).
75. FINRA Rule 4311(b)(4).
76. *See SEC v. Variable Annuity Life Ins. Co. of America*, 359 U.S. 65, 69-73 (1959).

Hypothetical Two

Carmen wants to make sure that her interns understand how the broker-dealer industry operates. To test her interns, she has provided a list of five broker-dealers (provided below) and has asked them to categorize (e.g., whether it is full service or discount, market focused or functionally focused, insurance affiliated) and identify the business model(s) (wire house or independent broker-dealer) of the broker-dealers. Each intern must present his or her findings during the weekly seminar because Carmen believes that presentation skills, along with knowledge of the broker-dealer industry, are essential to success. Carmen also believes in conciseness. Therefore, each presentation is restricted to two minutes. Despite the short time frame, Carmen expects the interns to identify the characteristics and activities upon which their determinations are based.

1. LPL Financial Holdings, Inc.

2. Morgan Stanley

3. Loop Capital Markets, LLC

4. Commonwealth Financial Network

5. Securities Service Network, Inc.

IV. Functional Organization of a Broker-Dealer[77]

Figure 2.7

Front Office	Middle Office	Back Office
• Sales	• Customer (Investment) Accounting	• Purchase & Sale
• Trading	• Trade Processing Management	• Cashier
• Portfolio Management	• Compliance	• Corporate Action (Reorganization)
	• Risk Management	• Position Management
	• Client Services	• Margin
		• New Accounts
		• Accounting

A broker-dealer's operational infrastructure is very complex and, generally, highly automated. For purposes of illustration and ease of understanding, this chapter provides a high-level review of the typical functional component parts of a broker-dealer as though it were not connected to a financial conglomerate — that is, as if the bro-

---

77. The author realizes that the terms *front office*, *middle office*, and *back office* cannot be defined with precision because there is no accepted source that defines these terms in everyday usage. Therefore, in practical settings, verification of the meanings of these terms may be required.

ker-dealer were operating as a stand-alone organization. Although this discussion centers on a conceptual separation of broker-dealer operational infrastructure into the front, middle, and back offices, there is no bright-line delineation between the activities conducted among them.

A. Front Office

Figure 2.8

Front Office
- Sales
- Trading
- Portfolio Management

The front office is composed of revenue-producing departments whose primary goal is to sell the broker-dealer's services and products to its customers. In essence, the primary objective of front office activities is to recommend securities and to process orders. Accordingly, front office employees interact and manage the relationships with the broker-dealer's customers by taking orders and executing trades. The salesperson or trader enters customer orders and tracks the progress of each order as it is executed.[78] Front-office activities may be divided into two business categories: institutional and retail. The front office of a broker-dealer with institutional customers consists of salespeople, traders, portfolio managers, and researchers. Salespeople and traders service the broker-dealer's customers based on information obtained, from among other sources, the documents generated when the client opens her account with the broker-dealer.[79] They also record information about their contacts with their customers, including information provided by customers about their investment objectives, as well as recommendations made to each customer. However, each broker-dealer may organize its front office differently. In *Harding v. Wachovia Capital Markets LLC*, 2012 U.S. Dist. LEXIS 141827, pp. 2–3, the court described the broker-dealer's front office activities as follows:

> The front office employees are divided between the sales desk and the trading desk. The sales desk is responsible for marketing Wachovia products and originating and completing sales, both to internal Wachovia financial advisors

---

78. This information is contained in a trade blotter, which reports the trader's current position in every security she trades and on the trader's overall profit and loss. A blotter is a workflow tool that permits a trader to see the orders pending execution and to manage those orders through the execution process. Blotters are usually formatted spreadsheets with rows corresponding to individual orders and columns representing the components of the order. A blotter is a workflow representation of the current status of all the orders that a trader is supposed to work in the market at any instant.

79. See, Section IV.C.6 of this chapter for more information about the account opening process.

and to external investors and clients. The trading desk is responsible for trading securities, executing trades, and conducting risk management.... The compensation of front office sales and trading desk employees is significantly more than the compensation of the middle office operations employees.

The front office for institutional customers requires market information to provide appropriate services and products to the broker-dealer's institutional customers. Market information is required to make decisions regarding trades, including initiating a trade, and must be provided in real-time. Market information generally includes: current prices of securities in the marketplace; price history on selected securities (e.g., highs and lows); current news that may affect the clients' positions; recommendations made by the broker-dealer's research department based on the broker-dealer's internal research; as well as information obtained from market data vendors.

The broker-dealer's research and analytics[80] applications are also used to provide services and products to its institutional customers. Research and analytics are used to develop recommendations, rebalance portfolios, and identify risks for institutional customers. Such applications also may be used to perform a sensitivity analysis on customer portfolios to determine, for example, how a change in interest rates might affect a customer's portfolio and whether other strategies should be considered.

The front office for retail clients generally consists of registered representatives and their assistants and is supported by the research department, market information systems, portfolio managers (if any) and performance measurement (if any). Unlike institutional salespeople, registered representatives have direct, continuous contact with the broker-dealer's customers. Information gathered from customers allows the registered representatives to recommend suitable services and products to their customers. The registered representative, along with her sales assistant, must record information about her contacts with customers, including information provided by customers about their investment objectives, as well as recommendations of broker-dealer products and services to customers. The registered representative also relies on market information and reports from the broker-dealer's research department to make suitable recommendations to customers. The registered representative and her assistant are also responsible for entering manual orders and tracking the progress of each order as it is executed for each customer; computer systems supporting this activity provide real-time trade reporting on the current position in every security traded and the overall profit and loss.

---

80. Portfolio Analytics refers to the quantification of any portfolio using performance attribution, portfolio profiling, and global risk analysis. This enables clients to deconstruct a portfolio's sources of return. Portfolio Analytics systems measure financial metrics of currencies, economies, and industry sectors as well as fundamental factors such as size, growth, and P/E ratio. Risk components allow analysis and attribution of risk attributable to holding. *Portfolio Analytics*, DEFINE FINANCE, http://www.definefinance.com/portfolio-analytics.

Figure 2.9

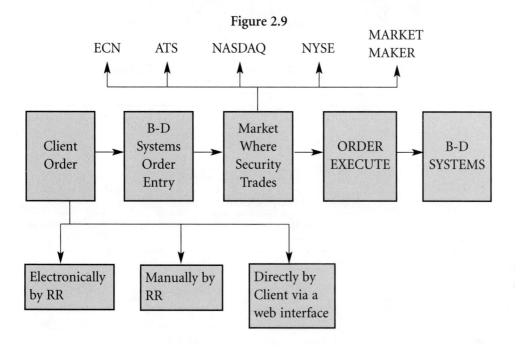

The broker-dealer's research personnel and portfolio managers use research and analytics computer applications to develop recommendations for asset allocation and to identify risk in customer portfolios. These computer applications allow researchers and portfolio managers to evaluate investment alternatives for the broker-dealer's customers. Generally, registered representatives with discretionary authority to trade on behalf of their clients do not have access to a portfolio management computer application, but do manage purchases and sales of securities for their customers.

However, in both the retail and institutional business, the trader is generally the person responsible for routing and executing orders. The primary goal of the trader is to obtain best execution. She does this by monitoring markets and market data. To obtain best execution, the trader must determine which trading venue or venues (NYSE, NASDAQ, etc.) should be selected to route the order, what order types should be employed, what portions of the total order should be exposed to the market and when, and what additional actions should be taken to ensure the order complies with best execution requirements.[81] See Figure 2.9.

---

81. *See* FINRA Rule 5310 and Chapter 14 of this textbook for a discussion of best execution requirements.

Table 2.1 Order Types

Order Type	Description
Buy Order	Order authorizing the purchase of a specific amount of securities.
Sell Order	Order authorizing the sale of a specific amount of securities.
Short Sell	Security is sold by a customer who does not currently own the security being sold.
Market Order	Order to buy or sell a security immediately at the best price available at the time the order is executed.
Day Orders	Order expires at the close of the exchange's trading day if it is not executed on the day the trade is entered.
Good 'til Canceled (GTC)	Open order that remains in force until it is executed or canceled by the customer.
Limit Order	Order where the customer sets her acceptable maximum buying price for a security or her acceptable minimum selling price for a security.
Stop Order (or Stop Limit Order)	Order to buy or sell a security that becomes effective as soon as a security reaches a certain price.
AON—All or Nothing	Instruction to fill all of the order or none of it.
FOK—Fill or Kill	Order specifying that the entire order must be filled immediately and if the entire order cannot be filled it is canceled.
IOC—Immediate or Cancel	Order instruction requiring the broker-dealer to immediately fill as much of the order as possible, and cancel the rest of the order.
NH—Not Held	Indicates that the broker or trader has discretion over the time and price and can take whatever time is needed to get a good execution.

Depending on the products and services offered by the broker-dealer, the front office may also include trading, investment banking, mergers and acquisitions, and research departments. The trading department handles all of the products that the broker-dealer trades for its own accounts. The investment banking department is responsible for assisting companies and municipalities in securing funding from various sources for a multitude of needs; this includes short-term borrowing needs and underwriting. The mergers and acquisitions department assists clients in locating and effecting consolidations of companies or divesting parts of an existing company. The research department analyzes companies, industries, the economy (fundamental research), and the market and stock movement patterns to discern correlations and trends (technical research) in order to maximize returns for the broker-dealer and its customers.

B. Middle Office

Figure 2.10

Middle Office
- Customer (Investment) Accounting
- Trade Processing Management
- Compliance
- Risk Management
- Client Services

The middle office acts as a liaison between the front office and back office. The middle office developed in the late 1960s and early 1970s to link front office and back office technology. Increased trading volume in the late 1960s overwhelmed the manual trading systems of broker-dealers resulting in a back-office crisis.[82] Many broker-dealers went bankrupt and others were forced into mergers with larger firms because they were unable to handle (clear and settle) a substantial increase in trading volumes. Broker-dealers began automating their back offices, one department after another, with available technology in order to handle this increased transaction volume. Eventually the back-office departments were electronically linked, but much of the original computer code used to automate back-office departments remain, even today. As the use of technology increased in the securities industry, broker-dealers also began to automate front-office functions; however, this automation of the front office occurred with current technology, while back-office technology was not comprehensively updated. Accordingly, as the use of technology increased and technology advanced, broker-dealers were forced to develop the middle office to link new front-office technology with back-office legacy systems. As a result, broker-dealer technology infrastructure in many instances contains outdated technology. In fact, outdated applications running on modern hardware continue to be a significant problem for the markets and create many of the challenges that result in slower change and seemingly unnecessary costs.

Given its history, there may not be a clear demarcation between middle-office functions and those of the front and back offices. However, middle-office functions involve supporting customers and, in particular, providing information that customers need to manage their positions and to make ongoing investment decisions. The middle office provides this support indirectly to customers. Direct interaction with customers, typically, is reserved to the front office. Also, some order management functions may be performed in the middle office. Order management includes tracking orders sent to various markets and the related executions that are received. Based on these customer support and order management activities, our discussion of the middle office

---

82. See Chapter 1 for more about the back-office crisis that led to the Securities Acts Amendments of 1975.

will include the following functions: Customer (Investment) Accounting, Trade Processing, Risk Management, Compliance, and Regulatory Reporting.

1. *Customer (Investment) Accounting*

The customer accounting function provides customers, both retail and institutional, with information about the securities and cash in their accounts. The two primary functions of customer accounting are: (1) to manage the customer's cash or near-cash positions, and (2) to manage the customer's holdings either directly in securities or in pooled investment funds, such as mutual funds. This means that the customer accounting function requires tracking changes in customers' holdings and value, which are reported to customers. Securities purchases result in increasing customer holdings and securities sales result in decreasing customer holdings. When securities are purchased there is a corresponding decrease in customer cash positions, and conversely, when securities are sold, there is a corresponding increase in customer cash positions. Adjustments for capital changes (e.g., stock splits, dividends, etc.) and price changes in securities holdings must also be reflected in the valuation of customer accounts. For example, the broker-dealer may credit securities holdings for customers who are buying or reduce securities holdings for customers who are selling if the customer has elected to keep its securities holdings in street name.[83] When the broker-dealer pays cash for a customer's purchase of securities, funds are taken from either the account of funds held for the customer at the broker-dealer or funds delivered to the broker-dealer by the customer for settlement. In summary, customer accounting encompasses all accounting required to support customers.

Middle office staff also use market information to research and update holdings and transactions. Changes and updates to customer holdings are posted to master files maintained by the broker-dealer. Broker-dealers must maintain master files or databases to process customer transactions and update customer holdings. Generally, this data is contained in three master files: Securities Master File, the Stock Record, and the Customer Information File. The Securities Master File ("SMF") contains data describing each security held, or recently held, by the broker-dealer and its clients. This descriptive or reference data includes the name of the security, the issuer of the security, the security's CUSIP number,[84] and other characteristics, such as maturity, dividend declaration, and interest payments. The Stock Record contains the position for each security at various points in time and its transaction history from changes in position.[85] The broker-dealer must maintain this information to comply with SEC

---

83. If the customer's securities holdings are not held in street name, then the broker-dealer transfers the customer's securities holdings as instructed by the customer. Rarely does the customer elect to have a physical securities certificate (if available), which requires registration in the customer name before forwarding to the customer.

84. CUSIP stands for Committee on Uniform Securities Identification Procedures; CUSIP numbers are used to uniquely identify most securities, including stocks and U.S. government and municipal bonds. A CUSIP number contains nine characters that include letters and numbers.

85. The Stock Record is maintained in the broker-dealer's Cashier's Department in its back office and is therefore examined in Section IV.C.2 of this chapter.

rules[86] that require it to segregate securities fully owned by customers in their cash accounts from securities owned by the broker-dealer.[87] The Customer Information File ("CIF") contains information about the broker-dealer's customers. This information includes names, addresses, and identifying numbers. The CIF also includes customer investment preferences and other information from the customer account-opening process.[88] Although the SMF, Stock Record, and CIF contain data about the broker-dealer's retail and institutional customers, much of the customer accounting performed by middle office staff is for the broker-dealer's retail customers.

Institutional customers most often either manage their own holdings or, more likely, entrust holdings to custodians. The broker-dealer's primary responsibility to institutional customers is to participate in the allocation process and affirmations, which are described below in the section on trade processing.

> Customer activities performed by the broker-dealer for retail customers are very different from those performed for institutional customers. Retail brokerage (generally identified as wealth management) is increasingly focused on managing assets for a fee based on assets-under-management rather than on commissions generated from transactions. As a result, broker-dealer computer systems must manage, and report on, both securities and funds owned by the customer left in street name. Wealth management requires software that tracks each customer's holdings and matches those holdings to the aggregate positions of the broker-dealer.

2. Trade Processing

Trade processing in the middle office involves activities that occur after execution but before clearing and settlement. The goal of these activities is to ensure that each trade clears and settles properly. If the trade fails to clear and settle, then the trade must be unwound. This is very costly for the broker-dealer.

Trade processing in the middle office consists of trade matching, confirmation, allocation, affirmation and settlement matching. Trade matching happens when counterparties to a trade (buyers and sellers of securities) match the details of executed trades to ensure that both sides to a trade agree in advance of settlement. Trade matching occurs on the street side (broker-dealer) and on the client-side of a trade. Street side matching occurs as a result of four types of trades: from the broker-dealer's inventory, on an exchange, verbally over-the-counter, and through an alternative trading system (ATS). Trade matching from the broker-dealer's inventory occurs when the broker-dealer's customer is the counterparty to a trade in a security in which the

---

86. *See* Exchange Act Rule 15c3-3, 17 C.F.R. §240.15c3-3.

87. Customer cash and margin accounts are examined in Section IV.C.5 of this chapter. Margin trading is discussed in Chapter 8.

88. The customer account opening process is examined in Section IV.C.6 of this chapter.

Depository Trust Company (DTC)

The DTC, established in 1973, was created to reduce costs and provide clearing and settlement efficiencies by immobilizing securities and making "book-entry" changes to ownership of the securities. Among other services, the DTC provides settlement for institutional trades, which typically involve money and securities transfers between custodian banks and broker-dealers.

---

broker-dealer maintains an inventory. This means that trade matching is done within the broker-dealer because the broker-dealer acts as both a broker and a dealer. Trade matching on an exchange occurs when two broker-dealers complete a trade on an exchange and the exchange records and reports the completed trade. Trade matching of verbal executions occurs when securities traded off an exchange require intervention from traders to match the details of a trade; both sides of the trade must conduct a post-trade match to ensure successful clearing and settlement. Trade matching on an ATS in many cases occurs immediately because ATSs are computer applications that provide broker-dealers an opportunity to find counterparties and to agree to a trade electronically. This means that the details of the trade are captured automatically at the time of execution.

Customers engage in trade matching upon receipt of confirmations from their broker-dealers. Confirmations contain the essential details of the trade, such as account, commission, the name of the security, price of the security, settlement date, order type, fees, and the broker-dealer's role in the trade (dealer or broker). Retail and Institutional customers use confirmations to match the trade confirmation to their original order. This process is designed to ensure that the customer's order was executed as directed and paves the way for successful clearing and settlement. Retail customers receive paper confirmations in the mail and must notify the broker-dealer of any errors or discrepancies promptly. Institutional customers generally use an automated system to receive electronic confirmations; they must receive electronic confirmations through the Depository Trust Company's (DTC)[89] automated system for securities held by the DTC. Automated confirmation systems route confirmations between investment managers, broker-dealers, and custodians. Omgeo-TradeSuite is the primary electronic trade confirmation system used in the United States, although there are others.

Trade processing for institutional customers requires allocation because they often buy and sell large quantities of a specific security (block trades) that they then must allocate across several accounts or portfolios. Preparation for settlement of block trades requires a separate confirmation from the broker-dealer identifying the exact account, amount, and settlement instructions. The process of trade allocation involves distributing all the trades required to completely or partially satisfy an order or group

---

89. The DTC is a subsidiary of the Depository Trust Clearing Corporation, a U.S. post-trade financial services company that provides clearing and settlement services to the financial markets.

of orders at an average price that is fair to all participants and satisfies any explicit regulatory obligations, such as best execution. The average price is weighted by the number of shares at each price and reflects the effective price obtained for the entire order. This process can be quite complex.

Historically, allocations were sent by fax, but most are now transmitted electronically using dedicated computer systems. These computer systems utilize a Standing Settlement Instruction database (SSI) to avoid sending detailed processing instructions with each transaction. The SSI is accessed by the broker-dealer to obtain instructions for allocating the trade in preparation for settlement.

Trade affirmation must be performed by institutional customers whose funds and securities are held by a custodian.[90] Institutional customers must give a positive instruction to the custodian to release their funds or their securities for settlement. Essentially, institutional customers must formally accept trades executed on their behalf by broker-dealers to allow the custodian to release funds or securities. When a trade is affirmed, the custodian is authorized to provide transfer instructions if the institutional customer is selling securities or payment instructions if the institutional customer is buying securities. Without affirmation, a trade will not settle.[91] Like other activities in trade processing, affirmation is automated.

Settlement matching is required to ensure that the settlement details are correct before the actual settlement occurs. Settlement matching occurs for single trades when the customer compares the order to its corresponding confirmation. For block trades, settlement matching occurs after the block trade has been allocated and affirmed.[92]

3. Compliance

Although historically compliance has been a middle-office function, it is a core management responsibility of a broker-dealer, which occurs throughout the organization. The broker-dealer compliance infrastructure must be designed to meet, at a minimum, three broad objectives:

- To operate in accordance with applicable securities laws (federal and state), rules promulgated by securities regulators, and SRO rules;
- To operate in accordance with customer instructions and investment objectives; and
- To operate in accordance with the broker-dealer's own internal policies and procedures.

Compliance activities and functions focus on the financial and operational functions of the broker-dealer, governed by applicable securities laws and SRO rules. Compliance

---

90. Some institutional customers, for example, pension funds, are required by law to hold their funds and securities at third-party institutions (such as banks) for safekeeping and administration.

91. Institutional customers, through contractual agreement, may authorize their custodians to affirm their trades on their behalf.

92. Settlement matching for block trades can also take place before allocation by matching the executed block trade to its corresponding order.

activities include reporting requirements, monitoring interactions with customers and counterparties, monitoring personnel conformity with business management guidelines, and ensuring required employee licensing and certifications. Financial compliance functions, among other things, require the broker-dealer to maintain net capital requirements established by the SEC, SROs, and clearing organizations.[93] Operational compliance functions require the broker-dealer to monitor its middle- and back-office activities to ensure that the broker-dealer performs in accordance with applicable securities laws and SRO rules, which continue to increase in number and complexity.[94] The regulatory requirements of the front, middle, and back offices are discussed in various chapters of this textbook. For example, operational compliance functions require the broker-dealer to ensure that it operates in accordance with instructions and investment objectives imposed by customers (including asset preferences and aversions, income distribution, and investment performance); corresponding regulatory requirements are examined throughout this textbook as compliance is the core subject matter.

Broker-dealers increasingly rely on technology to perform compliance activities and functions. Computerized systems are used to track the broker-dealer's activities throughout the organization and to archive information. Reports[95] are produced to evidence that the broker-dealer is meeting its many compliance obligations. In fact, many of the regulatory requirements discussed in this textbook are performed by specialized computer software and systems. Depending on the size of the firm, the compliance department may have a few or many employees. Smaller firms may outsource many of their compliance responsibilities. However, the broker-dealer remains legally responsible for compliance even if the compliance activities are outsourced.

Some broker-dealers have moved some compliance activities from the middle to the front office to be proactive rather than reactive. The broker-dealer is attempting to ensure compliance before, rather than after, the trade is executed. This trend and the computerization of compliance activities and functions are demonstrated by the description of compliance at Knight Capital Group, a leading wholesale market maker, in a FINRA administrative proceeding for failure to supervise.[96]

> To assist the firm's personnel with compliance issues and to ensure that the compliance department stayed familiar with the firm's operations, [the firm's chief compliance officer] testified that compliance department personnel sat amongst institutional sales traders and market makers during the day. Knight,

---

93. Net capital requirements are examined in Chapter 7.

94. For example, as of the date of publication of this textbook, all the rules required to implement the mandates of the Dodd-Frank Act of 2010 have yet to be adopted.

95. Reporting responsibilities are shared between the middle and back offices.

96. Knight Capital Group provided trade executions only to broker-dealers and institutional customers. All trading conducted by Knight was done on a principal basis, i.e., Knight bought or sold for its own (proprietary) accounts. *In the Matter of Department of Market Regulation, vs. John Patrick Leighton, and Kenneth D. Pasternak,* Decision No. CLG050021, 2010 FINRA 2010 WL 781457 (FINRA Mar. 3, 2010).

however, also utilized comprehensive automated compliance and order management systems. These systems automated the firm's protocols for compliance with order handling, short sales, and trade reporting requirements, and generated numerous exception reports.... Knight's systems were therefore designed to allow supervisory and compliance personnel to review all trades effected by Knight's market makers, including trades executed for institutional customers.... [T]he compliance department was required to periodically review a sampling of institutional trades, the size and frequency of that trading, and to meet with Knight's institutional sales traders and customers to discuss their business. *Id.* at p. 30.

4. Risk Management

Risk management, a classic middle-office function,[97] is deemed by the SEC and FINRA to be an essential component of the broker-dealer's business. Regulators have defined risk management as "the identification, management, measurement and oversight of various business risks and is part of a [broker-dealer's] internal control structure."[98] The broker-dealer is subject to various types of business risks, including funding and liquidity risks. Funding risk includes the possibility of the broker-dealer losing funding sources as a result of a broker-dealer specific event or systemic credit events, such as the financial crisis of 2008. Liquidity risk includes the possibility of unanticipated deterioration of the quality of assets held by the broker-dealer and contagion across markets and future earnings volatility that could affect the broker-dealer's liquidity positions. Funding and liquidity risk are intertwined and were of special concern during the financial crisis of 2008.

Regulators expect the broker-dealer to develop a risk management system to monitor and control for risks resulting from the broker-dealer's specific business activities. The risk management system must include policies and procedures that specify the level of funding and liquidity risk that the broker-dealer is willing to accept to meet its business goals; specifically, the broker-dealer must set appropriate funding and liquidity risk limits and evaluate existing risks presented by various markets and counterparties. Risk management systems must also include computer systems that can capture information about funding and liquidity exposure across all business lines. Reports generated by the broker-dealer's risk management computer systems— both quantitative and qualitative—generally summarize key measures of funding and liquidity, such as: (1) the amount of excess liquidity currently available; (2) inventory concentrations in related asset classes; (3) usage and limits of secured and unsecured lines of credit; (4) the maturity profile of available funding sources; and (5) the level of funding through particular markets and position concentrations for

---

97. Although it is a classic middle-office function, risk management can also be performed in the front office.

98. *Broker-Dealer Risk Management Practices Joint Statement*, NASD 704 (July 29, 1999), http://www.finra.org/web/groups/industry/ip/reg/notice/documents/notices/p004054.pdf.

certain counterparties.[99] Accordingly, risk management staff perform such functions as analyzing exposure across business lines, monitoring for early warning signs for potential funding and liquidity problems,[100] evaluating pricing decisions,[101] performing stress tests,[102] and maintaining and regularly updating contingency funding plans.[103]

The broker-dealer's risk management system must include an assessment of the impact of the failure of its affiliates, subsidiaries, or holding company. Specifically, unless the broker-dealer qualifies for an exemption,[104] it is subject to the risk assessment rules contained in Exchange Act Rules 17h-1T and 17h-2T. These rules were adopted by the SEC to assess the risk of the business activities of broker-dealer holding companies, affiliates, or subsidiaries that are reasonably likely to have a material impact on the financial or operational condition[105] of the broker-dealer.[106] Broker-dealers must make and keep specific records identified in Rules 17h-1T and 17h-2T, which concern its policies, procedures, or systems for monitoring and controlling financial and operational risks resulting from the activities of affiliates, subsidiaries, or holding

---

99. *Risk Management*: Funding and Liquidity Risk Management Practices, FINRA 3 (Nov. 2010), https://www.finra.org/web/groups/industry/ip/reg/notice/documents/notices/p122388.pdf.

100. Early warning signs or red flags of potential funding and liquidity problems include sudden difficulty in entering into longer-term funding arrangements, significant decline in earnings or projected earnings for the broker-dealer that could reduce the broker-dealer's perceived credit worthiness, and excess reliance on the use of customer assets. *See Risk Management*: Funding and Liquidity Risk Management Practices, FINRA 5 (Nov. 2010), https://www.finra.org/web/groups/industry/ip/reg/notice/documents/notices/p122388.pdf. Many of these issues will be discussed in Chapters 7 through 9, which examine books and records and net capital requirements for broker-dealers.

101. This includes periodically revaluating methodologies used to value the broker-dealer's assets to identify discrepancies between actual results and results obtained from the valuation methodologies. *Id.*, at p. 3.

102. Stress tests are designed to identify and quantify sources of potential liquidity strains and to analyze the effects of such strains on the broker-dealer's cash-flow, profitability, and solvency. Essentially, effective stress tests allow the broker-dealer to determine whether it has sufficient excess liquidity in the form of unencumbered and highly marketable securities to meet possible funding shortfalls without selling its assets at fire sale prices or depending on additional funding from credit-sensitive markets. *Id.*, at pp. 6–7.

103. *Id.* at p. 3.

104. Exemptions include broker-dealers that do not carry or clear customer assets, introducing broker-dealers that clear all transactions with and for customers on a fully disclosed basis with a clearing broker, that clear customer trades but do not hold customer funds or securities except to facilitate transactions and only for the time necessary to complete the transactions, that maintain capital of less than $20 million, and that maintain less than $250,000 in total capital. 17 C.F.R. §240.17h-1T(d).

105. This includes the broker-dealer's net capital, its liquidity, or its ability to finance its operations.

106. The Risk Assessment Program was established under the Market Reform Act of 1990 following the collapse of Drexel Burnham Lambert Group, Inc. (Drexel), the holding company parent of Drexel Burnham Lambert, Inc. (DBL), a registered broker-dealer. Drexel's collapse demonstrated that broker-dealers could encounter serious financial difficulty due to the loss of market confidence, loss of access to the capital markets, or failure of the registered broker-dealer's affiliates or the holding company itself.

companies that are reasonably likely to have a material impact on their financial or operational condition.[107]

Risk management for broker-dealers in today's global marketplace is complex and a constantly moving target. Extreme weaknesses in broker-dealer risk management systems were exposed in the financial crisis of 2008. The difficulty in conducting effective risk management to respond successfully to extreme events such as the 2008 financial crisis in the broker-dealer industry was noted in a March 2009 speech by Richard G. Ketchum, former chairman and CEO of FINRA, at SIFMA's[108] annual compliance and legal division's seminar.

> ... A certain amount of financial hubris set into the belief that modeling risk essentially crowded out, what people now term in various ways—as "black swans" ... or "fat tails."[109] Whatever term you may use, it is the consideration of what happens when that portion of risk at the tail end of the curve happens to manifest. We also now understand correlational risk as perhaps never before—the risk that if there is a two percent modeled risk of default in an asset, the occurrence of that event substantially causes the market in that entire asset class to cease to exist....
>
> In my short time in the industry, I participated in risk management exercises, and let me emphasize that I understand just how difficult that process is. But the painful lessons learned from the last 18 months cannot be forgotten. I will leave to the SEC and Fed to determine how leverage and capital requirements must be adjusted, but changes in the risk management process is equally important. First, scenario analyses need to be performed by independent risk managers that are not in love with the positions or the strategies.

---

107. Broker-dealers subject to the Risk Assessment rules must keep records and file with the Commission information including the holding company organizational chart, risk management policy information, consolidating and consolidated financial statements, securities and other financial product position data of material associated persons, and other categories of financial and securities related information, as specified in Exchange Act Rules 17h-1T and 17h-2T and Form 17-H, 17 C.F.R. § 240.17h-1T, 17 C.F.R. § 240.17h-2T, and 17 C.F.R. § 249.328T, respectively. Chapter 9 contains more information about the recordkeeping and reporting obligations required under Rules 17h-1T and 17h-2T.

108. SIFMA, the Securities Industry and Financial Markets Association, is a securities industry association that represents broker-dealers, banks, and asset managers in the United States. It is the U.S. regional member of the Global Financial Markets Association ("GFMA"). GFMA represents financial and capital market participants in the global financial markets.

109. Taleb, Nicolas Nassim, The Black Swan: The Impact of the Highly Improbable (Random House 2007), popularized one of the concepts of the work of Benoit B. Mandelbrot, a researcher of mathematical concepts, that financial markets do not follow normal probability distributions; instead, financial markets have a much higher probability of extreme events. This concept is referred to as fat-tailed distributions. Taleb theorized that because much of the pricing for financial markets depends on models that assume a normal distribution of prices, risk managers not only underestimate the probability of losses but compound the problem by convincing themselves and others that, had better risk-management tools been in place, no losses would have occurred. Taleb contends that whatever the quality of risk management, specific losses that cannot be reasonably predicted or mitigated will occur from time to time.

Second, scenarios must always evaluate cross-asset contagion risk. Third, the firm must react immediately when there are dramatic market and economic changes to reevaluate the exposures and maximum potential losses, with a careful appreciation of funding implications resulting from holding company exposures and careful concern as to how customers are being advised. And finally, this must be a task that is not delegated by the CEO and senior management of the broker-dealer no matter what the press of other business.[110]

5. Client Services

Although much of client services are performed in the front office, the middle office may assist in servicing customer needs. For example, the middle office may assist in the resolution of the broker-dealer's internal investigations and follow-up on new account documentation. Resolution of internal investigations requires tracking the investigation and helping the investigator gather the information needed to resolve the question or problem. For retail customers, client services may include providing confirmations, monthly statements, year-end tax reports, and a monthly newsletter containing general investment advice. For institutional customers, client services may include more extensive reporting, including daily transaction reports, monthly statements, and quarterly evaluations.

C. Back Office

Figure 2.11

Back Office
- Purchase & Sale
- Cashier
- Corporate Action (Reorganization)
- Position Management
- Margin
- New Accounts
- Accounting

The broker-dealer's back office processes its transactions and maintains its assets and liabilities. Specifically, back office activities include the extension of credit, maintenance of books and records, receipt and delivery of funds and securities, safeguarding of funds and securities, and production of confirmations and statements. Given the complexity and automation of back-office activities, this section is designed to provide a high level

---

110. Richard G. Ketchum, Chairman & CEO, FINRA, *Remarks From the SIFMA Compliance & Legal Division's Annual Seminar*, March 23, 2009, FINRA, https://www.finra.org/newsroom/speeches/032309-remarks-sifma-compliance-legal-divisions-annual-seminar

overview of broker-dealer back-office activities sufficient to provide context for under-standing the regulatory framework of broker-dealers examined in this textbook.

The broker-dealer's back office is organized into various departments, including purchase and sale (P&S), cashier, transfer, corporate actions (reorganization), position management (stock record), margin, income,[111] proxy,[112] accounting,[113] new accounts, and reporting/compliance.[114]

1. *Purchase and Sale Department*

The Purchase and Sale department (P&S) is the first line of defense against clearing and settlement errors and, therefore works closely with clearing corporations. Trade comparison and reconciliation is this department's primary focus. P&S functions include recording, street-side reconciliation, comparisons, and settlement. The recording function ensures that all trade executions have been properly posted in the broker-dealer's computer systems. This means that essential components of the trade—such as the net amount, security type, number of shares or units, commission, fees, and applicable taxes—are input correctly into the broker-dealer's books and records. Street-side reconciliation tracks all securities transactions and reconciles the broker-dealer's positions with the applicable clearing organization.[115] This process requires the clearing corporation to issue reports listing the trades reported by the broker-dealers from each side of the trade (broker and the contra broker[116]) and notes whether the trades are compared or uncompared. A trade is compared when both counterparties (broker and the contra broker) to the trade report identical information and no further action is required by either counterparty to the trade. This initial comparison occurs on trade date + 1.[117] If the trades are uncompared, both counterparties must check their trade tickets for errors and the erring party must send an adjustment to the applicable clearing organization no later than trade

---

111. The income department is responsible for receiving and distributing all cash dividends as well as interest payments.

112. The proxy department provides customers with the proxy notice, which is the official notice of specific issues requiring a vote by shareholders; it also contains a description of the shareholders' voting rights. Issues reflected in a proxy notice might include election of directors or ratification of the appointment of independent auditors. Most proxy activities are outsourced to vendors such as ADP.

113. The accounting department is responsible for the broker-dealer's bookkeeping and accounting report production. Reports produced by the accounting department are prepared in accordance with Generally Accepted Accounting Principles (GAAP). Accounting reports and other bookkeeping requirements are discussed in Chapter 9.

114. The broker-dealer's reporting and compliance obligations are discussed throughout this textbook and therefore are not discussed in detail in this chapter.

115. The appropriate clearing organization is determined based on the type of security. For example, corporate and municipal bonds and equities are cleared with the NSCC; government bonds are cleared with the FICC-GSD.

116. The contra broker is the broker-dealer participating on the other side of the trade.

117. This time frame assumes that the NSCC is the applicable clearing organization. Other clearing organizations have different clearing and settlement processes, but all use the same process of identifying compared and uncompared trades.

date + 2. P&S reconciles its trades against the trading activity displayed in the report issued by the applicable clearing organization. For example, if the NSCC is the applicable clearing organization, trading activity is processed through the NSCC's Continuous Net Settlement (CNS) system. Under CNS, rather than settling individual trades in a single security for each broker, one net deliver position for a single security for each broker is recorded and the net change for each broker for each compared traded is continuously calculated. CNS minimizes the movement of securities and money balances required to settle trades.[118] For example, if during a day of trading, Morgan Stanley purchases 1,000 shares of Twitter for one customer and sells 1,000 shares of Twitter for another customer, Morgan Stanley will have a zero net settlement in Twitter shares. This process occurs continuously throughout the day.[119]

Trade for Trade and Balance Order Settlement are available if the security is not a CNS-eligible security if both counterparties agree.[120] Trade for Trade Settlement requires the broker-dealer to deliver or receive traded securities directly to or from the broker-dealer with whom the trade was executed. For example, Success First buys 200 shares of XYZ from Morgan Stanley. On settlement date, Morgan Stanley delivers 200 shares of XYZ to Success First and Success First pays Morgan Stanley for the delivered 200 shares of XYZ. Balance Order Settlement occurs in the P&S when securities are not eligible for CNS and are processed alongside CNS in a similar manner. If a non-CNS trade is matched in CNS, it is reported on the compared trade report and a Balance Order is issued. If it is not matched, it is posted to the non-compared report for further investigation and resolution.

2. Cashier's Department

The Cashier's Department is responsible for a number of functions focused on trade settlement. The movement of securities and funds in the Cashier's Department concludes the trade settlement process. Activities performed in this department include receiving and delivering securities and funds (receive and deliver), balancing/reconciling the broker-dealer's securities positions with the DTC, maintaining the vault system, segregation of securities, bank loans, and account transfers. The broker-dealer's Receive and Deliver Master File (R&D File) is an accounting sub-ledger that maintains the settlement instructions for the broker-dealer's trading activity. The R&D File receives trade data from the broker-dealer's P&S, which instructs the Cashier's Department to

---

118. Under CNS, NSCC acts as a central counter-party; typically, CNS transactions that reach midnight of trade date +1 become guaranteed by NSCC.

119. The CNS process is continuous because it takes a firm's prior CNS Position into consideration in conjunction with the firm's new net trading activity when determining the firm's new CNS Position. Under Continuous Net Settlement, the determination of whether a firm is a net buyer or seller of securities begins with the firm's prior day closing CNS Position. The firm's prior day closing position is netted with the current day's net trading activity to determine the firm's new CNS Position.

120. CNS eligible securities include equities, corporate bonds, Unit Investment Trusts, and municipal bonds that are eligible at The Depository Trust Company (DTC).

deliver securities (sell trades) or to receive securities (buy trades). The R&D File provides specific information about the securities to be received or delivered, including the settlement date, the specific security issue to be settled, the quantity to be delivered or received, the settlement amount to be collected or paid, and the contra broker to whom the securities are to be delivered or from whom the securities are to be received.

The receive and deliver function balances and reconciles the broker-dealer's positions with the DTC on a daily basis. Differences between the DTC's and the broker-dealer's securities positions are identified as breaks. Each break must be researched and resolved with adjusting entries to the broker-dealer's books and records. If the break is caused by a failure to deliver a particular security by the counterparty, i.e., a fail, it can be resolved through the securities lending process, which is also a function performed in the Cashier's Department.

a. The Vault Department

The Vault Department is used to store and track physical securities certificates and other important documents. It is a large safe that must be fireproof and alarm protected. The Vault Department keeps track of all the physical receives and delivers and records what has gone in and out of the vault. Generally, only self-clearing broker-dealers have a securities vault on site. Customer securities stored in the vault are held in the broker-dealer's nominee name to facilitate ease of transfer.

b. Segregation

Rule 15c3-3 of the Exchange Act requires the broker-dealer to hold separately or segregate securities owned by the customer from its own securities. Before the Cashier's Department can deliver shares in settlement of a sell trade, it must know which of the securities it holds belong to its customers and which belong to the broker-dealer. A customer is considered to own securities once she pays for the securities in full. In essence, the broker-dealer is required to segregate securities for which customers have fully paid from other securities and cannot hypothecate[121] or sell them without the customer's permission.

The broker-dealer can only settle with excess securities—that is, securities that are not fully paid for by the customer. Before each and every delivery, the Cashier's Department must calculate its excess securities position. If excess securities are available for delivery, the delivery can be made. If excess securities are not available, the deficit is resolved by borrowing excess shares from another broker-dealer or by purchasing sufficient shares on the open market.[122] Of course, this means that the Cashier's Department is also responsible for lending to other broker-dealers who need securities to settle.

---

121. That is, pledge as collateral.
122. See Chapter 8 for more information about customer segregation rules.

c. Bank Loans

Broker-dealers may use short-term bank loans to finance their daily operating expenses. Excess securities are used as collateral for such loans. A broker-dealer may hypothecate or pledge excess securities as collateral to a bank to obtain short-term funding at reasonable rates. Generally, smaller broker-dealers use bank loans to finance daily operations. Larger broker-dealers have access to a cheaper source of funding for daily operations, such as stock lending or borrowing and tri-party repos.[123]

d. Account Transfers

The Cashier's Department is also responsible for customer account transfers between broker-dealers.[124] Transfers may involve individual securities or entire accounts. If an entire account is transferred, usually it is conducted through the Automated Customer Account Transfer System (ACATS), an NSCC service. ACATS provides for the orderly transfer of customer accounts between broker-dealers when directed to do so by the customer. It is designed to facilitate the customer account transfer process through automation and to safeguard the customer's investment assets. ACATS begins when the customer instructs her new broker-dealer to receive her account from her prior broker-dealer. The customer must provide the new broker-dealer with the account number to be transferred, the name of the beneficial owner or owners, the type of account (cash, margin, etc.), and the customer's tax identification or Social Security number. The entire ACATS process takes six business days to complete barring any complications.

3. Corporate Actions (Reorganization) Department

The Corporate Actions or Reorganization department (Reorg) is responsible for executing corporate actions that affect securities held by the broker-dealer for its customers. Certain actions taken by a corporation have investment consequences for customers holding the corporation's securities. These actions include corporate name changes, mergers between two or more entities, tender offers, distributions of corporate earnings (cash dividends,[125] stock dividends),[126] and stock splits.[127] The broker-dealer must ensure that the results of corporate actions are properly reflected in its customers' accounts.

Corporate actions may be categorized as mandatory or voluntary. A mandatory corporation action is one in which the issuer of the security has the right to insist that

---

123. See Chapter 8 for a discussion of the use of hypothecation and structured and tri-party repos.

124. In very large broker-dealers, the customer account transfer function may be a stand-alone department separate from the Cashier's Department.

125. A cash dividend is a distribution of corporate earnings paid by the corporation to its shareholder in cash as of a specified date.

126. A stock dividend is a distribution of corporate earnings paid by the company to its shareholders as of a specified date in the form of a distribution of the corporation's stock.

127. A stock split is a corporate action through which the corporation increases the number of shares outstanding by dividing the number of shares outstanding into smaller units of ownership. Each share outstanding is split into two or more shares.

the corporate action occur. Mandatory corporate actions include mergers,[128] acquisitions,[129] calls and redemptions,[130] liquidations,[131] and spinoffs.[132] A voluntary corporate action occurs when the holder of the security has the right to decide whether she wants to accept or reject a proposed corporate action. Voluntary corporate actions involve more risk for the broker-dealer because the broker-dealer must notify customers of the voluntary action and then collect responses within the specified period; failure to properly notify the customer or the issuer results in losses for the broker-dealer. Voluntary corporate actions include convertible bonds,[133] tender offers,[134] and warrants.[135]

The processing of corporate actions by the broker-dealer involves several distinct activities. These activities include event notification, entitlement determination, client notification, event posting, and reconciliation. Event notification generally comes from the broker-dealer's market data vendors. After event notification, entitlement determination is performed by checking the broker-dealer's position files to ascertain which accounts are likely to be affected. Client notification requires the broker-dealer to inform the customer of the corporate action event and, if it is voluntary, to explain the customer's choices with respect to the corporate action. Event posting occurs when the execution date is reached and the necessary entries are made to all applicable accounts. Reconciliation involves ensuring that the amount received or the shares on hand are the same as reflected in the broker-dealer's records. Any differences must be investigated and resolved.

4. Position Management (Stock Record) Department

The Position Management Department tracks the total number of securities owned by the broker-dealer and its clients. Specifically, Rule 17a-3(5) of the Exchange Act re-

---

128. A merger is a combination of the assets and liabilities of two or more companies into one legal entity through the exchange of equity.

129. In an acquisition, the shares of one issuer are canceled and the owners of the acquired issuer get new shares issued by the acquiring issuer.

130. When a bond is called, the issuer of the bond issues a call notice in accordance with the terms of the bond indenture. The owners of the bond must present the bond to the issuer for redemption. Bonds are usually called at a premium to the current market price. Redemptions may also occur when a bond matures.

131. A liquidation is the closing of a corporation and the distribution of the remaining assets. A distribution is made to the shareholders after all other liabilities have been satisfied.

132. A spinoff occurs when a portion of a company is separated from an existing company and established as a separate legal entity or when a firm owns shares in another corporation and distributes them to its shareholders. The new legal entity, if established as a corporation, has its own capital structure.

133. A conversion occurs when one security is exchanged for another, usually within the same issuer. A convertible bond can be exchanged for common shares in the same issuer.

134. A tender offer is a formal offer by one company or individual to buy the shares of another company with cash, securities, or a combination of both.

135. A warrant is a security that allows its owner to purchase the issuing corporation's stock at a certain price over a stated period, usually 10 to 20 years. It is a negotiable instrument and can be sold to another investor if the holder chooses not to exercise the warrant. They are often attached to another security as an inducement to investors and can usually be detached and traded separately.

Table 2.2. Success First's Position in EFG Shares

Account	Quantity Debits	Quantity Credits
DTC Position		-100,000
Customer A	+25,000	
Customer B	+50,000	
Customer C	+25,000	
Totals	+100,000	-100,000

quires the broker-dealer to create and maintain a detailed listing of the broker-dealer's securities holdings identified by account (customer or the broker-dealer itself), quantity, and location.[136] This requirement is reflected in the Stock Record. The Stock Record is a perpetual inventory system, using the dual entry method, designed to track the ownership and location of securities and must always balance. On the Stock Record, ownership of securities is designated by a debit or plus quantity. Accounts (broker-dealers and their customers) that have debit quantities on the Stock Record are said to have a long position; a long position is always based on ownership of the securities. The location of the security is designated by a credit or minus quantity. Accounts that have credit quantities on the Stock Record are said to have a short position. On the Stock Record the long position (debits) in a particular security must equal the short position (credits) in the same security. Specifically, for every ownership in a security there must be a location. Table 2.2 above reflects a stock record for Stock EFG at Success First.

Based on this Stock Record, Success First holds a total of 100,000 shares of EFG for the benefit of three customer accounts. All 100,000 shares are held on deposit at the DTC. All debits equal credits for the broker-dealer's position in EFG shares. Therefore, the Stock Record is in balance.

When debits do not equal credits, there is a break in the Stock Record. All breaks must be investigated and resolved. The number of breaks and the time required to resolve such breaks is an indicator of operating efficiency at the broker-dealer. The Stock Record department compiles a daily listing of breaks for each security held by the broker-dealer. Every department that processes the receipt and delivery of securities or that affects the location of a security affects the Stock Record.

5. Margin Department

The Margin Department manages the granting of credit to the broker-dealer's customers. Customers may purchase securities by paying for them in full or by borrowing a portion of the purchase price of the securities. A customer buys on margin when

---

136. The primary regulations affecting the Stock Record are Rule 15c3-3, Rule 17a-5, and the quarterly security counts to be made by certain broker-dealers. Chapters 8 and 9 contain more information about these rules.

she borrows a portion of the purchase price of a security. In a margin purchase, the customer pays for some of the acquired securities and uses the remaining newly purchased securities to finance the part of the purchase price that is still owed. The broker-dealer loans the remaining portion of the purchase price to the customer and uses the securities as collateral for the loan to the customer.[137] As with all loans, the customer must pay interest to the broker-dealer. For example,

Anita, a Success First customer, purchases 100 shares of ITI with a current market value (CMV) of $50 per share on margin:[138]

1. Anita buys 100 shares of ITI @ $50/share = $5,000 CMV

2. Anita pays for 50 percent of the purchase price = $2,500

3. Anita now owns $5,000 of ITI shares in her account and must pay interest on the $2,500 loaned to her by Success First to purchase ITI shares.

Margin Department functions include monitoring the status of each customer's account and ensuring compliance with federal and SRO rules governing the extension of credit to broker-dealer customers. These rules require maintenance minimums, i.e., they regulate the monetary level to which equity in a customer's account can fall after which the customer must deposit additional collateral in the form of cash or securities. Such rules also regulate the minimum amount of available cash or securities that a customer must have in her account to initiate a margin trade. In essence, the Margin Department monitors the margin position for each customer overnight and during the day in real-time. If the value of the securities and cash in a customer's margin account falls below the maintenance minimum, the broker-dealer must contact the customer to request additional funding. If the customer is unable to provide additional funding, the broker-dealer liquidates securities in the customer's margin account until the account can be brought back within minimum maintenance requirements.

6. New Accounts Department

The New Accounts Department is responsible for managing the process of opening new accounts for the broker-dealer's customers. A customer must open a securities account with the broker-dealer in order to buy and sell securities. The account opening process is designed to ensure completion of all required documentation needed to open an account with the broker-dealer, to know the customer's investment objectives and financial condition to avoid fraud, to comply with applicable securities laws, and to ensure that the customer understands the terms of her account.

---

137. Only certain securities are marginable, i.e., can be used as collateral by the broker-dealer to lend to the customer. Marginable securities include exchange-listed equities, OTC equities, listed corporate bonds, and U.S. government bonds. In addition, federal and SRO rules govern the amount of the loan to the customer by the broker-dealer. Chapter 8 contains more information about margin rules.

138. For illustrative purposes, the author has excluded any fees and taxes.

There are two general categories of customers opening accounts with broker-dealers—retail[139] and institutional.[140] In the account opening process for retail customers, forms needed to open the account include the account opening form, the client agreement, signature cards, and tax forms. The account opening form identifies the person opening the account and initiates the process of evaluating her credit history and investment knowledge and skills. It also states the customer's investment objectives; identifying the customer's investment objectives is critical in determining whether trading executed in the customer's account matches her investment objectives. Accordingly, the account opening form should be completed by the customer and signed by the broker-dealer, but this is not always the case. The information on the account opening form must also be verified by the New Accounts Department. Information required in the retail account opening form includes the customer's full name and address, Social Security number or taxpayer identification number, age, employment status, marital status, number of dependents, and net worth.

The retail account agreement is the legal contract between the customer and the broker-dealer. The terms of the account agreement are based on the type of account opened by the customer. The most common types of accounts opened by retail customers include cash,[141] margin,[142] and third-party[143] accounts. Each broker-dealer creates its own account agreement, but important terms common to the industry include an arbitration clause requiring arbitration of customer disputes with the broker-dealer, the broker-dealer's capacity as agent for the customer, and the right to use the customer's securities for securities lending without compensating the customer.

The institutional customer account requires specialized forms to reflect the legal status of the institutional entity. These forms include the institutional account opening form, corporate or legal status documentation, the account agreement, and signature cards. The institutional account opening form, among other things, identifies the person authorized to open the account on behalf of the institution and defines the institution's investment objectives. Corporate or legal status documentation includes documentation establishing that the legal entity is authorized, under applicable laws,

---

139. Retail customers are individuals who own securities. They trade through the broker-dealer's registered representatives or online.

140. Institutional customers are non-bank persons or organizations that trade securities in sufficiently large share quantities or dollar amounts that they qualify for preferential treatment and lower commissions, e.g., pension funds, mutual funds, etc.

141. Only cash transactions are permitted and all securities purchased must be paid in full on settlement date. No credit is provided.

142. The margin account allows the customer to use the securities in the account as collateral to purchase additional securities. A secured credit relationship is established between the customer and the broker-dealer. See Chapter 8.

143. Third-party accounts are used to give investment discretion to another party other than the customer and when the customer cannot legally make investment decisions. They include discretionary trading accounts (the broker-dealer is allowed to trade without receiving specific authorization from the customer) and custodial accounts (usually parent/child accounts, often established under the Uniform Gift to Minors Act or UGMA.

to operate and to trade securities. For example, if the institutional customer is a corporation, the corporation must present a certificate of incorporation to prove its legal existence; the corporation must also provide specific documentation that it is authorized to open a securities account, and specifically identify corporate personnel authorized to trade on its behalf.

Notes and Questions

1. Almost inevitably, any action that reduces risk limits the profit-making potential of participants, and they usually oppose the actions. For example, any efforts to increase capital requirements means participants cannot invest or trade with capital that is set aside. Efforts to increase capital requirements might originate from which functional unit of the broker-dealer's organization—the front, middle, or back office?

Hypothetical Three

Carmen has decided to test the interns in a manner similar to the Series 99 exam required by FINRA for operations professionals. The Series 99 Exam is designed to assess the competency of an entry-level representative to perform as an operations professional. However, Carmen sees that the interns have worked very hard to understand the materials she provided about the business side of broker-dealers and successfully performed other tasks that she assigned. To reward the interns, she has decided to conduct an oral exam, instead of a written exam, of the types questions on the Series 99 as provided below.

1. When does a trade settle?

    a. Upon execution

    b. At the time cash is exchanged for securities

    c. Upon confirmation between contra parties

    d. At the time the confirmation is received by the customer

2. Which department within a clearing firm or a self-clearing broker-dealer oversees the extension of credit to a customer?

    a. Purchase and Sales

    b. Banking

    c. Margin

    d. Settlement

3. A self-regulatory organization (SRO) is responsible for:

    a. the oversight of member firms and enforcing its rules.

    b. regulating that a fair number of consumers make a profit.

    c. regulating documentation standards across all broker-dealers.

    d. the oversight of market indexes.

4. Liquidity is the degree of ease with which assets can be:

    a. purchased on credit.

    b. converted into cash.

    c. used as collateral.

    d. transferred to other ownership.

5. Who maintains a fair and orderly market on the NYSE trading floor?

    a. Floor brokers

    b. Designated market makers

    c. Order book officials

    d. Market Makers

6. Which of the following activities is *not* performed in the Cashier's Department?

    a. Segregation

    b. Bank loans

    c. Account transfers

    d. Margin

Glossary

529 Plans — an investment vehicle in the United States with preferential tax treatment whose primary purpose is to facilitate saving for future higher education expenses.

A

Affiliates — any broker-dealers that are under common control with another company or a type of relationship between a broker-dealer and another company where either company owns less than a controlling quantity of ownership of another's voting securities.

Alternative Trading System — private trading systems that facilitate electronic trading. Like exchanges, ATSs bring together buyers and sellers of securities but, unlike exchanges, they do not engage in self-regulatory conduct, make markets, or provide a listing service for securities.

Automated Customer Account Transfer System (ACATS) — a system that provides for the orderly transfer of customer accounts between broker-dealers when directed to do so by the customer. It is designed to facilitate the customer account transfer process through automation and to safeguard the customer's investment assets.

B

Back Office — processes a broker-dealer's transactions and maintains its assets and liabilities. Back office activities include the extension of credit, maintenance of books and records, receipt and delivery of funds and securities, safeguarding of funds and securities, and production of confirmations and statements.

Best execution — requires a broker-dealer to seek the most favorable terms reasonably available under the circumstances for a customer's transaction.

C

Capital introduction — a service offered by prime brokers to assist their clients in raising capital by identifying potential investors. In practice, this is essentially a matchmaking service introduces hedge fund clients to potential investors to facilitate the fundraising process for the prime broker's hedge fund clients.

Clearing — requires a comparison of trade order details of the seller with those of the buyer to make sure that there is a common understanding of the terms of the trade. The resulting compared trade is cleared by essentially advising the seller and the buyer of their delivery and payment obligations

Clearing broker — performs clearing and settlement functions to complete securities transactions.

Consolidated tape — an electronic program that provides continuous, real-time last sale transaction data (volume and price) for exchange-listed securities.

Custodian — a financial institution that holds customers' securities for safekeeping so as to minimize the risk of their theft or loss.

Customer Information File — a computerized file that stores all pertinent information about a broker-dealer's customer's personal and account information including names, addresses, and investment objectives

D

Depository Trust Company — one of the world's largest securities depositories. The Depository Trust Company, founded in 1973 and based in New York City, is organized as a limited purpose trust company and provides safekeeping through electronic recordkeeping of securities balances. It also acts like a clearinghouse to process and settle trades in corporate and municipal securities.

Derivative Security — a type of security whose price is dependent upon or derived from one or more underlying assets. It is memorialized in a contract between two or more parties and it value is determined by the underlying asset. Examples include options, futures contracts, and swaps.

Designated Market Makers (DMM) — A market maker on the NYSE that is obligated to maintain fair and orderly markets for an assigned set of listed firms. Formerly known as specialists, the designated market maker is a point of contact for the listed company, and provides the company with information, such as the mood of traders and who has been trading the stock. Quotes offered by the DMM are on par with what floor brokers offer, and the DMM is obligated to quote at the national best bid or offer for a percentage of the time.

Discount broker-dealer—a broker-dealer who executes buy and sell orders for investors at relatively low commissions.

E

Exchange traded fund—a type of exchange-traded investment fund that must register with the SEC. Like mutual funds, ETFs allow investors to pool their money in a fund that invests in stocks, bonds, or other assets and to receive an interest in the pool. Unlike mutual funds, ETFs are traded on a national stock exchange at market prices that may not be the same as the net asset value of its shares, i.e., the value of the ETF's assets minus its liabilities divided by the number of shares outstanding

F

Federal Open Market Committee (FOMC)—The FOMC sets monetary policy for the Federal Reserve System and decides whether the Federal Reserve will join the Treasury Department in foreign exchange (FX) intervention. There are twelve voting members of the FOMC: the seven members of the Board of Governors and the presidents of five of the 12 Federal Reserve Banks. The president of the NY Fed is a permanent voting member in light of its unique activities in implementing monetary policy. The presidents of the other Federal Reserve Banks rotate serving one-year terms. By tradition, the chairman of the Board of Governors serves as chairman of the FOMC.

Floor broker—are NYSE members positioned on the floor of the NYSE at the point of sale during openings, closings and unique intra-day occurrences to execute trades. Floor brokers do not work exclusively for any Designated Market Maker on the NYSE and receive orders directly from various sources including broker-dealers, hedge funds, mutual funds, pension funds, day traders, and even some high-net worth individuals. Essentially, floor brokers execute agency orders and act as a market information gathering and delivery service for their customers

Front Office—is composed of revenue-producing departments whose primary goal is to sell the broker-dealer's services and products to its customers. In essence, the primary objective of front office activities is to recommend securities and to process orders. Front office employees interact and manage the relationships with the broker-dealer's customers by taking orders and executing trades.

Full-service broker-dealer—A broker that provides a large variety of services to its customers, including research and advice, retirement planning, tax tips, etc.

G

General obligation bond—a municipal bond backed by the credit and "taxing power" of the issuing jurisdiction rather than the revenue from a given project.

I

Independent broker—offers middle and back office services for a fee to investment professionals memorialized in an independent contractor agreement. The investment professional establishes her own financial services firm and associates with the IBD to meet the financial services needs of her customers, which may include providing investment advice as well as insurance products.

Institutional Customer—are non-bank persons or organizations that trade securities in sufficiently large share quantities or dollar amounts that they qualify for preferential treatment and lower commissions, e.g., pension funds, mutual funds, etc.

Introducing broker-dealer—a broker-dealer that has determined to enter into a business relationship with another broker-dealer (generally much larger than the introducing broker-dealer) to perform certain functions in connection with trading for itself and its customers. This business relationship is memorialized in a contract generally identified as a clearing agreement. The two parties to such clearing agreements are identified as the introducing broker-dealer and the carrying or clearing broker-dealer.

Investment banker—a broker-dealer that assists companies in raising capital in the public securities market. Investment bankers, among other things, advise companies as to the appropriateness of raising capital by conducting a public offering of their securities, the likely price of their securities should they determine to offer them to the public, and the types of investors that might be interested in purchasing their securities. They also market and sell the company's securities to potential investors subsequent to their determination to conduct a public offering.

L

Liquidity—the ability to quickly convert an investment portfolio or a security position to cash with little or no loss in value.

M

Margin agreements—an agreement signed by a broker-dealer's customer to permit the customer to engage in margin trading. Under the federal securities laws, a broker-dealer that loans money to a customer to finance securities transactions is required to provide the customer with written disclosure of the terms of the loan, such as the rate of interest and the method for computing interest. The broker-dealer must also provide the customer with periodic disclosures informing the customer of transactions in the account and the interest charges to the customer.

Margin loans—loans made by broker-dealers to their customers to finance the customer's securities transactions.

Margin trading—permits the customer to purchase securities by borrowing part of the purchase price from her broker-dealer.

Market maker—a broker-dealer that stands ready to buy and sell a particular stock on a regular and continuous basis at a publicly quoted price. Generally, a market maker must be ready to buy and sell at least 100 shares (a round lot) of any stock in which they make a market.

Merchant bank—negotiated private equity investment by financial institutions (including broker-dealers) in the unregistered securities of either privately or publicly held companies.

Middle office—a function at a broker-dealer that involves supporting customers in managing their positions and making ongoing investment decisions. Generally, middle office employees do not have direct contact with the broker-dealer's customers.

N

National Best Bid—the best (highest) available bid price offered by the broker-dealer to customers when customers sell securities to the broker-dealer. Conversely, the highest price at which a broker-dealer is willing to purchase a particular security from a customer.

National Best Offer—the best (lowest) available ask price offered by the broker-dealer to customers when customers want to buy securities from the broker-dealer. Conversely, the lowest price at which a broker-dealer is willing to sell a security to a customer.

Net Capital Rule—that broker-dealers have sufficient liquid assets to cover their current indebtedness and are in a position to return customers' funds and securities upon reasonable demand. See Exchange Act Rule 15c3-1.

NYSE Open Book—refreshed every five seconds, is provided by NYSE to vendors and customers and displays the depth of the market in real time. It also discloses limit order interest at the best bid and offer as well as prices below the best bid and above the best offer.

O

Order Handling Rules of Regulation NMS—The Order Handling Rules of Regulation NMS consist of the Limit Order Rule and the Quote Rule. The Limit Order Display Rule requires that specialists and market makers who have received a limit order to publicly display the prices of a limit order if the price contained in the limit order is better than that specialist's or market maker's quoted price. The Quote Rule requires specialists and market makers to display the lowest price they will accept from a customer to sell the securities and the highest price they will pay a customer to purchase the securities. This is the so called quote.

P

Primary dealer—a broker-dealer that trades in the U.S. government securities market. The U.S. government securities market consists of securities issued or guaranteed by the U.S. government including bonds, bills (T-bills) and notes (T-notes). Primary dealers trade in U.S. government securities directly with the New York Federal Reserve.

Prime Brokerage—a registered broker-dealer that clears and finances customer trades executed by one or more other registered broker-dealers on behalf of the customer who is generally a hedge fund. The prime broker-arrangement is advantageous to the customer because the prime broker serves as a clearing facility and accountant for all the customer's trades wherever executed and acts as a central custodian for all the customer's securities and funds.

Proprietary Product—an investment product that is created, marketed, and sold by a particular broker-dealer or financial holding company.

Proprietary trading—when a broker-dealer buys or sells securities for direct gain with its own money instead of on behalf of a customer. Essentially, the firm has decided to profit from the market rather than from commissions resulting from executing customer trades.

R

Registered representative—a person who works for a broker-dealer that is registered with the Securities and Exchange Commission (SEC) and a member of FINRA and who acts as an account executive (sometimes called an investment advisor) for clients trading investment products such as stocks, bonds and mutual funds.

Registered Investment Adviser—a person or company registered with the Securities and Exchange Commission who engages in the business of advising others as to the value of securities or as to the advisability of investing in, purchasing, or selling securities.

Retail investor—a natural person who buys and sells securities for their personal account. Trading is usually conducted in relatively small amounts.

Revenue bond—a municipal bond supported by the revenue from a specific project, such as a toll bridge, highway or local stadium.

Risk arbitrage—is a transaction effected with a view to profit from the consummation of a merger, acquisition, tender offer or other similar transaction involving a recapitalization.

S

Securities lending—the act of loaning a stock, derivative, other security to an investor or broker-dealer. Securities lending requires the borrower to put up collateral in the form of cash or securities. When a security is loaned, the title and the ownership is also transferred to the borrower.

Securities Masterfile—a broker-dealer computer database describing each security held, or recently held, by the broker-dealer and its customers. This descriptive or reference data includes the name of the security, the issuer of the security, the security's CUSIP number, and other characteristics such as maturity, dividend declaration, and interest payments.

Security-based swaps—A security-based swap is any agreement, contract, or transaction that is a swap and that is based on a narrow-based security index, or a single security or loan, or any interest therein or on the value thereof, or the occurrence or non-occurrence of an event relating to a single issuer of a security or the issuers of securities in a narrow-based security index, provided that such event directly affects the financial statements, financial condition, or financial obligations of the issuer.

Security index—a statistical tool used to track the track the market by following a set basket of securities. For example, the S&P 500 is an index that tracks the performance of the Fortune 500 companies.

Self-regulatory organization—A non-governmental organization authorized by law to create and enforce industry regulations and standards.

Settlement—occurs with the actual delivery of securities to the buyer and the payment of money to the seller.

Stock Record—an electronic system that helps broker-dealers keep track of the positions, location and ownership of the securities they hold.

Subsidiary—a company whose outstanding voting securities are owned by another company in such a quantity that the latter company can exercise control over the former.

Supplemental Liquidity Providers—are broker-dealer market participants that use sophisticated high-speed computers and algorithms to create high volume on exchanges in order to add liquidity to the markets. As an incentive for providing liquidity, the exchange pays the SLP a rebate or fee.

Swap—is defined in Section 1(a) (47) of the Commodity Exchange Act (CEA) and quite is detailed and comprehensive, though certain agreements, contracts, and transactions are excluded from the definition. It includes, for example, interest rate swaps, commodity swaps, currency swaps, equity swaps and credit default swaps. Essentially it involves the exchange of one security for another to change the maturity or quality of securities for the respective parties. The exchange is of mutual benefit to the exchangers, e.g., in an interest rate swap, the exchangers gain access to interest rates available only to the other exchanger by swapping them.

T

Trade execution—the process of a broker sending a client's order to a market to be filled.

Two-sided obligation—the obligation of a market maker to buy or sell at their stated firm bid and ask for each security in which it makes a market.

W

Wire house—An term used to describe a type of business model for broker-dealers. A wire house broker-dealer is a full service broker-dealer with a national network of employees or individual investment professionals, some employing tens of thousands.

Chapter 3

Broker-Dealer Registration

Regulatory Authority

Securities Exchange Act of 1934 Sections 3(a)(4); 3(a)(5); 3(a) (12) (A); 3(a) (17); 3(a) (18); 12(g)(2)(D); 15(a), (b), and (c); 15A(b)(4); 15B; 15C; 19(d); 21(d)(3); 29(b); 30(b)

Exchange Act Rules 15a-6; 15b1-3; 15b3-1; 15b7-1

Securities Act of 1933 Sections 3(a)(3) and 3(a)(11)

Securities Act Rule 147

FINRA Rules 1010; 1013, 1014 1021; 1022; 1031; 1032; 1050; 1230(b)(6); 1250; 3110; 4360

Motivating Hypothetical

Business at Success First is going very well and the Board of Directors has unanimously voted to expand. Success First wants to expand rapidly but, unfortunately, members of the Board of Directors do not agree about the manner in which Success First should expand. However, all want Success First's expansion to be cost-effective. After many meetings, the Board of Directors, which consists of four inside directors and three outside directors, is seriously considering two options. Carmen Alvarez, CEO and director of Success First, along with Sidney Ratnam, CFO and director of Success First, and one of Success First's outside board members support option one. Tatum Chen, CCO and director of Success First, along with Josephine Wiseman, GC and director of Success First and one outside board member, support option two. Option One is to expand by purchasing a company that services other broker-dealers. Option two is to expand by hiring more salespeople and creating more branch offices. Option One requires Success First to purchase BD Advantage, <u>a company that acts as an intermediary between introducing broker-dealers and clearing broker-dealers.</u> Carmen and others supporting option one believe that purchasing BD Advantage is the most cost-effective way to expand because they believe that BD Advantage's business model does not require registration with the SEC or membership in FINRA. Therefore, they believe that acquiring BD Advantage <u>would result in a substantial increase</u> in Success First's revenues without significantly increasing its compliance costs, which are already considerable. Tatum and others supporting option two are not at all convinced that BD Advantage does not have to register with the SEC or become a member of FINRA. They believe that the second option will immediately generate greater revenues than option one and that compliance costs, in the long run, would not be appreciably higher, despite the initial registration costs for salespeople and additional branch offices. As you read the materials in Chapter 3 discussing registration requirements for broker-dealers, consider which option, as outside counsel, you would recommend to Success First?

The 2nd, needs to be registered.

I. Introduction

All broker-dealers are required to register with the SEC in order to effect securities transactions in the U.S. This registration requirement not only applies to the broker-dealer as an entity, but also to any person not associated with a broker-dealer who is acting in that capacity. Although the terms *broker* and *dealer* are generally used conjointly, they are two distinct terms under the federal securities laws. A broker is defined in § 3(a)(4) of the Exchange Act as "any person engaged in the business of effecting transactions in securities for the account of others." A dealer is defined in § 3(a)(5) of the Exchange Act as "any person engaged in the business of buying and selling securities ... for such person's own account through a broker or otherwise." This chapter first identifies the activities and functions that distinguish broker-dealers. It also describes the role of finders as intermediaries between broker-dealers who are not required to register with the SEC. The qualifications of broker-dealers to register with the SEC and to become members of, and to register their associated persons with, FINRA are reviewed; also, an overview of the registration process for broker-dealers and their associated persons is provided. The following cases discuss the broker-dealer registration requirement. *Roth v. SEC* describes the broker-dealer registration requirement and its purpose in the securities regulatory framework, and *SEC v. Offill* illustrates that no single element in determining whether an entity is required to register with the SEC is dispositive.

Roth v. SEC

22 F.3d 1108 (D.C. Cir. 1994)

Before SILBERMAN, SENTELLE, and HENDERSON, Circuit Judges.

Per curiam.

* * *

Petitioner Charles Roth seeks review of an order of the Securities and Exchange Commission ("SEC" or "Commission"), partially affirming final disciplinary action by the National Association of Securities Dealers ("NASD"). For the reasons set forth below, we deny the petition for review in all respects.

In 1988 the NASD began disciplinary proceedings against Roth, who was a registered representative with R.B. Marich, Inc., a member firm of the NASD. The NASD charged Roth with violating Art. III, §§ 1 & 40 of the NASD Rules of Fair Practice, which prohibit any person associated with a NASD member firm from effecting a private securities transaction unless the member firm is given prior written notice. Roth was also charged with violating Art. III, § 1 of the NASD Rules of Fair Practice, by failing to register himself as a broker-dealer pursuant to § 15(a)(1) of the Securities Exchange Act of 1934. The violations were alleged to have arisen out of Roth's participation in various insurance company securities sales on seven separate occasions between 1985 and 1986.

The NASD Board of Governors found that Roth had violated the rules pertaining to private securities transactions and broker-dealer registration. Roth was fined $ 510,038.13, suspended from associating with a member firm for six months, and ordered to requalify by examination as a registered representative. Roth appealed the decision of the NASD to the SEC.... The SEC vacated the NASD's sanction for one of the transactions and reduced Roth's total fine to $ 105,000, but otherwise upheld the findings and conclusions of the NASD.

Before this court, Roth argues that the NASD's penalty provisions and "private securities transactions" rules are unconstitutionally vague; that the SEC's interpretation of the private securities transactions rules and of § 15(a) of the Securities Exchange Act are erroneous; that substantial evidence does not support the SEC's factual conclusions that Roth effected private securities transactions and acted as a broker-dealer; and that his sentence is excessive. We find these challenges to be meritless, and affirm the SEC's order in all respects. Roth's arguments do not warrant separate discussion, with one exception: namely, that he was not required to register as a broker-dealer under § 15(a) since he was at all times a registered representative with R.B. Marich, Inc., a registered broker-dealer.

* * *

Section 15(a)(1) of the Securities Exchange Act provides in relevant part that

> It shall be unlawful for any broker or dealer which is ... a natural person not associated with a broker or dealer ... to effect any transactions in, or to induce or attempt to induce the purchase or sale of, any security ... unless such broker or dealer is registered [with the Commission].

Roth claims that the plain language of § 15(a)(1) exempts him from any duty to register as a broker-dealer, since he was a "natural person ... associated with a broker or dealer" when the six securities transactions in question took place. The SEC contends that § 15(a)(1)'s registration exemption for persons associated with a broker-dealer applies only if the person is acting within the "scope" of his or her association with the member firm. We evaluate Roth's statutory claim mindful of the fact that Congress delegated substantial authority to the Commission to set forth registration requirements for broker-dealers, and that an agency's interpretation of an ambiguous statute should be affirmed if reasonable and consistent with the statute's purpose....

The broker-dealer registration requirement serves as the "keystone of the entire system of broker-dealer regulation." A broker-dealer that has registered with the Commission is bound to abide by numerous regulations designed to protect prospective purchasers of securities, including standards of professional conduct, financial responsibility requirements, recordkeeping requirements, and supervisory obligations over broker-dealer employees. *See generally* David A. Lipton, *A Primer on Broker-Dealer Registration,* 36 Cath. U.L. Rev. 899 (1987). The interlocking requirements of registration and supervision act to ensure that "securities are [only] sold by a salesman who understands and appreciates both the nature of the securities he sells and his responsibilities to the investor to whom he sells." *Persons Deemed Not to Be Brokers,* Exchange Act Release No. 20,943 (May 9, 1984), 49 Fed. Reg. 20,512, 20,515 (1984).

The language of § 15(a)(1) does not make plain whether registered representatives like Roth are always exempt from registration as broker-dealers, or whether the exemption from broker-dealer registration extends only to those individuals subject to the supervisory relationship which normally accompanies association with a member firm. The SEC's resolution of this ambiguity is reasonable in light of the structure and evident purposes of the statutory scheme. Roth's contrary reading would leave the exemption with no reason to exist. Why would Congress exempt from registration those natural persons associated with a registered entity unless it reposed faith in the latter's supervision? If an individual is operating as a broker-dealer outside the course and scope of his employment, the employer's registration would seem to have little relevance.

The record clearly reflects that Roth conducted a private securities business completely separate from R.B. Marich's operations.[1] As Roth admitted in his submissions to the NASD, this arrangement allowed him to solicit clients and consummate transactions "autonomously," with "negligible" supervision from R.B. Marich and "without the licensing authority of a broker dealer." Roth's clients were accordingly deprived of the numerous regulatory protections afforded to purchasers and sellers of securities, either directly through broker-dealer registration or indirectly through a supervisory relationship with a member firm. Other circuits have found violations of the broker-dealer registration requirement when a securities salesman has acted outside the scope of his association with a member firm. *See, e.g., Securities & Exchange Comm'n v. Ridenour,* 913 F.2d 515, 517 (8th Cir. 1990) (bond salesman violated § 15(a)(1) by engaging in a series of undisclosed, private securities transactions as part of private bond business of which member firm had no knowledge or opportunity to supervise).

Because the SEC's interpretation and application of § 15(a)(1) in this case were reasonable and Roth's remaining challenges are meritless, we deny Roth's petition for review ...

_____

SEC v. Offil

2012 U.S. Dist. LEXIS 9369, Fed. Sec. L. Rep. (CCH) P96,723 (N.D. Tex. 2012)

* * *

_____

1. Illustratively, Roth corresponded with clients on stationery bearing only his name, billed clients in his own name, received payment in that fashion, kept separate records of customer transactions, and maintained offices separate from those of Marich.

I.

The SEC brings this enforcement against the following eleven defendants: Phillip W. Offill, Jr. ("Offill"), David B. Stocker ("Stocker"),[2] Curtis-Case, Inc. ("Curtis-Case"), Shane A. Mullholand ("Mullholand"), Ryan M. Reynolds ("Reynolds"), Timothy T. Page ("Page"), Steven P. Fischer ("Fischer"), RSMR Capital Group, Inc. ("RSMR"), Dissemination Services, LLC ("Dissemination"), Page Properties, LP ("Page Properties"), and ATN Enterprises, LLC ("ATN"), and three relief defendants Timothy B. Barham ("Barham"), Ballad Enterprises, Inc. ("Ballad"), and Bellatalia, LP ("Bellatalia"). The SEC alleges violation[] ... of § 15(a)(1) of the Securities Exchange Act of 1934 ("Exchange Act"). The alleged violation [] involve[s] the securities offerings of six companies as they transitioned from private to publicly traded companies.

The first two offerings at issue involved American Television and Film Company, Inc. ("ATFT") and Vanquish Productions, Inc. ("Vanquish"). The owners of ATFT and Vanquish sought to raise capital for their companies by taking them public. Mullholand and Reynolds, using Mullholand's company, Dissemination,[3] agreed to help take the companies public and raise up to $1 million for them by selling their newly-issued stock. Mullholand and Reynolds, through their companies, Dissemination and RSMR,[4] sold the companies' stock to raise capital and to pay for market awareness work conducted on behalf of the companies.... Stocker performed the legal work for the transactions. The companies also issued stock to Dissemination and RSMR as payment for their services. The stock was deposited into various brokerage accounts, from which many of the shares were then sold shortly thereafter.[5] During the initial days of trading, Reynolds bought some of the stock and encouraged friends and family to do the same.

The next two offerings at issue involved Ecogate, Inc. ("Ecogate") and Media International Concepts, Inc. ("Media International"). Page, through Lion Capital Holdings, Inc.[6] ("Lion Capital"), agreed to help take the two companies public. Page introduced Stocker to the companies to conduct the necessary legal work. Page paid the companies $42,500 and $25,000, respectively, in return for millions of their newly issued shares. Mullholand and Reynolds conducted a market awareness campaign for Ecogate, and after being introduced to Fischer by Barham,[7] hired Fischer's

---

2. [1] The court entered a final consent judgment as to Stocker on May 7, 2009.

3. [4] The profits from Dissemination were split evenly between Mullholand and Reynolds by checks paid to their private companies, Bach Investments, Inc. ("Bach") and Veruschka LLC ("Veruschka"), which is now relief defendant Bellatalia.

4. [5] RSMR is a holding company that Mullholand and Reynolds formed to make investments. Mullholand and Reynolds each owned 50% of RSMR.

5. [6] Both Mullholand and Reynolds had trading authority over an RSMR brokerage account at Bishop Rosen and over Dissemination brokerage accounts at Bishop Rosen and at four other brokerage firms. Mullholand primarily controlled these accounts, but Reynolds occasionally directed trading from the accounts when Mullholand was away.

6. [7] Page owned 76% of Lion Capital.

7. [8] Barham, acting through his company Ballad, was a business opportunity broker. He introduced parties who might be interested in working together, and he received 10% of the gross proceeds from any deals resulting from his introduction. Barham acted as a business opportunity broker for

company, ATN,[8] to conduct market awareness for Media International. Ecogate issued shares to Page, Dissemination, and TGWSS Ventures, LLC, a Texas company managed by Offill.[9] Offill transferred his shares to Stocker's company, Curtis-Case. Page, Dissemination, and Curtis-Case then sold their Ecogate shares to the market. Media International issued shares to Page, Dissemination, and Odyssey Contracting, a Texas company created by Offill. Odyssey Contracting also transferred its shares to Curtis-Case. After Dissemination paid ATN in the form of Media International stock, ATN sold its Media International shares to the public.

The fifth offering at issue involved Auction Mills, Inc. ("Auction Mills"). Mullholand, Reynolds, Dissemination, and RSMR raised money for Auction Mills by selling its shares after taking it public. Mullholand once again hired Fischer to conduct market awareness for Auction Mills, for which Fischer was paid in Auction Mills stock. Auction Mills issued shares to Dissemination, RSMR, and Crimson City Holdings, Inc. ("Crimson City"), a company created by Offill. Crimson City transferred its shares to Curtis-Case. Dissemination then issued part of its Auction Mills shares to ATN as payment for Fischer's work. ATN, RSMR, Dissemination, and Curtis-Case sold their Auction Mills shares to the public through their respective brokerage accounts.

The sixth offering at issue involved Custom Design Compressor Systems, Inc. ("CDCS"). Mullholand, Reynolds, RSMR, and Dissemination raised money for CDCS by assisting it in going public. Fischer conducted a market awareness campaign for CDCS. CDCS issued its shares to Classical Movement Holdings, Inc. ("Classical Movement"), another entity controlled by Offill. Classical Movement then transferred CDCS shares to Curtis-Case, ATN, Dissemination, RSMR, and Stocker. RSMR and ATN sold their shares through their respective brokerage accounts. ATN paid Ballad from money ATN made selling CDCS stock as payment for Barham's introducing Fischer to Mullholand and Reynolds....

* * *

IV

The SEC seeks summary judgment on its claim that defendants Reynolds, Mullholand, RSMR, Dissemination, Page, and Page Properties violated §15(a)(1) of the Exchange Act by acting as unregistered brokers and dealers.

A

Under 15 U.S.C. §78o(a)(1), it is

> unlawful for any broker or dealer ... to make use of the mails or any means or instrumentality of interstate commerce to effect any transactions in, or

---

Fischer from 2003 to 2005. Fischer paid Barham from the proceeds of the sale of the stock Fischer acquired as payment for his market awareness work.

8. [9] Fischer owned ATN, and often hired subvendors to conduct portions of the market awareness campaigns.

9. [10] Offill was a private securities attorney who assisted Stocker by creating entities that would initially invest in securities offerings.

> to induce or attempt to induce the purchase or sale of, any security ... unless such broker or dealer is registered.

Scienter is not an element of §78o(a)(1). *SEC v. Rabinovich & Assocs., LP*, 2008 U.S. Dist. LEXIS 93595, 2008 WL 4937360, at *5 (S.D.N.Y. Nov. 18, 2008); *see also Eastside Church of Christ v. Nat'l Plan, Inc.*, 391 F.2d 357, 361–62 (5th Cir. 1968) (without making finding of scienter, finding that defendant violated §78o(a)(1)). A broker is "any person engaged in the business of effecting transactions in securities for the account of others," 15 U.S.C. §78c(a)(4), and a dealer is:

> any person engaged in the business of buying and selling securities for such person's own account through a broker or otherwise, [but] does not include a person that buys or sells securities for [his] own account, either individually or in some fiduciary capacity, but not as a part of a regular business.

15 U.S.C. §78c(a)(5).

Section 15 of the Exchange Act does not define the phrase "engaged in the business." Various courts have described the conduct that constitutes being "engaged in the business" of "effecting transactions in, "or "buying and selling," securities. One court has held that "regularity of participation is the primary indicia of being engaged in the business." *SEC v. Kenton Capital, Ltd.*, 69 F.Supp.2d 1, 12 (D.D.C. 1998). Regularity of participation can be shown by "such factors as the dollar amount of securities sold ... and the extent to which advertisement and investor solicitation were used." *Id.* at 12–13 (discussing factors to consider when determining whether one is engaged in the business of a broker); *see also Mass. Fin. Servs. Inc., v. Sec. Investor Prot. Corp.*, 411 F. Supp. 411, 415 (D. Mass. 1976 ("Both definitions connote a certain regularity of participation in securities transactions at key points in the chain of distribution. Yet, neither definition is all-encompassing. Each excludes, either explicitly or by implication, a variety of functions.").

The Exchange Act likewise does not define "effecting transactions" for the purposes of being a broker. In determining whether a person "effected transactions," courts consider several factors, such as whether the person (1) solicited investors to purchase securities, (2) was involved in negotiations between the issuer and the investor, and (3) received transaction-related compensation ...

Exchange Act. "The distinction drawn between the broker and the finder or middleman is that the latter bring[s] the parties together with no involvement on [his] part in negotiating the price or any of the other terms of the transaction ..."A finder, however, will be performing the functions of a broker-dealer, triggering registration requirements, if activities include: analyzing the financial needs of an issuer, recommending or designing financing methods, involvement in negotiations, discussion of details of securities transactions, making investment recommendations, and prior involvement in the sale of securities." ...

Although there is not an abundance of binding case law defining broker and dealer, one Fifth Circuit case is illustrative. In *Eastside Church* the court held that the defendant was both a broker and a dealer for purposes of the Exchange Act. *Eastside Church*,

391 F.2d at 361–62. The defendant assisted churches in all the legal work associated with a bond plan, acted as a trustee and the financial agent of the property, and directed the bond sales program, making sales throughout the country. The court found the above activities "conclusively" established that the defendant was a broker. The court also held that the defendant was a dealer based solely on the fact that it "purchased many church bonds prior to the ones in question for its own account as a part of its regular business and sold some of them."

B

1

It is undisputed that Reynolds, Mullholand, RSMR, Dissemination, Page, and Page Properties were not registered with the SEC as brokers or dealers.... [The court] concludes that the SEC has introduced sufficient undisputed evidence to hold that they used the instrumentalities of interstate commerce in acting as unregistered[10] dealers.[11]

2

Page, however, does contest whether he is a dealer. He maintains that his involvement in the transactions does not amount to what other courts have found constitutes being "*engaged in the business* of buying and selling securities for [one's] own account." (emphasis added). Page cites in support cases that hold that one is only "engaged in the business" of buying and selling securities for his own account if he has been involved in regular solicitations involving large dollar amounts, which Page maintains he was not.[12]

The SEC responds with uncontested evidence showing that Page was "engaged in the business" of buying and selling securities. First, the evidence establishes that Page and Page Properties owned investment accounts at J. Alexander and Bishop Rosen. Despite Page's contentions to the contrary, a reasonable jury could only find that Page used his accounts to buy and sell the securities of multiple companies. The evidence shows that Page bought shares of both Ecogate and Media International, and Page's company, Lion Capital, received shares of Ecogate in connection with the company's work on the Ecogate offering. Shortly thereafter, Page sold these shares through his accounts at J. Alexander and Bishop Rosen. Second, the evidence establishes that, through the purchase and sale of the shares of three other companies not at issue in

---

10. [20] Mullholand, Reynolds, Dissemination, and RSMR used the instrumentalities of interstate commerce by using brokerage accounts in New York and California from Texas to sell shares of Texas companies. They were not registered with the SEC as brokers or dealers.

11. [21] Mullholand, Reynolds, Dissemination, and RSMR acted as dealers by engaging in the business of selling shares for their own accounts. Mullholand and Reynolds, through Dissemination and RSMR, purchased or received as compensation millions of shares of the six companies involved in the transactions at issue in this case, and sold those shares for substantial sums.

12. [22] The SEC and Page only cite cases that define "engaged in the business" of a broker, not a dealer. Thus the court focuses on the regularity of participation in the actions of a dealer, *see Massachusetts Financial Services*, 411 F. Supp. at 415, rather than on activities that courts have considered when determining whether someone is engaged in the business of a broker.

this case—NuEnergy, Inc. ("NuEnergy"), eCarfly, Inc. ("eCarfly"), and ConnectAJet.com ("ConnectAJet")—Page regularly participated in buying and selling of securities for his own account. Page received one million shares of NuEnergy stock directly from the company for his services promoting NuEnergy as part of a Rule 504 offering, 500,000 of which he gave to Mullholand and Reynolds for their market awareness campaign promoting NuEnergy. Page also purchased millions of shares of both eCarfly and ConnectAJet and began immediately selling the shares to the public. In response to the SEC's questioning about these transactions, Page asserted his *Fifth Amendment* rights and refused to respond.

The best indication of someone's being "engaged in the business" of a dealer is the "regularity of [his] participation" in the buying and selling of securities for his own account. *Mass. Fin. Servs.*, 411 F. Supp. at 415. The SEC has introduced unrebutted evidence that Page regularly bought and sold securities for his own account. Additionally, the transactions involved a substantial number of shares and money. Page and Page Properties sold more than three million shares of Ecogate and Media International for more than $250,000. Acting through various companies he controlled, Page bought ten million shares of both eCarfly and ConnectAJet, and received another million shares of NuEnergy, some of which he sold to the public. Moreover, Page was not buying and selling securities as an individual investor making isolated transactions, which would disqualify him as a "dealer" under the statute. Page not only bought and sold securities through his companies Page Properties and Lion Holdings, but also through Testre LP and Griffdom Enterprises, Inc.

Although there are few cases describing what actions courts should look to when determining whether a person is a dealer, the evidence described above would only enable a reasonable jury to find that Page's actions constitute "engag[ing] in the business" of buying and selling securities. In *Eastside Church* the Fifth Circuit held that the defendant was a dealer because it "purchased many church bonds prior to the ones in question for its own account as part of its regular business and sold some of them." *Eastside Church*, 391 F.2d at 361. Like the defendant in *Eastside Church*, Page bought and sold securities as part of his regular business, making him a dealer under 15 U.S.C. §78c(a)(5).

3

A party violates 15 U.S.C. §78o(a)(1) if he is an unregistered broker *or* dealer and effects transactions in, or induces or attempts to induce the purchase or sale of, any security. Because a reasonable jury could only find that defendants are unregistered dealers, the court grants the SEC's motion for summary judgment against defendants on its claim under §15(a)(1) of the Exchange Act.

———

The next two sections of this chapter will examine the specific elements required to establish whether an entity or person is acting as a broker or dealer. While in most cases the terms *broker* and *dealer* are used together, it is important to study these two terms separately because they are defined separately in the Exchange Act.

II. Who Must Register as a Broker?

Essentially, a broker-dealer acts as an agent by bringing together the buyer and seller of securities for a fee or commission. As previously noted, a broker is defined in § 3(a)(4) of the Exchange Act as "any person engaged in the business of effecting transactions in securities for the account of others." Specifically, a person acts as a broker and must register with the SEC, when: (1) engaged in the business; (2) of effecting transactions in securities; (3) for the account of others. This definition contains two undefined elements—"effecting transactions" and "engaged in the business." The courts and the SEC have defined these elements very broadly; as a result, the determination of broker status requiring registration is very fact dependent.

A. Effecting Transactions in Securities

The element of "effecting transactions in securities" is established by showing that the person participates in securities transactions at key points in the chain of distribution." The following no-action letter and case illustrate factors used to determine whether a person is "effecting transactions in securities."

2000 SEC No-Act LEXIS 660

Broker-Dealer Activities of Transfer Online, Inc.[13]

To: Securities & Exchange Commission
From: Lori Livingston, President
March 15, 2000

To whom it may concern:

I am seeking guidance/authority in regard to activities which have become possible through the ever increasing use of the internet by the companies which I act as transfer agent for, new clients and their shareholders.

I am a registered transfer agent with approximately 75 companies and growing. Transfer Online provides online access to Issuers and their shareholders at the companies [sic] website, www.transferonline.com. The website provides shareholders and Issuers the opportunity to access their records and communicate online in a way which had never been available to them before. As a result, there has been an ever increasing demand for a variety of services.

Over the years I have been a transfer agent it has not been uncommon to be asked to participate as a third party in a private transaction. The principal difference I am encountering now is the increasing interest and demand from Issuers and shareholders interested in using this service as an alternative to brokerage firms and to save money. Transfer Online has been transferring shares as the result of transactions as well as providing services by which to exchange the funds.

---

13. The order of the letters has been reversed for ease of understanding. The original document has the SEC letter first and the letter from Transfer Online requesting no action second.

We have not received any commissions or fees from these transactions and have only charged the usual transfer fee for the service. As the frequency of requests for these services and the interest in them grows I have turned to various sources in an attempt to be sure we are staying within existing rules and regulations. There has been no definitive answer and no historical precedent readily accessible for guidance.

The services I am providing and seeking to expand upon, are first and foremost an empowerment tool and opportunity for choice for the ordinary investor. Additionally, my services are relatively unchanged from the past except that the venue has moved to the internet where it gains more exposure, and, therefore demand. I have not given advise [sic], taken commission for the purchase or sale of securities, or charged the Issuer any additional fees for this service.

I have been unable to locate any existing documents or releases for guidance and am therefore seeking the advise [sic] of your office for comments. I would like to continue to offer this service to shareholders as they request it, but I do not wish in any way to compromise my position as a Transfer Agent.

Please let me know how I might proceed to satisfy any rules or regulations which might exist. I thank you in advance for any information you can provide.

SECURITIES AND EXCHANGE COMMISSION
WASHINGTON, D.C. 20549
May 3, 2000

Ms. Lori Livingston
Transfer Online, Inc.
227 SW Pine Street, Suite 300
Portland, OR 97204

Re: Broker-Dealer Activities of Transfer Online, Inc.

Dear Ms. Livingston:

This letter is in response to your correspondence dated March 15, 2000 sent via e-mail (a copy of which is enclosed). You requested guidance in regard to Transfer Online, Inc. ("Transfer Online"), a registered non-bank transfer agent, serving as a "third party" in private securities transactions "as an alternative to brokerage firms." Your correspondence indicates that Transfer Online has been transferring shares as a result of these transactions as well as providing services by which to exchange funds. Your correspondence also indicates that Transfer Online has received its "usual transfer fee" for these transactions. We have reviewed both your correspondence and information posted on Transfer Online's website, located at www.transferonline. com. We believe that Transfer Online is engaging in broker-dealer activity and should be registered as a broker-dealer pursuant to Section 15(b) of the Securities Exchange Act of 1934 ("Exchange Act").

Section 15(a) of the Exchange Act makes it unlawful for a broker or dealer "to effect any transactions in, or to induce or attempt to induce the purchase or sale of, any security (other than an exempted security or commercial paper, bankers' acceptances, or commercial bills) unless such broker or dealer is registered" with the Securities and Exchange Commission ("Commission"). Section 3(a)(4) of the Exchange Act defines a "broker" as a person, other than a bank, that is "engaged in the business of effecting transactions in securities for the account of others."

A person effects transactions in securities if he or she participates in such transactions "at key points in the chain of distribution." Such participation includes, among other activities, assisting an issuer to structure prospective securities transactions, helping an issuer to identify potential purchasers of securities, soliciting securities transactions (including advertising), and participating in the order-taking or order-routing process (for example, by taking transaction orders from customers). Factors indicating that a person is "engaged in the business" include, among others: receiving transaction-related compensation; holding oneself out as a broker, as executing trades, or as assisting others in settling securities transactions; and participating in the securities business with some degree of regularity. In addition to indicating that a person is "effecting transactions," soliciting securities transactions is also evidence of being "engaged in the business."

We believe that Transfer Online is a broker within the meaning of Section 3(a)(4) of the Exchange Act. Through the "Stock Trading Board" of its website, Transfer Online brings buyers and sellers of securities together, receiving a fee based on the completion of a transaction. The Stock Trading Board allows shareholders to post offers to sell shares in companies for which Transfer Online serves as transfer agent and who have "engaged" Transfer Online to "manage" the Stock Trading Board. Registered users of the site are able to accept posted offers or to make counter-offers through the website. Sellers in turn are able to respond to counter-offers through the website. Registered users have the option of joining a mailing list through which Transfer Online will notify them via e-mail of new postings of offers to sell shares on the Stock Trading Board.

Transfer Online also processes "buy/sell requests pursuant to the terms set by the buyers and sellers" and settles securities transactions. Specifically, once a buyer and seller have agreed to the terms of a transaction, Transfer Online removes the offer to sell from the Stock Trading Board and invoices the buyer for the purchase price. In addition, Transfer Online handles customer funds, requiring that buyers send payment for shares purchased through the website to Transfer Online "within 5 business days of confirmation."

* * *

In conclusion, we believe that Transfer Online may already be required to register as a broker-dealer with the Commission. For your convenience, we have enclosed a copy of Form BD (broker-dealer registration package).

Very truly yours,
Catherine McGuire
Chief Counsel

SEC v. Margolin

Fed. Sec. L. Rep. (CCH) ¶ 97,025 (S.D.N.Y. 1992)

OPINION AND ORDER

LEISURE, *District Judge*,

This is an action by the Securities and Exchange Commission (the "Commission") against Ronald Margolin ("Margolin"), Brown & Mueller Investments Ltd. ("BMI"), Roger B. Webb ("Webb"), Mark L. Lutz ("Lutz"), and CMB Capital Management, Inc. ("CMB Capital") (collectively, the "defendants") for having allegedly conducted a trading scheme in violation of the federal securities laws. It is alleged that, since approximately September 1991, defendants have engaged in a fraudulent securities scheme, commonly referred to as "free-riding," in which they placed trades for over $35 million worth of securities, but refused to pay for trades that were unprofitable. The Commission alleges that the defendants financed this multi-million dollar trading scheme by defrauding nine brokerage firms out of more than $640,000 which the brokers were forced to pay to cover the defendants' trading losses. The defendants allegedly concealed from brokers, through various omissions and misrepresentations, their plan to use the proceeds of matching trades to finance their transactions in violation of applicable margin regulations and then the defendants simply avoided reimbursing the brokerage firms when losses were incurred.

* * *

In the instant action, the free-riding scheme in which Margolin was allegedly involved consisted of ordered purchases and sales of millions of dollars of securities and, therefore, the illegal credit was substantial. Each time the defendants ordered a purchase they did not have enough money to pay for, they forced their brokers to unwittingly extend them credit in violation of Regulation T. Moreover, in connection with sales, brokers were forced to violate Regulation T in two ways: (1) each time defendants ordered a broker to sell securities they did not own, the defendants essentially forced the broker to lend them the securities that the broker sold for them; and (2) each time a broker was forced to cover an unsettled sale by "buying-in" shares, the broker was extending credit in the account....

* * *

(3) *Violation of Section 15(a)(1) of the Exchange Act*

Section 15(a)(1) of the Exchange, requires a broker or dealer to register with the Commission if it makes use of the jurisdictional means "to effect any transaction in, or to induce or attempt to induce the purchase or sale of, any security." Section 3(a)(4) of the Exchange Act, defines a "broker" as "any person engaged in the business of effecting transactions in securities for the account of others, but does not include a bank."

In the instant case, Margolin ... has participated in dozens of transactions for various clients, the Commission can demonstrate "regularity of business activity" which supports the statutory definition of broker or dealer. *See Massachusetts Financial Serv-*

ices, Inc. v. Securities Investor Protection Corp., 411 F. Supp. 411, 415 (D. Mass. 1976). The record also indicates that Margolin engaged in other conduct which provided evidence of brokerage activity such as receiving transaction-based compensation, advertising for clients, and possessing client funds and securities.

Accordingly, the Court finds that the Commission has made a substantial showing of likelihood of success on the merits with respect to their claim that Margolin operated as an unregistered broker in violation of Section 15(a)(1) of the Exchange Act ...

Figure 3.1 summarizes the types of activities that the courts and the SEC have identified as effecting transactions in securities by participating at key points in the chain of distribution. However, none of these activities are definitive. In addition, it is unclear whether all or a few of these activities are required to establish the element of effecting transactions in securities under § 3(a)(4) of the Exchange Act.

Figure 3.1. Broker Activities to Determine "Effecting Transactions in Securities"

- Advising or commenting on any possible or proposed transaction
- Soliciting securities transactions (including advertising)*
- Participating in negotiations between parties to a transaction
- Assisting investors with the closing of a transaction
- Handling, receiving, or directing any funds or securities involved in a transaction
- Selecting the market to which a securities transaction will be sent
- Participating in the order-taking or order-routing process (e.g., taking transaction orders from customers)

  * As we will see below, soliciting securities transactions is also evidence of being "engaged in the business."

B. Engaged in the Business

The element of "engaged in the business" is established through regularity of participation in purchasing and selling securities.[14] Courts and the SEC have noted the importance of three factors in determining whether there is regularity of participation in the purchase and sale of securities: (1) the number of transactions and customers; (2) the dollar amount of securities sold; and (3) the extent to which advertisement and investor solicitation were used.

---

14. Note that this is also an element in determining dealer status under § 3(a)(5) of the Exchange Act. See, *supra*, Section II of this chapter.

SEC v. Kenton Capital, Ltd.

69 F. Supp. 2d 1(D.C.C. 1998)

Colleen Kollar-Kotelly, District Judge

MEMORANDUM OPINION

This case involves alleged violations of the anti-fraud, securities registration, broker registration, and investment adviser registration provisions of the federal securities laws. The Securities and Exchange Commission ("SEC") filed an Amended Complaint stating five claims against Defendants Donald Wallace and Kenton Capital, LTD ("Kenton").... The Fourth Claim charges Defendants with violating section 15(a) of the Exchange Act.... Currently pending before the Court is the SEC's Motion for Summary Judgment against Wallace and Kenton ...

Kenton is an entity incorporated in the Cayman Islands, British West Indies. Donald Wallace is Kenton's president. Prior to his involvement with Kenton, Wallace worked for many years as a registered securities professional.

In 1994, Wallace was interested in raising money through short term bank instruments. In February 1995, Wallace met Jeffrey Carter, who claimed to have experience with such programs. After Carter introduced Wallace to some investors in the Cayman Islands, Wallace established Kenton and arranged for Carter to act as a consultant for the company. As president of Kenton, Wallace was a signatory on Kenton's bank account and signed contracts on Kenton's behalf. According to Carter, Wallace made all of Kenton's decisions.

On behalf of Kenton, Wallace and Carter began to search for trading programs and investors. From a hotel room in Little Rock, Arkansas, Carter contacted prospective investors about providing capital to Kenton. Carter sent agreements to three investors, which described trading programs with projected returns of 3750% per week for forty weeks ("the Carter program").... The agreements that Carter sent also ensured that the investment would be "returned to the investor no later than the end of the investment period" of one year and one day....

During initial negotiations to raise capital, Carter arranged with Atlantic Pacific Guarantee Corporation ("AP") that AP would provide bonds as insurance for investments.... Carter also contacted Harry Watson, who agreed to raise capital for Kenton through his company, Deltaur Partners. Watson and his partner, Tracy French, succeeded in bringing investors to Kenton....

In April 1995, Wallace and Carter met with Watson to discuss possible trading programs. Watson informed them that he believed Carter's program offering a 3750% return was "absolutely impossible" and would lose money. Wallace then asked Watson to recommend a "safe program" for Kenton to use instead. Watson suggested that Kenton contact John Silver, a trader that he knew in Germany. Wallace and Watson called Silver, and Silver proposed the following program ("the Silver program"): for $ 2 million, Silver would rent $ 100 million in U.S. Treasury bills, paying Kenton 7% per week and providing a bank guarantee on the principal. Silver would take the rented securities to a bank, borrow 90% of the face vale [sic], and then trade the borrowed amount in offshore investments. Wallace decided to use the Silver program …

After this meeting with Watson, Wallace revised the investment agreement that Carter had been sending to investors. Wallace sent investors a replacement contract, titled "Investment Advisor's Agreement." Soon afterward, a third contract was sent to investors, which was identical to the Investment Advisor's Agreement except that the title had been changed to "Joint Venture Agreement," and instead of offering "specialist investment advice" the Joint Venture Agreement offers "specialist investment information." These contracts did not specify a rate of return, and gave Kenton complete discretion as to how to invest the funds it collected.

These new contracts were accompanied by a document describing the Silver program, titled "Asset Leveraging. The Asset Leveraging Opportunity proposed that Kenton would pool investments in order to invest $ 100 million or more in "Bank Instrument Trading Programs." This would be accomplished when a "facilitator" leased U.S. treasuries at 2% per month, established an account with a brokerage house, and hypothecated the treasuries for 90% of their value. Through this program, the facilitator could generate 7% profits per week, provided that investors pledged at least $ 100,000 in cash. For every $ 100,000 invested, investors were promised $ 110,000 in profits per week for forty weeks. Wallace has stated that, to the best of his knowledge, such profits have never been achieved by any trading program … The agreement authorized Kenton to purchase an AP guarantee bond for the investor in order to ensure repayment within a year and a day. The contract relieved Kenton of responsibility for the performance of the bond and required the investor to investigate the bond company.

The Joint Venture Agreement also provided that investors pay fees and costs to Kenton "from the Investment Amount." These included a 10% finder's fee, a 15% administrative fee, and costs for arranging leveraging. Kenton also requested 50% of "any profits earned on the investment of the net proceeds of the Investment Amount."

On the basis of these representations, over forty investors pledged to invest in Kenton's trading program. The SEC claims that the Defendants actually collected $ 1,745,000 from twelve investors.

On April 26, 1995, Kenton learned that the SEC was investigating its trading program. At that time, Kenton had not yet entered a formal contract with a trader. On May 3, 1995, the SEC obtained a Temporary Restraining Order prohibiting Kenton from transferring any funds, thereby halting the trading program.

* * *

C. FOURTH CLAIM: VIOLATION OF THE BROKER REGISTRATION PROVISIONS OF THE EXCHANGE ACT

Section 15(a) of the Exchange Act makes it unlawful for brokers to offer securities without registering themselves with the SEC. A broker is "any person engaged in the business of effecting transactions in securities for the account of others." Defendants do not dispute that they were effecting transactions in securities for the account of others. Instead, they argue that they were not "engaged in the business" because their activities were not sufficiently regular. In support of this position, Defendants allege that Wallace had not worked in the securities industry in the years immediately prior to forming Kenton, and that Kenton itself did "no other business and has since shut down."

"Engaged in the business" is not defined by statute. Cases and SEC No-Action letters interpreting the phrase have indicated that regularity of participation is the primary indicia of being "engaged in the business." *See, e.g., SEC v. Margolin*, 1992 U.S. Dist. LEXIS 14872, 1992 WL 279735, (S.D.N.Y.) (citing *Massachusetts Fin. Servs., Inc. v. Securities Investor Protection Corp.*, 411 F. Supp. 411, 415 (D. Mass 1976)). Regularity of participation has been demonstrated by such factors as the dollar amount of securities sold, *see SEC v. National Executive Planners, LTD.*, 503 F. Supp. 1066, 1073 (M.D.N.C. 1980) ($ 4.3 million of securities sold); *UFITEC, S.A. v Carter*, 20 Cal. 3d 238, 571 P.2d 990, 142 Cal. Rptr. 279 (Cal. 1977) (several million dollars of securities sold); and the extent to which advertisement and investor solicitation were used, *see SEC v. Deyon*, 977 F. Supp. 510, 518 (D. Me. 1997) (substantial solicitation); *National Executive Planners*, 503 F. Supp. at 1073 (investors solicited actively); Joseph McCulley, SEC No-Action Letter, [1972-73 Transfer Binder Fed. Sec. L. Rep. (CCH) P 78,982, at 82,111 (Aug. 2, 1972) (advertising "on a single, isolated basis" is not enough, but more than that would require registration)). A corporation could be a broker even though securities transactions are only a small part of its business activity. *See UFITEC*, 571 P.2d at 994 (citing 2 Louis Loss, *Securities Regulation* 1295 (1961)).

As the SEC's supporting evidence indicates, Defendants' securities transactions were not a single, isolated transaction, but rather the first step in a larger enterprise. Kenton was established for the exclusive purpose of participating in trading programs. To that end, Defendants received pledges to invest from over forty individuals totaling $17,450,000, actually collecting $1,745,000 from twelve investors. In its representations to investors, Kenton held itself out as being engaged in the business, actively soliciting participation. On these facts, the Court finds that no triable issue exists as to whether Defendants' participation was regular enough to require registration. The SEC is entitled to summary judgment on this claim.

SEC v. Martino
255 F. Supp. 2d 268 (S.D.N.Y. 2003)

POLLACK, Senior District Judge.

Plaintiff Securities and Exchange Commission ("Commission") has moved for summary judgment against defendants Carol Martino ("Martino"), CMA Noel Ltd. ("CMA"), Gerard Haryman ("Haryman"), and JTM Limited ("JTM"). Defendant Martino, a former stock broker, is a recidivist securities law violator and convicted felon (for related tax evasion). This civil enforcement action concerns Martino's latest securities law violations. The Commission charges Martino with (1) flagrantly and repeatedly violating a 1992 Commission order barring her from associating with a broker or dealer (the "Bar Order"); (2) acting as an unregistered broker in violation of the federal securities laws; and (3) engaging in a scheme to manipulate the stock price of one of her largest brokerage clients, RMS Titanic, Inc. Defendant CMA was Martino's closely-held brokerage firm ... The Commission seeks against Martino and CMA disgorgement of their illegal brokerage commissions, an injunction against future securities law violations, and other relief.

* * *

II. *Martino and CMA's Post–Bar Order Brokerage Activities*

Notwithstanding the Martino Bar Order, and from April 1992 through at least 1995, Martino, through CMA, brokered more than $20 million in sales of stock by several United States companies to overseas investors, purportedly pursuant to Regulation S of the Securities Act.[15] CMA was a "Subchapter S corporation" of which Martino was "President and sole owner."[16] Martino conducted these transactions using the means of interstate commerce from offices located in New York and Florida (and other United States locations). She earned millions of dollars in brokerage "commissions" from sales of Regulation S stock of at least five companies: Viral Testing Systems Corporation ("VTS"), Chippewa Resources, Inc. ("Chippewa"), Computer Concepts Corporation ("Computer Concepts"), Lone Star Casino Corporation ("Lone Star"), and RMS Titanic, Inc. ("Titanic"). During the time period at issue, Martino and CMA were not registered with the Commission as brokers or dealers. The brokerage services that Martino provided between each of the U.S. companies listed above and their foreign customers who purchased Regulation S stock from them are mentioned below.

A. *VTS*

On April 1, 1992 (the same date that the Commission issued Martino's Bar Order), Martino executed an agreement with Teleconcepts Corporation (later known as "Viral Testing Systems Corporation") (collectively "VTS") to broker sales of VTS stock to foreign purchasers. Under the agreement, Martino was to act as "liaison between buyer and seller" and receive "10% of the gross proceeds" of the stock sales.... Martino brokered at least $10 million in VTS stock sales during the period 1992 through 1993, and she proved to be "instrumental" in the "placement" of VTS shares. For her services, Martino received at least $1 million in cash commissions (*i.e.,* 10% of the $10 million in VTS stock sales), plus at least 82,500 VTS stock shares. In an affidavit, Martino

---

15. [3] "Regulation S" permits United States issuers to offer and sell securities if *conducted totally outside* the United States while exempting such sales (*i.e.,* sales that comply with Regulation S's conditions) from the Securities Act's Section 5 prohibitions against the sale of unregistered securities conducted in any part in the United States. Martino specialized in brokering sales conducted in part in the United States of deeply-discounted stock of United States companies to foreign investors pursuant to Regulation S. During the time period at issue, resale of Regulation S stock was prohibited for only forty days, after which the foreign purchasers could sell the stock at U.S. market prices for a significant profit ...

16. [4] Because CMA essentially was Martino's alter ego, reference to them hereinafter is both synonymously as "Martino," unless otherwise indicated.

refers to her receipt of VTS stock as "commissions due ... in connection with the placement" of VTS shares.... Martino provided complete brokerage services regarding VTS stock sales, from soliciting potential purchasers, through completing the sales transactions....

B. *Chippewa Resources, Inc.*

On April 20, 1992 (three weeks after the Commission issued Martino's Bar Order), Martino executed an agreement with Chippewa Resources, Inc. ("Chippewa") to broker sales of its Regulation S stock made for overseas investors. Martino again was to act as "liaison between buyer and seller" of Chippewa stock.

Martino likewise provided complete brokerage services for Chippewa stock sales. She furnished potential purchasers with company information, including Chippewa Commission filings and press releases, and she maintained constant contact with her investors. Martino also advised Chippewa investors regarding the sale terms that Chippewa favored and even attempted to "pre-sell" Chippewa stock to investors. In substance, Martino performed all functions called for under her brokerage agreement with Chippewa.... Martino routinely communicated by the telephone and written correspondence ... (from her offices in Florida and New York).... In return for her services, Martino received "a percentage of the price at which the stock was sold." Martino brokered at least $3 million in Chippewa stock sales and earned at least $398,000 in commissions....

C. *Computer Concepts*

On April 24, 1993, Martino executed an agreement with ETR & Associates Incorporated ("ETR") to broker sales of Computer Concepts stock to overseas investors. Pursuant to that agreement, on May 1, 1993, Martino executed an agreement with Computer Concepts and ETR to act as "liaison between buyer and seller" and to:

> (a) Provide Financial information of [Computer Concepts] to brokers and dealers to identify prospective purchasers of securities located outside the United States, (b) interview [] and recommend [] appropriate broker dealers, selling groups and individuals, (c) advise [] and assist [] [Computer Concepts] in negotiations with the prospective buyers as to the terms and conditions of the sale of [the stock].

Under the agreement, Computer Concepts agreed to furnish Martino 1 million shares of Computer Concepts stock to "offer for sale to purchasers." Martino agreed to receive 20.5% of the proceeds of each sale. Throughout 1993 and 1994, Martino and Hallmark Trading Co. (another Martino-controlled entity), received "commission" payments for these services from Computer Concepts totaling more than $1.2 million.

D. *Lone Star*

In 1993, Martino executed a similar brokerage agreement with Lone Star. The agreement allowed Martino to "sell [Lone Star] shares on behalf of the company." Martino subsequently brokered at least $4.1 million in Lone Star stock sales and earned over $393,000 in cash commissions, plus 65,000 shares of Lone Star stock as a "5% commission."

E. *Titanic*

In May 1993, Martino executed an agreement with RMS Titanic Corp. ("Titanic") to broker sales of its stock to overseas investors. Under that agreement, Martino was to perform all duties normally associated with "the sale of securities," including "serving as a liaison between buyer and seller." Martino's Titanic Regulation S stock sales services further included:

> (a) Provision of financial information of [Titanic] to brokers and dealers to identify prospective purchasers of securities located outside the United States; (b) interviewing and recommending appropriate broker dealers, selling groups and individuals; (c) advising and assisting [Titanic] in negotiations with the prospective buyers as to the terms and conditions of the sale of [] securities.

Under the Titanic agreement, Titanic was to make available to Martino 2,500,000 shares of Titanic stock for placement overseas. *Id.* Martino was to sell the stock at a minimum price of $3.20 per share and to receive a "fee" of 10% of all sales, plus any excess revenue that Titanic received above $2.88 per share.... Martino subsequently brokered over $3.6 million in Titanic stock sales and earned cash commissions in excess of $780,000, plus 45,000 shares of Titanic stock....

* * *

II. *Martino and CMA Engaged in Illegal Brokerage Activities*

A. *Martino and CMA Violated Section 15(a) of the Exchange Act*

Martino, both directly and through CMA, brokered Regulation S stock sales without registering as a broker with the Commission. Thus, both Martino and CMA violated Section 15(a) of the Exchange Act.

Section 15(a) makes it unlawful for any "broker or dealer" to make use of any means of interstate commerce and "to effect any transactions in, or to induce or attempt to induce the purchase or sale of, any security" without registering as a broker with the Commission. The Exchange Act broadly defines "broker" as one who "engaged in the business of effecting transactions in securities for the account of others." In determining whether a particular individual or entity falls within this definition, courts consider whether the individual may be "characterized by 'a certain regularity of participation in securities transactions at key points in the chain of distribution.'" *SEC v. Hansen*, No. 83 Civ. 3692, 1984 WL 2413, at *10 (S.D.N.Y. Apr. 6, 1984) (quoting *Massachusetts Fin. Services, Inc. v. Securities Investor Protection Corp.*, 411 F.Supp. 411, 415 (D.Mass.) *aff'd*, 545 F.2d 754 (1st Cir. 1976))…. Courts also have considered whether the individual:

> 1) is an employee of the issuer; 2) received commissions as opposed to a salary; 3) is selling, or previously sold, the securities of other issuers; 4) is involved in negotiations between the issuer and the investor; 5) makes val-

uations as to the merits of the investment or gives advice; and 6) is an active rather than passive finder of investors....

During the time period at issue (April 1992 through 1995), neither Martino nor CMA were registered as brokers with the Commission. Nonetheless, and in violation of Section 15(a), both plainly acted as brokers. Martino was the sole owner of CMA, and solely controlled its activities. Thus, her and CMA's activities are one and the same for the purpose of this analysis. Martino and CMA regularly solicited overseas clients to purchase Regulation S stock from U.S. companies, and regularly acted as middlemen between the U.S. sellers and foreign purchasers to complete these transactions. Indeed, their activities satisfy each of the "broker" criteria described above.

From April 1992 through 1995, CMA and Martino regularly participated in securities transactions and did so "at key points in the chain of distribution." In fact, Martino was involved in every aspect of the numerous securities transactions at issue. Ilan Arbel (one of Martino's major foreign clients) testified that Martino was "all the time aware" of the status of his many Regulation S stock transactions, and that she continuously contacted Arbel to discuss his payment for the stock and his satisfaction with the transactions, as well as his receipt of purchase agreements.

CMA and Martino plainly were not employees of Martino's clients. Their written agreements with their U.S. clients describe "consulting" services that plainly are brokerage services. The agreements with Chippewa, VTS, Computer Concepts, and Titanic all allow CMA to serve as a "consultant" and "to perform such duties as are normally associated with the sale of securities." Martino's U.S. clients expressly considered her a "broker," not an employee. In correspondence to a third party, Montle (who represented several of Martino's U.S. clients) referred to Martino as "the broker on this transaction." Likewise, Josef Hettrich (one of Martino's major foreign clients) stated in an affidavit that he relied on Martino as his "broker" in connection with certain Lone Star transactions.

Martino and CMA received commissions (not a salary) for their services, and the five CMA agreements identified above plainly reference those commissions. In accordance with those agreements, CMA received a percentage of the proceeds of each sale that Martino brokered (in the form of either cash or stock). Moreover, Martino consistently and continuously referred to her compensation as "commissions."

CMA and Martino's transactions also were not isolated incidents. To the contrary, defendants participated in the sale of stock of numerous issuers over a period of several years. Martino entered into five agreements with U.S. companies and subsequently made concerted efforts to raise more than $20 million in four years for those companies.

Martino and CMA also assisted in negotiating the stock sales at issue. Under their written agreements, CMA agreed to act as the "liaison between the buyer and seller" and to "advise [] and assist [] ... in negotiations with the prospective buyers as to the terms and conditions of the sale of [the stock]." And Martino performed such services in each case. For example, Chippewa CEO Larson stated that Martino acted in accordance with her Chippewa brokerage agreement. Arbel stated that Martino advised him about Regulation S and encouraged Arbel to invest. And Josef Hettrich stated that he relied upon Martino as his "advisor" in connection with certain Lone Star transactions.

Martino actively sought investors. Martino agreed in each case to "solicit" purchases of Regulation S stock and actively did so. For example, Martino attempted to "pre-sell" Chippewa stock to investors, and she disseminated Chippewa press releases and Commission filings to attract potential purchasers of Chippewa stock. In correspondence to Titanic, Martino stated that her "selling efforts will be continuous." In addition, Arbel stated that Martino "tried to put both sides together," and that Martino repeatedly contacted him to encourage him to purchase stock.

Thus, Martino and CMA plainly acted as unregistered brokers in violation of 15 U.S.C. § 78o(a).

―――――

Receipt of transaction-based compensation related to securities transactions, although not determinative, is a key factor for the SEC in requiring an entity to register as a broker-dealer. Although the phrase "transaction-based compensation related to securities transactions" is not defined in the Exchange Act or any related rule, the SEC, in no-action letters, has defined "transaction-based compensation related to securities transactions" as charging fees to users or participating broker-dealers based, directly or indirectly, on (or retroactively modified as the result of) the size, value, or occurrence of any securities transactions that have taken place or are expected to take place in the future, or the amount of money deposited or maintained in the user's brokerage account. This definition is very broad and indicates that the SEC will look behind the words used to describe compensation arrangements to determine whether such arrangements are transaction-related. The SEC asserted its core regulatory concern about transaction-based compensation related to securities transactions in 1st Global, Inc., No-Action Letter, 2001 WL 499080 (May 7, 2001):

> Persons who receive transaction-based compensation generally have to register as broker-dealers under the Exchange Act because, among other reasons, registration helps to ensure that persons with a "salesman's stake" in a securities transaction operate in a manner consistent with customer protection standards governing broker-dealers and their associated persons, such as sales practice rules. That not only mandates registration of the individual who directly takes a customer's order for a securities transaction, but also requires registration of any other person who acts as a broker with respect to that order, such as the employer of the registered representative or any other person in a position to direct or influence the registered representative's securities activities.

Not every receipt of transaction-based compensation related to securities transactions results in requiring registration as a broker-dealer with the SEC. In *SEC v. Kramer*, the court determined that the defendant was not required to register as a broker-dealer with the SEC; although the defendant received compensation in relation to securities transactions, the court determined that such compensation was not transaction-based compensation related to securities transactions. As you read this case, identify the key factors considered by the court in ruling in favor of the defendant.

S.E.C. v. Kramer

778 F. Supp. 2d 1320 (M.D. Fla. 2011)

ORDER

STEVEN D. MERRYDAY, District Judge.

The Commission sues to permanently enjoin the defendant Kenneth R. Kramer from violating the broker registration requirement under Section 15(a)(1) of the Exchange Act....

* * *

II. Findings of Fact & Conclusions of Law

Kramer, a resident of Lake Worth, Florida, worked approximately forty years ago (beginning in 1969) "in the municipal bond business" as the vice-president of a company that sold municipal bonds. Later, Kramer became the president of another company that sold municipal bonds. Between 1976 and 1977, Kramer co-owned a company that sold "London Commodity Options" until Congress prohibited sale of the options in the United States. Kramer worked in the telecommunications industry and co-owned a company that installed telephone systems from 1982 to 1988. However, in 1988, Kramer pleaded guilty to a charge of wire fraud and conspiracy and later served twenty-eight months in prison. After his release in 1990, Kramer formed LCP Consultants, Inc.

Twenty years ago, Kramer and the defendant Baker became business associates and began working on projects together. At the time of Kramer and Baker's collaboration, Baker owned at least two companies, Affiliated Holdings, Inc., and Worldwide Associates, Inc. To formalize their business relationship, Kramer and Baker executed a written agreement in August, 2003. Kramer (as CEO of LCP Consultants) signed a "co[-]operative agreement" with Affiliated Holdings. Under the agreement, Kramer and Baker promised generally (1) to co[-]operate "in presenting to each other prospective merger and acquisition candidates, potential sources of investment and venture capital funding, and other forms of business opportunities...." and (2) to share any fee or "other compensation" resulting from "successful conclusion of a business arrangement...."[17]

---

17. [16] In 2005, Kramer and Baker entered another agreement entitled "consulting agreement" in which LCP Consulting (Kramer's company) retained Worldwide Associates (Baker's company) as a consultant. Under the agreement, Worldwide Associates (designated as the "Consultant") agreed to perform certain consulting services, which consisted (in relevant part) of (1) presenting "prospective acquisition targets, business opportunities, joint ventures[,] and any other form of revenue enhancements" to the "Company," LCP Consulting; (2) assisting "in the implementation of short range and long term strategic planning to fully develop and enhance ... assets, resources, products[,] and services"

Several months before signing the agreement with Kramer, Baker (in March, 2003) on behalf of Affiliated Holdings signed with Skyway Aircraft an agreement, in which Skyway Aircraft agreed to pay Baker a five-percent commission (1) on capital raised on behalf of the company, (2) on the purchase price of any acquisition or merger resulting from Baker's introducing Skyway Aircraft and a third party, and (3) on the total value of any contract brought to Skyway Aircraft by Baker. James Kent, the CEO of Skyway Aircraft, signed the agreement. Under the agreement, Baker facilitated a "reverse merger"[18] between Skyway Aircraft and another entity, a so-called "public shell." Skyway Aircraft was "the corporation that was formed in order to roll into the reverse merger," which resulted in Skyway Global LLC becoming the public company, Skyway Communications Holding Corp ("Skyway") in 2003.

Before and after becoming a public company, Skyway retained an array of "independent contractors," including Baker, to facilitate Skyway's finding "technology programs"; potential merger or acquisition candidates; and "investment houses, venture capital, wealthy individuals, [and] investment groups." Skyway provided each "finder" a folder of information about the company and (based on successful performance of the finder's agreement) compensation in Skyway shares. Brent Kovar, the president of Skyway from 2003 to 2005, met Baker after Baker (in 1998 or 1999) contacted Kovar's former company. Kovar understood that Baker was both a prospective investor and a representative of investors, and hired Baker as a "finder" after Kovar became the president of Skyway.

In mid-2003, Kovar met Kramer, who Kovar understood worked for Baker. As an employee of Baker's, Kramer contacted Kovar on a regular basis and sought press re-

---

of LCP Consulting; and (3) advising as to "the continued development [of] a customer relations program and ... stimulat[ing] interest in [LCP Consultants] by institutional investors and other members of the financial community." The consulting agreement obligated LCP Consultants to pay Worldwide Associates ten percent of any "funds raised or invested," the "purchase price of an [] acquisition or merger," or the "total value of a [] contract brought to [LCP Consultants]."

18. [18] In a "reverse merger," a privately held entity merges with a publicly traded "shell," and the merger renders publicly tradeable the private entity's shares. *S.E.C. v. Surgilight, Inc.,* 2002 WL 31619081, *1 n. 1 (M.D.Fla.2002) (Sharp, J.). As *S.E.C. v. M & A West, Inc.,* 2005 WL 1514101, *2 (N.D.Cal.2005) (Walker, J.), explains:

A "reverse merger," as used herein and in the parties' papers, is a transaction in which a private operating corporation (a "private" company) merges into a corporation whose stock has previously been offered to the public (a "public" company). Typically, the public company will at the time of the reverse merger be a "shell" company with minimal assets and liabilities and no actual operations. To complete the securities aspect of the reverse merger, the public shell company will exchange its treasury stock (along with, perhaps, shares from its stockholders) for all outstanding shares of the private company, and in consideration, the shareholders who control the public shell company will transfer most of their shares in the shell company to the owners of the private company. Often the public shell company will take on the name formerly used by the private company, and operations will carry on as before, except the formerly private company is now an issuer of publicly traded securities. The overall transaction thus provides a way for the private company effectively to offer its stock to the public in a more expedient and cost-effective manner than conducting an initial public offering.

leases about Skyway and Skyway's accomplishments. In response and if Skyway had issued a new press release, Kovar directed Kramer to Skyway's web site. Kovar understood that Kramer assisted Baker in Baker's efforts for Skyway but lacked personal knowledge of the details of Kramer's conduct. Baker, on the other hand, became a trusted and driving force behind Skyway's business. In addition to orchestrating the reverse merger, Baker introduced Skyway to broker-dealers and invited potential investors both to Skyway's aircraft demonstrations and to Skyway's headquarters.

After Baker's introducing Kramer to Skyway in 2003, Kramer and Skyway (through Kent [Skyway's CEO]) developed an understanding that Skyway would pay Kramer for introducing a potential investor to Skyway if the potential investor decided to invest. Shortly thereafter, Kramer introduced Nick Talib to Baker and Skyway. A friend of Kramer's, Gary Johnson, became acquainted with Talib, who was a registered broker living in Arkansas and who sold Johnson shares of Skyway. Talib eventually traveled to Florida, and Kramer drove Talib from the airport to a restaurant where Talib and Kramer met Baker. Talib, Baker, and Kramer traveled to Skyway's headquarters and introduced Talib to Kovar. After the introduction, Baker, Talib, and Kovar adjourned to a conference room, and Kramer received a tour of Skyway's facility. Talib eventually raised approximately $14 million in capital for Skyway by selling shares of Skyway to investors. As a result of Kramer's introducing Talib to Baker and Skyway, Skyway paid Kramer between $189,000.00 and $200,000.00 in "the form of periodic checks." The first payment to Kramer from Skyway for the Talib introduction occurred in December, 2003.

Because Kramer thought that Skyway was a good investment and because Baker asked Kramer to tell people about Skyway, Kramer (1) bought shares in Skyway through his brokerage account and (2) encouraged certain others to read a press release about Skyway and to visit Skyway's web site. Thus, when Skyway issued a press release, Kramer recommended that people read the press release. Kramer told some of his friends, including Barry Krohn, Seymour Cohen, Bob Herko, Lino Morris, Jeffrey Steinig, and Allen Katz,[19] about Skyway and shared his opinion that Skyway was a good investment. For example, Katz (a retired employee of Oppenheimer) and Kramer (a long-time neighbor of Katz) often discussed investments. Kramer told Katz that Kramer thought Skyway "might be a good deal" and that Kramer had visited Skyway's headquarters. Katz later purchased shares of Skyway. Kramer also talked about Skyway to his attorney, Allen Denowitz, and his doctor, Allen Sklover, both of whom later purchased shares. Kramer discussed Skyway with his two sons, one of whom purchased shares. Additionally, Cohen, Herko, Herko's son, Steinig, Steinig's brother, and Morris

---

19. [32] Krohn and Kramer, friends since childhood, habitually speak on the phone at least once or twice a day. Cohen and Kramer were partners in "the commodity business" and became friends in 1976. Herko and Kramer met over forty years ago when Kramer was "in the municipal bond business" and became re-acquainted approximately ten years ago when Herko visited Florida. After becoming re-acquainted, Herko and Kramer talked on the phone once or twice a week. Morris and Kramer became friends fifteen years ago and speak on the phone once or twice a week. Steinig and Kramer became friends thirty-two years ago. Rohatynsky and Kramer became friends ten years ago and talk on the phone once a week, at most.

purchased Skyway shares. Krohn purchased Skyway shares after Kramer's mentioning Skyway to Krohn, Kramer's recommending that Krohn evaluate the company, and Krohn's reviewing information about Skyway. After purchasing shares, Krohn (similar to Kramer) talked to people about Skyway and directed people to Skyway's web site. Based on Krohn's evaluation of Skyway, Krohn advised certain others that Skyway was both a good company and worth considering as an investment. Of the people with whom Krohn discussed Skyway, approximately four or five purchased shares. Each person (with whom either Kramer or Krohn spoke) purchased Skyway shares from a registered broker who received a commission based on the purchase.

At some point, Baker requested from Kramer information about (1) who purchased Skyway shares, (2) from whom the person purchased the Skyway shares, and (3) the number of shares purchased. In exchange, Baker offered to pay Kramer twenty percent of the number of shares that each person bought.[20] Accordingly, after Kramer's friends and acquaintances purchased shares through a registered broker, Kramer received from Baker (through Baker's company, Affiliated Holdings) additional shares in Skyway. Similarly, after Cohen, Krohn, Herko, Steinig, and others talked to people about Skyway, each received from Baker additional shares of Skyway. For example, when Katz purchased shares in Skyway, Kramer reported Katz's purchase to Baker, and Kramer received from Baker additional shares of Skyway. Similarly, when Krohn reported to Kramer (who reported to Baker) a purchase of Skyway shares, Krohn received from Baker additional shares of Skyway. Each report described purchases by individuals through registered brokers such as Scottrade, E*trade, and Merrill Lynch. The fax cover page of a report states that "the number below represents balance owed after stock delivery" and lists a number of shares "owed" followed by the name, address, and social security number of the recipient (e.g., Kramer, Cohen, Krohn, and others).

By the time Skyway petitioned for bankruptcy in 2005, Kramer had earned approximately $700,000.00 from his Skyway shares, and Krohn had earned approximately $75,000.00 from his Skyway shares. Kramer at no time either registered with the Commission or obtained a securities license.

In this action, the Commission argues that Kramer acted as an unregistered broker of Skyway securities.... "Broker" means "any person engaged in the business of effecting transactions in securities for the accounts of others."[21] The Commission bears the burden of proving by a preponderance of the evidence a violation of Section 15(a). *S.E.C. v. Ginsburg*, 362 F.3d 1292, 1298 (11th Cir.2004).

The Exchange Act is intended "to protect investors ... through regulation of transactions upon securities exchanges and in over-the-counter markets" against manipulation of share prices. The broker-dealer registration requirement is "of the utmost

---

20. [39] As to why Baker sought the reported information (and was willing to pay Kramer, Krohn, and others for the reports) neither Kramer nor Krohn provided an explanation, aside from Baker's requesting the information.

21. [47] The defendant agrees that this action involves a security (shares of Skyway), that Kramer's conduct involves the use of a "means or instrumentality of interstate commerce," and that Kramer never registered with the Commission.

importance in effecting the purpose [] of the [Exchange] Act," because registration facilitates both discipline "over those who may engage in the securities business" and oversight "by which necessary standards may be established with respect to training, experience, and records."

Because the Exchange Act defines neither "effecting transactions" nor "engag[ing] in the business," an array of factors determines whether a person qualifies as a broker under Section 15(a). The most frequently cited factors, identified in *S.E.C. v. Hansen*, 1984 WL 2413, *10 (S.D.N.Y.1984), consist of whether a person (1) works as an employee of the issuer, (2) receives a commission rather than a salary, (3) sells or earlier sold the securities of another issuer, (4) participates in negotiations between the issuer and an investor, (5) provides either advice or a valuation as to the merit of an investment, and (6) actively (rather than passively) finds investors. *See also Cornhusker Energy Lexington, LLC v. Prospect St. Ventures*, 2006 WL 2620985, *6 (D.Neb.2006) (Bataillon, J.) … *S.E.C. v. Margolin*, 1992 WL 279735 (S.D.N.Y.1992) (Leisure, J.) (finding evidence of "brokerage activity" in the defendant's "receiving transaction-based compensation, advertising for clients, and possessing client funds and securities.")…. *Cornhusker* describes "transaction-based compensation" as "one of the hallmarks of being a broker-dealer." 2006 WL 2620985 at *6 (stating that "[t]he underlying concern has been that transaction-based compensation represents a potential incentive for abusive sales practices that registration is intended to regulate and prevent."). In other words, transaction-based compensation is the hallmark of a salesman. By contrast, a person's recommending a particular investment or participating in a negotiation typically occurs in an array of different commercial activities and professional pursuits, including brokering.

* * *

In another case, *S.E.C. v. Corporate Relations Group, Inc.*, 2003 WL 25570113 (M.D.Fla.2003) (Antoon, J.), the Commission alleged that a "stock promotion firm" violated Section 15(a). The firm "published investment-related material ranging from one-page faxes to the monthly full-color magazine, *Money World*" and, in exchange for a fee, agreed (1) to promote a security in one of the firm's publications, (2) to forward an investor inquiry about the security to a registered broker, and (3) to direct the firm's "broker relations executives" ("BREs") to both contact the registered broker and encourage the broker to sell the security. According to two former BREs, the BREs also counseled an inquiring investor to purchase a security featured in the firm's publications. If a BRE submitted proof that the investor purchased the security from a broker, the BRE received a commission from the firm based on the sale. On summary judgment, *Corporate Relations Group* holds that the firm (not the BREs) acted as an unregistered broker in violation of Section 15(a), because the firm "actively sought investors, … recommended securities to investors through registered [brokers], and … [paid] transaction-based compensation for stock sales."

In contrast, *S.E.C. v. M & A West, Inc.*, 2005 WL 1514101 (N.D.Cal.2005) (Walker, J.), grants summary judgment *sua sponte* in favor of a defendant on the Commission's Section 15(a) claim. The undisputed facts established that the defendant facilitated and participated in reverse mergers. Specifically, the defendant worked with the shareholders of a private company (1) to identify "suitable public shell companies," (2) to prepare documents for the reverse merger, and (3) to co-ordinate the parties to the reverse merger. Upon successful completion of a reverse merger, the defendant received compensation in cash and securities. Rejecting the Commission's argument that the defendant's conduct amounted to broker activity, *M & A West* finds that:

> Th[e] [Commission's] factual recitation capped with an ipse dixit sheds no light on why [the defendant]'s activities—commonly associated with para-legals (who draft documents), lawyers (who draft documents and orchestrate transactions), businessmen (who identify potential merger partners) and op-portunists (who like to take a small cut of a big transaction), none of whom is commonly regarded as a broker—add up to [the defendant's] being a bro-ker. In particular, no assets were entrusted to [the defendant], and the Com-mission identifies no evidence that he was authorized to transact "for the account of others" (aside from his fiduciary authority over [the] accounts [of entities controlled by him]). Although [the defendant] was in the business of facilitating securities transactions among other persons, the Commission cites no authority for the proposition that this equates to "effecting transac-tions in securities for the account of others."

Following *M & A West,* a series of cases identified a limited, so-called "finder's ex-ception" that permits a person or entity to " 'perform a narrow scope of activities without triggering the b[r]oker/dealer registration requirements.' " *Salamon v. Teleplus Enterprises, Inc.,* 2008 WL 2277094, *8 (D.N.J.2008) (Walls, J.) (quoting *Cornhusker,* 2006 WL 2620985 at *6); *Salamon v. CirTran Corp.,* 2005 WL 3132343, *2–*3 (D.Utah 2005) (Stewart, J.). "Merely bringing together the parties to transactions, even those involving the purchase and sale of securities, is not enough" to warrant broker reg-istration under Section 15(a). Rather, the evidence must demonstrate involvement at "key points in the chain of distribution," such as participating in the negotiation, analyzing the issuer's financial needs, discussing the details of the transaction, and recommending an investment. *Cornhusker,* 2006 WL 2620985 at *6. Even if the "finder" receives a fee "in proportion to the amount of the sale"—i.e., a percentage of the total payment rather than a flat fee—the Commission (in a series of "no-action" let-ters) "has been willing to find that there was no need for registration...." David A. Lipton, 15 Broker–Dealer Regulation § 1:18 (explaining, however, that payment of a flat fee "does not insure that the payment will be regarded as non[-]commission com-pensation."); *but see Brumberg, Mackey & Wall, P.L.C.,* SEC No-Action Letter, 2010 WL 1976174 (May 17, 2010) (stating that "any person receiving transaction-based compensation in connection with another person's purchase or sale of securities typ-ically must register as a broker-dealer or be an associated person of a registered bro-ker-dealer."). The distinction between a finder and a broker, however, remains largely unexplored, and both the case law and the Commission's informal, "no-action" letter advice is highly dependent upon the facts of a particular arrangement....

In the trial of this action, the Commission argued that Kramer's conduct qualified as broker activity subject to Section 15(a) because Kramer (1) received transaction-based compensation, (2) actively solicited investors (by distributing promotional material and directing people to Skyway's web site), (3) advised investors about Skyway (by telling people that Skyway was a good company and suggesting that people read Skyway's press releases), (4) used a "network" of associates to promote Skyway, (5) demonstrated a regularity of participation (through the money that Kramer earned and the two-years over which the conduct occurred), (6) promoted the shares of other issuers, and (7) earned commissions rather than a salary as a Skyway employee. In response, Kramer asserted that Kramer (1) never sold a share of stock, (2) never "engaged in the business of effecting securities transactions for the accounts of others," (3) talked about investments in the manner that people talk about sports or politics, (4) talked to only some of Kramer's relatives and close friends about Skyway, (5) acted as a finder by introducing Talib to Skyway, and (6) reported purchases of Skyway shares to Baker because Baker requested the information and because Baker agreed to pay Kramer (with Baker's Skyway shares) for collecting the information.... Kramer stipulated to receiving payment from Skyway as a result of the Talib introduction and admitted receiving shares of Skyway from Baker based on Kramer's reports to Baker of Skyway purchases. Kramer admitted telling his friends and intimates about Skyway (to generate "market awareness") and directing attention to Skyway's web site and press releases. However, Kramer repeatedly disputed the Commission's use of the term "network" to refer to his friends and denied that any of Kramer's agreements with Baker pertained to Skyway or to Kramer's reports to Baker.

* * *

Kramer received so-called transaction-based compensation in two distinct instances. The first instance involved Nick Talib. Skyway hired Baker as an independent contractor to facilitate Skyway's finding both a potential merger or acquisition candidate and other financing. As a developing company, Skyway hired many independent contractors to find both financing and technology. Skyway never hired Kramer. However, after Baker informed Kramer about Skyway, Kramer developed an understanding that Kramer would receive compensation for Kramer's introducing a potential investor to Skyway. Additionally, Baker and Kramer had an ongoing business relationship governed by a "co-operative agreement," which obligated each party to share a potential business opportunity and any resulting compensation. When Kramer's friend, Gary Johnson, told Kramer about Talib (a registered broker) and Talib's interest in Skyway, Kramer arranged a meeting between Talib, Baker, and Skyway. The evidence establishes that the extent of Kramer's involvement in the Talib transaction consisted of arranging the meeting and providing transportation for Talib from the airport to Skyway's headquarters. Talib eventually raised a substantial amount of financing for Skyway by selling shares to investors, and both Baker and Kramer received a payment from Skyway based on the success of the introduction.

In this instance, Kramer's conduct consisted of nothing more than bringing together the parties to a transaction. The Commission presented no evidence that Kramer either participated in the negotiation, discussed the detail of the transaction, analyzed the financial status of Skyway, or promoted an investment in Skyway to

Talib or to Talib's investors. In fact, the evidence shows that, after introducing Talib to Baker and driving Talib to Skyway's headquarters, Kramer received a tour of the facility while Baker and Kovar adjourned to a conference room with Talib. Kramer's minimal involvement in the Talib transaction is not susceptible to the description "engaged in the business of effecting transactions in securities for the accounts of others." No evidence shows that Kramer possessed authority over the accounts of others or sought to influence Talib's authority over the accounts of others. In fact, the Commission presented evidence neither of Kramer's communicating with Talib (beyond facilitating the introduction to Skyway) nor of Kramer's communicating with Talib's investors about Skyway. Rather, the only available inference from the evidence is that Talib sought an introduction to Skyway, Talib convinced investors to entrust him with assets, Talib effected securities transactions for those investors, and Talib earned commissions. Kramer's introduction of Talib was an ephemeral, remote, and isolated initiative. Kramer's receiving transaction-based compensation for introducing Talib to Skyway cannot, without additional evidence, qualify Kramer a broker under Section 15(a).

Kramer also received compensation from Baker based on Kramer's reporting to Baker purchases of Skyway shares. The Commission argues (1) that Kramer received compensation because Baker directed Kramer to promote Skyway; (2) that, to accomplish the task, Kramer employed a "network" of associates to promote Skyway shares; and (3) that, in turn, Kramer (and each of his associates) received Skyway shares upon proof that a purchase occurred.

The evidence shows that Kramer told a small but close group (each susceptible to description as either a friend or an intimate) about Skyway and opined that Skyway seemed like a good investment. According to the Commission, the nature of Kramer's relationship with each person is irrelevant to the broker analysis under Section 15(a). However, the broker analysis under Section 15(a) (as developed in *Hansen, Martino,* and other cases) permits examination of a wide array of factors, including those factors already identified in applicable precedent. In the absence of a statutory definition of either "effecting securities transactions" or "engaged in the business," certain factors determine whether a person qualifies as a broker. One factor may evidence broker activity while another factor suggests the absence of broker activity. Accordingly, the nature of a person's relationship with another (although not determinative, of course) may support either the absence or the presence of broker activity.

In this instance, the evidence establishes that Kramer discussed Skyway with his lawyer, his doctor, Krohn, Cohen, Herko, Morris, Steinig, Katz, and his son. The full measure of Kramer's "advice" to, or "solicitation" of, this array of Kramer's intimate friends and family consisted of Kramer's (1) sharing his opinion that Skyway was a good company and a good investment and (2) directing attention to Skyway's web site and press releases. Some of Kramer's intimate friends and family (1) purchased Skyway shares and (2) talked to other people about Skyway. Baker, whom Skyway retained as a consultant, requested that Kramer collect and send to Baker reports of purchases of Skyway shares. In exchange for the reports, Baker paid Kramer and some of Kramer's intimate friends with Baker's shares of Skyway.[22] Odd, but true. Odd, but not "broker" activity.

The Commission presented no additional, admissible evidence that Kramer either (1) sold a share of Skyway; (2) participated in the purchase and sale of a Skyway security; (2) provided advice or other information about the investment; (3) advertised or distributed promotional material for Skyway; (4) sponsored a seminar or social event at which Kramer promoted Skyway; (5) sold the security of another issuer; (6) hired employees to contact potential investors about Skyway; (7) called a potential investor (i.e., someone other than one of Kramer's intimate friends); or (8) encouraged a broker to sell Skyway securities. Rather, the Commission's evidence against Kramer leads inexorably to the conclusion (1) that, at most, Kramer (and Krohn and others) exhibited conduct similar to an associated person of an unregistered broker and (2) that in this instance the unregistered broker, if anyone, was either Bruce Baker or Baker's company, Affiliated Holdings. Baker executed a written contract with Skyway to find financing for Skyway; Baker promoted Skyway to Kramer, Talib, and others; Baker became intimately involved in Skyway's financial transactions, including the Talib transaction and the reverse merger; Baker received transaction-based compensation from Skyway; and Baker paid Kramer, Krohn, and others to tell people about Skyway and to send reports of Skyway share purchases.

This instance is analogous to *Corporate Relations Group* to the extent that, through Affiliated Holdings, Baker (similar to the firm in *Corporate Relations Group*) (1) agreed for a fee to promote an issuer's securities, (2) forwarded an investor inquiry either to a broker or directly to the issuer, and (3) hired employees to help accomplish each task. However, unlike the BREs in *Corporate Relations Group*, Kramer, Krohn, and the others who received payments from Baker neither (1) contacted a broker and encouraged the broker to sell Skyway securities, (2) fielded investor inquiries, nor (3) counseled an investor to purchase shares of Skyway. Nonetheless, assuming that Kramer's sharing his opinion—that Skyway was a "good company" and a "good deal"—equates to investment advice, the Commission presents insufficient evidence from which to conclude that Kramer's conduct in this instance is somehow materially different from a BRE in *Corporate Relations Group*. In other words, *Corporate Relations Group* found that the firm—not a BRE—acted as an unregistered broker and, in this instance, the evidence against Kramer fails to show conduct comparable (either in nature or in extent) to either the firm or the BREs in *Corporate Relations Group*.

In sum, neither applicable precedent nor the statutory language permits the conclusion, based on the admissible evidence presented in this action, that Kramer acted as an unregistered broker in violation of Section 15(a). In this instance, the Commission fails to show by a preponderance of the evidence that Kramer "engaged in the business of effecting transactions in securities for the accounts of others."

---

22. [53] Neither Kramer nor Krohn could articulate the reason for Baker's requesting the reports, which contain information likely available from a better source for a lesser or no charge.

Notes and Questions

1. As discussed above in *Kramer,* both the courts and the SEC, through issuance of no-action letters, have recognized an exemption from the registration requirement of § 15(a) for limited activities. *Salamon v. Teleplus Enterprises, Inc.,* Fed. Sec. S. Rep. P 94,742 (N.J.D.C. 2008) involved a claim to rescind a contract based on a violation of Section 15(a) and the denial of summary judgment based on conflicting evidence of broker conduct. In *Teleplus Enterprises,* the parties disputed whether a consultant hired by an issuer qualified as a "finder" or as an unregistered broker. The issuer argued that the consultant qualified as a broker because the consultant (1) claimed a 10 percent commission based on financing received by the issuer as a result of the consultant's finding an investor for the issuer, (2) solicited potential investors, (3) participated in negotiations, and (4) provided advice to the issuer. The consultant asserted that he participated neither in negotiating nor in structuring the deal after the consultant introduced the investor to the issuer. Based on *Kramer,* would the consultant in *Teleplus Enterprises* be a finder or an unregistered broker? → *An unregistered broker given (3) & (4). Enough for*

2. As noted, the phrase "engaged in the business of effecting transactions in securities" in the definition of broker in § 3(a)(4) of the Exchange Act is not defined in the Exchange Act. In struggling to define this phrase, which requires registering with the SEC, the SEC and the courts distinguish between brokers and finders. A finder is defined in various SEC no-action letters as a person who places potential buyers and sellers of securities in contact with one another for a fee. However, the Exchange Act does not contain an exception for finders. Identify SEC policies that support distinguishing between a broker required to register under § 15(a) of the Exchange Act and a finder not required to register with the SEC.
   ↳ Needing regulation and protection versus not.

Hypothetical One

Success First has come to you for advice about a potential acquisition, BD Advantage. It is concerned that it might have to register the company as a broker with the SEC based on its activities. Carmen Alvarez, Success First's president, believes that the company would be a great acquisition to expand Success First's business lines. The general counsel of Success First, Josephine Wiseman, is concerned because of the potential for a significant increase in compliance expenses, if the SEC determines that BD Advantage is a broker and therefore is required to register with the SEC under § 15(a). The president of Success First describes the business of BD Advantage as follows. BD Advantage is in the business of referring registered brokers (introducing brokers) to a registered broker that clears trades (clearing broker) for introducing brokers under a fully disclosed clearing agreement. BD Advantage's service allows the introducing brokers to constitute a group, which enables them to qualify for discounts in transaction fees; the clearing brokers treat such introducing brokers as a group and aggregates their transactions for fee purposes. As consideration for the referrals, the clearing broker pays BD Advantage a fee based on the number of transactions generated from the group of introducing brokers. BD Advantage has no contact with any customers of the introducing brokers and does not in any way influence a customer's choice of broker or securities. The introducing brokers execute all trades for their customers. Specifically, BD Advantage is referring brokers, not customers, to a clearing broker. It is also not involved in any way with advising customers, executing trades, or delivering funds or securities. It merely organizes the introducing brokers and provides them a way to reduce their costs, while at the same time bringing new brokers to the clearing broker. Must BD Advantage register with the SEC?

III. Who Must Register as a Dealer?

Section 3(a)(5) of the Exchange Act defines a dealer as any person engaged in the business of buying and selling securities for her own account through a broker or otherwise and as part of a regular business. Therefore, registration as a dealer with the SEC is required if two elements are established: (1) buying and selling securities for one's own account and (2) being engaged in the business of buying and selling securities for one's own account as part of a regular business. Both of these elements must be established to require registration as a dealer with the SEC under § 15(a)(1). The first element means that the person must purchase or sell securities as principal, i.e., the person must execute a principal transaction. A principal transaction is executed when a person sells from an existing inventory of securities that she already owns or when she executes a riskless principal transaction. A riskless principal transaction occurs when the dealer, after receiving an order to buy (or sell) from a customer, purchases (or sells) the security from (or to) another person in a contemporaneous offsetting transaction. Essentially, in riskless principal transactions the dealer sustains no risk that the price of the security will fluctuate adversely, because both the purchase and sale of the security occur contemporaneously. The second element "engaged in the business" is similar to the element "engaged in the business" required to establish broker status requiring registration. However, it differs slightly because the factors used to establish this element under the definition of *dealer* are not necessarily the same. For example, to meet the definition of *dealer*, there must be a regular customer base, a holding out as buying and selling securities at a regular place of business, and a regular turnover of business with investors (or other broker-dealers if acting as a market maker).

Eastside Church of Christ v. National Plan, Inc.

391 F.2d 357 (5th Cir. 1968)

Opinion

GRIFFIN B. BELL, Circuit Judge:

The appellants, seven churches, are seeking recovery against the two appellees, National Plan, Inc. and its president and principal owner, Robert H. Knox. The churches, asserting that they never received payment for certain bonds which they issued and which were purchased by National, claim that they are entitled to recover the bonds still in National's possession and damages for any which National has transferred to innocent purchasers. National answers that the bonds are valid and subsisting obligations of the churches. The District Court agreed with National. Unfortunately we cannot finally resolve the question in full. We affirm in part; but, because of a basic error of law in the District Court in the area of securities regulation, the case must be reversed in part and remanded for further proceedings.

* * *

II.

This leaves for decision whether appellees or either of them are liable to the churches, or any of them, by reason of the breach as claimed of an additional section of the Securities Exchange Act, § 15(a)(1), or of the rules promulgated thereunder, Rules 15c1-4 and 15c2-4. National Plan proceeded for declaratory judgment on the premise that the bonds were exempt from regulation under the securities law; hence National Plan was exempt from registration, and that it need only show that it was a holder in due course to establish that the churches were obligated on the bonds.

The District Court concluded that the bonds were exempt securities under the Exchange Act and that there was no violation of the registration provisions of that Act by National. In addition, the judgment provides if there were violations of any securities law in connection with the bond transactions, they did not materially deny the churches any protection which the law was designed to afford. As will be seen, these two holdings are incorrect and require reversal....

This brings us to the pertinent facts. National acquired the bonds in the following manner. Paden, a church contractor, agreed to construct buildings for each of the appellant churches. To finance the construction of the buildings, the churches issued bearer bonds to Paden, either selling them to him outright or delivering them to him as agent to sell, or as the church witnesses said, 'to place' the bonds on behalf of the churches. The churches claim that Paden was obligated to remit to them the full face value of the bonds, without commission, either promptly or, in the case of certain bonds, as the money would be needed for construction of the buildings. Paden sold bonds in the face amount of $215,750 to National at a discount. In the case of a few the discount was ten per cent; in the case of most, fifteen per cent. National, as directed by Paden, paid for the bonds either directly to Paden or to a company called World Oil & Gas of Delaware, Paden having told National that World Oil & Gas would absorb the discount and pay Paden the full face value of the bonds as he needed it for the church construction projects. The evidence was that Paden failed to remit to the churches on the National purchases.

The churches entrusted Paden with the bonds. They issued the bonds in negotiable form. They printed on the face of each bond: 'This is a bearer bond and as such may be transferred by delivery'. In addition, each bond bore the certificate that payment had been received for the bond but, of course, with respect to those bonds purchased by National on the representation from Paden that he was acting as agent for the churches in an effort to sell the bonds, National knew that the churches had not been paid.

The churches claim that National purchased the bonds in violation of three provisions of the federal securities laws. First, they assert that National was an unregistered broker-dealer and, accordingly, that National's purchase of the bonds violated § 15(a)(1) of the Act, prohibiting an unregistered broker-dealer from effecting securities transactions.... The churches claim that, as a result of th[is] violation [], National's purchases of the bonds are void under § 29(b) of the Exchange Act, thus entitling the churches to the relief sought.

We consider first the failure of National to register and the result which ensues because of § 15(a)(1) of the Act. It was stipulated that National had not registered as either a broker or dealer under the Act, that the mails were used in the transactions in question and that they took place in interstate commerce.

We are concerned with the Securities Exchange Act of 1934. Section 12(g)(2)(D) of that Act contains an exemption of church bonds, but that exemption, again, relates only to their registration, it does not relate to the antifraud or broker-dealer registration provisions. There is simply no exemption in the Exchange Act from these provisions even when the broker or dealer is handling church bonds.

The District Court did not decide whether National was a broker or a dealer within the meaning of the Exchange Act. This question was not reached due to the erroneous view that church bonds were exempt securities even for the purposes of the broker-dealer registration provisions.... Section 3(a)(5) of the Exchange Act defines a dealer as any person engaged in the business of buying and selling securities for his own account, through a broker or otherwise. The evidence demands a finding that National was so engaged. National purchased many church bonds prior to the ones in question for its own account as a part of its regular business and sold some of them. Thus National was a ... dealer within the meaning of the Act.

It follows that the purchases which National made from the appellant churches through their agent Paden were in violation of § 15(a)(1) of the Exchange Act ... The question next arises whether appellants may void these transactions because National acted in violation of § 15(a)(1) of the Act. Section 29(b) of that Act provides that 'every contract made in violation of any provision of this chapter or any rule or regulation thereunder ... shall be void ... as regards the rights of any person who, in violation of any such provision, rule, or regulation, shall have made or engaged in the performance of any such contract ...'. There are certain exceptions to this voiding provision but none is applicable here. Section 29(b) also contemplates civil suit for relief by way of rescission and damages where the transactions are void.

Without more, it appears that appellants may void these transactions but National contends that appellants are nevertheless not entitled to relief unless they can establish that any harm which they suffered was caused by National's failure to register. However, the Act requires only that appellants be in the class of persons whose interest the Act was designed to protect. In our view a more stringent requirement would be contrary to the express mandate of § 29(b).

Under § 15(a)(1), National was prohibited from effecting the transactions here involved and thus violated the Act by entering into those transactions. Under the voiding provision of § 29(b), it is sufficient to show merely that the prohibited transactions occurred and that appellants were in the protected class. We have found no case precisely in point but a similar voiding provision in 26(b) of the Public Utility Holding Company Act of 1935, 15 U.S.C.A. § 79z(b), has been construed in accord with our holding. (citations omitted).

The harsh remedy which this view dictates, even under the circumstances of this case where the churches chose the unfaithful agent, seems to be what Congress intended. The fact that Congress removed certain violations from the voiding sanction of § 29(b) lends support to our construction of § 29(b) in this case. The requirement that brokers and dealers register is of the utmost importance in effecting the purposes of the Act. It is through the registration requirement that some discipline may be exercised over those who may engage in the securities business and by which necessary standards may be established with respect to training, experience, and records.

Appellees urge that such consequences are inequitable in light of the conduct of the churches is turning the bonds over to Paden as their agent for the purposes of sale and collection of the proceeds therefrom. They contend that the churches should account for the monies paid to Paden by National but which were not paid to the churches by Paden. This does not follow in light of the voiding provision. The transactions were void ab initio and National must account for such of the bonds as were owned by the churches and for which the churches have not been paid.

III.

Because of our holding that those transactions involving purchases from the churches are void due to National's failure to register, the case must be remanded to the District Court for further findings and conclusions....

―――――――

The SEC considers many factors in determining whether a person is required to register as a dealer. Similar to factors considered in establishing that registration as a broker is required, factors considered in establishing dealer status are not determinative; the analysis of whether a person is a dealer under § 3(a)(5) of the Exchange Act depends upon all of the relevant facts and circumstances. See Figure 3.2 for a nonexhaustive listing of such factors.

Finally, persons associated with a registered broker-dealer are required to register with FINRA. The term *associated person of a broker-dealer* or *person associated with a broker-dealer* is defined in § 3(a)(18) of the Exchange Act. An associated person is defined as all employees of the broker-dealer engaged in the broker-dealer's securities business as well as its partners and directors. It also includes any person or entity that directly or indirectly controls, is controlled by, or under common control with the broker-dealer. The term does not include employees or other persons whose func-

Figure 3.2. Factors Establishing Dealer Status Identified by the SEC

- Underwriting;
- Acting as a market maker or specialist on an organized exchange or trading system;
- Acting as a de facto market maker whereby market professionals or the public look to the firm for liquidity; or
- Buying and selling directly to securities customers together with conducting any of an assortment of professional market activities, such as providing investment advice, extending credit, and lending securities in connection with transactions in securities, and carrying a securities account.

tions are solely clerical or ministerial. The registration requirements of associated persons are discussed below in Section V of this chapter.

Notes and Questions

1. Dealer versus Trader Distinction. The SEC recognizes that the distinction between a dealer requiring registration under 15(a)(1) and an individual trading on behalf of herself, who is not required to register, may blur in practice. In *SEC v. Ridenour*, 913 F.2d 515 (1990), Ridenour argued that he need not register as a dealer under § 15(a)(1) based on a series of private transactions in municipal bonds and corporate securities that he executed on his own behalf from 1979 to 1981. The court required Ridenour to register because his level of activity during this period made him more than an active investor. "Ridenour attempted to obtain and keep a regular clientele for his 'private' bond deals, which he negotiated out of his office at Dean Witter, albeit on his own behalf." *Id.,* at 517. In addition, in SEC No-Action Letter, *Stephen V. Hart,* 1980 SEC No-Act LEXIS 3020 (Mar. 6, 1980), the SEC stated that "[a]lthough the definition of 'dealer' seeks to exclude from its scope a person who buys or sells securities for his own account as an ordinary trader and not as part of a regular business, it is sometimes difficult to distinguish when a person is a trader as opposed to a dealer. Isolated transactions for one's own account will not subject a person to the requirement of registration as a 'dealer in securities,' particularly when a person's securities activities are relatively minor measured against his other activities and he does not have memberships in exchanges or associations of dealers and does not provide the services to others that dealers customarily supply to customers. This is a matter of interpretation based on all the relevant facts."

2. In *SEC v. American Institute Counselors, Inc.*, Fed. Sec. L. Rep. ¶ 95,388, 1975 WL 440, *17, the court, citing 2 Loss, Securities Regulation (2d ed. 1961) p. 1295–96, noted that "[i]t is well established that: "the phrase ('engage in the busi-

ness') connotes a certain regularity of participation in purchasing and selling activities rather than a few isolated transactions ... and there is likewise nothing in the concept of a 'business' which precludes a person from being a broker or dealer because he handles, with regularity, only a single issue of securities." 2 Loss, Securities Regulation (2d ed. 1961) p. 1295–96.

3. In *UFITEC, S.A. v. Carter*, 571 P.2d 990, 994 (1977), the court noted that one could be required to register as a dealer pursuant to § 15(a)(1), even if the securities transactions are a relatively small part of an entity's business. UFITEC argued that it was not a broker or dealer because its securities transactions were a relatively small part of its investment banking and placement activity; accordingly, it was not "engaged in the business" for either itself or others within the meaning of §§ 3(a)(5) or 3(a)(4) of the Exchange Act. However, its securities business constituted several million dollars and UFITEC charged a commission for its service. The court found that "[t]he phrase 'engaged in the business' connotes a certain regularity of participation in purchasing and selling securities, but there is no requirement such activity be a person's principal business or principal source of income." The SEC reiterated the court's finding in SEC No-Action Letter, *Joseph McCulley Sales*, 1972 SEC No-Act. LEXIS 3229.

IV. Exemptions from Broker-Dealer Registration

There are only a few narrow exemptions from the registration requirement of Section 15(a). These exemptions include: (1) broker-dealers whose business is exclusively intrastate; (2) certain broker-dealers dealing in excluded and exempted securities; (3) certain foreign broker-dealers or non-U.S. domiciled broker-dealers. However, exemption from the registration requirement of § 15(a) does not exempt the broker-dealer from the antifraud provisions of § 15(c) of the Exchange Act. Section 15(c) applies to broker-dealers who make use of the instrumentality of interstate commerce. Section 3(a)(17) of the Exchange Act defines interstate commerce and this definition includes the "intrastate use of 'a telephone or other interstate means of communication ...'"

A. Intrastate Broker-Dealers

Broker-dealers whose business is exclusively intrastate and who do not make use of any facility of a national securities exchange are exempt from the registration requirements of § 15(a). However, this exemption is used infrequently because of the extremely narrow interpretation of this exemption by the SEC and the courts. This exemption requires the broker-dealer to only effect transactions in securities within the state in which it is located and all aspects of the securities transaction must be within the broker-dealer's state. The broker-dealer and its customers, as well as the issuer, must be located in only one state; this also means that the issuer must be a resident of, and perform all of its business activities in, the same state as the broker-dealer. The SEC uses § 3(a)(11) and Rule 147[23] of the Securities Act as guidance in determining when an issuer is deemed to be a resident of, and doing business within, a state. Section 3(a) (11) of the Securities Act exempts securities from the registration requirements of § 5 of the Securities Act if they are "part of an issue offered and sold only to persons resident within a single State or Territory, where the issuer of such security is a person resident and doing business within or, if a corporation, incorporated by and doing business within, such State or Territory." In addition, the broker-dealer cannot deal in securities that are traded on a national exchange. This confines the broker-dealer's business to residents and relatively small issuers of a single state. In addition, the SEC has stated that information posted on the Internet that is accessible in another state would be considered the use of an instrumentality of interstate commerce, thus triggering registration under § 15(a).

Securities and Exchange Commission (S.E.C.)
In the Matter of Capital Funds, Inc.

File No. 8-10968.
Promulgated August 20, 1964

FINDINGS AND OPINION OF THE COMMISSION

The issues raised in these proceedings pursuant to Sections 15(b) and 15A(b)(4) of the Securities Exchange Act of 1934 ('Exchange Act') are whether we should deny or permit withdrawal of the application for registration as a broker and dealer of Capital Funds, Inc. ('applicant' or 'Capital'), and whether we should find Austin E. Gatlin and his wife Erma S. Gatlin, officers, directors and principal stockholders, each a cause of any order of denial which may be entered against applicant.

After hearings, at which the Gatlins were present and testified, the hearing examiner submitted a recommended decision in which he found that respondents had committed willful violations of the Securities Acts as alleged in the order for proceedings, and he recommended that we deny the application and find the Gatlins causes of the denial. Applicant filed exceptions and a brief. Our findings are based on an independent review of the record.

I

From about April to December 1962, Capital acted as underwriter on a best efforts basis with respect to a public offering at $5 per share of 60,000 shares of stock of Peoples Loan and Investment Co., Inc. ('Peoples'). Gatlin was general manager of Peoples, in which he and his wife through Capital had a controlling interest, and Capital shared Peoples' offices in Ft. Smith, Arkansas. The public offering of Peoples stock was assertedly limited to residents of Arkansas, and no registration statement with respect to it was filed under the Securities Act of 1933, purportedly in reliance on the ex-

---

23. Rule 147 was adopted "to provide more objective standards upon which responsible local businessmen intending to raise capital from local sources may rely in claiming the section 3(a) (11) exemption." 17 C.F.R. § 230.147.

emption from registration accorded certain intrastate offerings under Section 3(a)(11) of that Act.

We find, however, as did the hearing examiner, that in at least two instances Peoples stock was sold by a salesman in Capital's employ to persons who were, and were also known to be, residents of Oklahoma. Applicant seeks to escape the consequences of these sales to nonresidents by asserting that the transactions represented sales by the salesman of his personally owned shares and not sales by Capital. The salesman testified that he subscribed for 1,000 shares in the middle or latter part of June 1962; that he thereafter concluded he could not pay for the shares; and that after discussion with Gatlin he arranged to sell the shares to the two nonresidents. The first such sale was made on July 2, and the second on September 13, 1962.

The hearing examiner rejected the contention that the salesman had become the bona fide owner of the 1,000 shares, and in our opinion the record amply supports the examiner's conclusion. The salesman never paid for the stock and never received any stock certificates; according to the respondents' own version of the transactions the salesman concluded within a matter of only days after he had assertedly subscribed for the shares that he could not pay for them; respondents have been unable to produce any subscription form signed by the salesman; the usual subscription form used by Capital in its sales on behalf of Peoples was signed by one of the out-of-State purchasers; and the payments by both such purchasers were made to Peoples. Moreover, although Mrs. Gatlin was in charge of the records, applicant has been unable to explain the fact that the stock certificate ostensibly issued in June 1962 to the salesman, on the basis of subscriptions allegedly executed by him at that time, bears a number higher than those on certificates issued to the nonresidents who purchased in July, and August 1962.

* * *

II

The hearing examiner found that applicant, although not registered as a broker-dealer with us, engaged in a securities business which was not exclusively intrastate.

Applicant was incorporated in Oklahoma in March 1961. It registered as a broker-dealer in that State in April 1961, and beginning in May 1961 acted as underwriter on a best efforts basis with respect to a public offering at $2 per share of 100,000 shares of stock of Lawton Loan and Investment Corporation stated to be limited to residents of Oklahoma. Thereafter applicant established an additional office in Arkansas, and in January 1962 it obtained a certificate of authority to do business in that State and in March 1962 obtained a license as an Arkansas securities dealer. Applicant claims it discontinued securities transactions in Oklahoma and limited its activities in Oklahoma to the loan business before it opened its office in Arkansas. However, applicant continued to be qualified as a securities dealer in both States and, as we have already noted, during the period April, to December 1962, applicant acted as underwriter with respect to the public offering of Peoples stock to residents of Arkansas, in the course of which at least two sales were made to residents of

Oklahoma. Moreover, the record shows that applicant made some sales of securities to a resident of Missouri, and that it purchased from a resident of Texas some shares of Peoples stock which it thereafter sold to residents of Oklahoma. Applicant's contention, that those transactions constituted investment activity and therefore should be disregarded in determining the character of its business, must be rejected.

Under all the circumstances, we agree with the hearing examiner's finding that applicant's business was not exclusively intrastate, and accordingly conclude that applicant, aided and abetted by the Gatlins, willfully violated Section 15(a) of the Exchange Act in using the mails and interstate facilities to effect transactions in securities when it was not registered as a broker-dealer pursuant to Section 15(b).

* * *

V

In view of the nature and extent of the wilful violations we conclude, as did the hearing examiner, that it is in the public interest to deny rather than permit the withdrawal of the application for registration as a broker-dealer. We also find that the Gatlins, who managed and directed applicant's affairs and operations, are each a cause of the denial.

B. Commercial Paper Exemption

Broker-dealers who deal exclusively in commercial paper are exempt from the registration requirement of § 15(a)(1). Specifically, § 15(a)(1) does not require broker-dealers to register if their business is exclusively in an "exempted security or commercial paper, bankers' acceptances, or commercial bills." Commercial paper, bankers' acceptances, or commercial bills are short-term financial instruments used to finance short-term cash needs of a business. For example, commercial paper consists of short-term (not more than 270 days), prime quality notes used to finance short term obligations such as accounts receivables and inventories. They are also identified as exempted securities under § 3(a)(3) of the Securities Act. Bankers' acceptances are also short-term financial instruments endorsed by a bank, which obligate the bank to pay the instrument on the due date (generally 30–180 days); these instruments are used in international trade and are only endorsed by the bank if it is comfortable with the buyer's financial strength and stability. Commercial bills are bills of exchange[24] issued by commercial organizations to raise funds to pay short-term obligations.

However, certain broker-dealers are required to register with the SEC even if transacting business exclusively in exempted securities. The term *exempted security* is defined in § 3(a) (12) (A) of the Exchange Act and is extensive. Exempted securities

-----

24. A bill of exchange is a written, unconditional order by the drawer to the drawee to pay a certain sum either immediately or on a fixed date for the payment of goods or services. The drawee accepts the bill by signing it, which converts it into a post-dated check and a binding contract.

identified in § 3(a) (12) (A) include U.S. government securities and municipal securities. However, even though § 15(a) would seemingly exempt broker-dealers dealing exclusively in U.S. government and municipal securities, such broker-dealers are still required to register with the SEC. Broker-dealers transacting business exclusively in U.S. government securities are required to register with the SEC pursuant to § 15C of the Exchange Act. Brokers transacting business in municipal securities are required to register under § 15(a) because § 3(a) (12) (B)(ii) of the Exchange Act states that municipal securities shall not be deemed to be "exempted securities" for the purposes of section 15 of the Exchange Act; dealers transacting business exclusively in municipal securities must register with the SEC pursuant to § 15B of the Exchange Act. Accordingly, broker-dealers transacting business exclusively in U.S. government securities and municipal securities are required to register with the SEC.

C. Foreign Broker-Dealer Exemption

In general, foreign broker-dealers, i.e., non-U.S. broker-dealers, are required to register with the SEC unless they qualify for an exemption. The definitions of broker and dealer are not based on location, but on securities transactions with U.S. citizens. In addition, the definition of "interstate commerce includes trade, commerce, transportation, or communication ... between any foreign country and any State, or between any State and any place or ship outside thereof." Combined, these provisions establish the jurisdictional means (using interstate commerce to effect securities transactions) for subjecting foreign broker-dealers to the registration requirements of § 15(a) of the Exchange Act. In addition, § 30(b) of the Exchange Act, which excludes the application of the Exchange Act to any person that transacts a securities business "without the U.S.," has been held unavailable in securities transactions: (1) that occur in a U.S. securities market; (2) if offers and sales are made abroad to U.S. persons or in the U.S. to facilitate sales of securities abroad; or (3) if the U.S. is used as a base for securities fraud perpetrated on foreigners. Essentially, the SEC asserts that "a broker-dealer operating outside the physical boundaries of the United States, but using the U.S. mails, wires, or telephone lines to trade securities with U.S. persons located in [the U.S.], would not be, in the words of section 30(b), 'transact[ing] a business in securities without the jurisdiction of the United States.[25] The goal is to protect U.S. citizens where it is reasonable to expect the protections of the U.S. broker-dealer regulatory framework.

In light of the internationalization of broker-dealer activities, Rule 15a-6 was adopted to provide clear guidance to foreign broker-dealers engaged in transactions with U.S. citizens about whether such interactions required registration as a broker-dealer under § 15(a) of the Exchange Act. Rule 15a-6 defines the term foreign broker-dealer as:

> any non-U.S. resident person (including any U.S. person engaged in business as a broker or dealer entirely outside the United States, except as otherwise

---

25. *Registration Requirements for Foreign Broker-Dealers,* (Jul. 18, 1989) 54 FR 30013, (Rel. No. 34-27017) p. 11.

permitted by this rule) that is not an office or branch of, or a natural person associated with, a registered broker or dealer, whose securities activities, if conducted in the United States, would be described by the definition of "broker" or "dealer" in sections 3(a)(4) or 3(a)(5) of the Act.

Essentially, a foreign broker-dealer is a non-U.S. resident person, not associated with a registered broker-dealer, engaged in the business of effecting securities transactions for others or for his own account. In addition, the SEC asserts that this definition "expressly includes any U.S. person engaged in business as a broker or dealer entirely outside the United States."

Rule 15a-6 allows: (1) nondirect contacts between foreign broker-dealers and U.S. investors, (2) direct contacts between foreign broker-dealers and certain U.S. investors through intermediaries, and (3) direct contacts between foreign broker-dealers and certain other persons directly.

1. Nondirect Contacts

Paragraph (a)(1) of Rule 15a-6 exempts a foreign broker-dealer from registration under § 15(a) if it effects an unsolicited trade for a U.S. investor. According to the SEC, "registration is [not] necessary if U.S. investors have sought out foreign broker-dealers outside the United States and initiated transactions in foreign securities markets entirely of their own accord.... U.S. investors would have little reason to expect these foreign broker-dealers to be subject to U.S. broker-dealer requirements. Moreover, requiring a foreign broker-dealer to register as a broker-dealer with the [SEC] because of unsolicited trades with U.S. persons could cause that foreign broker-dealer to refuse to deal with U.S. persons under any circumstance."

The prohibition on solicited transactions also includes the distribution of research reports to U.S. investors. Although the term *solicit* is not defined in Rule 15a-6, it has been interpreted by the SEC to include research reports. The SEC believes that research reports constitute a solicitation when the basic purpose of providing the research report is to generate transactional business for the broker-dealer. Paragraph (a)(2) of Rule 15a-6 prescribes the manner in which research reports may be used without being deemed a solicitation and therefore a prohibited activity under Rule 15a-6.

Rule 15a-6 permits a foreign broker-dealer to give research reports to major U.S. institutional investors and to effect transactions in the securities discussed in the research reports under specified conditions. Rule 15a-6 defines a major U.S. institutional investor as a U.S. institutional investor[26] that has, or has under management, total assets in excess of $100 million or a registered investment adviser with total assets

---

26. A U.S. institutional investor is a person that is: (i) a registered investment company under § 8 of the Investment Company Act of 1940; or (ii) a bank, savings and loan association, insurance company, business development company, small business investment company, or employee benefit plan under Rule 501(a)(1) of Regulation D of the Securities Act; a private business development company under Rule 501(a)(2) of the Securities Act; a 501(c)(3) organization under the Internal Revenue Code; or a trust under Rule 501(a)(7)(17) of the Securities Act.

under management in excess of $100 million. Specifically, Rule 15a-6(2) provides an exemption from registration for foreign broker-dealers that furnish research reports to major U.S. institutional investors if: (1) the research report does not recommend the use of the foreign broker-dealer to effect trades in any security and (2) the foreign broker-dealer does not initiate follow-up contact with major U.S. institutional investors receiving the research, or otherwise attempt to induce the purchase or sale of any security by major U.S. institutional investors. However, if the foreign broker-dealer has an existing relationship[27] with a registered broker-dealer, all transactions in securities resulting from the provision of research reports must be effected through the registered broker-dealer.

The exemption from registration for research reports distributed to major U.S. institutional investors does not include soft dollar arrangements. Soft dollar arrangements include agreements to provide research with the express or implied understanding that customers (in this case major U.S. institutional investors) will pay for the research by directing trades to the broker-dealer that result in a specified level of commission dollars. Moreover, if a foreign broker-dealer participates in a soft dollar arrangement, the SEC will presume that it has induced purchases and sales of securities even if the securities were not related to the particular research provided. This means the exemption in paragraph (a)(2) of Rule 15a-6 would no longer be available.

2. Direct Contacts

Rule 15a-6 allows foreign broker-dealers to have direct contacts with U.S. institutional investors and major U.S. institutional investors under certain conditions without being required to register under § 15(a)(1). The rule distinguishes between the type of direct contact allowed with respect to whether the foreign broker-dealer is contacting a U.S. institutional investor or a major U.S. institutional investor. Contacts between associated persons of foreign broker-dealers and U.S. institutional investors cannot occur without the participation of an associated person of a registered broker-dealer in each such contact. Participation of an associated person of a registered broker-dealer is not necessary in contacts between major U.S. institutional investors and foreign broker-dealers. The SEC believes that major U.S. institutional investors have the requisite "skills and experience to assess independently the integrity and competence of the foreign broker-dealers …". However, all transactions that occur as a result of direct contacts between U.S. institutional investors and major U.S. institutional investors and foreign broker-dealers must be executed by a registered broker-dealer.[28]

---

27. Rule 15a-6(3)(a)(iii) requires that the relationship be with a registered broker-dealer that agrees to be responsible for effecting the transactions on behalf of the U.S. investor, issuing required confirmations and statements to the investor, extending or arranging credit to investors, maintaining the required books and records under Rules 17a-3 and 17a-4, complying with the net capital rule, and safeguarding funds and securities resulting from the transactions effected on behalf of the U.S. investor.

28. The registered broker-dealer is responsible for issuing confirmations and account statements. In addition, it is responsible for the extension of credit in connection with the securities transactions

This requirement facilitates SEC regulation of broker-dealer financial responsibility and the effective enforcement of U.S. securities laws. In addition, the foreign broker-dealer must agree to service of process through the registered broker-dealer[29] and to provide information and documents requested by the SEC in connection with its enforcement activities. Also, the registered broker-dealer is required to review such transactions for possible violations of U.S. securities laws. Finally, Rule 15a-6 imposes certain requirements on associated foreign persons of foreign broker-dealers who are allowed to contact U.S. institutional investors and major U.S. institutional investors. Associated foreign persons must conduct all their securities activities outside of the U.S. but are allowed to visit U.S. institutional investors and major U.S. institutional investors within the U.S. as long as they are accompanied by an associated person of a registered broker-dealer who has agreed to take responsibility for all communications with such investors and to effect all securities transactions resulting from such communications. In addition, associated foreign persons must not be subject to statutory disqualification in their home jurisdictions.[30]

Rule 15a-6 also allows direct contact between foreign broker-dealers and certain persons in the United States. without participation of a registered broker-dealer as an intermediary. These persons include registered broker-dealers, certain international organizations, foreign persons temporarily in the U.S. with bona fide pre-existing relationships with the foreign broker-dealer, foreign agencies or branches of U.S. persons permanently located outside of the U.S., and non-resident U.S. citizens. Rule 15a-6 specifies the types of international organizations with whom the foreign broker-dealer may have direct contacts; they include The African Development Bank, the Asian Development Bank, the Inter-American Development Bank, the International Bank for Reconstruction and Development, the International Monetary Fund, the United Nations, and their agencies, affiliates, and pension funds. With respect to foreign agencies or branches of U.S. persons permanently located outside of the United States, all securities transactions must take place outside of the United States. In addition, although direct contacts between non-resident U.S. citizens and foreign broker-dealers are permitted, the foreign broker-dealer must not direct its selling efforts toward identifiable groups of U.S. citizens resident abroad, e.g., the U.S. military and U.S. embassy personnel.

The no-action request granted to Chase Capital Markets, although granted before the adoption of Rule 15a-6, is an example of the exemption permitted in Rule 15a-6 from the registration requirement of § 15(a) of the Exchange Act.

---

and for maintaining books and records required under Exchange Act Rules 17a-3 and 17a-4. All such records must be maintained in the United States.

29. This includes proceedings initiated by the SEC and SROs. The registered broker-dealer must maintain a written record of any such contents made by the foreign broker-dealer.

30. See § 3(a)(39) of the Exchange Act. Statutory disqualification includes, among others, persons expelled or suspended from FINRA membership or from association with a broker-dealer and persons subject to an SEC or FINRA order denying or suspending membership with FINRA. In addition, the registered broker-dealer is responsible for obtaining information about sanctions imposed by foreign securities authorities against the foreign broker-dealer and its associated persons.

Chase Capital Markets US Milbank, Tweed, Hadley & McCloy[31]

S.E.C. Release No. 91 (Jul. 28, 1987)

We are writing on behalf of The Chase Manhattan Corporation ("Chase") to request assurance that the staff will not recommend that the Commission take enforcement action under Section 15(a) of the Securities Exchange Act of 1934 (the "Exchange Act") if certain of Chase's direct or indirect foreign subsidiaries, authorized under local and applicable Federal banking law to act as securities professionals abroad ("Foreign Subsidiaries"), do not register in the United States as broker-dealers under the circumstances described below.

Background. Chase Manhattan Capital Markets Corporation ("CMCMC") is a wholly owned, operating subsidiary of Chase owned through several subsidiaries of Chase, including The Chase Manhattan Bank, N.A. (the "Bank"). CMCMC, which is organized under the laws of the State of Delaware, is registered as a broker-dealer with the Commission and is a member of the National Association of Securities Dealers (the "NASD"). CMCMC is authorized, pursuant to notice to the Office of the Comptroller of the Currency under 12 C.F.R. §5.34, to provide securities brokerage service for institutional customers nationwide and investment advisory services for institutional customers nationwide either for a fee or as an incident to brokerage services provided by CMCMC. Copies of the notice and the response are enclosed for your convenience. At this time CMCMC provides investment advice to such customers only incidentally to brokerage services under Section 202(a) (11) (C) of the Investment Advisers Act of 1940.

Among the securities which CMCMC may recommend to its U.S. institutional customers from time to time are seasoned debt and equity securities of foreign sovereign and foreign private sector issuers (such as gilt-edge bonds, Sterling securities and Eurobonds) trading in the secondary market abroad ("Foreign Securities"). CMCMC will not, and indeed under applicable banking law may not, participate in the distribution of securities (other than those eligible for underwriting by national banks) in the United States or abroad. With respect to Foreign Securities for which CMCMC receives an order, whether as a result of a recommendation or otherwise, CMCMC's activity will be limited to acting as agent for the customer (or as agent for the customer and for the counterparty from whom the Foreign Security is obtained, which may be another broker or dealer including affiliates). CMCMC expects to execute on behalf of its customers (with disclosure to the customer) a portion of its Foreign Securities transactions with Foreign Subsidiaries (which may be market-makers). For example, transactions in the following securities may be executed with the below-specified Foreign Subsidiaries, which are London-based broker-dealers and market-makers: Eurosecurities, with Chase Manhattan Euro Securities Limited and with Chase Investment Bank Limited; sterling securities (e.g., Eurosterling securities, moneymarket instruments, debentures, preference stocks, loan stocks, local govern-

---

31. The order of the letters has been reversed. In the original document the SEC's response letter comes before the request.

ment stocks and sterling debt instruments generally), with Chase Manhattan Securities and with Chase Manhattan Gilts Limited; equity securities and convertible issues, with Chase Manhattan Equities Limited and with Chase Manhattan Securities; and British government securities ("gilts"), with Chase Manhattan Gilts Limited. In many such cases, the order would be filled by the Foreign Subsidiary on the International (London) Stock Exchange. Neither CMCMC nor any Foreign Subsidiaries intend to act as market-makers in Foreign Securities in the United States. The Foreign Subsidiaries do not have offices in the United States and do not underwrite or distribute securities in the United States. Foreign Subsidiaries would sell securities to, and purchase securities from, U.S. persons only insofar as the Subsidiaries received unsolicited orders therefor abroad.

Proposed Activity. Foreign Subsidiaries which are broker-dealers in Foreign Securities typically provide foreign customers with research on foreign issuers and their securities and on Foreign Securities markets generally. CMCMC proposes to provide to CMCMC's U.S. institutional customers research furnished to CMCMC by certain Foreign Subsidiaries which are not registered as broker-dealers with the Commission, under CMCMC's own name, with the source of the research identified as required by NASD Rules. In addition to furnishing such written research materials to its customers, CMCMC proposes to make knowledgeable employees of the Foreign Subsidiaries providing such research available to CMCMC's customers by telephone to provide further information regarding foreign securities markets generally and/or specific issues. A registered representative employed by CMCMC will participate in any such telephonic communication for the entire duration of such communication and will identify the employer of the foreign person who participates in the call. In no case will any such telephonic communication be initiated by the employee of the Foreign Subsidiary. Any order resulting from such conversations will be taken by a registered representative of CMCMC and filled as described above.

Discussion. In two relevant no-action letters, the staff of the Commission has taken the position that a foreign broker-dealer is not required to register with the Commission if it generates orders for foreign securities by furnishing investment research to U.S. registered broker-dealers (including affiliates) for dissemination to U.S. customers. We believe that the proposed arrangements between CMCMC and the Foreign Subsidiaries relating to the purchase and dissemination in the United States of investment research and advice are similar to those described in such no action letters. While these letters dealt with dissemination of purchased foreign written research, CMCMC proposes to disseminate research under the supervision of registered persons which is both oral and written in form and purchased from a foreign securities affiliate.

CMCMC will disseminate the research under its own name and will identify the source of the information, and any telephonic communications with employees of Foreign Subsidiaries will be with the participation of a registered representative employed by CMCMC. Since CMCMC has no discretionary accounts, investment decisions whether or not to purchase or sell Foreign Securities which are the subject of research reports or advice provided by CMCMC will be made solely by the institutional customers. Orders for Foreign Securities from U.S. customers will be taken by a registered representative of CMCMC (and not by employees of the Foreign Subsidiaries). CMCMC, in its capacity as broker, will execute the orders with the Foreign Subsidiaries or with other unaffiliated broker-dealers and market-makers in accordance with applicable U.S. legal and regulatory requirements. CMCMC would be responsible for confirming all transactions, for paying funds or delivering securities to its customers, and for all other aspects of its U.S. customers' transactions.

As a registered broker-dealer, CMCMC is subject to a broad scheme of regulations applicable to registered broker-dealers under the Exchange Act, including the prohibitions against manipulative, deceptive or fraudulent devices or contrivances contained in Section 15(c) of that Act and the series of rules thereunder. In addition, as an NASD member, CMCMC must comply, among other things, with the NASD's Rules of Fair Practice and the standards of commercial honor and just and equitable principles of trade embodied therein.

Should the Commission, in furtherance of its statutory responsibilities, request information with respect to any transaction of CMCMC involving research provided by a Foreign Subsidiary, Chase will cause the Foreign Subsidiary to furnish information relating to any such research, and where such information results in an order filled by CMCMC through such Foreign Subsidiary, Chase will use its best efforts to cause such Foreign Subsidiary to provide relevant trading data related to such order and to provide additional requested information to the Commission subject to the necessity of obtaining, or causing the appropriate Foreign Subsidiary to obtain, the consent of such Subsidiary's customer authorizing the Foreign Subsidiary to provide additional requested information to the Commission and subject to any local regulatory constraints.

For the reasons discussed above, it is our view that the proposed arrangements between CMCMC and Foreign Subsidiaries would not require any Foreign Subsidiary to register as a broker-dealer with the Commission under the Exchange Act. Therefore, we request on behalf of Chase, CMCMC and the Foreign Subsidiaries that the staff of the Commission confirm that it will not recommend to the Commission that any action be taken pursuant to the Exchange Act to require registration of any Foreign Subsidiary as a broker-dealer if Foreign Subsidiaries enter into the proposed arrangements with CMCMC described above.

If you have any questions or need any additional information concerning the foregoing, please do not hesitate to telephone me . . .

Very truly yours,
Frank C. Puleo

* * *

Dear Mr. Puleo:

This is in response to your letter of April 24, 1987, in which you request, on behalf of The Chase Manhattan Corporation ("Chase"), the staff's advice regarding the applicability of section 15(a) of the Securities Exchange Act of 1934 ("Exchange Act") to proposed activities of certain Chase direct and indirect foreign subsidiaries that are authorized under local and applicable Federal banking law to act as securities professionals abroad ("Foreign Subsidiaries"). On the basis of your letters and conversations with the staff, I understand the facts to be as follows.

Chase Capital Markets Corporation ("Chase Capital Markets U.S.") is a wholly-owned, operating subsidiary owned by Chase through several subsidiaries of Chase, including The Chase Manhattan Bank, N.A. ("Bank"). Chase Capital Markets U.S., which is organized under the laws of the State of Delaware, is registered as a broker-dealer with the Commission and is a member of the National Association of Securities Dealers, Inc. ("NASD"). Chase Capital Markets U.S. is authorized, pursuant to notice to the Office of the Comptroller of the Currency under 12 C.F.R. §5.34, to provide securities brokerage service for U.S. institutional customers nationwide and investment advisory services for U.S. institutional customers nationwide either for a fee or as an incident to brokerage services provided by Chase Capital Markets U.S. Presently, Chase Capital Markets U.S. provides investment advice to such customers only incidentally to brokerage services under section 202(a)(11)(C) of the Investment Advisers Act of 1940. Chase Capital Markets U.S. does not participate in the distribution of securities, (other than those eligible for underwriting by national banks), in the United States or abroad.

Proposed Activity

Among the securities that Chase Capital Markets U.S. may recommend to its U.S. institutional customers from time to time are seasoned debt and equity securities of foreign sovereign and foreign private sector issuers, such as gilt-edge bonds, Sterling securities and Eurobonds, trading in the secondary market abroad ("Foreign Securities"). With respect to Foreign Securities for which Chase Capital Markets U.S. receives an order, whether as a result of a recommendation or otherwise, Chase Capital Markets U.S.'s proposed activity will be limited to acting as agent for the customer, or as agent for the customer and for the counterparty from whom the Foreign Security is obtained, which may be another broker or dealer, including affiliates.

Chase Capital Markets U.S. proposes to execute on behalf of its customers, with disclosure to the customer, a portion of its Foreign Securities transactions with Foreign Subsidiaries, which may be market makers. For example, transactions in the following securities may be executed with the below-specified Foreign Subsidiaries, which are London-based broker-dealers and market makers: Eurosecurities, with Chase Manhattan Euro Securities Limited and with Chase Investment Bank Limited; Sterling securities (e.g., Eurosterling securities, moneymarket instruments, debentures, preference stocks, loan stocks, local government stocks and Sterling debt instruments generally), with Chase Manhattan Equities Limited and with Chase Manhattan Securities; and British government securities ("gilts"), with Chase Manhattan Gilts Limited. In many such cases, the order would be filled by the Foreign Subsidiary on the International (London) Stock Exchange. Neither Chase Capital Markets U.S. nor any Foreign Subsidiaries intend to act as market makers in the

Foreign Subsidiaries in the United States. The Foreign Subsidiaries do not have offices in the United States and do not underwrite or distribute securities in the United States.

Foreign Subsidiaries that are broker-dealers in foreign securities typically provide foreign customers with research on foreign issuers and their securities and on Foreign Securities markets generally. Chase Capital Markets U.S. proposes to provide to Chase Capital Markets U.S.'s U.S. institutional customers research furnished to Chase Capital Markets U.S. by certain Foreign Subsidiaries that are not registered as broker-dealers with the Commission. The research will be provided under Chase Capital Markets U.S.'s own name, with the source of the research identified as required by NASD rules. In addition to furnishing such written research materials to its customers, Chase Capital Markets U.S. also proposes to make knowledgeable employees of the Foreign Subsidiaries providing such research available to Chase Capital Markets U.S.'s customers by telephone to provide further information regarding specific issues or foreign securities markets generally. A registered representative employed by Chase Capital Markets U.S. will participate in any such telephone communication for the entire duration of such communication and will identify the employer of the foreign person who participates in the call. In no case will any employee of the Foreign Subsidiary initiate such telephonic communication. Any order resulting from such conversations will be taken by a registered representative of Chase Capital Markets U.S. and filled as described above.

Foreign Subsidiaries will sell securities directly to, and purchase securities from U.S. domiciled persons, institutional or otherwise, only insofar as the Foreign Subsidiaries receive unsolicited orders. If a U.S. domiciled customer receives research produced by a Foreign Subsidiary or is otherwise solicited in the U.S. by a Foreign Subsidiary, any transactions resulting from the research provided, or other forms of solicitation, will be carried out according to the terms of this letter, thereby ensuring that the U.S. customer effects its transctions (*sic*) through Chase Capital Markets U.S.

Chase Capital Markets U.S. has no discretionary accounts; therefore, investment decisions regarding the purchase or sale of Foreign Securities that are the subject of research reports or advice provided by Chase Capital Markets U.S. will be made solely by the U.S. institutional customers. Orders for Foreign Securities from U.S. customers will be taken by a registered representative of Chase Capital Markets U.S., not by employees of the Foreign Subsidiaries. Chase Capital Markets U.S., in its capacity as broker, will execute the orders with the Foreign Subsidiaries or with other unaffiliated broker-dealers and market makers in accordance with applicable U.S. statutory and regulatory requirements. Chase Capital Markets U.S. will be responsible for confirming all transactions, for paying funds or delivering securities to its customers, and for all other aspects of its U.S. customers' transactions.

You represent that should the Commission, in furtherance of its statutory responsibilities, request information with respect to any transaction of Chase Capital Markets U.S. involving research provided by a Foreign Subsidiary, Chase will cause the Foreign Subsidiary to furnish information relating to any such research. Where such information results in an order filled by Chase Capital Markets U.S. through such Foreign Subsidiary, Chase will use its best efforts, to the full extent permissible under applicable statutory and regulatory provisions, to obtain, or to cause such Foreign Subsidiary to provide, relevant trading data related to such order and to provide additional requested information to the Commission subject to the necessity of obtaining, or causing the appropriate Foreign Subsidiary to obtain, the consent of such Foreign Subsidiary's customer authorizing the Foreign Subsidiary to provide additional requested information to the Commission and subject to any local regulatory constraints.

On the basis of the foregoing, the staff of the Division of Market Regulation would not recommend enforcement action against the Foreign Subsidiaries if they engage in the activities described above without registering as broker-dealers in accordance with Section 15(b) of the Exchange Act. This is a staff position regarding enforcement action only and does not express any legal conclusions regarding the issues presented in your request. This position is based solely upon the representations you have made. Different facts or circumstances may result in a different response.

* * *

Sincerely,
Amy Natterson Kroll
Attorney
Office of Chief Counsel

———

Hypothetical Two

Your law firm, engaged principally in the practice of corporate and securities law, has been approached by an existing client to assist in raising funds to finance its operations and development. This particular client currently generates significant revenue for your firm. Your client has asked you to sign an agreement that would require you to introduce your client to individuals and entities who may have an interest in providing financing to your client through investments in equity or debt instruments issued by your client. In return for this service, the client would pay your firm an amount equal to a percentage of the gross amount your client raised as a result of your introductions. Your firm's proposed role would be limited to the introduction of your client to a limited number of your firm's contacts who may have an interest in providing funds to your client. Your firm will not: (1) engage in any negotiations whatsoever on behalf of your client and any such contact; (2) provide any such contact with any information about your client that may be used as the basis for any negotiations for funding to be provided to your client; (3) have any responsibility for, nor make any recommendations concerning the terms, conditions, or provisions of any agreement between your client and any such contact providing funding for your client; and (4) provide any assistance to any such contact or your client with respect to any transactions involving the financing of operations and development for your client. The lead partner and owner of your firm wants to know if assisting this client will require registration as a broker with the SEC. How would advise him?

There do not appear to be any reasons requiring registration as a broker with the SEC but would advise there may be ethical issues since receiving money.

Page 123: need both elements for a dealer and can only prove 2nd, not 1st

V. The Registration Process for Broker-Dealers and their Associated Persons

The SEC registration process is governed by § 15(b) of the Exchange Act. Section 15(b) prescribes the manner in which broker-dealers must register with the SEC pursuant to § 15(a). The SEC is authorized to require broker-dealers to register by filing an application prescribed by the SEC. The application specified by the SEC is the Uniform Application for Broker-Dealer Registration or Form BD. The Form BD requires the applicant to submit various types of information and is composed of a primary document, disclosure reporting pages (DRPs), and supporting schedules (Schedules A–E). The information requested in the primary document includes the broker-dealer's legal status and organization (partnership, LLC, or corporation), where it intends to engage in the securities business, SRO memberships, and arrangements (if any) with third parties for clearing and settlement services and/or maintenance of books and records. Question 11 in the Form BD requests information about the disciplinary history of the applicant or its control affiliate[32] and requires the applicant to provide the details of such events on the appropriate DRPs; there are several categories of events disclosed in DRPs: (1) criminal actions; (2) regulatory actions (actions initiated by the SEC, SRO, or state securities regulatory authority); (3) civil actions in any domestic or foreign court; (4) Bankruptcy or SIPC actions; (5) denial, pay out, or revocation initiated by a bonding company; and (6) unsatisfied judgments or liens. Schedules A and B to Form BD require the applicant to list its direct and indirect owners and executive officers. Schedule C is used to update information in Schedules A and B, and Schedule D provides additional space for explaining certain "yes" answers in items 1–13 of the primary document of the Form BD, e.g., the identification of any organization or individual that wholly or partially finances the business of an applicant.

The SEC is required within 45 days of the filing date of an application for registration, by order, to grant registration or to institute proceedings to determine whether the registration should be denied. However, the SEC's order granting registration cannot become effective until the broker-dealer has become a member of a registered securities association, e.g., FINRA. In addition, § 15(b)(8) of the Exchange Act prohibits any registered broker-dealer from effecting any transactions in, or inducing

---

32. A control affiliate is any other individual or organization that directly or indirectly controls, is under common control with, or is controlled by, the *applicant*, including any current employee except one performing only clerical, administrative, support, or similar functions, or who, regardless of title, performs no executive duties or has no senior policy-making authority

purchases or sales of, securities unless it is a member of FINRA or effects transactions in securities solely on a national securities exchange of which it is a member. In practice, this means that FINRA performs most of the activities to determine whether the applicant has the ability to comply with applicable securities laws and SRO rules. In fact, the Form BD is filed with the SEC, FINRA, and corresponding state securities regulatory authorities using the Central Registration Depository or Web CRD, which is operated by FINRA.[33]

The importance of filing, and maintaining, a complete and accurate Form BD cannot be overstressed. The Form BD is a report filed with the SEC and thus can be the basis of a violation of the federal securities laws as illustrated in the following SEC administrative proceeding.

In the Matter of Michael W. Crow

S.E.C. Release No. 376 (Apr. 22, 2009)

BRENDA P. MURRAY, Chief Administrative Law Judge.

* * *

Findings of Fact and Conclusions of Law

The Division filed a First Amended Complaint in the United States District Court for the Southern District of New York on August 17, 2007. The named Defendants were Crow, Duncan Capital LLC, Duncan Capital Group LLC, Fuchs, Robert MacGregor, and seven Relief Defendants.... Crow founded Duncan Capital LLC in 2002, and, in February 2004, he changed the name to Duncan Capital Group LLC (together, Duncan Capital Group). Crow controlled the operation and management of Duncan Capital Group, and it was not registered with the Commission.[34] Duncan Capital's primary business was to provide financial advisory services to small cap companies, including assisting such companies to raise capital.

In March 2004, Fuchs and Crow created a new entity, Duncan Capital LLC, and it merged with a registered broker dealer, Rockwood, Inc. The result was Duncan Capital LLC (Duncan Capital).

The Complaint alleged, among other things, that

> From November 2003 through at least December 2004 (the "Relevant Period"), defendant Crow, an individual previously enjoined by the United States District Court for the Southern District of California from future violations of the anti-fraud provisions of the federal securities laws, and previously sanctioned by the Commission, unlawfully acted as an unregistered principal of defendant Duncan Capital, a registered broker-dealer. Crow con-

---

33. Web CRD is the central licensing and registration system for the U.S. securities industry and its regulators. It contains the registration records of registered broker-dealers, and the qualification, employment, and disclosure histories of their associated persons.

34. [4] M.W. Crow Family LP, a Relief Defendant in the civil action, wholly owned Duncan Capital Group for most of the relevant period.

trolled virtually every significant aspect of Duncan Capital's operations and received the vast majority of its profits. Yet Duncan Capital's regulatory filings falsely and improperly omitted to state both Crow's control of the firm and his prior regulatory history.

Following a seven-day bench trial, U.S. District Court Judge Colleen McMahon issued Findings of Fact and Conclusions of Law on November 5, 2008, and a Final Judgment on November 13, 2008. The Final Judgment found that "[Crow] aided and abetted violations of Sections 15(a), 15(b)(1) and 15(b)(7) of the Exchange Act [15 U.S.C. §§ 78o(a), 78o(b)(1) and 78o(b)(7)], and Rules 15b3-1 and 15b7-1 promulgated thereunder [17 C.F.R. §§ 240.15b3-1 and 15b7-1]."

The court's Findings of Fact and Conclusions of Law found that, during the relevant period, Crow was a person associated with Duncan Capital, a registered broker-dealer; Crow acted as an unregistered broker and generally oversaw Duncan Capital's brokerage activities; Crow was Chairman and Chief Executive Officer of Duncan Capital Group; and Crow was an owner and manager of an investment adviser, B&P Management LLC. During the relevant period, Crow, although not a registered principal of Duncan Capital, controlled virtually every significant aspect of Duncan Capital's operations and received the vast majority of its profits. Duncan Capital was a placement agent for approximately twenty securities offerings, from which it raised over $100 million for the issuers, and Crow received millions in cash compensation and warrants.

The court permanently restrained and enjoined Crow and his officers, agents, servants, etc. from aiding and abetting any violation of Sections 15(a), 15(b)(1), and 15(b)(7) of the Exchange Act and Exchange Act Rules 15b3-1 and 15b7-1.

The court found Crow and Duncan Capital Group jointly and severally liable and ordered them to pay disgorgement of ill-gotten gains of $1,562,337, together with prejudgment interest, ... for a total of $1,999,752.87. The court also found Crow and others jointly and severally liable and ordered them to disgorge ill-gotten gains of $3,903,474, together with prejudgment interest, ... for a total of $4,996,351.... The court ordered Crow to pay a civil monetary penalty, pursuant to Section 21(d)(3) of the Exchange Act, in the amount of $250,000.

Judge McMahon found that:

> There is no assurance that Crow can be trusted in the future to comply with securities laws. Crow has not acknowledged any wrongdoing. He had been enjoined once already and has acted in breach of the terms of that consent agreement with the SEC. In his actions at [Duncan Capital and Duncan Capital Group], he has demonstrated a willingness to disregard the advice of counsel and he took steps to cover up what he was actually doing. His conduct was egregious and he acted with scienter. In addition, he perjured himself in this court.

* * *

Based on the findings of fact and conclusions of law set forth above, I Order that, pursuant to Section 15(b) of the Securities Exchange Act of 1934 and Section 203(f) of the Investment Advisers Act of 1940, Michael W. Crow is barred from association with any broker, dealer, or investment adviser.

Notes and Questions

1. **Successor registration.** Section 15(b)(2) and Rule 15b1-3 allow successor registration. Successor registration occurs when one broker-dealer succeeds to, and continues the business of, another broker-dealer already registered under § 15(b). The registration of the predecessor broker-dealer remains effective as the registration of the successor broker-dealer, if the successor files an application for registration on Form BD within 30 days after succession, and the predecessor broker-dealer files a notice of withdrawal from registration on Form BDW. Given the facts of *In the Matter of Michael W. Crow,* does this procedure provide a pathway for fraud? In *Crow*, Fuchs and Crow created a new entity, Duncan Capital LLC, and it merged with a registered broker-dealer, Rockwood, Inc.

   [handwritten: → No since Duncan had to be registered before the merger to properly withdraw.]

2. **Amendments to Form BD.** The Form BD is a dynamic document. This means that the broker-dealer is responsible for keeping the information in the Form BD current and to file accurate supplementary information on a timely basis. In addition, the execution page requires the broker-dealer to consent to service of process to any actions brought by the SEC and any SRO, as well as any application for a protective decree filed by the SIPC. Accordingly, a full paper Form BD with the applicant's notarized signature is required with the initial filing with the CRD.

A. FINRA Membership

In practice, the process for obtaining FINRA membership and registering with the SEC is, in effect, the same. Under § 15(b), SEC registration cannot become effective until an applicant becomes a member of FINRA. This means that FINRA initially evaluates all applicants to determine whether they meet the requirements for registration under § 15(b) by assessing whether the applicants meet FINRA's membership requirements. However, the SEC has final authority over whether an applicant becomes a registered broker-dealer and a member of FINRA. Section 19(d) of the Exchange Act authorizes the SEC to review SRO actions denying membership, either on its own motion or on the applicant's motion.

1. FINRA Membership Application Process

The FINRA membership application process is extensive. It covers meeting initial membership standards, updating, and renewing membership. Accordingly, this discussion is confined to key parts of the process for meeting initial membership standards. Figure 3.3 summarizes steps in the membership application process.

Electronic forms referenced in Figure 3.3 must be submitted using FINRA's Firm Gateway. The Firm Gateway is a computer portal that allows the broker-dealer access to FINRA computer applications for regulatory compliance, including the new mem-

---

Figure 3.3. Membership Application Process

- Request reservation of broker-dealer firm name
- Determine and pay applicable fees (e.g., application, examination, and registration fees)
- Submit hard copies of a notarized Form BD, a New Organization Super Account Administrator Entitlement Form, a Member Firm Email Notification Contact Form
- Complete the following electronic forms: Form U4, Form BR, Form BD, and Form NMA
- Submission of fingerprints for each of the broker-dealer's associated persons

---

ber application and Web CRD. However, in order to access the Firm Gateway, the applicant must submit hard copies of a notarized Form BD, a New Organization Super Accountant Administrator Entitlement Form & FINRA Entitlement Agreement ("SAA/FEA"), and a Member Firm Email Notification Contact Form. The SAA/FEA must be submitted by the applicant in order to access FINRA's Firm Gateway and therefore its computer application for new member applicants. The Member Firm Email Notification Form enables the applicant to receive certain e-mail notifications from FINRA about its associated persons, e.g., when an associated person is within days of a continuing education requirement.

A key form submitted in the new member application process using the Firm Gateway is the NMA. Form NMA is an interactive application used by the applicant to submit information to FINRA about, among other things, its contractual and business relationships, facilities, maintenance of adequate net capital, and supervisory structure. Form NMA contains 12 sections modeled after the first 12 standards of FINRA's Standards of Admission enumerated in NASD Rule 1014. See Figure 3.4.

Figure 3.4. Form NMA Categories

- Overview of Applicant
- Licenses and Registrations
- Compliance with Securities laws, Just and Equitable Principles of Trade
- Contractual and business relationships
- Facilities
- Communications and Operational Systems
- Maintaining Adequate Net Capital
- Financial Controls
- Written Procedures
- Supervisory Structure
- Books and Records
- Continuing Education

FINRA membership requirements are enumerated in its NASD Rule Series 1010 (Membership Proceedings). The key provisions in this rule series are NASD Rules 1013 (New Member Application and Interview) and 1014 (Department[35] Decision). NASD Rule 1013 contains definitions, filing instructions, and information and document requirements. Of particular importance to a successful membership application is the preparation of the broker-dealer's business plan required in NASD Rule 1013(a)(1)(E). The business plan must comprehensively describe all material aspects of the broker-dealer's business, including future business expansion plans. Specifically, NASD Rule 1013(a)(1)(E) requires the business plan to include information about the applicant's present and projected financial condition, marketing plan, and organizational structure; present and future sources of capital; and technology to be employed. See Figure 3.5 for a list of some of the specific documents that must be included in the business plan.

Figure 3.5. NASD Rule 1013(a)(1)(E) Document Requirements

1. Trial balance, balance sheet, supporting schedules, and computation of net capital
2. Monthly projection of income and expenses
3. Description of the nature and source of the applicant's capital, with supporting documentation
4. Description of financial controls
5. Organizational chart
6. Intended location and principal place of business and all other offices
7. A list of the types of securities offered and sold and types of retail or institutional customers to be solicited
8. Description of methods and media used to develop a customer base and to offer and sell products and services (includes Internet, telephone solicitations, seminars, or mailings)
9. Description of the business facilities, including copy of any proposed or final lease
10. Description of the communications and operational systems used to conduct business with customers and other broker-dealers and plans to ensure business continuity
11. Number of markets to be made, the type and volatility of the products, and the anticipated maximum inventory positions
12. Contractual commitments, e.g., underwritings
13. Plans to distribute or maintain securities products in proprietary positions and risks, volatility, degree of liquidity, and speculative nature of the products
14. A list of all associated persons
15. Documentation of any regulatory, remedial, criminal, or civil actions against the applicant or any associated person that is not reported in the CRD

---

35. Department refers to the staff in FINRA's Department of Member Regulation.

The applicant must also submit a description of its supervisory system, along with a copy of its written supervisory procedures. Specifically, NASD Rule 1013(a)(1)(N) requires a copy of the applicant's internal operating procedures, internal inspections plan, written approval process, and qualifications investigations required by FINRA Rule 3110. The applicants' written supervisory procedures (WSP) are essential for facilitating compliance with applicable federal securities laws and SEC and SRO rules. In effect, it is a comprehensive compliance manual containing policies and procedures that address the broker-dealer's business activities, as well as transactions effected between the broker-dealer and any affiliate. WSP requirements are specified in FINRA Rule 3110, which is examined in Chapter 4. However, FINRA requires the applicant to submit the Written Supervisory Procedures Review Checklist ("Checklist") with its application to ensure coverage of selected key topics in the applicant's WSP. Although the outline of topics in the Checklist is not all-inclusive, FINRA reviews the Checklist and the WSP, along with other information, to determine whether the applicant meets FINRA's Standards for Admission enumerated in NASD Rule 1014. See Figure 3.6 for a summary of FINRA's Standards for Admission.

An in-person interview is required after the applicant has submitted the application. Specifically, NASD Rule 1013(b)(1) requires FINRA's Department of Member Regulation to conduct a membership interview with representatives of the broker-dealer before making a decision. The focus of the interview is FINRA's determination of the applicant's ability to meet the Standards for Admission contained in NASD Rule 1014. This means that discussion during the interview will consist of substantially all aspects of the applicant's proposed business for which it will have regulatory and compliance responsibilities; for example, the applicant's supervisory structure and the background and experience of its supervisory (principals) and non-supervisory personnel (representatives) would be discussed during the membership interview.

FINRA must grant the application for membership if the applicant and its associated persons meet each of the standards for admission in NASD Rule 1014(a). If the applicant does not meet one or more of the standards for admission, FINRA may grant the application and impose restrictions designed to address any deficiencies or deny the application. However, a presumption exists that the application should be denied if the applicant or its associated persons is subject to: (1) a permanent or temporary adverse action with respect to a registration or licensing determination; (2) a pending, adjudicated, or settled regulatory action or investigation by the SEC, CFTC, SRO, unpaid arbitration settlements or awards, or a civil action for damages or an injunction or a criminal action; (3) a termination for cause or a permitted resignation by an associated person after an alleged violation of federal or state securities laws or FINRA rules; (4) an indication that the applicant or an associated person otherwise poses a threat to public investors based on information provided by a state or federal authority or SRO.

Figure 3.6. Summary of FINRA's Standards for Admission

1. Complete and accurate application and supporting documents
2. Applicant and associated persons must have all required licenses and registrations
3. Applicant and associated persons are capable of complying with federal securities laws and FINRA rules
4. Applicant has established all contractual arrangements and business relationships necessary to engage in its proposed securities business
5. Adequate facilities to initiate operations and to comply with federal securities laws and FINRA rules
6. Adequate communications and operational systems to conduct its business operations and to provide reasonably for business continuity
7. Maintain a level of net capital in excess of minimum net capital sufficient to support applicant's business operations
8. Financial controls to ensure compliance with federal securities laws and FINRA rules
9. Compliance, supervisory, operational, and internal control practices and standards consistent with practices and standards regularly employed in the securities business
10. Supervisory system and compliance procedures designed to prevent and detect violations of the federal securities laws and FINRA rules.
11. A recordkeeping system, along with sufficient staff, to comply with federal, state, and SRO recordkeeping requirements
12. Training needs assessment and written training plan that complies with continuing education requirements imposed by federal securities laws and FINRA rules
13. FINRA does not possess any information indicating that applicant will avoid compliance with the federal securities laws and FINRA rules
14. The application and all supporting documents otherwise are consistent with federal securities laws and FINRA rules

---

2. Registration of Associated Persons

Individuals who are associated persons of a broker-dealer and engaged in the broker-dealer's investment banking and securities business must register with FINRA. Generally, associated persons are employees of broker-dealers but, as discussed earlier in this chapter, they also may be partners, directors, controlling persons, and independent contractors. Broker-dealers must supervise the securities activities of their personnel regardless of whether they are considered employees or independent contractors.[36] Thus, FINRA registration of individuals who work for registered broker-dealers is specific to the employing broker-dealer who, in turn, is responsible for their supervision, i.e., ensuring compliance with federal securities laws and FINRA rules. Only those associated persons engaged in the broker-dealer's investment banking and securities business are required to register with FINRA. This means that broker-dealer personnel whose functions are solely and exclusively: (1) clerical or ministerial; (2) related to the broker-dealer's need for nominal corporate officers; or (3) for capital participation are not required to register with FINRA. In addition, individuals who are associated persons of broker-dealers generally are not required to register separately with the SEC.

FINRA identifies two broad categories of registration—representatives and principals. In addition, there are subcategories within these two broad categories of registration based on the type of functions performed in the broker-dealer's business. See Figure 3.7. NASD Rule 1031 defines a representative as an associated person of a broker-dealer who is "engaged in the investment banking or securities business [of the broker-dealer] including the functions of supervision, solicitation or conduct of business in securities or … in the training … for any of these functions …" Broker-dealers are prohibited from registering representatives with FINRA "where there is no intent to employ …" them in the broker-dealer's investment banking or securities business. However, there is an exception to this prohibition for associated persons who perform legal, compliance, internal audit, back-office operations, or similar responsibilities along with associated persons who perform administrative support functions for a broker-dealer's registered personnel.

A principal is an associated person of a broker-dealer who is actively engaged in the management of the broker-dealer's investment banking or securities business. NASD Rule 1021 specifically includes supervision, solicitation, conduct of business, or training of associated persons in this category. It also expressly identifies associated persons that must be designated as principals in the broker-dealer business, including officers, partners, managers of offices of supervisory jurisdiction,[37] and directors of corporations. Similarly, broker-dealers may not register associated persons as principals if there is no intent to employ them in their investment banking or securities business. Also, like the representative category, there is an exception to this prohibition for associated persons performing legal, compliance, or similar responsibilities for the broker-dealer's registered personnel. See Figure 3.7 for a partial listing of registered principal subcategories. NASD Rule 1021 requires broker-dealers to have at least two officers or partners who are registered as principals with respect to each aspect of the broker-dealer's investment banking and securities business.

All representatives and principals must pass qualification examinations that are administered by FINRA. These examinations are organized by series and the content depends upon the type of activities performed in the broker-dealer's investment bank-

---

36. Independent contractor status is generally defined under state law.

37. *See* Notes and Questions, Note 7, *infra*.

Figure 3.7.

NASD Rule 1032. Categories of Representative Registration	
Subcategory	Required Examination
General Securities Representative	Series 7
Limited Representative— Investment Company and Variable Contracts Products	Series 6
Limited Representative—Direct Participation Programs	Series 22
Limited Representative—Corporate Securities	Series 62
Securities Trader	Series 57
NASD Rule 1022. Categories of Principal Registration	
Subcategory	Required Examination
General Securities Principal	Series 24
Limited Principal—Financial and Operations	Series 27
Limited Principal—Introduction Broker/Dealer Financial and Operations	Series 28
Limited Principal—Investment Company and Variable Contracts Products	Series 26
Limited Principal—Direct Participation Programs	Series 39
Limited Principal—General Securities Sales Supervisor	Series 9 and 10

ing or securities business. The examinations are designed to demonstrate proficiency (a minimum level of understanding and expertise) appropriate to the functions to be performed by the representative or principal. *See* Figure 3.7. In addition, all representatives and principals are subject to continuing education requirements specified in FINRA Rule 1250.

The broker-dealer registers its associated persons as representatives and principals by electronically filing the Uniform Application for Securities Industry Registration or Transfer ("Form U4") with FINRA. The information required in Form U4 is extensive and includes the associated person's physical characteristics (e.g., eye color, height), residential history, employment and educational history, other businesses, and SRO registrations. Most important, Item 14 of Form U4 requires disclosure of the associated person's disciplinary history, e.g., criminal, regulatory, and civil proceedings; customer complaints; and prior terminations of employment based on allegations of improper behavior. It also requires disclosure of the associated person's personal financial information, including bankruptcy proceedings and unsatisfied judgments. Accordingly, the associated person must sign a paper copy of the Form U4, which must be retained by the broker-dealer, in addition to the electronic submission to FINRA through Web CRD. Only a portion of the information contained in the Form U4 is made publicly available through BrokerCheck, which is available on FINRA's web site. Like the Form BD, the Form U4 is a report—failure to ensure that all information is current and accurate may result in a violation of FINRA rules.

Notes and Questions

1. **Operations Professionals.** FINRA Rule 1230(b)(6) contains an additional representative registration category and qualification examination for certain operations (back office) personnel. It requires registration of individuals identified as covered persons in the rule who are engaged in, responsible for, or supervising certain of the broker-dealer's operations functions (covered functions). The rule identifies three categories of covered persons—(a) senior management directly responsible for covered functions; (b) any person designated by senior management to be responsible for approving the work of other persons in direct furtherance of covered functions; and (c) persons with the authority to commit a broker-dealer's capital or any material contract in direct furtherance of covered functions. Covered functions include client on-boarding (customer account data and document maintenance), receipt and delivery of securities and funds, trade confirmation and account statements, stock/loan securities lending, approval of pricing models used for valuations, financial control (including general ledger and treasury), and defining and approving business requirements for sales and trading systems and security requirements for information technology. FINRA believes that "unregistered individuals who perform and oversee member operations functions … play an integral role in the business of the [broker-dealer], and their activities often have a meaningful connection to client funds, accounts, and transactions." Does FINRA Rule 1230(b)(6) represent excessive regulation of persons already subject to FINRA registration and examination requirements? Review FINRA Rule 1230(b)(6)(D) and FINRA Regulatory Notice 11-33 and identify registered personnel eligible to register as Operations Professionals without taking Series 99, the operations professional qualification examination.

2. **Registration of Research Analysts.** NASD Rule 1050 requires broker-dealers to register their associated persons who function as research analysts. A research analyst is defined as an associated person whose primary job function is to provide investment research and who is primarily responsible for preparing the substance of a research report or whose name appears on a research report. What are the registration requirements listed in NASD Rule 1050 for registration of research analysts?

3. **Lapse in Registration.** FINRA specifically prohibits broker-dealers from maintaining the registration of any person no longer active in a broker-dealer's securities business. An associated person's registration lapses if he or she has not been active in the broker-dealer's business for two years. This means that the associated person must requalify by taking the appropriate qualification examinations again to be employed in the securities industry.

4. **SIPC Membership.** All registered broker-dealers must be members of SIPC unless the broker-dealer conducts its business outside of the United States; its securities business is exclusively in investment company shares, variable annuities, or insurance products; or it provides only investment advisory services.

5. **State Registration.** Generally, a broker-dealer is required to register in any state in which it does business. However, this registration is primarily ministerial as a result of the passage of the National Securities Markets Improvement Act of 1996 ("NSMIA"). NSMIA pre-empted state regulation of broker-dealer capital, custody, margin, financial responsibility, books and records, bonding, and financial or operational reporting requirements. The state registration process in most states consists only of the submission of the Form BD through the Web CRD and payment of the requisite fee. However, broker-dealers that effect transactions in a state in contravention of a state's registration requirements may be subject to administrative actions by the state. In addition, customers may have the right to rescind all transactions if the broker-dealer fails to register in the state. Review the North American Securities Administration Association's ("NASAA") web site. How does it assist in determining broker-dealer registration requirements for each state? Must broker-dealers register in, for example, the State of Maryland?

6. **Fidelity Bonds.** FINRA Rule 4360 requires registered broker-dealers doing business with the public to maintain blanket fidelity bond coverage. The fidelity bond must include a cancellation rider stating that the insurance carrier will use its best efforts to promptly notify FINRA if the bond is canceled, terminated, or substantially modified. The amount of the fidelity bond is specified in FINRA Rule 4360 and is based on the broker-dealer's net capital. What are the areas in which the fidelity bond must provide coverage against loss and have insuring agreements?

7. **Branch Office Registration.** Broker-dealers must register each of their branch offices with FINRA. Registration requires the broker-dealer to file Form BR using Web CRD. The two categories of branch office registration are FINRA Office of Supervisory Jurisdiction ("OSJ") and non-OSJ branch offices. An OSJ is any office at which one or more of the following functions take place: (1) order execution or market making; (2) structuring of public offerings or private placements; (3) maintaining custody of customers' funds or securities; (4) final acceptance of new accounts; (5) review and endorsement of customer orders; and (6) final approval of retail communications used by a broker-dealer's associated persons. OSJs must have at least one on-site supervisor who is a registered principal with the broker-dealer. The main office of a broker-dealer is always considered an OSJ and has supervisory jurisdiction and responsibility over all of the broker-dealer's non-OSJ branch offices. FINRA Rule 3110(f)(2) defines a branch office as any location where one or more associated persons of a broker-dealer regularly conducts a securities business. What types of locations are not branch offices under FINRA Rule 3110(f)(2)?

Hypothetical Three

Angela Bennett, the branch manager at Success First's West Palm Beach, Florida, branch has decided to hire an assistant representative. Janice Goodall has interviewed for the position. Janice has some experience because she worked for another broker-dealer three years ago, accepting customer orders. Janice believes that in light of her past experience, she should be compensated based on the number or size of transactions effected for Success First's customers. She also would like to receive an annual bonus for her work. Janice is not sure whether she is required to take and pass a qualification exam to work as an assistant representative for Success First. Angela takes a deep breath and discusses the job qualifications for the position of assistant representative at Success First. What does she say to Janice? Must Janice take and pass a qualification examination? May Janice receive transaction-based compensation?

① PAGE 150

No, according to 1042.

Yes, all representatives including assistant representatives. PAGE 150 ②

Unless ③ which do not think applies.

Chapter 4

Supervisory Responsibilities of Broker-Dealers

Regulatory Authority

Securities Exchange Act of 1934 Sections 15(b)(4)(E) and 15(b)(6)

FINRA Rules 2330, 3110, 3120, 3130, 3220, 3240, and 3270

Municipal Securities Rulemaking Board Rules G-27

Motivating Hypothetical

Carmen Alvarez, Success First's CEO, and the board of directors have now unanimously agreed to significantly grow Success First's business; and all but Josephine, Success First's general counsel, agree that the best way to expand the business is to use the independent contractor business model. They believe that Success First should purchase NeverLast, a registered broker-dealer already using the independent contractor business model. NeverLast has approximately 1,100 registered representatives, who are allowed to engage in business activities other than buying and selling securities. About 50 percent of NeverLast's registered representatives engage in some type of business activity outside the firm, such as selling insurance or financial planning. Between 10 and 20 percent of NeverLast's registered representatives work outside their assigned offices regularly, and about five percent never go to the office. In addition, most of NeverLast's branch offices, located throughout the United States, are staffed by two or three registered representatives. Carmen asserts that purchasing NeverLast will allow Success First to reduce its liability but greatly increase its client base because under the independent contractor model, independent contractors are responsible for their own overhead, such as office space and utilities. However, Josephine disagrees. She believes that purchasing NeverLast will significantly increase Success First's liability because its independent contractor business model does not facilitate reasonable supervision. She believes that it will be more difficult to keep track of the non-branch offices and outside business activities of NeverLast's associated persons. For example, NeverLast's independent contractor model, given the large number of widely dispersed registered representatives, would require Success First to maintain a record of those who operate regularly from unregistered locations and inspect those locations on a regular schedule. Josephine points out that the SEC and

FINRA apply the same supervision rules to all registered representatives, whether they are independent contractors or employees. Josephine worries that the increase in compliance costs and potential liability might negate the anticipated growth in earnings from such an expansion.

Part I: Supervision Under the Federal Securities Laws
I. Introduction

Broker-dealers are required to establish and maintain effective systems of supervision. The SEC asserts that the obligation of broker-dealers to establish and maintain effective systems of supervision is a key component of the regulatory framework for broker-dealers. It believes that, in such a system of self-policing, broker-dealer employees engaged in supervision are in the best position to detect and to prevent fraudulent activities that could harm investors. In essence, the primary responsibility of compliance—assuring that the firm's operation complies with sound business practices and the rules and regulations of all regulatory bodies—rests with the broker-dealer's management.[1]

Section 15(b)(4)(E) of the Securities Exchange Act of 1934 (Exchange Act) authorizes the SEC to sanction broker-dealers who have "failed reasonably to supervise, with a view to preventing violations of the provisions of [the Exchange Act]..., another person who commits" violations of the federal securities laws. Section 15(b)(6) confers the same authority with respect to persons associated with the broker-dealer. Thus, both sections are required to sanction the broker-dealer as an entity and its employees, including senior management and owners, for failure reasonably to supervise. While Section 15(b)(4)(E) does not prescribe a single standard for determining reasonable supervision, it does contain a safe harbor, which serves as a guideline for a legally sufficient supervisory system. To qualify for the safe harbor contained in Section 15(b)(4)(E)(i)–(ii), the broker-dealer, prior to the violation committed by its associated person, must have established procedures, and a system for applying such procedures, that would reasonably be expected to prevent and detect, insofar as practicable, any such violation by [an associated person] ... and [the broker-dealer] has reasonably discharged the duties and obligations incumbent upon him by reason of such procedures and system without reasonable cause to believe that such procedures and system were not being complied with.

---

1. *See Supervisory Responsibilities of a Broker-Dealer Manager,* Exchange Act Release No. 34-8404, 1968 WL 87260 (Sept. 11, 1968). Although supervision is a key component of the regulatory framework for broker-dealers, only the SEC may bring enforcement actions for failure to supervise under §§ 15(b)(4)(E) and 15(b)(6). Courts have held that there is no private right of action under these provisions. *See Synder v. Newhard, Cook & Co., Inc.,* 764 F. Supp. 612, 615 (D. Colo. 1991).

II. Development of Failure to Supervise

Until the enactment of the Securities Acts Amendments of 1964, failure to supervise was not an independent ground for imposing sanctions against broker-dealers under the federal securities laws. It was only after the enactment of sections 15(b)(4)(E) and 15(b)(6) that the SEC had an express, independent statutory basis to impose sanctions for failure to supervise against firms and their associated persons. However, even before the 1964 Amendments, the SEC maintained that Supervisory personnel of a broker-dealer firm had a responsibility to supervise employees and that revocation or other appropriate sanctions may be imposed upon a broker-dealer whose employee commits violations [of the federal securities laws].[2]

Before the 1964 Securities Acts Amendments, the SEC used Section 15(b)(4)(D) as a basis for imposing sanctions on broker-dealers and their associated persons for supervisory deficiencies. Section 15(b)(4)(D) authorizes the SEC to bring enforcement proceedings against broker-dealers and their associated persons if either have willfully violated any provisions of the Securities Act of 1933, the Investment Advisers Act of 1940, the Investment Company Act of 1940, the Commodity Exchange Act, [the Securities Exchange Act of 1934], the rules or regulations under any of such statutes, or the rules of the Municipal Securities Rulemaking Board, or is unable to comply with any such provisions.[3]

The SEC applied Section 15(b)(4)(D) to broker-dealers whose employees committed violations of the federal securities laws by using the common law doctrine of *respondeat superior*. However, the authority conferred in Section 15(b)(4)(D) regarding failure to supervise was not express; that is, it did not, among other things, expressly authorize the SEC to initiate administrative proceedings against a firm's employees and, as previously noted, did not establish supervisory deficiency as an independent violation. *In the Matter of Reynolds & Co.* illustrates the SEC's use of Section 15(b)(4)(D) to bring failure to supervise cases prior to the enactment of Sections 15(b)(4)(E) and 15(b)(6).

---

2. 29 Fed. Reg. 13455, 13459 (Sept. 30, 1964).

3. In the 1964 Amendments, Section 15(b)(4)(D) was Section 15(b)(5)(D) and did not include the Commodity Exchange Act and the Municipal Securities Rulemaking Board. It read as follows: "The Commission shall, after appropriate notice and opportunity for hearing, by order censure, deny registration to, suspend for a period not exceeding twelve months, or revoke the registration of, any broker *or* dealer if it finds that such censure, denial, suspension, or revocation is in the public interest and that such broker or dealer, whether prior or subsequent to becoming such, or any person associated with such broker or dealer, whether prior or subsequent to becoming so associated ... has willfully violated any provision of the Securities Act of 1933, or of the Investment Advisers Act of 1940, or of the Investment Company Act of 1940, or of this title, or of any rule or regulation under any of such statutes." Act of Aug. 20, 1964, Pub. L. No. 88-467, 78 Stat. 565 (emphasis added) ("provid[ing] ... improved qualification and disciplinary procedures for registered brokers and dealers").

In the Matter of Reynolds & Co.

39 S.E.C. 902 (May 25, 1960)

These are consolidated proceedings to determine, among other things, whether, pursuant to Section 15(b) of the Securities Exchange Act of 1934 ('Exchange Act'), we should revoke the registration as a broker and dealer of Reynolds & Co. ('registrant'), a partnership; whether, pursuant to Section 15A (l)(2) of that Act, we should suspend or expel registrant from membership in the National Association of Securities Dealers, Inc. ('NASD'), a registered securities association; whether, under Section 19(a)(3) of the Act, we should suspend or expel registrant and its partners from membership in certain national securities exchanges; and whether, under Section 15A (b)(4) of that Act, we should find that William R. Rice and John G. White, partners in registrant, Robert B. Whittaker, Wilson M. Dodd, and Wilfred C. Aldous, branch managers, and Wesley J. Roland, Elmer J. Stefany, and Patrick H. Coleman, Jr., employees, are each a cause of any order of revocation, suspension or expulsion which may be entered.

The order for proceedings relating to registrant, as amended, alleges, among other things, that between December 1, 1953 and January 9, 1959, registrant, together with or aided and abetted by certain partners, branch managers, and employees, induced excessive trading in customers' accounts, effected transactions in customers' accounts without their consent, and made false and misleading statements of material facts in inducing the purchase by customers by certain securities, in willful violation of the anti-fraud provisions of the Securities Act of 1933 ('Securities Act') and the Exchange Act and rules thereunder, ... The order further alleges that registrant, through lack of supervision and internal control, permitted the above activities and the misappropriation of funds of customers by one of its salesmen.

The transactions under consideration occurred primarily in the branch offices of registrant located in Carmel, California, Chicago, Illinois, San Francisco and Berkeley, California, and Minneapolis, Minnesota.

TRANSACTIONS IN THE CARMEL OFFICE

The violations charged with respect to registrant's Carmel office involve excessive trading in four investment accounts of customers between January 1954 and January 1959. Two of the accounts were opened about January 1954, one by a Mrs. D, a widow and semiretired real estate broker with limited securities experience, and the other by a Mr. A, a veterinarian's assistant who had obtained the capital for his account as a result of the termination of a trust of which he was a beneficiary and who had no securities experience. These customers subsequently gave Coleman, a salesman, discretionary authority to effect transactions in their account. This authority, at first oral, was put in written form in August 1954. At Coleman's request the customers paid him special fees for looking after their accounts. The third account was opened in May 1956, by Mr. P, a semi-retired poultry raiser and farmer, and his wife, a former schoolteacher, who verbally gave Coleman authority to buy and sell for their account. The fourth account was opened in January 1957, by Dr. L and his wife, retired physicians, at which time Dr. L advised Coleman that he had been in ill health and gave Coleman full responsibility for the management of the account.

All four of these accounts were grossly overtraded in the light of the character of the accounts. In Mrs. D's account, an average investment of $57,310 was turned over 29 times in a period of 46 months.[4] Purchases totaling $1,664,572 and sales totalling $1,651,907 were effected in this account. Of 318 'in-and-out' transactions in this account,[5] approximately 158 were completed within 30 days, with 22 being completed on the same or the following day. The net realized and unrealized loss in the account was $35,986, and registrant charged $26,852 in commissions.

In Mr. A's account, a cash deposit of $66,012 was turned over 34.47 times in 56 months. Purchases totalled $2,275,715 and sales $2,253,440. Of 507 in-and-out transactions, 34 were completed on the same or next day, and around 200 others within 30 days. The net loss in the account was $19,847, and registrant obtained $38,428 in commissions.

In Mr. and Mrs. P's account an average investment of $15,175 was turned over 27.38 times in 28 months. Coleman effected 114 purchases in this account for a total of $415,475 and the same number of sales for a total of $401,575. Of 98 in-and-out transactions, about 42 were completed within 30 days, with 15 being completed on the same or the next day. The customer sustained a net loss of $6,200, and registrant charged $7,555 in commissions.

The account of Dr. L and his wife had an average investment of $59,961 which was turned over 5.63 times in 16 months. There were 82 purchases totalling $337,511, and 90 sales totalling $322,218. Of 58 in-and-out transactions, 24 were completed within 30 days, with 14 of them being completed on the same or next day. The account lost $11,591, and registrant received $5,542 in commissions.

Even apart from the discretionary authority given to Coleman, in view of the trust and confidence reposed in him by the customers, Coleman and registrant assumed a fiduciary obligation to effect transactions in the accounts with an eye single to the best interests of the customers. It is evident that this obligation was disregarded by the effecting of an excessive number of transactions in the customers' accounts in order to produce commissions for registrant and Coleman.

Rice, the managing partner of registrant's west coast branch offices and manager of the San Francisco office, had been informed in August 1954, that Coleman was engaging in discretionary trading in the accounts of Mrs. D and Mr. A pursuant to oral authority. Under a rule (now Rule 408) of the New York Stock Exchange, of which registrant and its partners were members, written authorization of the customer

---

4. The turnover rate is computed by dividing the aggregate amount of the purchases by the average cumulative monthly investment, the latter representing the cumulative total of the net investment in the account at the end of each month, exclusive of loans, divided by the number of months under consideration.

5. The term "in-and-out" transaction refers to the purchase of a security and its subsequent sale, or the short sale of a security and the subsequent purchase to cover the short position.

is required with respect to any discretionary power and all orders in a discretionary account must be initialed and approved by a partner. In addition to the failure to obtain written authorization, the transactions in the two accounts had been effected without any initialling or approval by a partner. These circumstances alone should have prompted Rice to inquire into Coleman's activities. However, Rice's only action was to direct the obtaining of written authorizations from the two customers and he did not either direct any surveillance or control of Coleman's activities or initial or approve any of the subsequent transactions in those accounts.

Rice asserts that he felt he could not initial the orders because the San Francisco office where he was located did not receive the statements of customers' accounts in the other California offices at that time. He states that he therefore arranged with registrant's director of compliance in September 1954, that discretionary orders of the Carmel office should be initialed by a New York partner and, to make this possible, such orders were to be marked discretionary. However, registrant's records indicate that none of the orders received in the New York office were marked as discretionary, and the partners in the New York office who would normally initial discretionary orders do not recall being advised by the director of compliance to initial any such orders.

The trading activities in Mrs. D's and Mr. A's accounts were from time to time called to the attention of Rice and Aldous, manager of the Carmel office, by the office's co-manager, who pointed out that, while Coleman was handling relatively few accounts, he was making as much in commissions as other registered representatives who were handling many more. On several occasions Rice and Aldous discussed the volume of trading in those accounts with Coleman, who took the position that as long as the accounts were making money, the volume of trading was unimportant. Rice and Adlous agreed with that position, and did not require any change in Coleman's method of handling the accounts.

The conclusion is inescapable that Rice depended upon Aldous to supervise Coleman, and Aldous in turn merely relied upon Coleman's integrity. Rice was aware of the volume of transactions in the four accounts and knew that at least in the case of Mrs. D and Mr. A a relationship of trust and confidence had existed between them and Coleman. Under the circumstances it was incumbent upon him to make such personal inquiry as was necessary to verify the facts and make certain that there were no improprieties in the handling of the accounts.

TRANSACTIONS IN THE CHICAGO OFFICE

The charges relating to fraudulent activities in the Chicago office involve the effecting of transactions in customers' accounts by an employee in that office without authorization by the customers and his forging of customers' names. It is alleged that between March 1, 1955 and May 1, 1957, Stefany, Whittaker, and White caused these fraudulent practices by failing properly to supervise this employee ...

The unauthorized transactions described involved a course of conduct extending over more than a year. During this period, various circumstances came to the attention of supervisory personnel which should have resulted in the detection of the employee's fraudulent activities ... Stefany, Whittaker, and White failed to perform their supervisory responsibilities in this respect.

TRANSACTIONS IN THE SAN FRANCISCO AND BERKELEY OFFICES

The alleged violations resulting from activities in registrant's San Francisco and Berkeley offices involve false and misleading statements by Roland, assistant manager of the Berkeley office, and other employees of registrant in inducing the purchase by customers of stock in six mining companies ('mining companies').... From April 1, 1954 to April 30, 1955, registrant purchased as agent for customers a total of 5,175,932 shares of stock of the mining companies, out of 17,000,000 shares outstanding.

Roland told customers, among other things, that the stock was the 'hottest thing' he had ever seen or handled, that it was 'going up tomorrow' and that 'the sky was the limit.' Roland failed to disclose to customers to whom he recommended the purchase of stock of the mining companies that he was at the same time selling shares of such stock which he himself owned and that..., he and the other employees deliberately withheld execution of customers' buy orders until the market price of the stock of the mining companies had increased as a result of the inclusion at their direction of increasingly higher bids in the over-the-counter quotations ...

Registrant and its supervisory personnel knew that Roland and other employees were recommending shares of the mining companies to their customers despite registrant's stated policy against encouraging customer investment in low-priced speculative securities. They were also aware of the large volume of business being done by these employees in the stock of the mining companies.

Dodd, manager of the Berkeley office in which Roland was employed, was also derelict in his supervisory duties. He failed to ascertain what literature was being used by Roland and to examine it. Further, Dodd allowed Roland to negotiate for the purchase or sale of the stock of the mining companies with other dealers directly by telephone rather than sending such orders through registrant's order room.... Allowing Roland to place orders and negotiate with other broker-dealers by telephone constituted a lack of proper supervision by Rice and Dodd.

CONDUCT IN THE MINNEAPOLIS OFFICE

It is alleged in the amended order for proceedings, for consideration upon the issue of the public interest, that through lack of adequate supervision registrant permitted a salesman in its Minneapolis office to misappropriate customers' funds.... The practice of giving the salesman, without question, checks drawn on the accounts of customers would not have been permitted under an effective system of internal control and supervision.

CONCLUSIONS AS TO VIOLATIONS

The activities in registrant's branch offices which have been described demonstrate serious and extensive misconduct by employees in those offices and grave deficiencies *no Safe Harbor*

in the supervision and internal control exercised by registrant and the individual … respondents over such employees.

In the light of these considerations we are of the opinion that, where the failure of a securities firm and its responsible personnel to maintain and diligently enforce a proper system of supervision and internal control results in the perpetration of fraud upon customers or in other misconduct in willful violation of the Securities Act or the Exchange Act, for purposes of applying the sanctions provided under the securities laws such failure constitutes participation in such misconduct, and willful violations are committed not only by the person who performed the misconduct but also by those who did not properly perform their duty to prevent it.

Accordingly, we conclude that registrant, together with or aided and abetted by Rice, White, Whittaker, Dodd, Stefany, Aldous, Coleman, and Roland, willfully violated the anti-fraud provisions in the respects discussed above, …

———

In the Matter of Reynolds demonstrates the lack of express statutory authority to sanction broker-dealers and their supervisory employees for failing to prevent the conduct of primary violators (person who actually violated a provision of the federal securities laws). The SEC was forced to assert that the supervisors participated in the conduct by failing to prevent the conduct of the primary violators — a tortured theory at best, because it required the SEC to use the common law doctrine of *respondeat superior* to hold both the firm and its supervisory employees liable under the Exchange Act for violations they had not committed, but had only failed to stop.

The adoption of Sections 15(b)(4)(E) and 15(b)(6) meant that the SEC no longer had to rely primarily on the theory of *respondeat superior* to impose sanctions for failure to supervise. It now had a clear basis upon which to directly sanction individual supervisors employed by broker-dealers along with the broker-dealer. In a speech before the Practicing Law Institute about the Securities Acts Amendments of 1964, Commissioner Hugh F. Owens stated that:

> The Amendments [gave] the Commission authority, for the first time, to proceed administratively against individuals who have violated the Federal securities laws without being required to join their employers or associates. The N.A.S.D. [was] also given this express authority for the first time. They also allow the Commission to impose sanctions other than suspension or expulsion from a national securities association or revocation of registration. These include censure, bar or suspension from association with a broker-dealer and suspension of registration, in addition to the 'all-or-nothing' alternatives in the prior provisions of the law. These two changes make it possible to cull out the individual 'bad apples' without injuring innocent co-workers or supervisors, and to impose sanctions upon individuals, as well as upon firms and their principals, which more nearly fit the offense charged. The Amendments make it clear that supervisors may not be found to be re-

sponsible for violations committed in spite of reasonable efforts on their part to prevent them.

After the Securities Acts Amendments of 1964, the SEC has several legal theories available to prosecute failure to supervise cases. First, section 15(b)(6) (now codified as Section 15(b)(6)(A)) allows the SEC to sanction an individual supervisor associated with the broker-dealer who fails to satisfy the requirements of Section 15(b)(4)(E), i.e., who fails reasonably to supervise the primary violator. Second, the SEC can sanction the broker-dealer for violations by the primary violator along with the broker-dealer's individual supervisors under the theory of *respondeat superior*. Third, the SEC can sanction the broker-dealer for failure reasonably to supervise under Section 15(b)(4)(E).

Although Sections 15(b)(4)(E) and 15(b)(6)(A) authorize the SEC to sanction broker-dealers and their supervisory employees who have failed reasonably to supervise, reasonable supervision is not defined in these sections nor anywhere else in the Exchange Act. However, the safe harbor contained in section 15(b)(4)(E)(i)–(ii) allows the broker-dealer and its supervisory employees to avoid liability for failure reasonably to supervise if appropriate supervisory procedures and systems have been established and neither the broker-dealer nor its supervisory personnel have reason to believe that failure to comply with the procedures and systems has not occurred.[6] In addition, it is not clear whether Congress intended that the safe harbor contained in Section 15(b)(4)(E)(i)–(iii) should preclude the SEC from using the explicit *respondeat superior* provisions contained in the preamble of Section 15(b)(4), which still allow a broker-dealer to be sanctioned for violations by its associated persons.

> The Commission, by order, shall censure, place limitations on the activities, functions, or operations of, suspend for a period not exceeding twelve months, or revoke the registration of any broker or dealer if it finds, on the record after notice and opportunity for hearing, that such censure, placing of limitations, suspension, or revocation is in the public interest and that such *broker or dealer, whether prior or subsequent to becoming such, or any person associated with such broker or dealer, whether prior or subsequent to becoming so associated.*... (emphasis added). 15 U.S.C. § 78o(b)(4).

The legislative history of Section 15(b)(4)(E) suggests that the SEC is not prohibited from using the *respondeat superior* provisions in the preamble of Section 15(b)(4) as a basis to impose liability for failure reasonably to supervise. In *Armstrong, Jones & Co. v. SEC*, 421 F.2d 359 (6th Cir. 1970), *cert. denied*, 398 U.S. 958 (1970), the court held that Section 15(b)(4)(E) does not displace the doctrine of *respondeat superior* as a basis for imposing sanctions for failure reasonably to supervise. In doing so, the court noted the long history of the SEC's use of the doctrine of *respondeat superior* to sanction broker-dealers for willful violations of its agents and that the adoption of Section 15(b)(4)(E) did not limit the SEC's power to discipline a broker-dealer for its employees' acts. *Id.* at 362. However, critics have asserted that, as a matter of

---

6. See Section IV for a discussion of reasonable supervision.

policy, the SEC should not use the doctrine of *respondeat superior* to avoid the safe harbor contained in Section 15(b)(4)(E) (i)–(ii), which provides that no person shall be deemed to have failed reasonably to supervise any other person, if—

(i) there have been established procedures, and a system for applying such procedures, which would reasonably be expected to prevent and detect, insofar as practicable, any such violation by such other person, and

(ii) such person has reasonably discharged the duties and obligations incumbent upon him by reason of such procedures and system without reasonable cause to believe that such procedures and system were not being complied with.

It has been argued that, as a policy matter, it is not appropriate for the SEC to utilize its *respondeat superior* authority, rather than Section 15(b)(4)(E), in its administrative proceedings so as to circumvent the reasonable supervision defense contained in Section 15(b)(4)(E)(i)–(ii). In supporting this contention, scholars have recognized that no supervision system can be 100 percent successful, and therefore, for the SEC to bring a failure to supervise case on a theory that excludes Section 15(b)(4)(E)'s safe harbor is unfair and contrary to one of the SEC's key missions—to promote investor protection. Moreover, broker-dealers should be allowed to use the safe harbor defense that Congress specifically made available in Section 15(b)(4)(E)(i)–(ii). It seems that the SEC agrees with these critics and commonly uses 15(b)(4)(E) to bring failure to supervise cases rather than the common law doctrine of *respondeat superior*. Finally, there is no private right of action under Sections 15(b)(4(E) and 15(b)(4)(6) for a person harmed as a result of a broker-dealer's or its associated person's failure reasonably to supervise.

 However, a private right of action is available under Section 20(a) of the Exchange Act, which deals with control person liability. Section 20(a) provides a means for holding a controlling party liable for violations of the federal securities laws by its agents. For example, the broker-dealer (the controlling party) who controls a primary violator, its employee (the agent of the broker-dealer), may be held liable under Section 20(a) of the Exchange act if it did not act in good faith and if it induced the violation. Section 20(a) provides that,

Every person who, directly or indirectly, controls any person liable under any provision of this chapter or of any rule or regulation thereunder shall also be liable jointly and severally with and to the same extent as such controlled person to any person to whom such controlled person is liable..., unless the controlling person acted in good faith and did not directly or indirectly induce the act or acts constituting the violation or cause of action.[7]

---

7. Section 15(a) of the Securities Act contains a similar provision concerning liability of controlling persons. "Every person who, by or through stock ownership, agency, or otherwise, or who, pursuant to or in connection with an agreement or understanding with one or more other persons by or through stock ownership, agency, or otherwise, controls any person liable under Section 11 or 12 [of the Securities Act], shall also be liable jointly and severally with and to the same extent as such controlled person to any person to whom such controlled person is liable, unless the controlling person had no knowledge of or reasonable grounds to believe in the existence of the facts by reason of which the liability of the controlled person is alleged to exist." 15 U.S.C. 77o(a) (2015).

The following case demonstrates the use of Section 20(a) to hold supervisors liable for the violations of their employees in a private right of action.

Hollinger v. Titan Capital Corp.
914 F.2d 1564 (9th Cir. 1990)

WILLIAM A. NORRIS, Circuit Judge:

Emil Wilkowski, a dishonest securities salesman, embezzled money entrusted to him by four clients. As a result, Wilkowski was convicted of criminal securities fraud and grand theft. In this civil action for alleged violations of federal securities and state laws, the victimized investors seek to recover their losses from a brokerage firm and a financial counseling firm with which Wilkowski was associated. The district court granted summary judgment to both defendants, which plaintiffs now appeal.

* * *

To hold Titan liable under § 20(a), appellants must first establish that Titan was a "controlling person" within the meaning of the statute.[8]

* * *

A

The SEC, as amicus curiae, joins appellants in arguing that the district court erred in holding that Titan could not be held vicariously liable as a "controlling person" under § 20(a) for Wilkowski's misdeeds. We agree. Today we hold that a broker-dealer is a controlling person under § 20(a) with respect to its registered representatives.

First, the SEC notes that this circuit and other circuits have interpreted the securities laws to impose a duty on broker-dealers to supervise their registered representatives.[9] In *Zweig*, we noted that Congress adopted § 20(a) in an attempt to protect the investing public from representatives who were inadequately supervised or controlled:

> Purchasers of securities frequently rely heavily for investment advice on the broker-representative handling the purchaser's portfolio. Such representatives traditionally are compensated by commissions in direct proportion to sales. The opportunity and temptation to take advantage of the client is ever present. To ensure the diligence of supervision and control, the broker-dealer is held vicariously liable if the representative injures the investor through violations of Section 10(b) or the rules thereunder promulgated. The very

---

8. The SEC has defined "control" to mean: "[T]he possession, direct or indirect, of the power to direct or cause the direction of the management and policies of a person, whether through the ownership of voting securities, by contract, or otherwise." 17 C.F.R. § 230.405 (2014).

9. *See, e.g., Zweig v. Hearst Corp.*, 521 F.2d 1129, 1134-35 (9th Cir. 1975), *cert. denied*, 423 U.S. 1025 (1975); *accord Paul F. Newton & Co. v. Tex. Commerce Bank*, 630 F.2d 1111, 1120 (5th Cir. 1980); *Marbury Mgmt., Inc. v. Kohn*, 629 F.2d 705, 716 (2d Cir. 1980), *cert. denied*, 449 U.S. 1011 (1980).

nature of the vast securities business, as it has developed in this country, militates for such a rule as public policy and would seem to suggest strict court enforcement.

521 F.2d at 1135.

The SEC argues that the representative/broker-dealer relationship is necessarily one of controlled and controlling person because the broker-dealer is required to supervise its representatives. This requirement arises from § 15 of the 1934 Act, which the SEC has interpreted as authority to impose sanctions on broker-dealers who have failed to provide adequate supervision of their registered representatives. (citations omitted).

Second, the SEC argues that as a practical matter the broker-dealer exercises control over its registered representatives because the representatives need the broker-dealer to gain access to the securities markets. Again, the SEC points to § 15(a) of the 1934 Act, which provides that a person cannot lawfully engage in the securities business unless he or she is either registered with the NASD [] as a broker-dealer or as a person associated with a broker-dealer. Because a sales representative must be associated with a registered broker-dealer in order to have legal access to the trading markets, the broker-dealer always has the power to impose conditions upon that association, or to terminate it. The broker-dealer's ability to deny the representative access to the markets gives the broker-dealer effective control over the representative at the most basic level. Moreover, because the broker-dealer is required by statute to establish and enforce a reasonable system of supervision to control its representatives' activities, the broker-dealer necessarily exerts ongoing control over the types of transactions made by the representative and her ways of handling clients' accounts.

In contrast to the SEC's position, the district court's reasoning implied that even if Titan had the power to deny Wilkowski access to the trading markets or was required by statute to supervise his securities transactions, Titan still should not be considered a controlling person under § 20(a) because Wilkowski was an independent contractor, not an agent. We find no support in the statutory scheme for such a restrictive definition of controlling person that would exclude independent contractors, and thus, we do not distinguish for purposes of § 20(a) between registered representatives who are employees or agents and those who might meet the definition of independent contractors.

In sum, § 20(a) of the Act provides that a person cannot lawfully engage in the securities business unless he is either registered as or associated with a broker-dealer, and we see no basis in the statutory scheme to distinguish between those associated persons who are employees and agents on the one hand, and those who are independent contractors on the other. To exclude from the definition of controlling person those registered representatives who might technically be called independent contractors would be an unduly restrictive reading of the statute and would tend to frustrate Congress' goal of protecting investors. Thus, we reject the argument that broker-dealers can avoid a duty to supervise simply by entering into a contract that purports to make the representative, who is not himself registered under the Act as a broker-dealer, an "independent contractor."[10]

To summarize, we hold that a broker-dealer is a controlling person under § 20(a) with respect to its registered representatives ...

B

Titan also argues that it was not a controlling person because it was not a "culpable participant" in Wilkowski's deeds ...

The district court, citing earlier cases from our circuit, agreed with Titan and ruled that a broker-dealer is not a "controlling person" under § 20(a) unless the plaintiff proves that the broker-dealer was a "culpable participant" in the violation

Today, however, we hold that a plaintiff is *not* required to show "culpable participation" to establish that a broker-dealer was a controlling person under § 20(a).[11] The statute does not place such a burden on the plaintiff. Section 20(a) provides that a "controlling person" is liable "unless [he] acted in good faith and did not directly or indirectly induce the act or acts constituting the violation or cause of action." 15 U.S.C. § 78t(a). Thus, the statute premises liability solely on the control relationship, subject to the good faith defense. According to the statutory language, once the plaintiff establishes that the defendant is a "controlling person," then the defendant bears the burden of proof to show his good faith.

Today we return to what had once been the law of our circuit, namely that § 20(a) requires the defendant to prove his good faith. Now, we make clear that in an action based on § 20(a), the defendant who is a controlling person, and not the plaintiff, bears the burden of proof as to defendant's good faith. Thus, a plaintiff need not make a showing as to defendant's culpable participation; rather, a defendant has the burden of pleading and proving his good faith.

To summarize, a broker-dealer controls a registered representative for the purposes of § 20(a). By recognizing this control relationship, we do not mean that a broker-dealer is vicariously liable under § 20(a) for all actions taken by its registered representatives. Nor are we making the broker-dealer the "insurer" of its representatives,

---

10. The contract between Titan and Wilkowski provided:

> 7. *Contractor's Freedom from Company Controls.* The Company has no right to control or direct the Contractor in the sales of securities, not only as to the result to be accomplished by the work but also as to the details and means by which the result is accomplished, excepting [oversight and instructions required to comply with securities laws].... [T]he Contractor is completely free from the will and control of the Company not only as to what shall be done, but how it shall be done.

R.E. at 311-12.

11. Today's holding, however, is reached in the context of the broker-dealer/registered representative relationship exclusively. We do not address the question of whether in other contexts the first prong of the *Buhler* and *Christoffel* test for determining a "controlling person," namely that of power and influence, may be applied. A person may, of course, be a controlling person without being a broker-dealer. *See, e.g., Zweig,* 521 F.2d at 1132.

which is a result we rejected in *Christoffel* as going beyond the scope of the vicarious liability imposed upon a broker-dealer by § 20(a). The mere fact that a controlling person relationship exists does not mean that vicarious liability necessarily follows. Section 20(a) provides that the "controlling person" can avoid liability if she acted in good faith and did not directly or indirectly induce the violations. By making the good faith defense available to controlling persons, Congress was able to avoid what it deemed to be an undesirable result, namely that of insurer's liability, and instead it made vicarious liability under § 20(a) dependent upon the broker-dealer's good faith.[12]

C

Contrary to the district court's ruling, the broker-dealer cannot satisfy its burden of proving good faith merely by saying that it has supervisory procedures in place, and therefore, it has fulfilled its duty to supervise. A broker-dealer can establish the good faith defense only by proving that it "maintained and enforced a reasonable and proper system of supervision and internal control." (citations omitted) Accordingly, the district court erred in ruling that because "Titan had adopted rules for accepting investment payments and for supervising a contractor's compliance with securities laws and regulations," it had satisfied its duty to supervise. Should Titan choose to rely upon the good faith defense, then it must carry its burden of persuasion that its supervisory system was adequate and that it reasonably discharged its responsibilities under the system. The evidence below raised material issues of fact as to whether Titan's supervision of Wilkowski was sufficient to entitle Titan to the good faith defense. Summary judgment was, accordingly, improper.

Notes and Questions

1. *Tests used by Courts to identify the control person.* There is a split in the circuits as to the appropriate test to use to determine when one person is a control person of the primary violator. The two tests used by the various circuits are the Potential Control Test and the Culpable Participation Test. The Potential Control Test, used by the Eighth and Ninth Circuits, requires plaintiffs to establish that the alleged control person: (1) actually exercised control over the operations of the corporation or person in general and that (2) the defendant possessed the power to control the specific transaction or activity upon which the primary violation is predicated, but is not required to prove that this specific power to control was exercised. *See Metge v. Baehler,* 762 F.2d 621 (8th Cir. 1985). The Culpable Participation test, used by the Second, Third, and Fourth Circuits, requires the plaintiff to show:

---

12. The broker-dealer may also, of course, rely on a contention that the representative was acting outside of the broker-dealer's statutory "control." For example, Titan could argue that when appellants entrusted their money to Wilkowski they were not reasonably relying upon him as a registered representative of Titan, but were placing the money with Wilkowski for purposes other than investment in markets to which Wilkowski had access only by reason of his relationship with broker-dealer Titan.

(1) control of the primary violator by the alleged controlling person and (2) that the alleged controlling person was a culpable participant in the specific fraud perpetrated by the primary violator. *See SEC v. First Jersey Sec., Inc.,* 101 F.3d 1450, 1472 (2d Cir. 1996).

2. *Broker-dealer controlling person liability under § 20(a) and the SEC.* Section 15(b)(4)(E) authorizes the SEC to discipline broker-dealers that fail reasonably to supervise their associated persons or employees. What is the relationship of the broker-dealer's duty to supervise and its exposure to controlling person liability under Section 20(a)? → Liability is solely based on the control relationship, subject to good faith.

3. *Relationship of Controlling Person Liability to Common Law Secondary Liability.* Failure to supervise may also form the basis for a suit based on negligence or other common law causes of action. In this context, the question of whether Section 20(a) is the exclusive remedy for supervisory cases is significant because, unless Section 20(a) is the exclusive remedy, it will only shield a defendant broker-dealer from liability from claims under the Exchange Act, and not from tort claims for fraud, negligent misrepresentation, and similar claims governed by different standards of joint or vicarious liability. There is a division of authority regarding whether Section 20(a) displaces common law agency principals, including *respondeat superior*. Many circuits have held that Section 20(a) is not an exclusive remedy. Prior to 1990, the Ninth Circuit held that Section 20(a) was an exclusive remedy. However, it reversed its previous holding and decided *en banc* that Section 20(a) does not preempt common law vicarious liability. *Hollinger v. Titan Capital Corp.,* 914 F.2d 1564, 1577 (9th Cir. 1990), *cert. denied* 499 U.S. 976 (1991):

> After reexamination of the issue as an en banc court, we are now satisfied that "the 'controlling person' provision of Section 20(a) was not intended to supplant the application of agency principles in securities cases, and that it was enacted to expand rather than to restrict the scope of liability under the securities laws." *Marbury Management,* 629 F.2d at 712; *accord Paul F. Newton & Co.,* 630 F.2d at 1118 (The legislative "history does not reflect any congressional intent to restrict secondary liability for violations of the acts to the controlled persons formula.").

> Section 20(a), which was modelled after the controlling person provision of § 15 of the Securities Act of 1933, 15 U.S.C. § 77, was intended "to prevent evasion" of the law "by organizing dummies who will undertake the actual things forbidden."[13] In other words, § 20(a) was intended to impose liability on controlling persons, such as controlling shareholders and corporate officers, who would not be liable under *respondeat superior* because they were

---

13. Stock Exchange Practices: Hearings on S. Res. 84 (72d Cong.) and S. Res. 56 and S. Res. 97 (73d Cong.) Before the Senate Comm. on Banking and Currency, 73d Cong., 1st Sess. 6571 (1934) (statement of Thomas G. Corcoran, in the office of counsel for the Reconstruction Finance Corporation and one of the drafters of the Securities Act of 1934).

not the actual employers. Thus, in enacting § 20(a), Congress expanded upon the common law, and in doing so, created a defense (the good faith defense) that would be available only to those who, under common law principles of *respondeat superior*, would have faced no liability at all.

Only if both *respondeat superior* and § 20(a) are available is the statutory scheme comprehensive and the public protected by the federal securities laws. "To allow a brokerage firm to avoid secondary liability simply by showing ignorance, purposeful or negligent, of the acts of its registered representative contravenes Congress' intent to protect the public, particularly unsophisticated investors, from fraudulent practices." *Paul F. Newton & Co.*, 630 F.2d at 1118–19. When both remedies are available, then the agent who personally committed the wrong is primarily liable (based on proof of his actions or omissions, and on scienter when required); the principal who acts through the agent (assuming the agent is acting within the scope of his agency) is secondarily liable; and other persons who are not subject to *respondeat superior* but who nevertheless control the wrongdoer can be held liable under § 20(a). Because the liability of persons under § 20(a) represents an extension of liability, beyond that imposed by the common law, such persons are afforded statutory defenses not available in the principal-agent context. Controlling persons may thus avoid liability under § 20(a) by demonstrating that they acted in "good faith" within the meaning of that section.

4. A more recent example of the use of Section 20(a) in the context supervision occurred in the protracted case of *SEC v. Pasternak and Leighton*, 561 F. Supp. 2d 459 (D.N.J. 2008). In this case, the SEC asked the court to enjoin defendants, among other things, "from controlling any person that is in a position to violate Exchange Act Sections 15(c)(1)(A) and 17(a) and Exchange Act Rule 17a-3[.]" According to the court, the purpose of Section 20(a) of the Exchange Act is to impose liability on persons who were able to directly or indirectly exert influence on the policy and decision-making process of others. The SEC sought to assert liability as a controlling person pursuant to Section 20(a) of the Exchange Act against Pasternak, the CEO, president, and chairman of the board of Knight, the broker-dealer.[14] The Court, using the Culpable Participant Test, enumerated the required elements to impose control liability under Section 20(a): (1) the defendant must be a controlling person; (2) the controlled person must have violated the securities laws; (3) the defendant must be a culpable participant in the fraud in that he directly or indirectly induced the underlying violation; and (4) the defendant did not act in good faith. It is unclear whether Section 20(a)

---

14. The SEC also asserts violation of FINRA rules, but not FINRA Rule 3010. FINRA also brought a proceeding against the defendants but it sought to impose liability based on FINRA 3010 for respondents' failure reasonably to supervise. It seems that the SEC chose not to allege failure reasonably to supervise under Sections 15(b)(4)(E) and 15(b)(6) in its complaint because it would have been difficult to argue that Knight had not established, implemented, and maintained a reasonable supervisory system.

requires scienter; six circuits have determined that Section 20(a) does not require scienter; however, the Third and Fourth Circuits have held that Section 20(a) does require scienter. In order to avail himself of the affirmative defense of good faith under Section 20(a), the defendant must prove that "he exercised due care in his supervision of the violator's activities in that he maintained and enforced a reasonable and proper system of supervision and internal controls." (citations omitted). The Court determined that defendant Pasternak did not have control person liability under Section 20(a) because the SEC failed to establish all the requisite elements. How may *Pasternak and Leighton* be distinguished from *Hollinger*, if at all, in determining when a supervisor may have control person liability under Section 20(a)? → *The burden is shifted onto Hollinger & away from P&L.*

5. *Relationship between Rule 14e-3 and the Duty to Supervise.* Although rarely used by the SEC in failure to supervise cases, Section 14(e) of the Exchange Act and Rule 14e-3 promulgated thereunder provide an affirmative defense for broker-dealers charged with failure to supervise under Sections 15(b)(4)(E) and 15(b)(6) in the context of tender offers. Section 14(e) and Rule 14e-3 govern transactions by persons in possession of material nonpublic information in tender offers. Subsection (a) of Rule 14e-3 enumerates the elements of a primary violation, and subsection (b) of Rule 14e-3 states the availability of an affirmative defense against liability for the broker-dealer employing the individual violator under Section 15(b)(4)(E). The SEC articulated its views on this safe harbor in *Koppers Company, Inc. v. American Express Co.,* 689 F. Supp. 1413, 1416 (W.D. Pa. 1988), recognizing that a blanket proscription would prevent multi-service financial institutions from engaging in their various roles, therefore the Commission built into the rule an exception. Under that exception, no violation of Rule 14e-3(a) occurs if an institution engaged in the securities business can show, first, that the individuals making investment decisions for a transaction about which the institution possesses confidential information did not know the information and, second, that the institution has implemented reasonable procedures to ensure that such individuals would not violate Rule 14e-3(a). These procedures may include, but are not limited to: (i) those that restrict any purchase, sale, and causing any purchase and sale of any such security or (ii) those that prevent such individual(s) from knowing such information. Specific procedures recognized by the SEC include information barriers, restricted lists, and watch lists. *Id.* at 1416.

6. *The Relationship between the Insider Trading and Securities Fraud Enforcement Act (ITSFEA) and Duty to Supervise in Section 15(b)(4)(E).* ITSFEA requires broker-dealers to adopt supervisory policies and procedures designed to prevent insider trading. In order to avoid liability for failure to supervise, Section 3(b)(2) of ITSFEA requires the broker-dealer to establish, maintain, and enforce policies and procedures designed to prevent the misuse of non-public material information and to update such policies and procedures as required. Section 3(b) of ITSFEA was designed to complement existing Self-Regulatory Organization ("SRO") supervisory requirements and Section 15(b)(4)(E).

Table 4.1. Summary — Supervisory Liability

Statute	Description	Private Right of Action
§ 15(b)(4)(E)	Authorizes the SEC to sanction broker-dealers who have failed reasonably to supervise their associated persons with a view to preventing violations of the federal securities laws.	NO
§ 15(b)(4)(E)(i)–(ii)	Provides a safe harbor for broker-dealers from liability for deficient supervision.	NO
§ 15(b)(4)(6)	Authorizes the SEC to directly hold associated persons of broker-dealers liable for deficient supervision.	NO
§ 20(a)	Provides joint and several liability for every person who, directly or indirectly, controls any person who has violated the federal securities laws.	YES
§ 14(3) and Rules 14e-(a) and (b) promulgated thereunder	Provides an affirmative defense for broker-dealers charged with failure to supervise under Sections 15(b)(4)(E) and 15(b)(6) in the context of tender offers.	YES
§ 3(b) of ITFSEA	Requires broker-dealers to adopt supervisory policies and procedures designed to prevent insider trading.	YES

Hypothetical One

John DoGood is a registered representative and employee of Success First. He works out of Success First's West Palm Beach, Florida, office and has been an employee for 15 years. Currently, the West Palm Beach office has eight registered representatives in addition to DoGood, and all report to Angela Bennett, the branch manager. Bennett, in turn, reports to the regional manager, Naomi Watts, who is responsible for the southeast region. Investors invested money through JD investments, Inc., an entity that DoGood controlled. In connection with these investments, DoGood sold promissory notes to investors, listing JD investments as the borrower. Instead of investing the money in JD investments, however, DoGood misappropriated the funds for his personal use, spent the money in other ways, or simply transferred money among other investors to prevent them from discovering the fraud. Identify theories of liability that can be asserted against Success First, Bennett, and Watts.

III. Elements of Failure Reasonably to Supervise

A supervisor has failed reasonably to supervise under Sections 15(b)(4)(E) and 15(b)(6) when the SEC finds, by a preponderance of the evidence, that: (1) another person violated a provision of the federal securities laws, (2) that person was subject to the supervision of the supervisor, and (3) the supervisor failed reasonably to supervise that person with a view to preventing her violations. In order to establish a violation of Sections 15(b)(4)(E) and 15(b)(6), it must be determined that the broker-dealer and/or one of its employees or associated persons is a supervisor of a person who has violated a provision of the federal securities laws. However, there is no definition of the term *supervisor* in the Exchange Act, and even the SEC has struggled to provide a clear and consistent definition of the term *supervisor* under Sections 15(b)(4)(E) and 15(b)(6) since the enactment of the Securities Act Amendments of 1964.

A. Who Is a Supervisor?

Historically, the SEC has attempted to provide meaningful guidance as to who is a supervisor. This is necessary because one can only fail reasonably to supervise if there is—as stated in the statute—someone subject to your supervision. While it may be fairly straightforward to determine who is a supervisor at the first level of supervision with respect to the registered representative, it becomes more difficult when going up the chain of command and more difficult still when determining whether compliance personnel are supervisors within the meaning of Sections 15(b)(4)(E) and 15(b)(6). As a result, the SEC's failure-to-supervise cases may be divided into two general categories—line supervisors and non-line supervisors. Line supervisors supervise employees in their direct chain of command including employees engaged in revenue-generating activities. Non-line supervisors supervise employees not in their direct chain of command and may include employees engaged in the compliance function of the broker-dealer. However, the SEC has consistently held that partners,

Figure 4.1. Duty to Supervise

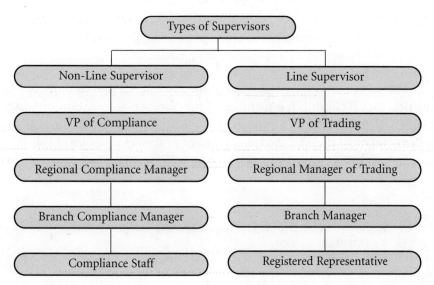

branch managers, and other supervisory personnel of a broker-dealer have a responsibility to supervise employees and that revocation of the broker-dealer's registration with the SEC, or other appropriate sanctions, may be imposed upon a broker or dealer whose employees violate that responsibility.

1. Line Supervisors

Line supervisors are persons who are in a direct supervisory chain of command above the principal violator. According to the SEC:

> [w]hen you are in the direct supervisory line, you are presumptively assumed to be a person who is a supervisor of the wrongdoer. The presumption arises from the very nature of your responsibilities and authority; from the fact that in most organizations persons in the direct chain of command are given both the authority and the ability to influence the conduct of lower level employees.[15]

a. Branch Managers

Determining whether a person is a supervisor depends on whether, under the facts and circumstances of a particular case, that person has the requisite degree of responsibility, ability, or authority to affect the conduct of the employee whose behavior is at issue. The SEC attempts to provide guidance regarding when, under the facts and circumstances, a person becomes a line supervisor and thus is liable if he or she fails reasonably to supervise. The branch manager is the first level in the chain of command in a broker-dealer's organization. Branch managers are key supervisors who have responsibility for the supervision and control of all sales and operational activities of the branch offices of the broker-dealers.[16] It is fairly settled law that a branch manager of a broker-dealer is a line supervisor and, therefore, subject to liability for deficient supervision.

In the Matter of the Application of Christopher J. Benz

Admin. Proc. File No. 3-8986 (Mar. 26, 1997)

I.

Christopher Benz, formerly manager of the Los Angeles branch office of Gilford Securities, Inc. ("Gilford"), a member of the National Association of Securities Dealers, Inc. ("NASD") appeals from NASD disciplinary action. The NASD found that Benz violated Article III, Sections 1 and 27 of the NASD Rules of Fair Practice ("Rules") in that Benz failed adequately to supervise a registered representative of

---

15. Mary L. Schapiro, *Remarks to the SIA Compliance and Legal Seminar, Orlando, Florida*, in FED. SEC. L. REP. No. 1548, Mar. 31, 1993, at 6.

16. *See* NYSE, PATTERNS OF SUPERVISION: A GUIDE TO THE SUPERVISION AND MANAGEMENT OF REGISTERED REPRESENTATIVES AND CUSTOMER ACCOUNTS 33–35 (1982).

Gilford and failed to enforce Gilford's supervisory procedures. The NASD censured Benz, fined him $7500, assessed costs, and required that Benz requalify as a general securities principal before again acting in a principal capacity.[17] Our findings are based on an independent review of the record.

II.

In January 1990, Christopher Benz was hired to work on Gilford's trading desk in New York. In July 1991, Gilford's president and chief executive officer, Ralph Worthington, asked Benz to become the branch manager of the Los Angeles office of Gilford. In preparation for assuming the responsibilities of branch manager, Benz spent two days with Gilford's most senior branch manager who worked at Gilford's Connecticut office, had conversations with Gilford's financial staff, and passed the NASD's Series 24 principal examination. Benz also had several conversations with Worthington about the Los Angeles office which Worthington characterized as "kind of a mess." Worthington warned Benz that one registered representative in the Los Angeles office, Elias Argyropolous, could be "tricky" and could cause headaches.

Benz commenced his duties as branch manager in August 1991. Benz began to be concerned about Argyropolous's activities in March 1992 when Benz received a subpoena from this Commission related to trades made by Argyropolous. Benz also noticed unusually high numbers of margin calls in the accounts of Argyropolous's clients. Benz contacted Worthington, who told Benz to monitor the situation.

Between March and December 1992, Benz received more customer complaints about Argyropolous, as well as document requests from different stock exchanges relating to Argyropolous's accounts. Benz discussed the complaints with Worthington and with Argyropolous. Benz continued to see unusual margin activity in Argyropolous's accounts.

In December 1992, Benz drafted a memo to Worthington detailing his concerns about Argyropolous's activities. Benz noted, for example, that Argyropolous "continually over-purchased" for his clients and that his clients were not meeting their "house" margin calls. As a result, many of Argyropolous's customers' accounts were being liquidated. Benz also suggested that Argyropolous's clients were not aware of the "illegality or potential consequences" of not meeting their margin calls. Benz stated his belief that Argyropolous was engaging in free-riding in an attempt to make up for earlier losses suffered by his clients. As a result of this memo, Worthington called Argyropolous to New York for a meeting, at which time Argyropolous assured Worthington that he would pay closer attention to the correct handling of his accounts.

---

17. The complaint also named as respondents Gilford, Gilford's president and chief executive officer, Ralph Worthington, and Elias Argyropolous, the registered representative whose underlying conduct was at issue. These three respondents settled with the NASD. Gilford and its president and chief executive officer were each censured, and fined $30,000. Gilford further agreed to improve and publish internally the firm's amended supervisory procedures. The registered representative's settlement resulted in a censure, a bar in all capacities, and a $200,000 fine (with collection efforts on the fine suspended unless and until he seeks to become associated with a member firm).

When Benz returned from a holiday vacation in early January 1993, he discovered that Argyropolous had made a large number of purchases in yet another stock while he was gone and that some of the accounts of Argyropolous's clients were heavily margined. He notified Worthington who advised him to ensure that the customers were going to pay for the trades.[18]

In early July 1993, Benz notified Worthington that he was resigning and left the firm a few weeks later.

III.

Article III, Section 27 of the Rules requires a member to establish, maintain, and enforce a supervisory system with written procedures. Each registered representative must be adequately monitored by a supervisor.

Benz does not assert that he took sufficient action to meet these requirements. Rather, Benz contends that, although his title was "branch manager," he merely reported to Worthington, who actually controlled the Los Angeles office from New York.[19] The record does not support this contention. Benz performed the functions of a branch manager including: 1) reviewing order tickets, account statements, brokers' family-related accounts, and margin activity; 2) approving new accounts; 3) reviewing and responding to customer complaints; and 4) approving cross-trades in customer accounts. He also admitted that he reviewed incoming mail for the office, and he held himself out in correspondence as the branch manager.

* * *

Benz further argues that he did not have authority to supervise Argyropolous and that he could not fire him without Worthington's approval. Firm officials, however, can be responsible for a failure to supervise even if they lack the ability to hire and fire.[20] Worthington testified that Benz had authority to hire and fire all employees in the Los Angeles branch office.[21] Moreover, Benz admitted in his testimony before the NASD that he had authority to supervise the remaining registered representatives— other than Argyropolous—in the Los Angeles office.

---

18. The NASD found that Argyropolous engaged in a wide variety of sales practice abuses and manipulative and deceptive devices during the time that Benz was his supervisor, including unauthorized trades, unsuitable recommendations, sharing losses with customers, guaranteeing customers against losses, and engaging in wash sales and matched orders.

19. Benz contends that, because Argyropolous produced large revenue for Gilford, Worthington was unwilling to supervise him too closely.

20. *See* Conrad C. Lysiak, 51 S.E.C. 841, 844 (1993), *aff'd*, 47 F.3d 1175 (9th Cir. 1995) (unpublished opinion).

21. Worthington noted, however, that he would have wanted notice before someone as senior as Argyropolous was fired. Benz asserts that Worthington shaded this testimony in order to obtain a good settlement of the NASD's disciplinary action against Worthington and Gilford. Regardless of whether Benz had authority to hire and fire, he was responsible for adequately supervising Argyropolous.

Notes and Questions

1. The NASD's disciplinary action taken in *Benz* was sustained (*See* Exchange Act Release No. 38440, Mar. 26, 1997) even though the branch manager claimed not to have the authority to hire and fire registered representatives in his branch office. In *In the Matter of Arthur James Huff*, Exchange Act Release No. 29017, 1991 WL 296561 (Mar. 28, 1991), two SEC commissioners, in a concurring opinion, stated that the most important element in failure to supervise cases is the extent to which an employee had particular authority and responsibility for the salesperson's violative conduct " ... and had the employee[] wished to exercise it could have prevented the salesperson[] from continuing [his/her] activities in those areas in which the [employee] exercised that authority and responsibility, *even if [the employee] did not have the power to fire, demote or reduce the pay of the salesperson[] in question.*" (emphasis added). Does this mean that these elements—the authority to hire and fire—are not required in determining who is a line supervisor under Sections 15(b)(4)(E) and 15(b)(6) of the Exchange Act? → Yes, merely a factor.

2. Under the federal securities laws, a branch manager is deemed to be a supervisor of the registered representatives employed in the branch manager's branch office. *See In the Matter of Sandra Logay*, Exchange Act Release No. 159, 2000 WL 95098 (Jan. 28, 2000). In *Logay* the administrative law judge concluded that the definition of a *supervisor* under the federal securities laws is extremely broad and that Logay's position as branch office manager at her firm made her responsible for the direct supervision of the registered representatives in her branch office. *Id.* at 21. Why are branch managers considered the first line of defense in the broker-dealer regulatory framework? → Since they are key supervisors who have responsibility for the supervision & control of all sales & operational activities of the

3. What types of responsibilities are performed by branch managers? branch offices of the bd.
   ↳ Since they have so much responsibility. ◁

b. Regional Managers

Supervisory status also attaches to line supervisors of the firm above the position of branch manager. This means that other firm employees in the chain of supervision in addition to the firm's branch manager may be held liable for deficient supervision. In many cases, this includes regional and home office employees engaged in the firm's business activities (typically retail). The key element is whether the wrongdoer is subject to the person's supervision, i.e., whether that person has the requisite degree of responsibility, ability, or authority to affect the conduct of the employee whose behavior is at issue. This determination, in most instances, is based on the facts and circumstances of the particular case. The following case illustrates the determination of line supervisory status and consequent liability of line supervisors at the middle management level.

In the Matter of George J. Kolar

Initial Decision Rel. No. 152, Administrative Proceeding File No. 3-9570

The United States Securities and Exchange Commission (Commission) instituted these proceedings on March 27, 1998, pursuant to Sections 15(b), 19(h), and 21B of the Securities Exchange Act of 1934 (Exchange Act). The Order Instituting Proceedings (OIP) alleges that George J. Kolar, while employed at Dean Witter Reynolds, Inc. (Dean Witter), a registered broker-dealer, failed reasonably to supervise a registered representative subject to his supervision, within the meaning of Section 15(b)(4) of the Exchange Act. The registered representative is alleged to have committed willful violations of Sections 5(a), 5(c), and 17(a) of the Securities Act of 1933 (Securities Act) and Sections 10(b), 15(a)(1), and 15(c)(1) of the Exchange Act, as well as Commission Rules 10b-5 and 15c1-2.

The OIP alleges that, from approximately January 1992 through June 1995, Mr. Kolar was the manager of Dean Witter's branch office at Southfield, Michigan, and also supervised the branch manager of Dean Witter's Troy, Michigan, branch office and the registered representatives in the Troy office. It further alleges that Mr. Kolar failed reasonably to supervise Dean C. Turner, a registered representative in the Troy branch office, with a view toward preventing Mr. Turner's violations of the federal securities laws.

The OIP charges that Mr. Turner sold approximately $13.6 million in promissory notes issued by Lease Equities Fund, Inc. (LEF) to the customers of Dean Witter, and that the notes were not registered with the Commission and were not approved by Dean Witter for sale to its customers. It also maintains that the notes were part of a "Ponzi" scheme, that Mr. Turner offered and sold the notes without conducting any due diligence inquiry, and that he made misrepresentations of, and omitted to state, material facts to investors concerning the use of investor funds, the source of funds to be repaid to investors, the risks associated with the securities, the collateral for the securities, and the returns to be realized. The OIP further alleges that Mr. Turner's customers lost at least $10 million due to the fraudulent nature of the notes.

The OIP asserts that, beginning in August 1992, Respondent Kolar received a "red flag" in the form of a complaint made to him by an individual who provided certain financial services to clients of Dean Witter. According to the OIP, the complainant told Mr. Kolar that Dean Turner had been selling LEF securities to his customers at Dean Witter. After receiving the "red flag," the OIP asserts, Mr. Kolar did not take any steps to investigate the complaint, other than relying on Mr. Turner's unverified representation that he did not solicit or sell LEF securities to his customers.

* * *

Mr. Kolar maintains that his involvement with Mr. Turner and the events at issue are limited to one isolated incident in August 1992. At that time, Mr. Kolar, who was not even located in the same branch office as Mr. Turner, immediately reacted to information about Mr. Turner that he received from a person unknown to him by reporting that information to his own supervisor. Respondent asserts that he then made the inquiries of Mr. Turner that he was directed to make by his supervisor, after that supervisor had consulted with Dean Witter's Law Department. Those inquiries involved an interview of Mr. Turner and review of corroborative income tax documentation from him. Mr. Kolar then reported the results of these inquiries to his supervisor, and was not told to do anything further. Respondent contends that the charges should be dismissed.

* * *

FINDINGS OF FACT

Respondent Kolar

Mr. [George J.] Kolar has been affiliated with Dean Witter since 1981 … Dean Witter reassigned Mr. Kolar to Detroit from February 1992 through June 1995. At all times relevant to this case, he held the title of Detroit metropolitan area manager and wore three hats: first, he supervised the firm's focus market program in the Detroit area; second, he managed Dean Witter's Southfield, Michigan, branch office, with twenty-five brokers; third, he supervised other branch offices at Troy, Dearborn, and downtown Detroit. Each of these three offices also had its own on-site branch manager; collectively, the four Detroit-area offices had 120 registered representatives. During this period, Mr. Kolar was a full-time manager; he had very few customers of his own, and did not earn commission income.

From February 1992 through June 1995, Mr. Kolar also supervised, on an overall basis, the branch office managers at Dearborn, Detroit, and Troy. During this period, the Troy branch office manager reported directly to Mr. Kolar. Mr. Kolar visited the Troy branch office every six to eight weeks, and spoke by telephone with the Troy branch office manager as frequently as business required—sometimes two or three times per day, sometimes only once a week. Such conversations involved sales and marketing issues (frequently) and operations and compliance issues (occasionally). On his visits to the Troy branch, Mr. Kolar also talked to the brokers and reviewed the office ledgers.

During this period, Mr. Kolar participated in hiring, disciplinary, and firing decisions as to registered representatives at the Troy branch. He did not have the last word in such matters, but did have input, and his views carried weight with Dean Witter's midwest regional director in Chicago. Mr. Kolar was not simply a messenger between the Troy branch manager and the midwest regional director.

Dean Turner

From August 1990 to December 1995, Dean C. Turner was a registered representative and vice president of Dean Witter at the firm's Troy branch office.

Before joining Dean Witter, Mr. Turner was a registered representative at another broker-dealer. He informed one customer that he was switching firms because "he had an arrangement with Dean Witter by which he didn't have to push conventional products" but "was free to seek good solid investments on his own"). He told another customer that, at Dean Witter, he would have "special situations that weren't available to everybody." He advised clients and associates that Dean Witter had "bought him out ... because they wanted him and his portfolio," that he had received a "very very good offer," and a "signing bonus." The Troy branch manager told Dean Witter's Compliance Department that he was "very excited" about recruiting Mr. Turner "and the potential business [he] can bring to Dean Witter."

Thomas O'Neil, Raymond Basile

At all relevant times, Thomas C. O'Neil was Dean Witter's midwest regional director, with an office in Chicago, Illinois. He exercised overall supervisory responsibility for the operation of sixty to seventy branch offices in an eleven state area.... In thirty-seven years of professional experience, Mr. O'Neil has encountered approximately six cases of "selling away." In most such episodes, the matter came to the firm's attention by customer complaint, after the investments in question had proven unsuccessful. Management then confronted the offending brokers, who confessed, and were terminated.

Raymond A. Basile managed Dean Witter's Troy branch office from August 1990 to February 1996. In this capacity, he was Dean Turner's immediate day-to-day supervisor. At all relevant times, there were fifty to sixty brokers in the Troy office. Mr. O'Neil removed Mr. Basile from this position as a result of the LEF matter. From February 1996 through the date of hearing, Mr. Basile has been central division manager for Dean Witter's Mutual Fund Division.

Before Mr. Kolar arrived in Detroit in February 1992, and after Mr. Kolar left Detroit in June 1995, Mr. Basile reported directly to Mr. O'Neil.

Mr. Basile hired Dean Turner early in his tenure as Troy branch manager, with input from and approval by Mr. O'Neil During the interview process, Mr. Turner told Mr. Basile that he was an investor in LEF notes and that he had friends and associates who were also investors in LEF notes. He was advised by Mr. Basile that he could not offer or sell those instruments to Dean Witter customers. Although Mr. Turner later requested and received Dean Witter's approval for certain of his outside investments, including T. P. Investment Corporation and Genesis Secured Prime Plus Limited Partnership, there is no documentary evidence that he sought the required approval to invest in or hold LEF notes.

LEF Notes

LEF was a Michigan corporation, organized in 1988, with its office in Milford, Michigan. Its stock was owned by NBF. William Malek was president of both corporations. LEF was liquidated in February 1996, after several creditors filed an involuntary bankruptcy petition.

LEF leased equipment to small and medium size businesses that could not get conventional financing. An investor would loan money to LEF in exchange for a promissory note from LEF to the investor, requiring LEF to pay back the principal and interest at a fixed rate over a period of time ... LEF told investors that its promissory notes were backed by collateral in the form of LEF's rights to payments under the equipment leases held by LEF or assigned to LEF. In fact, only some LEF notes were backed by collateral; many others were not.

Most notes were for terms of twenty to sixty months. Face value of the notes ranged from $10,000 to $500,000. From 1991 to 1995, fixed interest rates ranged from seven percent to fifteen percent. In one case, the return was twenty-four percent, which the investor described as a gift from Mr. Turner.

LEF notes were sold between 1989 and 1995 by several individuals ... in addition to Messrs. Malek [former president and co-owner of National Business Funding, Inc. (NBF) an LEF affiliate, and], Turner ... *At no time did NBF or LEF file a securities registration statement with the Commission.*

* * *

I find that LEF was operating as a "Ponzi" scheme by late 1992, [and that b]y October 1995, over 100 investors had purchased LEF notes, many of them on more than one occasion. At that time, LEF owed investors in its notes approximately $11 to $14 million.

Turner's Sale of LEF Notes

Mr. Turner sold LEF promissory notes from 1990 through 1995. For a brief time in 1993, he was also vice president and secretary of LEF. He knew before starting his employment at Dean Witter that Dean Witter had not approved the LEF notes and would not authorize him to sell them.

In the summer of 1992, Mr. Turner asked that he no longer receive wages from LEF, reportable on IRS Form W-2. He told Mr. Malek that he wanted to switch from payroll income to investment income, reportable on IRS Form 1099, because he did not want Dean Witter to know he was receiving compensation from another source.

August 1992

At all relevant times, Michael Czerny was a representative of CIGNA Financial Advisors, Inc. (CIGNA), one of several companies that marketed estate planning and insurance products to Dean Witter customers. In the late 1980s and early 1990s, Mr. Czerny, like Dean Turner, was moonlighting in the offer and sale of NBF and LEF notes.

In 1991, about ten or twelve investors to whom Mr. Czerny had sold NBF notes were not receiving timely payments from LEF. Mr. Czerny believed that Mr. Malek was paying off investors brought to NBF and LEF by Dean Turner, in preference to paying off those introduced by Mr. Czerny. In addition, there had been bad blood between Mr. Czerny and Mr. Turner, stemming from an incident several months earlier in which Mr. Turner had accused Mr. Czerny of stealing his clients. That allegation had been relayed to Mr. Czerny through an unidentified Dean Witter regional vice president in Chicago. The episode had effectively ended Mr. Czerny's ability (and desire) to gain referrals under the Dean Witter-CIGNA business arrangement.

Mr. Czerny then contacted Mr. Kolar and identified himself as a CIGNA representative. The two men disagree on just about everything that happened next. Mr. Kolar testified that they had a five minute telephone conversation, but never met in person; and that Mr. Czerny's accusations against Mr. Turner were strictly limited to "selling away." For his part, Mr. Czerny testified that the initial five minute telephone conversation was followed by a face-to-face meeting in Mr. Kolar's office, lasting forty-five to sixty minutes. At this in-person meeting, Mr. Czerny testified that he laid out not only his "selling away" allegations, but also informed Mr. Kolar about the cash flow difficulties at LEF and his suspicions that Dean Turner controlled the payments to LEF investors. At this time, Mr. Kolar did not have any concerns about Mr. Czerny's credibility.

Mr. Kolar took notes of his conversation with Mr. Czerny, and recorded them on his day timer for August 14, 1992. The notes read as follows:

> *Got a call from Mike Czerny of CIGNA. Client that Dean Turner recommended to Mike said he got some private equipment leases from Dean Turner. The partnerships were put into a pension account. The clients involved are Don Dixon, Melvyn Eder, Dr. Abbott. The company that Dean got them through is named National Business Funding — SEC registered as Lease Equities Fund. Mike says he has a copy of a 1099 made out to Dean for the calendar year 1991 for $57,000. Mike says he will make copies of everything and drop it off at the office early next week ...*

Mr. Kolar told Mr. Czerny that he would handle the situation. He further stated that he would call the Troy branch manager that day. Mr. Kolar did try to inform Mr. Basile that afternoon, but he was out of town. Mr. Basile promptly learned of the allegations from Mr. Kolar when he returned to the office the following Monday.

At the same time, Mr. Kolar also sought the advice of Mr. O'Neil in Chicago. Although Mr. Kolar testified that he briefed both Mr. O'Neil and Mr. Basile by reading his notes of the Czerny conversation "verbatim," neither Mr. O'Neil nor Mr. Basile could recall Mr. Kolar's making specific identification of Mr. Czerny as the complaining outside vendor.

After consulting with Dean Witter's Law Department, Mr. O'Neil told Mr. Kolar that he and Mr. Basile should interview Mr. Turner. He left it to Messrs. Kolar and Basile to formulate the questions they would put to Mr. Turner. He further stated that "a very productive avenue" of inquiry would be to question Mr. Turner about LEF and to have him bring his personal income tax returns to the meeting. According to both Messrs. Kolar and Basile, their meeting with Dean Turner took place on August 18, 1992, and lasted two to three hours. Mr. Turner brought his 1991 income tax return, as requested. Mr. Kolar chaired the meeting, which was confrontational and abrasive from the start. Both managers asked Mr. Turner personal questions about his background, where (other than at Dean Witter) he made his money, and what his wife did for a living.

Mr. Turner acknowledged that he was an investor in LEF notes, and that fellow members of his country club (who were Dean Witter customers) were also LEF investors. He denied selling LEF notes to anyone.... Messrs. Kolar and Basile testified that they also reviewed the 1991 joint federal income tax return of Mr. Turner and his spouse. They described the tax return and the accompanying schedules as thirty to forty pages in length. They did not find a Schedule C, reflecting profit and loss from business activities. They also did not find W-2 wage income reflecting earned income from NBF or LEF. They did find numbers on Schedule B of the return that "matched perfectly" what they were looking for—interest or dividend income from NBF in the approximate amount of $57,000. Mr. Basile prepared summary notes at the close of the meeting; ... Mr. Basile's notes state:

> *Ray Basile, George Kolar and Dean Turner in my office discussed outside interests, outside CIGNA rep advised. He has not solicited any outside limited partnerships since joining Dean Witter. The 1099 information was his interest earned, not commissions. Discussed with Tom O'Neil, George and Ray. Dean stated that he had no involvement in Lease Equities other than as an investor.*

David Disner is a certified public accountant from West Bloomfield, Michigan. He has prepared the tax returns of Dean Turner for ten years. He provided a copy of the federal income tax return he prepared for Mr. Turner and his spouse for calendar year 1991. Among other things, that return shows that Mr. Turner did not file his 1991 tax return on April 15, 1992, but sought an automatic four-month extension that allowed him to file as late as August 17, 1992—one day before the Kolar-Basile-Turner meeting. Additionally, the tax return prepared by Mr. Disner shows that Mr. Turner had reportable 1991 wage income from NBF of $34,282. This amount was posted to line 7 of IRS Form 1040, and is consistent with the Form W-2 issued by NBF's bookkeeper. The tax return provided by Mr. Disner also shows on Schedule B, Interest and Dividend Income, that the combined interest and dividend income of Mr. Turner and his wife for 1991 was far less than the $57,533.69 that Mr. Kolar and Mr. Basile state they saw in their review of the return on August 18. Finally, Mr. Disner posted the 1099-MISC income of $57,533.69 to Mr. Turner's tax return on Schedule C, Profit and Loss from Business, as part of the gross receipts or sales.

After Mr. Kolar and Mr. Basile had interviewed Mr. Turner, they dismissed him from the room. The two managers then held a fifteen to twenty minute telephone conversation with Mr. O'Neil, summarizing their meeting. They told Mr. O'Neil they had examined Mr. Turner's 1991 income tax return and found evidence of investment income from LEF, but no sign of earned income from LEF.... The three managers collectively concluded that Mr. Turner was not selling LEF notes, but was an investor in LEF notes. Based on Mr. Turner's cooperation and explanations, his demeanor at the meeting, the absence of prior discipline or customer complaints, and their examination of his income tax return, they concluded that he was not "selling away." They jointly decided not to proceed further.

1993 and 1994: LEF's Cash Flow Difficulties Get Worse

In 1993, LEF loaned $500,000 to a start-up company named "JET-U.S." Shortly thereafter, JET-U.S. failed, and the company ceased operations. LEF lost not only its $500,000 loan, but also an additional $500,000 in legal fees in connection with the transaction.

At about the same time, Mr. Turner and Mr. Malek started their own cable television service company, NBF Cable Systems, Inc. (NBF Cable), in Ft. Lauderdale,

Florida. LEF loaned over $2 million to NBF Cable to cover high capitalization costs and litigation expenses incurred by NBF Cable.

In a separate transaction, Joseph Cole, another Dean Witter broker in the Troy office, and Derrick Suciu, who was then a trust investment officer at the First National Bank of Pittsburgh (First National), discussed LEF promissory notes as an investment for the bank. Eventually, Mr. Suciu purchased about $8 million in LEF promissory notes for the bank's account.

In mid-1994, after a bank audit, officials at First National notified Mr. Malek that the LEF notes were inappropriate investments. The bank demanded immediate repayment. Mr. Malek negotiated with the bank officials, and reached an agreement to repay approximately $4.8 million. LEF acquired the funds to repay the bank by soliciting individual investors.

From August through November 1994, Mr. Turner solicited at least three such investors, and raised at least $1.4 million, to pay LEF's debt to First National. Among other things, Mr. Turner told these prospective investors that LEF had the opportunity to buy back some leases from the bank at a discount, without telling them that LEF was actually indebted to the bank for nearly $4.8 million and that the bank was demanding immediate repayment. He said that the investment was a "*really sweet deal*," a "*slam dunk, no brainer*," and that the investors "*cannot lose*"; that the loans were backed by the State of Michigan and therefore were guaranteed; that Dean Witter's accounting staff had told him that it was allowable for an individual investor to margin his pension account to enter the transaction; and that the leases could be obtained at a good rate if they were purchased quickly.

At this juncture, Mr. Malek began to falsify documents, issue leases without collateral, and use the same collateral for different leases.

1995: The "Ponzi" Scheme Collapses

In the Spring and Summer of 1995, LEF began failing to meet its payment obligations on many of the notes to investors. During this time, Mr. Turner was frequently in contact with Mr. Malek or his office assistants to determine whether LEF had sufficient funds available so he could decide which customers' checks from LEF he could deposit into their bank accounts. If investors inquired of Mr. Turner about the late payments, he would offer excuses, such as telling them the payments were merely delayed because a storm had disabled LEF's computers, or because his own assistant at Dean Witter was out sick. In some cases, Mr. Turner tried to convince investors that LEF was still a sound company. He continued to sell LEF promissory notes to investors through August 1995.

In late August 1995, Mr. Basile learned that the back office staff at the Troy branch office had been experiencing difficulties in clearing several LEF and NBF checks. On August 25, 1995, the Compliance Department, which had been auditing the Troy branch, requested Mr. Basile to obtain additional information from Mr. Turner about his outside financial interests, including LEF. Mr. Basile interviewed Mr. Turner, who again denied that he had any affiliation with LEF, and also denied that he had solicited Dean Witter clients to invest in LEF. With respect to the large number of checks going to LEF from Dean Witter, and coming from LEF to Dean Witter, Mr. Turner explained that LEF was run by a friend who referred clients to him. The branch manager reported these denials and explanations to Dean Witter's Compliance Department in a memorandum dated September 18, 1995.

In the Autumn of 1995, after LEF had failed to meet its payment obligations, Mr. Turner attempted to convince his major customers to surrender their LEF notes, so that a new company could be formed which would be given a lien on the assets of LEF. While attempting to persuade investors to accept this agreement, Mr. Turner falsely told one investor that other investors had signed on to the plan, in order to convince her to follow suit. The reorganization plan did not take place.

Several creditors filed an involuntary bankruptcy petition against LEF on December 15, 1995. After a hearing, the corporation was liquidated. The earliest customer lawsuits were also filed in December 1995, amid considerable publicity in the local press.

* * *

CONCLUSIONS OF LAW

Section 15(b)(6) of the Exchange Act, in conjunction with Section 15(b)(4), provides that the Commission may sanction a supervisor for failure reasonably to supervise a person subject to his supervision, with a view to preventing violations of the Securities Act, the Exchange Act, or the Commission's implementing rules and regulations. In order to sanction Mr. Kolar in this case, the Division must prove that Mr. Turner violated at least one of the statutory provisions or regulations identified in the OIP, that he was subject to Mr. Kolar's supervision, and that Mr. Kolar failed reasonably to supervise Mr. Turner with a view to preventing the violations.

In addition, while Mr. Turner's "selling away" strongly suggests that he violated Dean Witter policies and the rules of various self-regulatory organizations, the OIP does not identify specific rules or require me to drawing conclusions as to any such rule violations. "Selling away," by itself, has not been shown to be a *per se* violation of any of the Securities Act or Exchange Act provisions or Commission rules identified in the OIP, and suggestions to the contrary by the Division and its expert witness remain unproved.

Turner Willfully Violated Sections 5(a) and 5(c) of the Securities Act

Section 5(a) of the Securities Act provides that, unless a registration statement is in effect as to a security, it shall be unlawful for any person, directly or indirectly, to sell the security through the use of any means or instrumentality of transportation or communication in interstate commerce or of the mails.

No registration statement for LEF notes was ever filed with the Commission Mr. Turner offered and sold LEF notes to various investors through the use of the mails and the telephone. He certainly intended to do so. The Division has thus established a *prima facie* case.

Turner Willfully Violated Section 15(a)(1) of the Exchange Act

It is undisputed that Mr. Turner was not registered as a broker or dealer at any time relevant to this case. Because Mr. Turner sold LEF notes privately, only to Michigan residents, and only on behalf of LEF, a Michigan issuer, Respondent argues in his posthearing brief that Mr. Turner's activities were "exclusively intrastate," and that he was therefore not required to register as a broker or dealer. Respondent also contends that Mr. Turner need not have registered independently, because he was already a person associated with Dean Witter, itself a registered broker-dealer, and he was acting within the scope of his employment in the sale of LEF notes.

The Division has shown that Mr. Turner violated Section 15(a)(1). However, the parties have not cited, and I have not found, any *contested* cases in which the Commission has sanctioned a supervisor for failing to supervise where the underlying violation by the registered representative is the failure to register as a broker or dealer under Section 15(a)(1). *Cf. SECO Sec., Inc.*, 49 S.E.C. 873, 875 n.3 (1988). *Such a holding would be counter-intuitive, as the stated need for the individual to register is grounded in the lack of opportunity to supervise. If there is a lack of opportunity to supervise, … it is not clear how there can also be a failure reasonably to supervise. For these reasons, Mr. Kolar's liability for failure to supervise will not be based on Mr. Turner's underlying violation of Section 15(a)(1).*

Turner Was "Subject to" Kolar's Supervision

While the law governing alleged failure to supervise by a branch office manager is fairly settled, it has been evolving with respect to broker-dealer employees who are line supervisors above the branch office manager level, or who are staff officials within a firm, such as heads of functional areas, compliance officers, and general counsel. The Division argues that the case law defining a supervisor under the federal securities laws is extremely broad, and that its proper application here should reach beyond Mr. Basile, the Troy branch office manager, to Mr. Kolar, the metropolitan area manager. Citing the Commission's Settlement Order and Report of Investigation in *John H. Gutfreund*, 51 S.E.C. 93, 113 (1992), it contends that a supervisor is anyone who "has a requisite degree of responsibility, ability or authority to affect the conduct of the employee whose behavior is at issue."

Mr. Kolar contends that Dean Turner was never "*subject to his supervision*" within the meaning of Section 15(b)(4)(E) of the Exchange Act. Pointing to the concurring views of two Commissioners in *Arthur James Huff*, 50 S.E.C. 524, 530–37 (1991), Respondent argues that "control" is the essence of supervision, and that he lacked control over Mr. Turner because he never had the power to hire, fire, reward, or punish him. Pointing to *Louis R. Trujillo*, 49 S.E.C. 1106, 1110 (1989), Respondent also maintains that he had only limited advisory authority with respect to Mr. Turner's supervision. He urges me to hold that his "participation" in group managerial decisions and the fact that Mr. O'Neil had "high regard" for his opinions are insufficient as a matter of law to confer supervisory responsibility. Finally, Mr. Kolar argues that *Gutfreund* should not be used to evaluate his supervisory authority here because: (1) it represents a settlement, as opposed to a litigated case; and (2) "if" it imposes a new standard of supervisory responsibility, due process prohibits its retroactive application to conduct occurring in August 1992, four months before that Settlement Order and Report of Investigation were issued.

The Commission has not specifically addressed whether other aspects of the *Huff* concurrence, beyond Part VI, are consistent with *Gutfreund*. Part III of the *Huff* concurrence, on which Mr. Kolar relies, expresses the "power to control" in varying terms. At one point, it references the line manager's "power to hire *or* fire, *and* to reward *or* punish." 50 S.E.C. at 532 (emphasis added). Shortly thereafter, it identifies supervisors as presumptively those who have "the authority and the responsibility to hire *and* fire *and* reward *and* punish." *Id.* (emphasis added). In contrast, *Lysiak*, citing *Gutfreund*, states that the lack of authority to hire and fire is "far from dispositive." 51 S.E.C. at 844.

It is inappropriate to twist that analysis here to hold that those who are obviously line supervisors—branch managers (Mr. Basile), metropolitan area managers (Mr. Kolar), and regional directors (Mr. O'Neil)—need not be deemed supervisors.

Using pre-*Huff* case law as a point of reference, Mr. Turner was subject to Mr. Kolar's control because Mr. Kolar was his second-level line supervisor. Using the *Huff* concurrence as a point of reference, Mr. Kolar had the authority to control Mr. Turner. Using the *Gutfreund* report of investigation as a point of reference, Mr. Kolar had significant ability to affect Mr. Turner's conduct. Mr. Kolar was the Detroit metropolitan area manager, with overall supervisory responsibility for the operation of four branch offices, including Troy, and their registered representatives, including Mr. Turner. His regular visits and telephone calls to these branch offices, along with his review of paper work and his contact with the registered representatives at the branches, confirms his own recognition of the breadth of his supervisory duties. He was considered a supervisor with a full range of authority, and not a mere messenger, by Mr. O'Neil. There is no ambiguity in Mr. O'Neil's testimony about the four Detroit area branch managers: "They reported to George ... Period." Mr. Kolar was also recognized as a supervisor with full authority to control, by the Dean Witter staff. When Mr. Czerny asked for the name of an official "with some authority" to discuss his concerns about Dean Turner and LEF, he was referred to Respondent. Mr. Kolar participated in the decision to discipline Troy branch representatives, including Mr. Alito. He was simply not credible in minimizing his own supervisory role over all aspects of the four Detroit area branch offices. The fact that he could not hire, fire, reward, or discipline "on his own," but shared such responsibilities with other supervisors, is not dispositive. It has long been the Commission's view that a Respondent is not relieved of his supervisory obligations just because other officials at a registered broker-dealer firm share responsibility for supervising the firm's sales agents. *Robert J. Check*, 49 S.E.C. 1004, 1008 (1988). Likewise, the notion that an individual can successfully defend against failure to supervise liability on the grounds that the firm lacked clear lines of responsibility for its officers was discredited in *Patrick v. SEC*, 19 F.3d 66, 68 (2d Cir. 1994) (NYSE hearing panel conclusion to that effect reversed by NYSE Board of Directors). I therefore conclude that Mr. Turner was "subject to" Mr. Kolar's supervision from February 1992 through June 1995. Mr. Basile, the Troy branch office manager, was also "subject to" Mr. Kolar's supervision during this same period, as alleged in the OIP.

Notes and Questions

1. The administrative law judge's (ALJ) initial decision in *Kolar* was appealed to the SEC in 2002. *In the Matter of George J. Kolar*, 77 S.E.C. Docket 2944 (Jun. 26, 2002). In this decision, the SEC made clear that it had never adopted the views expressed in the *Huff* concurrence, i.e., that control is the essence of supervision. Instead, the SEC reiterated the rule stated in *Gutfreund* that "determining if a particular person is a 'supervisor' depends on whether, under the facts and circumstances of a particular case, that person has a requisite degree of responsibility, ability or authority to affect the conduct of the employee whose behavior is at issue." *Gutfreund*, 51 S.E.C. 93, 113 (1992).

2. In *Kolar* the administrative law judge (ALJ) found that Turner engaged in the business of being a broker-dealer without being registered as a broker-dealer pursuant to section 15(a)(1). Sections 15(b)(4)(E) and 15(b)(6) of the Exchange Act base liability for failure reasonably to supervise on a substantive violation of the federal securities laws (including the Exchange Act) by an associated person subject to supervision. Seemingly, this violation by Turner would suffice as a basis for liability for failure reasonably to supervise. In *SECO Sec., Inc.*, 49 S.E.C. 873, 875 n.3 (1988), the SEC based liability under sections 15(b)(4)(E) and 15(b)(6) on a violation of section 15(a)(1) by a registered representative. Why did the ALJ determine that a violation of section 15(a)(1) by Turner was not a basis for liability under sections 15(b)(4)(E) and 15(b)(6)? Was the ALJ's decision in conflict with established SEC policy?

[handwritten: To potentially limit how many they were making liable.]

[handwritten: No, since seeking to protect consumers.]

Hypothetical Two

In early 2013, Thomas Jane became an administrative manager to the branch manager of Success First's NYC office. The duties assigned to Jane included administrative matters and several compliance functions. With respect to compliance, Jane was required to review proposed new accounts, investigate customer complaints, and review daily activity reports of customer transactions. Although Jane was given substantial responsibility for detecting problems, he was given only limited authority to correct them. Only the NYC branch manager was able to take significant action when a salesperson became a compliance problem. Only the NYC branch manager had the power to discharge, suspend, or fine a registered representative, place a written censure in a registered representative's record, or restrict a registered representative's activities as a precautionary measure. Jane essentially performed a surveillance role by serving as the branch manager's eyes and ears, providing information on the basis of which the branch manager might or might not choose to act. One registered representative singled himself out as a major compliance problem. This particular registered representative extended a customer beyond his means, forcing a margin call liquidation; he also refused to execute a sell order and churned the customer's account. Are Jane and the NYC branch manager supervisors of the registered representative under Sections 15(b)(4)(E) and 15(b)(6)?

[handwritten margin: · requisit authority / had a degree of responsibility / · authority to effect the conduct]

[handwritten: Not Jane.]

[handwritten: Yes supervisor.]

[handwritten: Yes both are given Jane's extensive responsibility concerning detection. Hiring is only one consideration.]

c. Other Line Managers

Other managers in functional areas of broker-dealer operations, excluding compliance, have also been determined to be supervisors under Sections 15(b)(4)(E) and 15(b)(6). The following case illustrates failure-to-supervise liability in a context other than retail sales, i.e., registered representatives dealing directly with the investing public. The primary violator was a research analyst who issued favorable research reports on issuers that were investment banking clients of his firm. His supervisors were not branch managers, but directors of functional units of the firm.

In the Matter of John B. Hoffman and Kevin J. McCaffrey

Administrative Proceeding File No. 3-11930 (May 19, 2005)

On the basis of this Order and Respondents' Offers, the Commission finds[22] that:

FACTS

Respondents

John B. Hoffmann, age 64, entered the securities industry in 1964 as a research analyst with Smith Barney. He became director of U.S. equity research at Smith Barney in approximately 1988 and director of Global Research in 1995. After Smith Barney merged with Salomon Brothers in 1997 to form Salomon Smith Barney, Inc. ("SSB"), Hoffmann was director of Global Equity Research at SSB until February 2003.

Kevin J. McCaffrey, age 41, is a registered representative. He entered the securities industry in 1988 as a general securities representative. He joined Smith Barney as head of New York institutional equity sales in 1994 and became deputy director of equity research in 1995. McCaffrey became director of U.S. Equity Research at SSB after Smith Barney merged with Salomon Brothers. He continued in that position until October 2002. Since January 2003, McCaffrey has been employed by Citigroup Alternative Investments LLC ("CAI"), which is registered with the Commission as an investment adviser. Until January 2005, McCaffrey served as the Head of Global Sales for CAI. He presently is engaged in developing CAI's business outside the United States.

Other Relevant Entity

Citigroup Global Markets, Inc. ("CGM"), formerly known as Salomon Smith Barney, Inc. ("SSB"), is a New York corporation with its headquarters and principal executive offices in New York, New York. It is a wholly-owned subsidiary of Citigroup Inc. CGM engages in a full service securities business, including retail and institutional sales, investment banking services, trading, and research. CGM is, and during the relevant period was, registered with the Commission as a broker-dealer and investment adviser.[23]

---

22. [1] The findings contained herein are made pursuant to the Respondents' respective Offers of Settlement and are not binding on any other person or entity in this or any other proceeding.

23. [2] Because it was known as Salomon Smith Barney during the period when the conduct described herein occurred, this Order refers to the firm hereafter as "SSB."

Summary

In 2000 and 2001 (the "relevant period"), John Hoffmann, as the director of Global Equity Research, and Kevin McCaffrey, as director of U.S. Equity Research at SSB, were supervisors of Jack B. Grubman ("Grubman"), once one of the most prominent research analysts at SSB and on Wall Street.

Hoffmann and McCaffrey failed to supervise Grubman adequately with a view to preventing him from publishing fraudulent research on Focal Communications Corp. ("Focal") and Metromedia Fiber Networks, Inc. ("Metromedia Fiber"). During the same period, Grubman also published research on RCN Communications, Williams Communications Group, Level 3 Communications, Adelphia Business Solutions, and XO Communications that violated NASD Inc. and New York Stock Exchange Inc. ("NYSE") advertising rules.[24] Each of these firms was an SSB investment banking client. In particular, with respect to these companies, Hoffmann and McCaffrey failed to respond adequately to red flags that Grubman made unreasonable research assumptions that led him to publish unrealistically bullish ratings and price targets.

During the relevant period, Hoffmann and McCaffrey were aware of potential conflicts of interest posed by Grubman's involvement in the firm's telecommunications ("telecom") investment banking activities and were aware of Grubman's importance to the firm's telecom investment banking franchise. Hoffmann and McCaffrey failed to respond adequately to red flags concerning investment banking pressure on Grubman not to downgrade the firm's banking clients.

Hoffmann and McCaffrey Were Supervisors of Grubman

During the relevant period, Respondents were supervisors of Grubman. All U.S. equity research analysts, including Grubman, reported directly to McCaffrey, as director of U.S. Equity Research, and McCaffrey reported to Hoffmann, as director of Global Equity Research. Hoffmann was a member of the management committee at SSB.

Hoffmann and McCaffrey both participated in the process of Grubman's annual performance review and in determining Grubman's salary and bonus.... Grubman ... played a significant role in attracting investment banking business for SSB from telecom companies he covered.... Grubman earned approximately $20.2 million in salary,

---

24. [3] NASD Rule 2210 and NYSE Rule 472 (the "advertising rules"), require members' communications with the public to have a reasonable basis and not contain exaggerated or unwarranted claims. In addition, NASD Rule 2110 and NYSE Rules 401 and 476 require member firms to observe high standards of commercial honor and just and equitable principles of trade in their business dealings. As described in SEC v. Jack Benjamin Grubman, No. 03 Civ. 2938 (WHP) (S.D.N.Y.) (Complaint, filed April 28, 2003), during the relevant period, Grubman issued certain research reports on RCN Communications, Williams Communications Group, Focal, Level 3 Communications, Adelphia Business Solutions, and XO Communications that were not based on principles of fair dealing and good faith, did not provide a sound basis for evaluating facts regarding these companies' business prospects, contained exaggerated or unwarranted claims about these companies, and/or contained opinions for which there was no reasonable basis. As a result of this conduct, Grubman violated NASD Rules 2110 and 2210 and NYSE Rules 401, 472, and 476.

bonus, and deferred compensation in 2000 … making him the highest paid analyst at SSB.…

Grubman Issued Fraudulent and Misleading Research on Certain Telecommunications Companies

As described in *SEC v. Jack Benjamin Grubman*, No. 03 Civ. 2938 (WHP) (S.D.N.Y.) (Complaint, filed April 28, 2003), Grubman and SSB issued fraudulent research reports on two companies, Metromedia Fiber Networks, Inc., and Focal Communications Corp., that, among other things, presented an unrealistically optimistic picture that overlooked and minimized the risk of investing in these companies, predicted substantial growth in the companies' revenues and earnings without a reasonable basis, did not disclose certain material facts about these companies, and contained material misstatements about the companies. As a result of this conduct, Grubman aided and abetted SSB's violations of Section 15(c) of the Exchange Act and Rule 15c1-2 thereunder. Grubman also published research on RCN Communications, Williams Communications Group, Focal, Level 3 Communications, Adelphia Business Solutions, and XO Communications that violated NASD and NYSE advertising rules. Each of these seven companies was an investment banking client of SSB …

Respondents' Failure to Supervise

Section 15(b)(6) of the Exchange Act, incorporating by reference Section 15(b)(4)(E) of the Exchange Act, authorizes the Commission to sanction a person who is associated, or at the time of the alleged misconduct was associated, with a broker or dealer if it finds that the sanction is in the public interest and the person "has failed reasonably to supervise, with a view to preventing violations of the [federal securities laws], another person who commits such a violation, if such person is subject to his supervision."

A failure to supervise can arise when an individual acting in a supervisory capacity fails to take adequate steps to prevent a person under their supervision from aiding and abetting violations of the federal securities laws. (citations omitted).

"[D]etermining if a particular person is a 'supervisor' depends on whether, under the facts and circumstances of a particular case, that person has a requisite degree of responsibility, ability or authority to affect the conduct of the employee whose behavior is at issue." *In the Matter of John H. Gutfreund, et al.*, 51 S.E.C. 93, 113, Exchange Act Release No. 31554 (Dec. 3, 1992). "The supervisory obligations imposed by the federal securities laws require a vigorous response even to indications of wrongdoing." *Id.* at 108. "In large organizations it is especially imperative that those in authority exercise particular vigilance when indications of irregularity reach their attention.… Red flags and suggestions of irregularities demand inquiry as well as adequate follow-up and review. When indications of impropriety reach the attention of those in authority, they must act decisively to detect and prevent violations of the federal securities laws." *Kantor*, 51 S.E.C. at 447 (internal quotations omitted).

Hoffmann and McCaffrey failed reasonably to supervise Grubman, a person subject to their supervision within the meaning of Section 15(b)(4)(E) of the Exchange Act …

with a view to preventing him from aiding and abetting SSB's violations of Section 15(c) of the Exchange Act and Rule 15c1-2 thereunder by issuing fraudulent research....

Hypothetical Three

·No red flags

Success First has a research unit responsible for conducting research on both global and domestic securities. The research is used by Success First's registered representatives to make recommendations to their clients and is, sometimes, posted on its web site. However, most importantly, the unit publishes research on existing and prospective investment banking clients of Success First. The research unit is composed of seven analysts who report directly to Andrew Melnick, managing director of research. Melnick, in turn, reports directly to Jack Graham, senior managing director of research. Alice Walters works as an analyst at Success First and is frequently interviewed on major financial news outlets about securities that she follows; in addition, she has played a major role in attracting and retaining investment banking clients for Success First. Although Walters doesn't report directly to Graham, as head of research, Graham had ultimate responsibility for the people under him. In addition, Graham and Melnick participated in the process of Walters' annual performance review and in determining Walters' salary and bonus. Recently, however, Melnick discovered that Walters has issued fraudulent research reports about certain Success First investment banking clients because some of her research reports contained exaggerated or unwarranted claims and opinions for which there was no reasonable basis. It is unclear whether Melnick reported Walters' fraudulent behavior to Graham. Is Graham Walter's supervisor under Sections 15(b)(4)(E) and 15(b)(6)?

Graham
↑
Melnick

Walter

⤷ Yes given ✳ on page 191.

d. Senior Management

Senior executives have been held liable for failure to supervise employees down the chain of command. Generally, they have the highest authority at a broker-dealer and therefore have the power to hire, fire, and otherwise control the behavior of their associated persons. Although all senior executives are not line supervisors, CEOs and presidents are generally deemed to be line supervisors despite the existence of several levels of management between them and the primary violator. The SEC's view is that chief executive officers (CEOs) and presidents have supervisory responsibilities for ensuring a firm-wide system of proper supervision and for delegating supervisory functions to qualified personnel.

The SEC unequivocally affirmed its view that CEOs and presidents are supervisors and therefore subject to liability for failure to supervise in *In the Matter of John H. Gutfreund*. This decision clearly expressed the SEC's view that liability under section 15(b)(4)(E) included liability for deficient supervision by a senior supervisor of lower-level supervisors subject to the senior supervisor's supervision. *Gutfreund* is a definitive case in determining liability under section 15(b)(4)(E) for both line and non-line supervisors and has been widely followed. Its implications for non-line supervisors will be discussed in section III(A)(2) of this chapter.

In the Matter of John H. Gutfreund, Thomas W. Strauss, and John W. Meriwether

Exchange Act Release No. 31,554 (Dec. 3, 1992)

A. FACTS

1. Brokerage Firm Involved

Salomon Brothers Inc. ("Salomon") is a Delaware corporation with its principal place of business in New York, New York. At all times relevant to this proceeding, Salomon was registered with the Commission as a broker-dealer pursuant to Section 15(b) of the Exchange Act. Salomon has been a government-designated dealer in U.S. Treasury securities since 1939 and a primary dealer since 1961.

2. Respondents

John H. Gutfreund was the Chairman and Chief Executive Officer of Salomon from 1983 to August 18, 1991. He had worked at Salomon since 1953. Thomas W. Strauss was the President of Salomon from 1986 to August 18, 1991. During that time period, Strauss reported to Gutfreund. He had worked at Salomon since 1963.

John W. Meriwether was a Vice Chairman of Salomon and in charge of all fixed income trading activities of the firm from 1988 to August 18, 1991. During that period, Meriwether reported to Strauss. During the same period, Paul W. Mozer, a managing director and the head of Salomon's Government Trading Desk, reported directly to Meriwether.

* * *

4. Summary

In late April of 1991, three members of the senior management of Salomon — John Gutfreund, Thomas Strauss, and John Meriwether — were informed that Paul Mozer, the head of the firm's Government Trading Desk, had submitted a false bid in the amount of $3.15 billion in an auction of U.S. Treasury securities on February 21, 1991. The executives were also informed by Donald Feuerstein, the firm's chief legal officer,[25] that the submission of the false bid appeared to be a criminal act and, although not legally required, should be reported to the government. Gutfreund and Strauss agreed to report the matter to the Federal Reserve Bank of New York. Mozer was told that his actions might threaten his future with the firm and would be reported to the government. However, for a period of months, none of the executives took action to investigate the matter or to discipline or impose limitations on Mozer. The information was also not reported to the government for a period of months. During

---

25. The determination of Feuerstein's status as a supervisor under 15(b)(4)(E) and 15(b)(6) of the Securities Exchange Act is discussed under non-line supervisors in Section III(A)(2) of this chapter.

that same period, Mozer committed additional violations of the federal securities laws in connection with two subsequent auctions of U.S. Treasury securities.

The Respondents in this proceeding are not being charged with any participation in the underlying violations. However, as set forth herein, the Commission believes that the Respondents' supervision was deficient and that this failure was compounded by the delay in reporting the matter to the government.

5. The Submission of Two False Bids in the February 21, 1991 Five-Year U.S. Treasury Note Auction

For a considerable period of time prior to the February 21, 1991 auction, the Treasury Department had limited the maximum bid that any one bidder could submit in an auction of U.S. Treasury securities at any one yield to 35% of the auction amount. On February 21, 1991, the Treasury Department auctioned $9 billion of five-year U.S. Treasury notes. Salomon submitted a bid in its own name in that auction at a yield of 7.51% in the amount of $3.15 billion, or 35% of the auction amount.[26] In the same auction, Salomon submitted two additional $3.15 billion bids at the same yield in the names of two customers: Quantum Fund and Mercury Asset Management. Both accounts were those of established customers of Salomon, but the bids were submitted without the knowledge or authorization of either customer. Both bids were in fact false bids intended to secure additional securities for Salomon. Each of the three $3.15 billion bids was prorated 54% and Salomon received a total of $5.103 billion of the five-year notes from the auction, or 56.7% of the total amount of securities sold at that auction.

After the auction results were announced, Paul Mozer, then a managing director in charge of Salomon's Government Trading Desk, directed a clerk to write trade tickets "selling" the $1.701 billion auction allocations received in response to the two unauthorized bids to customer accounts in the names of Mercury Asset Management and Quantum Fund at the auction price. Mozer at the same time directed the clerk to write trade tickets "selling" the same amounts from those accounts back to Salomon at the same price. These fictitious transactions were intended to create the appearance that the customers had received the securities awarded in response to the unauthorized bids and had sold those securities to Salomon.

---

26. The Treasury Department adopted the 35% limitation in July of 1990 after Salomon submitted several large bids in amounts far in excess of the amount of securities to be auctioned. Prior to July of 1990, the Treasury Department had not placed limitations on the amount of bids that could be submitted but had limited the maximum amount that any single bidder could purchase in an auction to 35% of the auction amount.

The Salomon bids which led to the adoption of the 35% bidding limitation were submitted at the direction of Paul Mozer. Mozer was angered by the adoption of the new bidding limitation and he expressed his disagreement with the decision to adopt the new rule to officials at the Treasury Department and in several news articles. Mozer also registered his anger through his bidding activity in the Treasury auction the following day. In an auction for $8 billion of seven-year U.S. Treasury notes on July 11, 1990, Mozer entered 11 bids at the maximum 35% amount at successive yields between 8.60% and 8.70%. The successful bids in the auction were between 8.55% and 8.58%, and the bids submitted by Mozer were intended as protest bids.

Under Salomon's internal procedures, the trade tickets written by the clerk resulted in the creation of customer confirmations reflecting the purported transactions. Mozer directed the clerk to prevent the confirmations from being sent to either Mercury Asset Management or Quantum Fund. As a result, the normal procedures of Salomon were overridden and confirmations for the fictitious transactions were not sent to either Mercury Asset Management or Quantum Fund.

6. The Submission of a bid in the February 21, 1991 Auction by S.G. Warburg and the Treasury Department's Investigation of That Bid and the Salomon False Bid

In the February 21, 1991 five-year note auction, S.G. Warburg, a primary dealer in U.S. Treasury securities, submitted a bid in its own name in the amount of $100 million at a yield of 7.51%. The 7.51% yield was the same yield used for the unauthorized $3.15 billion Mercury bid submitted by Salomon. At the time the bids were submitted, S.G. Warburg and Mercury Asset Management were subsidiaries of the same holding company, S.G. Warburg, PLC. Because the unauthorized Mercury bid was for the maximum 35% amount, the submission of the $100 million bid in the name of S.G. Warburg meant that two bids had apparently been submitted by affiliated entities in an amount in excess of 35% of the auction.

The Treasury Department officials did not know that one of the bids had been submitted by Salomon without authorization from Mercury....

After reviewing facts concerning the corporate relationship between Mercury Asset Management and S.G. Warburg, the Treasury Department determined to treat the two firms as a single bidder in future auctions of U.S. Treasury securities. The Treasury Department conveyed that decision in a letter dated April 17, 1991 from the Acting Assistant Commissioner for Financing to a Senior Director of Mercury Asset Management in London. The April 17 letter noted that a $3.15 billion bid had been submitted by Salomon on behalf of Mercury Asset Management in the five-year U.S. Treasury note auction on February 21, 1991, and that S.G. Warburg had also submitted a bid in the same auction, at the same yield, in the amount of $100 million. The letter noted that Mercury Asset Management and S.G. Warburg were subsidiaries of the same holding company and stated that the Treasury Department would thereafter "treat all subsidiaries of S.G. Warburg, PLC as one single entity for purposes of the 35 percent limitation rule." Copies of the letter were sent to Mozer and to a managing director of S.G. Warburg in New York.

7. Receipt of the April 17, 1991 Treasury Department Letter by Salomon

Mozer received the April 17 letter during the week of April 21, 1991. On April 24, he spoke with the Senior Director at Mercury Asset Management who had also received the April 17 letter. Mozer told the Senior Director that the submission of the $3.15 billion bid in the name of Mercury Asset Management was the result of an "error" by a clerk who had incorrectly placed the name of Mercury on the tender form. Mozer told the Senior Director that he was embarrassed by the "error," which he said had been "corrected" internally, and he asked the Senior Director to keep the matter confidential to avoid "problems." The Senior Director indicated that such a course of action would be acceptable. The Mercury Senior Director was not aware that the submission of the bid was an intentional effort by Salomon to acquire additional securities for its own account.

8. Mozer's Disclosure to John Meriwether of the Submission of One False Bid

Mozer then went to the office of John Meriwether, his immediate supervisor, and handed him the April 17 letter. When Meriwether was finished reading the letter, Mozer told him that the Mercury Asset Management bid referred to in the letter was in fact a bid for Salomon and had not been authorized by Mercury. After expressing shock at Mozer's conduct, Meriwether told him that his behavior was career-threatening, and he asked Mozer why he had submitted the bid. Mozer told Meriwether that the Government Trading Desk had needed a substantial amount of the notes, that there was also demand from the Government Arbitrage Desk for the notes, and that he had submitted the false bid to satisfy those demands.

Meriwether then asked Mozer if he had ever engaged in that type of conduct before or since. Mozer responded that he had not. Meriwether told Mozer that he would have to take the matter immediately to Thomas Strauss. Mozer then told Meriwether of his conversation with the Mercury Senior Director in which he had told that individual that the bid was an "error" and had asked him to keep the matter confidential. Meriwether listened to Mozer's description of the conversation, but did not respond. He then gave the letter back to Mozer and Mozer left the office.

9. Discussions Among Senior Management

Meriwether then called Thomas Strauss. Strauss was not in, but he returned Meriwether's call later that day. Meriwether told Strauss that Mozer had informed him that he had submitted an unauthorized customer bid in an auction of U.S. Treasury securities. Strauss indicated that they should meet to discuss the matter first thing the next morning.

Meriwether met with Strauss at 9:15 a.m. the following morning, April 25, in Strauss' office. Prior to the meeting, Strauss had arranged for Donald Feuerstein, the firm's chief legal officer, to attend, and Feuerstein was in Strauss' office when Meriwether arrived. Meriwether began the meeting by describing his conversation with Mozer the previous day.

When Meriwether was finished, Feuerstein said that Mozer's conduct was a serious matter and should be reported to the government. Feuerstein asked to see a copy of the April 17 letter.... After some discussion about the letter, Strauss said he wanted to discuss the matter with Gutfreund, who was then out of town, and the meeting ended.

A meeting was then held early the following week, on either Monday, April 29 or Tuesday, April 30, with Gutfreund. The meeting was attended by Meriwether, Feuerstein, Strauss and Gutfreund and was held in Strauss' office. Meriwether summarized his conversation with Mozer. Meriwether also indicated that he believed that the incident was an aberration and he expressed his hope that it would not end Mozer's career at Salomon.

After Meriwether's description, Feuerstein told the group that he believed that the submission of the false bid was a criminal act. He indicated that, while there probably was not a legal duty to report the false bid, he believed that they had no choice but to report the matter to the government. The group then discussed whether the bid should be reported to the Treasury Department or to the Federal Reserve Bank of New York. The hostile relationship that had developed between Mozer and the Treasury Department over the adoption of the 35% bidding limitation in the Summer of 1990 was noted, as was the role of the Federal Reserve Bank of New York as Salomon's regulator in the area of U.S. Treasury securities, and the group concluded that the preferable approach would be to report the matter to the Federal Reserve Bank of New York. The meeting then ended.

At the conclusion of the meeting, each of the four executives apparently believed that a decision had been made that Strauss or Gutfreund would report the false bid to the government, although each had a different understanding about how the report would be handled. Meriwether stated that he believed that Strauss would make an appointment to report the matter to Gerald Corrigan, the President of the Federal Reserve Bank of New York. Feuerstein stated that he believed that Gutfreund wanted to think further about how the bid should be reported. He then spoke with Gutfreund the next morning. Although the April 17 letter had been sent from the Treasury Department, Feuerstein told Gutfreund that he believed the report should be made to the Federal Reserve Bank of New York, which could then, if it wanted, pass the information on to the Treasury Department. Strauss stated that he believed that he and Gutfreund would report the matter in a personal visit with Corrigan, although he believed that Gutfreund wanted to think further about how the matter should be handled. Gutfreund stated that he believed that a decision had been made that he and Strauss, either separately or together, would speak to Corrigan about the matter.

Aside from the discussions referred to above regarding reporting the matter to the government, there was no discussion at either meeting in late April about investigating what Mozer had done, about disciplining him, or about placing limits on his activities. There was also no discussion about whether Mozer had acted alone or had been assisted by others on the Government Trading Desk, about whether false records had been created, about the involvement of the Government Arbitrage Desk, which Mozer had said had sought securities from the auction, or about what had happened with the securities obtained pursuant to the bid. Similarly, there was no discussion about whether Salomon had violated the 35% bidding limitation by also submitting a bid in its own name.

For almost three months, no action was taken to investigate Mozer's conduct in the February 21 auction. That conduct was investigated only after other events prompted an internal investigation by an outside law firm, as is discussed below. During the same period, no action was taken to discipline Mozer or to place appropriate limitations on his conduct. Mozer's employment by Salomon was terminated on August 9, 1991, after an internal investigation had discovered that he had been involved in additional improper conduct.

Each of the four executives who attended the meetings in late April placed the responsibility for investigating Mozer's conduct and placing limits on his activities on someone else. Meriwether stated that he believed that, once he had taken the matter of Mozer's conduct to Strauss and Strauss had brought Feuerstein and Gutfreund into the process, he had no further responsibility to take action with respect to the false bid unless instructed to do so by one of those individuals. Meriwether stated that he also believed that, though he had the authority to recommend that action be taken to discipline Mozer or limit his activities, he had no authority to take such action unilaterally. Strauss stated that he believed that Meriwether, who was Mozer's direct supervisor, and Feuerstein, who was responsible for the legal and compliance activities of the firm, would take whatever steps were necessary or required as a result of Mozer's disclosure. Feuerstein stated that he believed that, once a report to the government was made, the government would instruct Salomon about how to investigate the matter. Gutfreund stated that he believed that the other executives would take whatever steps were necessary to properly handle the matter. According to the executives, there was no discussion among them about any action that would be taken to investigate Mozer's conduct or to place limitations on his activities.

10. Violations After Disclosure by Mozer to Management

After Mozer's disclosure of one unauthorized bid on April 24, 1991, he submitted two subsequent unauthorized bids in auctions of U.S. Treasury securities.

a. The April 25, 1991 Five-Year U.S. Treasury Note Auction

On April 25, 1991, the U.S. Treasury auctioned $9 billion of five-year U.S. Treasury notes. Salomon submitted a bid in that auction for $3 billion, just under the maximum 35% amount of $3.15 billion. Salomon also submitted a $2.5 billion bid in the name of Tudor Investment Corporation ("Tudor"). A bid of only $1.5 billion had been authorized by Tudor, however, and the tender form submitted by Salomon was thus false in the amount of $1 billion. The bid by Salomon in its own name and the unauthorized portion of the Tudor bid totalled $4 billion, or 44.4% of the auction amount.

The $2.5 billion bid on behalf of Tudor was prorated 84% and $2.1 billion of five-year notes was awarded in response to the bid. Trade tickets were written providing the entire $2.1 billion auction allocation to Tudor after the auction. At Mozer's instruction, a trade ticket was then written "selling" $600 million of the notes back to Salomon on the auction day at the auction price. The five-year notes were "sold" from Tudor to Salomon at the auction price even though the price of the notes had risen above that price by the time of the transaction.

b. The May 22, 1991 Two-Year U.S. Treasury Note Auction

On May 22, 1991, the U.S. Treasury auctioned $12.255 billion of two-year U.S. Treasury notes. Salomon submitted a $2 billion bid in that auction on behalf of Tiger Management Corporation ("Tiger"). A bid of only $1.5 billion had been authorized by Tiger, and the tender form submitted by Salomon was thus false in the amount of $500 million.

The $2 billion bid submitted on behalf of Tiger was accepted in full. After the auction results were announced, Tiger was provided with $1.5 billion of the $2 billion allocation provided in response to its bid. The remaining $500 million was not provided to Tiger but was transferred internally to a proprietary trading account on the Government Trading Desk at Salomon.

The activities described above with respect to the April 25, 1991 and the May 22, 1991 auctions of U.S. Treasury securities violated Sections 10(b) and 17(a) of the Exchange Act and Rules 10b-5, 17a-3, and 17a-4 thereunder. There is no evidence that the respondents or Feuerstein knew of the submission of the false bids in the February 21, April 25 and May 22, 1991 auctions.

11. The Delay in Reporting the False Bid to the Government

There was no disclosure to the government of the false bid in the February 21, 1991 auction prior to August 9, 1991, when the results of the internal investigation were first made public.

In mid-May, after it had become clear to Feuerstein that the false bid had not yet been reported, Feuerstein met with Gutfreund and Strauss and urged them to proceed with disclosure as soon as possible. He was told by both that they still intended to report the matter. He also again [on May 23, 1991] discussed with Strauss his belief that the bid should be reported to the government as soon as possible. Feuerstein also spoke with Gutfreund in early June and again urged him to report the matter to the government.

Strauss and Gutfreund also discussed the matter of reporting the bid on several occasions during this period. On at least one occasion, Strauss also urged Gutfreund to decide how to handle the matter and to proceed with disclosure to the government. Gutfreund indicated on these occasions that he still intended to report the false bid to the government. Gutfreund stated that he believed, however, that the false bid was a minor aberration, and that the reporting of the bid was not a matter of high priority.

As noted above, in the auction on May 22, 1991 for two-year U.S. Treasury notes, Salomon and two customers bid for and received approximately 86% of the two-year notes. On May 30, press reports mentioned Salomon by name in connection with a rumored short squeeze in the two-year notes.

In early June, Strauss spoke by telephone with a senior official of the Treasury Department. Strauss told the official that the firm was aware of the Department's interest in the May 22, 1991 auction and was willing to discuss the matter with the Department. Following Strauss' call, Gutfreund arranged to meet with officials of the Treasury Department to discuss Salomon's role in the May 22, 1991 auction.

On June 10, 1991, Gutfreund met with an Under Secretary of the Treasury and other Treasury Department officials in Washington, D.C. During the meeting, Gutfreund told the Treasury Department officials that he believed that the firm had acted properly in connection with the May 22, 1991 auction, and he indicated that the firm would cooperate with any inquiries by the Department into the matter. While the focus of the discussion at the meeting was the May 22, 1991 auction, Gutfreund did not disclose to the Treasury Department officials that he knew that a false bid had been submitted in the February 21, 1991 five-year note auction by the head of the firm's Government Trading Desk, the same individual responsible for the firm's activities in connection with the May two-year note issue.

On June 19, Meriwether, Strauss and Gutfreund met to discuss the allegations concerning the May 22, 1991 two-year note auction. At that meeting, Strauss and Gutfreund decided that disclosure of the unauthorized customer bid in the February 21, 1991 auction should be delayed until more information could be obtained about Salomon's activities in the May two-year note auction. No decision was made about how much time should elapse before a report was made. While Gutfreund and Strauss were under the general impression that someone in the legal department was reviewing the May 22, 1991 auction, there was not any discussion about any specific efforts or inquiries that would have to be undertaken before a report could be made. There were also no efforts or inquiries underway at that time to investigate Mozer's conduct in the February 21, 1991 auction. Feuerstein was not informed of or present at the meeting and was not informed of the decision to delay the disclosure.

For the next several weeks, there was not any further consideration of reporting the unauthorized bid in the February 21, 1991 auction to the government. Some discussion about limiting Mozer's activities did occur in late June with respect to the auction for June two-year U.S. Treasury notes. On the day of the auction, Strauss and Gutfreund told Mozer that he should not bid in an aggressive or high-profile manner in the auction because of the attention which had been focused on Salomon's role in the May two-year auction.

12. The Internal Investigation

In early July, Salomon retained a law firm to conduct an internal investigation of the firm's role in the May 22, 1991 two-year note auction ... The law firm was not informed of the false bid submitted in the February 21, 1991 auction. Sometime during the week of July 8, the attorneys learned that one of Salomon's customers in the May two-year note auction, Tiger Management Corporation, had apparently sold $500 million of a $2 billion auction award to Salomon on the day of the auction at the auction price, and that trade tickets for the transaction did not exist.

On July 12, attorneys from the law firm interviewed Thomas Murphy, who was then the head trader on the Government Trading Desk. In connection with questions about customer authorization for the $500 million portion of the $2 billion Tiger award sold to Salomon on the day of the auction, Murphy was asked whether there had been similar types of problems in the past. Murphy said that he could not answer the question without speaking to the Salomon attorney who was present. Murphy and the attorney then left the room. When they returned, Murphy did not answer the question but continued with the interview.

When the interview was over, Feuerstein met with the attorneys from the law firm for a previously-scheduled status meeting. During that meeting, Feuerstein and the attorneys discussed the questions concerning authorization for the $500 million portion of the Tiger award. Feuerstein then informed the attorneys that Salomon had submitted an unauthorized customer bid in the February 21, 1991 five-year note auction. The attorneys and Feuerstein agreed that the scope of the internal investigation should be broadened, and a decision was made that the law firm would expand the investigation to include a review of all auctions for U.S. Treasury notes and bonds since the July 1990 adoption by the Treasury Department of a 35% bidding limitation.

During the review that was conducted between July 15 and early August, the law firm discovered a $1 billion false bid in the December 27, 1990 auction of four-year U.S. Treasury notes, a second $3.15 billion false bid in the February 21, 1991 auction, a $1 billion false bid in the February 7, 1991 auction of thirty-year U.S. Treasury bonds, the failure to disclose the $485 million when-issued position in the May 22, 1991 auction, and questions concerning customer authorization for the bid submitted in the name of Tudor in the April 25, 1991 auction.[27] The results of the internal investigation were reported to Feuerstein on August 6 and to other members of senior management of Salomon, including Gutfreund, Strauss, and Meriwether, on August 7.

On Sunday, August 18, at a special meeting of the Board of Directors of Salomon Inc., Gutfreund and Strauss resigned their positions with Salomon and Salomon Inc., and Meriwether resigned his position with Salomon. On August 23, 1991, Feuerstein resigned his position as Chief Legal Officer of Salomon.

13. The Commission's Action

Among other things, the complaint charged that Salomon had submitted or caused to be submitted ten false bids in nine separate auctions for U.S. Treasury securities between August of 1989 and May of 1991. The false bids alleged in the complaint totalled $15.5 billion and resulted in the illegal acquisition by Salomon of $9.548 billion of U.S. Treasury securities.

Simultaneously with the filing of the action, Salomon and Salomon Inc. consented, without admitting or denying the allegations of the complaint, to the entry of a Final Judgment of Permanent Injunction and Other Relief. The Judgment required, among other things, that Salomon pay the amount of $290 million, representing a payment of $190 million to the United States Treasury as civil penalties and asset forfeitures and a payment of $100 million to establish a civil claims fund to be administered by a Fund Administrator appointed by the Court.

On May 20, 1992, the Commission also instituted and settled, pursuant to an Offer of Settlement submitted by Salomon, an administrative proceeding against the firm pursuant to Section 15(b) of the Exchange Act. In that proceeding, the Commission found that Salomon had failed, in connection with the facts described in

---

27. As with the false bids submitted in the February 21, 1991 auction, the false bids in the December 27, 1990 and February 7, 1991 auctions were accompanied by fictitious sales of auction allocations received in response to the false bids to accounts in the names of customers and then back to Salomon, all at the auction price. In addition, in each of those instances, the normal procedures of Salomon were also overridden and confirmations for the fictitious transactions were not sent to the customers.

this Order, reasonably to supervise a person subject to its supervision with a view to preventing violations of the federal securities laws.

B. FINDINGS

1. Legal Principles

Section 15(b)(4)(E) of the Exchange Act authorizes the Commission to impose sanctions against a broker-dealer if the firm has:

> failed reasonably to supervise, with a view to preventing violations [of federal securities laws], another person who commits such a violation, if such person is subject to his supervision.

Section 15(b)(6) of the Exchange incorporates Section 15(b)(4)(E) by reference and authorizes the Commission to impose sanctions for deficient supervision on individuals associated with broker-dealers.

The principles which govern this proceeding are well-established by the Commission's cases involving failure to supervise. The Commission has long emphasized that the responsibility of broker-dealers to supervise their employees is a critical component of the federal regulatory scheme.[28]

2. The Failure to Supervise

As described above, in late April of 1991 three supervisors of Paul Mozer—John Meriwether, Thomas Strauss, and John Gutfreund—learned that Mozer had submitted a false bid in the amount of $3.15 billion in an auction of U.S. Treasury securities.... As a result, although there may be varying degrees of responsibility, each of the supervisors bears some measure of responsibility for the collective failure of the group to take action.

Under the circumstances of this case, the failure of the supervisors to take action to discipline Mozer or to limit his activities constituted a serious breach of their supervisory obligations. Gutfreund, Strauss and Meriwether thus each failed reasonably to supervise Mozer with a view to preventing violations of the federal securities laws.

As Chairman and Chief Executive Officer of Salomon, Gutfreund bore ultimate responsibility for ensuring that a prompt and thorough inquiry was undertaken and that Mozer was appropriately disciplined. A chief executive officer has ultimate affirmative responsibility, upon learning of serious wrongdoing within the firm as to any segment of the securities market, to ensure that steps are taken to prevent further violations of the securities laws and to determine the scope of the wrongdoing. He failed to ensure that this was done.

Once improper conduct came to the attention of Gutfreund, he bore responsibility for ensuring that the firm responded in a way that recognized the seriousness and urgency of the situation. In our view, Gutfreund did not discharge that responsibility.

Strauss, as the President of Salomon, was the official within the firm to whom Meriwether first took the matter of Mozer's misconduct for appropriate action. As

---

28. Smith Barney, Harris Upham & Co., Exchange Act Release No. 21,813 (March 5, 1985).

its president, moreover, Strauss was responsible for the operations of Salomon as a brokerage firm.[29] ... Strauss retained his supervisory responsibilities as the president of the brokerage firm, and he failed to discharge those responsibilities.

Meriwether was Mozer's direct supervisor and the head of all fixed-income trading activities at Salomon. Meriwether had also been designated by the firm as the person responsible for supervising the firm's fixed-income trading activities, including the activities of the Government Trading Desk. As a result, until he was instructed not to carry out his responsibilities as Mozer's direct supervisor, Meriwether was required to take appropriate supervisory action.

Notes and Questions

1. Although the SEC emphasized in *Gutfreund* that line senior executives were unequivocally supervisors under sections 15(b)(4)(E) and 15(b)(6), it asserted in a previous case, *Arthur James Huff*, Exchange Act Release No. 29017 (March 28, 1991), Part VI, that " ... in each situation a person's actual responsibilities and authority, rather than, for example, his or her 'line' or non-line' status, will determine whether he or she is a 'supervisor'..." The SEC defines a line supervisor as one who has the power to hire, fire, reward and punish the primary violator. Does this conflict with its conclusions about the supervisory status of Gutfreund and Strauss?

   [handwritten margin note: No since the violation was significant.]

2. Even prior to *Gutfreund*, the SEC maintained that senior line executives of broker-dealers, such as CEOs, are supervisors under Sections 15(b)(4)(E) and (6) of the Exchange Act. In *James Michael Brown*, Exchange Act Release No. 31223, 1992 WL 275520 (Sept. 23, 1992), the SEC affirmed a FINRA decision that held that James Michael Brown, the president and CEO of an inactive broker-dealer, was responsible for violations of recordkeeping and reporting requirements even though he contended that he had no control over the firm, was not paid for his services, and lacked hiring, firing, and check-writing authority. The SEC asserted that even if Brown's contentions were accurate, he was still a senior line supervisor and therefore could be held liable for deficient supervision under Sections 15(b)(4)(E) and (6) of the Exchange Act. "[The SEC has] consistently stated that the president of a firm *is responsible for* its compliance efforts *unless and until he reasonably delegates a particular* function to another person at the firm and neither knows nor has reason to know that such person is not performing his duties." The SEC determined that Brown's title alone sufficed to determine the scope of his supervisor responsibility. To reiterate this point in *James Michael Brown*, the SEC expressly referenced *Kirk A. Knapp*, Exchange Act Release No. 30391, 1992 WL 40436 (Feb. 21, 1992) in which it held "once a president accepts that title,

---

29. As we noted in *Universal Heritage Investments Corporation*, Exchange Act Release No. 19308, 1982 WL 525157, *5 (Dec. 8, 1982): "The president of a corporate broker-dealer is responsible for compliance with all of the requirements imposed on his firm unless and until he reasonably delegates particular functions to another person in that firm, and neither knows nor has reason to know that such person's performance is deficient."

he [is] required to fulfill the obligations attached to his office, for so long as he occupie[s] the position ..." Also, In *Signal Sec. Inc.*, Exchange Act Release No. 43350, 2000 WL 1423891 (Sept. 26, 2000), the SEC stated that " ... [R]esponsibility for the supervisory function of a registered broker-dealer is incumbent upon the most senior members of management. Senior management has a duty not only to provide a meaningful supervisory structure, but also to actively monitor and enforce it. It is incumbent upon management to ensure that branch managers, registered representatives, or any other firm employees do not ignore procedures." (citations omitted).

3. Federal courts have supported the SEC's view of the supervisory responsibilities of senior executives. In *In Sheldon v. SEC*, 45 F.3d 1515, 1517 (2d Cir. 1995), the court explicitly stated a senior executive's responsibility for ensuring a firm-wide system of proper supervision and appropriate delegation: The president of a corporate broker-dealer is responsible for compliance with all of the requirements imposed on his firm unless and until he reasonably delegates particular functions to another person in that firm, and neither knows nor has reason to know that such person's performance is deficient. *See also Patrick v. SEC*, 19 F.3d 66 (2d Cir. 1994).

4. Finally, in a recent decision, the SEC seems to have expanded the basis for the types of primary violations that can be used to sustain liability for deficient supervision under Section 15(b)(4)(E) in the context of line supervisors. In 1999, the ALJ in *Kolar* refused to premise liability for failure reasonably to supervise on a violation of Section 15(a)(1), which requires registration as a broker-dealer in order to engage in a securities business in the United States. Specifically, the ALJ asserted that "[s]uch a holding would be counter-intuitive, as the stated need for the individual to register is grounded in the lack of opportunity to supervise. For these reasons, Mr. Kolar's liability for failure to supervise will not be based on Mr. Turner's underlying violation of Section 15(a)(1)." If there is a lack of opportunity to supervise, ... it is not clear how there can also be a failure reasonably to supervise." Essentially, if the registered representative failed to register as a broker-dealer under section 15(a)(1), he could not have a supervisor and thus there would be no opportunity for deficient supervision. The ALJ's logic in *Kolar* has not precluded the SEC from recently asserting deficient supervision under Section 15(b)(4)(E) based on a primary violation of Section 15(a)(1) for failure to register as a broker-dealer as illustrated by the following case.

In the Matter of Jack C. Smith, Jr.

Administrative Proceeding File No. 3-14229, Exchange Act Release No. 34-63834
(Feb. 3, 2011)

Summary

* * *

Respondent

1. Jack C. Smith, Jr., age 61, resides in San Diego, California. Smith has had an ownership interest in Torrey Pines since November 1987, and during the relevant

period, he was president, chief executive officer, and had overall supervisory responsibility for the firm. In 2009, Smith sold the majority of his ownership interest in Torrey Pines.

Other Relevant Entity and Person

2. **Torrey Pines Securities, Inc.** is a broker-dealer headquartered in Del Mar, California. Torrey Pines has been registered with the Commission since 1985....

3. **Dennis Lee Keating, II**, age 46, resides in Highland, Utah. In April 2006, Keating joined Torrey Pines as a part-owner and registered representative, working in and supervising the Corona, California branch office. Keating resigned from Torrey Pines in November 2008, and sold his ownership interest. Keating was permanently enjoined on June 28, 2010 for violations of the securities and broker-dealer registration and antifraud provisions, specifically Sections 5(a), 5(c), and 17(a) of the Securities Act of 1933, and Sections 10(b) and 15(a) of the Exchange Act and Rule 10b-5 thereunder. (citation omitted) On July 6, 2010, the Commission barred Keating from associating with a broker-dealer or investment adviser. (citation omitted).

Background

4. Smith formed Torrey Pines in 1987 and was its sole owner until 2006 when Keating and a third individual purchased interests in Torrey Pines. These three individuals remained part-owners from 2006 through 2008. During the relevant period, Smith was the president and chief executive officer and had overall supervisory responsibility for the firm. Torrey Pines is headquartered in Del Mar, California, and had four branch offices, three in California and one in Florida.

Keating's Unregistered Offering

5. Keating joined Torrey Pines in April 2006, opening the Torrey Pines Corona, California branch office (the "Corona Office"). Keating, along with an office assistant, and, for a short time, one other representative, worked in the Corona Office. Keating had overall supervisory responsibility for the Corona Office.

6. In August 2006, Keating formed a privately-held company and until April 2007, he raised over $17 million from friends, family, and Torrey Pines's customers in a private, unregistered offering of securities. Until at least November 2008, Keating also continued lulling investors with false assurances that they would receive a return on their investments. Keating acted as an unregistered broker-dealer in violation of Section 15(a) of the Exchange Act, as he conducted the offering outside the scope of his employment with Torrey Pines.

Smith Failed to Establish Reasonable Procedures and Systems to Supervise Keating; Keating Left to Supervise Himself

7. During the relevant period, according to Torrey Pines' written supervisory procedures manual (the "Manual"), Smith was responsible for establishing the firm's supervisory policies and procedures, as well as systems to implement them, at Torrey Pines. In practice, Smith also had the ability and authority to establish

policies and procedures, and to implement supervisory systems that would apply to Keating.

8. Smith failed to establish reasonable policies and procedures to assign responsibility for supervising Keating. When Keating became a part-owner of Torrey Pines, Smith did not revise the Manual or create other policies or procedures for Keating to be supervised reasonably at the firm's Corona Office. Although Smith delegated to the resident manager the responsibility of supervising Keating's trading activities, no one other than Keating oversaw the other daily activities of the Corona Office. No one reviewed Keating's daily correspondence or telephone calls, other than in cursory annual audits. Smith's delegation of most of the Corona Office's daily responsibilities to Keating resulted in Keating supervising himself. If Keating had not been left to supervise himself, his outside sales activities, which violated Section 15(a) of the Securities Exchange Act likely would have been prevented and detected.

* * *

Violations

11. As a result of the conduct described above, Keating violated Section 15(a) of the Exchange Act.

12. Section 15(b)(4)(E) of the Exchange Act requires broker-dealers reasonably to supervise persons subject to their supervision, with a view toward preventing violations of the federal securities laws. *See, e.g., Dean Witter Reynolds, Inc.,* Exchange Act Release No. 46578 (Oct. 1, 2002). The Commission has emphasized that the "responsibility of broker-dealers to supervise their employees by means of effective, established procedures is a critical component in the federal investor protection scheme regulating the securities markets." *Id.* Section 15(b)(4)(E) of the Exchange Act provides for the imposition of a sanction against a broker or dealer who "has failed reasonably to supervise, with a view to preventing violations of the securities laws, another person who commits such a violation, if such other person is subject to his supervision." Section 15(b)(6)(A)(i) incorporates by reference Section 15(b)(4)(E) and provides for the imposition of sanctions against persons associated with a broker-dealer.

13. As a result of the conduct described above, Smith failed reasonably to supervise Keating within the meaning of Section 15(b)(4)(E) of the Exchange Act, ... when he failed to supervise Keating with a view to preventing and detecting violations of Section 15(a) of the Exchange Act.

Hypothetical Four

Bennett has discovered another errant registered representative in Success First's West Palm Beach office. During the period from October 2012 through late October 2013, Julie Kolowski misappropriated more than $2 million from about 30 customers of her outside business, including approximately 20 clients who were Success First customers for part of that period. From her hiring by Success First through her October 2013 termination, Kolowski operated her Success First securities business, as well as her 401(k) and payroll services businesses, from an off-site office under the name of CAI. Kolowski misrepresented to some investors that CAI was a registered broker-dealer, and she persuaded them to open or continue accounts with her at CAI. Kolowski directly received customer funds, payable to Kolowski and/or CAI, for the purpose of purchasing securities and other investments in those accounts. Shortly after Kolowski went to work for Success First, Bennett received a letter from the Pennsylvania State Securities Commission in response to Kolowski's license application inquiring whether Success First was aware of Kolowski's disciplinary history, which included a past customer arbitration and financial judgments. Bennett notified Watts, her regional director, about Kolowski's disciplinary history, who in turn notified his senior managing director. Subsequently, the senior managing director met with Tatum and Alvarez to discuss, among other things, Kolowski's prior disciplinary history. At that time Success First had never hired a registered representative with a disciplinary history; consequently, procedures did not require heightened supervision of registered representatives who had a history of sales practice or compliance-related complaints or concerns. In the meantime, while waiting for a response from upper management about Kolowski's disciplinary history, Bennett received a complaint from one of Kolowski's customers that the customer had not received a confirmation of a stock purchase and had not received account statements, except for some that Kolowski had sent him. Bennett's investigation of the customer complaint relied primarily on her conversations with Kolowski. She did not contact the customer directly. She did, however, forward the results of her investigation up the management chain. About one month after Bennett dealt with the Kolowski customer complaint, she received a response signed by Watts, the senior managing director, Tatum, and Alvarez, instructing her to fire Kolowski. Identify Kolowski's supervisors.

2. Non-Line Supervisors

The majority of SEC administrative proceedings against broker-dealers for deficient supervision are against *line* supervisors, i.e., supervisors in the direct chain of command. In these proceedings, the ability to determine who is responsible for overseeing a particular employee is fairly straightforward. At most broker-dealers, persons in the direct chain of command are given both the authority and ability to influence the conduct of the lower-level employees. However, in the context of non-line supervisors, it becomes much more difficult to determine lines of authority and responsibility. Moreover, many broker-dealers do not have simple linear supervisory systems. In cases where there are parallel or collateral responsibilities shared by different individuals, it becomes much more difficult to establish whether a broker-dealer employee is a supervisor. The difficulty lies in the wording of the statute itself:

> Section 15(b)(4)(E) authorizes the SEC to impose sanctions, if the firm or its employee has failed reasonably to supervise … another person who com-

mits a violation of the federal securities laws, if such person is "subject to his supervision."

Initially, the SEC struggled with the meaning of the phrase "subject to his supervision." It has emphasized that failure to supervise cases require a case-by-case analysis of the particular facts and circumstances presented and that neither the individual's job title nor the broker-dealer's organizational chart is determinative. The SEC's struggle with determining when a non-line employee is a supervisor under Sections 15(b)(4)(E) and 15(b)(6) is illustrated in the following case.

In the Matter of Arthur James Huff

Exchange Act Release No. 29017, 1991 WL 296561 (Mar. 28, 1991)

Chairman BREEDEN and Commissioner ROBERTS:

I.

Arthur James Huff, a vice president and senior registered options principal ("SROP") in the New York headquarters compliance department of PaineWebber Incorporated ("PW"), appeals from the decision of an administrative law judge. The law judge found that, between July 1979, when Huff first joined PW, and May 1980, Huff failed to exercise reasonable supervision over (1) Dennis E. Greenman, a salesman in PW's Miami, Florida branch office, with a view to preventing Greenman's violations of antifraud provisions, and (2) Philip Huber, branch manager of that office, with a view to preventing Huber's deficient supervision of Greenman. Greenman was a registered representative of PW from September 1978 until May 1980, when his employment with PW terminated. The law judge concluded that Huff should be suspended from association with any broker or dealer for 60 days.

II.

It is undisputed that Greenman, the "biggest producer" in PW's Miami office and ranked nationally by PW as its fifth largest producer of commissions, engaged in a massive securities fraud in which he used investors' funds without their authorization for options trading, incurring heavy losses. In order to conceal those losses from customers, Greenman employed various deceptive devices. He intercepted customers' account statements and sent them fictitious ones, arranging for the genuine statements to be sent to fictitious addresses including post office boxes that he controlled and incorrect or non-existent street addresses. The fictitious statements generally showed monthly rates of return ranging from 5% to 7%. Greenman did not even open accounts at PW for some of the customers participating in his program, depositing their funds instead in the accounts of other customers participating in the program. His customers suffered total losses of some $7.6 million. Greenman also went to great lengths to deceive PW with respect to his activities.

Prior to Huff's arrival at the firm in July 1979, Greenman had been the cause of considerable concern to the PW compliance department. Between January and June, it undertook a review of all of his activities. Among other things, compliance prepared a profit and loss analysis of about ten Greenman accounts, reviewed activity letters that were sent out over his signature, prepared a memorandum outlining Greenman's options trading system, and investigated the circumstance that Greenman's accounts included a number of customers with post office box or identical addresses. The compliance department review of Greenman's activities culminated in a June meeting in New York at which Ray Vass, compliance director, other members of his department, and a member of PW's legal staff met with Huber and Greenman. By the end of that meeting, Vass had concluded that all of the concerns that had been raised regarding Greenman's accounts had been satisfactorily resolved, subject to Greenman's providing certain account documentation to the legal department. The documentation was subsequently supplied, and the accounts were approved by the legal department.

As noted above, Huff joined PW in July 1979. His duties included the development, implementation and oversight of firm-wide procedures in the options area. Shortly after Huff's arrival, Vass, his immediate supervisor, gave him the thick compliance department file on Greenman and his options trading program. Vass instructed Huff to keep on top of Greenman's activities and to follow through if any question arose concerning Greenman. Huff familiarized himself with the contents of the file and monitored Greenman's accounts on a selected basis. However, he was aware that the questions previously raised with respect to Greenman had been resolved to the satisfaction of Vass and the compliance department. For that reason, he did not consider Greenman "a compliance concern" at that time.

III.

Section 15(b)(6) of the Securities Exchange Act, incorporating Section 15(b)(4)(E) by reference, provides that this Commission may sanction any person associated with a broker-dealer if we find that such person "failed reasonably to supervise, with a view to preventing [securities] violations ... another person who commits such a violation, if such other person is subject to his supervision". Section 15(b)(4)(E) further provides that no person shall be deemed "to have failed reasonably to supervise any other person" if he "reasonably discharged the duties and obligations incumbent upon him by reason of [his firm's] procedures" *and* had no reasonable basis for believing that those procedures were not being followed.

As set forth below, we cannot find that Huff failed reasonably to perform the supervisory duties with respect to Greenman that were vested in him by Vass.[30] We conclude that the Division of Enforcement has not sustained its burden of showing that, under all the circumstances, Huff failed to exercise reasonable supervision with a

---

30. To the extent that Huff's arguments may be read to contend that Greenman was not "subject to his supervision" because of the function Huff performed in the PW organization, we need not and do not rule on that contention. Rather, we assume for purposes of this opinion that Huff had a supervisory relationship vis-a-vis Greenman.

view to preventing Greenman's antifraud violations. Thus we deem it unnecessary to determine whether Greenman was a person "subject to [Huff's] supervision" within the meaning of the statute.[31]

IV.

As noted above, Section 15(b)(4)(E) provides that no person shall be held responsible for deficient supervision if he "reasonably discharged the duties and obligations incumbent upon him by reason of [his firm's] procedures and system". Thus, different supervisors may have different responsibilities depending on how each firm devises its compliance program.

Under the particular circumstances of this case, we cannot conclude that Huff's overall discharge of "the duties and obligations incumbent upon him by reason of [PW's] procedures and system" fell below a standard of reasonableness so as to amount to a failure to supervise within the meaning of Section 15(b)(4)(E) of the Securities Exchange Act.[32]

V.

As noted above, the law judge also found that Huff failed to exercise reasonable supervision over Huber with a view to preventing Huber's deficient supervision of Greenman. However, that finding is inconsistent with applicable statutory provisions. As set forth above, Section 15(b)(6) of the Exchange Act, incorporating Section 15(b)(4)(E) by reference, provides that persons associated with broker-dealers may be sanctioned for failing reasonably to supervise, "with a view to preventing violations [of the securities acts and rules thereunder], another person who commits such a violation". (Emphasis supplied). However, *deficient supervision by a subordinate is not a "violation"* on the basis of which the subordinate's superior can be disciplined. The statute [Sections 15(b)(4) and 15(b)(6)] lists separate and distinct bases for disciplining associated persons. That list includes injunctions, convictions, violations of the securities acts and rules, and deficient supervision. Thus the statute—indeed, the very sections at issue—clearly distinguishes between violations and supervisory deficiencies. We accordingly conclude that Huber's deficient supervision was not a "violation"

---

31. The law judge's finding that Greenman was such a person was in large part based on a Chicago Board Options Exchange rule calling for SROP supervision of customer accounts and orders relating to options contracts. The rule was amended effective April 25, 1980. However, it is not determinative of the issue.

32. The concurring opinion states that we have not directly addressed the issue of whether Huff was Greenman's supervisor. As noted above, we expressly found it unnecessary to reach that issue. Hence we make no finding in that regard. The concurring opinion also states that Huff's performance "hardly provides a model of how supervisors ought to behave." Under our disposition of this matter, the issue is not whether Huff was a model supervisor, but whether his supervision was reasonable under all the attendant circumstances. We conclude that it was. Indeed, had Huff done any less than he did in this case by way of following up on Greenman's accounts, our disposition of this matter might well have been different.

within the meaning of Section 15(b)(4)(E). Thus it is not a statutory basis for sanctioning Huff.

VI.

The charges against Huff have not been sustained. Accordingly, these proceedings must be dismissed.

Commissioners LOCHNER and SCHAPIRO concur in part and file a separate opinion. Commissioner FLEISCHMAN did not participate in this matter.

Commissioners LOCHNER and SCHAPIRO:

We concur in the Commission's decision to dismiss the proceedings against Huff, but write separately in order to state our view that Greenman was not subject to the supervision of Huff for purposes of Section 15(b)(4)(E) of the Exchange Act.[33]

I.

Greenman was a salesperson in PaineWebber's Miami branch office who defrauded his customers of more than seven million dollars through unauthorized options trading. Greenman's immediate supervisors, PaineWebber's branch manager and regional manager for the Miami office, have previously been sanctioned by the Commission for failing reasonably to supervise Greenman. *The issue in this case is whether Huff, a member of PaineWebber's compliance department in New York, should also be held statutorily responsible for the supervision of Greenman.*

The Commission's opinion does not directly address in any detail whether Huff was Greenman's supervisor; rather it apparently assumes Huff was, and then concludes that he reasonably performed the duties with respect to Greenman that were assigned to him by PaineWebber.... We prefer to ask, first, whether Huff was a supervisor. Since we find that he was not, we need not reach the question of whether his performance in his job met the statutory standard.

II.

The Commission's statutory authority directly to sanction individuals for supervisory failures was granted by the Securities Acts Amendments of 1964. Prior to that time, an individual supervisor could be sanctioned only if the firm was found to have committed a violation, and the supervisor was found to have been the "cause" of the firm's violation.[34] In 1963, the Special Study of the Securities Markets noted the need for greater supervision by broker-dealers over their increasingly far-flung branch offices and salespersons,[35] and the Commission subsequently requested

---

33. We concur in Part V of the Commission's opinion, which concludes that Huber's deficient supervision of Greenman was not a "violation" within the meaning of Section 15(b)(4)(E), and it therefore is not a statutory basis for sanctioning Huff.

34. *See, e.g.*, Reynolds & Co., 39 S.E.C. 902, 905, 917 (1960).

35. *See* Report of the Special Study of the Securities Markets of the SEC (1963), reprinted in H.R.Doc. 95, 88th Cong., 1st Sess. (1963), pt. 1 at 290–91, 328.

greater authority from Congress to proceed directly against individuals for failures to supervise.[36]

Prior to sending a legislative request to Congress, the Commission sought the views of a securities industry liaison group on a draft of the proposed legislation. The draft legislation provided merely that a broker-dealer employee could be sanctioned for "failing reasonably to supervise" a person who committed a violation. In response to an industry request for greater clarification concerning the scope of the supervisory requirement, the Commission amended its legislative request to specify that a broker-dealer employee could not be sanctioned for failing reasonably to supervise a person who committed a violation unless that person was "subject to the supervision" of the broker-dealer employee. Congress ultimately included this language in Section 15(b)(4)(E) of the Exchange Act, with both the Senate and House reports on the legislation noting that "a supervisory person would be responsible only if the employee who violated [the securities] laws was subject to his supervisory jurisdiction."

Unfortunately, the legislative history provides little guidance as to what was intended by the phrase "subject to the supervision". For the phrase to have any meaning, however, the least that can be said is that it has some limiting effect on the individuals whom the Commission can sanction, even if they fail reasonably to supervise.

The Commission has recognized that substantial and affirmative responsibilities are placed on those who have a duty to supervise. The Commission has stated that such persons must "exercise particular vigilance when indications of irregularity reach their attention." As the phrase "failure to supervise" itself indicates, the violation frequently is an act of omission, rather than commission. With the benefit of hindsight, it is often possible to identify many who, if they had only exercised particular vigilance, could have prevented or terminated another's violation. The statute does not indicate an intention to hold mere bystanders to this exacting standard, however. The statute requires a supervisory relationship and such a relationship can only be found in those circumstances when, among other things, it should have been clear to the individual in question that he was responsible for the actions of another and that he could take effective action to fulfill that responsibility. Basic notions of fairness and due process reinforce this conclusion.

In our view, the most probative factor that would indicate whether a person is responsible for the actions of another is whether that person has the power to control the other's conduct. This view is supported by the common meaning of the term "supervision", when used in the employment relationship to which the statute refers and by the statutory language "subject to his supervision" which also seems to emphasize control. Admittedly, there are a number of other aspects of supervision. Control, however, is the essence of supervision, and it is unlikely that anyone would consider his or her self another's employment "supervisor" if he or she did not have authority to control the other's actions.

---

36. *See* S. Rep. No. 379, 88th Cong., 1st Sess. 44–45, 75–76 (1963).

III.

Our reading of Section 15(b)(4)(E) to require the power to control is also supported by the Commission's decisions in the twenty-seven years since the provision's enactment. The vast majority of these cases involve broker-dealer employees who had what is commonly referred to as "line" responsibility for the violator. These employees, beginning with branch managers and proceeding up the "line", at least in a large firm like PaineWebber, to regional managers and their head office superiors (and ultimately to the Board of Directors), have clear and direct authority and responsibility to control the conduct of salespersons, including the power to hire or fire, and to reward or punish. Whatever the precise meaning of supervision in a particular case, these powers clearly are a very substantial part of it. Thus, employees in a broker-dealer's administrative structure are, at least presumptively, supervisors of those whom they have the authority and the responsibility to hire and fire and reward and punish.

Outside the context of line supervisors, however, it becomes much more difficult to ascertain clear lines of authority and responsibility, and there are only a handful of cases in which the Commission has proceeded against a broker-dealer employee for failing to supervise a salesperson for which the employee did not have line responsibility, i.e., where the power to hire, fire, reward and punish was not present.[37] The Commission's reluctance to pursue such cases against persons other than line supervisors is appropriate, in our view, given the likelihood that persons other than line supervisors would not have the requisite control over the supervised person.

In each of the cases in which the Commission concluded that a non-line employee was a supervisor, the Commission made a detailed factual analysis of the non-line employee's authority and responsibility within the administrative structure of the broker-dealer. This analysis, in fact, turns on the ability of these specific non-line employees to control at least some critical aspects of the behavior of the persons supervised.

For example, in *Tennenbaum* the non-line employee found to be a "supervisor" headed a broker-dealer's options department and had sole authority to permit salespersons to handle discretionary options accounts. After permitting a particular salesperson to handle discretionary accounts, many facts came to Tennenbaum's attention indicating that the salesperson had committed violations that were directly related to the risks involved with discretionary options accounts. The Commission rejected Tennenbaum's argument that he did not have supervisory authority over the salesperson because he did not occupy a line position. However, the Commission did find that Tennenbaum nonetheless had control over the salesperson's violative conduct.

Of critical importance is the fact that Tennenbaum had sole authority to permit a salesman to handle discretionary options accounts. As Tennenbaum reiterated several times during the hearings, his "only power" over Graham was the power to

---

37. *See Gary W. Chambers*, Securities Exchange Act Release No. 27975, 1990 WL 311827 (May 1, 1990); *Robert J. Check*, Securities Exchange Act Release No. 26367, 1988 WL 902613 (Dec. 16, 1988); *Michael E. Tennenbaum*, Securities Exchange Act Release No. 18429, 1982 WL 31984 (Jan, 19, 1982).

revoke that permission. Registrant had a general rule prohibiting discretionary options accounts, which Tennenbaum acknowledged was necessary because of the unusual litigation risks they posed for the firm.... Once Tennenbaum had given Graham his approval, he assumed responsibility for ensuring that this grant of authority, over which he continued to exercise control, was not being abused. (Emphasis added).

Another example of the Commission's emphasis on the particular authority and responsibility of a non-line employee to control violative conduct is provided by *Check*, in which the non-line employee was the manager of a broker-dealer's mutual fund sales department. The underlying violations were failures by salespersons properly to process mutual fund sales orders. With language very similar to that in *Tennenbaum*, the Commission rejected Check's argument that he did not have supervisory obligations because he did not occupy a line position. Supervisory obligations were found, instead, in Check's ability to control behavior of salespersons in the specific category of activity in which the violations took place.

Check was uniquely positioned to exercise effective supervisory control in the specialized area of mutual fund sales, and, as indicated above, he did exercise control on certain occasions when he received inconsistent information on sales orders. It was Check ... who by his control over mutual fund orders had the power and obligation to see to it that customers received benefits to which they were entitled, and Check who had, and sometimes exercised, the power to reject mutual fund orders. (Emphasis added)

An important element in these cases is the extent to which they focus on the fact that the employees had particular authority and responsibility for the salespersons' violative conduct (apparently even more so than did the branch and regional managers who were also responsible for supervision of the salespersons), and had the employees wished to exercise it could have prevented the salespersons from continuing their activities in those areas in which they exercised that authority and responsibility, even if they did not have the power to fire, demote or reduce the pay of the salespersons in question. In *Tennenbaum* it was the power to control the salesperson's ability to deal with discretionary options accounts, and in *Check* it was the power to exercise control over approving salespersons' mutual fund sales orders. Even though they were non-line employees, Tennenbaum and Check exercised control over the violative conduct involved. If the salespersons' violations in these cases had been unrelated to those particular powers, it seems evident that the Commission would not have found the individuals responsible for failures to supervise.

IV.

In light of the statutory language and history, and the Commission's prior decisions, we believe that a supervisor for purposes of Section 15(b)(4)(E) *ought* to be defined by the Commission as a person at a broker-dealer who has been given (and knows or reasonably should know he has been given) the authority and the responsibility for exercising such control over one or more specific activities of a supervised person which fall within the Commission's purview so that such person could take effective action to prevent a violation of the Commission's rules which involves such activity or activities by such supervised person.

An analysis of Huff's authority and responsibility at PaineWebber indicates that Greenman was not subject to Huff's supervision. Because Huff was not in the line of authority at PaineWebber to hire, fire, reward or punish Greenman, Huff should be held to be a statutory supervisor of Greenman only if, in light of all relevant facts and circumstances, he knew or should have known that he had the authority and responsibility within the administrative structure of PaineWebber to exercise such control over Greenman's activities that he could have prevented Greenman's violations.

Huff was certainly never clearly told he had the requisite authority and responsibility. Unlike in *Tennenbaum* and *Check*, where the non-line employees had direct authority to control the violative behavior involved, it does not appear that Huff had the authority or responsibility to direct Greenman to discontinue his practice of providing questionable account documentation and to sanction Greenman if he failed to comply. The authority and responsibility to exercise control over account documentation clearly lay with PaineWebber's branch managers and regional managers, and Huff had no particular authority or responsibility for this matter.

V.

The administrative law judge found two principal sources for his holding that Greenman was subject to Huff's supervision: (1) Huff's position as PaineWebber's senior registered options principal ("SROP"); and (2) the duties assigned to Huff by Vass, particularly Vass' handing of Greenman's file to Huff with instructions to stay on top of the matter. We find neither persuasive.

The only authorities that the law judge cited for holding an SROP responsible were a self-regulatory organization ("SRO") rule, an interpretation of that rule, and, in particular, a draft of an SRO educational handbook on options transactions. Huff's position as PaineWebber's SROP, however, does not provide a great deal of guidance concerning Huff's authority and responsibility to exercise control over Greenman's violative conduct. First, SRO rules are not determinative of an individual's supervisory responsibilities, and the Commission has historically declined to rely on them for that proposition. Second, the SRO rules plainly indicate that an SROP's primary responsibility is to establish appropriate procedures for overall supervision of the firm's options activities, not to supervise individual salespersons. Third, the meaning and legal significance of the draft SRO handbook's discussion of an SROP's responsibility for "overall supervision and control" of a firm's options activities is unclear at best. Fourth, Vass' memo disputing the handbook's discussion would have made it very clear to Huff that, at least as far as his superior was concerned, Huff did not have supervisory responsibility for Greenman. Fifth, Greenman's fraud, while associated with options accounts, was not particularly related to the options matters for which Huff, as PaineWebber's SROP, was responsible, such as approving options accounts and enforcing options position limits. None of this suggests Huff had or knew he had authority and responsibility for Greenman's actions, as opposed to general oversight duties in connection with certain options matters.

The fact that Vass delivered Greenman's file to Huff with instructions to stay on top of the matter and follow through on any problems is clearly insufficient to bring Greenman within Huff's supervision, based on the administrative structure of PaineWebber. First, the language Vass used was hardly a clear grant of authority and responsibility. The evidence indicates that several members of the PaineWebber compliance department in addition to Huff had substantial responsibility for Greenman. For example, Vass himself often handled Greenman-related matters or assigned them to other members of the compliance department. This tends to reduce the significance of Vass giving Greenman's file to Huff.

Second, a large number of files in addition to Greenman's were delivered to Huff at the time he assumed his new job. It is not clear that Vass intended that Huff give the Greenman matter substantially greater attention than all of the other matters that were passed on to him. Nor was it clear exactly what responsibility Vass gave to Huff for any of those files. Moreover, for the six months prior to Huff's arrival at PaineWebber, the compliance department had been reviewing Greenman's activities. The compliance department's review had specifically focused on the documentation for Greenman's accounts, and such documentation ultimately was reviewed and approved by PaineWebber's legal department. Thus, before Huff arrived, several others, including Huff's direct supervisor, Vass, had apparently concluded that Greenman's accounts were in order. The fact that the compliance department had recently concluded its review of Greenman's activities tends to reduce the extent to which Huff would have believed that he was particularly responsible for inquiring into Greenman's accounts, as compared to fulfilling his other compliance responsibilities.

VI.

We do not find that Huff was not Greenman's supervisor merely because of Huff's position as a staff compliance officer (i.e., he was not one of Greenman's "line" supervisors); however his lack of authority to affect Greenman's violative behavior (by firing, demoting or disciplining him or by any other means) is, it seems to us, the most compelling factor in determining whether Huff was Greenman's supervisor, irrespective of what department Huff worked in. Given the absence of such authority, we merely find that, based on the facts in this record, Huff was never clearly given authority or responsibility for any of Greenman's violative activities and that Huff's authority otherwise to control Greenman's violative conduct was, for all practical purposes, nonexistent. Thus Huff was not Greenman's supervisor for purposes of Section 15(b)(4)(E).

Notes and Questions

1. In *Huff*, the SEC, relying on statutory language and its prior decisions, asserts that a supervisor for purposes of Sections 15(b)(4)(E) and 15(b)(6) should be

defined as a person at a broker-dealer who has been given (and knows or reasonably should know he has been given) the authority and the responsibility for exercising such control over one or more specific activities of a supervised person that fall within the SEC's purview so that such person could take effective action to prevent a violation of the federal securities laws and rules that involve such activity or activities by such supervised person. How does this definition compare to the definition of line supervisor previously prescribed by the SEC, i.e., the person at a broker-dealer must have the authority to hire, fire, reward and punish the primary violator? The SEC made clear in its decision rendered in the appeal of *Kolar* that it had never adopted the views expressed in the *Huff* concurrence, i.e., that control is the essence of supervision. In the *Kolar* appeal, the SEC reiterated the rule stated in *Gutfreund* that "determining if a particular person is a 'supervisor' depends on whether, under the facts and circumstances of a particular case, that person has a requisite degree of responsibility, ability or authority to affect the conduct of the employee whose behavior is at issue." *Gutfreund*, 51 S.E.C. 93, 113 (1992).

[handwritten: → More narrow now.]

2. According to *Huff*, the most probative factor that would indicate whether a person is responsible for the actions of another is whether that person has the power to control the other's conduct. Does this conflict with the SEC's determination that deficient supervision by a supervisory subordinate is not a basis for liability under Sections 15(b)(4)(E) and 15(b)(6)? The SEC stated that the ALJ's conclusion that Huff failed to exercise reasonable supervision over Huber, Greenman's branch manager, with a view to preventing Huber's deficient supervision of Greenman was not a basis for imposing liability for failure to supervise. "Thus the statute—indeed, the very sections at issue—clearly distinguishes between violations and supervisory deficiencies." *Huff*, 1991 WL 296561 at * 5. Does the SEC's conclusion conflict with its assertion that the critical factor in determining who is a supervisor, and therefore has liability, is the person's control over the activities in question? If yes, would not this include supervisors of supervisors? Has the SEC seemingly avoided this conundrum by designating all persons involved in controlling the actions of the primary violator, even if they are supervisors of supervisors, as supervisors of the primary violator? See *Gutfreund, infra*. Moreover, if a senior supervisor assumes a hands-on-role in dealing with a supervisory problem, so much so that the senior supervisor makes all decisions regarding the problem, does an intermediate supervisor continue to have any supervisory authority over the problem employee?

[handwritten: → Yes, appears to.]
[handwritten: → Yes]
[handwritten: → Yes]
[handwritten: → Yes]
[handwritten: → Yes]

3. In *Michael E. Tennenbaum*, Exchange Act Release No. 18429, 1982 WL 31984 (Jan. 19, 1982), the SEC sanctioned a non-line supervisor, Michael E. Tennenbaum, for failure to supervise. The SEC found that Tennenbaum, a general partner and SROP of a broker-dealer, failed to exercise reasonable supervision over a salesman who had churned customers' options accounts over which he exercised discretion. Tennenbaum was not the salesman's line supervisor, but was recognized by the broker-dealer's compliance department as the supervisor of discretionary options trading and considered himself to have "personal regulatory responsibility" in the area. *Id.* at 5. Critical to the SEC's determination that Ten-

nenbaum was a supervisor was the fact that he had sole authority to permit a salesman to handle discretionary options accounts, i.e., Tennenbaum had the authority to stop the fraudulent activity by refusing to allow the salesman to engage in options trading.

4. In *Robert J. Check*, Exchange Act Release No. 26367, 1988 WL 902613 (Dec. 16, 1988), Check contended that he did not have supervisory duties because he did not have a line position and because the branch managers were responsible for supervising the broker-dealer's salesman and the compliance department was in charge of supervising the branch managers. Check was the manager of the broker-dealer's mutual fund sales department; several of the salesmen overcharged customers who purchased mutual funds. The SEC rejected Check's argument and held that the fact that other officials at the firm shared responsibility for supervising the salesman did not relieve Check of his supervisory duties. Specifically, the SEC found that Check "by his control over mutual fund orders had the power and control to see to it that customers received the benefits to which they were entitled" and was "uniquely positioned to exercise effective supervisory control in the specialized area of mutual fund sales." *Check*, 1988 WL 902613, at *1.

a. Compliance Officers and Legal Counsel

Compliance officers and legal counsel may also be subject to liability for failure to supervise under Sections 15(b)(4)(E) and 15(b)(6). Some commentators assert that they are inherently vulnerable because of their responsibilities for establishing reasonable supervisory systems and ensuring that such systems are implemented and maintained effectively. However, compliance officers and legal counsel are not subjected to liability based solely on their job titles.

As illustrated in *Huff*, the SEC has endeavored to identify the basis upon which compliance officers and legal counsel will be held liable for failure to supervise. It has consistently asserted that such non-line managers will be held liable when they have the authority and responsibility to control one or more of the activities of the person being supervised who has committed the violation. In a 1993 article, former SEC Director of Enforcement, William R. McLucas identified three principles that the SEC used to determine whether to impose failure-to-supervise liability on compliance officers and legal counsel: (1) proceedings alleging deficient supervision must be analyzed on a case-by-case basis; (2) the facts and circumstances must warrant a conclusion that the prospective supervisor had the authority and/or responsibility or control over one or more of the activities of the person being supervised; and (3) the job title is not determinative in assessing liability.[38] The McLucas article was published after the SEC issued the *Gutfreund* decision, which included a 21(a) report designed to clarify the SEC's views on when it would impose liability on compliance and legal

---

38. William R. McLucas and Jeffrey Hiller, *The* Salomon *Case and the Supervisory Responsibilities of Lawyers and Compliance Personnel,* INSIGHTS (May 1993).

personnel for failure to supervise, *i.e.*, when such personnel would be deemed supervisors under Sections 15(b)(4)(E) and 15(b)(6) of the Exchange Act. However, these principles were used by the SEC in the case below, decided nine months before *Gutfreund*, to impose liability on an individual serving as chief compliance officer and general counsel of a broker-dealer.

In the Matter of First Albany Corporation, John T. Batal and Michael R. Lindburg

Exchange Act Release No. 30515, (Mar. 25, 1992)

I.

The United States Securities and Exchange Commission ("Commission") deems it appropriate and in the public interest that public administrative proceedings be instituted pursuant to Sections 15(b) and 19(h) of the Securities Exchange Act of 1934 ("Exchange Act") against First Albany Corporation ("First Albany"), John T. Batal ("Batal") and Michael R. Lindburg ("Lindburg") to determine whether First Albany, Batal and Lindburg failed reasonably to supervise persons subject to their supervision with a view to preventing violations of the Securities Act of 1933 ("Securities Act"), the Exchange Act and the rules promulgated thereunder.

In anticipation of these proceedings, First Albany, Batal and Lindburg have submitted Offers of Settlement which the Commission has determined to accept.... First Albany, Batal and Lindburg consent to the entry of the findings and remedial sanctions set forth below.

II.

[T]he Commission makes the following findings:

A. The Respondents

First Albany has been registered with the Commission as a broker-dealer since 1953, and is primarily engaged in providing retail brokerage services. First Albany ... maintains approximately 20 retail sales offices in New York and New England, employing approximately 200 brokers. Its executive offices and largest sales office are located in Albany, New York.

Batal has been a registered representative from 1959 to the present. Since August of 1985, he has been employed by First Albany. At all times relevant to this matter, Batal was the Branch Manager of First Albany's branch office in Boston.

Lindburg was an Assistant U.S. Attorney in the Western District of New York from 1979 to 1981. From 1984 to 1986, he was Vice President and General Counsel of the Boston Stock Exchange. In 1986, he became Vice President and General Counsel of First Albany Corporation. From April, 1988 through December, 1990, he was also Chief Compliance Officer of First Albany Corporation.

B. Summary

This matter arises from First Albany's failure to adequately supervise a former registered representative ("the registered representative") that First Albany employed at its Boston, Massachusetts office, with a view towards preventing violations of the federal securities laws and regulations. During the period from April, 1988, when he joined First Albany, to April, 1989, the registered representative engaged in certain acts, conduct and practices that violated Section 17(a) of the Securities Act, Section 10(b) of the Exchange Act and Rule 10b-5 thereunder. These violations involved activity that was intended to create a false or misleading appearance of active trading in the stock of Central Co-Operative Bank ("Central"), and the misappropriation of funds from a customer's account.

The registered representative's violative activities were able to occur because First Albany lacked adequate supervisory and compliance policies and procedures, and lacked an adequate system for applying those supervisory and compliance procedures that were in place. In addition, Batal and Lindburg failed to discharge adequately their supervisory responsibilities. Batal and Lindburg failed to supervise adequately with a view toward preventing violations by the registered representative of the federal securities laws.

C. The Registered Representative's Misconduct

Shortly before he joined First Albany in April, 1988, the registered representative's customers held 798,000 shares of Central, which was 44% of the outstanding shares and 57% of the approximate float of outstanding shares. From the point when he joined First Albany in April, 1988 to April, 1989, the registered representative's customers held as few as 411,425 shares (in April, 1988) and as many as 777,658 shares (in April, 1989) of Central stock at First Albany. During that one year period, the registered representative executed 64 cross trades[39] in his customers' accounts, 10 of which were also wash sales[40], involving a total of approximately 920,000 shares of Central. In executing certain of these cross trades and wash sales, the registered representative intended to create a false or misleading appearance of active trading in Central stock.

In most cases, the registered representative either solicited one side of the transaction and executed the other side on a discretionary basis, or executed both sides of the transaction on a discretionary basis. Accordingly, these transactions violated a First Albany trading restriction that prohibited him from soliciting purchases of Central, as described below in more detail. The registered representative attempted to prevent First Albany from discovering this violation by marking all order tickets "unsolicited." When customers occasionally complained to the registered representative about unauthorized transactions in their accounts, or when trades were made in accounts with insufficient margin equity, the registered representative cancelled the trade and rebilled it to another account. Although such corrections ordinarily occur

---

39. A cross trade occurs when an order is entered for the purchase (or sale) of a security with the knowledge that an order of substantially the same size, at substantially the same time, and at substantially the same price, for the sale (or purchase) of that security, has been or will be entered by or for the same or different parties.

40. A wash sale is a transaction in a security, which involves no change in the beneficial ownership thereof.

infrequently, the registered representative cancelled and rebilled over 70 Central trades, 7 of which were cross trades.

In addition, the registered representative made 13 unauthorized withdrawals totalling $129,500 from one of his customer's brokerage account, and converted these funds to his own use. The registered representative also transferred without authorization $12,000 from the same customer's account to another customer's account. The registered representative accomplished this scheme by using forged letters purportedly authorizing the withdrawals and transfers.

D. First Albany's Supervisory Failures

As discussed below, Lindburg and Batal failed reasonably to supervise the registered representative with a view to preventing violations of the federal securities laws and regulations. First Albany is liable for certain of these failures because it lacked adequate supervisory and compliance policies and procedures, including a sufficient system of review to determine whether the existing policies and procedures were followed.

Although a member of the compliance department reviewed the daily trading activity of First Albany's registered representatives, none of the firm's trading reports specifically identified cross trades or wash sales. Due to the absence of those capabilities within the trading reports (or of other procedures achieving substantially equivalent results) the execution of cross trades and wash sales for the purpose of creating a false or misleading appearance of active trading went undetected and unprevented. In the circumstances of the multi-branch brokerage business conducted by First Albany, the absence of any such procedures rendered First Albany's supervisory and compliance policies inadequate.

In addition, First Albany's Policies and Procedures Manual required the Branch Manager to approve order ticket changes, for example, for cancels and rebills, only after determining the facts necessitating the change, and to oversee the hand delivery of disbursements. First Albany's system of follow up and review to determine whether Batal exercised his responsibilities consisted of asking him during the annual internal compliance audit what his procedures were, which was inadequate. Repeated cancellations and rebills give rise to the necessity for additional procedures and specification of responsibility for review.

Similarly, there were no procedures beyond the branch level that were reasonably designed to review the branch manager's fulfillment of his responsibility to detect and prevent the violation of a trading restriction imposed on the registered representative. When the registered representative joined First Albany, the firm restricted him from soliciting additional purchases of Central because his customers collectively owned a concentrated position in Central with a large margin debt, and the firm did not want to extend more credit. However, First Albany implemented no procedures that vested supervisory responsibility, or a system of follow up and review, to detect and prevent violations of the restriction imposed on the registered representative, even where, as here, such violations might be expected to result in violations of applicable law and rules.

* * *

F. Lindburg's Supervisory Failures

At First Albany, Lindburg as Chief Compliance Officer was responsible for ensuring that registered representatives complied with firm policy. Lindburg had the power to take disciplinary action against a registered representative who violated firm policy by removing commissions and imposing small fines.

Although he knew that the registered representative was restricted from soliciting purchases of Central, Lindburg failed to take any actions or put in place or implement any procedures, either at the Boston branch or in the Compliance Department, to provide a sufficient system of review to determine whether this restriction was enforced, even after he had reasonable cause to believe that the registered representative had violated this restriction. In September, 1988, in connection with an NASD inquiry directed to First Albany concerning the trading of Central, Lindburg requested an explanation from the registered representative as to whether the Central transactions in his customers' accounts over a three month period were solicited or unsolicited. The registered representative replied in writing that the transactions were unsolicited. This response was forwarded to Lindburg by Batal, with a note suggesting that it be shortened before forwarding to the NASD. Lindburg accepted the registered representative's statement that all the trades were unsolicited without performing any further inquiry. The volume of the trading (more than 100 trades) over a three-month period, however, necessitated further inquiry.

Four months later, in December, 1988, Lindburg learned from an annual compliance audit conducted that month that most of the order tickets in the Boston office did not indicate whether a transaction was solicited or unsolicited, and that the corresponding confirmation almost always carried the legend "unsolicited." The Compliance Department requested a response from the Branch Manager detailing steps taken to correct the deficiency. The Branch Manager, however, failed to comply with this request. Lindburg did not take any further action to determine whether the registered representatives in the Boston branch complied with firm policy requiring accurate completion of order tickets, and Lindburg thereby failed reasonably to supervise registered representatives, who were subject to his supervision.

Lindburg failed to respond reasonably to another apparent indication that the registered representative was engaged in improper conduct: the registered representative's repeated cancelling and rebilling of Central trades. On May 20, 1988, Lindburg attended a meeting with the registered representative, during which the registered representative's cancels and rebills were discussed. Some time later, the Margin Department Manager told Lindburg that the cancelling and rebilling activity by the registered representative was "unexplainable." Lindburg, however, failed to perform an inquiry reasonable in light of the history and circumstances.

In early October, 1988, based on the Margin Department Manager's recommendation, Lindburg notified the registered representative that he had to obtain the prior approval of the Margin Department for all margin purchases of Central (as well as two other stocks which were actively traded by the registered representative). In order to obtain approval, the account was required to have sufficient buying power to meet the margin requirement for the new purchase. The Margin Department Manager was responsible for enforcing the restriction by not approving any trade in which there was insufficient buying power to meet the margin requirement. For approximately one month, the Margin Department Manager enforced the procedure, and the trading which led to the procedure abated. Between November 25, 1988 and April 24, 1989, however, seventeen trades in two of the registered representative's customers' accounts generated margin calls in violation of this procedure. After the Margin Department Manager told Lindburg that the registered representative was not following the procedure, Lindburg failed either to perform a reasonable inquiry, or to establish any other procedure to determine whether the registered representative complied with firm margin policy, and Lindburg thereby failed reasonably to supervise the registered representative.

* * *

I. Conclusion

The Commission finds that First Albany, Batal and Lindburg failed reasonably to supervise the registered representative, who was subject to their supervision, with a view to preventing violations of Section 17(a) of the Securities Act, Section 10(b) of the Exchange Act and Rule 10b–5 thereunder, within the meaning of Sections 15(b)(4)(E) and 15(b)(6) of the Exchange Act.

———

Although *First Albany* held a chief compliance officer and general counsel of a broker-dealer liable for failure to supervise [for the first time], it was not explicit as to why such personnel were deemed to be supervisors. That is, under what facts and circumstances are compliance and legal personnel, especially a broker-dealer's chief legal counsel and/or chief compliance officer, held liable for failure to supervise under Sections 15(b)(4)(E) and 15(b)(6) of the Exchange Act. In *Gutfreund*, the SEC attempted to provide clarity as to when it would hold a broker-dealer's chief legal officer and/or chief compliance officer liable for failing to supervise a primary violator in the 21(a) report issued in conjunction with its decision.

In the Matter of John H. Gutfreund, Thomas W. Strauss, John W. Meriwether

Exchange Act Release No. 31554 (Dec. 3, 1992)

* * *

C. DONALD M. FEUERSTEIN[41]

Donald Feuerstein, Salomon's chief legal officer, was informed of the submission of the false bid by Paul Mozer in late April of 1991, at the same time other senior executives

———

41. See section III(A)(1)(d), for a full recitation of the facts of *Gutfreund*.

of Salomon learned of that act. Feuerstein was present at the meetings in late April at which the supervisors named as respondents in this proceeding discussed the matter. In his capacity as a legal adviser, Feuerstein did advise Strauss and Gutfreund that the submission of the bid was a criminal act and should be reported to the government, and he urged them on several occasions to proceed with disclosure when he learned that the report had not been made. However, Feuerstein did not direct that an inquiry be undertaken, and he did not recommend that appropriate procedures, reasonably designed to prevent and detect future misconduct, be instituted, or that other limitations be placed on Mozer's activities. Feuerstein also did not inform the Compliance Department, for which he was responsible as Salomon's chief legal officer, of the false bid.[42]

Unlike Gutfreund, Strauss and Meriwether, however, Feuerstein was not a direct supervisor of Mozer at the time he first learned of the false bid. Because we believe this is an appropriate opportunity to amplify our views on the supervisory responsibilities of legal and compliance officers in Feuerstein's position, we have not named him as a respondent in this proceeding. Instead, we are issuing this report of investigation concerning the responsibilities imposed by Section 15(b)(4)(E) of the Exchange Act under the circumstances of this case.

Employees of brokerage firms who have legal or compliance responsibilities do not become "supervisors" for purposes of Sections 15(b)(4)(E) and 15(b)(6) solely because they occupy those positions. Rather, determining if a particular person is a "supervisor" depends on whether, under the facts and circumstances of a particular case, that person has a requisite degree of responsibility, ability or authority to affect the conduct of the employee whose behavior is at issue.[43] Thus, persons occupying positions in the legal or compliance departments of broker-dealers have been found by the Commission to be "supervisors" for purposes of Sections 15(b)(4)(E) and 15(b)(6) under certain circumstances.

In this case, serious misconduct involving a senior official of a brokerage firm was brought to the attention of the firm's chief legal officer. That individual was informed of the misconduct by other members of senior management in order to obtain his advice and guidance, and to involve him as part of management's collective response to the problem. Moreover, in other instances of misconduct, that individual had directed the firm's response and had made recommendations concerning appropriate disciplinary action, and management had relied on him to perform those tasks.

Given the role and influence within the firm of a person in a position such as Feuerstein's and the factual circumstances of this case, such a person shares in the

---

42. In late May or early June, Feuerstein did speak with the head of the Compliance Department about the need to develop compliance procedures with respect to the firm's activities in government securities.

43. Although it did not represent an opinion of the Commission, the concurring opinion in *Arthur James Huff*, Exchange Act Release No. 29017, 1991 WL 296561 (Mar. 28, 1991), is consistent with this principle. The operative portion of that opinion, Part VI, explains that in each situation a person's actual responsibilities and authority, rather than, for example, his or her "line" or "non-line" status, will determine whether he or she is a "supervisor" for purposes of Sections 15(b)(4)(E) and (6).

responsibility to take appropriate action to respond to the misconduct. Under those circumstances, we believe that such a person becomes a "supervisor" for purposes of Sections 15(b)(4)(E) and 15(b)(6). As a result, that person is responsible, along with the other supervisors, for taking reasonable and appropriate action. It is not sufficient for one in such a position to be a mere bystander to the events that occurred.

Once a person in Feuerstein's position becomes involved in formulating management's response to the problem, he or she is obligated to take affirmative steps to ensure that appropriate action is taken to address the misconduct. For example, such a person could direct or monitor an investigation of the conduct at issue, make appropriate recommendations for limiting the activities of the employee or for the institution of appropriate procedures, reasonably designed to prevent and detect future misconduct, and verify that his or her recommendations, or acceptable alternatives, are implemented. If such a person takes appropriate steps but management fails to act and that person knows or has reason to know of that failure, he or she should consider what additional steps are appropriate to address the matter. These steps may include disclosure of the matter to the entity's board of directors, resignation from the firm, or disclosure to regulatory authorities.[44]

These responsibilities cannot be avoided simply because the person did not previously have direct supervisory responsibility for any of the activities of the employee. Once such a person has supervisory obligations by virtue of the circumstances of a particular situation, he must either discharge those responsibilities or know that others are taking appropriate action.

Notes and Questions

1. Although the SEC asserted in *Gutfreund* that employees of brokerage firms who have legal or compliance responsibilities do not become "supervisors" for purposes of Sections 15(b)(4)(E) and 15(b)(6) solely because they occupy those positions, this determination is made on a case-by-case basis using the standard that the chief legal officer is a supervisor if she becomes involved in management's collective response to the problem. Is this standard helpful? Does the standard allow determination of supervisor status *ex ante*?

2. Why did the SEC decide not to hold Feuerstein liable for failure to supervise, when it previously held Lindburg liable for failure to supervise in *First Albany* under Sections 15(b)(4)(E) and 15(b)(6)? Both were general counsels at their respective firms and presumably had the requisite degree of responsibility, ability, or authority to affect the conduct of the employee whose behavior was at issue. Does it matter that Feuerstein's job title was General Counsel, while Lindburg's title was General Counsel and Chief Compliance Officer? According to the McLucas article, the SEC used the

[Handwritten annotations: "→No" next to question 1; "↘No" below question 1; "→ Given the corporate structure Feuerstein was compliance for all & not really a supervisor" next to question 2; "↓ Partially" below]

---

44. Of course, in the case of an attorney, the applicable Code of Professional Responsibility and the Canons of Ethics may bear upon what course of conduct that individual may properly pursue.

Gutfreund decision " … to amplify [its] views on the supervisory responsibilities of legal and compliance officers in Feuerstein's position …" instead of naming him as a respondent. In *Gutfreund*, the SEC clearly states that " … Feuerstein was not a direct supervisor of Mozer at the time he first learned of the false bid …" However, once Feuerstein was " … informed of the misconduct by other members of senior management in order to obtain his advice and guidance …" and involved as part of management's collective response to the problem, he became a supervisor under sections 15(b)(4)(E) and 15(b)(6). The SEC also stated that Feuerstein had on previous occasions " … directed the firm's response and had made recommendations concerning appropriate disciplinary action, and management had relied on him to perform those tasks.… Given the role and influence within the firm of a person in a position such as Feuerstein's and the factual circumstances of this case, such a person shares in the responsibility to take appropriate action to respond to the misconduct. Under those circumstances, … such a person becomes a 'supervisor' for purposes of Sections 15(b)(4)(E) and 15(b)(6). As a result, that person is responsible, along with the other supervisors, for taking reasonable and appropriate action …" Is the SEC's reasoning helpful? Was this necessary after its *First Albany* decision?

↳ No   ↳ No

3. How does the standard enumerated in *Gutfreund* to determine when compliance and legal personnel may be held liable as supervisors under sections 15(b)(4)(E) and 15(b)(6) differ, if at all, from the standard enumerated in the concurring opinion in *Huff* regarding such personnel? In *Huff*, Commissioners Lochner and Shapiro stated that "[i]n light of the statutory language and history, and the Commission's prior decisions, we believe that a supervisor for purposes of Section 15(b)(4)(E) ought to be defined by the Commission as a person at a broker-dealer who has been given (and knows or reasonably should know he has been given) the authority and the responsibility for exercising such control over one or more specific activities of a supervised person which fall within the Commission's purview so that such person could take effective action to prevent a violation of the Commission's rules which involves such activity or activities by such supervised person." However, as noted earlier, the SEC has repudiated the view expressed in this concurrence. Moreover, Commissioner Schapiro, in a 1993 speech, basically disavowed her concurrence in *Huff* in which she concluded that Huff was not a supervisor for purposes of Sections 15(b)(4)(E). According to Commissioner Schapiro, " … my reference to these particular powers was never intended to indicate a de facto limiting principle, whereby an individual who did not possess the power to hire, fire, reward or punish, could insulate himself from the reach of the statute. Rather, the message of *Huff's* concurring opinion is that a non-line employee may be a supervisor of a particular employee when he or she has the authority and responsibility to exercise some degree of control over the salesperson's conduct, knows or should know that she is vested with this authority, and in fact could have influenced the violative behavior if she had exercised her control." Remarks of Commissioner Mary L. Schapiro, SIA Compliance and Legal Seminar, Mar. 24 1993.

Creates nondirect situations where they can become liable if they become involved.

4. In *Gary W. Chambers*, Exchange Act Release No. 27963, 1990 WL 311728 (Apr. 30, 1990), Chambers, a Senior Vice President of Compliance and Operations at a broker-dealer, was assigned specific supervisory responsibilities. Moreover, he was responsible for ensuring that his firm adopt and maintain adequate supervisory and compliance procedures. Although he drafted a compliance manual, he failed to establish a system designed to implement the procedures contained in the compliance manual. The SEC found that "Chambers compiled the FIS [his broker-dealer] Manual of Compliance Policies and Procedures (the "Manual"), which purported to establish supervisory and compliance policies and procedures for FIS and to institute a system for applying such procedures. In the administrative structure of FIS, the supervisory and compliance procedures contained in the Manual were not reasonably designed to prevent and detect ... fraudulent activities. Further, Chambers failed to discharge the duties and obligations incumbent upon him by reason of such procedures, and he knew or should have known that no system was implemented within FIS for the application of such procedures by other officers and managers of FIS. Within the administrative structure of FIS, Chambers had an obligation to supervise ... and Chambers' deficient supervision allowed ... violations ... by registered representatives of the federal securities laws." Is *Chambers* an easier case to make under Sections 15(b)(4)(E) and 15(b)(6) than *Huff*? Does the *Chambers* case indicate a continuation of the standards enumerated by the SEC for determining supervisory liability for legal and compliance personnel in *Huff* and *Gutfreund*?

[handwritten margin note: → No, since dealing with their own manual.]

[handwritten margin note: → Yes.]

   Most recently, the SEC's attempts to determine when legal and compliance personnel should be held liable for deficient supervision failed completely. The Commissioners were unable to agree whether the broker-dealer's chief legal officer should be held liable for failure reasonably to supervise under Sections 15(b)(4)(E) and 15(b)(6), thus rendering the ALJ's decision null and void. Although the ALJ determined that the chief legal officer was a supervisor, on appeal the SEC commissioners could not reach a decision. It is interesting to note that one of the dissenters in *Huff*, Mary Schapiro, was the Chairman of the SEC when the SEC Commissioners were unable to agree whether the general counsel was a supervisor in the following case.

In the Matter of Theodore W. Urban

Exchange Act Rel. No. ID-402 (Sept. 8, 2010)

INITIAL DECISION

On October 19, 2009, the Securities and Exchange Commission (Commission or SEC) issued an Order Instituting Proceedings (OIP) pursuant to Section 15(b) of the Securities Exchange Act of 1934 (Exchange Act) and Section 203(f) of the Investment Advisers Act of 1940 (Advisers Act). The OIP alleges that Theodore W. Urban (Urban), Ferris, Baker Watts, Inc.'s (FBW), General Counsel, Executive Vice President, and a voting member of the FBW Board of Directors (Board), the Executive Committee of the Board (Executive Committee), and the Credit Committee failed reasonably to supervise Stephen Glantz (Glantz), a broker, with a view to detecting and preventing Glantz's violations of Section 17(a) of the Securities Act of 1933 (Securities Act) and Section 10(b) of the Exchange Act and Rule 10b-5 thereunder.

Facts

Urban

Urban ... became General Counsel at Ferris & Company, Inc. (Ferris & Company) in 1984, where he was the firm's only lawyer, it had one compliance officer, and he shared a secretary with Ferris.

In 2003 through 2005, Urban headed three FBW departments: Compliance, Human Resources, and Internal Audit and reported to Roger Calvert (Calvert), CEO. The Legal and Compliance departments at FBW were viewed as one entity. Urban saw their functions as serving the regulatory compliance and legal needs of the firm and basically providing legal and compliance advice to anyone and everyone within the firm. Urban denies the allegations in the OIP.

FBW Board and Executive Committee

FBW, a registered broker-dealer and a registered investment adviser, specialized in the stocks of local community banks and other smaller companies' stocks.

In the period 2003-05, the Board was composed of George B. Ferris, Jr. (Ferris), Chairman, Calvert, Louis J. Akers (Akers), Wendy Gildemeister (Gildemeister), Sherry A. Gordon (Gordon), Craig Hartman (Hartman), Kevin Rast (Rast), Steven L. Shea (Shea), Adrian Teel (Teel), Urban, and Gail Winslow (Winslow), and it met six times a year. Two retail brokers rotated on the Board for periods of time. The Executive Committee was everyone except Gildemeister, Teel, Winslow, and the retail brokers. The Executive Committee and the Board considered policy issues; they did not consider matters involving problems with retail brokers, which they expected Retail Sales & Service (Retail Sales) and Compliance to resolve.... Problems with brokers did not come before the Board because Compliance and the department in which there was an issue handled specific personnel issues. No Board member who testified could recall the Board ever considering an issue of broker misconduct, except where an arbitration decision or settlement cost FBW money.... The Board did not consider any issue without Calvert's approval, and, if an issue got to the Board, people looked to Calvert for how they should vote.

During this same period, FBW had Written Supervisory Procedures in place, and the Board regularly received information on large margin accounts that always included several of Glantz's customers, and it approved salary advances for Glantz.

The Executive Committee and the Board learned of investigations by the Commission and the Justice Department and a lawsuit concerning Glantz's activities in October 2006.

FBW and Glantz

Calvert was President and CEO of FBW from 2003 through 2005, but Akers, head of Retail Sales, was the most powerful person at the firm. Calvert gave Akers autonomy and deferred to him on issues involving Retail Sales. One Board member could not recall Calvert ever overruling Akers. Akers had been with FBW since 1989, but was forced to step down as CEO, in December 2001, when the firm learned of his significant gambling debts and tax problems. FBW loaned Akers $1.3 million and appointed him Vice Chairman of the Board and head of Retail Sales.

Akers was a big physical presence, a domineering personality, who was engaging to some and a bully to others. Akers was aggressive towards everyone, he yelled at people, and he was always determined that his positions prevailed. Akers's relationship with Patricia Centeno (Centeno), Chief Compliance Officer and Compliance Director in the period January 1, 2003, until March 30, 2004, was contentious and adversarial. Centeno testified of multiple incidents in which Akers thwarted her compliance efforts. In an incident that occurred after she left FBW, but which supports her position, Akers described the Compliance Director as a member of Hitler's Third Reich and a Compliance branch examiner as Frankenstein's lab assistant, Igor, at a fairly large meeting of branch managers in 2005. Akers also joked that the good news was that FBW sold Compliance to Merrill Lynch. Akers's disparaging, unsupportive views of Compliance were well known among his subordinates. Calvert heard about Akers's comments but took no action.

Akers and Patrick Vaughan (Vaughan), Assistant Head of Retail Sales, recruited Glantz to FBW in 2002.[45] Glantz began working at FBW's Beachwood, Ohio, office (Beachwood) in January 2003. On December 31, 2002, his official start date, Glantz received an upfront $800,000 signing bonus, which was considered high, embodied in a promissory note forgivable over a five-year period negotiated by Akers and Vaughan. Calvert testified he did not remember hearing of Glantz before January 2003; however, Calvert had dinner in Baltimore with Glantz, Vaughan, and DePalma, a FBW broker who recommended that FBW hire Glantz, on May 31, 2002.

Akers had grown the retail operation substantially and, in 2003-05, Retail Sales accounted for 70 to 75% of FBW revenues. Akers's power derived, in part, from the fear of some that he would take the big-producing brokers with him if he left the firm, and he supervised branch managers, branch management, and branch personnel. Glantz knew that Akers liked his high production and the syndicate business he was bringing to FBW, and he thought Akers liked him personally. Glantz spoke with Akers at least once a week. They had lunch or dinner on occasion, and Mrs. Akers, a real estate agent, helped him buy a home.

The unanimous evidence is that Akers had unquestioned overall authority over Retail Sales, he did not tolerate interference by anyone, even Calvert, and it was the

---

45. According to Glantz, he had made $500,000 his last year at Advest, but he switched firms because he had terrible gambling and drug habits and needed money. The record does not indicate how Glantz was able to meet FBW's requirement that new employees pass a drug test. Glantz testified that he used cocaine, alcohol, and opiates (Percocet, Vicodin, and Xanax) daily at times while employed at FBW, and he was diagnosed as bipolar in 2006. Urban had no knowledge of Glantz's drug use. Glantz credited his recovery to a nine-month residential drug treatment program offered by the Federal Bureau of Prisons.

responsibility of Retail Sales to supervise and to address problems with retail brokers. Gordon, who worked for Akers, testified to an experience where she went to discuss something with Calvert, who specified a day when Akers was supposed to be at the Hunt Valley branch office (Hunt Valley). However, Akers was in the Baltimore office (Baltimore), and Calvert was very nervous because Akers was in Urban's office and could observe Gordon talking with Calvert in Calvert's office. Gordon knew Calvert was concerned because Akers would be upset if he thought Calvert was interfering with a Retail Sales employee. Calvert told Gordon that their conversation never happened. On another occasion, Calvert told Gordon never to bring anything to the Board that did not have Akers's approval.

Akers and Vaughan considered Glantz a valuable broker because he was a top revenue producer, he could sell new issues, and he was a source of stock sold by syndicates for which there was significant broker demand. In the year ended December 31, 2003, Glantz ranked number seven in production among 252 FBW sales people. For FBW's fiscal year that ended February 29, 2004, Glantz was ranked number six. In the fiscal year that ended February 28, 2005, he ranked number two.

FBW Committees

FBW had several significant committees. The Cost Control Committee, composed of Ferris, Calvert, Akers, and Hartman, reviewed the firm's operational and administrative costs. Ferris did not like the firm to spend money. If Ferris saw a cost in a monthly management report that he thought was high, Calvert, through the Cost Control Committee, would get an explanation from the manager. In mid-2002, shortly before the relevant period, the Cost Control Committee required Urban to justify the staffing costs of the Legal and Compliance Departments.

The Credit & Risk Committee (Credit Committee) consisted of Calvert, Hartman, Urban, and Gildemeister. In 2003 and part of 2004, everyone on the Credit Committee was also on the Board, and everyone but Gildemeister was also on the Executive Committee. Tomiko Turpin (Turpin), Credit Risk Manager, took minutes until she left around June February 2004. Charles W. McNeilly (McNeilly) took over as Credit Risk Manager in January and became a member of the Credit Committee. Everyone on the Credit Committee, which dealt mainly with unusual situations involving the extension of margin credit, reported to Calvert. McNeilly reported to Urban and Hartman, and he worked on special projects for Calvert with whom he talked more or less daily.

The Credit Committee acted as a group. Calvert considered Urban the focal point of Credit Committee communications and Urban was the person who handled communications with outside parties. McNeilly provided the Credit Committee members on a regular basis, perhaps weekly, statements that showed, among other things, accounts in which the firm had margin exposure, a list of accounts of concern, and securities with large concentrations on margin. Glantz's accounts were consistently among the firm's largest margin debits.

The Del Buono Memo

In April or May 2003, Centeno told Urban that she and Sandra A. Del Buono (Del Buono), the person in Compliance assigned to Beachwood, had concerns about Glantz's supervision, and they were looking at trading in Innotrac, particularly by the IPOF Fund, and use of margin by Glantz's customers. Urban directed her to keep gathering information and to consolidate their thoughts for discussion for Credit Committee consideration.

On May 28, 2003, the Credit Committee considered a May 23, 2003, memorandum, "Trading Activity in Innotrac Corp. (INOC), IPOF Fund Account," that Centeno had Del Buono send to her, Urban, and Calvert, with copies to Gildemeister, Hartman, Turpin, Rick Leatherbarrow (Leatherbarrow), Sharon Pennington (Pennington), and Vaughan (Del Buono Memo). The Del Buono Memo was an effort by Centeno to have the Credit Committee consider the IPOF Fund account. She addressed the Del Buono Memo to Calvert and other senior members of the firm so they could not claim later that they were not aware of Glantz and the IPOF Fund situation.

The Del Buono Memo described concerns about the trading activity and use of margin in the IPOF Fund account, the status of the Innotrac common stock, and Glantz's trading Innotrac stock in the account. It noted that FBW customers owned approximately 40% of Innotrac's total float and 19% of the outstanding shares. The Del Buono Memo showed at least seven Glantz customer accounts that had very large concentrations of Innotrac stock. The accounts of some respected FBW brokers, including Usry and Dyer held Innotrac, but no account came close to the amount of Innotrac held in the IPOF Fund. Innotrac's 52-week low per share price was $1.50 on October 11, 2002, and the 52-week high was $6.65 on May 6, 2003. Innotrac's price rose in 2003.

The Del Buono Memo stated that the IPOF Fund account had a $9.381 million margin debit balance, which continued to increase while the account purchased the stock of Innotrac and that the IPOF Fund qualified as a control person of Innotrac. It noted that Vaughan denied Glantz's representation that he had discussed the IPOF Fund in detail with Vaughan. In Centeno's view, the IPOF Fund was controlling the price of Innotrac stock, and its accumulation of shares in small lots almost daily resulted in raising the price. The Del Buono Memo advised that: "The Compliance Department believes that the Firm needs to address the potential issues and arrive at some decisions regarding the concerns noted," and "[w]ithout question, there is and has been a breakdown is [sic] the supervisory responsibilities and who shares or owns supervisory responsibility over the activity in the [IPOF Fund] account and Mr. Glantz."

As a result of the Del Buono Memo, FBW suspended purchases of Innotrac by the IPOF Fund and it placed the Regulation T (Reg.-T) requirement at 60% and a maintenance requirement of 60% on Innotrac in the IPOF Fund account.

Urban believed that the Credit Committee directed him to: (1) address the IPOF Fund's filing requirements, and (2) speak with Retail Sales and Usry about Glantz's supervision and his accounts. Following the Credit Committee meeting, Urban accomplished getting the IPOF Fund and Dadante to make the necessary Schedule 13G and Form 3 filings, he confirmed with Wasserman that the IPOF Fund was not a control person of Innotrac, and that it was an Ohio limited partnership. In June through August 2005, Urban received communications from Wasserman about a visit to Innotrac headquarters and conversations with the company's officers and counsel from a respected Atlanta firm that indicated positive financial results and the likelihood that Innotrac would be capable of doing an underwriting.

Within a week or so of the Credit Committee's consideration of the Del Buono Memo, Urban, Akers, Vaughan, Centeno, and Del Buono had a conference call to discuss Centeno's and Del Buono's concerns. Urban's recollection is that Akers and Vaughan agreed to talk to Weaver in Beachwood about Glantz's supervision, and Akers challenged the Del Buono Memo's assertion that the IPOF Fund did not hold quality stocks. Centeno's recollection is that Akers attacked the memorandum's credibility, yelled and screamed, and was abusive primarily to Urban.

As further follow-up, Urban spoke with Weaver, and he met with Glantz in Baltimore on June 4, 2003, at which time they discussed the IPOF Fund account reporting requirements, the Vinocur account, and supervision. Also on June 4, 2003, Urban sent an email to Vaughan, noting his communication with Weaver and discussion with Glantz, and requesting that Akers and/or Vaughan speak with him before their dinner with Glantz the next day. Urban told Centeno that Calvert understood everything and was "on board," and he consistently directed her to monitor the situation and to bring her findings to him.

On June 9, 2003, Urban traveled to Ohio and met with Glantz and Weaver separately. Those discussions clarified that Weaver was supposed to supervise the accounts for which Glantz used the account numbers BW99 and BWA4 (Beachwood), and Usry was to supervise those Glantz accounts with the IS34 number (Institutional Sales). Urban had a conversation with Usry in which he acknowledged supervision of Glantz's practices while he was on the Institutional Sales desk.

The 2003 Annual Branch Compliance Inspection for Beachwood (Compliance Inspection) evidenced concern, "[a]s noted in an earlier memorandum," that the branch manager may not be able to adequately supervise Glantz who split his time between Retail Sales in Beachwood and Institutional Sales in Baltimore.

On August 28, 2003, Gildemeister informed the Credit Committee by email that the IPOF Fund had a margin debit of almost $9 million, that Dadante had opened another partnership account in the name of GSGI, that accounts at FBW held over 25% of the outstanding shares of Innotrac, and that seven Glantz accounts held Innotrac on margin. On Aug 20, 2003, the IPOF Fund had a total value of $26.1 million, of which $16.7 million was concentrated in Innotrac, and a margin balance of $10.3 million. The value of assets other than Innotrac was $9.4 million, which was insufficient to cover the margin debit in violation of the Credit Committee's conditions. If it had become necessary to sell the Innotrac stock to satisfy a margin call, it would likely have destroyed the value of the stock. The Orchen Pension Plan account had Innotrac as 92% of its holdings and had a 40% maintenance requirement on the stock following firm policy.

Glantz had signed off on the GSGI account for Dadante to circumvent the restriction not to buy any more Innotrac in the IPOF Fund account. Trades occurred in the GSGI account before Glantz signed the new account form and Weaver signed the client application, and manipulation, by way of wash sales, occurred in the account. Urban replied to Gildemeister's email almost immediately, noting that he had preliminary discussions with Calvert and that the Credit Committee would meet that day. The Credit Committee put in an alternative test to address the concentration of Innotrac in the IPOF Fund account, the GSGI account was closed, and Gildemeister alerted Operations to watch for Dadante's name on account forms. According to Urban, the Credit Committee required that the value of non-Innotrac securities and 10% of the market value of Innotrac stock in the IPOF Fund account had to be equal to or greater than the margin debit. Also, FBW's Margin Department was to monitor the margin maintenance requirements.

On September 4, 2003, Urban traveled to Hunt Valley to discuss with Akers, Vaughan, and Glantz the GSGI incident, margin, and possible manipulative trading in the IPOF Fund account, concentrations of Innotrac in other accounts, and whether Innotrac stock had value. Urban wanted to cut off purchases of Innotrac, but Akers noted the amount of business that the IPOF Fund generated and, to keep the account happy, suggested allowing cash purchases of Innotrac. According to Urban, Vaughan said that someone needed to call Vinocur and get some level of assurance. Akers and Vaughan assured Urban that they would "get on Mr. Weaver to exercise his supervisory responsibilities at the branch level," and he believed they also told him that Glantz would be moving to Baltimore, where William Spencer (Spencer), an effective manager, was the branch manager.

In September 2003, the Credit Committee increased the margin requirement on the IPOF Fund to 60% on Innotrac stock and it also increased the margin requirement to 40% on any account that held Innotrac stock.

Credit Committee Reaction to the IPOF Fund Owning More Innotrac Stock

On January 22, 2004, Centeno informed Urban that the IPOF Fund owned 26.37% of Innotrac's stock and that Innotrac had changed its bylaws to allow the IPOF Fund to acquire up to 40% of Innotrac stock. On January 29, 2004, Del Buono forwarded to Centeno and Urban an email from Leatherbarrow, titled "IPOF & the emperor's new clothes," characterizing the IPOF Fund as a ticking time bomb and noting that, if people realized that Innotrac stock was worthless, the value of the other securities in the IPOF Fund account would likely be diminished by over a half a million dollars. Leatherbarrow testified that he meant if Innotrac became worthless; he did not believe Innotrac stock was worthless. Leatherbarrow believed that the IPOF Fund's trading activity was driving the price of Innotrac. Centeno feared that the margin balance in the IPOF Fund would leave FBW with an unsecured debt. She sensed that Urban was becoming more concerned but he continued to believe that FBW had the right controls in place.

Urban was surprised and dismayed by the information in the January emails, particularly that the IPOF Fund's margin debit had grown to above $16 million, and he immediately went into Calvert's office and found that Calvert did not know the information either. The Margin group in the Operations Department had failed to apply the restrictions that the Credit Committee had applied to the account in September 2003.

On February 4, 2004, Urban sent an email, requesting that the Credit Committee meet the following day to revisit the IPOF Fund account, which it had not considered since September 2003. Attached to the email was a memorandum, with a copy to Vaughan, informing them that Innotrac had changed certain of its corporate provisions and now the IPOF Fund could acquire up to 40% of Innotrac shares and that, as of that date, the IPOF Fund had a margin debit of over $18 million and an account value of over $47 million, including Innotrac shares valued at over $35 million.[46] Urban urged the Credit Committee to "revisit this account immediately" because the restrictions imposed on purchases of Innotrac were ineffective, other holdings in the account were not of high quality and some were illiquid, FBW did not have much information about the account's exit strategy from Innotrac or the creditworthiness of the IPOF Fund except for its FBW holdings. Urban noted that other Glantz accounts were substantial holders of Innotrac and that he concluded there "continues to be a lack of clear definition as to who has day-to-day supervisory responsibility" for Glantz.

On February 4, 2004, Calvert, in a memorandum, informed Belgrade of additional restrictions on trading in Innotrac in the IPOF Fund. Shea did note that the following occurred that when Belgrade showed him Calvert's memorandum: "this was a disaster waiting to happen but it's not going to come back on us. Shea told Belgrade to go back and look at his paycheck, that Belgrade was getting paid too much money to worry about things like this." Shea never disclosed any concerns about the IPOF Fund to Urban.

The Credit Committee met on February 5, 2004, at which time it prohibited the IPOF Fund from purchasing Innotrac and adopted five other points set out in a memorandum Urban drafted. When Urban wrote the February 4, 2004, memorandum, he became aware that the assurances he received from Akers, Vaughan, and Weaver, that Retail Sales would address concerns about Glantz's supervision had not happened and Glantz had not transferred to Baltimore where he would be supervised by Spencer.

Calvert agreed that Urban's February 4, 2004, memorandum to the Credit Committee was the second time in less than twelve months that he was informed in writing that there were supervisory responsibility issues related to Glantz. Calvert and Urban had regular conversations on a variety of issues. Calvert testified that Urban never came to

---

46. Urban furnished Calvert with material on the IPOF Fund account in advance of the meeting. On a daily basis, in the period November 3, 2003, through February 3, 2004, the IPOF Fund owned an average of 34.59% of the shares of Innotrac in the market. Before the Credit Committee meeting, Urban informed Glantz in writing that, per their discussion, Glantz would not accept any additional orders for Innotrac effective February 5, 2004, until the Credit Committee reviewed the IPOF Fund account.

him on the issue of Glantz's supervision. "It was never on one of my pending sheets. It was never something that I viewed as my responsibility to be followed up on."

Dealings with Glantz in 2004

On November 12, 2004, Sraver and Silbert wrote a thirteen-page memorandum to Urban and Haas to establish concerns about Glantz's trading. For example, Vinocur was a widow/homemaker with three dependents and annual income of less than $200,000. She was an unsophisticated investor with an account balance of $2.6 million and a margin balance of $1.5 million. Her account was classified as an institutional account, and nineteen trades occurred in the account in September 2004. The memorandum raised concerns about the unsolicited nature of the trades, the amount of the commissions, the appropriateness of the trades given the investment objectives in the Vinocur account and similar questions about trading in twelve other Glantz accounts. The memorandum questioned cross-selling 50,000 shares of Innotrac stock among Glantz's accounts in September 2004, which could have indicated an attempt to manipulate the stock price. The memorandum states:

> Based on our conversation with William Spencer, Horace Usry and Mark Weaver, and review of supervisory records and reports, it is our impression that the appropriate supervisory oversight is currently not in place for Mr. Glantz.

On November 30, 2004, Urban met with Silbert, Sraver, and Haas to discuss the November 12 memorandum. Urban was very concerned. Glantz was the primary focus of the meeting. Sraver wrote a memorandum, dated December 7, 2004, to Spencer, memorializing what Urban wanted conveyed to Spencer on supervising Glantz. The memorandum, which was never sent, would have required the Vinocur and Ziemba & Thatcher to be moved to strictly Retail Sales, and for Spencer to talk to Vinocur without Glantz present, and to sit with Glantz weekly to discuss his business. Urban thought that Glantz had new Baltimore retail numbers and that Spencer had been reviewing activity in Glantz's accounts since late February or March 2004. Usry was to be responsible for only truly institutional accounts.

Urban testified that his recollection is the memorandum was not sent to Spencer because Silbert learned of some intervening trades that concerned him in early December 2004. In fact, Silbert learned on December 3, 2004, that Glantz purchased 77,000 shares of Innotrac for the Gildenhorn Trust (Gildenhorn was Glantz's uncle), Vinocur, and Ziemba & Thatcher accounts, and that the IPOF Fund sold Innotrac shares on the same day. Silbert informed Urban, who directed him to get an explanation. Silbert and Haas met with Glantz on December 10, 2004. Glantz lied and told Urban he did not know who at Advest was arranging certain trades.[47] Urban met with Boo, Leatherbarrow, and possibly Haas about Glantz's purchases and was dis-

---

47. Glantz testified that, in fact, he had worked out the trades with Dadante and Salem so that Dadante could meet a margin call from Advest and that he had told this to Akers and Vaughan. They told him not to do it again and that they would take care of it. Glantz asked Akers to get Compliance

tressed when Leatherbarrow contradicted Glantz's explanation for the purchases.[48] Urban also directed Haas and Silbert to call the three clients as soon as possible and find out what they knew of the transactions. Urban testified that he told Calvert about the trades and asked that he not inform Akers because Compliance was going to communicate directly with customers.

At Urban's direction, Silbert called Glantz's customers—Gildenhorn, Vinocur, and Ziemba & Thatcher—in mid-December 2004. The clients told Silbert they knew nothing about the recent trades in their accounts, but they were not surprised because they entrusted their accounts to Glantz. Two of the clients knew nothing about margin and the third said he had been trying to get Glantz to reduce the size of the margin debit. Urban was surprised, disappointed, and dumbfounded that Weaver had not communicated with these retail customers. Glantz recalled Urban telling him that the IPOF Fund could not continue to sell to Glantz's other clients at FBW and that FBW would have to file a Form RE-3 to disclose Glantz's unauthorized trading.

Special Supervision

Urban recalled meeting with Akers, Vaughan, and Haas in his office on December 14, 2004, to discuss Glantz's future at FBW, but Haas recalled that the meeting occurred on December 16. At the meeting, Urban and Haas recommended that Glantz be terminated. Akers was vehemently opposed and screamed at Urban in a loud, angry manner, complaining about the fact that Silbert had contacted Glantz's customers and criticizing Silbert's description of those conversations as inaccurate. Akers accused Compliance of going on a witch-hunt to cause harm to Glantz and called one of the clients to confirm. Akers questioned Urban for wanting to drive a good producer out of the firm. Urban got visibly angry at Akers's verbal attack and shouted in defense of Compliance. The meeting was sufficiently loud that someone from several offices away came and shut the door. Urban's recollection is that Akers and Vaughan, who supported Akers, left the meeting with the matter unresolved.

The following day, December 15, 2004, Urban wrote Akers and Vaughan a memorandum, recommending that they terminate Glantz immediately. Urban's memorandum noted that Glantz's business was heavily concentrated in a limited number of accounts that carry significant margin debits and that a large percentage of his business involved short-term holdings typically with little customer benefit but sig-

---

and Silbert "off his back," which Glantz testified Akers did for a while. Akers and Vaughan did not share Glantz's disclosure with Urban.

48. Later, on April 4, 2005, when the IPOF Fund made a Form 4 filing, Leatherbarrow wrote Urban an email, confirming that the IPOF Fund account at Advest sold Innotrac to several of Glantz's clients in December 2004. Urban directed Leatherbarrow to examine whether there was a correlation between activity in the IPOF Fund accounts at other places and the IPOF Fund at FBW, but none was found. Urban had asked Glantz in December if he knew who at Advest originated the sales, but Glantz continued to insist that he did not know.

nificant commissions. It stated that, as they were aware, Glantz had essentially been unsupervised for the entire two years he was with FBW.

Urban's memorandum detailed the Innotrac purchases from Advest that Glantz made for the accounts of Gildenhorn, Vinocur, and Ziemba & Thatcher and that these customers did not initiate the purchases, although FBW had no written authorization for trading by Glantz. It noted that trading in the accounts exposed Glantz and FBW to potential claims of churning. The memorandum stated that Glantz had "no credibility and does not appear to deserve any." In response to arguments that Akers made at the meeting on December 14, Urban stated that he had agreed to consider retaining Glantz based on concerns that FBW could better manage issues, particularly concerns about Innotrac stock if Glantz remained with FBW, but that Urban had changed his mind because: (1) Glantz could not be trusted; (2) the Innotrac situation was beyond Glantz's control; and (3) Glantz had committed reportable offenses so it was better for FBW to take the strongest possible initiative at the present time.

Urban's recollection is that Akers came to his office on December 16 or 17, 2004, for a second, shorter, and uncontentious discussion. Akers made clear that he would not terminate Glantz and he appealed for a different resolution. Urban testified that he still believed termination was appropriate, but Akers insisted on special supervision and, if Akers would not accept his advice, special supervision was probably the next best thing. Urban concluded that there was a reasonable chance that Akers's special supervision of Glantz would succeed because his experience was that Akers accomplished those Compliance actions with which he agreed. Akers had a redemptive trait based on his personal experience, and he took brokers with personal problems under his wing to help them with some success. Akers acknowledged to Urban that other people had not paid sufficient attention to Glantz, but that he would make it happen, and Urban believed him.

Glantz and Akers signed a Special Supervision Memorandum, dated and effective on January 11, 2005, that warned failure to conform would result in immediate termination....

Someone in Akers's management position did not usually assume the labor-intensive responsibilities of special supervision of a broker. Glantz testified that Akers told him to calm down and let things blow over and to comply with the special supervision requirements.

Glantz began working at Hunt Valley, where Akers had his main office, under Akers's supervision in January 2005, ... After he was on special supervision, many of Glantz's accounts continued to appear on the Activity Report as aggressively trading speculative stocks in accounts that had growth and income investment objectives.... Brent did not do anything with the information because Akers told him he was supervising Glantz.

On February 4, 2005, in an email to Akers with a copy to Haas, Glantz claimed he had satisfied all thirteen conditions of special supervision, and that, "PER [AKERS] AND T. URBAN OK," will work at Hunt Valley, Beachwood, or his laptop. Glantz claimed that Urban gave him permission to work at Beachwood while visiting his children, but Urban testified he never approved Glantz working out of Beachwood when he was on special supervision. On November 2, 2005, Haas told Weaver that Glantz was returning to Beachwood and that Weaver would take over special supervision from Akers, but Glantz never returned to Beachwood.

On June 29, 2005, Boo [head of NASDAQ trading and market making for FBW] wrote Urban about an unusual purchase by Dadante of Innotrac stock in the IPOF Fund and stated that "the customer's approach to this order raises warning flags that could point to attempted price manipulation." Leatherbarrow was concerned about manipulation; Urban said he needed to think about it, but that he would give Boo directions before leaving for vacation. Neither Boo nor Leatherbarrow could recall any follow up by Urban. In the summer of 2005, Urban asked Boo to begin selling Innotrac in a way that would not impact the market price.

On June 30, 2005, Urban sent Calvert a copy of the Annual Compliance Report (Compliance Report) mandated by the NYSE and NASD that Compliance prepared and Urban reviewed and signed. Calvert signed the Annual Compliance and Supervision Certification (CEO Compliance Certification) required by NASD Rule 3013(b) that basically stated that FBW had processes in place to reasonably meet NASD and Municipal Securities Rulemaking Board rules and federal securities laws and regulations, and attached the Compliance Report. The Compliance Report has a section on supervision that does not mention any specific problems with brokers.

On August 29, 2005, Calvert asked Urban the status of Glantz's supervision. On November 16, 2005, Calvert informed Hartman that Akers had authority to grant Glantz a second $200,000 advance against salary, but, in the future, Calvert did not want new advances until old advances had been paid ...

On December 8, 2005, Glantz submitted his resignation to FBW. An agreement between FBW and Glantz, negotiated by Wasserman representing Glantz and Urban representing FBW, provided that FBW would submit a "clean" U-5 form, indicating that Glantz's departure from FBW was without cause, without any reasons stated, and no derogatory information. Glantz agreed to pay FBW $430,000 owed on his forgivable loans and other obligations, cooperate on customer claims, and give an exit interview. Glantz needed a clean Form U-5 to receive a signing bonus from another firm. Glantz left FBW at the end of 2005 and joined Sanders, Morris, Harris.

As the result of law suits initiated after Glantz left FBW, FBW paid $7.2 million to the receiver of the IPOF Fund and paid about $1.285 million to Glantz's customers.

Steering Committee

The Steering Committee's purpose was to examine the facts surrounding Glantz's activities as a rogue broker and make recommendations to the Board, and to manage the Justice Department and Commission investigations.

According to Teel, the Steering Committee had two bases for recommending that the Board place Urban on paid administrative leave and later negotiate a termination agreement consisting of a resignation and a severance package with Urban. It found that Urban could be potentially culpable because he did not bring to the Board issues concerning Glantz, including the IPOF Fund or Innotrac stock. Second, Calvert lacked confidence in Urban. Calvert was angry that he signed the CEO Compliance Certification that included a Compliance Report which did not mention the IPOF Fund. Urban, however, believed, based on NASD pronouncements and conversations with colleagues, that the CEO Compliance Certification was to assure regulators that the firm had policies and procedures in place, and the Compliance Report was not to document instances where the policies and procedures did, or did not, work.

Urban's Evidence

The overwhelming evidence is that Urban was not responsible and had no authority for hiring, assessing performance, assigning activities, promoting, or terminating employment of anyone, outside of the people in the departments he directly supervised. FBW required that Compliance check on new registered representatives with regulatory issues in their background, and Compliance reviewed Glantz's record because it had some items. Urban signed off on hiring Glantz because his Form U-4 contained nothing unusual. Glantz's Central Registration Depository record showed ten items related to the sale of limited partnerships in the 1980s, bankruptcy in 1992— divorce related, and one non-material item. Glantz had no problems while employed at Advest, his most recent employer, which was considered a good firm. Outside of a few items, such as getting an account "locked down" because of ongoing illegal activities or not allowing a person with lots of items on his or her CRD to be hired, Compliance offered recommendations to FBW's business entities.

Urban did not believe he was Glantz's supervisor or that he had authority to hire, fire, discipline, or direct the conduct of Retail Sales personnel without the concurrence of Akers or someone in Retail Sales management. For example, Urban testified, "[I]f there was an issue that compliance came to me saying that they had been advising [Retail Sales] to do A, B or C and their advice wasn't being followed, if I spoke with [Akers], there was a greater chance that the advice would be followed." Urban testified that Compliance could recommend that a broker be placed on special supervision but someone had to agree to exercise special supervision.

FBW's Written Supervisory Procedures, show Urban as the supervisor of "All Employees;" however, Centeno, who drafted the procedures, testified that "[a]ll employees indicated that Ted was in charge of providing legal advice to all employees, not that he supervised all employees." Moreover, a PowerPoint presentation dated November 8, 2005, states that the Legal and Compliance Department "*[r]ecommends* appropriate remedial action whenever deviations from the policies and procedures are detected" (emphasis added).

Throughout the 2003-05 period, the FBW Legal and Compliance functions were lightly staffed. When FBW had about 700 employees and about 275 brokers, the Legal Department had two lawyers: Urban and Dana Gloor, and Compliance had about seven or eight people.

* * *

There is no dispute that Urban was very busy and had limited staff. The minutes of the Executive Board meeting on September 12, 2005, show Urban reporting on five of ten topics.

At the Division's direction, FBW calculated that, for fiscal years 2003 through 2005, Urban received $13,706.82 as a bonus from the revenue pool created by Glantz's activities at FBW. The estimate is a calculation from various sources reflecting Glantz's earnings that went into a bonus pool from which Urban derived some benefit. However, the calculation is suspect because the bonus pool component, "Innotrac Commission Revenues," includes commissions earned by FBW brokers in addition to Glantz, and "Innotrac Trading Revenues" could include amounts from non-FBW customers.

Arguments of the Parties

The Division argues that it has shown by a preponderance of the evidence that Glantz violated the antifraud provisions of the federal securities laws, and that Urban had supervisory responsibility over Glantz and failed reasonably to supervise him with a view to preventing those violations. The Division notes that in *Gutfreund*, the CLO was not a line supervisor and others shared supervisory responsibility; still, he was a supervisor because he had the requisite degree of responsibility, ability, or authority to affect the person's conduct when senior management informed him of the misconduct to obtain his advice and guidance and to involve him as part of management's collective response to the problem. The Division notes that, in *Kirk Montgomery*, 55 S.E.C. 485, 500 (2001), the Commission declared a chief compliance officer a supervisor because it was sufficient if the person plays a significant, even if shared, role in the firm's supervisory structure and that his authority was subject to countermand at a higher level. The Division maintains that there is a long line of cases in which individuals with less authority than Urban have been found to have failed to supervise.

A major thrust of the Division's case is that Urban comes within the scope of Section 15(b) of the Exchange Act and Section 203(f) of the Advisers Act because he failed to respond reasonably to red flags that Glantz's conduct was illegal. It is the Division's position, citing *Gutfreund*, that once Urban became involved in addressing the red flags, he was obligated to respond vigorously and that he failed to do so.

The Division contends that Urban was required to take concerns about Glantz's conduct to FBW's Board or Executive Committee, and, if they did not act, he was required to resign and report the matter to regulatory authorities. It believes that Urban acted recklessly in ignoring repeated red flags and in missing opportunities to detect and prevent Glantz's fraud and significant investor losses. It maintains that Urban's supervisory failures were egregious and recurrent and occurred over a period of nearly three years.

Urban argues that Glantz was not subject to his supervision, his actions were reasonable under the circumstances, and the Division is not entitled to the relief it seeks. Urban maintains that the following actions he took were reasonably designed to prevent Glantz's illegal conduct: encouraging Compliance to inquire into the IPOF Fund and ensuring that the Credit Committee considered the IPOF Fund; recommending that the Credit Committee restrict credit to the IPOF Fund and that the IPOF Fund make required Commission filings; urging increased vigilance of Glantz by Retail Sales and other business managers; instructing Compliance to perform additional diligence on Glantz; advocating strongly for Glantz's termination and causing Compliance to make a NYSE filing as to Glantz; and advocating for strict terms of special supervision after senior business managers refused to terminate Glantz.

Urban contends that a failure to supervise cannot be found where his reasonable actions were frustrated by Glantz's consistent lies, the failure of FBW business executives to fulfill their responsibilities, and Akers's and Vaughan's refusal to accept his advice, including terminating Glantz.

Conclusions

Urban was credible.

Based on my observations of Urban's demeanor during his testimony and comparing his responses with other evidence in the record, I judge him to be honest and credible. Not one witness had concerns about his honesty, and persons, who worked with him for long periods of time both at FBW and in a civic endeavor with which he was involved for many years, were unanimous on his honesty and high ethical standards. Centeno, who worked very closely with Urban for ten years and who strongly disagreed with him at times, respects him and considers him absolutely honest and ethical. The Division's expert noted, "[l]iterally every witness that I heard that testified talked about [Urban's] integrity and his desire to do the right thing. I never heard anybody suggest anything to the contrary."

Allegation—Urban failed reasonably to supervise Glantz with a view to detecting and preventing Glantz's alleged violations of Section 17(a) of the Securities Act and Section 10(b) of the Exchange Act and Exchange Act Rule 10b-5.

Exchange Act Section 15(b)(6)(A)(i), in conjunction with Section 15(b)(4)(E), authorizes the Commission, if it is in the public interest, to censure, place limitations on the activities or functions, suspend for a period not to exceed twelve months, or bar from association with a broker or dealer, or from participating in an offering of penny stock, a person associated with a broker or dealer who "has failed reasonably to supervise, with a view to preventing violations of the provisions of such statute, rules, and regulations, another person who commits such a violation, if such other person is subject to his supervision."

No person is deemed to have failed reasonably to supervise any other person if:

(i) there have been established procedures, and a system for applying such procedures, which would reasonably be expected to prevent and detect, insofar as practicable, any such violation by such other person, and

(ii) such person has reasonably discharged the duties and obligations incumbent upon him by reason of such procedures and system without reasonable cause to believe such procedures and system were not being complied with.

Reaching a determination on the legal issue requires conclusions on several factual issues, which I will do seriatim. The first two issues are whether it has been shown that Glantz committed violations of the federal securities statutes and regulations, and whether Urban was his supervisor.

Glantz violated the federal securities statutes, rules, and regulations while associated with FBW.

The preponderance of the evidence is that Glantz violated the anti-fraud provisions of the federal securities laws, and rules and regulations thereunder. This conclusion is based on Glantz's guilty plea to one count of securities fraud in *United States v. Glantz*, No. 1:07-CR-464 (N.D. Ohio Sept. 26, 2007), and Glantz's admissions of deliberate fraud, manipulation, and unauthorized and self-serving behavior in handling specific customer accounts in the period 2003 through 2005, which are supported by other evidence in the record.

Gutfreund

The Commission's views of who should be considered a supervisor among non-line personnel are set out in *Gutfreund*, which has carried considerable precedential clout since it was issued in 1992. In *Gutfreund*, CLO Feuerstein informed the three members of senior management that the submission of a false bid in an auction of U.S. Treasury securities by the head of the firm's Government Trading Desk, Paul Mozer (Mozer), was a criminal act which, while not required, should be reported to the government. *Gutfreund*, 51 S.E.C. at 108. Following the disclosure, neither Feuerstein nor the three executives investigated or disciplined Mozer or informed the government of the criminal acts for a number of months, during which the illegal activities continued. *Id.* at 98-101. Although not a decision, but a report of investigation issued pursuant to Section 21(a) of the Exchange Act, the Commission has cited *Gutfreund* favorably in many decisions. (Citations omitted.)

Before beginning a point-by-point analysis of *Gutfreund*, there are significant factual differences that distinguish the two situations that are relevant in reaching a conclusion on the allegations. *Gutfreund* is very different factual[y] from this situation i[n] the following material respects. In the period 2003 through 2005, Glantz was a respected broker whose conduct was only suspect by some. *Gutfreund* involved known criminal conduct. In hindsight, Centeno's suspicions about Glantz were right on the mark, but, in 2003-04, they were only suspicions. FBW's Written Supervisory Procedures specified branch managers as the initial level of supervision, and Urban believed that FBW operated in this manner.

In the entire time Glantz was employed at FBW, not one branch manager in any retail office where Glantz was located—Weaver (Beachwood), Spencer (Baltimore), or Brent (Hunt Valley), who had available and should have reviewed detailed descriptions of Glantz's transactions in his customer accounts—came to Urban with concerns about Glantz. Glantz's Retail Sales supervisors, Akers and Vaughan, consistently represented that they were supervising Glantz. Usry, Glantz's supervisor on his institutional transactions, made the same representations. Not one customer of Glantz complained about Glantz to Compliance and, when Compliance contacted three customers, they all knew Glantz was trading in their accounts, they were not knowledgeable about margin, but no one asked that Glantz be removed as his or her broker. The Credit Committee members had the Del Buono Memo and other information, and met frequently on matters involving Glantz. In addition to Urban, Credit Committee members, Calvert, Hartman, and Gildemeister, were on the Board and, as members, they received additional financial reports that showed Glantz had several accounts with enormous margin debits. In spite of information about Glantz, the enormous margin debit of the IPOF Fund, and concerns about Innotrac, no one—not Calvert, Akers, Vaughan, Shea, Usry, nor Hartman—ever came to Urban to voice concerns about Glantz's conduct and possible manipulation. As late as April 2004, Glantz was in good standing with Calvert who invited him to attend several Credit Committee meetings and believed he could help FBW solve the IPOF Fund debit problems.

In *Gutfreund*, after senior management officials were explicitly informed of an illegal act, they did not discuss among themselves any actions to investigate Mozer's conduct or to place limitations on Mozer for several months; Feuerstein's role was that of a bystander, and he did not inform the Compliance Department of the situation. *Gutfreund*, 51 SEC at 113. This situation is unlike *Gutfreund* in that Urban was not a bystander, he took actions, and he shared information. Compliance began scrutinizing Glantz and the IPOF Fund shortly after Glantz joined FBW. Urban made no attempt to keep those concerns secret. Compliance, through Centeno and Del Buono, raised most of the issues that are the basis of the charges against Urban to the Credit Committee, most prominently in May 2003, less than five months after Glantz was recruited to FBW by Retail Sales.

Perhaps the most significant difference between the posture of Urban and Feuerstein in *Gutfreund* is that almost all the business leaders at FBW either lied to Urban or kept information from him, and people with clear supervisory responsibility over Glantz did not carry out their supervisory responsibilities. The undisputed evidence is that managers at FBW told Urban that Glantz was being supervised. Vaughan represented that Usry was supervising Glantz's Institutional Sales, but, according to Glantz, Usry had refused to accept supervisory responsibility, and Shea, Usry's boss, testified he knew nothing about Institutional Sales supervising Glantz. Akers assured Urban he would exercise special supervision of Glantz and he did not do so.

In addition to misrepresentations about supervision, Urban also had to deal with other instances of dishonest conduct by high management officials at FBW that were not present in *Gutfreund*. Shea's comments to Belgrade in February 2004, indicate that he thought the IPOF Fund was a disaster waiting to happen, but the head of Equity Capital Markets did not share those concerns with Urban. According to Glantz, Akers and Vaughan knew that he purchased Innotrac for his client accounts to benefit Dadante in December 2004, but they did not share this information with Urban.

Urban was Glantz's supervisor.

Gutfreund set out the following test for who is a supervisor:

> [D]etermining if a particular person is a "supervisor" depends on whether, under the facts and circumstances of a particular case, that person has a requisite degree of responsibility, ability or authority to affect the conduct of the employee whose behavior is at issue. Thus, persons occupying positions in the legal or compliance departments of broker-dealers have been found by the Commission to be "supervisors" for purposes of Sections 15(b)(4)(E) and 15(b)(6) under certain circumstances.

* * *

Given the role and influence within the firm of a person in a position such as Feuerstein's and the factual circumstances of this case, such a person shares in the responsibility to take appropriate action to respond to the misconduct. Under those circumstances, we believe that such a person becomes a "supervisor" for purposes of Section 15(b)(4)(E) and 15(b)(6). As a result, that person is responsible, along with the other supervisors, for taking reasonable and appropriate action. It is not sufficient for one in such a position to be a mere bystander to the events that occurred. (citations omitted)

In *Gutfreund*, Feuerstein was considered to be Mozer's supervisor within the meaning of Exchange Act Sections 15(b)(4)(E) and 15(b)(6) because he was informed of serious misconduct by "senior management in order to obtain his advice and guidance and to involve him as part of management's collective response to the problem," and, under the factual circumstances, he shared responsibility to take appropriate action to respond to the misconduct. Since Urban was not Glantz's supervisor in the sense that he did not have the power normally associated with supervision, the issue becomes whether, under these facts and circumstances, Urban had the "requisite degree of responsibility, ability or authority to affect" Glantz's conduct.

In *Montgomery*, the Commission found it sufficient that a person played "a significant, even if shared, role in a firm's supervisory structure," and "[t]he fact that he 'share[d] in the responsibility to take appropriate action to respond to ... misconduct,' or that his authority was subject to countermand at a higher level, does not negate a finding that he had supervisory responsibility." 55 S.E.C. at 500-02, citing *Gutfreund* and *James J. Pasztor*, 54 S.E.C. 398 at 409 n.28 (1999) (Supervisor not "relieved of responsibility because he had to report to [firm president who] could overrule his decisions.").

Even though Urban did not have any of the traditional powers associated with a person supervising brokers and the facts and circumstances of his situation are very different than in *Gutfreund* and its progeny, the case law dictates that Urban be found to be Glantz's supervisor. As General Counsel, Urban's opinions on legal and compliance issues were viewed as authoritative and his recommendations were generally followed by people in FBW's business units, but not by Retail Sales. Urban did not direct FBW's response to dealing with Glantz, however, he was a member of the

Credit Committee, and dealt with Glantz on behalf of the committee. I agree with the opposing experts, Paulukaitis and Steinberg, that the language in *Gutfreund*, taken literally, would result in Glantz having many supervisors because many people at FBW acted to affect Glantz's conduct in a variety of different ways.

Exchange Act Sections 15(b)(4)(E)(i) and (ii).

In summary, Exchange Act Section 15(b)(4)(E)(i) provides that: (1) no person will be deemed to have failed reasonably to supervise any other person if there are supervisory procedures being appl[ed], which could reasonably be expected to detect and prevent the violations; and (2) the person discharging his or her duties and obligations under the supervisory procedures had no reasonable cause to believe they were not being complied with.

FBW had established supervisory procedures in place and Urban believed that they were being followed in the 2003 through 2005 period. My review of the evidence is that Urban performed his responsibilities in a cautious, objective, thorough, and reasonable manner. He believed people were carrying out their responsibilities and he repeatedly prodded them to do so to assure that Glantz was being adequately supervised. When he concluded in December 2004, that FBW's supervisory procedures were not being complied with and that Glantz's conduct was unacceptable, he moved to terminate Glantz.

I find that Urban did not fail to supervise Glantz given the provisions of Exchange Act Section 15(b)(4)(E)(i).

Notes and Questions

1. The ALJ's decision in *Urban* was appealed to the SEC. However, only two Commissioners, Commissioners Aguilar and Paredes, heard the appeal. They were evenly divided as to whether, among other issues, Urban was a supervisor under Sections 15(b)(4)(E) and 15(b)(6). Commissioners Walter and Gallagher and Chairman Schapiro did not participate. This means that the ALJ's initial decision is of no effect. According to SEC Rule of Practice 411(f), 17 C.F.R. §201.411(f), in the event a majority of participating Commissioners do not agree to a disposition on the merits, the initial decision shall be of no effect, and an order will be issued in accordance with this result.

2. In Urban, the ALJ used the standard enumerated in *Gutfreund* to determine whether a non-line employee is a supervisor under Sections 15(b)(4)(E) and 15(b)(6). Is the *Gutfreund* standard too broad? Would anyone in compliance or legal personnel be a supervisor under this standard? → Yes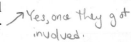

3. Would Urban have been deemed a supervisor if the ALJ had used the standard enumerated in *Huff* for determining when a non-line employee is a supervisor under Sections 15(b)(4)(E) and 15(b)(6) and therefore liable for failure reasonably to supervise another employee subject to his or her supervision? → Yes

Hypothetical Five

James Andrews works in the largest NYC office of Success First and is the largest producer in the NYC region. Shortly before Andrews joined Success First in April, 2012, his customers held 798,000 shares of Durham Inc., which was 44 percent of the outstanding shares and 57 percent of the approximate float of outstanding shares. From the point when Andrews joined Success First in April 2012 to April,2013, Andrews executed 64 cross-trades in his customers' accounts, 10 of which were also wash sales, involving a total of approximately 920,000 shares of Durham, representing 65 percent of the approximate float of Durham's outstanding shares. Andrews executed these cross-trades and wash sales, to create a false or misleading appearance of active trading in Durham stock. In most cases, Andrews either solicited one side of the transaction and executed the other side on a discretionary basis, or executed both sides of the transaction on a discretionary basis. Accordingly, these transactions violated a Success First trading restriction that prohibited Andrews from soliciting purchases of Durham because his customers collectively owned a concentrated position in Durham with a large margin debt at Success First. Andrews attempted to prevent detection of this violation by marking all order tickets "unsolicited."

In response to a FINRA inquiry to Success First concerning the trading in Durham, Josephine Wiseman (Success First's general counsel) through Malak Johnson (Success First's chief compliance officer) requested an explanation from Andrews as to whether the Durham transactions were solicited or unsolicited. Wiseman as general counsel had the power to take disciplinary action against a registered representative who violated firm policy by removing commissions and imposing small fines. Andrews replied in writing that the transactions were unsolicited; Wiseman and Malak accepted Andrews's statement without performing any further inquiry. Four months later, Wiseman and Johnson learned from an annual compliance audit that most of the order tickets in the NYC office did not indicate whether a transaction was solicited or unsolicited, and that the corresponding confirmation almost always carried the legend "unsolicited." Later Wiseman, through Johnson, notified Andrews that he had to obtain the prior approval of Success First's margin department for all margin purchases of Durham. However, after the margin department manager told Wiseman and Johnson that Andrews was not following this margin policy, Wiseman did not perform any inquiry or establish any other procedure to determine whether Andrews complied with this margin policy. Is Wiseman Andrew's supervisor under Sections 15(b)(4)(E) and 15(b)(6)?

b. Delegation of Supervisory Responsibilities

Supervisors may delegate some of their supervisory responsibilities to other employees of the broker-dealer. Delegates, along with their supervisors, may have liability for failure reasonably to supervise. Liability for delegates under Sections 15(b)(6)(E) and 15(b)(6) may rest on the scope of their supervisory responsibilities. In *Louis R. Trujillo*, Exchange Act Rel. No. 26,635, 1989 WL 992646 (Mar. 16, 1989), a branch manager delegated certain of his supervisory responsibilities to Trujillo, his administrative manager. Trujillo's supervisory duties included reviewing new accounts, investigating customer complaints, and reviewing daily activity reports of customers' transactions. Although Trujillo's performance of his delegated supervisory duties was questionable, the SEC held that Trujillo was not liable for failure reasonably to supervise. The SEC stated:

> Critical to our decision in this case is the limited scope of Trujillo's authority. Trujillo's functions were largely advisory. His primary job was to apprise [the branch manager] of situations that needed his attention, and it was up to the [branch manager] to decide what action, if any, should be taken. It was [the branch manager] who had the power to discharge, restrict, or otherwise take effective action against [the registered representative]. *Id.* at *4.

c. Policy

Bringing charges against compliance and legal personnel raises the policy question of whether the SEC is improperly using its enforcement authority against those it should instead be supporting. Some commentators assert that such proceedings do fundamental damage to the securities industry personnel on whom the SEC primarily relies for compliance with the federal securities laws. Generally, the role of legal and compliance personnel at broker-dealers is to provide advice and guidance about the application of laws, including federal securities laws and regulations, to the broker-dealer's business activities.

In fact, the SEC seemingly recognized this argument as expressed by then-Director of Enforcement William R. McLucas in the McLucas/Hiller article:

> ... from a policy perspective, the argument is that such enforcement proceedings are self-defeating, in effect doing damage to the very segment of the securities industry that is responsible for the first level of effective law enforcement.... The reaction to the *Feuerstein* 21(a) Report by the industry has thus far been one of concern and resentment over a level of liability which people in positions of responsibility and authority similar to *Feuerstein* believe is misplaced. The objective, however, of holding an individual in this type of position to account is not to intimidate responsible compliance personnel into avoiding involvement in solving problems. Nor is the agency trying to set impossible-to-achieve standards of accountability. Rather, the Commission is making it clear that when such personnel are responsible within the firm for responding to very real problems, they are as accountable as others if they fail to respond reasonably.

This policy debate still continues 20 years later with respect to holding legal and compliance personnel liable under Sections 15(b)(e) and 15(b)(6). SEC Commissioner Gallagher, in a speech on February 24, 2012, raised many of the same issues as former enforcement director McLucas; he acknowledged that clarity in the area of liability for failure to supervise for legal and compliance personnel remains a challenge:

The question of what makes a legal or compliance officer a supervisor, however, remains disturbingly murky. In searching for clarity on the issue, however, we must be mindful of the importance of the legal and compliance role and, critically, the ability of legal and compliance personnel to carry out their responsibilities.

* * *

Unfortunately, robust engagement on the part of legal and compliance personnel raises the specter that such personnel could be deemed to be "supervisors" subject to liability for violations of law by the employees they are held to be supervising. This creates a dangerous dilemma. A compliance officer or in-house attorney who stays ensconced in a dark corner of the firm drafting policies and sending out memoranda, but never interacting with the individuals governed by those policies or the recipients of those memos, risks diminished effectiveness or even irrelevance; but such a person would reduce his or her potential liability as a supervisor. On the other hand, the more engaged a firm's legal counsel or compliance personnel become — the more they bring their expertise to bear in addressing important, real-world compliance issues and in providing real-time advice for concrete problems the firms and their employees face — the more likely they are to be deemed to be playing a supervisory role. Thus, the Commission's position on supervisory liability for legal and compliance personnel may have had the perverse effect of increasing the risk of supervisory liability in direct proportion to the intensity of their engagement in legal and compliance activities.

Any understanding of the issue must begin with the fact that broker-dealer or investment adviser compliance and legal personnel are, by default, *not* supervisors but rather *providers of support* for the firm's other employees. We're not talking about widget factories here — the business of regulated entities inherently involves regulatory issues at every turn. Almost every facet of broker-dealer and investment adviser "business" issues are also regulatory issues, and accordingly the Commission and the SROs should want legal and compliance in the discussion about most issues....

In contrast to Commissioner Gallagher's perspective, Commissioner Schapiro provides another perspective regarding the efficacy of prosecuting non-line and/or compliance professionals:

Legal and compliance officers [should not be given] an automatic "out" from liability, because they do not, in many instances, possess the ability to hire, fire, reward, or punish. If those powers were all that mattered, the Commission would find itself in the position of allowing persons who are on notice of the occurrence of violative behavior, *and* are in a position to influence the outcome, to merely stand by and let it happen. Whether you are the chairman or president of the firm, an in-house lawyer or someone with lesser authority, the Commission should not in my opinion absolve you of the responsibility to act when you see that the house is on fire, and you are in possession of some part of the hose.... the independence of these professionals is not compromised by holding them accountable for their own conduct, if the circumstances so warrant. Moreover, independence, while certainly a virtuous quality, should not become a roadblock to enforcement of our laws.

Notes and Questions

> *Stunts involvement*

1. Why shouldn't senior compliance officials (including a broker-dealer's general counsel) be held accountable for deficient supervision? Isn't accountability desirable with respect to all supervisors at broker-dealers? → No.

> *Yes.*

2. Is there a viable argument to support the contention that compliance and legal employees of a broker-dealer are, by definition, not supervisors? That by definition such employees are supervisors? ↳ No.

C. Reasonable Supervision

Section 15(b)(4)(E) describes reasonable supervision using the three basic categories enumerated in its safe harbor. First, reasonable supervision requires the broker-dealer to establish reasonable procedures. Second, the broker-dealer must have a system for applying its procedures that would reasonably be expected to prevent and detect "insofar as practicable," violations of the federal securities laws by itself, its employees, and other associated persons. Third, the broker-dealer must reasonably discharge the supervisory duties enumerated in its supervisory procedures and system; reasonable discharge of supervisory duties means that the broker-dealer has no cause to believe that its supervisory procedures and system are not being complied with. There is, however, no one standard, uniform set of procedures and system of implementation that all broker-dealers can adopt and thereby automatically fall within the protections of the safe harbor in Section 15(b)(4)(E). Each broker-dealer must determine the type of supervisory procedures and system of implementation that is appropriate for its particular lines of business. As the SEC noted in *Trujillo*, "what are appropriate procedures varies, depending on what would be considered reasonable under the particular circumstances." This means that reasonable supervision will differ, depending on the organizational structure and lines of business of the particular broker-dealer.

1. Reasonable Supervisory Procedures

Neither the SEC nor FINRA have explicitly stated the type of supervisory procedures and system of implementation that constitute reasonable supervision. They have only provided guidance—FINRA more so than the SEC—about the types of supervisory procedures and implementing systems that comply with Sections 15(b)(4)(E) and 15(b)(6).[49] The SEC's guidance, in its administrative proceedings and cases initiated

---

49. See Section III.B.1 of this chapter for a detailed discussion of FINRA guidance on reasonable supervisory procedures and systems.

against broker-dealers, has identified certain common concerns and themes as to the types of activities that constitute reasonable procedures that comply with Sections 15(b)(4)(E) and 15(b)(6).

One common theme is that supervisory procedures, which rely solely on the representations of the employee involved in possible wrongdoing are not considered reasonable. In other words, the supervisor cannot simply take the word of the registered representative when confronted with evidence of possible wrongdoing in a customer's account. At the very least, the supervisor should verify the representations of the registered representative by contacting the customer. In *Bache Halsey Stuart Shields, Inc. et al.*, Exchange Act Rel. No. 19725 (May 3, 1983), the SEC asserted that a branch manager could not conduct an adequate inquiry into wrongdoing when he relied solely on representations made by the registered representative in response to inquiries concerning certain trading executed by the registered representative.

Relying solely on the representations of the registered representative would not suffice, even if the registered representative had significant skill and experience in a particular area. In such circumstances, active monitoring of the customer's account is required. Moreover, if the supervisor is aware of prior improprieties, heightened supervisory procedures should be implemented and tailored specifically to detecting and preventing the registered representatives' past improprieties. In *Robert J. Prager*, Exchange Act Rel. No. 51,974 (Jul. 6, 2005), at *11, the SEC stated that " ... [w]e also have emphasized the need for heightened supervision when a firm chooses to have associated with it a person who has known regulatory problems or customer complaints."

Another common theme is that reasonable supervisory procedures must be established with respect to all aspects of the broker-dealer's business. This encompasses two basic categories: (1) all employees of the broker-dealer engaged in securities activities and (2) the broker-dealer's business operations. The first category includes every employee, including senior management, and any salesperson with an independent contractor arrangement with the broker-dealer. In *Howe Barnes Inv. Inc.*, Exchange Act Rel. No. 37,707 (Sept. 23, 1996), the SEC asserted that a broker-dealer must have reasonable supervisory procedures in place for senior management. The SEC also noted that such procedures cannot be structured in reliance on the sophistication of the broker-dealer's customers. In *Howe Barnes*, the firm structured its supervisory procedures in reliance, in part, on the expectation that, because most of the registered representative's customers were institutional customers, such customers would be more alert to improper sales practices than retail or less sophisticated customers. Category one also includes any salesperson with an independent contractor arrangement with the broker-dealer. In *William v. Giordano*, Exchange Act Rel. No. 36,742, (Jan. 19, 1996), the SEC stated that it " ... does not recognize the concept of 'independent contractors' for purpose of the Exchange Act, even if an arrangement with an associated person satisfies the criteria for 'independent contractor' status for other purposes: To the extent that a firm forms a relationship with an independent contractor, that firm would be responsible for either (1) ensuring that the independent contractor was registered as a broker-dealer or (2) assuming the supervisory responsibilities attendant to a relationship with an associated person." Outside of the federal securities laws, generally parties enter into independent contractor arrangements to purchase services or products from another party, without any rights to control or supervise the related activity. Such arrangements have both economic and legal incentives, including avoidance of certain labor laws and reduction of the broker-dealer's tax liability. However, allowing true independent contractor status, i.e., no right for the broker-dealer to control or supervise the independent contractor, would undermine the regulatory framework of broker-dealers, particularly the reasonable supervision requirement under Sections 15(b)(4)(E) and 15(b)(6).

The second category, the broker-dealer's business operations, requires the broker-dealer to adopt reasonable supervisory procedures for every aspect of its business. This category includes the broker-dealers' sales practices and back-office operations. Sales practices encompass procedures used to sell the financial products of the broker-dealer. The supervisor must ensure that such procedures and therefore the sales practices used by employees comply with the federal securities laws and SRO rules. In the following case, the broker-dealer was sanctioned for failure to adopt reasonable supervisory procedures when selling one of its financial products.

In the Matter of TD Ameritrade, Inc.

Exchange Act Release No. 63,829 (Feb. 3, 2011)

I.

The Securities and Exchange Commission ("Commission") deems it appropriate and in the public interest that public administrative proceedings be, and hereby are, instituted pursuant to Section 15(b) of the Securities Exchange Act of 1934 ("Exchange Act") against TD Ameritrade, Inc. ("Respondent").

III.

On the basis of this Order and Respondent's Offer, the Commission finds that:

* * *

Respondent

1. Respondent, a New York corporation headquartered in Omaha, Nebraska, is a broker-dealer registered with the Commission pursuant to Section 15(b) of the Exchange Act and is a member of the Financial Industry Regulatory Authority. Respondent is a wholly-owned subsidiary of TD Ameritrade Online Holdings Corp. Respondent was formed as a result of the consolidation of retail brokerage operations of Ameritrade, Inc. and TD Waterhouse Investor Services, Inc. following Ameritrade Holding Corporation's acquisition of TD Waterhouse Group, Inc. on January 24, 2006.

Facts

The RYP Fund and the Current Status of Fund Redemptions to Respondent's Customers

2. The RYP Fund was a diversified mutual fund that sought to provide higher returns than a money market fund while seeking to maintain a net asset value ("NAV")

of $1.00. The RYP Fund generally invested in instruments comparable to those of a money market fund, except that it purchased longer-term investments to generate higher returns.

3. As described in the Fund's Form N-Q filed August 26, 2008 for the quarter ended June 30, 2008, among the Fund's investments was commercial paper issued by Lehman Brothers Holdings, Inc. ("Lehman"). The Reserve wrote down these Lehman investments to a value of zero on September 16, 2008, after Lehman filed for bankruptcy the preceding day. As a result, the Fund's NAV fell to $0.97. The Reserve ceased to honor redemption requests for the Fund and, on October 9, 2008, announced that the Fund would be liquidated. On October 24, 2008, the Commission issued an order under Section 22(e)(3) of the Investment Company Act of 1940 permitting the RYP Fund to suspend redemptions as of October 8, 2008. Since then, and as part of the RYP Fund's plan to liquidate its assets, the Fund has made five separate distributions to Fund shareholders totaling approximately $1.1 billion, representing the return of approximately 95 percent of shareholders' principal. The Fund has retained approximately $39 million for possible future distribution.

4. During the relevant period, Respondent's representatives offered and sold two classes of shares in the RYP Fund to customers: Class R shares (RYPQX) and Class Treasurer's shares (RYPTX). As of July 2008, most of the total amount invested in these two classes of shares was held by Respondent's customers. Thousands of Respondent's customers continue to hold a majority of the Fund's shares in these classes.

Respondent Begins Offering the Fund

5. During the latter part of 2006, and in response to customer requests, Respondent sought to identify a higher yielding alternative to money market funds. After researching products that might meet this need, Respondent selected the RYP Fund.

6. In connection with the rollout of the Fund, Respondent designed a compilation of training materials specific to the Fund. These materials, which included the Fund prospectus, accurately characterized the Fund, emphasized that the Fund was not a money market fund, and described the various risks associated with investing in the Fund. After the training materials had been distributed in January 2007, Respondent authorized many of its representatives to offer the RYP Fund to customers.

7. Thereafter, throughout the relevant period, Respondent's representatives offered and sold the RYP Fund through the following four sales channels: (1) the Branch Offices; (2) the National Branch; (3) the Fixed Income Guidance Group ("FIGG"); and (4) Investor Services. Respondent's representatives and managers received no enhanced compensation for selling the Fund relative to other products offered and sold by Respondent.

The Violative Sales Practices of Respondent's Representatives

8. During the relevant period, representatives within the four sales channels at times mischaracterized the Fund as a "money market fund," an "enhanced money market fund" or a "higher yielding money market." Respondent's representatives also at times equated the Fund to money market funds in terms of "safety and liquidity"

or stated that the Fund was insured by the Federal Deposit Insurance Corporation or the Securities Investor Protection Corporation. Other times, representatives offered the Fund in response to a customer's specific request for a money market fund or an instrument with similar risk, without discussing the nature or risks of the Fund. As described above, Fund-specific training materials that accurately characterized the Fund and that described the various risks associated with investing in the Fund were available for these representatives' review and use when selling this product.

Respondent's Procedures and Systems for Applying Such Procedures to Prevent and Detect Its Representatives' Violative Conduct

Training and Education Regarding the Fund

9. Respondent first trained some of its representatives on how to offer the RYP Fund beginning in January 2007 after Respondent had determined to allow its representatives to recommend the Fund.

10. Respondent's procedures provided that the representatives' direct managers were to conduct in-person training sessions with their respective groups of representatives using the written training materials. Beginning in January 2007, Respondent disseminated the training materials via email to all managers in the Branch Offices, the National Branch, and the FIGG with instruction to train their respective groups. However, Respondent did not disseminate such materials to all managers within the Investor Services sales channel at that time. Rather, various Investor Services managers received the training materials on an ad hoc basis throughout 2007 without any specific instruction to train the representatives they managed. Representatives within Investor Services were generally unfamiliar with the prescribed procedures by which representatives were to recommend sales of the Fund.

11. Despite its training efforts, Respondent had no system to implement procedures during the relevant period that was reasonably designed to ensure that representatives actually received the training from their managers and understood the materials. Respondent did not take adequate steps, such as providing additional training, refresher courses, or continuing education on the RYP Fund, to ensure that its representatives understood this product. While the FIGG conducted a training session in June 2008 regarding short-term instruments, including the RYP Fund, that representatives could offer, the training materials used at this training session mischaracterized the RYP Fund as a money market fund.

12. Many new hires whom Respondent employed after the initial dissemination of the training materials did not receive training about the Fund. Respondent did not include information regarding the RYP Fund as part of the curriculum that Respondent used for purposes of its training program for new hires.

13. As set forth above, although Respondent developed materials and procedures to train its representatives specifically regarding the Fund, it did not have a system to implement such procedures which was reasonably designed to prevent and detect the representatives' violative conduct.

Supervisory Oversight and Review

14. During the relevant period, Respondent's four sales channels employed different supervisory structures and procedures for the review of trades, including purchases of the RYP Fund.

15. At the time Respondent disseminated the training materials in January 2007, all of its Branch Offices and its National Branch were separately designated as an Office of Supervisory Jurisdiction ("OSJ"). According to Respondent's policies and procedures, the representatives' direct managers were responsible for reviewing any solicited trades in the RYP Fund and were required to review other available documentation to ensure that the trades were suitable for customers. However, the procedures did not require managers to perform any supervisory review to ensure that representatives provided proper disclosures to customers regarding the Fund.

16. In March 2007, Respondent changed its branch office supervisory structure by removing the OSJ designation from all but one of the branch offices and creating a centralized, independent branch supervision and controls group which then became the registered OSJ for the branch offices. This group functioned through four Divisional Operations Managers ("DOMs"), each of whom had direct oversight over one of the four regions in which the branch offices operated and one of whom also assisted the National Branch with its supervision.

17. In conjunction with this restructuring, Respondent revised its written supervisory procedures for the Branch Offices and National Branch to place primary responsibility upon the DOMs for reviewing sales of the RYP Fund. The DOMs' review focused upon ensuring that representatives updated suitability information for each account to determine whether the Fund was suitable for the purchasing customer, but these reviews did not focus on whether representatives had provided the proper disclosures regarding the Fund.

18. Subsequently during the relevant period, Respondent revised the procedures by which the DOMs conducted their review of the Fund transactions. Specifically, Respondent implemented a computer-based system that was intended to assist management's supervisory review of customer transactions. Regarding Fund transactions, the system generated various exception reports for further review by the DOMs based upon certain rules. However, the system was incapable of reviewing Fund transactions to determine whether representatives had made proper disclosures regarding the Fund. As a result, and as with Respondent's earlier procedures, these revised procedures were not reasonably designed to prevent and detect any misrepresentations or omissions by Respondent's representatives.

19. During the relevant period, the FIGG was designated as a separate OSJ and had a supervisory structure and procedures separate from the National Branch and Branch Offices. For most of the period, the FIGG did not employ any procedures for supervisory review of its representatives' sales of the Fund. In June 2008, the FIGG implemented procedures for review of Fund solicited transactions that mirrored the suitability reviews implemented in Respondent's National Branch and Branch Offices.

The FIGG's supervisory review of Fund transactions was also not reasonably designed to prevent and detect the representatives' violative conduct.

20. During the relevant period, Investor Services was also designated as a separate OSJ and had its own set of supervisory procedures. However, Investor Services did not have established procedures for the supervisory review of solicited transactions in the Fund to determine whether representatives provided customers with proper disclosures. While Investor Services revised its procedures in August 2007 to require supervisory review of solicited orders in general, this review focused primarily on a suitability analysis for an exchange traded fund that Respondent began offering at that time. During the relevant period, Respondent did not implement supervisory procedures within Investor Services reasonably designed to identify representatives' misrepresentations and omissions regarding the RYP Fund.

21. As set forth above, Respondent did not have policies and procedures regarding supervisory oversight and review of its representatives' solicited trades in the RYP Fund which were reasonably designed to prevent and detect violative conduct by its representatives.

Violations

Respondent's Representatives Violated Section 17(a)(2) of the Securities Act

22. As a result of the sales practices concerning the RYP Fund as described above, Respondent's representatives violated Section 17(a)(2) of the Securities Act, which prohibits the offer or sale of any securities by the use of any means or instruments of transportation or communication in interstate commerce or by use of the mails, directly or indirectly, to obtain money or property by means of any untrue statement of a material fact or any omission to state a material fact necessary in order to make the statements made, in light of the circumstances under which they were made, not misleading.

Respondent Failed Reasonably to Supervise Its Representatives

23. Section 15(b)(4)(E) of the Exchange Act requires broker-dealers to supervise reasonably, with a view to preventing violations of the federal securities laws, persons subject to their supervision. The responsibility of broker-dealers to supervise reasonably their employees by means of effective, established procedures is a critical component of the federal regulatory scheme. (Citations omitted).

24. As described above, Respondent failed to have a system to implement procedures for the training and education of its representatives regarding the RYP Fund which would reasonably be expected to prevent and detect violative conduct by its representatives. In addition, Respondent failed to establish policies and procedures for the supervisory oversight and review of its representatives' solicited trades in the RYP Fund which would reasonably be expected to prevent and detect violations by the representatives.

25. Because Respondent's representatives violated Section 17(a)(2) of the Securities Act, and Respondent failed to implement adequate policies and procedures and a system for applying established procedures reasonably designed to prevent or detect

such violations, Respondent failed reasonably to supervise its representatives within the meaning of Section 15(b)(4)(E) of the Exchange Act.

————

2. *Supervisory System*

Reasonable supervision requires the broker-dealer to have an adequate system in place to implement its procedures effectively. The SEC has stated that "establishment of policies and procedures alone is not sufficient to discharge supervisory responsibility. It is also necessary to implement measures to monitor compliance with those policies and procedures."[50] This system for applying the broker-dealer's procedures must be comprehensive and capable of determining whether all levels of supervisory responsibility are operating effectively. Determining whether the system is reasonable depends, among other things, on the number of the broker-dealer's employees, and its business lines. It is crucial that the system be capable of monitoring whether supervisory delegation at all levels of supervisory responsibility is functioning in accordance with the broker-dealer's established procedures and policies. This means that the system must include mechanisms for monitoring supervisory responsibilities delegated to both line supervisors (from the branch manager to the president/CEO) and non-line supervisors; and from the compliance staff to the chief compliance manager and/or CLO.

The branch manager is generally the first level of delegated supervisory responsibility that must be addressed by a compliant supervisory system. The system must include a mechanism for determining whether the branch manager is carrying out her responsibilities delineated in the broker-dealer's written procedures and policies. In *Alan Charles Refkin, David Barry Harberson and Scott Michael Flanagan,* Exchange Act Rel. No. 26,312 (Nov. 25, 1988), the SEC suggested that an effective system for determining whether the branch manager is performing her delegated supervisory responsibilities with respect to registered representatives subject to her supervision should include daily review of all trade tickets, periodic review of registered representatives' commission reports, and approval of the execution of transactions involving amounts of money over a specified level.

However, the broker-dealer's supervisory system cannot rely solely on the branch manager, but must include sufficient checks to ensure that the branch manager is functioning adequately. The SEC considers a system that relies solely on the branch manager to be tantamount to having no supervisory system at all.[51] In addition, an effective supervisory system for larger broker-dealers requires a regional supervisor and a compliance department with the requisite authority to take action. The regional supervisor must take an active role in ensuring that the branch manager is complying

————

50. Spear Leads & Kellogg, L.P., Exchange Act Release No. 48199, 3002 WL21688753 at *7 (July 21, 2003).

51. W. McLucas & W. Morse, *Liability of a Branch Office Manager for Failure to Supervise,* 23 Rev.Sec. & Commod. Reg. 1, 2 (Jan 10, 1990).

with the broker-dealer's procedures and policies. That is, the regional supervisor must, at a minimum, monitor the branch manager's activities. A supervisory system that complies with the federal securities laws and FINRA rules, depending on the size of the broker-dealer, may also include home office supervision and a centralized compliance system.

Compliance personnel, sometimes deemed the third level of supervision, must have the ability to enforce their orders and restrictions to be a useful component of the supervisory system. This means that the broker-dealer's compliance department must have the resources and power to perform meaningful compliance. In *Prudential-Bache Sec. Inc.*, Exchange Act Rel. No. 22, 755, (Jan. 2, 1986), the SEC stated:

> A firm must have adequate procedures to assure that trading restrictions issued by its Compliance Department are not ignored by the branch managers or other personnel. A firm's Compliance Department is an important means for assuring adherence by its employees to the federal securities laws. A broker-dealer is not meeting its supervisory obligations if its Compliance Department can be disregarded or otherwise rendered ineffective by a branch manager.

Adequate resources for the compliance department requires that it have sufficient staff in relation to the broker-dealer's number of employees. As the broker-dealer's business expands, it must also increase the number of staff in compliance in relation to its number of registered representatives. In *First Affiliated Securities, Inc.* Exchange Act Rel. No. 23,335 (Jun. 18, 1996), the SEC found that a primary cause of the firm's deficient supervisory system was that the firm had only one compliance employee to monitor 80 branch offices and 250 registered representatives.[52] The SEC ordered the broker-dealer, among other things, to increase the number of employees in its compliance department from one to five. Adequate resources also include full-time employment and non-commission-based compensation for compliance employees. In *Brooks, Weinger, Robbins & Leeds, Inc.*, Exchange Act Rel. No. 2625 (Feb. 9, 1987), the SEC ordered the broker-dealer to employ a full-time compliance director, whose compensation would not be commission-based and who would have the authority to hire sufficient compliance personnel to staff a reorganized compliance department. It also ordered the reorganized compliance department to perform an annual compliance review of each of the broker-dealer's branch offices. After the financial crisis of 2008, Chairman Schapiro issued an open letter to CEOs of broker-dealers encouraging them "to ensure that, in the event a firm's sales force expands, the firm's supervisory and compliance infrastructure retains sufficient size and capacity ..." Chairman Schapiro issued her letter in an environment in which broker-dealers were engaging in a vigorous recruiting program for registered representatives by using large up-front bonuses and enhanced commissions. Chairman Schapiro was concerned that such practices would enhance risks to investors because the registered representatives might feel the pressure to sell unsuitable products to investors in order to earn

---

52. *See also* First Colonial Sec. Grp., Inc., Exchange Act Release No. 43349, 2000 WL 1424081 (Sept. 26, 2000).

increased commissions.[53] However, this was not the first time that the SEC was forced to grapple with the failure of large broker-dealers to provide adequate resources for their compliance departments along with the authority to impose and enforce their orders and restrictions. For example, Prudential, formerly known as Prudential-Bache Securities Inc., was sanctioned several times for deficient supervision based on its failure to provide adequate resources for its compliance department and the authority to enforce compliance orders and restrictions. Prudential was sued by the SEC in 1986 for deficient supervision and again in 1993 because it failed to comply with the 1986 order.

In the Matter of Prudential Securities Inc.

Exchange Act Release No. 33,082 (Oct. 21, 1993)

I.

The Securities and Exchange Commission ("Commission") deems it appropriate and in the public interest that public proceedings be instituted pursuant to Sections 15(b), 19(h) and 21C of the Securities Exchange Act of 1934 ("Exchange Act") against Prudential Securities Incorporated ("PSI" or the "firm"). In anticipation of these proceedings, PSI has submitted an Offer of Settlement which the Commission has determined to accept.... PSI, by its Offer of Settlement, without admitting or denying the Commission's statements of fact, findings or conclusions, consents to the entry of this Order Instituting Public Proceedings, Making Findings and Imposing Sanctions ("Order").

* * *

III.

FACTS

A. RESPONDENT

PSI, a wholly-owned subsidiary of Prudential Securities Group, Inc., is registered with the Commission pursuant to Section 15(b) of the Exchange Act. PSI is a full service broker-dealer and a member of the Municipal Securities Rulemaking Board ("MSRB") and all the major exchanges. The New York Stock Exchange, Inc. ("NYSE") is the firm's designated examining authority. PSI has approximately 6,000 registered representatives in 325 retail branch offices.

B. UNDERLYING VIOLATIONS

This proceeding involves two separate matters. The first matter involves PSI's violations of the antifraud provisions of the federal securities laws, Section 17(a) of the Securities Act of 1933 ("Securities Act"), Section 10(b) of the Exchange Act and Rule 10b–5 thereunder, in connection with its offer and sale of limited partnership interests and other proprietary products originated, sponsored and marketed by its

---

53. Letter from Mary L. Schapiro, SEC Chairman, to CEOs of broker-dealers (Aug. 31, 2009), available at: http://www.sec.gov/news/press/2009/2009-189-letter.pdf.

Direct Investment Group between January 1, 1980 and December 31, 1990, and PSI's failure to adequately supervise its Direct Investment Group [DIG].

The second matter results from PSI's failure in certain respects to adopt, implement or maintain procedures sufficient to achieve compliance with the requirements of a prior Commission order regarding improved supervision,[54] and PSI's failure to adequately supervise ten former PSI registered representatives in nine branch offices whose conduct included improper sales practices in connection with retail customer accounts.

IV.

A. SUMMARY OF PSI'S LIMITED PARTNERSHIP RELATED SALES PRACTICE VIOLATIONS

From 1980 through 1990, PSI sold approximately $8 billion of interests in more than 700 different limited partnership offerings to investors throughout the United States.[55]

B. BACKGROUND

The approximately $8 billion PSI raised in limited partnerships was invested principally in real estate, oil and gas producing properties, and aircraft leasing ventures. Limited partnership investors generally have suffered significant losses in recent years due to, among other factors, declining prices for these assets. Moreover, in many instances, the partnerships have substantially reduced or altogether ceased making cash distributions to their limited partners.

C. DIG'S ORGANIZATION, AND ORIGINATION AND MARKETING ACTIVITIES

PSI's participation in limited partnership offerings was handled by DIG which was, for most of the relevant period, a unit of the firm's Retail Sales Group. Between 1980 and approximately 1990, DIG, in conjunction with at least 68 different co-sponsors, caused PSI to participate in the origination or sale of more than 700 different limited partnership offerings. PSI functioned variously as underwriter, selling agent, and/or sole or co-general partner in connection with each of these offerings.

In its New York headquarters, DIG operations were divided among various sections including for most of the relevant period: Origination/Due Diligence — responsible for developing the investment concept into a limited partnership product, in conjunction with PSI's co-sponsors; Asset Management — responsible for carrying

---

54. On January 2, 1986, the Commission issued an Order Instituting Consolidated Proceedings Pursuant to Section 15(b)(4) and (6) of the Securities Exchange Act of 1934 and Findings, Opinion and Order in Prudential-Bache Securities, Inc., 48 SEC 372 (1986) (the "Prior Order"), which describes the consolidated proceedings in Prudential-Bache Securities, Inc., (8-27154), Admin.Pro. No. 3-6600 (the "Captain Crab" matter) and Prudential-Bache Securities, Inc., Sam Kalil, Jr., John Solomon, and James Moore, (8–27154), Admin.Pro. No. 3-6601.

55. This aspect of the proceeding relates to PSI's sale of securities originated, offered or sold by, through or in conjunction with PSI's Direct Investment Group. The vast majority of these offerings consisted of public and private placement limited partnerships. This unit also participated in the origination and marketing of a limited number of grantor trusts and real estate investment trusts. These various investments are hereinafter referred to collectively as "Limited Partnership Interests."

out PSI's responsibilities as sole or co-general partner of the limited partnerships it sponsored, and monitoring PSI's co-sponsors who functioned in that capacity; and Marketing—responsible for limited partnership-related promotional efforts nationwide.

The goal of DIG was to promote limited partnership sales. Once a limited partnership offering had been structured, DIG's marketing personnel generated a wide variety of selling tools to promote its sale throughout PSI's vast retail branch office network. DIG personnel located in DIG's New York headquarters and in PSI's various regional offices prepared "promotional" materials directed to registered representatives. DIG also distributed information to PSI's sales force through other PSI publications. Many individual brokers also prepared their own sales materials derived in whole or in part from information supplied by DIG, which they provided directly to customers. In addition, PSI's co-sponsors had their own marketing operations which produced a substantial amount of promotional materials for use by PSI's brokers in selling limited partnerships. PSI did not adequately review the materials DIG generated internally or those materials prepared by PSI's co-sponsors.

During most of the relevant period, the principal DIG marketing officers were known as Regional Coordinators. Normally, each DIG Regional Coordinator was allocated a Regional Marketing Specialist and several staff assistants. Although physically located in PSI's various regional headquarters, DIG Regional Coordinators reported directly to the head of DIG in New York, rather than to the firm's Regional Directors, who were otherwise responsible for the overall activities of the branch offices located within their regions. DIG Regional Coordinators and their staffs made sales presentations and distributed sales literature and promotional materials to branch office personnel in person, through inter-office mail and other internal communication systems. Their activities were outside PSI's regular supervisory and compliance structure and received little supervision or monitoring from any personnel outside of DIG.

D. OVERVIEW OF DIG PROMOTIONAL MATERIALS

Many DIG promotional pieces directed to PSI's sales force were in standardized formats which were adapted for use in numerous offerings.[56] DIG supplemented this printed information with oral presentations to registered representatives over a nationwide inter-office telephone communications system and at periodic meetings, conferences and seminars throughout the country.... As "proprietary products," most direct investment limited partnerships were available exclusively through PSI and, at the time of the purchase, there were rarely any sources of information outside of the firm concerning these products. Brokers relied on the printed and oral infor-

---

56. For example, DIG generated many of the following materials directed to registered representatives for each limited partnership offering: a so-called "Fact Sheet," regional "DI Sales Action Worksheet" and "DIG Product Snapshots," and numerous miscellaneous items such as presentation outlines, seminar invitations, telephone scripts, and prospecting guides. PSI and its co-sponsors also distributed several periodic publications containing product descriptions, performance updates, sales commission rates and other sales incentive information.

mation they received to ascertain limited partnership characteristics such as potential returns, suggestions for potentially suitable investors and the risks attendant to the investment.

PSI expected brokers to use DIG promotional materials in their oral sales presentations to customers and to rely on their contents. Brokers were not required, and frequently were not encouraged to read prospectuses. Prospectuses were viewed by many registered representatives as "legal documents" that they were required to provide to customers, but which were to be orally supplemented and explained pursuant to the promotional materials provided by the firm. Purchasers of DIG-sponsored public limited partnership offerings typically received prospectuses only after they had committed to purchase the product.

* * *

H. IN MANY INSTANCES, PSI BROKERS IGNORED SUITABILITY DETERMINATIONS

DIG's marketing approach generally was to ignore individual suitability considerations and promote the sale of limited partnerships to virtually every PSI customer. DIG promotional materials contained numerous statements such as "this product is suitable for every customer in your book" and "is there any reason you could not invest $10,000 or $20,000 in this limited partnership?" DIG also stressed that its promotional materials were adaptable for most investors, including stock buyers, bond buyers, CD investors, commodities traders, active accounts, or those who buy for the long term.

As a result, PSI recommended and sold limited partnerships to tens of thousands of investors for whom they were not suitable.

I. ANTIFRAUD VIOLATIONS ARISING OUT OF PSI'S OFFER AND SALE OF LIMITED PARTNERSHIP INTERESTS

The Commission has repeatedly stressed the obligation of broker-dealers to assure that retail sales activities comply with the antifraud provisions of Section 17(a) of the Securities Act, Section 10(b) of the Exchange Act and Rule 10b–5 thereunder. (citations omitted)

1. False Statements and Omissions

PSI made material misstatements and omissions in the sale of limited partnership interests relating, among other things, to the nature, potential yields, safety, and purported liquidity of the investments.

In many instances, PSI failed adequately to disclose significant risks attendant to limited partnerships such as the absence of a reliable secondary market, the qualified nature of guarantees, and inherent conflicts of interest.

Investors had few if any reliable sources of information other than PSI concerning the limited partnerships they were purchasing and were therefore vulnerable to misleading sales presentations from brokers willing to disregard the unsuitability of the recommended security for the purchaser.

These practices violated the antifraud provisions of Section 17(a) of the Securities Act, Section 10(b) of the Exchange Act and Rule 10b–5 thereunder. (Citations omitted.)

2. Suitability

In many instances, PSI failed to make required determinations, in recommending and selling limited partnerships, that the investments were suitable for investors in light of their individual financial status and investment goals. PSI also recommended, often in disregard of their individual needs and financial goals, that investors, including some who were elderly or retired, transfer money from investments with relatively little risk of loss of principal to speculative, illiquid limited partnerships. As a result, PSI violated Section 17(a) of the Securities Act, Section 10(b) and Rule 10b–5 thereunder. (citations omitted).

J. FAILURE TO SUPERVISE DIG

PSI established an operating unit which, over a ten-year period, facilitated the sale of approximately $8 billion in limited partnership interests to hundreds of thousands of investors nationwide. PSI permitted this unit to operate outside of the firm's existing supervisory and compliance structure. As a result, PSI's sales force sold limited partnerships to thousands of customers using materially false and misleading misrepresentations and omissions, in violation of the antifraud provisions of the federal securities laws.

Section 15(b)(4) of the Exchange Act authorizes the Commission to sanction broker-dealers who fail reasonably to supervise, with a view to preventing violations of the federal securities laws.

The responsibility of broker-dealers to supervise their employees by means of effective, established procedures is a critical component of the federal investor protection scheme regulating securities markets.

As the Commission has observed: "[I]n large organizations it is especially imperative that the system of internal control be adequate and effective."

PSI failed adequately to oversee its DIG unit to ensure that the sales presentations of registered representatives — persons subject to its supervision and control — were accurate, consistent with prospectus disclosure, and otherwise complied with applicable rules and regulations. PSI's supervisory failures permitted violations to continue for years.

PSI did not adequately review, supervise or control DIG personnel with a view towards preventing the creation, distribution and use of false and misleading promotional materials in selling limited partnerships. DIG, headquartered in New York and with personnel located nationwide, operated outside of PSI's regular supervisory and compliance structure. DIG marketing personnel made sales presentations and distributed materials to PSI's retail sales force with little supervision or monitoring from any personnel outside of DIG.

V.

A. SUMMARY OF PSI'S FAILURE TO REASONABLY SUPERVISE CERTAIN BRANCH OFFICE ACTIVITIES AND FAILURE TO ACHIEVE COMPLIANCE WITH A PRIOR COMMISSION ORDER

This aspect of the proceeding pertains to PSI's failure to reasonably supervise various PSI employees in certain branch offices with a view to preventing violation of the antifraud provisions of the federal securities laws, and its failure in certain respects to adopt, implement or maintain procedures sufficient to achieve compliance with the Commission's Prior Order. The violations described herein are separate from the DIG-related violations described above. PSI registered representatives in nine branch offices violated the antifraud provisions of the federal securities laws through improper sales practices, including unauthorized and unsuitable trading and churning.

Pursuant to the Prior Order, the firm agreed to certain undertakings to adopt, implement and maintain adequate supervisory procedures. One of the principal undertakings required PSI to hire an independent outside Consultant to review its compliance procedures and adopt either his specific recommendations for improved supervision or equivalent alternative procedures. PSI retained an independent outside Consultant who performed a national compliance review. The Consultant was required to recommend, and PSI was required to adopt, implement and maintain adequate procedures, revising existing procedures as required, to provide for the regular and systematic supervision and monitoring of branch office activities designed to prevent and detect violations of applicable state and federal securities laws. Pursuant to the Consultant's recommendations, the firm established a number of new or improved compliance procedures. However, in several important respects, PSI failed to adopt, implement or maintain certain procedures sufficient to achieve compliance with requirements imposed by the Prior Order. This matter presents some of the same types of violations and supervisory failures that gave rise to the Prior Order.

The Prior Order also directed the firm to comply with its undertaking to adopt, implement and maintain procedures designed to assure that violations and failures to comply with firm policies and procedures identified by firm audits were promptly remedied. The procedures adopted by PSI did not adequately comply with this undertaking. PSI also failed to comply with its undertaking to vest compliance directives with authority.

B. CHURNING, UNSUITABLE RECOMMENDATIONS AND MISREPRESENTATIONS BY REGISTERED REPRESENTATIVES

Registered representatives in nine PSI offices defrauded customers through a variety of schemes including churning.[57] Examples of the various violations are described below.

---

57. "Churning" occurs when a broker exercising control over the volume and frequency of trading, abuses his customer's confidence for personal gain by initiating transactions which are excessive in view of the character of the account. Its hallmarks are disproportionate turnover, frequent in and out trading, and large brokerage commissions. (citations omitted).

* * *

6. The Chesterfield, Missouri Branch Office

Between November 1990 and May 1992, the firm failed to reasonably supervise a registered representative in the firm's Chesterfield, Missouri branch office who effected unauthorized transactions in speculative stocks which were excessive and unsuitable. A number of his customers were widows, elderly, retired and often financially unsophisticated. Unsuitable margin accounts were opened for several customers. Many customers did not realize that a margin account had been opened. The registered representative proceeded to trade speculative stocks without the consent of his customers. When the customers brought these trades to the registered representative's attention, he misrepresented that the trades had been cancelled or that the account statements were erroneous due to computer breakdowns.

At times the registered representative also misrepresented that he was investing the customers' funds in securities when, in fact, he used the funds for other purposes, including payment to other customers as reimbursement for losses sustained by trading activities in their accounts.

One example of fraud involves an account held jointly by a 90-year-old widow living in a nursing home and her son. Her investment objective was conservative. The funds in the account constituted her entire life savings and, combined with her social security benefits, were the only source of income to pay the costs of her nursing home. The registered representative churned her account, engaged in excessive and unsuitable trading on margin, and diminished the principal of the account by approximately $70,000 between November 1990 and June 1992.

Although these customer accounts appeared on PSI's active account reports, they were not contacted by PSI's Branch Office Managers as required.

The registered representative's misconduct at the Chesterfield, Missouri branch illustrates several failures to detect and prevent improper sales practices. By 1991, 16 complaints against the registered representative had been filed by customers alleging misconduct at his prior firm. PSI's Compliance and Registration Departments were aware of the complaints. In all, approximately 28 complaints concerning his conduct at his prior employer were filed against the registered representative while he worked at PSI. Nonetheless, there was inadequate follow-up by PSI to increase supervision of the registered representative.

The registered representative engaged in frequent transactions in speculative stocks and low grade bonds. During his 18 month employment at PSI, 18 of his customers appeared a total of 33 times on the active account reports, amounting to almost 17% of all the branch's active accounts during the period. At least five of the customers were not contacted personally as required. In addition, there were significant delays when personal contact was made — an average delay of over two months and, in some cases, over six months.

* * *

D. PSI'S FAILURE TO REASONABLY SUPERVISE

1. Duty to Supervise Branch Offices

The Commission has repeatedly warned broker-dealers that it will not tolerate lax supervisory policies and procedures, particularly the supervision of retail sales activities in branch offices. "The responsibility of broker-dealers to supervise their employees by means of effective, established procedures is a critical component of the federal investor protection scheme regulating securities markets." (citations omitted)

The Commission has also insisted that broker-dealers achieve "adequate follow-up and review when a firm's own procedures detect irregularities or unusual trading activity in a branch office." That system must also be sufficient to determine that any delegated responsibility to supervise is being diligently exercised. The adoption of regulations, policies and procedures without the adoption of "a sufficient system of review to determine whether the existing policies and procedures were followed" exalts form over substance and is ineffective to protect the investing public.

The failure to have policies mandating a sufficient system for testing and Branch Office Manager follow-up on problems discovered during audits is the equivalent to having no system for compliance at all. It is not sufficient for a broker-dealer to establish a system of supervisory procedures which relied solely on supervision by Branch Office Managers.

2. Overview of PSI's Branch Office Supervisory Failures

* * *

The firm failed to have adequate procedures in place to ensure that Branch Office Managers and other supervisors adhered to compliance procedures ...

The firm did not adopt adequate supervisory procedures above the Branch Office Manager level. For example, the firm did not implement procedures identifying the supervisory steps that Regional Directors were to take to supervise the Branch Office Managers in their region. No job descriptions for Regional Directors delineating their supervisory responsibilities were ever adopted. In addition, the firm did not implement procedures outlining how senior management in the Retail Branch Group should supervise the Regional Directors or requiring compliance reports from Branch Office Managers or Regional Directors.

These failures contributed to and were a cause of the violations described herein and demonstrate that the firm failed to reasonably supervise the registered representatives who committed the underlying violations.

3. The Prior Order and PSI's Failure to Achieve Compliance with It

The Prior Order was the fifth time since June 1982 that the Commission found PSI and its predecessor firm to have failed in their supervisory responsibilities.[58] The Commission stressed the relevance of this fact:

---

58. *See* Prudential-Bache Securities, Inc., Exchange Act Release No. 34-20380 [1983–1984 Transfer Binder] [Fed.Sec.L.Rep. (CCH) ¶ 83,455 (November 17, 1983); Bache Halsey Stuart Shields, Inc., Exchange Act Release No. 34-19725 [1982–1983 Transfer Binder] Fed.Sec.L.Rep. (CCH) ¶ 83,350 (May

Such a past history of supervisory behavior is clearly germane when reviewing Prudential–Bache conduct in the matter at issue in this case. Many of the same facts and supervisory deficiencies common to those prior proceedings are again present in the two separate matters embraced by the instant consolidated proceedings. Moreover, certain procedures which Prudential–Bache had been ordered to implement to remedy those deficiencies were not followed in this matter.

The Prior Order made specific findings regarding PSI's supervisory deficiencies and required the firm to comply with its representations and undertakings designed to remedy those deficiencies. PSI failed in certain respects to adopt, implement or maintain effective procedures sufficient to achieve compliance with the Prior Order as discussed herein. These failures were a contributing cause of the underlying violations.

a. Failure to Achieve Compliance with Certain Recommendations of the Consultant

The firm entered into an undertaking to retain an independent outside Consultant and to "adopt, implement and maintain any and all policies and procedures recommended by the Consultant" or "alternative procedures designed to achieve the same objective or purpose as that recommended by the Consultant." The Consultant completed his review and issued his Report in July 1986. As discussed herein, PSI did not follow certain important recommendations of the Consultant.

(1) Branch Procedures Concerning Active Accounts

The Consultant recommended that PSI alter its procedures concerning Branch Office Manager review of active accounts in several respects, including the establishment of a requirement that Branch Office Managers personally contact the customer at the first appearance of the customer's account on the active account report and at "appropriate intervals" thereafter. The Consultant further recommended that the firm should "alter its procedures so as to assure greater compliance with [the personal contact] requirement" and "so as to better achieve more comprehensive surveillance of active accounts."

PSI failed to comply with these Consultant's recommendations in several respects: the active account procedures actually adopted were often not complied with; the firm failed to implement effective procedures to monitor Branch Office Manager compliance with the procedure; and when certain PSI officials became aware of such noncompliance, they failed to take timely and effective action to achieve compliance.

As the Consultant observed, the active account procedure is the primary surveillance tool by which Compliance monitors Branch Office Manager supervision of registered representatives regarding improper sales practices. Apart from the branch office audits, which generally occur annually, it was the only procedure PSI had to document Branch Office Manager supervisory activities in this area. The firm's Com-

---

3, 1983); Bache Halsey Stuart Shields, Inc., Exchange Act Release No. 34-19003 [1982 Transfer Binder] Fed.Sec.L.Rep. (CCH) ¶ 83,249 (August 24, 1982); Bache Halsey Stuart Shields, Inc., Exchange Act Release No. 34-18796, 25 SEC Docket 721 (June 8, 1982); Prudential-Bache Securities, Inc., Exchange Act Rel. No. 34-22755 [1985–1986 Transfer Binder] Fed.Sec.L.Rep. (CCH) ¶ 83,948 (January 2, 1986).

pliance Manual requires the Branch Office Manager to review the accounts which appear for the first time on the active account report, discuss the account with the registered representative, personally contact the customer to reasonably determine that the trading in the account is consistent with the customer's investment objectives and financial resources, document his review on an active account review form and forward the form to Compliance. Without the documentation, Compliance cannot adequately monitor Branch Office Manager supervision of the broker handling the account.

Although the staff's investigation of this matter commenced in May 1990, the firm's own analysis showed that at least 40 branches continued to have significant deficiencies as late as July 1991. The firm had notice at least as early as July 1989 of widespread failure to comply with the active account procedure, yet failed to timely remedy the deficiencies. Although adherence to the procedure improved substantially over time, deficiencies in this area continued until early 1992.

(2) Compliance Department Authority (Compliance Directives)

In the Prior Order, the Commission specifically observed that "Prudential–Bache had no policy, practice or guidelines setting forth the appropriate action to be taken, such as informing the Law Department, when a branch manager chose to disobey the Compliance Department's trading restrictions." The Commission also observed that "[a] broker-dealer is not meeting its supervisory obligations under the federal securities laws if its Compliance Department can be disregarded or otherwise rendered ineffective by a branch manager." In response to these Commission criticisms the Consultant recommended:

> A specific policy directive should be issued announcing that Compliance Department decisions take precedence and remain in force and effect unless and until reversed by the General Counsel after consultation with the Compliance department, the relevant Regional Director and the President of Retail Group, if necessary or appropriate. The policy directive also should emphasize that the General Counsel has the ultimate and final responsibility for all compliance decisions and his decisions remain final unless revoked or revised by the Chief Administrative Officer or Chief Executive Officer.

The firm's updated Compliance Manual adopted this recommendation. However, the firm did not define "Compliance Department decisions" and did not give Compliance sufficient authority to enforce its decisions. For several years, Compliance requests, instructions and directives to the Regional Directors and Branch Office Managers to follow the active account procedure were not effectively complied with. Because of these and other problems outlined herein, the firm never effectively implemented this fundamental recommendation of the Consultant.

b. PSI's Failure to Achieve Compliance with Its Undertaking to Remedy Failures Uncovered by Audits

Pursuant to the Prior Order, PSI entered into an undertaking to implement and maintain procedures designed to assure that all failures and violations identified by the firm's audits would be remedied within 30 days after the completion of the audit report. PSI auditors routinely sent their reports to senior PSI officials in the Retail Branch Group, the Audit Department, the Law Department, and the Compliance Department. The audit reports informed senior management officials of the Branch Office Managers' failures to comply with the firm's active account procedures. In these reports, Branch Office Managers represented that they had or would remedy deficiencies identified by the audits. Although the Compliance Director sent memoranda to the Regional Directors and took steps to follow up, the firm failed to take timely and effective action to remedy the systemic problem.

The firm had no effective procedures defining specific responsibility for correction of audit deficiencies or outlining specific corrective steps to be taken. In addition, there were defects in the firm's audit approach in that the firm did not require any effort to correct active account deficiencies retroactively. The firm's procedures addressed only the issue of how deficiencies should be corrected prospectively. For example, the Branch Office Manager in the Atlanta (Piedmont) branch was not required to contact customers or review accounts that had previously appeared on active account reports. The firm overly relied upon the Branch Office Managers' representations that active account deficiencies had been or would be corrected. Moreover, the firm had no procedures requiring the Branch Office Manager to increase supervision when deficiencies were identified or requiring that branches with audit deficiencies be examined more frequently. This lack of procedures resulted in audit deficiencies not being corrected in an effective and timely manner, which was a significant factor in the firm's failure to detect and prevent fraud.

Notes and Questions

1. The SEC's order in *Prudential Securities* was extensive and demonstrated a framework for a reasonable supervisory system for large broker-dealers. The SEC required *Prudential's* board to establish a Compliance Committee, of no fewer than three people, responsible for overseeing its compliance with the SEC's order, federal securities laws, and rules of applicable SROs. In addition, the Compliance Committee was to report, at least quarterly, on its activities to the board. The Compliance Committee also had authority to enforce compliance with Compliance Directives issued by *Prudential's* Director of Compliance. The SEC's order specifically defined a Compliance Directive as:

    (A) any instruction from the Compliance Department, designated as such, to any PSI employee(s) to cease any activity or course of conduct or to affirmatively take action to comply with federal and state securities laws, the rules and regulations of all national securities exchanges, the MSRB, and self-regulatory organizations of which PSI is a member, or PSI's policies and procedures embodied in its Compliance Manual or other Compliance Department publications; or

(B) any other instruction from the Compliance Department to any PSI employee(s) designated as a Compliance Directive.

In Section VII.C of the SEC's 1993 Order, The SEC directs *Prudential* to perform specific activities and reporting structures with respect to compliance. Identify and describe some of the reporting structures required in the SEC's order in *Prudential Securities.*

[handwritten: → To ensure there was an overarching compliance structure]

[handwritten: • That corrections were retroactive.]

[handwritten: • To follow the advice of the consultant.]

3. *Reasonable Discharge of Supervisory Duties*

The SEC will sanction a broker-dealer if it fails to discharge reasonably its supervisory duties even if it has an adequate supervisory system in place. Many failure-to-discharge cases may be organized into two general categories: (1) The supervisors fail to follow established procedures and (2) the supervisors fail to react to "red flags." Supervisors may fail to follow established procedures for a myriad of reasons. Perhaps the procedures failed to state clearly the allocation of responsibility between supervisors, supervisors were inadequately trained, or supervisors were just plain negligent. It is also important that senior management indicate clearly the importance of maintaining an adequate supervisory system in order to encourage a culture of compliance at the firm.[59] This means that compliance should be just as important to the broker-dealer as profits.

Red flags or warning signs are numerous and may depend on the broker-dealer's lines of business. Red flags consist of the types of activities that suggest that misconduct may be occurring at the broker-dealer. The cause of failure to react to red flags may be the same as failure to follow established procedures. Basically, supervisors must be alert to possible trouble or warning signs and respond in an adequate manner. In addition, the SEC has identified certain patterns of activity that constitute red flags, i.e., that warrant further investigation by supervisors.

Examples of red flags include:

- An unusually high level of aggressive trading, a substantial portion of which was on margin and in conflict with the customer's investment goals and objectives and limited financial resources.

- Identification by compliance of accounts as accounts with high commissions and active trading.

- An unusually large number of margin calls and liquidations.

- Generation of a large percentage of the registered representatives' commissions from a relatively small number of customers.

- Trading by the registered representative in a customer account that is inconsistent with the customer's investment objectives, age, and financial status.

- A registered representative who fails to take a vacation.

---

59. For an example of a broker-dealer that has encouraged a culture of compliance see *Urban* in section I of this chapter.

Inevitably, the supervisory system is only as good as the broker-dealer's employees. The broker-dealer relies on its employees to reasonably discharge their supervisory duties. Identify in the following case whether the supervisor's failure to discharge his supervisory duties was due to failure to follow established procedures and/or failure to react to red flags.

In the Matter of Raymond James Financial Services, Inc., J. Stephen Putman and David Lee Ullom

Initial Decision Release No. 296 (Sept. 15, 2005)

ISSUES

1. Whether Raymond James and Mr. Putnam failed reasonably to supervise Dennis Herula (Mr. Herula), a person subject to their supervision, with a view to preventing or detecting Mr. Herula's violations of Section 17(a) of the Securities Act and Section 10(b) of the Exchange Act and Rule 10b-5 thereunder.

FINDINGS OF FACT

Brite Business Corporation

Brite Business Corporation (Brite Business) was a non-public company set up to defraud investors. Michael Clarke (Mr. Clarke) originated Brite Business in the United Kingdom. Mr. Clarke "began soliciting investors through Brite Business S.A., a British Virgin Islands company, which was established in December 1997." Mr. Clarke's acquaintance Johan C. Hertzog (Mr. Hertzog) brought in Martin D. Fife (Mr. Fife), who agreed to manage client funds. Mr. Fife allegedly had influential friends and accoutrements of wealth, including a residence on Central Park West in New York City. In April 1999, Mr. Fife arranged for Charles Sullivan (Mr. Sullivan) to incorporate Brite Business. In 2000, Mr. Fife, Mr. Hertzog, Robert M. Wachtel (Mr. Wachtel), and Mr. Clarke, represented that they were on Brite Business's board. Mr. Fife and Mr. Sullivan represented that they were Brite Business's president and vice president, respectively.[60] From April 1999 until it was dissolved around March 2001, Brite Business was a Delaware corporation with an office address in New York City. Beginning in October 1999, Brite Business maintained investor funds in brokerage accounts at Raymond James's Cranston, Rhode Island, branch office (Cranston branch office).

From 1999 through 2002, Brite Business engaged in a fraudulent offering scheme, run by Mr. Fife and others, in which it represented that investments of a minimum

---

60. According to Brite Business, Mr. Fife, a Lehigh University graduate, was a trustee of each of the Dreyfus Funds and one of the most respected investment bankers in South Africa. Mr. Clarke gained extraordinary marketing expertise in the telecommunications industry as an area manager for British Telecom. Mr. Wachtel, Brite Business's representative for North, South, and Central America, "converted, leveraged, compounded and traded assets for some of the most well-known and influential industrialists, financial magnates such as the world-renowned gold trader, Mr. Jack Lazar." Mr. Sullivan served for eight years as Chairman of the National Football League.

of one million dollars could earn double digit interest per month. Brite Business represented that when it accumulated $100 million it would "leverage" the funds to purchase T-bills, or some other government issue, and without leaving the Brite Business account those deposits would earn astronomical returns. It was not clear what Brite Business intended to do with the investment proceeds or how it would be able to pay such astronomical returns. Some understood that Brite Business intended to use the funds as a credit enhancer allowing it to borrow more funds, while others believed that international entities would pay astronomical sums to be allowed to show Brite Business's funds to "enhance their balance sheet." At least one investor believed that Brite Business would deposit his funds at "Bank Raymond James," and would use pooled funds to buy T-bills, which would enable Brite Business to borrow from other sources and earn more than the T-bill rate on the pooled $100 million. All investors believed the investment involved no risk of capital.

Raymond James

Raymond James is registered with the Commission as a broker-dealer pursuant to Section 15(b) of the Exchange Act ...

Raymond James "is an independent contractor firm that introduces its business into Raymond James & Associates, Inc.," and its primary regulator is the National Association of Securities Dealers (NASD). Raymond James & Associates, Inc., (R.J. & Associates), a member of the New York Stock Exchange, performs the research, execution, clearing, bookkeeping, and is responsible for servicing all customer accounts at Raymond James. R.J. & Associates has clearing relationships with forty-four other broker-dealers, in addition to Raymond James. These two broker-dealers conduct the majority of the business of the holding company.

During the relevant period, August 1999 through December 2000, Raymond James had from 1,100 to 4,000 registered representatives, who were allowed to engage in business activities other than buying and selling securities. About fifty percent of Raymond James's registered representatives engaged in some type of business activity outside the firm, such as selling insurance or financial planning. Between ten to twenty percent of Raymond James's registered representatives worked outside their assigned offices regularly, and about five percent never went to the office.

The NASD applies the same rules to all registered representatives whether they are independent contractors or employees. This proceeding involves the Cranston branch office, part of the securities division of Raymond James. Most of Raymond James's approximately 550 branch offices located throughout the United States were staffed by two or three registered representatives. Under NASD rules, Raymond James designated the Cranston branch office as an Office of Supervisory Jurisdiction (OSJ), which required that it have a registered principal.

Mr. Putnam

Mr. Putnam, sixty-two years old, graduated from Bowdoin College in 1965, and served with the Army in Vietnam. Mr. Putnam was with his family's securities firm, F.L. Putnam, from 1968 until 1981, and in 1979 was chairman of the board of directors of the NASD. Mr. Putnam's Form U-4 shows five items in the late 1970s or early 1980s: two offers of settlement and three acceptance, waiver & consents. These matters involved allegations of failure to supervise, failure to maintain net capital, "integration with respect to a tax incentive investment," and excessive mark-ups. The result in almost each instance was a censure and a fine of $1,000 or $1,500, which F.L. Putnam paid. Mr. Putnam did not pay anything personally.

In July 1983, Mr. Putnam became president and chief executive officer (CEO) of Robert Thomas. He became an executive vice president and board member of the holding company in about 1987. When Raymond James was created in January 1999, Mr. Putnam became president, chief operating officer, and a director. Mr. Putnam reported to the CEO. Mr. Putnam's responsibilities included direct oversight of the securities division, which included the Cranston branch office. Mr. Putnam supervised the activities of the branch offices in conjunction with Raymond James's Compliance Department (Compliance Department).

David Ullom

Mr. Ullom, a graduate of Pennsylvania State University, began working in the securities industry in 1970. From 1974 until 1991, Mr. Ullom was an owner and the CEO of Barclay Investments, a broker-dealer with three offices and twenty registered representatives. Mr. Ullom first met Mr. Putnam in the 1970s when Mr. Ullom and some associates from Barclay Investments became a division of F.L. Putnam. Mr. Ullom considered Mr. Putnam a friend and contacted Mr. Putnam in 1991 when he was looking for a position.

Mr. Ullom had no significant regulatory violations when he signed a Registered Representative Agreement with Robert Thomas on June 7, 1992. In 1994, when he became the principal of the Robert Thomas office in Rhode Island, Mr. Ullom held the following licenses: general securities, financial principal, general principal, options principal, municipal principal, and investment adviser. The Independent Sales Associate Agreement he signed with Robert Thomas in 1994 provided that Mr. Ullom was an independent contractor with Robert Thomas.

The terms of the Independent Sales Associate Agreement required Mr. Ullom to maintain an office, to bear the expenses, to be responsible for assuring that registered representatives in the office adhered to all applicable regulations, cooperated with audits, and to indemnify Raymond James against any liability arising from his conduct, or that of a registered representative in the office. Mr. Ullom managed Raymond James's Cranston branch office as an independent contractor, Foxhill Management (Foxhill), with a checking account in the name of "Foxhill d/b/a Raymond James Financial Services." The Foxhill account was the operating account for the Cranston branch office, and the account statements for 1999 and 2000 were in the Foxhill file at the Cranston branch office. Foxhill, a Rhode Island C corporation, provided office space, utilities, staff support, employee benefits, and "interfaced with Raymond James for purposes of receiving commission dollars back that had been generated." Signs in the Cranston branch office identified only Raymond James. All mailings, account documents, and client payments were to Raymond James. Mr. Ullom could hire registered representatives subject to Raymond James's approval.

In 1995, Mr. Ullom settled an allegation that a registered investment adviser he co-owned had mischaracterized revenue. The Commission Order found that Mr. Ullom: (1) made false statements to a Rhode Island Department of Business Regulation examiner; (2) directed the investment adviser's bookkeeper to alter financial documents; (3) distributed a brochure with misleading information; (4) violated Section 207 of the Investment Advisers Act by making untrue statements of material fact in a report filed with the Commission; and (5) knew, or acted with reckless disregard for whether his actions were part of an overall activity that was improper and provided substantial assistance to the adviser's violations. When it accepted the settlement, the Commission knew Mr. Ullom was managing a broker-dealer branch office. The Commission censured Mr. Ullom; ordered him to cease and desist; fined him $10,000; ordered him to retake and pass the general securities principal examination before any future association with an investment adviser in a supervisory capacity; and attached conditions to Mr. Ullom's ownership of more than twenty percent of an investment adviser. The Commission's Order did not restrict Mr. Ullom's activities with a broker-dealer or investment adviser.

The Independent Sales Associate Agreement defined "Other Associates" as qualified registered representatives who enter independent contractor relationships with Raymond James. In the independent contractor relationship, each registered representative in the Cranston branch office had a direct contractual relationship with Raymond James, and a relationship with Foxhill. Raymond James took between ten and twenty-five percent of the commissions earned by registered representatives in the Cranston branch office. Raymond James forwarded the remainder monthly to the Foxhill account to be disbursed roughly twenty-five percent to Foxhill and fifty percent to the registered representatives. Raymond James terminated Mr. Ullom in November 2001 for failure to supervise.

I find Mr. Ullom totally lacking in credibility. He frequently changed his testimony after he was confronted with contradictory prior testimony or exhibits. Mr. Ullom lied and withheld information from Mr. Putnam, and he assisted Mr. Herula's fraudulent activities.

Dennis Herula

Mr. Herula is a fifty-eight-year-old high school graduate who attended college and served in the military. Mr. Herula claims to have been associated with "Kemper, Merrill Lynch, Shearson Lehman Brothers, Oppenheimer, W.C. Roney & Company, E.F. Hutton" in his twenty or more years in the securities industry. Mr. Ullom forwarded Mr. Herula's application to become associated with Robert Thomas to the Compliance Department in August 1999. Robert Thomas checked Mr. Herula's criminal record, his financial background, and with his prior employers before hiring him. In the materials the Compliance Department reviewed, Mr. Herula had no serious reported complaints in ten years of industry experience. Mr. Ullom knew Mary Lee Capalbo (Ms. Capalbo) was married to Mr. Herula. Mr. Putnam terminated Mr. Herula on December 26, 2000, effective the first business day of January 2001.

The Registered Representative Agreement (Agreement) between Raymond James and Mr. Herula provided that: (1) Mr. Herula was being retained by Mr. Ullom as an independent contractor pursuant to an Independent Sales Associate Agreement between Raymond James and Mr. Ullom; (2) the Agreement did not create an agency, employment, or joint venture relationship; and (3) Mr. Herula had "the right to solicit and engage in the purchase and sale for [Raymond James] approved securities with the general public, and engage in other business activities except to the extent such activities are subject to the rules, regulations and interpretations of Regulatory Authorities." As branch manager, Mr. Ullom was Mr. Herula's first-level supervisor in 1999 and 2000.

In August and September 1999, Mr. Herula worked in the Cranston branch office during normal business hours. For the remainder of 1999, Mr. Herula came to the office late in the day or at night because he said he was caring for his ill wife. Mr. Ullom claims that he allowed Mr. Herula to work from his home and other locations in accord with Raymond James's policies. Beginning in January 2000, Mr. Ullom claims that Mr. Herula came to the office about once a month because he said he was traveling and raising funds for Brite Business, an outside business activity that Raymond James allowed. Mr. Herula came into the Cranston branch office about once a month in the first half of 2000, and a total of four times between May and December 2000. According to Mr. Ullom, this was unusual for a registered representative, but because the accounts Mr. Herula handled were very conservative accounts, they did not require frequent client contact.

Raymond James and Brite Business

Mr. Ullom, on behalf of Mr. Herula, requested that Mr. Putnam meet with Brite Business, about a business opportunity for Raymond James from people with substantial assets. At the time, Mr. Herula had been associated with Raymond James for about two months and had fifteen to twenty client accounts, the largest with assets of about $2 million.

Mr. Putnam was on the holding company's Capital Markets Committee, and was told that Brite Business would deposit $5 million in a Raymond James account. On October 19 and 20, 1999, Mr. Herula sent Mr. Putnam the resumes of Ian Doidge (Mr. Doidge), Principal & Practice Leader, Global Asset Services Group, Arthur Andersen Business Consulting (Arthur Andersen), Toronto, and Mr. Fife. Mr. Putnam called Arthur Andersen and confirmed that Mr. Doidge was at the phone number he provided. Mr. Putnam believed that Brite Business was a legitimate business enterprise based on Mr. Doidge's position with Arthur Andersen, Mr. Fife's credentials, and Brite Business's $5 million deposit.

During the week of October 20, 1999, Mr. Putnam, assembled an ad hoc committee composed of John C. Maynard (Mr. Maynard), a vice president with Raymond James Trust Company (R.J. Trust); Thomas R. Tremaine (Mr. Tremaine), vice president and treasurer at R.J. & Associates; Jeff Julien (Mr. Julien), chief financial officer at the holding company; John Kritsas (Mr. Kritsas) and John Walsh (Mr. Walsh) from R.J. & Associates. This committee met with Mr. Herula and Mr. Doidge, representing

Brite Business, at Raymond James's headquarters. Mr. Ullom was not invited but attended the meeting.

The meeting lasted less than an hour. Mr. Putnam understood that Brite Business was involved in construction in foreign jurisdictions. Brite Business proposed that Raymond James participate in its activities by: (1) loaning money for purchase of Treasuries; (2) holding a trust; (3) doing the transactions such as the purchase of Treasury bonds or securities; and (4) having R.J. Trust hold the assets in escrow as well as the trust receipt. Brite Business described a series of transactions in the range of $50 to $100 million each where United States Treasuries (Treasuries) would enter the United States from England and be leveraged so that the asset side of Brite Business's balance sheet would be increased. Brite Business proposed placing the Treasuries and other funds under a trust arrangement, which would protect the funds and allow the transaction to be unwound. These activities would supposedly allow Brite Business some tax advantages. Supposedly, the interest cost of the borrowing would be a tax benefit as it would offset income earned abroad. Mr. Doidge said that the offsetting increase in liabilities did not matter for this particular strategy. However, he claimed that he could not disclose the tax implications in detail because of confidentiality issues. The meeting participants were told the strategy was proprietary to Arthur Andersen and that Raymond James did not have to be concerned about what happened inside the "black box." In his investigative testimony, Mr. Putnam acknowledged that there were several renditions of the "balance sheet enhancement," but that it was a tax strategy and involved "depositing money into some sort of an escrow, buying some treasuries, doing either a repo or a reverse repo with a bank." Mr. Putnam testified that one issue was whether Raymond James would be willing to make a loan. In an e-mail sent on January 17, 2000, Mr. Putnam described the transaction as follows:

> It involved moving treasuries from England to the U.S. and creating a loan from one group to another through [Raymond James] and then doing a repo on the instruments with the proceeds going into a trusteed bank account and the transactions being able to be unwound every ninety days. It was suggested that [Raymond James] would be the custodian of the bonds, do the transactions, trustee the account, and have an [Investment Management Program for Advisory Clients] arrangement with respect to the account. We were told this had something to do with a balance sheet for a deal or deals. Arthur Andersen's representative assured us that the money was not fraudulent and that the money came from good sources. The principal Martin Fife sits on the boards of several Dreyfus Funds and his wife has been the Deputy Mayor of NY and he appears to be quite connected.

This transaction would have been very unusual for R.J. Trust, which provided only personal fiduciary trust services to Raymond James's clients. Mr. Maynard attended the meeting in place of his boss, David Ness (Mr. Ness), the head of R.J. Trust, and described Brite Business's proposal as a complicated tax shelter that involved debt-financed purchase of Treasuries.

The ad hoc committee met only once soon after the October 1999 meeting to discuss the proposal. Everyone was skeptical about the proposal and questioned Brite Business's motives. The consensus was that Raymond James should not get involved in something they did not fully understand. Mr. Putnam indicated that the transaction did not sound like something Raymond James would involve itself with. In an e-mail on October 29, 1999, Mr. Walsh wrote to Mr. Putnam and others, "My gut feeling on this deal is bad. Let's continue to proceed very cautiously."

Mr. Putnam testified that some people jumped to conclusions about what occurred in October but that the ad hoc committee: (1) did not take a formal vote and reject the transaction; (2) reached a consensus to do more discovery but would not commit to the transaction; and (3) had healthy skepticism, but was willing to look at subsequent proposals from Brite Business. The size of the transaction was beyond Raymond James's normal transaction size. Brite Business also wanted to start the transaction before the end of 1999. Mr. Putnam testified that the proposal considered in October became moot within days because of its size, complexity, and Brite Business's desire to complete it by year end. Following the October meeting, Mr. Maynard and Mr. Tremaine looked at whether there were some parts of the transaction that Raymond James could be comfortable with. For example, on October 25, 1999, Mr. Maynard reported that Brite Business thought "[Mr. Putnam's] suggestion will work" and R.J. Trust might be able to hold the cash for Brite Business.

On October 25, 1999, Brite Business opened a cash account at Raymond James with a $5 million deposit. Mr. Herula was the account representative, and Mr. Ullom approved the new account form. The Corporate Resolution accompanying the New Account Form was signed by Brite Business Assistant Secretary, Farouk Alam Khan; President, Mr. Fife; Chairman & CEO, Mr. Hertzog; and trader, Mr. Doidge. Mr. Putnam believed that Raymond James knew its client, Brite Business, "quite well." On October 26, 1999, Brite Business entered an Investment Management Program for Advisory Clients (IMPAC), which provided that Raymond James would be paid $250,000 for investment advisory services.

On November 9, 1999, Mr. Ullom called Mr. Ness and yelled at him complaining that Raymond James would lose the Brite Business transactions to First Union Bank "because the folks in the home office were concerned about minor details." Mr. Ullom claimed that Mr. Maynard had behaved in an unprofessional manner at the October meeting with Brite Business and had lost Raymond James the business. Mr. Ullom also told Mr. Ness that Brite Business was a big client and that R.J. Trust had one more chance to get the job done.

Mr. Ness informed Mr. Maynard of Mr. Ullom's criticisms, which Mr. Maynard denied. Mr. Maynard was so taken aback by Mr. Ullom's actions that he learned through business contacts that Brite Business had contacted First Union Bank with the same deal and First Union Bank had "sent them packing." Contrary to the representations of Mr. Ullom and Mr. Herula, the deal made no sense to First Union Bank and it had "distinctly not" done the deal. Mr. Maynard relayed this information to Mr. Ness, Mr. Putnam, Mr. Julien, Mr. Kritsas, and Mr. Tremaine.

On November 10, 1999, upon learning this information, Mr. Ness e-mailed Mr. Putnam and stated that he found the fact that First Union Bank had not done the deal "particularly disturbing since it potentially casts some question in the direction of [Brite Business's] principals." Mr. Tremaine was convinced that Raymond James should not participate "at any level." Mr. Tremaine's comment referred to the transaction Brite Business proposed in October.

On November 9, 1999, in an e-mail to Mr. Putnam, Mr. Julien, Mr. Kritsas, and Mr. Tremaine, Mr. Ness: (1) asked whether Mr. Ullom was a significant producer with experience in sophisticated transactions; (2) criticized the quality of the escrow agreement that Mr. Ullom had sent him for Brite Business; (3) stated that Brite Business's current proposal did not pass "the smell test either," i.e., as an aggressive tax shelter; and (4) stated it was too difficult "to understand the economic justification of the deal." Mr. Ness questioned the economic justification for the deal, the "C Team player" involved, and worried about being the only one with clean hands in a dirty deal and aggressive tax shelter. In a November 10, 1999, response, Mr. Putnam did not adopt Mr. Ness's concerns. Rather, Mr. Putnam stated that he understood that "the first deal was done with First Union"; that Mr. Ullom had "run a brokerage firm and been responsible for underwriting multi-million dollar deals"; and he questioned whether the reference to "C Team players" was to the English broker, an alleged participant, whom Raymond James was unable to identify.

On November 10, 1999, Mr. Ness responded to a draft agreement from Mr. Ullom concerning a Brite Business transaction. In the transaction, Raymond James would act as an escrow agent where Brite Business borrowed funds from a bank. Mr. Ness viewed Brite Business's November proposal as only using R.J. Trust as an escrow agent, where Brite Business's October proposal would have had Raymond James lend funds, serve as an escrow agent, and do securities transactions.

On December 9, 1999, when Brite Business had about $12.3 million in its Raymond James brokerage account, Raymond James filled a Brite Business order to purchase $115 million of Treasuries on margin. In effect, Raymond James lent Brite Business approximately $103 million, with the United States Treasuries as security. Considering the liquidity of Treasuries, the risk to Raymond James was minimal. This purchase was a "highly unusual transaction" for Raymond James because of its size, and was likely the largest margin purchase of Treasuries that Raymond James had ever executed.

The transaction was unusual because of its size, but principally because it resulted in a loss to Brite Business, in that the coupon on the Treasuries was less than the lending rate, which created a negative spread. Mr. Putnam was satisfied that persons representing Brite Business were sophisticated investors who understood the transaction and wanted it to happen. Kevin A. Carreno (Mr. Carreno), one of three Raymond James principals who could approve such a large trade, approved the transaction and subsequently informed Mr. Putnam of the transaction. Operating persons in Raymond James's government bond department handling the purchase were upset that the order arrived late on a Friday afternoon, without any advance notice, which gave them little time to arrange adequate financing to close the transaction. On December 13, 1999, Mr. Tremaine informed Mr. Putnam that "[a]t this point I do not want to do another trade of this size in this account. Once we fully contemplate the impact [on operations and the firm's cash and capital position] we can then discuss."

Mr. Putnam was not concerned by the transaction, which he considered to be in the normal course of business. Mr. Putnam was not concerned that the transaction was part of the balance sheet enhancement program because he understood the purchase was in connection with a repurchase agreement that Brite Business had with the Bank of New York, and that the securities were being delivered to that institution.[61] Mr. Herula gave Mr. Putnam this information after the purchase of the Treasuries. On December 16, 1999, Mr. Herula mentioned that Mr. Fife would be depositing an additional $22 million in the Brite Business account, and that Mr. Fife had provided a reference to Bill Britt, who had a portfolio of $100 million. Mr. Putnam urged Mr. Fife to sell the Treasuries when the reverse repurchase transaction did not occur by January 1, 2000, because he was concerned that regulators might fault Raymond James for the margin interest Brite Business was paying. Mr. Fife, however, assured Raymond James that he wanted the arrangement to continue. Mr. Putnam, Mr. Augenbraun, Mr. Carreno, and Mr. Tremaine did not understand the purchase of Treasuries as indicating participation by Raymond James in the transactions that Brite Business proposed in October 1999.

Around December 13, 1999, Mr. Putnam told Mr. Carreno that Brite Business was involved in balance sheet enhancement and that Brite Business might bring some managed accounts to Raymond James.[62] On December 16, 1999, Mr. Putnam indicated to Mr. Tremaine, Dennis Zank (Mr. Zank) and Mr. Van Sayler, from R.J. & Associates, that Mr. Fife appeared to be using a tax strategy using Treasuries, and that if Mr. Fife's relationship with Raymond James was going to be more than a treasury trade, perhaps "Tom [James] or Tremaine and me" should meet with Mr. Fife.

On December 20, 1999, the Compliance and Standards Committee of the holding company (C&S Committee), chaired by Thomas James (Mr. James), the chairman and CEO of the holding company, discussed what standards should apply for processing large-size trades on margin. Mr. Putnam, who was also on the C&S Committee, was in London and missed the meeting.

On December 20, 1999, Mr. DiGirolamo informed Mr. Putnam, Mr. Greene, and Mr. Zank that the C&S Committee: (1) noted apparent failures on the bond desk and in the margin department in approving Brite Business's $115 million margin purchase of Treasuries; (2) questioned why the trade was done since the client was paying more

---

61. Mr. Putnam understood that as part of the repurchase agreement, the Bank of New York would buy the Brite Business Treasuries held at Raymond James. Brite Business would receive any amounts over the amounts owed in margin interest, and Brite Business would agree to repurchase the Treasuries from the Bank of New York at a later date at a fixed price.

62. Mr. Putnam was referring to the situation where an outside investment adviser provides the advice and Raymond James provides the record keeping. This is one of Raymond James's principal businesses, and is different from IMPAC where the financial adviser advises the client.

in margin interest than it was receiving in interest; (3) questioned why the trade was placed after a committee declined an earlier strategy; and (4) questioned whether the trade should stay on Raymond James's books and wondered if "there was some sort of scam going on." Mr. DiGirolamo commented that without knowing all the details "this smells a little fishy." Mr. Putnam believes the C&S Committee would have been satisfied if he had been present to explain that Mr. Fife was a sophisticated and knowledgeable client who was being advised by Arthur Andersen. However, several people who had looked at Brite Business's proposals were on the C&S Committee. Mr. Putnam had expressed concerns about Brite Business's motives for the Treasury transaction to Mr. DiGirolamo, Mr. Van Sayler, Mr. Zank, and Mr. James. On December 21, 1999, the C&S Committee approved a policy that any retail order for fixed income securities in excess of $1 million must be referred by the trading desk to the Compliance Department for approval prior to execution. The policy was further modified by raising the amount to $5 million, substituting customer relations for the Compliance Department, and specifying the transaction referred to margin purchases.

Mr. James informed Mr. Putnam on January 8, 2000, that he was strongly biased "to not do any trade or participate in any strategy that we do not understand. Thus, unless the Arthur Andersen and Holland [&] Knight people can convince the original committee to do the transaction, I want no other parts of it executed here." Mr. James understood that those who looked at the transaction in October concluded that Raymond James should not do the transaction, but "then the first phase occurred anyway." Mr. Putnam replied that: (1) he too was leery of doing any transaction that involves large number and appears illogical; (2) the original transaction Brite Business proposed in October was moot; (3) following his trip to New York the ad hoc committee would convene to consider Brite Business's proposals; and (4) the throw-off in personal business from Brite Business could be significant for the branch and the firm. Mr. James replied that a participant on the ad hoc committee informed him that it had rejected the transaction, and Mr. James did not want another step taken without a super majority vote of the ad hoc committee, and that at least one person was "more than nervous."

On January 7, 2000, Mr. Herula sent Mr. Putnam an e-mail describing an additional transaction that Brite Business would like to do with Raymond James that included a trust account. On January 12, 2000, Mr. Putnam and Barry Augenbraun (Mr. Augenbraun), senior vice president and corporate secretary of the holding company, an attorney and C&S Committee member, met with Mr. Fife and others at Mr. Fife's home, a large penthouse on Central Park West in New York City. The purpose of the meeting was to learn more about Brite Business, the new Brite Business proposal, and to meet Mr. Fife and other Brite Business principals. Mr. Augenbraun also wanted to determine why Brite Business had purchased Treasuries on margin in December 1999. At the January 2000 meeting, representatives of Brite Business presented an elaborate business plan from a package with Arthur Andersen's name on the cover. Brite Business's plan was to create new corporations, similar to Brite Business, to finance construction projects where Treasuries would be used to enhance the corporate balance sheets. There was no discussion of high-yield trading programs or high rates of return. Farouk Khan represented that he was involved in a bank in the Middle East. Mr. Doidge and Nick Gatto, an attorney with Holland & Knight, represented that balance sheet enhancement had been used in other places, that Sunoco used it in a bidding process, and that it was done all the time.

On January 17, 2000, Mr. Putnam sent ten people at Raymond James a: (1) description of the New York meeting, which included a description of a complex transaction that involved an encumbered pool of cash that would convince certain people that Brite Business was large enough to bid on certain jobs; and (2) recommendation from himself and Mr. Augenbraun that Raymond James "not become any further involved in these transactions. Mr. Putnam believes that the transactions Raymond James rejected had nothing to do with Brite Business's purchase of Treasuries. Mr. James and Mr. Maynard informed Mr. Putnam that they agreed with the decision. Mr. Putnam informed Mr. Fife that Raymond James would not be interested in the transaction Brite Business proposed in January, and suggested that Mr. Fife contact Bear Stearns, because it did a lot of aggressive work in the fixed-income area.[63] Neither Mr. Augenbraun nor Mr. Putnam saw any need to terminate Brite Business's brokerage account at Raymond James based on the meeting in New York.

Mr. Putnam believed that Raymond James should continue to "see if there was something [Raymond James] could do that we would feel comfortable doing with" Brite Business. A relationship with Brite Business offered the potential of large fees for Raymond James and the possibility of additional advisory business from wealthy friends and associates of Mr. Fife. Mr. Putnam might have rejected Brite Business out of hand, except that the people associated with Brite Business appeared to have substantial wealth, which could translate into new business for Raymond James.

On January 18 and 19, 2000, Mr. Herula communicated with Mr. Putnam, advancing support for the balance sheet enhancement program and projected that Raymond James would receive a large new account as a referral. Mr. Putnam was not able to obtain confirmation on the legitimacy of balance sheet transactions from two references supplied by Mr. Herula and Brite Business. On January 19, 2000, Mr. Herula informed Mr. Putnam that a new unnamed account was considering depositing $100 million to purchase an "RJ Bank CD," or another product that "we may wish to structure for him." "The purpose would be to assist Brite [Business] by margining or borrowing against the product." Mr. Herula asked for Mr. Putnam's help in salvaging the relationship. Mr. Putnam responded on January 19, 2000, that "[i]f this is the only thing they would do I can't see a problem but you mentioned some other transactions including a loan to Brite Business." Mr. Putnam talked with the referral from this transaction, professional investors "who would be purchasing bonds in large amounts, keeping a very large balance with" Raymond James. On January 28, 2000, Mr. Fife requested Mr. Putnam's assistance in establishing a line of credit at Raymond James or another institution for fixed

---

63. Mr. Augenbraun believed that Mr. Putnam was going to inform Mr. Fife to wind down the Brite Business account so that Raymond James was not extending credit on the purchase of Treasuries.

income trading by a new special purpose corporation. Mr. Putnam rejected the request on February 1, 2000, because the note issued by a new special purpose corporation backed by assets in escrow and an insurance bond would not be considered a marginable security.

Mr. Ullom informed Mr. Putnam on February 29, 2000, that Mr. Fife was raising money and Brite Business would possibly sell the Treasuries it had purchased on margin.[64] Mr. Putnam approved the sale of the Treasuries on February 29, 2000, but he and Mr. Zank questioned whether it made sense to do so a week before the maturity date of March 9, 2000. Mr. Zank commented, "I'm not sure why one would sell with maturity so close. However, I haven't understood this trade from the get go, so a sale at this time wouldn't surprise me."

On March 5, 2000, Mr. Herula sent Mr. Putnam an e-mail informing him that: (1) Brite Business planned to deposit substantial funds into its Raymond James account and that it may need to escrow with a third party; (2) Brite Business may need to purchase T-bills; and (3) he was developing additional business from a money manager that may bring in a $100 million deposit. On March 7, 2000, at Mr. Putnam's request, Mr. Ness agreed to look at whether R.J. Trust would serve as an escrow for a portion of Brite Business funds.

On March 13, 2000, Mr. Fife directed Mr. Herula to buy $100 million in Treasuries in the "Brite Business margin account" for the purpose of offsetting a substantial tax benefit elsewhere. Mr. Putnam did not consider this proposed Treasury purchase as related to Brite Business's "balance sheet enhancement program." Mr. Putnam considered the March proposal as standing alone. Mr. Putnam would not allow Brite Business to purchase additional Treasuries on margin so he rejected the transaction. Mr. Putnam did not want another situation like December when Raymond James's books showed Brite Business paying margin interest on a Treasury purchase, a situation that lacked economic sense. On March 15, 2000, Mr. Van Sayler informed Mr. Putnam that he believed that Mr. Herula "misrepresented the facts on this situation to the desk." Mr. Putnam asked for details and Mr. Van Sayler did not provide them. At the same time, Mr. Putnam approved Brite Business's purchase of $10 million of Treasuries for cash.

Supervision and Compliance at Raymond James

Pursuant to Rule 3030 of the NASD, Raymond James required persons conducting business outside the firm to file a form with the branch manager and the Compliance Department stating the nature of their outside activities. Mr. Putnam and Mr. Ullom knew in August 1999 that Mr. Herula was attempting to raise funds from commercial banks for Brite Business, and that this activity required that a form be filed. Raymond

64. Mr. Ullom did not tell Mr. Putnam that, on the same day, he had approved a letter of authorization (LOA) transmitting $10 million from the Brite Business account to Beehive International, LLC (Beehive), and a LOA transmitting $100,000 to Bill Britt representing "interest and is final payment to close out Britt/Beehive investment." Raymond James's Customer Accounts notified Mr. Putnam of the $10 million transfer to Beehive because it was a third-party distribution and it was unable to verbally confirm with Mr. Fife.

James has no form or memoranda on file showing that it was aware that Mr. Herula was conducting this outside business activity. Mr. Ullom did not file a Request for a Non Branch Location for Mr. Herula, which Raymond James required when a registered representative was conducting business from his home. Mr. Ullom did not know of any special procedures or compliance policies that Raymond James had in place for supervising registered representatives who worked outside the office. Raymond James had a long-standing policy that all outgoing written communications from registered representatives, including e-mails and facsimiles, had to be approved in advance by the branch manager. Raymond James always prohibited the use of Raymond James stationery for business outside of Raymond James. Mr. Ullom never inspected or reviewed Mr. Herula's work locations outside the Cranston branch office. Mr. Putnam did not know that Mr. Herula spent considerable or significant time away from the Cranston branch office.

Excluding provisions of the money laundering statutes, Raymond James's procedures for disbursing funds from an account had the sole objective of assuring that the client authorized the transfer of funds. The branch manager and registered representative are responsible for knowing the client and what type of business the client is conducting. Raymond James believes it has no right to question why a client is making a disbursement or whether the funds in the account belonged to the client.

Raymond James considered the transfer of funds to an unrelated or third-party account to be an out-of-the-norm transfer.

Between January 1999 and March or April 2000, what had been Robert Thomas's and was now Raymond James's securities division and what had been IMR's and was now Raymond James's investment management division, operated two separate compliance departments. Mr. Carreno was director of compliance at Raymond James's securities division and financial institutions division from January 1, 1999, until March 2000. Mr. Carreno reported to Mr. Putnam. To monitor both the securities division and the financial institutions division, the Compliance Department was staffed with only sixteen employees. Mr. Carreno testified that Robert Thomas had about 1,100 registered representatives located in 300 offices of supervisory jurisdiction.

Mr. Carreno considered the 1995 settlement Mr. Ullom entered with the Commission in 1995, and decided following discussions with Mr. Ullom and his counsel, that Robert Thomas should not subject Mr. Ullom to additional supervisory procedures. In making his decision, Mr. Carreno considered that Mr. Ullom's actions did not result in losses to clients, the bookkeeping entry involved was $1,800, and the Commission did not restrict Mr. Ullom's activities as a registered representative.

When the Robert Thomas and IMR compliance departments merged in about April 2000, Mr. DiGirolamo became chief of compliance for all Raymond James divisions. It appears that when Mr. DiGirolamo took charge, he applied the supervisory policies of IMR to the entire firm. Mr. DiGirolamo installed a new structure for the securities division in which a regional compliance officer reported to an associate director, who then reported to him. Mr. DiGirolamo reported to Tony Greene (Mr.

Greene), Raymond James's CEO and chairman. Mr. DiGirolamo had no involvement with Mr. Herula or Brite Business in 1999 and 2000.

Raymond James used its branch managers as its first line of defense against illegal activities by registered representatives. Raymond James required that branch managers pass either the branch managers exam or the general securities principal exam. Raymond James's Compliance Department had three major areas: (1) internal audits; (2) account monitoring, which included exceptions reports; and (3) dealing with customer complaints. The Compliance Department's role was to: (1) educate financial advisers and staff on rules, regulations, and policies; (2) conduct branch office audits; and (3) review exception reports and report results to supervisors. Raymond James conducted oversight of its branch offices by daily reviews of all business and an annual surprise audit conducted by its Branch Audit Department. Additional audits were performed if Raymond James had special concerns or special circumstances existed. The branch audit was the means of determining whether the supervisory practices were, in fact, being carried out. Broker-dealers depend on effective compliance audits to ensure their branch managers are supervising appropriately.

According to Mr. Carreno, Raymond James's Internal Supervisory Procedures (Supervisory Procedures) was a summary of the supervisory procedures at Raymond James. Raymond James had more detailed written procedures and there were also NASD rules. The Supervisory Procedures provided that a branch manager was to review and approve any business communication written by a registered representative to a member of the public, and a copy was to be retained in the branch files for review by the Internal Audit Department. Letters that were to be sent to three or more people were to be forwarded to the Compliance Department for review and approval. Registered representatives were to send all business related e-mails from the Cranston branch office to Mr. Ullom for his review. Registered representatives were prohibited from acting as an agent for a client, or an individual, without permission in writing from Raymond James. Registered representatives were also prohibited from raising, or agreeing to raise, money for any company, or individual, other than as an independent contractor for Raymond James, without written permission. The Supervisory Procedures also required branch offices to submit a monthly Compliance Report to the Compliance Department. The Supervisory Procedures contained a single sheet of Procedures for Raymond James Financial Services, Inc., Outside Activity, and a Request to Engage in Outside Activity (Form 1790) to be submitted to the Compliance Department. In some cases, the Compliance Department reviewed the Form 1790. Mr. Herula's activities in raising funds for Brite Business was the type of business activity that required a Form 1790, however; he never filed one. Every registered representative, including Mr. Herula, certified annually that he or she knew and understood Raymond James's compliance policies.

During the relevant period, the NASD and Raymond James required that any location where a registered representative worked as a primary or regular work location, other than the branch office, should be registered as a satellite office. In 1999-2000, the four room Cranston branch office had five or six registered representatives and only three desks. This space allocation was possible because Mr. Herula and three other registered representatives did not work at the branch office. The evidence is that only Mr. Ullom and Jason Ullom, his son, worked from the Cranston branch office in 1999-2000. Raymond James depended: (1) on the voluntary submission of requests for a non-branch location to inform them that a registered representative was working regularly from home; and (2) on the branch manager to make sure that correspondence and documentation for business activity conducted outside the office came through the office to which the registered representative was assigned. The Compliance Department was never notified that Mr. Herula worked almost entirely from locations other than the Cranston branch office. In his investigative testimony, Mr. DiGirolamo testified that branch managers were not required to report that a registered representative worked regularly from home, and acknowledged that Raymond James did not know the number of registered representatives working from home. At the hearing, however, Mr. DiGirolamo changed his testimony based on his review of the auditor's questionnaire. He testified that branch managers were asked during the 2000 audit if any registered representatives were working regularly outside the branch office. Mr. DiGirolamo's present position is that if the registered representative was regularly working at a location other than a branch office in 1999 and 2000, Raymond James required disclosure so that it could register the location as a satellite office with the NASD. Donald Runkle (Mr. Runkle), who became Raymond James's chief compliance officer in May 2004, acknowledged that prior to 2003, Raymond James did not maintain a list of who it believed worked at unregistered locations.

In accordance with Raymond James's policy, Mr. Ullom allowed Mr. Herula to work from locations other than the Cranston branch office. Raymond James allowed this and, in keeping with NASD requirements, insisted that locations outside the branch office could not be advertised, that all correspondence be sent from the branch office, and all files be maintained at the branch office. Mr. Carreno testified during the investigation that Raymond James did not require a registered representative to obtain approval to work from home. At the hearing, however, Mr. Carreno testified that Raymond James asked branch managers to fill out a form when a registered representative was going to operate regularly from home. Mr. Ullom never inspected or reviewed Mr. Herula's work locations outside the Cranston branch office. He was also unaware of any special procedures or compliance policies that Raymond James had in place for supervising registered representatives who worked outside the office.

The files in the Cranston branch office did not contain copies of correspondence from Mr. Herula. Mr. Herula testified that he worked out of his home offices from mid-December 1999, until he left Raymond James, and that his files contained copies of all his unauthorized correspondence.

Mr. Ullom and the registered representatives in the Cranston branch office signed a form annually representing that they observed the company's ethics policies, and its financial adviser business procedures. Mr. Ullom did not have Mr. Herula submit a Request to Engage in Outside Activity for his work raising funds for Brite Business.

Mr. Ullom testified that this was because Raymond James knew of Mr. Herula's attempts to arrange loans for Brite Business.

Raymond James's had Operations Manuals for compliance available in hard copy and online during the relevant period. The Compliance Department established parameters for situations that required review from a compliance perspective and the clearing firm produced computer generated exception reports showing these situations (exception reports). During the relevant period, R.J. & Associates periodically provided Raymond James's Compliance Department with over fifty different exception reports. On a monthly basis, the Compliance Department sent Mr. Ullom and other branch managers, MARS reports, which were a summary of exception reports applicable to the specific branch. The branch manager was required to review the MARS reports and perform any investigation that was required.

Sending the MARS reports to the branch offices, "didn't relieve the [C]ompliance [D]epartment from doing what it needed to do with the exception report" from a compliance perspective. The MARS reports for March, April, May, August, September, and October 2000, noted that the Brite Business and Mary Lee Capalbo, Esq., Special Client, a related account, issued third-party checks for millions of dollars, and/or transferred millions of dollars between accounts at Raymond James.

Raymond James's Notice of Mr. Herula's Unauthorized Correspondence and Other Information

Throughout the relevant period Mr. Herula signed and transmitted correspondence on Raymond James letterhead to investors in Brite Business. Mr. Herula signed most of this correspondence on Raymond James letterhead as Financial Consultant or Investment Manager. On November 28, 1999, Mr. Herula sent Brite Business, by facsimile, from the Cranston branch office, a form letter with three paragraphs of unauthorized representations and guarantees. This material appears in much of his later correspondence on behalf of Brite Business. Mr. Ullom denies he knew of this form letter, and agrees that no one at Raymond James was aware of it until a similar unauthorized letter appeared in March 2000.

Mr. Herula was not put on formal heightened supervision status by Mr. Putnam or the Compliance Department. Mr. Putnam thought heightened supervision would have been unusual based on a single piece of unauthorized correspondence and where Mr. Herula, in Mr. Putnam's view, was naïve. Mr. Putnam directed Mr. Ullom to monitor Mr. Herula's activities closely and to review Mr. Herula's correspondence. Mr. Putnam believed that Mr. Ullom knew he had "to get on top of [Mr. Herula's] correspondence," and that Mr. Ullom had placed Mr. Herula on enhanced monitoring. Mr. Putnam did not follow up to assure that Mr. Ullom was supervising Mr. Herula appropriately.

Mr. Putnam never sent internal auditors to the Cranston branch office to review Mr. Herula's correspondence. Raymond James's auditors are instructed to look for correspondence ... unauthorized correspondence can be the basis for further investigation. No one from Raymond James's headquarters came to the Cranston branch office to interview Mr. Herula or review his correspondence file....

R.J. & Associates's Client Services Department informed Mr. Putnam of the transfers to and from the restricted Brite Business account. Raymond James followed its procedures and established that the person controlling the account authorized each transfer. Mr. Putnam did not stop transfers from the Brite Business restricted account or question Mr. Ullom about them; no one at Raymond James called for more information on transfers of more than a million dollars from a restricted account to non-restricted accounts at Raymond James, and then to accounts outside Raymond James.

CONCLUSIONS OF LAW

1. Supervision of Mr. Herula

Arguments of the Parties

The Division maintains that Raymond James failed to adequately supervise Mr. Herula because its agent, Mr. Ullom, failed to do so. The Division argues that it is insufficient for a broker-dealer to establish a system of supervisory procedures that relies solely on supervision by branch managers, and that Raymond James was required to provide checks to ensure that the first-line supervisor was functioning adequately. The Division contends that broker-dealers conducting business through off-site offices cannot adequately discharge their supervisory obligations when there is no inspection of off-site locations. The Division charges that Raymond James had essentially no policies or procedures in place for supervising registered representatives working outside the branch office. It claims that Raymond James failed to keep track of who was working off-site, or how they were being monitored. The Division claims that Raymond James had no systems in place to ensure that Mr. Ullom was examining Mr. Herula's off-site office, monitoring Mr. Herula's correspondence, or providing additional scrutiny once red flags were discovered as to Mr. Herula's unauthorized activities.

The Division further alleges that Raymond James acted unreasonably by failing to take adequate steps to investigate or terminate Mr. Herula's illegal activities until approximately $16.4 million in investor funds were misappropriated or otherwise dissipated. The Division faults Raymond James for: (1) not reviewing the operating account as part of the Cranston branch office audit; (2) not having written procedures for placing registered representatives on heightened supervision, and for not placing Mr. Herula on heightened supervision; and (3) not investigating transfers from the Brite Business account to the employee-related Mary Lee Capalbo Esq., Special Client account.

The Division views the three procedures that Raymond James claims to have used to ensure compliance—the internal audit, the monthly compliance reports, and exception reports—as largely ineffective. It notes that: (1) the internal audit and the monthly compliance reports place undue reliance on self-reporting; (2) the internal auditor lacked information or resources necessary to perform a meaningful audit; and (3) no one in the compliance department reviewed the exceptions reports for accuracy and there is no evidence that the majority of suspicious trades that appeared on the exceptions reports were reviewed.

Next, the Division argues that Mr. Putnam, Mr. Ullom, and other Raymond James executives failed to respond reasonably to the following events that raised red flags suggesting that Mr. Herula was engaged in inappropriate activities.

* * *

3. The fact that Mr. Herula continued to urge Raymond James to stay involved and consider proposals from Brite Business after the ad hoc group came to a consensus that it would not do the transaction Brite Business proposed.

4. The suspicions of persons at Raymond James and affiliates in November 1999 on learning that Mr. Herula and Mr. Ullom had falsely represented that First Union Bank had agreed to the Brite Business transaction.

5. The purchase on margin of approximately $115 million of U.S. Treasuries by Brite Business in December 1999 that made no economic sense.

* * *

8. In January 2000, Mr. Ullom became aware that Mr. Herula had sent an e-mail from his Raymond James account soliciting an investor to deposit $100 million at Raymond James. Mr. Herula signed the e-mail as a Raymond James representative and stated that Brite Business agreed to ensure a ten percent return on the investment.

* * *

11. Beginning in December 1999, until he was fired in December 2000, Mr. Herula worked out of an apartment in Cranston that had a computer, a fax machine, a copier, a scanner, telephones, and copies of correspondence. No one at Raymond James ever inspected this office. Beginning in October 2000, Mr. Herula began working at an office he set up in his home in Tiburon, California.

12. From January 2000 through March 2000, Mr. Herula signed an e-mail as a Raymond James registered representative using his Raymond James account, soliciting an investor to deposit $100 million at Raymond James in connection with Brite Business. Mr. Herula forwarded the e-mail to Mr. Ullom. In the same period, Mr. Herula engaged in correspondence with Mr. Al Bloushi in which he made false representations.

* * *

14. The unexplained activity in the Brite Business and Mary Lee Capalbo accounts, which included multi-million dollar deposits promptly followed by transfers to related and third-party accounts, coupled with the suspicious nature of Brite Business's balance sheet enhancement program, and its purchase of Treasuries, constitute indicia of money laundering that should have triggered further investigation.

Finally, the Division argues that Mr. Putnam had actual knowledge of multiple red flags that alerted him to Mr. Herula's suspicious activities, yet he failed to respond to them. The Division argues that Mr. Putnam cannot excuse his failure to supervise Mr. Herula by claiming that he relied on Mr. Ullom because: (1) Mr. Putnam did not develop a system to ensure that Mr. Ullom was monitoring Mr. Herula; (2) Mr.

Putnam should have known that Mr. Ullom's supervision of Mr. Herula was deficient; and (3) as the president of a corporate broker-dealer, Mr. Putnam was ultimately responsible for all the firm's requirements.

Raymond James represents that throughout the relevant period it had procedures and systems in place that were reasonably designed to prevent and detect securities law violations. Raymond James insists that these supervisory procedures were in accord with NASD Conduct Rule 3010-Supervision. Raymond James argues that the failure to detect wrongful conduct does not by itself establish a failure to supervise. Raymond James maintains that it reasonably discharged its supervisory duties and obligations and had no reasonable cause to believe that the procedures and systems were not being followed. Raymond James argues, further, that a broker-dealer's branch manager is its first line of defense and that its reliance on Mr. Ullom was reasonable. According to one Raymond James expert, the branch manager is responsible for making sure that everything is done properly and that nothing unauthorized is released. Raymond James notes that when it hired Mr. Ullom to manage the Cranston branch office, he had no prior record of supervisory problems. Mr. Ullom was an experienced manager, and Mr. Putnam had known him for many years. Raymond James cites expert testimony to support its position that broker-dealers customarily rely on branch managers to enforce their supervisory rules and regulations.

Raymond James insists that it had no cause to believe that its supervisory procedures were being violated. It cites various written materials such as operations manuals, newsletters, an Intranet digest that addressed compliance, a dedicated compliance staff, and training for its twenty-eight compliance professionals. Raymond James stresses its efforts at oversight including over seventy types of exception reports, branch office compliance reports, and branch audits.

Raymond James denies the existence of any red flags that would have put it on notice of Brite Business's prime bank scheme.

Raymond James insists that, during the relevant period and at present, its procedures for: (1) supervising off-site locations; (2) reviewing branch office operating accounts; (3) disbursing or transferring funds from accounts; and (4) placing registered representatives on heightened supervision, met or exceeded industry standards. Raymond James reiterates, as it did throughout the hearing, that a broker-dealer's duty of supervision is imposed to protect the investing public and is owed only to its customers, not to third parties. In support, it refers to NASD Rule 3010.

Raymond James maintains that it was deceived about the nature of Mr. Herula's outside business activities, that these activities did not involve Raymond James's business, and did not trigger any supervisory responsibility for the firmIt notes that the NASD has addressed the issue of "non-member business conducted by an associated person" in Rules 3030 and 3040. An associated person may be involved in non-member business in two categories: outside business activities and private securities transactions. According to Raymond James, by definition then, a registered representative's outside business activity is not the business of the member firm.

Mr. Putnam maintains that the Division's so-called red flags did not suggest the fraud that occurred. Mr. Ullom, the key in a reasonable system of supervision, was actively involved in the fraud and withheld critical information from Mr. Putnam and Raymond James.

Mr. Putnam argues that several issues must be considered when assessing the reasonableness of his supervision of Mr. Herula. Mr. Putnam denies that he was responsible for the adoption and implementation or design of Raymond James's supervisory procedures in his position as president and chief operating officer. The CEO of Raymond James did not delegate responsibility for the adoption and implementation of the firm's compliance procedures or responsibility for the firm's supervisory system to him. Second, Mr. Putnam delegated to Mr. Ullom the job of gathering all Mr. Herula's correspondence, placing Mr. Herula under close scrutiny, and reporting any problems. Mr. Putnam had a reasonable expectation that Mr. Ullom would do as he was directed.

Conclusions

Section 15(b) of the Exchange Act provides that the Commission may sanction any person associated with a broker or dealer or the broker-dealer itself, if it finds that such person or broker-dealer "failed reasonably to supervise, with a view to preventing violations of [the securities laws], another person who commits such a violation, if such other person is subject to their supervision." Exchange Act Section 15(b) further provides that no person shall be deemed to have failed reasonably to supervise if: (1) procedures, and a system for applying those procedures, have been established, which would reasonably be expected to prevent and detect any such violation; and (2) the person has reasonably discharged the duties and obligations incumbent upon him by reason of [his firm's] procedures and system and had no reasonable basis for believing that those procedures were not being followed. Ultimately, the test is whether the supervision was reasonable under the circumstances.

The fact that Raymond James's CEO did not formally delegate to Mr. Putnam responsibility for the design, adoption and implementation of Raymond James's supervisory procedures does not change the fact that Mr. Putnam was responsible for supervising Mr. Herula. Mr. Putnam controlled Mr. Herula's activities. From August 1999 until at least February 2000, Mr. Carreno reported to Mr. Putnam. Raymond James's Compliance Manual showed Mr. Putnam had responsibility for hiring financial advisers within branch offices, and for sales management branch management oversight. Mr. Putnam had the power to fire Mr. Herula, which he did, finally, in December 2000. I find that Mr. Putnam was Mr. Herula's supervisor throughout the relevant period.

During the relevant period, Raymond James did not have procedures in place which would reasonably be expected to prevent and detect antifraud violations by its registered representatives or a system for applying those procedures. Furthermore, neither Raymond James nor Mr. Putnam reasonably discharged the duties and obligations incumbent upon them by reason of the procedures and systems that existed.

At the time Robert Thomas and IMR merged in January 1999, each company had separate and different compliance programs. After the firms merged, Raymond James operated two separate compliance programs for several months. During these months, the separate programs were headed by two different compliance directors. The two compliance departments merged in March or April 1999, under the leadership of Mr. DiGirolamo. A new compliance manual for the merged company was not produced until May 2000. It appears that in March 2000, Raymond James did not have specific heightened supervision policies but it did have procedures to deal with extraordinary situations, which Mr. Carreno called enhanced supervision. Mr. Putnam indicated that under Raymond James's procedures at the time of the Lanciano letter, the branch, not the individual, was placed on heightened supervision. A meeting was held every quarter to review either the individual or branch where someone was in heightened supervision status. The process is not structured to disclose outside business activities. The evidence is that Raymond James's first written heightened supervision policies for registered representatives occurred in October 2001.

The evidence does not support Raymond James's and Mr. Putnam's position that they reasonably relied on Mr. Ullom to carry out their supervisory responsibilities. The Commission has repeatedly warned that procedures that rely solely on supervision by branch managers are insufficient (citations omitted).

Raymond James retained Mr. Ullom as a supervisor knowing that he settled a proceeding with the Commission in which Mr. Ullom was found to have: (1) given false information to a state securities examiner; (2) directed an employee of an investment adviser he co-owned to alter documents that Mr. Ullom submitted to state authorities; and (3) filed a Form ADV with the Commission that contained false information. The settlement found that Mr. Ullom violated the Advisers Act; willfully aided and abetted violations by the investment adviser; and caused the investment adviser's violations. It was patently unreasonable for Raymond James to rely on Mr. Ullom in a position, which the experts agree was Raymond James's "first line of defense," and someone Raymond James relied on to make sure everything was done properly, when in 1995 Mr. Ullom deliberately submitted false information to securities regulatory agencies (citations omitted).

In addition to adopting effective procedures for supervision, broker-dealers must also "provide effective staffing, sufficient resources, and a system of follow up and review to determine that any responsibility to supervise delegated to compliance officers, branch managers, and other personnel is being diligently exercised." The system must provide sufficient checks "to insure that the first line of compliance, the branch manager, [is] functioning adequately." "The need for central control increases, not decreases, as the branch offices become more numerous, dispersed, and distant.

Raymond James's Compliance Department relied on the branch manager's monthly compliance reports, the annual internal audit, and exception reports as tools to accomplish supervision. Each of these instruments is a valid means of supervision, but Raymond James failed to use them in a reasonable or effective manner. Mr. Ullom submitted compliance reports monthly to the Compliance Department. There is no evidence that Raymond James independently verified the contents of the reports. This case provides ample evidence that a monthly compliance report submitted by the branch manager representing that he has discharged his responsibilities, which is not subject to any verification, is a self-serving document without any value. It was unreasonable for Raymond James to accept that the information in Mr. Ullom's monthly compliance report was true without any type of verification.

Under the circumstances, Raymond James's internal compliance audit of the Cranston branch office in 2000 was not an effective procedure to prevent and detect violations. Raymond James's characterization of the process as "an audit" is a misnomer. Raymond James did not reasonably prepare Mr. Wegner for the audit. According to Mr. Wegner, who I find to be a knowledgeable and credible witness, much of the audit was "just a review of procedures and systems in place at the branch." Mr. Wegner testified that he would have liked to have known any concerns regarding the branch office he was auditing and would have given emphasis to those areas during the audit. Raymond James did not inform Mr. Wegner that Mr. Herula had a business relationship with Brite Business, that Mr. Herula had sent out unauthorized correspondence, or that Mr. Herula worked outside the Cranston branch office throughout 2000. Mr. Wegner testified that he would have liked to have known that Mr. Herula was working for Brite Business. In addition, Mr. Wegner was not aware that: (1) a third party had made a claim for the funds in an account where Mr. Herula was the registered representative; (2) the president of Raymond James had put a restriction on the Brite Business account where Mr. Herula was the registered representative; or (3) Mr. Herula was almost fired in July 2000 for sending unauthorized correspondence. Mr. Wegner believes that anything that resembles a complaint should be in the branch office compliant file ...

Because Mr. Wegner did not know that Mr. Herula did not come to the office throughout 2000, he accepted Jason Ullom's false answer that no registered representatives worked outside the Cranston branch office. Mr. DiGirolamo did not think notice of problems with unauthorized correspondence was necessary if the branch manager believed the problem had been resolved. Mr. Wegner was unaware, and could not report, that Mr. Herula never returned the Financial Advisor Annual Compliance Interview questionnaire he left for him because, under Raymond James's procedures, Mr. Wegner's responsibility for the audit ended when he submitted his report to the Compliance Department.

Raymond James did not follow NASD Notice to Members 98-38 (Notice 98-38), issued May 1998, which states that a member's supervisory responsibility includes maintaining a record of the location of all unregistered offices. Notice 98-38 cites NASD Rule 3010I as requiring that members conduct inspections of unregistered locations in accordance with a regular schedule. Raymond James's expert testified that he saw nothing to indicate that Raymond James had an inspection schedule. The evidence is that Raymond James did not have accurate information about the actual work locations of the approximately five or six registered representatives assigned to the Cranston branch office. Jason Ullom told Mr. Wegner that there were no registered representatives working outside the office. Mr. Ullom, however, testified that three of the six registered representatives, excluding Mr. Herula, did not regularly work at the Cranston branch office. Even accepting that NASD's notices to members are advisory, given Raymond James's large number of widely dispersed registered representatives, I find that it should have maintained a record of those who operated regularly from unregistered locations and inspected those locations on a regular schedule.

The unanimous evidence is that no one at Raymond James, except Mr. Ullom who is not credible, saw a connection between the transactions Brite Business proposed and Brite Business's purchase of Treasuries, or suspected that Brite Business was an illegal enterprise.

Based on his demeanor and responses to cross examination, I find that Mr. Putnam gave credible, candid testimony. The record, however, contains no reasonable explanation why Mr. Putnam excused Mr. Herula's violations of Raymond James's rules against unauthorized correspondence as naïve errors when Mr. Herula had more than twenty years of experience in the securities industry. In addition, Mr. Putnam knew that Mr. Herula was raising funds for Brite Business. Given this knowledge, it was unreasonable for Mr. Putnam to rely completely on Mr. Ullom to ensure that Mr. Herula was in compliance and to accept, without verification, Mr. Ullom's representations that the oral reports in May 2000 did not involve Brite Business representatives. (the Commission has often expressed its views that a system of supervisory procedures which rely solely on the branch manager is insufficient).

Mr. Putnam and Mr. DiGirolamo held widely different views on the role of the Compliance Department. These differences prevented implementation of Raymond James's supervisory procedures. Mr. Putnam appears to believe that the Compliance Department operated independently without input from him. In contrast, Mr. DiGirolamo, viewed the Compliance Department's role as a support function for senior management, and that senior management had to approve any disciplinary action. Mr. Putnam never told the Compliance Department to place Mr. Herula on heightened supervision because if the Compliance Department "had wanted to put him on heightened supervision, [Mr. DiGirolamo] could do so, you know, if he felt it was appropriate."

Mr. Putnam did not inform Mr. DiGirolamo, or anyone in the Compliance Department, about Mr. Herula's unauthorized letters. Mr. Putnam did not suggest closer scrutiny of Mr. Herula's activities because "the internal auditors don't report to me. That is a compliance function, so I would not be telling the internal auditors anything." As a result, Raymond James's Compliance Department was unaware of any questions or concerns regarding Mr. Ullom's supervision of Mr. Herula during the relevant period. From January through August 2000, Mr. Putnam and Mr. Ullom knew that Mr. Herula sent unauthorized e-mails and at least three pieces of unauthorized correspondence, and Mr. Putnam knew of one suspect oral representation by Brite Business. The Compliance Department detected none of these happenings through its compliance efforts and Mr. Herula's supervisors did not provide it with this information.

The restrictions Mr. Putnam placed on the Brite Business account following the Lanciano letter were meaningless. Mr. Putnam expert viewed them as "simply an informational check." The record shows nothing that would cause Mr. Putnam to be so confident that he would not seek confirmation that Mr. Herula was being closely supervised. On these facts, Mr. Putnam did not act reasonably. He should have asked the Compliance Department to investigate whether Mr. Herula was acting legitimately and whether Mr. Ullom was closely supervising Mr. Herula.

It is impossible to reconcile the evidence in this record that Raymond James's system of supervision met or exceeded industry standards and/or Raymond James exercised reasonable supervision. The overwhelming evidence requires a different conclusion.

For all the reasons stated, I find in these circumstances that Raymond James and Mr. Putnam failed to reasonably supervise Mr. Herula, a person subject to their supervision, with a view to preventing or detecting Mr. Herula's violations of Section 17(a) of the Securities Act and Section 10(b) of the Exchange Act and Rule 10b-5.

Notes and Questions

1. This administrative proceeding follows a related civil proceeding in the United States District Court for the District of Rhode Island. *SEC v. Dennis S. Herula, et al.*, C.A. No. 02-154 ML (D.R.I.). On October 17, 2002, the district court entered a Final Judgment and enjoined Mr. Herula from further violations of the antifraud provisions of the federal securities laws and ordered him to pay disgorgement and prejudgment interest totaling $18,941,665.63. On January 27, 2003, the district court entered a Final Judgment and enjoined Ms. Capalbo from further violations of the antifraud provisions of the federal securities laws and ordered her to pay disgorgement and prejudgment interest totaling $19,292,102.14. The court also ordered Mr. Herula and Ms. Capalbo to each pay civil monetary penalties of $250,000. On October 18, 2004, Mr. Herula pleaded guilty to criminal charges of wire fraud that included misrepresentations to investors, money laundering, and bankruptcy fraud brought by the U.S. Attorney in Rhode Island. Mr. Herula was sentenced to 188 months and ordered to make restitution of more than $13 million.

2. The *Raymond James* decision states that a reasonable supervisory system requires independent verification of compliance reports submitted by branch managers. How would a broker-dealer implement such a system? Does this decision also require independent verification of outside business reports from registered repre- → Yes sentatives? How might this be accomplished? → Have a branch responsible for this.

Like a web.

Hypothetical Six

Success First has decided to expand using the independent contractor model. However, in an effort at compromise with Josephine's concern for increased liability with this type of business model, Carmen has decided to test the waters by entering into an independent contractor relationship with a small broker-dealer with only one location. This broker-dealer is owned and operated by Shemika Oliver and employs six registered representatives. The terms of the Agreement between Success First and Ms. Oliver require Ms. Oliver to maintain an office, to bear the expenses, to be responsible for assuring that registered representatives in the office adhere to all applicable regulations, cooperate with audits, and to indemnify Success First against any liability arising from Ms. Oliver's conduct, or that of any registered representative in the office. Ms. Oliver manages the office as an independent contractor in the name of SM Management with a checking account in the name of SM Management d/b/a/ Success First. The SM Management checking account is the operating account for this office. SM Management, a Delaware C corporation, provides office space, utilities, staff support, and employee benefits. SM Management interfaces with Success First in order to receive commission dollars generated by Ms. Oliver and the six registered representatives. However, signs in this office identify only Success First. In addition, all mailings, account documents, and client payments are to Success First. Ms. Oliver has authority to hire registered representatives subject to Success First's approval.

Ms. Oliver allows registered representatives to work from home and to engage in business activities other than buying and selling securities, such as selling insurance or financial planning. At least two of the registered representatives never come to work at the office. Also, one of the registered representatives has a disciplinary history.

List five supervisory procedures and identify corresponding systems that would facilitate implementation of a reasonable supervisory system for Success First's independent contractor relationship with SM Management.

Part II: Supervision Under FINRA Rules
IV. FINRA Supervison

Figure 4.2

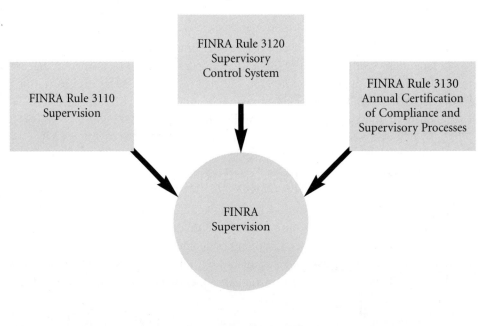

A. Introduction to FINRA Supervisory Requirements

Supervisory obligations of broker-dealers are central to effective oversight by FINRA of its member broker-dealers. FINRA requires all member broker-dealers to establish and maintain a comprehensive supervisory system that is reasonably designed to achieve compliance with applicable securities laws and FINRA rules. FINRA's supervision requirements, unlike the supervisory requirements under Exchange Act Sections 15(b)(4)(E) and 15(b)(6), are far more comprehensive and impose an affirmative obligation on broker-dealers to establish supervisory systems and procedures for their own activities, as well as the activities of their associated persons. Essentially, FINRA's supervision rules provide meaningful guidance to broker-dealers regarding reasonable supervision under the broker-dealer regulatory framework.

The crux of FINRA's supervision requirements consists of three complementary and interrelated rules: FINRA Rule 3110 Supervision; FINRA Rule 3120 Supervisory Control System; and FINRA Rule 3130 Annual Certification of Compliance and Supervisory Processes. These rules require broker-dealers to establish and maintain supervisory systems and procedures reasonably designed to achieve compliance with the federal securities laws, FINRA rules, and the rules of the Municipal Securities Rulemaking Board ("MSRB"). FINRA Rule 3130 requires the chief executive officer to certify that the broker-dealer has created effective processes to establish, maintain, review, and modify (as necessary) its policies and procedures to achieve compliance with applicable FINRA rules, MSRB rules, and federal securities laws and regulations. Essentially, FINRA Rule 3130 certification means that the broker-dealer has complied with the requirements of FINRA Rule 3110, which provides factors that must be considered in establishing a reasonable and effective supervisory system. FINRA Rule 3120 requires the broker-dealer to test, verify, and modify (as needed) its supervisory procedures to ensure compliance with applicable federal securities laws and FINRA rules. FINRA's supervision requirements anticipate a supervisory structure, which "consists of process, supervision, and adoption of policies and procedures, and testing and amendment of such policies and procedures."[65] Effective compliance with FINRA's supervision rules requires each broker-dealer to assess and evaluate its lines of business, management, and operations. Essentially, instead of prescribing uniform supervisory procedures for all member firms, FINRA has required its complex and diverse membership to develop supervisory systems and written supervisory policies and procedures that are "tailored" to each broker-dealer's business. In this model, the broker-dealer retains the ultimate responsibility for properly supervising its business and its associated persons in an ever-changing regulatory environment. To discharge this responsibility, broker-dealers must regularly assess changes in their businesses and in regulatory requirements to ensure compliance. These requirements are summarized in Table 4.2 below.

---

65. *Supervisory Controls: SEC Approves New Rules and Rule Amendments Concerning Supervision and Supervisory Controls*, FINRA (Oct. 2004), https://www.finra.org/web/groups/industry/@ip/@reg/@notice/documents/notices/p011633.pdf.

Table 4.2. FINRA Supervision

	FINRA Rule 3110 Supervision	FINRA Rule 3120 Supervisory Control System	FINRA Rule 3130 Annual Certification of Compliance and Supervisory Processes
Summary	• Establish and maintain a supervisory system. • Reflection of the supervisory system in the written supervisory procedures (WSPs). • Internal inspections.	• Establish, maintain, and enforce a supervisory control system, including written supervisory control procedures (SCPs). • Test and verify, create and amend supervisory procedures.	• Designate and identify CCOs • CEO and CCO meeting(s) • CEO Certification
Timing	Ongoing.	At least annually, testing and verification of the supervisory procedures must take place.	Annual certification.
Meeting	Participation of each registered representative and registered principal in an annual compliance meeting or interview.	None required.	At least annually, a meeting between the CEO and CCO to discuss the certification, compliance efforts, and a discussion of compliance issues and plans for new business areas.
Designation and Identification	Designate and maintain, on an internal record, the names of all individuals designated as supervisory personnel and the effective dates.	Designate and identify to FINRA one or more principals who shall enforce supervisory control policies and procedures.	Designate and identify to FINRA CCOs on Schedule A of the Form BD.
Report	After a review and inspection of an office, an internal inspection report must be produced regarding the testing and verification of the firm's policies and procedures. At a minimum, the report must include the testing and verification of supervisory policies and procedures regarding changes in customer accounts, safeguarding of funds and securities, and maintenance of books and records.	The designated principal(s) must create a report, at least annually, that describes the firm's supervisory control, results of the testing and verification of the supervisory procedures, identified exceptions of significance, and actions taken in response such as amended or newly created supervisory procedures.	A report must be produced prior to the certification for review by the CEO that documents the firm's processes for establishing, maintaining, reviewing, testing, and modifying compliance policies reasonably designed to comply with applicable regulations. The report must be submitted to the firm's board of directors and audit committee.

1. FINRA Review of Supervisory Systems and Written Supervisory Procedures

FINRA reviews the supervisory procedures, systems, and controls for broker-dealers at three key points, starting with when broker-dealers apply to obtain membership, when they seek to expand operations or other business activities, and as part of the examination process. Requirements at these three key points underscore the importance of supervision in self-regulation.

a. New Membership Application Process

A member firm's supervisory system is initially reviewed when a firm applies to become a member of FINRA by participating in the New Membership Application (NMA) process.[66] The failure to have an adequate supervisory system consisting of written supervisory policies and procedures and a supervisory control system with operational and internal controls reasonably designed to detect and, to the extent practicable, prevent violations of applicable laws, regulations and rules may result in a denial of membership. To obtain membership in FINRA, a prospective member firm must demonstrate compliance with 14 criteria outlined in NASD Rule 1014(a), including subsection (9) requiring compliance, supervisory, operational and internal control practices and standards, and subsection (10) requiring a supervisory system, written supervisory procedures, internal operating procedures and compliance procedures.

b. Continuing Member Application Process

A broker-dealer must participate in the Continuing Membership Application ("CMA") process prior to a "material change" in its business. Examples of a material change in the broker-dealer's business include a change of ownership or control and changes in, or expansions of, the broker-dealer's business. The CMA process requires the broker-dealer to provide information and documentation about its supervisory personnel for any material change in its business, along with a description of the supervisory and compliance procedures the broker-dealer will establish to comply with FINRA Rule 3110.

c. Examinations

FINRA examines the supervisory procedures and supervisory systems of its member broker-dealers. All broker-dealers are examined at least once every four years and more often depending on FINRA's risk assessment of the broker-dealer's business. In these examinations, FINRA examines closely the supervisory structure and written supervisory procedures of the broker-dealers to determine whether its internal controls are appropriate for the broker-dealer's business and personnel, whether the procedures are being maintained and updated as appropriate, and finally, whether the procedures are being enforced. Supervisory failures discovered through the examination process may result in disciplinary action and sanctions.

---

66. *See* Chapter 3 for more information on the NMA process.

Notes and Questions

1. Does requiring firms to supervise registered representatives and ultimately bear the responsibility for their activities promote fair and efficient regulation or increase the cost of business, which is eventually passed on to the retail investor?

2. FINRA-imposed sanctions for failure to supervise depend on the severity of the misconduct and can range from settlements in the form of Acceptance, Waiver, and Consent (AWC) to expulsion or bar from membership.[67] If disciplinary actions involving a failure-to-supervise violation are settled in the form of an AWC letter, broker-dealers are typically required to revise written supervisory procedures to correct the deficiencies noted. FINRA's Sanction Guidelines discuss four separate violations resulting from inadequate supervision: (1) the failure to discharge supervisory obligations, (2) failure to comply with the taping rule, (2) failure to supervise, and (3) deficient written supervisory procedures.

3. When determining sanctions for a failure to supervise, FINRA also takes into consideration the presence or absence of three factors: (1) whether the broker-dealer disregarded red flags that necessitated further inquiry and whether the associated persons involved in the violative conduct attempted to conceal the misconduct; (2) the nature and quality of the underlying violation; and (3) the type of procedures and internal controls and the supervisor's implementation of such procedures. Where there is a systematic or prolonged supervision failure or the presence of other violative conduct, the broker-dealer may be suspended or barred from membership.

B. Elements of Supervision

Figure 4.3

Establish and Maintain a Supervisory System **+** Reflect the Supervisory System in the WSPs **+** Conduct Internal Inspections **=** **Rule 3110**

---

67. FINRA Rule 9216 permits FINRA's Department of Enforcement and Department of Market Regulation to enter into a letter of Acceptance, Waiver and Consent (AWC) if they believe a violation has occurred and the broker-dealer or the associated person does not dispute the violation. By accepting a proposed AWC letter, the broker-dealer and/or the associated person is "accepting a finding of violation, consenting to the imposition of sanctions, and agreeing to waive such [broker-dealer's] or associated person's right to a hearing before a Hearing Panel or, if applicable, an Extended Hearing Panel, and any right of appeal to the National Adjudicatory Council, the SEC, and the courts, or to otherwise challenge the validity of the letter, if the letter is accepted." The AWC letter, if accepted by the National Adjudicatory Counsel, is considered the complaint, answer and decision in the disciplinary matter.

1. *Supervisory System*

FINRA Rule 3110 requires broker-dealers to establish and maintain a supervisory system and to document the supervisory system in their written supervisory procedures ("WSPs"). Minimum components of such a supervisory system, in addition to WSPs, include designating: (1) principals responsible for supervision; (2) offices of supervisory jurisdiction ("OSJ"); (3) OSJ/non-OSJ branch supervisors; (4) supervisors for registered representatives and other associated persons; and (5) adequately qualified supervisory personnel by training or experience. A reasonable supervisory system also requires the broker-dealer to conduct an annual compliance meeting and to perform internal inspections.

a. Written Supervisory Procedures

FINRA Rule 3110(a)(1) and (b) require each member broker-dealer to "establish, maintain, and enforce" written supervisory procedures to supervise both the activities of its associated persons and the types of business in which the broker-dealer engages. These written supervisory procedures must document the broker-dealer's supervisory system and be available at each OSJ and each location from which supervisory activities are conducted. Broker-dealers must also maintain a record of all supervisory personnel and the effective dates of their supervisory responsibilities for at least three years. Broker-dealers have a continuing obligation to amend written supervisory procedures in a "reasonable time" when changes occur in their supervisory system, lines of businesses, or regulatory requirements. In addition to the written supervisory procedures, broker-dealers must designate appropriate supervisory principals.

b. Principal Designation Rule and Registered Principal Requirement

FINRA Rule 3110(a)(2) requires the designation of principals responsible for supervision at a broker-dealer. These principals must be "appropriately registered" and must have the "authority" to supervise each of the broker-dealer's lines of business. The designated principal must be registered with FINRA as a registered principal by passing the Series 24 General Securities Principal examination, which tests the applicants' understanding of broker-dealer management and supervision.[68] FINRA Rule 3110(a)(6) further requires that all registered persons in supervisory positions either qualify by experience or training to supervise their areas of supervisory responsibility.

Registered Principals are those associated persons engaged in the management of the broker-dealer and can include managers of OSJs, partners, sole proprietors, corporate directors, and officers. They are actively engaged in the management of the broker-dealer's investment banking or securities business, including training of associated persons.[69] FINRA Rule 3110(a)(4) requires the member broker-dealer to des-

---

68. See Chapter 3 for more information on registration requirements for broker-dealers.
69. *See*, NASD Rule 1021(b).

ignate one or more appropriately registered principals in each OSJ and branch office with the authority to oversee the broker-dealer's supervisory responsibilities. Registered Principals are typically disclosed on Schedule A of the Form BD, which requires the broker-dealer applicant to disclose its direct owners and executive officers, such as the chief executive officer, chief financial officer, chief operations officer, chief legal officer, chief compliance officer, director, and control persons.[70]

In addition to designating appropriately registered principals, broker-dealers must also designate Offices of Supervisory Jurisdiction ("OSJ").

c. Designation of Office of Supervisory Jurisdiction (OSJ)

FINRA Rule 3110(a)(3) requires the registration and designation of branch offices or OSJs if the broker-dealer conducts business in multiple locations. A broker-dealer may have a main office and branch offices to serve its clients. The main office and each of the branch offices may be designated as an OSJ if the OSJ designation is required under Rule 3110(f). FINRA Rule 3110(f)(1) requires the designation of OSJ status if a location engages in certain functions of regulatory significance, such as executing orders, maintaining customer funds and/or securities; market-making activities; structuring of public offering or private placement transactions; final approval of new accounts or advertising or sales literature used by associated persons; reviewing and approving of customer orders or the supervision of associated persons located at one or more other branch offices. In addition, FINRA Rule 3110.02 requires the broker-dealer to register a location as an OSJ if: (a) there is regular contact with public customers; (b) there are a substantial number of registered persons conducting securities activities or are otherwise supervised, at the location; (c) the location is geographically distant from another OSJ of the broker-dealer; (d) the broker-dealer's registered persons are geographically dispersed; and (e) securities activities at the location are diverse or complex.

d. Supervisory Reporting Assignments

FINRA Rule 3110(a)(5) requires that each registered person be assigned to either a registered principal or a qualified registered representative with the responsibility for supervising the assigned person. This rule contemplates a supervisory structure wherein not all supervisors need to be registered principals. FINRA's supervision requirement, in essence, requires broker-dealers to build a multi-tiered supervisory structure designed to detect and prevent potential violations. Moreover, broker-dealers must make a reasonable effort to determine that all supervisory personnel are

---

70. See Chapter 3 for more information about the Form BD. http://www.goodwinprocter.com/Publications/Newsletter-Articles/Financial-Services-Articles/2011_06/~/media/6341FDA2F3324 D7797AC3C0117EE8D57.pdf (showing "proposed FINRA supervision rules"); Practising Law Institute, http://seclawcenter.pli.edu/wp-content/uploads/2011/03/Kirsch-Broker-Dealer-Supervision.pdf; Federal Register, http://www.federalregister.gov/articles/2011/06/29/2011-16232/self-regulatory-organizations-financial-industry-regulatory-authority-inc-notice-of-filing-of (providing a notice of proposed supervisory rule change).

qualified to perform their assigned responsibilities. However, under no circumstances should a registered person be permitted to supervise his own activities.

e. Annual Compliance Interview or Meeting

Broker-dealers must conduct a compliance interview or meeting with its registered persons at least annually. Many broker-dealers meet the annual compliance meeting or interview requirement by requiring registered persons to complete an annual compliance questionnaire; the questionnaire may include questions about changes in registration status, opening of outside securities accounts, whether the registered person was subject to any criminal or regulatory action, borrowed or loaned money to any customers, etc....[71] The broker-dealer is not required to conduct an in-person interview or meeting. Many broker-dealers have also used webcasts to conduct annual compliance interviews or meetings with registered persons located in dispersed geographic locations.[72]

The obligation to maintain adequate supervisory systems is an ongoing requirement, especially with the addition of business lines and branch offices. In *Department of Market Regulation v. Yankee Financial Group, Inc.,* a small broker-dealer added new personnel, engaged in a new line of business, and opened two new locations. While reviewing this case, consider the types of changes a broker-dealer must make to its supervisory system when it adds business lines and branch offices.

Department of Market Regulation v. Yankee Financial Group, Inc.

No. CMS030182, 2006 NASD Discip. LEXIS 21 (Aug. 4, 2006)

I. Background

Since Yankee's formation in 1986, Kresge has been the Firm's president, chief executive officer, [compliance officer] and 95 percent owner. During the relevant period of time, Kresge was registered with Yankee in several capacities, including general securities representative, general securities principal, and financial and operations principal.

Yankee has been a registered broker-dealer since August 1986. During the relevant period, Yankee's main office was in Bay Shore, New York. Between 1986 and 2001, Yankee's business primarily involved municipal and government bonds and mutual funds. As described in more detail below, Yankee experienced a major change in the nature of its operations when it opened two new offices, one in Melville and the other in Brooklyn, New York, in 2001.

---

71. *See Annual Compliance Questionnaire*, QUEST CE, https://learn.questce.com/firmelement/files/ACQSample.pdf (accessed Mar. 13, 2016).

72. *See* Letter from Afshin Atabaki, FINRA Assistant General Counsel, to Evan Charkes, Citigroup Managing Director, *available at* http://www.finra.org/Industry/Regulation/Guidance/InterpretiveLetters/P018026 (last modified Nov. 30, 2006). *See also* FINRA Rule 3110.04.

II. Facts

A. Yankee Opens an Office in Melville, New York

In early 2001, Yankee, acting through Kresge, reached an agreement with Kenneth Gliwa ("Gliwa") and Robert Stelz ("Stelz"), principals of Glenn Michael Financial, Inc. ("Glenn Michael"), to buy Glenn Michael's branch office in Melville, New York. In March 2001, Yankee bought the Melville office, adding approximately 50 representatives to Yankee's existing 10 to 12 representatives. At that time, the Melville office's business consisted of municipal bonds, mutual funds, listed equities, and a small amount of penny stock business.

After the acquisition of the Melville office, Kresge continued to work in Bay Shore, and Gliwa and Stelz continued to work in Melville. Kresge remained Yankee's president, compliance officer, and 95 percent owner, and he visited the Melville office once every 10 to 14 days. Stelz became the manager of the Melville office. Gliwa, who was registered as a general securities representative, a general securities principal, and an equity trader, was assigned responsibility for the Firm's trading. Both Stelz and Gliwa continued to service their own customers.

B. Yankee Opens an Office in Brooklyn, New York

In or around August 2001, Gliwa informed Kresge about a client, Joseph Masone ("Masone"), who knew of some unhappy representatives looking to switch firms. A meeting was held to discuss adding these representatives at a location that was to be a new Yankee office. At the meeting, Masone introduced Kresge, Stelz, and Gliwa to Joseph Ferragamo ("Ferragamo"). Ferragamo explained that he was registered with Valley Forge Securities, Inc. ("Valley Forge")…. Ferragamo stated that he was the spokesperson for several brokers who wanted to leave Valley Forge and suggested Gary Giordano ("Giordano") could serve as the branch manager of a new Yankee office.

At a meeting in September 2001, Kresge and Gliwa met with Ferragamo, Masone, and Michael Trotta ("Trotta"), the chief executive officer of Silver Star Foods ("Silver Star"). Kresge did not know Trotta, and no one asked why he was there. At or soon after this second meeting, an agreement was reached to open a Yankee office in Brooklyn. Kresge testified that Ferragamo financed the Brooklyn office and guaranteed the payment of its expenses. The terms also provided that Yankee would receive 15 percent of the Brooklyn office's commissions and a $25 per ticket charge. No records were created to document Ferragamo's financing role or the override arrangement.

At Ferragamo's recommendation, Kresge hired Giordano to be the manager of the Brooklyn office. As manager, Giordano was responsible for handling the day-to-day office operations, hiring brokers subject to Kresge's approval, and supervising the office, which included signing off on new accounts, conducting suitability reviews, training representatives regarding sales practices, and monitoring transactions and "back office" functions. Around September 2001, Ferragamo asked Kresge not to register him with Yankee, first claiming that the new office had limited funds to do so, but then claiming that he wanted to avoid being held jointly and severally liable with his former firm in a "minor" NASD arbitration matter in which he was named. Kresge agreed not to register Ferragamo.

* * *

C. Fraudulent Sales and Unsuitable Recommendations

The Brooklyn office opened in October 2001. Immediately thereafter, hundreds of customer accounts were transferred to Yankee from Valley Forge and L.H. Ross. From October 2001 until April 2002, the Brooklyn representatives solicited members of the public to purchase large quantities of securities in three companies: Silver Star, Western Media Group, Corp. ("Western Media"), and Golden Chief Resources, Inc. ("Golden Chief"). In total, approximately 147 Yankee customers invested $6.3 million in Silver Star, $1.6 million in Western Media, and $500,000 in Golden Chief. The financial statements of all three of these issuers contained going concern opinions. The record amply demonstrates that all three over-the-counter securities were highly speculative.

Ten Yankee customers testified how Brooklyn representatives [...] solicited them to purchase these three securities. Finding the customers' testimony to be credible, the Hearing Panel found that the Brooklyn brokers solicited investments using material omissions and misrepresentations, with scienter, in violation of Section 10(b) of the Securities Exchange Act of 1934 ("Exchange Act"), Exchange Act Rule 10b-5, and NASD Conduct Rules 2120 and 2110. Specifically, the Hearing Panel found that Yankee representatives made no risk disclosures, "enthusiastically gave false information about the companies' prospects and stability at a time when those companies' losses were mounting and when their auditors placed 'going concern' qualifications on their financial statements," and "used ... boiler-room type tactics such as creating a false sense of urgency to invest, claiming to be investing themselves or for family members, and making baseless price predictions."[73] The Hearing Panel further concluded that the Brooklyn brokers' recommendations of these securities to such customers were unsuitable, in violation of Conduct Rule 2310 and IM-2310-2[74]. In so holding, the Panel found that the brokers ignored their customers' financial information and investment objectives, failed to assess their customers' risk tolerance, and lacked a reasonable basis for believing that these securities were suitable for their clients. We affirm these findings.

* * *

---

73. [3] For example, [a registered representative] frequently urged WB, an 84-year old customer, to buy shares of Silver Star, Western Media, and Golden Chief, predicting that the price of each would dramatically increase, such as his claim that Golden Chief would rise from $.88 per share to as high as $8 to $15 per share. [A registered representative] told customer JL, a 66-year old retiree, that he was involved in Silver Star, that he and his parents were investing in it, and that it was relatively safe. Up to four times per week, [the registered representative] called JL and pressured him to invest, telling him "[g]et money any way you can, borrow it, do it anyway you can do, but you really ought to put a lot of money in it because I think it's going to go up a lot." ...

74. NASD rule 2310 is now FINRA Rule 2111. Suitability.

E. Yankee's Supervisory System for the Brooklyn Office

1. Supervisors and Compliance Officers

As explained above, Kresge purported to delegate primary supervisory responsibility over the Brooklyn office to Giordano. Kresge also purported to delegate to Gliwa, who remained in the Melville office, responsibility to supervise both Giordano's execution of his supervisory duties and Giordano's conduct with his own book of clients. Gliwa also remained responsible for supervising Yankee's order execution function, which now included trades called in to Melville from Brooklyn. According to Kresge, Giordano was to "bother" Gliwa or Kresge only if there was a problem.

From October 2001 to December 2001, Kresge served as Yankee's compliance officer. During this period, Brooklyn brokers, through aggressive sales practices, sold nearly $3 million of Silver Star alone. Kresge testified that Gliwa was overwhelmed with work and had visited the Brooklyn office just two or three times.

2. Written Supervisory Procedures

In adding the Melville office, Kresge took an old supervisory procedures manual that the Melville office had been using and taped "Yankee" on the cover. Assuming that the Melville representatives already had copies, Kresge did not ask Gliwa to distribute the manual. When the Brooklyn office opened, Kresge did not provide Giordano with a compliance manual, assuming, apparently without asking, that Gliwa would. Neither the Melville nor the Brooklyn representatives received a copy of the supervisory procedures manual.

3. Supervision of the Brooklyn Office

Kresge viewed the Brooklyn office as an independent and separate entity. Tellingly, he claimed he had no awareness of what was occurring there. From October to December 2001, Kresge paid just three visits to that office, during which he did not review any files, talk to any brokers, or discuss any customer complaints. Kresge did not know whether the Brooklyn brokers were trained on suitability or sales practices. In investigative testimony, Kresge testified that he never asked Gliwa how the Brooklyn office was doing "compliance wise" or what Gliwa looked at when he reviewed order tickets. Kresge also believed that neither Gliwa nor Stelz had ever reviewed any Brooklyn customer accounts....

* * *

IV. Discussion

A. Failure to Supervise

The Hearing Panel found that Yankee and Kresge failed to establish a supervisory system and failed to supervise the Brooklyn office, in violation of Conduct Rules 3010[75] and 2110.[76] We affirm the Hearing Panel's findings.

---

75. This rule is now FINRA Rule 3110. Supervision.
76. This rule is now FINRA Rule 2010. Standards of Commercial Honor and Principles of Trade.

1. Respondents Failed to Establish a Reasonable System of Supervision

Conduct Rule 3010(a) provides that "[e]ach member shall establish and maintain a system to supervise the activities of each registered representative and associated person that is reasonably designed to achieve compliance with applicable securities laws and regulations and with applicable NASD rules." The requirement to comply with this rule is not limited to the member firm itself. As president, Kresge was responsible for "compliance with all the requirements imposed on his firm unless and until he reasonably delegates particular functions to another person in that firm, and neither knows nor has reason to know that such person's performance is deficient." *William H. Gerhauser, Sr.*, 53 S.E.C. 933, 941 (1998).... There is no evidence that Kresge delegated ultimate responsibility to establish the Firm's reasonable system of supervision to anyone else.

In 2001, Yankee added two new locations, a substantial number of new personnel, and, for the first time, the sale of speculative, unlisted, over-the-counter stocks. Respondents' failure to modify (or at least consider whether they needed to modify) Yankee's procedures in light of these dramatic changes was inconsistent with their obligations. Most significantly, Yankee's transformation from a firm that sold only bonds and mutual funds to one that also sold speculative, unlisted securities marked a fundamental shift in the risk profile of Yankee's business. Sales of such products involve heightened regulatory responsibilities and a corresponding need for heightened supervision. At the first sign that the Brooklyn representatives were selling such securities, Kresge should have known that the Firm's supervisory system was insufficient. As explained below, respondents failed to design a reasonable system of supervision that accounted for these major changes.

a. Respondents Failed to Designate the Brooklyn Office as an Office of Supervisory Jurisdiction

Respondents failed to designate the Brooklyn office as an Office of Supervisory Jurisdiction ("OSJ"), as required by Conduct Rule 3010(a)(3). Certain types of activities, set forth in Rule 3010(g)(1), "are sufficiently vested with regulatory significance that the locations where members conduct these types of activities require special recognition and attention." Some of these activities occurred in Brooklyn. Kresge testified that Giordano was reviewing and approving new accounts and customer orders. *See* Rule 3010(g)(1)(D), (E). The record also shows that Kresge was aware that Giordano supervised two brokers in the Staten Island executive suite. *See* Rule 3010(g)(1)(G) (defining an OSJ to include any office that has "responsibility for supervising the activities of persons associated with the member at one or more other branch offices"). Moreover, a member firm is required to designate offices as OSJs "as it determines to be necessary in order to supervise its registered representatives and associated persons." Rule 3010(a)(3). Among the relevant considerations is "whether registered persons at the location engage in retail sales or other activities involving regular contact with public customers." Rule 3010(a)(3)(A). Given that the Brooklyn representatives engaged in retail sales of a new, and particularly risky, product line for Yankee, respondents were required to designate the Brooklyn office as an OSJ.

b. Respondents Failed to Make Reasonable Efforts to Determine That Supervisory Personnel Were Qualified

Conduct Rule 3010(a)(6) requires "[r]easonable efforts to determine that all supervisory personnel are qualified by virtue of experience or training to carry out their assigned responsibilities." Kresge did not make reasonable efforts to determine that Giordano was qualified to supervise the Brooklyn office. Ferragamo recommended Giordano for the position of Brooklyn branch manager. In considering Giordano, Kresge was required to determine that Giordano understood, and could effectively conduct, his required responsibilities. Kresge did interview Giordano and review his CRD record. Kresge also testified that he asked Giordano about his employment history. Had he conducted an effective investigation, Kresge would have learned that from November 1997 to September 2001, Giordano was employed by five different firms. Kresge generally agreed that a broker changing firms frequently in a relatively short period would be a "red flag of a potential compliance issue." Kresge checked to see if Giordano's firm was on NASD's Taping Rule list,[77] but Kresge admitted that he had never heard of the firms Giordano had worked for. Kresge also was not sure if he reviewed Giordano's examination history at the time. Asked whether he ever asked Giordano how long he had been a principal, Kresge evasively testified that he asked Giordano if he understood compliance procedures and how to carry them out.

Had Kresge conducted a reasonable due diligence investigation concerning Giordano's qualifications, he would have learned that Giordano passed his general securities representative and principal qualification examinations in December 1997 and March 2001, respectively, passing the latter just six months before he began managing the Brooklyn office. The fact that a person has passed the appropriate licensing examination "does not, in and of itself, qualify a supervisor." Moreover, Kresge's reliance on Giordano's self-description of his qualifications was not sufficient, since Kresge could "confirm the representations without having to undertake extreme or excessive efforts." Kresge did not even ensure that Giordano received a copy of what was serving as Yankee's written supervisory procedures. Moreover, once the Brooklyn office opened, Kresge took no steps to monitor Giordano, except, as explained below, to assign a person (Gliwa) to monitor him who did not have the time and possibly the qualifications to do so effectively. Kresge admitted that he did not even know if the Brooklyn representatives had received any training concerning suitability or sales practices. As the Commission has held, "it is not sufficient for the person with overarching supervisory responsibilities to delegate supervisory responsibility to a subordinate, even a capable one, and then simply wash his hands of the matter until a

---

77. [14] Conduct Rule 3010(b)(2) (the "Taping Rule") requires broker-dealers that hire a certain percentage of their representatives from "Disciplined Firms," as defined in Rule 3010(b)(2)(J), to establish, maintain, and enforce special written procedures for supervising the telemarketing activities of its registered persons, including tape-recording all telephone conversations between the member's registered persons and both existing and potential customers. NASD maintains a list of Disciplined Firms as well as firms that are subject to the Taping Rule.

problem is brought to his attention.... Implicit is the additional duty to follow-up and review that delegated authority to ensure that it is being properly exercised."

Likewise, respondents failed to investigate reasonably whether Gliwa was qualified to serve as a supervisor for Giordano. While assigning someone to supervise Giordano was certainly the right idea, "[a] member's obligation to determine whether a supervisor is properly qualified to fulfill his or her supervisory duties is an ongoing obligation." By December 2001, Kresge was aware that Gliwa was having difficulty fulfilling his supervisory duties. Kresge testified that, during the October 2001 to December 2001 period, Gliwa, who maintained his own book of clients, was "wearing seven or eight hats," was "overwhelmed with work," and visited the Brooklyn office only "two or three times." Kresge never discussed with Gliwa what he would look for when reviewing order tickets, was aware that Gliwa never conducted regular reviews of Brooklyn trades or customers' accounts for suitability, and knew that, prior to NASD's investigation, Gliwa had never rejected any orders. At one point ... Kresge [was informed] that Gliwa was incompetent as a supervisor and "doesn't get it." But despite these warnings about Gliwa's qualifications, respondents never delivered a copy of the written supervisory procedures to Gliwa and kept him on as a supervisor of the Brooklyn office. We agree with the Hearing Panel, which found that "[b]ecause Kresge knew of Gliwa's supervisory deficiencies, [the] continued delegation to [Gliwa] of supervisory authority was not reasonable."

c. Respondents Failed to Ascertain the Qualifications of the Brooklyn Representatives

Conduct Rule 3010(e) provides that "[e]ach member shall have the responsibility and duty to ascertain *by investigation* the good character, business repute, qualifications, and experience of any person prior to making such a certification in the application of such person for registration with [NASD]." (Emphasis added.) NASD has indicated that, at a minimum, members must review an applicant's Uniform Application for Securities Industry Registration or Transfer ("Form U4") and Uniform Termination Notice for Securities Industry Registration ("Form U5"), review the applicant's CRD history, and contact the applicant's previous employers. Firms also should consider using best hiring practices, including obtaining explanations regarding any customer complaints and regulatory actions to determine the merit, to the extent practicable, of each before hiring, and asking about any pending proceedings, customer complaints, regulatory investigations, or arbitrations not listed in CRD. As indicated above, a firm's president is responsible for compliance with this requirement unless and until it is reasonably delegated.

Viewed under these standards, Kresge's efforts to investigate the Brooklyn brokers were woefully insufficient. Kresge claimed that he contacted NASD to ensure that adding these representatives would not result in changes to Yankee's restrictive agreement. Yet Kresge did not contact the prospective representatives' employers. Kresge interviewed all of the representatives, except [one].and asked the questions contained on Form U4, but nothing beyond that. Although Kresge reviewed the applicants' CRD records, all that mattered to him was whether they were registered as general securities representatives, had any disclosures, or worked for a firm that was on

NASD's list of firms subject to the Taping Rule, which he explained was his "barometer of quality" for a firm. Kresge admitted that he was not concerned with the amount of the applicants' experience and did not check to see which, or how many, firms had employed the applicants. When reviewing Ferragamo's CRD record, Kresge did not check to determine the capacity in which Ferragamo was registered or to see what examinations he had passed.

As a result, Kresge hired a number of brokers for the Brooklyn office with questionable histories. Kresge conceded that he was not aware that [several of the Brooklyn registered representatives] had previously switched firms numerous times within short periods. Moreover, those same individuals previously worked for firms that, as of September 2001, either were Disciplined Firms for purposes of the Taping Rule or subject to that rule, despite Kresge's claim that he checked to see if the brokers' previous firms were subject to the Taping Rule. Although Kresge allowed Ferragamo to work as an unregistered principal, Kresge failed to learn that Ferragamo had been registered only as a corporate securities representative, had never been registered as a general securities representative or principal, and twice failed the general securities representative examination. Had Kresge exerted minimal investigative efforts, he would have discovered this troubling information.

Kresge also evidently did not learn that Ferragamo was the subject of two pending customer arbitration matters, which were not reported in CRD until November 2001 and August 2002, that claimed damages totaling $190,000 allegedly caused by unauthorized transactions, breaches of contract and fiduciary duty, negligence, and unsuitable recommendations.

d. Respondents Failed to Establish Reasonably Designed Procedures

Rule 3010(a) requires that each member establish and maintain a supervisory system "that is reasonably designed to achieve compliance with applicable securities laws." Although the Firm had written supervisory procedures, the procedures were not distributed to anyone in Melville or Brooklyn. A concomitant duty is that a firm should determine whether heightened supervisory procedures are necessary for any of its registered representatives "with a recent history of customer complaints, final disciplinary actions involving sales practice abuse or other customer harm, or adverse arbitration decisions." Respondents employed [Lawrence] Dugo, who was the subject of a pending arbitration matter when he was hired and who had a prior felony conviction for a drug-related offense, and [David] Anderson, who was the subject of numerous complaints lodged by Yankee customers as early as November 2001. Despite this, respondents failed to require heightened supervisory procedures for these two employees until April 2002, six months after the Brooklyn office opened.

For all of these reasons, we affirm the Hearing Panel's findings that respondents failed to establish and maintain a reasonable system of supervision, in violation of Conduct Rules 3010 and 2110.

2. Respondents Failed to Supervise the Brooklyn Office

Market Regulation further alleged, and the Hearing Panel found, that respondents failed to supervise the activities in the Brooklyn office. We affirm the Hearing Panel's findings.

As an initial matter, we find that Kresge was responsible at all times not only for establishing a supervisory system, but also for supervising the Brooklyn office. The Commission has "long maintained that 'final responsibility for supervision of the trading activities of a member firm of NASD rests with the firm's president, unless the president reasonably delegates the duties to someone else and has no reason to know that person is not properly performing the delegated duties.'" The record does not demonstrate that Kresge's purported delegations of supervisory authority were reasonable.

Although Kresge purported to put Giordano in charge of the Brooklyn office and Gliwa in charge of monitoring Giordano, based upon all of the circumstances, these were unreasonable delegations of supervisory authority. As explained in detail above, Kresge failed to conduct a reasonable investigation into Giordano's qualifications, leaving Kresge with no sufficient basis to conclude that Giordano was capable of supervising an entire office. Furthermore, Kresge knew that Gliwa's performance of his supervisory responsibilities was deficient. Moreover, after this supervisory scheme was established, ample red flags soon appeared, demonstrating that these supervisors were not fulfilling their responsibilities, as further explained below.

Kresge was responsible for "reasonable supervision," a standard that "is determined based on the particular circumstances of each case." The SEC has held that "red flags and suggestions of irregularities demand inquiry as well as adequate follow-up and review."

Respondents argue that Kresge was ignorant of the problems in the Brooklyn office, asserting that Giordano and Gliwa deliberately concealed evidence of the sales practice problems. The record, however, demonstrates that Kresge knew, or should have known, of a number of red flags, but took no action. After the first meeting with Masone and Ferragamo, Stelz, the Melville office manager, was concerned enough to advise Kresge to check out Masone's background. Moreover, Ferragamo resisted being registered for reasons that ostensibly included a desire to avoid being held liable in an arbitration matter pending against him. Ferragamo described the brokers he wanted to bring with him to Yankee as disgruntled, and the brokers whom Kresge ultimately hired included persons who had moved frequently to and from disciplined firms, several persons with little relevant experience, and one person who was the subject of a pending arbitration.

The red flags continued after the Brooklyn office opened. Contrary to Ferragamo's representation that his business primarily involved listed stocks, the Brooklyn representatives immediately began selling speculative Over-the-Counter Bulletin Board ® stocks. Kresge was aware of the large volume and speculative nature of Brooklyn's business, given that he reviewed commission runs and saw Brooklyn-generated order tickets, and that Yankee received significant commission overrides and ticket charges. Scott Gomolak, who worked at the trading desk, testified that he sought Kresge's approval for certain orders for Silver Star placed by Brooklyn brokers, and Kresge admitted seeing a ticket for a very large order of Silver Star. In fact, around November 2001, Stelz warned Kresge that the Brooklyn office's trading of "cheap stocks" needed to be monitored closely. Moreover, Yankee started receiving complaints concerning the Brooklyn brokers[...] and Kresge himself fielded complaints from Montani about Yankee brokers lying to Valley Forge customers. Kresge knew of, and had approved, the Staten Island office. Kresge also was aware that Masone, who was not registered with Yankee, was frequently in the Melville office, used the telephones, and delivered documents between Melville and Brooklyn.

Faced with these red flags, Kresge should have been actively monitoring the activities in Brooklyn. Instead, Kresge paid little attention. Kresge visited the Brooklyn office just three times in the first three months of its operation. Kresge relied on various persons to supervise the Brooklyn office.... Yet Kresge never asked Gliwa how the Brooklyn office was doing compliance-wise; did not know whether the Brooklyn brokers were trained on suitability or sales practices; knew that neither Gliwa nor Stelz had reviewed any customer accounts; never ensured [the] recommendation to tape record the Brooklyn brokers was implemented; and remained ignorant about how Giordano distributed the 85 percent share of Brooklyn's commissions or whether these payments were accurately reflected on the books and records of the broker-dealer. Kresge claimed that he was not alarmed about the pending arbitration matter against Ferragamo and was evasive when asked whether he further investigated it. And when Kresge saw the large order for Silver Star, his only concern was whether the client had money to cover the trade. Had respondents responded to the litany of red flags, they might have brought the improper sales activity to an end more quickly.

The cases that respondents cite in support of their argument that they did not fail to supervise are distinguishable. For example, in *Arthur J. Huff*, 50 S.E.C. 524 (1991), the SEC dismissed allegations that a principal in a compliance department failed to supervise a representative who engaged in a massive securities fraud. When the principal joined the firm, he inherited responsibility to monitor the representative, whom the compliance department had already investigated to its satisfaction, and there were no new developments that raised questions. When a problem did surface, the principal conducted an investigation and recommended that the representative be fired. *Id.* at 528-29. The Commission also dismissed the allegations in *Louis R. Trujillo*, 49 S.E.C. 1106 (1989), that a supervisory employee had failed to supervise a representative who engaged in repeated violations of antifraud provisions. In *Trujillo*, the supervisor had limited authority to correct problems he detected. Despite that limited authority, the supervisor detected and reported numerous concerns about the problematic representative and ultimately went over his own supervisor's head when appropriate remedial action was not taken. In *Juan C. Schidlowski*, 48 S.E.C. 507 (1986), the Commission dismissed allegations that a president had failed to supervise activities that involved sales of securities before the effective date of registration. In that case, there was no indication that the president was aware of the irregularities or that the person in charge of the sales, also a high level manager, could not be trusted. In contrast to *Huff, Trujillo,* and *Schidlowski,* Yankee and Kresge had ample authority to supervise the Brooklyn office, had plenty of reasons to be concerned about Giordano and Gliwa ... [who] took little action to detect problems, and did not respond appropriately if at all to the red flags and warning signs until months after the Brooklyn office opened.[78]

Accordingly, the preponderance of the evidence demonstrates that Yankee and Kresge failed to reasonably supervise the Brooklyn office, in violation of Conduct Rules 3010 and 2110.

* * *

C. Respondents' Liability for the Yankee Representatives' Violations of NASD Conduct Rules

The Hearing Panel found that Yankee and Kresge were liable for the Brooklyn representatives' violations of NASD's suitability and antifraud rules, and, as a result, violated the high standards of commercial honor and just and equitable principles of trade required of NASD members and their associated persons.[79] We affirm the Hearing Panel's decision to hold Yankee responsible for these violations. As the Commission has held, "[i]t is well-established that a firm may be held accountable for the misconduct of its associated persons because it is through such persons that a firm acts." Accordingly, we affirm the Hearing Panel's decision that Yankee is liable for the Brooklyn representatives' violations of NASD's antifraud, suitability, and fair dealing rules.

We also affirm the Hearing Panel's decision to hold Kresge accountable for the Brooklyn brokers' violations of NASD's suitability and antifraud rules. Our finding in this regard is separate and apart from our finding above that Kresge failed to supervise, in violation of Conduct Rule 3040. Kresge was president of his firm and accordingly had an overarching responsibility for his firm's regulatory obligations. It is axiomatic that "the president of a brokerage firm is responsible for his firm's compliance with all applicable requirements unless and until he reasonably delegates a

---

78. [22] As explained above, there is abundant evidence that the Brooklyn representatives engaged in fraudulent solicitations and made unsuitable recommendations. We nevertheless note that "[a] determination that a respondent has violated NASD's supervisory rule is not dependent on a finding of a violation by those subject to the respondent's supervision." *Prager,* 2005 SEC LEXIS 1558, at *47 (*citing NASD Notice to Members 98-96* (Dec. 1998)).

79. [40] Conduct Rule 2120 provides that "[n]o member shall effect any transaction in, or induce the purchase or sale of, any security by means of any manipulative, deceptive or other fraudulent device or contrivance." Conduct Rule 2310 requires that a member, "[i]n recommending to a customer the purchase, sale or exchange of any security, ... shall have reasonable grounds for believing that the recommendation is suitable for such customer." Conduct Rule 2110 requires that a "member, in the conduct of his business, shall observe high standards of commercial honor and just and equitable principles of trade." NASD Rule 115 extends the requirements of NASD rules to persons associated with a member.

particular function to another person in the firm, and neither knows nor has reason to know that such person is not properly performing his or her duties."

NASD's antifraud and suitability rules are *member firm* requirements. We, therefore, find that it is consistent with *Knapp* to hold Kresge personally responsible for the Yankee representatives' violations of NASD's antifraud and suitability rules, especially given the reckless manner in which he carried out his responsibilities in connection with the Brooklyn office. Kresge played an active role in creating the environment for violative activities by the Brooklyn-based representatives, turning a blind eye to the questionable qualifications and histories of the participants involved despite having a duty to ascertain their qualifications, and failing to put in place a reasonable system of supervision. Kresge also recklessly ignored the numerous red flags that predictably followed. Given the extent to which Kresge abdicated his responsibilities as president when approving the composition of the Brooklyn office and its putative supervisors, it was an extreme departure from the standards of care for Kresge simply to walk away almost as if this situation were someone else's problem. Moreover, had he been fulfilling his supervisory responsibilities, Kresge would have had ample and clear reasons to know that the Brooklyn-based brokers were not complying with applicable antifraud and suitability rules, especially considering the reckless way in which he staffed the Brooklyn office.

Accordingly, we affirm the Hearing Panel's decision to hold Yankee and Kresge liable for the Brooklyn representatives' violations of Conduct Rules 2120, 2310, and IM-2310-2.

VI. Sanctions

... [W]e expel Yankee and we bar Kresge in all capacities.

———

Notes and Questions

1. One of the principal considerations in determining whether a failure to supervise violation has occurred is whether the supervisor ignored "red flags" that should have resulted in additional supervisory scrutiny. What were the red flags that should have demonstrated to Kresge that Gliwa was deficient in his discharge of the supervisory responsibilities delegated to him? → So busy, unable to handle.

2. The National Adjudicatory Council pointed out that Giordano—from November 1997 to September 2001—was employed by five different broker-dealers. Why should frequent changes from one broker-dealer to another by a registered representative in a short period be considered a red flag? → Likely problems so switching places

3. The National Adjudicatory Council ("NAC") found that the respondents failed to establish heightened supervisory procedures for Lawrence Dugo (CRD# 2555823). Why did the NAC determine that heightened supervisory procedures were necessary for Dugo? Review the disclosure events section of Dugo's BrokerCheck report by visiting http://www.finra.org/BrokerCheck/.

Past disciplinary history

4. Yankee Financial Group, Inc., received several customer complaints in 2001 and 2002 regarding the conduct of its associated persons. None of these complaints were reported to FINRA. Review FINRA Rule 4530 to determine the steps the broker-dealer should have taken with regard to its customer complaints. Assume all customer complaints were written complaints. ↳ *Must submit a disclosure.*

There should have been a system that follows up.

5. Review disciplinary proceeding No. 2009020383002 using FINRA's Disciplinary Actions Online database, which concluded with the respondents, Cantone Research Inc., and its Chief Compliance Officer ("CCO") Christine L. Cantone, submitting an Offer of Settlement for their supervisory violations. Due to the CCO's failure to detect red flags and take further supervisory action, a registered representative continued to engage in a scheme selling fictitious investments resulting in the misappropriation of more than $1.6 million. Review the case and identify the "red flag" warnings that should have resulted in additional supervisory scrutiny.

Accepted registered representatives words regarding questionable activity.
· No follow up review for suspicious transactions.
· Allowed retention of account (by registered representative) at another firm.

C. Special Supervisory Procedures

While FINRA's supervision rules require broker-dealers to develop a supervisory system and written supervisory procedures in accordance with the types of businesses in which they engage, in certain areas broker-dealers must be aware of special supervisory procedures.

1. *Deferred Variable Annuities*[80]

A deferred variable annuity is a contract between an investor and an insurance company in which the insurance company promises to make periodic payments to the investor at a future date stated in the contract. A deferred variable annuity offers several investment options to the investor, but typically investment options are mutual funds that invest in stocks, bonds, money market instruments, or some combination thereof. This investment option means that the investor's periodic payments depend on the performance of the investment options chosen by the investor, although some deferred variable annuities may guarantee a particular minimum level of annuity payments for an additional fee. Essentially, investors purchase deferred variable annuities to receive periodic payments for life, a death benefit, and tax deferred investment growth. However, in purchasing a deferred variable annuity, the investor may incur various charges in addition to the purchase price, including initial sales loads, surrender charges, fees for transferring between investment options, and fees and expenses of underlying investment funds.

---

80. Variable annuities are regulated by the SEC as well as the state insurance commissions. In *SEC v. Variable Annuity Life Ins. Co.*, 359 U.S. 65 (1959), the Supreme Court held variable annuity contracts are securities and thus must be registered with the SEC. *See generally Joint SEC/NASD Report on Examination Findings Regarding Broker-Dealer Sales of Variable Ins. Products*, FINRA (June 2004), http://www.finra.org/web/groups/industry/@ip/@reg/@guide/documents/industry/p010368.pdf (analyzing the practice of broker-dealers selling variable insurance to investors); *Variable Annuities: What You Should Know*, SEC, http://www.sec.gov/investor/pubs/varannty.htm.

FINRA has expressed regulatory concerns regarding the sale of deferred variable annuities by broker-dealers. These concerns include unsuitability for investor liquidity needs, high fees and expenses eroding possible investment gains, and high commissions leading broker-dealers to engage in excessive switching or exchanges between available investment options. FINRA adopted additional supervisory requirements to address these concerns. If a broker-dealer or its associated person recommends the purchase or exchange of deferred variable annuities, then, in addition to meeting the supervisory requirements contained in FINRA Rules 3110, 3120, and 3130, it also must comply with FINRA Rule 2330. FINRA Rule 2330 requires the broker-dealer to establish and maintain specific written supervisory procedures for recommending purchases and exchanges of deferred variable annuities. Among other requirements, the broker-dealer must implement surveillance procedures to determine whether any of its associated persons have high rates of effecting exchanges and adopt policies and procedures reasonably designed to implement corrective measures to address inappropriate exchanges of deferred variable annuities. FINRA Rule 2330 also prohibits the broker-dealer from recommending the purchase or exchange of a deferred variable annuity, unless it has a reasonable basis to believe that the transaction is suitable for the customer and that the customer has been informed, generally, of the various features of deferred variable annuities, including potential surrender charges; a tax penalty if the customer sells or redeems before reaching age 59 1/2; market risk; and whether the customer would benefit from features such as tax-deferred growth, annuitization, or a death or living benefit. In addition, a broker-dealer must develop and document specific training policies or programs reasonably designed to ensure that associated persons who effect, and registered principals who review, transactions in deferred variable annuities comply with all provisions of FINRA Rule 2330 and understand the material features of deferred variable annuities.

2. 529 College Savings Plans

The purchase and sale of state-sponsored 529 plans must meet the Municipal Securities Rulemaking Board rules and regulations, which are enforced by FINRA. Named after Section 529(b) of the Internal Revenue Code, 529 College Savings Plans, typically established by states, are considered by the SEC to be municipal fund securities. All municipal fund securities transactions must be supervised by a municipal securities principal or limited principal (Series 53 or Series 51) and must meet all applicable MSRB rules, including MSRB Rule G-27, regarding supervision. FINRA has taken action against broker-dealers for failing to establish and maintain adequate supervisory procedures for the purchase of municipal securities. Often, supervisory violations result when a broker-dealer fails to establish supervisory procedures for 529 plans that require consideration of state income tax benefits in the suitability analysis, as demonstrated in the following Acceptance, Waiver and Consent letter (AWC) entered into by Merrill Lynch.

Financial Industry Regulatory Authority
Letter of Acceptance, Waiver and Consent
NO. 20090189070

Merrill Lynch, Pierce, Fenner & Smith Inc. (Nov. 23, 2010)

* * *

FACTS AND VIOLATIVE CONDUCT

a. 529 Plans and Merrill Lynch's 529 Plan Sales

529 plans are tax-advantaged investment programs designed to help finance qualified higher education costs. All 529 plans offer the same federal tax advantages, including tax deferral on earnings. Approximately half of the states offer state income tax deductions and/or other benefits based on investments by residents in their state's 529 plan, and five states offer state income tax deductions and/or other benefits regardless of which 529 plan the resident invests in. Some states offer 529 plans directly, others offer the 529 plans through designated broker-dealers, and some states offer their plans both directly and through designated broker-dealers. In addition, each plan has different costs, expenses, investment options and other plan features.

From June 2002 through February 2007, Merrill Lynch sold over $3 billion of 529 plans.

b. Merrill Lynch Failed to Establish and Maintain Adequate Procedures Related to the Sale of 529 Plans

From June 2002 through February 2007, Merrill Lynch required registered representatives to consider potential state tax benefits offered by a state in which a client resided as one of a variety of factors before recommending an out of state 529 plan. However, during the period June 2002 through February 2007, Merrill Lynch failed to establish and maintain specific procedures reasonably designed to achieve compliance with industry suitability standards related to the sale of 529 plans. The Firm's written supervisory procedures did not adequately ensure that the Firm's registered representatives were considering customer state income tax benefits during their 529 suitability analyses. The Firm failed to establish and maintain written supervisory procedures requiring supervisors to perform and document reviews to determine if registered representatives were complying with suitability requirements before recommending a 529 plan purchase. Moreover, Merrill Lynch did not have effective procedures relating to documenting its suitability determinations in connection with the sale of 529 plans.

c. Violations

From June 2002 through February 2007, Merrill Lynch failed to establish and maintain supervisory systems and procedures, including written supervisory procedures, reasonably designed to achieve compliance with industry suitability standards related to the sale of 529 plans.

529 plans are municipal securities. As a result, when offering and selling 529 plans, regulated firms must comply with the applicable rules of the MSRB. MSRB Rule G-27 requires that regulated firms supervise the conduct of the municipal securities ac-

tivities of the firm and its associated persons to ensure compliance with MSRB rules and the federal securities laws, and that firms adopt, maintain and enforce written supervisory procedures reasonably designed to ensure that municipal securities activities are in compliance. Merrill Lynch's conduct, as described above, was in violation of MSRB Rule G-27.

———

3. Heightened Supervisory Procedures

Heightened supervisory procedures are required in the supervision of complex products and registered representatives with a disciplinary history due to customer complaints, disciplinary actions, and/or adverse arbitration decisions.

a. Complex Products

The solicitation of retail customers in the purchase and sale of complex products must be properly supervised. FINRA does not define the term complex product, but such a product "may include a security or investment strategy with novel, complicated or intricate derivative-like features such as structured notes, inverse or leveraged exchange-traded funds, hedge funds and securitized products, such as asset-backed securities." Although FINRA does not provide a definition of a complex product, broker-dealers are encouraged to evaluate product complexity and risk to investors, reasoning that "complexity of a product often necessitates more scrutiny and supervision...." While adherence to specific requirements are unnecessary, FINRA has set forth certain best practices in FINRA Regulatory Notice 12-03 wherein complex products require "enhanced oversight" consisting of internal controls and procedures for the approval of the initial sale and a post-approval review. The approval of the sale of complex products consists of making a "reasonable basis suitability determination" to determine the potential risks and rewards associated with the transaction. The post-approval review requires reassessment of the complex features of a product to determine whether changes in the risk profile of the investment necessitates changes in the supervisory system.

b. Registered Representatives

Heightened supervisory procedures are required for registered persons with a history of customer complaints, disciplinary actions, and/or adverse arbitration decisions. At a minimum, heightened supervisory procedures require the member firm to review the facts and circumstances of each event and determine whether the firm's supervisory and training system are adequate to address the deficiencies and issues presented by the registered person's disciplinary record. While typically the member firms retain the discretion to determine the type of heightened supervisory procedures implemented, they must obtain FINRA's approval to employ an individual who is statutorily disqualified[81] from registration with FINRA. As demonstrated in *In the Matter of the Association of X*, these heightened supervisory requirements can be very specific.

———

81. Statutory disqualification is defined in § 3(a)(39) of the Exchange Act, 15 U.S.C. § 78o(c)(a)(39), and includes, among others, persons expelled or suspended from FINRA membership or from asso-

In the Matter of the Association of X as a General Securities Representative with the Sponsoring Firm

Redacted Decision
SD11007
2011

Introduction

On March 24, 2009, the Sponsoring Firm filed a Membership Continuance Application ("MC-400" or "the Application") with FINRA's Department of Registration and Disclosure, seeking to permit X, a person subject to a statutory disqualification, to associate with the Sponsoring Firm as a general securities representative. For the reasons explained below, we approve the Sponsoring Firm's Application.

The Statutorily Disqualifying Event

X is statutorily disqualified due to FINRA's acceptance, in 2006, of a Letter of Acceptance, Waiver and Consent ("AWC") finding that X willfully failed to disclose material information on his Uniform Application for Securities Industry Registration or Transfer ("Form U4"). Specifically, the AWC found that X failed to disclose two civil judgments against him on his Form U4 on five separate occasions between March 2002 and August 2004. The AWC also found that X failed to provide his member firm with written notice, or obtain prior authorization of, his participation in certain private securities transactions, in violation of NASD Rules 3040 and 2110. FINRA suspended X in all capacities for six months and fined him $10,000. X served the FINRA suspension from November 2006, until May 2007, and he paid the fine in full. X is currently unemployed.

X's Proposed Business Activities and Supervision

The Sponsoring Firm proposes to employ X in the Sponsoring Firm's home office in City 1 as a general securities representative. X's compensation will be entirely commissions based. X testified that his business will focus primarily on institutional businesses and high net worth individuals in the Indian-American community.

The Sponsoring Firm proposes that the Proposed Supervisor will be X's primary on-site supervisor. The Proposed Supervisor qualified as a general securities representative in 1997 and as a general securities principal in 1998. The Proposed Supervisor also registered as an options principal in 2003, and passed the uniform securities agent state law examination in 1998 and the uniform investment adviser law examination in 2007. The Proposed Supervisor has been employed with the Sponsoring Firm since October 2006. Prior to that time, he was associated with three other firms. The Proposed Supervisor currently supervises one other individual, and at the hearing the Proposed Supervisor and the Sponsoring Firm represented that the Proposed Supervisor will not be compensated by overrides from X's transactions.

---

ciation with a broker-dealer and persons subject to an SEC or FINRA order denying or suspending membership with FINRA.

The Sponsoring Firm also proposes that when the Proposed Supervisor is not available, Employee 2, the Sponsoring Firm's chief compliance officer, will supervise X.

Discussion

... [B]ased on the facts presented to us in the record, we find that the proposed primary on-site supervisor, the Proposed Supervisor, is qualified. He has been in the securities industry since 1997 without any disciplinary history, and he qualified as a general securities principal in 1998. He will be located in the same office as X, and X will sit immediately outside of the Proposing Supervisor's office (which will permit him to closely monitor all of X's activities). Further, the Proposed Supervisor supervises only one other individual, and we find credible the Proposed Supervisor's testimony that he will be able to supervise X pursuant to heightened supervisory conditions and that he fully understands the responsibility that he is undertaking in doing so.

We are satisfied that the following heightened supervisory procedures will enable the Sponsoring Firm to reasonably monitor X's activities on a regular basis:[82]

1. The Sponsoring Firm will amend its WSPs to state that the Proposed Supervisor is the primary supervisor responsible for X.*

2. If the Proposed Supervisor is on vacation or out of the office for an extended period, Employee 2 will act as X's interim supervisor.*

3. X will work the same hours as the Proposed Supervisor. The Proposed Supervisor or the alternate supervisor will be in the office at all times that X is in the office.*

4. X will not maintain discretionary accounts.

5. X will not act in a supervisory capacity.*

6. The Sponsoring Firm will not allow X to conduct any outside business activities or private securities transactions.*

7. The Sponsoring Firm will review and pre-approve each of X's customer securities accounts, prior to opening of the account by X. Account paperwork will be documented as approved with a date and signature maintained at the Sponsoring Firm's home office. Documents pertaining to the review and approval of such accounts will be segregated for ease of review during any SD [Statutory Disqualification] examination.*

8. The Proposed Supervisor will review and approve X's orders after execution, or as soon as practicable, on a T+1 basis. The Proposed Supervisor will evidence his review by initialing the reports, and keep copies of the reports in a separate file for ease of review during any SD examination.*

9 X agrees that he shall not: (a) share accounts with others; (b) split or share with others any commissions (other than his standard commission split with the Sponsoring Firm, as outlined in his employment agreement); (c) receive

---

82. [7] The items that are denoted by an asterisk are heightened supervisory conditions for X and are not standard operating procedures of the Sponsoring Firm.

overrides on the commissions, fees, or profits generated by others. In order to ensure compliance with these prohibitions, the Proposed Supervisor will review each account and trade (as indicated in conditions nos. 7 and 8) to ensure that X is complying with the stipulations of this condition.*

10. All complaints pertaining to X, whether verbal or written, will be immediately referred to the Proposed Supervisor for review, and then to the Compliance Department. The Proposed Supervisor will prepare a memorandum to the file as to what measures he took to investigate the merits of the complaint (e.g., contact with the customer) and the resolution of the matter. Documents pertaining to these complaints should be kept segregated for ease of review during an SD examination.*

11. X agrees not to engage in the following activities: training or advising registered representatives or persons seeking to become registered representatives. X also agrees to conduct all business solely in English.*

12. The Sponsoring Firm will only permit X to conduct business at the Sponsoring Firm's office in City 1, State 2, which is the principal place of business of the Sponsoring Firm and where X's designated supervisor, the Proposed Supervisor, is located.*

13. The Proposed Supervisor will review X's incoming correspondence (including email), upon its arrival and review outgoing correspondence before it is sent.*

14. For the purposes of client communication, X will only be allowed to use an email account that is held at the Sponsoring Firm, with all emails being filtered through the Sponsoring Firm's email system. If X receives a business-related email message in another email account outside the Sponsoring Firm, he will immediately deliver that message to the Sponsoring Firm's email account. X will inform the Sponsoring Firm of all outside email accounts that he maintains. The email messages are to be preserved and kept segregated for ease of review during any statutory disqualification examination.*

15. For the duration of X's statutory disqualification, the Sponsoring Firm will obtain prior approval from Member Regulation before changing the permanent supervisor of X from the Proposed Supervisor to another person.*

16. The Proposed Supervisor must certify quarterly (March 31st, June 30th, September 30th, and December 31st) to the Compliance Department of the Sponsoring Firm that the Proposed Supervisor and X are in compliance with all of the above conditions of heightened supervision to be accorded X.*

17. The plan of heightened supervision will be forwarded to and maintained by the Sponsoring Firm's chief compliance officer.

———

4. *Taping Rule*

FINRA Rule 3170, known as the "Taping Rule," was developed in response to supervisory concerns that arise when a member firm hires a large number of registered persons who previously worked at disciplined firms.[83] The Taping Rule applies if a certain percentage of registered persons, depending on the size of the broker-dealer, were previously employed with a disciplined broker-dealer—40 percent for small broker-dealers (five to nine total registered persons) and 20 percent for large broker-dealers (at least 20 total registered persons). Unless an exemption from compliance with the Taping Rule is granted, broker-dealers must establish special written procedures to supervise the telemarketing activities of its registered representatives. These procedures must provide for the tape-recording of conversations between registered persons and existing or potential customers. The tape-recordings must be retained for at least three years from creation. Also, appropriate procedures must be implemented for reviewing the tape-recordings, and such procedures must be tailored to the broker-dealer's business lines, size, customers, and structure.

Complying with the taping rule may raise state and federal legal issues. For example, there are often state notice and consent laws that affect implementation of the taping rule.[84] In FINRA Notice to Members 98-52, FINRA states that the best practice for broker-dealers subject to the Taping Rule is to notify their registered persons and customers that their telephone calls are being tape recorded. This practice is recommended to facilitate broker-dealer compliance with applicable federal and state civil and criminal statutes governing the tape recording of conversations.

Financial Industry Regulatory Authority
Letter of Acceptance, Waiver and Consent

No. 2006003684702
Carlton Capital, Inc. (Oct. 6, 2008)

* * *

On February 17, 2006, Carlton Capital began tape recording telephone calls pursuant to the "Taping Rule," NASD Rule 3010(b)(2).[85]

In 2006, Carlton Capital maintained two parallel telephone systems in order to circumvent the Taping Rule—representatives dialing out on an area code 646 line

---

83. These disciplined firms can also include firms that have been expelled from membership or participation in any securities industry SRO or that have had their registrations revoked by the SEC.

84. *See Dep't of Enforcement v. Mission Sec. Corp.*, Case No. 2006003738501 (Dec. 18, 2008), http://www.finra.org/web/groups/industry/@ip/@enf/@adj/documents/ohodecisions/p118004.pdf; *Dep't of Enforcement v. Mission Sec. Corp.*, Compl. No. 2006003738501 (Feb. 24, 2010), http://www.finra.org/web/groups/industry/@ip/@enf/@adj/documents/nacdecisions/p120983.pdf; *Mission Sec. Corp.*, Exchange Act Release No. 63453 (Dec. 7, 2010), http://www.sec.gov/litigation/opinions/2010/34-63453.pdf; *NASD Notice to Members 98-*52, FINRA (Aug. 17, 1998), http://www.finra.org/web/groups/industry/@ip/@reg/@notice/documents/notices/p004858.pdf; *Fin. Indus. Regulatory Auth. Letter of Acceptance, Waiver & Consent*, Case No. 2006003684702 (Nov. 5, 2008), http://disciplinaryactions.finra.org/viewdocument.aspx?DocNB=13136; *NASD Notice to Members 97-19*, NASD (Apr. 1997), http://www.complinet.com/file_store/pdf/rulebooks/nasd_9719.pdf.

85. Recodified as FINRA Rule 3170.

were recorded, while representatives who selected an area code 212 line were not. Carlton Capital intentionally gave certain representatives access to the unrecorded lines, which these representatives knew to be unrecorded and which the representatives used to communicate with Firm customers.

In 2006, the Firm also routinely allowed representatives to talk to and accept orders from customers on cell phones and other unrecorded lines when the representatives were out of the office, which was about 20 percent of the time. Finally, while the Firm did retain the tape recordings of telephone calls made on the 646 lines in 2006, it did not catalog them by registered person as required. Starting in January 2007, Carlton Capital installed a USB-based taping system that recorded telephone calls to the hard drives of the computers on representatives desks. Employees were informed that only the President of the Firm was permitted access to the telephone recordings, but the data was not password protected and the Firm backed-up the data only once a year.

The system Carlton Capital installed in January 2007 did not comply with the Taping Rule, as evidenced by the fact that, in October 2007, Carlton Capital sought to access the recorded telephone calls of a representative it suspected of conducting business away from the Firm and discovered that his telephone calls from January to October 2007 had been deleted, likely by the representative himself.

Accordingly, Carlton Capital violated NASD Conduct Rules 3010(b)(2) and 2110.

---

5. Supervision when Outsourcing

Broker-dealers often contract with third-party providers or vendors for assistance in performing business operations and meeting regulatory responsibilities. This practice of outsourcing allows broker-dealers to focus on their core business and obtain expertise without hiring internal staff, which may be costly. Outsourcing has a long history in the securities industry, with FINRA Rule 4311 permitting introducing broker-dealers to enter into clearing agreements with clearing broker-dealers. According to a survey conducted by FINRA in October 2004, outsourcing has expanded from clearing agreements to other areas such as "accounting/finance (payroll, expense account reporting, etc.), legal and compliance, information technology (IT), operations functions (*e.g.*, statement production, disaster recovery services, etc.), and administration functions (e.g., human resources, internal audits etc.)."[86] The survey found that two-thirds of the third-party providers were regulated either by FINRA, NYSE, Federal Reserve or the Office of the Comptroller of the Currency and that the remaining third-party vendors were unregulated entities.

Outsourcing an activity or function to a third party does not relieve the broker-dealer of its regulatory responsibilities regarding the outsourced activity. A broker-

---

86. *Outsourcing: Members' Responsibilities When Outsourcing Activities to Third-Party Service Providers*, FINRA 2 (July 2005), http://www.finra.org/web/groups/industry/@ip/@reg/@notice/documents/notices/p014735.pdf.

dealer may not outsource its supervisory and compliance activities away from its direct control. These activities, even if a broker-dealer outsources to a third party, require the development of a supervisory system and written supervisory procedures to ensure compliance with applicable rules and regulations. Supervisory and compliance activities are "covered activities" and include activities such as order taking, handling of customer funds and securities, and other activities that, if performed by the broker-dealer, would be subject to requirements of FINRA Rules 3110 and 3120. FINRA guidance regarding outsourcing contemplates due diligence as the cornerstone of the outsourcing arrangement. If a broker-dealer anticipates outsourcing a covered activity, it must first have policies and procedures to determine the appropriateness of the outsourcing. When determining the appropriateness of outsourcing, the broker-dealer must consider factors such as its ability and capacity to comply with existing and future regulations along with the financial, reputational, and operational impact on the broker-dealer should the third-party service provider fail to perform in any way. The broker-dealer must also consider the potential impact of outsourcing on its responsibility to provide adequate services to its customers, including potential losses to the firm's customers; the regulatory status of the third-party provider; any affiliation or other corporate relationship between the broker-dealer and the third-party service provider; and any other factors pertinent to the broker-dealer's analysis based on its business structure, the activity or function to be outsourced, and the third-party service providers being considered.[87] If the outsourcing of a covered activity is appropriate, the broker-dealer must then conduct a due diligence analysis to determine the fitness and ability of the prospective third-party service provider to perform the outsourced activities. Even after the selection of a third-party service provider, the broker-dealer must monitor the performance and assess the ongoing fitness and capacity of the third-party service provider to perform the outsourced activities.

FINRA and other applicable regulators must have complete access to the work product of the third-party service provider. This means that any third-party providers conducting covered activities will be considered associated persons of the broker-dealer.

The importance of having adequate supervisory policies and procedures regarding outsourcing to third-party service providers was illustrated in the initial public offering of Vonage Holdings Corp ("Vonage"), a provider of cloud communications services for businesses and consumers. Vonage customers opened accounts with the lead underwriters of its IPO — Citigroup Global Markets, UBS, and Deutsche Bank — to participate in the directed share program (DSP). DSPs are company-sponsored programs that allow qualified parties with a relationship to the company to acquire shares at the IPO price. Under the DSP, the three investment banks sold 4.2 million shares to Vonage customers. When the third-party service provider sent incorrect commu-

---

87. *Principles on Outsourcing of Fin. Servs. for Mkt. Intermediaries*, INT'L ORG. OF SEC. COMM'NS 3 (Feb. 2005), http://www.cmvm.pt/CMVM/Cooperacao%20Internacional/Docs%20Iosco/Documents/ioscopd187.pdf.

nications to Vonage's customers, the investment banks were unaware of the incorrect communications and did not know how many of Vonage's customers received the communications. Citigroup Global Markets led the group with 7,000 DSP customer accounts and sales of approximately $2.5 million shares.

Financial Industry Regulatory Authority
Letter of Acceptance, Waiver and Consent
NO. 20060054506-01
Citigroup Global Markets Inc. (Sept. 22, 2009)

* * *

FACTS AND VIOLATIVE CONDUCT

The Underwriting of the Vonage IPO

CGMI was one of three lead underwriters for the initial public offering of 31,250,000 stock of Vonage on May 24, 2006. As part of the offering, 13.5 percent of the stock offered was reserved by Vonage for sale to approximately one million of its customers, in a directed share program ("DSP"). CGMI was responsible for selling approximately 2.5 million shares in the Vonage DSP and a total of 7,031,250 shares in the Vonage IPO. To participate in the DSP, eligible Vonage customers were required to open a limited-purpose brokerage account at one of the underwriters. Over 7,000 accounts were opened at CGMI by customers to participate in the Vonage IPO through the DSP.

Shares sold pursuant to the DSP were purchased from Vonage by CGMI and sold to customers through the accounts the customers had opened at the firm. CGMI received approximately $2 million in compensation for its activities in connection with the Vonage DSP, including writing discounts and commissions for the sale of DSP shares. The underwriters collectively received approximately $4 million for their activities in connection with the DSP.

Because of the large number of expected DSP participants, Vonage and the underwriters agreed that the DSP should be administered through an on-line, electronic platform. None of the underwriters had the requisite in-house technological ability to administer such a platform, so the Third Party Company was engaged to maintain the DSP website. Vonage contracted directly with the Third Party Company for its work on the DSP project, and CGMI was not a party to that contract. CGMI agreed that most communications to DSP participants, including DSP participants who opened accounts with CGMI, would be conducted through the website which was administered by the Third Party Company. These communications were to include the acceptance of offers, the provision of information about share allocations, and communications about money owed by the customers to CGMI for allocated shares.

CGMI had written supervisory procedures for directed share programs. Its Directed Share Program Manual stated that a team of its representatives "is responsible for contacting participants to confirm their allocations[,]" either by "speaking directly with the participants or sending a system generated e-mail." The Manual also stated that CGMI's representatives must "communicate the price per share, number of shares allocated and total amount due" to DSP participants. However, CGMI did not follow these procedures in connection with the Vonage DSP. CGMI also had written supervisory procedures for outsourcing, but also did not follow those procedures in connection with the Vonage DSP.

The Vonage DSP Website

Eligible Vonage customers who wanted to purchase IPO shares through the DSP were required to use the Vonage DSP website. After opening a brokerage account at one of the three underwriters, eligible customers could submit conditional offers through the website to purchase at least 100 and no more than 5,000 shares from one of the underwriters. This conditional offer constituted an offer to purchase from the underwriters up to the number of shares of stock specified in the offer, at any price within the initial public offering range set forth on the Vonage DSP website. Upon the posting of an acceptance notice and share allocation to a customer's DSP website, the underwriters would accept the customer's offer and the customer would be obligated to purchase the number of shares allocated at the IPO price.

The deadline for DISP participants to submit conditional offers for the Vonage DISP was May 19, 2006.

After that date, customers were prohibited from making new conditional offers, although a customer could withdraw an existing conditional offer until it was accepted by the underwriter and shares were allocated to the customer.

The Vonage IPO

On May 23, 2006, the Securities and Exchange Commission declared Vonage's statement effective, and the price for shares in the IPO was set at $17 a share. Conditional offers submitted by DSP participants were then accepted and the Third Party Company ran a computer program to determine IPO allocations that would be provided to DSP Participants. At approximately 5:24 p.m. on May 23, 2006, the "My Offer Summary" section of the main menu page, and the pricing page, of the Vonage DSP website were updated to include a line entitled "Your Allocation." At that point, the line included text, in red, which stated that "allocations have not been made." Participants were instructed to "check back soon."

At approximately 5:33 p.m., an e-mail was sent from the DSP website to Vonage DSP participants entitled "Vonage IPO Information: Pricing and Allocation Imminent." The e-mail stated that the registration statement had been declared effective and the IPO price had been determined. The email also advised participants that they could withdraw their conditional offer "until an acceptance notification is posted on the [DSP] website," which was "expected to occur shortly." Finally, the e-mail stated that "[t]he posting of an acceptance notification will constitute the underwriters' acceptance of your conditional offer."

At approximately 6:09 p.m., the Vonage DSP website was updated with a new message under the "Announcements" section on the summary page. The new message was entitled "Allocation Confirmation[.]" Under the "Allocation Confirmation" title, the website stated that the price for the IPO had been set, and it also advised users that if they were allocated shares, they would be required to pay the underwriter with which they opened a limited-purpose brokerage account within three business days. At that time, the "Your Allocation" line on the user's homepage remained unchanged and stated that "allocations have not been made" and that users should "check back soon."

The Incorrect Allocation Messages

IPO Allocations were released to the DSP website at approximately 7:43 p.m. on May 23, 2006. Shares were allocated to approximately 11,613 different accounts. Over 2.5 million shares were allocated to the 7,242 accounts that had been opened at CGMI to participate in the IPO.

Once the allocations were released, DSP participants could see how many shares they had and how much they owed for those shares, in the "Your Allocation" section of the website. This information was posted in red.

However, because of an error by the Third Party Company in disabling a server when the allocation program was run, some DSP participants whose offers to purchase shares had been accepted saw messages on the website incorrectly stating that they had not been allocated any shares. DSP participants affected by this error saw a message incorrectly stating they had been allocated "0 shares at $17" and that "You Owe: $0."

At the time the share allocations were posted on the DSP website, CGMI was also provided information about which of its customers had been allocated shares, how many shares those customers had been allocated, and how much the customers owed CGMI for the shares. However, CGMI did not begin to separately communicate this information to its customers until the second day of trading, when CGMI began to call customers who had not paid for their shares.

CGMI Becomes Aware That Customers Are Affected

On the first day of trading of Vonage stock, May 24, 2006, the value of Vonage's shares declined from $17 per share to $14.85 per share. On the second day of trading, May 25, 2006, the price of the stock declined further and closed at $13 per share.

By May 25, 2006, CGMI was aware that customers were complaining that they had been told they had not been allocated any IPO shares, when in fact they had received allocations. The customer complaints prompted a CGMI representative on the Vonage DSP project team to send a series of e-mails on May 25, 2006 to the Third Party Company and to senior personnel at CGMI about the potential causes of the provision of the incorrect information and how many customers might be affected.

In addition, later in the evening on May 25, the CGMI representative forwarded a customer's complaint to his counterparts at the other lead underwriters. In the e-mail, the CGMI representative stated that the Third Party Company had estimated that approximately 70 customers had seen the incorrect information stating that they had not received share allocations, and that "[t]hese 70 people may, therefore, not know they have allocations[, w]hich may be a good reason for making out-bound calls." A representative from one of the other lead underwriters responded that he "spoke to at least three people with this problem, and there may have been others who were not escalated to me[,]" that "[t]he problem seemed to be a caching issue[,]", and that "[i]f they hit refresh, it would still show zero shares, but if I had them logout and back in, the allocations showed correctly …"

While the Third Party Company provided the CGMI representative with a list of 70 CGMI customers who logged onto the website, the CGMI representative was unable to use the list and, the Third Party Company did not provide additional information to the CGMI representative at that time. When the CGMI representative made further requests for information, representatives of the Third Party Company told him that it could not provide information about its database because its contract was with Vonage, and not with CGMI. CGMI did later receive certain information that it requested from the Third Party Company concerning transactions of customers who complained that they had seen incorrect share allocations on the Vonage DSP website. As CGMI later learned, numerous customers may have been affected.

Upon learning the information described above, CGMI did not take sufficient action to determine the cause and extent of the dissemination of incorrect information to its customers through the website. For instance, CGMI did not make calls to customers to determine if they saw incorrect allocation information on the VCDSP website or were harmed by relying on that incorrect information.

In fact CGMI did not know the cause of the incorrect information about share allocations on the Vonage DSP website and did not learn what had caused the problem until the Third Party Company's investigation was completed a number of months later. At that time, CGMI learned that the incorrect allocation information was provided to certain customers as the result of a mistake by the Third Party Company. The Third Party Company reported to CGMI that its investigation had revealed that an employee of the company had failed to reset one of the servers.

CGMI Violated NASD Rules 3010 and 2110 by Failing to Establish Adequate Supervisory Procedures or Systems for Outsourced Communications with Its Customers

NASD Rule 3010 requires firms to establish, maintain, and enforce supervisory systems, including, written procedures, that are reasonably designed to achieve compliance with applicable securities laws and regulations.

Rule 3010 applies to activities undertaken by a member firm directly as well as those that are outsourced to third parties. As FINRA reminded firms in Notice to Members 05-48 ("Members' Responsibilities When Outsourcing Activities to Third-Party Providers") issued in July 2005, "outsourcing an activity or function to a third party does not relieve members of their ultimate responsibility for compliance with all applicable federal securities laws and regulations and [FINRA] and MSRB rules regarding the outsourced activity or function." As noted in NTM 05-48, firms have a "continuing responsibility to oversee, supervise, and monitor the service provider's performance of covered activities" — "functions that, if performed directly by members, would be required to be the subject of a supervisory system and written supervisory procedures pursuant to Rule 3010."

CGMI allowed a third party to communicate with its customers through the Vonage DSP website about the sale of IPO shares to those customers through accounts at CGMI. Those activities should have been subject to CGMIs supervisory systems and procedures, even if performed on behalf of the firm by a third party. CGMI failed, however, to establish or implement adequate supervisory procedures or systems regarding the activities of the Third Party Company in communicating with CGMIs customers about the sale of Vonage securities through the Vonage DSP website.

CGMI also failed to respond adequately when it became aware that incorrect information about IPO allocations may have been provided to customers. When the zero allocation issue arose, GGMI was unable to take effective action to address the problems that were caused by the provision of incorrect information. At the time, CGMI did not know what allocation information had been communicated to its customers or how many customers may have been affected by the problem. CGMI also failed to take steps prior to the IPO to require that the Third Party Company maintain sufficient records of its communications with CGMI's customers about the IPO and IPO allocations. CGMI did not, for example, require that the Third Party Company maintain copies of screenshots or other records that would have reflected statements made on the website to customers about IPO allocations. CGMI also did not know, and could not promptly determine, the cause of the problem, whether an error had occurred, and if so how to correct the error. CGMI was therefore unable to investigate or remedy the problem or respond adequately to customer complaints. In fact, it was a number of months before CGMI was able to learn the cause of the problem, when the Third Party Company reported the results of its investigation. Because of technological limitations of the website, the Third Party Company reported, the Third Party Company was unable to determine how many customers were affected, or what allocation information had been conveyed to certain customers.

Responding promptly to these problems was important because certain customers did not know for several days that they had received allocations of shares in the IPO. As a result, those customers may not have paid attention to the price of Vonage stock in the first few days of trading. By the time some of those customers later learned that they had been allocated shares, the price of Vonage stock had declined significantly from the IPO price. When those customers later sold their shares, they incurred losses.

CGMI also failed to ensure that FINRA had the same access to the work of the Third Party Company for CGMI that FINRA would have had if CGMI had performed the work directly. For example, in its investigation, FINRA requested that employees of the Third Party Company testify under oath, in a transcribed interview, about the Vonage DSP and the process of allocating shares and communicating share allocation information to customers. However, the Third Party Company representatives provided only unsworn and untranscribed interviews, and CGMI and the other lead underwriters were unable to arrange for employees of the Third Party Company to testify under oath, and in transcribed sessions, as requested by FINRA. In addition, FINRA requested that CGMI provide certain information about the workings of the Vonage DSP website to assist in identifying customers who might have been provided incorrect information about share allocation. However, CGMI was not able to provide that information or obtain it from the Third Party Company to provide to FINRA without a confidentiality agreement, which was not acceptable to FINRA.

Based on the foregoing, CGMI failed to establish and maintain supervisory procedures or systems regarding the outsourcing of communications with its customers that were reasonably designed to achieve compliance with NASD rules. As a result, CGMI violated NASD Rules 3010 and 2110....

———

D. Supervisory Control System and Procedures

The following case demonstrates a weakness in the broker-dealer supervisory system — that of supervising the supervisors. On January 11, 2002, Frank D. Gruttadauria, a former branch manager of the Cleveland, Ohio, office of the now-defunct Lehman Brothers, Inc., mailed a letter to the FBI confessing to fraudulent conduct and misappropriation of client funds over a 15-year period and disappeared.[88] A month later he turned himself in to the FBI. Neither the broker-dealers with whom he was associated, the NYSE, or the SEC uncovered the fraudulent conduct in the 15-year period before the broker turned himself in. As you read the case, consider what types of supervisory controls may have facilitated detection of Gruttadauria's violative conduct.

In the Matter of Lehman Brothers, Inc., Respondent

Release No. 34-48336/August 14, 2003
ADMINISTRATIVE PROCEEDING
File No. 3-11217

Summary

1. Respondent failed reasonably to supervise Frank D. Gruttadauria ("Gruttadauria") with a view to preventing and detecting his violations of the federal securities laws during the 15-month period that it employed him from October 2000 to January 2002. From 1987 to January 2002, while employed at a series of five different registered broker-dealers, Gruttadauria defrauded over 60 customers by lying about purchases

———

88. *See Accused of $300 Million Theft, Broker Surrenders*, N.Y. TIMES, Feb. 11, 2002, http://www.nytimes.com/2002/02/11/business/accused-of-300-million-theft-broker-surrenders.html.

and sales of securities, misappropriating funds and securities, and sending falsified account documents. By the time that Gruttadauria confessed generally to his fraudulent conduct in a letter to the Federal Bureau of Investigation on January 11, 2002, he had misappropriated over $115 million from customers over a period of 15 years—transferring most of the money to other customers to cover withdrawal requests—and overstated account values by more than $280 million.

Respondent

2. Respondent Lehman Brothers, Inc., a direct subsidiary of Lehman Brothers Holdings, Inc., is a Delaware corporation registered with the Commission as a broker-dealer pursuant to Section 15(b) of the Exchange Act. Lehman Brothers has its principal place of business in New York, New York and maintains approximately 52 branch offices throughout the United States and worldwide.

Other Relevant Person

3. Frank D. Gruttadauria, 45, was the manager of Lehman Brothers' Cleveland, Ohio branch office from October 2000 through January 2002. Gruttadauria was also a registered representative of Lehman Brothers throughout this period. Gruttadauria became an associated person of Lehman Brothers upon Lehman Brothers' acquisition of certain assets of the retail brokerage business of SG Cowen Securities Corporation ("SGC") in October 2000. From January 1984 through October 2000, Gruttadauria was employed as a registered representative at several other broker-dealers, including SGC from July 1998 through October 2000, and SGC's predecessor beginning in 1989. From 1990 through October 2000, Gruttadauria was also the branch manager for the Cleveland branch of SGC and its predecessor.

4. On August 29, 2002, Gruttadauria pled guilty to, among other things, federal charges of securities and mail fraud in connection with his fraudulent conduct. On November 14, 2002, Gruttadauria was sentenced to seven years of confinement.

Gruttadauria's Misconduct

5. In October 2000, Lehman Brothers acquired certain assets of SGC's retail brokerage business. Among the assets of that brokerage business was the branch office in Cleveland, Ohio, of which Gruttadauria was the branch office manager ("BOM"). Gruttadauria had also been among the top-producing brokers at SGC nationwide.

6. Since 1987, Gruttadauria had been defrauding dozens of customers through various means. He lied to some of those customers about purchases and sales of securities in their accounts and the performance of those accounts, often telling these customers that their accounts contained a wide variety of holdings worth millions of dollars when, in fact, the accounts contained only a few thousand dollars. He falsely told some customers that he used the funds that they deposited into their accounts to buy securities when, in fact, he misappropriated those funds. In a few instances, Gruttadauria induced customers to give him funds to open an account and simply misappropriated the funds. Gruttadauria also told a number of customers from whom he did not misappropriate funds or securities that their accounts were more valuable than the accounts actually were. When those customers sought to with-

draw the inflated amounts, Gruttadauria misappropriated funds from other customer accounts to satisfy those withdrawal requests.

7. Gruttadauria used most of the misappropriated funds to conceal and perpetuate the fraudulent acts in which he was engaging. In most instances, he transferred funds or securities deposited by some customers for investment purposes to other customers or their designees, either directly or through an intermediary brokerage or bank account. Virtually all of these transfers were used to satisfy withdrawal requests made by customers to whom Gruttadauria falsely represented that they had sufficient funds to make the transfers out of their own accounts, but whose accounts had been depleted or had fewer assets than Gruttadauria had reported.

8. To further conceal his false representations and misappropriations, Gruttadauria created and sent many of the defrauded customers falsified account statements and other documents that vastly overstated the actual value of the accounts, reflected holdings that did not exist, reflected purchases or sales of securities that had never occurred, and failed to disclose unauthorized withdrawals from the accounts. Gruttadauria caused the actual brokerage statements for some of these customers to be mailed, without the knowledge or authorization of these clients, to entities or post office boxes under his control. The account address information Lehman Brothers received from SGC included these unauthorized mailing addresses.

9. By the time that Lehman Brothers employed Gruttadauria in October 2000, he had misappropriated at least $94 million from over 40 customers. He had led the customers to whom he had been sending falsified account statements and other documents to believe that they had over $294 million in their accounts when, in fact, they had less than $30 million in those accounts.

10. During his employment with Lehman Brothers, Gruttadauria misappropriated in total approximately $21.5 million from the accounts of seven customers, with about $19 million coming from one customer and about $2 million from another customer. Gruttadauria transferred over $19 million of the misappropriated funds to a bank account under his control and disbursed the money to other customers who had made requests for withdrawals out of their depleted accounts. In over ten instances, Gruttadauria transferred monies from a customer's brokerage account at Lehman Brothers to another customer or that customer's designee without using the intermediary bank account.

11. During this period, Gruttadauria also sent falsified account statements to approximately 40 clients representing almost 60 accounts. Gruttadauria had already misappropriated all or most of the funds from the majority of these accounts before Lehman Brothers employed him. Of the clients receiving falsified account statements, over 30 also received funds that Gruttadauria had misappropriated from other accounts. Gruttadauria transferred misappropriated funds to about 18 other customers who did not receive falsified account statements.

12. On January 11, 2002, Gruttadauria disappeared, leaving a letter with the Federal Bureau of Investigation in which he confessed to the general outlines of his fraudulent

conduct. At that time, the last falsified account statements that Gruttadauria had sent to clients showed that their accounts were worth over $285 million, when the actual Lehman Brothers statements for those accounts showed an aggregate balance of less than $2 million. About a month later, Gruttadauria surrendered to the Federal Bureau of Investigation.

13. As a result of the conduct described above, Gruttadauria, during the period that Lehman Brothers employed him, violated Section 17(a) of the Securities Act of 1933 and Section 10(b) of the Exchange Act and Rule 10b-5 thereunder, which prohibit fraudulent conduct in connection with the offer, purchase or sale of securities.

Lehman Brothers' Failure to Supervise

Background

14. The failure of Lehman Brothers reasonably to supervise Gruttadauria occurred in a context that itself created an inherent risk that Gruttadauria would not be adequately supervised. Gruttadauria was a producing BOM, which means that he was responsible both for the overall supervision of the Cleveland branch and for his own retail brokerage customers. The procedures Lehman Brothers had in place at the Cleveland branch when it employed Gruttadauria required the firm to assign a person with a Series 8 registration to oversee all of the retail brokerage activity in the Cleveland branch, including activity for those customers serviced by Gruttadauria. Lehman Brothers assigned two persons within the Cleveland branch to those responsibilities. It assigned the administrative manager to oversee day-to-day sales activity and the operations manager to review and approve requests for third-party disbursements. Although these individuals interacted periodically with others outside of the Cleveland branch, by choosing persons in the Cleveland branch subordinate to Gruttadauria to oversee his daily retail brokerage activity, Lehman Brothers structured its supervisory and compliance functions in a manner that created an inherent risk that Gruttadauria would not be adequately supervised. As BOM, Gruttadauria had input within the Cleveland branch relating to personnel matters, such as salaries, bonuses, and continued employment of the branch staff, including that of the two persons assigned to oversee his activities as a broker. This type of authority can lead to conflicts of interest that, in turn, can compromise the ability of those subordinate to the BOM to oversee adequately the BOM's activity. This structure may have been a contributing factor in the supervisory failures described below.

A. Failure to Supervise Gruttadauria as a Producing Branch Office Manager

15. Lehman Brothers failed reasonably to supervise Gruttadauria's conduct as a producing BOM. Although Lehman Brothers had procedures addressing the review of outgoing and incoming correspondence, Gruttadauria was able to evade that review because Lehman Brothers did not have an adequate system for applying these procedures to Gruttadauria, who as a producing BOM had access to a facsimile machine and the office's postage meter.[89] Gruttadauria's facsimile machine, which only he and

---

89. [5] Respondent's procedures required the review by the branch administrative manager of all incoming correspondence before distribution to the registered representatives and an after-the-fact review each month of a random sample of outgoing correspondence, with each registered represen-

his sales assistants were authorized to use, was located outside of his office. Gruttadauria represented to the compliance staff that he used this machine only for transmitting and receiving confidential internal administrative correspondence such as performance evaluations. However, Gruttadauria also used this facsimile machine to evade the review of outgoing and incoming correspondence, by using it to send and receive correspondence in furtherance of his fraudulent activity. Additionally, because he was the BOM, Gruttadauria also had a key to the otherwise secure area, known as the cage, which contained the branch office's postage meter. Gruttadauria used this key to evade the review of his outgoing correspondence that contained falsified account statements by, on a monthly basis, entering the cage after working hours, and placing a stack of sealed envelopes containing the falsified statements directly on top of the postage meter for mailing. These unreviewed statements were mailed out the next morning with Lehman Brothers' official envelopes and postage markings.

B. Other Failures to Supervise Gruttadauria

1. *Failures Related to the Monitoring and Use of Personal Computers*

16. Lehman Brothers did not have supervisory procedures expressly for monitoring the use of personal computers that were separate from the firm's company-wide computer system.[90] Unlike the company-wide system, such personal computers do not have built-in safeguards against creating false account data. At SGC and throughout the period that Lehman Brothers employed him, Gruttadauria had a personal computer that was networked to similar computers used by his two sales assistants, but not to the company-wide system. Gruttadauria ostensibly used this computer system as an electronic posting book, into which he had his sales assistants enter trading data and out of which he generated reports reflecting a client's holdings and year-end profit and loss statements for tax preparation purposes. However, Gruttadauria also used this computer system to generate the falsified account statements that he mailed to many of his defrauded customers. Thus, Lehman Brothers did not have procedures reasonably designed to prevent and detect Gruttadauria's generation of falsified account statements on personal computers.

2. *Failures Related to Third-Party Transfers*

17. A crucial component of Gruttadauria's fraudulent conduct was misappropriating funds and securities out of customer accounts and then transferring them into an intermediary bank account or directly to other customers or their designees. This type of transfer is known as a third-party transfer because the assets at issue change ownership. Under certain circumstances pertinent here, Lehman Brothers' procedures for

---

tative's correspondence subject to a review at least annually. The practice in the Cleveland branch was that the administrative manager actually reviewed outgoing correspondence before it was sent out. Once the administrative manager approved the correspondence, the broker or his or her assistant would place the correspondence in an unsealed envelope in a mail bin to be picked up by the mailroom staff, who would later seal the envelope and affix the postage using a machine.

90. [6] To the extent that a broker or sales assistant used a personal computer to generate client correspondence, that correspondence was subject to the review procedures described in footnote 5.

third-party disbursements required a Series 8 manager, other than the initiating broker, to confirm such transfers directly with the client out of whose account the disbursement was to occur. However, Lehman Brothers did not have an adequate system for applying its procedures for the processing and approval of third-party transfers. Lehman Brothers failed to detect or prevent Gruttadauria from making over $21 million in unauthorized third-party transfers, a number of them over $1 million.

3. *Failures Related to Account Documentation*

18. A brokerage firm is responsible for the accuracy of the account documentation that it maintains for its customers. The addresses on the account documentation that Lehman Brothers received from SGC for certain of the defrauded customers of Gruttadauria had been falsified by him prior to the time that he joined Lehman Brothers. Although Lehman Brothers endeavored to convert the former SGC accounts to its own accounts by re-opening them using Lehman Brothers' documentation procedures, which included procedures to confirm customer addresses, Lehman Brothers lacked an adequate system for ensuring that these procedures were applied to these accounts in a timely fashion.

19. In addition, Lehman Brothers lacked an adequate system for applying its procedures for generating exception reports concerning accounts with post office box and "care of" mailing addresses and following-up on these reports. Lehman Brothers' procedures required its examiners to generate reports reflecting the accounts each broker had with "care of" addresses or post office box addresses and review those reports with a view towards identifying patterns and conducting appropriate follow-up. Gruttadauria diverted account statements for at least 16 accounts to the same post office box in the name of an accounting firm that did not exist. Of those 16 accounts, at least 11 were captioned as "care of" accounts. Lehman Brothers did not implement its procedures in a fashion that ensured that these accounts of Gruttadauria's were identified and appropriate follow-up conducted.

4. *Conclusions*

For the reasons stated in paragraphs 1-19, Lehman Brothers failed reasonably to supervise Gruttadauria with a view to preventing or detecting his violations of the federal securities laws.

————

Notes and Questions

1. After the Gruttadauria incident, Lehman Brothers hired a consultant to review its current practices and to develop policies and procedures designed specifically to address the supervision of a producing BOM.

2. Testifying before the Subcommittee on Oversight and Investigations of the Congressional Committee on Financial Services, Lori Richards, then-Director of the SEC's Office of Compliance Inspections and Examinations, highlighted best prac-

tices for detecting and preventing misappropriation of customer funds and securities: verify address changes with the customer; review changes of address and changes to customer account information; special attention to P.O. boxes and addresses other than home addresses; confirm customer authorization of the transfer of funds; review for unusual activity; investigate unusual activity; independent supervision and review of activity by producing managers; control over account statements, letterheads, and mail facilities; provide customers with account information on-line; supervise employees' use of personal electronic devices; and routinely review compliance with policies and procedures. Would these procedures have assisted in detecting Gruttadauria's fraudulent conduct? → *Likely no, need change in supervisory structure.*

In response to the Gruttadauria matter, FINRA created and amended certain rules and interpretive materials in 2004 and the SEC granted accelerated approval to these supervisory control amendments.[91] These supervisory control amendments addressed the deficiencies noted in the Gruttadauria matter, and prescribed a "new regulatory supervisory scheme consist[ing] of process, supervision, and adoption of policies and procedures, and testing and amendment of such policies and procedures."[92] These changes resulted in the adoption of two new rules: NASD Rule 3012 Supervisory Control System (Now FINRA Rule 3120) requiring an annual review and testing of a broker-dealer's supervisory system and FINRA Rule 3130 Annual Certification of Compliance and Supervisory Processes requiring certification by the CEO attesting to the broker-dealer's compliance and supervisory controls. Commenters have noted that these new aspects of the supervision requirements, requiring internal control reviews and senior management's certification, are similar to the requirements of the Sarbanes-Oxley Act of 2002 for public issuers.[93]

Figure 4.4

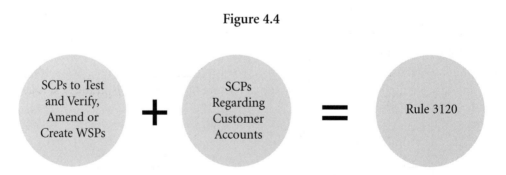

---

91. *See* NTM 04-71 for more information on all the rule amendments and rules created as part of FINRA's Supervisory Control Amendments.

92. *Id.*

93. *See* David F. Freeman, Jr., *Designing & Implementing an Effective Compliance Program for Mut. Funds, Inv. Advisers, & Broker-Dealers*, ALI-ABA COURSE OF STUDY 2 (June 16, 2006), http://files.ali-aba.org/thumbs/datastorage/skoobesruoc/pdf/CL089_chapter_04_thumb.pdf.

1. Testing and Verification of Supervisory Control Procedures (SCP)

FINRA Rule 3120 requires broker-dealers to designate and specifically identify to FINRA one or more principals who must establish, maintain, and enforce a system of supervisory control policies and procedures (SCPs) that test and verify whether its supervisory procedures are designed to comply with applicable securities laws and regulations and FINRA rules. Also, the designated principal must amend or create additional supervisory procedures where the need is identified by testing and verification. An annual report must be filed with the broker-dealer's senior management that documents in detail the broker-dealer's system of supervisory controls, the summary of its testing and verification results, including any significant identified exceptions, and any additional or amended supervisory procedures created in response to the test results.

Broker-dealers may satisfy the testing and verification requirement in whole or in part through a self-assessment, internal audit, or inspection process. While firms must engage in testing and verification annually, there is no requirement that all the broker-dealer's policies and procedures be tested and verified; the broker-dealer may use sampling or risk-based methodologies to test a subset of its policies and procedures.

2. Rule 3130 CEO Certification

FINRA Rule 3130 requires the chief executive officer ("CEO") of the broker-dealer to annually certify that the broker-dealer has in place processes reasonably designed to achieve compliance with applicable FINRA rules, MSRB rules, and federal securities laws and regulations. The certification includes an attestation to a supervisory control system that is modified as required and periodically tested for effectiveness. FINRA Rule 3130 also requires the broker-dealer to designate and specifically identify to FINRA on Schedule A of the Form BD one or more principals to serve as a chief compliance officer ("CCO"). The rule designates the CCO as a primary advisor to the broker-dealer on its "overall compliance scheme and the particularized rules, policies and procedures." It also requires the CCO to have "an expertise in the process of: (1) gaining an understanding of the products, services or line functions that need to be the subject of written compliance policies and written supervisory procedures; (2) identifying the relevant rules, regulations, laws and standards of conduct pertaining to such products, services or line functions based on experience and/or consultation with those persons who have a technical expertise in such areas of the [broker-dealer's] business; (3) developing, or advising other business persons charged with the obligation to develop, policies and procedures that are reasonably designed to achieve compliance with those relevant rules, regulations, laws and standards of conduct; (4) evidencing the supervision by the line managers who are responsible for the execution of compliance policies; and (5) developing programs to test compliance with the [broker-dealer's] policies and procedures." In essence, the role of the CCO is to have regular and significant interaction with senior management regarding the broker-dealer's comprehensive compliance program to enable the CEO to make the annual certification required under FINRA Rule 3130.

The broker-dealer's processes for establishing, maintaining, and reviewing its policies and procedures must be evidenced in a report, which is reviewed by the CEO,

CCO, and such other officers as deemed necessary by the broker-dealer to make the certification required by FINRA Rule 3130. This report must be submitted to the broker-dealer's board of directors and audit committee.

E. Internal Inspections

FINRA Rule 3110(c) requires broker-dealers to conduct internal inspections of their businesses at least annually. These inspections must be reasonably designed to detect and prevent violations of, and to achieve compliance with, applicable securities laws and regulations and FINRA rules; the examination of customer accounts to detect and prevent irregularities or abuses is expressly required. All inspections must be reduced to writing and maintained by the broker-dealer for at least three years. If applicable, written inspection reports must include testing and verification of the broker-dealer's policies and procedures in the specified areas, including safeguarding of customer funds and securities, supervision of supervisory personnel, transmittals of funds or securities from customers to third-party accounts, and changes of customer account information. Required inspection cycles are based on the type of location, size of the broker-dealer's business, and the complexity of products offered. See Table 4.3 below for a summary of mandated inspection cycles.

Table 4.3. Rule 3110(c) Internal Inspection Cycles

Inspection Cycle	Location Type	Comment
Every year	• Offices of supervisory jurisdiction • Supervisory branch offices *(a branch office that supervises one or more non-branch locations)*	
Every three years	• Non-supervisory branch offices	More frequent inspection required depending on the assessment of the below 3110(c)(1)(B) factors: • Nature and complexity of the securities activities for which the location is responsible; • Volume of business done; • Number of associated persons assigned to the location.
Periodically (maybe longer than three years)	• Non-branch locations (*unregistered locations*)	More frequent inspection required depending on the assessment of the below 3110(c)(1)(C) factors: • Nature and complexity of the securities activities for which the location is responsible; • Nature and extent of contact with customers.

The broker-dealer must have procedures reasonably designed to prevent inspections from being compromised due to conflicts of interest that may be present with respect to the location being inspected. Conflicts of interest may include economic, commercial, or financial interests in the associated persons and businesses being inspected. Specifically, the broker-dealer must ensure that the person conducting the inspection is not an associated person assigned to the location being inspected or directly or indirectly supervised by an associated person at the location.

Notes and Questions

1. FINRA recommends that broker-dealers conduct unannounced branch office inspections to prevent document concealment or destruction. However, FINRA's examinations of broker-dealers begin with data collection prior to examiners arriving for the on-site portion of the examination.

2. The majority of broker-dealers registered with FINRA are classified as "small," i.e., broker-dealers with 150 registered representatives or fewer, often with principals serving in multiple roles. What types of supervisory challenges are faced by a small broker-dealer without a compliance department where principals must serve in multiple roles? Are the challenges faced by small broker-dealers similar to those faced by large broker-dealers with compliance departments but with a greater number of registered representatives and geographically dispersed offices?

[handwritten margin note: Less heirarchical structure. One on "top" & many to manage below.]

[handwritten note: → Yes, similar but different.]

Hypothetical Seven

Joan Chen, a registered representative with Success First, a week after moving from a studio into a home in a posh gated community with country club style living amenities, was informed that Success First will conduct an internal inspection of her primary residence. Joan is registered with and sometimes works from the local branch office. For convenience, she works from home calling customers located all over the country, emailing her clients from her work computer, and executing trades through the Success First's secured trading platform. Joan does not meet with her customers at her home. Joan argues that it is an invasion of her privacy for Success First to inspect her home and that primary residences like hers are exempt from the branch office definition unless it is specifically registered as such. May the Success First proceed with an internal inspection of Joan's primary residence? What, if any, concerns may the Success First have about this inspection?

[handwritten margin note: → If a warrant yes.]

[handwritten note: → Less invasive forms of determining compliance.]

F. Review of Correspondence and Transactions

The broker-dealer's written supervisory procedures must include policies and procedures to review correspondence and internal communications related to its investment banking or securities business. FINRA Rule 3110(b)(4) requires review of incoming and outgoing written (including electronic) correspondence to ensure that customer complaints, instructions, and funds and securities are handled in accordance with the broker-dealer's procedures and applicable FINRA rules and federal securities laws. Similarly, the broker-dealer also must review its internal communications for compliance. Review of correspondence and internal communications must be conducted by a designated registered principal;[94] this designation must be evidenced in writing (electronically or on paper). FINRA Rule 3110.06 permits risked-based review of correspondence and internal communications. Risked-based review means that all of the broker-dealer's correspondence and internal communications will not be reviewed before distribution or use. Accordingly, the procedures of a member employing risked-based principles must include education and training of its associated persons about the broker-dealer's procedures governing correspondence. The broker-dealer must document its education and training and must conduct surveillance and follow-up to ensure implementation of such procedures. Evidence of the broker-dealer's review of its correspondence and internal communications must include the name of the reviewer, specifically identify correspondence and internal communications reviewed, the date of review, and any actions taken by the broker-dealer in the event significant regulatory issues are discovered. FINRA Rule 3110.07 states that "[m]erely opening a communication is not sufficient review." Finally, FINRA Rule 3110.09 requires retention of the broker-dealer's correspondence and internal communications for three years, the first two years in an easily accessible place.

The broker-dealer's supervisory procedures for the handling of customer complaints must include procedures to capture, acknowledge, and respond to such complaints. This requirement only applies to written customer complaints. This means that to ensure broker-dealer accountability, the customer must reduce all complaints to writing.

FINRA Rule 3110 requires the broker-dealer's supervisory procedures to include review by a registered principal, evidenced in writing, of all transactions relating to its investment banking and securities business. The review process must be reasonably designed to identify trades that may violate the provisions of the Exchange Act or FINRA rules prohibiting insider trading and manipulative and deceptive devices in its accounts and the accounts of its associated persons. Suspicious transactions must be promptly investigated to determine whether a violation has occurred. If the investigation uncovers a violation, the broker-dealer must submit a report, signed by a senior officer, detailing the results, and the report must include any internal disciplinary action taken and any referral to the SEC or other regulatory authority. In addition, the broker-dealer must submit a quarterly report

---

94. The designated principal may delegate certain functions to a non-registered person, but remains ultimately responsible for effective review of the broker-dealer's correspondence and internal communications.

to FINRA, signed by a senior officer, describing each internal investigation initiated in the previous calendar quarter that includes, among other things, the status of each open internal investigation and the identity of the security, trades, accounts, and associated persons or family members involved in each investigation. FINRA Rule 3110.05 permits risk-based review of the broker-dealer's transactions as long as its risk-based review is reasonably designed to provide sufficient information on areas of the broker-dealer's business that pose the greatest number and risk of violations.

G. Supervisory Responsibilities Relating to the Conduct of Associated Persons

FINRA Rules address certain types of conduct directly related to the broker-dealer's associated persons. These rules include procedures for monitoring the outside business activities of associated persons, borrowing from or lending to customers, influencing or rewarding the employees of others, and examining the private securities transactions of associated persons.

1. Outside Business Activities (FINRA Rule 3270)

Broker-dealers must monitor and evaluate the outside business activities in which their associated persons engage. FINRA Rule 3270 requires the broker-dealer to establish procedures that require its associated persons to provide written notice to, and if necessary obtain permission from, the broker-dealer regarding their outside business activities. Specifically, FINRA Rule 3270 prohibits the associated person from acting as an employee, independent contractor, sole proprietor, officer, director, or partner of another person in any business activity outside the scope of the relationship with her broker-dealer unless the associated person has provided written notice to the broker-dealer. This notice must be provided regardless of whether the associated person receives compensation in connection with her outside business activity. Upon receipt of a written notice from its associated person, the broker-dealer must consider whether the proposed outside business activity will compromise the associated person's responsibilities to the broker-dealer or its customers, or be viewed by the broker-dealer's customers or the public as part of the broker-dealer's business. Based on its review, the broker-dealer must evaluate the advisability of imposing specific conditions or limitations on, or prohibiting, its associated person's outside business activity. Associated persons must not engage in outside business activities for compensation without providing prior written notice to, and obtaining permission from, the broker-dealer. Also, the broker-dealer is required to evaluate the proposed outside business activity to determine whether it should be treated as an outside securities activity subject to the requirements of FINRA Rule 3280 (see below). Finally, the broker-dealer must keep a record of its compliance with FINRA Rule 3270, and these records must be preserved for at least three years after the associated person's employment, and any other connection with the broker-dealer, has terminated.

2. Borrowing from or Lending to Customers (FINRA Rule 3240)

FINRA Rule 3240 permits certain borrowing and lending arrangements between the broker-dealer's associated persons and its customers under specified conditions. The broker-dealer must have written procedures allowing such arrangements that conform to the requirements of FINRA Rule 3240. Accordingly, the broker-dealer's written procedures may permit its associated persons to borrow money from, or to lend money to, certain types of customers: (1) members of the associated person's immediate family;[95] (2) financial institutions or other entities or persons that regularly arrange or extend credit in the ordinary course of business; (3) registered persons of the same broker-dealer; (4) customers with whom the associated person has a personal relationship (outside of the broker-dealer customer relationship) such that the loan would not have been given in the absence of the personal relationship between the customer and the associated person; (5) customers with whom the associated person has a business relationship (outside of the broker-dealer customer relationship) on which the lending arrangement is based. The associated person must notify, and obtain prior approval from, its broker-dealer in writing to participate in borrowing and lending relationships with customers who are registered persons with its employing broker-dealer and when the borrowing or lending arrangement is based on a personal relationship or outside business relationship (outside the scope of the broker-dealer customer relationship) with the customer. Notification and prior approval is not required under FINRA Rule 3240 for borrowing and lending arrangements between the associated person and his immediate family. The broker-dealer's procedures may, but are not required to, mandate notification and prior approval for lending and borrowing arrangements between its associated persons and customers who are financial institutions, or other entities arranging or extending credit in their ordinary course of business, as long as the arrangement is made on terms that the customer would normally make to the general public. FINRA Rule 3240.01 requires broker-dealers to preserve all written pre-approvals of permitted borrowing and lending arrangements for at least three years after the date that such arrangements have terminated, or for at least three years after the associated person's association with the broker-dealer has terminated.

3. Influencing or Rewarding Employees of Others (Rule 3220)

FINRA Rule 3220 restricts the amount of gratuities or gifts that a broker-dealer or its associated persons may provide to another person on an annual basis. The gratuity or gift may not exceed $100 per person per year. Specifically, a broker-dealer or its associated persons is not permitted to give gratuities or gifts to another person where the payment relates to the business of the recipient's employer. Ac-

---

95. The term immediate family is defined in FINRA Rule 3240(c) as the associated person's parents, grandparents, mother-in-law or father-in-law, husband or wife, brother or sister, brother-in-law or sister-in-law, son-in-law or daughter-in-law, children, grandchildren, cousin, aunt or uncle, or niece or nephew, and any other person whom the [associated] person supports, directly or indirectly, to a material extent.

cording to FINRA, Rule 3220 is designed to protect against improprieties that might arise when broker-dealers or their associated persons give substantial gifts or payments to employees of a customer or a counterparty. However, payments made pursuant to a *bona fide* written employment contract are expressly excluded. In addition, broker-dealers must keep separate records detailing all payments or gratuities given and any employment compensation paid to persons pursuant to FINRA Rule 3220.

4. *Private Securities Transactions (FINRA Rule 3280)*

Associated persons of broker-dealers are not permitted to engage in private securities transactions unless they comply with FINRA Rule 3280. The term *private securities transactions* is defined in the rule as "any securities transaction outside the regular course or scope of an associated person's employment with a [broker-dealer]."[96] The associated person must provide written notice to her employer broker-dealer before engaging in any private securities transaction. The written notice provided to the employer broker-dealer must describe the proposed transaction in detail, the associated person's proposed role, and whether selling compensation has or may be received in connection with the transaction. *Selling compensation* is defined in FINRA Rule 3280(e)(2) as any compensation paid from whatever source in connection with the purchase or sale of a security, including finder's fees, securities or rights to acquire securities, rights of participation in profits, tax benefits, or expense reimbursements. If the associated person receives, or may receive, selling compensation, the broker-dealer must approve or disapprove the private securities transaction in writing. Broker-dealer approval of an associated person's private securities transaction that involves selling compensation must be recorded on the broker-dealer's books and records and supervised as if the transaction were executed on behalf of the broker-dealer. Private securities transactions in which the associated person does not receive selling compensation do not require broker-dealer approval, but the broker-dealer must promptly acknowledge notice provided by its associated person of such transactions and may require its associated person to adhere to specified conditions in connection with her participation in the transaction.

Hypothetical Eight

Ben Moxen, an associated person at Success First, borrowed $25,000 at eight percent interest from Lisa Lender, a wealthy socialite known for her lavish parties and live-in models. Success First requires its associated persons to provide prior notification and to obtain written approval before engaging in any borrowing and lending arrange-

---

96. Transactions subject to the notification requirements of NASD Rule 3050, transactions among immediate family members (as defined in FINRA Rule 5130) for which no associated person receives any selling compensation, and personal transactions in investment company and variable annuity securities are expressly excluded from the definition of private securities transaction under FINRA Rule 3280.

ments except those involving immediate family members or financial institutions regularly engaged in the business of providing credit. Ben repays the loan from Lisa within two years as agreed. Lisa, shortly after Ben has repaid the loan, files a customer complaint alleging that Ben recommended unsuitable investments. During the investigation of Lisa's complaint, Success First discovers the prior lending arrangement between Ben and Lisa. Ben asserts that the lending arrangement between he and Lisa complies with FINRA Rule 3240 and the policies of Success First because Lisa has entered into lending arrangements with other members of the general public. Specifically, Lisa has previously loaned money to her maid to start a Fast Maids LLC franchise, her butler's daughter for tuition for culinary school, and to her favorite neighborhood beauty salon to expand her business. These lending arrangements, including the loan to Ben, were memorialized in a contract written by Lisa's attorney. Lisa's lending arrangements varied with terms of two to three years and interest rates between six percent and eight percent. The interest from Lisa's lending arrangements represented a small portion of her income. Does Ben's prior lending arrangement violate FINRA Rule 3240? *See* FINRA Regulatory Notice 04-14.

> ↳ No. Even though might fit under 340 (4) & (5) the facts do not suggest it was notified & approved as required.

Chapter 5

Broker-Dealers and Public Offerings of Securities

Regulatory Authority

Securities Act of 1933 Sections 2(a)(10)–(11), 4(3), 5, 6, 7, and 10

Securities Act Rules 134, 135, 137, 138, 139, 141(a), 144A, 153, 163, 163A, 164, 168, 169, 172, 173, 174, 405, 424(b), 430, 430A, 433, 473, 501, Regulation M

Securities Exchange Act of 1934 Sections 3(a)(11), 10(b), 15(c)(2), 28(e)

Exchange Act Rules 10b-9, 10b-10, 15c2-4, 15c2-8, 15c6-1(c)

FINRA Rules 2210, 2262, 2269, 2711, 5110, 5121, 5130, 5131, 5141, 5160, 5190, 5280

Motivating Hypothetical

Success First's IPO business is doing quite well. It has acted as an underwriter or selling group participant in several tech IPOs during the first quarter of this year and business seems on track to continue its upward trend. It appears that acting as managing underwriter for Gaagle, Inc.'s IPO, a major dot-com company, has substantially boosted its reputation on the street. Its business as a managing underwriter in hot IPOs has increased by 30 percent over the last year. To meet this new business demand, the board of directors has authorized Carmen Alvarez, CEO of Success First, to hire a senior managing director to manage its IPO business. Carmen has hired Alicia Luigi to be Success First's new senior managing director. Alicia comes to Success First with a storied pedigree. She graduated in the top five percent of her class from Howard University School of Law. Alicia also has an M.B.A. from Howard University School of Business and graduated first in her class. Alicia has worked on Wall Street with major investment banks for the last five years and is excited about the opportunity to manage and grow Success First's IPO business.

I. Introduction

Broker-dealers are integral to the public offering of securities as underwriters and selling group members. This chapter focuses on the regulation of broker-dealer activities in the public offering process for equity securities. Sections 5, 6, 7, and 10 of the Securities Act and the corresponding rules most relevant to broker-dealer activities in the public offering process will be reviewed. In addition, the regulatory framework for broker-dealers participating either as underwriters or members of the selling (dealer) group in the three periods of a public offering will be discussed. Next, the regulation of broker-dealer activities during and around a public offering such as stabilization and passive market making will be examined. Finally, specific FINRA rules governing broker-dealer activities in initial public offerings of equity securities will be considered.

II. Overview of the Public Offering Process and Regulation Basics

A. Role of a Broker-Dealer in the Public Offering of Securities

Broker-dealers acting as underwriters assist companies in raising capital in the public securities market. Companies raise capital in the public securities markets by selling their securities to public investors. Broker-dealers, among other things, advise the companies as to the appropriateness of raising capital by conducting a public offering of their securities, the likely price of their securities should they determine to offer them to the public, and the types of investors that might be interested in purchasing their securities. They also market and sell the company's securities to potential investors subsequent to their determination to conduct a public offering. Overall, the broker-dealer attempts to aid the company in making potential investors willing to buy its securities.

The broker-dealer often acts as an underwriter as part of a syndicate. A syndicate is a group of other broker-dealers who have agreed to participate as underwriters in the public offering. A common form of underwriting is a firm commitment offering. In a firm commitment offering, the syndicate purchases the company's securities and then sells the securities to public investors. Also, members of the syndicate agree to make a market in the company's securities after the completion of the public offering, thus supporting a liquid market for the company's securities. Many broker-dealers that participate in public offerings, such as Goldman Sachs and Morgan Stanley, are quite well known and have a wealth of contacts with institutional investors, securities dealers, and investors.

A company that wants to sell its securities in a public offering must go through the complex process of registering its securities with the SEC. The registration process requires the company or issuer to file and distribute mandatory disclosure documents containing information about the company, such as its management, financial condition, the securities that it intends to offer to public investors and its arrangement with the underwriters participating in the offering. The Securities Act requires a company to file a registration statement with the SEC containing this information. The Securities Act governs the registration process, along with the content of the registration statement. The specific sections of the Securities Act, and underlying rules, that govern broker-dealer activities during the registration process, are discussed later in Section C.4 of this chapter.

B. Overview of the Securities Act and the Registration Process

The purpose of the Securities Act is to provide potential investors with a reliable source of information upon which to make an informed investment decision, along with adequate time to review such information. Thus, it is essentially a disclosure statute that focuses on the offering and distribution of securities. Disclosure is accomplished by requiring the company to provide certain information about itself and its securities in the form of a registration statement. The SEC requires that the information contained in a registration statement be complete and accurate, but it does not guarantee either. This means that the SEC does not approve or judge the quality of the company's securities; it only insists that the issuer disclose all required facts about itself and its securities. As underwriters, broker-dealers occupy a unique position that enables them to discover and compel disclosure of essential facts in the registration statement. In general, the information disclosed in the registration statement includes a description of the company's business and properties; a description of the security to be offered for sale; information about the management of the company; and financial statements audited by independent accountants. Registration statements are available to the public after filing with the SEC on the SEC's EDGAR database, accessible at www.sec.gov.

Broker-dealers are directly affected by provisions of the Securities Act governing public offerings when they are acting as underwriters and members of the selling group. The Securities Act requires all offers and sales of securities to be registered with the SEC, unless there is an applicable exemption. Section 5 of the Securities Act prohibits public offers of a company's securities before a company has filed a registration statement relating to that transaction and prohibits sales of those securities unless there is an effective registration statement. Sections 5 and 8 of the Securities Act set forth the procedure for registration and sections 7 and 10 of the Securities Act specify the information that must be disclosed. Sections 3 and 4 of the Securities Act describe the types of securities and securities transactions that are exempt from the registration requirement of Section 5. Sections 11 and 12 of the Securities Act set forth the liability provisions arising from failing to comply with section 5, as well as any misrepresentations or omissions in the prospectus, which is the portion of the registration statement that must be distributed to public investors. Section 17 of the Securities Act prohibits fraudulent or deceitful practices in connection with the offer or sale of securities.[1] Broker-dealer liability for misrepresentations or omissions of material information in the registration statement is reviewed in Chapter 6 of this textbook.

The rules under the Securities Act governing communications and other activities during and around the registration process are known as the gun-jumping rules. A detailed description of what is permitted and prohibited under the gun-jumping rules is provided later in the in the discussion of the activities performed by underwriters participating in a public offering of securities. Advances in technology and resulting

---

1. Section 17(a) of the Securities Act applies whether or not the securities or securities transaction is required to be registered under Section 5. In addition, there is no private right of action under Section 17(a); only the SEC can bring an action based on a violation of Section 17(a).

changes in market structure led the SEC, in 2005, to modernize the gun-jumping rules ("2005 Offering Reforms"). Among other things, the 2005 Offering Reforms reduced or eliminated Securities Act communication restrictions for companies already required to make extensive disclosures to the SEC under the Exchange Act. The SEC adopting release for the 2005 Offering Reforms illustrates the impact of technology on disclosure during the registration process and the focus on disclosure in investor decision making.

Securities Offering Reform

Securities Act Release No. 8591
August 3, 2005

I. Introduction

A. Overview

* * *

The rules we are adopting today continue the evolution of the offering process under the Securities Act that began as far back as 1966, when Milton Cohen noted the anomaly of the structure of the disclosure rules under the Securities Act and the Exchange Act and suggested the integration of the requirements under the two statutes. Mr. Cohen's article was followed by a 1969 study led by Commissioner Francis Wheat and the Commission's Advisory Committee on Corporate Disclosure in 1977. These studies eventually led to the Commission's adoption of the integrated disclosure system, short-form registration under the Securities Act, and Securities Act Rule 415 permitting shelf registration of continuous offerings and delayed offerings.

The Commission's attention to the offering and communications processes under the Securities Act continued more recently. ... In July 1996, the Advisory Committee on the Capital Formation and Regulatory Processes delivered its report to the Commission. Its principal recommendation was that the Securities Act registration and disclosure processes be more directly tied to the philosophy and structure of the Exchange Act through the adoption of a system of "company registration." Under company registration, the focus of Securities Act and Exchange Act registration and disclosure would move from transactions to issuers, and corollary steps would be taken to provide for disclosure and registration of individual offerings within the company registration framework

... [T]he Commission issued a concept release regarding regulation of the securities offering process. The release sought input on a number of significant issues, including:

* * *

- Whether adjustments to the roles and responsibilities of traditional "gatekeepers" in the Securities Act offering process, such as underwriters and accountants, should be made in light of increases in the speed of and other evolutions in the offering process; ...

* * *

B. Background

1. Advances in Technology

As we noted in the Proposing Release, significant technological advances over the last three decades have increased both the market's demand for more timely corporate disclosure and the ability of issuers to capture, process, and disseminate this information. Computers, sophisticated financial software, electronic mail, teleconferencing, videoconferencing, webcasting, and other technologies available today have replaced, to a large extent, paper, pencils, typewriters, adding machines, carbon paper, paper mail, travel, and face-to-face meetings relied on previously. The rules we are adopting today seek to recognize the integral role that technology plays in timely informing the markets and investors about important corporate information and developments.

2. Exchange Act Reporting Standards

The role that a public issuer's Exchange Act reports play in investment decision-making is a key component of the rules we are adopting today. Congress recognized that the ongoing dissemination of accurate information by issuers about themselves and their securities is essential to the effective operation of the trading markets. The Exchange Act and underlying rules have established a system of continuing disclosure about issuers that have offered securities to the public, or that have securities that are listed on a national securities exchange or are broadly held by the public. The Exchange Act rules require public issuers to make periodic disclosures at annual and quarterly intervals, with other important information reported on a more current basis. The Exchange Act specifically provides for current disclosure to maintain the timeliness and adequacy of information disclosed by issuers, and we have significantly expanded our current disclosure requirements ...

A public issuer's Exchange Act record provides the basic source of information to the market and to potential purchasers regarding the issuer and its management, business, financial condition, and prospects. Because an issuer's Exchange Act reports and other publicly available information form the basis for the market's evaluation of the issuer and the pricing of its securities, investors in the secondary market use that information in making their investment decisions. Similarly, during a securities offering in which an issuer uses a short-form registration statement, an issuer's Exchange Act record is very often the most significant part of the information about the issuer in the registration statement.

* * *

We are adding a new category of issuer — a "well-known seasoned issuer" — that will be permitted to benefit to the greatest degree from the modifications to our rules we are adopting today regarding communications and the registration processes.

* * *

B. Other Categories of Issuers

We also are using existing categories of issuers, including seasoned issuers, unseasoned Exchange Act reporting issuers, and non-reporting issuers, in the new rules regarding communications and the registration process. A seasoned issuer is an issuer that is eligible to use Form S-3 ... to register primary offerings of securities pursuant to General Instructions I.B.1 I.B.2, I.B.5, or I.C. of Form S-3 ...

An unseasoned issuer is an issuer that is required to file reports pursuant to Section 13 or Section 15(d) of the Exchange Act, but does not satisfy the requirements of Form S-3 ... for a primary offering of its securities. A non-reporting issuer is an issuer that is not required to file reports pursuant to Section 13 or Section 15(d) of the Exchange Act, regardless of whether it is filing such reports voluntarily.

* * *

III. Communications Rules

A. Communications Requirements Prior to Today's Rules and Amendments

The Securities Act restricts the types of offering communications that issuers or other parties subject to the Act's provisions (such as underwriters) may use during a registered public offering. The nature of the restrictions depends on the period during which the communications are to occur.... Violations of these restrictions generally are referred to as "gun jumping," and we use the term "gun-jumping provisions" in this release to describe the statutory provisions of the Securities Act that set forth these restrictions

B. Need for Modernization of Communications Requirements

1. General

[T]he gun-jumping provisions of the Securities Act were enacted at a time when the means of communications were limited and restricting communications (without regard to accuracy) to the statutory prospectus appropriately balanced available communications and investor protection. The gun-jumping provisions were designed to make the statutorily mandated prospectus the primary means for investors to obtain information regarding a registered securities offering.

The capital markets, in the United States and around the world, have changed very significantly since those limitations were enacted. Today, issuers engage in all types of communications on an ongoing basis, including, importantly, communications mandated or encouraged by our rules under the Exchange Act, rules or listing standards of national securities exchanges, ... Modern communications technology, including the Internet, provides a powerful, versatile, and cost-effective medium to communicate quickly and broadly. The changes in the Exchange Act disclosure regime and the tremendous growth in communications technology are resulting in more information being provided to the market on a more nondiscriminatory, current, and ongoing basis.

* * *

C. Overview of Communications Rules

Today, we are adopting rules that relate to the following:

- Regularly released factual business information;

- Regularly released forward-looking information;

- Communications made more than 30 days before filing a registration statement;

- Communications by well-known seasoned issuers during the 30 days before filing a registration statement;

- Written communications made in accordance with the safe harbor in Securities Act Rule 134; and

- Written communications (other than a statutory prospectus) made by any eligible issuer after filing a registration statement.

* * *

The new and revised rules we are adopting establish a communications framework that, in some cases, will operate along a spectrum based on the type of issuer, its reporting history, and its equity market capitalization or recent issuances of fixed income securities. Thus, under the rules we are adopting, eligible well-known seasoned issuers will have freedom generally from the gun-jumping provisions to communicate at any time, including by means of a written offer other than a statutory prospectus. Varying levels of restrictions will apply to other categories of issuers. We believe these distinctions are appropriate because the market has more familiarity with large, more seasoned issuers and, as a result of the ongoing market following of their activities, including the role of market participants and the media, these issuers' communications have less potential for conditioning the market for the issuers' securities to be sold in a registered offering. Disclosure obligations and practices outside the offering process, including under the Exchange Act, also determine the scope of communications flexibility the rules give to issuers and other offering participants.

C. The Broker-Dealer in the Public Underwriting Process

This section reviews the broker-dealer's activities when acting as an underwriter in a public offering. Specifically, when is a broker-dealer deemed to be an underwriter under the Securities Act and what can a broker-dealer do under the gun-jumping rules when it is acting as an underwriter in a public offering? Keep in mind, however, that before becoming subject to the gun-jumping rules, the broker-dealer must be deemed an underwriter under the Securities Act.

1. The Underwriter

Broadly speaking, an underwriter is someone who participates in the distribution of the issuer's securities between the issuer and the public. Typically, underwriters are professionals who are able to evaluate the financial condition and business prospects of the issuer and play a vital role in providing information to prospective investors. Moreover, prospective investors rely on the underwriter's expertise and reputation and reasonably expect that the underwriter has conducted an investigation of the offering in which it is involved. In Chapter 6, we will see that this expectation is embodied in the regulatory framework in Sections 11 and 12 of the Securities Act, under which underwriters are held liable for misrepresentations and omissions in the issuer's registration statement.

The term *underwriter* is defined in Section 2(a)(11) of the Securities Act as "[A]ny person who has purchased from an issuer with a view to, or offers or sells for an issuer in connection with, the distribution of any security, or participates or has a direct or indirect participation in any such undertaking, or participates or has a participation in the direct or indirect underwriting of any such undertaking ..."

Typically, a broker-dealer becomes an underwriter by purchasing an issuer's securities with a view to distributing the issuer's securities or by participating in a distribution of the issuer's securities. Underwriter status is more easily determined when the broker-dealer enters into a written agreement with the issuer to purchase its securities for the purpose of selling them to public investors. Such arrangements are discussed in detail in the next section of this chapter. Underwriter status is less clear, however, when there is no such written agreement, but rather the broker-dealer participates, directly or indirectly, in an offering of the issuer's securities to public investors. The courts and the SEC have interpreted the term *underwriter* broadly and have accorded underwriter status to broker-dealers who neither purchased nor sold the issuer's securities; the broker-dealers are deemed statutory underwriters because they have participated in the purchase, offer, or sale of an issuer's securities with a view toward distributing such securities. Participation necessary for underwriter status has been defined as some act performed by the broker-dealer that facilitates the distribution of the issuer's securities. The following case illustrates the factors used by the court, and the broad interpretation of Section 2(a)(11), in determining underwriter status.

Special Situations Fund, III, L.P. v. Cocchiola

Fed. Sec. L. Rep. P 94,459 (D.N.J. 2007)

WALLS, Senior District Judge.

The plaintiffs, Special Situations Fund, III, L.P. and Special Situations Cayman Fund, L.P., move for partial summary judgment under Fed.R.Civ.P. 56.... The motion is granted in part and denied in part.

* * *

The plaintiffs in this action are two institutional investors, Special Situations Fund, III, L.P. and Special Situations Cayman Fund, L.P. (collectively the "Special Situations plaintiffs" or the "plaintiffs"). The Special Situations plaintiffs purchased 250,000 newly-issued Suprema Specialties, Inc. ("Suprema") common stock shares, worth $2 million, from the lead stock underwriter, Hobbs Melville Securities Corp. ("Hobbs Melville"), in an August 2000 secondary stock offering (the "2000 Offering"). Special

Situations alleges that its purchase of these shares resulted from false and misleading statements in Suprema's public filings.

Suprema was a New York corporation that manufactured, processed, imported, and marketed cheese products. Headquartered in Paterson, New Jersey, Suprema had processing plants in New Jersey, California, New York, and Idaho. Suprema was founded in 1983 as a non-public corporation, and went public in 1991. It was listed on the NASDAQ exchange in 1993. After showing impressive growth in the late 1990s, Suprema made a secondary stock offering of 1.2 million shares of common stock in 2000....

The plaintiffs allege that the spectacular growth in sales and receivables Suprema reported from 1999 to 2001 was the result of a fraudulent scheme to inflate revenues. In this scheme, Suprema sold cheese products to fictitious buyers, who resold the cheese to fictitious suppliers. In turn, these suppliers resold the cheese to Suprema. For the most part, no actual cheese changed hands; when it did, the cheese products were of a much lower grade than Suprema represented. The volume of fraudulent sales transactions led creditors to increase Suprema's line of credit, which allowed Suprema to further, enlarge the circular sale scheme. In August 2000, Suprema sold $8.6 million of Suprema shares and certain shareholders sold $1.5 [million] of their Suprema shares to the public through certain underwriters in the 2000 Offering. From late 1998 to late 2000, as the company's reported sales and revenues grew, Suprema's share price doubled. In September 2001, shortly before the 2001 Offering.... Fortune Magazine named Suprema the twenty-third fastest growing small company in America.

On December 21, 2001, Suprema announced an internal investigation of its reported financial results. Shortly thereafter, the NASDAQ exchange suspended the trading of Suprema shares. On January 25, 2002 Suprema announced that it had retained the outside accounting firm Deloitte & Touche, LLP to assist in its investigation. On February 24, 2002 Suprema filed for Chapter 11 bankruptcy protection. On March 20, 2002 the bankruptcy proceeding was converted to Chapter 7 liquidation.

This motion for summary judgment concerns only certain defendants who were members of what the Special Situations plaintiffs characterize as an "underwriting syndicate" that underwrote the 2000 Offering. The Special Situations plaintiffs claim that documents relating to the 2000 Offering, including the prospectus and registration statement, contained misrepresentations and omissions of material facts, and assert claims against the underwriters of that offering ...

The Special Situations plaintiffs allege that the syndicate that underwrote the 2000 offering was led by Hobbs Melville and included seven other underwriters: Auerbach, Pollak & Richardson, Inc. ("Auerbach"); Girard Securities, Inc. ("Girard"); Mercer Partners, Inc. ("Mercer"); Oberweis.net ("Oberweis"); Paulson Investment Company Inc. ("Paulson"), Westminster Securities Corporation ("Westminster"); [and] Westport Resources Investment Services, Inc. ("Westport").

The Special Situation plaintiffs bring these motions for partial summary judgment against the five remaining members of the underwriting syndicate: Girard, Oberweis, Paulson, Westminster, and Westport. The plaintiffs seek summary judgment on two separate issues. First, they ask the Court to rule that each of these five companies was an "underwriter" as defined under the Securities Act.[2]

DISCUSSION

II. Are the defendants underwriters as defined by the Securities Act?

The Special Situations plaintiffs ask the Court to grant summary judgment that Paulson, Oberweis, Westminster, Westport, and Girard are underwriters under the Securities Act. The plaintiffs claim that Paulson and Oberweis are underwriters because they purchased stock shares from Suprema and distributed those shares to the public. In contrast, the plaintiffs do not contend that Westminster, Westport, and Girard actually sold shares to the public. Nevertheless, they maintain that these three defendants are underwriters because they participated in the offering and in the direct or indirect underwriting of the offering.

A. Section 2(11) of the Securities Act

"An underwriter is commonly understood to be a 'person who buys securities directly or indirectly from the issuer and resells them to the public, or performs some act (or acts) that facilitates the issuer's distribution.'" *In re WorldCom, Inc. Securities Litigation,* 346 F.Supp.2d 628, 662 (S.D.N.Y.2004) (citations omitted). Section 2(11) of the Securities Act expressly defines the term "underwriter" for the purposes of that Act as:

> ... any person who *has purchased from an issuer with a view to, or offers or sells for an issuer in connection with, the distribution of any security,* or *participates or has a direct or indirect participation in any such undertaking,* or *participates or has a participation in the direct or indirect underwriting of any such undertaking;* but such term shall not include a person whose interest is limited to a commission from an underwriter or dealer not in excess of the usual and customary distributors' or sellers' commission. As used in this paragraph the term "issuer" shall include, in addition to an issuer, any person directly or indirectly controlling or controlled by the issuer, or any person under direct or indirect common control with the issuer. 15 U.S.C. 77b(a)(11) (emphasis added).

From this section, it is apparent Congress defined broadly the term "underwriter" in the Securities Act. The term most clearly includes persons who purchased a security from an issuer with a view to its distribution and persons who offered or sold the security for an issuer in connection with its distribution. It also includes persons who "'participate in,' [ ] have 'direct or indirect participation in,' or [ ] have a 'participation

---

2. [3] The Special Situation plaintiffs bring these motions for partial summary judgment against the five remaining members of the underwriting syndicate: Girard, Oberweis, Paulson, Westminster, and Westport. The plaintiffs seek summary judgment on two separate issues. First, they ask the Court to rule that each of these five companies was an "underwriter" as defined under the Securities Act. 15 U.S.C. § 77k(a). To have a cause of action against any of the alleged members of the underwriting syndicate under this provision of section 11, a plaintiff must first prove that person is an "underwriter." *See In re Global Crossing, Ltd. Securities Litig.,* 313 F.Supp.2d 189, 212 (S.D.N.Y.2003).

in the direct or indirect underwriting of,' (1) the purchase of the [security] with a view to distribution, or (2) the offer or sale of the [security] in connection with [its] distribution." Harden. In short, an underwriter is one who "participates in the transmission process between the issuer and the public." *Ingenito v. Bermec Corp.*, 441 F.Supp. 525, 536 (S.D.N.Y.1977).

A 1933 House of Representatives committee report better explains the categories of underwriters encompassed by the statute's definition of the term:

> The term is defined broadly enough to include not only the ordinary underwriter, who for a commission promises to see that an issue is disposed of at a certain price, but also includes as an underwriter the person who purchases an issue outright with the idea of then selling that issue to the public. The definition of underwriter is also broad enough to include two other groups of persons who perform functions, similar in character, in the distribution of a large issue. The first of these groups may be designated as the underwriters of the underwriter, a group who, for a commission, agree to take over pro rata the underwriting risk assumed by the first underwriter. The second group may be termed participants in the underwriting or outright purchase, who may or may not be formal parties to the underwriting contract, but who are given a certain share or interest therein.

H.R. Rep. 73-85, at 13 (1933). A later House conference report explains how the Senate amendment to the House bill limited the scope of the term to those who actually "participate" in the offering. Contrary to the implication of the House report, the term "underwriter" does not encompass those who merely have an "interest" in the offering.

> The [Senate's] substitute amends the definition of underwriter contained in the House bill so as to make clear that a person merely furnishing an underwriter money to enable him to enter into an underwriting agreement is not an underwriter. Persons, however, who participate in any underwriting transaction or who have a direct or indirect participation in such a transaction are deemed to be underwriters. The test is one of participation in the underwriting undertaking rather than that of a mere interest in it. H.R. Conf. Rep. 73-152, at 24 (1933).

Judicial interpretation of the statutory definition, though hardly comprehensive, further clarifies the statutory definition of "underwriter." To be an underwriter under the Securities Act, it is not necessary for a person to undertake the risk that they will be left holding unsold shares. In other words, the term "underwriter" in the Securities Act includes persons who take part in both "firm commitment" and "best efforts" offerings. *Dale v. Rosenfeld*, 229 F.2d 855, 857 (2nd Cir.1956). Nor must a party actually sell shares to the public to be an underwriter under the Securities Act, mere participation in an offering is enough. *Harden v. Raffensperger, Hughes & Co., Inc.*, 65 F.3d 1392, 1400-01 (7th Cir.1995); *SEC v. Intern'l Chem. Dev. Corp.*, 469 F.2d 20, 32 (10th Cir.1972). Finally, courts have held that a person need not derive any financial benefit from his participation in the distribution of security to be considered an underwriter. *Intern'l Chem. Dev. Corp.*, 469 F.2d at 33.

Courts have also interpreted what "participation" means in the context of the statutory definition of underwriter. The Seventh Circuit has interpreted the phrases "participate in" and "participation" in section 2(11) to mean "engage in steps necessary to the distribution of securities":

> [I]n *SEC v. Van Horn*, 371 F.2d 181 (7th Cir.1966), we commented ... that "the statutory definition [of underwriter, contained in section 2(11)] specifically covers every person who participates in a distribution of securities." 371 F.2d at 188.... We subsequently noted that *Van Horn* suggests that the term 'underwriter' is broad enough to encompass all persons who engage in steps necessary to the distribution of securities." *SEC v. Holschuh*, 694 F.2d 130, 139 n.13 (7th Cir.1982) (considering section 5 liability, but declining to rule on scope of section 2(11)). Other courts have interpreted section 2(11) in similar fashion. *See also Intern'l Chem. Dev. Corp.*, 469 F.2d at 33 (person whose "participation was a vital aspect in the steps necessary to the distribution" is underwriter under section 2(11)); [] *SEC v. N. Am. Research and Dev. Corp.*, 280 F.Supp. 106, 126 (S.D.N.Y.1968), *aff'd in part and vacated in part on other grounds,* 424 F.2d 63 (2d Cir.1970) (person who listed security in "Pink Sheets," a function essential to distribution and ordinarily performed by underwriter, is underwriter precluded from exemption under section 4(1) of the Securities Act).

Courts have held that certain actions do constitute participation under section 2(11). For instance, a person who takes part in the actual preparation of the registration statement or prospectus is an underwriter. *See In re Activision Sec. Litig.*, 621 F.Supp. 415, 424 (N.D.Cal.1985). A person who, motivated by increasing the value of shares he is holding, solicits brokers in various parts of the country and distributes sales literature, is considered an underwriter. *N. Am. Research*, 280 F.Supp. at 127. The General Counsel of the SEC, in a 1938 opinion letter, implied that a "person enjoying substantial relationships with the issuer or underwriter, or engaging in the performance of any substantial functions in the organization or management of the distribution" would be considered an underwriter by virtue of participating in the issue.[6] *Opinion of General Counsel relating to Rule 142*, Sec. Act Release No. 1862, 1938 WL 31127 (Dec. 14, 1938).

Courts have also found that certain actions do not necessarily constitute participation under section 2(11). Marginal participation, such as limited solicitation of purchases or distribution of sales literature without compensation, *N. Am. Research*, 280 F.Supp. at 128, or simply writing sales literature, *see id.*, does not necessarily make someone an underwriter. *See also McFarland v. Memorex Corp.*, 493 F.Supp. 631, 645–46 (N.D.Cal.1980) (warrantholders who (1) had no indirect or direct interest in underwriting, (2) did not bear risk in sale of shares to public, and (3) did not hold themselves out as experts able to evaluate financial condition of issuing company did not "participate" in the issue, and so were not underwriters).

In itself, that a person is listed as an underwriter in a prospectus or registration statement does not require, as a matter of law, a court to find that the person is an underwriter. *See In re: Sec. Am. Corp. Sec. Litig,* No. 81 C 3910, 1985 WL 2266, at *4 (N.D.Ill. Aug. 9, 1985) (defendant who accepted offer to participate in stock offering and then withdrew, but name remained listed in prospectus, granted summary judgment because not underwriter); *see also Re Comstock-Dexter Mines, Inc.,* SEC Release No. 33-2691, 1941 SEC LEXIS 229 (October 23, 1941) (defendant contracted by issuer to supervise stock sales not necessarily underwriter where plaintiff had not demonstrated that defendant had supervised or solicited sales). However, a factfinder could find that persons who were identified in the prospectus as an underwriter *and* arranged to have their stock included in a registration statement are underwriters. *Byrne v. Faulkner, Dawkins, & Sullivan,* 550 F.3d 1303, 1312 (2d Cir.1977).

B. Analysis

The Special Situations plaintiffs have introduced numerous pieces of evidence to support their contention that all five members of the alleged underwriting syndicate—Girard, Westminster, Westport, Paulson, and Oberweis—acted as underwriters of the 2000 Offering. Suprema's August 24, 2000 prospectus (the "Prospectus") lists Girard, Westminster, Westport, Paulson, Oberweis, and Mercer[3] as underwriters who each agreed to purchase 75,000 Suprema shares, subject to "approval of certain legal matters by counsel and to certain other conditions." A document, filed with the SEC on or about July 24, 2000, titled the "Underwriting Agreement," states that Suprema "proposes to issue and sell to the several Underwriters named in Schedule I hereto" 1 million shares of its stock. However, Schedule I of the Underwriting Agreement lists only one underwriter, Hobbs Melville Securities Corp., which is described in the agreement as the "representative" of the "several underwriters."

1. Girard

The Special Situations plaintiffs argue that Girard was an underwriter under section 2(11) because Girard participated in the offering and in the direct or indirect underwriting of the offering. However, aside from the Prospectus and Underwriting Agreement, they produce no evidence to gauge Girard's involvement in the 2000 Offering. Plaintiffs' counsel asserts that he served their first request for document on Girard's counsel in August 2006, and, as of February 2, 2007, Girard has produced no documents in response. In response to the plaintiffs' motion for summary judgment, Girard argues that the evidence introduced by the plaintiffs is insufficient to show that no material issue of fact exists with respect to its participation in the offering.

The Court concludes that the Special Situations plaintiffs have not met their burden of proof. The Prospectus and Underwriting Agreement are ambiguous, and do not clearly demonstrate the extent of Girard's actual participation in the 2000 Offering. On this evidence, a reasonable jury could well determine that the plaintiffs have not

---

3. [8] The Prospectus also states Hobbs Melville and Auerbach, the now-defunct principal underwriters of the 2000 Offering, agreed to purchase a total of 750,000 shares from Suprema and certain selling shareholders. Hobbs Melville and Auerbach are described as "representatives" for the other five underwriters.

proved that Girard participated in the offering or in the underwriting of the offering. There exists a genuine, material issue of fact. Summary judgment against Girard is denied on this issue.

2. Westminster and Westport

Similarly, the Special Situations plaintiffs argue that Westminster and Westport are underwriters because they participated in the offering or in the underwriting of the offering. With respect to Westminster, the plaintiffs also rely on several additional pieces of evidence which they argue support summary judgment in their favor. They submit: (1) a copy of a document entitled "Agreement Among Underwriters," signed by John D. Fine, described as a Westport V.P., on August 16, 2000, which states that Westport confirms its agreement to purchase Suprema shares as provided by the "Underwriting Agreement"; (2) two facsimiles, dated August 24 and August 25, 2000, sent from Hobbes Melville to Westport, which state that Westport's final underwriting participation is 75,000 shares and its9 final retention amount is 0 shares; (3) a November 20, 2000 letter from Hobbs Melville to Westport stating that a check for $2,350.00 enclosed with the letter represents Westport's underwriting fee for its participation in the Suprema offering; and (4) a copy of a November 20, 2000 check for $2,350.00, signed by James Carrazza, drawn on Hobbs Melville's Citibank account and payable to Westport.

Westport points out that it was not identified as an underwriter anywhere in the original registration statement for the 2000 Offering filed with the SEC on May 10, 2000, or in either of the two amended registration statements filed on May 24 and July 24, 2000.

As to Westminster, the plaintiffs introduce evidence substantially similar to that introduced with respect to Westport. This evidence includes: (1) an undated copy of the "Agreement Among Underwriters" discussed above, signed by James M. Carrazza, identified as the CEO of Hobbs Melville, and by John P. O'Shea, identified as the president of Westminster; (2) an August 25, 2000 Westminster facsimile transmittal sheet from John O' Shea to James Carrazza of Melville which states that the signed Agreement among Underwriters is attached and thanking Carrazza for "the opportunity to participate in this placement"; (3) August 24 and August 25, 2000 facsimiles from Hobbes Melville to Westminster stating that Paulson's final underwriting participation is 75,000 shares and its final retention amount is 0 shares; and (4) a Westminster document entitled "Detail Cash Receipts by Date Paid," which appears to show that Westminster received $2350 from Hobbs Melville on November 29, 2000.

The Special Situations plaintiffs have not demonstrated that no material issues of fact exist that Westport or Westminster underwrote the 2000 Offering. To be sure, the plaintiffs have provided more evidence to demonstrate Westport and Westminster participated in the offering than they did with regard to Girard. But viewing that evidence in the light most favorable to Westport and Westminster, the Court concludes that the plaintiffs have not met their burden. The nature and extent of Westminster's and Westport's involvement in the 2000 Offering remains ambiguous because the plaintiffs are unable to point to particular actions these defendants took to facilitate the offering. The plaintiffs have not demonstrated that a reasonable jury would be compelled by plaintiffs' evidence to find that Westminster or Westport participated in the 2000 Offering. Summary judgment on this issue is denied.

3. Paulson and Oberweis

The Special Situations plaintiffs argue that Paulson and Oberweis were underwriters of the 2000 Offering because they purchased and sold Suprema shares to the public.

The plaintiffs introduced several documents, in addition to the Prospectus and Underwriting Agreement, relating to Paulson and Oberweis. With respect to Paulson they introduced: (1) an undated copy of the "Agreement Among Underwriters," signed by Tracy H. Parker for Paulson; (2) a signed July 18, 2000 letter from Tracy Parker of Paulson to Hobbs Melville wherein she expresses Paulson's interest in participating in the offering[4]; (3) an August 24 and August 25, 2000 facsimiles from Hobbes Melville to Paulson stating that Paulson's final underwriting participation is 75,000 shares and its final retention amount is 35,000 shares[5]; (4) trade tickets and order confirmations produced by Paulson which appear to demonstrate that Paulson purchased 35,000 shares of Suprema stock at $7.60 per share on August 25, 2000 and that Paulson's clients in turn purchased or ordered 35,000 shares of Suprema stock at $8 per share, the offering price[6]; (5) an August 28, 2000 letter from Hobbs Melville to Paulson which appears to show that Paulson is to pay Hobbs Melville $266,000 on August 30, 2000 for 35,000 Suprema shares purchased at $7.60 per share; and (6) a November 20, 2000 letter from Hobbes Melville to Paulson stating that a check for $2,350.00 was enclosed with the letter and represents Paulson's underwriting fee for its participation in the Suprema offering.

With regard to Oberweis, the plaintiffs have introduced: (1) an undated copy of an identical "Agreement Among Underwriters," signed by James W. Oberweis, the president of Oberweis.net; (2) an August 24, 2000 facsimile from Hobbes Melville to Oberweis stating that Oberweis's final underwriting participation is 75,000 shares and its final retention amount is 70,000 shares[7]; (3) an account summary produced by Oberweis which shows that on August 30, 2000 Oberweis purchased 70,000 Suprema shares at $7.60 per share and sold 70,000 Suprema shares at $8 per share; (4) an August 28, 2000 letter from Hobbs Melville to Oberweis which appears to show that Oberweis is to pay Hobbs Melville $266,000 on August 30, 2000 for 70,000 Suprema shares purchased at $7.60 per share.

On the basis of the evidence listed above, the Court finds that the plaintiffs have met their burden and shown that there exists no genuine, material issue of fact that

---

4. [10] Specifically, Parker writes: "I would like to raise our indication of interest in Suprema Specialties to 37,000 shares. We would also be interested in participating as an underwriter for up to $500,000. [...] We appreciate any consideration you can give us in this offering and look forward to working with you."

5. [11] A handwritten note on this letter reads: "All sold clear DTC 221 PAUL Thank you!"

6. [12] Some of the tickets and orders are dated August 25, 2000, and others are not dated.

7. [13] A handwritten note on this letter reads: "All sold clear DTC 221 PAUL Thank you!"

Paulson and Oberweis acted as underwriters by selling Suprema shares to the public during the course of the 2000 Offering.... Accordingly, the Court grants summary judgment to the Special Situations plaintiffs against Paulson and Oberweis on this issue.

Notes and Questions

1. *Selling Shareholders as Statutory Underwriters.* In *In re Activision Securities Litigation,* 621 F. Supp. 415 (1985), the court determined that selling shareholders should be liable as statutory underwriters only if they participate in the distribution process of the securities offering. The court reasoned as follows:

    > Regulations were carefully constructed under the Securities Act of 1933 so that securities would not be released for sale to the public until the registration statement is effective and all the requirements for its preparation have been met. In a case of firm commitment underwriting, as here, all shares for distribution are purchased by the underwriting group for sale to the public. The Underwriting Agreement and Prospectus show that the purchase by the underwriting syndicate included the shares to be issued by the company and the selling shareholder shares. The selling shareholders do not participate in the distribution process by merely selling their shares to the underwriter. In their capacity as selling shareholders they do not participate in the registration statement process. On these facts no purpose is served in holding them liable under § 11.

    Does the court's reasoning in *Activision* conflict with the court's broad interpretation of the meaning of *underwriter* in *Special Situations Fund, III, L.P.*? Should the reasoning in *Activision* only apply in a firm commitment underwriting? Firm Commitment underwritings are described in Section C.2. below.

2. *Participation versus a Purchase or Sale of a Security.* In *Harden v. Raffensperger Hughes and Co., Inc.*, the court opined that a purchase or sale was not necessary to establish underwriter status under Section 2(a)(11). Purchasers of the notes issued by Firstmark, a financial services company, filed a class action lawsuit against Raffensperger. Raffensperger was a qualified independent underwriter who only performed due diligence on the registration statement and recommended a minimum yield. Raffensperger performed this service because Firstmark was a member of FINRA, which required its members to retain a qualified independent underwriter to perform due diligence when issuing Firstmark's own securities. Purchasers of the Firstmark notes claimed that the registration statement contained material falsehoods and omitted material facts and that Raffensberger, as a statutory underwriter under Section 2(a)(11) was liable under Section 11(a)(5) of the Securities Act. Raffensperger moved for summary judgment on the ground that it was not an "underwriter" because it neither offered, purchased, sold, nor distributed the Firstmark notes. The court stated that underwriter status under Section 2(a)(11) could also be found if Raffensberger

participated, directly or indirectly, in the underwriting of: (1) the purchase of the Firstmark notes or (2) the offer or sale of the notes with a view to, or in connection with, their distribution. The court held that it was clear that Raffensperger qualified as an underwriter because his actions were necessary to the distribution of the Firstmark notes. Does this interpretation of the term *underwriter* serve to facilitate disclosures to investors, enabling them to make informed investment decisions?

3. *Section 4(a)(1) of the Securities Act Exemption.* The definition of *underwriter* in Section 2(a)(11) can include individual investors who are not broker-dealers or investment banks. Such individuals generally participate in a chain of transactions through which securities move from an issuer to the public. Section 4(a)(1) contains an exemption for the private investor unrelated to the issuer who later wishes to sell restricted securities, which he purchased from the issuer.

4. *Finders as Underwriters.* Finders, in the underwriting context, bring together potential issuers (sellers) and broker-dealers (buyers) for a fee. Statutory underwriter status may result from such activities if they involve evaluation of the offering or participation in negotiations. In a No-Action letter issued to F. Willard Griffith, II (avail. Oct. 2, 1974), [1974–1975 Transfer Binder] Fed. Sec. L. Rep. (CCH) P79,994 regarding underwriter status, the staff of the Division of Corporation Finance determined that it would not recommend an enforcement action based on finder activities. Mr. Griffith proposed to introduce parties who wished to negotiate mergers, consolidations, or other acquisitions of businesses or assets, and also persons who wanted to negotiate transactions in particular securities. Mr. Griffith would identify such parties through the receipt of written inquiries from subscribers to a publication, which he would distribute through the mails to subscribers and others. The publication described the business assets or securities sought and the proposed terms of the transaction. Prospective parties would be identifiable by code number only. If a response was generated, Mr. Griffith would introduce the parties, but would not become involved in the negotiations between the parties. In addition, all written communications would prominently mention that Mr. Griffith made no effort to ascertain the accuracy of information provided by prospective parties, did not undertake any advisory, evaluative, or decision-making function, and did not represent that the proposed transaction was lawful. The staff of the Division of Corporation Finance determined that Mr. Griffith would not be a statutory underwriter when conducting his activities as long as, through the use of Mr. Griffith's services, an issuer did not seek to effect a public distribution of securities by using Mr. Griffith to solicit indications of interest.

2. Types of Underwriting Arrangements

When acting as an underwriter, the broker-dealer and the issuer sign an underwriting agreement. The underwriting agreement is a contractual arrangement between the broker-dealer and the issuer under which the broker-dealer agrees to sell the issuer's securities either as an agent or as a principal. Types of underwriting agreements include: (1) firm commitment, (2) best efforts, (3) all-or-none, or (4) minimum-maximum (mini-max). In a firm commitment underwriting agreement, the broker-dealer acts as a principal because it is contractually obligated to purchase the securities from the issuer. The purchase price of the securities is less than the subsequent offering price and the broker-dealer will profit on the difference between the purchase price from the issuer and the subsequent offering price to public investors (the spread or gross underwriting profit). Accordingly, the broker-dealer purchases securities from the issuer at a discount from the subsequent offering price under firm commitment underwriting agreements. The issuer is willing to accept proceeds at a discount to the offering price for certainty regarding the amount of the proceeds it receives from the offering. The risk of being able to sell the securities at the offering price shifts from the issuer to the underwriter and there is a charge against the broker-dealer's net capital.[8] To ameliorate this risk, firm commitment underwriting agreements generally include a market-out clause for the broker-dealer. Market-out clauses relieve the underwriter of liability if it decides not to complete the offering based on a calamitous or near-calamitous event. The SEC has identified some types of market-out clauses as inappropriate when based on: (1) the occurrence of non-material events affecting the issuer or the securities market in general, or (2) an inability to market the securities.

A best-efforts underwriting agreement between the broker-dealer and the issuer simply requires the broker-dealer to use its best efforts to sell the issuer's securities. Best-efforts underwriting agreements generally specify a period in which the broker-dealer will exercise its best efforts to sell the issuer's securities. Unlike a firm commitment underwriting, the broker-dealer is under no obligation to purchase the issuer's securities. The broker-dealer is acting merely as an agent for the issuer. Remuneration for the broker-dealer is a commission—a portion of each sale is withheld. Proceeds from sales of the issuer's securities are forwarded to the issuer by the broker-dealer less the amount of the negotiated commission. Because the broker-dealer is under no obligation to purchase the issuer's securities, there is no charge against the broker-dealer's net capital.

In all-or-none underwriting agreements, the broker-dealer agrees to sell all of the issuer's securities and no less than all. Like the best-efforts underwriting agreement, the broker-dealer acts as the issuer's agent. The risk of failing to sell out the entire offering rests with the issuer, not the broker-dealer, thus there is no charge against the broker-dealer's net capital. Unlike a best-efforts underwriting agreement, the broker-dealer does not receive an underwriting commission if it fails to sell out the entire offering. Generally, all-or-none underwriting agreements contain a time limit for the offering, perhaps 30 to 90 days; some also include 30-day extensions at the election of the broker-dealer, the issuer, or both.

---

8. The broker-dealer's required minimum net capital is discussed in Chapter 7.

Mini-Max underwriting agreements require the sale of a minimum amount of the issuer's securities during the offering. The offering is completed when the maximum, minimum, or some amount between the maximum and minimum of the issuer's securities are sold. Essentially, a specified minimum must be sold and the offering may continue for a specified period in order to reach the maximum. The broker-dealer is acting as agent for the issuer and is remunerated by commission. If the minimum amount of the issuer's securities is not sold, collected funds are returned to subscribers (or investors).

All conditional offerings require the broker-dealer to maintain funds collected on behalf of the issuer in an escrow account or a depository bank. Failure to do so constitutes fraud under § 15(c)(2) and Rule 15c2-4 of the Exchange Act. Rule 15c2-4 requires the broker-dealer to deposit all consideration received by the broker-dealer during such offerings promptly in an escrow account or depository bank. There must be a written agreement with the depositary bank that it will transmit all funds held in the account to the issuer when the condition occurs. Rule 10b-9 of the Exchange Act requires the broker-dealer to refund funds collected from subscribers if the broker-dealer fails to reach the condition; failure to do so constitutes fraud under § 10(b) of the Exchange Act and Rule 10b-9 promulgated thereunder.

FINRA Rule 5110 requires broker-dealers to file underwriting arrangements relating to public offerings with FINRA. In fact, the offering cannot begin until the underwriting arrangements have been filed, reviewed, and approved by FINRA. FINRA Rule 5110 also prohibits participation in offerings in which the underwriting terms and conditions are unfair or unreasonable. For example, the maximum amount of compensation considered fair and reasonable generally will vary directly with the amount of risk to be assumed by participating broker-dealers (firm commitment or best efforts) and inversely with the dollar amount of the offering proceeds. The rule also prohibits arrangements specifying any payment of commissions or reimbursement of expenses directly to the underwriter and related persons prior to commencement of the public sale of the securities being offered, except for reasonable advances against out-of-pocket expenses anticipated to be incurred. The broker-dealer must reimburse the issuer to the extent that such expenses were not actually incurred. There are also restrictions on non-cash compensation such as gifts, meals, and entertainment, which may be included in the underwriting arrangement and other related agreements.

3. The Underwriting Syndicate

Public offerings of any type are generally conducted through an underwriting syndicate for the purpose of distributing the financial responsibility and risk of the public offering. An underwriting syndicate is an association of broker-dealers bound together under contract for a specified period for the purpose of selling the issuer's securities to public investors. Large contractual commitments require large amounts of capital. Assistance from other broker-dealers is required both for capital and in the distribution process.

Generally, the underwriting syndicate consists of the managing underwriter, the co-underwriters (if any), and the dealer group. The managing underwriter enters into an underwriting agreement directly with the issuer. The co-underwriters enter into an agreement among underwriters directly with the managing underwriter. Both the managing underwriter and the co-underwriters incur statutory liability for the offering under Sections 11 and 12 of the Securities Act. The dealer group enters into a dealer agreement directly with the underwriter. However, the dealer group does not incur statutory liability as an underwriter. Section 2(a)(11) exempts broker-dealers participating as dealers from underwriter status: "such term shall not include a person whose interest is limited to a commission from an underwriter or dealer, not in excess of the usual and customary distributors' or sellers' commission." This means that the managing underwriter must limit the compensation of broker-dealers participating in the dealer group to an amount not in excess of the usual and customary distributors' or sellers' commission.

The phrase "usual and customary distributor's or sellers' commission" is defined in Rule 141(a) of the Securities Act to mean "a commission or remuneration, commonly known as a spread.... Which is not in excess of the amount usual and customary in the distribution and sale of issues of similar type and size; and not in excess of the amount allowed to others ... for comparable service in the distribution of the particular issue." Moreover, Rule 141(a) of the Securities Act makes clear that this exclusion is available only to broker-dealers who purchase the issuer's securities from the underwriter for resale to the public. Generally, dealer group compensation is usually no more than 50 to 60 percent of the principal or co-underwriter's commission or discount. Members of the dealer group may include other broker-dealers in the distribution and reallow a portion of their commission to the other broker-dealers. By custom, the reallowance is 50 percent of the dealer group's compensation. It is also industry practice to limit the number of securities being offered through dealers to an amount not exceeding approximately 10 percent to any one dealer. In addition, FINRA Rule 5160 requires selling syndicate agreements or selling group agreements to state the price at which the securities are to be sold to the public or the formula by which the price can be ascertained—along with selling concessions, if allowed.

The following case illustrates the development of, and activities performed by, underwriting syndicates. It also discusses the origins of many of the major investment bankers, some of whom still exist today, and the basis for excluding the underwriting syndicate from U.S. antitrust laws.

United States v. Morgan

118 F. Supp. 621 (S.D.N.Y. 1953)

MEDINA, Circuit Judge.

Introduction

This is a civil action in equity to restrain the continuance of certain alleged violations of Sections 1 and 2 of the Sherman Act, ... It is charged that defendants entered into a combination, conspiracy and agreement to restrain and monopolize the securities business of the United States and that such business was thereby unreasonably restrained and in part monopolized.

The 'securities business'... is defined ... to include new issues, and secondary offerings registered with the Securities and Exchange Commission under the Securities Act of 1933, ... of securities of domestic and foreign business corporations and foreign governmental units and foreign municipalities, offered to or placed with investors in the United States ...

[I]t is charged in the complaint that in 1915 'the modern syndicate method of distributing securities was invented by defendant banking firms and their predecessors,' and that defendants agreed that with certain modifications this method should be utilized by defendants to stabilize the business 'by fixing and controlling the prices, terms, and conditions of purchase, sale and resale of securities.' This 'device' is said to be manipulated by defendants in various ways, all as part of the general plan or scheme.

Thus we turn to the evolution and growth of the investment banking business and the way it functions in the modern American scheme of financial affairs....

[I]t has been conclusively established, as already stated, that the syndicate system as a means of issuing and distributing security issues was in use at least as early as the 1890's; and in this early period price maintenance was to some extent used, as it was appreciated even in those days that the problem of placing upon the market a large bulk of new securities required careful management and planning lest the very quantity involved should depress the price and make distribution within a reasonable time difficult if not impossible....

The evolution of the investment banking industry in the United States is illustrated by the early phases of the development of two of the defendant investment banking firms, Goldman, Sachs & Co. and Lehman Brothers.

Goldman, Sachs & Co. traces its origin back to the year 1869, when Marcus Goldman started a small business buying and selling commercial paper. In the year 1882, he was joined in that business by Samuel Sachs, and at that time the firm, which had been known as Marcus Goldman, became M. Goldman & Sachs. In the year 1885, when additional partners joined the firm, the firm became Goldman, Sachs & Co., and has continued as such from then on to today. At that time, it was very difficult for small manufacturers and merchants to get capital with which to operate, so Goldman, Sachs & Co. developed the business of buying their short-term promissory notes, thus furnishing them with needed capital, and selling these notes to banks or other investors. This commercial paper business prospered and continued to expand in the 1880's and 1890's and, by the time of the year 1906, when the opportunity first arose for Goldman, Sachs & Co. to underwrite some financing for United Cigar Manufacturers, now known as the General Cigar Company, the firm had established many contacts all over the country with merchants and manufacturers. During this period, also, partners of Goldman, Sachs & Co. took frequent trips to Europe, because at that time it was difficult to raise capital for American enterprises in the financial markets of this country, and they entered into arrangements with European bankers, whereby they would lend money in this country for their account.

Likewise, the firm of Lehman Brothers traces its ancestry back to about 1850. Since then, a series of partnerships, formed from time to time upon the withdrawal or death of partners or the addition of new ones, has conducted business under the name of Lehman Brothers. The firm had prospered greatly as 'cotton bankers,' and, years before the turn of the century, it had established its headquarters in New York City.

In the late 1890's and the early 1900's, the prime securities were railroad bonds and real estate mortgages. The public utilities business had not as yet achieved great importance, and, consequently, public utility securities were generally looked upon with disfavor. Railroad and public utility financing was handled by a small number of firms. The railroad financing was done to a considerable extent by Kuhn, Loeb & Co., J. P. Morgan & Co., Vermilye & Co. and August Belmont; and a large percentage of the capital was furnished by French and German underwriters. The public utility financing was done to a large extent by Harris, Forbes & Co., which had become a specialist in the securities of companies providing power and light. Harris, Forbes & Co. was becoming known as an underwriter which understood and knew how to solve the problems of those companies, and had the knack of raising capital for the growing industry. There was an open field in certain light industrial and retail store financing which had been neglected or overlooked.

After the beginning of this century, as family corporations grew larger and needed more capital for expansion, or when the head of a family died and money was needed to pay inheritance taxes, it became increasingly apparent that commercial paper, which was short-term money, was insufficient to meet the capital requirements of those small enterprises. At about this time, Goldman, Sachs & Co., desirous of entering the business of underwriting securities, conceived the idea of inducing privately owned business enterprises to incorporate and to launch public offerings of securities. In the early 1900's it was considered undignified to peddle retail store securities, but Goldman, Sachs & Co. believed that, with the growth in size of family corporations and other privately owned business enterprises, there would be a market on a national basis for their security issues. The problems involved in offering securities to the public, where no securities were previously outstanding in the hands of the public, were new and difficult of solution, and different from the problems involved in the underwriting of bonds of a well known railroad. The sale of retail or department store securities required a different market.

When the opportunity arose in the year 1906 for Goldman, Sachs & Co. to underwrite the financing of United Cigar Manufacturers, it was unable to undertake the entire commitment alone, and could not get the additional funds which it needed to underwrite from commercial banks or other underwriters, as they would not at that time underwrite this type of securities. Henry Goldman prevailed upon his friend Philip Lehman of Lehman Brothers to divert some of his capital from the commodity business and to take a share in the underwriting. The result was that the two firms, Goldman, Sachs & Co. and Lehman Brothers, became partners in the underwriting of the financing of United Cigar Manufacturers.

In the period from the year 1906 to the year 1917, Goldman, Sachs & Co. and Lehman Brothers together underwrote the financings of many enterprises which had a small and humble beginning, but which later grew to very great size, among them being United Cigar Manufacturers, Sears, Roebuck & Co., B. F. Goodrich Company, May Department Stores Company and F. W. Woolworth Company.

There thus grew up between these two firms an informal, oral arrangement whereby they, as partners or joint adventurers, purchased security issues directly from issuers, and divided equally the profit which was realized from their sale.

There was then no network of securities dealers throughout the country, such as there is at the present time. In or about the year 1905 or 1906, there were only about five investment banking houses which had a national distribution system for securities: Lee Higginson & Co.; N. W. Harris & Co.; N. W. Halsey & Co.; Kidder, Peabody & Co.; and William Salomon & Co. Investment banking houses such as J. P. Morgan & Co., Kuhn, Loeb & Co., and William A. Read & Co. were underwriters of securities primarily in the New York market. Up to about the year 1912 or 1915, there were approximately only two hundred and fifty securities dealers in the entire United States, most of whom were concentrated in the eastern and middle eastern parts of the country. It was not until the time of the launching of the Liberty Loan[9] in the year 1917 that we find a large number of independent dealers engaged in the business of distributing securities throughout the country.

As there was no network of securities dealers on a nation wide scale, the underwriters sold as many securities as they could directly to individual investors, and the sale of security issues generally was not completed rapidly. For example, it took Goldman, Sachs & Co. and Lehman Brothers three months to sell the Sears, Roebuck & Co. security issue which they underwrote in the year 1906, and, in many other instances, it took the underwriters much longer to complete the distribution of security issues. The personnel of the distributing organizations was small, and their operations were concentrated in the eastern and northeastern parts of the country. The purchase and banking groups were characteristically organized to last for a period of one year, and the manager had broad powers to extend the period. This power to extend was frequently exercised by the manager; there are records of such groups continuing from two to five years or longer. Investment banking firms kept lists of investors, and, whenever they underwrote a security issue, they would go directly to the investors and try to sell them that particular security. It was common for an investment banker to purchase an entire issue directly from the issuer at stated price, and that banker alone would sign the purchase contract with the issuer. Generally, the investment banker's agreement to purchase represented a firm obligation. This investment banker would then immediately organize a larger group, composed of a limited number of investment banking firms, which was sometimes called a 'purchase syndicate,' whereby he would, in effect, sub-underwrite his risk by selling the securities which he had

---

9. The Liberty Loan Act was enacted to authorize the issuance and sale of war bonds to aid in financing World War I. The goal was to sell not just to institutional investors but to the common man.

purchased alone from the issuer to this larger group, at an increase or 'step-up' in price. The investment banker who purchased the entire issue directly from the issuer was known as the 'originating banker' or 'house of issue.' The originating banker became a member and the manager of the 'purchase syndicate.' Goldman, Sachs & Co. is said to be one of the first investment banking firms to develop this method of underwriting securities …

Other investment bankers used the same method to underwrite the securities of large industrial enterprises, railroads and utilities. As business enterprises in this country grew in size, and as the amounts of capital required by these enterprises became larger, sometimes a second group, more numerous than the 'purchase syndicate,' would be formed in order to spread still wider the risk involved in the purchase and sale of the securities. The 'purchase syndicate' would then sell the securities which it had purchased at an increase in price from the originating banker to this second larger group, which was sometimes called a 'banking syndicate,' at another increase or 'step-up' in price. The originating banker and the other investment banking firms, which were members of the 'purchase syndicate,' usually became members of the 'banking syndicate' and the originating banker became its manager. The transfer of the securities to the 'purchase syndicate' and then to the 'banking syndicate' was practically simultaneous with the original purchase of the securities from the issuer by the originating banker.

Even at a time before there was any delegation of powers to any particular one of the original purchasers, according to the testimony of Harold L. Stuart of Halsey, Stuart & Co., 'there was an agreement between the houses to buy them and to sell them and to maintain a price' which was even then called a 'public offering price.'

It is evident that the various steps which were taken, including use of the purchase and banking groups above described, were all part of the development of a single effective method of security underwriting and distribution, with such features as maintenance of a fixed price during distribution, stabilization and direction by a manager of the entire coordinated operation of originating, underwriting and distributing the entire issue.

This evolution of the syndicate system was in no sense a plan or scheme invented by anyone. Its form and development were due entirely to the economic conditions in the midst of which investment bankers functioned. No single underwriter could have borne alone the underwriting risk involved in the purchase and sale of a large security issue. No single underwriter could have effected a successful public distribution of the issue. The various investment bankers combined and formed groups, and pooled their underwriting resources in order to compete for business. These groups of investment bankers were not combinations formed for the purpose of lessening competition. On the contrary, there could have been no competition without them. Unless investment bankers combined and formed such groups there would have been no underwriting and no distribution of new security issues. Perhaps the English system, which seems superior in the view of some, has many advantages. But the investment banking business in America grew and developed and prospered according to an indigenous American Pattern.

Thus in these early times we find investment bankers employing trained experts who spend much of their time developing plans and designing the set-ups of issues of securities which will be especially suitable for the needs of a particular issuer, at a particular time and under particular circumstances. We find groups forming for the purposes of competition, sometimes small groups developing into larger ones. And we find the already well developed shaping up of the syndicate system, with features of price maintenance and stabilization and broad powers delegated to the managers in connection with distribution and otherwise, not as a means of merely merchandizing securities, as one would buy and sell hams and potatoes, as suggested by government counsel, but rather as a means of integrating the steps of purchase and distribution necessary to the attainment of the ultimate goal of channeling the savings of investors into the coffers of the issuer as a single unified, integrated transaction. No longer does the issuer bear the risk alone and distribute its securities by agents selling on a commission basis. The pattern of performing a series of interrelated services by the investment banker, including the formulation of the plan and method to be pursued in raising the money, the undertaking of the risk and the distribution of the security issue as a whole, has already emerged.

II. Between World War I and the Securities Act of 1933

In the following decade [after 1923] there was an unprecedented expansion of industrial and business enterprises, an increase in the number and geographical distribution of investors; and the use of the corporate form was adopted more and more widely. As domestic business units increased in size and number, the demands for investment capital reached a magnitude never before experienced.

J. P. Morgan & Co. was the leading firm. But all the great publicly owned banks were in the investment banking business, first for their own account and later indirectly through either subsidiary or affiliated corporations formed for the purpose. Dillon Read, Lee Higginson, the old Kidder Peabody and Blair appear to have been perhaps the best known names in all-around business. Kuhn Loeb together with J. P. Morgan & Co. were leaders in railroads, in which field older firms such as Speyer, J. & W. Seligman, and Ladenburg Thalmann were also important. Bonbright, Harris Forbes, Halsey Stuart and Coffin & Burr were leaders in public utilities. Lehman and Goldman Sachs were leaders in merchandising and other fields.

There were three types of these selling syndicates ... used throughout the 1920's ... The first type was known as the 'unlimited liability selling syndicate.' In this group, each member agreed to take a pro rata share in the purchase of the security issue by the selling syndicate from the previous group, at a stated price, and to take up his share of any unsold securities, which remained in the syndicate at the time of its expiration. The syndicate agreement stated the terms upon which the offering to the public was to be made. Each member was given the right to offer securities to the public, and he received a stated commission on all confirmed sales. However, regardless of the amount of securities which he sold, he still retained his liability to take up his proportionate share of unsold securities. The undivided syndicate combined selling with the assumption of risk; therefore, both houses with distributing ability and houses with financial capacity, but without distributing ability, were included in the syndicate. Usually, a banking group was not organized where this type of selling syndicate was to be used. The purchase group sold the security issue directly to the selling syndicate.

The dealers who did the actual selling of the securities objected to the 'unlimited liability selling syndicate,' as they were compelled to take up in their proportionate shares the securities, which the other dealers, who were members of the selling syndicate, were unable to sell. Consequently, the second type of selling syndicate, which was known as the 'limited liability selling syndicate,' subsequently was developed. This syndicate operated in much the same manner as the undivided syndicate, except that the obligation of each member was limited to the amount of his commitment, and, when he distributed that amount, he was relieved of further liability. Each member retained his proportionate liability for the costs of carrying the securities, shared in the profits or losses of the trading account, and was liable for such other expenses as occurred after the purchase from the purchase or banking group. A banking group was usually organized where the 'limited liability selling syndicate' was to be used.

The 'limited liability selling syndicate' gradually evolved into the third type of selling syndicate, which was simply known as the 'selling group.' The 'selling group' differed from the 'limited liability selling syndicate' in that its members relieved themselves of all liability for carrying costs, the trading account and other expenses. Each member of the 'selling group' was concerned only with expenses connected with the actual retail distribution of securities. The financial liability of the member was restricted to selling or taking up the amount of securities for which he subscribed. Usually, a large banking group was organized where the 'selling group' was to be used. The banking group took over the liability for carrying costs, the trading account and other expenses.

In all of these types of selling syndicates, the members acted as principals, and not as agents of the manager, in distributing securities to the public. The syndicate agreement specified the price at which the securities were to be sold, and it was a violation of the agreement for a member to sell at any other price. The manager traded in the open market during the period of distribution in order to maintain the public offering price. Through such stabilizing operations, the manager sought to prevent any securities, which had been sold by dealers, from coming back into the market in such a manner as to depress the public offering price. It was felt that with respect to the securities which appeared in the market, the members of the selling syndicate had not performed their function of 'placing' with investors, for which they were paid a selling commission; and, consequently, 'repurchase penalties' were provided for, whereby the manager had the right to cancel the selling commission on the sale of those securities which he purchased in the market at or below the public offering price. Under most agreements, the manager had the option of either cancelling the selling commission on the sale of the securities, or of requiring the member who sold the securities to take them up at their cost to the trading account. Records of the serial numbers of securities were kept, and the securities which appeared in the market were thus traced to the dealers who sold them. Stabilizing operations and the repurchase penalty were used in all of the three types of selling syndicates which prevailed throughout this period. However, where a 'selling group' was used, it became more and more common practice to restrict the re-purchase penalty to the cancellation of commissions.

The operations of the 'selling syndicate'... were directed by the manager whose general supervisory function over the whole machinery of purchase and distribution was continued. Even in the earlier period provisions for maintenance of the public offering price by persons to whom title had passed had been included in some agreements.

III. Further Developments 1933–1949

[A] long series of hearings, under the auspices of various committees of the Congress, ... resulted in the Banking Act of 1933 (known also as the Glass-Steagall Act), the Securities Act of 1933 and the Securities Exchange Act of 1934 ... [t]hese statutes, together with the Public Utility Holding Company Act of 1935 and the Maloney Act, effective June 25, 1938, which added Section 15A to the Securities Exchange Act of 1934, and authorized the organization of the National Association of Securities Dealers, Inc. (NASD), under the supervision of the SEC, which followed, effected changes of the most radical and pervasive character; and these changes were made with a complete and comprehensive understanding by the Congress of current methods of operation in common use in the securities issue business.

Institutions which had previously engaged both in commercial and deposit banking on the one hand and investment banking on the other were required to elect prior to June 16, 1934, which of the two functions they would pursue to the exclusion of the other. This resulted in the complete elimination of the commercial banks and trust companies from the investment banking business; and the various bank affiliates were dissolved and liquidated.

The elaborate procedures which now became necessary in connection with the sale of new issues of securities were at first implemented by the Federal Trade Commission and then, upon the creation of the Securities and Exchange Commission, transferred to it. The regulation of the securities business which followed with such salutary and beneficial results has been one of the significant developments of our time.

As of the end of 1949 only 7 of the defendant firms had a capital of 5 million dollars and larger, 8 a capital of between 2 and 5 millions and 2 a capital of between 1 and 2 millions. Nor could any of them use all of their capital or borrowing power for underwritings, as each was engaged in other activities which tied up a part of their capital funds and they were all subject to certain regulations of the SEC and the various exchanges which promulgated rules and regulations affecting the amount of capital available for underwriting.

Section 11 of the Securities Act of 1933 imposed on each underwriter a civil liability, for any omission or misstatement of a material fact in the registration statement ... The liability ... plus the transfer taxes made it necessary for the underwriters to abandon the purchase of security issues jointly or jointly and severally, and resulted in the purchase by the various underwriters in severalty, which has been the prevailing method ever since....

The form in which underwriting transactions commonly took place from the passage of the Banking and Securities legislation up to the present time is that of a purchase or 'underwriting agreement' between the issuer and the underwriters represented by the manager, and an 'agreement among underwriters.'

The manager, like the originating banker or manager in the previous periods, handles the negotiations with the issuer and supervises the whole process of underwriting and distribution.

* * *

IV. How the Investment Banker Functions

The actual design of the issue involves preparation of the prospectus and registration statement, with supporting documents and reports, compliance with the numerous rules and regulations of the SEC or ICC or FPC and the various Blue Sky Laws passed by the several States. In view of the staggering potential liabilities under the Securities Act of 1933 this is no child's play, as is known only too well by the management of issuers.

[T]he investment banker will try to get as much of the business as he can Thus he may wind up as the manager or co-manager, or as a participant in the group of underwriters with or without an additional selling position; or he may earn a fee as agent for a private placement or other transaction without any risk-bearing feature.

Thus we find that in the beginning there is no 'it.' The security issue which eventuates is a nebulous thing, still in future. Consequently the competition for business by investment bankers must start with an effort to establish or continue a relationship with the issuer.

The tentative selection of an investment banker to shape up the issue and handle the financing has now been made; and there ensues a more or less prolonged period during which the skilled technicians of the investment banker are working with the executive and financial advisers of the issuer, studying the business from every angle, becoming familiar with the industry in which it functions, its future prospects, the character and efficiency of its operating policies and similar matters.

At last the issue has been cast in more or less final form, the prospectus and registration statement have been drafted and decisions relative to matters bearing a direct relation to the effective cost of the money, such as the coupon or dividend rate, sinking fund, conversion and redemption provisions and serial dates, if any, are shaped up subject to further consideration at the last moment. The work of organizing the syndicate, determining the participation positions of those selected as underwriters and the making up of a list of dealers for the selling group or, if no selling group is to be used, the formulation of plans for distribution by some other means, have been gradually proceeding, practically always in consultation with the issuer, who has the final say as to who the participating underwriters are to be. The general plans for distribution of the issue require the most careful and expert consideration, as the credit of the issuer may be seriously affected should the issue not be successful. Occasionally an elaborate campaign of education of dealers and investors is conducted.

Thus, if the negotiated underwritten public offering route is to be followed, we come at last to what may be the parting of the ways between the issuer and the investment banker—negotiation relative to the public offering price, the spread and the price to be paid to the issuer for the securities. These three are inextricably interrelated. The stating point is and must be the determination of the price at which the issue is to be offered to the public. This must in the very nature of things be the price at which the issuer and the investment banker jointly think the security can be put on the market with reasonable assurance of success; and at times the issuer, as already indicated in this brief recital of the way the investment banker functions, will for good and sufficient reasons not desire the public offering price to be placed at the highest figure attainable.

Once agreement has been tentatively reached on the public offering price, the negotiation shifts to the amount of the contemplated gross spread. This figure must include the gross compensation of all those who participate in the distribution of the issue: the manager, the underwriting participants and the dealers who are to receive concessions and re-allowances. Naturally, the amount of the spread will be governed largely by the nature of the problems of distribution and the amount of work involved. The statistical charts and static data indicate that the amount of the contemplated gross spreads is smallest with the highest class of bonds and largest with common stock issues, where the actual work of selling is at its maximum. While no two security issues are precisely alike and they vary as the leaves on the trees, it is apparent that the executive and financial officers of issuers may sit down on the other side of the bargaining table confidently, and without apprehension of being imposed upon, as data relating to public offering prices, spreads, and net proceeds to issuers from new security issues registered under the Securities Act of 1933 are all public information which are publicized among other means by the wide distribution of the prospectuses for each issue.

And so in the end the 'pricing' of the issue is arrived at as a single, unitary determination of the public offering price, spread and price to the issuer.

I. Did the Seventeen Defendant Investment Banking Firms Use the Syndicate System as a Conspiratorial Device in Connection with Any Integrated Over-all Combination?

There are in evidence about 1,300 underwriting papers, colloquially referred to as 'syndicate agreements.' They cover a period of well upwards of thirty years, some of them much older, and they contain a great variety of provisions relative to price maintenance, the trading account or stabilization, withholding commissions (the so-called 'penalty' clauses), uniform concessions and re-allowances, authorizations to the manager to act for the group in such matters as group sales, dealer sales, syndicate and price termination, extension or price reduction and so on. I have spent many weeks studying these syndicate agreements and my conclusion, based on the evidence as a whole, is that, in the drafting and use of these agreements these defendant firms acted as separate entities and were motivated solely by normal, ordinary business considerations. These firms played their several parts, just as did other prominent and leading investment banking houses, in the evolution of the syndicate system as described in the preliminary portion of this opinion devoted to the history of the investment banking business. Different firms had different policies, and these are often reflected in the draftsmanship by some of the leading law firms, who sometimes entertained different views on questions of law. At times the forms of agreement used by a single firm on various occasions differ markedly one from another. There is a conspicuous lack of uniformity. Indeed, Morgan Stanley eliminated price maintenance clauses from its underwriting and selling agreements as long ago as 1938; it gave up selling agreements entirely in 1946; and its withholding commissions clause, for failure to place securities with investors, was for a time eliminated from its underwriting agreements and later restored. Price maintenance clauses were omitted from Harriman Ripley agreements in 1943. There are a bewildering variety of clauses used from time to time in their syndicate agreements by the other defendant firms.

Of course there is a certain fundamental similarity in those features which are characteristic of the system. In view of the evolution of the syndicate system over the years how could it be otherwise. The underwriters are formed into a group, broad powers are delegated to the manager, there are provisions for group and dealer sales and with respect to concessions, re-allowances and so on. In a moment we shall find that all these similarities and others are reflected in the forms, registration statements, prospectuses and reports required by the SEC pursuant to the authority of the Congress. But government counsel would have me believe that the very variety of the clauses used by the different defendant firms is some evidence of subtle connivance; that some changes were due to fear engendered by this or that investigation or by the filing of the brief in the PSI[10] case by the Antitrust Division of the Department of Justice attacking the single-price security offering as violative of the Sherman Act. Doubtless the filing of this brief attacking price maintenance clauses, stabilization clauses and the rest did cause a near-panic among some investment bankers, both defendants and non-defendants. And why not? It is not a very pleasant prospect for a business man, who thinks he has been complying with the law, and who has been following as best he can the directions of the Congress and the SEC, to find himself fact to face with a possible indictment and the onerous expense connected with defending oneself against an antitrust charge. But the reaction of the different defendant firms to the filing of that brief was as various and sometimes as contradictory as could well be imagined. Some continued as before, some did not. Even Halsey, Stuart & Co. gave up using price maintenance clauses for a year or so and then came back to them because Stuart thought they could not do business without them.

* * *

---

10. The Antitrust Division of the Department of Justice filed a brief in the PSI case attacking the single-price security offering as violative of the Sherman Act.

The modern syndicate system in general use today by the investment banking industry is nothing more nor less than a gradual, natural and normal growth or evolution by which an ancient form has been adapted to the needs of those engaged in raising capital. By no stretch of the imagination can it be considered a scheme or plan or device to which investment bankers have from time to time adhered. There is nothing conspiratorial about it; nor, on the record now before me, can these defendant firms or anyone fairly be said to have formed at any time any combination or conspiracy to operate under the syndicate system.

The utility and reasonableness of the entire operation, and the fact that functionally it serves a legitimate business and trade-promoting purpose, is amply demonstrated by its unchallenged growth by a gradual process of evolution over a period of a half-century, more or less.

Furthermore, the syndicate system has no effect whatever on general market prices, nor do the participating underwriters and dealers intend it to have any. On the contrary, it is the general market prices of securities of comparable rating and quality which control the public offering price, as explained in the preliminary part of this opinion. Whether by bringing out one issue or many, none of these defendants nor any group of them acting together, have ever, so far as appears in this record, been so foolhardy as to attempt to control or in any manner affect general price levels in the securities market. The particular issue, even if a large one, is but an infinitesimal unit of trade in the ocean of security issues running into the billions, which constitutes the general market.

Of even greater significance are the basic underlying characteristics of the relationship between the issuer, the investor and the group of underwriters and dealers, who together serve the issuer in making the single, entire, unitary transaction possible by shaping up the issue, underwriting the risk and planning and carrying out the distribution.

* * *

It matters not whether the members of the team be called 'partners,' 'quasi-partners,' 'joint adventurers' or what not; the significant fact vis-a-vis the Sherman Act is that they are acting together in a single, integrated, unitary, cooperative enterprise, the purpose of which is not 'raising, fixing, pegging, or stabilizing the price' of anything, nor the exercise of any manner of control over general market prices, but solely the distribution of a new security issue in an orderly manner.

It is upon the basis of these facts, peculiar to the business of raising new capital for issuers, whether by syndicates of underwriters proceeding in negotiated transactions or by public sealed bidding, that the Congress and the SEC evidently arrived at the same conclusion that I arrive at, namely, that the fixed-price type of public offering of new securities viewed in the large, and on the basis of methods now in common use by the investment banking industry, gives no offense to the Sherman Act.

———

4. *Putting It All Together—the Registration Statement, the Gun-Jumping Rules, and the Underwriter*

Figure 5.1

Statute or Rule	Application
5(a) of the Securities Act	No sales of securities until the registration statement is effective.
5(c) of the Securities Act	No offers of securities until the registration statement is filed.
Rule 135 of the Securities Act	Allows short, factual notices about the proposed offering.
Rule 138 of the Securities Act	Research Reports—allows broker-dealer to underwrite one type of a reporting issuer's securities, while providing regular course research on another type of the issuer's securities.
Rule 139 of the Securities Act	Issuer-Specific Research Reports and Industry Research Reports.
Rule 137 of the Securities Act	Safe harbor for distribution of research reports for broker-dealers not participating in the offering (analysts).
Rule 163 of the Securities Act	Permits Well-Known Seasoned Issuers (WSKIs) to make offers during the pre-filing period.
Rule 163A of the Securities Act	Establishes a safe harbor for communications made more than 30 days prior to the filing of the registration statement.
Section 5(d) of the Securities Act	Test the Waters for certain companies defined as Emerging Growth Companies.
Section 6(e) of the Securities Act	Confidential filing of the registration statement.
FINRA Rule 5280	Prohibits trading ahead of research reports.
FINRA Rule 5121	Prescribes conditions for public offerings in which the broker-dealer has a conflict of interest.

This section provides an overview of the public offering of an issuer's securities from the prospective of the broker-dealer. Accordingly, the focus is on the laws, regulations, and rules governing the activities of broker-dealers during a public offering of an issuer's securities. Where necessary for clarification, issuer-specific rules and regulations are also reviewed.

Broker-dealers acting as underwriters or members of the selling group must comply with the gun-jumping rules, which govern their activities during a public offering of an issuer's securities. The gun-jumping rules consist of rules promulgated pursuant to Section 5 of the Securities Act. Unless there is an available exemption, Section 5 prohibits the offer or sale of securities to the public unless the transaction is registered with the SEC. Moreover, the public offering of an issuer's securities is governed by the registration process prescribed in Section 5 and the gun-jumping rules; the broker-dealer is a major participant in the registration process, which requires the issuer to file a registration statement with the SEC. The form of the registration statement is prescribed by the SEC and provides essential facts about the issuer and the securities being offered to the public to facilitate informed decision making by investors. The SEC will declare the registration statement effective upon its determination of sufficient disclosure of information about the issuer and its securities. The SEC rarely examines all the registration statements it receives nor evaluates the merits of offerings.

The registration process under Section 5 is organized by three time periods. The periods are: (1) the pre-filing period; (2) the waiting period; and (3) the post-effective period. The pre-filing period begins before the filing of the registration statement and ends with the filing of the registration statement; generally, during this period all offers to sell or offers to buy are prohibited. The waiting period commences with the filing of the registration statement and ends when the registration statement becomes effective; offers are allowed, subject to restrictions, but sales are prohibited during the waiting period. The post-effective period begins when the registration statement becomes effective and ends when the offering is completed; during this period, broker-dealers acting as underwriters and part of the selling group are permitted to make offers and sales as long as certain information is provided. Figure 5.2 depicts these periods with the corresponding subsections of Section 5 of the Securities Act.

Figure 5.2. The Operation of Section 5 of the Securities Act

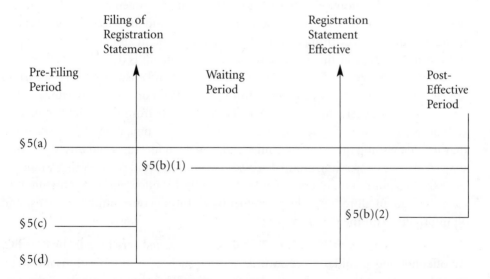

a. The Pre-Filing Period

The pre-filing period begins at least when the broker-dealer and the issuer reach an understanding that the broker-dealer will act as its managing underwriter. It ends upon the filing of the registration statement with the SEC. Some guidance as to the beginning of the pre-filing period is provided by Rule 163A of the Securities Act; Rule 163A is an issuer safe harbor that permits issuer communications made more than 30 days prior to the filing of the registration statement with the SEC.

During the pre-filing period, section 5(a) prohibits all sales of the issuer's securities and section 5(c) prohibits any offers of the issuer's securities. Although the broker-dealer cannot assess investor interest in the issuer's securities during the pre-filing period because offers are prohibited, there are many other activities performed by the broker-dealer to facilitate a successful offering. Most important, the broker-dealer and the issuer, along with their counsel and experts, work together to prepare the registration statement. A working group is formed that includes the issuer's management, the issuer's outside counsel, the issuer's board of directors, any selling shareholders and their counsel, the managing underwriter, the co-managing underwriters (if any), the selling group, the underwriter's counsel, and the issuer's independent public accounting firm (the Working Group).

The managing underwriter conducts an organizational meeting with other members of the Working Group to allocate responsibilities required for successful completion of the offering. The organizational meeting specifically addresses a proposed timetable for preparing and completing the registration statement and projected effective date, as well as a plan for completing the required due diligence (due diligence and corresponding liability is examined in Chapter 6). Although the issuer's management and counsel take the lead in drafting the registration statement, the managing underwriter and its counsel must review the registration statement. In addition, the managing underwriter and its counsel prepare the underwriting documents, including the underwriting agreement, agreement among underwriters, and the selected dealer's agreement. The final underwriting agreement and the agreement among underwriters are not executed until near the time the registration statement is declared effective. The managing underwriter also obtains a CUSIP number and ensures that the securities are eligible for book-entry settlement through the DTC or other depositories. The underwriter's counsel may request specified documents from the issuer required to conduct the underwriter's due diligence. In addition to document review, due diligence may include visiting the issuer's facilities and in-person meetings and interviews with management. The working group discusses the need to avoid conduct that would violate the prohibition on offers under Section 5(c); this effort includes obtaining information about all recent public statements, all future communication plans, and all information on the issuer's website.

The term *offer*, defined in § 2(a)(3), has been construed very broadly by the SEC. An offer not only includes express words of offer, such as communications including the term *offer*, but may include any communications and publications about the proposed offering designed to condition the market, i.e., to arouse public interest in the issuer or in its securities before receiving the required disclosures contained in the registration statement to facilitate informed investor decision making. Section 2(a)(3) states, in part, that,

The term "sale" or "sell" shall include every contract of sale or disposition of a security or interest in a security, for value. The term "offer to sell," "offer for sale," or "offer" shall include every attempt or offer to dispose of, or solicitation of an offer to buy, a security or interest in a security, for value.... The terms defined in this paragraph and the term "offer to buy" as used in subsection (c) of section 5 shall not include preliminary negotiations or agreements between an issuer ... and any underwriter or among underwriters who are or are to be in privity of contract with an issuer ...

In the Matter of Carl M. Loeb, Rhoades & Co.
38 S.E.C. 843 (1959)

FINDINGS AND OPINION OF THE COMMISSION

* * *

The orders for proceedings allege that commencing on September 17, 1958, registrants and Grant offered to sell shares of stock of Arvida Corporation ("Arvida") when no registration statement had been filed as to such securities, in willful violation of Section 5(c) of the Securities Act of 1933 ("Securities Act").

The Offering of Arvida Stock

Arvida was incorporated in Florida on July 30, 1958, pursuant to plans developed over the preceding four or five months to provide for the financing and development of the extensive real estate holdings of Arthur Vining Davis ("Davis") in southeastern Florida. In April 1958 each of the registrants was approached by representatives of Davis, and thereafter, in May and June 1958, as a result of discussions[,] a plan was developed under which certain of Davis' properties would be placed in a new corporation to be financed in large part through a public offering of securities by an underwriting group proposed to be managed by registrants.

* * *

On September 16 and 17, 1958, meetings were held in New York at which the proposals of registrants for the financing were placed in final form and submitted to representatives of Davis for transmission to him. At this time it was decided to issue an additional press release. Grant drafted such a release on the evening of September 17 and, on September 18 submitted it to officers of Arvida, representatives of Davis, [registrants] and counsel for the proposed underwriters, obtaining the approval of all of them. Later that day, Davis approved registrants' financing proposals, and public relations counsel for Loeb Rhoades was called in to arrange for distribution of the release in New York.

The release, which was issued on the letterhead of Loeb Rhoades, stated that Arvida, to which Davis was transferring his real estate, would be provided with $25 million to $30 million of additional capital through an offering of stock to the public, and that Arvida would have assets of over $100,000,000 "reflecting Mr. Davis' investment" and the public investment. It referred to a public offering scheduled within 60 days through a nationwide investment banking group headed by registrants' and to the transfer from Davis to Arvida of over 100,000 acres "in an area of the Gold Coast" in three named Florida counties and contained a brief description of these properties including reference to undeveloped lands and to "operating properties."

The release identified the principal officers of Arvida and stated that Arvida proposed to undertake a "comprehensive program of orderly development," under which some of the lands would be developed "immediately into residential communities" and others would be held for investment and future development as the area expands. It closed with a reference to the attraction of new industry and the place Arvida would assume in the "further growth of Southeastern Florida."

Officers of Arvida were anxious to have the release issued promptly. Public relations counsel advised Loeb Rhoades that, in order to make sure that the story appeared in three prominent New York newspapers, which coverage Loeb Rhoades wanted, it would be advisable, in view of newspaper deadlines, to call reporters from these papers to Loeb Rhoades' office. This was done on the afternoon of Thursday, September 18. The reporters asked certain questions which Grant undertook to answer. He disclosed that the offering price of the stock would be in the vicinity of $10 or $11 per share and gave certain information about Davis and his career but declined to answer questions concerning Davis' reasons for entering into the transaction, the extent of mortgage indebtedness, the capitalization of Arvida, its balance sheet, and the control of the corporation. His stated reason for refusing to answer these questions was that he did not wish to go beyond the release which had been approved by all interested parties.

Copies of the release were also delivered to other New York newspapers and to the principal wire services. The substance of the release and the information supplied by Grant appeared in the three New York newspapers on September 19, 1958, and in numerous other news media throughout the country.

The Impact of Section 5(c) of the Securities Act

Section 5(c) of the Securities Act, as here pertinent, prohibits offers to sell any security, through the medium of a prospectus or otherwise, unless a registration statement has been filed. Section 2(3) defines "offer to sell" to include "every attempt or offer to dispose of, or solicitation of an offer to buy, a security for value."

The broad sweep of these definitions is necessary to accomplish the statutory purposes in the light of the process of securities distribution as it exists in the United States. Securities are distributed in this country by a complex and sensitive machinery geared to accomplish nationwide distribution of large quantities of securities with great speed. Multi-million dollar issues are often over-subscribed on the day the securities are made available for sale. This result is accomplished by a network of prior informal indications of interest or offers to buy between underwriters and dealers and between dealers and investors based upon mutual expectations that, at the moment when sales may legally be made, many prior indications will immediately materialize as purchases. It is wholly unrealistic to assume in this context that "offers" must take any particular legal form. Legal formalities come at the end to record prior understandings, but it is the procedures by which these prior understandings, embodying investment decisions, are obtained or generated which the Securities Act was intended to reform....

[W]e have made clear our position that the statute prohibits issuers, underwriters and dealers from initiating a public sales campaign prior to the filing of a registration statement by means of publicity efforts which, even though not couched in terms of an express offer, condition the public mind or arouse public interest in the particular securities....

We accordingly conclude that publicity, prior to the filing of a registration statement by means of public media of communication, with respect to an issuer or its securities, emanating from broker-dealer firms who as underwriters or prospective underwriters have negotiated or are negotiating for a public offering of the securities of such issuer, must be presumed to set in motion or to be a part of the distribution process and therefore to involve an offer to sell or a solicitation of an offer to buy such securities prohibited by Section 5(c). Since it is unlawful under the statute for dealers to offer to sell or to offer to buy a security as to which registration is required, prior to the filing of a registration statement, dealers who are to participate in a distribution likewise risk the possibility that employment by them of public media of communication to give publicity to a forthcoming offering prior to the filing of a registration statement constitutes a premature sales activity prohibited by Section 5(c)....

Brokers and dealers properly and commendably provide their customers with a substantial amount of information concerning business and financial developments of interest to investors, including information with respect to particular securities and issuers. Section 5, nevertheless, prohibits selling efforts in connection with a proposed public distribution of securities prior to the filing of a registration statement and, as we have indicated, this prohibition includes any publicity which is in fact part of a selling effort. Indeed, the danger to investors from publicity amounting to a selling effort may be greater in cases where an issue has "news value" since it may be easier to whip up a "speculative frenzy" concerning the offering by incomplete or misleading publicity and thus facilitate the distribution of an unsound security at inflated prices. This is precisely the evil which the Securities Act seeks to prevent.

Securities Act Release No. 3844

Securities and Exchange Commission (Oct. 8, 1957)

Re: PUBLICATION OF INFORMATION PRIOR TO OR AFTER THE EFFECTIVE DATE OF A REGISTRATION STATEMENT

* * *

It is necessary ... that corporate management, counsel, underwriters, dealers and public relations firms recognize that the Securities Acts impose certain responsibilities and limitations upon persons engaged in the sale of securities and that publicity and public relations activities under certain circumstances may involve violations of the securities laws and cause serious embarrassment to issuers and underwriters in connection with the timing and marketing of an issue of securities. These violations not only pose enforcement and administrative problems for the Commission, they may also give rise to civil liabilities by the seller of securities to the purchaser.

Absent some exemption, Section 5(c) of the Securities Act of 1933 makes it unlawful for any person directly or indirectly to make use of any means or instruments of interstate commerce or of the mails to offer to sell a security unless a registration statement has been filed with the Commission as to such security.

The terms "sale," "sell," "offer to sell" and "offer for sale" are broadly defined in Section 2(3) of the Act and these definitions have been liberally construed by the Commission and the courts.

It follows from the express language and the legislative history of the Securities Act that an issuer, underwriter or dealer may not legally begin a public offering or initiate a public sales campaign prior to the filing of a registration statement. It apparently is not generally understood, however, that the publication of information and statements, and publicity efforts, generally, made in advance of a proposed financing, although not couched in terms of an express offer, may in fact contribute to conditioning the public mind or arousing public interest in the issuer or in the securities of an issuer in a manner which raises a serious question whether the publicity is not in fact part of the selling effort....

Example #1

An underwriter-promoter is engaged in arranging for the public financing of a mining venture to explore for a mineral which has certain possible potentialities for use in atomic research and power. While preparing a registration statement for a public offering, the underwriter-promoter distributed several thousand copies of a brochure which described in glowing generalities the future possibilities for use of the mineral and the profit potential to investors who would share in the growth prospects of a new industry. The brochure made no reference to any issuer or any security nor to any particular financing. It was sent out, however, bearing the name of the underwriting firm and obviously was designed to awaken an interest which later would be focused on the specific financing to be presented in the prospectus shortly to be sent to the same mailing list.

The distribution of the brochure under these circumstances clearly was the first step in a sales campaign to effect a public sale of the securities and as such, in the view of the Commission, violated Section 5 of the Securities Act.

––––––

The SEC has adopted several rules and added subsection (d) to Section 5 of the Securities Act to identify exceptions to the broad definition of an offer under Section 2(a)(3) for broker-dealers participating in public offerings. The following discussion focuses on those rules—Rules 138 and 139—and Section 5(d) of the Securities Act.

Rule 138 allows broker dealers participating in public offerings of reporting issuers (issuers required under the Exchange Act to file reports with the SEC) to publish research reports about certain of the reporting issuers' securities. A research report is defined in Rule 405 of the Securities Act as a written communication that includes information, opinions, or recommendations about an issuer's securities or an analysis of a security or an issuer, whether or not it provides information reasonably sufficient upon which to base an investment decision. Specifically, broker-dealers participating in a public offering of the reporting issuer's common stock are permitted to publish research about the same reporting issuer's fixed income securities, and vice versa, as long as the broker-dealer publishes such research in its regular course of business. For example, if the broker-dealer publishes research solely about the reporting issuer's common stock, or debt securities or preferred stock convertible into its common stock , it can participate in the reporting issuer's public offering of solely non-convertible debt securities or non-convertible, non-participating preferred stock; if the research report relates solely to the reporting issuer's non-convertible debt securities or non-convertible, non-participating preferred stock, it can participate in the reporting issuer's public offering of solely common stock, or debt securities or preferred stock convertible into the reporting issuer's common stock.

According to the SEC, "[t]he underlying premise of Rule 138 is that there is less opportunity to condition the market when a broker or dealer is underwriting one type of security but providing regular course research on the other type (for example, underwriting an offering of equity securities while providing research on debt securities)."[11] In addition, reporting issuers must be current in their periodic Exchange Act reports, and this safe harbor is not available for blank check companies, shell companies and penny stock issuers. Research reports distributed in reliance upon Rule 138 are exempt from the broad definition of offer contained in Section 2(a)(3) of the Securities Act and therefore do not violate Section 5(c) of the Securities Act. In summary, broker-dealers are allowed to publish research reports about reporting companies as shown in Figure 5.3.

Figure 5.3. Rule 138 of the Securities Act

If Research Report	Then Offering
• Relates solely to issuer's common stock, or debt securities or preferred stock convertible into its common stock	• Can only involve the issuer's non-convertible debt securities or non-convertible, non-participating preferred stock
• Relates solely to issuer's non-convertible debt securities or non-convertible, non-participating preferred stock	• Can only involve issuer's common stock, or debt securities or preferred stock convertible into its common stock

Rule 139 allows broker-dealers to continue to publish research reports[12] during the pre-filing period without violating the prohibition on offers in Section 5(c) under

---

11. *Securities Offering Reform*, Release No. 8501 (2004).
12. The definition of research reports is the same for Rules 138 and 139.

specified conditions. These conditions are based on the of type research report being issued, combined with the type of reporting issuer. Recall that compliance with the gun-jumping rules is based on issuer type: Non-reporting issuers, Unseasoned issuers, Seasoned issuers, and Well-Known Seasoned Issuers (WKSI). The two categories of research reports that are allowed under Rule 139 about issuers during the pre-filing period are determined, in part, by issuer type, i.e., whether the issuer during the pre-filing period is a non-reporting issuer, an unseasoned issuer, a seasoned issuer, or a

Figure 5.4. Issuer-Specific Research Reports

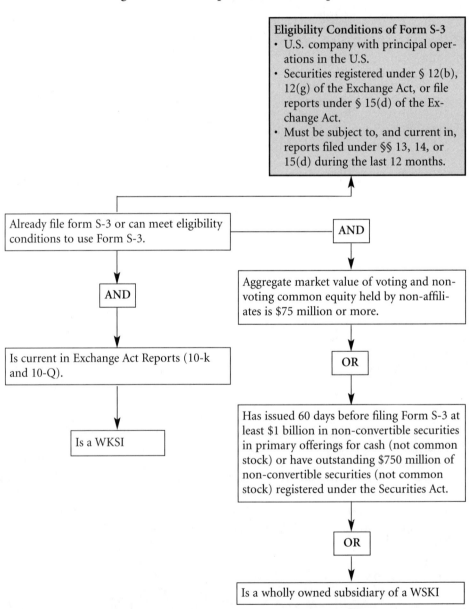

WKSI. Furthermore, the research reports are divided into two categories: Issuer-specific research reports and industry research reports. Issuer-specific research reports are research reports about the specific issuer currently participating in a public offering. Industry research reports are research reports discussing the issuer currently participating in a public offering along with other companies in the same industry. Figure 5.4 depicts issuer requirements to allow the broker-dealer to publish Issuer-specific research reports while participating in a public offering about the same issuer. In addition, the broker-dealer must publish such reports in the regular course of its business and must have already published research reports about the same issuer; the broker-dealer cannot initiate or reinitiate publication of research reports about the company.

Unlike issuer-specific research reports, the industry research report safe harbor in Rule 139 applies to all issuers reporting pursuant to Sections 13 or 15(d) of the Exchange Act except blank check, shell, and penny stock issuers. Figure 5.5 depicts requirements that permit broker-dealers to publish industry research reports while participating in a public offering about the same issuer. The broker-dealer continues to be prohibited from initiating or reinitiating coverage and cannot give the issuer subject to the public offering materially greater space or prominence over other companies mentioned in the industry research report.

Figure 5.5. Industry Research Reports. Rule 139

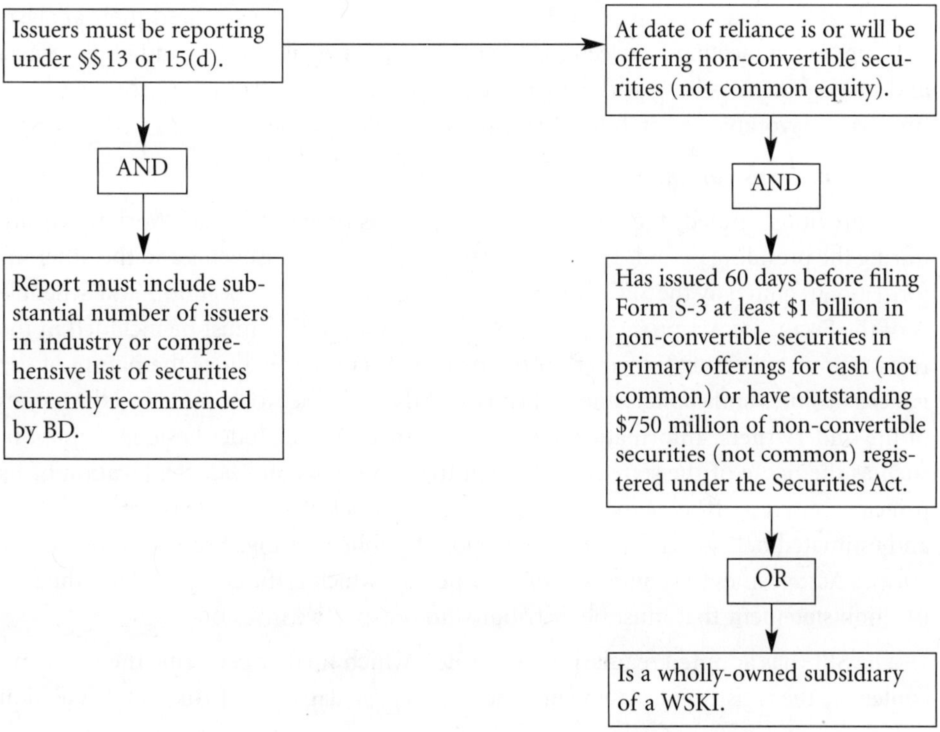

Section 5(d) allows broker-dealers participating or contemplating participating in a public offering for an emerging growth company (EGC) to engage in oral or written communications with certain potential investors without violating the prohibition against offers during the pre-filing period. EGCs are companies whose annual gross revenues are less than $1 billion. Potential investors must be either Qualified Institutional Buyers (QIBs) or institutions that are accredited investors. QIBs are defined in Rule 144A of the Securities Act and include institutions that own and invest on a discretionary basis at least $100 million in securities of non-affiliated issuers such as insurance companies, registered investment advisers, and mutual funds. QIBs may also be registered dealers acting for their own account or other QIBs that own and invest on a discretionary basis at least $10 million of securities of non-affiliated issuers. Banks with an audited net worth of at least $25 million and that own and invest at least $100 million in securities of non-affiliated issuers are also QIBs. Accredited investors are defined in Rule 501 of Regulation D of the Securities Act and include institutions such as banks and insurance companies, registered broker-dealers, and entities in which all of the equity owners are individual accredited investors. Individual accredited investors include persons not related to the issuer who have a net worth in excess of $1,000,000 (excluding their primary residence) as well as individuals whose income exceeds $200,000 ($300,000 if the person has a spouse) in each of the two most recent years with a reasonable expectation of reaching the same income level in the current year. Communications with QIBs and accredited investors regarding a contemplated public offering must be accompanied by a prospectus that meets the requirements of Section 10(a) of the Securities Act (written communications meeting the requirements of a Section 10 prospectus are discussed throughout the remainder of this chapter). In addition, unlike other issuers, EGC status allows underwriters and their analysts to be present in meetings between underwriters and potential investors and underwriters and management as long as the analyst does not engage in prohibited conduct, e.g., promising favorable research for investment banking business.

i. The Registration Statement

As previously noted, the registration statement is prepared by the Working Group during the pre-filing period. It consists of two parts—the prospectus and the other information required by the SEC that is not part of the prospectus. Section 7 and Schedule A of the Securities Act prescribe the general information that must be included in the registration statement. Information required by Section 7 includes the nature of the issuer's business and capitalization, the price of the securities to be sold, and the names of the underwriters. Information required by Schedule A includes basic information, such as the name of the state under which the issuer is organized, the location of its principal business office, names and addresses of underwriters and the issuer's directors, and estimated net proceeds from the proposed public offering. Section 10 of the Securities Act specifies the content of the prospectus, which is the component of the registration statement that must be distributed to prospective investors.

The SEC has adopted regulations and rules, which further prescribe the form and content of the registration statement. The primary regulations and rules are Regulation

C, Regulation S-K, and Regulation S-X under the Securities Act. These regulations are used to complete the various registration forms prescribed by the SEC, which contain issuer and transaction eligibility requirements. Regulation C contains technical requirements for filing the registration statement, such as the form and content, use of contents, filing fees, and amendments. Regulation S-K prescribes the specific disclosure information that must be included in the prospectus, such as descriptions of the issuer's business and property, management and compensation, risk factors, and securities being offered. Regulation S-X sets forth the form and content of, and requirements for, financial statements in the registration statement. Financial statements are deemed to include all notes to the financial statements and all related schedules.

Section 6 of the Securities Act governs the filing of the registration statement with the SEC. Among other things, it describes the method of filing and states the required filing fees. It also requires, except as noted below, that all registration statements filed with the SEC be publicly available upon filing. However, Section 6(e) permits EGCs, prior to their initial public offering date, to confidentially submit a draft registration statement for non-public review by the SEC. The EGCs' registration statement must be made public no later than 21 days before the EGC conducts a roadshow. Roadshows occur in the waiting period and are discussed below.

Finally, one of the most important roles of the underwriter during the pre-filing period is to conduct due diligence, i.e., to verify the facts about, and the value of, the issuer's business represented in the registration statement. Due diligence activities and the underwriter's corresponding liability are examined in Chapter 6.

Notes and Questions

1. In general, all registration statements filed with the SEC are available to the public, except confidential submissions from EGCs. Most registration statements are filed electronically using the SEC's Electronic Data Gathering, Analysis, and Retrieval System (EDGAR). EDGAR performs automated collection, validation, indexing, acceptance, and forwarding of submissions by companies required to file forms with the SEC. EDGAR is located on the SEC's web site at: http://www.sec.gov/edgar.shtml.

2. FINRA Rule 5280 prohibits the broker-dealer from trading ahead of research reports, including those distributed under Rules 138 and 139 of the Securities Act. Specifically, the broker-dealer must establish, maintain, and enforce policies and procedures reasonably designed to restrict information flow between research department personnel to prevent trading department personnel from using non-public advance knowledge for the benefit of the broker-dealer.

3. FINRA Rule 5121 governs broker-dealer activities when a broker-dealer has a conflict of interest in an entity's public offering. Conflicts of interest exist when, among other things, the securities are to be issued by the member broker-dealer; the issuer controls, or is controlled by, the member broker-dealer or its associated persons;

at least five percent of the offering proceeds (excluding underwriting compensation) will be used to reduce or retire the balance of a loan extended by the member broker-dealer; or, as a result of the public offering, the member broker-dealer will be an affiliate of the issuer or will become publicly owned. Control is defined in subparagraph (6) of FINRA Rule 5280 and means beneficial ownership of 10 percent or more of the outstanding common equity, distributable profits or losses, outstanding preferred equity, or the power to direct the management or policies of an entity. FINRA Rule 5280 requires broker-dealers participating in public offerings of securities with conflicts of interest to meet one of two conditions. The first condition requires prominent disclosure of the nature of the conflict of interest in the prospectus, procurement of a broker-dealer to act as a managing underwriter that does not have a conflict of interest nor a disciplinary history, and that the securities offered have a bona fide public market; if the preceding conditions are not met, then the securities offered must be investment-grade rated or be in the same series that have equal rights and obligations as investment-grade rated securities. The second condition requires a qualified underwriter to participate in the preparation of the registration statement exercising the usual standards of due diligence and prominent disclosure in the prospectus of the nature of the conflict of interest, name of the qualified independent underwriter, and a brief statement about the role and responsibilities of the qualified independent underwriter. FINRA Rule 5121 is also applicable during the waiting period.

4. Rule 135 of the Securities Act is an issuer safe harbor that excludes certain notices that comply with its provisions from being deemed an offer and therefore violating Section 5 of the Securities Act. It can be used by the issuer or by those acting on behalf of the issuer, which includes the underwriter. Rule 135 provides very limited protection because it removes from the definition of *offer* only short, factual notices of a proposed public offering. Specifically, the notice may contain only the information enumerated in Rule 135, which includes identifying the issuer, the amount and basic terms of the offered securities, the purpose of the offering, and the anticipated timing of the offering. It cannot, however, identify the underwriter by name.

5. Rule 137 of the Securities Act provides a safe harbor for broker-dealers that are not participating in an issuer's public offering of securities, but who publish or distribute research about the issuer's securities. Non-participating broker-dealers are permitted to distribute research about the public offering. They are not considered being engaged in a distribution and therefore are not considered underwriters in the public offering about which they only distribute research. This safe harbor applies to securities under registration of any issuer, including non-reporting issuers (excluding blank check companies, shell companies, and penny stock issuers). Rule 137 is available only to broker-dealers (and their affiliates), and, if different, the person (and any affiliate) that has published the report who: (1) is not participating and does not propose to participate in the registered offering of the issuer's securities; (2) is not receiving and has not received con-

sideration in connection with the research report from the issuer of the securities, a selling security holder, any participant in the distribution of the securities, or any other person interested in any of such securities; and (3) publishes or distributes the research report in the regular course of its business.

Hypothetical One

Success First is the managing underwriter for the initial public offering of Justin-Time, Inc. ("JustinTime"), a time management company and non-EGC issuer. Justin-Time plans to file its registration statement for its IPO on Form S-1. You have been hired as outside counsel for Success First to review the preliminary prospectus for compliance with applicable SEC rules. To prepare for your review of the preliminary prospectus, you have ordered your new associate, AttheReady Johnson, to obtain information required in the prospectus for the item numbers listed in Table 5.1 by identifying the applicable sections of Regulation S-K and Regulation S-X and briefly summarizing the required information.

Table 5.1

Prospectus Item No.	Applicable Regulation
Item 2	
Item 7	
Item 11(c)	
Item 11(e)	

b. The Waiting Period

Figure 5.6

Statute/Rule	Description
Section 5(a) of the Securities Act	Prohibits sales of securities unless a registration statement is in effect
Section 5(b)(1) of the Securities Act	Prohibits use of any prospectus relating to a security for which a registration statement has been filed unless it meets the requirements of Section 10 of the Securities Act
Rule 473 of the Securities Act	Delaying Amendments for registration statement that has not become effective. Tolls the 20-day automatic effective date for the registration statement in § 8(a) of the Securities Act.
Section 10(b)	Allows for Section 5(b)(1) purposes a prospectus that omits in part or summarizes information; this is the preliminary prospectus
Rule 430 of the Securities Act	Defines preliminary prospectus
Rule 15c2-8 of the Exchange Act	Preliminary prospectus delivery requirements

The waiting period begins with the filing of the registration statement and ends when the SEC declares the registration statement effective. The purpose of the waiting period from the broker-dealer's perspective is to solicit indications of interest from prospective investors, i.e., to gauge investor sentiment for the issuer's securities. Essentially, this is when the underwriting syndicate and the issuer market the offering. It is also the time when the SEC reviews and issues comments on the registration statement. Pursuant to Section 8(a), registration statements will go effective 20 days after filing unless an amendment is filed to restart the 20-day period. This 20-day period is rarely sufficient for the SEC to complete its review of the registration statement and for the issuer to respond to deficiencies in the registration statement identified by the SEC. Rule 473 of the Securities Act addresses this problem by allowing the inclusion of a prescribed legend on the bottom of the front cover page of the registration statement that tolls the 20-day period indefinitely, thereby eliminating the necessity for filing amendments solely for the purpose of restarting the 20-day period in Section 8(a). Moreover, issuers and underwriters are reluctant to distribute the prospectus (including the preliminary prospectus discussed below) until all deficiencies identified by the SEC not related to pricing are satisfactorily addressed. Rule 473 delaying amendments are generally used when conducting initial public offerings ("IPOs").

From the SEC's perspective, the rules and regulations governing the waiting period are designed to provide investors with the material information needed to make an informed investment decision and with the time to review such materials. Although § 5(a)'s prohibition of sales remains. However, offers, but not sales, of the issuer's securities are permitted if information to make an informed investment decision is available to prospective investors. The prospectus—part one of the registration statement—is used to provide information to investors for informed decision making. Section 5(b)(1) of the Securities Act prohibits the use of any prospectus for which a registration statement has been filed unless it meets the requirements of Section 10 of the Securities Act. Section 10(b) allows the use, for Section 5(b)(1) purposes, of a prospectus that omits in part or summarizes information in accordance with SEC rules, i.e., a preliminary prospectus. Rule 430 of the Securities Act defines a preliminary prospectus as a document that satisfies the requirements of Section 10 of the Securities Act; it expressly permits the omission of the following information in the preliminary prospectus: (1) the offering price; (2) the underwriters' and dealers' discounts and commissions; and (3) the amount of proceeds, conversion rates, call prices, or "other matters depending upon the offering price." The preliminary prospectus plays an especially important role with respect to IPOs because it is the primary written communication used to deliver information about a non-reporting issuer to prospective investors during the waiting period. The preliminary prospectus also allows the underwriting syndicate and the issuer to market the offering without violating Section 5(b)(1) of the Securities Act. In addition, it is not necessarily part of the registration statement for liability purposes under Section 11 of the Securities Act (Section 11 liability is discussed in Chapter 6).

Rule 15c2-8 of the Exchange Act mandates preliminary prospectus delivery requirements for broker-dealers participating in public offerings. Broker-dealers participating in an IPO must deliver a copy of the preliminary prospectus to every person they expect will receive a confirmation of sale 48 hours before sending the confirmation. In addition, broker-dealers participating in a public offering are required to deliver a preliminary prospectus to any person who makes a written request for a preliminary prospectus between the filing date and a reasonable time prior to the effective date of the registration statement. Rule 15c2-8 also requires broker-dealers participating in a public offering to take reasonable steps to make available a copy of the preliminary prospectus (including amendments promptly after filing) to each of their associated persons who are expected to solicit customer orders before such associated persons make any solicitations. Moreover, the managing underwriter is required to take reasonable steps to provide all members in the underwriting syndicate with sufficient copies of each preliminary prospectus, including amendments. Failure to meet the preliminary prospectus requirements of Rule 15c2-8 is deemed a deceptive practice or fraudulent act under the Exchange Act.

i. Other Communications Allowed during the Waiting Period

The SEC has adopted several rules to address issuer and underwriter communications during the waiting period. Rule 405 of the Securities Act defines communication as any communication that is written, printed, a radio or television broadcast, or a graphic communication. A graphic communication includes, but is not limited to, audiotapes, videotapes, facsimiles, CD-ROM, electronic mail, web sites, and widely distributed messages using computers, computer networks, and other forms of computer data compilation. A graphic communication does *not* include a communication that originates live, in real-time to a live audience and that does not originate in recorded form, despite the fact that it is transmitted through graphic means.

The following discussion focuses on safe harbors for the underwriting syndicate. It is organized into three categories: (1) Written communications, (2) Live roadshows and other oral offers, and (3) free writing prospectuses. Similar to the pre-filing periods, permitted communications during the waiting period are based on the type of issuer, e.g., non-reporting, reporting, seasoned, and WKSI. As noted in Figure 5.7, Rules 138 and 139, previously discussed in section II.C.4.a. of this chapter, continue as effective safe harbors for research reports during the waiting period.

Figure 5.7

Statute/Rule of the Securities Act	Description
Rule 138	Research Reports—allows broker-dealer to underwrite one type of a reporting issuer's securities, while providing regular course research on another type of the issuer's securities.
Rule 139	Issuer-Specific Research Reports and Industry Research Reports.
Rule 134	Limited content communications defined as not a prospectus.
Section 5(d)	Test the waters.

c. Rule 134 Communications

Rule 134 is a safe harbor that excludes from the definition of prospectus certain communications about the offering and the issuer distributed during the waiting period. This means that communications or notices complying with Rule 134 do not violate § 5. Rule 134 can only be used if a registration statement has been filed with the SEC and is available to the public on EDGAR. Accordingly, Rule 134 is not available to EGCs during the confidential registration statement submission process with the SEC. Rule 134 allows disclosure, among other things, of the issuer's legal and business location (including the address, phone number, and e-mail address of the issuer's principal place of business), the amount and type of security to be offered, the business of the issuer, and the price of the security. It also allows disclosure of the names of the underwriting syndicate, their roles in the offering, a description of marketing events (e.g., roadshows, which are discussed below), and a description of the procedures used by the underwriters to conduct the offering. However, Rule 134 prohibits communications that contain a detailed term sheet for the securities being offered; term sheet information is confined to the "title of the security or securities and the amount or amounts being offered, which title may include a designation as to whether the securities are convertible, exercisable, or exchangeable, and as to the ranking of the securities." In addition, Rule 134 communications must contain a legend stating that the securities in the offering cannot be sold until the registration statement becomes effective and from whom a preliminary prospectus may be obtained. However, this legend is not required if the communication is accompanied, or preceded, by a preliminary prospectus or if the Rule 134 communication only states from whom a preliminary prospectus may be obtained, identifies the security, states the price, and by whom orders will be executed.

Rule 134 also allows solicitation of offers to buy from investors, or requests to investors of whether they might be interested in the security if a preliminary prospectus accompanies or precedes the communication. If the Rule 134 communication is electronic, the preliminary prospectus requirement can be satisfied by providing an active hyperlink to the prospectus in the electronic communication. Communications soliciting such offers or indications of interest must contain a statement that no offer can be accepted and no part of the purchase price can be received until the registration statement has become effective and that the offer to buy may be withdrawn or revoked prior to acceptance by the underwriter, without obligation or commitment of any kind.

d. Live Roadshows and Other Oral Offers

The roadshow is the primary marketing effort during the waiting period. It is designed to introduce the issuer and its management to potential investors (generally institutional investors) and is typically conducted after all of the SEC comments have been resolved. A traditional roadshow is defined in Rule 433(h)(4) of the Securities Act as "an offer ... that contains a presentation regarding an offering by one or more members of the issuer's management ... and includes discussion ... of the issuer, ... management, and the securities being offered ..." The issuer's senior management, the managing underwriter, and other members of the underwriting syndicate make a series of presentations about the strengths of the issuer and respond to investor questions about the proposed offering in various cities over a period of one to two weeks to generate interest in the public offering.

Traditional roadshows are live, i.e., they involve face-to-face meetings between participants at which, generally, only the preliminary prospectus is distributed. Traditional roadshows are considered to be oral offers; oral offers are not written communications and therefore not a prospectus under § 2(a)(10) and do not violate § 5(b)(1)'s preliminary prospectus requirement. In addition, during this period members of the underwriting syndicate make telephone calls and meet individually with prospective institutional investors. Similarly, these types of activities are oral and therefore are not prospectuses under 2(a)(10). As such, they do not violate § 5(b)(1). Traditional roadshows, telephone calls, and individual meetings to discuss the offering with investors are part of the underwriters' process of "building the book" in a public offering.

EGCs are only permitted to conduct a traditional roadshow if they are no longer requesting confidential treatment of their registration statement. Specifically, the EGC must make its registration statement public at least 21 days prior to conducting a traditional roadshow. There was some confusion regarding whether test-the-waters communications could also be viewed as coming within the Rule 433(h)(4) definition of roadshow. The SEC has clarified that test-the-waters communications by an EGC with QIBs and institutional accredited investors are not deemed to be a roadshow, and therefore would not trigger the public filing requirement of an EGCs registration statement.

Roadshows may also be electronic. Rule 433(h) defines a bona fide electronic roadshow as a "written communication transmitted by graphic means that contains a presentation by one or more officers of an issuer or other persons in an issuer's management ..." Electronic roadshows are written communications that are not part of the preliminary prospectus. Accordingly, they are free writing prospectuses governed by Rules 164 and 433 of the Securities Act discussed in the following section.

e. Free-Writing Prospectus

A free writing prospectus is any "written communication ... that constitutes an offer to sell or a solicitation of an offer to buy the securities related to a registered offering that is used after the registration statement ... is filed.... and that [does] not meet the definition of a statutory prospectus (preliminary or final) under § 10. Two other terms integral to the definition of a free-writing prospectus are defined in Rule 405 — written communication and graphic communication. The term *written communication* includes printed, broadcast and graphic communications. The term *graphic communications* includes all forms of electronic media such as e-mails, web sites, CD-ROMS, videotapes, and "substantially similar messages widely distributed" over a variety of electronic communication networks. Whether a free writing prospectus satisfies the § 5(b)(1) informational requirements is governed by Rules 164 and 433 of the Securities Act. If the requirements of Rule 433 are met, Rule

164 states that the free writing prospectus is treated as a § 10(b) or preliminary prospectus for purposes of § 5(b)(1). This means that offering participants, including underwriters, may use the broadcast (including telecast) and print media, the Internet, and other electronic media in addition to the registration statement to market the offering as long as such materials satisfy the requirements of a free writing prospectus.

The use and requirements of free writing prospectuses are governed by Rules 164 and 433, which must be read together. Both rules are available to underwriting participants along with issuers. Rule 164, among other things, identifies the types of issuers permitted to use free writing prospectuses by excluding certain issuers. Rule 433 prescribes the conditions that must be satisfied in order for a free writing prospectus to satisfy § 5(b)(1) informational requirements, and thus to be used in the marketing effort. Rule 164 expressly excludes, among others, reporting issuers who are delinquent in their reporting requirements under §§ 13 or 15(d), blank check companies, shell companies, penny stock issuers, issuers subject to pending stop orders, and issuers subject to regulatory actions prohibiting violation of the antifraud provisions of the federal securities laws. Otherwise, seasoned issuers and WKSIs are permitted to use free writing prospectuses after a registration statement has been filed that includes a prospectus that complies with Section 10 of the Securities Act (e.g. a preliminary prospectus under § 10(b)). In addition, Rule 163 of the Securities Act permits WKSIs to use a free writing prospectus in the pre-filing period; essentially, WKSIs may distribute free writing prospectuses in all three periods of the public offering process without violating the gun jumping rules. Non-reporting issuers and unseasoned issuers are permitted to use free writing prospectuses only if preceded, or accompanied, by a preliminary prospectus that includes a price range.

The information in a free writing prospectus must not conflict with information in the filed registration statement. A legend is required that states that a registration statement has been filed with the SEC in connection with the offering and how the registration statement may be obtained. The legend may also provide an e-mail address and web site and corresponding Internet address with the location of the registration statement on the web site. If the issuer is a reporting issuer, information in the free writing prospectus must not conflict with information in any of the issuer's periodic and current reports (e.g., Form 10-K or Form 10-Q filings with the SEC).

A free writing prospectus must be filed by the issuer and any offering participant (e.g., the underwriter) with the SEC no later than the date it is first used, unless there is an exemption. A free writing prospectus prepared, or referred to, by the issuer must be filed with the SEC. The issuer is also required to file any free writing prospectus that contains information about the issuer that is prepared on its behalf by any offering participant (e.g., the underwriter). However, a free writing prospectus that is prepared by a third party that is based on, or derived from, issuer information does not have to be filed with the SEC. The issuer must also file a free writing prospectus describing the final terms of the offering within two days of the later of the date final terms were established and the date of first use. Any offering participant, such as the underwriter, must file with the SEC any free writing prospectus that it uses, or refers to, in relation to the offering and that is distributed in a manner reasonably designed to lead to its broad unrestricted dissemination. However, the SEC does not require either the issuer or any offering participant to file a free writing prospectus that contains information already filed with the SEC in a previously filed free writing prospectus or prospectus.

FINRA Rule 2210, which governs broker-dealer communications with the public, may also apply in the waiting period to communications made in connection with a public offering. Sales materials, in certain circumstances, used to market the public offering must also be filed with the FINRA Advertising Department for review and approval prior to first use. In light of this requirement, some broker-dealers may require the managing underwriter to file all such communications with FINRA even though FINRA Rule 2210 may not require the managing underwriter to do so. In addition, FINRA Rule 2210 requires review of broker-dealer communications with the public by appropriate personnel at the broker-dealer prior to submission to the FINRA Advertising Department.

i. Media Publications or Broadcasts and Issuer Web Sites

Free writing prospectuses (which by definition are written offers) can take many forms and, as long as they meet the requirements of Rule 433, will be deemed to be 10(b) prospectuses that satisfy Section 5(b)(1). Information on the issuer's web site about the offering, including hyperlinks on the issuer's web site to a third party's web site, must satisfy the requirements of Rule 433 or will constitute an illegal offer. However, a free writing prospectus does not encompass historical issuer information located in a separate section of the issuer's web site and that is not included in the prospectus for the offering.

Media publications or broadcasts may also be used in connection with an offering and will comply with section 5(b)(1) if they satisfy the requirements in Rule 433. In order to satisfy the requirements of Rule 433, however, the issuer and underwriter must not pay for the media publication or broadcast and the issuer must file a copy with the SEC with the legend specified in Rule 433 within four days of dissemination or when the issuer or underwriter becomes aware of the media publication or broadcast. If, however, the issuer or underwriter pays for the media publication or broadcast (e.g., an infomercial or written advertisement), and the issuer is non-reporting or unseasoned, a statutory preliminary prospectus must precede or accompany the media publication or broadcast. Seasoned issuers that prepare and pay for a media publication or broadcast are only required to have their most recent statutory prospectus on file with the SEC.

Electronic roadshows are written communications under Rule 405 and therefore must satisfy the requirements of a free writing prospectus. Filing of an electronic roadshow that is a free writing prospectus with the SEC is required for IPOs of common equity or convertible equity securities, unless the issuer makes at least one version of a bona fide electronic roadshow available without restriction to the public, using electronic media such as the Internet.

Hypothetical Two

As managing underwriter for JustinTime's IPO, Success First is preparing to conduct a roadshow in connection with the upcoming IPO. Success First has decided to use several FWPs to assist in its marketing efforts to solicit offers for JustinTime's securities. Alicia Luigi, senior managing director at Success First, wants to make sure that the FWPs prepared by her staff meet the use and content requirements permitted for FWPs under applicable rules of the Securities Act. She has asked Monique Oliver, a second-year associate in Success First's legal department, to identify the applicable rules and to summarize the corresponding requirements in table format. This is Monique's first IPO legal assignment, and she wants to do well. Monique is a bit nervous because Alicia has told her that she needs this information "yesterday."

Notes and Questions

1. *SEC review of the Registration Statement.* Registration statements are selectively reviewed by SEC staff in its Division of Corporation Finance ("CorpFin"). This review process does not evaluate the merits of securities or their issuers; it merely seeks to determine whether the issuer has provided all the disclosure required by the applicable forms and rules. The review process does not guarantee that disclosure is complete and accurate because this responsibility lies with the issuer and others who prepared the registration statement. CorpFin staff may conduct one of three types of reviews: (1) a full review of the entire registration statement; (2) a financial statement review, which includes review of financial statements and related disclosures; and (3) a targeted issue review in which specific items of the registration statement are examined for compliance with applicable accounting standards and/or other requirements of the federal securities laws. Potential deficiencies in the registration statement are addressed by comment letters issued by CorpFin staff. Comment letters may require the issuer, and others who participated in the preparation of the registration statement (e.g., the underwriter), to provide additional supplemental information, revise disclosure, or provide additional or different disclosure. The issuer's response to CorpFin's comment letter will determine the number of comment letters required to address all staff questions and concerns about the disclosure in the registration statement and thus the time required for the registration statement to become effective. Although CorpFin staff comments are not legally binding, failure to address all issues identified in comment letters will delay effectiveness, at a minimum, or be the basis for a Division of Enforcement investigation and/or a Commission stop order proceeding.

2. Investigations by the SEC are private until the SEC files an order initiating an enforcement action against an issuer. Is the issuer required to disclose such an investigation by the SEC while it is in registration? *See* D. Stuart and D. Wilson, *Disclosure Obligations under the Federal Securities Laws in Government Investigation,* 64 Bus. Law. 973 (2009).

3. *Directed Share Programs.* Directed Share Programs ("DSPs"), sometimes called "friends and family" programs, include issuer or underwriter-directed allocation of a portion of an IPO (usually no more than 5%) at the IPO price to issuer employees, vendors, customers, and others with a friendly or business relationship with the issuer. DSPs represent a reward to friends of the issuer by allowing such persons to benefit from the anticipated price appreciation of the IPO. DSPs can involve written offers to sell and violate § 5(a) if they constitute a binding commitment to purchase before the registration statement has been declared effective.

4. *Issuer Safe Harbors.* Rules 168 and 169 of the Securities Act are issuer safe harbors available in both the pre-filing and waiting periods of which the broker-dealer should be aware. They are important because they allow issuers to disseminate certain business information that the issuer would normally release to conduct business. Rule 168 allows issuers required to file reports under Section 13(a) or 15(d) of the Exchange Act to continue to disseminate regularly released factual or forward-looking business information. Rule 169 allows non-reporting issuers to disseminate factual business information, but not forward-looking information. Factual business information, such as advertisements or information about the issuer's products and services, is included in these safe harbors.

5. *FINRA Rule 2262, Disclosure of Control Relationship with Issuer and FINRA Rule 2269, Disclosure of Participation or Interest in Primary or Secondary Distribution.* FINRA Rule 2262 requires a broker-dealer to disclose to its customer if a control relationship exists between the issuer and the broker-dealer before the customer purchases or sells such issuer's security. This disclosure must be in writing. FINRA Rule 2269 requires the broker-dealer to disclose in writing its participation or interest in a primary or secondary distribution to its customer before the customer completes any securities transaction in such primary or secondary distribution. How do these rules apply, if at all, during the waiting period?

6. *FINRA Rule 2210, Communications with the Public.* FINRA Rule 2210 specifies FINRA's requirements for the filing, content, approval, and record-keeping requirements of sales literature used by broker-dealer offering participants that are filed as free writing prospectuses with the SEC pursuant to Rule 433(d)(1)(ii) of the Securities Act (because they are intended to be broadly disseminated). This means that such sales literature must be filed, reviewed, and approved by the FINRA Advertising Department within 10 business days of first use. In addition, the content of such sales literature must comply with the content standards specified in paragraph (d) of Rule 2210. For example, broker-dealers must ensure that statements in such communications are clear and not misleading within the

context in which they are made, and that they provide balanced treatment of risks and potential benefits. In addition, such communications must be based on principles of fair dealing and good faith, must be fair and balanced, and must provide a sound basis for evaluating the facts in regard to the particular security being offered to the public.

f. Post-Effective Period

Figure 5.8

Statute or Rule	Application
5(b)(1) of the Securities Act	No offers of securities unless preceded or accompanied by a §10(b) prospectus.
5(b)(2) of the Securities Act	No sale or delivery of securities unless preceded or accompanied by a §10(a) [final] prospectus.
2(a)(10) of the Securities Act	Allows distribution of sales literature after the registration statement has been declared effective by excluding such written communications from definition of prospectus as long as it is preceded or accompanied by a §10(a) [final] prospectus.
Rule 430A of the Securities Act	Permits registration statement to be declared effective without certain underwriting compensation information and amount of proceeds if the offering is a cash offering.
Rule 424(b)	Missing information from the prospectus permitted under Rule 430A must be filed no later than two business days following earlier of price determination date or first use of registration statement.
Rule 172	Access equals delivery of final prospectus.
Rule 173	
Rule 10b-10 of the Exchange Act	Confirmation of sale.
Rules 164/433	Free writing prospectus.

The post-effective period commences when the SEC declares the registration statement effective. During this period, the issuer and underwriters and selling group can continue to make offers and to make sales of securities. However, the requirements of §5(b)(1) still apply. In addition, the issuer, underwriter, and selling group can now make sales subject to the delivery requirements of §5(b)(2). Offering participants also may disseminate supplemental sales literature and written investment information (free writing) during the post-effective period as long as a final prospectus accompanies or precedes the dissemination of such free writing. Once the original allotment of securities has been sold and the offering has been completed, the closing takes place. There are also post-closing events, which consist of the remaining tasks required to complete the registration process.

As we examine the prospectus delivery requirements in this section, you will note that the prospectus is the singular disclosure document mandated by the federal securities laws to provide investors with the material information required to make an informed investment decision. However, before reviewing prospective delivery requirements, it should be noted that Rule 430A of the Securities Act allows the registration statement to be declared effective using a prospectus with the omission of certain pricing information. Specifically, the registration statement may be declared effective with a prospectus that does not include:

> [I]nformation with respect to the public offering price, underwriting syndicate, underwriting discounts or commissions, discounts or commissions to dealers, amount of proceeds, ... delivery dates, and terms of the securities dependent upon the offering date; ...

Rule 430A may only be used in a cash public offering and Rule 424(b) of the Securities Act requires the missing information to be filed with the SEC no later than the second business day following the earlier of the date of price determination of the securities being offered or the date the prospectus is first used after the registration statement has been declared effective. Failure to file in accordance with the time frame of Rule 424(b) means that the underwriters must amend the registration statement and again, request that the SEC declare it effective. Any sales prior to the effectiveness of the amended registration statement would violate Section 5 of the Securities Act. Rule 430A is often used to provide flexibility to the underwriting syndicate in negotiating and finalizing the offering price and terms of the offering. This flexibility allows the issuer and managing underwriter to account for changing market conditions and to select the actual pricing day most favorable for the offering. In addition, a change in volume or price that represents no more than a 20 percent change in the maximum aggregate offering price is permitted under Rule 430A. Accordingly, the underwriter avoids the necessity of filing of a pricing amendment to the prospectus, thus decreasing the duration of its liability under § 11 of the Securities Act (broker-dealer civil liability is discussed in Chapter 6).

i. Prospectus Delivery Requirements

A significant responsibility of broker-dealers during the post-effective period is delivery of a final statutory prospectus to purchasers that complies with Section 10(a) of the Securities Act. In fact, §§ 5(b)(1) and (2) operate together to facilitate receipt of a complete final statutory prospectus by purchasers of securities in public offerings. As previously noted, § 5(b)(1) prohibits written communications, including media publications or broadcasts, unless they qualify as § 10 prospectuses. Although § 5(b)(1) encompasses both § 10(a) (final) and § 10(b) (preliminary) prospectuses, it will be reviewed below in the section discussing permissible free writing in the post-effective period (i.e., traditional free writing). Section 5(b)(2) provides that, before a security can be delivered for sale, it must be preceded or accompanied by a final statutory prospectus. Rule 172(b) states that the prospectus delivery requirements under § 5(b)(2) are met if the conditions specified in Rule 172(c) are met. Rule 172(c) conditions include: (1) an effective registration statement that is not subject to any pending stop order suspending the registration statement or to an examination to determine whether a stop order should be issued; (2) neither the issuer, nor underwriter, or any participating dealer is subject to a pending cease-and-desist proceeding; and (3) the issuer has filed a § 10(a) prospectus with the SEC or has made a good faith and reasonable effort to do so within the time frame required under Rule 424(b) of the Securities Act, or will do so as soon as practicable. In recognition of technological advances and changes in market structure, Rule 173 of the Securities Act allows the delivery requirement of a § 10(a) prospectus to be met by providing notice of the availability of a § 10(a) or final prospectus filed with the SEC, i.e., access equals delivery, no later than two business days after the sale of the security. A Rule 173 notice is expressly exempt from the prohibitions of § 5(b)(1).

Rule 15c2-8 of the Exchange Act sets forth prospectus delivery requirements specifically for the underwriter and members of the selling group. During the post-effective period the underwriter and any member of the selling group must provide a copy of the final prospectus to any person making a written request and to any associated person participating in the distribution who is expected to solicit customers before the associated person solicits any customers. In addition, the managing underwriter must provide a copy of the final prospectus to all broker-dealers participating in the distribution or trading in the security to enable them to comply with the requirements of §§ 5(b)(1) and 5(b)(2). However, the prospectus delivery requirement in § 5(b)(2) may be met with respect to transactions between broker-dealers if the transaction is effected on a national securities exchange, NASDAQ, or an ATS; securities of the same class as the securities that are the subject of the transaction are being traded; the registration statement is effective (includes a § 10(a) prospectus) and not subject to a stop order or examination; and neither the issuer nor any underwriter or participating dealer is the subject of a pending cease-and-desist order. Violation of Rule 15c2-8 is a fraudulent act.

Even broker-dealers who are not participating as underwriters or as members of the selling group have prospectus delivery requirements during the post-effective period. Although § 4(3) of the Securities Act provides an exemption from the prospectus delivery requirements of § 5(b), Rule 174 of the Securities Act, in conjunction with § 4(3), establishes periods when the § 4(3) exemption is not available. Section 4(3) exempts compliance with the requirements of § 5 for transactions by a dealer (including those no longer acting as an underwriter with respect to the public offering), except transactions that take place prior to the expiration of 40 days after the effective date of the registration statement or after the first date upon which the security was offered to the public, whichever is later. The 40 days is extended to 90 days if the public offering is an IPO. Rule 174, combined with § 4(3), establish prospectus delivery requirements for broker-dealers who are acting as dealers, but *are not* acting as underwriters in the offering. These prospectus delivery requirements are as shown in Figure 5.9:

Figure 5.9

Number of Days	Type of Issuer
0	Issuer is an Exchange Act Reporting Company pursuant to §§ 13 or 15(d) immediately prior to the filing of the registration statement
25	Issuer is a not an Exchange Act Reporting Company pursuant to §§ 13 or 15(d) but will be listed on a registered national securities exchange (e.g., NYSE or NASDAQ) or authorized for inclusion in an electronic inter-dealer quotation system sponsored and governed by FINRA as of the offering date (i.e., the later of the effective date of the registration statement or the first date on which the security is bona fide offered to the public)
40	Issuer is not an Exchange Act Reporting Company, will not be listed on a registered national securities exchange or authorized for inclusion in an electronic inter-dealer quotation system sponsored and governed by FINRA, and the offering is not an initial public offering
90	Issuer is conducting an initial public offering

In addition, Rule 153 of the Securities Act provides an exemption from the prospectus delivery requirements of §5(b)(2) for sales to broker-dealers who are members of a registered national exchange, a FINRA trading facility, or an ATS. Rule 153 satisfies the "preceded by a prospectus" requirement in §5(b)(2) for transactions where §10(a) prospectuses have been delivered to the exchange, FINRA trading facility, or ATS for redelivery to its members (or subscribers) upon their request. Rule 153 applies to sales to members of a registered national exchange, FINRA trading facility, or an ATS occurring prior to 40 days after the effective date of the registration statement or the first date upon which the security was bona fide offered to the public, whichever is later. The availability of the Rule 153 exemption presumes that the registered national exchange, FINRA trading facility, or ATS has requested sufficient copies to meet its members' request and the issuer or underwriter has complied with all such requests. In addition, the registration statement filed with the SEC cannot be subject to a pending stop order proceeding or examination to determine whether a stop order should be issued, and neither the issuer, nor underwriter, or participating dealer can be subject to a pending cease-and-desist order.

ii. Free Writing or Supplemental Sales Literature

The federal securities laws permit supplemental sales literature, including broadcast media, or other "free writing" to be delivered to investors during the post-effective period, so long as it is accompanied or preceded by a §10(a) or final prospectus. Section 2(a)(10)(a) removes such free writing from the definition of prospectus even though it does not conform to a §10 prospectus. Accordingly, use of such material does not violate §5(b)(1). Free writing under §2(a)(10)(a) antedates free writing prospectuses, which were part of the 2005 Securities Offering Reform, and is excluded from the definition of a free writing prospectus in Rule 405. As such, there are no legend, filing, or record retention requirements for free writing. This means that broker-dealers, along with issuers, are permitted to send sales literature and other written communications to potential investors during the post-effective period as long as they include or are preceded by a § 10(a) prospectus. By definition, free writing under § 2(a)(10) is only permitted during the post-effective period. Despite the fact that the content of free writing is not restricted by rule or statute, it is subject to the anti-fraud provisions of the federal securities laws. Although Rules 138 and 139 exclude certain broker-dealer research reports from the prospectus requirements, FINRA Rule 2711 imposes a quiet period on such research reports if made by a broker-dealer acting as manager or co-manager, underwriter, or dealer of a public offering. Specifically, managers or co-managers of a public offering may not issue research reports or make public appearances on behalf of the issuer for 40 days following the date of offering of an initial public offering or for 10 days following the date of offering for a secondary offering; underwriters and dealers (excluding managers and co-managers) participating in an initial public offering are prohibited from issuing such research reports or making public appearances on behalf of the issuer for 25 days after an initial public offering.

iii. Confirmations

Section 5(b)(2) requires each broker-dealer participating in a public offering to provide each purchaser with a confirmation of sale that is accompanied by or preceded by a copy of the final § 10(a) prospectus. Without an exemption, this confirmation of sale would violate § 5(b)(1) of the Securities Act because it does not conform to a § 10 prospectus. Rule 172(a) of the Securities Act provides an exemption from the requirements of § 5(b)(1) for a confirmation of sale that contains only the information specified in Rule 10b-10 of the Exchange Act and notices provided pursuant to Rule 173 of the Securities Act. Rule 10b-10 information includes the date and time of the transaction; the identity, price, and number of shares sold; the broker-dealer's status in the transaction (i.e., whether it acts as agent or principal); and the broker-dealer's compensation for executing the transaction.

iv. Regulation M

Regulation M under the Exchange Act (Rules 100–105) governs the activities of underwriters, among others, in public offerings of securities to prevent price manipulation during the offering. Essentially, underwriters and the selling group must refrain from purchasing (or causing others to purchase) securities during the distribution in a manner that materially affects the price of the security. Regulation M only applies to a distribution of securities, which is defined broadly in Rule 100 as an offering of securities, whether or not subject to registration under the Securities Act, that is distinguished from ordinary trading transactions by the magnitude of the offering and the presence of special selling efforts and selling methods. Regulation M contains a general prohibition that states "it shall be unlawful for a distribution participant ... to bid for, purchase, or attempt to induce any person to bid for or purchase, a covered security during the applicable restricted period. A covered security means any security that is the subject of a distribution, or any reference security. The applicable restricted period is determined by the trading volume of the security and the issuer's public float. Restricted period means:

(1) For any security with an ADTV [average daily trading volume] value of $100,000 or more of an issuer whose common equity securities have a public float value of $25 million or more, the period beginning on the later of one business day prior to the determination of the offering price or such time that a person becomes a distribution participant, and ending upon such person's completion of participation in the distribution; and

(2) For all other securities, the period beginning on the later of five business days prior to the determination of the offering price or such time that a person becomes a distribution participant, and ending upon such person's completion of participation in the distribution ..."

Essentially, the restricted period for an IPO is between one business day before determining the offering price and the completion of participation in the distribution and, for all other types of offerings, begins five business days before determining the offering price.

ADTV is defined in Rule 100 to mean "the worldwide average daily trading volume during the two full calendar months immediately preceding, or any 60 consecutive calendar days ending within the 10 calendar days preceding, the filing of the registration statement ..." However, the SEC has not designated a source for determining ADTV. Instead, the offering participant must have a reasonable basis for believing that the source used is reliable. The SEC also has not specified the method for calculating ADTV, but has stated that the offering participant may use any reasonable and verifiable method.

The Issuer's public float must be determined in the manner set forth on the front page of Form 10–K as to the aggregate market value of common equity securities held by non-affiliates of the issuer. The instruction on the front page of Form 10-K requires the issuer to state the aggregate market value of the voting and non-voting common equity held by non-affiliates computed by reference to the price at which the common equity was last sold, or the average bid and asked price of the common equity, as of the last business day of the registrant's most recently completed second fiscal quarter. This definition applies even if the issuer is a non-reporting company.

There are several exceptions to compliance with Regulation M for the underwriter and selling group, which allow them to perform the activities required to conduct a public offering. First, the restrictions in Regulation M do not apply to actively traded equity securities. An actively traded equity security has an ADTV value of at least $1 million where the issuer's common equity securities have a public float value of at least $150 million. Regulation M also does not apply to exempt securities as defined in § 3(a)(12) [e.g., government securities such as U.S. Treasury bills). Moreover, transactions among the underwriting syndicate and between the underwriter and the issuer effected in connection with the public offering are exempt from the requirements of Regulation M; however, this exemption is only available if the transactions are not effected on a national registered securities exchange, through an inter-dealer quotation system, or through an ECN. In addition, research meeting the requirements of Rules 138 and 139 of the Securities Act is also exempt from the requirements of Regulation

M. Accordingly, members of the underwriting syndicate and selling group may continue, in the normal course of business, to distribute research reports regardless of whether the recipients of such research are customers or have previously received research from the broker-dealer.

Rule 105 of Regulation M prohibits, with some exceptions, any person from selling short a security that is the subject of a public offering and purchasing the security in the offering from an underwriter or broker-dealer participating in the offering, if such short sale was effected during a specified period before determination of the offering price. Specifically, the specified period is the shorter of the five business days before the offer price is determined or beginning with the initial filing of the registration statement and ending on the day when the offer price is determined. The SEC adopted Rule 105 to prevent artificial distortion of the market price for a security and to allow the market to function as an independent pricing mechanism. Exceptions to Rule 105 include bona fide purchases and offerings that are not conducted on a firm commitment basis.

FINRA Rule 5190 specifies notification requirements for complying with Regulation M. Broker-dealers acting as offering participants must notify FINRA of the commencement of the applicable restricted period (one or five business days) and the basis for their determination. They must also identify the distribution participants no later than the business day prior to the first complete trading session of the applicable restricted period. Broker-dealers are also required to notify FINRA about pricing, including the basis for pricing, no later than the close of business the next business day following the pricing of the distribution. If the broker-dealer determines that the security is actively traded and therefore not subject to a restricted period, it must notify FINRA and provide the basis for this determination. The broker-dealer must also notify FINRA of penalty bids and syndicate covering transactions (see section II.C. below) in connection with an offering of an OTC Equity Security prior to engaging in such activity. Generally, the managing underwriter submits notifications to FINRA.

v. The Closing

The closing is a formal meeting that occurs at the conclusion of the offering. It typically happens within three to four business days because Rule 15c6-1(c) of the Exchange Act permits the closing of firm commitment underwritings for cash to take place on the fourth business day after pricing, if pricing occurs after 4:30 P.M. Eastern Time. Attendees at the closing include the underwriters, counsel for the underwriters and the issuer, the auditor, the registrar, and the transfer agent. The underwriters pay for the securities sold in the offering and the issuer releases the securities certificates, unless the issuer uses a book entry system. Documents exchanged during the meeting include: (1) a legal opinion from the issuer's counsel that, among other things, states that the issuer is validly incorporate and in good standing and that counsel believes there is no misrepresentation or omission of a material fact in the registration statement; (2) a legal opinion from the underwriters' counsel as to the legality of the offering based on a limited investigation as to the accuracy of the registration statement; (3) certifications to the underwriters from certain of the issuer's senior officers that, among other things, there is no SEC stop order pending or threatened, the disclosures in the registration statement are true, and the representations and warrants of the issuer in the underwriting agreement are true; (4) a comfort letter from the auditor stating, among other things, that they are unaware of any material, adverse change in the issuer's financial condition or results of operations as set forth in the prospectus; and (5) any other documents requested by the attendees.

Notes and Questions

1. *Modified Dutch Auction.* A modified Dutch auction is a Dutch auction in which underwriters participate. In a Dutch auction the issuer accepts bids from potential investors and each bid lists a desired quantity of the security and the price that the investor is willing to pay for the security. The issuer evaluates the bids and sells its securities for the highest price at which it can sell all the securities in the offering ("the clearing price"). Each investor with an offer at or above the clearing price then receives its requested shares at the clearing price, which may be lower than other prices shown on the compiled bid list. A modified Dutch auction is one in which either an underwriter participates or the issuer has the option to decouple the offering price from the clearing price. The purpose of the Dutch auction is to provide equal access to potential investors and to alleviate concerns of underpricing an IPO. Google used a modified Dutch auction for its IPO in 2005: did it leave money on the table, i.e., sell its shares at a lower price than necessary to sell all of its shares? See https://www.sec.gov/Archives/edgar/data/1288776/000119312504073639/ds1.htm.

2. Regulation M, Rule 103, allows passive market making by broker-dealers offering participants with certain restrictions. 17 C.F.R. §242.103. Identify and describe these restrictions.

3. *Stabilization and Regulation M.* Rule 104 of Regulation M permits the underwriting syndicate and selling group to make bids or purchases of securities necessary to maintain the price of the security during the offering. This type of activity is defined in Rule 100 as stabilizing, i.e., the placing of any bid, or the effecting of any purchase, for the purpose of pegging, fixing, or otherwise maintaining the price of a security. However, stabilizing for manipulative purposes at a price resulting from unlawful activity is prohibited. In addition, the placing of more than one stabilizing bid in any one market at the same price at the same time is prohibited. Rule 104 permits a stabilizing bid to be initiated, maintained, reduced, or raised based on the current price in the principal market for the security, as long as the bid does not exceed the offering price of the security or a stabilizing bid in the principal market of the security. Identify policies that support the practice of permitting stabilization during public offerings.

4. *Over-Allotment Option.* An over-allotment option allows the underwriters to purchase additional shares in addition to the original commitment for a specified period after the registration statement becomes effective. The underwriters may need additional shares due to overselling the original commitment of shares, i.e., to cover a short position. The underwriters may exercise this option multiple times for up to 30 days after the registration statement is declared effective. The additional shares subject to the over-allotment option are included in the registration statement.

D. FINRA Regulation of Initial Public Offerings

FINRA Rules 5130, 5131, and 5141 regulate broker-dealer activities during the public offering process for new issues or initial public offerings of equity securities. FINRA Rule 5130 (Restrictions on the Purchase and Sale of Initial Equity Offerings) is designed to prohibit certain broker-dealer activities that adversely affect the integrity of the public offering process for IPOs of equity securities. FINRA Rule 5131 (New Issue Allocations and Distributions) specifically addresses broker-dealer abuses in the allocations and distributions of IPOs. FINRA Rule 5141 (Sale of Securities in a Fixed Priced Offering) generally prohibits broker-dealers that participate in fixed price offerings (securities offered at a stated public offering price) from offering or granting any securities from the offering below the public offering price to anyone other than the underwriting syndicate and selling group.

FINRA Rule 5130 attempts to protect the integrity of the public offering process for new issues or IPOs of equity securities by ensuring that broker-dealers make a bona fide public offering at the public offering price, do not withhold securities in a public offering for their own benefit and do not take advantage of their insider position at the expense of public investors. Accordingly, its prohibitions do not apply to the activities of the underwriting syndicate or the selling group that are incidental to conducting the IPO for new issues or initial equity public offerings. In general, FINRA Rule 5130 prohibits broker-dealers and their associated persons from selling a new issue in an IPO to an account in which certain restricted persons have a beneficial interest, a broker-dealer and its associated person have a beneficial interest, and from continuing to hold new issues acquired as an underwriter or member of a selling group, except as otherwise permitted under the Rule. A new issue is expressly defined in Rule 5130 as any IPO of an equity security defined in § 3(a)(11) of the Exchange Act (*See* Box 5.1 defining equity securities under Rule 5130) made pursuant to a registration statement or offering circular; Rule 5130 specifically excludes, among others, offerings of exempted securities (e.g., municipal securities), preferred securities, and registered investment companies (e.g. mutual funds).

Box 5.1. Equity Security Defined under FINRA Rule 5130
[§ 3(a)(11) of the Exchange Act].

The term equity security means any stock or similar security; or any security future on any such security; or any security convertible, with or without consideration, into such a security, or carrying any warrant or right to subscribe to or purchase such security; or any such warrant; or any other security which the [SEC] shall deem to be of similar nature and consider necessary or appropriate by such rules and regulations as it may prescribe in the public interest or for the protection of investors, to treat as an equity security.

The term *restricted person* under Rule 5130 is broad in scope and focuses on those participating in the public offering process that are in the best position to engage in abusive activities during the public offering process. Consequently, the definition of *restricted person* expressly includes broker-dealers, broker-dealer personnel and agents engaged in the investment banking or securities business, finders and fiduciaries, portfolio managers, the immediate family members of such entities and individuals, and persons owning more than 10 percent of a broker-dealer (*See* Box 5.2, Restricted Persons under Rule 5130). Rule 5130, in general, allows the issuer to make allocation decisions to restricted persons, other than broker-dealers and finders and fiduciaries for the managing underwriter, including accounts controlled by them or immediate family members. The goal is to remove any involvement or influence of broker-dealers and their finders and fiduciaries participating in IPOs of new issues of equity securities from the issuer's allocation decisions. In addition, the issuer is exempted from the prohibitions of Rule 5130 if it has a directed share program meeting the requirements specified in section d(3) of Rule 5130 (e.g., the class of participants do not include a disproportionate number of restricted persons).

Box 5.2. Restricted Persons. FINRA Rule 5130

— FINRA BD members or other BDs
— BD Personnel: Officer, director, agents, immediate family member (includes person's parents, in-laws, children, persons receiving/providing material support)
— Finders/fiduciaries, including immediate family members, of managing underwriter
— Portfolio managers and immediate family members
— Persons owning a BD: Any direct owner or executive officer that owns at least 10%; any indirect owner that owns at least 10%; any direct owner that owns at least 10% of an Exchange Act reporting company, not listed on an exchange; any indirect owner that owns at least 25% of an Exchange Act reporting company not listed on an exchange
— Any immediate family member of a person owning a BD unless person owning BD does not materially support/receive support from immediate family member; is not owner or Affiliate of BD selling new issue to immediate family member; and no ability to control the allocation of the new issue

---

In addition, Rule 5130 has other general exemptions to facilitate its focus on abusive practices in the purchase and sale and allocation of initial equity public offerings. These include preconditions for selling a new issue to any account and general exemptions for sales and purchases for specified accounts. Before selling a new issue to any account, the broker-dealer must in good faith have obtained a representation from the beneficial owner or a conduit (bank broker-dealer or investment adviser) of the account that it is eligible to purchase new issues in compliance with Rule 5130. Also, accounts generally exempted from compliance with Rule 5130 include investment companies registered with the SEC, insurance investment accounts, accounts organized under the Employee Retirement Income Security Act (ERISA), and tax-exempt charitable organization accounts organized under Section 501(c)(3) of the Internal Revenue Code.

FINRA Rule 5131 ("Rule 5131") identifies and prohibits specific abusive practices during the public offering process for new issues. The prohibited practices include quid pro quo allocations, spinning, flipping, and certain pricing and trading practices, including required terms for lock-up agreements. Rule 5131 prohibits quid pro quo allocations of a new issue by a broker-dealer as a means of obtaining excessive compensation from the recipient for other services provided by the broker-dealer. This prohibition applies to all services provided by the broker-dealer, including trading services. However, Rule 5131 is not intended to prohibit legitimate quid pro quo activities; that is, it is not intended to prohibit a broker-dealer from allocating new issue shares to a customer because the customer has separately retained the broker-dealer for other services as long as the customer has not paid excessive compensation in relation to the services provided. Spinning involves the allocation of shares of a new issue by the broker-dealer to any account in which an executive officer or director of an issuer or a person materially supported by such persons has a beneficial interest and is a current, former, or prospective investment banking client of the broker-dealer. Spinning is prohibited because FINRA believes that such allocations have the potential to divide the loyalty of the executive officers or directors (agents of the issuer) from the issuer (the principal) because executive officers or directors are often in a position to retain broker-dealers on behalf of the issuers that they serve. The spinning prohibitions do not apply to written issuer-directed allocation decisions in which broker-dealers have no involvement or influence, to certain types of accounts (e.g., ERISA, insurance companies, and investment companies registered with the SEC), and to accounts in which the beneficial interests of executive officers and directors of the issuer (including persons materially supported by such persons) in the aggregate do not exceed 25 percent of such accounts.

Rule 5131 also prohibits the unfair imposition of penalty bids by the managing underwriter against syndicate members whose customers engage in flipping. Flipping is the practice of selling new issues into the secondary market at a profit within 30 days following the offering date. The managing underwriter imposes penalty bids on syndicate members whose customers engage in flipping because such sales create downward pressure on the secondary market-trading price of the new issue. A penalty bid allows the managing underwriter to reclaim the selling concession for allocations to syndicate members whose customers engage in flipping. Consequently, underwriting agreements may contain a provision that imposes a penalty bid on syndicate members whose customers engage in flipping. According to FINRA, penalty bids, independent of underwriter-imposed syndicate penalty bids, are sought by some broker-dealers from their associated persons (registered representatives) when their customers flip a new issue and this practice has the potential of favoring institutional investors at the expense of retail investors. "FINRA believes that it is only appropriate for a firm to recoup a particular broker's compensation for selling a new issue in connection with a customer's decision to flip a security when the firm itself is required to forfeit its compensation to the managing underwriter(s)."[13] Rule 5131 prohibits any broker-dealer or persons associated with a broker-dealer from imposing penalty bids for flipping unless the managing underwriter of the new issue has assessed a penalty bid on the entire underwriting syndicate. Under Rule 5131 the broker-dealer is required to establish, maintain, and enforce policies and procedures reasonably designed to ensure that investment banking personnel of the broker-dealer have no involvement or influence in the broker-dealer's new allocation decisions.

Rule 5131 also focuses on certain pricing and trading prices that occur in new issue public offerings. The book-running lead manager of the underwriting syndicate must provide certain disclosures to the issuer's pricing committee, or its board of directors, to facilitate greater transparency about the demand for the issuer's securities during the public offering process. This disclosure requires regularly reporting indications of interest of institutional investors, along with their names and number of shares and the aggregate demand of retail investors. In addition, after settlement date, the book-running lead manager of the underwriting syndicate must submit a report detailing the final allocation of shares to institutional investors, including the names and number of shares purchased by each and the aggregate sales to retail investors.

Rule 5131 also requires that lock-up agreements that restrict the transfer of the issuer's shares by its officers and directors also include their issuer-directed shares. In addition, if such lock-up agreements are released or waived, the book-running lead managing underwriter must notify the issuer within two business days before the release or waiver and announce the impeding release or waiver through a major news service unless the shares are transferred without consideration and the new owner agrees to be bound by the same lock-up agreement. The agreement among underwriters must also include a provision that requires (to the extent not inconsistent with Regulation M of the Securities Act) any shares trading at a premium to the public offering price of a new issue that are returned to a syndicate member after secondary market trading begins be used to offset the existing syndicate short position or if no syndicate short position exists, the syndicate member must either: (1) offer returned shares at the public offering prince to unfilled customers' orders randomly

---

13. FINRA Regulatory Notice 10-60, *Approval of New Issue Rule* (November 2010).

or (2) sell the returned shares on the secondary market and donate the profits to an unaffiliated charitable organization anonymously. Without this requirement in the agreement among underwriters regarding returned shares for new issues trading at a premium to the IPO price, the syndicate member reallocating such shares would be able to confer an almost instantaneous and risk-free profit.

Finally, Rule 5131 prohibits broker-dealers from accepting a market order for the purchase of shares in a new issue before secondary market trading begins in order to protect investors against unreasonable increases in the price of the new issue in the secondary market. The absence of an established trading market allows for the potential of a wide variance between the public offering price and the price of the new issue when secondary market trading begins. Instead, investors are permitted to place limit orders prior to the commencement of trading of the new issue shares in the secondary trading market to guard against unreasonable variances between the public offering price and the secondary market price.

FINRA Rule 5141 ("Rule 5141") is designed to protect the integrity of fixed priced offerings and therefore applies to any public offering in addition to IPOs of new issues. Rule 5141 prohibits broker-dealers and their associated persons that participate in the distribution of a fixed price public offering from offering or granting any securities at a reduced price below the public offering price to anyone that is not a member of the underwriting syndicate or selling group. The term "fixed price offering" is defined in Rule 5141 to mean the offering of securities at a stated public offering price in a public offering, whether or not the offering is registered, but excludes public offerings of exempted securities, municipal securities, or redeemable shares of registered investment companies offered at prices determined by the net asset value of the securities (e.g., mutual funds). The term "reduced price" is defined broadly to encompass many forms of remuneration in exchange for securities in the offering. Accordingly, a reduced price may be obtained, among other ways, by awarding selling concessions, discounts or other allowances, credits, rebates, fee reductions, and sales of products or services below reasonable commercially available rates for similar products and services in exchange for securities in the offering. However, Rule 5141 does permit the purchase of research by selling securities in the public offering provided the person or account pays the stated public offering price for the securities and the research is provided pursuant to § 28(e) of the Exchange Act.[14]

---

14. Section 28(e)(3) of the Exchange Act defines the brokerage and research services that are protected. The statute states that a person provides brokerage and research services insofar as he —
(A) furnishes advice, either directly or through publications or writings, as to the value of securities, the advisability of investing in, purchasing, or selling securities, and the availability of securities or purchasers or sellers of securities;
(B) furnishes analyses and reports concerning issuers, industries, securities, economic factors and trends, portfolio strategy, and the performance of accounts; or
(C) effects securities transactions and performs functions incidental thereto (such as clearance, settlement, and custody) or required in connection therewith by rules of the Commission or a self-regulatory organization of which such person is a member or person associated with a member or in which such person is a participant.

Notes and Questions

1. FINRA Rules 5130 and 5110 require broker-dealers to file specified information with FINRA using its Distribution Manager. The Distribution Manager is an electronic filing platform designed to capture certain information about firm-commitment IPOs under Rules 5130 and 5110. The broker-dealer designated by the underwriting syndicate reports underwriting commitments and retentions on behalf of the underwriting syndicate. Specifically, the designated broker-dealer, among other things, is required to submit the names of the underwriters, the anticipated effective date, and retention information for each underwriter by completing the Initial Distribution Form (IDF) in the Distribution Manager. The designated broker-dealer must also submit the final list of distribution participants and their underwriting commitment and retention amounts no later than three business days after the offering date. This information is reviewed by the Corporate Financing Department at FINRA.

Hypothetical Three

Success First's IPO business continues to grow. Carmen is congratulating herself for hiring Alicia, who is doing a wonderful job in growing and managing Success First's IPO business. Success First has another new customer, Fells Point Luxury Cruises, Inc., ("Fells Point"), which needs capital to expand into a new market. Currently it offers Alaskan cruises, but now has an opportunity to break into the Caribbean market if sufficient funds can be raised to buy two new luxury cruise ships, approximately $30,000,000. Fells Point has decided to issue its securities to the public for the first time to raise the required capital and has selected Success First as its managing underwriter. The registration statement, prepared using Form S-1, has been filed with the SEC. Fells Point expects the SEC to declare the registration statement effective tomorrow. The prospectus includes a bona fide estimate of a maximum aggregate offering price of $7–$10 per share. The SEC declares the registration statement effective and Success First determines that the price at which Fells Point will be able to sell its securities is $6 per share. Will Fells Point have to file a pricing amendment to the prospectus? Review Securities Act Rules 430A and 424(b).

Chapter 6

Broker-Dealer Civil Liability in Public Offerings[1]

Regulatory Authority

Securities Act of 1933 Sections 11, 12(a)(1), 12(a)(2)

Securities Act Rules 159, 159A, 176, 436

Motivating Hypothetical

Although extremely pleased with the substantial increase in Success First's IPO business and with Alicia's management, Success First's board of directors ("BOD") is concerned about increasing litigation costs resulting from its IPO business. Josephine Wise, a director and Success First's general counsel, is especially concerned about what she believes to be a steady increase in litigation in connection with Success First's IPO business. The number of IPOs in which Success First acted as managing underwriter, or participated in the underwriting syndicate, has grown from 50 last year to 100 this year, an astonishing increase of 100 percent. Success First acted as managing underwriter in 25 of last year's IPOs and in 75 of this year's IPOs. However, of the 25 IPOs in which Success First acted as managing underwriter (solely responsible for conducting due diligence for the underwriting syndicate) last year there have been four lawsuits alleging violations of §§ 11, 12(a)(1) and 12(a)(2) of the Securities Act. All four of these lawsuits were resolved in favor of Success First on motions to dismiss. Of the 75 IPOs in which Success First acted as managing underwriter this year, seven lawsuits have been filed alleging violations of §§ 11, 12(a)(1) and 12(a)(2). So far, five of these lawsuits have been resolved in favor of Success First on motions to dismiss. However, two of the lawsuits survived Success First's motions to dismiss. Although discovery is ongoing, Josephine is quite concerned because she believes that at this point the probability of these actions being resolved in favor of Success First is low. Josephine and Carmen (director and CEO of Success First) are concerned about whether the quality of Success First's performance of its due diligence obligations

---

1. Broker-dealer civil liability under § 17 of the Securities Act is examined in Chapter 10, which covers broker-dealer fraud under the anti-fraud provisions of the federal securities laws. It is not covered in this chapter because there is no implied private right of action under § 17. *See, e.g., Barnes v. Resource Royalties, Inc.,* 795 F.2d 1359, 1365, fn.7 (8th Cir. 1986), *cert. denied sub nom.,* McPherson v. Barnes, 493 U.S. 1077 (1990).

411

contributed significantly to the initiation of the two lawsuits that survived Success First's motions to dismiss. The BOD has directed Josephine to analyze these two lawsuits and determine why Success First was not successful in its motions to dismiss. She has been directed to prepare a written report to the BOD that includes an analysis of Success First's current policies and procedures governing the performance of its due diligence obligations. The BOD believes that the quality of Success First's due diligence is an integral component in the resolution of lawsuits alleging violations of §§ 11, 12(a)(1), and 12(a)(2). Although the BOD understands that lawsuits are inevitable in the IPO business, it would like to increase Success First's percentage of success in favorably resolving these types of actions on motions to dismiss. Josephine believes that establishing, implementing, and monitoring supervisory and operational policies and procedures for the due diligence process when Success First acts as managing underwriter will significantly reduce the probability that Success First will be sued for material misrepresentations and omissions in the registration statement and increase the probability of motions to dismiss in such lawsuits being resolved in favor of Success First.

I. Introduction

This chapter explores the broker-dealer's civil liability in public offerings under §§ 11 and 12 of the Securities Act. Sections 11 and 12 allow the purchaser-investor to sue the broker-dealer for material misstatements or omissions made in connection with public offerings, as well as failure to conduct a public offering in compliance with the provisions of § 5 of the Securities Act. This means that there is a private right of action under §§ 11 and 12. In addition, only the civil liability of the broker-dealer will be discussed, even though § 11 expressly identifies other possible defendants along with the broker-dealer. These provisions work together to incentivize the broker-dealer to ensure that investors obtain the information required to make an informed investment decision by holding them accountable for failing to do so.

II. Section 11

Section 11 of the Securities Act imposes civil liability on broker-dealers acting as underwriters for material misrepresentations and omissions contained in a registration statement, which has been declared effective by the SEC. Unlike other antifraud provisions under the federal securities laws, § 11 expressly identifies broker-dealers participating as underwriters in a public offering as defendants. Specifically, § 11 permits a purchaser of securities to sue underwriters for material misrepresentations and omissions in a registration statement that has been declared effective. Although § 11 is an antifraud provision, it does not require proof of scienter. Consequently, liability may be imposed on the underwriter for unintentional or negligent material misrepresentations or omissions. In fact, as discussed later in this chapter, there are relatively few elements required to establish a cause of action under § 11. However, the seemingly broad scope of a cause of action based on § 11 is limited by the requirements that investors, or purchasers of securities, must meet to bring suit under § 11, i.e., to obtain standing to sue.

A. Standing

Section 11 requires the plaintiff to trace the securities purchased to a specific registration statement that has been declared effective in order to obtain standing to sue. This means that the investor must show that the specific shares he purchased were sold as part of the public offering under the registration statement that contained the material misrepresentation or omission. Although the first of the following two cases does not identify a broker-dealer as a defendant, both of these cases illustrate how the standing requirement of § 11 may limit its usefulness as an antifraud tool for investors, especially in the secondary market. As you read these cases, consider whether the courts' interpretation of the phrase "any person acquiring such security" has reduced the effectiveness of § 11 as an antifraud provision.

Hertzberg v. Dignity Partners
191 F.3d 1076 (9th Cir. 1999)

W. FLETCHER, Circuit Judge

* * *

BACKGROUND

On February 14, 1996, Dignity filed a registration statement for an initial public offering of approximately 2.7 million shares of common stock. Hertzberg asserts, on behalf of a class of persons who purchased Dignity stock between February 14, 1996, and July 16, 1996, that the registration statement contained materially false and misleading statements and omitted material facts. He seeks damages under Section 11 as well as under other provisions of the federal securities laws.

Dignity was in the business of making "viatical settlements." It purchased the rights to the proceeds of life insurance policies from individuals with terminal illnesses, and in exchange paid lump sums to the individuals and assumed responsibility for payment of premiums. The amounts Dignity paid to the individuals were based on their estimated life expectancies, and the profits Dignity received depended on the accuracy of those estimates. Nearly all of the individuals from whom Dignity purchased its rights had AIDS.

By 1995, new drugs and treatments for AIDS became available, and many of the individuals with whom Dignity had contracted began to live longer than expected. Hertzberg alleges that, as a consequence, the value of Dignity's business was in jeopardy because it could not collect the life insurance proceeds as rapidly as expected, it had to pay premiums for longer periods than expected, and it could no longer estimate with accuracy the life expectancy of the persons with whom it contracted.

Hertzberg alleges that the owners of this privately held company saw the prospect of their entire investment disappearing and decided to liquidate much of their holding by taking the company public. According to Hertzberg, the financial statements in Dignity's registration statement were misleading because they misrepresented the true worth of the business. Hertzberg alleges that shortly before the offering Dignity adopted the accrual method of accounting, under which Dignity counted the potential proceeds from a particular policy as income as soon as it purchased the rights, rather than when it actually received the proceeds. Hertzberg further alleges that this new accounting method was misleading because it hid the facts that Dignity was taking longer to collect on those policies and that Dignity could no longer accurately estimate when individuals would die. Finally, Hertzberg alleges that Dignity violated Section 11 by failing to disclose its inability to make accurate estimations of life expectancies, the "adverse trends" experienced in 1995, and the fact that its accrual ... accounting method did not comport with Generally Accepted Accounting Principles.

After the facts concerning the lengthened life expectancies for AIDS patients became public knowledge, Dignity's stock fell from the initial offering price of $ 12 a share to about $ 6. In June of 1995, less that five months after the beginning of the initial public offering, Dignity announced an anticipated quarterly loss of $ 10 million, and a month later announced that it would abandon the viatical settlement business. As a result of these announcements, the stock fell to $ 1 a share before settling at about $ 2 at the time the action was filed.

Dignity moved to dismiss Hertzberg's Section 11 claims because the named plaintiffs had not purchased their shares "in" the registered offering. The district court, ruling from the bench, held that because the named plaintiffs purchased their stock more than 25 days after the registration statement was filed, they did not have standing to bring an action under Section 11. It therefore dismissed their Section 11 claims.

* * *

[W]e reverse.

DISCUSSION

We review the district court's interpretation of Section 11 *de novo* ... Section 11(a) provides that where a material fact is misstated or omitted from a registration statement accompanying a stock filing with the Securities and Exchange Commission, "any person acquiring such security" may bring an action for losses caused by the misstatement or omission. The district court read this phrase as if it had been written, "any person acquiring such security *on the first day of an initial public offering or in the twenty-five day period thereafter.*" This reading adds a significant limitation not found in the original text.... The limitation on "any person" is that he or she must have purchased "such security." Clearly, this limitation only means that the person must have purchased a security issued under that, rather than some other, registration statement. *See Barnes v. Osofsky*, 373 F.2d 269 (2d Cir. 1967). While it might present a problem of proof in a case in which stock was issued under more than one registration statement, the only Dignity stock ever sold to the public was pursuant to the allegedly misleading registration statement at issue in this case. Thus, as long as Hertzberg is suing regarding this security, he is "any person purchasing such security," regardless of whether he bought in the initial offering, a week later, or a month after that.

* * *

Other circuits that have addressed this issue agree with our reading of the text and have uniformly allowed for recovery by purchasers in the aftermarket. *Versyss Inc. v. Coopers and Lybrand*, 982 F.2d 653, 657 (1st Cir. 1992), *cert. denied*, 508 U.S. 974, 125 L. Ed. 2d 665, 113 S. Ct. 2965 (1993) (Section 11 "is remarkably stringent where it applies, readily imposing liability on ancillary parties to the registration statement (like accountants) for the benefit *even of purchasers after the original offering*") (emphasis added); *Barnes, supra*, 373 F.2d 269 (2d Cir. 1967); *Columbia General Inv. Corp. v. SEC*, 265 F.2d 559, 562 (5th Cir. 1959) ("Persons other than those who purchase the new stock under the Registration may be affected in point of fact and may, under certain circumstances, have remedies in point of law for misrepresentations in a Registration").…

However, we note that even if we were to find the wording of the statute ambiguous, the legislative history supports Hertzberg's reading of Section 11.

The House Report accompanying the version of the bill that ultimately became the Securities Act of 1933 provides:

> the civil remedies accorded by [Section 11] are given to all purchasers … regardless of whether they bought their securities *at the time of the original offer or at some later date*, provided, of course, that the remedy is prosecuted within the period of limitations provided by section 13.

H.R. Rep. No. 73-85, at 22 (emphasis added). By expressly referring to purchasers who bought their securities "at some later date" other than "at the time of the original offer," the Report makes it clear that purchasers in the aftermarket are intended to have a cause of action under the Section. Similarly, when Congress amended Section 11 in 1934 to add a requirement of proof of reliance on the registration statement if there had been an intervening earning statement, the House Report stated:

> The basis of this provision is that in all likelihood the purchase and price of the security purchased after publication of such an earning[sic] statement will be predicated upon that statement rather than upon the information disclosed upon registration.

H.R. Rep 73-1838 at 41. By referring to purchases after publication of an earning statement, the Report makes clear that purchasers in the aftermarket are within the group of purchasers provided a cause of action by Section 11.… Dignity also cites pieces of the legislative history that show Congress meant Section 11 to deal with new offerings of securities. But that issue has never been in dispute. As discussed above, all the stock ever publicly issued by Dignity was sold in the single offering at issue in this case. The difficulties of tracing stock to a particular offering present in some cases are thus not present here.

* * *

REVERSED AND REMANDED.

———

Krim v. pcOrder.com

402 F.3d 489 (5th Cir. 2005)

Patrick E. Higginbotham, Circuit Judge:

Investors who purchased stock in pcOrder.com brought this consolidated securities action under Section[ ]11 ... of the Securities Act of 1933 against defendants pcOrder.com, its directors, its controlling shareholder Trilogy Software, and its investment bankers (collectively "PCOrder"), alleging that the registration statements filed with the Securities and Exchange Commission were false and misleading. The district court concluded that, with one exception, the investors lacked Section 11 standing because they could not trace their stock to the registration statements in question.... We affirm.

I

PcOrder conducted an initial public offering of pcOrder.com stock on February 26, 1999, and a secondary public offering on December 7, 1999. In connection with each offering PCOrder filed a registration statement with the SEC.

Several holders of pcOrder.com stock filed multiple lawsuits against PCOrder under Section 11 of the Securities Act of 1933, which provides a right of action to "any person acquiring" shares issued pursuant to an untrue registration statement. The plaintiffs alleged that the registration statements were false and misleading by indicating that pcOrder.com had a viable business plan, had an ability to generate and report accurate operating and financial information, and was not competing with Trilogy Software for revenue. The district court consolidated the actions and appointed Lead Plaintiffs. The Lead Plaintiffs sought to have a class action certified and have themselves designated as class representatives.

In its October 21, 2002, order denying class certification, the district court first found that none of the Lead Plaintiffs purchased their stock during the public offerings — that is, they were "aftermarket" purchasers.[2] However, it held that Section 11 is available not only to those who purchased their stock during the relevant public offerings, but also to aftermarket purchasers as long as the stock is "traceable" back to the relevant public offering.

The district court then considered whether Lead Plaintiffs Beebe, Dr. Burke, and Petrick could trace their stock back to either of the two public offerings. The district court found that the approximately 2.5 million shares issued in the pcOrder.com IPO were registered in a stock certificate in the name of Cede & Co., the nominee of the

———

2. [4] The "aftermarket," also termed the "secondary market," is the "securities market in which previously issued securities are traded among investors." Black's Law Dictionary 990 (8th ed. 2004).

Depository Trust Company. The court found that, on April 19, 1999, when Beebe purchased 1000 of these "street name" shares, the pool of street name stock still contained only the IPO stock. Therefore, because all of his stock was *necessarily* IPO stock, Beebe was able to satisfy the traceability requirement and establish standing.

In contrast, the court concluded that standing was lacking for Dr. Burke and Petrick. By the end of June 1999 when Dr. Burke purchased 3000 shares, the court found that non-IPO shares—specifically, insider shares—had entered the street name certificate and intermingled with the IPO shares, but that IPO shares still comprised 99.85% of the pool. Subsequent to the December 7, 1999, secondary public offering, Dr. Burke made additional purchases and Petrick also purchased a number of shares at a time when IPO and SPO shares (collectively "PO stock") constituted 91% of the market. Appellants' expert acknowledged that there is no way to track individual shares within a pool once it becomes contaminated with outside shares.

In light of the intermingling of PO and non-PO stock in the market at the time of their purchases—even though PO stock was the overwhelming majority—the district court held that Dr. Burke and Petrick could not demonstrate that their shares were traceable to the public offering registration statements. In reaching this conclusion, the court considered expert testimony indicating that, given the number of shares owned by each Lead Plaintiff and the percentage of PO stock in the market, the probability that each Lead Plaintiff owned at least one share of PO stock was very nearly 100%. However, the court held that this did not satisfy the traceability requirement because the "Lead Plaintiffs must demonstrate *all* stock for which they claim damages was actually issued pursuant to a defective statement, not just that it might have been, probably was, or most likely was, issued pursuant to a defective statement." The district court noted that, "otherwise, 'all persons who held stock in street name on and after the offering date could claim a proportional interest in the shares.'"

Having found that Dr. Burke and Petrick lacked Section 11 standing, the court concluded that they could not serve as class representatives and denied class certification.... The court then dismissed Beebe's claim as moot because PcOrder had offered Beebe a settlement equal to his full recovery under the statute. Having disposed of the suits, the district court ... entered final judgment in favor of PcOrder.

Appellants challenge the district court's rulings regarding standing ...

III

A.

Appellants argue that Dr. Burke, Mrs. Burke, and Petrick can establish Section 11 standing by proffering nothing more than statistics indicating a high mathematical probability, based on the number of shares purchased by each individual and the number of PO shares in the market, that at least some of their shares were issued pursuant to the challenged registration statement. We disagree

We turn first to the language of the statute. In general, the Securities Act of 1933 ("Securities Act") "is concerned with the initial distribution of securities." Section 11 of the Securities Act, imposing civil liability for public offering of securities pursuant to a false registration statement, permits "any person acquiring such security" to sue. While Section 11's liability provisions are expansive—creating "virtually absolute" liability for corporate issuers for even innocent material misstatements—its standing provisions limit putative plaintiffs to the "narrow class of persons" consisting of "those who purchase securities that are the direct subject of the prospectus and registration statement."

In *Rosenzweig v. Azurix Corp.*, we recently held that aftermarket purchasers do not inevitably lack standing. The district court here foreshadowed this in holding that Section 11's "language suggests a much broader class of potential plaintiffs than those who literally purchased their shares in the challenged offering." Indeed, the plain language of the statute confers standing on "any person acquiring such security," and there is no reason to categorically exclude aftermarket purchasers, " 'so long as the security was indeed issued under *that* registration statement and not another.' " As such, aftermarket purchasers seeking standing must demonstrate the ability to "trace" their shares to the faulty registration. As one court explained:

> To be able to take advantage of the lower burden of proof and almost strict liability available under §11, a plaintiff must meet higher procedural standards. The most significant of the procedural standards is the requirement that a plaintiff be able to trace the security for which damages are claimed to the specific registration statement at issue.

In *Rosenzweig*, we further held that this traceability requirement is satisfied, as a matter of logic, when stock has only entered the market via a single offering. We did not speculate on what other methods might be available to satisfy the traceability requirement for aftermarket purchases, but we were careful to note the Supreme Court's concern "that the Securities Act remain anchored to its original purpose of regulating only public offerings."

Appellants, as aftermarket purchasers, assert that they can also demonstrate standing by showing a very high probability that they each have at least one PO share. Appellants argue that their statistical determinations, being over 50%, demonstrate by a preponderance of the evidence, that it is "more likely than not," that their shares are traceable to the public offerings in question.

We are persuaded that accepting such "statistical tracing" would impermissibly expand the statute's standing requirement. Because any share of pcOrder.com stock chosen at random in the aftermarket has at least a 90% chance of being tainted, its holder, according to Appellants' view, would have Section 11 standing. In other words, *every* aftermarket purchaser would have standing for every share, despite the language of Section 11, limiting suit to "any person acquiring *such* security." As the district court found, it is "likely that any street name shareholder can make a similar claim with regard to *one* share." This cannot be squared with the statutory language—that is, with what Congress intended. We decline the invitation to reach further than the statute.

The fallacy of Appellants position is demonstrated with the following analogy. Taking a United States resident at random, there is a 99.83% chance that she will be from somewhere other than Wyoming. Does this high statistical likelihood alone, assuming for whatever reason there is no other information available, mean that she can avail herself of diversity jurisdiction in a suit against a Wyoming resident? Surely not.

In limiting those who can sue to "any person acquiring such security," Congress specifically conferred standing on a *subset* of security owners (unless of course, as in *Rosenzweig*, all shares in the market are PO shares). To allow Appellants to satisfy the tracing requirement for aftermarket standing in this case with the proffered statistical methodology would contravene the language and intent of Section 11....

Appellants point out that, given the fungible nature of stocks within a street name certificate, it is virtually impossible to differentiate PO shares from non-PO shares.

However, as we have explained, Section 11 *is* available for anyone who purchased directly in the offering and any aftermarket purchasers who can demonstrate that their shares are traceable to the registration statement in question—*e.g.* when, as with Beebe, there had only been one offering at the time of purchase. When Congress enacted the Securities Act of 1933 it was not confronted with the widespread practice of holding stock in street name that Appellants describe as an impediment, absent our acceptance of statistical tracing, to invoking Section 11. That present market realities, given the fungibility of stock held in street name, may render Section 11 ineffective as a practical matter in some aftermarket scenarios is an issue properly addressed by Congress. It is not within our purview to rewrite the statute to take account of changed conditions. In the words of one court, Appellants' arguments may "have the sound ring of economic reality but unfortunately they merely point up the problems involved in the present scheme of statutory regulation."

In *Barnes v. Osofsky*, the Second Circuit confronted an intermingled stock pool not unlike the one we face today. In that case, two individuals challenged the settlement of a class action alleging Section 11 violations in a secondary public offering. The challengers, who purchased stock after the SPO, were unable to trace a portion of their shares to the SPO as opposed to the preexisting shares on the market. They objected to a provision of the settlement "limiting the benefits of the settlement to persons who could establish that they purchased securities issued" in the SPO. The court was not deterred by the reality that this "eliminated those who purchased after the issuance of the allegedly incomplete prospectus but could not so trace their purchases," because Section 11 "extends only to purchases of the newly registered shares." While not addressing the question before us today, *Barnes* is nonetheless instructive.

Plaintiffs in that case urged a broad reading of Section 11 to cover anyone purchasing stock after the SPO—whether or not it was traceable to the SPO. Not unlike the concerns expressed by Appellants in the instant case, the plaintiffs in *Barnes* argued as follows:

> Once it is agreed that § 11 is not limited to the original purchasers, to read that section as applying only to purchasers who can *trace the lineage* of their shares to the new offering makes the result turn on mere accident since most

trading is done through brokers who neither know nor care whether they are getting [tainted] or [clean] shares.... It is often impossible to determine whether previously traded shares are [clean] or [tainted], and that tracing is further complicated when stock is held in margin accounts in street names since many brokerage houses do not identify specific shares with particular accounts but instead treat the account as having an undivided interest in the house's position.

The court rejected these arguments and rejected the plaintiffs' broad reading of Section 11's standing requirement as "inconsistent with the over-all statutory scheme" and "contrary to the legislative history." The same is true of Appellants' view today.

* * *

Congress conferred standing on those who *actually* purchased the tainted stock, not on the whole class of those who *possibly* purchased tainted shares — or, to put it another way, are at risk of having purchased tainted shares ... Appellants here cannot meet the statutory standing requirement of Section 11 merely by showing that they jumped into a potentially polluted "pool" of stock.

Unquestionably, principles of probability are powerful tools, when deployed in appropriate tasks. Unquestionably, the statistics in this case indicate a high probability that a person purchasing a given number of shares will obtain at least one tainted share. However, these general statistics say nothing about the shares that a specific person *actually* owns and have no ability to separate those shares upon which standing can be based from those for which standing is improper. The task before the district court was to determine, by a preponderance of the evidence, whether and in what amount a plaintiff's shares are tainted, not whether the same number of shares drawn at random would likely include at least one tainted share. Understood in this light, statistical tracing is not up to the task at hand.

In sum, aftermarket purchasers seeking Section 11 standing must demonstrate that their shares are traceable to the challenged registration statement. We are not persuaded that the statistical tracing method advanced today is sufficient to satisfy this traceability requirement.

Notes and Questions

1. Both *Hertzberg* and *Krim* conclude that a purchaser of securities in the aftermarket is not precluded from obtaining standing to sue under § 11. The term *aftermarket* describes the secondary market, which is the securities market in which previously issued securities are traded among investors. Why is it more difficult for the purchaser to establish standing when an issuer has conducted both initial and secondary public offerings?

2. *Krim* notes that the practice of holding stock in street name has become widespread. Has this practice diminished the effectiveness of § 11 as an antifraud tool for investors against broker-dealers?

Hypothetical One

Success First acted as lead underwriter in the initial public offering of JustGo.com in June 2015. It also acted as lead underwriter in a public offering of JustGo.com's shares in January 2016. Unfortunately, neither of the registration statements used in connection with the June 2015 and January 2016 offerings disclosed that JustGo.com's CEO, Henry James, was convicted of drunk driving in Atlanta, Georgia, in May 2015. Elaine Smith purchased 1,000 shares of JustGo.com through Success First on February 1, 2016. Elaine's shares are held in street name. This means that her securities are held through her broker-dealer, Success First, therefore, she does not own the actual physical securities, but rather, she owns a securities entitlement in the aggregate number of shares of JustGo.com or fungible bulk, controlled by Success First. Jane wants to sue Success First along with the issuer under § 11 because JustGo.com's registration statements for both offerings contained a material omission. Can Elaine establish that she has standing in connection with either or both of the JustGo.com's public offerings?

B. Elements of a § 11 Cause of Action

Section 11 imposes strict liability for fraud against broker-dealers acting as underwriters in public offerings without requiring the establishment of certain traditional elements when alleging securities fraud. For example, proof of scienter and causation is not required. In addition, the plaintiff does not have the burden of proving reliance on a material misrepresentation or omission unless the issuer has made public an earnings statement covering a period of at least 12 months beginning after the effective date of the registration statement. In summary, the plaintiff is not required to prove scienter, fraud, or negligence by the seller, nor is the plaintiff required to establish that he relied on the misrepresentation or omission or that his loss was a direct result of the misrepresentation or omission. Specifically, section 11 requires establishing the following elements:

1. An effective registration statement (i.e., a registration statement filed with, and declared effective by, the SEC);

2. The purchaser of the security must trace the security to a registration statement;

3. The registration statement must contain a misstatement or omission (where there is a duty to disclose); and

4. The misstatement must be material (materiality is discussed in Chapter 12 and is defined in *TSC Industries, Inc. v. Northway,* 426 U.S. 438 (1976) as the existence of a "substantial likelihood that the disclosure [or omission] … would have been viewed by the reasonable investor as having significantly altered the 'total mix' of information made available.").

Material misstatements and omissions in the registration statement are determined as of the date that the SEC declares the registration statement effective. However, different parts of the registration statement may have different effective dates and therefore different dates on which liability under § 11 commences, i.e., § 11 imposes liability on "any part of the registration statement when that part became effective." For example, filing a post-effective amendment to the registration statement establishes a new effective date under § 11 for the information contained in the amendment, thereby increasing liability exposure. In many cases, the part of the registration statement requiring amendment is the prospectus, which is made in the form of a prospectus supplement filed with the SEC after the initial effective date. This prospectus supplement is considered part of the registration statement and resets the effective date for the part of the registration statement to which the prospectus supplement relates. Moreover, a broker-dealer that becomes an underwriter in a public offering after the registration statement has been declared effective is only liable under § 11 as of the date it became an underwriter; it does not have § 11 liability as of the effective date of the registration statement.

In addition, plaintiff's success in bringing a § 11 claim may be adversely affected by the special pleading requirements of fraud actions brought under the federal securities laws despite the fact that it imposes strict liability for innocent and/or negligent conduct. The Private Securities Litigation Reform Act of 1995 (PSLRA) requires plaintiffs to plead securities fraud allegations with particularity. This means that plaintiffs must, among other things, state the facts constituting the alleged securities fraud violations and the facts evidencing scienter, i.e., the defendants' intent to defraud. Typically, because § 11 claims do not require proof of scienter, the heightened pleading requirements of the PSLRA are inapplicable. Instead, pleadings in § 11 complaints only need to satisfy the notice pleading standard in FRCP 8(a). However, if the pleadings in a § 11 claim "sound in fraud," the plaintiff may be subject to the heightened pleading requirements of FRCP Rule 9(b). Although not as stringent as the heightened pleading requirements of the PSLRA, Rule FRCP 9(b) requires § 11 claims that sound in fraud to state with particularity the circumstances constituting fraud or mistake, but malice, intent, and other conditions of a person's mind (e.g., scienter) may be alleged generally. Courts are not always clear on the meaning of *sound in fraud*, but many make this determination by assessing whether the plaintiff alleges an intent to defraud. The following case discusses these issues along with the difficulties in bringing a successful § 11 claim against broker-dealers in the context of a motion to dismiss.

———

In re Ariad Pharms., Inc. Secs. Litig.

2015 U.S. Dist. LEXIS 36818

WILLIAM G. YOUNG, United States District Judge.

MEMORANDUM AND ORDER

I. INTRODUCTION

This is a shareholder class action brought by Joseph Bradley, the City of Fort Lauderdale Police & Fire Retirement System, Pension Trust Fund for Operating Engineers and Automotive Industries Pension Trust Fund, and William A. Gaul, D.M.D. (collectively, "the Lead Plaintiffs"), on behalf of themselves and all similarly-situated shareholders, against ARIAD Pharmaceuticals, Inc. ("ARIAD"), several officers and directors of ARIAD (Chief Executive Officer Harvey Berger, Chief Financial Officer Edward Fitzgerald, Chief Medical Officer Frank Haluska, and Chief Scientific Officer Timothy Clackson) ("the Individual Defendants," together with ARIAD, the "ARIAD Defendants"), and seven underwriters. The underwriter defendants are J.P. Morgan Securities LLC, Cowen and Company, LLC, Jefferies & Company, Inc., BMO Capital Markets Corp., Leerink Swann LLC, RBC Capital Markets, LLC, and UBS Securities LLC (collectively, "the Underwriters").

The Lead Plaintiffs bring this proposed class action on behalf of themselves and all other persons or entities who purchased or acquired (1) any publicly-traded ARIAD securities between December 12, 2011 and October 30, 2013 (the "Class Period"), or (2) any of ARIAD's common stock pursuant or traceable to the secondary offering that occurred on or about January 24, 2013 ("2013 Stock Offering") and were damaged thereby. They allege that the ARIAD Defendants made a series of false and misleading statements and omissions in regards to the safety, efficacy, and commercial prospects of ARIAD's main product, a cancer medication called ponatinib, which is used to treat chronic myeloid leukemia. As a result of these statements and omissions, the Lead Plaintiffs allege that the price of ARIAD common stock traded at artificially high values, while ARIAD concealed the full extent of adverse events arising from their clinical trials. Arguing that the Individual Defendants knew the full extent of the negative results stemming from the ongoing clinical trials, the Lead Plaintiffs ... bring a claim against the ARIAD Defendants and the Underwriters under Section 11 of the Securities Act of 1933 ("Section 11") for alleged misstatements and omissions in stock offering materials.

The ARIAD Defendants and the Underwriters seek dismissal of all claims against them.

* * *

B. Facts Alleged[3]

ARIAD is a biotechnology company based in Cambridge, Massachusetts, specializing in the development and sale of cancer drugs. For several years, the company primarily has focused on developing the drug ponatinib, also known as Iclusig, as a treatment for chronic myeloid leukemia ("CML"). In particular, ARIAD focused on developing a front-line drug to compete with existing drugs to treat CML, noting that front-line drugs are more lucrative products than second-line drugs (explaining that front-line drugs "typically outsell second-line treatments by many orders of magnitude"). In the course of seeking approval by the U.S. Food and Drug Administration

---

3. [1] The factual pleadings were divided into two parts, the first relating to the Exchange Act claims and the second relating to Section 11 claims.... The complaint is structured as two independent parts, and the second part contains no statements incorporating by reference any statements from the first part of the complaint. The analysis and conclusions regarding the Section 11 claims are based solely on the pleadings made in the second part of the complaint. The facts relevant to both sets of claims are summarized in this section.

("FDA"), ARIAD commenced a clinical trial on September 13, 2010, referred to by the parties as the PACE 2 trials. The trial was "designed to assess the efficacy and safety of ponatinib in a larger subject group" consisting of "second-line" CML patients, meaning those with a demonstrated resistance to other, more established treatments. The PACE 2 protocol provided for 449 test subjects to be treated with a recommended daily dose of 45 milligrams of the drug. Seeking funding for their ongoing clinical trials, ARIAD held its first of two stock offerings in December 2011, raising $258,000,000.

On June 4, 2012, ARIAD announced favorable interim results at a medical conference, citing "clear evidence of a favorable safety and tolerability profile in ponatinib in resistant or intolerant CML patients." ARIAD also submitted an interim report to the FDA containing data through the end of July 2012 (the "July 2012 Interim Report"). The results of this interim report documented adverse cardiovascular events in test subjects, including the incidence of "serious arterial thrombosis" in eight percent of patients.

Shortly after the submission of the July 2012 Interim Report, ARIAD began a new clinical trial (the "EPIC" trial), which "was designed to support FDA approval of ponatinib in newly-diagnosed, never-treated CML patients, a.k.a. 'front-line' CML." The prescribed dosage for the EPIC trial was also 45 milligrams daily.

On December 14, 2012, ARIAD filed a Form 8-K and announced in a press release that the FDA had granted accelerated approval to market ponatinib for second-line use (noting that the FDA relied on and publicized the data evinced in the July 2012 Interim Report). This press release included the list of serious adverse events that had occurred, including an eight percent occurrence of "serious arterial thrombosis" and four percent occurrence of serious congestive heart failure, with four fatalities. The FDA's approval was conditioned on two requirements: first, that each bottle of ponatinib include a "black box" warning label disclosing the occurrence of serious adverse cardiovascular events in users, and second, that ARIAD submit follow-up PACE 2 data to the FDA. A "black box" warning is the strongest warning level for a prescription drug under FDA guidelines. The same day as the press release, ARIAD's share price fell twenty-one percent.

One month later, ARIAD conducted a public secondary offering of common stock ("the Offering") on January 24, 2013, with the intention that the proceeds of the Offering be earmarked for developing and manufacturing ponatinib. In connection with the Offering, the Underwriters prepared materials, including a prospectus supplement, to accompany existing materials such as a shelf registration statement, a prospectus, and a number of SEC filings (collectively, "the Offering Materials"). ARIAD issued 15,307,000 shares in the Offering and raised $310,000,000.

In August 2013, ARIAD submitted follow-up data from the PACE 2 trials to the FDA. The new data, which covered the trial period from August 2012 to August 2013, "showed [among other things] that the rate of serious arterial thrombosis associated with ponatinib had increased from 8 [percent] to 11.8 [percent] in the time since" July 2012.

Two months later, ARIAD announced that the FDA had terminated the EPIC trial, foreclosing ponatinib's approval for front-line use, which resulted in a stock value drop of forty-one percent. Shortly thereafter, ARIAD announced that the FDA had suspended marketing of ponatinib, resulting in a further forty-four percent drop in market value. The FDA disclosed a number of serious adverse side effects occurring in ponatinib patients and stated that "[a]t this time, [the] FDA cannot identify a dose level or exposure duration that is safe."

After the Class Period ended, ARIAD announced on December 20, 2013 that the FDA was now allowing the marketing and distribution of ponatinib under a new label which included additional language on vascular occlusive events and heart failure. This re-labeling significantly narrowed the eligible population of CML-patients, as it was relegated for third and fourth-line usage. The FDA issued independent safety findings on December 18, noting that "similar rates of serious vascular events have not been observed in several other drugs of this class."

II. ANALYSIS: Claims Against the Defendant ARIAD

A. Standard of Review

1. The Motion to Dismiss Standard

Under the Federal Rules of Civil Procedure, a complaint must contain "a short and plain statement of the claim showing that the pleader is entitled to relief." Fed. R. Civ. P. 8(a)(2). To survive a Rule 12(b)(6) motion to dismiss, a complaint must contain sufficient factual matter, accepted as true, to "state a claim to relief that is plausible on its face." *Bell Atl. Corp. v. Twombly*, 550 U.S. 544, 570, 127 S. Ct. 1955, 167 L. Ed. 2d 929 (2007). A mere recital of the legal elements supported only by conclusory statements is not sufficient to state a cause of action. *Id.* at 555.

2. Standard of Review in Securities Actions

In many securities actions, a heightened pleading standard applies. This is so because claims alleging fraud are subject to the stricter standards of Federal Rule of Civil Procedure 9(b), and because the Private Securities Litigation Reform Act ("PSLRA"), (citation omitted) imposes an even more rigorous standard on scienter allegations, a required element of fraud claims under Section 10 of the Exchange Act. (citation omitted). PSLRA, enacted as a "check against abusive litigation by private parties," requires that plaintiffs "state with particularity both the facts constituting the alleged violation, and the facts evidencing scienter, i.e., the defendant's intention 'to deceive, manipulate, or defraud.'" *Tellabs, Inc. v. Makor Issues & Rights, Ltd.*, 551 U.S. 308, 313, 127 S. Ct. 2499, 168 L. Ed. 2d 179 (2007) (internal citation omitted).

Plaintiffs pleading a violation of Section 11 of the Securities Act, however, typically "need only satisfy the notice-pleading standard of Fed. R. Civ. P. 8(a)," since scienter is not an element of Section 11. The First Circuit recognizes one exception to the "relatively minimal burden" of pleading a Section 11 claim: when the allegations supporting a Section 11 claim sound in fraud, ... they are subject to the heightened requirements of Rule 9(b). "[C]ourts must ensure that [Section 11 allegations] truly do 'sound in fraud' before the heightened pleading standard ... attaches."

The Plaintiffs' Section 11 claims, however, do not sound in fraud.... ("Lead Plaintiffs do not allege or intend to allege any claims or assertions of fraud in connection with their claims in this section of the Complaint, which are rooted exclusively in theories of innocent and/or negligent conduct to which the strict liability provision[] of the []§ 11 ... apply...."). Although the first part of the complaint contains extensive allegations of fraudulent representations and concealment by ARIAD and its management, there are no allegations in the second part of the complaint suggesting that any of the Underwriters affirmatively knew of or attempted to cause incomplete and misleading disclosures in the Offering Materials. The second part of the complaint addressing the Section 11 claims, then, is subject to the ordinary pleading standard applicable to a Rule 12(b)(6) motion to dismiss ... *See In re WebSecure, Inc. Sec. Litig.*, 182 F.R.D. 364, 367 (D. Mass 1998) (O'Toole, J.) (holding that Section 11 claims against underwriters do not sound in fraud because "[n]owhere in the complaint is there any allegation of scienter with regard to the underwriter defendants").

* * *

III. ANALYSIS: Claims Against the Underwriters Defendant [sic]

The Plaintiffs allege that the ARIAD and Underwriter Defendants are liable under Section 11 of the Securities Act of 1933 for alleged misstatements and omissions in stock offering materials. ARIAD and the Underwriter Defendants seek dismissal of all Section 11 claims against them on the basis that the Plaintiffs lack standing and that they fail to state a claim.

A. Legal Standard: Section 11 and Section 15 of the Securities Act

Section 11 of the Securities Act creates a cause of action empowering purchasers of securities offered under a false or misleading registration statement to sue certain enumerated parties. Specifically, the statute "impos[es] a stringent standard of liability on the parties who play a direct role in a registered offering," a category which includes participating underwriters. As mentioned above, the Section 11 claims in this action do not sound in fraud and are subject to the ordinary pleading standards under Rule 12 of the Federal Rules of Civil Procedure....

B. Standing

The ARIAD Defendants and Underwriters challenge the Plaintiffs' standing to bring Section 11 claims against them. According to the Underwriters, the Plaintiffs have not sufficiently alleged that they purchased ARIAD shares issued under the challenged 2013 Offering, as opposed to ARIAD shares issued in previous stock offerings.

Section 11 confers standing only on persons who acquired the specific securities issued under the challenged registration statement. This requirement is satisfied whether the plaintiff purchased shares in the public offering itself or in the secondary market, so long as the plaintiff can trace the origin of his shares back to the offering in dispute. It follows that a person holding shares issued in a different, undisputed offering does not have standing to join a Section 11 action, as he cannot be said to have relied on the purportedly fraudulent registration materials.

At the motion to dismiss stage, the relevant issue for the Court to analyze is whether the Plaintiffs adequately have pled that they purchased securities traceable to the challenged offering. The parties in this action disagree as to the appropriate standard of pleading. The Plaintiffs contend that general allegations, akin to notice pleading, are sufficient in the First Circuit. But the Underwriters argue that in the wake of *Bell Atlantic Corp. v. Twombly*, 550 U.S. 544, 127 S. Ct. 1955, 167 L. Ed. 2d 929 (2007), and *Ashcroft v. Iqbal*, 556 U.S. 662, 129 S. Ct. 1937, 173 L. Ed. 2d 868 (2009), more is required.

1. This Court's Rule Prior to *Twombly* and *Iqbal*

Case law preceding the publication of *Twombly* and *Iqbal* shows that in the District of Massachusetts prior to 2007, this issue was settled by a line of cases analyzing the impact of *Gustafson v. Alloyd Co., Inc.*, 513 U.S. 561, 115 S. Ct. 1061, 131 L. Ed. 2d 1 (1995), on Section 11 standing.[4] This Court's practice has been to hold general allegations sufficient to survive a motion to dismiss for lack of standing.

2. Developments Since *Twombly* and *Iqbal*

Jurisprudence is emerging in at least one other circuit holding that Section 11 standing must be pled with greater particularity than the standard articulated above. The most prominent decision promulgating this interpretation recently was rendered by the Ninth Circuit in *In re Century Aluminum Co. Sec. Litig.*, 729 F.3d 1104 (9th Cir. 2013). In that case, the Ninth Circuit observed that although general allegations of traceable stock purchases were "probably" sufficient to survive a motion to dismiss before 2007, "*Iqbal* and *Twombly* moved us away from a system of pure notice pleading."

The Ninth Circuit applies this principle by requiring particular factual specificity when the plaintiffs hold shares that could have been issued in any one of multiple stock offerings. Under *In re Century Aluminum*, this standard expressly cannot be satisfied by a "conclusory allegation" that plaintiffs purchased stock directly traceable to a particular offering. Because "experience and common sense tell us that ... [such] aftermarket purchasers usually will <u>not</u> be able to trace their shares back to a particular offering," plaintiffs must "allege facts from which we can reasonably infer that their situation is different."

The *In re Century Aluminum* plaintiffs attempted to accomplish this by showing that they purchased shares during periods of extreme change in trading volume and stock price, likely attributable to the issuance of new shares flooding the secondary market. *Id.* at 1108. But the Ninth Circuit ruled that such evidence was insufficient to support a reasonable inference that the plaintiffs' shares were traceable to any par-

---

4. [6] In the wake of *Gustafson*, this Court and other sessions in the District of Massachusetts determined that holders of securities "traceable to" a fraudulent offering had Section 11 standing even if they did not directly purchase those securities from the issuer at the time of the offering. In coming to this conclusion, this Court and its colleagues consistently denied motions to dismiss for lack of standing in favor of plaintiffs who had made only allegations, without more, that their shares were traceable to a contested offering. These rulings indirectly affirm that general allegations of the kind pled in this action were enough to survive a motion to dismiss.

ticular offering. "[T]he 'obvious alternative explanation' [was] that [the shares] could instead have come from the pool of previously issued shares. Plaintiffs' allegations [were] consistent with their shares having come from either source." *Id.* (citing *Twombly*, 550 U.S. at 567). Without "facts tending to exclude the possibility that the alternative explanation is true," the plaintiffs' explanation was "merely *possible* rather than plausible."

At the district court level, a split on this issue is emerging. In addition to the decisions of district courts bound by this precedent, at least two district court decisions outside of the Ninth Circuit have endorsed a similar approach to pleading Section 11 standing. Recent decisions of other district courts, however, hold that general allegations of traceability continue to be sufficient to allege Section 11 standing.…

The Defendants more or less urge this Court to disregard any decision relying on pre-*Twombly* and pre-*Iqbal* cases. *Twombly* and *Iqbal* did not, however, so fundamentally alter the Rule 8 pleading standards so as to render all prior pleading jurisprudence immaterial. Surely the district court decisions holding that general allegations continue to suffice post-*Twombly* and *Iqbal* recognized those Supreme Court precedents. Those courts simply reached a conclusion different from the Ninth Circuit as to the effect of *Twombly* and *Iqbal* on Section 11 standing allegations.

3. Maintaining the Court's Previous Rule

In the absence of additional guidance or evidence that the Ninth Circuit is not an outlier among circuits on this issue, this Court takes a conservative approach to the Underwriters' challenge and hews to the established pre-*Twombly* standard. This Court holds that general allegations that the Plaintiffs hold traceable shares are sufficient to plead standing under Section 11, even if those allegations are unaccompanied by more specific corroborating allegations.

Under this rule, the Plaintiffs' complaint passes muster, and the Court DENIES the ARIAD and Underwriter Defendants' motion to dismiss for lack of standing.

C. Material Misstatements and Omissions

The Underwriters argue in the alternative that the Plaintiffs have failed to allege actionable misstatements or omissions made in the Offering Materials. To make out a Section 11 violation, the Plaintiffs "need only show a material misstatement or omission to establish [their] prima facie case." The First Circuit has identified four elements that must be alleged: "(1) that [the company's] prospectus contained an omission; (2) that the omission was material; (3) that defendants were under a duty to disclose the omitted information; and (4) that such omitted information existed at the time the prospectus became effective."

In their complaint, the Plaintiffs refer to misstatements and omissions in three areas: (1) the alleged increasing incidence of "serious cardiovascular adverse events" related to ponatinib throughout 2012 … (2) the alleged infeasibility of the recommended prescribed 45 milligram dose of ponatinib in the majority of patients, and (3) the allegedly dwindling potential of ponatinib's approval for front-line use. The Plaintiffs additionally allege that the Offering Materials failed to disclose "that the incidence of adverse cardiovascular events in PACE 2 had or was reasonably expected to have a material … unfavorable impact on … revenues," in violation of Item 303 of Regulation S-K.

According to the Underwriters, all material information related to these claims and existing as of January 2013 was fully and accurately disclosed.…

1. Trends in Adverse Cardiovascular Events

The parties disagree as to whether information about adverse cardiovascular events related to ponatinib was fully disclosed in the Offering Materials. The Underwriters assert that such information was fully disclosed because the Offering Materials expressly incorporated, among other things, the results of ARIAD's July 2012 Interim Report on the progress of its PACE 2 trials. The Plaintiffs counter that the Offering Materials contained no information on PACE 2 results between July 2012, the cut-off date of the interim report, and January 2013, the time of the stock offering. During this time, the Plaintiffs say, the incidence of adverse events was worsening, which would have been material to prospective investors.

a. The July 2012 Interim Results

It is undisputed that at the time of the January 2013 Stock Offering, the information available to investors about a possible link between ponatinib and adverse cardiovascular events was not uniformly positive. Recall that one month before the offering, on December 14, 2012, ARIAD issued a press release announcing the FDA's limited approval of the drug with a serious "black box" warning on its label. The announcement of this development made public the results from the July 2012 Interim Report on the progress of the PACE 2 clinical trials, as that report was the basis for the FDA's decision to grant conditional approval. According to the Plaintiffs' complaint, the July 2012 Interim Report "showed an increase in both adverse and 'serious' adverse cardiovascular events in patients taking ponatinib." Accordingly, the drug's black box warning was required to list several types of adverse cardiovascular events experienced by ponatinib-treated patients and specifically disclose that "serious arterial thrombosis occurred in 8 [percent] of … patients."

b. August 2013 Results as a Basis for Alleging Trends Between July 2012 and January 2013

The Underwriters vigorously attest that these developments and underlying data were fully disclosed in the Offering Materials. The Plaintiffs do not dispute this, but they point out that by the time of the stock offering, ARIAD had collected approximately six months of additional clinical trial data beyond July 2012, none of which was provided to participating investors. The December disclosure that eight percent of patients experienced arterial thrombosis was, according to the Plaintiffs, only a "snapshot in time of adverse event data" as of July 2012, "reveal[ing] nothing about the trends or uncertainties then known to Defendants" as of January 2013. The Plaintiffs' complaint and brief go on to allege that the PACE 2 data from July 2012 through January 2013 was unfavorable and "gave rise to material, adverse facts, trends, and uncertainties" requiring disclosure, "including that adverse events were increasing over time."

These characterizations are based on a report submitted to the FDA in August 2013, providing eleven months of follow-up data on the PACE 2 clinical trials after July 2012. The August 2013 report showed, for example, "that the rate of serious arterial thrombosis associated with ponatinib had increased from 8 [percent] to 11.8 [percent] in the time since the July 2012 Interim PACE 2 Report."

The Underwriters point out that the August 2013 report provides aggregated data from both before and after the January 2013 stock offering. The Plaintiffs' allegations rely on the report's results without differentiating between pre- and post-offering data. According to the Underwriters, this lack of specificity prevents the Court from being able to draw a reasonable inference that the adverse trends established as of August 2013 were known as of January 2013.

c. Pleading Standard Under *Shaw*

The Underwriters' argument is a compelling one. Even though Rule 9(b) pleading standards do not apply here, this Court has held that when a complaint pleads "the alleged nondisclosure of information premised on a subsequent announcement or disclosure of such information," such allegations "address matters of projection or forecast to which a stricter standard of pleading attaches." Such heightened pleading is required in the First Circuit because of the risk that "the plaintiff's claim of nondisclosure may be indistinguishable from a claim that the issuer should have divulged its internal predictions about what would come of the undisclosed information." *Shaw*, 82 F.3d at 1211 (1st Cir. 1996). Thus, while allegations that disclosure was required in "relat[ion] to a specific, verifiable fact" are accepted as true under the classic dismissal standard, allegations that information should have been disclosed as "a matter of judgment or projection" are not entitled to the same benefit of the doubt.

Since the Plaintiffs' allegations regarding adverse cardiovascular events fall in the latter category, the question for the Court to resolve is whether "the allegedly undisclosed information is sufficiently remote in time or causation from the ultimate events of which it purportedly forewarned." *Shaw*, 82 F.3d at 1211. That means determining whether the increasing trend in adverse cardiovascular events "is of such a nature that it is reasonable to infer its existence at the time of the Offering from a disclosure some eight months later."

d. Fact-Specific Analysis

"As desirable as bright-line rules may be, this question cannot be answered by reference to such a rule." *Shaw*, 82 F.3d at 1210. Previous decisions addressing this subject turn on fact-intensive and contextual analysis....

The instant case presents a close call. On the one hand, the six months of data collected from August 2012 to January 2013 represents a significant, albeit not overwhelming, portion of the three-year PACE 2 study, and it covers half of the period tracked by the August 2013 follow-up study that caused the FDA to suspend sales and marketing of the drug. Further, the FDA's October 2013 safety announcement referred to an "increasing rate and pattern" of adverse events and warned that "[i]n some patients, fatal and serious adverse events have occurred as early as 2 weeks after starting

Iclusig [ponatinib] therapy." Given the alleged importance of ponatinib to ARIAD, it is likely that the progress of the PACE 2 was closely monitored, meaning that any trends presenting in the data likely would be known almost immediately. These facts are consistent with a conclusion that ARIAD knew at the time of the Offering that the prognosis for ponatinib was even worse than the July 2012 results suggested.

On the other hand, it is common sense that data collected over too short of an interval cannot be a basis for reliable conclusions about something so complex and multivariable as a cancer treatment drug. If the Offering had occurred two weeks after the July 2012 interim report cut-off date, it is unlikely that the Plaintiffs would claim a Section 11 violation for the omission of two weeks of follow-up data. The question is therefore as follows: is six months of follow-up data enough to trigger a reasonable inference that a reliable trend was evident?

One possible touchstone could be the actions of the FDA. Again, the FDA based its December 2012 decision to approve ponatinib with a black box warning on ARIAD's results from July 2012.... In so doing, the agency did not examine data collected between July 2012 and the time of its decision. It instead required ARIAD to submit follow-up data over a twelve-month window after the interim report. This might suggest that in the FDA's judgment, data from July to December 2012 was not likely to be sufficient to alter the agency's assessment of ponatinib's safety profile.[5] The Court might reason from this that data over nearly the same time period, July 2012 to January 2013, similarly could not have been relied on to draw sound conclusions about ponatinib's safety.

Further, the Plaintiffs plead few facts that would allow the Court to infer with any particularity how troubling the PACE 2 results were at the time of the Offering. The Complaint contains, for example, no allegations describing the nature of the rate of increase in adverse cardiovascular events. It could be that the incidence of such events steadily increased throughout the clinical trial, such that ARIAD could reasonably expect that results would only worsen beyond the disclosed July 2012 results. But it could also be that the adverse reactions to ponatinib presented at irregular intervals throughout the three-year trial, or that the majority of adverse events occurred at the tail end of the study after prolonged use of ponatinib.

Given these uncertainties, the Court rules that the PACE 2 results as of August 2013 do not support a reasonable inference that materially adverse trends—beyond what was disclosed in the July 2012 Interim Report—existed at the time of the Offering a full eight months prior. It is certainly possible that negative trends already had manifested in the data by that point, but absent more factual detail about the specific results collected through January 2013, these pleadings "stop [] short of the line between possibility and plausibility."

---

5. [7] The FDA's actions could also suggest, however, nothing more than the fact that it is a government agency with limited resources to monitor pharmaceutical clinical trials. It could be that the agency does not have much capacity to check up on the progress of drug trials at intervals shorter than twelve months.

The Court rules that the complaint does not allege facts sufficient to support a reasonable inference that a materially worsened trend in adverse cardiovascular events existed in the PACE 2 trials at the time of the Offering.

2. Dosage Reductions

Plaintiffs further allege that the Offering Materials omitted material information regarding the dosages of ponatinib administered to patients in ARIAD's clinical trials. Specifically, the Offering Materials allegedly failed to disclose that the drug was toxic at the 45 mg dose; that the PACE 2 data in the July 2012 Interim Report showed that 73 [percent] of PACE 2 patients were given a less efficacious, lower dose in order to reduce adverse events and continue to tolerate the drug, or taken off ponatinib altogether; that therefore the more effective 45 mg "recommended dose" was not a feasible dose that could be maintained; and that follow-up data from the PACE 2 trial showed that patients continued to receive reduced doses of ponatinib.

The Underwriters seek dismissal of claims based on these alleged omissions, arguing that the Plaintiffs' assertions here either are insufficiently pleaded or were fully disclosed in the Offering Materials.

a. "Toxic" and "Not a Feasible Dose"

Two of the Plaintiffs' alleged omissions are but conclusory allegations. The complaint does not plead any specific facts to support its allegations that the recommended 45 milligram dose of ponatinib was "toxic" or "not a feasible dose that could be maintained." The Plaintiffs' most concrete allegation in this area, that many patients had their dosage adjusted downward from 45 milligrams, does not support an inference that the 45 milligram dose was toxic or infeasible—particularly if, as is suggested in the complaint, some patients did maintain the recommended dosing regimen. (referring to the PACE 2 interim results showing that 73 percent of patients received lower doses of ponatinib, implying that 27 percent of patients were able to maintain 45 milligram doses).

Without allegations laying out, for example, the clinical standard for toxicity, ponatinib's relationship to that standard at the 45 milligram dose, or other verifiable facts that ARIAD could have known that would make the drug "toxic," the Plaintiffs' allegations are baseless. . . .

The Court rules that there was no material misstatement or omission in the Offering Materials for failure to disclose that ponatinib was "toxic" or infeasible at the 45 milligram dose.

b. Dosage Reductions in July 2012 Interim Report

Second, the Plaintiffs allege that the Offering Materials failed to disclose that 73 percent of PACE 2 patients as of July 2012 were prescribed lower doses of ponatinib to mitigate adverse effects. The Underwriters contend "that this data was publicly disclosed prior to the Offering, including in materials that were incorporated into the Offering Materials." They refer to a number of sources that allegedly publicized the data, including (1) Full Prescribing Information prepared by the FDA published on the FDA's and ARIAD's websites, and referred to in a December 14, 2012 press release which was in turn incorporated into the Offering Materials; (2) a report of the FDA's Center for Drug Evaluation and Research ("CDER"), published on the FDA's website in late 2012; and (3) a December 14, 2012 conference call in which ARIAD's chief medical officer fielded questions from a number of investment analysts.

The Court is empowered, at the least, to take judicial notice of the FDA's Full Pre-scribing Information and the FDA CDER report as public records. Further, the Plain-tiffs do not address these documents in their reply brief, failing to challenge the public nature or authenticity of any of these documents. These records show that not only was the rate of down-dosing in the July 2012 Interim Report public knowledge by the time of the Offering, the statistic was at least indirectly incorporated into the Of-fering Materials.

The Court rules that as to dosage reduction data in the July 2012 Interim Report, no material omission was made from the Offering Materials.

c. Continued Dose Reductions After July 2012

The Plaintiffs allege that the Offering Materials were misleading because they failed to mention that patients in the PACE 2 study continued to have their ponatinib doses adjusted downward after July 2012. The Underwriters respond that the complaint "allege[s] no facts supporting this allegation of 'continued' dose reductions, let alone facts suggesting any such reductions were in any way different in frequency or scope from the reductions disclosed in the Offering Materials."

This element of the Plaintiffs' complaint is problematic for two reasons. First, as the Underwriters point out, the complaint contains virtually no facts that would sup-port a reasonable inference that dose reductions continued in the six months prior to the Offering. The complaint does not even refer in this context to the results of the August 2013 study, making the continued dose reductions claim even more lacking in support than the Plaintiffs' claim of increased adverse cardiovascular events. The only basis offered to support the allegation that dose reductions continued is a per-functory reference to confidential witnesses, but no elaboration beyond the single use of the term "CWs" is provided. The Plaintiffs do not offer more than a conclusory assertion of continued dose reductions.

Second, even if the Court accepts this unsubstantiated assertion as true, the allegation as pled does not make out a claim of material omission. As discussed in the preceding section of this memorandum, the rate of dose reductions in the PACE 2 interim results as of July 2012 was public and available to potential investors at the time of the Offering. It was also evident to investors from ARIAD's disclosures throughout 2012 that actual dose administration could be expected to depart from the planned recommended dose of 45 milligrams. Disclosing that the rate of dose adjustments remained the same be-tween July 2012 and January 2013 would have done nothing to "significantly alter[] the total mix of information made available" to investors. (citations omitted).

The Court rules that the complaint does not plead sufficient facts to support a reasonable inference that dose reductions continued at the same rate from July 2012 to January 2013, and also rules that even if continued dose reductions occurred, it was not a material omission to fail to disclose them in the Offering Materials.

3. Ponatinib's Potential for Front-Line Use

The third category of misrepresentations alleged by the Plaintiffs deals with ponatinib's prospects for "front-line" treatment of CML. ARIAD's Prospectus Supplement contained statements describing the company's "initial commercial strategy" to market ponatinib to "second-line" CML patients, and estimating global sales that "may reach $1 billion by 2018." According to the Plaintiffs, these statements were materially untrue because they did not disclose "that the drug's potential for front-line use was dramatically decreasing based on (1) the increasingly negative safety profile relating to cardiovascular events, and (2) the necessary down-dosing from the more effective 45 mg dose to the less effective 30 mg and 15 mg doses."

* * *

b. No Misrepresentation

This Court also rules that no actionable misrepresentation or omission has been made with regard to ponatinib's front-line potential. First, the Plaintiffs' allegation that ponatinib's front-line potential was rapidly declining at the time of the Offering, even if accepted as true, has no bearing on the truth of ARIAD's statement that its initial commercial strategy at the time of the Offering was to market ponatinib for second-line use.... In fact, the complaint pleads numerous facts confirming the truth of ARIAD's statement at the time of the Offering, e.g. that ponatinib was approved by the FDA for second-line use, and that the PACE trials assessing second-line use were much further along than the EPIC trial aimed at supporting front-line use. It is difficult to see how the truth of a statement regarding ARIAD's strategy in the present could be undermined by dim prospects for a completely different future strategy.[6]

The Court rules that no material misrepresentation or omission was made by the statement regarding ARIAD's "initial commercial strategy."

c. Forward-Looking Statements Under the PSLRA Safe Harbor

As for the statement regarding global sales projections identified by the Plaintiffs as misleading, the Court rules that the statements are protected by the safe harbor provisions of the PSLRA. Under the safe harbor, defendants such as the Underwriters cannot be held liable for forward-looking statements, as long as such a statement is

---

6. [8] The Underwriters go a bit too far, though, in arguing that "[n]othing in this [initial commercial strategy] statement ... made any projection concerning the drug's 'potential for front-line use.'" It could be argued, albeit not strongly, that an undisclosed decline in ponatinib's front-line potential made ARIAD's statement materially untrue because of the use of the word "initial." The framing of second-line use as merely an "initial" strategy could be read to imply that ARIAD's ultimate goal was to position ponatinib for front-line use. This implication would be materially untrue, then, if the drug's actual prospects for front-line use were as dismal as the Plaintiffs claim yet such data remained undisclosed. This is a tortured line of reasoning, however, and one that ignores the structure of the statement as an expression of present, not future, strategy.

"(i) identified as a forward-looking statement, and is accompanied by meaningful cautionary statements identifying important factors that could cause actual results to differ materially from those in the forward-looking statement; or (ii) immaterial." The statute further explains that the definition of a forward-looking statement includes:

> (A) a statement containing a projection of revenues, income (including income loss), earnings (including earnings loss) per share, ... or other financial items;
>
> (B) a statement of the plans and objectives of management for future operations, including plans or objectives relating to the products or services of the issuer;
>
> (C) a statement of future economic performance ... ; [or]
>
> (D) any statement of the assumptions underlying or relating to any statement described in subparagraph (A), (B), or (C)....

ARIAD's estimate in the prospectus supplement that global sales of ponatinib could reach $1,000,000,000 by 2018 plainly falls within this portion of the statute. It is a classic example of a projection of revenues, captured by the definition of a forward-looking statement ... The statement was also qualified by language referring investors to an extensive discussion in that same document of risk factors.... As the Plaintiffs advance no arguments even addressing the applicability of the PSLRA safe harbor, no further analysis is needed to conclude that the $1,000,000,000 revenue projection is a protected statement.

The Court rules that ARIAD's projected sales estimate for 2018 was a forward-looking statement protected by the PSLRA safe harbor.

4. Item 303 of Regulation S-K

Finally, the Underwriters seek to dismiss the Plaintiffs' Section 11 claim based on an alleged violation of Item 303 of SEC Regulation S-K. The goal of Item 303 is "to give the investor an opportunity to look at the company through the eyes of management, so that they may assess the financial condition and results of operations of the registrant, with particular emphasis on the registrant's prospects for the future." This requires management to "[d]escribe any known trends or uncertainties that have had or that the registrant reasonably expects will have a material favorable or unfavorable impact on net sales or revenues or income from continuing operations." A plausible complaint stating a failure to disclose such trends or uncertainties "must allege (1) that a registrant knew about an uncertainty before an offering; (2) that the known uncertainty is reasonably likely to have material effects on the registrant's financial condition or results of operation; and (3) that the offering documents failed to disclose the known uncertainty."

This part of the Plaintiffs' complaint fails for the same reasons discussed above. According to the complaint, Defendants were required to disclose: (i) that the incidence of adverse cardiovascular events in PACE 2 had or was reasonably expected to have a "material ... unfavorable impact on ... revenues," and (ii) to what extent that trend had impacted or was reasonably expected to impact ARIAD's revenue.

These assertions rehash insufficient allegations made earlier in the complaint. Because the results of the July 2012 Interim Report were made public prior to the Offering, only uncertainties stemming from developments between July 2012 and January 2013 can be the subject of an alleged Item 303 violation. Again, at this stage of the litigation, the only available data point for assessing what ARIAD further knew about adverse cardiovascular events in January 2013 comes from the company's August 2013 follow-up report. As was discussed earlier in greater detail, general reference to the PACE 2 results as of August 2013 is insufficient to support a reasonable inference that management knew of a worsening trend eight months earlier.

The Court rules that the complaint fails to allege facts sufficient to support a reasonable inference that the Offering Materials violated Item 303 of Regulation S-K.

C. Section 11 and 15 Claims Against the ARIAD Defendants

1. Standing

The ARIAD Defendants seek to dismiss the Plaintiffs' Section 11 claims against them on the basis that the Plaintiffs lack standing because they are unable to trace their shares to the January 24, 2013 secondary offering....

As discussed above, this Court adopts the pre-*Twombly* standard for Section 11 claims, which accepts general allegations that the Plaintiffs held traceable shares as sufficient to plead standing under Section 11, even if those allegations are unaccompanied by other facts.

2. Material Misstatements or Omissions

This Court references the discussion in Section III.B. above and rules that no inference of material misrepresentation or omission can be found against the ARIAD Defendants with regard to the Section 11 claims. In sum, this Court concludes that the supposed omission of six months of data, between the July 2012 Interim Report and the January 2013 Offering, offered no basis that cardiovascular adverse events were increasing or that there was a worsening trend in adverse events in the PACE 2 trial.

* * *

On the contrary, ARIAD disclosed the rates of serious cardiovascular events in their black box warning label in their December 2012 FDA approval announcement, making them publicly known, and incorporated this data into their January 2013 offering materials. The news of the eight percent rate of arterial thrombosis, which negatively affected ARIAD stock price upon announcement, had already been absorbed into the market at the time of the January Offering, and the Plaintiffs are unable to point to what adverse trends existed in the six months of PACE 2 study leading up to the offering. Accordingly, the Court rules that no material misstatements or omissions can be established against the ARIAD Defendants with regard to the Section 11 claims, and GRANTS the ARIAD Defendants' motion to dismiss based on a failure to state a claim under Section 11.

* * *

IV. CONCLUSION

As to the Underwriters' motions, the Court DENIES the motion to dismiss for lack of standing, and GRANTS the Underwriters' motion to dismiss for failure to state a claim pursuant to Federal Rule of Civil Procedure 12(b)(6).

———

Notes and Questions

1. Under *Ariad,* what must the plaintiff do to ensure the availability of FRCP 8(a) when alleging a violation of § 11 to avoid the more stringent pleading requirement of FRCP 9 in constructing the complaint?

2. Does § 11 require plaintiff to allege state of mind or intent?

3. Must § 11 claims be brought within one year after discovery of an untrue statement or omission, and in no case more than three years after the subject securities were offered to the public?

Hypothetical Two

Success First, along with its customer, Alpha, Inc., has been sued in a class action lawsuit in connection with its role as lead underwriter in Alpha's initial public offering. Plaintiffs seek to hold Success First and Alpha liable under § 11 because the registration statement for its IPO understated and omitted material facts regarding Alpha's bad debt reserves. Specifically, Plaintiffs allege that Alpha's registration statement omitted that Alpha was having difficulty collecting certain receivables (some were more than 270 days old) and that some were uncollectible; that it falsely represented that its credit risk with regard to its account receivables was limited because Alpha had policies in place to ensure that sales were made to customers with high credit standing; and that it falsely represented that it calculated its bad debt reserves based on standard quantitative measures. On the last day of the class period, Alpha announced its quarterly financial results and disclosed that it had decided to write off approximately $111 million in outstanding accounts receivable. Following these disclosures, Alpha's share price dropped by 66 percent and it filed for bankruptcy the following month. Plaintiffs alleged that Alpha's bad debt reserves were materially understated and that Success First knew and/or disregarded with deliberate recklessness the true facts regarding Alpha's bad debt reserves throughout the class period; in addition, plaintiffs' complaint regarding their § 11 claims repeatedly and explicitly exclude any allegations of fraud. In fact, the section of plaintiffs' complaint alleging violation of § 11 is separate from, and not incorporated into, other sections of its complaint alleging fraud.

Success First has made a motion to dismiss in response to plaintiffs' complaint asserting that plaintiffs have failed to state a claim under § 11 because their complaint has failed to allege the elements required to state a cause of action under § 11. In addition, Success First asserts that plaintiffs' complaint should be subjected to the pleading requirements of FRCP Rule 9(b) [fraud must be pleaded with particularity] because its § 11 allegations sound in fraud. Will Success First be successful in its motion to dismiss?

C. Defenses

The broker-dealer has several defenses to § 11 liability enumerated in the statute. One defense is to resign. Section 11(b)(1) allows the broker-dealer to resign before the effective date of the registration statement; this resignation must be in writing and provided to the SEC and, of course, the issuer. The broker-dealer may also avoid liability if the registration statement, or a part of it, became effective without his knowledge, or upon becoming aware of effectiveness, the broker-dealer acts forthwith, resigns, advises the SEC, and provides reasonable public notice that the registration statement became effective without his knowledge. This, in effect, places the broker-dealer in the position of acting as a whistleblower. The broker-dealer may also avoid liability by establishing that plaintiffs had actual knowledge of the alleged misrepresentation or omission in the registration statement. Section 11(a) prohibits liability if the purchaser had actual knowledge of the misrepresentation or omission at the time that she acquired the security. The broker-dealer, of course, has the burden of establishing the purchaser's actual knowledge. Finally, the broker-dealer has a "due diligence" defense under §§ 11(b)(3)(A) and (C).

1. Due Diligence

The underwriter's due diligence defense is the primary defense used by broker-dealers against § 11 lawsuits. The requirements to establish the due diligence defense are based on two categories of information contained in the registration statement — expertised or non-expertised. Expertised information in the registration statement is prepared by an expert such as an accountant; the accountant prepares and certifies the portion of the registration statement that contains an issuer's financial statements. Other experts that may prepare and certify information in the registration statement include engineers and appraisers. Non-expertised information in the registration statement is all information prepared by non-experts — for example, the CEO or CFO of an issuer. Interestingly, neither the underwriter nor the underwriter's counsel is considered an expert under § 11. With respect to expertised information in the registration statement, a successful due diligence defense requires a broker-dealer to sustain the burden of proof that it "had no reasonable ground to believe and did not believe, at the time such part of the registration statement became effective, that the statements therein were untrue or that there was an omission to state a material fact required to be stated therein or necessary to make the statement therein not misleading...." With respect to non-expertised information in a registration statement, the broker-dealer must establish that it had "after reasonable investigation, reasonable ground to believe and did believe, at the time such part of the registration statement became effective, that the statements therein were true and that there was no omission to state a material fact required to be stated therein or necessary to make the statement therein not misleading." Further, § 11(d) defines "what constitutes reasonable investigation and reasonable ground for belief ... [as] that required of a prudent [person] in the management of [his or her] own property." Table 6.1 summarizes a broker-dealer's due diligence defense requirements.

Table 6.1. Broker-Dealer Due Diligence Defense Requirements

	Non-Expertised	Expertised
Broker-Dealer	Reasonable Investigation, Reasonable Ground to Believe, and Did Believe Material Statements True and No Omissions	Reasonable Ground to Believe and Did Believe Material Statements True and No Omissions
Standard of Reasonableness	Prudent Person in the Management of His/Her Own Property	Prudent Person in the Management of His/Her Own Property

SECURITIES ACT OF 1933, Release No. 5275; SECURITIES EXCHANGE ACT OF 1934, Release No. 9671
THE OBLIGATIONS OF UNDERWRITERS, BROKERS AND DEALERS IN DISTRIBUTING AND TRADING SECURITIES, PARTICULARLY OF NEW HIGH RISK VENTURES (FILE NO. S7-450)

In Exchange Act Release No. 9671, the SEC described the importance and function of the underwriter's due diligence defense in § 11(b) in the securities regulatory framework for facilitating adequate and accurate disclosure in the public offering process as follows,

> The availability (to the underwriters and others) of a due diligence defense appears to reflect a congressional policy to change and improve the standards of conduct to which persons associated with the distribution of securities are to be held by imposing upon them standards of "honesty, care and competence." Indeed, the primary function of Section 11 may not be the compensation of investors. It appears rather, that the section may have been designed by Congress to assure adherence to high standards of conduct through the "in terrorem" nature of the liabilities. It was believed that, in the desire to avoid liability, the persons subject to Section 11 would exercise the "honesty, care and competence" necessary to assure the accuracy of the statements in the registration statement.

* * *

> The underwriter's status is unique among those involved in the distribution of securities, in that, other than experienced securities lawyers, he is likely to be the only one experienced in making a due diligence investigation. The underwriter is able to call upon business or technical experts during the course of the investigation; and often is reimbursed for the expenses of his investigation.

Also unique is the importance of the underwriter in the distribution of the securities. His role is central as the intermediary between the issuer and the investing public. Correspondingly, the public looks to the underwriter for protection and expects him to verify the accuracy of the statements in the registration statement. As the Commission observed in *The Richmond Corporation*:

By associating himself with a proposed offering, an underwriter impliedly represents that he has made such an investigation in accordance with professional standards. Investors properly rely on this added protection which has a direct bearing on their appraisal of the reliability of the representations in the prospectus.

Moreover, the underwriter is unique in that he is the person who can most easily assume a posture which may be seen as adverse to the company, at least for purposes of the due diligence investigation. Because the underwriter is usually not legally committed to the underwriting until at or about the effective date of the registration statement (subject to terms of the underwriting agreement providing for certain events which may terminate such commitments), and because the participation of the underwriter is central to the successful distribution of the securities, the underwriter is peculiarly able to demand access to information which verifies the statements in the registration statement.

The underwriter's ability to make an investigation, and the public expectation that he will do so, emphasize the importance of his due diligence inquiry which would require exercising a degree of care reasonable under the circumstances to assure the substantial accuracy of representations made in the prospectus. The underwriter may not always rely on the truthfulness of all the information supplied by the issuer. "Such reliance ... [does] not constitute discharge of the duty to exercise reasonable care...." Rather, "the underwriters must make some reasonable attempt to verify the data submitted to them." Of course, the nature and extent of verification which is required will vary with the circumstances, but an essential element of every investigation is the independent nature of the verification by the underwriter.

———

As noted in the SEC's release, and discussed in the following case, a reasonable investigation under the standard in § 11(c) will vary under the circumstances.

Escott v. BarChris Construction Corp.

283 F. Supp. 643 (S.D.N.Y. 1968)

McLEAN, District Judge.

This is an action by purchasers of 5 1/2 per cent convertible subordinated fifteen year debentures of BarChris Construction Corporation (BarChris) ...

The action is brought under Section 11 of the Securities Act of 1933. Plaintiffs allege that the registration statement with respect to these debentures filed with the Securities and Exchange Commission, which became effective on May 16, 1961, contained material false statements and material omissions....

At the time relevant here, BarChris was engaged primarily in the construction of bowling alleys, ... The introduction of automatic pin setting machines in 1952 gave a marked stimulus to bowling. It rapidly became a popular sport, with the result that "bowling centers" began to appear throughout the country in rapidly increasing numbers. BarChris benefited from this increased interest in bowling. Its construction operations expanded rapidly. It is estimated that in 1960 BarChris installed approximately three per cent of all lanes built in the United States....

BarChris's sales increased dramatically from 1956 to 1960. According to the prospectus, net sales, in round figures, in 1956 were some $800,000, in 1957 $1,300,000, in 1958 $1,700,000. In 1959 they increased to over $3,300,000, and by 1960 they had leaped to over $9,165,000....

In general, BarChris's method of operation was to enter into a contract with a customer, receive from him at that time a comparatively small down payment on the purchase price, and proceed to construct and equip the bowling alley. When the work was finished and the building delivered, the customer paid the balance of the contract price in notes, payable in installments over a period of years. BarChris discounted these notes with a factor and received part of their face amount in cash.

The factor held back part as a reserve.

In 1960 BarChris began a practice which has been referred to throughout this case as the "alternative method of financing." In substance this was a sale and leaseback arrangement. It involved a distinction between the "interior" of a building and the building itself, i.e., the outer shell. In instances in which this method applied, BarChris would build and install what it referred to as the "interior package." Actually this amounted to constructing and installing the equipment in a building. When it was completed, it would sell the interior to a factor, James Talcott Inc. (Talcott), who would pay BarChris the full contract price therefor. The factor then proceeded to lease the interior either directly to BarChris's customer or back to a subsidiary of BarChris. In the latter case, the subsidiary in turn would lease it to the customer.

Under either financing method, BarChris was compelled to expend considerable sums in defraying the cost of construction before it received reimbursement.[7] As a consequence, BarChris was in constant need of cash to finance its operations, a need which grew more pressing as operations expanded.

In December 1959, BarChris sold 560,000 shares of common stock to the public at $3.00 per share....

---

7. [4] Under the sale and leaseback arrangement, Talcott paid part of the price to BarChris as the work progressed.

By early 1961, BarChris needed additional working capital. The proceeds of the sale of the debentures involved in this action were to be devoted, in part at least, to fill that need.

The registration statement of the debentures, ... was filed with the Securities and Exchange Commission on March 30, 1961 ... [and] became effective on May 16....

By that time BarChris was experiencing difficulties in collecting amounts due from some of its customers.... As time went on those difficulties increased....

In October 1962 BarChris came to the end of the road. On October 29, 1962, it filed in this court a petition for an arrangement under Chapter XI of the Bankruptcy Act ...

The Debenture Registration Statement

* * *

The underwriters were represented by the Philadelphia law firm of Drinker, Biddle & Reath. John A. Ballard, a member of that firm, was in charge of that work, assisted by a young associate named Stanton....

The registration statement in its final form contained a prospectus as well as other information. Plaintiffs' claims of falsities and omissions pertain solely to the prospectus, not to the additional data.

The prospectus contained, among other things, a description of BarChris's business, a description of its real property, some material pertaining to certain of its subsidiaries, and remarks about various other aspects of its affairs. It also contained financial information. It included a consolidated balance sheet as of December 31, 1960, with elaborate explanatory notes. These figures had been audited by Peat, Marwick. It also contained unaudited figures as to net sales, gross profit and net earnings for the first quarter ended March 31, 1961, as compared with the similar quarter for 1960. In addition, it set forth figures as to the company's backlog of unfilled orders as of March 31, 1961, as compared with March 31, 1960, and figures as to BarChris's contingent liability, as of April 30, 1961, on customers' notes discounted and its contingent liability under the so-called alternative method of financing.

Plaintiffs challenge the accuracy of a number of these figures. They also charge that the text of the prospectus, apart from the figures, was false in a number of respects, and that material information was omitted....

* * *

Summary

For convenience, the various falsities and omissions ... are recapitulated here. They were as follows:

1.   1960 Earnings
      (a) Sales
      As per prospectus $9,165,320

Correct figure $8,511,420

Overstatement $653,900
(b) Net Operating Income
As per prospectus $1,742,801
Correct figure $1,496,196

Overstatement $246,605
(c) Earnings per Share
As per prospectus $.75
Correct figure $.65
Overstatement $.10

2.   1960 Balance Sheet

        Current Assets

        As per prospectus $4,524,021
        Correct figure $3,914,332

        Overstatement $609,689

3.   Contingent Liabilities as of
        December 31, 1960 on Alternative
        Method of Financing

        As per prospectus $750,000
        Correct figure $1,125,795
        Understatement $375,795
        Capitol Lanes should have been
        shown as a direct liability $325,000
4.   Contingent Liabilities as of April $30, 1961

        As per prospectus $825,000
        Correct figure $1,443,853
        Understatement $618,853
        Capitol Lanes should have been
        shown as a direct liability $314,166

5.   Earnings Figures for Quarter ending
        March 31, 1961

        (a) Sales

	As per prospectus	$2,138,455
	Correct figure	$1,618,645
	Overstatement	$519,810
	(b) Gross Profit	
	As per prospectus	$483,121
	Correct figure	$252,366
	Overstatement	$230,755

6. Backlog as of March 31, 1961
    As per prospectus $6,905,000
    Correct figure $2,415,000
    Overstatement $4,490,000

7. Failure to Disclose Officers' Loans
    Outstanding and Unpaid on May
    16, 1961 $ 386,615

8. Failure to Disclose Use of Proceeds
    in Manner not Revealed in Prospectus

    Approximately $1,160,000

9. Failure to Disclose Customers'
    Delinquencies in May 1961 and
    BarChris's Potential Liability with Respect Thereto

    Over $1,350,000

10. Failure to Disclose the Fact
    that BarChris was Already Engaged,
    and was about to be More Heavily
    Engaged, in the Operation of
    Bowling Alleys

                    * * *

The "Due Diligence" Defenses

Section 11(b) of the Act provides that:

" … no person, other than the issuer, shall be liable … who shall sustain the burden of proof—

                    * * *

(3) that (A) as regards any part of the registration statement not purporting to be made on the authority of an expert … he had, after reasonable investigation,

reasonable ground to believe and did believe, at the time such part of the registration statement became effective, that the statements therein were true and that there was no omission to state a material fact required to be stated therein or necessary to make the statements therein not misleading; ... and (C) as regards any part of the registration statement purporting to be made on the authority of an expert (other than himself) ... he had no reasonable ground to believe and did not believe, at the time such part of the registration statement became effective, that the statements therein were untrue or that there was an omission to state a material fact required to be stated therein or necessary to make the statements therein not misleading...."

Section 11(c) defines "reasonable investigation" as follows:

"In determining, for the purpose of paragraph (3) of subsection (b) of this section, what constitutes reasonable investigation and reasonable ground for belief, the standard of reasonableness shall be that required of a prudent man in the management of his own property." Every defendant, except BarChris itself, to whom, as the issuer, these defenses are not available, and except Peat, Marwick, whose position rests on a different statutory provision, has pleaded these affirmative defenses. Each claims that (1) as to the part of the registration statement purporting to be made on the authority of an expert (which, for convenience, I shall refer to as the "expertised portion"), he had no reasonable ground to believe and did not believe that there were any untrue statements or material omissions, and (2) as to the other parts of the registration statement, he made a reasonable investigation, as a result of which he had reasonable ground to believe and did believe that the registration statement was true and that no material fact was omitted. As to each defendant, the question is whether he has sustained the burden of proving these defenses. Surprising enough, there is little or no judicial authority on this question. No decisions directly in point under Section 11 have been found.

Before considering the evidence, a preliminary matter should be disposed of. The defendants do not agree among themselves as to who the "experts" were or as to the parts of the registration statement which were expertised. Some defendants say that Peat, Marwick was the expert, others say that BarChris's attorneys, Perkins, Daniels, McCormack & Collins, and the underwriters' attorneys, Drinker, Biddle & Reath, were also the experts. On the first view, only those portions of the registration statement purporting to be made on Peat, Marwick's authority were expertised portions. On the other view, everything in the registration statement was within this category, because the two law firms were responsible for the entire document.

The first view is the correct one. To say that the entire registration statement is expertised because some lawyer prepared it would be an unreasonable construction of the statute. Neither the lawyer for the company nor the lawyer for the underwriters is an expert within the meaning of Section 11. The only expert, in the statutory sense, was Peat, Marwick, and the only parts of the registration statement which purported to be made upon the authority of an expert were the portions which purported to be made on Peat, Marwick's authority.

The parties also disagree as to what those portions were. Some defendants say that it was only the 1960 figures (and the figures for prior years, which are not in controversy here). Others say in substance that it was every figure in the prospectus. The plaintiffs take a somewhat intermediate view. They do not claim that Peat, Marwick expertised every figure, but they do maintain that Peat, Marwick is responsible for a portion of the text of the prospectus, i.e., that pertaining to "Methods of Operation," because a reference to it was made in footnote 9 to the balance sheet.

Here again, the more narrow view is the correct one. The registration statement contains a report of Peat, Marwick as independent public accountants dated February 23, 1961. This relates only to the consolidated balance sheet of BarChris and consolidated subsidiaries as of December 31, 1960, and the related statement of earnings and retained earnings for the five years then ended. This is all that Peat, Marwick purported to certify. It is perfectly clear that it did not purport to certify the 1961 figures, some of which are expressly stated in the prospectus to have been unaudited.

Moreover, plaintiffs' intermediate view is also incorrect. The cross reference in footnote 9 to the "Methods of Operation" passage in the prospectus was inserted merely for the convenience of the reader. It is not a fair construction to say that it thereby imported into the balance sheet everything in that portion of the text, much of which had nothing to do with the figures in the balance sheet.

I turn now to the question of whether defendants have proved their due diligence defenses....

* * *

The Underwriters and Coleman

The underwriters other than Drexel made no investigation of the accuracy of the prospectus. One of them, Peter Morgan, had underwritten the 1959 stock issue and had been a director of BarChris. He thus had some general familiarity with its affairs, but he knew no more than the other underwriters about the debenture prospectus. They all relied upon Drexel as the "lead" underwriter.

Drexel did make an investigation. The work was in charge of Coleman, a partner of the firm, assisted by Casperson, an associate. Drexel's attorneys acted as attorneys for the entire group of underwriters. Ballard did the work, assisted by Stanton.

On April 17, 1961 Coleman became a director of BarChris. He signed the ... registration statement in its final form, filed on May 16. He thereby assumed a responsibility as a director and signer in addition to his responsibility as an underwriter.

The facts as to the extent of the investigation that Coleman made may be briefly summarized. He was first introduced to BarChris on September 15, 1960. Thereafter he familiarized himself with general conditions in the industry, primarily by reading reports and prospectuses of the two leading bowling alley builders, ... These indicated that the industry was still growing. He also acquired general information on BarChris by reading the 1959 stock prospectus, annual reports for prior years, and an unaudited statement for the first half of 1960. He inquired about BarChris of certain of its banks and of Talcott and received favorable replies.

The purpose of this preliminary investigation was to enable Coleman to decide whether Drexel would undertake the financing.... Coleman was sufficiently optimistic about BarChris's prospects to buy 1,000 shares of its stock, which he did in December 1960.

On January 24, 1961, Coleman held a meeting with Ballard, Grant [BarChris's attorney] and Kircher [BarChris's treasurer], among others. By that time Coleman had about decided to go ahead with the financing, although Drexel's formal letter of intent was not delivered until February 9, 1961 (subsequently revised on March 7, 1961). At this meeting Coleman asked Kircher how BarChris intended to use the proceeds of the financing. In reply to this inquiry, Kircher wrote a letter to Coleman dated January 30, 1961 outlining BarChris's plans. This eventually formed the basis of the application of proceeds section in the prospectus.

Coleman continued his general investigation. He obtained a Dun & Bradstreet report on BarChris on March 16, 1961. He read BarChris's annual report for 1960 ...

By mid-March, Coleman was in a position to make more specific inquiries. By that time Grant had prepared a first draft of the prospectus, consisting of a marked-up copy of the January 1961 warrant prospectus. Coleman attended the meetings to discuss the prospectus with BarChris's representatives. The meetings were held at Perkins, Daniels' [Law firm at which Grant was a partner] office on March 20, March 23 and March 24, 1961. Those present included Grant or his partner McCormack and Kircher for the company, and Coleman, Casperson and Ballard for the underwriters. Logan, Peat, Marwick's manager of the 1960 audit, was present at one of the meetings.

* * *

Coleman and Ballard asked pertinent questions and received answers which satisfied them. Among other things, the following transpired.

Logan explained some of the 1960 figures, including the reserve for bad debts, which he considered adequate.

There was a discussion of the application of proceeds section. It was not changed in any respect material here.

As to the backlog of orders on hand, Ballard said that the figure, not then available, must be "hard and fast," not "puffy." Grant and Kircher "concurred."

There was talk about the 15 to 25 per cent down payment figure. Kircher said that this was accurate.

More important for our purposes, there was a discussion of the one-half of one per cent figure with respect to BarChris's past experience in repurchasing discounted customers' notes. Kircher said that this figure was "conservative." Ballard inquired whether, regardless of what past experience had been, there was "any real chance that you see of being forced to take any [alleys] back in the future?" Kircher's answer was "negative."

The alternative method of financing was explained. Kircher said that BarChris's contingent liability was only 25 per cent.

There was talk about operating alleys. Kircher said that BarChris did not operate any. Coleman and Ballard inquired whether BarChris built alleys on speculation, i.e., without any customer's contract for them. Kircher said BarChris did not.

There was discussion of officers' loans. Kircher said that the $155,000 had been repaid and that no further officers' loans were contemplated. Coleman said that this was wise, for loans from officers "indicated financial instability of the company."

Coleman did not participate personally in any further meetings of this sort. Casperson attended some and reported to Coleman. Ballard advised Coleman as to what he was doing.

After Coleman was elected a director on April 17, 1961, he made no further independent investigation of the accuracy of the prospectus. He assumed that Ballard was taking care of this on his behalf as well as on behalf of the underwriters.

In April 1961 Ballard instructed Stanton to examine BarChris's minutes for the past five years and also to look at "the major contracts of the company."[8] Stanton went to BarChris's office for that purpose on April 24. He asked Birnbaum for the minute books. He read the minutes of the board of directors and discovered interleaved in them a few minutes of executive committee meetings in 1960. He asked Kircher if there were any others. Kircher said that there had been other executive committee meetings but that the minutes had not been written up.

Stanton read the minutes of a few BarChris subsidiaries. His testimony was vague as to which ones. He had no recollection of seeing the minutes of Capitol Lanes, Inc. or Biel or Parkway Lanes, Inc. He did not discover that BarChris was operating Capitol or that it planned to operate Bridge and Yonkers.

As to the "major contracts," all that Stanton could remember seeing was an insurance policy. Birnbaum told him that there was no file of major contracts. Stanton did not examine the agreements with Talcott. He did not examine the contracts with customers. He did not look to see what contracts comprised the backlog figure. Stanton examined no accounting records of BarChris. His visit, which lasted one day, was devoted primarily to reading the directors' minutes.

On April 25 Ballard wrote to Grant about certain matters which Stanton had noted on his visit to BarChris the day before, none of which Ballard considered "very earth shaking." As far as relevant here, these were (1) Russo's [Executive vice president of BarChris] remark as recorded in the executive committee minutes of November 3, 1960

---

8. [23] Stanton was a very junior associate. He had been admitted to the bar in January 1961, some three months before. This was the first registration statement he had ever worked on.

to the effect that because of customers' defaults, BarChris might find itself in the business of operating alleys; (2) the fact that the minutes of Sanpark Realty Corporation were incomplete; and (3) the fact that minutes of the executive committee were missing.

On May 9, 1961, Ballard came to New York and conferred with Grant and Kircher. They discussed the Securities and Exchange Commission's deficiency letter of May 4, 1961 which required the inclusion in the prospectus of certain additional information, notably net sales, gross profits and net earnings figures for the first quarter of 1961. They also discussed the points raised in Ballard's letter to Grant of April 25. As to the latter, most of the conversation related to what Russo had meant by his remark on November 3, 1960. Kircher said that the delinquency problem was less severe now than it had been back in November 1960, that no alleys had been repossessed, and that although he was "worried about one alley in Harlem" (Dreyfuss), that was a "special situation." Grant reported that Russo had told him that his statement on November 3, 1960 was "merely hypothetical." On the strength of this conversation, Ballard was satisfied that the one-half of one per cent figure in the prospectus did not need qualification or elaboration.

As to the missing minutes, Kircher said that those of Sanpark were not significant and that the executive committee meetings for which there were no written minutes were concerned only with "routine matters."

It must be remembered that this conference took place only one week before the registration statement became effective. Ballard did nothing else in the way of checking during that intervening week.

Ballard did not insist that the executive committee minutes be written up so that he could inspect them, although he testified that he knew from experience that executive committee minutes may be extremely important. If he had insisted, he would have found the minutes highly informative, as has previously been pointed out.

Ballard did not ask to see BarChris's schedule of delinquencies or Talcott's notices of delinquencies, or BarChris's correspondence with Talcott.

Ballard did not examine BarChris's contracts with Talcott. He did not appreciate what Talcott's rights were under those financing agreements or how serious the effect would be upon BarChris of any exercise of those rights.

Ballard did not investigate the composition of the backlog figure to be sure that it was not "puffy." He made no inquiry after March about any new officers' loans, although he knew that Kircher had insisted on a provision in the indenture which gave loans from individuals priority over the debentures. He was unaware of the seriousness of BarChris's cash position and of how BarChris's officers intended to use a large part of the proceeds. He did not know that BarChris was operating Capitol Lanes.

Like Grant, Ballard, without checking, relied on the information which he got from Kircher. He also relied on Grant who, as company counsel, presumably was familiar with its affairs.

The formal opinion which Ballard's firm rendered to the underwriters at the closing on May 24, 1961 made clear that this is what he had done. The opinion stated:

"In the course of the preparation of the Registration Statement and Prospectus by the Company, we have had numerous conferences with representatives of and counsel for the Company and with its auditors and we have raised many questions regarding the business of the Company. Satisfactory answers to such questions were in each case given us, and all other information and documents we requested have been supplied. We are of the opinion that the *data presented* to us are accurately reflected in the Registration Statement and Prospectus and that there has been omitted from the Registration Statement no material facts *included in such data*. Although *we have not otherwise verified* the completeness or accuracy of the information furnished to us, on the basis of the foregoing and with the exception of the financial statements and schedules (which this opinion does not pass upon), we have no reason to believe that the Registration Statement or Prospectus contains any untrue statement of any material fact or omits to state a material fact required to be stated therein or necessary in order to make the statements therein not misleading."

Coleman testified that Drexel had an understanding with its attorneys that "we expect them to inspect on our behalf the corporate records of the company including, but not limited to, the minutes of the corporation, the stockholders and the committees of the board authorized to act for the board." Ballard manifested his awareness of this understanding by sending Stanton to read the minutes and the major contracts. It is difficult to square this understanding with the formal opinion of Ballard's firm which expressly disclaimed any attempt to verify information supplied by the company and its counsel.

In any event, it is clear that no effectual attempt at verification was made. The question is whether due diligence required that it be made. Stated another way, is it sufficient to ask questions, to obtain answers which, if true, would be thought satisfactory, and to let it go at that, without seeking to ascertain from the records whether the answers in fact are true and complete?

I have already held that this procedure is not sufficient in Grant's case. Are underwriters in a different position, as far as due diligence is concerned?

The underwriters say that the prospectus is the company's prospectus, not theirs. Doubtless this is the way they customarily regard it. But the Securities Act makes no such distinction. The underwriters are just as responsible as the company if the prospectus is false. And prospective investors rely upon the reputation of the underwriters in deciding whether to purchase the securities.

There is no direct authority on this question, no judicial decision defining the degree of diligence which underwriters must exercise to establish their defense under Section 11.

There is some authority in New York for the proposition that a director of a corporation may rely upon information furnished him by the officers without independently verifying it. *See Litwin v. Allen*, 25 N.Y.S.2d 667 (Sup. Ct. 1940).

In support of that principle, the court in *Litwin* (25 N.Y.S.2d at 719) quoted from the opinion of Lord Halsbury in, *Dovey v. Cory* (1901) App. Cas. 477, 486, in which he said:

> "The business of life could not go on if people could not trust those who are put into a position of trust for the express purpose of attending to details of management."

Of course, New York law does not govern this case. The construction of the Securities Act is a matter of federal law. But the underwriters argue that *Litwin* is still on point, for they say that it establishes a standard of reasonableness for the reasonably prudent director which should be the same as the standard for the reasonably prudent underwriter under the Securities Act.

In my opinion the two situations are not analogous. An underwriter has not put the company's officers "into a position of trust for the express purpose of attending to details of management." The underwriters did not select them. In a sense, the positions of the underwriter and the company's officers are adverse. It is not unlikely that statements made by company officers to an underwriter to induce him to underwrite may be self-serving. They may be unduly enthusiastic. As in this case, they may, on occasion, be deliberately false.

The purpose of Section 11 is to protect investors. To that end the underwriters are made responsible for the truth of the prospectus. If they may escape that responsibility by taking at face value representations made to them by the company's management, then the inclusion of underwriters among those liable under Section 11 affords the investors no additional protection. To effectuate the statute's purpose, the phrase "reasonable investigation" must be construed to require more effort on the part of the underwriters than the mere accurate reporting in the prospectus of "data presented" to them by the company. It should make no difference that this data is elicited by questions addressed to the company officers by the underwriters, or that the underwriters at the time believe that the company's officers are truthful and reliable. In order to make the underwriters' participation in this enterprise of any value to the investors, the underwriters must make some reasonable attempt to verify the data submitted to them. They may not rely solely on the company's officers or on the company's counsel. A prudent man in the management of his own property would not rely on them.

It is impossible to lay down a rigid rule suitable for every case defining the extent to which such verification must go. It is a question of degree, a matter of judgment in each case. In the present case, the underwriters' counsel made almost no attempt to verify management's representations. I hold that that was insufficient.

On the evidence in this case, I find that the underwriters' counsel did not make a reasonable investigation of the truth of those portions of the prospectus which were not made on the authority of Peat, Marwick as an expert. Drexel is bound by their failure. It is not a matter of relying upon counsel for legal advice. Here the attorneys were dealing with matters of fact. Drexel delegated to them, as its agent, the business of examining the corporate minutes and contracts. It must bear the consequences of their failure to make an adequate examination.

The other underwriters, who did nothing and relied solely on Drexel and on the lawyers, are also bound by it. It follows that although Drexel and the other underwriters believed that those portions of the prospectus were true, they had no reasonable ground for that belief, within the meaning of the statute. Hence, they have not established their due diligence defense, except as to the 1960 audited figures.

The same conclusions must apply to Coleman. Although he participated quite actively in the earlier stages of the preparation of the prospectus, and contributed questions and warnings of his own, in addition to the questions of counsel, the fact is that he stopped his participation toward the end of March 1961. He made no investigation after he became a director. When it came to verification, he relied upon his counsel to do it for him. Since counsel failed to do it, Coleman is bound by that failure. Consequently, in his case also, he has not established his due diligence defense except as to the audited 1960 figures.

––––––

As noted in *Escott*, an underwriter's due diligence is generally coordinated and performed by its counsel. This is so, even though the underwriter's counsel has no §11 liability. The underwriter's counsel acts as the agent of the underwriter in the process of conducting due diligence and if it fails to conduct adequate due diligence, §11 liability is imposed solely on the underwriter.

Escott also left open the question of whether all members of the underwriting syndicate are held to the same standard of reasonable investigation as the managing underwriter, even though they are bound by the managing underwriter's due diligence activities. However, courts later confirmed that members of the underwriting syndicate may rely on an adequate investigation conducted by the managing underwriter. *See Competitive Assoc., Inc. v. Int'l Health Sciences, Inc.*, 1975 U.S. Dist. LEXIS 14230., p. 19. However, the reliance on the managing underwriter by other syndicate members must be reasonable. In addition, Rule 176(g) of the Securities Act provides that the determination of whether an underwriter conducts a reasonable investigation depends on "the type of underwriting arrangement, the *role of the particular person as an underwriter*, and the availability of information with respect to the registrant." (emphasis added).

As discussed earlier, adequate due diligence with respect to the expertised portion of the registration statement generally does not require an investigation. Instead, the broker-dealer is required to have a reasonable ground to believe, and does believe, that the registration statement does not contain any material misstatements or omissions. Specifically, the broker-dealer may rely on the expert for the expertised portion of the registration statement. Of course, the broker-dealer cannot rely on the expert for the expertised portion of the registration statement if it fails to disclose all material information to the expert. *See Flecker v. Hollywood Entertainment Corp.*, 1997 U.S. Dist. LEXIS 5329. However, even if the broker-dealer has not concealed information from the expert, it may be required to conduct its own investigation with respect to the expertised portion of the registration statement. Compare the following two cases.

In re Software Toolworks, Inc. Securities Litigation
38 F.3d 1078 (9th Cir. 1994)

CYNTHIA HOLCOMB HALL, Circuit Judge:

In this case, we again consider the securities-fraud claims raised by disappointed investors in Software Toolworks, Inc., who appeal the district court's summary judgment in favor of auditors Deloitte & Touche and underwriters Montgomery Securities and PaineWebber, Inc. We affirm in part, reverse in part, and remand.

In July 1990, Software Toolworks, Inc., a producer of software for personal computers and Nintendo game systems, conducted a secondary public offering of common stock at $18.50 a share, raising more than $71 million. After the offering, the market price of Toolworks' shares declined steadily until, on October 11, 1990, the stock was trading at $5.40 a share. At that time, Toolworks issued a press release announcing substantial losses and the share price dropped another fifty-six percent to $2.375.

The next day, several investors ("the plaintiffs") filed a class action alleging that Toolworks, auditor Deloitte & Touche ("Deloitte"), and underwriters Montgomery Securities and PaineWebber, Inc. ("the Underwriters") had issued a false and misleading prospectus and registration statement in violation of section[] 11 ... of the Securities Act of 1933 ("the 1933 Act").... Specifically, the plaintiffs claimed that the defendants had (1) falsified audited financial statements for fiscal 1990 by reporting as revenue sales to original equipment manufacturers ("OEMs") with whom Toolworks had no binding agreements, (2) fabricated large consignment sales in order for Toolworks to meet financial projections for the first quarter of fiscal 1991 ("the June quarter"), and (3) lied to the Securities Exchange Commission ("SEC") in response to inquiries made before the registration statement became effective.

Toolworks and its officers quickly settled with the plaintiffs for $26.5 million. After the completion of discovery, the district court granted summary judgment in favor of the Underwriters on all claims and in favor of Deloitte on all claims other than one cause of action under section 11. The district court held that (1) the Underwriters had established a "due diligence" defense under section[] 11 ... as a matter of law, (2) Deloitte had made no material misrepresentations or omissions, other than the OEM revenue statements, on which liability under section[] 11 ... could attach.... The plaintiffs ... filed a timely appeal....

* * *

We ... address the plaintiffs' claims against the Underwriters under section[] 11 ... of the 1933 Act. Section 11 imposes liability "[i]n case any part of [a] registration statement ... contain[s] an untrue statement of a material fact or omit[s] to state a material fact required to be stated therein or necessary to make the statements therein not misleading...."

Liability under section[] 11 ... properly may fall on the underwriters of a public offering. Underwriters, however, may absolve themselves from liability by establishing a "due diligence" defense. Under section 11, underwriters must prove that they "had, after reasonable investigation, reasonable ground to believe and did believe ... that the statements therein were true and that there was no omission to state a material fact required to be stated therein or necessary to make the statements therein not misleading."

The district court held that the Underwriters had established due diligence as a matter of law and, accordingly, issued summary judgment against the plaintiffs on the section 11 ... claim[]. On appeal, the plaintiffs contend that due diligence is so fact-intensive that summary judgment is inappropriate even where underlying historical facts are undisputed. The plaintiffs further contend that, in any event, the district court erred by ignoring disputed issues of material fact in this case. We hold that, in appropriate cases, summary judgment may resolve due diligence issues but that, in this case, the district court erred by granting summary judgment in favor of the Underwriters on several claims.

* * *

The plaintiffs next assert that a material issue of fact exists regarding whether the Underwriters diligently investigated, or needed to investigate, Toolworks' recognition of OEM revenue on its financial statements. The plaintiffs claim that the Underwriters "blindly rel[ied]" on Deloitte in spite of numerous "red flags" indicating that the OEM entries were incorrect and that, as a result, the district court erred in granting summary judgment.

An underwriter need not conduct due diligence into the "expertised" parts of a prospectus, such as certified financial statements. Rather, the underwriter need only show that it "had no reasonable ground to believe, and did not believe ... that the statements therein were untrue or that there was an omission to state a material fact required to be stated therein or necessary to make the statements therein not misleading." The issue on appeal, therefore, is whether the Underwriters' reliance on the expertised financial statements was reasonable as a matter of law.

As the first "red flag," the plaintiffs point to Toolworks' "backdated" contract with Hyosung, a Korean manufacturer. During the fourth quarter of fiscal 1990, Toolworks recognized $1.7 million in revenue from an OEM contract with Hyosung. In due diligence, the Underwriters discovered a memorandum from Hyosung to Toolworks stating that Hyosung had "backdated" the agreement to permit Toolworks to recognize revenue in fiscal 1990. The plaintiffs claim that, after discovering this memorandum, the Underwriters could no longer rely on Deloitte because the accountants had approved revenue recognition for the transaction.

If the Underwriters had done nothing more, the plaintiffs' contention might be correct. The plaintiffs, however, ignore the significant steps taken by the Underwriters after discovery of the Hyosung memorandum to ensure the accuracy of Deloitte's revenue recognition. The Underwriters first confronted Deloitte, which explained that it was proper for Toolworks to book revenue in fiscal 1990 because the company had contracted with Hyosung in March, even though the firms did not document the agreement until April. The Underwriters then insisted that Deloitte reconfirm, in writing, the Hyosung agreement and Toolworks' other OEM contracts. Finally, the Underwriters contacted other accounting firms to verify Deloitte's OEM revenue accounting methods.

Thus, with regard to the Hyosung agreement, the Underwriters did not "blindly rely" on Deloitte. The district court correctly held that, as a matter of law, the Underwriters' "investigation of the OEM business was reasonable."

b.

The plaintiffs next assert that the Underwriters could not reasonably rely on Deloitte's financial statements because Toolworks' counsel, Riordan & McKinzie, refused to issue an opinion letter stating that the OEM agreements were binding contracts. This contention has no merit because, contrary to the plaintiffs' assertions, Toolworks had never requested the law firm to render such an opinion. The plaintiffs attempt to infer wrongdoing in such circumstances is patently unreasonable. The district court correctly granted summary judgment in favor of the Underwriters on this issue.

c.

Finally, the plaintiffs assert that, by reading the agreements, the Underwriters should have realized that Toolworks had improperly recognized revenue. Specifically, the plaintiffs claim that several of the contracts were contingent and that it was facially apparent that Toolworks might not receive any revenue under them. As the Underwriters explain, this contention misconstrues the nature of a due diligence investigation:

> [The Underwriters] reviewed the contracts to verify that there was a written agreement for each OEM contract mentioned in the Prospectus-not to analyze the propriety of revenue recognition, which was the responsibility of [Deloitte]. Given the complexity surrounding software licensing revenue recognition, it is absurd to suggest that, in perusing Toolworks' contracts, [the Underwriters] should have concluded that [Deloitte] w[as] wrong, particularly when the OEM's provided written confirmation.

We recently confirmed precisely this point in a case involving analogous facts: "[T]he defendants relied on Deloitte's *accounting decisions* (to recognize revenue) about the sales. Those expert decisions, which underlie the plaintiffs' attack on the financial statements, represent precisely the type of 'certified' information on which section 11 permits non-experts to rely." *WOW II,* 35 F.3d at 1421; *see also In re Worlds of Wonder Sec. Litig.,* 814 F.Supp. 850, 864-65 (N.D.Cal.1993) ("It is absurd in these circumstances for Plaintiffs to suggest that the other defendants, who are not accountants, possibly could have known of any mistakes by Deloitte. Therefore, even if there are errors in the financial statements, no defendant except Deloitte can be liable under Section 11 on that basis.")

Thus, because the Underwriters' reliance on Deloitte was reasonable under the circumstances, the district court correctly granted summary judgment on this issue....

Thus, we hold that the district court properly granted summary judgment in favor of the Underwriters on the section 11 ... issue[] regarding their due diligence investigation into Toolworks' ... description of OEM revenue.

————

In re Worldcom, Inc. Securities Litigation

346 F. Supp. 2d 628 (S.D.N.Y. 2004)

COTE, District Judge.

This Opinion addresses issues related to an underwriter's due diligence obligations. Following the conclusion of fact discovery, several of the parties in this consolidated securities class action arising from the collapse of WorldCom, Inc. ("WorldCom") have filed for summary judgment. This Opinion resolves the motions for summary judgment filed by Lead Plaintiff for the class, who seeks a declaration that certain of the WorldCom financials incorporated in the registration statements for two World-Com bond offerings contained material misstatements; and by the underwriters for those same bond offerings, who seek a declaration that they have no liability for any false statements in the WorldCom financials that accompanied the registration statements or for the alleged omissions from those registration statements.

It is undisputed that at least as of early 2001 WorldCom executives engaged in a secretive scheme to manipulate WorldCom's public filings concerning WorldCom's financial condition. Because those public filings were incorporated into the registration statements for the two bond offerings, the underwriters are liable for those false statements unless they can show that they were sufficiently diligent in their investigation of WorldCom in connection with the bond offerings. Through these motions, the Lead Plaintiff emphasizes that the underwriters did almost no investigation of WorldCom in connection with their underwriting of the bond offerings for the company, and because they did essentially no investigation, will be unable to succeed with their defense that they were diligent. The Lead Plaintiff contends moreover that there were "red flags" that should have led the underwriters to question even the audited financials filed by WorldCom.

For their part, the underwriters emphasize that WorldCom management concealed the fraud from almost everyone within WorldCom, from WorldCom's outside auditor, and from the underwriters themselves. They assert that they were entitled to rely on WorldCom's audited financial statements as accurately describing the company's financial condition, and also on the comfort letters that WorldCom's outside auditor [Arthur Andersen] provided for the unaudited financial statements....

* * *

WorldCom announced a massive restatement of its financials on June 25, 2002. It reported its intention to restate its financial statements for 2001 and the first quarter of 2002. According to that announcement, "[a]s a result of an internal audit of the company's capital expenditure accounting, it was determined that certain transfers from line cost expenses[9] to capital accounts during this period were not made in accordance with generally accepted accounting principles (GAAP)." The amount of transfers was then estimated to be over $3.8 billion. Without the improper transfers, the company estimated that it would have reported a net loss for 2001 and the first quarter of 2002....

The plaintiffs allege that the Underwriter Defendants violated Section[] 11 ... of the Securities Act of 1933....

* * *

[The underwriters] argue in particular that they were entitled to rely on WorldCom's audited financial statements and had no duty to investigate their reliability unless they had reasonable grounds to believe that they were not accurate, and that they were also entitled to rely on the "comfort letters" from WorldCom's auditor for the interim unaudited WorldCom financial statements....

* * *

WorldCom's Accounting Strategies

WorldCom's single largest operating expense was its line costs. This item accounted for roughly half of its expenses and was so material that it was reported as a separate line item on its financial statements. WorldCom's ratio of line cost expense to its revenue was called the E/R ratio, was used as a measurement of its performance, and was also publicly reported in its SEC filings. The lower the ratio, the better the performance....

[S]enior management in WorldCom manipulated the public reports of World-Com's line costs beginning in the first quarter of 2001 through shifting a portion of them to capital expenditures accounts, and ... this manipulation was criminal. The manipulation reduced the reported line costs and resulted in a lower E/R ratio....

The capitalization fraud began on Friday, April 20, 2001, when Troy Normand, WorldCom's Director of Legal Entity Reporting in General Accounting, directed that line costs be reduced by $771 million by booking that amount of line costs in an entry labeled "prepaid capacity." Between that day and Tuesday, April 24, WorldCom personnel allocated the line costs expenses to WorldCom's two tracker stocks[10] and other business units. This manipulation was necessary to make the E/R ratio for the first quarter of 2001 "fairly consistent" with the E/R ratio for the prior quarter.

---

9. [1] Line costs, which are transmission costs.... were the single largest operating expense incurred by WorldCom.

10. [10] On November 1, 2000, WorldCom announced a plan to separate its businesses and create two publicly traded tracking stocks: WorldCom, which would reflect the performance of WorldCom's "core high-growth data," Internet, hosting and international businesses; and MCI, which would reflect the performance of its high cash flow consumer, small business, wholesale long-distance voice and dial-up Internet access operations.

Andersen was unaware of the manipulation of line costs through this capitalization scheme.... The improper capitalization of line costs continued through the first quarter of 2002. WorldCom's internal audit department had completed its last audit of World-Com's capital expenditures in approximately January of 2002, and had not uncovered any evidence of fraud. In May of 2002, it began another audit of the company's capital expenditures. The fraudulent capitalization of line costs was uncovered as a result of a May 21 meeting between the company's internal auditors and the WorldCom director in charge of tracking capital expenditures. During that meeting the director used the term "prepaid capacity" to explain the difference between two sets of schedules that he was being shown. The auditors were unfamiliar with the term. After asking questions of several people about "prepaid capacity," Eugene Morse, a member of WorldCom's internal audit group, used a new software tool to investigate WorldCom's books and was able to uncover the transfer of line costs to capital accounts in a matter of hours.

Andersen and the 1999 Form 10-K

* * *

In its lengthy description of the regulatory environment, the 1999 Form 10-K noted that.... [l]ine costs "as a percentage of revenues" for 1999 were reported to be 43% as compared to 47% for 1998. "Overall decreases are attributable to changes in the product mix and synergies and economies of scale resulting from network efficiencies achieved from the continued assimilation of MCI," and other companies into the Company's operations.... the "principal components of line costs are access charges and transport charges." It added that WorldCom's "goal is to manage transport costs through effective utilization of its network, favorable contracts with carriers and network efficiencies made possible as a result of expansion of the Company's customer base by acquisitions and internal growth...." Andersen consented to the inclusion of its March 24, 2000 audit report in the Form 10-K.... [and] represented [that] In our opinion, based on our audit..., the financial statements referred to above present fairly, in all material respects, the financial position of MCI WorldCom, Inc. and subsidiaries as of December 31, 1999..., in conformity with accounting principles generally accepted in the United States.

* * *

2000 Offering

On May 24, 2000, WorldCom conducted a public offering of debt securities by issuing approximately $5 billion worth of bonds ("2000 Offering"). It filed a registration statement dated April 12, 2000, and prospectus supplement dated May 19, 2000 (collectively "2000 Registration Statement") that incorporated by reference among other things the WorldCom Form 10-K for the year ending December 31, 1999, and its Form 10-Q for the quarter ended March 31, 2000. SSB [Salomon Smith Barney] was the book runner and, with J.P. Morgan, was the co-lead manager.[11]

---

11. [19] A book runner is responsible for pricing the offering and allocating shares to institutional and retail investors. A lead manager determines the amount of shares reserved for its own sales efforts and the amount of the offering for other members of the syndicate.

The April 12, 2000 Registration Statement ... explained that it was part of a registration statement that was filed with the SEC using a " 'shelf' registration process."

> Under this process, we may sell any combination of the debt securities described in this prospectus in one or more offerings up to a total dollar amount of $15,000,000,000. This prospectus provides you with a general description of the securities we may offer. Each time we sell securities, we will provide a prospectus supplement that will contain specific information about the terms of that offering. The prospectus supplement may also add, update or change information contained in this prospectus....

The 2000 Registration Statement included a section labeled "experts." It explained that the year-end WorldCom consolidated financial statements have been audited by Arthur Andersen LLP, independent public accountants, as indicated in their report with respect thereto, and are included in the MCI WorldCom's Annual Report on Form 10-K for the year ended December 31, 1999, and are incorporated herein by reference, in reliance upon the authority of such firm as experts in accounting and auditing in giving such reports.

* * *

Andersen created an undated worksheet in connection with WorldCom's first quarter 2000 unaudited financial statement. The worksheet was an eleven-page Andersen form entitled "U.S. GAAS Review of Interim Financial Statements of a Public Company," and was a vital step in preparing a "comfort letter" for a company.... A "comfort letter" for the first quarter 2000 unaudited financial statement is dated May 19, is eight pages long, and indicates that it is written at the request of WorldCom. In it, Andersen reaffirms its audits, including those incorporated in the 2000 Registration Statement. It warns that having not audited any financial statements for any period subsequent to December 31, 1999, it is unable to express any opinion on the unaudited consolidated balance sheet of WorldCom as of March 31, 2000, or the results of operations or cash flows as of any date subsequent to December 31, 1999.... Andersen represented that nothing had come to its attention as a result of that work [preparing the comfort letter] that caused Andersen to believe that "[a]ny material modifications should be made to the unaudited condensed consolidated financial statements [for the first quarter of 2000], incorporated by reference in the Registration Statement, for them to be in conformity with generally accepted accounting principles" or that "[t]he unaudited condensed consolidated financial statements ... do not comply as to form in all material respects with the applicable accounting requirements of the Act and the related published rules and regulations." The letter concludes that it is offered to "assist the underwriters in conducting and documenting their investigation" of the affairs of WorldCom in connection with the offering of securities covered by the 2000 Registration Statement....

The Underwriter Defendants' Credit Assessment of WorldCom as of Early 2001

[S]everal of the Underwriter Defendants downgraded WorldCom as a credit risk in February 2001.... On February 22, Bank of America downgraded WorldCom's credit rating from 3 to 4, citing its lack of revenue growth, margin deterioration, the likelihood that WorldCom revenue from its long-distance business would continue to decline ... On February 27, a J.P. Morgan document reflects that the bank reduced its internal "senior unsecured" risk rating for WorldCom from A2 to BBB1 because of WorldCom's "weakened credit profile and continued pressure on its MCI long-distance business segment."

* * *

Within weeks of these decisions to downgrade WorldCom's credit rating, the Underwriter Defendants had to consider whether to participate in WorldCom's restructuring of its credit facility, which was a line of credit extended to WorldCom by several of the banks, and whether to compete for investment banking positions in the bond offering that WorldCom hoped to undertake that Spring.... There is evidence that several of the Underwriter Defendants decided to make a commitment to the restructuring of the credit facility and to attempt to win the right to underwrite the 2001 Offering, while at the same time reducing their own exposure to risk from holding WorldCom debt by engaging in hedging strategies, such as credit default swaps.[12]

2000 Form 10-K

With respect to long-distance services, the document reported that revenue fell in 2000 in absolute terms and as a percentage of total WorldCom revenues..., line costs were shown as a decreasing percentage of revenues for each year from 1998 to 2000, beginning with 45.3% in 1998, and ending at 39.6% in 2000.... a result of increased data and dedicated Internet traffic.

2001 Offering

Through the 2001 Offering WorldCom issued $11.9 billion worth of notes. The May 9, 2001 registration statement and May 14, 2001 prospectus supplement (collectively, "2001 Registration Statement") for the 2001 Offering incorporated WorldCom's 2000 10-K and first quarter 2001 Form 8-K dated April 26, 2001.... On May 9, a banker from J.P. Morgan and two Cravath attorneys spoke by telephone with Sullivan [Worldcom's CFO] and Stephanie Scott of WorldCom and with representatives of Andersen.... Sullivan [did not] disclose the $771 million capitalization of line costs.

Discussion

* * *

I. Legal Framework

* * *

A.   Section 11

---

12. [29] A credit default swap enables a lender to hedge its exposure to a borrower. The lender enters into a swap contract and pays a premium for credit default protection to the swap seller. In the event of a failure to pay, the swap seller agrees to pay the lender the value of the loan. If there is no failure to pay, the lender has lost only the premium.

B.   Section 12

* * *

Section 11 of the Securities Act "was designed to assure compliance with the disclosure provisions of the Act by imposing a stringent standard of liability on the parties who play a direct role in a registered offering...." As a result, such parties will be found to have violated Section 11 whenever "material facts have been omitted or presented in such a way as to obscure or distort their significance...." Section 11 provides an affirmative defense of "due diligence," which is available to defendants other than the issuer of the security.... The standard that applies to this defense varies depending on whether the misleading statement in the registration statement is or expressly relies on an expert's opinion....

II. Lead Plaintiff's Motion for Partial Summary Judgment

With respect to the 2000 Registration Statement, the Lead Plaintiff's motion is addressed to the reporting of line costs and depreciation and amortization. With respect to the 2001 Registration Statement, the Lead Plaintiff's motion is addressed to the reporting of line costs, capital expenditures, and assets and goodwill.

The Underwriter Defendants concede that the reporting of line costs and capital expenditures for the first quarter of 2001 was false. They resist summary judgment regarding the falsity of any other line of financial reporting with respect to the 2000 and 2001 Registration Statements. They assert that Andersen's professional judgment regarding certain items has not been shown to be unreasonable.... The Underwriter Defendants argue in addition that the Lead Plaintiff's motion does not address their affirmative defense of due diligence and their entitlement to rely on Andersen's audits and comfort letters.

* * *

III. The Underwriter Defendants' Motion for Summary Judgment; The Financial Statements

The Underwriter Defendants move for summary judgment with respect to the financial statements that were incorporated into the Registration Statements. They assert that there is no dispute that they acted reasonably in relying on Andersen's audits and comfort letters. The Underwriter Defendants contend that they were entitled to rely on WorldCom's audited financial statements and had no duty to investigate their reliability so long as they had "no reasonable ground to believe" that such financial statements contained a false statement. They also assert that they were entitled to rely in the same way on Andersen's comfort letters for the unaudited quarterly financial statements incorporated into the Registration Statements.

A. Role of the Underwriter

Underwriters must "exercise a high degree of care in investigation and independent verification of the company's representations." Overall, "[n]o greater reliance in our self-regulatory system is placed on any single participant in the issuance of securities than upon the underwriter." Underwriters function as "the first line of defense" with respect to material misrepresentations and omissions in registration statements. As a consequence, courts must be "particularly scrupulous in examining the[ir] conduct." (citations omitted).

B. The "Due Diligence" Defenses

* * *

There is a different standard that applies when a Section 11 defendant is entitled to rely upon the opinion of an expert. "[A]s regards any part of the registration statement purporting to be made on the authority of an expert," a defendant other than that expert will not be liable if he demonstrates that *he had no reasonable ground to believe and did not believe,* at the time such part of the registration statement became effective, *that the statements therein were untrue* or that there was an omission to state a material fact required to be stated therein or necessary to make the statements therein not misleading...."[T]he standard of reasonableness shall be that required of a prudent man in the management of his own property."

Courts have [labeled this] the reliance [defense] permitted by the statute on an expert's statement.... [I]t is settled that an accountant qualifies as an expert, and audited financial statements are considered expertised portions of a registration statement....

In order for an accountant's opinion to qualify as an expert opinion under Section 11(b)(3)(C), there are three prerequisites. First, it must be reported in the Registration Statement. Second, it must be an audit opinion. Finally, the accountant must consent to inclusion of the audit opinion in the registration statement.

In an effort to encourage auditor reviews of interim financial statements, the SEC acted in 1979 to assure auditors that their review of unaudited interim financial information would not subject them to liability under Section 11. The SEC addressed the circumstances in which an accountant's opinion can be considered an expert's opinion for purposes of Section 11(b) and made it clear that reviews of unaudited interim financial statements do not constitute such an opinion. Under Rule 436[of the Securities Act], where the opinion of an expert is quoted or summarized in a registration statement, or where any information contained in a registration statement "has been reviewed or passed upon" by an expert, the written consent of the expert must be filed as an exhibit to the registration statement. Yet written consent is not sufficient to convert an opinion or review into an expertised statement. Rule 436 provides that notwithstanding written consent, *"a report on unaudited interim financial information ... by an independent accountant who has conducted a review of such interim financial information shall not be considered a part of a registration statement prepared or certified by an accountant* or a report prepared or certified by an accountant within the meaning of sections 7 and 11" of the Securities Act.

* * *

In sum, underwriters can rely on an accountant's audit opinion incorporated into a registration statement in presenting a defense under Section 11(b)(3)(C). Underwriters may not rely on an accountant's comfort letters for interim financial statements in presenting such a defense. Comfort letters do not "expertise any portion of the registration statement that is otherwise non-expertised."

Section 11explicitly absolve[s] [an underwriter] of the duty to investigate with respect to "any part of the registration statement purporting to be made on the authority of an expert" such as a certified accountant if "he had no reasonable ground to believe and did not believe" that the information therein was misleading. This provision is in the Act because, *almost by definition, it is reasonable to rely on financial statements certified by public accountants ...*

Nevertheless, underwriters' reliance on audited financial statements may not be blind. Rather, where "red flags" regarding the reliability of an audited financial statement emerge, mere reliance on an audit will not be sufficient to ward off liability.... Where such red flags arise, a duty of inquiry arises ... Rather ... in order to be entitled to the reliance defense under Section 11, a defendant must show that he had "no reasonable ground to believe and did not believe" that the statements within the registration statement that were made on an expert's authority were untrue. Any information that strips a defendant of his confidence in the accuracy of those portions of a registration statement premised on audited financial statements is a red flag, whether or not it relates to accounting fraud or an audit failure. What is at stake under Section 11 is ... the accuracy and completeness of the statements in the registration statement.

* * *

G. The Application of the Law to This Motion

* * *

1. Audited Financial Statements

The Underwriter Defendants contend that they were entitled to rely on Andersen's unqualified "clean" audit opinions for WorldCom's 1999 and 2000 Form 10-Ks as expertised statements under Section 11(b)(3)(C). Their motion for summary judgment on their reliance defense is denied.

a. 2000 Registration Statement

The Lead Plaintiff points to one issue that it contends gave the Underwriter Defendants a reasonable ground to question the reliability of WorldCom's 1999 Form 10-K. According to the computations presented by the Lead Plaintiff, WorldCom's reported E/R ratio was significantly lower than that of the equivalent numbers of its two closest competitors, Sprint and AT & T.[13] The Lead Plaintiff argues that, in the extremely competitive market in which WorldCom operated, that discrepancy triggered a duty to investigate such a crucial measurement of the company's health. The Lead Plaintiff has shown that there are issues of fact as to whether the Underwriter De-

---

13. [47] WorldCom's E/R ratio was 43%. The expert for the Lead Plaintiff calculates that AT & T's equivalent ratio was 46.8% and Sprint's was 53.2%.

fendants had reasonable grounds to believe that the 1999 Form 10-K was inaccurate in the lines related to the E/R ratio reflected in that filing.

The Underwriter Defendants argue that the difference in the E/R ratios was insufficient as a matter of law to put the Underwriter Defendants on notice of any accounting irregularity. In support of this, they point to the fact that this difference was publicly available information and no one else announced a belief that it suggested the existence of an accounting fraud at WorldCom.

The fact that the difference was publicly available information does not absolve the Underwriter Defendants of their duty to bring their expertise to bear on the issue. The Underwriter Defendants do not dispute that they were required to be familiar with the Exchange Act filings that were incorporated by reference into the Registration Statement. If a "prudent man in the management of his own property" upon reading the 1999 Form 10-K and being familiar with the other relevant information about the issuer's competitors would have questioned the accuracy of the figures, then those figures constituted a red flag and imposed a duty of investigation on the Underwriter Defendants. A jury would be entitled to find that this difference was of sufficient importance to have triggered a duty to investigate the reliability of the figures on which the ratio was based even though the figures had been audited.

b. 2001 Registration Statement

The Lead Plaintiff points to three issues that it contends imposed upon the Underwriter Defendants a duty to investigate the reliability of WorldCom's 2000 Form 10-K. They are the discrepancy between WorldCom's E/R ratio and that of its competitors; the deterioration in the MCI long-distance business, which the Lead Plaintiff alleges should have caused them to question the accuracy of WorldCom's reported assets; and Ebbers' personal financial situation, which gave him both the motive and opportunity to inflate WorldCom's stock price through manipulation.

[T]he issue in connection with the reliance defense is not whether the red flag information was well known, but whether the red flags existed and imposed a duty upon the Underwriter Defendants under the "prudent man" standard to inquire of WorldCom and/or Andersen about the reporting of WorldCom's assets because the Underwriter Defendants had a reasonable ground to believe that the reporting of assets may have been inaccurate.

ii. Ebbers' Personal Finances

* * *

The issue here is whether the Underwriter Defendants' knowledge of Ebbers, including his financial circumstances, gave them reason to believe the WorldCom audited financial statements were inaccurate. Without some evidence that the Underwriter Defendants had reason to believe that Ebbers was untrustworthy, his dependence on WorldCom's financial health, even though extraordinary, is insufficient to constitute a red flag that he may have caused a manipulation of WorldCom's financial statements.

iii. E/R Ratio

The Underwriter Defendants rely on many of the arguments that they made regarding the E/R ratio in connection with the 2000 Registration Statement. The Lead Plaintiff has shown that there are issues of fact as to whether the discrepancy in the WorldCom E/R ratio, when compared to comparable companies' E/R ratios, was sufficient to cause a prudent man to make an inquiry regarding the accuracy of the 2000 Form 10-K.

2. Interim Financial Statements

The Underwriter Defendants contend that ... they were entitled to rely on Andersen's comfort letters for WorldCom's unaudited interim financial statements for the first quarter of 2000 and 2001 so long as the Lead Plaintiff is unable to show that the Underwriter Defendants were on notice of any accounting red flags.... The Underwriter Defendants argue that if they are not entitled to rely on a comfort letter, the costs of capital formation in the United States will be substantially increased since underwriters will have to hire their own accounting firms to rehash the work of the issuer's auditor. Nothing in this Opinion should be read as imposing that obligation on underwriters or the underwriting process. The term "reasonable investigation" encompasses many modes of inquiry between obtaining comfort letters from an auditor and doing little more, on one hand, and having to re-audit a company's books on the other. Nonetheless, if aggressive or unusual accounting strategies regarding significant issues come to light in the course of a reasonable investigation, a prudent underwriter may choose to consult with accounting experts to confirm that the accounting treatment is appropriate and that additional disclosure is unnecessary.... If red flags arise from a reasonable investigation, underwriters will have to make sufficient inquiry to satisfy themselves as to the accuracy of the financial statements, and if unsatisfied, they must demand disclosure, withdraw from the underwriting process, or bear the risk of liability.

Notes and Questions

1. Broker-dealer defendants were successful in avoiding liability by asserting the reliance defense in *Software* but unsuccessful in doing so in *Worldcom*. Why?

2. In *Worldcom* the broker-dealers acted as underwriters in a shelf registration. Shelf registration is the process by which securities are registered to be offered or sold on a delayed or continuous basis and allows a single registration statement to be filed for a series of offerings. It is advantageous to the issuer because it significantly reduces the time and expense necessary to prepare public offerings and permits the issuer to offer the security to the market in a matter of hours. Shelf registration also allows the incorporation by reference of information contained in the issuer's previous filings under the Exchange Act. Why did shelf registration and incorporation by reference trigger concerns among underwriters about performing adequate due diligence? How does Rule 176 of the Securities Act address this concern?

3. Is the actual knowledge defense in § 11(a) a meaningful defense for a broker-dealer? How will the broker-dealer show that plaintiff had actual knowledge of the material misrepresentation or omission? Generally, § 11 claims are brought as class actions. Does this make it even more difficult for broker-dealers?

Hypothetical Three

Compvision Corporation ("Compvision") a Massachusetts high-technology company, made an initial public offering of securities on August 14 of this year. Success First was part of the underwriting syndicate in this firm-commitment underwriting in which Compvision sold $600 million of securities. Six weeks after the IPO, Compvision announced that its revenues and operating results for the third quarter would be lower than expected. The price of Compvision's stock fell by 30 percent within a day of this announcement. On the day after this announcement, the first investor suit was filed. Compvision and the IPO underwriters, which included Success First, were sued under § 11 of the Securities Act of 1933. The complaint alleged a violation of § 11 because the prospectus for the IPO: (1) distorted Compvision's earning trends; (2) omitted disclosure of known uncertainties affecting Compvision's operating results; (3) omitted disclosure of the increasing likelihood that Compvision would not meet its internally projected results; (4) omitted disclosure of known declines in the demand for its services and products; and (5) omitted disclosure of software development problems. The underwriting syndicate plans to assert its due diligence defense under § 11. In conducting due diligence, the underwriting syndicate failed to continue to investigate Compvision up to the effective date of the offering and relied on Compvision's assurances as to its financial condition, although the underwriting syndicate had access to all available financial information. Did the underwriters meet their due diligence requirement under § 11 for the non-expertised and expertised portions of the registration statement? In addition, may Success First rely on managing underwriter to perform the required due diligence?

D. Damages

Section 11 expressly provides for the measure of damages. In § 11(e), damages are equal to the difference between the price that the plaintiff purchaser paid for her shares (but not exceeding the offering price) and one of three possibilities depending on whether, and if, the purchaser sold her shares.

1. If the purchaser sold her shares before the § 11 law suit was filed, then damages equal the difference between the purchase price and the price at which the purchaser sold her shares (but not exceeding the offering price);

2. If the purchaser has not sold her shares at the conclusion of the § 11 lawsuit, then damages equal the difference between the purchase price and the value of her shares at the time of the filing of the § 11 lawsuit (but not exceeding the offering price); or

3. If the purchaser sold her shares after the filing of the § 11 lawsuit but before judgment, then damages equal the difference between the purchase price and the price at which the purchaser sold her shares, if the amount of damages is less than the purchase price minus the sale price before the filing of the § 11 lawsuit (but not exceeding the offering price).

Figure 6.1. Measure of Damages § 11(e)

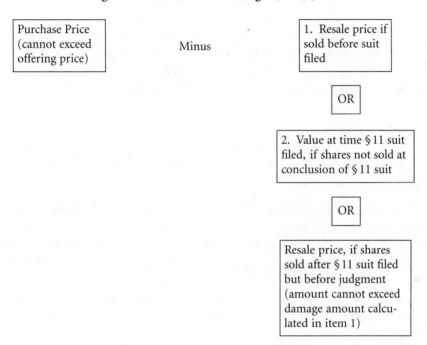

Section 11(g) caps the amount of damages recoverable from the broker-dealer to the price at which the security was offered to the public. However, this damages cap does not apply if the underwriter knowingly received some benefit directly or indirectly from the issuer not received by all other underwriters similarly situated in proportion to their respective interests in the offering. Also, assessment of costs, including attorney's fees, against the underwriter is allowed under § 11(e) if the court believes that any defense offered by the underwriter is without merit.

The term *value* used to prescribe damages in § 11(e) is not defined and, thus, is left to the courts to determine. While value would seemingly be the market price at the time the lawsuit was filed, this is not always the case. In addition, value determination, in many cases, occurs when the defendant is attempting to reduce damages in a § 11 lawsuit by establishing a negative causation defense, i.e., proving that the diminution in value is caused by factors other than the material misrepresentations and omissions contained in the registration statement.

NECA–IBEW Health & Welfare Fund v. Goldman Sachs & Co.
693 F.3d 145 (2d Cir. 2012)

* * *

Plaintiff NECA–IBEW Health & Welfare Fund ("NECA" or the "Fund") sued alleging [a] violation[] of § 11 ... of the Securities Act on behalf of a putative class consisting of all persons who acquired certain mortgage-backed certificates (the "Certificates") underwritten by defendant Goldman Sachs & Co. and issued by defendant GS Mortgage Securities Corp. ("GS Mortgage"). The Certificates were sold in 17 separate Offerings through 17 separate Trusts pursuant to the same Shelf Registration Statement, but using 17 separate Prospectus Supplements. NECA alleges that the Shelf Registration Statement contained false and misleading statements that were essentially repeated in the Prospectus Supplements....

In October 2007, NECA purchased $390,000 of the Class A2A Certificates of the GSAA Home Equity Trust 2007–10 (the "2007–10 Certificates") directly from Goldman Sachs in a public offering. In May 2008, it purchased approximately $50,000 of the Class 1AV1 Certificates from Group 1 of the GSAA Home Equity Trust 2007–5 (the "2007–5 Certificates")....

NECA alleges that the Offering Documents contained false and misleading information about the underwriting guidelines of the mortgage loan originators, the property appraisals of the loans backing the Trusts, and the risks associated with the Certificates.[14] ... For example, NECA alleges that ... [t]he statements in the Shelf Registration Statement were rendered misleading, ... by the Offering Documents' failure to disclose that the originators of the loans backing the Trusts falsely inflated (or coached borrowers falsely to inflate) their income; steered borrowers to loans exceeding their borrowing capacity; and approved borrowers based on "teaser rates" knowing they would be unable to afford payments once the rates adjusted. NECA further alleges that the originators allowed non-qualifying borrowers to be approved for loans they could not afford under exceptions to the underwriting standards based on so-called "compensating factors" when such "compensating factors" did not exist or did not justify the loans. Nor, allegedly, did the Offering Documents disclose that appraisers were ordered by loan originators to give predetermined, inflated appraisals to ensure loan approval; that the "comparable properties" used to generate appraisals were not comparable; and that property appraisals did not, in fact, conform to [Uniform Standards of Professional Appraisal Practice]. As a result of these abusive practices, NECA alleges, approximately 35%–40% of the loans in the 2007–5 Trust and 30–35% of the loans in the 2007–10 Trust were made with no determination of the borrower's ability to repay. And at least 47% of the loans in the 2007–5 Trust, and at least 41% of those in the 2007–10 Trust, were based on property value appraisals that were inflated by 9% or more.

---

14. [4] [A]t the same time they [Goldman Sachs] were selling the Certificates as "investment grade" instruments, Goldman Sachs was placing exotic bets via credit-default swaps that residential mortgages similar to those backing the Certificates would default.

* * *

[T]he district court held that NECA failed to allege "a cognizable loss" under § 11. It reasoned that NECA's allegation that it was exposed to greatly enhanced risk with respect to both the timing and amount of cash flow under the Certificates was insufficient to plead injury because of the Offering Documents' "specific warning ... about the possibility ... that the [C]ertificates may not be resalable." ... Observing that asset-backed securities are "'primarily serviced by the cash flows of a discrete pool of receivables or other financial assets, either fixed or revolving, that by their terms convert into cash within a finite time period,'" the court held that "NECA must allege the actual failure to receive payments due under the Certificates" in order to "allege an injury cognizable under Section 11."

NECA appealed.... [contending that ... the district court erred ... in requiring it to plead an out-of-pocket loss in order to allege injury under § 11....

* * *

We turn now to NECA's contention that the district [court] erred in concluding that it failed to allege cognizable damages under § 11. While a plaintiff need not plead damages under § 11, it must satisfy the court that it has suffered a cognizable injury under the statute. Section 11 permits a successful plaintiff to recover "the difference between the amount paid for the security" and either

> (1) *the value thereof as of the time such suit was brought,* or (2) the price at which such security shall have been disposed of in the market before suit, or (3) the price at which such security shall have been disposed of after suit but before judgment if such damages shall be less than [the measure of damages defined in subsection (1)].

15 U.S.C. § 77k(e) (emphasis added). In *McMahan & Co. v. Wherehouse Entertainment, Inc.,* 65 F.3d 1044 (2d Cir.1995), this Court provided guidance on the meaning of "value" in § 11(e): First, "the term ... was intended to mean the security's true value after the alleged misrepresentations are made public. Second, although "in a market economy, when market value is available and reliable, market value will always be the primary gauge of a [security's] worth," the value of a security may not be equivalent to its market price. Congress' use of the term "value," as distinguished from the terms "amount paid" and "price" indicates that, under certain circumstances, the market price may not adequately reflect the security's value.... However, "even where market price is not completely reliable, it serves as a good starting point in determining value." Thus, under § 11, the key is not, as the district court concluded and as defendants contend, market price; the key is value.

NECA, as it was required to do, plausibly pled a cognizable injury—a decline in value—under § 11. NECA alleged that "the value of the [C]ertificates ha[d] diminished greatly since their original offering, as ha[d] the price at which members of the Class could dispose of them[,] ... caus[ing] damages to the plaintiff and the Class." It supported this assertion of injury with the following well-pleaded facts: that the rating agencies "put negative watch labels on the Certificate[s] ... and downgraded previously-assigned ratings" and that holders were "exposed to much more risk with respect to both the timing and absolute cash flow to be received than the Offering Documents represented." The latter allegation was rendered plausible by the complaint's extensive allegations regarding loan originators' failure to determine, in a significant number of cases and contrary to their underwriting guidelines, "whether the borrower's monthly income ... will be sufficient to enable the borrower to meet its monthly obligations on the mortgage loan and other expenses related to the property." Drawing the requisite inferences in plaintiff's favor, it is not just plausible — but obvious — that mortgage-backed securities like the Certificates would suffer a decline in value as a result of (1) ratings downgrades and (2) less certain future cash flows. Thus, NECA plausibly alleged a "difference between the amount paid for the [Certificates]" and "the value thereof as of the time [its] suit was brought."

Defendants argue, and the district court reasoned, that plaintiff suffered no loss because the Complaint did not allege any missed payment from the Trusts and the Fund admitted that no payments had been missed. But basic securities valuation principles — discounting future cash flows to their present value using a rate of interest reflecting the cash flows' risk — belie the proposition that a fixed income investor must miss an interest payment before his securities can be said to have declined in "value." The reasonable inference from NECA's allegations is that, because the loans backing the Certificates were riskier than defendants represented, the future cash flows to which NECA was entitled under the Certificates required a higher discount rate once the Offering Documents' falsity was revealed, resulting in a lower present value. Put differently, the revelation that borrowers on loans backing the Certificates were less creditworthy than the Offering Documents represented affected the Certificates' "value" immediately, because it increased the Certificates' credit risk profile. In this analysis, whether Certificate-holders actually missed a scheduled coupon payment is not determinative....

Neither is the existence or liquidity of a secondary market. The district court determined that, because plaintiff "knew [the Certificates] might not be liquid, it [could] not allege an injury based upon the hypothetical price of the Certificates on a secondary market at the time of suit." *NECA–IBEW,* 743 F.Supp.2d at 292. We have three problems with this conclusion. First, NECA alleged the existence of a secondary market. Second, the district court's analysis conflates liquidity risk and credit risk. While plaintiff may have assumed liquidity risk when it purchased the Certificates, it did not assume the heightened credit risk associated with mortgage collateral allegedly far riskier than the Offering Documents represented. Both risks may tend to depress a security's price, but that does not prevent a damages expert from isolating their respective contributions to a given price decline. And NECA was not required to prove the precise amount of any damages at the pleading stage. Indeed, § 11 works the other way: It presumes that any diminution in value is attributable to the alleged misrepresentations, and places the burden on defendants to *disprove* causation. ("[I]f the defendant proves that any portion or all of [plaintiff's] damages represents other than the depreciation in value of such security resulting from such part of the registration statement[ ] with respect to which [defendant's] liability is asserted, ... such portion of or all such damages shall not be recoverable."); *In re Morgan Stanley Info. Fund,* 592 F.3d at 359 n. 7.[15]

Third, the district court also conflated the price of a security and its "value." The absence of an "actual market price for [a security] at the time of suit" does not defeat an investor's plausible claim of injury from misleading statements contained in that security's offering documents. The value of a security is not unascertainable simply because it trades in an illiquid market and therefore has no "actual market price." Indeed, valuing illiquid assets is an important (and routine) activity for asset managers, an activity typically guided by Statement 157 of the Financial Accounting Standards Board ("FAS 157").[16] Moreover, the fact that financial valuation may be difficult or "involve[ ] the exercise of judgment"—as defendants observe to be the case with the "complex asset-backed instruments at issue here"—does not render plaintiff's allegations of loss of value fatally conclusory.

For these reasons, the judgment of the district court dismissing plaintiff's §11 claim[ ] is vacated and ... reinstated. On remand, the court should afford plaintiff leave to replead, *inter alia,* "the price at which [the 2007–10 Class 1AV1 Certificates] shall have been disposed of after suit but before judgment," ...

III. Section 12

A. Section 12(a)(1)

The broker-dealer incurs liability under §12(a)(1) for any violation of §5 of the Securities Act as a statutory seller. Specifically, §12(a)(1) imposes strict liability against any person who offers or sells a security in violation of §5 of the Securities Act. This strict liability provision is designed to ensure compliance with the registration requirements for securities contained in §5 of the Securities Act. Section 12(a)(1) defendants also include anyone who solicits the purchase of securities based on the statutory definitions of the terms offer and sell contained in §2(a)(3) of the Securities Act. Section 2(a)(3) defines the terms "offer to sell", "offer for sale", or "offer" as "every attempt or offer to dispose of, or solicitation of an offer to buy, a security ..." as long as a purchase has occurred.

A buyer may recover under §12(a)(1) by proving that: (1) no registration statement involving the securities was in effect at the time of the sale; (2) under the language of the statute, the defendant was a person who sold or offered to sell (solicit) the se-

---

15. [15] It may well be that, ultimately, the Fund will recover nothing because defendants will prove that any diminution in value is attributable to, *e.g.,* (1) illiquidity, (2) the global financial crisis, or (3) a widening of credit spreads rather than defendants' misrepresentations. But that is irrelevant to whether plaintiff has alleged, at the pleading stage, a cognizable injury under the statute.

16. [16] Under the "fair value hierarchy" established by FAS 157, the highest priority "input" for valuing assets and liabilities is quoted prices in active markets for identical assets or liabilities. FAS 157 at 12. If such "Level 1" inputs are not available, "Level 2" inputs, such as quoted prices for similar assets or liabilities in active markets, should be used. *Id.* at 12–15. And if "Level 2" inputs are not available—such as when there is "little, if any, market activity for the asset or liability at the measurement date"—"unobservable" "Level 3" inputs, such as model assumptions that take market participant assumptions into account, should be used.

curities; and (3) a means of interstate commerce was used in the sale of securities. Although § 12(a)(1) requires privity of contract between the buyer and the seller, this concept has been expanded from the notion of the passing of title between a seller and a buyer to include third parties such as intermediaries who act as agents for the owner of the security and actively participate in the solicitation of the buyer of the securities even if there is no passing of title to the security between the broker-dealer and the buyer. The following case explores the concept of statutory seller under § 12(a)(1) with respect to broker-dealers and other third parties.

———

Pinter v. Dahl

486 U.S. 622 (1988)

Justice BLACKMUN delivered the opinion of the Court.

* * *

The controversy arises out of the sale prior to 1982 of unregistered securities (fractional undivided interests in oil and gas leases) by petitioner Billy J. "B.J." Pinter to respondents Maurice Dahl and Dahl's friends, family, and business associates. Pinter is an oil and gas producer in Texas and Oklahoma, and a registered securities dealer in Texas. Dahl is a California real estate broker and investor, who, at the time of his dealings with Pinter, was a veteran of two unsuccessful oil and gas ventures. In pursuit of further investment opportunities, Dahl employed an oil field expert to locate and acquire oil and gas leases. This expert introduced Dahl to Pinter. Dahl advanced $20,000 to Pinter to acquire leases, with the understanding that they would be held in the name of Pinter's Black Gold Oil Company and that Dahl would have a right of first refusal to drill certain wells on the leasehold properties. Pinter located leases in Oklahoma, and Dahl toured the properties, often without Pinter, in order to talk to others and "get a feel for the properties." Upon examining the geology, drilling logs, and production history assembled by Pinter, Dahl concluded, in the words of the District Court, that "there was no way to lose."

After investing approximately $310,000 in the properties, Dahl told the other respondents about the venture. Except for Dahl and respondent Grantham, none of the respondents spoke to or met Pinter or toured the properties. Because of Dahl's involvement in the venture, each of the other respondents decided to invest about $7,500.

Dahl assisted his fellow investors in completing the subscription-agreement form prepared by Pinter. Each letter-contract signed by the purchaser stated that the participating interests were being sold without the benefit of registration under the Securities Act.... Dahl received no commission from Pinter in connection with the other respondents' purchases.

When the venture failed and their interests proved to be worthless, respondents brought suit ... seeking rescission under § 12(1) of the Securities Act for the unlawful sale of unregistered securities....

The District Court, after a bench trial, granted judgment for respondent-investors ... A divided panel of the Court of Appeals for the Fifth Circuit affirmed.... The Court of Appeals next considered whether Dahl was himself a "seller" of the oil and gas interests within the meaning of § 12(1) ... [T]he court declined to hold that Dahl was a "seller" for purposes of § 12(1)....

Because of the importance of the issues involved to the administration of the federal securities laws, we granted certiorari....

In determining whether Dahl may be deemed a "seller" for purposes of § 12(1), such that he may be held liable for the sale of unregistered securities to the other investor-respondents, we look first at the language of § 12(a)(1).... That statute provides, in pertinent part: "Any person who ... offers or sells a security" in violation of the registration requirement of the Securities Act "shall be liable to the person purchasing such security from him." This provision defines the class of defendants who may be subject to liability as those who offer or sell unregistered securities. But the Securities Act nowhere delineates who may be regarded as a statutory seller, and the sparse legislative history sheds no light on the issue. The courts, on their part, have not defined the term uniformly.

At the very least, however, the language of § 12(1) contemplates a buyer-seller relationship not unlike traditional contractual privity. Thus, it is settled that § 12(1) imposes liability on the owner who passed title, or other interest in the security, to the buyer for value. Dahl, of course, was not a seller in this conventional sense, and therefore may be held liable only if § 12(1) liability extends to persons other than the person who passes title.

A

In common parlance, a person may offer or sell property without necessarily being the person who transfers title to or other interest in, that property. We need not rely entirely on ordinary understanding of the statutory language, however, for the Securities Act defines the operative terms of § 12(a)(1). Section 2(a)(3) defines "sale" or "sell" to include "every contract of sale or disposition of a security or interest in a security, for value," and the terms "offer to sell," "offer for sale," or "offer" to include "every attempt or offer to dispose of, or solicitation of an offer to buy, a security or interest in a security, for value." Under these definitions, the range of persons potentially liable under § 12(1) is not limited to persons who pass title. The inclusion of the phrase "solicitation of an offer to buy" within the definition of "offer" brings an individual who engages in solicitation, an activity not inherently confined to the actual owner, within the scope of § 12...."The statutory terms ["offer" and "sell"], which Congress expressly intended to define broadly, ... are expansive enough to encompass the entire selling process, including the seller/agent transaction." ... See Rubin v. United States, 449 U.S. 424, 430 (S. Ct. 1981) ("it is not essential under the terms of the [Securities Act] that full title pass to a transferee for the transaction to be an 'offer' or a 'sale'"). In addition, liability is imposed only on the buyer's immediate seller....

The purchase requirement clearly confines § 12 liability to those situations in which a sale has taken place. Thus, a prospective buyer has no recourse against a person who touts unregistered securities to him if he does not purchase the securities.... The requirement, however, does not exclude solicitation from the category of activities that may render a person liable when a sale has taken place. A natural reading of the statutory language would include in the statutory seller status at least some persons who urged the buyer to purchase. For example, a securities vendor's agent who solicited the purchase would commonly be said, and would be thought by the buyer, to be among those "from" whom the buyer "purchased," even though the agent himself did not pass title ...

The applicability of § 12 liability to brokers and others who solicit securities purchases has been recognized frequently since the passage of the Securities Act. It long has been "quite clear," that when a broker acting as agent of one of the principals to the transaction successfully solicits a purchase, he is a person from whom the buyer purchases within the meaning of § 12 and is therefore liable as a statutory seller.... Had Congress intended liability to be restricted to those who pass title, it could have effectuated its intent by not adding the phrase "offers or" when it split the definition of "sell" in § 2(3).

An interpretation of statutory seller that includes brokers and others who solicit offers to purchase securities furthers the purposes of the Securities Act-to promote full and fair disclosure of information to the public in the sales of securities. In order to effectuate Congress' intent that § 12(1) civil liability be *in terrorem* ... the risk of its invocation should be felt by solicitors of purchases. The solicitation of a buyer is perhaps the most critical stage of the selling transaction. It is the first stage of a traditional securities sale to involve the buyer, and it is directed at producing the sale. In addition, brokers and other solicitors are well positioned to control the flow of information to a potential purchaser, and, in fact, such persons are the participants in the selling transaction who most often disseminate material information to investors. Thus, solicitation is the stage at which an investor is most likely to be injured, that is, by being persuaded to purchase securities without full and fair information. Given Congress' overriding goal of preventing this injury, we may infer that Congress intended solicitation to fall under the mantle of § 12(1).

Although we conclude that Congress intended § 12(1) liability to extend to those who solicit securities purchases, we share the Court of Appeals' conclusion that Congress did not intend to impose rescission based on strict liability on a person who urges the purchase but whose motivation is solely to benefit the buyer. When a person who urges another to make a securities purchase acts merely to assist the buyer, not only is it uncommon to say that the buyer "purchased" from him, but it is also strained to describe the giving of gratuitous advice, even strongly or enthusiastically, as "soliciting." Section 2(3) defines an offer as a "solicitation of an offer to buy ... for value." The person who gratuitously urges another to make a particular investment decision is not, in any meaningful sense, requesting value in exchange for his suggestion or seeking the value the titleholder will obtain in exchange for the ultimate sale. The language and purpose of § 12(1) suggest that liability extends only to the person who successfully solicits the purchase, motivated at least in part by a desire to serve his own financial interests or those of the securities owner. If he had such a motivation, it is fair to say that the buyer "purchased" the security from him and to align him with the owner in a rescission action....

B

Petitioner is not satisfied with extending § 12(1) primary liability to one who solicits securities sales for financial gain. Pinter assumes, without explication, that liability is not limited to the person who actually parts title with the securities, and urges us to validate, as the standard by which additional defendant-sellers are identified, that version of the "substantial factor" test utilized by the Fifth Circuit before the refinement espoused in this case. Under that approach, grounded in tort doctrine, a nontransferor § 12(1) seller is defined as one "whose participation in the buy-sell transaction is a substantial factor in causing the transaction to take place." The Court of Appeals acknowledged that Dahl would be liable as a statutory seller under this test....

There is no support in the statutory language or legislative history for expansion of § 12(1) primary liability beyond persons who pass title and persons who "offer," including those who "solicit" offers. Indeed, § 12's failure to impose express liability for mere participation in unlawful sales transactions suggests that Congress did not intend that the section impose liability on participants' collateral to the offer or sale....

The deficiency of the substantial-factor test is that it divorces the analysis of seller status from any reference to the applicable statutory language and from any examination of § 12 in the context of the total statutory scheme. Those courts that have adopted the approach have not attempted to ground their analysis in the statutory language. Instead, they substitute the concept of substantial participation in the sales transaction, or proximate causation of the plaintiff's purchase, for the words "offers or sells" in § 12. The "purchase from" requirement of § 12 focuses on the defendant's relationship with the plaintiff-purchaser. The substantial-factor test, on the other hand, focuses on the defendant's degree of involvement in the securities transaction and its surrounding circumstances. Thus, although the substantial-factor test undoubtedly embraces persons who pass title and who solicit the purchase of unregistered securities as statutory sellers, the test also would extend § 12(1) liability to participants only remotely related to the relevant aspects of the sales transaction. Indeed, it might expose securities professionals, such as accountants and lawyers, whose involvement is only the performance of their professional services, to § 12(1) strict liability for rescission. The buyer does not, in any meaningful sense, "purchas[e] the security from" such a person....

[T]he substantial-factor test introduces an element of uncertainty into an area that demands certainty and predictability.... None of the courts employing the approach has articulated what measure of participation qualifies a person for seller status, and logically sound limitations would be difficult to develop.... We find it particularly unlikely that Congress would have ordained *sub silentio* the imposition of strict liability on such an unpredictably defined class of defendants....

C

We are unable to determine whether Dahl may be held liable as a statutory seller under § 12(1). The District Court explicitly found that "Dahl solicited each of the other plaintiffs (save perhaps Grantham) in connection with the offer, purchase, and receipt of their oil and gas interests." We cannot conclude that this finding was clearly erroneous. It is not clear, however, that Dahl had the kind of interest in the sales that make him liable as a statutory seller. We do know that he received no commission from Pinter in connection with the other sales, but this is not conclusive. Typically, a person who solicits the purchase will have sought or received a personal financial benefit from the sale, such as where he "anticipat[es] a share of the profits, or receives a brokerage commission." But a person who solicits the buyer's purchase in order to serve the financial interests of the owner may properly be liable under § 12(1) without showing that he expects to participate in the benefits the owner enjoys.

The Court of Appeals apparently concluded that Dahl was motivated entirely by a gratuitous desire to share an attractive investment opportunity with his friends and associates. This conclusion, in our view, was premature. The District Court made no findings that focused on whether Dahl urged the other purchases in order to further some financial interest of his own or of Pinter. Accordingly, further findings are necessary to assess Dahl's liability....

———

Successful plaintiffs under § 12(a)(1) are entitled to rescission or damages if they no longer own the security. If the plaintiff still owns the security, she is entitled to the return of the purchase price of the security with interest upon tender of the security to the broker-dealer. If she no longer owns the security, the broker-dealer is liable for damages based on the difference between the plaintiff's purchase price and sale price.

The broker-dealer has no defenses under § 12(a)(1). However, § 13 of the Securities Act does impose a statute of limitations of one year from discovery and three years from the sale of the security.

Notes and Questions

1. After *Pinter*, liability under § 12(a)(1) may be established if the broker-dealer (or other third party) solicited the securities transaction with the expectation of receiving a financial benefit. This means that underwriters and broker-dealers may be held liable under § 12(a)(1). Liability may attach if, for example, they are in contact with investors, directly or indirectly, by telephone, by participating in roadshows, and by having their name on the prospectus or free writing prospectuses.

2. It is unclear whether aiding and abetting liability is available in an action under § 12(a)(1) after *Pinter*. *See Wilson v. Saintine Exploration and Drilling Corp.*, 872 F.2d 1124, 1127 (2d Cir. 1989); *Royal American Managers, Inc. v. IRC Holding Corp.*, 885 F.2d 1011, 1017 (2d Cir. 1989); *Schlifke v. Seafirst Corp.*, 866 F.2d 935, 942 (7th Cir. 1989); *In re Craftmatic Securities Litigation*, 890 F.2d 628, 636–37 (3d Cir. 1989).

B. Section 12(a)(2)

Section 12(a)(2) is an antifraud provision for material misstatements and omissions made in the prospectus, or in an oral communication, in connection with a public offering. Like § 12(a)(1), privity of contract is required between the purchaser and the broker-dealer with the same expansion, i.e., privity of contract includes not only the passing of title between a seller and a buyer, but it also includes intermediaries acting as agents for the owner of the security who actively participate in the solicitation of the buyer even in the absence of the passing of title between the broker-dealer and the buyer. In addition, in *Gustafson v. Alloyd Co.,* 513 U.S. 561, the Supreme Court restricted § 12(a)(2) as a cause of action only to public offerings. However, courts have differed as to whether *Gustafson* has restricted § 12(a)(2) to initial public offerings or public offerings in general, i.e., secondary market trades during the period requiring the distribution of prospectuses under Rule 159 of the Securities Act. Compare the following two cases.

In re Sterling Foster and Co., Inc. Securities Litigation
222 F. Supp. 2d 216 (E.D.N.Y. 2002)

MEMORANDUM OF DECISION AND ORDER

Spatt, District Judge.

* * *

1. The Overall Scheme

The claims in this case arise from the public offerings of six companies: Advanced Voice Technologies, Inc. ("Advanced Voice"), Com/Tech Communication Technologies, Inc. ("Com/Tech"); Embryo Development Corporation ("Embryo"); Applewoods, Inc. ("Applewoods"); Lasergate Systems, Inc. ("Lasergate") (collectively, the "Issuer Defendants"); and ML Direct, Inc. ("ML Direct") (collectively, the "defendant companies"). Sterling Foster, a registered broker-dealer and a member of the National Association of Securities Dealers, Inc., ("NASD") underwrote the offerings for each company except ML Direct, whose offering was underwritten by a different investment bank, Patterson Travis, Inc. ("Patterson Travis"). The public offerings of Advanced Voice, Com/Tech, Embryo, Applewoods, and ML Direct were initial public offerings ("IPO"), while the Lasergate offering was a secondary offering.

Prior to each offering, certain company insiders and principal stockholders ("Selling Securityholders") purchased a substantial amount of stock, sometimes almost as much as was being offered to the public, in each of the defendant companies.... The Selling Securityholders purchase their stock for no more than $1.00 per share while the same securities were being offered to the public for roughly $5.00 per share. Most of the Selling Securityholders agreed not to sell their shares for at least one year following the offering unless they received written permission from Sterling Foster to do so. These "lock-up agreements" were disclosed in the Issuer Defendants' prospectuses.

However, Sterling Foster, Adam Lieberman ("Lieberman"), the company's president; Randolph Pace ("Pace"), the individual who is alleged to have secretly controlled the company; and Alan Novich ("Novich"), an attorney, entered into secret agreements with the Selling Securityholders. According to these undisclosed arrangements, shortly after the registration statements of the defendant companies became effective, Sterling Foster would release the Selling Securityholders from their lock-up agreements and would purchase the Selling Securityholders' shares at prices ranging from $1.50 to approximately $3.00 per share in order to cover a short position Sterling Foster intended to assume in the aftermarket. The plaintiff alleges that the prospectuses and registration statements distributed by Sterling Foster, Lieberman, Pace, and Novich were materially false and misleading because although they registered the shelf shares and lock-up agreements, they failed to disclose the secret arrangements between the Selling Securityholders and Sterling Foster. According to the plaintiffs, Sterling Foster customers purchased their securities in the defendant companies without the knowledge that Sterling Foster would release the Selling Securityholders from their lock-up agreements and purchase the shelf shares at deeply discounted prices.

In regard to the offerings themselves, [plaintiffs does] ... not specifically allege which plaintiffs purchased shares in an IPO as opposed to in the aftermarket. However, [plaintiffs do] set forth the dates on which the plaintiffs purchased their respective shares, and one could infer from that information that some plaintiffs might have purchased shares in the initial offering.

[W]hen the registration statements of the defendant companies became effective, and perhaps prior to those dates, Sterling Foster's sales force of 150 registered representatives ... engaged in a massive and aggressive selling campaign designed to artificially inflate the price of the defendant companies' stock through the use of, among other things, "boiler room" sales practices. Hawley, Paulson, and Sterling Foster's other registered representatives told potential customers that: (1) the stocks underwritten by Sterling Foster were "oversubscribed" because so many investors were interested in purchasing the stocks; (2) large institutions were about to buy large blocks of the stock; and (3) the stock being sold was going to reach a target price within a matter of days....

The plaintiffs also allege that Sterling Foster, Lieberman, Hawley, Paulson, and the other registered representatives failed to provide the plaintiffs with copies of the prospectuses for the Issuer Defendants; led the plaintiffs to believe that they were purchasing securities in an initial public offering, when in fact the plaintiffs were purchasing the securities in the aftermarket at substantially higher prices; concealed excessive mark-ups that the defendants were receiving for the sale of shares; and misrepresented that the offering price was the purchase price. Sterling Foster also discouraged its customers from selling their shares by telling them that such action would cause the price of the shares to decline. At times, Sterling Foster failed to effect or avoided effecting sell orders and told its registered representatives that if they wanted to keep their commissions, they must prevent their customers from selling the securities for at least 30 days. Sterling Foster itself purchased a substantial number of securities on the open market shortly after each defendant company's offering, thereby decreasing the number of shares available to the public....

When the share price and demand reached certain levels, Sterling Foster satisfied the demand it had created by selling shares to the public at the prices it had artificially inflated. Sterling Foster often sold shares it did not own and, in some situations, sold twice the number of securities that had been sold to the public in the offering.... Sterling Foster covered its short positions by releasing the Selling Securityholders from their lock-up agreements and purchasing their shelf shares at prices ranging from $1.50 to $3.00 per share, as per the terms of the secret agreements.

* * *

1. Standing

* * *

Section 12(a)(2) of the Securities Act grants buyers an express cause of action for rescission against sellers who make material misstatements or omissions "by means of a prospectus." In *Gustafson v. Alloyd Co., Inc.,* 513 U.S. 561, 115 S.Ct. 1061, 131 L.Ed.2d 1 (1995), the Supreme Court was presented with the question of whether "this right of rescission extends to a private secondary transaction, on the theory that recitations in the purchase agreement are part of a 'prospectus.' *Gustafson* did not involve a public offering or the issue of whether aftermarket purchasers have standing to sue under Section 12(a)(2). Rather, *Gustafson* involved the purchase of a company pursuant to a purchase agreement and contract of sale. When the company's earnings were lower than the estimates relied upon in negotiating the purchase price, the buyers filed suit seeking rescission of the contract pursuant to Section 12(a)(2) on the ground that the contract of sale was a "prospectus."

The Court held that the "word 'prospectus' is a term if [*sic*] art referring to a document that describes a public offering of securities by an issuer or controlling shareholder." The Court concluded that the private sales contract did not fall within this definition and, therefore, was not a prospectus for the purposes of Section 12(a)(2). The Court also indicated, in *dicta,* that a Section 12(a)(2) suit may only be maintained by a person who purchased the stock in the offering under the prospectus. In particular, the Court stated, "The intent of Congress and the design of the statute require that § 12(a)(2) liability be limited to public offerings." The Court also stated that "the liability imposed by § 12(a)(2) cannot attach unless there is an obligation to distribute the prospectus in the first place."

Courts in this Circuit have applied the rationale of this *dicta* to reach what is now the predominate conclusion that purchasers in private or secondary market offerings are precluded from bringing actions under Section 12(a)(2)....

The plaintiffs have not presented the Court with a persuasive reason to depart from the holdings of these cases. In a conclusory argument that spans just over one page, the plaintiffs simply claim that *Gustafson* does not restrict aftermarket purchasers from suing under Section 12(a)(2)....

In light of the fact that the plaintiffs have not put forth a compelling reason to depart from the numerous decisions by the courts in this circuit, this Court adopts this position and finds that plaintiffs have standing to sue under Section 12(a)(2) only if they claim to have purchased their securities in the various public offerings rather than in the secondary markets. The members of each subclass allege that they purchased their securities "pursuant to and traceable to" the respective prospectus. However, none of the plaintiffs asserts that the securities were purchased during the offering.

Some of the purchase dates listed in the complaint are close enough in time to suggest that the plaintiffs could have made their purchases in the offering.... Nevertheless, in the Court's view, the plaintiffs should specify at the pleading stage whether they made these purchases in the offering or in the secondary market. Accordingly, because the plaintiffs fail to allege that they purchased the securities in a public offering, as opposed to in the aftermarket, their Section 12(a)(2) claims are dismissed....

Feiner v. SS&C Technologies, Inc.

47 F. Supp. 2d 250 (D. Conn. 1999)

This securities action arises out of an initial public offering ("IPO") of shares in SS & C Technologies, Inc. ("SS & C") that was underwritten by Alex. Brown & Sons Incorporated ("Alex. Brown") and Hambrecht & Quist LLC ("Hambrecht & Quist"). The lead plaintiffs, all of whom purchased shares of SS & C during the period from May 31, 1996 through August 1, 1996, have moved this court pursuant to Fed.R.Civ.P. 23(c)(1) for an order certifying this suit as a class action. Defendants oppose the motion on a number of grounds. They argue first that plaintiffs' proposed class is impermissibly broad because it includes people who, having purchased shares in the aftermarket rather than in the IPO, lack standing to sue under Section[] ... 12(2) of the Securities Act of 1933.... For the following reasons, the lead plaintiffs' motion to certify a class is GRANTED.

I. DISCUSSION

Defendants' contention that the class should be limited to people who purchased shares during their initial distribution is without merit....

Defendants' "initial distribution" argument fails with regard to plaintiffs' § 12(a)(2) claim ... Section 12(a)(2) does not require that shareholders purchase their securities during the initial distribution of shares, but only that plaintiffs "purchase their shares directly from a seller who makes use of a false or misleading prospectus." The statute draws no express distinction between shares purchased in the initial distribution and shares purchased in the aftermarket. Instead, the statute requires only that a plaintiff have purchased a security, from a seller, pursuant to a misleading prospectus.

The Supreme Court's statement in *Gustafson v. Alloyd* that "§ 12(a)(2) liability [is] limited to public offerings" is not to the contrary. In *Gustafson,* the Court was drawing a distinction between public offerings and private ones, not between public offerings and aftermarket purchases. The central question in *Gustafson* was whether a purchase agreement used in connection with a private placement of securities could be considered a "prospectus" within the meaning of § 12(a)(2). The Court answered that question in the negative, holding that the term "prospectus" is "confined to documents related to public offerings by an issuer or its controlling shareholders." Therefore, the Court's statement that "§ 12(a)(2) liability [is] limited to public offerings" cannot be read to exclude aftermarket trading. By using the term "public offerings," the Court was simply distinguishing offerings in which the filing of a prospectus is required under the securities laws, i.e., public offerings, from those in which no prospectus need be filed, i.e., private placements. ("By and large, only public offerings ... require the preparation and filing of registration statements. It follows, we conclude, that a prospectus ... is confined to documents *related* to public offerings by an issuer or its controlling shareholders.") (emphasis added). The Court did not go further and address the question presented here, namely whether, within the context of a public offering, § 12(a)(2) liability attaches to only the initial distribution of securities or to certain aftermarket trading as well.

This court now holds that § 12(a)(2) extends to aftermarket trading of a publicly offered security, so long as that aftermarket trading occurs "by means of a prospectus or oral communication." This is not to say that a prospectus need in fact have been delivered for a purchaser to have a § 12(a)(2) claim. Rather, all that is necessary is that delivery of a prospectus have been required under the statutory and regulatory framework. *See Gustafson,* 513 U.S. at 570, 115 S.Ct. 1061 ("[T]he liability imposed by § 12(a)(2) [ ] cannot attach unless there is an obligation to distribute the prospectus in the first place....."). Under this framework, delivery of a prospectus is required for a fixed number of days after the registration statement becomes effective, even if the initial distribution of shares has already been completed. To limit § 12(a)(2) liability to the initial distribution would eviscerate this requirement. Under such a reading of § 12(a)(2), the statutory and regulatory framework would require that a prospectus be delivered for a certain number of days after the beginning of an offering, but would not require that the statements in that prospectus be truthful and non-deceptive. Moreover, the express language of § 12(a)(2) limits misrepresentations in connection with the sale of a security "by means of a prospectus," not "in a public offering." The court therefore rejects defendants' argument that § 12(a)(2) liability is limited to shares purchased in an initial distribution. Instead, the court holds that § 12(a)(2) liability is coextensive with the statutory and regulatory prospectus-delivery requirements.

In this case, the statutory and regulatory framework required that a prospectus be delivered for all transactions in SS & C common stock by Hambrecht & Quist or Alex. Brown within 25 days of the offering date. Any sale by an underwriter requires the delivery of a prospectus until such time as the initial distribution of shares is complete. In this case, it is undisputed that the initial distribution was complete on May 31, 1996, the first day of the IPO. Therefore, to the extent that Hambrecht & Quist or Alex. Brown made sales after this date, they did so not in their capacity as underwriters, but in their capacity as ordinary "dealers." *See* 15 U.S.C. § 77d(3) (defining "dealer" to include "an underwriter no longer acting as an underwriter in respect of the security involved in such transaction."). A sale by a dealer requires the delivery of a prospectus if the sale takes place within 90 days of the effective date of the registration statement for initial offerings, or within 40 days for secondary offerings, or within a shorter period set by the Securities and Exchange Commission (the "SEC"). Regulations adopted by the SEC have reduced the time period to 25 days after the offering date, provided that: (1) the security was not subject to § 13 or § 15(d) of the 1934 Act; and (2) as of the offering date, the security was listed on a registered national securities exchange or authorized for inclusion in a qualified electronic inter-dealer quotation system. 17 C.F.R. § 230.174(d). Here, SS & C stock was not subject to § 13 or § 15(d), and was sold on a national securities exchange. Therefore, the reduced, 25-day period applies. Because the security's registration statement became effective on May 31, 1996, Hambrecht & Quist and Alex. Brown were required to deliver the prospectus any time that they sold the security up until the end of the day on June 25, 1996.

Not all members of the proposed class who purchased SS & C stock within the 25-day period have standing to bring a claim against Hambrecht & Quist or Alex. Brown under § 12(a)(2), however. Section 12(a)(2) further requires that plaintiffs "purchase their shares directly from a seller who makes use of a false or misleading prospectus." The term "seller" encompasses not only anyone who stands in privity with a purchaser, but also anyone "who successfully solicits the purchase [of a security], motivated at least in part by a desire to serve his own financial interests or those of the securities owner." *Pinter v. Dahl*, 486 U.S. 622, 646, 108 S.Ct. 2063, 100 L.Ed.2d 658 (1988) ... In order to fall within this second category of seller, a defendant must have "actually solicited" the purchase by the plaintiffs. Therefore, a defendant's mere status as an underwriter is not sufficient to make it a seller to all purchasers for purposes of § 12(a)(2).

In this case, only certain members of the proposed class have standing to bring a § 12(a)(2) claim against Hambrecht & Quist or Alex. Brown. Plaintiffs concede that this was a "firm commitment" underwriting, i.e., one in which SS & C sold all of the shares that were issued in the IPO to the underwriters, who, in turn, sold all of the shares directly to the investing public. Because Hambrecht & Quist and Alex. Brown owned all of the shares, any sale made by either of them in the initial distribution would pass title directly to the purchaser. Therefore, any purchaser in the initial distribution stands in privity with either Hambrecht & Quist or Alex. Brown and has a § 12(a)(2) claim against them on that basis. Similarly, if either Hambrecht & Quist or Alex. Brown reacquired shares in aftermarket trading and then resold them on the aftermarket within the 25-day period, any purchaser of the resold shares would also have standing to bring a 12(a)(2) claim. In addition, to the extent that Hambrecht & Quist and Alex. Brown acted as dealers [*sic* brokers] for third parties in aftermarket trading, plaintiffs who purchased from them in that capacity on or before June 25, 1996 have § 12(a)(2) standing. *See Cortec Indus., Inc. v. Sum Holding L.P.*, 949 F.2d 42, 50 (2d Cir.1991) ("Section 12 liability has since the enactment of the Securities Act been applied to brokers and others who solicit securities purchases on a regular basis.").

Purchasers who did not acquire their shares directly from either Hambrecht & Quist or Alex. Brown, however, lack § 12(a)(2) standing. Such purchasers did not acquire their shares "directly from a seller who makes use of a false or misleading prospectus." Any argument by plaintiffs that standing to sue belongs to everyone who purchased SS & C shares within the class period is thus without merit. Under § 12(a)(2), "only a defendant from whom the plaintiff purchased securities may be liable." *Cortec Indus., Inc. v. Sum Holding L.P.,* 949 F.2d 42, 49 (2d Cir.1991). Therefore, proposed class members who purchased shares of SS & C from someone other than Hambrecht & Quist or Alex. Brown have no standing to sue either of them under § 12(a)(2).

That said, plaintiffs have not demonstrated that all class members have standing to bring ... a ... § 12(a)(2) claim. For example, someone who purchased shares during the 25-day period, but did not purchase those shares from Hambrecht & Quist or Alex. Brown, would not have standing to sue either of those defendants under § 12(a)(2).... [T]he court will certify a subclass, consisting of those plaintiffs who ... have standing to sue under § 12(a)(2). For the reasons discussed above, the subclass shall consist of everyone who purchased SS & C common stock from Hambrecht & Quist or Alex. Brown from May 31, 1996 through and including June 25, 1996.

––––––

Notes and Questions

1. Although § 12(a)(2) is an antifraud provision, it does not require proof of scienter. The elements that must be established to sustain a violation of § 12(a)(2) are: (1) An offer or sale of a security; (2) by use of an instrumentality of interstate commerce; and (3) by means of a prospectus or oral communication, which includes a material misstatement or omission. Section 12(a)(2) does not have a causation requirement, but the requirement that the offer or sale of a security is done by means of a prospectus or oral communication has been interpreted by the courts to imply a weak causal element.

––––––

Sanders v. John Nuveen & Co., Inc.
619 F.2d 1222 (7th Cir. 1980)

Tone, Circuit Judge.

The issue we decide on this appeal is whether plaintiff class members have established their claims under § 12(2) of the Securities Act of 1933. Holding that they have, we affirm the district court's judgment in their favor....

Plaintiff class consists of forty-two purchasers of unsecured short term promissory notes aggregating $1,612,500 issued by Winter & Hirsch, Inc. (WH), a consumer finance company. The purchases were made from John Nuveen & Co., Inc. during a seven-month period immediately preceding WH's default on the notes in February 1970....

Nuveen was the exclusive underwriter of the WH notes, which were sold, like other commercial paper, through its branch offices throughout the United States. As the underwriter, it bought the notes from WH and resold them to customers at a profit. According to the head of Nuveen's commercial paper department, Nuveen sold commercial paper, including the notes of WH, on the basis "that there should be no question but what the paper will be paid at maturity."

Nuveen prepared and circulated to prospective customers "commercial paper reports" on the WH commercial paper that it held for sale. Three members of the plaintiff class testified to having received copies of these reports before they bought WH notes. Two other members testified to having received commercial paper reports, but could not swear to having received them before making their purchases. Nine class members, including the three who had received reports before purchasing, testified that, when they bought their WH notes, Nuveen salesmen made oral statements about the quality of the notes. There was no evidence of oral communications to any other class members. All class members received the usual written confirmations advising them that they had purchased certain described notes and that Nuveen had sold the notes as principal.

WH's default was the product of a fraud it perpetrated with the connivance of the certified public accountants who audited its financial statements and rendered opinions thereon. In summary, over a period of ten years WH continually issued financial statements in which accounts receivable were overstated and some of its indebtedness was omitted. By 1970 WH's financial statements overstated accounts receivable by some $14,000,000 and failed to reflect some $1,750,000 of indebtedness. When the notes in issue in this case were purchased by members of the plaintiff class, WH's liabilities exceeded its assets.

Nuveen was not aware of the fraud and held "the mistaken but honest belief that financial statements (of WH) prepared by certified public accountants correctly represented the condition of" WH. It accordingly proceeded to sell the WH notes and also to issue commercial paper reports thereon that reflected the false WH financial statements....

After WH had dishonored the notes sold to the plaintiff class members, it was taken over by its creditors. They established the WH Liquidating Trust, liquidated WH, and over a period of time distributed the proceeds of the liquidation to creditors, including members of the plaintiff class, who received through these distributions approximately two-thirds of the amounts they paid Nuveen for the notes. The judgment appealed from is for the unpaid balance of the purchase price of the notes and prejudgment interest thereon.

I.

Defendant's first argument is that recovery by thirty-three of the forty-two class members is defeated by the absence of evidence of receipt by them of "a prospectus or oral communication" meeting the requirements of § 12(2). That section imposes liability on (a)ny person who ... (o)ffers or sells a security ... by means of a prospectus or oral communication, which includes an untrue statement of a material fact or omits to state a material fact necessary in order to make the statements, in light of the circumstances under which they were made, not misleading....

Liability is in favor of "the person purchasing such security from" the person who offers or sells the security. The purchaser must not have known of the untruth or omission.

Plaintiffs contend that several kinds of communications satisfied the prospectus or oral communication requirement of the statute. We need consider only one, the commercial paper reports.

Defendants admit that the reports were prospectuses and that they were false and misleading. The reports repeated the false financial information contained in the WH financial statements. Also, they stated that the figures were from a detailed audit when in fact the auditors' opinions stated that no detailed audit had been made.

Defendants' only response to this argument is that, except as to the three members proved to have received copies of reports before their purchases, the reports had no "causal relationship" with the sales of the WH notes.

Although the "by means of" language in the statute requires some causal connection between the misleading representation or omission and plaintiff's purchase, defendants' interpretation of that standard is much too stringent. It is well settled that § 12(2) imposes liability without regard to whether the buyer relied on the misrepresentation or omission.... To require a plaintiff to have received a commercial paper report before purchasing, as defendants would have us do, would tend toward erroneously imposing a reliance requirement.[17]

The statutory language, as amplified by the legislative history, indicates that a plaintiff need not prove that he ever received the misleading prospectus. The statute imposes liability in favor of a purchaser on any person who "(o)ffers or sells a security ... by means of a prospectus or oral communication" that is misleading. Although the statute explicitly requires privity between plaintiff-purchaser and defendant-seller, its terms do not require that the particular sale to an individual plaintiff be directly by means of the prospectus alleged to be misleading. The causal connection contemplated by the statute is revealed in the House Report on the bill that, after changes

---

17. In *Demarco v. Edens*, 390 F.2d 836 (2d Cir. 1968), the court rejected in dictum the argument that recovery could not be had under § 12(2) because the "offering circulars" in question were not received by the buyers until after the confirmations of sales had been received. The court reasoned that such a requirement would introduce an element of reliance not mandated by the statute.

However, one could require proof of receipt of a misleading prospectus or oral communication to show not that the buyer relied on the information in deciding to purchase, but that the vendor sold the security to the individual plaintiff "by means of" the misleading communication. Indeed, in *Demarco* the defendants specifically disclaimed a reliance argument before the district court, contending instead that since the prospectus was in no way employed in the transaction, they had not sold to plaintiffs "by means of" the prospectus. Nevertheless, the district court found liability appropriate essentially as an ancillary enforcement mechanism for the SEC regulation requiring that, with respect to some securities exempted from registration, the offering circular be sent before the confirmation. Demarco v. Edens, (1966–67 Transfer Binder) Fed. Sec. L. Rep. (CCH) ¶ 91,856, at 95924, 95933–34 (S.D.N.Y. Dec. 13, 1966).

not relevant here, became the Securities Act of 1933. See generally Landis, The Legislative History of the Securities Act of 1933, 28 Geo.Wash.L.Rev. 29 (1959). Referring to §§ 11 and 12, the two sections imposing civil liabilities, the report declared that statements issued in connection with the sale of securities, although they may never actually have been seen by the prospective purchaser, because of their wide dissemination, determine the market price of the security which in the last analysis reflects those manifold causes that are the impelling motive of the particular purchase. The connection between the statements made and the purchase of the security is clear, and, for this reason, it is the essence of fairness to insist upon the assumption of responsibility for the making of these statements. H.R.Rep.No.85, 73d Cong., 1st Sess. 10 (1933), reprinted at 2 LEGISLATIVE HISTORY OF THE SECURITIES ACT OF 1933 AND SECURITIES EXCHANGE ACT OF 1934, Item 18 (J. Ellenberger & E. Mahar, compilers, 1973) (hereinafter cited as Legislative History).

Defendants argue that this is not "an open market trading case where dissemination of information to some buyers or sellers can have an impact upon the market price and thus affect transactions by people who never saw the documents." The attempted distinction lacks substance. Even though short term commercial paper is not ordinarily traded in the same way as stock and instruments of indebtedness of publicly held companies, the price it will bring depends upon the financial condition of the issuer relative to that of other issuers and the going interest rates in the money market. In that sense there is a market price. A prospectus that reports on the issuer's financial condition affects that price. In the case at bar, publication of WH's true financial condition would have caused a total collapse of the market for its notes.

Thus, it is enough that the seller sold by means of a misleading prospectus securities of which those purchased by the plaintiff were a part. The false and misleading WH commercial paper reports issued by Nuveen therefore satisfy the statute's requirement of a false or misleading prospectus "by means of" which the security was sold, regardless of whether all plaintiff class members received copies of those reports.

––––––

In addition, the SEC adopted Rule 159 to clarify when the broker-dealer incurs liability under § 12(a)(2). Under Rule 159, the broker-dealer incurs liability for a prospectus or oral statement that contains a material misrepresentation or omission only at the time of sale. Any information conveyed to the purchaser after the time of sale is irrelevant. This timing rule applies to both the broker-dealer and the purchaser. The timing rule also affects the broker-dealer's ability to terminate a contract of sale and create a new contract, i.e., to terminate and reform a contract of sale that is consistent with the anti-waiver provisions of the federal securities laws; the procedure to terminate and reform a contract of sale would result in the purchaser's right to damages under the old contract ceasing to exist. Accordingly, any such procedure must be by mutual agreement, i.e., both the broker-dealer and purchaser must agree to terminate the old contract and enter into a new contract of sale.

The broker-dealer may be liable for free writing prospectuses under Section 12(a)(2) under certain circumstances. Liability may be incurred by the broker-dealer for misrepresentations or omissions in a free writing prospectus regardless of whether it is required to be filed with the SEC. However, the SEC adopted Rule 159A of the Securities Act to make clear that the broker-dealer is not responsible for all free writing prospectuses used in connection with a particular offering. Liability is incurred by the broker-dealer under § 12(a)(2) for a free writing prospectus if the broker-dealer:

1. used or referred to the free writing prospectus in offering or selling the securities to purchaser;

2. offered or sold the securities to the purchaser and participated in planning for the use of that free writing prospectus by other offering participants and such free writing prospectus was used or referred to in offering or selling securities to the purchaser by one or more of such offering participants;[18] or

3. under the conditions for use of the free writing prospectus in Rule 433 of the Securities Act, the broker-dealer is required to file the free writing prospectus with the SEC.

In essence, the broker-dealer will not be considered to offer or sell securities by means of a free writing prospectus solely because another person has used or referred to the free writing prospectus or filed the free writing prospectus with the SEC. It will only be liable under § 12(a)(2) for a free writing prospectus if the broker-dealer itself has used the free writing prospectus with respect to its purchasers and for those it has used and widely disseminated.

Accordingly, § 12(a)(2) requires the broker-dealer to carefully monitor the information actually provided to investors who purchase securities from it in a public offering.

C. Defenses and Damages under § 12(a)(2)

Unlike § 12(a)(1), the broker-dealer may assert three defenses to avoid liability under § 12(a)(2). First, the broker-dealer may prove that the purchaser knew of the material misstatement or omission at the time of sale, and purchased the security anyway. Second, the broker-dealer may prove that it did not know of the material misrepresentation or omission, and with the exercise of reasonable care could not have known. Third, the broker-dealer has a negative causation defense; § 12(b) permits the broker-dealer to reduce its damages by proving that all or some portion of the decline in value of the securities was due to some cause other than the material misstatement or omission in the prospectus or oral communication. However, like § 12(a)(1), claims under § 12(a)(2) are subject to the statute of limitations of one year from discovery and three years from the sale of the security imposed under § 13 of the Securities Act. With respect to the first defense—purchaser knowledge—Rule

---

18. The SEC stated that "[w]e do not intend that the typical inter-syndicate arrangement providing for sales out of the syndicate 'pot' falls within this provision, unless the arrangement contemplates use of free writing prospectuses in a manner described in [Rule 159A]."

159 again provides that the purchaser must know of the material misrepresentation or omission at the time of sale. However, the second defense, broker-dealer knowledge of the material misrepresentation or omission at the time of sale, required clarification by the SEC.

Section 12(a)(2) requires the broker-dealer to sustain the burden of proof that "[it] did not know, and in the exercise of reasonable care could not have known, of ..." the material misrepresentation or omission contained in the prospectus or oral communication. The standard of reasonable care in § 12(a)(2) is not as stringent as the due diligence defense in § 11, which requires a reasonable investigation by the broker-dealer in the non-expertised portion of the registration statement. In *John Nuveen & Co. v. Sanders*, 450 US 1005, 1008-1009 (Powell, J. dissenting from denial of cert.), the Court stated the SEC's view that the standard of reasonable care under § 12(a)(2) and the requirement of a reasonable investigation under § 11 are indeed two different standards, with § 12(a)(2) being less stringent.

> In providing standards of care under the 1933 Act, Congress thus used different language for different situations. "Reasonable *investigation*" is required for registered offerings under § 11, but nothing more than "mer[e] ... "reasonable *care*' " is required by § 12(2).... "Investigation" commands a greater undertaking than "care."

Moreover, in a brief filed in this case with the Court of Appeals, the SEC expressly stated its reasoning for concluding that the standard of care under § 12(2) is less demanding than that prescribed in § 11:

> [I]t would be inconsistent with the statutory scheme to apply precisely the same standards to the scope of an underwriter's duty under Section 12(2) as the case law appropriately has applied to underwriters under Section 11. Because of the vital role played by an underwriter in the distribution of securities, and because the registration process is integral and important to the statutory scheme, we are of the view that a higher standard of care should be imposed on those actors who are critical to its proper operations. Since Congress has determined that registration is not necessary in certain defined situations, we believe that it would undermine the Congressional intent — that issuers and other persons should be relieved of registration — if the same degree of investigation were to be required to avoid potential liability whether or not a registration statement is required. Brief for SEC in Nos. 74-2047 and 75-1260 (CA7), *Sanders III*, at p. 69.

Plaintiffs' recovery under § 12(a)(2) is the same as under § 12(a)(1). They are entitled to rescission or damages if they no longer own the security. If the plaintiff still owns the security, she is entitled to the return of the purchase price of the security with interest upon tender of the security to the broker-dealer. If she no longer owns the security, the broker-dealer is liable for damages based on the difference between the plaintiff's purchase price and sale price.

Chapter 7

The Net Capital Rule

Regulatory Authority

Securities Exchange Act of 1934 Sections 8(b), 10(b), 15(c), 15(c)(3), 15A(b)(1)–(3), 15A(g), 17(a)

Exchange Act Rules 15c3-1, 15c3-3, 17a-3, 17a-11

FINRA Rules 4110(e), 4120, 4140, 4160, 4360, 4521

Motivating Hypothetical

Due to increased regulation spurred by the continuing adoption of new rules and regulations by both federal regulators and FINRA to implement the Dodd-Frank Act, Success First has determined that it needs to hire 10 additional compliance employees. Success First has decided that it will hire recent law school graduates and train them using its new trainee program. Success First believes that using a training program will ensure loyalty and the depth of knowledge of the broker-dealer industry deemed necessary by Success First. The training program provides a basic understanding of the financial responsibility requirements under federal securities laws and FINRA rules. The program was established by the Training Program Committee, whose members include Sidney Ratnam, chief financial officer; Tatum Chen, chief operations officer; and Malak Johnson, chief compliance officer. Josephine Wiseman, general counsel of Success First, acts as advisor to the committee. Modules in the financial responsibility unit of the training program include net capital and the customer protection rule. Trainees successfully completing the program will be hired after a mandatory 14-month probationary program. John DoGoode, a 10-year registered representative working in compliance, has been assigned to mentor the trainees.

I. Introduction

The net capital rule is a critical regulatory tool for the SEC and SROs because it reflects the current liquidity status of the broker-dealer and facilitates investor protection. The purpose of the net capital rule is to ensure that the broker-dealer has a prescribed cushion of net liquid assets over liabilities so that it is at all times sufficiently liquid to promptly meet the reasonable demands of its customers. A prescribed level of liquidity is necessary because of the nature of the broker-dealer business model, which relies heavily on cash and securities to finance business on a daily basis. Investor protection requires the broker-dealer to rely less on customer funds and securities as the primary means of financing its business. The net capital rule, along with other financial responsibility rules, is designed to decrease broker-dealer reliance on customer funds and securities as a primary means of financing the broker-dealer's business. Accordingly, the net capital rule has been the principal means of protecting investors from broker-dealer insolvencies or other financial problems. It is interesting to note, however, that despite its importance, there appears to be no demonstrable statistical analysis to support the level of net liquid assets required under the net capital rule.

The net capital rule has evolved over the years and become increasingly complex. This is to be expected in light of the ever-changing nature of the securities industry and the liquidity concept at the core of the net capital rule—that broker-dealers have sufficient liquid assets to cover their current indebtedness and are in a position to return customers' funds and securities upon reasonable demand. Section II of this chapter provides an overview of the evolution of the net capital rule from its inception until the adoption of the Uniform Net Capital Rule in 1975. Section III of this chapter reviews the Uniform Net Capital Rule as it was initially adopted in 1975. An understanding of how the net capital rule has evolved since its inception provides a conceptual basis for understanding the current Uniform Net Capital Rule, which is reviewed in Section IV of this chapter.

II. The Net Capital Rule: 1942–1974

The origin of today's net capital rule began in 1934 with the enactment of Section 8(b) of the Exchange Act. As enacted in 1934, Section 8(b) provided that:

> It shall be unlawful for any member of a national securities exchange, or any broker or dealer who transacts a business in securities through the medium of any such member, directly or indirectly to permit in the ordinary course of business as a broker his aggregate indebtedness[1] to all other persons, including customers' credit balances (but excluding indebtedness secured by exempted securities), to exceed such percentage of the net capital (exclusive of fixed assets and value of exchange membership) employed in the business, but not exceeding in any case 2,000 percent, as the Commission may by rules and regulations prescribe as necessary or appropriate in the public interest or for the protection of investors.

Congress chose to use the ratio method in dealing with the financial responsibility of broker-dealers by imposing a ratio of 20:1. Essentially, for every $20 of aggregate indebtedness, the broker-dealer must have one dollar of net capital. The legislative history of Section 8(b) does not provide a demonstrable statistical basis for setting the net capital requirement at 20:1. At this stage, the calculation of net capital was

---

1. All liabilities of the broker-dealer.

relatively simple; net capital was determined by subtracting fixed assets and the value of the broker-dealer's exchange membership from net worth.[2] According to the SEC, Section 8(b) demonstrated Congress' intention to prohibit the continuing operation of a broker-dealer if its ratio of aggregated indebtedness to net capital exceeded 20:1 to protect customers from broker-dealer insolvency. However, Section 8(b) only applied to broker-dealers who were members of national exchanges and to broker-dealers who transacted business through broker-dealers who were members of national exchanges. Broker-dealers who transacted business exclusively in the over-the-counter markets were not subject to Section 8(b)'s net capital requirement.

Although the SEC never adopted rules as authorized under Section 8(b), the following case demonstrates how the SEC applied Section 8(b) to exchange member broker-dealers and broker-dealers transacting business through such firms.

Securities and Exchange Commission v. Lawson

24 F.Supp. 360 (D. Md. 1938)

CHESNUT, District Judge.

In this case the Securities and Exchange Commission filed its bill of complaint against the defendant, William P. Lawson, on July 30, 1938, to enjoin certain alleged illegal practices prohibited by the provisions of ... section 8, par. (b) of the Securities Exchange Act of 1934, 15 U.S.C.A. §78h(b).

* * *

Section 8(b) of the Securities and Exchange Act of 1934, section 78h(b) of 15 U.S.C.A., provides that,

'It shall be unlawful for any member of a national securities exchange, or any broker or dealer who transacts a business in securities through the medium of any such member, directly or indirectly—

* * *

'(b) To permit in the ordinary course of business as a broker his aggregate indebtedness to all other persons, including customers' credit balances * * * to exceed such percentage of the net capital * * * employed in the business, but not exceeding in any case 2,000 per centum, as the Commission may b [y] rules and regulations prescribe as necessary or appropriate in the public interest or for the protection of investors'

Findings of Fact.

I. At all times herein mentioned the defendant William P. Lawson was and now is an inhabitant and resident of the City of Baltimore, within the District of Maryland.

* * *

III. From on or about December 1, 1937 to on or about July 30, 1938, the defendant transacted business in securities as a broker and dealer within the meaning of the Se-

---

2. Net worth is calculated using the formula: Total Assets – Total liabilities = Net Worth.

curities Exchange Act of 1934, 15 U.S.C.A. § 78a et seq., through the medium of a member of a national securities exchange, and permitted in the ordinary course of his business as a broker his aggregate indebtedness to all other persons, including customers' credit balances (but excluding indebtedness secured by exempted securities) to exceed two thousand per centum of the net capital employed in the business in that the defendant was insolvent. From July 30, 1938 to August 13, 1938, the defendant's continuation of his business was in the course of closing it out only.

IV. At the time of the commencement of this action the defendant owed his customers a net amount of approximately $91,753.18 in money and securities, of which amount $78,716.38 represented customers' securities which had been sold by the defendant, and which should have been in the defendant's possession for delivery to the customers, but were not in his possession or under his control; and $13,036.80 represented customers' free cash credit balances not available for them. Since then the defendant has liquidated his business as broker and dealer and has secured releases from his customers by delivering to them money and securities representing approximately one-third of his indebtedness to customers, and personal promissory notes representing the remaining two-thirds of such indebtedness, some of which are secured. The defendant between July 30 and August 13, 1938 has completely closed out his stock brokerage and securities business, has dismissed all his employees, terminated his office lease, and given up all facilities for conduct of the business; and has given notice to the public to that effect. It is not his present intention to resume such business and there is no likelihood that he will do so.

On these facts the CONCLUSIONS OF LAW are:

* * *

III. That at the time of the commencement of this action the defendant was engaged in acts and practices which constituted violations of section 8(b) of the Securities Exchange Act of 1934.

IV. That the plaintiff is entitled to a final decree enjoining and restraining the defendant from the acts and practices constituting violations of ... section 8(b) of the Securities Exchange Act of 1934 set forth in the foregoing findings of fact or acts and practices of similar purport or object.

* * *

For these reasons I have concluded that a decree should be signed in usual form (but without allowance of costs to either party, as the statute so provides) for a perpetual injunction against the defendant to enjoin the illegal practices complained of ...

———

Four years later, Congress enacted section 15(c)(3) of the Exchange Act, which, authorized the SEC to use its rulemaking power to impose financial responsibility requirements (including net capital requirements) on broker-dealers who were not members of an exchange or contracting business through an exchange member. In essence, Section 15(c)(3) authorized the SEC to impose net capital requirements on broker-dealers who transacted business exclusively in the over-the-counter markets. As enacted in 1938, 15(c)(3) provided that:

> No broker or dealer shall make use of the mails or of any means or instrumentality of interstate commerce to effect any transaction in, or to induce or attempt to induce the purchase or sale of, any security (other than an exempted security, or commercial paper, bankers' acceptances, or commercial bills) otherwise than on a national securities exchange, in contravention of such rules and regulations as the Commission may prescribe as necessary or appropriate in the public interest or for the protection of investors to provide safeguards with respect to *the financial responsibility of brokers and dealers* (emphasis added).

Before the SEC could utilize its new rulemaking authority under 15(c)(3), the NASD attempted to impose minimum net capital requirements on over-the-counter broker-dealers. The NASD proposed to restrict membership on the basis of a fixed minimum net capital requirement of $5,000 for broker-dealers dealing with the public and a minimum net capital requirement of $2,500 for broker-dealers not dealing directly with the public.[3] However, for the reasons discussed in the following case, the SEC prohibited the NASD from imposing minimum net capital requirements as a condition for membership and, instead, adopted its own net capital rule in 1942.

In the Matter of National Association of Securities Dealers, Inc.

Release No. 34-3322 (Oct. 28, 1942)

(Securities Exchange Act of 1934 — Section 15A)

RULES OF NATIONAL SECURITIES ASSOCIATIONS.

A national securities association registered under Section 15A of the Securities Exchange Act of 1934 as amended, having proposed to amend its bylaws to provide for minimum capital requirements as a condition of membership, *held* the proposed amendment is not in conformance with the requirements of that section, and disapproved.

OPINION OF THE COMMISSION

National Association of Securities Dealers, Inc. (NASD) is an organization of brokers and dealers in the over-the-counter markets. Its membership of 2,600 is composed of firms of all sizes, located in many parts of the country. The association is registered with us as a national securities association under Section 15A of the Securities Exchange Act of 1934.[4]

---

3. Nothing in the record indicates any statistical basis for the selection of these minimum net capital requirements.

4. [1] Relevant portions of Section 15A will be set forth in the course of this opinion. The section, often called the Maloney Act, because Senator Francis Maloney of Connecticut introduced it into the Senate, was enacted in 1938 and has been incorporated into the Securities Exchange Act as an amendment thereto.

NASD has brought before us a proposed amendment to its bylaws, which would require as a condition of membership that all members and prospective members have a fixed minimum net capital of $5,000, if they deal directly with customers, and a minimum of $2,500 if they do not effect certain transactions directly with the public ...

This amendment was proposed by the board of governors of the association pursuant to the powers vested in the governors by the association's bylaws. According to the bylaws, proposals must be approved by a majority of those voting, provided that a majority of all members vote.

A total of 1,933 votes were cast with respect to the proposal. Approximately 700 members did not vote. Of the 1,933 votes cast, 1,197, a clear majority of those voting, and approximately 45 percent of the total membership, voted in favor of the rule and 738 voted against it.[5]

In submitting the proposal to its membership, NASD distributed an open ballot, which required a statement of the voter's firm name and the signature of its executive representative. This type of ballot was criticized by some of those who appeared before us in opposition to the rule. It has been charged that but for the open ballot the proposal would not have been approved by a majority, and it is suggested that the necessity of signing the ballot may have influenced some of the small dealers to vote in favor of the proposal or to refrain from voting at all, in order to avoid possible discrimination.

The bylaws of NASD do not expressly require a secret ballot for this type of proposal, and the association has in the past, in submitting amendments to its membership, used the signed, open type of ballot.

Upon consideration of all the circumstances, it is our view that charges of unworthy motives in the selection of the type of ballot are unwarranted. However, we are constrained to add that it now seems, largely as a matter of hindsight, that the use of a secret ballot would have been preferable.

* * *

The question for decision then, is this: Is the proposed restriction of membership in the public interest or for the protection of investors, and will it carry out the purposes of the Maloney Act?

We are completely convinced that in proposing the rule and urging us and its membership to approve it, the governors of the NASD were actuated by no improper or hidden motives; that their only purpose was to safeguard the industry and the investor—a desirable end to which the NASD has already made notable contributions. We think also that fairness to the NASD requires us to say that when the rule was first

---

5. [2] Of the 738 who voted against the rule, 691 represented firms whose personnel consisted of from 1 to 5 persons. Of the 700 who did not vote, approximately 530 represented firms whose membership consisted of between 1 and 6 persons. Thus it appears that a large number of those not voting represented small firms.

discussed the Commission was inclined to view it favorably. This however, was a purely tentative view, and a close study of the proposal and of the problems associated with it, and careful consideration of all the facts and all the arguments, which have been presented for and against the rule, have forced the conclusion that the proposed rule does not conform to the statutory standards. Therefore we must disapprove it.

In our opinion permitting the registration of NASD, we called attention to the lack of provisions designed to insure the safe capital position of its members. *National Association of Securities Dealers, Inc.*, 5 S.E.C. 627 (1939). We then said:

> The Commission hopes that the applicant will undertake within the not too distant future the task of insuring itself of its members' solvency. Of course, it must be borne in mind that the Commission may find it necessary to promulgate its own rules as to the financial condition of all registered brokers and dealers, whether or not members of the Association.

Since this opinion was promulgated, the Association has been assiduous in ascertaining the financial condition of its members and has acted in a number of cases where insolvency was discovered, and it may very well be that our statement prompted the Association in some degree to propose the pending amendment.

The proposed amendment is inconsistent with the general purpose of the Act. The associations covered by the Act were intended to be thoroughly democratic. The Act very pointedly requires the rules of an association to provide that *any* broker or dealer who uses the mails or instrumentalities of interstate commerce to buy and sell securities may become a member. (Section 15A (b)(3)). It affords to brokers and dealers refused admission, suspended, expelled or otherwise disciplined, the right to appeal to us. (Section 15A (g)).

Mr. Chief Justice Eicher, formerly Chairman of this Commission, while a member of the Committee on Interstate and Foreign Commerce of the House of Representatives, and Chairman of the subcommittee charged with the consideration of the Maloney Bill, stated for the Committee in its report on the bill:

> The broad purpose of this paragraph [Section 15A (b)(3)] is to make sure that all brokers and dealers who conduct an honest and responsible business shall be eligible for membership in some association.

Former Commissioner Mathews stressed to the Senate Committee charged with the bill the importance of 'open membership' in associations. He pointed out that membership—

> ... Is a valuable business right, and if it is to be given to members of these associations and to the associations as such, for the guidance of members, it is important that we do not have a monopolistic association. The association must be open to the fellow who is willing to conduct his business decently.

According to the NASD's own estimate, adoption of the rule may result in the expulsion of over one-fourth of its membership. To permit that result we should find clear authority for the rule in the statute. The Maloney Act provides no express basis for rules prescribing capital requirements as a condition of membership and its legislative history makes it quite clear that Congress specifically rejected minimum capital requirements as inappropriate for national associations. The Senate Committee on Banking and Currency, while considering the Maloney Bill, was presented with an express proposal to prescribe capital requirements. No such requirement was incorporated into the Act. The failure to do so was, without doubt, deliberate. The necessity of broad membership bases had been specifically brought to the attention of Congress. That Congress regarded such requirements as appropriate for *general* application is indicated by the fact that, contemporaneously with the passage of the Maloney Act, Congress enacted Section 15(c) of the Securities Exchange Act. That section authorizes the Commission to prescribe capital requirements of *general* application in the over-the-counter securities industry.

Further, Sections 15A (b)(1) and (2), applicable to this case, require that an association have a sufficient 'number of members' and that it be 'so organized' and 'of such a character' as to comply with the provisions and carry out the purposes of the Act. The expulsion of small firms and the limitation of the NASD to representation of larger firms is an inevitable result of the proposed rule, and the loss of so large a segment of its membership, merely because the firms are small, vitally and adversely affects the organization and character of the NASD as representative of the over-the-counter industry. No matter what state jurisdictions and exchanges may require, the legislation to which a national securities association must conform clearly intends that size shall not be a criterion of selection of membership or a basis of distinction in bringing to investors the advantage of cooperative regulation.

THE COMMISSION'S RULE

The need for general rules to achieve customer protection against financially unsafe brokers and dealers has been apparent to us for some time and we believe this an appropriate occasion to announce our rule under Section 15(c)(3).

Under this section the Commission may choose between various methods of providing for financial responsibility. It can, as the NASD has proposed to do, require brokers and dealers to maintain a fixed minimum net capital. On the other hand, it can, as it proposes to do, require the maintenance of a ratio of 1 to 20 between net capital and aggregate indebtedness. In making its choice of methods the Commission is motivated by a number of factors.

First, in dealing with the problem of financial responsibility as it relates to members of national securities exchanges and brokers and dealers who do business through such members, Congress has used the ratio method and it has prescribed a ratio between net capital and aggregate indebtedness similar to that provided in our rule.

Secondly, whatever might be said for the benefits of the minimum capital rule as a safeguard against insolvency, any standard of net capital so adjusted as to permit small, honest brokers and dealers to remain in business might be totally inadequate in many cases. For example, a net capital of $5,000 means little in the case of a dealer whose liabilities run into millions.

The argument has been made that some minimum capital requirement should exist which will be applicable to all brokers and dealers who do business with the public and which will, in effect, place a floor under financial responsibility. We do not need to decide the merits of this argument.

The problem of a proper minimum capital for brokers and dealers has been met in part by the laws of the various States, some of which impose such requirements on persons being [in] business within their jurisdiction.

Moreover, the Commission, in collaboration with various State commissioners and representatives of the securities industry, has prepared, and is about to promulgate, Rule X–17A–5 which will require that all registered brokers and dealers file with the Commission at least once a year a financial statement which in some cases must be certified by an independent accountant. The reports received under this rule will, for the first time, afford us an opportunity to study the financial condition of all registered brokers and dealers and the knowledge thus obtained should be extremely helpful if, at some future date, the Commission determines that the public interest requires change in the method of prescribing capital requirements.

The rule now adopted by the Commission provides that no broker or dealer shall permit his aggregate indebtedness to all other persons (exclusive of indebtedness secured by exempted securities) to exceed 2,000 percent of his net capital (exclusive of fixed assets and value of exchange memberships). After this rule becomes effective there will be placed upon every person engaged in the securities business a limitation upon his power to obligate himself which will vary with the nature and volume of business transacted. Thus there will be extended to *all* brokers and dealers who extend credit to customers or carry money or securities for the account of customers or owe money or securities to customers substantially the same requirements now imposed upon members of national securities exchanges and brokers and dealers who do business through such members by Section 8(b) of the Securities Exchange Act. In all cases, the requirement that borrowings and other indebtedness shall not exceed 2,000 percent of *net* capital will provide a minimum cushion of 5 percent of the aggregate indebtedness of the broker or dealer as a margin of safety to his customers. The value of exchange memberships and fixed assets will be available to customers and other creditors as an added protection. If experience indicates that the ratio is wrong—that the minimum cushion should be increased—it can be changed.

In the near future the Commission will publish for comment a proposed rule defining the terms 'net capital' and 'aggregate indebtedness' as used in the new rule. The Commission.... will refrain from adopting the defining rules until the industry has had an opportunity to express itself and to point out such changes as may be needed to bring about a workable rule.

———————

As initially adopted,[6] Rule 15c3-1 did not apply to broker-dealers who did not extend credit and did not carry money or securities for customers. This exemption only applied to a narrow group of broker-dealers — generally broker-dealers owned by insurance companies. In addition, the SEC later announced that Rule 15c3-1 did not apply to members of the New York Stock Exchange and certain other exchanges because the exchanges' net capital requirements were more stringent than those contained in the SEC's Rule.

The net capital rule did not become effective until November 9, 1944, when the SEC defined critical terms used in the rule. These terms included *aggregate indebtedness*, *net capital*, *exempted securities*, and *customer*. Aggregate indebtedness was defined as illustrated in Figure 7.1:

Figure 7.1

Aggregate Indebtedness defined
• Total money liabilities in connection with any transaction
• Minus
◦ Indebtedness secured by exempted securities
◦ Amounts segregated in accordance with the Commodities Exchange Act rules and regulations
◦ Liabilities on open contractual commitments

In addition, Rule 15c3-1 expressly included certain items in the broker-dealers' total money liabilities as described in Figure 7.2.

---

6. As adopted on October 29, 1942, the SEC's net capital rule, Rule X15c3-1, provided that:
   (a) No broker or dealer shall permit his aggregate indebtedness to all other persons (exclusive of indebtedness secured by exempted securities) to exceed 2000 per centum of his net capital (exclusive of fixed assets and value of exchange memberships).
   (b) The provisions of this rule shall not apply to any broker or dealer who (1) does not extend credit to any person to whom he sells or for whom he purchases any securities, and (2) does not carry money or securities for the account of customers or owe money or securities to customers, except as an incident to transactions with or for customers which are promptly consummated by payment or deliver; Provided, that credit shall not be deemed to be extended by reason of a bona fide delayed delivery of any such security against full payment of the entire purchase price thereof upon such delivery within thirty-five (35) days after such purchase.
   (c) This rule shall not become effective until further order of the Commission, and, in any event, not earlier than January 1, 1943.

Figure 7.2

Money Borrowed by the Broker-Dealer
Money Payable Against securities loaned by the Broker-Dealer
Money Payable against securities failed to receive[1]
Customers'[2] Free Credit Balances[3]
Credit Balances in Customers' Accounts having Short Positions in Securities
Equities in Customers' Commodities Futures Accounts

1. Money payable against securities failed to receive are generated when a buying broker fails to receive purchased securities by the settlement date.

2. Customer was defined as every person except a partner. The rule defined *partner* in the context of broker-dealers organized as partnerships, because only a partner who has agreed in writing that the equity in any accounts he may maintain with such broker-dealer be included as partnership property.

3. Free Credit balances are securities and cash that customers are entitled to obtain upon demand.

Rule 15c3-1 defined *net capital* as the broker-dealer's total assets minus total liabilities, or net worth, reduced by certain non-liquid assets and haircuts (a reduction in the current market value of securities held to reflect volatility and risk). See Figure 7.3.

Figure 7.3. Net Capital

```
    Total Assets
  − Total Liabilities
    Net Worth
  + Unrealized Profits
  − Unrealized Losses
  − Fixed Assets and other assets that cannot be readily converted to cash
  − Haircuts
    Net Capital
```

Rule 15c3-1 expressly includes in this category: net market value of real estate; furniture and fixtures; exchange memberships; prepaid rent, insurance, and expenses; unsecured advances and loans to partners, officers, directors, employees, and salespeople; customers' unsecured notes and accounts; and deficits in customers' accounts, except in bona fide cash accounts within the meaning of section 4(c) of Regulation T of the Board of Governors of the Federal Reserve System.

At this point in the history of the net capital rule, the adoption of Rule 15c3-1, combined with existing Section 8(b), imposed a minimum net capital requirement on all broker-dealers, except those who did not carry customers' securities or cash and did not extend credit. However, enforcement of net capital requirements against exchange member broker-dealers remained with the exchanges.

Notes and Questions

1. In its order granting the registration of the NASD in 1939 as an SRO, *National Association of Securities Dealers, Inc.*, 5 S.E.C. 627 (1939), the SEC noted:

   > There are, however, no rules whatsoever concerning the solvency of members or requiring any regular or periodic inspections on the part of the association of a member's books or the submission, on the part of a member, of his financial statement to the association or to an independent firm of auditors acting for the association. The Commission regrets that the association has not seen fit, initially, to adopt any such rules for the protection of investors. The Commission feels that it must emphasize the lack of such rules, lest the public be misled into thinking that membership in the applicant association in any way connotes solvency; as far as the rules of the association are concerned an insolvent broker or dealer might join and continue in membership without ascertainment of his condition by the association through an investigation of his books, unless one of its business conduct committees should conduct a special investigation. The Commission hopes that the applicant will undertake, within the not too distant future, the task of assuring itself of its members' solvency. Of course it must be borne in mind that the Commission may find it necessary to promulgate its own rules as to the financial condition of all registered brokers and dealers, whether or not members of the association.

   Does this observation indicate that the SEC expected the NASD, in the not-too-distant future, to adopt something similar to the NYSE's net capital rule, which, at the time, was also an SRO registered with the SEC? Why didn't the SEC approve the NASD's attempt to impose net capital requirements on its members in *In the Matter of National Association of Securities Dealers, Inc.*, Rel. No. 34-3322 (Oct. 28, 1942)?

2. In the SEC's original Rule 15c3-1, were there any types of over-the-counter broker-dealers that were exempt from its requirements?

3. The SEC also amended Rule 15c3-1 to permit the exclusion of a satisfactory subordination agreement in computing aggregate indebtedness and the inclusion of a satisfactory subordination agreement when computing net capital. SEC Exchange Act Release No. 5156 (Apr. 11, 1955). A satisfactory subordination agreement required a writing; subordination of any right of the lender to demand or receive payment to the claims of present and future general creditors of the broker-dealer could not be canceled at the will of either party; could not have a term of less than one year; and could not be terminated by mutual consent if the effect would be to reduce the net capital of the broker-dealer below the minimum amount required under Rule 15c3-1. In addition, default in the payment of interest or in the performance of covenants or conditions could not result in acceleration — the instrument was required to show on its face that it was subject to a subordi-

nation agreement and that any securities or other property loaned to the broker-dealer under the subordination agreement could be used by the broker-dealer as part of its capital and was subject to the risks of its business. Why should subordinated loans, which must be repaid at some point in the future, be used to increase the net capital of the broker-dealer?

————

The net capital rule was significantly revised again in 1965 as a result of the *Report of Special Study of Securities Markets* (Special Study)[7] conducted by the SEC in 1963. Congress directed the SEC to conduct a broad study of the securities markets, including the adequacy of investor protection. The Special Study noted that the current net capital ratio requirements were insufficient for the protection of investors and the operation of an efficient market. It also found that a disproportionate number of violations of SEC rules were committed by broker-dealers with limited capital, and that broker-dealers with "low capital were involved in a high proportion of revocation proceedings and that [broker-dealers] with net capital smaller than $5,000 [had] a significantly higher chance of falling into net capital difficulties under the [SEC's] ratio rule than those with a greater amount." As a result, the Special Study recommended that broker-dealers engaged in a general securities business be required to maintain minimum net capital of $2,500 for each branch office and $500 for each salesperson.[8]

Among the reasons cited by the Study were the following:

> First, the securities business involves dealing with other people's funds, and no firm handling or having custody of customers' funds and securities should have such a small amount of its own resources in the business that customers' assets may, in fact, become the principal working capital of the firm. Secondly, the smooth and speedy functioning of market mechanisms requires members of the financial community to have confidence in each other's stability and responsibility, and this in turn requires each of such persons to have sufficient capital to have adequate personnel, resources and equipment so that each may rely upon the other's ability to do business responsibly. Third, if the liability to customers resulting from violations of state and federal law is to be a deterrent to improper conduct by broker-dealers, they should not be judgment proof, but rather should have a substantial financial stake in their business.[9]

Based on the Special Study, the SEC adopted minimum dollar net capital requirements for broker-dealers, in addition to the existing net capital ratio requirement. However, in contrast to the Special Study recommendations, the SEC chose to impose

———

7. Report of Special Study of Securities Markets of the Securities and Exchange Commission, H.R. Doc. No. 88-95, pt. 1 (1963).

8. *Id.* at 161–62.

9. *Id.* at *passim*.

a minimum dollar net capital requirement of $5,000 for broker-dealers engaged in a general securities business; a $2,500 minimum dollar net capital requirement was imposed on broker-dealers who did not hold customers' funds or securities and whose businesses were limited to the sale and redemption of mutual funds, the sale of securities for customers to obtain funds for immediate reinvestment in mutual funds, and the solicitation of accounts for certain insured savings and loan associations.

Also, the exemption from the requirements of Rule 15c3-1 was narrowed considerably based on the Special Study. Prior to the 1965 amendments, broker-dealers were exempt from the requirements of Rule 15c3-1 if: (1) their securities business was limited to acting as an agent for an issuer in soliciting subscriptions for securities of the issuer; (2) they promptly transmitted all funds and securities in connection with customer transactions; and (3) they did not hold customers' funds or securities or owe funds or securities to customers. Amended Rule 15c3-1 limited the exemption only to broker-dealers who were also licensed as insurance agents and: (1) whose securities business was only limited to selling variable annuity contracts as agent for the issuer; (2) who promptly transmitted all funds and delivered all variable annuity contracts; (3) who did not otherwise hold customer funds or securities or owe money or securities to customers; and (4) who dealt with issuers of variable annuity contracts who filed an undertaking with the SEC stating that the issuer assumed responsibility for all valid claims arising out of the broker-dealers' activities.

The SEC also imposed additional requirements concerning satisfactory subordination agreements. Amended Rule 15c3-1 required the broker-dealer to file two copies of the subordination agreement within 10 days with the SEC with a statement of the name and address of the lender, a description of the business relationship between the broker-dealer and the lender, and whether the broker-dealer carried funds or securities for the lender about the time at which the broker-dealer and the lender entered into the subordination agreement. This filing requirement with the SEC was designed to facilitate enforcement of satisfactory subordination agreements between broker-dealers and their lenders.

The net capital rule was amended again because of the significant backlog of fails to deliver resulting from the Paperwork Crisis of 1967, along with the 1969-70 market downturn. Tremendous increases in trading volume restricted the ability of broker-dealers to clear and settle accounts by settlement date. Failure to settle by settlement date caused broker-dealers' fails-to-deliver accounts to contain numerous open items and subjected selling broker-dealers to the risk that broker-dealers on the other side of the transaction might experience financial difficulties prohibiting settlement.

> It was noted that the fundamental problem [arose] from the many steps involved in the handling of certificates and in the settlement and completion of trades. This problem [was] not confined to broker-dealers alone but involve[d] the entire securities industry—institutions, banks, transfer agents and others who participate[d] in the securities market.[10]

---

10. Exchange Act Release No. 8341, 1968 WL 88040 (June 20, 1968).

The SEC addressed this problem by amending Rule 15c3-1 to require varying deductions, up to 30 percent,[11] from the contract price of each item in the selling broker-dealers' securities fails-to-deliver account based on the period in which the item remained outstanding. This amendment also applied to broker-dealers who were members of an exchange if the exchange did not subject the broker-dealer to a similar requirement.

The Paperwork Crisis resulted in a study conducted by the SEC: *The Study of Unsafe and Unsound Practices of Brokers and Dealers December 1971*, which led to more significant amendments to the net capital rule. These amendments included an early warning system for net capital deficiencies, reduced the net capital ratio, and established minimum dollar net capital requirements based on the nature of the broker-dealer's business. The early warning system for net capital deficiencies consisted of four major provisions. The first provision required the broker-dealer to provide immediate telegraphic notice to the SEC, and the appropriate SRO, when its net capital was less than the required minimum, regardless of which net capital requirement applied.[12] The second provision required a broker-dealer to file a report furnishing data about its financial and operational condition when its net capital ratio was in excess of 1,200 percent (or total net capital was less than 120 percent of its required minimum or 12:1) within 15 days after the end of each month; this report was required until the broker-dealer's net capital ratio was not in excess of 1,200 percent for three consecutive months. The third provision required the broker-dealer to provide immediate telegraphic notice to the SEC and its SRO if it was not making and keeping current books and records and required the broker-dealer, within 48 hours of such a notice, to file a written report enumerating steps taken to correct the situation. The fourth provision of the early warning system required the broker-dealer's SRO to notify the SEC if the SRO learned that a member broker-dealer had failed to give notice or to file a report as required under the first three provisions of the early warning system.

The Paperwork Crisis and resulting study also led the SEC to reduce the net capital ratio to a maximum ratio of aggregate indebtedness to net capital of 8:1 for broker-dealers during their first year of operation. In addition, broker-dealers who held funds and securities of, or owed funds or securities to, customers were required to maintain a minimum dollar net capital of $25,000; broker-dealers who promptly transmitted all funds and delivered all securities in connection with their activities and did not otherwise hold funds or securities for, or owe funds or securities to, customers were required to maintain a minimum dollar net capital of $5,000.[13] The ex-

---

11. Deducting 10 percent of the contract price of each item in the securities fails to deliver account which is outstanding 40 to 49 calendar days; deducting 20 percent of the contract price of each item in the securities fails to deliver account which is outstanding 50 to 59 calendar days; and deducting 30 percent of the contract price of each item in the securities fails to deliver account which is outstanding 60 or more calendar days.

12. The Uniform Net Capital Rule was not established until 1975. Accordingly, broker-dealers were subject to varying net capital rules established by the SEC and certain exchanges.

13. This amendment did not change the minimum net capital requirement of $2,500 for broker-dealers engaged in the sale and redemption of redeemable securities of registered investment companies.

emption from Rule 15c3-1 for broker-dealers who were members of exchanges was continued, but was conditioned on the exchanges' net capital ratios and dollar minimums being at least equal to the SEC's new requirements in the amendment.

III. Adoption of the Uniform Net Capital Rule

Effective September 1, 1975, the SEC adopted a Uniform Net Capital Rule, which eliminated the fragmented regulation of broker-dealer net capital requirements.[14] Prior to the adoption of the Uniform Net Capital Rule, broker-dealers who were members of the major exchanges operated under one set of net capital requirements, while smaller broker-dealers were subject to the SEC's net capital requirements. The SEC noted specifically that:

> while the exchanges sought to provide a sound capital base for their members, some of them were unable in the 1968-1970 period to cope with the threats to the financial solvency of certain of their members. Furthermore, the lines of responsibility for administering the [net] capital rules were not always clear, and at times affirmative action was not taken to enforce the provisions of the net capital rules. Interpretations were made which undercut protective features of the net capital rules with a consequence that firms which would have been in violation of the Commission's net capital rule continued to function and expose customers to loss due to broker-dealer insolvency. The securities industry was compelled to pay a high price for the financial weaknesses of these members. The funding of the $140 million New York Stock Exchange trust fund to cover customer losses was borne by the industry.

The Uniform Net Capital Rule continued to impose a maximum ratio of aggregate indebtedness to net capital that a broker-dealer must maintain, the minimum dollar net capital requirement based on the nature of the broker-dealer's business, and introduced an alternative standard ratio to compute a broker-dealer's minimum net

---

See Net Capital of Certain Broker-Dealers; Restricted Rates and Minimum Requirements, Exchange Act Release No. 9633, 1972 WL 125506 (June 14, 1972).

14. Certain specialists were excluded at this time. For example, stock exchange specialists who only dealt with other exchange members, broker-dealers, and specialists and market makers in options were exempt from the Uniform Net Capital Rule. The approved exchanges were the American Stock Exchange, Boston Stock Exchange, Midwest Stock Exchange, New York Stock Exchange, Pacific Stock Exchange, PBW Stock Exchange, and the Chicago Board Options Exchange. The SEC deemed the rules and regulatory procedures at these exchanges to be at least as stringent as the Uniform Net Capital Rule. However, after the 1987 Market Break, the Uniform Net Capital Rule was applied to exchange specialists in 1988. Municipal securities broker-dealers were also subject to the Uniform Net Capital Rule. *See* Net Capital Requirements for Brokers and Dealers, Exchange Act Release No. 26402, 1988 WL 1000048 (Dec. 28, 1988).

capital requirement in addition to the aggregate indebtedness standard ratio. Under the Uniform Net Capital Rule, the maximum ratio of aggregate indebtedness to net capital requirement was reduced from 20:1 to 15:1 and the minimum dollar net capital requirement was amended as shown in Figure 7.4.

Figure 7.4. Minimum Dollar Net Capital Requirement

Minimum Net Capital Dollar Requirement	Eligibility
$5,000	Broker-Dealers who engage in sale of mutual funds on a direct wire order basis and certain floor brokers who effect but do not clear transactions for other broker-dealers.
$50,000	Broker-Dealers who write and endorse options where such options are not listed on a registered national securities exchange.
$25,000 or $2,500 per security with a maximum requirement of $100,000 or a 15:1 ratio, whichever is greater.*	Broker-dealers who act as market makers in securities.

* For securities with a market value of less than $5 per share the minimum requirement for each security was $500. *See Adoption of Amendments to Rule 15c3-1 and Adoption of an Alternative Net Capital Requirement for Certain Brokers and Dealers*, Exchange Act Release No. 11497, 1975 WL 162992 (June 26, 1975).

The Uniform Net Capital Rule increased the complexity of the determination of net capital requirements by, among other things, changing requirements to compute aggregate indebtedness and net capital as shown in Figure 7.5.

Figure 7.5. Changes to Aggregate Indebtedness

Item	Explanation
Indebtedness Collateralized by Exempted Securities	Option of charging net capital by an amount equal to 4% of any indebtedness collateralized by exempted securities in lieu of including the amount of such indebtedness in the computation of aggregate indebtedness.
Deferred Income Taxes	May be excluded from aggregate indebtedness.

The Uniform Net Capital Rule also established the alternative standard ratio to determine minimum net capital in addition to the aggregated indebtedness standard ratio. The alternative standard ratio was based largely on the Formula for Determination of Reserve Requirements of Broker-Dealers (Reserve Formula) under Rule 15c3-3. Use of the Reserve Formula under Rule 15c3-3 to determine minimum net capital requirements represented a change of focus by the SEC from solely broker-dealer liquidity to more direct protection for customers' funds and securities. Rule 15c3-3 limited broker-dealers' use of customers' funds and securities to financing customers' transactions; essentially, it prohibited use of customers' funds and securities to finance any part of a broker-dealer's business unrelated to servicing customers. If a broker-dealer chose to determine its minimum net capital requirement using the alternative standard ratio in 1975, it was required to maintain minimum net capital equal to the greater of $100,000 or four percent of aggregate debit items included in the Reserve Formula.[15]

After the adoption of the Uniform Net Capital Rule in 1975, the SEC continued to amend the rule to ensure adequate liquidity for the protection of investors. Significant amendments included allowing the use of revolving subordinated loans, the elimination from the Reserve Formula of securities borrowed from customers under certain circumstances,[16] increasing the required minimum net capital amount,[17] and making the Uniform Net Capital Rule applicable to all specialists except those operating as options market makers on the floors of the national securities exchanges.[18]

IV. The Current Uniform Net Capital Rule

The current Uniform Net Capital Rule (UNCR) remains quite complex, but maintains its focus on liquidity. Although paragraph (a)(2) of Rule 15c3-1 specifies minimum dollar levels of net capital that a broker-dealer must maintain, the broker-dealer's minimum net capital requirement is the greater of the minimum dollar levels specified paragraph (a)(2) or one of two ratio tests described in paragraph (a)(1) — the aggregate indebtedness standard ratio or the alternative standard ratio. However, determining a broker-dealer's required minimum net capital often is subject to disagreement between the broker-dealer and its examining authorities despite the UNCR's specificity because judgment is required in its application. Figure 7.6 provides an overview of the determination of a broker-dealer's minimum net capital requirement.

---

15. Rule 15c3-3 and its Reserve Formula are discussed in greater detail in Section IV.C. of this chapter.

16. *See Net Capital Requirements for Brokers and Dealers*, Exchange Act Release No. 18737, 1982 WL 529283 (May 13, 1982).

17. *See Net Capital Rule*, Exchange Act Release No. 31511, 1992 WL 356004 (Nov. 24, 1992).

18. *See Net Capital Requirements for Brokers and Dealers*, Exchange Act Release No. 32737, 1993 WL 307496 (Aug. 11, 1993).

Figure 7.6.

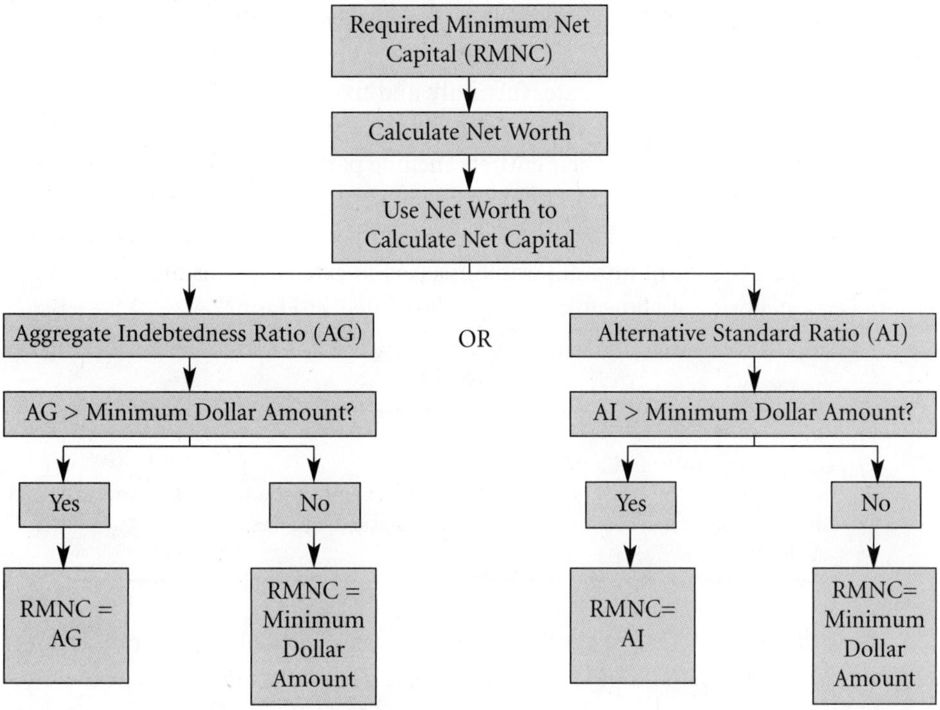

A. Computation of Net Capital

The first step in determining the broker-dealer's minimum net capital requirement is to calculate its net capital. Net capital is defined in paragraph (c)(2) of the UNCR and begins with calculating the broker-dealer's net worth. This requires subtracting the broker-dealer's total liabilities from its total assets. Next, the broker-dealer's net worth is adjusted to arrive at a figure that approximates the broker-dealer's net capital by: (1) subtracting all non-allowable assets, i.e., assets that cannot be readily converted into cash and (2) subtracting securities haircuts, i.e., a percentage of the market value of securities and commodities held in the broker-dealer's proprietary accounts to reflect market risk. This computation is summarized in Figure 7.7.

Figure 7.7. Computation of Net Capital

Total Assets
– <u>Total Liabilities</u>
Net Worth
– Non-allowable Assets
– Securities Haircuts
+ <u>subordination agreements</u>
Net Capital

1. Non-Allowable Assets

Rule 15c3-1's list of non-allowable assets is extensive and includes assets that are excluded in their entirety as well as partially. Non-allowable assets that are excluded in their entirety, include real estate, furniture and fixtures, exchange memberships, prepaid rent, prepaid insurance, goodwill, and organization expenses. Non-allowable assets that are not excluded in their entirety include partly secured receivables, which are allowable to the extent of the value of their corresponding collateral, and marketable securities, which are allowable at current market value less their corresponding haircut. Because the list of non-allowable assets is so extensive, it is more efficient to enumerate categories of allowable assets as illustrated in Figure 7.8.

Figure 7.8

Allowable Assets
- Secured receivables and liquid assets
- Partially secured receivables—allowable to the extent of the value of collateral
- Marketable securities—allowable at current market value less haircuts
- Fails to deliver

Broker-dealers generate receivables in connection with customer transactions, clearing organizations, and other broker-dealers. The broker-dealer may have a receivable arising from accounts held for customers and other broker-dealers and accounts held at clearing organizations for the broker-dealer. For example, a receivable may result from a customer in the customer account arising from margin trading. Also, repurchase agreement transactions with other broker-dealers may generate a secured or partly secured receivable from the borrowing broker-dealer.

2. Securities Haircuts

Haircuts are designed to account for the price volatility, lack of liquidity, and risk of the particular security or commodity. This means that the amount of the haircut varies by class of security. Moreover, the SEC is consistently revising the required haircuts in the UNCR based on market experience, with the risk of the various classes of securities and commodities. The UNCR prescribes differing haircut amounts for a variety of classes of securities (See Figure 7.9 below) and contains catch-all provisions to account for classes of securities not specified in the UNCR. In addition, if a security does not have a ready market,[19] it is subject to a 100 percent haircut or deduction from the broker-dealer's net capital.

---

19. Paragraph (c)(11) of the UNCR defines a ready market as including a recognized established securities market in which there exist independent bona fide offers to buy and sell so that a price reasonably related to the last sales price or current bona fide competitive bid and offer quotations can be determined for a particular security almost instantaneously and where payment will be received in settlement of a sale at such price within a relatively short time conforming to trade custom. Securities used as bank collateral will also be deemed to have a ready market under certain circumstances. 17 C.F.R. §240.15c3-1(c)(11) (2014).

Figure 7.9. Classes of Securities

Class of Security	Characteristics
U.S. Government Securities	Security issued or guaranteed as to principal or interest by the U.S. or any agency thereof; maturity date determines haircut percentage.
Municipal Securities	Security issued by a municipality and maturity date determines haircut.
Canadian Debt Obligations	Security issued or unconditionally guaranteed as to principal and interest by the Government of Canada.
Investment Company Securities	Redeemable securities of an investment company registered under the Investment Company Act of 1940.
Commercial Paper, Bankers Acceptances, and Certificates of Deposit	Short-term debt obligations with maturities not exceeding nine months with only a minimal amount of credit risk, or are guaranteed or issued by a bank; maturity date determines haircut percentage.
Nonconvertible Debt Securities	Have a fixed interest rate, a fixed maturity date, and only a minimal amount of credit risk; maturity date determines haircut percentage.
Convertible Debt Securities	Fixed rate of interest, a fixed maturity date, and is convertible into an equity security.
Cumulative, Non-Convertible Preferred Stock	Must rank prior to all other classes of stock of the same issuer, have minimal amount of credit risk, and may not be in arrears as to dividends.

Calculating haircuts can be quite complex. For example, the required haircut for equity securities traded on a national exchange is as follows:

> [T]he deduction shall be 15 percent of the market value of the greater of the long or short positions and to the extent the market value of the lesser of the long or short positions exceeds 25 percent of the market value of the greater of the long or short positions, the percentage deduction on such excess shall be 15 percent of the market value of such excess. 17 C.F.R. §240.15c3-1(c)(vi)(J).

First, a haircut equal to 15 percent of the market value of whichever is greater—the aggregate long positions or the aggregate short positions—must be taken. If the long positions exceed the short positions, 15 percent must be deducted from the value of the long positions. Next, it must be determined the extent to which the value of the lesser of the long or short positions (the position that does not receive the 15 percent deduction) exceeds 25 percent of the greater of the long or short positions (the position that received the 15 percent deduction). An additional haircut of 15 percent must be taken of this excess value. For example, assume that a broker-dealer has positions in only two stocks: a $1 million long position in Student, Inc. and a $500,000 short position in Professor, Inc. Since the long position is greater than the short position, a 15 percent haircut ($150,000) must be taken on the long position in Student, Inc. Since the $500,000 position in Professor, Inc. exceeds 25 percent of the $1 million long position in Student, Inc. ($ 250,000), an additional haircut must be taken equal to 15 percent of the excess value of $250,000 ($500,000 − $250,000) or $37,500 (250,000 × .15) for a total haircut of $187,500 ($150,000 + $37,500).

The UNCR also includes deductions on open contractual commitments in the broker-dealer's proprietary accounts. Open contractual commitments include underwriting, when distributed contracts,[20] the writing or endorsement of puts and calls, and aged fails to deliver contracts. For example, for aged fails to deliver contracts, the required haircut is determined by the class of securities involved and must be deducted from the contract value of each fails to deliver contract that is outstanding five business days or longer.[21]

Deductions for undue concentration of securities in a broker-dealer's proprietary accounts are also required. Deductions for undue concentrations is required if a particular security represents more than 10 percent of the broker-dealer's net capital before other haircuts are taken that are required under the UNCR.

3. The Ratio Tests

As discussed earlier in this chapter, determining required minimum net capital requires the calculation of one of two ratio tests — the aggregate indebtedness ratio and the alternative standard ratio. If the result of either of these ratios is less than the minimum dollar levels specified in paragraph (a)(2) of the UNCR, then the broker-dealer's required minimum net capital is the specified minimum dollar level. Again, calculation of these ratios requires first determining the broker-dealer's net capital as defined in paragraph (c)(2) of the UNCR (net worth reduced by non-allowable assets and securities haircuts). Generally, smaller broker-dealers choose the aggregate indebtedness ratio because the required minimum net capital is less than that required under the alternative standard ratio.

a. Aggregate Indebtedness Standard

After calculating the broker-dealer's net capital, its aggregate indebtedness must be calculated in order to determine its required minimum net capital. The UNCR prohibits a broker-dealer from allowing its aggregate indebtedness to exceed 1,500

---

20. Securities trade on a when distributed basis when they have been announced, but not yet issued. When distributed is a conditional transaction when securities have been authorized but not yet issued. The transaction is settled only after the security has been issued. Treasury securities, stock splits, and new issues of stocks and bonds may be traded on a when distributed basis.

21. If the fails-to-deliver contract involves a municipal security, the required haircut must be deducted if the contract is outstanding 21 business days or longer.

percent of its net capital (15:1). See Figure 7.10. However, during the first 12 months of operation, the broker-dealer's aggregate indebtedness cannot exceed 800 percent of its net capital (8:1).

Figure 7.10. Aggregate Indebtedness Standard

Aggregate indebtedness/net capital ≤ 15:1

Aggregate Indebtedness is defined in the UNCR as the total money liabilities of a broker-dealer arising in connection with any transaction whatsoever. However, certain items related to broker-dealers as opposed to customer activities are specifically excluded from the definition of aggregate indebtedness. These exclusions include indebtedness adequately collateralized by securities, which are carried long by a broker-dealer and which have not been sold, or indebtedness in the form of a secured demand note adequately collateralized by securities. Most important, while a broker-dealer is allowed to exclude certain liabilities from its aggregate indebtedness, the liability must still be included as a liability on the broker-dealer's balance sheet. This means that such liabilities reduce the broker-dealer's net worth and therefore its net capital. The following SEC No-Action Letter discusses the aggregate indebtedness standard ratio and how the broker-dealer's failure to include liabilities excluded from aggregate indebtedness as a liability on the broker-dealer's balance sheet in calculating its net worth affect the determination of a broker-dealer's minimum net capital requirement.

Mid America Financial Services, Inc.

1982 SEC No-Act LEXIS 2979
(Nov. 8, 1982)

June 17, 1982

Congressman Larry Winn
Room 2268
Rayburn House Office Bldg.
Washington, D. C. 20515

Dear Larry:

Please excuse me for taking your valuable time but I need your help.

I am enclosing copies of various rules of the Securities and Exchange Commission. If I have misinterpreted the rules we will be forced to give up our livlihood [sic].

I am attaching a copy of various sections of Chapter II 240.15c3-1 which defines some of the terminology of this rule on which my disagreement with the Securities and Exchange Commission hinges.

Aggregate Indebtedness—The term "aggregate indebtedness" shall be deemed to mean the total money liabilities of a Broker or Dealer arising in connection with any transaction whatsoever and includes among other things, money borrowed etc.

Exclusions from Aggregate Indebtedness—Indebtedness adequately collateralized by securities which are carried long by the broker or dealer and which have not been sold or by securities which collateralize a secured Demand note etc.

Attached is a copy of Appendix D to Rule 15c3-1 and a copy of a secured demand note so that you may see how confusing it is. I particularly call your attention to marked paragraphs on pages 56 through 59 of Appendix D to Rule 15c3-1.

I am also enclosing a copy of a letter dated May 18th received from the Securities and Exchange Commission Regional Office at Fort Worth, Texas and take issue with the following categories.

* * *

Net Capital

I disagree with the calculation of net capital in that there is no mention in the Rule of non-Aggregate Indebtedness and somehow it seems rather ridiculous to say non total liabilities and list as a liability somewhere else as was done by their calculation in arriving at net worth. The Net Capital problem apparently occurred due to the fact that I took the collateral for the Secured Demand Note (4,500 shares Broad Street Investing), and Frank & Velma's 400 shares Standard Oil of Calif., and 303 shares Howell Petroleum Corporation (which secured the loan) to the bank and used as collateral in order to secure a loan for the Corporation; which according to Appendix D page 58 I understood I could do. The SEC contends that this is a liability against Net Capital even though it is an exclusion from Aggregate Indebtedness: but according to my understanding Aggregate Indebtedness includes all liabilities, including money borrowed and this was an exclusion from Aggregate Indebtedness.

* * *

I have been in the Investment Business in KANSAS since 1962 with many clients who have become personal friends and have never had any complaints.

Please let me hear from you as to what the true interpretation of these rules are. The staff of the SEC will be hear [sic] at the law library in the Johnson County Courthouse June 22nd.

Your help will be greatly appreciated.

Sincerely

Velma L. Randall, President
Mid America Financial Services, Inc.

Mr. Matthew R. Schneider
Director of Legislative Affairs
Securities and Exchange Commission
500 North Capitol St.
Washington, DC 20549

Dear Mr. Schneider:

I have been in contact with Mrs. Velma Randall of Mid America Financial Services, Inc. of Olathe, Kansas on a matter involving the SEC.

There is disagreement between the regional office of the SEC in Fort Worth and Mrs. Randall on the interpretation of SEC rule 240.15c3-1. The Fort Worth office has written her notifying her of the violations and a meeting will occur on June 22 in Olathe to discuss the matter.

Mrs. Randall strongly disagrees with the interpretation of the Fort Worth office and would like some assistance from the Washington office. She will have to close her business if the interpretation holds.

Enclosed you will find documents which I hope will explain the situation. I would appreciate any assistance in having the matter reviewed by the SEC.

Most sincerely,

Larry Winn, Jr. Member of Congress
ENCLOSURE

October 7, 1982
The Honorable Larry Winn, Jr.
U.S. House of Representatives
Washington, D.C. 20515

Dear Congressman Winn:

This is in response to Mid America Financial Services, Inc.'s ("Mid America") letter addressed to you requesting your assistance in relieving it from unnecessary regulatory burdens imposed by the Commission's financial responsibility program, particularly Rules 15c3-1 ... adopted under the Securities Exchange Act of 1934 (the "Act").

We understand that the circumstances which prompted Mid America's request are as follows: Mid America is a registered SECO broker-dealer and a member of the Boston Stock Exchange. As a registered broker-dealer, Mid America is subject to the Commission's financial responsibility rules. Mid America was the subject of a routine Commission examination conducted on April 7, 1982 which disclosed the following deficiencies:

(1) The examiner's computation of Mid America's net capital as of February 28, 1982 reflected a deficiency in its required net capital of $12,775. A deficiency had existed since at least December 31, 1981. Thus, by effecting securities transactions while the firm's net capital was below the required minimum, Mid America had violated Section 15(c)(3) of the Act and Rule 15c3-1 promulgated thereunder.... and net capital computations for January and February 1982 could not be located.

In addition, Mid America's annual audited statement as of December 31, 1981 contained a material error in the computation of net capital. The computation reflected net capital of $70,689; the calculation however improperly treated a bank loan of $57,500 ...

* * *

The Commission's prior examination of Mid America's books and records conducted on February 2, 1981 revealed the exact deficiencies in Mid America's operations as those already enumerated.

It appears that Mid America's major complaint relates to the examiner's computation of the firm's net capital. The discrepancy between the firm and the examiner's computation of net capital revolves around the appropriate net capital treatment to be accorded a $57,500 bank loan. The bank loan in question is collateralized by securities owned by Mrs. Randall, Mid America's President, and mutual funds of a subordinated lender worth $50,000 which were deposited with Mid America as collateral for a subordinated Secured Demand Note ("SDN"). In short, Mid America used the SDN collateral along with the securities of its President to secure a bank loan to the corporation. Mid America apparently claims the bank loan should be excluded not only from the computation of its "aggregate indebtedness," but should also be excluded from the firm's liabilities in computing its "net worth." Since the question concerns an apparent misinterpretation of the net capital rule, a brief discussion of the rule seems appropriate.

The net capital rule prohibits a broker or dealer from incurring "aggregate indebtedness" in excess of 1500% of its "net capital" as those terms are defined in the rule. Hence, the rule requires two computations: one for "net capital" and the second for "aggregate indebtedness." The rule is designed among other things to ensure that brokers and dealers have sufficient liquid assets to pay off their customers claims on demand.

In general, the term "net capital" means the net worth (i.e., assets minus *liabilities*) of a broker or dealer, computed in accordance with generally accepted accounting principles. From this amount, a broker-dealer must subtract the value of assets not readily convertible into cash, such as buildings and furniture. In essence, this leaves a base of essentially highly liquid assets to pay off all liabilities. The broker or dealer then subtracts prescribed percentages of the market value of securities owned by the broker or dealer ("haircuts"), to account for unforeseen future market declines. Liabilities properly subordinated to all claims of the customers are added back to net worth in making the computation. After making other technical adjustments prescribed by the rule, the final figure is the broker-dealer's net capital.

The term "aggregate indebtedness" is defined as the total money liabilities of a broker or dealer in connection with any transaction whatsoever, except certain specifically excluded items. From the aggregate indebtedness figure, the amount of net capital a firm is required to have is determined. The more liabilities the broker or dealer has, the greater its required net capital.... However, the aggregate indebtedness figure is not directly used in determining a firm's net capital. In essence, it is used to determine aggregate customer exposure.

As to Mid America's specific situation, Mid America is correct in stating that it could rehypothecate the securities pledged as collateral to secure a SDN to secure any indebtedness of the broker or dealer. Furthermore, Mid America is correct in stating that the $57,500 bank loan is excluded from the firm's aggregate indebtedness, since among the obligations specifically excluded from aggregate indebtedness are indebtedness adequately collateralized by securities which collateralize a SDN pursuant to Appendix D to the net capital rule. Thus, while it is true that the rule allows Mid America to exclude from its aggregate indebtedness a liability adequately collateralized by securities which collateralize a SDN, that liability nonetheless must still be included as a liability on the firm's balance sheet, since it must repay the bank. As such, it results in a reduction of the firm's net worth. Hence, Mid America incorrectly assumed that the liability represented by the bank loan should be added to the firm's net worth. However, as noted above, the exclusion of the bank loan from the firm's aggregate indebtedness will have the effect of reducing the firm's required net capital.[22]

In conclusion, the bank loan in question is excluded from Mid America's aggregate indebtedness. However, the loan represents a liability that should be accounted for on the firm's balance sheet, which in turn results in a reduction of the firm's net worth. Thus, Mid America, since December 31, 1981, has been operating with a net capital deficit and pursuant to Section 15(c)(3) of the Act must cease doing business until it complies with the provisions of the net capital rule.

* * *

In its letter, Mid America states that the Commission's overall regulatory program makes it virtually impossible for smaller broker-dealers like itself to survive. The Commission since its inception has been aware of the need to evaluate the costs and competitive impact of its regulations on small broker-dealers. In recent years, in adopting new rules or amending others the Commission has attempted to tailor regulatory requirements to particular business practices to avoid unnecessary impositions on broker-dealers. In this regard, all of the Commission's major financial responsibility rules contain provisions which lessen the regulatory requirements on small broker-dealers without impairing investor protection. For instance, under the uniform net capital rule, Rule 15c3-1, certain broker-dealers who do not generally hold customer funds or securities need only have a minimum net capital of $5,000 rather than $25,000 which is required of those larger broker-dealers engaging in a general securities business....

* * *

If you have any specific questions or problems with these rules, please do not hesitate to write or to call me.

Yours truly,

Nelson S. Kibler
Assistant Director

———

22. The firm apparently confused the liabilities to the secured demand lender which is added back to net worth in computing net capital with the liability to the bank which like all other liabilities must be subtracted from assets in computing net worth, but is not added back to net worth in computing net capital.

b. The Alternative Standard Ratio

A broker-dealer may elect to use the Alternative Standard Ratio to determine its required minimum net capital instead of the Aggregate Indebtedness Standard ratio. Under the Alternative Standard ratio, a broker-dealer must not allow its net capital to be less than the greater of $250,000 or two percent of aggregate debit items; the computation of aggregate debit items is governed by the Reserve Formula in Exhibit A to Rule 15c3-3,[23] with certain amendments as described in Figure 7.11.

Figure 7.11. Amendments to Reserve Formula Required by Alternative Standard Ratio

Rule 15c3-1	Amendment
(a)(1)(ii)(A)	In lieu of the one percent reduction of debit balances in customers' cash and margin accounts (excluding unsecured accounts and accounts doubtful of collection) required by Note E of Exhibit A to Rule 15c3-3, a three percent reduction in such aggregate debit items is required;
(a)(1)(ii)(B)	The market value of short security count differences and short securities and credits in all broker-dealer suspense accounts must be included if more than seven business days old. Exhibit A to Rule 15c3-3 generally requires inclusion if such items are more than 30 days old.
(a)(1)(ii)(C)	Exclude credit balances in accounts for amounts payable for U.S. government securities, commercial paper, bankers' acceptances and certificates of deposit that have not yet been received and any related debit items from the Exhibit A to Rule 15c3-3 requirement for three business days; and
(a)(1)(ii)(D)	Adjust the net capital computation by deducting from net worth one percent of the contract value of all failed to deliver contracts or securities borrowed that were allocated to failed to receive contracts of the same issue and that were excluded from Items 11 or 12 of Exhibit A to Rule 15c3-3.

Interestingly, the amendments to the Reserve Formula stated in paragraph (a)(1)(ii)(A) of the UNCR require the broker-dealer to take a three percent reduction in the Reserve Formula debit items before calculating the two percent minimum net capital requirement. However, the SEC states that the two percent minimum net capital requirement is based on the Reserve Formula debit items before the three percent reduction required by paragraph (a)(1)(ii)(A) of the UNCR. The broker-dealer must compute the Reserve Formula on a weekly basis. In addition, if a broker-dealer chooses to use the Alternative Standard ratio to determine its required minimum net capital, it must notify its examining authority and must continue to use the Alternative Standard ratio unless the SEC approves a change. In light of the fact that the least amount of required minimum net capital using the Alternative Standard ratio is $250,000, it is generally used by large clearing broker-dealers.

---

23. Rule 15c3-3, the Customer Protection Rule, is discussed in Section IV.C. of this chapter.

4. *Minimum Dollar Amounts of Net Capital*

As previously noted, the UNCR specifies minimum dollar amounts of net capital that a broker-dealer must maintain. These minimum dollar amounts effectively act as the floor in the range of minimum required net capital if the result of the ratio test (aggregate indebtedness and alternative standard ratios) is less than the specified minimum dollar amounts in the UNCR. The minimum dollar amounts of net capital are based on the nature of the broker-dealer's business and whether it handles customer funds or securities. Table 7.1 (see next page) provides an overview of minimum dollar amounts of net capital required under the UNCR.

Hypothetical One

Tatum Chen, Success First's COO, has been approached by a friend, Joanie Corzine, who has decided to set up her own broker-dealer. Corzine has decided that she will introduce customers on a fully disclosed basis. She will also receive customer funds and securities but will remit them immediately to her clearing broker-dealer. Corzine's firm will also participate in firm commitment underwritings but will not purchase shares related to firm commitment underwritings in which the firm participates. She has come to Chen for advice about determining the minimum dollar amount of net capital required based on her firm's activities. What should Chen tell her?

5. *Subordinated Agreements*

A subordination agreement documents an investment in a broker-dealer for the purpose of increasing its net capital. Subordination agreements are advantageous to investors because of the higher interest rates available under such agreements. However, the higher interest rates reflect the higher risk in the event of broker-dealer insolvency. The effect of the subordination agreement is to prohibit repayment to the investor until all other creditors of the broker-dealer are paid. This means that any claims by the investor must be subordinate to claims of other parties against the broker-dealer, including its customers and employees. The terms of subordination agreements are regulated strictly because they allow the broker-dealer to increase its net capital, thereby increasing the amount of business it can generate. Appendix D to the UNCR prescribes the terms of acceptable subordination agreements, i.e., those that can be used to increase a broker-dealer's net capital. FINRA also regulates subordination agreements under Rule 4110(e) by imposing requirements in addition to those prescribed in Appendix D[24] and provides standard forms for subordinated loan agreements and secured demand notes and attestations that comply with Appendix D to the UNCR. FINRA must approve all subordination agreements before they become effective. Rules governing subordination agreements for contributions to increase net capital are designed to ensure that the cash and securities contributed remain

---

24. See below under Section IV.B. Financial Responsibility under FINRA Rules.

Table 7.1. Minimum Dollar Amounts of Net Capital Required Under the UNCR

Minimum Dollar Level	Broker-Dealer Business Type
$250,000	Brokers-dealers that carry customer or broker-dealer accounts and receive or hold funds or securities for such persons.
$100,000	Broker-dealers' transactions as dealer (as principal for its own account) are limited to the purchase, sale, and redemption of redeemable securities of registered investment companies or of interests or participations in an insurance company separate account, whether or not registered as an investment company.
$100,000	Broker-dealers acting as dealers (i.e., effecting more than 10 transactions in any one calendar year for their own account).
$50,000	Broker-dealers that introduce transactions and accounts of customers or other broker-dealers to another registered broker-dealer that carries such accounts on a fully disclosed basis; the introducing broker-dealer may receive but cannot hold the securities of customers or other broker-dealers. May also participate in firm commitment underwritings but cannot purchase shares related to such an underwriting.
$25,000	Broker-dealers engaged in the sale of redeemable shares of registered investment companies and certain other share accounts. Must promptly transmit all funds and promptly deliver all securities received and may not otherwise hold funds or securities for, or owe money or securities to, customers.
$5,000	Broker-dealer does not hold funds or securities for, or owe funds or securities to, customers and does not carry accounts of, or for, customers. Cannot act as dealer unless it engages in riskless principal transactions.
$2,500 for each security in which a market is made ($1,000 if the market value of the stock is $5 or less) not to exceed $1,000,000 and not less than either the aggregated indebtedness standard ratio or the alternative standard ratio.	Market Makers
$20,000,000	OTC derivatives dealer
$150,000,000	Primary dealer
$150,000	Municipal securities brokers' brokers: Broker-Dealer acting exclusively as an undisclosed agent in the purchase or sale of municipal securities for a registered broker-dealer or a registered municipal securities dealer; who has no customers; and does not maintain any municipal securities in its proprietary or other accounts.

with the broker-dealer for some reasonable length of time and cannot be withdrawn when the broker-dealer experiences financial or operational difficulties.

There are two types of subordination agreements: a Subordinated Loan Agreement ("SLA") and a Secured Demand Note ("SDN"). An SLA is created when an investor lends cash to a broker-dealer; the SLA discloses the terms of the loan (interest rate, repayment, parties, etc.). The investor cannot restrict the broker-dealer's use of the cash. An SDN is a promissory note[25] in which the investor agrees to loan cash to a broker-dealer on demand (i.e., without prior notice) during the term of the note. The investor must provide collateral to the broker-dealer generally in the form of securities. The investor retains beneficial ownership of the collateral, but the securities must be in the possession of the broker-dealer and registered in the broker-dealer's name. The investor cannot sell or otherwise use the collateral unless securities of equal or greater value are substituted and deposited with the broker-dealer. All contributions of securities must be made pursuant to an SDN arrangement. The investor must give sufficient securities so that when the securities are discounted, the net value of the securities will be equal to or greater than the amount of the SDN. The rate of the required discount is specified in Exhibit D to the UNCR and varies (as high as 30%) based on the type of securities used as collateral. If the pledged securities decline in value so that their discounted value is less than the face amount of the SDN, the investor is required to deposit additional securities with the broker-dealer; failure to do so allows the broker-dealer to sell some or all of the securities pledged by the investor. The broker-dealer may also sell the pledged securities if it makes a demand under the SDN and the investor fails to provide the broker-dealer with the cash. In addition, the broker-dealer can use the pledged securities as collateral, i.e., it may borrow money from another party using the securities the investor has pledged as collateral under an SDN as collateral for the new loan as the broker-dealer did in *Mid America*. All securities pledged as collateral under an SDN, including excess collateral, are subordinated to the claims of the broker-dealer's customers and creditors. This means that if the broker-dealer becomes insolvent, the investor's ability to retrieve her collateral may be at risk.

Notes and Questions

1. *The Early Warning Rule.* Rule 17a-11 provides an "early warning" to the SEC and FINRA when a broker-dealer's net capital declines below specified levels or in other instances that indicate the existence of financial or operational difficulties. The rule imposes a duty on broker-dealers to report net capital and other operational problems and to file reports regarding those problems within certain periods. With respect to net capital there are three early warning levels.[26] First, a

---

25. This means that it is shown as an asset on the broker-dealer's balance sheet.

26. Rule 17a-11(c)(4) prescribes an early warning net capital level for OTC derivatives that is not discussed because the legal framework regarding derivatives is beyond the scope of this textbook.

broker-dealer that has elected to compute its required minimum net capital under the Aggregate Indebtedness Standard ratio must give notice if its aggregated indebtedness exceeds 1200 percent of its net capital. Second, a broker-dealer that computes its required minimum net capital under the Alternative Standard ratio is required to give notice if its net capital falls below five percent of its aggregate debit items computed in accordance with the Reserve Formula under Rule 15c3-3. Third, a broker-dealer that computes its net capital under either ratio is required to give notice if its total net capital declines below 120 percent of its minimum requirement. A broker-dealer must also give notice if it is insolvent, if it fails to make and keep current books and records as required under Rule 17a-3, and if there is any material weakness discovered by the broker-dealer or its accountant in its internal controls with respect to compliance. All notices must be provided to the SEC and the broker-dealer's designated examining authority (generally FINRA) and must be transmitted by telegraphic notice or facsimile transmission promptly or within 24 to 48 hours. How does the early warning rule support the SEC's and FINRA's regulatory objectives?

2. Paragraph (c)(2)(i)(F) of the UNCR requires a broker-dealer, in calculating net capital, to include any liabilities that are assumed by a third party if the broker-dealer cannot demonstrate that the third party has the resources — independent of the broker-dealer's income and assets — to pay the liabilities. A broker-dealer can demonstrate the adequacy of the third party's financial resources by maintaining records such as the third party's most recent audited financial statements, tax returns or regulatory filings containing financial reports. Does obtaining financial information from such third parties facilitate regulation of broker-dealer financial responsibility?

3. Paragraph (c)(2)(i)(G) of the UNCR requires a broker-dealer to treat as a liability any contribution of capital to the broker or dealer that is (1) under an agreement that provides the investor with the option to withdraw it, or (2) that is intended to be withdrawn within a period of one year of contribution. Does this conflict with the UNCR's provisions regarding subordinated loan agreements? Is it necessary?

4. *Temporary Restrictions on Capital Withdrawals.* Under paragraph (e)(3) of the UNCR, the SEC may restrict, for up to 20 business days, any withdrawal by a broker-dealer of equity capital or unsecured loan or advance to a stockholder, partner, sole proprietor, member, employee, or affiliate as the SEC deems necessary or appropriate in the public interest or consistent with the protection of investors when the withdrawal may be detrimental to the financial integrity of the broker-dealer, or may unduly jeopardize the broker-dealer's ability to repay its customer claims or other liabilities that may cause a significant impact on the markets or expose customers or creditors to loss.

5. *Exemptions to the Uniform Net Capital Rule.* There are very few exemptions from the requirements of the UNCR for broker-dealers. Of course, the SEC has the authority to exempt broker-dealers from the requirements of the UNCR. However, it will only do so if the broker-dealer establishes to the satisfaction of the SEC

that the special nature of its business, its financial position, and the safeguards established for the protection of its customers' funds and securities makes compliance with the UNCR unnecessary. However, certain specialists and floor brokers are exempt. A specialist is exempt if it only conducts business as an options market maker on a national securities exchange; is a member in good standing and subject to the capital requirements of a national securities exchange; only transacts business with other broker-dealers registered under the Exchange Act or who are members of a national securities exchange; and is not a clearing member of The Options Clearing Corporation and whose securities transactions are effected through and carried in an account cleared by another broker-dealer registered with the SEC. Certain floor brokers may elect to be exempt from the requirements of the UNCR. However, they must be members in good standing of a national securities exchange and cannot engage in activities that would otherwise require compliance with the UNCR. If floor brokers elect to be exempt from the requirements of the UNCR, they must comply with another financial responsibility standard specified in the UNCR. This financial responsibility standard requires that the value of the floor broker's exchange membership must not be less than $15,000[27] and the rules of the floor broker's exchange must require that the proceeds from the sale of the floor broker's exchange membership must be subject to the prior claims of the exchange, the exchange's clearing corporation, and those arising directly from the closing out of contracts entered into on the floor of the exchange.

B. Financial Responsibility under FINRA Rules

FINRA RESPONSIBILITY RULES
FINRA Rule 4110. Capital Compliance
FINRA Rule 4120. Regulatory Notification and Business Curtailment
FINRA Rule 4140. Audit
FINRA Rule 4160. Verification of Assets
FINRA Rule 4521. Notifications, Questionnaires and Reports

FINRA's financial responsibility rules are designed to support the SEC's UNCR and other financial responsibility requirements. Essentially, FINRA's financial responsibility rules establish criteria promoting the permanence of a broker-dealer's capital, require the review and approval of certain material financial transactions, establish criteria intended to identify a broker-dealer approaching financial difficulty, and monitor a broker-dealer's financial and operational condition.

---

27. Or an amount equal to the excess of $15,000 over the value of the exchange membership is held by an independent agent in escrow.

1. *FINRA Rule 4110. Capital Compliance*

FINRA Rule 4110(a) authorizes FINRA to prescribe greater minimum net capital requirements than those applicable under the UNCR for its carrying and clearing member broker-dealers. Specifically, FINRA is authorized to restore or increase minimum net capital requirements when deemed necessary for the protection of investors or in the public interest, including more stringent treatment of items used in computing minimum net capital requirements. For example, FINRA may raise applicable haircuts or treat certain assets as non-allowable in computing net capital. FINRA cannot, however, reduce minimum net capital requirements below those specified in the UNCR. FINRA anticipates that Rule 4110(a) will be used in limited circumstances because it is designed to address threats to broker-dealer capital such as unanticipated systemic market events and undue concentration in illiquid products.

Paragraph (b) of Rule 4110 authorizes FINRA to direct any member broker-dealer to suspend all or a portion of its business operations during any period in which it is not in compliance with the UNCR. Paragraph (b)(1) is self-operative; this means that a broker-dealer, without any direction from FINRA, is automatically required to suspend all business operations if it fails to meet its minimum net capital requirement. In addition, FINRA may issue a notice of non-compliance under paragraph (b)(2) of Rule 4110.

Paragraph (c) of Rule 4110 specifies conditions under which FINRA may prohibit any member broker-dealer from withdrawing equity capital. Paragraph (c)(1) prohibits a broker-dealer from withdrawing contributed equity capital for one year, unless otherwise permitted by FINRA; this does not apply to withdrawal of profits except as provided in paragraph (c)(2) of Rule 4110. Paragraph (c)(2) applies only to carrying or clearing broker-dealers,[28] and prohibits withdrawal of capital to pay dividends or similar distributions and unsecured advancements or loans to owners or employees that would exceed 10 percent of the broker-dealer's excess net capital in any 35 rolling calendar-day period on a net basis.[29]

Paragraph (d) of FINRA Rule 4110 supports permanence of net capital by prohibiting a broker-dealer from entering into certain types of arrangements that would increase its tentative net capital[30] by more than 10 percent without the prior authorization of FINRA. Arrangements expressly enumerated in paragraph (d) are sale-and-leaseback arrangements with respect to any of the broker-dealer's assets and sale, factoring, or financing arrangements with respect to unsecured accounts receivable,

---

28. However, FINRA Rule 4110.02 states that all requirements that apply to clearing and carrying broker-dealers also apply to broker-dealers operating under the exemptive provisions of Rule 15c3-3(k)(2)(i) that clear customer transactions or hold customer funds in a bank account.

29. The calculation of 10 percent of excess net capital is based on the broker-dealer's net capital position as reported in its most recently filed FOCUS Report and the broker-dealer must assure itself that the excess net capital reported on its most recent FOCUS Report has not materially changed since the time it was filed. *Financial Responsibility: SEC Approves Consolidated FINRA Rules Governing Financial Responsibility*, FINRA 09-71, 7, n.9 (Feb. 8, 2010).

30. Paragraph (c)(2) of the UCNR defines the term *tentative net capital* as the net capital of a broker-dealer before deducting the securities haircuts required under (c)(2)(vi).

which would increase the broker-dealer's tentative net capital by 10 percent or more. Paragraph (d)(1)(A) only applies to carrying and clearing members. Paragraph (d)(1)(B)(1) prohibits the sale or factoring of customer debit balances by carrying broker-dealers, irrespective of amount, without FINRA's prior written authorization. Paragraph (d)(2) applies only to clearing and carrying broker-dealers and prohibits a broker-dealer from entering into any loan agreement, the proceeds of which exceed 10 percent of its tentative net capital, that is intended to reduce the deduction in computing net capital for fixed assets and other assets that cannot be readily converted into cash. Paragraph (d)(3) restricts the amount of all sale-and-leasebacks, factoring, financing, loans, and similar arrangements that the broker-dealer may consummate without obtaining FINRA's prior written authorization if the aggregate amount of such arrangements exceeds 20 percent of the broker-dealer's tentative net capital. Paragraph (d)(4) applies to all broker-dealers because it implements a requirement of paragraph (c)(11)(ii) of the UNCR determining whether securities have a ready market as, among other things, securities accepted as collateral for a bank loan to the broker-dealer. The securities must be submitted and acceptable to FINRA before the securities may be deemed to have a ready market. Factors used by FINRA to determine whether such securities have a ready market include whether the bank would have sole recourse under the agreement and whether the term of the loan is at least one year. According to FINRA, a determination of whether the securities have a ready market generally can be made within approximately one week.[31]

Paragraph (e) of FINRA Rule 4110 specifies requirements for subordinated loan agreements and loans made to general partners of broker-dealers that are partnerships. Specifically, paragraph (e)(1) implements Appendix D of the UNCR[32] by requiring compliance with the provisions of Appendix D in addition to standards that FINRA may require to ensure the continued financial stability and operational capability of a broker-dealer. In addition, the broker-dealer must confirm that any applicable provisions of the Securities Act of 1933 and/or state Blue Sky laws have been satisfied; FINRA may require the broker-dealer to submit evidence of such compliance prior to approval of the subordinated loan agreement. Paragraph (e)(2) addresses contribution of capital in the form of subordinated loans by general partners of broker-dealers. If the broker-dealer's general partner enters into any secured or unsecured borrowing to contribute capital to the broker-dealer, the loan agreement must be approved by FINRA in order for the proceeds to be used in computing the broker-dealer's net capital. The broker-dealer must submit a signed copy of the subordinated loan agreement, which must have a term of at least 12 months and include a provision that estops the lender from having recourse to the broker-dealer's assets. Moreover, FINRA may require additional documents to determine whether to approve the sub-

---

31. *Financial Responsibility: SEC Approves Consolidated FINRA Rules Governing Financial Responsibility*, FINRA 09-71, 3 (Feb. 8 2010).

32. Appendix D to the UNCR, 17 C.F.R. 240.15c3-1d, requires, among other things, that all subordination agreements be found acceptable by the broker-dealer's examining authority (FINRA) before they become effective.

ordinated loan agreement depending on the type of lender, e.g., an individual, bank, estate, trust, corporation, partnership, etc.

2. FINRA Rule 4120. Regulatory Notification and Business Curtailment

FINRA Rule 4120 addresses conditions that require regulatory notifications and business curtailment in the context of identifying a broker-dealer approaching financial difficulty. Paragraph (a) requires carrying and clearing broker-dealers to notify FINRA within 24 hours if certain financial triggers occur, including: (1) Net capital is less than 150 percent of the broker-dealer's minimum dollar net capital requirement; (2) if the broker-dealer uses the Aggregate Indebtedness Standard, its aggregate indebtedness is more than 1,000 percent of its net capital; and (3) if the broker-dealer uses the Alternative Standard, its net capital is less than five percent of aggregate debit items computed in accordance with the Reserve Formula in Exhibit A of Rule 15c3-3.

Paragraph (b) of Rule 4120 addresses circumstances under which FINRA deems it necessary to prohibit a broker-dealer from expanding its business. Paragraph (b)(1) is self-operative, applies only to carrying and clearing broker-dealers, and requires the broker-dealer to refrain from expanding its business during any period in which it reaches the financial triggers enumerated in Rule 4120(a)(1). Paragraph (b)(2) of FINRA Rule 4120 authorizes FINRA to restrict any broker-dealer's ability to expand its business for any financial or operational reason by issuing a notice under FINRA Rule 9557; notices under FINRA Rule 9557 give the broker-dealer the right to request an expedited hearing.

Paragraph (c) of Rule 4120 addresses circumstances under which FINRA would require a broker-dealer to reduce its business. Paragraph (c)(1) is self-operative and applies only to clearing and carrying broker-dealers and requires a reduction in business that enables available capital to exceed the standards enumerated in Rule 4120(a) when certain conditions continue to exist for more than 15 consecutive business days, including: (1) Net capital is less than 125 percent of a broker-dealer's minimum dollar net capital requirement or greater; (2) if subject to the Aggregate Indebtedness Standard, the broker-dealer's aggregate indebtedness is more than 1,200 percent of its net capital; and (3) if subject to the Alternative Standard, the broker-dealer's net capital is less than four percent. FINRA or the broker-dealer must have known of these conditions for at least five consecutive business days. In addition, paragraph (c)(2) authorizes FINRA to require a broker-dealer to reduce its business for any financial or operational reason by issuing a notice, which affords the right of an expedited hearing to the broker-dealer.[33] The term *business reduction* is defined in Paragraph (c)(3) and includes activities such as paying all or a portion of free credit balances to customers, delivering all or a portion of a customer's fully paid securities in the broker-dealer's possession, introduction of all or a portion of the broker-dealer's business to another

---

33. FINRA Rule 4120.01 provides examples of conditions under which FINRA might exercise its discretion of 4120(b)(2) and (c)(2).

broker-dealer on a fully disclosed basis, reducing the size or modifying the composition of a broker-dealer's inventory and reducing or ceasing market making, closing one or more existing branch offices, restricting payment of salaries or other sums to the broker-dealer's owners and other associated persons, liquidating or closing customer and/or proprietary transactions, and accepting only unsolicited customer orders.

3. FINRA Rule 4140. Audit

FINRA Rule 4140 authorizes FINRA to require an audit by an independent accountant of a broker-dealer's accounts or a review of its procedures under certain circumstances. Such circumstances include concerns regarding the accuracy or integrity of the broker-dealer's financial statements, books and records, or prior audited financial statements. If the broker-dealer fails to provide the required report, FINRA is authorized to impose a late fee of $100 for each day that the report is not timely filed up to a maximum of 10 business days.

4. FINRA Rule 4160. Verification of Assets

FINRA Rule 4160 was designed to ensure that FINRA could independently verify assets maintained by a broker-dealer at a non-member financial institution. A broker-dealer, when notified by FINRA, may not continue to have custody or retain record ownership of assets at a non-member financial institution that fails promptly to provide written verification of such assets at FINRA's request. While FINRA may request such independent verification, it generally cannot compel a financial institution that is not a member to comply with its request. If the non-member financial institution fails to comply with FINRA's request, the broker-dealer must transfer such assets within a reasonable period. FINRA Rule 4160 does not apply to a broker-dealer's proprietary assets that are treated as non-allowable assets under the UNCR.

5. FINRA Rule 4521. Notifications, Questionnaires, and Reports

FINRA Rule 4521 authorizes FINRA to request certain financial and operational information from broker-dealers. Under paragraph (a), FINRA has blanket authority to require carrying or clearing broker-dealers, including their correspondents, to submit financial and operational information necessary for FINRA to conduct its surveillance and examination responsibilities. Paragraph (c) requires carrying and clearing broker-dealers to notify FINRA no more than 48 hours after their tentative net capital has declined 20 percent or more from the amount reported in their most recent FOCUS Report.[34] Paragraph (d) addresses customer margin accounts and requires a broker-dealer carrying such accounts to submit a report containing, on a settlement date basis: (1) the total of all debit balances in securities margin accounts; and (2) the total of all free credit balances contained in customer cash or margin accounts. A late fee is imposed in the amount of $100 per day if the information in Rule 4521 is not timely filed, up to a maximum of 10 business days. In addition, any report

---

34. FOCUS Reports are discussed in Chapter 9.

filed that contains material inaccuracies is deemed not to have been filed until a corrected copy has been resubmitted.

Notes and Questions

1. How does FINRA Rule 4160 provide incentives for the non-member and the broker-dealer to comply with FINRA's regulatory function of supporting financial responsibility through verification of assets?

2. Why would FINRA allow required asset transfers to be effected within a reasonable period?

3. Under FINRA Rule 4360, broker-dealers required to join SIPC to have fidelity bond coverage. Broker-dealers are allowed to have a deductible of up to 25 percent of the coverage purchased. However, any deductible elected by that broker-dealer that is greater than 10 percent of the coverage purchased must be deducted from the broker-dealer's net worth in the calculation of net capital under the UNCR. However, Rule 15c3-1 does not specifically reference the SRO deductible requirements as a charge to net worth. This inconsistency is addressed in the UNCR by requiring the broker-dealer to deduct from its net worth the amount specified by the broker-dealer's designated examining authority relating to its fidelity bond coverage.

C. The Customer Protection Rule

Rule 15c3-3 was adopted by the SEC in 1972 to protect customer funds and securities held by broker-dealers. It was based on Congress' directive in Section 15(c)(3) of the Exchange Act to strengthen financial responsibility requirements for broker-dealers. In effect, it forbids broker-dealers from using customer assets to finance any part of their businesses unrelated to servicing customers. Like the UNCR, Rule 15c3-3 grew out of the Paperwork Crisis of 1968–1970, but focused specifically on the protection of customer funds and securities held by broker-dealers. In particular, Congress was concerned about broker-dealers using customer funds and securities to finance their proprietary businesses, such as underwriting and proprietary trading (e.g., market making). During the Paperwork Crisis, many broker-dealers were unable to locate and/or return customer free credit balances, i.e., securities and cash that customers were entitled to upon demand.[35]

Rule 15c3-3 applies only to carrying broker-dealers, i.e., broker-dealers that maintain custody of customers' funds and securities. The term *carrying broker-dealer* ex-

---

35. Free credit balances are defined in 17 C.F.R. 240.15c3-3(a)(8) — Funds payable by a broker-dealer to its customers on demand. They may result from cash deposited by the customer to purchase securities, proceeds from the sale of securities or other assets held in the customer's account, or earnings from dividends and interest on securities and other assets held in the customer's account. Broker-dealers may, among other things, pay interest to customers on their free credit balances or offer to routinely transfer (sweep) them to a money market fund or bank account.

cludes broker-dealers who promptly transmit all customers' funds and securities received in connection with securities transactions and do not otherwise hold funds or securities for, or owe money or securities to, their customers. Broker-dealers who do not carry margin accounts for customers and who effectuate all transactions between themselves and their customers through bank accounts designated as "Special Account for the Exclusive Benefit of Customers" ("Customer Reserve Account") are also excluded. Finally, broker-dealers whose activities are limited to the purchase, sale, and redemption of redeemable securities in registered investment companies and insurance company-affiliated broker-dealers engaging in securities transactions on behalf the insurance company as part of the insurance company's insurance business are also exempt from the requirements of Rule 15c3-3.

The meaning of the term *customer* is essential to the implementation of Rule 15c3-3 and thus is defined in the rule. A customer is any person from whom or on whose behalf a broker-dealer has received or acquired or holds funds or securities for the account of that person. Other broker-dealers, municipal securities, and broker-dealers are not customers under Rule 15c3-3. The term *customer* also excludes general partners, directors, and principal officers of the broker-dealer and any other person who has a claim for property or funds against the broker-dealer, which is part of the capital of the broker-dealer or is subordinated to the claims of creditors of the broker-dealer.[36]

1. Meeting the Requirements of Rule 15c3-3

Rule 15c3-3 requires a broker-dealer who maintains custody of customer funds and securities to take two primary steps to safeguard such assets. The first step requires the broker-dealer to maintain physical possession or control over customers' fully paid and excess margin securities. The second step requires the broker-dealer to maintain a reserve of cash or qualified securities in an account at a bank that is at least equal in value to the net cash owed to customers, including cash obtained from the use of customer securities.

a. Step One: Physical Possession or Control

The carrying broker-dealer must maintain physical possession or control over customers' fully paid and excess margin securities. The terms *fully paid securities* and *excess margin securities* are defined in Rule 15c3-3(a)(3) and (a)(5), respectively. The term *fully paid securities* includes all securities carried for the account of a customer in a special cash account as defined in Regulation T (12 CFR § 220.1 et seq.)[37]

---

36. The term *customer* also excludes certain persons with claims for security futures products held in a futures account or a counterparty who has delivered collateral to an OTC derivatives dealer. Rule 15c3-3(a)(1)(i)-(iv). However, the regulatory framework for OTC derivatives is beyond the scope of this textbook.

37. Authority and purpose. Regulation T (this part) is issued by the Board of Governors of the Federal Reserve System (the Board) pursuant to the Securities Exchange Act of 1934 (the Act) (15 U.S.C.78a et seq.). Its principal purpose is to regulate extensions of credit by brokers and dealers; it

as well as securities carried for the customer in a margin account, or any special account under Regulation T, that have no loan value for margin purposes (12 CFR § 220.8) and all margin equity securities that are fully paid; however, the term fully paid securities does not apply to any securities purchased in transactions for which the customer has not made full payment. The term *excess margin securities* includes securities carried for the account of a customer in a margin account[38] having a market value in excess of 140 percent of the total debit balances in the customer's margin account.

The broker-dealer must promptly obtain and maintain physical possession or control over customers' fully paid and excess margin securities. Physical possession or control requires the broker-dealer to hold such customer securities in specified locations, free of liens or any other interest that could be exercised by a third party to secure an obligation of the broker-dealer. Customer securities held by the carrying broker-dealer are not assets of the carrying broker-dealer. Rather, the carrying broker-dealer holds customer securities in a custodial capacity and the possession and control requirement is designed to ensure that the carrying broker-dealer treats them in a manner that allows for their prompt return upon customer demand. Because customer securities today are rarely held in certificate form or at the offices of the broker-dealer with a direct relationship with the customer, subsection (c) of Rule 15c3-3 defines control, i.e., it designates the manner and types of institutions in which customers' securities are deemed to be in the control of the carrying broker-dealer. Permissible locations include a bank, as defined in section 3(a)(6) of the Exchange Act and a clearing agency. The bank must be supervised by a U.S. federal or state bank regulator.[39]

b. Step Two: Reserve Accounts

i. Special Reserve Account for the Exclusive Benefit of Customers

The carrying broker-dealer must maintain a reserve of cash or qualified securities[40] in an account at a bank that is at least equal in value to the net cash owed to customers, including cash obtained from the use of customer securities. This account must be titled "Special Reserve Bank Account for the Exclusive Benefit of Customers" ("Customer Reserve Bank Account"). According to the SEC, the purpose of giving the account this title is to alert the bank and creditors of the carrying broker-dealer that

---

also covers related transactions within the Board's authority under the Act. It imposes, among other obligations, initial margin requirements and payment rules on certain securities transactions.

38. Rule 15c3-3(a)(4) defines *margin securities* as those securities carried for the account of a customer in a margin account and refers to section 4 of Regulation T, 12 CFR § 220.4, to define a customer margin account.

39. The SEC may designate a foreign depository, foreign clearing agency or foreign custodian bank as a satisfactory control location for securities upon application by the broker-dealer or on its own motion. *See* 17 C.F.R. § 240.15c3-3(c)(4) (2014).

40. Qualified securities are securities issued by the U.S. government or securities of which the principal and interest are guaranteed by the U.S. government. *See* 17 C.F. R. § 240.15c3-3(a)(6) (2014).

this account is to be used to meet the carrying broker-dealer's obligations to customers, not the claims of general creditors, in the event the carrying broker-dealer must be liquidated in a formal proceeding. The amount of net cash owed to customers is computed according to the Reserve Formula in Exhibit A to Rule 15c3-3. This is the same formula, with adjustments, used to calculate minimum net capital requirements using the Alternative Standard ratio under the UNCR. Under the Reserve Formula, the carrying broker-dealer adds up customer credit items (e.g., cash in customer securities accounts) and then subtracts from that amount customer debit items (e.g., margin loans). If credit items exceed debit items, the net amount must be on deposit in the customer reserve account in the form of cash and/or qualified securities.

The Reserve Formula is designed to isolate customer cash by the carrying broker-dealer so that an amount equal to the net liabilities to customers is held as a reserve in the form of cash or qualified securities. Customer cash is a balance sheet item of the carrying broker-dealer. The establishment of the Customer Reserve Account effectively prevents the carrying broker-dealer from using customer funds for proprietary business activities, such as investing in securities. According to the SEC, the goal is to put the carrying broker-dealer in a position to be able to readily meet its cash obligations to customers by requiring the carrying broker-dealer to make deposits of cash and/or qualified securities into the Customer Reserve Account in the amount owned to customers. For example:

If a carrying broker-dealer holds $100 for customer A, the carrying broker-dealer can use that $100 to finance a security purchase of customer B. The $100 the broker-dealer owes customer A is a credit in the formula and the $100 customer B owes the carrying broker-dealer is a debit in the formula. Under the Reserve Formula, there would be no requirement to maintain cash and/or qualified securities in the Customer Reserve Account. However, if the carrying broker-dealer did not use the $100 held in customer A's account for this purpose, there would be no offsetting debit and, the carrying broker-dealer would need to have on deposit in the Customer Reserve Account cash and/or qualified securities in an amount at least equal to $100.

The Reserve Formula only permits the carrying broker-dealer to offset customer credit items with customer debit items. This ensures that the carrying broker-dealer only uses customer cash to facilitate customer transactions (e.g., financing customer margin loans and borrowing securities to make deliveries of securities that customers have sold short), not its proprietary business activities.

ii. Special Reserve Account for Brokers and Dealers

Carrying broker-dealers that carry accounts that hold proprietary securities and cash of other broker-dealers ("PAB accounts")[41] also must maintain a reserve of cash or qualified securities in an account at a bank that is equal to or greater than the

---

41. Broker-dealers are not within the definition of customer for purposes of Rule 15c3-3. Also, Rule 15c3-3(a)(16) defines the term PAB account as a proprietary securities account of a broker or dealer ... other than a delivery-versus-payment account (delivery of securities will only occur if a payment occurs) or a receipt-versus-payment account (buyer's payment for securities is due at the

amount that credits exceed debits as calculated using the Reserve Formula.[42] This account must be titled "Special Reserve Bank Account for Brokers and Dealers" ("PAB Reserve Bank Account").

When initially enacted, Rule 15c3-3 did not require maintenance of cash reserves for PAB accounts. However, the SEC subsequently amended Rule 15c3-3 to require a separate cash reserve account at a bank for PAB accounts because of the broader definition of customer under the SIPA, which includes PAB account holders as customers. As SIPA customers, broker-dealers have the right to a pro-rata share of the customer property,[43] but are not entitled to receive an advance from the SIPC fund. The treatment of PAB account holders as SIPA customers but not as customers under Rule 15c3-3 increased the risk that, in the event a carrying broker-dealer was liquidated under SIPA, the claims of SIPA customers (i.e., customers and PAB account holders) would exceed the amount of customer property available, and thereby expose the SIPC fund and potentially SIPA customers to losses. The SEC also noted that if customer property was insufficient to satisfy all SIPA claims and losses were incurred, the PAB account holders could be placed in financial distress resulting in adverse impacts to the securities markets beyond those resulting from the failure of a particular carrying broker-dealer. The entitlement of PAB account holders to a pro rata share of the fund of customer property places all SIPA customers at risk if the carrying broker-dealer does not establish a PAB reserve account for excess credits owed to PAB account holders. In addition, it had been a long-standing practice for carrying broker-dealers to use securities in PAB accounts in their business activities. As amended, Rule 15c3-3 attempts to close the gap between SIPA and prior Rule 15c3-3 by requiring carrying broker-dealers to: (1) perform a separate reserve computation using the Reserve Formula; (2) establish and fund a separate reserve account for the benefit of PAB account holders; and (3) obtain and maintain physical possession or control of non-margin securities carried for PAB accounts unless the carrying broker-dealer has provided written notice to the PAB account holder that it will use those securities in the ordinary course of its securities business, and has provided an opportunity for the PAB account holder to object to such use.[44] In essence, the goal of amended Rule 15c3-3 is to create a process that protects Rule 15c3-3 customers and PAB account holders from risk of loss of a failed carrying broker-dealer.

---

time securities are delivered); however, the term does not include an account that has been subordinated to the claims of creditors of the carrying broker or dealer.

42. However, if a U.S. broker-dealer decides to subordinate its claims to assets in its PAB account to the claims of other creditors of the carrying broker-dealer, it will not be able to include those assets as allowable for its own net capital computation. *See* 17 C.F.R. § 240.15c3-1(c)(2)(iv)(E)(1) (2014).

43. Customer property includes those securities positions that are held for customers and the cash that is owed to customers. 15 U.S.C. 78lll(4) (2012).

44. Under Rule 15c3-3(b)(5) the carrying broker-dealer is affirmatively required to maintain possession and control of non-margin securities unless the broker-dealer has provided written notice to the PAB account holder. This is unlike fully paid securities and cash of customers, which is not allowed to be used in the carrying broker-dealer's business activities whatsoever.

2. Reserve Bank Account Computations, Deposits, and Withdrawals

Generally, computation of the amount of the required reserve must be made weekly on the last business day at the end of the business day.[45] The required reserve amount must be deposited in the bank within two days of making the computation and no later than one hour after the bank opens for business. However, carrying broker-dealers whose aggregate indebtedness does not exceed 800 percent (8:1) and who maintain customer funds not exceeding $1 million are allowed to compute the required reserve for the Customer Reserve Bank Account monthly, but must deposit 105 percent of the required reserve amount. In addition, carrying broker-dealers who do not maintain customer accounts and do not conduct a proprietary trading business, may also compute the required reserve amount for the PAB Reserve Bank Account on a monthly basis. However, if such a carrying broker-dealer is required to deposit additional qualified securities or cash in the PAB Reserve Bank Account, it must make the reserve bank account computation weekly until four successive weekly computations are made in which the carrying broker-dealer is not required to deposit additional cash or qualified securities. Carrying broker-dealers must make and maintain a record of each reserve bank account computation. The carrying broker-dealer must notify the SEC and its SRO by telegram immediately, if it fails to make deposits to the reserve accounts as required by the Reserve Formula computation. In addition, in keeping with the goal of prohibiting broker-dealers from using customer funds and securities to finance proprietary activities, the carrying broker-dealer may use credits related to PAB accounts to finance customer debits, but it cannot use customer credits to finance PAB debits.

Rule 15c3-3 prescribes the types of banks in which the carrying broker-dealer maintains Customer Reserve Bank Accounts and PAB Reserve Bank Accounts. The carrying broker-dealer must exclude any cash deposited with an affiliated bank when determining required minimum deposits. Carrying broker-dealers must either deposit qualified securities or move their accounts to non-affiliated banks. The SEC believes that the reserve requirement may be undermined if a holding company becomes insolvent, resulting in adverse consequences to both the affiliated bank and its broker-dealer subsidiary. In addition, cash deposits held at non-affiliated banks must be excluded when determining required minimum deposits to the amount of which the deposit exceeds 15 percent of the bank's equity capital as reported by the bank in its most recent Call Report.[46] This requirement serves to protect against bank failures by avoiding the situation where a carrying broker-dealer's cash deposits constitute a

---

45. Carrying broker-dealers may compute required reserve amounts on a daily basis. If deposits are required, they must be made within two days, no later than one hour after the bank opens for business.

46. The equity line requirement in the Call Report effectively excludes U.S. branches of foreign banks [even though they may meet the definition of Bank under Section 3(a)(6) of the Exchange Act] from holding cash deposits for reserve accounts because there is no equity capital line for such entities in the Call Report. The SEC intentionally excluded U.S. branches of foreign banks because their deposits generally are not FDIC-insured. The FDIC protects depositors' funds in the event of the financial failure of their bank or savings institution.

substantial portion of the bank's deposits because it directly addresses potential impairment of the bank's ability to quickly return the deposit to the carrying broker-dealer. Consequently, larger carrying broker-dealers that maintain large amounts of cash in their Customer Reserve Bank Accounts and PAB Reserve Bank Accounts generally use more than one non-affiliated bank.

Customer Reserve Bank Accounts and PAB Reserve Bank Accounts must be kept separate from all other accounts of the carrying broker-dealer maintained at the bank for the carrying broker-dealer. The carrying broker-dealer must obtain a written notification from each bank that it was informed that all cash and/or qualified securities held by the bank in Customer Reserve Bank Accounts and PAB Reserve Bank Accounts must be kept separate. In addition, the carrying broker-dealer must have a written contract with the bank in which it agrees not to re-lend or hypothecate securities deposited into reserve accounts, nor use cash in such accounts as collateral in lending to carrying broker-dealers. This means that the bank cannot use the securities in its business and is designed to provide a measure of protection by requiring that the securities will be available to the carrying broker-dealer in the event of bank financial difficulty or insolvency. However, cash deposits in reserve bank accounts may be freely used in the course of the bank's commercial activities.[47]

The carrying broker-dealer may make withdrawals from Customer Reserve Accounts and PAB Reserve Accounts only when deposits exceed the minimum required deposit as computed under the Reserve Formula Rule. The amount remaining in such accounts must equal the required deposit at the time of the withdrawal. This determination is the responsibility of the carrying broker-dealer. The bank is permitted to presume that the broker-dealer has determined that the withdrawal does not reduce cash and/or qualified securities in reserve accounts below the required minimum deposit. The carrying broker-dealer must make and maintain a record of the computation used to determine its eligibility for the withdrawal.

a. Free credit balances

Rule 15c3-3 defines and requires special treatment of customer free credit balances. Special treatment is required because free credit balances consist of funds payable by a broker-dealer to its customers on demand resulting from, among other things, cash deposited by the customer to purchase securities, proceeds from the sale of securities or other assets held in the customer's account, or earnings from dividends and interest on securities and other assets held in the customer's account. In other words, free credit balances consist of money that belongs to the customer, not the carrying broker-dealer. Rule 15c3-3 defines free credit balances as:

> Liabilities of a broker or dealer to customers which are subject to immediate cash payment to customers on demand, whether resulting from sales of securities, dividends, interest, deposits or otherwise ... [and] also includes, if

---

47. Cash is fungible and is the primary funding source for most banks.

subject to immediate cash payment to customers on demand, funds carried
in a securities account pursuant to a self-regulatory organization portfolio
margining rule ...

Carrying broker-dealers may pay interest to customers on their free credit balances
or offer to routinely transfer (sweep) them to a money market fund or a bank
account. Rule 15c3-3 is designed to ensure that customers understand the consequences of transferring free credit balances to various products—e.g., a money market fund or an interest-bearing bank account—and have a sufficient opportunity
to make an informed decision. For example, money market shares are securities and
receive up to $500,000 in SIPA protection in the event of broker-dealer failure, while
bank deposits as cash receive up to $250,000 from the FDIC in the event of bank
failure.

Paragraph (j) of Rule 15c3-3 prescribes conditions under which carrying broker-
dealers are permitted to deal with customer free credit balances. Carrying broker-
dealers must notify customers in writing about their free credit balances. Specifically,
the carrying broker-dealer must provide each customer with a written statement informing the customer of the amount due and that the funds are payable on demand.
If the customer decides to have free credit balances transferred to a Sweep Program
or a bank account, this direction must be given to the carrying broker-dealer in
writing. The carrying broker-dealer is only permitted to invest or transfer a customer's
free credit balances to another account or institution by written authorization; the
authorization must describe the manner, terms, and conditions of the handling of
the customer's free credit balances.

Paragraph (j)(2)(ii) of Rule 15c3-3 deals specifically with the transfer of customers'
free credit balances to, and between, Sweep Programs offered by the carrying broker-dealer. The term Sweep Program is defined in Rule 15c3-3; it is a service offered
by a carrying broker-dealer that allows customers to automatically transfer their
free credit balances to either a money market mutual fund, or to a bank account
that is FDIC-insured. The customer must provide written consent for such transfers
after the carrying broker-dealer provides information about the general terms and
conditions about products available through its Sweep Program and that available
products may change. If the carrying broker-dealer decides to make changes to the
terms and conditions of products in its Sweep Program, change products entirely,
or change the customer's investment from one product to another, the carrying
broker-dealer must adequately describe such changes, provide written notice 30
days before any such change, and describe available options should the customer
not accept the change. This notice requirement is designed to ensure that the customer will have time to evaluate available options before changes are made to the
carrying broker-dealer's Sweep Program. The carrying broker-dealer must also give
the customer notices and disclosures about its Sweep Program required by its SRO
and advise the customer in quarterly statements that free credit balances can be liquidated on order and proceeds can be returned to the customer's securities account
or directly to the customer.

The following case illustrates operation of Rule 15c3-3 and enforcement against the owner of the broker-dealer for aiding and abetting the violation of Rule 15c3-3 by his firm.

SEC v. Goble

682 F.3d 934 (11th Cir. 2012)

Cox, Circuit Judge:

The Securities and Exchange Commission ("SEC") brought this civil enforcement action against Richard L. Goble after he orchestrated a plan to manipulate the amount of money his company was required to set aside to safeguard customer assets. The district court conducted a five-day bench trial to consider the SEC's claims. The court found Goble liable for committing securities fraud in violation of § 10(b) of the Securities and Exchange Act of 1934 (the "Exchange Act"), 15 U.S.C. § 78j(b), and Rule 10b–5, 17 C.F.R. § 240.10b–5. The court also found that Goble aided and abetted violations of the Customer Protection Rule, 15 U.S.C. § 78*o*(c)(3); 17 C.F.R. § 240.15c3–3, and the books and records requirements of the Exchange Act, 15 U.S.C. § 78q(a); 17 C.F.R. § 240.17a–3. According to the court, Goble directed one of his employees to record a fake purchase of a money market fund in his company's books. And each of Goble's violations arose out of this single sham transaction. The court enjoined Goble from future violations of the securities laws and permanently restrained him from seeking a securities license or engaging in the securities business.

On appeal, Goble challenges the district court's holding on liability and the propriety of the resulting injunction. He argues that the district court erred by concluding that he committed § 10(b) securities fraud. If we reverse this securities fraud count, Goble believes his aiding and abetting violations must be reversed as well. After reviewing the record and having the benefit of oral argument, we agree with Goble that the facts as found by the district court do not support securities fraud liability and we reverse the court's judgment on this claim. However, it is also clear from the district court's factual findings that Goble aided and abetted violations of the Exchange Act, so we affirm the judgment finding liability on these counts.

I. BACKGROUND

Goble founded North American Clearing, Inc. ("North American"), a securities and clearing brokerage firm, in 1995. While he had no officially designated regulatory or supervisory responsibilities at North American, he sat on the corporation's board of directors, actively participated in North American's day-to-day operations, and in effect controlled a 100% interest in the company. Clearing firms like North American process trades for smaller and less capitalized brokers and dealers. At the time the SEC filed its complaint, North American acted as the clearing firm for about forty small brokerage firms and cleared transactions for more than 10,000 customer accounts valued at more than $500 million.

A variety of SEC regulations governed North American's operations. Central to this case is the Customer Protection Rule. This Rule is designed to protect broker-dealer customers in the event the brokerage firm becomes insolvent. It requires that brokerage firms establish a separate Reserve Bank Account ("Reserve Account") to hold an amount of cash adequate to reimburse customers if the firm fails. 17 C.F.R. § 240.15c3–3(e)(1). The Rule also dictates that firms use the regulation's Reserve Formula to calculate the balance they must maintain in the Reserve Account. *Id.*

The specifics of the Reserve Formula are fairly arcane, but its operation is straightforward. On a weekly basis, firms must balance customer credits against customer debits. 17 C.F.R. § 240.15c3–3(e)(3). Subject to some adjustments, the Rule requires that firms hold an amount equal to the excess of credits over debits in the Reserve Account. 17 C.F.R. § 240.15c3–3a. As defined by the regulations, "customer credits" captures the amount the firm owes its customers while "customer debits" refers to amounts the customers owe the firm. If, after the firm makes the reserve computation, it discovers that the Reserve Account balance is higher than the amount required by the Reserve Formula, the firm may make a withdrawal from the Reserve Account. 17 C.F.R. § 240.15c3–3(g).

During late 2007 and early 2008, North American faced declining revenues, and it struggled to meet its operating expenses and make the required contributions to the Reserve Account. To make up for the shortfall, North American drew on an existing loan secured by customer securities. Because customer securities collateralized the loan, however, the Reserve Formula dictated that North American deposit more money into the Reserve Account when it increased the loan balance. Thus, drawing on the loan only exacerbated North American's cash flow problem.

In March of 2008, the Financial Industry Regulatory Authority, Inc. ("FINRA") began an on-site audit of North American and remained there as the events precipitating this case transpired. During the audit, FINRA examiners uncovered irregularities in North American's reserve computations. Timothy Ward,[48] North American's Chief Financial Officer who had responsibility for North American's financial reporting and preparing the weekly reserve computation, characterized these irregularities as the result of his own mistakes and miscalculations. The examiners helped Ward correct these mistakes, and they remained on-site conducting regular reviews of North American's books and records.

By May of 2008, the cash flow problem at North American was severe. On May 13, Goble sought a $5 million unsecured loan to rectify the firm's negative financial spiral. When Goble was unable to procure the loan, he directed Ward to record a $5 million money market purchase in North American's books. But no such purchase had been made. The purpose of this sham transaction was to make it appear on paper that North American could withdraw money from the Reserve Account. Had there been a real purchase of money market funds, it would have decreased the amount of the required balance in the Reserve Account. The day after Ward recorded the sham purchase he made an interim reserve calculation using the faulty numbers

---

48. The SEC's complaint charged Ward and Goble as codefendants. Prior to trial, however, Ward settled with the SEC. He testified as a witness for the SEC at Goble's trial.

created by the sham transaction. This computation showed that North American could withdraw $3.4 million from the Reserve Account. Bruce Blatman[49] (North American's President and CEO) and Goble signed a wire request to move $3.4 million from the Reserve Account into North American's settlement account. After the funds transferred, the FINRA examiners quickly discovered a discrepancy created by the sham money market purchase and demanded an explanation.

As a result, Ward and Blatman discussed the May 13th sham transaction with the examiners. At the insistence of the examiners, Ward returned the $3.4 million to the Reserve Account and prepared a revised reserve computation. The revised computation showed that North American needed to deposit an additional $1.8 million into the Reserve Account. In the following days, it became clear that North American could not meet the reserve requirement, and Ward and Blatman decided to wind down North American's affairs after consultation with FINRA and the SEC.

A few days later, the SEC filed its complaint in this case against North American, Bruce Blatman, Timothy Ward, and Richard Goble for violations of the securities regulations. The complaint alleged that North American violated the Customer Protection Rule at § 15(c)(3) of the Exchange Act and Rule 15c3–3 thereunder, and that North American violated the Exchange Act's books and records requirements at § 17(a) and Rule 17a–3 thereunder. It maintained that Goble, Blatman, and Ward aided and abetted these violations. The complaint also alleged that each of the defendants violated the anti-fraud provision at § 10(b) of the Exchange Act and Rule 10b–5 thereunder.

The SEC settled with North American, Blatman, and Ward, but the district court held a five-day bench trial on the claims against Goble. The court concluded that Goble aided and abetted North American's Customer Protection Rule and books and records violations. It also held that Goble's actions concerning the sham money market transaction violated § 10(b) of the Exchange Act and Rule 10b–5. The injunction also permanently restrained Goble from violating the Customer Protection Rule, the books and records requirements, § 10(b), and Rule 10b–5. Goble appeals, challenging the court's decision on liability and the injunction.

II. ISSUES ON APPEAL

Goble raises the following five issues: … whether he can be liable for aiding and abetting North American's violations of the Customer Protection Rule and the Exchange Act's books and records requirements if there is no underlying securities fraud. …

* * *

B. Aiding and Abetting Violations

The court also found Goble liable for aiding and abetting North American's violations of the Customer Protection Rule and the Exchange Act's books and records requirements. The Customer Protection Rule directs that a specific balance be maintained in a segregated account. There is no question North American failed to maintain

---

49. Like Ward, Blatman was also named as a codefendant. He too settled with the SEC and testified for the SEC at Goble's trial.

the balance required by the Rule. The books and records requirements at §17(a) of the Exchange Act, 15 U.S.C. §78q(a), and Rule 17a–3, 17 C.F.R. §240.17a–3 thereunder, required North American to maintain accurate records. Goble does not dispute that North American failed to comply with these regulations. Instead, he claims that no primary securities fraud violation supports his aiding and abetting liability. But this argument misses the mark.

Exchange Act §20(e), 15 U.S.C. §78t(e), allows the imposition of aiding and abetting liability against "any person that knowingly or recklessly provides substantial assistance to another person in violation of a provision of [the Exchange Act], or of any rule or regulation issued" thereunder. 15 U.S.C. §78t(e). Thus, to impose aiding and abetting liability under §20(e) there must be: (1) a primary violation of the securities laws; (2) the aider and abettor must have knowledge of the primary violation; and (3) the aider and abettor must provide substantial assistance in the commission of the primary violation.

There is no question that primary violations of the Customer Protection Rule and the books and records requirements occurred at North American. And, the testimony offered at trial supports the district court's finding that Goble had knowledge of and assisted these primary violations. Ward testified that Goble ordered him to enter the sham money market transaction in North American's books despite Ward's counsel that this would violate the regulations. Goble also directed Ward to complete the interim reserve computation after the sham transaction was on the books. Based on this interim reserve computation, Goble signed a wire transfer request to move money out of the reserve account. These facts clearly show that Goble knew his actions surrounding the May 13th sham money market transaction would violate the books and records requirements and the Customer Protection Rule and that he substantially assisted in the violation of these regulations. The district court did not err by finding him liable for aiding and abetting these violations.

IV. CONCLUSION

We affirm the court's judgment that Goble aided and abetted North American's violations of the Customer Protection Rule and books and records requirements of the Exchange Act. We reverse the court's conclusion that Goble committed securities fraud in violation of §10(b)

Notes and Questions

1. Why was Goble charged with aiding and abetting a violation of Rule 15c3-3, instead of being charged directly?

Hypothetical Two

Jane Plain was hired by Success First on a probationary basis to work for Sidney Ratnam, Success First's Chief Financial Officer. Ratnam wants to test Plain's knowledge of the Reserve Formula under the Customer Protection Rule. He poses this hypothetical to Plain: If Success First holds $100 for Customer D, but wants to finance a security purchase for Customer E for $100, may Success First use Customer D's $100 to finance a security purchase for Customer E for $100 under the Reserve Formula without having to maintain cash and/or qualified securities in the Customer Reserve Bank Account? What if Success First wanted to use Customer D's $100 to finance a proprietary security purchase?

Chapter 8

Margin Regulation

Regulatory Authority

Securities Exchange Act of 1934 Sections 7(a)-(c), 8, 15(c)(2), 15(e)

Exchange Act Rules 8c-1, 15c2-1, 15c3-3

Federal Reserve Board Regulations U and T

FINRA Rules 4210, 4220, 4230, 4314, 4330

Motivating Hypothetical

Success First's training program about a broker-dealer's financial responsibility requirements under the federal securities laws and FINRA rules is now in week three. Members of the Training Program Committee are quite pleased with its operation and the progress of Success First's new hires—10 law students from the local law schools. It seems that the training program is achieving its stated goal—ensuring loyalty and the depth of knowledge needed about the broker-dealer industry from Success First's perspective. So far, all of the trainees have done well in the training program and are on track to become permanent employees of Success First. The topic of this week's module is margin regulation. John DoGoode, the mentor of the 10 trainees, is especially excited about margin regulation because he believes that it is profitable for both Success First and its customers. Josephine Wiseman, Success First's general council, is especially concerned about ensuring that the trainees understand the mechanics of margin trading and its regulatory framework. In her experience, many customers and broker-dealers do not understand that the rules and regulations governing margin trading are designed to ensure comprehension of the risks of margin trading by both the broker-dealer and its customers. Often, both the broker-dealer and the customer focus on the higher profits obtained through leverage and not the attendant risks.

I. Introduction

Margin trading involves the use of credit (a loan) to purchase securities. Both broker-dealers and customers may engage in the purchase of securities using margin. In essence, the customer borrows a portion of the purchase price of the securities and the purchased securities serve as collateral for the loan or extension of credit. Margin trading is regulated, i.e., margin regulation limits the amount of credit that broker-dealers may extend to their customers and to other broker-dealers to purchase securities. The regulation of margin is shared between the Federal Reserve Board, the SEC, and SROs, including FINRA. First, however, it is necessary to understand how margin trading is conducted, along with its benefits and risks, in order to comprehend the margin regulatory framework. The following investor guidance issued by FINRA describes margin trading, and its corollary, short selling,[1] from the customer's perspective and identifies three categories of margin regulation.

Purchasing on Margin, Risks Involved With Trading in a Margin Account

* * *

Use of Margin Accounts

A customer who purchases securities may pay for the securities in full or may borrow part of the purchase price from his or her securities firm. If the customer chooses to borrow funds from a firm, the customer will open a **margin account** with the firm. The portion of the purchase price that the customer must deposit is called margin and is the customer's initial equity in the account. The loan from the firm is secured by the securities that are purchased by the customer. A customer may also enter into a short sale through a margin account, which involves the customer borrowing stock from a firm in order to sell it, hoping that the price will decline. Customers generally use margin to leverage their investments and increase their purchasing power. At the same time, customers who trade securities on margin incur the potential for higher losses.

Margin Requirements

The terms on which firms can extend credit for securities transactions are governed by federal regulation and by the rules of FINRA and the securities exchanges. This investor guidance focuses on the requirements for marginable equity securities, which includes most stocks. Some securities cannot be purchased on margin, which means they must be purchased in a cash account, and the customer must deposit 100 percent of the purchase price. In general, under Federal Reserve Board Regulation T, firms can lend a customer up to 50 percent of the total purchase price of a stock for new, or initial, purchases.

The rules of FINRA and the exchanges supplement the requirements of Regulation T by placing "**maintenance**" margin requirements on customer accounts. Under the

---

1. The regulatory framework governing short selling is discussed in Chapter 13, Market Regulation.

rules of FINRA and the exchanges, as a general matter, the customer's equity in the account must not fall below 25 percent of the current market value of the securities in the account. Otherwise, the customer may be required to deposit more funds or securities in order to maintain the equity at the 25 percent level. The failure to do so may cause the firm to force the sale of—or liquidate—the securities in the customer's account in order to bring the account's equity back up to the required level.

Margin Transaction—Example

For example, if a customer buys $100,000 of securities on Day 1, Regulation T would require the customer to deposit margin of 50 percent or $50,000 in payment for the securities. As a result, the customer's equity in the margin account is $50,000, and the customer has received a margin loan of $50,000 from the firm. Assume that on Day 2 the market value of the securities falls to $60,000. Under this scenario, the customer's margin loan from the firm would remain at $50,000, and the customer's account equity would fall to $10,000 ($60,000 market value less $50,000 loan amount). However, the minimum maintenance margin requirement for the account is 25 percent, meaning that the customer's equity must not fall below $15,000 ($60,000 market value multiplied by 25 percent). Since the required equity is $15,000, the customer would receive a maintenance margin call for $5,000 ($15,000 less existing equity of $10,000).

Firm Practices

Firms have the right to set their own margin requirements—often called "house" requirements—as long as they are higher than the margin requirements under Regulation T or the rules of FINRA and the exchanges. Firms can raise their maintenance margin requirements for specific volatile stocks to ensure there are sufficient funds in their customers' accounts to cover large price swings. These changes in firm policy often take effect immediately and may result in the issuance of a maintenance margin call. Again, a customer's failure to satisfy the call may cause the firm to liquidate a portion of the customer's account.

Margin Agreements and Disclosures

If a customer trades stocks in a margin account, the customer needs to carefully review the margin agreement provided by his or her firm. A firm charges interest for the money it lends its customers to purchase securities on margin, and a customer needs to understand the additional charges he or she may incur by opening a margin account. Under the federal securities laws, a firm that loans money to a customer to finance securities transactions is required to provide the customer with written disclosure of the terms of the loan, such as the rate of interest and the method for computing interest. The firm must also provide the customer with periodic disclosures informing the customer of transactions in the account and the interest charges to the customer.

Additional Risks Involved with Trading on Margin

There are a number of additional risks that all investors need to consider in deciding to trade securities on margin. These risks include the following:

You can lose more funds than you deposit in the margin account. A decline in the value of securities that are purchased on margin may require you to provide additional funds to the firm that has made the loan to avoid the forced sale of those securities or other securities in your account.

The firm can force the sale of securities in your account. If the equity in your account falls below the maintenance margin requirements under the law—or the firm's higher "house" requirements—the firm can sell the securities in your account to cover the margin deficiency. You will also be responsible for any short fall in the account after such a sale.

The firm can sell your securities without contacting you. Some investors mistakenly believe that a firm must contact them for a margin call to be valid, and that the firm cannot liquidate securities in their accounts to meet the call unless the firm has contacted them first. This is not the case. As a matter of good customer relations, most firms will attempt to notify their customers of margin calls, but they are not required to do so.

You are not entitled to an extension of time on a margin call. While an extension of time to meet initial margin requirements may be available to customers under certain conditions, a customer does not have a right to the extension. In addition, a customer does not have a right to an extension of time to meet a maintenance margin call.

———

II. The Regulatory Framework for Trading on Margin

A. The Purpose of the Regulatory Framework for Trading on Margin

The regulatory framework for trading on margin is based on Section 7 of the Exchange Act, which states that the purpose of margin regulation is to prevent the excessive use of credit for the purchase or carrying of securities. In essence, the margin regulatory framework is designed to protect the overall economy by regulating the amount of credit used in the securities markets for speculation and, therefore, diverted away from more productive uses. Contrary to popular belief, the primary purpose of margin regulation is not the protection of small investors as noted in the following case.

Stonehill v. Sec. Nat'l Bank
68 F.R.D. 24 (S.D.N.Y. 1975)

ROBERT L. CARTER, District Judge.

This action concerns a series of loans which allegedly violated the margin requirements of Regulation U, 12 C.F.R. § 221.1 *et seq.*, promulgated by the Federal Reserve

Board pursuant to §7 of the Securities Exchange Act of 1934, 15 U.S.C. §78g. All of the parties now move for summary judgment.

The Pleadings

Plaintiff Maurice L. Stonehill's amended complaint alleges that on or about January 21, 1970, plaintiff agreed to lend 24,000 shares of Jeanette Corporation ('Jeanette') common stock to defendant John B. Fowler, Jr.; that Stonehill agreed that the Jeanette stock was to be used by Fowler as collateral for a loan to provide working capital for Fowler and J. S. Love & Co., Inc. ('J. S. Love'), a duly registered broker-dealer of which Fowler was chairman, chief executive officer and stockholder; that plaintiff agreed that the working capital was to be used 'to buy, sell, and trade registered securities * * * and to purchase such securities under certain underwritings;' that defendant Security National Bank ('Security') is the successor in interest of Royal National Bank of New York ('Royal'); and that Fowler pledged plaintiff's 24,000 shares of Jeanette stock as collateral for a loan of $225,000 from Royal to Fowler for the benefit of Fowler and J. S. Love.

The first court [sic] of the amended complaint asserts that Royal's loan to Fowler violated Regulation U and §7 of the Exchange Act. Regulation U provides that no bank shall grant any loan in an amount exceeding a certain percentage of the value of stock pledged as collateral (the 'maximum loan value') where the purpose of the loan is to 'purchase or carry' margin stock.

Court [sic] 1 alleges that Fowler and J. S. Love used the proceeds of the loan for the purpose of purchasing or carrying margin stock; that Royal knew or should have known that the proceeds would be used for that purpose; that the amount of the loan exceeded the maximum loan value of the 24,000 Jeanette shares; that Fowler defaulted on payment of the loan; and that Security still holds the Jeanette collateral. Count 1 seeks a declaratory judgment declaring the loan to Fowler void as a violation of Regulation U, and an injunction ordering Security to return the 24,000 Jeanette shares to Stonehill free of all liens and claims.

* * *

Discussion

Before considering the alleged violations of Regulation U on the merits, the court must determine whether plaintiff as a guarantor has a right of action under Regulation U, and the nature of his obligation, if any, under the guarantee.

Right of Action by Guarantor

In determining whether a guarantor should have a right of action, the nature of the right accorded a *borrower* must first be examined. In *Serzysko v. Chase Manhattan Bank*, 290 F.Supp. 74 (S.D.N.Y.1968), *aff'd mem.*, 409 F.2d 1360 (2d Cir.), *cert. denied*, 396 U.S. 904, 90 S.Ct. 218, 24 L.Ed.2d 180 (1969) the leading decision on Regulation U, the court held that there was a dual basis for the borrower's action. The borrower's declaratory action to void the loan and his *defense* to the bank's action to enforce the obligation both rest on §29(b) of the Exchange Act, 15 U.S.C. §78cc (b). That section provides that any contract which violates the Act or regulations thereunder is void as regards the rights of the violator.[2] *See Cooper v. Union Bank*, 354 F.Supp. 669, 682 (C.D. Cal.1973).

The borrower's action for damages, on the other hand, is based on §286 of the Restatement of Torts (1934), which gives a private tort action for violation of a statute to one who is within the class of persons intended to be protected by the statute.[3] 290 F.Supp. At 88–90. *Remar v. Clayton Securities Corp.*, 81 F.Supp. 1014 (D.Mass.1949); *Goldman v. Bank of Common-wealth*, 467 F.2d 439, 446 (6th Cir. 1972), *aff'g* 332 F.Supp. 699 (E.D.Mich.1971); *see Grove v. First National Bank of Herminie*, 352 F.Supp. 1250, 1252 (W.D.Pa.1972), *aff'd*, 489 F.2d 512 (3d Cir. 1973).

However, an examination of the legislative history of §7 has led courts to ... [Note that] ... it is clear that protection of the borrower-investor was not the primary legislative objective in enacting the margin provisions:

> 'The main purpose of these margin provisions * * * is not to increase the safety of security loans for lenders. Banks and brokers normally require sufficient collateral to make themselves safe without the help of law. *Nor is the main purpose even protection of the small speculator by making it impossible for him to spread himself too thinly*—although such a result will be achieved as a by-product of the main purpose.' (Citations omitted).

The 'main purpose' of the margin rules was to regulate the volume of credit flowing into the securities market:

> 'The main purpose is to give a Government credit agency an effective method of reducing the aggregate amount of the nation's credit resources which can be directed by speculation into the stock market and out of other more desirable uses of commerce and industry—to prevent a recurrence of the pre-crash situation where funds which would otherwise have been available at normal interest rates for uses of local commerce, industry and agriculture,

---

2. Section 29(b) provides in pertinent part:

(b) Every contract made in violation of any provision of this chapter or of any rule or regulation thereunder, and every contract (including any contract for listing a security on an exchange) heretofore or hereafter made, the performance of which involves the violation of, or the continuance of any relationship or practice in violation of, any provision of this chapter or any rule or regulation thereunder, shall be void (1) as regards the rights of any person who, in violation of any such provision, rule, or regulation, shall have made or engaged in the performance of any such contract.

3. Section 286 of the Restatement of Torts provides in pertinent part:

§286. VIOLATIONS CREATING CIVIL LIABILITY.

The violation of a legislative enactment by doing a prohibited act, or by failing to do a required act, makes the actor liable for an invasion of an interest of another if:

(a) the intent of the enactment is exclusively or in part to protect an interest of the other as an individual; ... and

(d) The violation is a legal cause of the invasion, and the other has not so conducted himself as to disable himself from maintaining an action.

were drained by far higher rates into security loans and the New York call market.' (Citations omitted).

In its *Report of Special Study of Securities Markets*, 88th Cong., 1st Sess. Ch. X, 9 (1963), the SEC similarly stated that its primary concern in respect of the margin rules is *not* to protect the small investor from loss, but to prevent speculative swings in securities prices:

> '* * * [T]he Commission's primary concern is the efficacy of security credit controls in preventing speculative excesses that produce dangerously large and rapid securities price rises and accelerated declines in the prices of given securities issues and in the general price level of securities. Losses to a given investor resulting from price declines in thinly margined securities are not of serious significance from a regulatory point of view. When forced sales occur and put pressures on securities prices, however, they may cause other forced sales and the resultant snowballing effect may in turn have a general adverse effect upon the entire market.'

————

Essentially, the purpose of margin regulation can be summarized as follows. First and foremost, it is designed to protect the overall economy by restricting the amount of credit allowed for financing securities transactions. Second, margin regulation protects the U.S. business system from "excessive speculation, resulting in sudden and unreasonable fluctuations in the prices of securities which (a) cause alternately unreasonable expansion and unreasonable contraction of the volume of credit available for trade, transportation, and industry in interstate commerce, (b) hinder the proper appraisal of the value of securities and thus prevent a fair calculation of taxes owing to the United States and to the several States by owners, buyers, and sellers of securities, and (c) prevent the fair valuation of collateral for bank loans and/or obstruct the effective operation of the national banking system and Federal Reserve System."[4] Third, and of least importance, is protecting the small investor from an unreasonably high risk of loss.

B. The Regulation of Trading on Margin

Trading on margin is regulated by limiting the amount of credit that may be extended to purchase securities. These limits or margin requirements may be divided into two categories: (1) Initial margin and (2) Maintenance margin. Initial margin is the portion of the purchase price for securities that the customer must pay in cash or securities to make the initial purchase of the security. Maintenance margin is the amount of equity that the customer must keep in her margin account to avoid a margin call. Section 7 of the Exchange Act authorizes the Federal Reserve Board to regulate both initial and maintenance margin but the Federal Reserve Board has only exercised

---

4. 15 U.S.C. § 78b (3) (2012).

its authority with respect to initial margin. Maintenance margin requirements are determined by SROs and broker-dealers. Maintenance margin requirements set by broker-dealers must be equal to, but are generally greater than, maintenance margin requirements set by SROs. Broker-dealers usually require higher maintenance margin requirements than SROs because they want to ensure payment of loans extended for purchasing securities and to avoid margin calls, which may have an adverse impact on their net capital. The SEC has the authority to enforce the provisions of the Exchange Act and the rules adopted thereunder and, therefore, to enforce the rules adopted by the Federal Reserve Board that regulate margin requirements. The Exchange Act also requires the SROs to enforce the Exchange Act and the rules adopted thereunder along with adopting SRO rules that enforce the federal securities laws, including margin requirements.

1. *Federal Margin Regulation: Initial Margin*

The Federal Reserve Board is authorized to adopt regulations to enforce the margin requirements in Section 7 of the Exchange Act. Section 7(a) of the Exchange Act authorizes the Federal Reserve Board to set initial and maintenance requirements based on a standard of "[a]n amount not greater than whichever is the higher of: (1) 55 per centum of the current market price of the security, or (2) 100 per centum of the lowest market price of the security during the preceding thirty-six calendar months, but not more than 75 per centum of the current market price." However, Section 7(b) of the Exchange Act allows the Federal Reserve Board to make changes from this standard at its discretion in order to, among other things, prevent the excessive use of credit to finance transactions in securities. The Federal Reserve Board used margin requirements to effect monetary policy between 1934 and 1974 by frequently changing initial margin requirements to control market speculation and fluctuations in business activity. It no longer uses margin requirements as a tool to effect monetary policy and initial margin has remained constant at 50 percent of the current market value of a security since approximately 1974. Section 7(c) of the Exchange Act authorizes the Federal Reserve Board to regulate the extension and arranging of margin loans, or any extension of credit to customers, by broker-dealers. Specifically, a broker-dealer may extend, or arrange for, credit to purchase securities to customers only with collateral and the collateral must be securities designated by the Federal Reserve Board or exempted securities.[5] The Federal Reserve Board also regulates lenders, other than broker-dealers, that extend, or arrange for, credit to purchase securities.

a. Regulation T

The Federal Reserve Board adopted Regulation T ("Reg T") to set initial margin requirements and payment rules on transactions in margin securities as authorized under Section 7 of the Exchange Act. Margin securities are securities designated by

---

5. The term *exempted securities* is defined in Section 3(a) (12) of the Exchange Act and includes U.S. government securities.

the Federal Reserve Board as eligible for use as collateral in margin transactions. See Figure 8.1 for a list of margin securities.

Figure 8.1

Margin Securities — Reg T 12 C.F.R. § 220.2
Any security registered or having unlisted trading privileges on a national securities exchange
Any security listed on the NASDAQ Stock Market
Any non-equity security (see § 3(a)(11) of Exchange Act)
Any security issued by either an open-end investment company or unit investment trust registered under Section 8 of the Investment Company Act of 1940
Any foreign margin stock
Any debt security convertible into a margin security

The initial margin requirement varies depending on the type of margin security. For example, the initial margin requirement for a margin equity security that is not an exempted security is the greatest of 50 percent of its current market value or the percentage set by the SRO where the trade occurs. The initial margin requirement for an exempted security, a non-equity security, a money market mutual fund, or exempted securities mutual fund is the margin required by the broker-dealer in good faith.[6]

Reg T also governs margin requirements for short sales.[7] A short sale occurs when a customer sells a security she does not own and must borrow the security from her broker-dealer. Short sales are normally settled by the delivery of a security borrowed by the customer. At some time subsequent to settlement, the customer closes out the position by returning the borrowed security to the lender broker-dealer, typically by purchasing securities on the open market. Customers engage in short selling because they believe that the price of the security sold short will fall and enable them to buy it back at the lower price and make a profit. The initial margin requirement in a short sale for a non-exempted equity security is 150 percent of the current market value of the security, or 100 percent of the current market value if a security convertible into the security sold short is held in the customer's margin account. The initial margin requirement in a short sale for an exempted security or a non-equity security is 100 percent of the current market value plus the margin required by the broker-dealer in good faith.

Reg T requires all financial relations between a customer and broker-dealer be recorded in a margin account or special purpose accounts. The special purpose ac-

---

6. Good faith is defined in part 220.2 of Reg T as the amount of margin a creditor would require in exercising sound credit judgment and may require some investigation of the borrower, depending on the circumstances.

7. The regulatory framework for short sales is reviewed in Chapter 13, Market Regulation.

counts include the special memorandum account (SMA) and the cash account. All transactions not specifically authorized for inclusion in one of the other special purpose accounts must be recorded in the margin account. In a margin account, any margin deficiency must be paid within one payment period, i.e., two business days after the end of the three-business day settlement cycle[8] for equities or five business days. Failure to deposit the required securities or cash within the required payment period means that the broker-dealer must liquidate sufficient securities in the customer's account to meet the margin call, unless the margin deficiency is less than $1,000. The payment period may be extended by the broker-dealer's SRO, but the broker-dealer must liquidate securities in the customer's margin account if she fails to make a deposit sufficient to eliminate the margin deficiency. An SMA may be created in conjunction with a margin account to hold, among other things, excess margin (more margin than required by Reg T), dividend and interest payments, and excess cash (e.g., proceeds of a sale of securities not required to be maintained in a margin account). See Example 8.1 below.

Example 8.1. How Excess Margin Is Created

A customer opens a margin account and purchases 100 shares of ABC at $55. The total cost of the purchase is $5,500. Reg T requires the customer to post initial margin of 50 percent, or $2,750. The customer's account looks like the following:	
Market Value	$5,500 (100 ABC @ $55)
Debit Balance (Margin Loan from Broker-dealer)	–$2,750
Customer Equity	$2,750
Assume that the price of ABC stock goes up to $65 per share. If everything remains the same, the margin account looks as follows and the customer now has excess margin of $1,000 ($3,750–$2,750):	
Market Value	$6,500 (100 ABC @ $65)
Debit Balance/(Margin Loan from Broker-dealer)	–$2,750 (owed to broker-dealer)
Customer Equity	$3,750

In a customer cash account, the broker-dealer may buy or sell securities for the customer under specified conditions. The broker-dealer may buy for or sell to any customer if there are sufficient funds in her cash account, or the broker-dealer may accept in good faith the customer's agreement that she will promptly make full cash payment for the security before selling it. The broker-dealer may buy from or sell for any customer any security if the security is held in the cash account, or the broker-dealer accepts in good faith the customer's statement that the security is owned by

---

8. Exchange Act Rule 15c6-1 defines the payment cycle for equities as trade date plus three business days.

the customer or the customer's principal, and that it will be promptly deposited in the account.[9] Full cash payment must be received within one payment period, i.e., within five business days. A broker-dealer may not permit a customer to use the proceeds of the sale of a security in order to meet the applicable payment requirement. This practice, known as freeriding, is prohibited based on the theory that a customer who sells securities before having the cash to pay for them is actually borrowing money to invest; Reg T requires such transactions to be conducted in a margin account. Engaging in freeriding requires the broker-dealer to freeze, or place a hold on, the customer's account for 90 days (90-day settled-funds-only freeze) that prohibits the customer from investing funds from stock sales until the sales settle (trade date plus three business days). An example of permissible and impermissible (freeriding) transactions in a customer cash account are provided below in Example 8.2.

Example 8.2. Permissible Transaction in a Cash Account*

Business Day 1	Business Day 2	Business Day 3	Business Day 4
Sell ABC.	Buy XYZ with the sale proceeds.	No action taken.	Funds from the sale of ABC are received, Sell XYZ.

* Remember that settlement requirements vary based on the type of security. For example, the settlement date for mutual funds is one business day.

Impermissible Freeriding in a Cash Account

Business Day 1	Business Day 2	Business Day 3	Business day 4
Sell ABC.	Buy XYZ with the sale proceeds.	Sell XYZ.	Funds from the sale of ABC are received.

As illustrated in Example 8.2, impermissible freeriding in a cash account means that the customer is allowed to buy and sell XYZ with the proceeds from the sale of ABC before she receives the funds from the sale of ABC. This type of trading must be conducted in a margin account.

2. SRO Regulation: Maintenance Margin

SROs primarily regulate maintenance margin; however, FINRA requires a minimum amount of equity, or minimum margin, to establish a margin account for a customer. FINRA Rule 4210 prescribes requirements for the extension of credit by broker-dealers that offer margin accounts to customers, as permitted in accordance with Reg T. The Minimum margin requirement under FINRA Rule 4210 requires the customer to deposit cash and/or securities of at least $2,000 in order to establish a margin account.[10]

---

9. Other permissible transactions include selling an option as part of a covered option transaction.

10. The minimum amount for pattern day traders is $25,000. A pattern day trader is a customer who executes four or more "day trades" within five business days, provided that the number of day

Maintenance margin requirements, the minimum amount of margin that a broker-dealer is required to maintain in a customer's account, are also contained in FINRA Rule 4210 and vary based on the type of security.[11] Maintenance margin requirements under the rule are set forth in Figure 8.2.

Figure 8.2. Maintenance Margin Requirements under FINRA Rule 4210*

Twenty-five percent of the current market value of all margin securities, as defined in Section 220.2 of Reg T.
$2.50 per share or 100 percent of the current market value, whichever amount is greater, of each stock "short" in the account selling at less than $5.00 per share; plus
$5.00 per share or 30 percent of the current market value, whichever amount is greater, of each stock "short" in the account selling at $5.00 per share or above; plus
Five percent of the principal amount or 30 percent of the current market value, whichever amount is greater, of each bond "short" in the account.
100 percent of the current market value for each non-margin eligible equity security held "long" in the account.

* Margin requirements for security futures and other derivatives are beyond the scope of this textbook.

FINRA Rule 4210 also requires broker-dealers to formulate their own margin requirements. Such requirements cannot be less than the requirements in Rule 4210 and must include procedures for reviewing limits and types of credit extended to customers and the need for instituting higher margin requirements and collateral deposits than are required by Rule 4210.

Like Reg T, FINRA Rule 4210 prohibits freeriding in cash accounts. No broker-dealer may permit a customer to make a practice of effecting transactions in a cash account where the cost of securities purchased is met by the sale of the same securities. In addition, the broker-dealer cannot permit a customer to make a practice of selling securities in a cash account, which are to be received against payment from another broker-dealer where such securities were purchased and are not yet paid for. Any broker-dealer transferring an account subject to a Reg T 90-day freeze to another member must inform the receiving broker-dealer of the 90-day freeze.

FINRA has prescribed recordkeeping and reporting requirements for margin accounts held by broker-dealers. FINRA Rule 4220 specifies daily recordkeeping requirements of initial and maintenance margin calls that are issued by broker-dealers. FINRA Rule 4230 requires clearing broker-dealers to file a monthly report indicating

---

trades represents more than six percent of the customer's total trades in the margin account for that same five-business-day period. FINRA Rule 4210(f) (8) (B) (ii).

11. Maintenance margin requirements for fixed income, warrants and option securities, U.S. government securities, highly rated foreign sovereign debt securities, and non-equity securities are also prescribed under FINRA Rule 4210.

all broker-dealers for which it clears that have overall ratios of requests for extensions of time to meet margin calls to total transactions for the month (the extension-of-time-ratio) that exceed a percentage specified by FINRA currently set at two percent. Clearing broker-dealers must submit this report for months even when no broker-dealer for which it clears exceeds the extension-of-time ratio.

a. Portfolio Margin

Paragraph (g) of FINRA Rule 4210 regulates portfolio margin in contrast to Reg T or strategy-based margin requirements. Portfolio margin brings a more risk-sensitive approach to establishing margin requirements. For example, in a diverse portfolio some positions may appreciate and others depreciate in response to a given change in market prices. The portfolio margin methodology recognizes offsetting potential changes among the full portfolio of related instruments. This links the margin required to the risk of the entire portfolio as opposed to the individual positions on a position-by-position basis. Most important, portfolio margin is beneficial for investors because it may result in lower margin requirements for customers with well diversified portfolios.

Some Key Differences between Reg T Margin and Portfolio Margin

Reg T Margin	Portfolio Margin
Position- and strategy-based (for options) margin. Conservative portfolios have the same margin requirements as risky portfolios.	Portfolio- and risk-based margin. Conservative portfolios have lower margin requirements compared to riskier portfolios.
Minimum equity requirement of $2,000.	Minimum equity requirement greater than $2,000 (generally $100,000–$150,000). Minimum equity amount for unlisted derivatives is at least $5 million.
Differing initial and maintenance margin requirements, which means that additional capital is needed to enter the position.	Initial and maintenance margin requirements are the same. No additional capital is needed to enter a position.
50% initial margin, 25% maintenance margin.	Margin varies based on eligible product, but no higher than 15%.
Does not account for correlation between similar types of indexes or ETFs.	Accounts for correlation between similar types of indexes and ETFs.

Portfolio margin is a methodology for calculating a customer's margin requirement by determining the maximum loss the customer's portfolio would incur under adverse market scenarios. Calculating the customer's margin requirement using this methodology is very complex and must be determined using a pricing model approved by the SEC. Currently, the only theoretical pricing model approved by the SEC is the Theoretical Intermarket Margin System, or TIMS, developed by the Options Clearing Corporation (OCC). Using TIMS, the stock would be stressed across a range of percentage returns specified in FINRA Rule 4210(g) (2); for stocks the range is from -15% to +15%. The margin requirement is determined by finding the maximum net loss across all the scenarios examined. This means initial and maintenance margin are combined into a single margin requirement, which is generally lower than the margin required under Reg T. See Example 8.3 below.

Example 8.3. Portfolio Margin

For ease of illustration, assume that the customer has a portfolio containing 100 shares of Amazon, Inc. (ticker AMZN) trading at $560 per share. AMZN will be stressed along the range of -15% to 15% from its current price:

Stressed Stock Move	-15%	-12%	-9%	-5%	-2%	0%	2%	5%	9%	12%	15%
Scenario Price	$476.00	$492.80	$509.60	$532.00	$548.80	$560	$571.20	$588.00	$610.40	$627.20	$644.00

FINRA Rule 4210 restricts the use of portfolio margin to portfolios consisting of specified financial instruments. Specifically, broker-dealers may apply the portfolio margin requirements to all margin equity securities, among other financial instruments.[12] The broker-dealer cannot use portfolio margin in Individual Retirement Accounts (IRAs).

FINRA Rule 4210 also restricts the use of portfolio margin to certain participants and prior approval by FINRA is required. Broker-dealers may use portfolio margin in their proprietary margin accounts, but only certain customers are eligible. For example, in order for customers to be eligible to use portfolio margin, they must be approved to sell uncovered options transactions, even though their portfolio does not contain such financial instruments. Qualifying customers using this standard means that broker-dealers must implement specific procedures for accounts engaging in portfolio margining, including minimum equity requirements and maximum credit limits per account.

Broker-dealers have required such customers to maintain a minimum equity, ranging from $100,000 to $150,000 in their accounts. If the minimum equity or margin requirement is not met by the customer, the broker-dealer must require the customer to deposit additional cash and/or securities to meet these requirements; if the customer cannot do so, the broker-dealer must liquidate securities in the account to meet the specified minimum requirements. Moreover, the broker-dealer must deduct the amount of the deficiency from its net capital until the deficiency is satisfied or until sufficient securities in the customer's account are liquidated to cure the deficiency. Broker-dealers are prohibited from allowing customers to make a practice of meeting a margin deficiency by liquidation. In addition, on or before the initial transaction in the portfolio margin account, the broker-dealer must provide the customer with a special written disclosure statement describing the nature and risks of portfolio

---

12. All trading in portfolio margin accounts must comply with FINRA Rule 2630, as applicable, which prescribes options trading restrictions for broker-dealers.

margin; the customer must provide a written acknowledgement of receipt, which must be maintained by the broker-dealer.

Portfolio margin has a direct impact on a broker-dealer's net capital. A broker-dealer must not allow aggregate portfolio margin requirements to exceed 10 times its net capital or 10:1 for any period exceeding three business days. If it does exceed 10:1, the broker-dealer must cease opening new portfolio margin accounts until portfolio margin requirements decline. In addition, a broker-dealer must notify the SEC and FINRA immediately by telegraph or by facsimile.

Broker-dealers must have written procedures to monitor the risk of portfolio margin accounts. These procedures must be designed to maintain a comprehensive written risk analysis methodology for assessing the potential risk to the broker-dealer's capital over a specified range of possible market movements of positions maintained in portfolio margin accounts. The risk analysis methodology must specify the computations to be made, the frequency of computations, the records to be reviewed and maintained, and the employee responsible for this risk function. The risk analysis methodology must be filed with FINRA and submitted to the SEC prior to implementing portfolio margin.

Notes and Questions

1. There is no private right of action under Section 7 of the Exchange Act, nor Regulation T promulgated thereunder. In 1970, Congress amended Section 7 to make it unlawful for customers to accept credit in violation of federal margin requirements. *See* Judge Friendly's dissent in *Pearlstein v. Scudder & German*, 429 F.2d 1136, 1145, arguing against allowing a private right of action under Section 7 of the Exchange Act and regulations promulgated thereunder. Should the burden of compliance be apportioned equally between broker-dealer and customer in light of the purpose of margin regulation? → No, customer is much less knowledgeable.

2. FINRA Rule 4210 is long and complex. It contains margin requirements for various types of securities and accounts. For example, when two or more accounts are carried for a customer, the maintenance margin is determined on the net position of the accounts, provided the customer has consented that the money and securities in each of such accounts may be used to carry or pay any deficit in all such accounts. Moreover, the rule prohibits a broker-dealer from permitting a customer to make a practice of either deferring the deposit of cash or securities beyond the time when such transactions would ordinarily be settled or cleared, or meeting the margin required by the liquidation of the same or other commitments in the account; however, the prohibition on liquidations does not apply to accounts in compliance with the equity required under Rule 4210 or if the account is carried on an omnibus basis as prescribed by Reg T.

3. Margin requirements for day traders. FINRA Rule 4210 identifies special margin requirements for day traders and pattern day traders. Under the rule, day trading

is defined as the purchasing and selling or the selling and purchasing of the same security on the same day in a margin account.[13] Whenever day trading occurs in a customer's margin account, the special maintenance margin requirement is 25 percent for margin-eligible equity securities and 100 percent for non-margin-eligible equity securities and is based on the cost of all the day trades made during the day. Margin requirements for pattern day traders are higher still. A pattern day trader is any customer who executes four or more day trades within five business days.[14] Pattern day traders are subject to a minimum equity requirement of $25,000, which must be deposited in the account before the customer may continue day trading and must be maintained in the customer's account at all times. Moreover, if a pattern day trader customer fails to meet a special margin maintenance call by the fifth business day, on the sixth business day only, broker-dealers are required to deduct from net capital the amount of the unmet special margin maintenance call.

Hypothetical One

John DoGoode is a registered representative in Success First's home office and works in the margin department. Alice DeWitt is an existing customer of Success First but has now decided to open a margin account by purchasing 1,000 shares of EFG, which is traded on NASDAQ. EFG is currently trading at $100 per share. DeWitt makes the initial purchase of EFG at $100 per share for a total purchase price of $100,000. What is the initial margin requirement for DeWitt's purchase of 1,000 shares of EFG at $100 per share? John DoGoode makes this determination using the table below.

[handwritten annotations: = $20,000; $40; 500 shares × stock $/share = purchase price; purchase price; margin requirement; 65% × $20,000 = $13,000; 1,000 × $100 = $100,000; 25% ($100,000) = $25,000; 1,000 × $85 = $85,000; 25% ($85,000) = $21,250; $100 × 1,000 = $100,000; Side calculation = $25,000]

Account: Alice DeWitt

Market Value:	$100,000 (1,000 EFG @ $100)
Debit Balance (Margin Loan from Success First):	$0,000
DeWitt's Equity:	$0,000
Initial Margin:	$0,000
Maintenance Margin:	$25,000

Assume that the price of EFG shares decreases to $85 per share. Must John DoGoode issue a margin call? In other words, has the equity in DeWitt's account fallen

[handwritten: Yes. No]

---

13. Day trading does not occur in a margin account if a long security position is held overnight and sold the next day prior to any new purchase of the same security or if a short security position is held overnight and purchased the next day prior to any new sale of the same security. FINRA Rule 4210(f)(8)(B)(i).

14. If the number of trades is six percent or less of total trades for the five-business-day period, the customer will not be considered a pattern day trader. FINRA Rule 4210(f)(8)(ii).

below the required level of maintenance margin? Does Customer DeWitt have excess margin in her account?

3. Hypothecation

The hypothecation rules are an integral part of the margin regulatory framework because they restrict the broker-dealer's ability to pledge customers' securities in their custody. Sections 8 and 15(c) (2) of the Exchange Act authorize the SEC to adopt hypothecation rules in order to protect customers' funds and securities held by broker-dealers. Section 8 of the Exchange Act states that it is unlawful for any registered broker-dealer, member of a national securities exchange, or broker-dealer who transacts a business in securities through the medium of any member of a national securities exchange to:

> (a) In contravention of such rules and regulations as the Commission shall prescribe ... to hypothecate or arrange for the hypothecation of any securities carried for the account of any customer under circumstances (1) that will permit the commingling of his securities without his written consent with the securities of any other customer, (2) that will permit such securities to be commingled with the securities of any person other than a bona fide customer, or (3) that will permit such securities to be hypothecated, or subjected to any lien or claim of the pledgee, for a sum in excess of the aggregate indebtedness of such customers in respect of such securities.

> (b) To lend or arrange for the lending of any securities carried for the account of any customer without the written consent of such customer or in contravention of such rules and regulations as the Commission shall prescribe for the protection of investors.

Section 15(c) (2) authorizes the SEC to define and prescribe rules to prevent fraudulent acts, such as the unlawful pledging of customers' securities:

> (c) Use of manipulative or deceptive devices; contravention of rules and regulations (2)(A) No broker or dealer shall make use of the mails or any means or instrumentality of interstate commerce to effect any transaction in, or to induce or attempt to induce the purchase or sale of, any security (other than an exempted security or commercial paper, bankers' acceptances, or commercial bills) otherwise than on a national securities exchange of which it is a member, in connection with which such broker or dealer engages in any fraudulent, deceptive, or manipulative act or practice, or makes any fictitious quotation.

Opening a margin account subjects customers to hypothecation of their securities. In other words, the customer's securities are pledged against a loan from the broker-dealer for money to complete a transaction, i.e., to purchase securities. Hypothecation generally arises through margin trading. When a customer trades on margin, any common stock, cash, or securities in its margin account (customer property) can be considered as collateral for the money borrowed to effect securities transactions. In addition, the broker-dealer can borrow or loan securities in the customer's account up to the value of the amount the customer borrowed. The hypothecation rules are designed to regulate the use of customer property as collateral by the broker-dealer to protect the customer from risk of loss.

Before the adoption of the hypothecation rules, broker-dealers entered into agreements with customers that allowed them to commingle customer securities with their own securities. They were also allowed to borrow more against a customer's margin securities than the customer actually owed to the broker-dealer. As discussed in Chapter 2, the broker-dealer business model includes borrowing. Banks or other lenders collateralize loans to broker-dealers by holding a specific lien against the particular securities earmarked for each loan. In addition, lenders may hold general liens against securities in the broker-dealer's possession for the total amount of all of the loans extended to the broker-dealer, a portion of which represents borrowings on the broker-dealer's own securities to finance its proprietary trading activities. General liens were held against all securities deposited as collateral by the broker-dealer, which included customer securities, thus subjecting customers to risk of loss should the broker-dealer experience financial difficulties or become insolvent.

Rules 8c-1 and 15c2-1 were adopted to limit the amount of customers' securities that may be hypothecated and to prohibit hypothecation of customer securities that have been paid for in full without the customer's consent. The proscriptions of Rules 8c-1 and 15c2-1 mirror one another, are designed to work together to apply to all broker-dealers,[15] and prohibit broker-dealers from engaging in the following activities without first obtaining consent from their customers: (1) commingling of securities of different customers as collateral for a loan; (2) commingling a customer's securities with a broker-dealer's own securities under the same pledge; and (3) pledging a customer's securities for more than the customer owes, i.e., the customer's aggregate indebtedness to the broker-dealer. Further, Rule 15c2-1 expressly identifies violation of the hypothecation rules as a "fraudulent, deceptive, or manipulative act or practice."

The SEC has brought many cases for violation of the hypothecation rules, but there have also been a few criminal cases. The following case illustrates a violation of Rule 8c-1 and use of the federal securities laws to bring a criminal case.

United States v. Schwartz
464 F.2d 499 (2d Cir. 1972)

Clarie, District Judge:

The appellant was convicted after a trial by the court of having conspired to violate § 8(c) of the Securities Exchange Act of 1934 (the "Act"), 15 U.S.C. § 78h(c),[16] and

---

15. Not just those that are members of an exchange or who conduct business through members of exchanges as stated in Section 8 of the Exchange Act.

16. [1] 15 U.S.C. § 78h(c) (2012) provides in pertinent part:

It shall be unlawful for any member of a national securities exchange, or any broker or dealer who transacts a business in securities through the medium of any such member, directly or indirectly.... (c) In contravention of such rules and regulations as the Commission

Rule 17 C.F.R. §240.8c-1, which prohibit the unlawful hypothecation of securities by brokers or dealers, who transact a business through a national exchange. The trial court found that appellant had unlawfully caused Armstrong & Co., Inc., a broker-dealer, to hypothecate securities "carried for the account of" its customers, so that said securities were subjected to a lien in excess of the aggregate indebtedness of the customers on such securities. The appellant was sentenced to pay a fine of $2,500 pursuant to §32(a) of the Act, 15 U.S.C. §78ff, and 18 U.S.C. §371. We affirm that conviction.

Armstrong & Co., Inc. (Armstrong) was organized in 1960 by Robert Edens and Bruce Armstrong, and registered with the Securities and Exchange Commission (SEC) as a broker-dealer. Schwartz, an attorney, who had extensive experience in the securities field, acted as counsel for Armstrong which was the underwriter on several stock issuances. It was Schwartz's participation in the underwriting of a stock issuance for Triangle Instrument Co., Inc. (Triangle) that brought about this prosecution. **Appellant was more than simply the firm's legal counsel; he was intimately involved in its business activities, even extending credit by exchanging checks with the firm on occasion, so that it would have needed deposits upon which it could draw.**

Armstrong signed an underwriter's agreement with Triangle in which a Regulation A stock offering became effective September 15, 1961. It provided for the sale of 150,000 shares of Triangle stock at $2 per share, with "an all or nothing" proviso that required all of said shares to be sold within a 45-day period. In the event that this were not accomplished, all funds received from the shares were to be returned to the prospective purchasers without interest, and there would be no further obligation between the underwriter and the company. However, if the shares were sold within the required period, Armstrong was to pay over $230,000 to Triangle, and $70,000 was to be turned over to the underwriter to pay it a commission of 15% ($45,000) with the remaining $25,000 being used to cover expenses for accounting and legal fees.

The trial court found that at least 30,000 shares of stock were sold to individual customers of Armstrong and cash income in excess of $40,000 had been received for these shares. In addition, at least 70,650 shares were sold to brokers, who had not yet paid for them. At the end of the 45-day period, the Triangle issue had not been completely sold. When pressed by Triangle for a closing, Armstrong scheduled November 15, 1961, as the final date. Realizing that Armstrong did not have the $230,000 necessary to effect the closing, the appellant suggested that a loan be obtained from Sterling Factors. Principally through the efforts of defendant Schwartz, an agreement between Armstrong and Sterling was concluded for a loan of $115,000 secured by a pledge of the entire 150,000 shares of the stock with endorsements in blank. This agreement provided for repayment over a 4-week period, and for the release of the

---

shall prescribe for the protection of investors to hypothecate or arrange for the hypothecation of any securities carried for the account of any customer under circumstances ... (3) that will permit such securities to be hypothecated, or subjected to any lien or claim of the pledgee, for a sum in excess of the aggregate indebtedness of such customers in respect of such securities.

shares at the rate of $2 each. It was understood that all shares would be released, when the entire note had been paid.

Either prior to or at the closing, Armstrong paid over $40,000 directly to Triangle. This sum represented moneys which individual customers of Armstrong had paid for their purchase of Triangle stock. Schwartz was fully aware before the Sterling loan had been consummated, that Armstrong had sold a very substantial number of shares of this stock to customers other than broker-dealers, and that these stock customers had paid Armstrong in full.

Notwithstanding the Sterling loan, on November 15, the closing date, Armstrong was still short approximately $30,000 of the total sum due Triangle. Only by means of a loan subsequently negotiated by an officer of Armstrong was the necessary money finally obtained and the closing effected the following day. The trial court concluded that Schwartz's action in pledging all the shares of Triangle stock to Sterling Factors exposed the customers of Armstrong, who had paid full value for their shares of Triangle stock, to the risk that they might not receive the same, if Armstrong defaulted. In such event, they would be required to rely upon the general credit of Armstrong for the return of their money.[17]

Appellant's Claims

Appellant challenges his conviction on several grounds: ... (2) that the phrase "transacts a business" is so indefinite as to render 15 U.S.C. § 78h void for vagueness; (3) that the hypothecated securities were not "carried for the account of" Armstrong customers as required for a violation of 15 U.S.C. § 78h(c); (4) that the Government failed to establish the element of intent necessary for a conviction under § 32(a) of the Act, 15 U.S.C. § 78ff (a); ...

DISCUSSION OF ISSUES

* * *

Vagueness

The appellant's next contention is that § 8(c) of the Act is void for vagueness. He challenges primarily the application to his case of the jurisdictional phrase, "any broker or dealer who *transacts a business* in securities through the medium of any such member (of a national securities exchange)." We conclude that the trial court's construction of this term was proper, and that the phrase is sufficiently clear to satisfy due process requirements.

Appellant points out that that phrase, "transacts a business," was previously construed in a 1939 Federal Reserve Board decision, so as to bring within the purview

---

17. [4] Although not relevant to the legal charge against appellant, Armstrong defaulted on the payments to Sterling. Sterling released only some 38,000 shares against payments received from Armstrong. Finally, an arrangement was effected whereby Armstrong returned 25,000 shares of unsold Triangle stock to Triangle, which then paid $35,000 to Sterling in order to get release of the remaining 112,000 shares so that they could be distributed to the purchasers who had paid for them. (internal citation omitted)

of Regulation T any broker-dealer who conducted approximately 10% of its total securities business through the medium of members of a national securities exchange.[18] He argues that any subsequent construction of this phrase should limit the reach of the statute to those broker-dealers showing at least this 10% minimal factor. Since Armstrong's gross business in this area amounted to only 1% or less of its total transactions, appellant contends that § 8(c) of the Act is not applicable to him.

The trial court found that although Armstrong dealt primarily with over-the-counter securities, it regularly handled customers' transactions in securities listed on the major stock exchanges and transacted a modest business in such securities through members of the national securities exchanges. Although the business was only 1% or less, it was nevertheless a valued and material part of its overall business activities.

The trial court correctly concluded that Congress intended § 8(c) to apply to any broker or dealer, who transacted more than a trivial or *de minimis* business in securities through the medium of members of national securities exchanges. The very purpose of this Act was to provide remedial legislation, and it should be construed broadly, (citations omitted) in order to effect the congressional purpose of "insur(ing) the maintenance of fair and honest markets." 15 U.S.C. § 78b. (Citations omitted).

For the appellant's vagueness claim to be persuasive, it would have to meet the standards which this Court recently set out for use in evaluating a claim of statutory vagueness:

The applicable test is whether the language conveys 'sufficiently definite warning as to the proscribed conduct when measured by common understanding and practices.' *United States v. Petrillo*, 332 U.S. 1, 8, 67 S.Ct. 1538, 91 L.Ed. 1877 (1947). *See United States v. 16,179 Molso Italian .22 Caliber Winless Derringer Convertible Starter Guns*, 443 F.2d 463, 466 (2 Cir. 1971) (cert. denied, 404 U.S. 983, 92 S.Ct. 447, 30 L.Ed.2d 367 (1971)). A statute violates due process if 'men of common intelligence must necessarily guess at its meaning and differ as to its application.' *Connally v. General Construction Co.*, 269 U.S. 385, 391, 46 S.Ct. 126, 70 L.Ed. 322 (1926). Even in criminal cases, however, where the vagueness standard is most stringently applied, the statute must only present 'ascertainable standard(s) of guilt.' *Winters v. People of State of New York*, 333 U.S. 507, 515, 68 S.Ct. 665, 92 L.Ed. 840 (1948). As the Supreme Court stated in *Petrillo*:

> That there may be marginal cases in which it is difficult to determine the side of the line on which a particular fact situation falls is no sufficient reason to hold the language too ambiguous to define a criminal offense…. The Constitution does not require impossible standards. 332 U.S. at 7, 67 S.Ct. 1538. *United States v. Deutsch*, 451 F.2d 98, 113–114, (2d Cir. 1971), cert. denied 404 U.S. 1019, 92 S.Ct. 682, 30 L.Ed.2d 667 (1972).

---

18. [9] 25 Fed. Res. Bul. 961 (1939). Regulation T, 12 C.F.R. §§ 220.1 et seq., promulgated by the Federal Reserve Board pursuant to § 7(c) of the Act, 15 U.S.C. § 78g(c), deals with credit extensions by brokers and dealers. The phrase, "who transacts a business in securities through the medium of any such member (of a national securities exchange)" was removed from § 7(c) in a 1968 amendment.

The statutory phrase challenged here provides adequate notice to men of common intelligence as to its meaning and application. The term in question does not require that a substantial or principal part of the broker's business be conducted through members of the national securities exchanges, but only an ongoing regular portion thereof. The claim of statutory vagueness is therefore without merit.

Hypothecation of Stock

Appellant next contends that the Government has failed to prove an unlawful hypothecation within the purview of 15 U.S.C. §78h(c). He argues that the securities here were not "carried for the account of any customer" at the time of the pledge to Sterling Factors, and that therefore no hypothecation occurred.

Section 78h(c) and Rule 8c-1 proscribe the hypothecation of "securities carried for the account of any customer," when that hypothecation subjects those securities to any lien or claim of the pledgee for a sum in excess of the aggregate indebtedness of the customers in respect to such securities. Rule 8c-1 (b) (2) sets forth three separate definitions of the trade term, "securities carried for the account of any customer." The trial court found that each of these definitions was satisfied. Since we find that the transaction at bar satisfies at least the first definition, we need not consider the others.

Said Rule 8c-1(b) (2) provides:

"The term 'securities carried for the account of any customer' shall be deemed to mean:

"(i) Securities received by or on behalf of such member, broker or dealer for the account of any customer."

The thrust of the appellant's claims on this issue, is that these securities were not carried for the account of any customer, because at the time Triangle stock was pledged to Sterling, some of the stock issue was still unsold and some had not yet been paid for. He argues that if the securities were being carried by Armstrong for its customers at the time of the hypothecation, then Armstrong was purchasing these securities not yet sold to and paid for by the public, for its own account subject to the lien of Sterling. Appellant contends that under Regulation A, 17 C.F.R. §§230, 251 et seq., Armstrong was barred from taking down stock in its own name, until the entire stock issue was fully sold and paid for, by the funds of the public subscribers. In appellant's view, Armstrong cannot be said to have carried Triangle securities for the account of its customers at the time of the hypothecation; otherwise, Armstrong would have been in violation of Regulation A. Such an argument is fallacious, for even if the transaction in question did violate Regulation A, appellant cannot negatively explain away and attempt to justify the hypothecation violation, by pointing also to a Regulation A violation. The hypothecation here subjected the customers, who had paid for their stock, to precisely the kind of risk from which the statute and rule were intended to protect them. These securities which had been sold and paid for were in fact carried for the accounts of customers at the time of the pledge, within the meaning of the statute and rule.

Appellant also claims that Armstrong never "received" the shares, because Armstrong had transferred its interest in the Triangle shares to its pledgee, Sterling, on the day prior to issuance of the stock, when Armstrong delivered to Sterling stock powers signed in blank. The trial court concluded that "(i)f subsection (b) (2) (i) is in simplicity interpreted to include any security bought and paid for by a customer, that is so far 'received' by the broker that he is able to pledge it, then there is no problem in directly applying the statute" and rule to the hypothecation here.[19] Such a construction comports with the expressed Congressional intent to safeguard investors from irresponsible brokerage practices.[20] *Cf.* SEC v. Joiner Corp., 320 U.S. 344, 350–351, 64 S.Ct. 120, 88 L.Ed. 88 (1943).[21]

* * *

We have considered appellant's other contentions and find them without merit. The judgment of conviction is affirmed.

———

FINRA also has adopted rules that govern the lending and borrowing of customer securities in margin accounts. FINRA Rule 4330 prescribes the permissible use of customer securities held in margin accounts. Like the hypothecation rules, FINRA Rule 4330 requires the broker-dealer to obtain a customer's written authorization prior to lending securities that are held on margin for a customer and that are eligible to be pledged or loaned. However, the rule allows the broker-dealer to use a single customer-signed margin agreement or loan consent instead of requiring two separate agreements; If a single agreement is used, it must contain a legend in bold typeface placed directly above the signature line that states substantially that the customer, by

---

19. [12] Ruling on Motion to Dismiss the Indictment, at 10 (October 2, 1970). Judge Dooling also pointed out that:

> Armstrong's possession and control of the 150,000 shares was momentary and essentially notional or 'constructive' receipt and possession of the stock incident to and implicit in the Meadowbrook (the transfer agent)-Triangle delivery at Armstrong's behest of the certificates and the 'stock powers' to Sterling in satisfaction of Armstrong's obligation to do so created by Sterling's delivery of the $115,000 to Meadowbrook-Triangle.

Id. at 7.

20. [13] The Senate Report on the Securities Exchange Act of 1934 pointed out that:

> Severe financial losses have been sustained by investors from time to time in cases where a broker pledged his customers' securities for loans in excess of the aggregate indebtedness due him in respect of such securities, or pledged them along with his own securities to finance his private speculative commitments."

SEN. REP. No.792, 73rd Cong., 2d Sess. (1934), at 11. The House Report on the Act stated that:

> A broker is forbidden ... to pledge customers' securities ... under circumstances that will subject customers' securities to a lien in excess of the aggregate indebtedness of the customers. This means that a broker cannot risk the securities of his customers to finance his own speculative operations.

H.R. REP. No. 1383, 73rd Cong., 2d Sess. (1934), at 20.

21. [14] "[C]ourts will construe the details of an act in conformity with its dominating general purpose, will read text in the light of context and will interpret the text so far as the meaning of the words fairly permits so as to carry out in particular cases the generally expressed legislative policy." 320 U.S. at 350–351.

signing the agreement, acknowledges that the customer's securities may be loaned to
the broker-dealer or to others. Paragraph (b) of Rule 4330 specifies requirements for
borrowing customers' fully paid or excess margin securities. With respect to such securities carried for the account of a customer, a broker-dealer must comply with the
requirements of Rule 15c3-3 (140% limit of the value of excess margin securities.
See rehypothecation discussion in item 4 below), provide required notices to customers
under Section 15(e)[22] of the Exchange Act, and notify FINRA at least 30 days prior
to engaging in such transactions. In addition, the broker-dealer must conduct a reasonable investigation to determine whether it is suitable for the customer to enter
into transactions that involve securities loans. A reasonable investigation would
include, but is not limited to, determining the customer's financial situation and
needs, tax status, investment objectives, investment time horizon, liquidity needs,
and risk tolerance. This determination must be made prior to the customer entering
into the first securities lending transaction. The broker-dealer must also disclose in
writing to its customer that the protections of SIPC may not be available in the event
that the broker-dealer experiences financial difficulties or becomes insolvent. In addition, the customer must receive in writing information about the potential risks
involved in engaging in securities loan transactions including loss of voting rights,
limitations on the customer's right to sell loaned securities, and the broker-dealer's
right to liquidate such transactions in the event of broker-dealer insolvency.[23]

4. Rehypothecation

A broker-dealer engages in rehypothecation by reusing customer-pledged collateral
to secure its own trades and borrowings. In essence, the broker-dealer uses the same
collateral to support two separate borrowing transactions—the broker-dealer's margin
loan to its customer and loans made to the broker-dealer from other lenders. This is
obviously a risky practice, but broker-dealer rehypothecation activities are regulated
under the hypothecation rules as well as under Rule 15c3-3, which prohibits a broker-
dealer from rehypothecating an amount of a customer's collateral in excess of 140 percent of the customer's outstanding margin debt. For example, if a customer has
purchased $1,000 of securities on margin, the broker-dealer is required to collect 50
percent or $500 of the purchase price from the customer under Reg T. The broker-
dealer is allowed to rehypothecate up to 140 percent of the collateral, i.e., $700 ($500
x 140%). In effect, the $500 collateral used to collateralize the customer's margin loan
is also used by the broker-dealer to borrow up to $700 to fund operations. Rehypoth-
ecation is an inexpensive source of financing for the broker-dealer and often results in

---

22. Section 15(e) of the Exchange Act requires broker-dealers to provide notice to its customers
that they may elect not to allow their fully paid securities to be used in connection with short sales.
If a broker- dealer uses a customer's securities in connection with short sales, it must provide notice
to its customer that the broker-dealer may receive compensation in connection with lending the customer's securities.

23. *See also* Securities Loans and Borrowings, FINRA Rule 4314, which sets forth requirements
for securities lending and borrowings between broker-dealers and broker-dealers and non-FINRA
member firms.

lower margin interest rates for the customer. Thus, both parties benefit. However, because the collateral is used in two separate borrowing transactions, the customer has a much higher risk of losing the securities should the broker-dealer experience financial difficulties or become insolvent. The following case illustrates the risk of loss to customers, when the hypothecation rules and limits on rehypothecation are circumvented. It also notes a common practice among prime brokers of increasing leverage by transacting with entities outside of the U.S. who are not subject to the hypothecation rules and the limits of Rule 15c3-3. It is noteworthy that plaintiffs allege that violation of the hypothecation rules and Rule 15c3-3 resulted in violation of 10(b) and Rule 10b-5 of the Exchange Act, one of the antifraud provisions of the federal securities laws.

Capital Management Select Fund Ltd. v. Bennett

680 F.3d 214 (2012)

BACKGROUND

On an appeal from a grant of a motion to dismiss, we review *de novo* the decision of the district court. *See Staehr v. Hartford Fin. Servs. Group,* 547 F.3d 406, 424 (2d Cir.2008). We construe the complaint liberally, accepting all factual allegations in the complaint as true, and drawing all reasonable inferences in the plaintiff's favor. *Chambers v. Time Warner, Inc.,* 282 F.3d 147, 152 (2d Cir.2002).

a) *The Parties and Their Businesses*

Capital Management Select Fund Limited and other named appellants[24] are investment companies, which, along with members of the putative class, held assets in securities brokerage accounts with RCM. RCM is one of three principal operating subsidiaries of the now-bankrupt Refco, a publicly traded holding company that,

---

24. [2] This appeal arises from three separate actions that were consolidated at the pretrial phase: *VR Glob. Partners, L.P. v. Bennett,* No. 07 Civ. 8686, 2007 WL 4837764 (S.D.N.Y. filed Oct. 9, 2007) (the "VR Action"); *Capital Mgmt Select Fund Ltd. v. Bennett,* No. 07 Civ. 8688, 2007 WL 4837768 (S.D.N.Y. filed Oct. 9, 2007) (the "Capital Management Action"); and *RCM I,* 2007 WL 2694469 (S.D.N.Y. Sept. 13, 2007) (the "Class Action"). Lead plaintiffs in the original Class Action are Global Management Worldwide Ltd., Arbat Equity Arbitrage Fund Ltd., and Russian Investors Securities Ltd. All three lead plaintiffs in the Class Action are commonly controlled investment funds. Plaintiffs in the VR Action are VR Global Partners, L.P., Paton Holdings Ltd., VR Capital Group Ltd., and VR Argentina Recovery Fund, Ltd. (collectively "VR Plaintiffs"). In their complaint, VR Plaintiffs describe themselves as "private investment funds," each of which operates as either a limited liability partnership or limited liability company registered in Grand Cayman. Plaintiffs in the Capital Management Action are Capital Management Select Fund Ltd., Investment & Development Finance Corporation, and IDC Financial S.A. Capital Management is an investment company incorporated under the laws of the Bahamas. Investment & Development Finance is an investment company incorporated under the laws of the British Virgin Islands. IDC Financial is an investment company incorporated under the laws of Panama, RCM operated as a securities and foreign exchange broker that traded in over-the-counter derivatives and other financial products on behalf of its clients. Although RCM was organized under the laws of Bermuda and represented itself as a Bermuda corporation, it operated from New York at all relevant times. These operations were under the leadership of, and through a sales force of account officers and brokers employed by, its affiliated corporation, Refco Securities, LLC, ("RSL"), a wholly-owned subsidiary of Refco that operated as a U.S.-based broker-dealer registered with the SEC.

through its operating subsidiaries, provided trading, prime brokerage, and other exchange services to traders and investors in the fixed income and foreign exchange markets. Appellees are various former officers and directors of Refco and/or its affiliates (the "Refco Officer Defendants"), and Refco's former auditor, Grant Thornton, LLP.

b) *Brokerage Account Customer Agreements*

RCM Customers held securities and other assets in non-discretionary securities brokerage accounts with RCM pursuant to a standard form "Securities Account Customer Agreement" with RCM and RSL (the "Customer Agreement"). RCM Customers' securities and other property deposited in their accounts were not segregated but were commingled in a fungible pool. As a result, no particular security or securities could be identified as being held for any particular customer. Such a practice is common in the brokerage industry. *See Levitin v. PaineWebber, Inc.,* 159 F.3d 698, 701 (2d Cir.1998) ("Customer accounts with brokers are generally not segregated, *e.g.* in trust accounts. Rather, they are part of the general cash reserves of the broker."); U.C.C. §8–503 cmt. 1 ("[S]ecurities intermediaries generally do not segregate securities in such fashion that one could identify particular securities as the ones held for customers."); *Adoption of Rule 15c3-2 Under the Securities Exchange Act of 1934,* Exchange Act Release No. 34–7325, 1964 WL 68010, at *1 (1964) ("[W]hen [customers of broker-dealers] leave free credit balances with a broker-dealer the funds generally are not segregated and held for the customer, but are commingled with other assets of the broker-dealer and used in the operation of the business.").[25]

The Customer Agreement included a margin provision that permitted RCM Customers to finance their investment transactions by posting securities and other acceptable property held in their accounts as collateral for margin loans extended by RCM. Under the margin provision, RCM, upon extending a margin loan to a customer, had the right to use or "rehypothecate"[26] the customer's account securities and other property for RCM's own financing purposes. For example, RCM might pledge customers' securities as collateral for its own bank loans or sell the securities pursuant to repurchase agreements ("repos").[27] The parties dispute whether the re-

---

25. [3] We note that although Rule 15c3-does not require that customer funds be segregated and held for each customer, that rule was superseded in part by Rule 15c3-3. Rule 15c3-3 puts additional requirements on broker-dealers with regard to customers' securities, cash, and cash realized by the broker through the use of customer securities. In particular, that rule establishes standards for possession or control of fully-paid securities, requires specified levels of reserves that must be held by the broker-dealer with respect to customer cash and securities, and requires that those reserves be held in a separate account for the benefit of its customers. *See* Exchange Act Release No. 9856, 37 Fed. Reg. 25224 (Nov. 29, 1972).

26. [4] Rehypothecation technically refers to a broker's re-pledging of securities held in its customer's margin account as collateral for a bank loan. Similarly, a broker may sell the securities through a repurchase agreement, which is functionally equivalent to a secured loan.... Hereinafter we will refer to rehypothecation in the general sense—*i.e.,* a broker's use and/or pledging of its customer's margin account securities to obtain financing for its own transactions.

27. [5] A repurchase agreement is an agreement involving the simultaneous sale and future repurchase of an asset. In a typical repurchase agreement, the original seller buys back the asset at the

hypothecation rights were limited to securities serving as collateral or whether they also included securities that were excess collateral. We discuss this dispute, *infra.*

We briefly provide a generic background. From an ex ante perspective, such margin provisions provide distinct, but related, economic benefits to both the brokerage and its customers. For the customers, the margin provision provides the ability to invest on a leveraged basis and thereby earn amplified returns on their investment capital. As for the brokerage, the ability to rehypothecate its customers' securities presents, among other things, an additional and inexpensive source of secured financing. *See* Michelle Price, *Picking over the Lehman Carcass — Asset Recovery,* Banker, Dec. 1, 2008, *available at* 2008 WLNR 24064913 ("[Without rehypothecation rights] the prime broker would have to use its unsecured credit facilities, the cost of which is currently in the region of 225 to 300 basis points above that of secured credit.").

While these types of margin provisions provide economic benefits to both parties, like any creditor-debtor arrangement they also create counterparty risks. The brokerage bears the risk that its customers default on margin loans that could become undersecured due, for example, to a precipitous decline in the value of the posted collateral. Likewise, of course, the customers face the possibility that the brokerage, having rehypothecated its customers' securities, fails, making it unable to return customer securities after those customers meet their margin debt obligations.

Counterparty risks associated with margin financing have long been recognized by industry participants and regulators alike. In the United States, for example, margin financing has been subject to federal[28] and state[29] regulation, and, even longer still, to self-imposed limitations by brokers and self-regulating organizations.[30] In general, margin restrictions attempt to reduce the counterparty risk associated with margin financing by limiting the types of securities that can be posted by an investor as collateral for a margin loan and limiting the amounts that can be borrowed against that collateral.[31]

---

same price at which he sold it, with the original seller paying the original buyer interest on the implicit loan created by the transaction. *See In re Comark*, 124 B.R. 806, 809 n. 4 (Bankr. C.D. Cal. 1991).

28. [6] Federal regulation of margin financing for securities purchases was introduced in the 1913 Federal Reserve Act. *See* Board of Governors of the Federal Reserve System, *A Review and Evaluation of Federal Margin Regulations* 45 (1984). After the 1929 stock market crash, Congress imposed sweeping regulation of margin financing under the Exchange Act, 15 U.S.C. §§ 78a–78hh-1. Statutory authority for regulating margin financing was granted under Section 7 of the Act. *See id.* § 78g.

29. [7] State regulation of margin financing generally arises under Article 8 of the Uniform Commercial Code.

30. [8] The New York Stock Exchange ("NYSE") first established margin restrictions for exchange members in 1913 when it required its members to impose margin levels that were "proper and adequate." *See* Board of Governors of the Federal Reserve System, *supra* note 34, at 45. The NYSE currently restricts customer margin levels under NYSE Rule 431 which, *inter alia*, limits the amount of credit that can be used by a customer to purchase securities. *See* NYSE Rule 431.

31. [9] *See, e.g.,* Federal Reserve Board Regulation T, 12 C.F.R. § 200.1 *et seq.* (imposing initial and maintenance margin requirements on investors purchasing securities on margin); *see also* Federal Reserve Board Regulation U, 12 C.F.R. § 221.1 *et seq.* (similar margin restrictions applicable to banks

Similarly, at least in the United States, brokers' rehypothecation activities have long been restricted by federal[32] and state law,[33] and by rules promulgated by the principal stock exchanges.[34] These restrictions generally limit a broker's ability to commingle its customers' securities without their consent, and limit a broker's rehypothecation rights with respect to a customer's "excess margin securities" *i.e.*, securities not deemed collateral to secure a customer's outstanding margin debt, and "fully-paid securities," *i.e.*, securities in a cash account for which full payment has been made.[35]

The upshot of these restrictions is that in the United States, brokers and investors alike are limited in the amount of leverage that is available to amplify returns. However, since the development of globalized capital and credit markets, investors have sought to avoid these limitations by seeking unrestricted margin financing through, among other sources, unregulated offshore entities. *See, e.g., Metro-Goldwyn-Mayer, Inc. v. Transamerica Corp.,* 303 F.Supp. 1354 (S.D.N.Y.1969) (leveraged buyout of Metro–Goldwyn–Mayer financed through the Eurodollar market, thus avoiding U.S. margin restrictions); Martin Lipton, *Some Recent Innovations to Avoid the Margin Regulations,* 46 N.Y.U. L.Rev. 1 (1971). In recent years, U.S.-based broker-dealers have satisfied investor demand for unrestricted margin financing by providing financing to institutional investors—*e.g.,* hedge funds—through, *inter alia,* unregulated foreign affiliates that are not subject to U.S. margin or rehypothecation restrictions. *See* Noah Melnick et al., *Prime Broker Insolvency Risk,* Hedge Fund J., Nov. 2008 ("US prime brokers commonly rely on [foreign] unregulated affiliates for margin lending or securities; Sherri Venokur & Richard Bernstein, *Protecting Collateral against Bank Insolvency Risk—Part I,* Sept. 8, 2008, at 1 ("U.S. registered broker-dealers enter into derivatives transactions through their unregulated affiliates in order to reduce capital reserve requirements but also to be able to use counterparty collateral."); Roel C. Campos, SEC Comm'r, Remarks before the SIA Hedge Funds & Alternative Investments Conference (June 14, 2006) (noting that certain hedge fund financing is generally booked through foreign, unregulated affiliates).

In the instant case, RCM held itself out as, and the record indicates that at least some of the RCM Customers understood it to be, an unregulated offshore broker.

---

and other lenders); Federal Reserve Board Regulation X, 12 C.F.R. §224.1 *et seq.,* (similar margin restrictions applicable to margin loans not explicitly covered by other regulations).

32. [10] The SEC first restricted brokers' rehypothecation rights with the adoption of Rule 8c-1, 17 C.F.R. §240.8c-1, and Rule 15c2-1, 17 C.F.R. §240.15c2-1, in 1940. In general, these rules prohibit the following activities without first obtaining consent from the customer: (i) commingling of the securities of different customers as collateral for a loan; (ii) commingling a customer's securities with its own under the same pledge; and (iii) pledging a customer's securities for more than the customer owes. *See Statement of Commission Issued in Connection with the Adoption of Rules X-8C-1 and X-15-C2-1,* Exchange Act Release No. 2690, 11 Fed. Reg. 10982 (Nov. 15, 1940)

33. [11] *See* Report of Special Study of Securities Markets of the Securities and Exchange Commission, H.R. Doc. No. 88-95, pt. 1, at 406 (1963) (listing statutory hypothecation restrictions under the laws of Iowa, Michigan, Nebraska, and New York).

34. [12] *Id.* at 405–07 (listing rehypothecation restriction rules of the various exchanges).

35. [13] *See, e.g.,* SEC Rule 15c3-3, 17 C.F.R. §240.15c3-3 (prohibiting a broker from rehypothecating an amount of customer's collateral in excess of 140 percent of the customer's outstanding margin debt).

c) *The Lawsuit*

The event giving rise to this action is the collapse of Refco, RCM's now-bankrupt parent corporation. On October 20, 2005, a little more than two months after issuing an initial public offering of its stock, Refco announced a previously undisclosed $430 million uncollectible receivable and disavowed its financial statements for the previous three years. The uncollectible receivable stemmed, in part, from losses suffered by Refco and several of its account holders during the late 1990s. Rather than disclose its losses to the public and its investors at that time, Refco's management devised and implemented a "round robin" loan scheme to conceal the losses. The first part of this scheme involved Refco transferring its uncollectible receivables to the books of Refco Group Holdings, Inc. ("RGHI"), an entity owned and controlled by appellee-defendant Phillip R. Bennett, Refco's then-President, CEO, and Chairman. Then, in order to mask the magnitude and related-party nature of the RGHI receivable, a Refco entity (alleged by plaintiffs typically to be RCM) would extend loans to multiple unrelated third parties that would in turn lend the funds to RGHI to pay down the uncollectible receivables. In this manner, Refco effectively eliminated the uncollectible related-party receivable from its books just prior to each relevant financial period but would unwind the loans shortly thereafter. The transactions allegedly took place over the course of six years, between 1998 and 2004, and were never disclosed in Refco's public securities filings. By 2004, the RGHI receivable had grown to an amount alleged to be in excess of $1 billion. Prior to Refco's 2005 disclosure, beginning in late 2003, THL, a private equity investment fund that focuses on the acquisition of equity stakes in mid-to-large capitalization companies, began exploring investment opportunities in Refco, and ultimately completed a leveraged buyout in August 2004.

Following Refco's disclosure of its $430 million uncollectible receivable, customers holding accounts with RCM, including appellants, attempted to withdraw their assets from RCM. This began the proverbial "run on the bank," and, on October 13, 2005, Refco announced a unilateral 15-day moratorium on all RCM trading activities. On October 17, 2005, Refco, along with RCM and several other Refco affiliates, filed for Chapter 11 bankruptcy protection in the Southern District of New York. In a December 30, 2005 bankruptcy filing, RCM disclosed that it owed its customers approximately $4.16 billion, while holding only $1.905 billion in assets.

Along with a host of other plaintiffs who brought actions in the wake of Refco's collapse, on January 26, 2006, plaintiff-appellant Global Management Worldwide Limited, an investment fund organized under the laws of Bermuda, filed a putative class action on behalf of all brokerage customers of RCM who held securities with RCM and/or RSL between October 17, 2000 and October 17, 2005. On September 5, 2006, Global Management Worldwide filed a Consolidated Amended Class Action Complaint, in which Arbat Equity Arbitrage Fund Limited and Russian Investors Securities Limited, both "commonly controlled investment funds," were added as Co–Lead Plaintiffs of the putative class. The amended complaint named appellees as defendants. The complaint alleges that Refco's corporate officers caused RCM to improperly sell or lend securities and other assets from RCM Customers' trading accounts to various Refco affiliates in order to fund Refco's operations. The complaint further alleges that this practice was approved by, and well known to, all members of Refco senior management.

On September 13, 2007, the district court dismissed the putative class action suit for plaintiffs' failure to allege deceptive conduct. However, it granted plaintiffs leave to replead as to certain defendants ... On October 9, 2007, two separate groups of plaintiffs—one group associated with investment fund VR Global Partners, L.P., ("VR Plaintiffs"), and a second group associated with investment fund Capital Management Select Fund Ltd. ("CM Plaintiffs")—filed individual actions based on allegations similar to those raised in the putative class action complaint. Thereafter, on November 20, 2007, the district court consolidated all three actions for pretrial purposes, subsequent to which the lead plaintiffs in the putative class action filed a Second Amended Complaint.

In the consolidated action, all plaintiffs alleged violations of Sections 10(b) and 20(a) of the Exchange Act and Rule 10b-5 against all Refco Officer Defendants, and violations of Rule 10b–16 against all Refco Officer Defendants who, together with RCM and Refco, allegedly extended margin credit to RCM Customers without adequately disclosing RCM's use of Customer securities. 15 U.S.C. §§ 78j(b), 78*l* (Sections 10(b) and 20(a) of the Exchange Act); 17 C.F.R. §§ 240.10b-5, 10b-16 (Rules 10b-5 and 10b-16). In addition, VR Plaintiffs alleged violations of Section 10(b) and Rule 10b-5 as against Grant Thornton.

On August 28, 2008, the district court granted motions to dismiss filed by various Officer Defendants and Grant Thornton.... As a separate ground for dismissal, the court ruled that plaintiffs failed to adequately plead deceptive conduct through any affirmative act or misrepresentation, breach of fiduciary duty, or any other manner. *Id.* at 181–94.

Finally, as to RCM Customers' Section 20(a) claims, the court concluded that because plaintiffs could not bring a claim against any defendant for a primary violation of Section 10(b) and Rules 10b-5 and 10b-16, plaintiffs necessarily lacked standing to bring a controlling person action under Section 20(a). *Id.* at 195.

DISCUSSION

RCM Customers seek to recover under Section 10(b) of the Exchange Act.... RCM Customers assert that they were deceived by, *inter alia,* the terms of the Customer Agreement and RCM's written Trade Confirmations, RCM's written account statements, and oral representations by certain appellees.

a) *Section 10(b)*

We turn first to Section 10(b), which makes it unlawful to "use or employ, in connection with the purchase or sale of any security ... any manipulative or deceptive device or contrivance in contravention of such rules and regulations as the Commission may prescribe." The elements of a Section 10(b) claim are familiar to all federal courts. A plaintiff claiming fraud must allege scienter, "a mental state embracing intent to deceive, manipulate, or defraud," *Tellabs, Inc. v. Makor Issues & Rights, Ltd.,* 551 U.S. 308, 319, 127 S.Ct. 2499, 168 L.Ed.2d 179 (2007) (quoting

Ernst & Ernst v. Hochfelder, 425 U.S. 185, 193 n. 12, 96 S.Ct. 1375, 47 L.Ed.2d 668 (1976)), and must "state with particularity facts giving rise to a strong inference that the defendant acted with the required state of mind." A "strong inference of scienter" is one that is "more than merely 'reasonable' or 'permissible'—it must be cogent and compelling, thus strong in light of other explanations." *Tellabs,* 551 U.S. at 323–24, 127 S.Ct. 2499. This strong inference of scienter can be established by alleging either "(1) that defendants had the motive and opportunity to commit fraud, or (2) strong circumstantial evidence of conscious misbehavior or recklessness." *ECA & Local 134 IBEW Joint Pension Trust of Chi. v. JP Morgan Chase Co.,* 553 F.3d 187, 198 (2d Cir.2009).

* * *

Private actions may succeed under Section 10(b) if there are particularized allegations that the contract itself was a misrepresentation, *i.e.,* the plaintiff's loss was caused by reliance upon the defendant's specific promise to perform particular acts while never intending to perform those acts. *See Wharf (Holdings) Ltd. v. United Int'l Holdings, Inc.,* 532 U.S. 588, 121 S.Ct. 1776, 149 L.Ed.2d 845 (2001)

* * *

In the present case, there are no particularized allegations of fact supporting such an inference of deceptive intent at the time of execution of the Customer Agreements. Therefore, the requisite intent must be inferred, if at all, from the Customer Agreement itself and the nature of the alleged breach.

b) *The Customer Agreement as a Misrepresentation*

RCM Customers claim that they were deceived into believing that their securities and other assets would be safeguarded, and, in particular, that RCM would not rehypothecate excess margin or fully-paid securities. They allege that, in fact, RCM routinely rehypothecated all of its customers' securities, regardless of the customers' outstanding margin debt, and did so from the start of each customer's account. The allegations as to RCM's conduct are sufficient to satisfy the element of intent at the time of contract formation. The crux of the issue, therefore, is whether RCM's rehypothecation of securities even when they were not deemed collateral was so inconsistent with the provisions of the Customer Agreement that the Agreement was itself a deception.[36]

Section B of the Customer Agreement establishes the terms by which RCM would extend margin financing to RCM Customers, and provides in relevant part:

B. MARGIN

This Margin section applies in the event [RCM] finances any of your Transactions from time-to-time in Financial Instruments.

---

36. [15] There is no issue regarding the financial sophistication of the RCM Customers. They are investment funds with access to the finest advisory resources. Indeed, all plaintiffs have alleged that, from the outset, they knew of, and were sensitive to, the counterparty risk associated with a brokerdealers rehypothecation of its customers' securities

1. *Security Interest.* [RCM] reserves the right to require the deposit or maintenance of collateral (consisting of cash, United States government obligations or such other marketable securities or other property which may be acceptable to [RCM]) to secure performance of your obligations to [RCM].... To secure your obligations under Transactions entered into pursuant to this Agreement, you hereby grant to [RCM] and its affiliates (collectively, "Refco Entities") a first priority, perfected security interest in all of your cash, securities and other property (whether held individually or jointly with others) and the proceeds thereof from time-to-time in the possession or under the control of such Refco Entities, whether or not such cash, securities and other property were deposited with such Refco Entities.

2. *Rights and Use of Margin.* [RCM] shall have the right to loan, pledge, hypothecate or otherwise use or dispose of such cash, securities and other property free from any claim or right, until settlement in full of all Transactions entered into pursuant to this Agreement. [RCM's] sole obligation shall be to return to you such cash, like amounts of similar cash, securities and other property (or the cash value thereof in the event of any liquidation of collateral) to the extent they are not deemed to be collateral to secure Transactions entered into pursuant to this Agreement with any Refco Entities or have not been applied against obligations owing by you to Refco Entities, whether as a result of the liquidation of positions and any Transactions entered into pursuant to this Agreement or otherwise.

Section B.1 states that upon RCM's extension of margin financing to a customer—even a dime—RCM would obtain a "first priority, perfected security interest in all of [RCM Customers'] cash, securities and other property (whether held individually or jointly with others) and the proceeds thereof." Section B.1 also gave RCM the right to demand additional collateral in the event that a customer's collateral became insufficient to secure the customer's outstanding margin debt—if, for example, the value of the customer's securities collateral decreased in value such that RCM's margin loan was under-secured.

In addition, Section B.2 states that, if a customer's securities are no longer deemed collateral to secure the customer's outstanding margin debt, RCM was obligated to "return" such securities to the customer. It is evident that the promised "return" did not contemplate either securities or their value being returned to the actual possession of the RCM Customers. Margin accounts move up or down with both the buying and selling by the customer and the price movements of the collateral. The constant transfer of collateral back and forth between accounts in RCM's name or a customer's name would have imposed administrative costs on all parties, and no one argues that such constant transfers were required by the Customer Agreement. Moreover, all of the RCM Customers had to have been aware that, if RCM was not asking for more collateral, some of their securities were probably excess collateral. However, there is no allegation or indication that any RCM Customer ever noticed or complained about the lack of back-and-forth transfers.

In context, therefore, "return" must mean that, with respect to securities not deemed to be collateral, the customer could demand their return from the fungible pool. Moreover, in the case of a requested "return," RCM had the option of transferring physical securities or the "cash value thereof in the event of any liquidation of collateral." Thus, RCM, after rehypothecating all its customers' securities, could have satisfied a demand for "return" of excess securities by paying their cash value in lieu of the actual securities.

On review of the Customer Agreement, we conclude that it unambiguously warned the RCM Customers that RCM intended to exercise full rehypothecation rights as to the customers' excess margin securities.

Stripped of verbiage not pertinent to this dispute and substituting a crude and colloquial description for the specified collateral, Sections B.1 and 2 read:

B. *Margin*

This Margin section applies in the event [RCM] finances any of your Transactions ... in [your account].

1. *Security Interest.* [RCM] reserves the right to require ... [appropriate stuff as] collateral ... [T]o secure performance of your obligations to [RCM] ... you hereby grant to [RCM] ... a first priority, perfected security interest in all your [stuff] in the possession of ... [Refco Entities]....

2. *Rights and Use of Margin.* [RCM] shall have the right to ... use or dispose of such [stuff] free from any claim or right, until settlement in full of all Transactions.... [RCM's] sole obligation shall be to return to you such [stuff] ... to the extent [it is] not deemed to be collateral to secure Transactions....

Appellants' argument that the first use of "such [stuff]" in B.2 refers only to "stuff" deemed to be collateral is not consistent with the language of the agreement. The only referent for the first "such [stuff]" is "all your [stuff]" in B.1. Moreover, the second use of "such [stuff]" in B.2 is modified by "to the extent [it is] not deemed to be collateral," a most peculiar modifier if "such [stuff]" means only "stuff" deemed to be collateral.

RCM Customers also allege that RCM rehypothecated Customer assets at times that RCM Customers had no outstanding margin debt in breach of the Customer Agreement. However, the Customer Agreement provides only that the cash value of securities not deemed collateral shall be "return[ed]" to the customers, *i.e.,* recorded on RCM's books as money payable on demand to the particular customer. A perfectly plausible reading of the Agreement is that, on the occasions that some customers had no outstanding margin transactions, they had only a right to demand payment of the value of 100 percent of the securities that had been given to RCM.

There is, therefore, no disparity between the provisions of the Customer Agreement and RCM's conduct remotely supportive of a claim that the Agreement was a misrepresentation actionable under Section 10(b)....

* * *

c) *Consistency with Federal and State Law*

RCM Customers also contend that our interpretation of Section B.2 is inconsistent with federal and/or state law and that ambiguities in the Customer Agreement should be construed to comply with applicable legal rules. RCM Customers argue that RCM was subject to SEC Rules 15c3-1, 17 C.F.R. § 240.15c3-1, and 15c3-3, 17 C.F.R. § 240.15c3-3,[37] and New York state law, which would have limited RCM's rehypothecation rights with respect to excess margin securities. However, even assuming *arguendo* the existence of ambiguities in the Customer Agreement, we disagree.

The district court rejected these arguments regarding federal law based on our decision in *United States v. Finnerty,* 533 F.3d 143 (2d Cir.2008). *Finnerty* held that a defendant may be liable under Section 10(b) and Rule [10(b)(5)[*sic*] for violation of a NYSE rule only if the defendant had made a representation regarding compliance with the rule. *Finnerty,* 533 F.3d at 149–50. The district court concluded that because plaintiffs made no allegations that "RCM (or any Refco affiliate or employee) made any representation that RCM was subject to, or would comply with, any such regulations, much less [Rules 15c3-1 and 15c3-3]," RCM could not be found liable under Section 10(b) and Rule 10b-5 for violating Rules 15c3-1 and 15c3-3.

Here, more than simply remaining silent as to whether it was complying with U.S. law, RCM represented that it was *not* a U.S.-regulated company. Although RCM did state that it was subject to "all applicable laws" in the trade confirmations that simply raises the question of what laws were applicable. In short, RCM's alleged violation of federal law does not in and of itself constitute deceptive conduct.

The Security and Exchange Commission has expressed a concern, as *amicus curiae,* that affirming the district court in this regard will viscerate the so-called "shingle theory" of broker-dealer liability under Section 10(b, and will be inconsistent with our recent decision in *VanCook v. SEC,* 653 F.3d 130 (2d Cir.2011). We disagree.

Under the shingle theory, a broker makes certain implied representations and assumes certain duties merely by "hanging out its professional shingle." *Grandon v. Merrill Lynch & Co., Inc.,* 147 F.3d 184, 192 (2d Cir.1998).

However, the facts alleged in the instant matter do not, as asserted by appellant, give rise to liability based on "conduct inconsistent with an *implied* representation; specifically a broker-dealer's implied representation under the 'shingle theory' that it will deal fairly with the public in accordance with the standards of the profession."

---

37. [18] SEC Rule 15c3-1, the so-called Net Capital Rule, generally requires brokers and dealers to maintain sufficient capital to protect their customers from the firm's potential insolvency, *see* 17 C.F.R. § 240.15c3-1, and Rule 15c3-3, the so-called Customer Protection Rule, requires brokers and dealers to obtain and maintain physical possession or control of all fully paid and excess margin securities in a customer's account. *See* 17 C.F.R. § 240.15c3-3(b) (1). Under Rule 15c3-3, "excess margin securities" is defined as those securities in the customer's account whose market value exceeds 140 percent of the customer's outstanding margin debt. 17 C.F.R. § 240.15c3-3(a) (5). Thus, the Customer Protection Rule prohibits a broker from rehypothecating a customer's margin account securities in excess of 140 percent of the customer's outstanding margin debt.

Surely, RCM's affirmative representations that it was *not* a U.S.-regulated company trump any implied representation under the shingle theory.

* * *

In the instant case, RCM's Customer Agreement and its standard form Trade Confirmation expressly disclosed RCM's rehypothecation rights as well as RCM's status as an offshore unregulated entity. These disclosures were made in conjunction with a bargained-for agreement between sophisticated counter-parties that could be expected to understand the relevant benefits and risks. Thus, there is no liability under the shingle theory.

The terms of the Customer Agreement indicated that, insofar as RCM was acting as executing broker for its customers, RCM was not purporting to comply with the Rules in question but was relying on the safe harbor from broker registration provided under SEC Rule 15a-6, 17 C.F.R. § 240.15a-6. In general, Rule 15a-6 exempts from the federal broker-dealer registration requirements of Section 15(a) of the Exchange Act, 15 U.S.C. § 780, "foreign entities engaged in certain activities involving U.S. investors and securities markets." *See Registration Requirements for Foreign Broker–Dealers,* Exchange Act Release No. 27,017, 54 Fed.Reg. 30013, 30013 (July 18, 1989). In particular, Rule 15a–6(a)(3) exempts from registration foreign brokers that induce or attempt to induce trades in securities by "major U.S. institutional investors" and "U.S. institutional investors" so long as any trades are "effected through" a U.S.-registered broker-dealer and various conditions are met both by the foreign broker and the registered dealer that effects the trades. *See* 17 C.F.R. § 240.15a-6(a) (3) (i) (A).

* * *

Furthermore, the Customer Agreement's frequent references to RSL as "introducing" transactions to RCM on the customers' behalf clearly represented that trades executed at RCM for its customers would be "effected through" RSL to RCM in accordance with the requirements of Rule 15a–6(a)(3)(i)(A).

* * *

RCM Customers also assert that RCM was subject to New York General Business Law Section 339-e, which, in general, restricts a broker's rehypothecation rights with respect to fully-paid or excess margin securities. N.Y. Gen. Bus. Law § 339-e (McKinney 2004). RCM Customers argue that Section 339-e applies because Section H of the Customer Agreement and Paragraph 6 of the Trade Confirmation specified that the agreement would be governed by, and construed in accordance with, New York law.

The district court determined that Section H constituted a choice of law provision that governed only the Customer Agreement itself.... We agree with the district court. Section H neither created, nor represented, any affirmative obligations on RCM to conform to New York margin-lending restrictions. By its clear terms, the provision was included only as a choice of law and venue provision that would govern should any conflicts arise "out of or in connection with" the Customer Agreement.

Notes and Questions

1. As noted in *Capital Management*, hypothecation is regulated by federal and state laws. However, state law is preempted by federal law. See, *Levin v. PaineWebber, Inc.*, 159 F.3d 698, 704–07 (2d Cir. 1998). Section 15 (h) (1) of the Exchange Act expressly preempts state law covering broker-dealers' custody, margin, and financial responsibility requirements, but some state laws dealing with securities lending may apply to broker-dealers. In *St. Petersburgh v. Wachovia*, 2010 WL 2991431 (M.D. Fla. July 27, 2010), the court allowed a municipality's fiduciary duty claims to proceed in a situation involving the investment of cash collateral by broker-dealers and others from securities lending in bonds issued by Lehman Brothers Holding.

2. There is no implied private right of action under the hypothecation rules. *See Cohen v. Citibank, NA*, 1997 WL 88378 (1997). There is also no implied private right of action against SROs for failure to enforce their rules, including rules governing securities lending and borrowing, which serve to facilitate compliance with federal hypothecation rules. What was the basis for plaintiffs' cause of action in *Capital Management*? Did they allege a violation of the hypothecation rules?

   [handwritten: Loss of money & that was due to fraud.]
   [handwritten: ↳ Not directly.]

3. The SEC has held that failure to comply with the hypothecation rules may constitute violations of the antifraud provisions of the federal securities laws. In *In the Matter of Donald T. Sheldon*, 52 S.E.C. Docket 2496 (Nov. 18, 1992), a president of the broker-dealer was charged with failure to supervise [(Section 15(b) (4) (E) and (b) (6) of the Exchange Act] and fraud [Section 10(b) and Rule 10b-5]) as well as violation of the hypothecation rules, because he failed to disclose to customers that the firm violated the hypothecation rules. May customers bring a private right of action under Rule 10b-5 based on a violation of the hypothecation rules? *[handwritten: → Only if explicit since there is no implied private right of action under the hypothecation rules]*

[handwritten left margin: Perhaps but would make clearer to mitigate lawsuit possibility.]

Hypothetical Two

[handwritten left margin: Page 562 • Must comply with 140% limit of value of excess margin Securities]

[handwritten left margin: Page 561 Rule 4330]

Trainee Aba Owu has been asked to review the margin agreement between Success First and its customer Janice Lucky. The margin agreement allows hypothecation of securities in Lucky's margin account, including fully paid securities. Owu has been asked by DoGoode, her mentor, to ensure that the agreement as drafted complies with the hypothecation rules, including providing Lucky with required disclosures. A portion of the margin agreement is provided below. Owu really wants to do a good job so that she can survive her 14-month probationary period. Does the agreement comply with the hypothecation Rules and FINRA Rule 4330? Are there additional disclosures that Success First must make to Lucky to ensure compliance?

Margin Agreement

[handwritten: ↳ Would have a provision §5733 concerning sophistication of buyers]

[handwritten left margin: • Obtain written authorization from customer]

This Margin section applies in the event Success First finances any of your Transactions. Success First shall have the right to loan, pledge, hypothecate, or otherwise use or dispose of such cash, securities, and other property free from any claim or right, until settlement in full of all Transactions entered into pursuant to this Agreement. Success First's sole obligation shall be to return to you such cash, like amounts of similar cash, securities and other property (or the cash thereof in the event of any liquidation of collateral) to the extent they are not deemed to be collateral to secure Transactions entered into pursuant to this Agreement or have not been applied against obligations owing by you to Success First.

→ Specify whether complying with US law.

Chapter 9

Books, Records, and Reports

Regulatory Authority

Securities Exchange Act of 1934 17(a), 17(b), 17(h)

Exchange Act Rules 10b-10, 15c3-1d, 15c3-3, 13h-1, 17a-3, 17a-4, 17a-5, 17a-13, 17f-1, 17h-1T, 17h-2T

Exchange Act Regulation SHO Rule 200

FINRA Rules 2070, 2090, 4512, 4513, 4514, 4515, 4522, 4523, 4530, 4560

Municipal Securities Rulemaking Board ("MSRB) Rule G-8

Motivating Hypothetical

Malak Johnson, Success First's chief compliance officer, has been assigned to ensure that all participants in Success First's training program for newly hired registered representatives successfully complete the books and records portion of the Series 7 qualification examination. Malak believes that successful completion of his assigned task will mean a promotion to chief legal officer at Success First. Like Josephine Wiseman, Success First's current general counsel and chief legal officer, Malak has a law degree from a prestigious university (Howard University School of Law) and believes that he could do a much better job than Josephine. He has decided that the best way to make sure that the trainees pass is to have them take a practice exam after studying for a two-week period. He has been working diligently to compile study materials for the trainees to ensure that the trainees complete this portion of the exam with a high pass rate (greater than 70%). In fact, he has even written some of the study materials to ensure comprehensive coverage. To encourage the trainees to review the materials, he has procured a conference room that can only be used by the trainees for the next two weeks and that is always stocked with snacks and beverages. The two-week study period has commenced and Malak is anxiously waiting to administer the practice exam.

I. Introduction

Broker-dealers are required to make and keep certain books and records and make them available for examination by the SEC and appropriate SROs. These books and records and their examination are crucial regulatory tools for the SEC and SROs. Section 17(a) of the Exchange Act requires broker-dealers to make and keep certain records.

The content and maintenance of the books and records are prescribed in Rules 17a-3 and 17a-4 of the Exchange Act, respectively. In addition, section 17(b) of the Exchange Act expressly states that broker-dealer books and records are subject to examination by the SEC. The SEC has stated that, in combination, Rules 17a-3 and 17a-4 require broker-dealers to create, and preserve in an easily accessible manner, a comprehensive record of each securities transaction they effect and of their securities business in general. These requirements are integral to the Commission's investor protection function because the preserved records are the primary means of monitoring compliance with applicable securities laws, including antifraud provisions and financial responsibility standards. Exchange Act Rel. No. 47806 (May 7, 2003).

The SEC adopted Rules 17a-3 and 17a-4 of the Exchange Act in 1939 to capture the basic source documents and transaction records of broker-dealers. Rule 17a-3 is the SEC's principal recordkeeping provision. However, Rules 17a-3 and 17a-4 have been amended many times over the years to ensure that broker-dealer bookkeeping practices accurately reflect information needed to maintain their relevance as regulatory tools. Today, Rules 17a-3 and 17a-4 are quite extensive, thus this chapter will only cover certain sections of the rules.[1]

Some broker-dealers are not required to make and keep all of the records enumerated in Rules 17a-3 and 17a-4. A broker-dealer whose trading records are made and kept by another broker-dealer that acts as a clearing firm for its trading transactions is not required to keep its own set of such records.

This exemption also applies to broker-dealers whose trading records are made and kept by banks. Broker-dealers using banks as clearing firms must obtain from the bank a written agreement to the effect that the records are the property of the broker-dealer, must file a written undertaking with the SEC that such books and records are available for examination by the SEC,[2] and must, upon demand by the SEC, provide current copies of all such records.

---

1. A table containing a description of required books and records as well as how long and where they must be maintained is provided in the textbook library.

2. The written undertaking must include the following provisions: The undersigned hereby undertakes to maintain and preserve on behalf of [BD] the books and records required to be maintained and preserved by [BD] pursuant to Rules 17a-3 and 17a-4 under the Securities Exchange Act of 1934 and to permit examination of such books and records at any time or from time to time during business hours by examiners or other representatives of the Securities and Exchange Commission, and to furnish to said Commission at its principal office in Washington, D.C., or at any regional office of said Commission specified in a demand made by or on behalf of said Commission for copies of books and records, true, correct, complete, and current copies of any or all, or any part, of such books and records. This undertaking shall be binding upon the undersigned, and the successors and assigns of the undersigned. Nothing herein contained shall be deemed to relieve such member, broker, or dealer from the responsibility that such books and records be accurately maintained and preserved as specified in §§ 240.17a-3 and 240.17a-4, and 17 C.F.R. § 240.17a-3(b)(2).

Broker-dealers using banks to clear their trading transactions are not relieved of their responsibility to make and keep records in compliance with Rules 17a-3 and 17a-4. In addition, broker-dealers are not required to keep records for transactions involving certain types of securities, including sales of U.S. Tax Savings Notes, U.S. Defense Savings Stamps or U.S. Defense Savings Bonds, Series E, F, and G.

In addition, records of transactions in municipal bonds are deemed to comply with Rules 17a-3 and 17a-4 if they comply with Rule G-8 of the Municipal Securities Rulemaking Board.[3] Finally, broker-dealers are not required to keep records of transactions in security futures products and positions in futures accounts as long as the recordkeeping rules of the Commodity Futures Trading Commission (CFTC) apply, nor for cash transactions of $100 or less involving only subscription rights or warrants expiring within 90 days of their issuance.

FINRA also requires broker-dealers to make and keep books and records as required under its rules. FINRA rules require member broker-dealers to comply with books and recordkeeping requirements under the federal securities laws, including Rules 17a-3 and 17a-4. Significant FINRA rules regarding broker-dealer books and recordkeeping requirements will be noted as applicable. The remainder of this chapter provides an overview of broker-dealer books and recordkeeping requirements by category.

II. Financial and Business Records

A. Blotters

Blotters are records of original entry containing a daily account of all transactions of the broker-dealer and its customers. Broker-dealers must create and retain blotters that contain an itemized daily record of all purchases and sales of securities, all receipts and deliveries of securities (including certificate numbers), all receipts and disbursements of cash, and all other debits and credits.

The blotter must show the account for which each transaction was made, the name and amount of the securities, the unit and aggregate purchase or sale price, the trade date, and the name or other designation of the counterparty to the transaction.

Each record should reflect the activity as of the date it occurs and should be prepared no later than the following business day. Most broker-dealers create and maintain blotters electronically. Blotters must be kept for six years, the first two in an easily accessible place. An example of the content of a cash receipts & disbursements blotter is provided in Figure 9.1.

---

3. MSRB Rule G-8.

Figure 9.1. Cash Receipts and Disbursements Blotter

Purpose: A daily record of all receipts and disbursements of cash relating to the broker-dealer's business.
Required Contents:
Date funds were received
From whom funds were received
Date funds were disbursed
To whom funds were disbursed
Name of account to be debited or credited
Total dollars and cents debited or credited

B. Ledgers

Ledgers are records kept by account and are posted chronologically from information contained in the blotters. Rule 17a-3 requires the broker-dealer to create ledgers (or other records) for specified types of financial data. First, the broker-dealer must create a ledger reflecting all asset and liability, income and expense, and capital accounts; this record is usually identified as the broker-dealer's general ledger.

The general ledger enables the broker-dealer (or the SEC and/or FINRA) to determine its financial condition at any given time, and thus is used to compile the broker-dealer's trial balance. This ledger must be kept for six years, the first two in an easily accessible place. Next, the broker-dealer must create a ledger that itemizes separately for each cash and margin account of its customers, and the broker-dealer itself (including partners), all purchases, sales, receipts, and deliveries of securities and commodities and all other debits and credits for such accounts. These records also must be kept for six years, the first two in an easily accessible place.

In addition, there must be ledgers reflecting: (1) securities in transfer; (2) dividends and interest received; (3) securities borrowed and securities loaned; (4) monies borrowed and loaned (together with a record of the collateral and any substitutions of collateral); (5) securities failed to receive and failed to deliver; (6) long and short securities record (i.e., position book) differences arising from examination, count, verification, and comparison in accordance with SEC rules; and (7) repurchase and reverse repurchase agreements. These ledgers must be kept for three years, the first two in an easily accessible place. An example of the content of a monies borrowed and loaned ledger is shown in Figure 9.2.

Figure 9.2. Monies Borrowed and Loaned Ledger

Purpose: To show all monies borrowed or loaned and is maintained regardless of whether a customer's or the firm's securities are pledged as collateral.
Required Contents: Name of the bank, date the loan was made, interest rate, amount of loan, date the loan was paid.
An additional page, called a collateral record, should be provided for each loan. This record should contain the following: Number of shares or the principal amount of bonds, name of the securities used to secure the loan, certificate numbers of securities used as collateral for each particular loan.

FINRA Rule 4523 requires broker-dealers to designate an associated person to be responsible for each general ledger bookkeeping account. The assigned associated person must control and oversee entries into each general ledger account and determine that it is current and accurate as necessary to comply with all applicable FINRA rules and federal securities laws. The broker-dealer must maintain a record of the names of the associated person's assigned primary and supervisory responsibility for each general ledger account.

The assigned associated person must, as frequently as necessary, but at least monthly, review each account for accuracy and determine that aged or uncertain items are promptly identified for research and possible transfer to a suspense account.

The suspense account must be clearly identified, and each broker-dealer must record in the suspense account money charges or credits and receipts or deliveries of securities whose ultimate disposition is pending determination. The record must include all information known with respect to each item recorded in the suspense account. All records under FINRA Rule 4523 must be retained for a period of not less than six years in a format and media that complies with Exchange Act Rule 17a-4.

C. Trial Balance

A trial balance is a list of all open accounts in the broker-dealers' ledgers and their balances. The broker-dealer must keep a record of the proof of money balances in all ledger accounts in the form of trial balances. The trial balance is the starting point for the computation of aggregate indebtedness and net capital, which must be computed as of the date of the preparation of the trial balance. Trial balances must be prepared by the broker-dealer at least once a month and must be kept for three years, the first two in an easily accessible place. An example of a broker-dealer's trial balance is provided in Figure 9.3.

Figure 9.3. Trial Balance

Account Title	Debits	Credits
Cash in banks	$400,000,000	
Customer debits	40,000,000	
Customer credits		$115,000,000
Dividends payable		8,000,000
Syndicate payable		30,000,000
Furniture and fixtures (net)	12,000,000	
Advances and loans	20,000,000	
Good faith deposits	13,000,000	
Subordinated loans		40,000,000
Loans payable		30,000,000
Accrued expenses payable		7,000,000
Commission income		40,000,000
Trading account	130,000,000	
Investment account	100,000,000	
Real estate	50,000,000	
Mortgage payable		35,000,000
Interest receivables	5,000,000	
Capital account		465,000,000
Total	**$770,000,000**	**$770,000,000**

D. Securities Record

The securities record, often called the position book, must show the positions of securities that the broker-dealer carries for its own account and for its customers. It must reflect separately for each security all long and short positions as of the clearance date, i.e., the date when delivery is due.

It must also show the location of the long securities and the offsetting position of short securities, with the name and designation of the account where each security is carried. The securities record should show all positions resulting from purchases and sales transactions as of settlement date. It must be posted no later than the business day after settlement date or the date of securities movement. The securities record must be kept for six years, the first two in an easily accessible place.

In addition, FINRA Rule 4560 requires broker-dealers to report all gross short positions existing in each broker-dealer or customer account. This requirement includes broker-dealer accounts that resulted from a short sale[4] as well as where the transaction

---

4. Rule 200 of SEC Regulation SHO defines a short sale as any sale of a security that the seller does not own or any sale that is consummated by the delivery of a security borrowed by, or for the account of, the seller. 17 C.F.R. § 242.200 (2014).

that caused the short position was marked long due to the broker-dealer's or customer's net long position at the time of the transaction.

However, short positions resulting from short sales that were effected but have not reached settlement date by the given designated reporting settlement date, should not be included in the report for the given reporting cycle.

Short interest positions resulting from short sales that reached the expected settlement date, but failed to settle, must be included in the broker-dealer's report. In addition, broker-dealers must reflect company-related actions (e.g., dividends or distributions) in their short-interest reports adjusted as of the ex-date[5] of the corporate action.

E. Securities Counts, Verifications, and Comparisons

Rule 17a-13 of the Exchange Act requires carrying broker-dealers and those engaged in the lending and borrowing of customer cash and securities to periodically confirm the number and existence of the securities in their books and records.

At least once each quarter within a calendar year, the broker-dealer must physically examine and count all securities in its possession. It must also account for all securities subject to its control (i.e., not in its physical possession) by examining and comparing the supporting detail records with the appropriate ledger control accounts.

In addition, verification of securities subject to the broker-dealer's control must be conducted for securities that have been in transit for more than 30 days. The results of the securities counts and verifications must be compared with the broker-dealer's records and all unresolved differences must be recorded on its books and records within seven days of the count and verification.

However, no examination, count, verification, or comparison can be conducted within two months or more than four months following a prior examination, count, verification, or comparison. Associated persons regularly responsible for the care and protection of securities or for making or keeping records regarding securities held by, or subject to the control of, the broker-dealer are prohibited from conducting the required examinations, counts, verifications, or comparisons.

FINRA Rule 4522 reiterates the requirements of Rule 17a-13 but requires broker-dealers subject to the requirements of Rule 17a-13 to make more frequent examinations, counts, verifications, or comparisons "where prudent business practice would so require."[6] FINRA Rule 4522 also requires broker-dealers to receive position statements not less than once a month with respect to securities held by clearing corporations or custodians in order to reconcile all such securities and money balances by

---

5. The ex-date is the date on or after which a security is traded without a specific dividend or distribution.

6. FINRA Rule 4522(b). Greater frequency may be required for broker-dealers where there is a higher volume of activity.

comparing the clearing corporations' or custodians' position statements with the broker-dealer's books and records; all differences must be promptly resolved and, if not, all unresolved differences must be entered into a "Difference" account within seven business days of discovery.

The Difference Account must identify the unverified securities and reflect the number of shares or principal amount (long or short) of each security difference and the date of the security count that disclosed the difference.

F. Other Financial and Business Records

Rule 17a-4 of the Exchange Act, in addition to designating recordkeeping retention periods, establishes additional recordkeeping requirements concerning the broker-dealer's financial and business operations.

Required financial records include all records containing information in support of the broker-dealer's Financial and Operational Combined Uniform Single Report (FOCUS report). The broker-dealer's FOCUS report must be filed with the SRO designated as its examining authority using FORM X-17A-5.[7] The FOCUS report is divided into four parts.

Part I consists of two schedules that reflect the broker-dealer's financial condition and operational deductions from net capital. Schedule A (the Routine Report) reflects items on a monthly basis that reflect the financial condition of the broker-dealer, including net income, ownership equity, aggregate indebtedness, net capital, minimum net capital requirement, total credits and debits calculated under the Reserve Formula under Rule 15c3-3, and broker-dealer proprietary positions.

Schedule B (Supplemental Report) lists operational deductions from net capital (summarized as a line item on Schedule A) such as unresolved reconciling differences with correspondents, other broker-dealers, banks, and clearing organizations. Items contained in Part II include a statement of financial condition (total liabilities, assets, and ownership equity or a balance sheet); computation of net capital, computation of basic net capital requirement, aggregate indebtedness and other ratios; statement of income or loss; computation for the reserve requirements using the Reserve Formula under Rule 15c3-3; and a listing of ownership equity and subordinated capital proposed to be withdrawn within the next six months, which have not been deducted in the computation of net capital.

Part IIA is an abbreviated version of Part II and is used by noncarrying, nonclearing, and certain other broker-dealers. Part IIB contains information designed to evaluate the financial and operational condition of OTC derivatives dealers.[8] Part III requires information that identifies the broker-dealer (name, address, contact person) and the

---

7. FOCUS reports are deemed confidential and thus, generally, are not available on EDGAR. 17 C.F.R. § 240.17a-5(a) (3) (2014).

8. An analysis of the regulatory framework concerning the financial responsibility of OTC derivatives dealers is beyond the scope of this text.

broker-dealer's accountant with an oath and affirmation by the broker-dealer that the information and supporting schedules contained in the FOCUS report are true and correct and that neither the broker-dealer nor any partner or principal officer has any proprietary interest in any customer accounts except as so disclosed. Filing frequency of the FOCUS report depends on the nature and status of the broker-dealer. Broker-dealers that clear transactions or carry customers' accounts must file Part I of the FOCUS report within 10 days after the end of every month and Part II[9] within 17 business days after the end of every calendar quarter. Of course, the SEC and the SRO examining authority may require more frequent filing at their discretion.

FINRA Rule 4524 (Supplemental FOCUS Information) authorizes FINRA to require more detailed financial and operational information about a broker-dealer than is contained in the FOCUS Report. Broker-dealers, as designated by FINRA, must file additional financial or operational schedules or reports deemed necessary for the protection of investors or in the public interest.

The rule authorizes FINRA to designate the content, format, timing, and frequency of such filings in a Regulatory Notice filed with the SEC. Thus far, FINRA has adopted a new supplementary schedule—the Supplemental Statement of Income (SSOI). The SSOI requires the broker-dealer to provide a more detailed categorization of the revenue and expense line items that are on the Statement of Income (Loss) in Parts II and IIA[10] of the FOCUS report. This information is designed to assist FINRA to better understand a broker-dealer's revenue sources and expenses on an ongoing basis. The SSOI must be filed with FINRA within 20 business days of the end of each calendar quarter.

The broker-dealer must also file a Form Custody as part of its quarterly FOCUS report. This requirement is designed to elicit information as to whether and how a broker-dealer maintains custody of the cash and securities of customers and others, i.e., to enhance the SEC's oversight of the custody function of broker-dealers. The SEC determined this was necessary in light of the numerous enforcement actions involving misappropriation and misuse of customer assets. It also believes that Form Custody helps all regulators by providing current information about a broker-dealer's custodial activities and promoting compliance with applicable laws and rules, while enabling examiners to identify significant recent changes in a broker-dealer's custody practices.

Form Custody is comprised of nine line items eliciting information about a broker-dealer's custodial activities, a few of which require completion of charts and disclosure of custody-related information specific to the broker-dealer completing the form. If the broker-dealer introduces customer accounts on a fully disclosed basis to

---

9. There is an additional Schedule I that must be filed at the end of the fourth quarter as a supplement to the fourth quarter Part II, which provides overall information about the broker-dealer, such as the total number of public customers and the names of national securities exchanges of which the broker-dealer is a member.

10. The SSOI also requires similar financial information regarding commodities in Part II CSE. However, the regulatory framework for commodities is beyond the scope of this textbook.

another broker-dealer, the other broker-dealer's name and SEC registration and CRD numbers must be disclosed on Form Custody.

The same information is required if the broker-dealer introduces customer accounts on an omnibus basis. Form Custody also requires carrying broker-dealers to distinguish between customers and non-customers. Also, the broker-dealer must identify the location of securities, both within and outside of the United States. Most important, the broker-dealer must identify how frequently it reconciles its securities record with the records of the location at which the securities are held. Securities and cash carried for the accounts of customers and non-customers must be identified by type (U.S. equity securities, foreign equity securities, U.S. government debt, domestic corporate debt, etc.) and an approximate market value range must be provided.

The broker-dealer must state on Form Custody whether all securities it carries for the accounts of customers and non-customers are recorded on its securities record. If not, the broker-dealer must explain why not and provide an approximate market value of the unrecorded securities. Broker-dealers maintaining custody of customers' and non-customers' cash and securities must identify where, how, and by whom they are maintained. If such cash and securities are maintained by others, the broker-dealer must prepare a reconciliation between the records of the custody location and the broker-dealer's securities record.

Form Custody requires disclosure of each process used with respect to customers' free credit cash balances in cash accounts and non-customers free credit balances in securities accounts, e.g., whether they are included in the Reserve Formula Computation in Exhibit A of Rule 15c3-3, held in a bank account, or swept into a U.S. bank or money market fund.

Carrying broker-dealers must disclose the name and SEC registration and CRD numbers of broker-dealers for whom they act as a carrying broker-dealer and whether they perform this service on a fully disclosed or omnibus basis. Finally, the broker-dealer must disclose whether it is registered as an investment adviser; if so, it must identify all custodians used, disclose whether it is authorized to withdraw funds from, or effect transactions in, its adviser accounts, and whether its adviser client assets are recorded on its securities record. If the broker-dealer is an affiliate of an investment adviser, it must disclose whether it has custody of client assets of the investment adviser and the approximate U.S. dollar market value of the investment adviser client assets of which it has custody.

Every broker-dealer must file with the SEC and its applicable SRO an annual financial report audited by an independent public accountant registered with the PCAOB.[11] The annual financial report must contain: (a) a statement of financial condition; (b) a statement of income; (c) a statement of cash flows; (d) a statement of changes in stock-

---

11. Broker-dealers who are members of a national securities exchange, transact business solely with or for other members and do not carry margin accounts, credit balances, or securities for customers are not required to file the annual financial and compliance reports.

holders' or partners' or sole proprietor's equity, and a statement of changes in liabilities subordinated to claims of general creditors. All statements must be prepared in accordance with U.S. generally accepted accounting principles (GAAP) and must be in a format that is consistent with Part II or IIA of the FOCUS report. Supporting schedules that include a computation of net capital or the Reserve Formula must also be submitted along with the annual financial report. The broker-dealer must attach an affirmation attesting that, to the best of its knowledge and belief, the annual financial report is true and correct, signed by a senior officer of the broker-dealer.

The FOCUS Report, Form Custody, and the annual financial reports[12] are filed with FINRA using its eFOCUS system, FINRA's web-based application for filing FOCUS, Form Custody, and annual financial reports. The system allows a broker-dealer to enter and submit its financial information, to view historical information, and to generate line-item comparisons. The broker-dealer must be a registered user of FINRA's Firm Gateway and have entitlements to use eFOCUS. The Firm Gateway is an online regulatory compliance resource tool that provides consolidated access to FINRA applications along with broker-dealer-focused information.

Broker-dealers must also file an annual compliance report with the SEC.[13] The compliance report must disclose whether the broker-dealer has established and maintained internal controls reasonably designed to prevent or detect non-compliance with net capital requirements, reserve requirements, quarterly security counts, or any rule of the broker-dealer's SRO that requires account statements to be sent to customers. In addition, the annual compliance report must include a description of each material weakness in a broker-dealer's internal controls, along with any instance of noncompliance.

Rule 17a-5 defines material weakness as a deficiency in the broker-dealer's internal controls such that there is a reasonable possibility that non-compliance will not be prevented or detected on a timely basis. A deficiency exists when the design or operation of a control does not allow management or employees, in the normal course of performing their assigned functions, to prevent or detect noncompliance on a timely basis. The broker-dealer must attach an affirmation attesting that, to the best of its knowledge and belief, the compliance report is true and correct, signed by a senior officer of the broker-dealer.

In addition, the broker-dealer must preserve other business records under Rule 17a-4 as described in Figure 9.4. These records must be preserved for three years, the first two years in an easily accessible place.

---

12. However, the SEC and SIPC require broker-dealers to file hard copies of their annual financial reports directly.

13. A non-carrying broker-dealer claiming an exemption from Rule 15c3-3 must file an exemption report reviewed by its accountant; the exemption report must include the basis on which the broker-dealer claims the exemption (e.g., the broker-dealer promptly transmits all funds and securities and does not owe money or securities to its customers) and must include an affirmation signed by an authorized senior officer of the broker-dealer.

Figure 9.4

> **Other Business Records**
> • All checkbooks, bank statements, canceled checks and cash reconciliations
> • All bills receivable or payable (or copies), paid or unpaid, relating to the broker-dealer's securities business activities
> • Originals of all communications received and copies of all communications sent (and any approvals) by the broker-dealer (including inter-office memos) relating to its securities business activities, along with communications with the public subject to SROs' regulation (including sales scripts)
> • Branch office reconciliations and internal audit working papers
> • All guarantees of accounts, powers of attorney, other evidence of granting discretionary authority for any account, and copies of resolutions authorizing agents to act on behalf of a corporation
> • All written agreements, including agreements with respect to any account
> • Records mandated by Rule 15c3-3(d)(4) and (o) about the holding of fully paid and margin securities and securities futures products
> • Enterprise organization documents including (along with predecessor organizations) articles of incorporation or organization, minute books and certificate books, Form BDs, Form BDWs, all licenses (including registered representatives) and all amendments.

III. Trading Records

Broker-dealers must maintain records documenting trading for customers and for their own accounts. These documents are usually in the form of order tickets and must document the details of each order. Customer order tickets must show the terms and conditions of each order (and any modifications or instructions), the account for which it was entered, the time the order was received, the time of entry,[14] the price at which it was executed, the identity of the associated person (if any) responsible for the account, the identity of any other person who entered or accepted the order on the customer's behalf, a notation if the customer entered the order on an electronic system and, to the extent feasible, the time of execution or cancellation. In addition, customer orders must designate whether the broker-dealer entered them on the exercise of discretionary authority. Moreover, for customer orders, FINRA Rule 4515 requires the broker-dealer to place on the order form, before it is executed, the name or designation of the account for which such order is to be executed.

No changes to this information are allowed unless authorized by a qualified and registered principal of the broker-dealer; the principal must be personally informed of the essential facts, and approval of the change by the principal must be in writing. The record must also include the essential facts on which the principal relied to approve the change. Customer order tickets must be kept for three years, the first two in an easily accessible place.

---

14. Time of entry means the time the broker-dealer transmits the order for execution.

The broker-dealer must also create order tickets for its proprietary trading. These order tickets must show the price and, to the extent feasible, the time of execution. If the trade was with a customer other than another broker-dealer, the order ticket must also show the information required for a customer order. All order tickets must be kept for three years, the first two in an easily accessible place.

The broker-dealer must make and keep written confirmations of all trades, which must be distributed to customers at or before the completion of a transaction. This includes information about repurchase and reverse repurchase agreements and notices of all other debits and credits for securities, cash, and other items for customer accounts. Specifically, information contained in confirmations must include the date and time of the transaction;[15] the capacity of the broker-dealer (e.g., agent, principal, or market-maker); if the broker-dealer is acting as agent for the customer, the name of the person from whom the security was purchased or sold;[16] the amount of the broker-dealer's compensation, including payment for order flow;[17] the source and amount of any other transaction-based compensation, unless the payment is on other than a transactional basis; and the difference between the price to the customer and the broker-dealer's contemporaneous price for riskless principal trades.[18] Confirmations should be prepared no later than the business day after the transaction and may be prepared and disseminated electronically.

Rule 13h-1 requires broker-dealers to maintain records of all transactions effected by or through the accounts of large traders. A large trader (including all of its affiliates) is defined as a trader that has aggregate transactions in NMS securities[19] of: (a) 2 million shares or shares with a fair market value of $20 million on a calendar day; or (b) 20 million shares or shares with a fair market value of $200 million during a calendar month. Broker-dealers must also report large trader transactions electronically to the SEC, if requested, and perform a limited monitoring function to ensure compliance with Rule 13h-1. Under Rule 13h-1, large traders must obtain a unique large trader identification number (LTID),[20] which they must disclose to broker-dealers with respect to all of their accounts. The broker-dealer has an obligation to identify unregistered large traders, maintain records required under Rule 13h-1 for such traders, and inform them of their obligation to register and obtain an LTID if they have not done so already. The broker-dealer must retain these records for three years, the first two in an easily accessible place.

---

15. Or, must contain a statement that this information will be furnished upon written request from the customer. 17 C.F.R. § 240.10b-10 (2014).

16. Or, that this information will be furnished upon written request of the customer.

17. The source and nature for payment for order flow can be furnished upon written request to the broker-dealer.

18. There are other disclosure requirements for debt securities.

19. An NMS security means any security or class of securities for which transaction reports are collected, processed, and made available pursuant to an effective transaction reporting plan, or an effective national market system plan for reporting transactions in listed options.

20. LTIDs are obtained by filing a Form 13H.

IV. Customer Records

Broker-dealers must make and keep extensive records for customer accounts. For all accounts (including cash and margin accounts), the broker-dealer must make and keep a record indicating the name and address of the beneficial owner. In addition, margin accounts require a record of the signature of the beneficial owner. These records must be kept for three years, the first two in an easily accessible place. The account cards or records, which relate to the terms and conditions with respect to the opening and maintenance of all accounts, must also be preserved for at least six years after the closing of the account. There are additional records required if the customer is a natural person,[21] as noted in Figure 9.5.

Figure 9.5. Customer Account Records for Natural Persons

• Name, tax identification number, address
• Telephone number, date of birth
• Employment status (including occupation and whether the person is an associated person)
• Annual income, net worth (excluding value of primary residence)
• Investment objectives

However, under federal law, the information in Figure 9.6 is only required if the broker-dealer has been required to make a suitability determination within the past 36 months. In addition, the customer account record must identify the responsible associated person (if any) and whether the account was approved by a principal of the broker-dealer.

The broker-dealer must send the customer a copy of her account record (or documents with equivalent information) within 30 days of the opening of her account with a notice that she should correct and update information contained in her account record if necessary;[22] this too is only required if the broker-dealer has been required to make a suitability determination within the past 36 months. If the customer notifies the broker-dealer of a name, address, or investment objective change, the broker-dealer must send a notice of this change to the old address and to any joint owner and to the responsible associated person within 30 days of the broker-dealer's notice of the change.

For discretionary accounts, the broker-dealer must also keep a record containing the dated signature of each customer or owner granting the authority and the dated signature of each natural person to whom discretionary authority was granted.

The broker-dealer must maintain other account-related written agreements (e.g., margin agreements, options agreements, securities lending agreements, securities

---

21. A natural person excludes any account owned by a company, entity, government entity, or trust. However, the term *natural person* would include an account for a Uniform Gift/Transfer to Minor, an IRA, and a 401(k) account.

22. In addition, the information in Figure 9.6 must be sent thereafter to customers who are natural persons at intervals no greater than 36 months.

arbitration agreements, etc.) and such records must reflect that each customer received an executed copy. Customer account records for natural persons must be kept for six years after the earlier of the closing date of the account or of the replacement or updating of the information; all such records must be kept in an easily accessible place.

FINRA Rule 4512 specifies recordkeeping and retention requirements but differentiates these requirements between non-institutional and institutional accounts. Institutional accounts are defined as banks, savings and loan associations, insurance companies, registered investment companies, investment advisers registered with the SEC, or any person (including both natural persons and entities) with total assets of at least $50 million. However, unlike federal law, the broker-dealer must comply with FINRA Rule 4512's recordkeeping and retention requirements (summarized in Figure 9.6) even in the absence of a suitability determination.

Figure 9.6. FINRA Rule 4512. Customer Account Information

Non-Institutional Customers	Institutional Customers
Customer's name and address.	Customer's name and address.
Whether customer is of legal age.	
Name of associated person, if any, responsible for the account. Record must indicate scope of responsibility if multiple associated persons assigned to the account.	
Signature of the partner, officer or manager denoting that the account has been accepted in accordance with the broker-dealer's policies and procedures for acceptance of accounts.	Signature of the partner, officer or manager denoting that the account has been accepted in accordance with the broker-dealer's policies and procedures for acceptance of accounts.
If the customer is a corporation, partnership, or other legal entity, the names of any persons authorized to transact business on behalf of the entity.	If the customer is a corporation, partnership, or other legal entity, the names of any persons authorized to transact business on behalf of the entity.
Must make reasonable efforts to obtain before the initial transaction in the account: • Customer's tax identification or Social Security number; • Occupation of customer and name and address of employer; and • Whether customer is an associated person of another broker-dealer	
Discretionary accounts: • Customer must provide prior written authorization; acceptance of the account by the broker-dealer must be in writing and signed by the associated person responsible for supervising discretionary accounts.	Discretionary accounts: • Customer must provide prior written authorization; acceptance of the account by the broker-dealer must be in writing and signed by the associated person responsible for supervising discretionary accounts.

In addition, FINRA Rule 4512 requires compliance with FINRA Rules 2070 (Transactions Involving FINRA Employees) and 2090 (Know Your Customer). FINRA Rule 2070 requires a broker-dealer to provide duplicate account statements to FINRA of any FINRA employee account or any account in which trading is controlled by a FINRA employee; prohibits lending of money or securities to FINRA employees (excluding routine banking and brokerage activities); and prohibits receipt of anything above a nominal value ($100) by a FINRA employee who has responsibility for a regulatory matter involving the broker-dealer. FINRA Rule 2090 requires a broker-dealer to use reasonable diligence in ascertaining the essential facts about every customer (both non-institutional and institutional) and about the authority of each person acting on behalf of the customer.

The SEC details the complexity of the books and records that must be maintained by a broker-dealer in its complaint against Madoff's top lieutenant, Frank DiPascali. Interestingly, all of the books and records used to document transactions allegedly effected in Madoff's fraud, while tangible, were completely fictitious.

SEC v. Frank DiPascali, Jr.

Civ. Doc #09-CV-7085 (S.D.N.Y. 2009)

COMPLAINT

Plaintiff Securities and Exchange Commission ("Commission"), for its Complaint against defendant Frank DiPascali, Jr. ("DiPascali" or the "Defendant"), alleges:

SUMMARY

1.   For decades, DiPascali helped Bernard L. Madoff ("Madoff") conduct a massive securities and advisory fraud at Bernard L. Madoff Investment Securities LLC ("BMIS") that victimized thousands of investors before it collapsed, causing more than $64 billion in investor losses.

2.   A BMIS employee since 1975, DiPascali rose to become a key Madoff Lieutenant responsible for overseeing the bulk of the day-to-day operations of the unprecedented fraud that was run out of the 17th floor at BMIS' offices. DiPascali oversaw the mechanics of an entirely fictitious investment strategy, known as the "split-strike conversion," that BMIS claimed to be pursuing on behalf of its clients.

3.   DiPascali helped Madoff structure and record non-existent trades that were reflected on millions of pages of customer confirmations and account statements distributed each year. Not one of the trades purportedly executed as part of this strategy ever occurred. DiPascali also played a critical role in helping Madoff avoid detection of his scheme. DiPascali designed, developed and oversaw a wide and varying array of fictitious books and records—all prepared to conceal the scheme from investors, auditors and regulators.

* * *

VIOLATIONS

5.   By virtue of the conduct alleged herein, Defendant directly or indirectly, singly or in concert, has engaged in acts, practices, schemes and courses of business that violated ... 17(a) of the Exchange Act [15 U.S.C. § ... 78q(a)], and Rule[] ... 17a-3 thereunder [17 C.F.R. § ... 240.17a-3] ...

* * *

THE DEFENDANT

10.   DiPascali, age 52, resides in Bridgewater, New Jersey. DiPascali began working at BMIS in 1975 at the age of 19. After many years as a research clerk and then a trader, DiPascali was put in charge (by Madoff) of the build-out and computer installation in BMIS' new office space in the Lipstick Building at 885 Third Avenue in New York City in the mid-1980s. Later, at Madoff's direction, DiPascali became involved in, and eventually oversaw, the day-to-day operations of the bulk of BMIS' multi-billion dollar fraudulent scheme.

RELEVANT INDIVIDUALS AND ENTITIES

11.   Madoff, age 71, was, until recently, a resident of New York City and the sole owner of BMIS. Until December 11, 2008, Madoff, a former chairman of the board of directors of the NASDAQ stock market, oversaw and controlled the fraudulent investment adviser business at BMIS as well as the overall finances of BMIS. Madoff was charged civilly and criminally for his role in a multi-billion dollar Ponzi scheme. See, SEC v. Benard L. Madoff and Bernard L. Madoff Investment Securities LLC, No. 08-CV-10791 (S.D.N.Y.)(LLS)(the "Civil Action")(citations omitted) ...

12.   BMIS registered with the Commission as a broker-dealer in 1960 and as an investment adviser in September 2006. BMIS used to occupy floors 17-19 of the Lipstick Building in Manhattan, New York City. BMIS purportedly engaged in three different operations: investment adviser services; market-making services; and proprietary trading. BMIS is currently under the control of a trustee appointed pursuant to the Securities Investor Protection Act of 1970 (citations omitted).

FACTS

Background

* * *

B.   DiPascali's Early Career

17.   At least as early as the 1980s, DiPascali (together with other employees of BMIS) helped to fabricate various backdated and fictitious trades, often involving options, and to record them in investor account records for the purpose of generating phantom returns, hedges or tax events in those investors' accounts. DiPascali and others continued to help fabricate trades for this original group of accounts until the end of the fraudulent scheme in December 2008.

* * *

23.   [After 1992,] [t]o handle the volume, Madoff needed a more efficient and less labor intensive method of generating phony trade confirmations and account statements. Previously, BMIS had manually entered fictitious, backdated trades on an account-by-account basis. Madoff also needed an investment strategy that could credibly explain how he supposedly achieved specific target rates of return across hundreds of different accounts. DiPascali was instrumental in addressing both of these challenges.

* * *

24.   Madoff told most of BMIS' investors that he managed their accounts pursuant to the split-strike conversion strategy. In fact, Madoff's entire split-strike conversion strategy was a longstanding fraud. Every trade, every order ticket, every account statement, every confirmation and all other relevant records were fictitious.[23]

* * *

28.   Under DiPascali's oversight, BMIS' programmers organized the new accounts on a single IBM AS/400 computer. The accounts were set up so that one set of "trades" could be entered on an aggregate basis for all the accounts, and the computer would automatically allocate the fictitious trades, pro rata, to the various individual accounts. Once Madoff and DiPascali identified a basket trade that achieved the fictitious targeted return, the trade was proportionally replicated in each account automatically. The system then generated separate trade confirmations and account statements for each account based on its pro-rata share of the purported trading and carried forward the account holdings from month-to-month.

* * *

31.   Madoff instructed DiPascali to generate a credible annual return for the strategy, between 10 and 17%, although in the later years of the fraud the returns shifted towards the lower end of the range. Indeed, Madoff essentially promised some investors that they would enjoy a particular rate of return. To achieve these phantom returns, DiPascali closely monitored the basket and consulted with Madoff to ensure that the gains were appropriate—not too high or too low. Then, after several weeks of holding the position, Madoff directed DiPascali to sell off the basket and book a modest profit, averaging a return in the fraud's later years of about 1% per month. Since no actual purchase or sale took place, DiPascali could examine the historical prices of the securities comprising the basket and pick such date and pricing for the "sale" of the basket as was needed to achieve the targeted rate of return.

* * *

34.   Once Madoff decided to do a "basket trade," DiPascali (or his staff) provided key punch operators with the relevant pricing information and they then entered the data into the AS/400. The system then generated and printed hundreds of thousands

---

23. A number of preexisting friends and family accounts did not migrate to the new split-strike conversion strategy. These friends and family accounts continued to be handled on an account-by-account basis through December 2008, with DiPascali and others helping to select and create backdated and phony trades to fabricate returns.

of pages of confirmations (a separate one for each stock, for each account), which BMIS then mailed out to each investor. Millions of pages of paper and hundreds of hours of BMIS employee time were expended on these mailings each year.

* * *

40. DiPascali understood that the purported trading for these options accounts was fictitious. He knew that none of these securities was ever purchased. He knew that the transaction prices did not reflect actual transactions, but were picked after-the-fact to generate fictitious returns. He knew that there were no trade confirmations or account documentation coming from anywhere outside of BMIS that reflected the purported trading being shown in the client accounts.

* * *

43. Year after year, he directed that millions of pages of false account statements and trade confirmations be prepared and distributed to thousands of investors.

* * *

45. DiPascali knew that when investors sent in funds to BMIS for investment, the funds were deposited or wired into a bank account at JPMorgan Chase (the "703 Account"). He also knew that this account was not in any way reflected on the books and records (including the ledger) of BMIS's broker-dealer operation.

* * *

55. One reason the fraud was not detected for so long was DiPascali's considerable success in overseeing the creation of large quantities of false books and records that corroborated the fictitious trading.

56. In addition to allocating trades and generating trade confirmations and account statements, the AS/400 computer system housed and automatically generated books and records reflecting the phantom trading in the advisory accounts.

57. This computer and the books and records it generated were separate and distinct from the books and records for BMIS' market-making and proprietary trading operation, which in the later years used a different computer system.

58. Because no actual trading took place in the advisory accounts, the books and records generated by the AS/400 were incomplete and Madoff was concerned that they would raise doubts in the eyes of a regulator or auditor. For example, trade blotters and order tickets could not be generated by the AS/400 with credible execution times, counterparties or executing brokers.

59. In addition, the stock record for the advisory accounts did not reflect any real holdings and would not match the records held in BMIS' name at Depository Trust Corporation ("DTC"), which is the central securities depository in the United States.

60. Madoff and DiPascali, together with other BMIS employees, addressed these issues in a number of ways, often varying the approach depending on who was reviewing the records. Following are some examples of the methods they employed to avoid detection of the scheme during third party inquiries and examinations:

(a) Special Accounts. Although great effort was made to conceal the existence of advisory accounts to the fullest extent possible, some audits and regulatory inquiries required an acknowledgement that the business existed and the production of books and records to substantiate the activity in those accounts. However, Madoff was careful to avoid ever disclosing the scope and magnitude of the accounts, hiding the fact that there were several thousand accounts with aggregate values in excess of $50 billion. Accordingly, DiPascali helped Madoff devise a shifting subset of 10 to 25 accounts—the "special" accounts—which they deceptively presented as the universe of BMIS advisory accounts. DiPascali and others then prepared various fake books and records reflecting only this subset. This way, BMIS provided auditors and regulators with just enough information to make the phony books and records appear credible but not enough to appreciate the magnitude of the advisory business.

(b) Custody. Because securities were never purchased on behalf of investors, it was important to deflect inquiries into the custody of assets. One deceptive tactic was to claim that the assets were not custodied at BMIS because BMIS only functioned as an executing broker on an RVP/DVP (receive-versus-payment and delivery-versus-payment) basis. To substantiate this story, Madoff directed DiPascali and others to prepare alternate account statements and records for the special accounts. The alternate account statements excluded certain purported transactions and information that were inconsistent with an RVP/DVP arrangement. Madoff also directed DiPascali and others to change the titles for the special accounts to indicate that the assets were custodied elsewhere. For example, an account in the name of "John Doe" was changed to "European Bank for the benefit of John Doe" on the fictitious set of account statements and trade reports given to auditors or regulators. In this way, the assets were purportedly custodied at European Bank and there would be no reason to ask DTC for records reflecting BMIS holdings since the stock was held in street name at European Bank, not BMIS. Madoff even ordered that old, superseded BMIS stationary and letterhead be maintained indefinitely in case he had to fabricate records going back further in time.

(c) DTC Reports. For some investors and auditors, BMIS purported to hold custody of the advisory account assets. To address due diligence custody audits, Madoff directed DiPascali and others to create fake DTC reports. DiPascali and others spent substantial time and effort ensuring that these reports mimicked the layout, print font and paper-type of actual DTC reports. Madoff and DiPascali then made these fake DTC reports available to auditors for review. One investor was even shown the report onscreen at a computer terminal at BMIS and told that the computer was receiving a live feed from DTC.

(d) Shifting Counterparties. The advisory account records on the AS/400 did not reflect any counterparty information (because none existed). To respond to inquiries from regulators and auditors, however, DiPascali had to create credible trade blotters for the BMIS advisory business that included counterparty information. Including counterparties, however, created a risk of detection because the regulator or auditor might approach the counterparty for its corresponding records and compare the two. This risk was particularly acute for option trades because Madoff and DiPascali, when pressed about the volume or pricing of option positions, would explain that the option trading was not done on any exchange but directly with counterparties over-the-counter. To alleviate this risk, DiPascali, at Madoff's direction created a list of counterparties that were unlikely to be approached for verification. On the one hand, when regulators and auditors in the U.S. asked for the information, DiPascali provided a list of European financial institutions. On the other hand, when auditors for European investors asked for the information, DiPascali provided names of U.S. dealers. In addition to providing the list of names, DiPascali directed that fake trade blotters be prepared from only the "special" accounts to reflect fictitious trading with the various counterparties on the relevant list. These records were provided to regulators and auditors.

(e) Random Number Generator. BMIS received specific requests from regulators for order execution information for the advisory accounts. Since billions of dollars of fictitious trades were generally keyed into the AS/400 at one time, DiPascali could not use the data as it existed on the AS/400 because the order time would not be credible. Instead, he developed a report that would appear to reflect actual trading, at variable intervals and in different increments. To generate the report, DiPascali and others created and used a random number generator program to break up the massive trades into orders of variant sizes and prices and to randomly distribute the trades across different times. Furthermore, to avoid the possibility that the pricing at those intervals might not match the consolidated trading tape, DiPascali directed that the orders be "executed" during the early part of the day in Europe (the middle of the night in the U.S.). Madoff, DiPascali and others then represented that the single execution price reflected on the investor confirmations was an average price for trading purportedly done in the European market.

* * *

SIXTH CLAIM FOR RELIEF

Aiding and Abetting Violations of Section 17(a)
of the Exchange Act and Rule 17a-3
(Broker-Dealer Books and Records Violations)

87. As a registered broker-dealer, BMIS was required to make and keep certain books and records current and accurate pursuant to Section 17(a) of the Exchange Act [15 U.S.C. § 78q(a)] and Rule 17a-3 thereunder [17 C.F.R. § 240.17a-3].

88. BMIS failed to make and keep certain books and records current and accurate. BMIS, among other things, manufactured and maintained account statements, ledgers,

journals and other records reflecting fictitious securities holdings and fictitious securities transactions in investors' accounts.

89.   As a result, BMIS violated Section 17(a) of the Exchange Act and Rule 17a-3 promulgated thereunder [15 U.S.C. § 78q (a) and 17 C.F.R. § 240.17a-3].

90.   The Defendant knew that BMIS manufactured and maintained account statements, ledgers, journals and other records reflecting fictitious securities holdings and fictitious securities transactions in investors' accounts.

91.   By reason of the foregoing, and pursuant to Section 20(e) of the Exchange Act [15 U.S.C. § 78t (e)], the Defendant aided and abetted the violations of Section 17(a) of the Exchange Act [15 U.S.C. § 78q (a)] and Rule 17a-3 thereunder [17 C.F.R. § 240.17a-3]. Specifically, Defendant knowingly provided substantial assistance to BMIS in committing such violations.

Notes and Questions

1.   FINRA disciplined several broker-dealers for, among other things, failing to send to customers required notices concerning address changes and changes of investment objectives. *See* FINRA, News Release, *FINRA Fines Wachovia Securities and First Clearing $1.1 Million for Failing to Provide Required Notifications to Customers* (Mar. 24, 2009), available at: http://www.finra.org/Newsroom/News Releases/2009/P118173.

2.   The customer account records required in Rule 17a-3(a)(17)(i)(A) and (B) are only required if the broker-dealer makes a suitability determination currently or within the last 36 months.

3.   Rule 17a-3 does not expressly state that the broker-dealer must provide account statements regarding the transactions effected in the customer's account. However, most customers receive account statements at least quarterly. What is the legal basis for this action by the broker-dealer? Is it just gratuitous? → Yes, to show due

[handwritten margin note: To ensure compliance. ←]

[handwritten: diligence.]

4.   FINRA Rule 4514. Authorization Records for Negotiable Instruments Drawn from a Customer's Account. Broker-dealers and their associated persons are prohibited from obtaining or submitting negotiable instruments (checks, drafts, etc.) drawn on a customer's checking, savings, share, or similar account without the express written authorization of the customer. The customer's signature on the negotiable instrument may serve as the customer's authorization. However, if the customer's signature representing authorization is separate from the instrument, this authorization must be kept for three years following the date the authorization expires. How, if at all, does this rule assist FINRA in regulating its member broker-dealers?

[handwritten: ↳ If nothing signed no compliance.]

A. Employee Records

The broker-dealer must make and keep extensive records for associated persons. Much of this information is contained in FINRA's Central Registration Depository or CRD[24] and some of this information is available to the public through FINRA's BrokerCheck service.[25] Records for associated persons must be kept for three years, the first two in an easily accessible place, after the associated person has terminated his or her relationship with the broker-dealer. Associated person records must include the associated person's name,[26] address, Social Security number, date of birth, the starting date of employment or other association, and successfully completed qualification exams.[27] A complete, consecutive statement of all business connections for at least the preceding 10 years (full and part-time) must also be kept. The broker-dealer must have a listing for each associated person, which shows every office where the associated person regularly conducts a securities business. In addition, the associated person's records must include his or her CRD number and every internal identification number or code assigned, along with fingerprint cards and related information (if required).[28]

The broker-dealer must also maintain records of any denial of membership or registration, as well as any disciplinary actions taken by a state or federal regulator or SRO against the associated person or against the broker-dealer with whom the associated person is employed. Such records would include certain misdemeanors, criminal and civil actions, e.g., permanent or temporary injunctions; arrests or indictments for felonies; any misdemeanors pertaining to securities, commodities, banking, insurance or real estate; fraud (including tax fraud); false statements or omissions; and extortion.

Compensation records for each associated person must be created and maintained. Compensation records must show the purchase and sale of each security for which each associated person is compensated, including money compensation and a description of non-monetary compensation such as sales incentives, gifts, and trips.[29] All compensation-related agreements (including verbal agreements) dealing with the employment or contractual relationship between the broker-dealer and the associated person must be kept, including commission and concession schedules and the method by which compensation is determined. With respect to non-commission-based com-

---

24. FINRA operates Web CRD, the central licensing and registration system for the U.S. securities industry and its regulators. It contains the registration records of more than 6,800 registered broker-dealers and the qualification, employment, and disclosure histories of more than 660,000 active registered individuals.

25. The information distributed through BrokerCheck is simply a subset of the information contained in the CRD. Full access to CRD is available to federal or state regulators.

26. The associated person's records must also include any other names by which he or she has been known or has used.

27. See Chapter 3 for a discussion of broker-dealer qualification examinations.

28. Only those associated persons engaged in the broker-dealer's securities business are required to be fingerprinted and investigated. For example, the broker-dealers' general counsel would not be fingerprinted. Fingerprint cards are submitted to the Attorney General for processing. The fingerprint cards and corresponding processing information must be kept for three years after termination of employment or relationship with the broker-dealer.

29. For sales programs where non-cash compensation is awarded at the end of the year, a broker-dealer must only maintain records of the program, its criteria, and the recipients of the rewards.

pensation (not on a per trade basis), the broker-dealer must keep records for associated persons whose compensation is tied, directly or indirectly, to securities transactions. For example, a record is needed for a branch manager whose compensation is tied to the branch meeting certain sales goals. Compensation records for associated persons must be kept for three years, the first two in an easily accessible place.

The broker-dealer must make and keep a record of all written customer complaints against its associated persons.[30] Written customer complaints include electronic communications such as email. The record must contain the complaining customer's name, address, account number, date received, the name of any other associated person identified in the complaint, a description of the nature of the complaint, and the disposition of the complaint. The record must also show that the customer received the address and telephone number of the department to which the complaint was directed.

Customer complaint records must be kept for three years, the first two in an easily accessible place. Written customer complaints must be submitted to the CRD and may remain there indefinitely; such complaints can be accessed using FINRA's BrokerCheck service. FINRA Rule 4513 addresses customer complaints and their disposition at broker-dealers' offices of supervisory jurisdiction (OSJ).[31] Complaints initiated at OSJs may be maintained centrally as long as they are made available at the specific OSJ location when requested by FINRA. Unlike Rule 17a-3(a) (18), FINRA Rule 4513 requires customer complaint records to be maintained for at least four years.

V. Risk Assessment

Rule 17a-3(a) (23) requires certain broker-dealers to make and keep records documenting their credit, market, and liquidity risk management controls. Broker-dealers with more than $1 million in aggregate credit items as computed using the Reserve Formula of Rule 15c3-3 and more than $20 million in capital (including subordinated debt used as net capital under Rule 15c3-1d) must make and keep such records. Neither the rule nor the adopting release provides guidance on the particular types of policies and procedures required under the rule.[32] These records must be maintained for three years after the termination of use.

Section 17(h) of the Exchange Act requires broker-dealers to keep records concerning the financial and securities activities of the broker-dealers' associated persons whose business activities are reasonably likely to have a material impact on the broker-dealers' financial and operational condition, including its net capital, its liquidity,

---

30. An original of the customer complaint kept in the associated person's file is also acceptable.

31. Office of Supervisory Jurisdiction is an office designated by the broker-dealer as having supervisory responsibilities for agents. Its principal has final approval of new accounts, market making or structuring of public offerings.

32. *See* discussion of risk management controls for broker-dealers with market access under Rule 15c3-5 in Chapter 13 discussing market structure.

or its ability to finance its operations. Specifically, Section 17(h) provides that the records should concern the broker-dealer's policies, procedures, or systems for monitoring and controlling financial and operational risks to "[the broker-dealer] resulting from the activities of its material associated persons ... [and] authorizes the [SEC] to require broker-dealers to file summary reports...."[33]

The SEC adopted two rules and one form to implement the requirements of Section 17(h)—Rules 17h-1T and 17h-2T and Form 17-H. Rule 17h-1T sets forth specific recordkeeping requirements for risk assessment and provides guidelines to identify material associated persons of the broker-dealer that are subject to the rule's risk assessment recordkeeping and reporting requirements. Rule 17h-2T specifies reporting requirements, and their frequency, on Form 17-H filed with the SEC.

Only material associated persons are subject to the recordkeeping and reporting requirements of Rules 17h-1T and 17h-2T. Moreover, a material associated person is not a natural person. This means that the risk assessment rules only apply to affiliated entities of the broker-dealer. Rule 17h-1T contains several factors to be used by broker-dealers to identify affiliates subject to the risk assessment recordkeeping and reporting requirements. The factors are listed in Figure 9.7.

Figure 9.7. Factors to Determine Material Associated Person Status

> - The legal relationship between the broker or dealer and the affiliate;
> - The overall financing requirements of the broker-dealer and the affiliate, and the degree to which they are financially dependent on each other;
> - The degree to which the broker-dealer, or its customers, rely on the associated person for operational support or services in connection with the broker-dealer's business;
> - The level of risk present in the activities of the broker-dealer's affiliate; and
> - The extent to which the affiliate has the authority or the ability to cause a withdrawal of capital from the broker-dealer.

Rule 17h-1T requires broker-dealers to maintain and preserve two general categories of information about each material associated person. The first category concerns the organization and risk-management policies of the broker-dealer's holding company.

The second category involves the financial condition of the holding company, including financial statements, together with specialized categories of financial and securities activity-related data. The first category of information must include the organizational chart of the broker-dealer's holding company, showing all affiliated entities with specific identification of affiliates that are material associated persons.[34] The risk management policies must include written policies, procedures, or systems for the broker-dealer's:

---

33. Final Temporary Risk Assessment Rules, 57 Fed. Reg. 32159-01 (July 21, 1992).

34. Associated persons that exist solely for tax reasons or that are shell companies that produce little or no revenue may either be omitted from the chart or combined into a single entry to reduce the number of entries.

A. Method(s) for monitoring and controlling financial and operational risks to it resulting from the activities of any of its material associated persons;

B. Financing and capital adequacy, including information regarding sources of funding, together with a narrative discussion by management of the liquidity of the material assets, the structure of debt capital, and sources of alternative funding; and

C. Trading positions and risks, such as records regarding reporting responsibilities for trading activities, policies relating to restrictions or limitations on trading securities and financial instruments or products, and a description of the types of review conducted to monitor existing positions, and limitations or restrictions on trading activities.[35]

In addition, the broker-dealer must maintain and preserve a description of all material pending legal or arbitration proceedings involving a material associated person or the broker-dealer that are required to be disclosed by the broker-dealer's ultimate holding company under GAAP. This information should be updated quarterly only if there is a material change.

The risk assessment information required in the first category under Rule 17h-1T includes all financial data required to assess the risks to the broker-dealer caused by the activities of its material associated persons. The SEC believes that this information will enable it "to evaluate the broker-dealer's position in the holding company hierarchy as a whole, and will give an overview of the financial condition of the organization."[36]

The records required in Rule 17h-1T may be kept at either the material associated person or at a record storage facility located within the United States. In order to store such records with the material associated person or at a record storage facility, the material associated person or record storage facility must file a written undertaking with the SEC to the effect that the records will be treated as if the broker-dealer was maintaining the records in compliance with Rule 17h-1T (including that they be kept in an easily accessible place as stated in Rule 17a-4) and that it will permit the examination of such records by the SEC or its designees. However, the broker-dealer remains responsible for maintaining and preserving such records.

Rule 17h-2T requires this information to be filed on Form 17-H. Form 17-H must be filed with the SEC within 60 calendar days of the end of each fiscal quarter. The cumulative year-end financial statements required by Rule 17h-1T may be filed separately within 105 calendar days of the end of the fiscal year.

In addition, there are four categories of exemptive provisions in Section 17(h) and Rules 17h-1T and 17h-2T. The first category permits individual broker-dealers to apply to the SEC for an exemption from the requirements of the risk assessment rules. Section

---

35. 17 C.F.R. § 240.17h-1T(a)(1)(ii) (2014). If such policies, procedures, or systems do not exist, the broker-dealer must document, in writing, the absence of such policies.

36. Final Temporary Risk Assessment Rules, 57 FED. REG. at 12.

17(h) of the Exchange Act contains several factors that the SEC must consider when deciding whether to exempt an individual broker-dealer from the risk assessment rules. These factors include: (a) Whether the information required under the risk assessment rules is available from a supervisory agency, a state insurance commission or similar state agency, the CFTC, or a similar foreign regulator; (b) The primary business of any associated person; (c) The nature and extent of domestic or foreign regulation of the associated person's activities; (d) The nature and extent of the registered person's securities activities; and (e) With respect to the broker-dealer and its associated persons, on a consolidated basis, the amount and proportion of assets devoted to, and revenues derived from, activities in the U.S. securities markets.

The second category exempts limited-purpose mutual fund broker-dealers that are exempt from the provisions of the customer protection rule (Rule 15c3-3(k) (1)). Such broker-dealers must limit their activities to the purchase, sale, and redemption of redeemable securities of registered investment companies or of interests or participation in an insurance company separate account, whether or not registered as an investment company; the solicitation of share accounts for savings and loan associations insured by an instrumentality of the United States; and the sale of securities for the account of a customer to obtain funds for immediate reinvestment in redeemable securities of registered investment companies.

These types of broker-dealers include broker-dealers associated with insurance companies that are registered in order to offer variable annuity and other related products. The SEC believes that these types of broker-dealers pose limited systemic or customer risk and, therefore, remain exempt, regardless of the amount of their net capital. The third category exempts broker-dealers that do not carry customer accounts and whose net capital does not equal or exceed $20 million. The fourth category exempts broker-dealers who do carry customer accounts but whose net capital is less than $250,000.

A. Electronic Recordkeeping

In 1997, the SEC amended paragraph (f) of Rule 17a-4 to allow broker-dealers to store records electronically. Accordingly, for some time, most broker-dealers have maintained much of their records electronically. However, any system used by the broker-dealer must comply with every paragraph of Rule 17a-4(f).[37] Moreover, a broker-dealer must notify its examining authority prior to employing electronic storage media and represent to the SEC that the form of electronic storage media used complies with the definition of the term *electronic storage media* in Rule 17a-4. The term *electronic storage media* is defined in Rule 17a-4 as "any digital storage medium or system" that must:

(A) Preserve the records exclusively in a non-rewriteable, non-erasable format;

---

37. Rule 17a-4(f) also allows broker-dealers to maintain and preserve required records using micrographic media, i.e., on microfilm, microfiche, or any similar medium. 17 C.F.R. § 240.17a-4(f)(i) (2014).

(B) Verify automatically the quality and accuracy of the storage media recording process;

(C) Serialize the original and, if applicable, duplicate units of storage media, and time-date for the required period of retention the information placed on such electronic storage media; and

(D) Have the capacity to readily download indexes and records preserved on the electronic storage media to any medium acceptable under this paragraph (f) as required by the Commission or the self-regulatory organizations of which the member broker, or dealer is a member.

The broker-dealer's electronic storage system must at all times be available for examination by the SEC and SROs immediately in an easily readable projection or production of images. It must also be ready at all times to provide any facsimile enlargement of electronic records requested by the SEC, SROs, and state securities regulators. In addition, the broker-dealer must maintain a duplicate copy of all electronic records and the original records must be stored separately from the duplicate copy.

All electronic storage media or systems must be organized and indexed accurately, including the original and any duplicates. The broker-dealer must have such indexes available for examination and each index must be duplicated, with duplicate copies stored separately from the original index. Original and duplicate indexes must be preserved for the time required for the indexed records.

The broker-dealer must have an audit system to ensure the accuracy of records maintained in the form of electronic storage media. Specifically, the rule requires the audit system to be utilized when records are being entered or when changes to existing records are being made. An audit record is not required when a record is being accessed but cannot be altered by the reader of the record. The results of the audit system must be available at all times for examination by the SEC and SROs and must be preserved for the same period as the records being audited.

The broker-dealer is required to keep current all information necessary to download records and indexes stored on electronic storage media but may use a third-party vendor. If a third-party vendor is used, the broker-dealer could place in escrow and keep current a copy of the information necessary to access the format, i.e., the physical and logical file format of the electronic storage media, the field format of all different information types written on the electronic storage media, and the source code, together with the appropriate documentation and information necessary to access records and indexes.

Broker-dealers exclusively using electronic storage media for some or all of the preservation of records must have arrangements with at least one third-party provider with the ability to download information from their electronic storage system to another acceptable electronic storage medium as defined under Rule 17a-4(f). The third party provider must file an undertaking with the SEC that it will download information kept on the broker-dealer's electronic storage media to any medium acceptable under Rule 17a-4 and that it will take reasonable steps to provide access to information contained on the broker-dealer's electronic storage media. The undertaking must state specifically that if the broker-dealer fails to download information contained in its electronic storage media, the third-party provider will do so if requested by the SEC, SROs, or state securities regulators.

B. Other Reporting Requirements

FINRA Rule 4530 requires broker-dealers to report certain disciplinary events about themselves and their associated persons not initiated by FINRA. These events include findings by a regulatory body and quarterly statistical and summary information about customer complaints. The rule also requires broker-dealers to file with FINRA copies of specified criminal actions, civil actions and complaints, and arbitration claims. However, broker-dealers are not required to file findings and actions by FINRA against themselves and their associated persons.

Hypothetical One

Today is test day for the 10 trainees participating in the training program covering financial responsibility. The specific unit is Books and Records. John DoGoode has provided reading materials for the Books and Records unit and trainees must complete a multiple-choice exam to test their comprehension of the materials. Similar to the Series 7 qualification examination administered by FINRA, trainees will take the test on the class web site. A score of 70 percent constitutes passing. Failure to pass requires the trainee to retake the exam in 30 days. Passing the exam is required to continue in the training program.

 Question?

Notes and Questions

1. *Responsible Persons Records.* The broker-dealer must maintain a record of each principal responsible for establishing policies and procedures that are reasonably designed to ensure compliance with federal requirements or SRO rules that require acceptance or approval by a principal. In addition, the broker-dealer must maintain a list for each office that contains the name or title of each person who can explain the types and content of records maintained at the office. Responsible person records must be kept for six years, the first two in an easily accessible place. *Office* is defined in Rule 17a-3(h)(1) as any location where one or more associated persons regularly conducts the business of handling funds or securities or effecting any securities transactions. The broker-dealer is required to make and keep certain records at the office including blotters, order tickets, information on associated persons, and customer account records. Office records must be maintained at the office itself for the most recent two-year period or the broker-dealer can agree to keep them centralized and produce them promptly at the office at the request of the SEC, an SRO,

To ensure computers that don't use company computers are maintaining records properly.

or a state securities regulator. How do these records facilitate regulators' determination of broker-dealer compliance with applicable federal laws and SRO rules?

2. *Communications and Compliance Supervision Records.* The broker-dealer must make and keep a record showing that it has complied with applicable federal and SRO rules requiring a principal to approve its communications with the public. Such communications include advertisements and sales literature. It must also maintain all business-related communications (e.g., inter-office memos, emails, and tape recordings) including those approved by a principal. The record establishing approval by a principal must be kept for three years, the first two in an easily accessible place. In addition, the broker-dealer must keep each compliance, supervisory, and procedures manual (including updates, modifications, and revisions) describing the policies and practices of the broker-dealer with respect to compliance with applicable federal and SRO requirements for the supervision of its associated persons. These manuals must be kept for three years after the broker-dealer has ceased to use the manual.

3. *Lost or Stolen Securities.* Broker-dealers have reporting requirements with respect to certificated securities. Rule 17f-1(a)(6) defines *securities certificates* as any physical instrument that represents or purports to represent ownership in a security that was printed by or on behalf of the issuer, including canceled and counterfeit securities. Broker-dealers must report lost or stolen securities on Form X-17F-1A to the SEC and the FBI. Broker-dealers, to a limited extent, must inquire whether securities certificates they received have been reported as missing, lost, counterfeit, or stolen. Copies of Form X-17F-1A, any inquiry-related correspondence, and all agreements between reporting institutions regarding registration or other aspects of missing, lost, counterfeit, or stolen securities must be kept for three years. Under *When* what circumstances must transfer agents for securities be notified of lost, missing, or stolen securities? Read Rule 17f-1, 17 C.F.R. §240.17f-1.

4. *Broker-Dealer Internal Systems Records.* Broker-dealers operate internal trading systems that provide a mechanism for facilitating an agreement for the purchase or sale of a security between a customer and the broker-dealer or sponsor,[38] or between two customers of the broker-dealer or sponsor. Accordingly, a broker-dealer has substantial recordkeeping requirements under Rule 17a-3(a)(16). Records for such systems include the names of customers using the system (and their affiliation with the broker-dealer), daily summaries of trading (during and after regular trading hours), information on debt securities, counterparty identification, and time-sequenced records of transactions (e.g., execution date, time, price, size, and security traded). In addition, all notices distributed in connection with the broker-dealer's internal system must be maintained. For example, notices addressing hours of operations, system malfunctions, changes to system proce-

---

38. A sponsor is not a registered broker-dealer but has contracted with a broker-dealer to provide a facility for use by the broker-dealer and its customers. In other words, the sponsor acts as a system operator for the broker-dealer.

dures, and instructions pertaining to access must be kept. All records regarding the broker-dealer's internal trading systems must be kept for three years, the first two in an easily accessible place.

5. *Recordkeeping in the Cloud.* Recordkeeping in the Cloud should save broker-dealers considerable money because they avoid the costs of in-house IT by placing their applications and data on servers and systems maintained by other parties. Many broker-dealers take advantage of third-party service providers in the Cloud to archive e-mail, text messages, and other electronic documents, including financial transaction data, trade confirmations, order tickets, and net capital records. Does this outsourcing of recordkeeping comply with Rule 17a-4?

[handwritten] ↳ Yes so long notify change.

Chapter 10

Broker-Dealer Fraud

Regulatory Authority

Securities Act of 1933 Section 17(a)

Securities Exchange Act of 1934 Sections 10(b) and 15(c) (1)-(2)
Exchange Act Rule 10b-5

Motivating Hypothetical

The board of directors of Success First ("BOD") is very concerned about being accused of committing securities fraud. It realizes that broker-dealers are peculiarly subject to such claims given the nature of the securities business. When the market goes up, investors are happy because their investment portfolios are rising. Lately, the market has been steadily increasing. However, the BOD knows that it is only a matter of time before the market declines or becomes volatile. The BOD knows that when this happens customers who were previously happy will be unhappy because the value of their accounts will inevitably decline. The BOD wants to get ahead of this issue and be prepared for the possible claims that may be filed against Success First. Therefore, it has set up a special committee composed of Josephine Wiseman (director and general counsel of Success First), Carmen Alvarez (director and CEO), and Malak Johnson (chief compliance officer) to review Success First's entire book of business and evaluate it for possible exposure to liability for securities fraud. Josephine will lead the committee and expects that this assessment will take about three months to complete. She will prepare a report for the board. She will also start to vet outside counsel to represent Success First in possible securities arbitration claims filed by its customers with FINRA.

I. Introduction

The antifraud provisions of the federal securities laws apply to a range of broker-dealer misconduct in their dealings with customers and other market participants. Although there are several antifraud provisions under the federal securities laws, this chapter will focus on those most frequently used to combat fraudulent broker-dealer conduct: (1) Sections 15(c)(1) and (2) of the Exchange Act; (2) Section 17(a) of the

Securities Act; and (3) Section 10(b) of the Exchange Act.[1] Generally, these antifraud provisions can be established by proving essentially the same elements, but there are some differences. The work horse of the antifraud provisions for both regulators and private plaintiffs is § 10(b) and Rule 10b-5 promulgated thereunder. However, in addition to § 10(b) and Rule 10b-5, the SEC makes frequent use of § 15 of the Exchange Act and § 17(a) of the Securities Act in combating fraud committed by broker-dealers. This chapter explores the key differences in the scope of these antifraud provisions, reviews the elements of § 10(b) and Rule 10b-5, and then analyzes how these antifraud provisions are used by regulators and private plaintiffs to combat fraudulent broker-dealer conduct in the securities industry.

Sections 15(c)(1) and 15(c)(2) apply only to broker-dealers[2] and prohibit fraud in the purchase or sale of securities traded in the over-the-counter market.

(c) Use of manipulative or deceptive devices; contravention of rules and regulations

(1)(A) No broker or dealer shall make use of the mails or any means or instrumentality of interstate commerce to effect any transaction in, or to induce or attempt to induce the purchase or sale of, any security (other than commercial paper, bankers' acceptances, or commercial bills), ... by means of any manipulative, deceptive, or other fraudulent device or contrivance....

* * *

(2)(A) No broker or dealer shall make use of the mails or any means or instrumentality of interstate commerce to effect any transaction in, or to induce or attempt to induce the purchase or sale of, any security (other than an exempted security or commercial paper, bankers' acceptances, or commercial bills) otherwise than on a national securities exchange of which it is a member, in connection with which such broker or dealer engages in any fraudulent, deceptive, or manipulative act or practice, or makes any fictitious quotation....

Note that the primary difference between §§ 15(c) (1) and (2) is that the latter expressly prohibits fictitious quotations in the over-the-counter market. In addition, § 15(c) (2) (D) authorizes the SEC to define fraudulent conduct by rulemaking. The SEC has utilized this authority by adopting rules that specify certain broker-dealer

---

1. Section 9(a)(4) of the Exchange Act is also an antifraud provision. It prohibits fraudulent misstatements in the inducement of the purchase and sale of exchange-listed securities and requires proof that the broker-dealer know or have reason to know of the falsity of the statements. Although it is self-operative and permits a private right of action, it is used infrequently because of the limitations of § 9(f) of the Exchange Act. Section 9(f) of the Exchange Act requires the plaintiff to prove, in addition to the elements enumerated in § 9(a)(4), that the plaintiff purchased or sold the security at a price that was affected by the broker-dealer's manipulative acts, i.e., the plaintiff must prove causation. *See* Lowe v. Salomon Smith Barney, Inc., 206 F. Supp. 2d 442, 444 (W.D.N.Y 2002).

2. Subsections (B) and (C) of § 15(c)(1) expressly identify municipal securities dealers and government securities broker-dealers. The regulatory framework for municipal securities dealers and government securities broker-dealers is beyond the scope of this textbook.

conduct as fraud, including misrepresentations or omissions of material facts and excessive trading in discretionary accounts. However, the limitation of §§ 15(c) (1) and (2) to securities traded in the over-the-counter market means that it is used less frequently than § 17(a) of the Securities Act and § 10(b) of the Exchange Act by regulators to combat fraud.

Section 17(a) of the Securities Act prohibits fraud in the offer and sale of any security.

(a) Use of interstate commerce for purpose of fraud or deceit

It shall be unlawful for any person in the offer or sale of any securities ... by the use of any means or instruments of transportation or communication in interstate commerce or by use of the mails, directly or indirectly

(1) To employ any device, scheme, or artifice to defraud, or

(2) To obtain money or property by means of any untrue statement of a material fact or any omission to state a material fact necessary in order to make the statements made, in light of the circumstances under which they were made, not misleading; or

(3) To engage in any transaction, practice, or course of business which operates or would operate as a fraud or deceit upon the purchaser.

Section 17(a), unlike § 15(c), applies to any security that is offered and sold fraudulently by any person. In addition, § 17(a)(1) requires proof of scienter. Sections 17(a)(2) and 17(a)(3) may be violated by negligent conduct. In addition, the term *seller* is defined very broadly under § 17(a) so that the broker-dealer may be liable even if it doesn't own the security being sold as long as there is solicitation motivated by personal gain (anticipation of a share of the profits is sufficient to establish personal gain.). Finally, as we shall see below, § 17(a)(2) encompasses a broader scope of conduct than 10(b) and Rule 10b-5 because it does not require the seller of securities to actually make the false or misleading statement or omission. This means that an underwriter can be liable under § 17(a)(2) when selling securities by means of a false statement made by another person.

Section 10(b) prohibits fraud in the purchase or sale of any security.

It shall be unlawful for any person, directly or indirectly, by the use of any means or instrumentality of interstate commerce or of the mails, or of any facility of any national securities exchange—

* * *

(b) To use or employ, in connection with the purchase or sale of any security registered on a national securities exchange or any security not so registered, ... any manipulative or deceptive device or contrivance in contravention of such rules and regulations as the Commission may prescribe as necessary or appropriate in the public interest or for the protection of investors....

Section 10(b) is not self-operative and can only be violated by violating a rule adopted by the SEC. Thus, alleging a violation of § 10(b) requires an allegation of both § 10(b) and Rule 10b-5. Rule 10b-5 provides that:

It shall be unlawful for any person, directly or indirectly, by the use of any means or instrumentality of interstate commerce, or of the mails or of any facility of any national securities exchange,

(a) To employ any device, scheme, or artifice to defraud,

(b) To make any untrue statement of a material fact or to omit to state a material fact necessary in order to make the statements made, in the light of the circumstances under which they were made, not misleading, or

(c) To engage in any act, practice, or course of business which operates or would operate as a fraud or deceit upon any person,

in connection with the purchase or sale of any security.

The scope of § 10(b) and Rule 10b-5 is very broad. They apply to any security (OTC or exchange-listed) and any transaction that involves a security. They also apply to any person. Subsections (a) and (c) prohibit fraudulent or deceptive practices in the absence of a material misstatement or omission. This means that § 10(b) and Rule 10b-5 are used by regulators and private plaintiffs to assert claims against broker-dealers for various types of misconduct, such as churning, unauthorized trading, market manipulation, and recommending unsuitable securities.

II. Elements of § 10(b) and Rule 10b-5

The elements of a successful claim under § 10(b) and Rule 10b-5 depend upon whether the plaintiff is the SEC or a private plaintiff. See Table 10.1 below. The SEC is not required to prove three of the six elements.

Table 10.1. Elements of § 10(b) and Rule 10b-5 Claims

Element	SEC	Private Plaintiff
In connection with the purchase or sale of a security	✓	✓
Material misstatement or omission or other fraudulent device	✓	✓
Scienter	✓	✓
Reliance		✓
Loss Causation		✓
Damages (economic loss)		✓

In addition, private plaintiffs are subject to special pleading requirements. Section 21D(b)(1) of the Exchange Act requires private plaintiffs to identify with specificity the individuals making the material misrepresentations and the reasons such statements are misleading. Essentially, they must identify the who, when, where, and to whom the material misrepresentations or omissions were made. Section 21D(b)(2) of the Exchange Act requires private plaintiffs to allege facts that prove the defendant acted with a particular state of mind, i.e., scienter. In addition, Rule 9(b) of the Federal Rules of Civil Procedure ("FRCP 9(b)") require the SEC (and all plaintiffs) to plead fraud with this level of particularity, except that FRCP 9(b) allows scienter or state of mind to be pled generally. As we review the elements of § 10(b) and Rule 10b-5, consider how these heightened pleading requirements affect the probability of success for private plaintiffs.

A. In Connection with the Purchase or Sale of Any Security

The requirement that the fraud occur in connection with the purchase or sale of any security limits the class of persons that have standing to sue. Essentially, there must be a purchase or sale of a security and the purchase or sale must be related to the fraud. However, the courts have construed this requirement flexibly in both private causes of action and actions brought by the SEC, as illustrated in the following cases.

SEC v. Zandford
535 U.S. 813 (2002)

Justice STEVENS delivered the opinion of the Court.

The Securities and Exchange Commission (SEC) filed a civil complaint alleging that a stockbroker violated both § 10(b) of the Securities Exchange Act of 1934, and the SEC's Rule 10b-5, by selling his customer's securities and using the proceeds for his own benefit without the customer's knowledge or consent. The question presented is whether the alleged fraudulent conduct was "in connection with the purchase or sale of any security" within the meaning of the statute and the Rule.

I

Between 1987 and 1991, respondent was employed as a securities broker in the Maryland branch of a New York brokerage firm. In 1987, he persuaded William Wood, an elderly man in poor health, to open a joint investment account for himself and his mentally retarded daughter. According to the SEC's complaint, the "stated investment objectives for the account were 'safety of principal and income.'" The Woods granted respondent discretion to manage their account and a general power of attorney to engage in securities transactions for their benefit without prior approval. Relying on respondent's promise to "conservatively invest" their money, the Woods entrusted him with $419,255. Before Mr. Wood's death in 1991, all of that money was gone.

In 1991, the National Association of Securities Dealers (NASD) conducted a routine examination of respondent's firm and discovered that on over 25 separate occasions, money had been transferred from the Woods' account to accounts controlled by respondent. In due course, respondent was indicted in the United States District Court for the District of Maryland on 13 counts of wire fraud. The first count alleged that respondent sold securities in the Woods' account and then made personal use of the proceeds. Each of the other counts alleged that he made wire transfers between Maryland and New York that enabled him to withdraw specified sums from the Woods' accounts. Some of those transfers involved respondent writing checks to himself from a mutual fund account held by the Woods, which required liquidating securities in order to redeem the checks. Respondent was convicted on all counts, sentenced to prison for 52 months, and ordered to pay $10,800 in restitution.

After respondent was indicted, the SEC filed a civil complaint in the same District Court alleging that respondent violated § 10(b) and Rule 10b-5 by engaging in a scheme to defraud the Woods and by misappropriating approximately $343,000 of the Woods' securities without their knowledge or consent. The SEC moved for partial summary judgment.... Respondent filed a motion seeking discovery on the question whether his fraud had the requisite "connection with" the purchase or sale of a security. The District Court ... entered summary judgment against respondent....

The Court of Appeals for the Fourth Circuit reversed the summary judgment and remanded with directions for the District Court to dismiss the complaint.... The court then held that the civil complaint did not sufficiently allege the necessary connection because the sales of the Woods' securities were merely incidental to a fraud that "lay in absconding with the proceeds" of sales that were conducted in "a routine and customary fashion...." Respondent's "scheme was simply to steal the Woods' assets" rather than to engage "in manipulation of a particular security." Ultimately, the court refused "to stretch the language of the securities fraud provisions to encompass every conversion or theft that happens to involve securities." Adopting what amounts to a "fraud on the market" theory of the statute's coverage, the court held that without some "relationship to market integrity or investor understanding," there is no violation of § 10(b).

We granted the SEC's petition for a writ of certiorari, to review the Court of Appeals' construction of the phrase "in connection with the purchase or sale of any security." ...

In its role enforcing the Act, the SEC has consistently adopted a broad reading of the phrase "in connection with the purchase or sale of any security." It has maintained that a broker who accepts payment for securities that he never intends to deliver, or who sells customer securities with intent to misappropriate the proceeds, violates § 10(b) and Rule 10b-5. This interpretation of the ambiguous text of § 10(b), in the context of formal adjudication, is entitled to deference if it is reasonable.... For the reasons set forth below, we think it is. While the statute must not be construed so broadly as to convert every common-law fraud that happens to involve securities into a violation of § 10(b) ... neither the SEC nor this Court has ever held that there must be a misrepresentation about the value of a particular security in order to run afoul of the Act.

The SEC claims respondent engaged in a fraudulent scheme in which he made sales of his customer's securities for his own benefit. Respondent submits that the sales themselves were perfectly lawful and that the subsequent misappropriation of the proceeds, though fraudulent, is not properly viewed as having the requisite connection with the sales; in his view, the alleged scheme is not materially different from a simple theft of cash or securities in an investment account. We disagree.

According to the complaint, respondent "engaged in a scheme to defraud" the Woods beginning in 1988, shortly after they opened their account, and that scheme continued throughout the 2-year period during which respondent made a series of transactions that enabled him to convert the proceeds of the sales of the Woods' securities to his own use. The securities sales and respondent's fraudulent practices were not independent events. This is not a case in which, after a lawful transaction had been consummated, a broker decided to steal the proceeds and did so. Nor is it a case in which a thief simply invested the proceeds of a routine conversion in the stock market. Rather, respondent's fraud coincided with the sales themselves.

Taking the allegations in the complaint as true, each sale was made to further respondent's fraudulent scheme; each was deceptive because it was neither authorized by, nor disclosed to, the Woods. With regard to the sales of shares in the Woods' mutual fund, respondent initiated these transactions by writing a check to himself from that account, knowing that redeeming the check would require the sale of securities. Indeed, each time respondent "exercised his power of disposition for his own benefit," that conduct, "without more," was a fraud. In the aggregate, the sales are properly viewed as a "course of business" that operated as a fraud or deceit on a stockbroker's customer.

The benefit of a discretionary account is that it enables individuals, like the Woods, who lack the time, capacity, or know-how to supervise investment decisions, to delegate authority to a broker who will make decisions in their best interests without prior approval. If such individuals cannot rely on a broker to exercise that discretion for their benefit, then the account loses its added value. Moreover, any distinction between omissions and misrepresentations is illusory in the context of a broker who has a fiduciary duty to her clients....

In *United States v. O'Hagan*, 521 U.S. 642, 117 S.Ct. 2199, 138 L.Ed.2d 724 (1997), we held that the defendant had committed fraud "in connection with" a securities transaction when he used misappropriated confidential information for trading purposes. We reasoned that "the fiduciary's fraud is consummated, not when the fiduciary gains the confidential information, but when, without disclosure to his principal, he uses the information to purchase or sell securities. The securities transaction and the breach of duty thus coincide. This is so even though the person or entity defrauded is not the other party to the trade, but is, instead, the source of the nonpublic information. The Court of Appeals distinguished *O'Hagan* by reading it to require that the misappropriated information or assets not have independent value to the client outside the securities market. We do not read *O'Hagan* as so limited.

In the chief passage cited by the Court of Appeals for this proposition, we discussed the Government's position that "[t]he misappropriation theory would not ... apply to a case in which a person defrauded a bank into giving him a loan or embezzled cash from another, and then used the proceeds of the misdeed to purchase securities," because in that situation "the proceeds would have value to the malefactor apart from their use in a securities transaction, and the fraud would be complete as soon as the money was obtained." Even if this passage could be read to introduce a new requirement into § 10(b), it would not affect our analysis of this case, because the Woods' securities did not have value for respondent apart from their use in a securities transaction and the fraud was not complete before the sale of securities occurred.

[T]he SEC complaint describes a fraudulent scheme in which the securities transactions and breaches of fiduciary duty coincide. Those breaches were therefore "in connection with" securities sales within the meaning of § 10(b).[3] Accordingly, the judgment of the Court of Appeals is reversed, and the case is remanded for further proceedings consistent with this opinion.

Scottrade, Inc. v. BroCo Investments, Inc.

774 F. Supp. 2d 573 (S.D.N.Y. 2011)

RICHARD J. HOLWELL, District Judge:

This action presents a surprising question of first impression. Does a securities broker, whose customers have been defrauded, and who reimburses his customers—but to whom the customers have not assigned their claims, and who other than the reimbursements alleges no damages whatsoever—have standing to sue the alleged fraudsters for violations of Section 10(b) of the Securities Exchange Act of 1934, Exchange Act Rule 10b-5 promulgated thereunder, ... For the reasons discussed more fully below, and specifically because the Court concludes that the broker, Scottrade, Inc. ("Scottrade"), was not an "actual purchaser or seller of securities," the Court holds that the broker lacks standing to pursue those claims. The Court thus dismisses the claims for violations of Section 10(b), Rule 10b–5,

* * *

A. Background

Plaintiff Scottrade, an Arizona corporation ... is a securities broker-dealer registered with the United States Securities and Exchange Commission ("SEC"). As relevant to this action, Scottrade operates a website on which customers maintain accounts of securities and through which customers place orders to buy and sell securities. De-

---

3. [4] Contrary to the Court of Appeals' prediction, our analysis does not transform every breach of fiduciary duty into a federal securities violation. If, for example, a broker embezzles cash from a client's account or takes advantage of the fiduciary relationship to induce his client into a fraudulent real estate transaction, then the fraud would not include the requisite connection to a purchase or sale of securities. Likewise, if the broker told his client he was stealing the client's assets, that breach of fiduciary duty might be in connection with a sale of securities, but it would not involve a deceptive device or fraud.

fendant Genesis, a New York Limited Liability Company ... is also a securities broker-dealer registered with the SEC. Defendant BroCo Investments, Inc. ("BroCo")
is a corporation organized under the laws of Mauritius. Defendant Valery Maltsev is
BroCo's president. BroCo is not licensed to operate as a broker in the United States,
but appears to offer investment and/or brokerage services to its foreign customers.
BroCo also maintained an investment account with Genesis (the "BroCo/Genesis Account"), over which BroCo was the sole legal owner. BroCo pooled its customers'
funds in the BroCo/Genesis Account, and assigned its customers "user names" and
trading limits with which the customers could order trades by contacting Genesis directly. BroCo, however, and not its customers, took formal responsibility for the
trades in the account. Genesis would "regularly" generate reports of trading activity
in the BroCo/Genesis Account and transmit those reports to BroCo.

Between August 2009 and March 2010, Valery Vitalievich Ksendzov—not a defendant
in this action—allegedly carried out an elaborate "hack, pump, and dump" scheme
by which he made upwards of $650,000 dollars. Ksendzov, a BroCo customer, would
first purchase large blocks of thinly-traded domestic securities through the BroCo/Gen-
esis Account. Ksendzov then hacked[4] into the online brokerage accounts of Scottrade's
customers and entered huge numbers of buy orders in those Scottrade customer accounts
for the thinly-traded securities held under his "user name" in the BroCo/Genesis Account.
After the phony purchase orders drove up the price of the thinly traded securities,
Ksendzov would liquidate his positions for returns on investment as high as 32,000
percent. The Scottrade customer accounts were thereby presumably left with large
amounts of worthless illiquid stock that had been purchased at prices far above its value.

Scottrade alleges that Ksendzov's "trading activit[y] so consistently resulted in levels
of profitability that are unattainable in the absence of some form of fraud ... [that
defendants] Maltsev, BroCo and Genesis must have known, absent intentional disregard ... that Ksendzov's trading involved some form of illegal market manipulation."
Scottrade also alleges that BroCo and Genesis must have been aware of the fraud because Genesis would generate records of the trading activity in the BroCo/Genesis
Account and forward those records to BroCo.

After learning of the fraud, Scottrade "restored the customers' accounts to the state
they would have been in, but for the unauthorized transactions." The actual character
of that restoration, however, is not clear.... Scottrade alleges it "incurred" $1,464,690
in "losses" in the process.

* * *

Genesis moved to dismiss the complaint.... Scottrade moved for leave to file an
amended complaint based on new evidence....

* * *

C. Section 10(b) and Rule 10b-5 Claims

---

4. [3] "Essentially, hacking is the ability to bypass computer security protocols and gain access to
computer systems." *United States v. Petersen*, 98 F.3d 502, 504 n. 1 (9th Cir.1996).

Standing Requirement

"It is axiomatic that in order to have standing, a 10b–5 plaintiff in a private damages action must have been either a purchaser or seller of the securities that form the basis of the [ ] deceptive conduct." The "actual purchaser or seller" rule, articulated by the Second Circuit in *Birnbaum v. Newport Steel Corp.*, 193 F.2d 461 (2d Cir.1952), "was adopted by the Supreme Court as a bright-line rule in *Blue Chip Stamps v. Manor Drug Stores,* [421 U.S. 723, 95 S.Ct. 1917, 44 L.Ed.2d 539 (1975)]." *In re Refco Capital Markets, Ltd. Brokerage Customer Sec. Litig.*, 586 F.Supp.2d 172, 178–79 (S.D.N.Y.2008). In *Blue Chip Stamps*, "[t]he Court specifically rejected a shifting and highly fact-oriented disposition of the issue of who may bring a damages claim for violation of Rule 10b–5 and stated that such an approach would not be a satisfactory basis for a rule of liability imposed on the conduct of business transactions."

Nowhere in its complaint does Scottrade allege that it purchased or sold any securities. Instead Scottrade seems to allege that it provided the interface and systems by which defendants' and Ksendzov's purchases and sales occurred, and which eventually caused harm to Scottrade's customers. ("Scottrade's customers initiate orders to purchase or sell securities for their Scottrade accounts using online interfaces."); (Ksendzov " 'hacked' into the online brokerage accounts of Scottrade's customers ... to log on and enter orders to purchase the securities in which he had amassed a position.... [Ksendzov] had [no] authority to enter orders for the accounts of Scottrade's customers.").)[5] Indeed, Scottrade concedes that the losses were not felt by it due to its trading activity; but that those losses were instead the product of defendant's and Ksendzov's alleged scheme which used funds in accounts owned by Scottrade customers to purchase overvalued stock at increasingly inflated prices, and which left those accounts full of worthless stock. ("In effect, the perpetrators of 'hack, pump and dump' schemes steal money from the accounts in which the unauthorized orders have been placed.").) Scottrade only felt losses because it "restored the customers' accounts to the state they would have been in, but for the unauthorized transactions [and] Scottrade's losses incurred in doing so were at least $1,464,690."

---

5. [4] ("The relief sought is intended to compensate Scottrade for the losses it sustained in consequence of a so-called 'hack, pump and dump' scheme conducted in part through securities transactions effected or controlled by [defendants].")); ("Utilizing (without the owners' permission) user names and passwords that provide access to brokerage accounts of investors who handle their purchases and sales of securities through on-line interfaces with their brokerage firms' computers, perpetrators of 'hack, pump and dump' schemes place unauthorized orders to purchase shares of thinly traded securities for the brokerage accounts linked to the unwitting investors' user names."); ("The trading initiated by Ksendzov and effected or controlled by Maltsev, BroCo and Genesis ..."); (Ksendzov "entered unauthorized orders directing Scottrade to effect for the accounts of Scottrade's customers the transactions described."); (Scottrade "caused such orders to be executed."); (" ... the transactions Scottrade effected (pursuant to Ksendzov's unauthorized orders) for the accounts of the Scottrade customers ..."); ("In reliance upon the authenticity of those orders, Scottrade effected purchases and sales of securities."). Paragraphs 24, 31, and 43 suggests a congruence between "effect[ing]" of unauthorized trades on the one hand, and buying or selling on the other. As discussed in this opinion, *infra,* the two are not the same for the purposes of the "actual purchaser or seller" standing analysis.

The Court is therefore essentially faced with two questions. First, is Scottrade—an online broker that executed phony orders apparently placed by its customers, and then reimbursed its customers for those customers' losses on the trades—an "actual purchaser or seller" of securities in the traditional 10b–5 case? And second, can Scottrade assert "actual purchaser or seller" standing under any other theory?

Surprisingly, the Second Circuit and no court in this district has addressed these questions. But the Court finds the Second Circuit's decision in *Klein Co. Futures, Inc. v. Board of Trade of the City of New York*, 464 F.3d 255 (2d Cir. 2006) ("*Klein II*"), and district court cases *In re Refco Capital Markets, Ltd. Brokerage Customer Sec. Litig.*, 586 F.Supp.2d 172 (S.D.N.Y.2008), and *Manufacturers Hanover Trust Co. v. Smith Barney, Harris Upham Co., Inc.*, 770 F.Supp. 176 (S.D.N.Y.1991), persuasive; and finds that Scottrade was not here an "actual purchaser or seller" of securities.

In *Klein*, Klein was a "futures commission merchant ... [that] facilitated the trading and fulfilled certain obligations of its customers who traded through the [Board of Trade of the City of New York ('NYBOT')]," essentially acting "as a broker or agent that earned commissions for handling its customers [sic] trades." Klein's customers were required to maintain a certain level of equity in their accounts; and Klein was required, under federal statutes and NYBOT rules, to guarantee its customer's trades. Norman Eisler and his company First West, one of Klein's customers, manipulated settlement prices on certain futures and options eventually leading to a $4.5 million deficit in First West's account with Klein. Klein, as guarantor, took the $4.5 million hit, which eventually put Klein out of business.

Klein sued Eisler, First West, the NYBOT, and several other entities, for *inter alia* anti-fraud violations of the Commodity Exchange Act ("CEA"). The district ... dismissed on standing grounds and the Second Circuit affirmed. Section 22 of the CEA, like Section 10(b) and Rule 10b–5 of the Exchange Act, provides that "only *purchasers or sellers*" have standing. Klein, however, was not a purchaser or seller of the options contracts at issue, nor did it own those contracts. Instead, "Klein functioned merely as a broker or agent" that "handl[ed] its customers' trades." The trades at issue occurred on Klein's customers' accounts; no trading activity occurred on Klein's own account. It was First West, not Klein, that initiated the trades, and Klein had nothing to do with those decisions. Though Klein might have eventually had to guarantee account deficits, "Klein had no interest in any of the resulting profits or investments losses," resulting from First west's trades. Accordingly, Klein's damages were not the product of its activity as a purchaser or seller of securities; "[q]uite simply, it did not suffer its damages in the course of its trading activities on a contract market."

The case at bar presents the same standing requirement applied to almost the same factual scenario. Here, the alleged fraud of defendants and a non-defendant third party (Ksendzov) caused Scottrade's customers to engage in unauthorized purchases of securities. Though acting as a broker or agent that handled or "effected" customers' trades, much like Klein, Scottrade initiated no trades, did no trading activity itself, ordered no trades for its own account, and had no input concerning its customers' "decisions" to place orders. Furthermore, Scottrade had no direct interest in the resulting profits or losses on those trades; Scottrade's loss occurred only because it made its customers whole after those customers lost money due to, in part, Scottrade's own computer security failures. But as with the anti-fraud provisions of the CEA, standing under Section 10(b) requires that Scottrade itself have been an actual purchaser or seller of securities. Because Scottrade was not, it lacks standing in this case.

This holding finds support in this District's cases that have come closest to the issue when considering Section 10(b) claims. In *Manufacturers Hanover*, MHT was a stock transfer agent[6] whose employee stole stock certificates owned by MHT's customer DTC and entrusted to MHT. The employee then canceled DTC's stock certificates, reissued certificates to himself, and sold the stock. After discovering the fraud, MHT repurchased the stock in the market at its own expense of over $1 million, and returned that stock to DTC's account. DTC assigned all claims to MHT. MHT then sued the employee and the financial institutions that processed the employee's sales for Section 10(b) fraud, alleging *inter alia* that the institutions should have known fraud was afoot and would have been able to prevent the losses had they done proper investigations.

MHT argued it had standing as an actual purchaser or seller because (1) it stood in the shoes of DTC; (2) it possessed the stock certificates when they were stolen; (3) its employee's cancellation of the certificates operated as a securities sale; and (4) it was the sole injured party. The court disagreed. The Court found first that the facts did not present a purchase or sale of securities as much as a *theft* of stock certificates followed by a sale by the thief. Noting that "[a] conversion of securities does not become a purchase or sale of securities merely because the bailee reimbursed the loss," … the court stated, "[a] fraudulent change in ownership" does not "constitute sufficient basis for finding a sale of securities," and accordingly MHT lacked "purchaser or seller" standing. The Court went on to find that the fraud did not occur "in connection with" a purchase or sale of securities because "no investment decision [was] made by either DTC or MHT and no such decision was affected by any fraud on defendant's part."

As with *Manufacturers Hanover*, the fraud here involved no investment decision by Scottrade, no purchase or sale by Scottrade, and no losses for Scottrade other than due to its reimbursement of its clients. And like that case, Ksendzov's hacking activity sounds more in theft or conversion than in securities fraud; that Ksendzov used that theft to make profitable his own purchasing and selling activity does not, however, make *Scottrade* a purchaser or seller of securities.[7]

---

6. [5] A "stock transfer agent" is "entrusted with the custody and care of publicly traded stock certificates, in transferable form, by the owners or depositors of such stock certificates." *Manufacturers Hanover*, 770 F. Supp. at 178.

7. [6] To paraphrase *Manufacturers Hanover*: Scottrade's customers entrusted their accounts' security to the custody of Scottrade. Scottrade employed certain computer security systems to ensure the security of those accounts. The damage suffered by the customers and Scottrade flowed not from a decision to buy or sell securities but rather from the decision of Scottrade to employ its particular computer security systems. The customers relied upon Scottrade who in turn relied upon its computer security systems. Any breach by Ksendzov of those systems is not by itself sufficient to establish the basis for a federal securities claim, at least not by the executing broker.

A different but relevant situation was presented in *In re Refco Capital Markets, Ltd. Brokerage Customer Sec. Litig.*, 586 F.Supp.2d 172 (S.D.N.Y.2008). There plaintiffs were holders of "non-discretionary trading accounts at RCM [a brokerage firm], which meant that any transaction made by RCM on [plaintiffs'] behalf required their advance approval." RCM, however, purchased and sold the securities in plaintiffs' accounts without plaintiffs' approval, leading to "hundreds of millions of dollars in losses" in those accounts. The court found that plaintiffs were not actual purchasers or sellers of securities, and therefore lacked standing under Section 10(b), because of the "key fact" that RCM's trading activity was not done for plaintiffs' benefit but instead for its own.

Likewise here, Scottrade's customers' "trades," ordered by Ksendzov, were not made on *Scottrade's* behalf but instead on those customers' behalf. No trades were made for the benefit of Scottrade, the plaintiff here; and Scottrade bore the losses for those "trades" only because of its decision to make its customers whole. As Judge Lynch noted in *In re Refco*, "[i]n adopting the *Birnbaum* rule ... the Supreme Court itself recognized that the bright-line purchaser-seller requirement, strictly applied, would exclude certain classes of potential plaintiffs who may have legitimate claims of injury." Thus, "proper application of the [purchaser-seller rule] for standing to sue will undoubtedly prevent some otherwise meritorious claims from surviving motions to dismiss." Accordingly, though Scottrade's decision to restore its customers' accounts might be admirable, Scottrade is not a purchaser or seller for purposes of Section 10(b).

Scottrade argues that " 'there is authority in this [C]ircuit that a broker who purchases or sells as agent for his customer satisfies the purchaser-seller requirement.' " ... But *Odette*—a 1975 case decided before the Supreme Court's decision in *Blue Chip Stamps*—and the other cases Scottrade cites do not present the situation at bar. *Odette* held that standing existed because, as noted in *In re Refco*, the broker was acting as principal for its own account.

The authority cited by *Odette* for the proposition that brokers acting as agents for customers might be purchasers was *A.T. Brod Co. v. Perlow*, 375 F.2d 393 (2d Cir.1967). But *A.T. Brod* found that the broker had standing because it purchased securities for its customers and then turned around and demanded payment from those customers before delivering the securities, who did not pay and thereby caused the broker to suffer a loss when it resold the securities in the market. This situation—where an eventually non-paying customer orders securities and a broker buys the securities for the customer but takes a loss on its resale when the customer refuses to pay, or conversely where a clearing agent is required to guarantee a non-paying buyer's purchases and pay for and accept receipt from the seller of the securities involved for its own account—makes the broker or agent a "forced" or "compelled" purchaser or seller for purposes of Section 10(b) claims. But a "forced" or "compelled" purchaser or seller's standing is an exception to the "actual purchaser or seller" rule. *Gordon Partners v. Blumenthal*, No. 02 Civ. 7377, 2007 WL 431864, at *11 (S.D.N.Y. Feb. 9, 2007) ("The forced sale doctrine relaxes the requirement that only traditional purchasers or sellers of securities have standing to bring a Section 10(b) claim."). In any event, it does not apply to this case. Here, Ksendzov stole control of Scottrade's customers' accounts to make unauthorized purchases through Scottrade's online interface. Scottrade did not, however, solicit those customers' orders, place the trades, acquire the securities, and then seek payment for them before turning the securities over to the customers. Nor did Scottrade pay Genesis or any other party for its customers' fraudulent orders.

* * *

Because Scottrade does not satisfy the "actual purchaser or seller" standing requirement for Section 10(b) and Rule 10b–5 actions, those claims must be dismissed.

* * *

Genesis's motion to dismiss is GRANTED in its entirety, and all claims asserted against Genesis in this action are dismissed with prejudice. Scottrade's motion for leave to amend is DENIED in its entirety....

Hypothetical One

Josephine Wiseman, general counsel at Success First, has asked you, a newly hired associate, to compare two cases to determine whether the element "in connection with the purchase or sale of a security" could be established if it sustained losses in the event that the accounts of its online trading customers were hacked by a third party. She has directed you to prepare a memorandum that analyzes two cases to predict whether Success First would have standing to sue the third party if its online trading customers' accounts were hacked by a third party and Success First subsequently reimbursed them for their losses. Specifically, Wiseman has asked you to compare *Zandford* and *Scottrade,* noting the courts' reasoning for construing the "in connection with the purchase or sale of a security" element of Rule 10b-5 in each of the cases. Based on your comparative analysis of these two cases, is it possible to establish the "in connection with the purchase or sale of a security" element under Rule 10b-5 in favor of Success First?

B. Material Misstatement or Omission or Other Fraudulent Device

Section § 10(b) and Rule 10b-5 prohibit deception along with misstatements or omissions of material facts. Deception may take the form of a material misstatement or omission or may be "any device, scheme, or artifice to defraud" and any "act, practice, or course of business which operates or would operate as a fraud or deceit upon any person." The next case illustrates deception as a basic requirement in any successful action under § 10(b) and Rule 10b-5, even in the absence of a material misstatement or omission, and touches on the fiduciary obligation of broker-dealers.

Santa Fe Industries, Inc. v. Green
430 U.S. 462 (1977)

Mr. Justice WHITE delivered the opinion of the Court.

The issue in this case involves the reach and coverage of § 10(b) of the Securities Exchange Act of 1934 and Rule 10b-5 thereunder in the context of a Delaware short-form merger transaction used by the majority stockholder of a corporation to eliminate the minority interest.

I

In 1936, petitioner Santa Fe Industries, Inc. (Santa Fe), acquired control of 60% of the stock of Kirby Lumber Corp. (Kirby), a Delaware corporation. Through a series of purchases over the succeeding years, Santa Fe increased its control of Kirby's stock to 95%; the purchase prices during the period 1968-1973 ranged from $65 to $92.50 per share. In 1974, wishing to acquire 100% ownership of Kirby, Santa Fe availed itself of s 253 of the Delaware Corporation Law, known as the "short-form merger" statute. Section 253 permits a parent corporation owning at least 90% of the stock of a subsidiary to merge with that subsidiary, upon approval by the parent's board of directors, and to make payment in cash for the shares of the minority stockholders. The statute does not require the consent of, or advance notice to, the minority stockholders. However, notice of the merger must be given within 10 days after its effective date, and any stockholder who is dissatisfied with the terms of the merger may petition the Delaware Court of Chancery for a decree ordering the surviving corporation to pay him the fair value of his shares, as determined by a court-appointed appraiser subject to review by the court.

Santa Fe obtained independent appraisals of the physical assets of Kirby land, timber, buildings, and machinery and of Kirby's oil, gas, and mineral interests. These appraisals, together with other financial information, were submitted to Morgan Stanley & Co. (Morgan Stanley), an investment banking firm retained to appraise the fair market value of Kirby stock. Kirby's physical assets were appraised at $320 million (amounting to $640 for each of the 500,000 shares); Kirby's stock was valued by Morgan Stanley at $125 per share. Under the terms of the merger, minority stockholders were offered $150 per share.

The provisions of the short-form merger statute were fully complied with. The minority stockholders of Kirby were notified the day after the merger became effective and were advised of their right to obtain an appraisal in Delaware court if dissatisfied with the offer of $150 per share. They also received an information statement containing, in addition to the relevant financial data about Kirby, the appraisals of the value of Kirby's assets and the Morgan Stanley appraisal concluding that the fair market value of the stock was $125 per share.

Respondents, minority stockholders of Kirby, objected to the terms of the merger, but did not pursue their appraisal remedy in the Delaware Court of Chancery. Instead, they brought this action in federal court on behalf of the corporation and other minority stockholders, seeking to set aside the merger or to recover what they claimed to be the fair value of their shares. The amended complaint asserted that, based on the fair market value of Kirby's physical assets as revealed by the appraisal included in the information statement sent to minority shareholders, Kirby's stock was worth at least $772 per share.[8]

The complaint alleged further that the merger took place without prior notice to minority stockholders; that the purpose of the merger was to appropriate the difference between the "conceded pro rata value of the physical assets," and the offer of $150 per share to "freez(e) out the minority stockholders at a wholly inadequate price," and that Santa Fe, knowing the appraised value of the physical assets, obtained a "fraudulent appraisal" of the stock from Morgan Stanley and offered $25 above that appraisal "in order to lull the minority stockholders into erroneously believing that (Santa Fe was) generous." This course of conduct was alleged to be "a violation of Rule 10b-5 because defendants employed a 'device, scheme, or artifice to defraud' and engaged in an 'act, practice or course of business which operates or would operate as a fraud or deceit upon any person, in connection with the purchase or sale of any security.'" Morgan Stanley assertedly participated in the fraud as an accessory by submitting its appraisal of $125 per share although knowing the appraised value of the physical assets.

The District Court dismissed the complaint for failure to state a claim upon which relief could be granted. As the District Court understood the complaint, respondents' case rested on two distinct grounds. First, federal law was assertedly violated because the merger was for the sole purpose of eliminating the minority from the company, therefore lacking any justifiable business purpose, and because the merger was undertaken without prior notice to the minority shareholders. Second, the low valuation placed on the shares in the cash-exchange offer was itself said to be a fraud actionable under Rule 10b-5. In rejecting the first ground for recovery, the District Court reasoned that Delaware law required neither a business purpose for a short-form merger nor prior notice to the minority shareholders who the statute contemplated would be removed from the company, and that Rule 10b-5 did not override these provisions of state corporate law by independently placing a duty on the majority not to merge without prior notice and without a justifiable business purpose.

As for the claim that actionable fraud inhered in the allegedly gross undervaluation of the minority shares, the District Court observed that respondents valued their shares at a minimum of $772 per share, "basing this figure on the pro rata value of Kirby's physical assets." Accepting this valuation for purposes of the motion to dismiss, the District Court further noted that, as revealed by the complaint, the physical asset appraisal, along with other information relevant to Morgan Stanley's

---

8. [5] The figure of $772 per share was calculated as follows:
"The difference of $311,000,000 ($622 per share) between the fair market value of Kirby's land and timber, alone, as per the defendants' own appraisal thereof at $320,000,000 and the $9,000,000 book value of said land and timber, added to the $150 per share, yields a pro rata share of the value of the physical assets of Kirby of at least $772 per share. The value of the stock was at least the pro rata value of the physical assets."

valuation of the shares, had been included with the information statement sent to respondents within the time required by state law. It thought that if "full and fair disclosure is made, transactions eliminating minority interests are beyond the purview of Rule 10b-5," and concluded that the "complaint fail(ed) to allege an omission, misstatement or fraudulent course of conduct that would have impeded a shareholder's judgment of the value of the offer." The complaint therefore failed to state a claim and was dismissed.

A divided Court of Appeals for the Second Circuit reversed. It first agreed that there was a double aspect to the case: first, the claim that gross undervaluation of the minority stock itself violated Rule 10b-5; and second, that "without any misrepresentation or failure to disclose relevant facts, the merger itself constitutes a violation of Rule 10b-5" because it was accomplished without any corporate purpose and without prior notice to the minority stockholders.

As to the first aspect of the case, the Court of Appeals did not disturb the District Court's conclusion that the complaint did not allege a material misrepresentation or nondisclosure with respect to the value of the stock; and the court declined to rule that a claim of gross undervaluation itself would suffice to make out a Rule 10b-5 case. With respect to the second aspect of the case, however, the court fundamentally disagreed with the District Court as to the reach and coverage of Rule 10b-5. The Court of Appeals' view was that, although the Rule plainly reached material misrepresentations and nondisclosures in connection with the purchase or sale of securities, neither misrepresentation nor nondisclosure was a necessary element of a Rule 10b-5 action; the Rule reached "breaches of fiduciary duty by a majority against minority shareholders without any charge of misrepresentation or lack of disclosure."[9] The court went on to hold that the complaint, taken as a whole, stated a cause of action under the Rule:

> "We hold that a complaint alleges a claim under Rule 10b-5 when it charges, in connection with a Delaware short-form merger, that the majority has committed a breach of its fiduciary duty to deal fairly with minority shareholders by effecting the merger without any justifiable business purpose. The minority shareholders are given no prior notice of the merger, thus having no opportunity to apply for injunctive relief, and the proposed price to be paid is substantially lower than the appraised value reflected in the Information Statement."

We granted the petition for certiorari challenging this holding because of the importance of the issue involved to the administration of the federal securities laws. We reverse.

---

9. [8] The court concluded its discussion thus:
"Whether full disclosure has been made is not the crucial inquiry since it is the merger and the undervaluation which constituted the fraud, and not whether or not the majority determines to lay bare their real motives. If there is no valid corporate purpose for the merger, then even the most brazen disclosure of the fact to the minority shareholders in no way mitigates the fraudulent conduct."

II

The Court of Appeals' approach to the interpretation of Rule 10b-5 is inconsistent with that taken by the Court last Term in *Ernst & Ernst v. Hochfelder*, 425 U.S. 185, 96 S.Ct. 1375, 47 L.Ed.2d 668 (1976).

Ernst & Ernst makes clear that in deciding whether a complaint states a cause of action for "fraud" under Rule 10b-5, "we turn first to the language of § 10(b), for '(t)he starting point in every case involving construction of a statute is the language itself.'" ... The Court began with the principle that "(a)scertainment of congressional intent with respect to the standard of liability created by a particular section of the (1933 and 1934) Acts must ... rest primarily on the language of that section," and then focused on the statutory language of § 10(b) — "(t)he words 'manipulative or deceptive' used in conjunction with 'device or contrivance.'" The same language and the same principle apply to this case.

To the extent that the Court of Appeals would rely on the use of the term "fraud" in Rule 10b-5 to bring within the ambit of the Rule all breaches of fiduciary duty in connection with a securities transaction, its interpretation would, like the interpretation rejected by the Court in *Ernst & Ernest*, "add a gloss to the operative language of the statute quite different from its commonly accepted meaning." But, as the Court there held, the language of the statute must control the interpretation of the Rule:

> 'Rule 10b-5 was adopted pursuant to authority granted the (Securities and Exchange) Commission under § 10(b). The rulemaking power granted to an administrative agency charged with the administration of a federal statute is not the power to make law. Rather, it is "the power to adopt regulations to carry into effect the will of Congress as expressed by the statute." ... (The scope of the Rule) cannot exceed the power granted the Commission by Congress under § 10(b).'

The language of § 10(b) gives no indication that Congress meant to prohibit any conduct not involving manipulation or deception. Nor have we been cited to any evidence in the legislative history that would support a departure from the language of the statute. "When a statute speaks so specifically in terms of manipulation and deception, and when its history reflects no more expansive intent, we are quite unwilling to extend the scope of the statute ..." Thus the claim of fraud and fiduciary breach in this complaint states a cause of action under any part of Rule 10b-5 only if the conduct alleged can be fairly viewed as 'manipulative or deceptive' within the meaning of the statute.

III

It is our judgment that the transaction, if carried out as alleged in the complaint, was neither deceptive nor manipulative and therefore did not violate either § 10(b) of the Act or Rule 10b-5.

As we have indicated, the case comes to us on the premise that the complaint failed to allege a material misrepresentation or material failure to disclose. The finding of the District Court, undisturbed by the Court of Appeals, was that there was no "omission" or "misstatement" in the information statement accompanying the notice of merger. On the basis of the information provided, minority shareholders could either accept the price offered or reject it or seek an appraisal in the Delaware Court of Chancery. Their choice was fairly presented, and they were furnished with all relevant information on which to base their decision.

* * *

The judgment of the Court of Appeals is reversed, and the case is remanded for further proceedings consistent with this opinion.

———

Deception in the form of a material misstatement or omission requires determination of whether the statement or omission is material, a key concept under the federal securities laws.

Determining materiality in a § 10(b) and Rule 10b-5 action is a mixed question of law and fact. In *TSC Industries, Inc. v. Northway*, 426 U.S. 438 (1976), the Supreme Court stated that information is material if there is a "substantial likelihood that the disclosure ... would have been viewed by the reasonable investor as having significantly altered the 'total mix' of information available." This standard of materiality was adopted by the Supreme Court expressly for § 10(b) and Rule 10b-5 claims in the following case, along with an additional test for contingent or speculative events. As you read the case below, try to determine the formulation of the additional test for materiality and why it was necessary.

Basic Inc. v. Levinson
485 U.S. 224 (1988)

Justice BLACKMUN delivered the opinion of the Court.

This case requires us to apply the materiality requirement of § 10(b) of the Securities Exchange Act of 1934, and the Securities and Exchange Commission's Rule 10b-5, promulgated thereunder, in the context of preliminary corporate merger discussions....

I

Prior to December 20, 1978, Basic Incorporated was a publicly traded company primarily engaged in the business of manufacturing chemical refractories for the steel industry. As early as 1965 or 1966, Combustion Engineering, Inc., a company producing mostly alumina-based refractories, expressed some interest in acquiring Basic, but was deterred from pursuing this inclination seriously because of antitrust concerns it then entertained. In 1976, however, regulatory action opened the way to a renewal of Combustion's interest. The "Strategic Plan," dated October 25, 1976, for Combustion's Industrial Products Group included the objective: "Acquire Basic Inc. $30 million."

Beginning in September 1976, Combustion representatives had meetings and telephone conversations with Basic officers and directors, including petitioners here, concerning the possibility of a merger. During 1977 and 1978, Basic made three public statements denying that it was engaged in merger negotiations.[10] On December 18, 1978, Basic asked the New York Stock Exchange to suspend trading in its shares and issued a release stating that it had been "approached" by another company concerning a merger. On December 19, Basic's board endorsed Combustion's offer of $46 per share for its common stock, and on the following day publicly announced its approval of Combustion's tender offer for all outstanding shares.

Respondents are former Basic shareholders who sold their stock after Basic's first public statement of October 21, 1977, and before the suspension of trading in December 1978. Respondents brought a class action against Basic and its directors, asserting that the defendants issued three false or misleading public statements and thereby were in violation of § 10(b) of the 1934 Act and of Rule 10b-5. Respondents alleged that they were injured by selling Basic shares at artificially depressed prices in a market affected by petitioners' misleading statements and in reliance thereon.

On the merits, however, the District Court granted summary judgment for the defendants. It held that, as a matter of law, any misstatements were immaterial: there were no negotiations ongoing at the time of the first statement, and although negotiations were taking place when the second and third statements were issued, those negotiations were not "destined, with reasonable certainty, to become a merger agreement in principle."

The United States Court of Appeals for the Sixth Circuit ... reversed the District Court's summary judgment, and remanded the case. The court reasoned that while petitioners were under no general duty to disclose their discussions with Combustion, any statement the company voluntarily released could not be "so incomplete as to mislead." In the Court of Appeals' view, Basic's statements that no negotiations were taking place, and that it knew of no corporate developments to account for the heavy trading activity, were misleading. With respect to materiality, the court rejected the argument that preliminary merger discussions are immaterial as a matter of law, and held that "once a statement is made denying the existence of any discussions, even

---

10. On October 21, 1977, after heavy trading and a new high in Basic stock, the following news item appeared in the Cleveland Plain Dealer:

"[Basic] President Max Muller said the company knew no reason for the stock's activity and that no negotiations were under way with any company for a merger. He said Flintkote recently denied Wall Street rumors that it would make a tender offer of $25 a share for control of the Cleveland-based maker of refractories for the steel industry."

On September 25, 1978, in reply to an inquiry from the New York Stock Exchange, Basic issued a release concerning increased activity in its stock and stated that

"Management is unaware of any present or pending company development that would result in the abnormally heavy trading activity and price fluctuation in company shares that have been experienced in the past few days."

On November 6, 1978, Basic issued to its shareholders a "Nine Months Report 1978." This Report stated:

"With regard to the stock market activity in the Company's shares we remain unaware of any present or pending developments which would account for the high volume of trading and price fluctuations in recent months."

discussions that might not have been material in absence of the denial are material because they make the statement made untrue."

We granted certiorari, to resolve the split, among the Courts of Appeals as to the standard of materiality applicable to preliminary merger discussions ...

II

The Court ... explicitly has defined a standard of materiality under the securities laws, see *TSC Industries, Inc. v. Northway, Inc.*, 426 U.S. 438, 96 S.Ct. 2126, 48 L.Ed.2d 757 (1976), concluding in the proxy-solicitation context that "[a]n omitted fact is material if there is a substantial likelihood that a reasonable shareholder would consider it important in deciding how to vote." Acknowledging that certain information concerning corporate developments could well be of "dubious significance," the Court was careful not to set too low a standard of materiality; it was concerned that a minimal standard might bring an overabundance of information within its reach, and lead management "simply to bury the shareholders in an avalanche of trivial information—a result that is hardly conducive to informed decisionmaking." It further explained that to fulfill the materiality requirement "there must be a substantial likelihood that the disclosure of the omitted fact would have been viewed by the reasonable investor as having significantly altered the 'total mix' of information made available." We now expressly adopt the *TSC Industries* standard of materiality for the § 10(b) and Rule 10b-5 context.

III

The application of this materiality standard to preliminary merger discussions is not self-evident. Where the impact of the corporate development on the target's fortune is certain and clear, the *TSC Industries* materiality definition admits straightforward application. Where, on the other hand, the event is contingent or speculative in nature, it is difficult to ascertain whether the "reasonable investor" would have considered the omitted information significant at the time. Merger negotiations, because of the ever-present possibility that the contemplated transaction will not be effectuated, fall into the latter category.

A

Petitioners urge upon us a Third Circuit test for resolving this difficulty. Under this approach, preliminary merger discussions do not become material until "agreement-in-principle" as to the price and structure of the transaction has been reached between the would-be merger partners. By definition, then, information concerning any negotiations not yet at the agreement-in-principle stage could be withheld or even misrepresented without a violation of Rule 10b-5.

Three rationales have been offered in support of the "agreement-in-principle" test. The first derives from the concern expressed in *TSC Industries* that an investor not be overwhelmed by excessively detailed and trivial information, and focuses on the substantial risk that preliminary merger discussions may collapse: because such discussions are inherently tentative, disclosure of their existence itself could mislead investors and foster false optimism. The other two justifications for the agreement-in-principle standard are based on management concerns: because the requirement of "agreement-in-principle" limits the scope of disclosure obligations, it helps preserve the confidentiality of merger discussions where earlier disclosure might prejudice the negotiations; and the test also provides a usable, bright-line rule for determining when disclosure must be made.

None of these policy-based rationales, however, purports to explain why drawing the line at agreement-in-principle reflects the significance of the information upon the investor's decision. The first rationale, and the only one connected to the concerns expressed in *TSC Industries,* stands soundly rejected, even by a Court of Appeals that otherwise has accepted the wisdom of the agreement-in-principle test. "It assumes that investors are nitwits, unable to appreciate—even when told—that mergers are risky propositions up until the closing." Disclosure, and not paternalistic withholding of accurate information, is the policy chosen and expressed by Congress. We have recognized time and again, a "fundamental purpose" of the various Securities Acts, "was to substitute a philosophy of full disclosure for the philosophy of *caveat emptor* and thus to achieve a high standard of business ethics in the securities industry." The role of the materiality requirement is not to "attribute to investors a child-like simplicity, an inability to grasp the probabilistic significance of negotiations," but to filter out essentially useless information that a reasonable investor would not consider significant, even as part of a larger "mix" of factors to consider in making his investment decision.

The second rationale, the importance of secrecy during the early stages of merger discussions, also seems irrelevant to an assessment whether their existence is significant to the trading decision of a reasonable investor. To avoid a "bidding war" over its target, an acquiring firm often will insist that negotiations remain confidential, and at least one Court of Appeals has stated that "silence pending settlement of the price and structure of a deal is beneficial to most investors, most of the time."

We need not ascertain, however, whether secrecy necessarily maximizes shareholder wealth ... for this case does not concern the *timing* of a disclosure; it concerns only its accuracy and completeness.[11] We face here the narrow question whether information concerning the existence and status of preliminary merger discussions is significant to the reasonable investor's trading decision. Arguments based on the premise that some disclosure would be "premature" in a sense are more properly considered under the rubric of an issuer's duty to disclose. The "secrecy" rationale is simply inapposite to the definition of materiality.

The final justification offered in support of the agreement-in-principle test seems to be directed solely at the comfort of corporate managers. A bright-line rule indeed

---

11. [13] See *SEC v. Texas Gulf Sulphur Co.,* 401 F.2d 833, 862 (CA2 1968) (en banc) ("Rule 10b-5 is violated whenever assertions are made, as here, in a manner reasonably calculated to influence the investing public ... if such assertions are false or misleading or are so incomplete as to mislead ..."), cert. denied *sub nom. Coates v. SEC,* 394 U.S. 976, 89 S.Ct. 1454, 22 L.Ed.2d 756 (1969).

is easier to follow than a standard that requires the exercise of judgment in the light of all the circumstances. But ease of application alone is not an excuse for ignoring the purposes of the Securities Acts and Congress' policy decisions. Any approach that designates a single fact or occurrence as always determinative of an inherently fact-specific finding such as materiality, must necessarily be overinclusive or underinclusive. In *TSC Industries* this Court explained: "The determination [of materiality] requires delicate assessments of the inferences a 'reasonable shareholder' would draw from a given set of facts and the significance of those inferences to him ..." After much study, the Advisory Committee on Corporate Disclosure cautioned the SEC against administratively confining materiality to a rigid formula.[12] Courts also would do well to heed this advice.

We therefore find no valid justification for artificially excluding from the definition of materiality information concerning merger discussions, which would otherwise be considered significant to the trading decision of a reasonable investor, merely because agreement-in-principle as to price and structure has not yet been reached by the parties or their representatives.

B

The Sixth Circuit explicitly rejected the agreement-in-principle test, as we do today, but in its place adopted a rule that, if taken literally, would be equally insensitive, in our view, to the distinction between materiality and the other elements of an action under Rule 10b-5:

> "When a company whose stock is publicly traded makes a statement, as Basic did, that 'no negotiations' are underway, and that the corporation knows of 'no reason for the stock's activity,' and that 'management is unaware of any present or pending corporate development that would result in the abnormally heavy trading activity,' information concerning ongoing acquisition discussions becomes material *by virtue of the statement denying their existence....*

> ... In analyzing whether information regarding merger discussions is material such that it must be affirmatively disclosed to avoid a violation of Rule 10b-5, the discussions and their progress are the primary considerations. However, once a statement is made denying the existence of any discussions, even discussions that might not have been material in absence of the denial are material because they make the statement made untrue."

---

12. [14] Although the Committee believes that ideally it would be desirable to have absolute certainty in the application of the materiality concept, it is its view that such a goal is illusory and unrealistic. The materiality concept is judgmental in nature and it is not possible to translate this into a numerical formula. The Committee's advice to the [SEC] is to avoid this quest for certainty and to continue consideration of materiality on a case-by-case basis as disclosure problems are identified." House Committee on Interstate and Foreign Commerce, Report of the Advisory Committee on Corporate Disclosure to the Securities and Exchange Commission, 95th Cong., 1st Sess., 327 (Comm.Print 1977).

This approach, however, fails to recognize that, in order to prevail on a Rule 10b-5 claim, a plaintiff must show that the statements were *misleading* as to a *material* fact. It is not enough that a statement is false or incomplete, if the misrepresented fact is otherwise insignificant.

C

Even before this Court's decision in *TSC Industries,* the Second Circuit had explained the role of the materiality requirement of Rule 10b-5, with respect to contingent or speculative information or events, in a manner that gave that term meaning that is independent of the other provisions of the Rule. Under such circumstances, materiality "will depend at any given time upon a balancing of both the indicated probability that the event will occur and the anticipated magnitude of the event in light of the totality of the company activity." *SEC v. Texas Gulf Sulphur Co.,* 401 F.2d, at 849. Interestingly, neither the Third Circuit decision adopting the agreement-in-principle test nor petitioners here take issue with this general standard. Rather, they suggest that with respect to preliminary merger discussions, there are good reasons to draw a line at agreement on price and structure.

In a subsequent decision, the late Judge Friendly, writing for a Second Circuit panel, applied the *Texas Gulf* Sulphur probability/magnitude approach in the specific context of preliminary merger applied the Texas Gulf negotiations. After acknowledging that materiality is something to be determined on the basis of the particular facts of each case, he stated:

> "Since a merger in which it is bought out is the most important event that can occur in a small corporation's life, to wit, its death, we think that inside information, as regards a merger of this sort, can become material at an earlier stage than would be the case as regards lesser transactions — and this even though the mortality rate of mergers in such formative stages is doubtless high." *SEC v. Geon Industries, Inc.,* 531 F.2d 39, 47–48 (1976). We agree with that analysis.[13]

Whether merger discussions in any particular case are material therefore depends on the facts. Generally, in order to assess the probability that the event will occur, a factfinder will need to look to indicia of interest in the transaction at the highest corporate levels. Without attempting to catalog all such possible factors, we note by way of example that board resolutions, instructions to investment bankers, and actual negotiations between principals or their intermediaries may serve as indicia of interest. To assess the magnitude of the transaction to the issuer of the securities allegedly manipulated, a factfinder will need to consider such facts as the size of the two corporate entities and of the potential premiums over market value. No particular event or

---

13. [16] The SEC in the present case endorses the highly fact-dependent probability/magnitude balancing approach of *Texas Gulf Sulphur.* It explains: "The *possibility* of a merger may have an immediate importance to investors in the company's securities even if no merger ultimately takes place." The SEC's insights are helpful, and we accord them due deference.

factor short of closing the transaction need be either necessary or sufficient by itself to render merger discussions material.[14]

As we clarify today, materiality depends on the significance the reasonable investor would place on the withheld or misrepresented information. The fact-specific inquiry we endorse here is consistent with the approach a number of courts have taken in assessing the materiality of merger negotiations. Because the standard of materiality we have adopted differs from that used by both courts below, we remand the case for reconsideration of the question whether a grant of summary judgment is appropriate on this record.

————

The next case focuses on the use of the materiality standard adopted in *Basic* for § 10(b) and Rule 10b-5 actions in the context of statements and omissions made in connection with the purchase and sale of securities. As you read this case, try to identify factors used by the court in applying the standard of materiality adopted in *Basic* to the statements and omissions made by the broker-dealer's registered personnel. Note also that the court uses the same elements to establish violations of § 10(b) and Rule 10b-5 of the Exchange Act and § 17(a) of the Securities Act.

SEC v. Hasho

784 F. Supp. 1059 (S.D.N.Y. 1992)

EDELSTEIN, District Judge:

On December 13, 1990, the Securities and Exchange Commission (the "SEC") filed its complaint in this action alleging that defendants, ten registered representatives, engaged in unlawful high pressure sales of small highly speculative stocks, sometimes referred to in Wall Street parlance as "dogs," to unwary customers and caused trades to be entered in customer accounts without customer authorization. The SEC alleges that by such conduct, defendants violated Section 17(a) of the Securities Act of 1933 and Section 10(b) of the Securities Exchange Act of 1934, and Rule 10b-5, thereunder (the "anti-fraud provisions"). In essence, the SEC alleges that defendants engaged in a "boiler room" operation, which the Second Circuit has described as:

> A temporary operation established to sell a specific speculative security. Solicitation is by telephone to new customers, the salesman conveying favorable

———

14. [17] To be actionable, of course, a statement must also be misleading. Silence, absent a duty to disclose, is not misleading under Rule 10b-5. "No comment" statements are generally the functional equivalent of silence....

It has been suggested that given current market practices, a "no comment" statement is tantamount to an admission that merger discussions are underway. That may well hold true to the extent that issuers adopt a policy of truthfully denying merger rumors when no discussions are underway, and of issuing "no comment" statements when they are in the midst of negotiations. There are, of course, other statement policies firms could adopt; we need not now advise issuers as to what kind of practice to follow, within the range permitted by law. Perhaps more importantly, we think that creating an exception to a regulatory scheme founded on a prodisclosure legislative philosophy, because complying with the regulation might be "bad for business," is a role for Congress, not this Court.

earnings projections, predictions of price rises and other optimistic prospects without a factual basis. The prospective buyer is not informed of known or readily ascertainable adverse information; he is not cautioned about the risks inherent in purchasing a speculative security; and he is left with a deliberately created expectation of gain without risk.

On April 2, 1991, this Court proceeded to trial with defendants Ben Hasho, Mecca, and Yule.... The SEC offered the testimony of several customers of each defendant to support its allegations. These witnesses testified that defendants made several misstatements of fact, omitted certain information, and used other techniques to get them to invest in securities, including: (1) misleading statements by certain defendants about their past performances as registered representatives and unjustified predictions that their recommendations would produce future profits; (2) false statements by certain defendants that they possessed inside information; (3) false statements by certain defendants about the minimum amount of securities that customers were required to purchase; (4) omissions regarding risk factors, such as the speculative nature of securities and negative earnings of issuers; (5) baseless price predictions and profit guarantees; (6) misrepresentations about commissions.... Defendants Ben Hasho, Mecca and Yule primarily contend that they did none of the wrongful conduct alleged in the SEC's complaint. Defendant Vuono argues, and the other defendants also each contend, that he is not responsible for the conduct alleged in the SEC's complaint because he acted at the direction of his employer and obtained the information passed on to his customers from his employer.

This case reveals an outrageous abuse of trust by registered representatives who consistently preyed upon unsophisticated and unsuspecting customers through a myriad of misrepresentations, omissions, and other fraudulent devices for personal profit. Defendants' conduct here is akin to dealers of "three card monte" who prey upon unwary individuals by holding out the promise of easy money.... Defendants' contemptible conduct did more than harm their clients; their actions destroy investor confidence, pollute the environment for securities transactions, and bring disgrace and shame upon Wall Street.

Ben Hasho, Mecca, and Yule's contentions that they did none of the conduct alleged is incredible. Furthermore, while defendants' employers may have encouraged and fostered defendants' unlawful activities, this does not by any means give registered representatives license ... to violate the anti-fraud provisions of the securities laws. Registered representatives who engage in unlawful activity cannot point the finger at their employers to insulate themselves from liability....

FINDINGS OF FACT

Relevant Entities

Organized in November 1986, but now defunct, J.T. Moran & Co., Inc. ("J.T. Moran"), was a Delaware corporation that had its principal place of business in New York, New York. J.T. Moran was a wholly owned subsidiary of J.T. Moran Financial Corp. ("J.T. Moran Financial"). J.T. Moran was registered as a broker-dealer with the SEC, and, at all relevant times to this action, was a member of the National Association of Securities Dealers, Inc. J.T. Moran, which ceased operations in or about January 1990, employed approximately 600 registered representatives and maintained numerous branch offices in New York ...

* * *

II. The Defendants

A. Ben Hasho

Ben Hasho, a high school graduate, is 26 years old.... [B]ecame a registered representative at ... J.T. Moran from the beginning of 1988 to in or about January 1990....

B. Mecca

Mecca, a graduate of the State University of New York at Oswego, is 28 years old. He was a registered representative ... at J.T. Moran from in or about May 1988 through January 1990 ... Mecca was a sales supervisor at J.T. Moran.... Mecca, however, was not a licensed supervisor. In 1989, he failed the "Series 24" examination for the licensing of securities firm supervisors....

C. Yule

Yule, a graduate of Hofstra University with a bachelor's degree in business administration, is 26 years old.... From in or about May 1988 to in or about January 1990, Yule was a registered representative at J.T. Moran.

D. Vuono

Vuono, 25 years old, was employed as a registered representative at J.T. Moran's Long Island office from approximately December 1988 through January 1990.

* * *

V. Conduct

A. Misleading Statements Designed to Induce the Establishment of a Brokerage Account

In order to induce customers either to open brokerage accounts or to transfer their accounts to defendants' brokerage firms, defendants Ben Hasho and Mecca made misleading statements regarding their past performance as registered representatives and made baseless and unjustified predictions that their investment recommendations would produce future customer profits.

1. *Ben Hasho*

In or about October 1986, during Como's [a customer] first meeting with Ben Hasho, Ben Hasho told Como that "he had never lost a penny for any of his clients" and that he "values his customer's money as his own." Based upon Ben Hasho's representations, Como opened an account at First Jersey and made securities purchases through Ben Hasho.

2. *Mecca*

* * *

In or about April 1988, Mecca told Alexander [a customer] that J.T. Moran had a "good track record" for picking stocks and that, during his seven or eight years in the industry, Mecca's personal predictions have always been correct. Based upon Mecca's representations, Alexander opened an account and made securities purchases through J.T. Moran.

* * *

B. False Statements Regarding the Possession of Inside Information

On various occasions, defendants Mecca and Yule falsely stated or implied that they possessed material non-public information concerning various issuers in an effort to induce customer stock purchases. In fact, they did not possess such "inside" information.

1. *Mecca*

In or about September 1986, Mecca told Cherouvis [a customer] that he had inside information regarding International American Homes, Inc. ("International Home") and that based on this information Cherouvis should purchase shares of International Home.... When Cherouvis first started doing business with Mecca, he asked Mecca about risk factors contained in prospectuses provided to him in connection with Mecca's stock recommendations. During these conversations, Mecca responded that he, "had inside information that these [are] good stocks, I wouldn't make you a bad recommendation."

2. *Yule*

In or about January 1989, Yule recommended that Hirsch [a customer] purchase Med-Mobile common stock. During this telephone call, Yule told Hirsch in a whisper that he had been "at this meeting" where he had learned information that he could not discuss. Yule further told Hirsch that, based on this information, Yule knew that Med-Mobile "was really going to take off" and that Hirsch should buy as much of it as he could.

C. Misrepresentations Regarding Supply of Securities or Minimum Amount of Securities Available for Purchase

In order to induce a customer purchase of securities or to induce a customer to purchase large amounts of securities, defendants Mecca and Vuono misrepresented the minimum number of securities a customer had to buy in order to effectuate a trade. In or about July 1988, Mecca told Natoli [a customer] that he would not accept an order of Phonetel stock less than $10,000. In fact, other customers purchased shares of Phonetel in July 1988 in amounts far less than $10,000. Natoli eventually purchased less than $10,000 work [*sic*] of Phonetel after he told Mecca that he would not buy such a large amount.

D. Price Predictions and Other Misrepresentations and Omissions of Material Fact

Ben Hasho, Mecca, Yule, and Vuono made baseless price predictions regarding the future performance of various securities, misrepresented or omitted to disclose the speculative nature of securities, and omitted to disclose material information about securities recommended for purchase to customers. In addition, Ben Hasho, Mecca, and Yule guaranteed profits to customers and misrepresented that through defendants stock recommendations customers would recoup past losses.

1. *Ben Hasho*

* * *

In or about mid-1989, Ben Hasho recommended that Como [a customer] purchase Phonetel warrants. Ben Hasho failed to disclose that Phonetel had negative earnings, and that Phonetel warrants are a speculative investment. Ben Hasho told Como that Phonetel was about to enter into a new contract, and that the price of the warrants would rise from $7 per warrant to $10 or $12 in 30 days. Como testified that: "He guaranteed it to me because ... if he doesn't come through on this, I could come down to the office and 'kick him in the ass.' " Based upon Ben Hasho's representations, Como purchased 500 Phonetel warrants at $7 each on or about August 29, 1989. Ben Hasho's commission on the trade was approximately 5% of the purchase price.

* * *

2. *Mecca*

* * *

In or about May 1989, Mecca recommended that Lambiase [a customer] purchase $10,000 worth of Istec stock. Although Lambiase asked to see an Istec prospectus before he purchased, Mecca responded that he would send one, but that Liambiase "would have to invest right now ... in order to get a very good price." Lambiase also told Mecca that he needed to keep his capital liquid. In response, Mecca told Lambiase that the price of Istec stock would double and that Lambiase could get his money back in three months. Mecca did not disclose to Lambiase that Istec had lost $4.1 million for the year ended 1988. Lambiase testified that he agreed to purchase approximately $3,000 worth of Istec stock because, among other things, Mecca "seemed like he knew what he was talking about."

Following this purchase authorization, Lambiase decided that he did not want the stock and did not send a check for payment. Mecca called Lambiase for approximately two weeks and Lambiase did not return Mecca's telephone calls. When Mecca finally reached Lambiase, Lambiase told Mecca that he "just didn't want to invest that money at that time." Lambiase testified at trial that Mecca then, "started yelling and screaming and cursing at me" and told him that he had to purchase the stock. Lambiase then agreed to pay for the stock because he "felt a little guilty by then, and, you know, I felt bad for him." Mecca also told Lambiase, during this conversation, that the price of Istec was going to double in three months. The following day, Mecca drove to Lambiase's home in a "red Porsche" and picked up payment for the Istec shares. When Mecca picked up the check, he again told Lambiase that the price of Istec would double in three months. Lambiase, without receiving an Istec prospectus prior to his purchase, purchased 1,000 shares of Istec at $3.50 per share on or about June 5, 1989. In 1989, the bid price for Istec common stock never went above $4 1/8 per share. Mecca's commission on the trade was approximately 15% of the purchase price.

* * *

3. *Yule*

In or about November 1989, Yule recommended that Meyers [a customer] purchase American Network stock. Yule told Meyers that American Network would be in the "double digits" in approximately six months' time. During a conversation regarding American Network, Meyers informed Yule that he was diagnosed with a brain tumor and was going into the hospital for surgery to remove it. Meyers informed Yule that this operation was life threatening. Yule responded that American Network was "not a risk situation," and that an investment in American Network would protect Meyers' family. Based upon Yule's representations, Meyers purchased 1,000 shares of American Network at $2 5/8 per share on or about November 3, 1989. Yule's commission on the trade was approximately 14% of the purchase price.

* * *

4. *Vuono*

In or about January 1989, Vuono told Guggino [a customer] that the price of Med-Mobile warrants, then trading at $3.25 per share, would rise to between $4.50 and $5 per share in a few months. During this conversation, Vuono did not disclose to Guggino the fact of Med-Mobile's historical losses. When Guggino asked Vuono how he knew the price of Med-Mobile would rise, Vuono responded, "You know how to make pizzas. That's you job. And my job as stockbroker is to know things, to know what's going to be happening with the stocks." Based upon Vuono's representations, Guggino purchased 509 Med-Mobile warrants at $3.25 each. In 1989, the bid price for Med-Mobile common stock never exceeded $2 7/8? per share.

* * *

I. Failure to Sell or Difficulty Selling

On various occasions, defendants Ben Hasho, Mecca, Yule, and Vuono discouraged customer sell orders through high pressure sales tactics and through false and misleading statements, and at times refused to execute customer sell orders.

J. Defendants' Arguments

Defendants Ben Hasho, Mecca, and Yule argue in defense that they did none of the things alleged in the SEC's complaint.... I find that these three defendants' testimony regarding their dealings with customers was not credible. I find the argument that these three defendants engaged in none of the alleged activity incredible.... Like the other three defendants, Vuono refuses to accept blame for his conduct. Unlike the other three defendants, however, Vuono does not completely deny the SEC's allegations. Rather, he argues that J.T. Moran was to blame for his conduct. As is discussed in the conclusions of law, this does not excuse Vuono's conduct.

* * *

CONCLUSIONS OF LAW

Section 17(a) of the Securities Act, Section 10(b) of the Exchange Act, and Rule 10b-5, thereunder prohibit fraud in the offer or sale, or in connection with the purchase or sale, of securities.... The purpose of these provisions is "to substitute a philosophy of full disclosure for the philosophy of *caveat emptor,*" and thus to ensure that investors obtain disclosure of material facts in connection with their investment decisions regarding the purchase or sale of securities.

To establish liability under these provisions, the SEC must establish by a preponderance of the evidence: (1) a misrepresentation, or an omission (where there is a duty to speak), or other fraudulent device; (2) in the offer or sale, or in connection with the purchase or sale, of a security; (3) scienter on the part of a defendant; and (4) materiality, in the case of any misrepresentation or omission ... In addition, the SEC must show the use of any means or instruments of transportation or communication in interstate commerce, or of the mails, or any facility of any national securities exchange. Since the defendants communicated with customers through telephone calls and through confirmations and statements sent through the mails, the defendants utilized the mails, and other means of interstate commerce to perpetrate the frauds outlined in these findings.

Misrepresentation or Omission

The issue of the existence of a misrepresentation or omission, or other fraudulent device is a question of fact. This Court found a number of misrepresentations and omissions in the proposed findings of fact, including: (1) misleading statements by defendants Ben Hasho and Mecca about their past performances as registered representatives and unjustified predictions that their recommendations would produce future profits; (2) false statements by defendants Mecca and Yule that they possessed inside information; (3) false statements by defendants Mecca and Vuono relating to the supply of securities available for sale; (4) omissions by each defendant regarding risk factors, such as the speculative nature of securities and negative earnings of issuers; (5) baseless price predictions and profit guarantees made by each defendant; (6) misrepresentations by defendants Mecca, Yule and Vuono about their commissions ...

* * *

Material

The question of materiality is an objective one. "[M]ateriality depends on the significance the reasonable investor would place on the withheld or misrepresented information." The SEC must show that the information in question "would have been viewed by the reasonable investor to have changed the 'total mix' of information made available." Application of this standard requires a "delicate assessment of the inferences a reasonable shareholder would draw from a given set of facts and the significance of those inferences to him, and these assessments are peculiarly ones for the trier of fact." Material facts include "not only information disclosing the earnings ... of a company but also those facts which affect the probable future of a company and which may affect the desires of investors to buy, sell or hold the company's. As long as the information withheld or the misstatements made are material, positive proof of reliance is not necessary to establish violations of the anti-fraud provisions...." As set out in the findings of fact, defendants withheld material information and made several material misstatements to induce customers to purchase securities.

* * *

As described in the findings of fact, the four defendants failed to disclose material information about the issuers of securities they recommended to customers. Defendants failed to disclose risk factors and the past negative earnings of issuers. In addition, defendants either failed to disclose or misrepresented the speculative nature of the securities they recommended to customers. The failure to disclose such material information violates the anti-fraud provisions of the federal securities laws.

Failure to disclose the speculative nature of securities recommended or negative financial information about issuers, violate the anti-fraud provisions. An issuer's negative earnings are something to which a reasonable investor attaches importance. In fact, numerous customer witnesses in this case testified that they attached importance to such information.

During the course of telephone solicitations, the defendants made baseless price predictions, profit guarantees and told investors that they would recoup past investment losses if they followed the defendants' investment advice. The representation that an investment will recoup losses from previous investments is a price or profit prediction. Guarantees and predictions of substantial price rises with respect to securities are actionable absent a reasonable basis for the prediction. The fraud is not ameliorated where the positive prediction about the future performance of securities is cast as opinion or possibility rather than as a guarantee. Such material statements violate the anti-fraud provisions if no adequate basis existed for making such a statement. Since the defendants mostly recommended securities of unprofitable start-up corporations, of which defendants did no personal research, their price predictions and guarantees could not have had a reasonable basis in fact. Indeed, many of the recommendations went down in price substantially after the customer witnesses purchased these securities.

———

The next case distinguishes statements deemed opinions, (not actionable under the antifraud provisions) instead of acts, and reiterates that, under the antifraud provisions, there is no general duty to disclose. Note that the conduct at issue in this case occurred during the financial crisis of 2008. Why wasn't Wang successful in proving a material omission under the antifraud provisions?

Wang v. Bear Stearns Companies, LLC

14 F. Supp. 3d 537 (2014)

SWEET, District Judge.

Defendants Joe Y. Zhou ("Zhou") and Garrett Bland ("Bland") (collectively, the "Defendants") have moved pursuant to Federal Rules of Civil Procedure 9(b) and 12(b)(6) to dismiss the claims against them in the complaint filed on March 29, 2011 (the "Complaint") by plaintiff Vivine H. Wang ("Wang" or the "Plaintiff"). Upon the conclusions set forth below, the motion is granted and the Complaint is dismissed as to Zhou and Wang ...

* * *

Allegations of the Complaint

The Complaint makes the following allegations. Vivine Wang is an individual residing in California. [Joey] Zhou and [Garrett] Bland worked for Bear Stearns in its Century City, California office. Wang alleges that Zhou worked as a "broker-dealer, the agent of a broker-dealer, and/or an investment advisor" and Bland as a broker-dealer and/or investment advisor with the title of "Senior Managing Director."

Beginning in the mid-1990s, Zhou provided investment advice to the Wang family. In early 2008, after some time working with a different broker, Wang and her husband contacted Zhou and asked to "place some stock orders with Bear Stearns." Zhou told her that a new account would need to be opened, and then met with Wang to execute the necessary paperwork.

On February 29, 2008, Wang entered into a Customer Agreement with Bear Stearns, which set forth the terms and conditions on which Bear Stearns "open[ed] and maintain[ed]" her account. The Customer Agreement stated:

(a) A Bear Stearns entity will execute transactions accepted by it and/or will provide such other clearance, settlement and custody services in connection with the maintenance of your Account(s) at Bear Stearns.

(b) Bear Stearns is acting as a broker-dealer and custodian, and not as (1) an investment adviser under the Investment Advisors Act of 1940, or (2) a "fiduciary" as defined in Section 3(21) of the Employee Retirement Income Security Act of 1974, as amended ("ERISA") or Section 4975 of the Internal Revenue Code of 1986, as amended ("Code"), with respect to your Account(s) under this Agreement.... Neither Bear Stearns nor its employees are authorized to provide, and shall not provide, legal, tax or accounting advice or services and you will not solicit or rely upon any such advice from them whether in connection with transactions in any of your accounts or otherwise. You have consulted or will consult with your own technical, legal, regulatory, tax, business, investment, financial and accounting advisors to the extent you deem necessary in determining the investment and trading strategy appropriate, for you and the appropriateness of each transaction.

Shortly after the new account was opened, Roger Wang began placing verbal orders through Zhou for purchases of stock in financial companies. On March 6, 2008, he ordered 10,000 shares of Bear Stearns common stock ("BSC"). He placed additional orders for 20,000 BSC shares on March 10 and 11 respectively.

On March 11, 2008, Roger Wang attended a meeting (for the Asia Society) that was hosted at the offices of Bear Stearns in Century City, California. At this meeting Roger Wang was seated at a table with Bland. Bland is alleged to have told Roger Wang: "that Bear Stearns was financially sound, that its stock value should be at least

$85.00 per share, and that now was a great time to invest in the stock." In addition, Bland allegedly told Roger Wang "to buy as much BSC stock as he could."

Early in the week of March 10, rumors had begun to infiltrate the market about Bear Stearns's liquidity. On March 10, 2008, the Company's liquidity pool stood at $18.1 billion. At the end of the day on March 11, 2008, the Company's liquidity remained at $15.8 billion (adjusted for the release of customer protection funds) … well within the range of the preceding weeks.

Clients continued pulling their funds on March 12 and 13, drawing down the Company's liquidity pool. By the evening of Thursday, March 13, 2008, Bear Stearns's liquidity had declined to $2 billion. Because Bear Stearns could not open for business the next day without financing, it negotiated with JPMorgan for a $30 billion funding facility backstopped by the federal government. At 9:00 am on the morning of Friday, March 14, 2008, before the market opened, Bear Stearns issued a press release announcing the deterioration of its liquidity position, and the secured loan facility from JPMorgan. Following this release, the price of Bear Stearns stock fell from $57 per share to $30 per share.

At some point after the market opened on March 14, Roger Wang, allegedly unaware of Bear Stearns's press release, contacted Zhou and placed a verbal order for 200,000 additional shares of BSC. The order, however, was only "partially filled," and, as a result, Wang was to receive 100,000 shares of BSC at approximately $34 per share and "at no time that day or ever did … Zhou warn, caution, or advise Plaintiff or her husband against buying any more BSC stock." In placing this order on March 14, Roger Wang is also alleged to have relied on Bland's "favorable recommendation" from three days earlier.

Over the ensuing weekend, the loan facility did not calm the market's fears. On Sunday, March 16, 2008, Bear Stearns announced an agreement for JPMorgan to purchase the Company for the equivalent of $2 per share. According to the Complaint, this announcement is when the Wangs "learned of the fraud." The Wangs immediately stopped payment, "on the scheduled wire transfer for their final stock trades," and refused to pay for their purchases of BSC stock. The following day, March 17, a representative of Bear Stearns demanded payment from the Wangs, but was referred to their lawyer.

Based on these allegations, the Plaintiff has brought claims against the Defendants for violation of Securities Exchange Act of 1934, Section 10(b), and breach of fiduciary duty; conspiracy to induce breach of fiduciary duty, fraud and deceit and conspiracy to defraud.…

* * *

The Allegations of Section 10(b) Violations Are Inadequate

Wang's Section 10(b) allegations inadequately allege fraud with particularity, scienter, and reliance on any misstatements or omissions.

The Complaint does not plead fraud with particularity. With respect to Zhou, Plaintiff does not allege any affirmative misstatements. Instead, she alleges that Zhou failed to "caution or advise Plaintiff or her husband against buying any more BSC stock" on March 14, 2008 "or ever." However, "[s]ilence [i.e., an omission] absent a duty to disclose, is not misleading under Rule 10b-5." The Complaint does not adequately allege that Zhou had any duty to advise Wang or caution her about purchases of BSC shares in view of the disclaimer in the Customer Agreement that Wang signed.

It is not alleged that Zhou had a duty to speak in order to correct any prior statements. Zhou did not have a duty to correct any misstatement allegedly made by anyone else at Bear Stearns, since there is no allegation that he was involved in any way in the making of those statements.

Plaintiff concedes that the Complaint does not allege any affirmative misstatement by Zhou but has alleged that Zhou should have warned her not to purchase any additional BSC stock on Friday, March 14, 2008 in view of the 9 a.m. announcement that Bear Stearns's liquidity had significantly deteriorated and the firm was receiving extraordinary financing from JPMorgan. The Complaint also has alleged that the Bear Stearns press release on the morning of March 14 meant, "[i]n effect, Bear Stearns' credit facilities had essentially dried up, liquidity was in fact a huge problem, and the company was rapidly heading towards complete financial collapse."

Even if the allegedly omitted, publicly available information about Bear Stearns's financial condition on March 14 was material, Zhou had no duty to disclose that information to the Wangs. The Customer Agreement signed by Plaintiff specifically disclaimed any such duty. Plaintiff has contended' that the Customer Agreement only disclaimed fiduciary duties in the context of ERISA or retirement accounts, but the Customer Agreement is not so limited. It explicitly notes on the first page that "Bear Stearns is acting as a broker-dealer and custodian ... Brokerage activities are regulated under different laws and rules than advisory activities and generally do not give rise to the fiduciary duties that an investment adviser has to its clients."

Wang has alleged that Zhou placed certain orders for BSC stock at her husband's request and that Zhou was incentivized to commit fraud in order to earn commissions on the trades. Wang does not allege that Zhou received any greater commissions from Wang's purchases of Bear Stearns stock than he did from Wang's other stock purchases at this time, and such generalized allegations do not give rise to a strong inference of scienter.

In the absence of motive, the Plaintiff must provide "correspondingly greater" circumstantial allegations of scienter. Plaintiff has not alleged that Zhou was in possession of any material information about Bear Stearns's financial condition that was not publicly disclosed. Although Wang cites several "early warning signs such as that, on March 11, ING Group NV allegedly informed Bear Stearns that it was pulling $500 million in financing," there is no connection alleged between Zhou and those allegations nor an explanation for why a retail broker in the Bear Stearns's Los Angeles office would have had any knowledge of these events in real time. A corporation's knowledge cannot be attributed to every employee.

Wang does not dispute that she and her husband are highly sophisticated investors who placed unsolicited orders with Zhou for increasing amounts of BSC stock in

March 2008 as the rumors about Bear Stearns's financial condition intensified and its stock price dropped. Wang also does not dispute that she purchased BSC stock on March 14 following the public announcement of Bear Stearns's serious liquidity problems. Plaintiff's alleged reliance on Zhou is unreasonable as a matter of law.

Further, any omission by Zhou would only be actionable as fraud under § 10(b) to the extent it was "material." To establish materiality a plaintiff must demonstrate "a substantial likelihood that the disclosure of the omitted fact would have been viewed by the reasonable investor as having significantly altered the total mix of information *made available*." Wang fails to allege that a representation from Zhou regarding the instability of Bear Stearns would have affected the decision to purchase stock. Moreover, Wang has acknowledged that the substance of Zhou's alleged omission on March 14 had already been disclosed to the market at the time of the purchases that day. Any failure on Zhou's part to reference the release relating to the loan facility with JP Morgan in a later conversation with Roger Wang after the release cannot be material as a matter of law.

To the extent that Wang's claims against Zhou are based on a failure to "ever" caution her or her husband about buying more BSC shares, not just on March 14, Wang has not alleged with any particularity why omissions on other occasions were materially misleading.

With respect to Bland, Plaintiff claims that Bland represented to Roger Wang during a conference on March 11 that Bear Stearns was a sound investment, that "its stock value should be at least $85.00 per share, ... that [it] was a great time to invest in the stock," and that he would have purchased more shares at the time if he could. However, Bland's alleged statements are opinion. Prior cases have found statements virtually identical to Bland's to be inactionable as fraud:

- "[Bank] is in very good shape as it moves into its next stage of development."
- "[Company has a] strong balance sheet."
- "[Company is] in very good shape ... problems reflect what every other reinsurer faced. We have put it behind us ..."
- Plaintiffs "were going to make good money on new issues." and
- "[Bank] set the standard for best practices in risk management techniques"

Such corporate optimism has been held to be actionable only when the speaker provided "guarantees or ... specific statements of fact, ... or if [he] does not genuinely or reasonably believe them." Wang makes no allegation that Bland ever made any guarantees or specific statements of fact, and she provides no adequate allegation that Bland did not subjectively believe the statements when made....

In addition, Wang has failed to allege opportunity that either Zhou or Bland were actually in possession of, or had access to, material information about Bear Stearns's liquidity or the value of its stock price that had not already been publicly disclosed. Absent credible allegations that Zhou or Bland had access to nonpublic facts about

Bear Stearns's unfolding financial condition, Wang's claim cannot satisfy the PSLRA and the particularity requirements of Rule 9(b).

With respect to Bland, there is no circumstantial evidence from which to infer that Bland did not subjectively believe that March 11, 2008 was in fact a good time to invest in Bear Stearns. That Bland's prediction turned out to be wrong is not relevant. *** The "hallmark of an opinion is that it does not express 'matters of objective fact' which can be assessed against an 'objective standard' but instead conveys a belief or 'judgment' whose 'determination is inherently subjective.'" Bland's alleged statements reflect his own subjective beliefs. While the Plaintiff has contended it would be inappropriate to find that these statements were opinions as opposed to factual statements, such findings are routinely made by courts on motions to dismiss.

Plaintiff's allegations do not give rise to a plausible inference that Bland did not subjectively believe his alleged March 11, 2008 statements to Roger Wang about Bear Stearns. The contention that Bland must have known that Bear Stearns was in a precarious financial position because two lenders allegedly pulled a small amount of financing from Bear Stearns prior to March 11 fails to connect Bland to the withdrawals of financing and does not allege any facts demonstrating that Bland knew or should have known of those events....

Notes and Questions

1. *No General Duty to Disclose Material Non-Public Information.* In *Dirks v. SEC,* 463 U.S. 646, 647 (1983), the Supreme Court stated that there is no general duty to disclose material non-public information: "[T]here is no general duty to disclose before trading on material nonpublic information, and ... that a duty to disclose under § 10(b) does not arise from the mere possession of nonpublic market information ..." *Id.* At 654.

2. *Half-Truths May Be Materially Misleading.* In *SEC v. Gabelli,* 653 F.3d 49, 57 (2d Cir. 2011) *rev'd,* 133 S. Ct. 1216, 185 L. Ed. 2d 297 (2013) *and remanded to,* 518 Fed. Appx. 32 (2d Cir. 2013), the U.S. Supreme Court held that the District Court erred in dismissing claims under § 17(a) of the Securities Act and § 10(b) and Rule 10b-5 because "[t]he law is well settled ... that so-called 'half-truths'—literally true statements that create a materially misleading impression—will support claims for securities fraud." In *Gabelli,* Marc J. Gabelli and Bruce Alpert, while prohibiting most investors in their Gabelli Global Growth Fund ("GGGF") from engaging in a form of short-term trading called "market timing,"[15] secretly permitted one investor to market time the Fund in exchange

---

15. Market timing refers "to buying and selling mutual fund shares in a manner designed to exploit short-term pricing inefficiencies.... A mutual fund sells and redeems its shares based on the fund's net asset value ("NAV") for that day, which is usually calculated at the close of the U.S. markets at 4:00 P.M. Eastern Time. Prior to 4:00 P.M., market timers either buy or redeem a fund's shares if they

for an investment in a hedge fund managed by Gabelli. Alpert posted a memo on the GGGF website stating that GGGF identified and restricted or banned market timers from making further trades in its efforts to eliminate market timers. During this time period, Gabelli and Alpert permitted one customer to engage in market timing. Why was the memo posted on GGGF's web site materially misleading? Answer: the complaint plausibly alleges that a reasonable investor reading the Memorandum would conclude that the Adviser had attempted in good faith to reduce or eliminate GGGF market timing across the board, whereas, as Alpert well knew but failed to disclose, the Adviser had expressly agreed to let one major investor engage in a very large amount of GGGF market timing, in return for its investment in a separate hedge fund run by Gabelli. The District Court therefore erred in dismissing the Securities Act and Securities Exchange Act claims.

3. *Deceptive Conduct.* Deceptive conduct may include trading strategies and therefore violate the antifraud provisions of the federal securities laws. In *Orlando Joseph Jett*, Rel. No. 34-49366, 82 S.E.C. Dockett 1129 (Mar. 5, 2004), the SEC determined that Jett's trading strategy at his broker-dealer violated the antifraud provisions because it resulted in the recording of fictitious unrealized profits in the firm's books and records. Jett's " 'trading strategy' was a means of deceiving the brokerage firm that employed him about the profitability of his securities trading. Jett orchestrated the deception through a sequence of exchange instructions that he formulated and entered into [the brokerage firm's] computer system and through his false and misleading explanations of the source of his 'profits.' " Jett's "paper profits grossly distorted economic reality by showing profits of over $264 million when, in fact, there were losses of $74.7 million." Interestingly, Mr. Jett's conduct was not found to be securities fraud in the initial decision issued by the administrative law judge in an SEC proceeding (*In re Orlando Joseph Jett*, Initial Decisions Release No. 127, 1998 SEC LEXIS 1501, (July 21, 1998) and in a FINRA (f/k/a NASD) proceeding (1997 NASD Arb. LEXIS 1637) initiated by Kidder Peabody against Mr. Jett. Mr. Jett was a successful bond trader on Wall Street prior to his troubles at Kidder Peabody. However, the SEC's March 4, 2004, order above was enforced in *SEC v. Jett*, 514 F. Supp. 2d 532 (2007) and Jett was ordered to cease and desist from committing or causing any violations, or future violations of the antifraud provisions; barred from association with any broker-dealer, exchange, or member of a registered securities association (FINRA); to disgorge $8.21 million; and to pay a civil money penalty in the amount of $200,000.

4. In *Derek L. DuBois,* Exchange Act Rel. No. 48332, 2003 WL 21946858, DuBois, a registered representative with Baraban Securities, failed to disclose to his cus-

---

believe that the fund's last NAV is "stale," *i.e.,* that it lags behind the current value of a fund's portfolio of securities as priced earlier in the day. The market timers can then reverse the transaction at the start of the next day and make a quick profit with relatively little risk. *SEC v. Gabelli*, 653 F.3d at 53.

tomers that he was being paid by a stock promoter for the company whose shares he recommended. The SEC determined that Dubois's failure to disclose this information was an omission of a material fact in violation of the antifraud provisions of the federal securities laws. DuBois was paid $2,562 by the stock promoter to recommend the stock of the company that it promoted. The SEC stated that "the salesperson's recommendation of that investment might not be disinterested. DuBois' failure to disclose his arrangement deprived his customers of the opportunity to consider DuBois' own interest in recommending [the company's] stock."

Hypothetical Two

Customers have been complaining about Adam Stefura, a registered representative in Success First's Chicago Office, in connection with purchases of Freedom Golf, a small manufacturer of custom golf clubs and other equipment traded over-the-counter on OTC Markets Group. Unfortunately, Malak Johnson, Success First's chief compliance officer, has only recently discovered that Adam has a substantial ownership interest in Freedom Golf—he owns 60% of Freedom Golf's outstanding shares— which he did not disclose to Success First or his customers before he began recommending and selling Freedom Golf's shares to Success First's customers. Adam posted numerous Internet messages supportive of Freedom Golf stock urging people to buy it. Examples of the messages include:

> "I hear rumblings that some very powerful investor relations people are going to get involved here."

> "Pump up the volume!" "Get in now before the fireworks ..." "All aboard! This train is pulling out ..."

Adam also distributed an investor report for Freedom Golf containing favorable projections. The investor report contained projections for the next three years, showing rapidly increasing revenues with profits of $1.6 million, $4.5 million, and $13.5 million, respectively. The CEO of Freedom Golf told Adam that these numbers were realistic, but only if a certain infomercial about golf clubs was produced and marketed. Adam knew that the infomercial was never produced. Also, Adam was aware when he distributed the investor report and posted messages on the Internet that Freedom Golf's actual financial situation was dire. Freedom Golf has now filed for bankruptcy. Adam claims that his Internet postings and the investor report are not material misstatements or omissions because they merely reflect corporate optimism for the future of Freedom Golf. Josephine Wiseman, general counsel at Success First, has asked you, a newly hired associate, to determine whether Adam made material misrepresentations or omissions in connection with the sale of Freedom Golf's shares. As usual, Josephine requires this information as soon as possible.

C. Scienter

All plaintiffs must prove scienter in § 10(b) and Rule 10b-5 actions. This means that both regulators and private litigants must establish this element. *Scienter*, a type of state of mind, was required and defined in the case below as something more than negligence. As you read the case below, assess whether scienter requires a showing of actual intent.

Ernst & Ernst v. Hochfelder

425 U.S. 185 (1976)

* * *

I

Petitioner, Ernst & Ernst, is an accounting firm. From 1946 through 1967 it was retained by First Securities Company of Chicago (First Securities), a small brokerage firm and member of the Midwest Stock Exchange and of the National Association of Securities Dealers, to perform periodic audits of the firm's books and records. In connection with these audits Ernst & Ernst prepared for filing with the Securities and Exchange Commission (Commission) the annual reports required of First Securities under § 17(a) of the 1934 Act. It also prepared for First Securities responses to the financial questionnaires of the Midwest Stock Exchange (Exchange).

Respondents were customers of First Securities who invested in a fraudulent securities scheme perpetrated by Leston B. Nay, president of the firm and owner of 92% of its stock. Nay induced the respondents to invest funds in "escrow" accounts that he represented would yield a high rate of return. Respondents did so from 1942 through 1966, with the majority of the transactions occurring in the 1950's. In fact, there were no escrow accounts as Nay converted respondents' funds to his own use immediately upon receipt. These transactions were not in the customary form of dealings between First Securities and its customers. The respondents drew their personal checks payable to Nay or a designated bank for his account. No such escrow accounts were reflected on the books and records of First Securities, and none was shown on its periodic accounting to respondents in connection with their other investments. Nor were they included in First Securities' filings with the Commission or the Exchange.

This fraud came to light in 1968 when Nay committed suicide, leaving a note that described First Securities as bankrupt and the escrow accounts as "spurious." Respondents subsequently filed this action for damages against Ernst & Ernst in the United States District Court for the Northern District of Illinois under § 10(b) of the 1934 Act. The complaint charged that Nay's escrow scheme violated § 10(b) and Commission Rule 10b-5, and that Ernst & Ernst had "aided and abetted" Nay's violations by its "failure" to conduct proper audits of First Securities. As revealed through discovery, respondents' cause of action rested on a theory of negligent nonfeasance. The premise was that Ernst & Ernst had failed to utilize "appropriate auditing procedures" in its audits of First Securities, thereby failing to discover internal practices of the firm said to prevent an effective audit. The practice principally relied on was Nay's rule that only he could open mail addressed to him at First Securities or addressed to First Securities to his attention, even if it arrived in his absence. Respondents contended that if Ernst & Ernst had conducted a proper audit, it would have discovered this "mail rule." The existence of the rule then would have been disclosed in reports to the Exchange and to the Commission by Ernst & Ernst as an irregular procedure that prevented an effective audit. This would have led to an investigation of Nay that would have revealed the fraudulent scheme. Respondents specifically disclaimed the existence of fraud or intentional misconduct on the part of Ernst & Ernst.[16]

After extensive discovery the District Court granted Ernst & Ernst's motion for summary judgment and dismissed the action. The court rejected Ernst & Ernst's contention that a cause of action for aiding and abetting a securities fraud could not be maintained under § 10(b) and Rule 10b-5 merely on allegations of negligence. It concluded, however that there was no genuine issue of material fact with respect to whether Ernst & Ernst had conducted its audits in accordance with generally accepted auditing standards.

The Court of Appeals for the Seventh Circuit reversed and remanded, holding that one who breaches a duty of inquiry and disclosure owed another is liable in damages for aiding and abetting a third party's violation of Rule 10b-5 if the fraud would have been discovered or prevented but for the breach. The court reasoned that Ernst & Ernst had a common-law and statutory duty of inquiry into the adequacy of First Securities' internal control system because it had contracted to audit First Securities and to prepare for filing with the Commission the annual report of First Securities' financial condition required under § 17 of the 1934 Act and Rule 17a-5. The court further reasoned that respondents were beneficiaries of the statutory duty to inquire and the related duty to disclose any material irregularities that were discovered. The court concluded that there were genuine issues of fact as to whether Ernst & Ernst's failure to discover and comment upon Nay's mail rule constituted a breach of its duties of inquiry and disclosure and whether inquiry and disclosure would have led to the discovery or prevention of Nay's fraud.

We granted certiorari to resolve the question whether a private cause of action for damages will lie under § 10(b) and Rule 10b-5 in the absence of any allegation of "scienter" intent to deceive, manipulate, or defraud. We conclude that it will not and therefore we reverse.

* * *

During the 30-year period since a private cause of action was first implied under § 10(b) and Rule 10b-5, a substantial body of case law and commentary has developed as to its elements. Courts and commentators long have differed with regard to whether scienter a necessary element of such a cause of action is, or whether negligent conduct

---

16. [5] In their response to interrogatories in the District Court respondents conceded that they did "not accuse Ernst & Ernst of deliberate, intentional fraud," merely with "inexcusable negligence."

alone is sufficient. In addressing this question, we turn first to the language of § 10(b), for "(t) he starting point in every case involving construction of a statute is the language itself."

Section 10(b) makes unlawful the use or employment of "any manipulative or deceptive device or contrivance" in contravention of Commission rules. The words "manipulative or deceptive" used in conjunction with "device or contrivance" strongly suggest that § 10(b) was intended to proscribe knowing or intentional misconduct.

In its Amicus curiae brief, however, the Commission contends that nothing in the language "manipulative or deceptive device or contrivance" limits its operation to knowing or intentional practices.[17] In support of its view, the Commission cites the overall congressional purpose in the 1933 and 1934 Acts to protect investors against false and deceptive practices that might injure them. The Commission then reasons that since the "effect" upon investors of given conduct is the same regardless of whether the conduct is negligent or intentional, Congress must have intended to bar all such practices and not just those done knowingly or intentionally. The logic of this effect-oriented approach would impose liability for wholly faultless conduct where such conduct results in harm to investors, a result the Commission would be unlikely to support. But apart from where its logic might lead, the Commission would add a gloss to the operative language of the statute quite different from its commonly accepted meaning. The argument simply ignores the use of the words "manipulative," "device," and "contrivance" terms that make unmistakable a congressional intent to proscribe a type of conduct quite different from negligence. Use of the word "manipulative" is especially significant. It is and was virtually a term of art when used in connection with securities markets. It connotes intentional or willful conduct designed to deceive or defraud investors by controlling or artificially affecting the price of securities.

B

Although the extensive legislative history of the 1934 Act is bereft of any explicit explanation of Congress' intent, we think the relevant portions of that history support

---

17. [18] The Commission would not permit recovery upon proof of negligence in all cases. In order to harmonize civil liability under § 10(b) with the express civil remedies contained in the 1933 and 1934 Acts, the Commission would limit the circumstances in which civil liability could be imposed for negligent violation of Rule 10b-5 to situations in which (i) the defendant knew or reasonably could foresee that the plaintiff would rely on his conduct, (ii) the plaintiff did in fact so rely, and (iii) the amount of the plaintiff's damages caused by the defendant's conduct was definite and ascertainable. The Commission concludes that the present record does not establish these conditions since Ernst & Ernst could not reasonably have foreseen that the financial statements of First Securities would induce respondents to invest in the escrow accounts, respondents in fact did not rely on Ernst & Ernst's audits, and the amount of respondents' damages was unascertainable. Respondents accept the Commission's basic analysis of the operative language of the statute and Rule, but reject these additional requirements for recovery for negligent violations.

our conclusion that § 10(b) was addressed to practices that involve some element of scienter and cannot be read to impose liability for negligent conduct alone.

* * *

Neither the intended scope of § 10(b) nor the reasons for the changes in its operative language are revealed explicitly in the legislative history of the 1934 Act, which deals primarily with other aspects of the legislation. There is no indication, however, that § 10(b) was intended to proscribe conduct not involving scienter. The extensive hearings that preceded passage of the 1934 Act touched only briefly on § 10, and most of the discussion was devoted to the enumerated devices that the Commission is empowered to proscribe under § 10(a). The most relevant exposition of the provision that was to become § 10(b) was by Thomas G. Corcoran, a spokesman for the drafters. Corcoran indicated: "Subsection (c) (§ 9(c) of H.R. 7852 later § 10(b)) says, 'Thou shalt not devise any other cunning devices.'

"Of course subsection (c) is a catch-all clause to prevent manipulative devices. I do not think there is any objection to that kind of clause. The Commission should have the authority to deal with new manipulative devices." Hearings on H.R. 7852 and H.R. 8720 before the House Committee on Interstate and Foreign Commerce, 73d Cong., 2d Sess., 115 (1934).

This brief explanation of § 10(b) by a spokesman for its drafters is significant. The section was described rightly as a "catchall" clause to enable the Commission "to deal with new manipulative (or cunning) devices." It is difficult to believe that any lawyer, legislative draftsman, or legislator would use these words if the intent was to create liability for merely negligent acts or omissions. Neither the legislative history nor the briefs supporting respondents identify any usage or authority for construing "manipulative (or cunning) devices" to include negligence.

The legislative reports do not address the scope of § 10(b) or its catchall function directly. In considering specific manipulative practices left to Commission regulation, however, the reports indicate that liability would not attach absent scienter, supporting the conclusion that Congress intended no lesser standard under § 10(b).... There is no indication that Congress intended anyone to be made liable ... unless he acted other than in good faith. The catchall provision of § 10(b) should be interpreted no more broadly.

* * *

We also consider it significant that each of the express civil remedies in the 1933 Act allowing recovery for negligent conduct is subject to significant procedural restrictions not applicable under § 10(b). Section 11(e) of the 1933 Act, for example, authorizes the court to require a plaintiff bringing a suit under § 11, § 12(2), or § 15 thereof to post a bond for costs, including attorneys' fees, and in specified circumstances to assess costs at the conclusion of the litigation. Section 13 specifies a statute of limitations of one year from the time the violation was or should have been discovered, in no event to exceed three years from the time of offer or sale, applicable to actions brought under § 11, § 12(2), or § 15. These restrictions, significantly, were imposed by amendments to the 1933 Act adopted as part of the 1934 Act. Prior to amendment § 11(e) contained no provision for payment of costs. The amendments also substantially shortened the statute of limitations provided by § 13.

We think these procedural limitations indicate that the judicially created private damages remedy under § 10(b)—which has no comparable restrictions—cannot be extended, consistently with the intent of Congress, to actions premised on negligent wrongdoing. Such extension would allow causes of action covered by §§ 11, 12(2), and 15 to be brought instead under § 10(b) and thereby nullify the effectiveness of the carefully drawn procedural restrictions on these express actions. We would be unwilling to bring about this result absent substantial support in the legislative history, and there is none.

D

We have addressed, to this point, primarily the language and history of § 10(b). The Commission contends, however, that subsections (b) and (c) of Rule 10b-5 are cast in language which if standing alone could encompass both intentional and negligent behavior. These subsections respectively provide that it is unlawful "(t) to make any untrue statement of a material fact or to omit to state a material fact necessary in order to make the statements made, in the light of the circumstances under which they were made, not misleading ..." and "(t)o engage in any act, practice, or course of business which operates or would operate as a fraud or deceit upon any person...." Viewed in isolation the language of subsection (b), and arguably that of subsection (c), could be read as proscribing, respectively, any type of material misstatement or omission, and any course of conduct, that has the effect of defrauding investors, whether the wrongdoing was intentional or not.

We note first that such a reading cannot be harmonized with the administrative history of the Rule, a history making clear that when the Commission adopted the Rule it was intended to apply only to activities that involved scienter.[18] More importantly, Rule 10b-5 was adopted pursuant to authority grand [sic] the Commission under § 10(b).

---

18. [32] Apparently the Rule was a hastily drafted response to a situation clearly involving intentional misconduct. The Commission's Regional Administrator in Boston had reported to the Director of the Trading and Exchange Division that the president of a corporation was telling the other shareholders that the corporation was doing poorly and purchasing their shares at the resultant depressed prices, when in fact the business was doing exceptionally well. The Rule was drafted and approved on the day this report was received.... Although adopted pursuant to § 10(b), the language of the Rule appears to have been derived in significant part from § 17 of the 1933. There is no indication in the administrative history of the Rule that any of the subsections was intended to proscribe conduct not involving scienter. Indeed the Commission's release issued contemporaneously with the Rule explained:

> "The Securities and Exchange Commission today announced the adoption of a rule prohibiting fraud by any person in connection with the purchase of securities. The previously existing rules against fraud in the purchase of securities applied only to brokers and dealers. The new rule closes a loophole in the protections against fraud administered by the Commission by prohibiting individuals or companies from buying securities if they engage in fraud in their purchase." ...

The rulemaking power granted to an administrative agency charged with the administration of a federal statute is not the power to make law. Rather, it is "'the power to adopt regulations to carry into effect the will of Congress as expressed by the statute.'" Thus, despite the broad view of the Rule advanced by the Commission in this case, its scope cannot exceed the power granted the Commission by Congress under § 10(b).... When a statute speaks so specifically in terms of manipulation and deception, and of implementing devices and contrivances — the commonly understood terminology of intentional wrongdoing — and when its history reflects no more expansive intent, we are quite unwilling to extend the scope of the statute to negligent conduct.

The judgment of the Court of Appeals is

Reversed.

Mr. Justice BLACKMUN, with whom Mr. Justice BRENNAN joins, dissenting.

Once again, the Court interprets § 10(b) of the Securities Exchange Act of 1934, and the Securities a [sic] Exchange Commission's Rule 10b-5, restrictively and narrowly and thereby stultifies recovery for the victim.

* * *

No one questions the fact that the respondents here were the victims of an intentional securities fraud practiced by Leston B. Nay. What is at issue, of course, is the petitioner accountant firm's involvement and that firm's responsibility under Rule 10b-5. The language of the Rule ... seems to me, clearly and succinctly, to prohibit negligent as well as intentional conduct of the kind proscribed, to extend beyond common-law fraud, and to apply to negligent omission and commission. This is consistent with Congress' intent, repeatedly recognized by the Court, that securities legislation enacted for the purpose of avoiding frauds be construed "not technically and restrictively, but flexibly to effectuate its remedial purposes."

On motion for summary judgment, therefore, the respondents' allegations, in my view, were sufficient, and the District Court's dismissal of the action was improper to the extent that the dismissal rested on the proposition that suit could not be maintained under § 10(b) and Rule 10b-5 for mere negligence. The opposite appears to be true, at least in the Second Circuit, with respect to suits by the SEC to enjoin a violation of the Rule.... If negligence is a violation factor when the SEC sues, it must be a violation factor when a private party sues. And, in its present posture, this case is concerned with the issue of violation, not with the secondary issue of a private party's judicially created entitlement to damages or other specific reef [sic].

The critical importance of the auditing accountant's role in insuring full disclosure cannot be overestimated.... In this light, the initial inquiry into whether Ernst & Ernst's preparation and certification of the financial statements of First Securities Company of Chicago were negligent, because of the failure to perceive Nay's extraordinary mail rule, and in other alleged respects, and thus whether Rule 10b-5 was violated, should not be thwarted. But the Court today decides that it is to be thwarted;

and so once again it rests with Congress to rephrase and to re-enact, if investor victims, such as these, are ever to have relief under the federal securities laws that I thought had been enacted for their broad, needed, and deserving benefit.

———

As noted in Justice Blackmun's dissent, the SEC was not required to establish scienter in § 10(b) and Rule 10b-5 actions at the time that *Ernst* was decided. In fact, there was a conflict in the federal courts as to whether the SEC was required to establish scienter as an element under § 10(b) and Rule 10b-5 that was not resolved in *Ernst*. This conflict was resolved in *Aaron v. SEC*, 446 U.S. 680 (1980). In *Aaron*, the U.S. Supreme Court determined that scienter was a required element in SEC actions alleging violations of § 10(b) and Rule 10b-5. The Court also determined that, like § 10(b), SEC actions brought under § 17(a)(1) also required proof of scienter. However, actions brought under §§ 17(a)(2) and 17(a)(3) did not require proof of scienter because the Supreme Court determined that the language of these subparagraphs did not require a showing of intentional conduct. According to the Court, "since Congress drafted § 17(a) in such a manner as to compel the conclusion that scienter is required under one subparagraph but not under the other two, it would take a very clear expression in the legislative history of congressional intent to the contrary to justify the conclusion that the statute does not mean what it so plainly seems to say.... We find no such expression of congressional intent in the legislative history.... In the absence of a conflict between reasonably plain meaning and legislative history, the words of the statute must prevail." *Aaron*, at 697–699.

Although the Court in *Ernst* also reserved the question of whether a showing of recklessness was sufficient to establish scienter, all the circuit courts have determined that a showing of recklessness is sufficient. The circuit courts have been careful to distinguish recklessness from negligence. "Severe recklessness is limited to those highly unreasonable omissions or misrepresentations that involve not merely simple or even inexcusable negligence, but an extreme departure from the standards of ordinary care, and that present a danger of misleading buyers or sellers which is either known to the defendant or is so obvious that the defendant must have been aware of it." *See Rosenberg v. Gould*, 554 F.3d 962, 965 (11th Cir. 2009).

Finally, the element of scienter is subject to the heightened pleading standard of the PLSRA in private causes of action, but not in SEC enforcement actions. The PLSRA requires the plaintiff to state with particularity the facts that give rise to a strong inference that the defendant acted with scienter. In the following case, the court stated that under this heightened pleading standard "[a]n inference of scienter must be more than merely plausible or reasonable—it must be cogent and at least as compelling as any opposing inference of nonfraudulent intent." This standard must be met before discovery commences. It also illustrates the application of the heightened pleading standards of the PLSRA using the recklessness standard of scienter. How do these heightened pleading standards affect the success of private causes of action under § 10(b) and Rule 10b-5?

Tellabs, Inc. v. Makor Issues & Rights

551 U.S. 308 (2007)

Justice GINSBURG delivered the opinion of the Court.

This Court has long recognized that meritorious private actions to enforce federal antifraud securities laws are an essential supplement to criminal prosecutions and civil enforcement actions brought, respectively, by the Department of Justice and the Securities and Exchange Commission (SEC). Private securities fraud actions, however, if not adequately contained, can be employed abusively to impose substantial costs on companies and individuals whose conduct conforms to the law. As a check against abusive litigation by private parties, Congress enacted the Private Securities Litigation Reform Act of 1995.

Exacting pleading requirements are among the control measures Congress included in the PSLRA. The PSLRA requires plaintiffs to state with particularity both the facts constituting the alleged violation, and the facts evidencing scienter, *i.e.*, the defendant's intention "to deceive, manipulate, or defraud. This case concerns the latter requirement. As set out in § 21D (b)(2) of the PSLRA, plaintiffs must "state with particularity facts giving rise to a strong inference that the defendant acted with the required state of mind."

* * *

Petitioner Tellabs, Inc., manufactures specialized equipment used in fiber optic networks. During the time period relevant to this case, petitioner Richard Notebaert was Tellabs' chief executive officer and president. Respondents (Shareholders) are persons who purchased Tellabs stock between December 11, 2000, and June 19, 2001. They accuse Tellabs and Notebaert (as well as several other Tellabs executives) of engaging in a scheme to deceive the investing public about the true value of Tellabs' stock.

Beginning on December 11, 2000, the Shareholders allege, Notebaert (and by imputation Tellabs) "falsely reassured public investors, in a series of statements ... that Tellabs was continuing to enjoy strong demand for its products and earning record revenues," when, in fact, Notebaert knew the opposite was true. From December 2000 until the spring of 2001, the Shareholders claim, Notebaert knowingly misled the public in four ways. First, he made statements indicating that demand for Tellabs' flagship networking device, the TITAN 5500, was continuing to grow, when, in fact, demand for that product was waning. Second, Notebaert made statements indicating that the TITAN 6500, Tellabs' next-generation networking device, was available for delivery, and that demand for that product was strong and growing, when in truth the product was not ready for delivery and demand was weak. Third, he falsely represented Tellabs' financial results for the fourth quarter of 2000 (and, in connection with those results, condoned the practice of "channel stuffing," under which Tellabs flooded its customers with unwanted products). Fourth, Notebaert made a series of overstated revenue projections, when demand for the TITAN 5500 was drying up and production of the TITAN 6500 was behind schedule. Based on Notebaert's sunny assessments, the Shareholders contend, market analysts recommended that investors buy Tellabs' stock.

* * *

The Court of Appeals for the Seventh Circuit ... concluded that the Shareholders had sufficiently alleged that Notebaert acted with the requisite state of mind.

The Court of Appeals recognized that the PSLRA "unequivocally raise[d] the bar for pleading scienter" by requiring plaintiffs to "plea[d] sufficient facts to create a strong inference of scienter." In evaluating whether that pleading standard is met, the Seventh Circuit said, "courts [should] examine all of the allegations in the complaint and then ... decide whether collectively they establish such an inference." "[W]e will allow the complaint to survive," the court next and critically stated, "if it alleges facts from which, if true, a reasonable person could infer that the defendant acted with the required intent.... If a reasonable person could not draw such an inference from the alleged facts, the defendants are entitled to dismissal."

In adopting its standard for the survival of a complaint, the Seventh Circuit explicitly rejected a stiffer standard adopted by the Sixth Circuit, *i.e.,* that "plaintiffs are entitled only to the most plausible of competing inferences." ... We granted certiorari to resolve the disagreement among the Circuits on whether, and to what extent, a court must consider competing inferences in determining whether a securities fraud complaint gives rise to a "strong inference" of scienter.

II

* * *

In an ordinary civil action, the Federal Rules of Civil Procedure require only "a short and plain statement of the claim showing that the pleader is entitled to relief." Fed. Rule Civ. Proc. 8(a) (2). Although the rule encourages brevity, the complaint must say enough to give the defendant "fair notice of what the plaintiff's claim is and the grounds upon which it rests."

Prior to the enactment of the PSLRA, the sufficiency of a complaint for securities fraud was governed not by Rule 8, but by the heightened pleading standard set forth in Rule 9(b). Rule 9(b) applies to "all averments of fraud or mistake"; it requires that "the circumstances constituting fraud ... be stated with particularity" but provides that "[m]alice, intent, knowledge, and other condition of mind of a person may be averred generally. Courts of Appeals diverged on the character of the Rule 9(b) inquiry in § 10(b) cases: Could securities fraud plaintiffs allege the requisite mental state "simply by saying that scienter existed," or were they required to allege with particularity facts giving rise to an inference of scienter? Circuits requiring plaintiffs to allege specific facts indicating scienter expressed that requirement variously. The Second Circuit's formulation was the most stringent. Securities fraud plaintiffs in that Circuit were required to "specifically plead those [facts] which they assert give rise to a *strong inference* that the defendants had" the requisite state of mind. The "strong inference" formulation was appropriate, the Second Circuit said, to ward off allegations of "fraud by hindsight."

Setting a uniform pleading standard for § 10(b) actions was among Congress' objectives when it enacted the PSLRA. Designed to curb perceived abuses of the § 10(b) private action — "nuisance filings, targeting of deep-pocket defendants, vexatious discovery requests and manipulation by class action lawyers," — the PSLRA installed both substantive and procedural controls.... in § 21D (b) of the PSLRA, Congress "impose[d] heightened pleading requirements in actions brought pursuant to § 10(b) and Rule 10b–5."

Under the PSLRA's heightened pleading instructions, any private securities complaint alleging that the defendant made a false or misleading statement must: (1) "specify each statement alleged to have been misleading [and] the reason or reasons why the statement is misleading," and (2) "state with particularity facts giving rise to a strong inference that the defendant acted with the required state of mind." ...

The "strong inference" standard "unequivocally raise[d] the bar for pleading scienter," and signaled Congress' purpose to promote greater uniformity among the Circuits. But "Congress did not ... throw much light on what facts ... suffice to create [a strong] inference," or on what "degree of imagination courts can use in divining whether" the requisite inference exists. While adopting the Second Circuit's "strong inference" standard, Congress did not codify that Circuit's case law interpreting the standard. With no clear guide from Congress other than its "inten[tion] to strengthen existing pleading requirements," Courts of Appeals have diverged again, this time in construing the term "strong inference." Among the uncertainties, should courts consider competing inferences in determining whether an inference of scienter is "strong"? Our task is to prescribe a workable construction of the "strong inference" standard, a reading geared to the PSLRA's twin goals: to curb frivolous, lawyer-driven litigation, while preserving investors' ability to recover on meritorious claims.

III

A

We establish the following prescriptions: *First,* faced with a Rule 12(b)(6) motion to dismiss a § 10(b) action, courts must, as with any motion to dismiss for failure to plead a claim on which relief can be granted, accept all factual allegations in the complaint as true....

Second, courts must consider the complaint in its entirety, as well as other sources courts ordinarily examine when ruling on Rule 12(b)(6) motions to dismiss, in particular, documents incorporated into the complaint by reference, and matters of which a court may take judicial notice. The inquiry ... is whether *all* of the facts alleged, taken collectively, give rise to a strong inference of scienter, not whether any individual allegation, scrutinized in isolation, meets that standard.

Third, in determining whether the pleaded facts give rise to a "strong" inference of scienter, the court must take into account plausible opposing inferences. The Seventh Circuit expressly declined to engage in such a comparative inquiry. A complaint could survive, that court said, as long as it "alleges facts from which, if true, a reasonable person could infer that the defendant acted with the required intent"; in other words, only "[i]f a reasonable person could not draw such an inference from the alleged facts" would the defendant prevail on a motion to dismiss. But in § 21D (b) (2), Congress did not merely require plaintiffs to "provide a factual basis for [their] scienter allegations," *i.e.*, to allege facts from which an inference of scienter rationally *could* be drawn. Instead, Congress required plaintiffs to plead with particularity facts that give rise to a "strong" — *i.e.*, a powerful or cogent — inference.

The strength of an inference cannot be decided in a vacuum. The inquiry is inherently comparative: How likely is it that one conclusion, as compared to others, follows from the underlying facts? To determine whether the plaintiff has alleged facts that give rise to the requisite "strong inference" of scienter, a court must consider plausible, nonculpable explanations for the defendant's conduct, as well as inferences favoring the plaintiff. The inference that the defendant acted with scienter need not be irrefutable, *i.e.*, of the "smoking-gun" genre, or even the "most plausible of competing inferences." Recall in this regard that § 21D(b)'s pleading requirements are but one constraint among many the PSLRA installed to screen out frivolous suits, while allowing meritorious actions to move forward. Yet the inference of scienter must be more than merely "reasonable" or "permissible" — it must be cogent and compelling, thus strong in light of other explanations. A complaint will survive, we hold, only if a reasonable person would deem the inference of scienter cogent and at least as compelling as any opposing inference one could draw from the facts alleged.

B

Tellabs contends that when competing inferences are considered, Notebaert's evident lack of pecuniary motive will be dispositive. The Shareholders, Tellabs stresses, did not allege that Notebaert sold any shares during the class period. While it is true that motive can be a relevant consideration, and personal financial gain may weigh heavily in favor of a scienter inference, we agree with the Seventh Circuit that the absence of a motive allegation is not fatal. As earlier stated, allegations must be considered collectively; the significance that can be ascribed to an allegation of motive, or lack thereof, depends on the entirety of the complaint.

Tellabs also maintains that several of the Shareholders' allegations are too vague or ambiguous to contribute to a strong inference of scienter. For example, the Shareholders alleged that Tellabs flooded its customers with unwanted products, a practice known as "channel stuffing." But they failed, Tellabs argues, to specify whether the channel stuffing allegedly known to Notebaert was the illegitimate kind (*e.g.*, writing orders for products customers had not requested) or the legitimate kind (*e.g.*, offering customers discounts as an incentive to buy). We agree that omissions and ambiguities count against inferring scienter, for plaintiffs must "state with particularity facts giving rise to a strong inference that the defendant acted with the required state of mind." We reiterate, however, that the court's job is not to scrutinize each allegation in isolation but to assess all the allegations holistically. In sum, the reviewing court must ask: When the allegations are accepted as true and taken collectively, would a reasonable person deem the inference of scienter at least as strong as any opposing inference?

* * *

Justice SCALIA, concurring in the judgment.

I fail to see how an inference that is merely "at least as compelling as any opposing inference," can conceivably be called what the statute here at issue requires: a "strong inference." If a jade falcon were stolen from a room to which only A and B had access, could it *possibly* be said there was a "strong inference" that B was the thief? I think not, and I therefore think that the Court's test must fail. In my view, the test should be whether the inference of scienter (if any) is *more plausible* than the inference of innocence.*

* * *

Congress has expressed its determination in the phrase "strong inference"; it is our job to give that phrase its normal meaning. And if we are to abandon text in favor of unexpressed purpose, as the Court does, it is inconceivable that Congress's enactment of stringent pleading requirements in the Private Securities Litigation Reform Act of 1995 somehow manifests the purpose of giving plaintiffs the edge in close cases.... There is no indication that the statute at issue here was meant to relax the ordinary rule under which a tie goes to the defendant. To the contrary, it explicitly strengthens that rule by extending it to the pleading stage of a case.

* * *

I hasten to add that, while precision of interpretation should always be pursued for its own sake, I doubt that in this instance what I deem to be the correct test will produce results much different from the Court's. How often is it that inferences are precisely in equipoise? All the more reason, I think, to read the language for what it says.

* * *

Justice ALITO, concurring in the judgment.

I

In dicta ... the Court states that "omissions and ambiguities" merely "count against" inferring scienter, and that a court should consider all allegations of scienter, even nonparticularized ones, when considering whether a complaint meets the "strong inference" requirement. Not only does this interpretation contradict the clear statutory language on this point, but it undermines the particularity requirement's purpose of preventing a plaintiff from using vague or general allegations in order to get by a motion to dismiss for failure to state a claim. Allowing a plaintiff to derive benefit from such allegations would permit him to circumvent this important provision.

Furthermore, the Court's interpretation of the particularity requirement in no way distinguishes it from normal pleading review, under which a court naturally gives less weight to allegations containing "omissions and ambiguities" and more weight to allegations stating particularized facts. The particularity requirement is thus stripped of all meaning.

Questions certainly may arise as to whether certain allegations meet the statutory particularity requirement, but where that requirement is violated, the offending allegations cannot be taken into account.

II

I would also hold that a "strong inference that the defendant acted with the required state of mind" is an inference that is stronger than the inference that the defendant lacked the required state of mind.... Justice SCALIA's interpretation would align the pleading test ... with the test that is used at the summary-judgment and judgment-as-a-matter-of-law stages, whereas the Court's test would introduce a test previously unknown in civil litigation. It seems more likely that Congress meant to adopt a known quantity and thus to adopt Justice SCALIA's approach.

Notes and Questions

1. *Scienter and Economic Analysis.* In *Newton v. Merrill Lynch, Pierce, Fenner & Smith, Inc.,* 135 F.3d 266, 273 (3d Cir.), *cert. denied sub nom. Merrill Lynch, Pierce, Fenner & Smith, Inc. v. Kravitz,* 525 U.S. 811 (1998), the Third Circuit determined that scienter could be established based on an economic analysis of the relationship between the broker-dealer and its customer. In *Newton,* broker-dealers routinely executed retail customer trades at the NBBO when more favorable prices were available through private quotation services; the broker-dealers availed themselves of the more favorable prices. The Court stated that summary judgment was inappropriate because issues of fact existed because "a reasonable trier of fact [could] find that the [broker-dealers'] misrepresentation — namely, that they would execute plaintiffs' trades in a manner maximizing plaintiffs' economic gain — was at least reckless, if not intentional." *Id.* at 273.

2. *Customer Sophistication and Scienter.* Lack of customer sophistication may not establish scienter based on recklessness, i.e., highly unreasonable omissions or misrepresentations that involve not merely simple or even inexcusable negligence, but *an extreme departure from the standards of ordinary care,* and that present a danger of misleading buyers or sellers that is either known to the defendant or is so obvious that the defendant must have been aware of it. In *Congregation of the Passion, Holy Cross Province v. Kidder Peabody & Co.,* 800 F.2d 177, 182, the court found that even assuming lack of sophistication on the part of the church, the mere fact that the church was confused did not establish scienter. In *Congregation,* the church stated that confirmations received from transactions executed on its behalf were misleading because the church lacked the sophistication to understand the confirmations. *See also, Warren v. Reserve Fund, Inc.,* 728 F.2d 741, 745 (5th Cir. 1984). However, when the broker-dealer has a duty to explain, failure to do so is sufficient to establish scienter based on recklessness. *Vucinich v. Paine Webber Jackson and Curtis, Inc.,* 803 F.2d 454 (9th Cir. 1986). In *Vucinich,* the broker-dealer failed to explain the speculative nature of short selling to an investor in a way that she could

understand the risks. Vucinich was a housewife with three semesters of college majoring in home economics who had inherited stocks and cash from her parents.

3. *Circumstantial Evidence and Scienter.* Scienter may be established by circumstantial evidence, but there must be some factual basis giving rise to a strong inference of fraudulent intent or recklessness. In *Beard v. Sachnoff & Weaver, Ltd*, 941 F.2d 142, 143–144 (2d Cir. 1991), investors in a limited partnership, which operated a hotel, brought securities fraud claims against the limited partnership's counsel. The hotel later declared bankruptcy because the seller and principal guarantor of the hotel failed to perform. Counsel for the limited partnership failed to disclose that the seller and principal guarantor of the hotel had recently been convicted of mail fraud and conspiracy in a similar venture. The court found that "these allegations, taken together, establish a relatively strong inference that [counsel] was reckless in preparing the offering documents. Indeed, [counsel's] failure to mention [the] conviction in the initial offering memorandum could be considered reckless as a matter of law." *Id.* at 144. *See also, Phillips v. Kidder, Peabody & Co.*, 933 F. Supp. 303, 317 (S.D.N.Y. 1996).

Hypothetical Three

One of Success First's customers, John Lytle, along with his business partner, Andrew Knight, has been accused of committing securities fraud by the SEC. Knight is not Success First's customer. The SEC alleges that Lytle and Knight committed securities fraud by engaging in a prime bank fraud. In a prime bank fraud, the perpetrator solicits investments by telling prospective investors that the investors' money will be invested in high-yield bank-issued securities not available or even known to the general public. Success First is worried that it might be drawn into the case because it acted as custodian for the funds raised by Lytle and Knight. According to the SEC's complaint, Lytle and Knight raised $32 million from 31 investors. In his responsive answer to the SEC's complaint, Lytle asserts that the information that he disclosed to investors during the course of the fraud came solely from Knight, whom he trusted implicitly. Investors were told that they were investing in a no-risk trading program, that their investments were insured up to 196 percent of their original investment, that they would earn a return of 100 percent per week, and that their investments were being monitored by the Federal Reserve Board. However, Lytle and the SEC now know that Knight misappropriated several million dollars of the funds raised from investors to purchase, among other items, a gazebo and a custom-built piano. Josephine is concerned that Success First may be liable because it acted as custodian for the funds raised by Lytle and Knight. Lytle says that he had no reason not to trust his business partner of many years and therefore cannot have committed securities fraud because scienter cannot be established. Josephine, concerned about having Success First's reputation sullied, has asked two of the most experienced attorneys on her staff to research the case law and determine whether the SEC can establish scienter in the case. She is anxiously awaiting the court's ruling but must report to Success First's board of directors next week about any possible exposure to liability in this case.

D. Reliance

Reliance is a required element of a private action under §10(b) and Rule 10b-5. The SEC does not have to plead or prove reliance. In general, this means that, in order to recover, the private plaintiff must have actually and justifiably relied on the misrepresentation or omission. However, the U.S. Supreme Court's interpretation of this requirement is flexible. The following case illustrates the establishment of the reliance element in the context of a material omission. How did plaintiffs establish reliance on the material omission?

Affiliated Ute Citizens of Utah v. U.S.
406 U.S. 128 (1972)

Mr. Justice BLACKMUN delivered the opinion of the Court.

The Ute Partition Act pertained to the Ute Indian Tribe of the Uintah and Ouray Reservation in Utah. At the time of the Act's adoption the tribe had a membership of about 1,765, consisting of 439 mixed-bloods[19] and 1,326 full-bloods. Section 1 of the Act stated its purpose, namely "to provide for the partition and distribution of the assets of the ... Tribe ... between the mixed-blood and full-blood members thereof; for the termination of Federal supervision over the trust, and restricted property, of the mixed-blood members of said tribe; and for a development program for the full-blood members thereof, to assist them in preparing for termination of Federal supervision over their property." The estimated value of the cash, accounts receivable, and land owned by the tribe was $20,702,885. The tribe possessed additional assets consisting of oil, gas, and mineral rights (principally oil shale deposits underlying the reservation), and unadjudicated and unliquidated claims against the United States.

* * *

[T]he mixed-bloods, in 1956, organized AUC as an unincorporated association.... empowered its board of directors to delegate to corporations organized in accordance with the Act "such powers and authority as may be necessary or desirable in the accomplishment of the objects and purposes for which said corporations may be so organized."

---

19. [3] Counsel for the petitioners advised us at oral argument that the term 'mixed-blood' is a slur and is offensive and that the preferred description is 'terminated Utes.' Section 2 of the Act, however, defines as a 'full-blood' a member of the tribe 'who possesses one-half degree of Ute Indian blood and a total of Indian blood in excess of one-half, excepting those who become mixed-bloods by choice.... ' It defines as a 'mixed-blood' a member of the tribe who does not fall within the full-blood class, and one who becomes a mixed-blood by choice.... Inasmuch as the statute specifically employs the terms 'full-blood' and 'mixed-blood,' we feel compelled, for purposes of consistency and clarity, to do the same. No slur or offense whatsoever is intended.

UDC was incorporated in 1958 with the stated purpose "to manage jointly with the Tribal Business Committee of the full-blood members of the Ute Indian Tribe ... all unadjudicated or unliquidated claims against the United States, all gas, oil, and mineral rights of every kind, and all other assets not susceptible to equitable and practicable distribution to which the mixed-blood members of the said tribe ... are now, or may hereafter become entitled ... and to receive the proceeds therefrom and to distribute the same to the stockholders of this corporation...." UDC then issued 10 shares of its capital stock in the name of each mixed-blood Ute, a total of 4,900 shares. UDC and First Security Bank of Utah, N.A. (the bank), executed a written agreement dated December 31, 1958, by which the bank became transfer agent for UDC stock. UDC apparently also decided at this time not to deliver the certificates for its 137 shares to the shareholders but, instead, to deposit them with the bank; the bank was then to issue receipts to the respective shareholders. Counsel advised the bank that this was "because of some rather unfavorable experiences had in the Indian service with the loss of valuable instruments."

UDC's articles provided that if a mixed-blood shareholder determined to sell or dispose of his UDC stock at any time prior to August 27, 1964, that is, within 10 years from the date of the Partition Act, he was first to offer it to members of the tribe, both mixed-blood and full-blood, in a form approved by the Secretary; that no sale of stock prior to that date was valid unless and until that offer was made; and that if the offer was not accepted by any member of the tribe, the sale to a nonmember could then be made but at a price no lower than that offered to the members. The articles further provided that all UDC stock certificates should have stamped thereon a prescribed legend referring to those sale conditions. The certificates so issued bore that legend. In addition, each certificate had on its face, in red lettering, a warning that the certificate did not represent stock in an ordinary business corporation, that its future value or return could not be determined, and that the stock should not be sold or encumbered by its owner, but should be retained and preserved for the benefit of the shareholder and his family.

II

The Present Litigation

* * *

In February 1965 Anita R. Reyos and 84 other mixed-bloods sued the bank, two of the bank's employee-officers, John B. Gale and Verl Haslem, and certain automobile dealers, charging violations of the Securities Exchange Act of 1934 and of Rule 10b-5 of the Securities and Exchange Commission....

* * *

The claims center in the facts that the bank, by its agreement with UDC, was the transfer agent for UDC shares; that it had physical possession of all the stock certificates with their specific legend of caution and warning; that, because of the bank's possession, a shareholder's possible contact with, and awareness of, the legend was minimized; that the bank handled the documents implementing the first-refusal procedure;

and that the mixed-blood who contemplated the sale of his shares was compelled to deal through the bank.

In 1959, after the bank was retained as transfer agent, UDC's attorney wrote the bank advising it that UDC's directors, by formal minute, had instructed him to ask the bank "to discourage the sale of stock of the Ute Distribution Corporation by any of its stockholders and to emphasize and stress to the said stockholders the importance of retaining said stock." The letter further stated, "(W)e trust you will impress upon anyone desiring to make a transfer that there is no possible way of determining the true value of this stock."

The bank maintained a branch office in Roosevelt ... Defendants Gale and Haslem were the bank's assistant managers at Roosevelt.... With respect to most of the sales of UDC stock by the 12 plaintiffs to nonmembers of the tribe, either Gale or Haslem prepared and notarized the necessary transfer papers, including signature guarantees and the affidavits of the sellers to the effect that they were receiving not less than the price at which the shares had been offered to members of the tribe. The procedure with respect to the preparation and execution of these affidavits was informal at best. In at least one case the affidavit was signed in blank; in another Gale dissuaded the seller from reading the affidavit before she signed it.... Some of the affidavits do not accurately describe the sales to which they relate. Although they state that the sales were for cash, some sellers actually received second-hand automobiles or other tangible property. The superintendent relied on the recitals in the affidavits in preparing his authenticating certificates that were transmitted to the bank as transfer agent.

During 1963 and 1964 mixed-bloods sold 1,387 shares of UDC stock. All were sold to nonmembers of the tribe. Haslem purchased 50 of these himself (all after August 27, 1964), and Gale purchased 63 (44 before that date and 19 after). The 113 shares Haslem and Gale purchased constituted 8 1/3% of the total sold by mixed-bloods during those two years. The 12 plaintiffs sold 120 shares; of these Gale purchased 10 and Haslem purchased six.[20] They paid cash for the shares they purchased. Thirty-two other white men bought shares from mixed-bloods during the period.

In 1964 and 1965 UDC stock was sold by mixed-bloods at prices ranging from $300 to $700 per share. Shares were being transferred between whites, however, at prices from $500 to $700 per share. Gale and Haslem possessed standing orders from non-Indian buyers. About seven of these were from outside the State. Some of the prospective purchasers maintained deposits at the bank for the purpose of ready consummation of any transaction.

---

20. [14] On or about July 8, 1964, Gale bought five shares from Glen Reed at $350 per share. He sold them in August for $530 per share. After August 27, 1964, in three separate transactions, he purchased five shares from Letha Harris Wopsock. He sold three of these at a higher price; the record is silent as to whether he sold the other two at a price in excess of his cost. On or about August 31, 1964, Haslem bought five shares from Reed at $400 and resold them immediately. In November 1964 he purchased one share from Joseph Arthur Workman for $350. He transferred the Workman share to his brother. The record does not indicate Haslem's transfer prices.

The two men received various commissions and gratuities for their services in facilitating the transfer of UDC stock from mixed-bloods to non-Indians. Gale supplied some funds as sales advances to the mixed-blood sellers. He and Haslem solicited contracts for open purchases of UDC stock and did so on bank premises and during business hours. In connection with all this, the bank sought individual accounts from the tribal members.

The District Court concluded:

* * *

As to Gale and Haslem: The two men had devised a plan or scheme to acquire, for themselves and others, shares in UDC from mixed-bloods. In violation of their duty to make a fair disclosure, they succeeded in acquiring shares from mixed-bloods for less than fair value.

The District Court then ruled that each of the defendants, was liable to each of the 12 plaintiffs (32 transactions involving 122 shares).

The Court of Appeals reversed in substantial part. It held: ... Gale and Haslem personally liable, and the bank also, only with respect to a few sales; and, as to those sales, remanded the case on the issue of damages.

We consider, in turn, the posture of the several defendants.

* * *

B. Gale and Haslem.

* * *

[W]e conclude that the Court of Appeals viewed too narrowly the activities of defendants Gale and Haslem. We would agree that if the two men and the employer bank had functioned merely as a transfer agent, there would have been no duty of disclosure here. But, as the Court of Appeals itself observed, the record shows that Gale and Haslem "were active in encouraging a market for the UDC stock among non-Indians." They did this by soliciting and accepting standing orders from non-Indians. They and the bank, as a result, received increased deposits because of the development of this market. The two men also received commissions and gratuities from the expectant non-Indian buyers. The men, and hence the bank, as the Court found, were "entirely familiar with the prevailing market for the shares at all material times." The bank itself had acknowledged, by letter to AUC in January 1958, that "it would be our duty to see that these transfers were properly made" and that, with respect to the sale of shares, "the bank would be acting for the individual stockholders." The mixed-blood sellers "considered these defendants to be familiar with the market for the shares of stock and relied upon them when they desired to sell their shares."

Clearly, the Court of Appeals was right to the extent that it held that the two employees had violated Rule 10b-5; in the instances specified in that holding the record reveals a misstatement of a material fact, within the proscription of Rule 10b-5(2), namely, that the prevailing market price of the UDC shares was the figure at which their purchases were made.

We conclude, however, that the Court of Appeals erred when it held that there was no violation of the Rule unless the record disclosed evidence of reliance on material fact misrepresentations by Gale and Haslem. We do not read Rule 10b-5 so restrictively. To be sure, the second subparagraph of the rule specifies the making of an untrue statement of a material fact and the omission to state a material fact. The first and third subparagraphs are not so restricted. These defendants' activities, outlined above, disclose, within the very language of one or the other of those subparagraphs, a "course of business" or a "device, scheme, or artifice" that operated as a fraud upon the Indian sellers. This is so because the defendants devised a plan and induced the mixed-blood holders of UDC stock to dispose of their shares without disclosing to them material facts that reasonably could have been expected to influence their decisions to sell. The individual defendants, in a distinct sense, were market makers, not only for their personal purchases constituting 8 1/3% of the sales, but for the other sales their activities produced. This being so, they possessed the affirmative duty under the Rule to disclose this fact to the mixed-blood sellers. It is no answer to urge that, as to some of the petitioners, these defendants may have made no positive representation or recommendation. The defendants may not stand mute while they facilitate the mixed-bloods' sales to those seeking to profit in the non-Indian market the defendants had developed and encouraged and with which they were fully familiar. The sellers had the right to know that the defendants were in a position to gain financially from their sales and that their shares were selling for a higher price in that market.

Under the circumstances of this case, involving primarily a failure to disclose, positive proof of reliance is not a prerequisite to recovery. All that is necessary is that the facts withheld be material in the sense that a reasonable investor might have considered them important in the making of this decision....

Gale and Haslem engaged in more than ministerial functions. Their acts were clearly within the reach of Rule 10b-5. And they were acts performed when they were obligated to act on behalf of the mixed-blood sellers.

———

Another example of the flexible interpretation of the reliance element is the fraud on the market theory, which is available when the issuer's securities are traded in an efficient public market. The fraud on the market theory, a rebuttable presumption of reliance, was first enumerated in *Basic v. Levinson*:

> The fraud on the market theory is based on the hypothesis that, in an open and developed securities market, the price of a company's stock is determined by the available material information regarding the company and its business.... Misleading statements will therefore defraud purchasers of stock even if the purchasers do not directly rely on the misstatements.... The causal connection between the defendants' fraud and the plaintiffs' purchase of

stock in such a case is no less significant than in a case of direct reliance on misrepresentations.

The Court justified this fraud on the market presumption based on the Efficient Capital Market Hypothesis:

> The presumption is ... supported by common sense and probability. Recent empirical studies have tended to confirm Congress' premise that the market price of shares traded on well-developed markets reflects all publicly available information, and, hence, any material misrepresentations. It has been noted that "it is hard to imagine that there ever is a buyer or seller who does not rely on market integrity. Who would knowingly roll the dice in a crooked craps game? Indeed, nearly every court that has considered the proposition has concluded that where materially misleading statements have been disseminated into an impersonal, well-developed market for securities, the reliance of individual plaintiffs on the integrity of the market price may be presumed.... An investor who buys or sells stock at the price set by the market does so in reliance on the integrity of that price. Because most publicly available information is reflected in market price, an investor's reliance on any public material misrepresentations, therefore, may be presumed for purposes of a Rule 10b-5 action.

Recently, in the case below, the Court rejected an effort to overrule its fraud-on-the market presumption first enumerated in *Basic*. As you read this case, consider how the Court determines the existence of an efficient market and the impact of the ECMH on the Court's jurisprudence. In addition, how may a defendant rebut the *Basic* presumption of reliance?

Halliburton Co. v. Erica P. John Fund, Inc.

134 S. Ct. 2398 (2014)

Chief Justice ROBERTS delivered the opinion of the Court.

Investors can recover damages in a private securities fraud action only if they prove that they relied on the defendant's misrepresentation in deciding to buy or sell a company's stock. In *Basic Inc. v. Levinson*, 485 U.S. 224, 108 S. Ct. 978, 99 L.Ed.2d 194 (1988), we held that investors could satisfy this reliance requirement by invoking a presumption that the price of stock traded in an efficient market reflects all public, material information—including material misstatements. In such a case, we concluded, anyone who buys or sells the stock at the market price may be considered to have relied on those misstatements.

We also held, however, that a defendant could rebut this presumption in a number of ways, including by showing that the alleged misrepresentation did not actually affect the stock's price—that is, that the misrepresentation had no "price impact." The questions presented are whether we should overrule or modify *Basic*'s presumption of reliance and, if not, whether defendants should nonetheless be afforded an opportunity in securities class action cases to rebut the presumption at the class certification stage, by showing a lack of price impact.

I

Respondent Erica P. John Fund, Inc. (EPJ Fund), is the lead plaintiff in a putative class action against Halliburton and one of its executives (collectively Halliburton) alleging violations of section 10(b) of the Securities Exchange Act of 1934, and Securities and Exchange Commission Rule 10b-5. According to EPJ Fund, between June 3, 1999, and December 7, 2001, Halliburton made a series of misrepresentations regarding its potential liability in asbestos litigation, its expected revenue from certain construction contracts, and the anticipated benefits of its merger with another company—all in an attempt to inflate the price of its stock. Halliburton subsequently made a number of corrective disclosures, which, EPJ Fund contends, caused the company's stock price to drop and investors to lose money.

EPJ Fund moved to certify a class comprising all investors who purchased Halliburton common stock during the class period. The District Court found that the proposed class satisfied all the threshold requirements of Federal Rule of Civil Procedure 23(a): It was sufficiently numerous, there were common questions of law or fact, the representative parties' claims were typical of the class claims, and the representatives could fairly and adequately protect the interests of the class. And except for one difficulty, the court would have also concluded that the class satisfied the requirement of Rule 23(b)(3) that "the questions of law or fact common to class members predominate over any questions affecting only individual members." The difficulty was that Circuit precedent required securities fraud plaintiffs to prove "loss causation"—a causal connection between the defendants' alleged misrepresentations and the plaintiffs' economic losses—in order to invoke *Basic*'s presumption of reliance and obtain class certification. Because EPJ Fund had not demonstrated such a connection for any of Halliburton's alleged misrepresentations, the District Court refused to certify the proposed class. The United States Court of Appeals for the Fifth Circuit affirmed the denial of class certification on the same ground.

We granted certiorari and vacated the judgment, finding nothing in "*Basic* or its logic" to justify the Fifth Circuit's requirement that securities fraud plaintiffs prove loss causation at the class certification stage in order to invoke *Basic*'s presumption of reliance. "Loss causation," we explained, "addresses a matter different from whether an investor relied on a misrepresentation, presumptively or otherwise, when buying or selling a stock." We remanded the case for the lower courts to consider "any further arguments against class certification" that Halliburton had preserved.

On remand, Halliburton argued that class certification was inappropriate because the evidence it had earlier introduced to disprove loss causation also showed that none of its alleged misrepresentations had actually affected its stock price. By demonstrating the absence of any "price impact," Halliburton contended, it had rebutted *Basic*'s presumption that the members of the proposed class had relied on its alleged misrepresentations simply by buying or selling its stock at the market price. And without the benefit of the *Basic* presumption, investors would have to prove reliance on an individual basis, meaning that individual issues would predominate over common ones. The District Court declined to consider Halliburton's argument, holding that the *Basic* presumption applied and certifying the class under Rule 23(b) (3).

The Fifth Circuit affirmed. The court found that Halliburton had preserved its price impact argument, but to no avail. While acknowledging that "Halliburton's price impact evidence could be used at the trial on the merits to refute the presumption of reliance," the court held that Halliburton could not use such evidence for that purpose at the class certification. "[P]rice impact evidence," the court explained, "does not bear on the question of common question predominance [under Rule 23(b)(3)], and is thus appropriately considered only on the merits after the class has been certified."

We once again granted certiorari, this time to resolve a conflict among the Circuits over whether securities fraud defendants may attempt to rebut the *Basic* presumption at the class certification stage with evidence of a lack of price impact. We also accepted Halliburton's invitation to reconsider the presumption of reliance for securities fraud claims that we adopted in *Basic*.

II

Halliburton urges us to overrule *Basic*'s presumption of reliance and to instead require every securities fraud plaintiff to prove that he actually relied on the defendant's misrepresentation in deciding to buy or sell a company's stock. Before overturning a long-settled precedent, however, we require "special justification," not just an argument that the precedent was wrongly decided. Halliburton has failed to make that showing.

A

* * *

The reliance element " 'ensures that there is a proper connection between a defendant's misrepresentation and a plaintiff's injury.' " "The traditional (and most direct) way a plaintiff can demonstrate reliance is by showing that he was aware of a company's statement and engaged in a relevant transaction—*e.g.*, purchasing common stock—based on that specific misrepresentation."

In *Basic,* however, we recognized that requiring such direct proof of reliance "would place an unnecessarily unrealistic evidentiary burden on the Rule 10b-5 plaintiff who has traded on an impersonal market." That is because, even assuming an investor could prove that he was aware of the misrepresentation, he would still have to "show a speculative state of facts, *i.e.,* how he would have acted ... if the misrepresentation had not been made."

We also noted that "[r]equiring proof of individualized reliance" from every securities fraud plaintiff "effectively would ... prevent [ ] [plaintiffs] from proceeding with a class action" in Rule 10b-5 suits. If every plaintiff had to prove direct reliance on the defendant's misrepresentation, "individual issues then would ... overwhelm[ ] the common ones," making certification under Rule 23(b)(3) inappropriate.

To address these concerns, *Basic* held that securities fraud plaintiffs can in certain circumstances satisfy the reliance element of a Rule 10b-5 action by invoking a rebuttable presumption of reliance, rather than proving direct reliance on a misrepresentation. The Court based that presumption on what is known as the "fraud-on-the-market" theory, which holds that "the market price of shares traded on well-developed markets reflects all publicly available information, and, hence, any material misrepresentations." The Court also noted that, rather than scrutinize every piece of public information about a company for himself, the typical "investor who buys or sells stock at the price set by the market does so in reliance on the integrity of that price" — the belief that it reflects all public, material information. As a result, whenever the investor buys or sells stock at the market price, his "reliance on any public material misrepresentations ... may be presumed for purposes of a Rule 10b-5 action."

Based on this theory, a plaintiff must make the following showings to demonstrate that the presumption of reliance applies in a given case: (1) that the alleged misrepresentations were publicly known, (2) that they were material, (3) that the stock traded in an efficient market, and (4) that the plaintiff traded the stock between the time the misrepresentations were made and when the truth was revealed.

At the same time, *Basic* emphasized that the presumption of reliance was rebuttable rather than conclusive. Specifically, "[a]ny showing that severs the link between the alleged misrepresentation and either the price received (or paid) by the plaintiff, or his decision to trade at a fair market price, will be sufficient to rebut the presumption of reliance." So for example, if a defendant could show that the alleged misrepresentation did not, for whatever reason, actually affect the market price, or that a plaintiff would have bought or sold the stock even had he been aware that the stock's price was tainted by fraud, then the presumption of reliance would not apply. In either of those cases, a plaintiff would have to prove that he directly relied on the defendant's misrepresentation in buying or selling the stock.

B

Halliburton contends that securities fraud plaintiffs should *always* have to prove direct reliance and that the *Basic* Court erred in allowing them to invoke a presumption of reliance instead. According to Halliburton, the *Basic* presumption contravenes congressional intent and has been undermined by subsequent developments in economic theory. Neither argument, however, so discredits *Basic* as to constitute "special justification" for overruling the decision.

* * *

Halliburton's primary argument for overruling *Basic* is that the decision rested on two premises that can no longer withstand scrutiny. The first premise concerns what is known as the "efficient capital markets hypothesis." *Basic* stated that "the market price of shares traded on well-developed markets reflects all publicly available information, and, hence, any material misrepresentations." From that statement, Halliburton concludes that the *Basic* Court espoused "a robust view of market efficiency" that is no longer tenable, for " 'overwhelming empirical evidence' now 'suggests that capital markets are not fundamentally efficient.' " To support this contention, Halliburton cites studies purporting to show that "public information is often not incorporated immediately (much less rationally) into market prices."

Halliburton does not, of course, maintain that capital markets are *always* inefficient. Rather, in its view, *Basic*'s fundamental error was to ignore the fact that "'efficiency is not a binary, yes or no question.'" The markets for some securities are more efficient than the markets for others, and even a single market can process different kinds of information more or less efficiently, depending on how widely the information is disseminated and how easily it is understood. Yet *Basic*, Halliburton asserts, glossed over these nuances, assuming a false dichotomy that renders the presumption of reliance both underinclusive and overinclusive: A misrepresentation can distort a stock's market price even in a generally inefficient market, and a misrepresentation can leave a stock's market price unaffected even in a generally efficient one.

Halliburton's criticisms fail to take *Basic* on its own terms. Halliburton focuses on the debate among economists about the degree to which the market price of a company's stock reflects public information about the company—and thus the degree to which an investor can earn an abnormal, above-market return by trading on such information. That debate is not new. Indeed, the *Basic* Court acknowledged it and declined to enter the fray, declaring that "[w]e need not determine by adjudication what economists and social scientists have debated through the use of sophisticated statistical analysis and the application of economic theory." To recognize the presumption of reliance, the Court explained, was not "conclusively to adopt any particular theory of how quickly and completely publicly available information is reflected in market price." The Court instead based the presumption on the fairly modest premise that "market professionals generally consider most publicly announced material statements about companies, thereby affecting stock market prices." *Basic*'s presumption of reliance thus does not rest on a "binary" view of market efficiency. Indeed, in making the presumption rebuttable, *Basic* recognized that market efficiency is a matter of degree and accordingly made it a matter of proof.

The academic debates discussed by Halliburton have not refuted the modest premise underlying the presumption of reliance. Even the foremost critics of the efficient-capital-markets hypothesis acknowledge that public information generally affects stock prices. Halliburton also conceded as much in its reply brief and at oral argument. Debates about the precise *degree* to which stock prices accurately reflect public information are thus largely beside the point. "That the ... price [of a stock] may be inaccurate does not detract from the fact that false statements affect it, and cause loss," which is "all that *Basic* requires." Even though the efficient capital markets hypothesis may have "garnered substantial criticism since *Basic*," Halliburton has not identified the kind of fundamental shift in economic theory that could justify overruling a precedent on the ground that it misunderstood, or has since been overtaken by, economic realities.

Halliburton also contests a second premise underlying the *Basic* presumption: the notion that investors "invest 'in reliance on the integrity of [the market] price.'" Halliburton identifies a number of classes of investors for whom "price integrity" is supposedly "marginal or irrelevant." The primary example is the value investor, who believes that certain stocks are undervalued or overvalued and attempts to "beat the market" by buying the undervalued stocks and selling the overvalued ones. If many investors "are indifferent to prices," Halliburton contends, then courts should not presume that investors rely on the integrity of those prices and any misrepresentations incorporated into them.

But *Basic* never denied the existence of such investors. As we recently explained, *Basic* concluded only that "it is reasonable to presume that *most* investors—knowing that they have little hope of outperforming the market in the long run based solely on their analysis of publicly available information—will rely on the security's market price as an unbiased assessment of the security's value in light of all public information."

In any event, there is no reason to suppose that even Halliburton's main counterexample—the value investor—is as indifferent to the integrity of market prices as Halliburton suggests. Such an investor implicitly relies on the fact that a stock's market price will eventually reflect material information—how else could the market correction on which his profit depends occur? To be sure, the value investor "does not believe that the market price accurately reflects public information *at the time he transacts.*" But to indirectly rely on a misstatement in the sense relevant for the *Basic* presumption, he need only trade stock based on the belief that the market price will incorporate public information within a reasonable period. The value investor also presumably tries to estimate *how* undervalued or overvalued a particular stock is, and such estimates can be skewed by a market price tainted by fraud.

C

The principle of *stare decisis* has "'special force'" "in respect to statutory interpretation" because "'Congress remains free to alter what we have done.'" So too with *Basic*'s presumption of reliance. Although the presumption is a judicially created doctrine designed to implement a judicially created cause of action, we have described the presumption as "a substantive doctrine of federal securities-fraud law." That is because it provides a way of satisfying the reliance element of the Rule 10b-5 cause of action. As with any other element of that cause of action, Congress may overturn or modify any aspect of our interpretations of the reliance requirement, including the *Basic* presumption itself. Given that possibility, we see no reason to exempt the *Basic* presumption from ordinary principles of *stare decisis*.

To buttress its case for overruling *Basic,* Halliburton contends that, in addition to being wrongly decided, the decision is inconsistent with our more recent decisions construing the Rule 10b-5 cause of action. As Halliburton notes, we have held that "we must give 'narrow dimensions ... to a right of action Congress did not authorize when it first enacted the statute and did not expand when it revisited the law.'" Yet the *Basic* presumption, Halliburton asserts, does just the opposite, *expanding* the Rule 10b-5 cause of action.

Not so. In *Central Bank* and *Stoneridge,* we declined to extend Rule 10b-5 liability to entirely new categories of defendants who themselves had not made any material, public misrepresentation. Such an extension, we explained, would have eviscerated the requirement that a plaintiff prove that he relied on a misrepresentation made *by the defendant*. The *Basic* presumption does not eliminate that requirement but rather provides an alternative means of satisfying it. While the presumption makes it easier for plaintiffs to prove reliance, it does not alter the elements of the Rule 10b-5 cause of action and thus maintains the action's original legal scope.

* * *

Finally, Halliburton and its *amici* contend that, by facilitating securities class actions, the *Basic* presumption produces a number of serious and harmful consequences. Such class actions, they say, allow plaintiffs to extort large settlements from defendants for meritless claims; punish innocent shareholders, who end up having to pay settlements and judgments; impose excessive costs on businesses; and consume a disproportionately large share of judicial resources.

These concerns are more appropriately addressed to Congress, which has in fact responded, to some extent, to many of the issues raised by Halliburton and its *amici*. Congress has, for example, enacted the Private Securities Litigation Reform Act of 1995 (PSLRA), which sought to combat perceived abuses in securities litigation with heightened pleading requirements, limits on damages and attorney's fees, a "safe harbor" for certain kinds of statements, restrictions on the selection of lead plaintiffs in securities class actions, sanctions for frivolous litigation, and stays of discovery pending motions to dismiss. And to prevent plaintiffs from circumventing these restrictions by bringing securities class actions under state law in state court, Congress also enacted the Securities Litigation Uniform Standards Act of 1998, which precludes many state law class actions alleging securities fraud. Such legislation demonstrates Congress's willingness to consider policy concerns of the sort that Halliburton says should lead us to overrule *Basic*.

III

Halliburton proposes two alternatives to overruling *Basic* that would alleviate what it regards as the decision's most serious flaws. The first alternative would require plaintiffs to prove that a defendant's misrepresentation actually affected the stock price—so-called "price impact"—in order to invoke the *Basic* presumption. It should not be enough, Halliburton contends, for plaintiffs to demonstrate the general efficiency of the market in which the stock traded. Halliburton's second proposed alternative would allow defendants to rebut the presumption of reliance with evidence of a *lack* of price impact, not only at the merits stage—which all agree defendants may already do—but also before class certification.

A

As noted, to invoke the *Basic* presumption, a plaintiff must prove that: (1) the alleged misrepresentations were publicly known, (2) they were material, (3) the stock traded in an efficient market, and (4) the plaintiff traded the stock between when the misrepresentations were made and when the truth was revealed. Each of these requirements follows from the fraud-on-the-market theory underlying the presumption. If the misrepresentation was not publicly known, then it could not have distorted the stock's market price. So too if the misrepresentation was immaterial—that is, if it would not have "'been viewed by the reasonable investor as having significantly altered the "total mix" of information made available,'"—or if the market in which the stock traded was inefficient. And if the plaintiff did not buy or sell the stock after the misrepresentation was made but before the truth was revealed, then he could not be said to have acted in reliance on a fraud-tainted price.

The first three prerequisites are directed at price impact—"whether the alleged misrepresentations affected the market price in the first place."

* * *

Halliburton argues that since the *Basic* presumption hinges on price impact, plaintiffs should be required to prove it directly in order to invoke the presumption. Proving the presumption's prerequisites, which are at best an imperfect proxy for price impact, should not suffice.

Far from a modest refinement of the *Basic* presumption, this proposal would radically alter the required showing for the reliance element of the Rule 10b-5 cause of action. What is called the *Basic* presumption actually incorporates two constituent presumptions: First, if a plaintiff shows that the defendant's misrepresentation was public and material and that the stock traded in a generally efficient market, he is entitled to a presumption that the misrepresentation affected the stock price. Second, if the plaintiff also shows that he purchased the stock at the market price during the relevant period, he is entitled to a further presumption that he purchased the stock in reliance on the defendant's misrepresentation.

By requiring plaintiffs to prove price impact directly, Halliburton's proposal would take away the first constituent presumption. Halliburton's argument for doing so is the same as its primary argument for overruling the *Basic* presumption altogether: Because market efficiency is not a yes-or-no proposition, a public, material misrepresentation might not affect a stock's price even in a generally efficient market. But as explained, *Basic* never suggested otherwise; that is why it affords defendants an opportunity to rebut the presumption by showing, among other things, that the particular misrepresentation at issue did not affect the stock's market price. For the same reasons we declined to completely jettison the *Basic* presumption, we decline to effectively jettison half of it by revising the prerequisites for invoking it.

B

Even if plaintiffs need not directly prove price impact to invoke the *Basic* presumption, Halliburton contends that defendants should at least be allowed to defeat the presumption at the class certification stage through evidence that the misrepresentation did not in fact affect the stock price. We agree.

1

There is no dispute that defendants may introduce such evidence at the merits stage to rebut the *Basic* presumption. *Basic* itself "made clear that the presumption was just that, and could be rebutted by appropriate evidence," including evidence that the asserted misrepresentation (or its correction) did not affect the market price of the defendant's stock.

Nor is there any dispute that defendants may introduce price impact evidence at the class certification stage, so long as it is for the purpose of countering a plaintiff's showing of market efficiency, rather than directly rebutting the presumption. As EPJ Fund acknowledges, "[o]f course ... defendants can introduce evidence at class certification of lack of price impact as some evidence that the market is not efficient."

After all, plaintiffs themselves can and do introduce evidence of the *existence* of price impact in connection with "event studies"—regression analyses that seek to show that the market price of the defendant's stock tends to respond to pertinent publicly reported events. In this case, for example, EPJ Fund submitted an event study of various episodes that might have been expected to affect the price of Halliburton's stock, in order to demonstrate that the market for that stock takes account of material, public information about the company. The episodes examined by EPJ Fund's event study included one of the alleged misrepresentations that form the basis of the Fund's suit.

Defendants—like plaintiffs—may accordingly submit price impact evidence prior to class certification. What defendants may not do, EPJ Fund insists and the Court of Appeals held, is rely on that same evidence prior to class certification for the particular purpose of rebutting the presumption altogether.

This restriction makes no sense, and can readily lead to bizarre results. Suppose a defendant at the certification stage submits an event study looking at the impact on the price of its stock from six discrete events, in an effort to refute the plaintiffs' claim of general market efficiency. All agree the defendant may do this. Suppose one of the six events is the specific misrepresentation asserted by the plaintiffs. All agree that this too is perfectly acceptable. Now suppose the district court determines that, despite the defendant's study, the plaintiff has carried its burden to prove market efficiency, but that the evidence shows no price impact with respect to the specific misrepresentation challenged in the suit. The evidence at the certification stage thus shows an efficient market, on which the alleged misrepresentation had no price impact. And yet under EPJ Fund's view, the plaintiffs' action should be certified and proceed as a class action (with all that entails), even though the fraud-on-the-market theory does not apply and common reliance thus cannot be presumed.

Such a result is inconsistent with *Basic*'s own logic. Under *Basic*'s fraud-on-the-market theory, market efficiency and the other prerequisites for invoking the presumption constitute an indirect way of showing price impact. As explained, it is appropriate to allow plaintiffs to rely on this indirect proxy for price impact, rather than requiring them to prove price impact directly, given *Basic*'s rationales for recognizing a presumption of reliance in the first place.

But an indirect proxy should not preclude direct evidence when such evidence is available. As we explained in *Basic*, "[a]ny showing that severs the link between the alleged misrepresentation and ... the price received (or paid) by the plaintiff ... will be sufficient to rebut the presumption of reliance" because "the basis for finding that the fraud had been transmitted through market price would be gone." And without the presumption of reliance, a Rule 10b-5 suit cannot proceed as a class action: Each plaintiff would have to prove reliance individually, so common issues would not "predominate" over individual ones, as required by Rule 23(b)(3). Price impact is thus an essential precondition for any Rule 10b–5 class action. While *Basic* allows plaintiffs to establish that precondition indirectly, it does not require courts to ignore a defendant's direct, more salient evidence showing that the alleged misrepresentation did not actually affect the stock's market price and, consequently, that the *Basic* presumption does not apply.

2

The Court of Appeals relied on our decision in *Amgen* in holding that Halliburton could not introduce evidence of lack of price impact at the class certification stage. The question in *Amgen* was whether plaintiffs could be required to prove (or defendants be permitted to disprove) materiality before class certification. Even though materiality is a prerequisite for invoking the *Basic* presumption, we held that it should be left to the merits stage, because it does not bear on the predominance requirement of Rule 23(b)(3). We reasoned that materiality is an objective issue susceptible to common, class wide proof. We also noted that a failure to prove materiality would necessarily defeat every plaintiff's claim on the merits; it would not simply preclude invocation of the presumption and thereby cause individual questions of reliance to predominate over common ones. In this latter respect, we explained, materiality differs from the publicity and market efficiency prerequisites, neither of which is necessary to prove a Rule 10b–5 claim on the merits.

EPJ Fund argues that much of the foregoing could be said of price impact as well. Fair enough. But price impact differs from materiality in a crucial respect. Given that the other *Basic* prerequisites must still be proved at the class certification stage, the common issue of materiality can be left to the merits stage without risking the certification of classes in which individual issues will end up overwhelming common ones. And because materiality is a discrete issue that can be resolved in isolation from the other prerequisites, it can be wholly confined to the merits stage.

Price impact is different. The fact that a misrepresentation "was reflected in the market price at the time of [the] transaction"—that it had price impact—is "*Basic*'s fundamental premise." It thus has everything to do with the issue of predominance at the class certification stage. That is why, if reliance is to be shown through the *Basic* presumption, the publicity and market efficiency prerequisites must be proved before class certification. Without proof of those prerequisites, the fraud-on-the-market theory underlying the presumption completely collapses, rendering class certification inappropriate.

Our choice in this case, then, is not between allowing price impact evidence at the class certification stage or relegating it to the merits. Evidence of price impact will be before the court at the certification stage in any event. The choice, rather, is between limiting the price impact inquiry before class certification to indirect evidence, and allowing consideration of direct evidence as well. As explained, we see no reason to artificially limit the inquiry at the certification stage to indirect evidence of price impact. Defendants may seek to defeat the *Basic* presumption at that stage through direct as well as indirect price impact evidence.

But as explained, publicity and market efficiency are nothing more than prerequisites for an indirect showing of price impact. There is no dispute that at least such indirect proof of price impact "is needed to ensure that the questions of law or fact common to the class will 'predominate.'" That is so even though such proof is also highly relevant at the merits stage.

More than 25 years ago, we held that plaintiffs could satisfy the reliance element of the Rule 10b-5 cause of action by invoking a presumption that a public, material misrepresentation will distort the price of stock traded in an efficient market, and that anyone who purchases the stock at the market price may be considered to have done so in reliance on the misrepresentation. We adhere to that decision and decline to modify the prerequisites for invoking the presumption of reliance. But to maintain the consistency of the presumption with the class certification requirements of Federal Rule of Civil Procedure 23, defendants must be afforded an opportunity before class certification to defeat the presumption through evidence that an alleged misrepresentation did not actually affect the market price of the stock.

* * *

Justice THOMAS, with whom Justice SCALIA and Justice ALITO join, concurring in the judgment.

The implied Rule 10b-5 private cause of action is "a relic of the heady days in which this Court assumed common-law powers to create causes of action," We have since ended that practice because the authority to fashion private remedies to enforce federal law belongs to Congress alone. Absent statutory authorization for a cause of action, "courts may not create one, no matter how desirable that might be as a policy matter."

Basic Inc. v. Levinson, 485 U.S. 224, 108 S.Ct. 978, 99 L.Ed.2d 194 (1988), demonstrates the wisdom of this rule. *Basic* presented the question how investors must prove the reliance element of the implied Rule 10b-5 cause of action — the requirement that the plaintiff buy or sell stock in reliance on the defendant's misstatement — when they transact on modern, impersonal securities exchanges. Were the Rule 10b-5 action statutory, the Court could have resolved this question by interpreting the statutory language. Without a statute to interpret for guidance, however, the Court began instead with a particular policy "problem": for investors in impersonal markets, the traditional reliance requirement was hard to prove and impossible to prove as common among plaintiffs bringing 10b–5 class-action suits.

With the task thus framed as "resol[ving]" that "'problem'" rather than interpreting statutory text, the Court turned to nascent economic theory and naked intuitions about investment behavior in its efforts to fashion a new, easier way to meet the reliance requirement. The result was an evidentiary presumption, based on a "fraud on the market" theory that paved the way for class actions under Rule 10b–5.

Today we are asked to determine whether *Basic* was correctly decided. The Court suggests that it was, and that *stare decisis* demands that we preserve it. I disagree. Logic, economic realities, and our subsequent jurisprudence have undermined the foundations of the *Basic* presumption, and *stare decisis* cannot prop up the façade that remains. *Basic* should be overruled.

I

Understanding where *Basic* went wrong requires an explanation of the "reliance" requirement as traditionally understood.

"Reliance by the plaintiff upon the defendant's deceptive acts is an essential element" of the implied 10b-5 private cause of action. To prove reliance, the plaintiff must show "'transaction causation,'" *i.e.*, that the specific misstatement induced "the investor's decision to engage in the transaction." Such proof "ensures that there is a proper 'connection between a defendant's misrepresentation and a plaintiff's injury'"—namely, that the plaintiff has not just lost money as a result of the misstatement, but that he was actually *defrauded* by it. Without that connection, Rule 10b-5 is reduced to a "'scheme of investor's insurance,'" because a plaintiff could recover whenever the defendant's misstatement distorted the stock price—regardless of whether the misstatement had actually tricked the plaintiff into buying (or selling) the stock in the first place.

The "traditional" reliance element requires a plaintiff to "sho[w] that he was aware of a company's statement and engaged in a relevant transaction ... based on that specific misrepresentation." But investors who purchase stock from third parties on impersonal exchanges (*e.g.*, the New York Stock Exchange) often will not be aware of any particular statement made by the issuer of the security, and therefore cannot establish that they transacted based on a specific misrepresentation. Nor is the traditional reliance requirement amenable to class treatment; the inherently individualized nature of the reliance inquiry renders it impossible for a 10b-5 plaintiff to prove that common questions predominate over individual ones, making class certification improper.

Citing these difficulties of proof and class certification, the *Basic* Court dispensed with the traditional reliance requirement in favor of a new one based on the fraud-on-the-market theory. The new version of reliance had two related parts.

First, *Basic* suggested that plaintiffs could meet the reliance requirement "'indirectly,'" The Court reasoned that "'ideally, [the market] transmits information to the investor in the processed form of a market price.'" An investor could thus be said to have "relied" on a specific misstatement if (1) the market had incorporated that statement into the market price of the security, and (2) the investor then bought or sold that security "in reliance on the integrity of the [market] price," *i.e.*, based on his belief that the market price "'reflect[ed]'" the stock's underlying "'value,'"

Second, *Basic* created a presumption that this "indirect" form of "reliance" had been proved. Based primarily on certain assumptions about economic theory and investor behavior, *Basic* afforded plaintiffs who traded in efficient markets an evidentiary presumption that both steps of the novel reliance requirement had been satisfied—that (1) the market *had* incorporated the specific misstatement into the market price of the security, and (2) the plaintiff *did* transact in reliance on the integrity of that price. A defendant was ostensibly entitled to rebut the presumption by putting forth evidence that either of those steps was absent.

II

Basic's reimagined reliance requirement was a mistake, and the passage of time has compounded its failings. First, the Court based both parts of the presumption of reliance on a questionable understanding of disputed economic theory and flawed intuitions about investor behavior. Second, *Basic*'s rebuttable presumption is at odds with our subsequent Rule 23 cases, which require plaintiffs seeking class certification to "'affirmatively demonstrate'" certification requirements like the predominance of common questions. Finally, *Basic*'s presumption that investors rely on the integrity of the market price is virtually irrebuttable in practice, which means that the "essential" reliance element effectively exists in name only.

Basic based the presumption of reliance on two factual assumptions. The first assumption was that, in a "well-developed market," public statements are generally "reflected" in the market price of securities. The second was that investors in such markets transact "in reliance on the integrity of that price." In other words, the Court created a presumption that a plaintiff had met the two-part, fraud-on-the-market version of the reliance requirement because, in the Court's view, "common sense and probability" suggested that each of those parts *would* be met.

In reality, both of the Court's key assumptions are highly contestable and do not provide the necessary support for *Basic*'s presumption of reliance. The first assumption—that public statements are "reflected" in the market price—was grounded in an economic theory that has garnered substantial criticism since *Basic*. The second assumption—that investors categorically rely on the integrity of the market price—is simply wrong.

1

The Court's first assumption was that "most publicly available information"—including public misstatements—"is reflected in [the] market price" of a security. The Court grounded that assumption in "empirical studies" testing a then-nascent economic theory known as the efficient capital markets hypothesis. Specifically, the Court relied upon the "semi-strong" version of that theory, which posits that the average investor cannot earn above-market returns (*i.e.,* "beat the market") in an efficient market by trading on the basis of publicly available information.

The upshot of the hypothesis is that "the market price of shares traded on well-developed markets [will] reflec[t] all publicly available information, and, hence, any material misrepresentations." At the time of *Basic,* this version of the efficient capital markets hypothesis was "widely accepted."

This view of market efficiency has since lost its luster. As it turns out, even "well-developed" markets (like the New York Stock Exchange) do not uniformly incorporate information into market prices with high speed. "[F]riction in accessing public information" and the presence of "processing costs" means that "not all public information will be impounded in a security's price with the same alacrity, or perhaps with any quickness at all." For example, information that is easily digestible (merger announcements or stock splits) or especially prominent (Wall Street Journal articles) may be incorporated quickly, while information that is broadly applicable or technical (Securities and Exchange Commission filings) may be incorporated slowly or even ignored.

Further, and more importantly, "overwhelming empirical evidence" now suggests that even when markets do incorporate public information, they often fail to do so accurately. "Scores" of "efficiency-defying anomalies"—such as market swings in the absence of new information and prolonged deviations from underlying asset values—make market efficiency "more contestable than ever." Such anomalies make it difficult to tell whether, at any given moment, a stock's price accurately reflects its value as indicated by all publicly available information. In sum, economists now understand that the price impact *Basic* assumed would happen reflexively is actually far from certain even in "well-developed" markets. Thus, *Basic*'s claim that "common sense and probability" support a presumption of reliance rests on shaky footing.

2

The *Basic* Court also grounded the presumption of reliance in a second assumption: that "[a]n investor who buys or sells stock at the price set by the market does so in reliance on the integrity of that price." In other words, the Court assumed that investors transact based on the belief that the market price accurately reflects the underlying "'value'" of the security. The *Basic* Court appears to have adopted this assumption about investment behavior based only on what it believed to be "common sense." The Court found it "'hard to imagine that there ever is a buyer or seller who does not rely on market integrity. Who would knowingly roll the dice in a crooked crap game?'"

The Court's rather superficial analysis does not withstand scrutiny. It cannot be seriously disputed that a great many investors do *not* buy or sell stock based on a belief that the stock's price accurately reflects its value. Many investors in fact trade for the opposite reason—that is, because they think the market has under- or overvalued the stock, and they believe they can profit from that mispricing. Indeed, securities transactions often take place because the transacting parties disagree on the security's value.

Other investor's trade for reasons entirely unrelated to price—for instance, to address changing liquidity needs, tax concerns, or portfolio balancing requirements. These investment decisions—made with indifference to price and thus without regard for price "integrity"—are at odds with *Basic*'s understanding of what motivates investment decisions. In short, *Basic*'s assumption that all investors rely in common on "price integrity" is simply wrong.

The majority tries (but fails) to reconcile *Basic*'s assumption about investor behavior with the reality that many investors do not behave in the way *Basic* assumed. It first asserts that *Basic* rested only on the more modest view that "'most investors'" rely on the integrity of a security's market price. That gloss is difficult to square with *Basic*'s plain language: "An investor who buys or sells stock at the price set by the market does so in reliance on the integrity of that price." In any event, neither *Basic* nor the majority offers anything more than a judicial hunch as evidence that even "most" investors rely on price integrity.

The majority also suggests that "there is no reason to suppose" that investors who buy stock they believe to be undervalued are "indifferent to the integrity of market prices." Such "value investor[s]," according to the majority, "implicitly rel[y] on the fact that a stock's market price will eventually reflect material information" and "presumably tr[y] to estimate *how* undervalued or overvalued a particular stock is" by reference to the market price. Whether the majority's unsupported claims about the thought processes of hypothetical investors are accurate or not, they are surely beside the point. Whatever else an investor believes about the market, he simply does not "rely on the integrity of the market price" if he does not believe that the market price accurately reflects public information *at the time he transacts*. That is, an investor cannot claim that a public misstatement induced his transaction by distorting the market price if he did not buy at that price while believing that it accurately incorporated that public information. For that sort of investor, *Basic*'s critical fiction falls apart.

* * *

C

But in practice, the so-called "rebuttable presumption" is largely irrebuttable.

The *Basic* Court ostensibly afforded defendants an opportunity to rebut the presumption by providing evidence that either aspect of a plaintiff's fraud-on-the-market reliance—price impact, or reliance on the integrity of the market price—is missing. As it turns out, however, the realities of class-action procedure make rebuttal based on an individual plaintiff's lack of reliance virtually impossible. At the class-certification stage, rebuttal is only directed at the class representatives, which means that counsel only needs to find one class member who can withstand the challenge. After class certification, courts have refused to allow defendants to challenge any plaintiff's reliance on the integrity of the market price prior to a determination on classwide liability. One search for rebuttals on individual-reliance grounds turned up only six cases out of the thousands of Rule 10b-5 actions brought since *Basic*.

The apparent unavailability of this form of rebuttal has troubling implications. Because the presumption is conclusive in practice with respect to investors' reliance on price integrity, even *Basic*'s watered-down reliance requirement has been effectively eliminated. Once the presumption attaches, the reliance element is no longer an obstacle to prevailing on the claim, even though many class members will not have transacted in reliance on price integrity. And without a functional reliance requirement, the "essential element" that ensures the plaintiff has actually been defrauded, Rule 10b-5 becomes the very "'scheme of investor's insurance'" the *rebuttable* presumption was supposed to prevent. For these reasons, *Basic* should be overruled in favor of the straightforward rule that "[r]eliance by the plaintiff upon the defendant's deceptive acts" — actual reliance, not the fictional "fraud-on-the-market" version — "is an essential element of the § 10(b) private cause of action."

Notes and Questions

1. In Justice White's dissent in *Basic,* he noted that "For while the economists' theories which underpin the fraud-on-the-market presumption may have the appeal of mathematical exactitude and scientific certainty, they are — in the end — nothing more than theories which may or may not prove accurate upon further consideration. Even the most earnest advocates of economic analysis of the law recognize this." Is the Court equipped to use economic theory to develop legal rules as a basis of recovery without a staff composed of economists, experts in the Efficient Capital Market Hypothesis (ECMH), and the ability to test the validity of empirical market studies?

2. What are the prerequisites of the *Basic* presumption? Answer — a plaintiff must prove that: (1) the alleged misrepresentations were publicly known, (2) they were material, (3) the stock traded in an efficient market, and (4) the plaintiff traded the stock between when the misrepresentations were made and when the truth was revealed.

3. How can defendants deal with the fraud-on-the market theory at the class certification stage?

4. Why does the Court state that class actions cannot be brought without the fraud-on-the-market theory?

5. *Event Studies.* "The event study methodology is designed to investigate the effect of an event on a specific dependent variable. A commonly used dependent variable in event studies is the stock price of the company. The definition of such an event study will be 'a study of the changes in stock price beyond expectation (abnormal returns) over a period of time (event window). Abnormal returns are attributed to the effects of the event.' The event study methodology seeks to determine whether there is an abnormal stock price effect associated with an event. From this, the researcher can infer the significance of the event.

   The key assumption of the event study methodology is that the market must be efficient. Given an efficient market, the effects of the event will be reflected immediately in the stock prices of the company...."[21]

---

21. Wong Shou Woon, Introduction to the Event Study Methodology, available at http://users.telenet.be/webdesignsite/Bachelorproeven/Bronnen/analyst%20recommendations/introduction_to_the_Event_Study_Methodology%5B1%5D.pdf.

E. Loss Causation

Plaintiffs in a private cause of action under § 10(b) and Rule 10b-5 must prove loss causation. This element is codified in § 21D(b)(4) of the Exchange Act. Section 21D(b)(4) provides that the plaintiff has the burden of proving that the defendant's act or omission alleged to have violated § 10(b) and Rule 10b-5 must have caused plaintiff's loss. As you read the case below, consider how this requirement affects plaintiff's burden in the context of a security traded in an efficient market. Must the plaintiff allege that the price of the security declined after the truth became known to the public?

Dura Pharmaceuticals, Inc. v. Broudo
544 U.S. 336 (2005)

Justice BREYER delivered the opinion of the Court.

A private plaintiff who claims securities fraud must prove that the defendant's fraud caused an economic loss. We consider a Ninth Circuit holding that a plaintiff can satisfy this requirement — a requirement that courts call "loss causation" — simply by alleging in the complaint and subsequently establishing that "the price" of the security "*on the date of purchase* was inflated because of the misrepresentation." In our view, the Ninth Circuit is wrong, both in respect to what a plaintiff must prove and in respect to what the plaintiffs' complaint here must allege.

I

Respondents are individuals who bought stock in Dura Pharmaceuticals, Inc., on the public securities market between April 15, 1997, and February 24, 1998. They have brought this securities fraud class action.... against Dura and some of its managers and directors (hereinafter Dura) in federal court. In respect to the question before us, their detailed amended (181 paragraph) complaint makes substantially the following allegations:

(1) Before and during the purchase period, Dura (or its officials) made false statements concerning both Dura's drug profits and future Food and Drug Administration (FDA) approval of a new asthmatic spray device.

(2) In respect to drug profits, Dura falsely claimed that it expected that its drug sales would prove profitable.

(3) In respect to the asthmatic spray device, Dura falsely claimed that it expected the FDA would soon grant its approval.

(4) On the last day of the purchase period, February 24, 1998, Dura announced that its earnings would be lower than expected, principally due to slow drug sales.

(5) The next day Dura's shares lost almost half their value (falling from about $39 per share to about $21).

(6) About eight months later (in November 1998), Dura announced that the FDA would not approve Dura's new asthmatic spray device.

(7) The next day Dura's share price temporarily fell but almost fully recovered within one week.

Most importantly, the complaint says the following (and nothing significantly more than the following) about economic losses attributable to the spray device misstatement: *"In reliance on the integrity of the market, [the plaintiffs] … paid artificially inflated prices for Dura securities"* and the plaintiffs suffered *"damage[s]"* thereby.

The District Court dismissed the complaint. In respect to the plaintiffs' drug-profitability claim, it held that the complaint failed adequately to allege an appropriate state of mind, *i.e.,* that defendants had acted knowingly, or the like. In respect to the plaintiffs' spray device claim, it held that the complaint failed adequately to allege "loss causation."

The Court of Appeals for the Ninth Circuit reversed. In the portion of the court's decision now before us—the portion that concerns the spray device claim—the Circuit held that the complaint adequately alleged "loss causation." The Circuit wrote that "plaintiffs establish loss causation if they have shown that the price *on the date of purchase* was inflated because of the misrepresentation." It added that "the injury occurs at the time of the transaction." Since the complaint pleaded "that the price at the time of purchase was overstated," and it sufficiently identified the cause, its allegations were legally sufficient.

Because the Ninth Circuit's views about loss causation differ from those of other Circuits that have considered this issue, we granted Dura's petition for certiorari. We now reverse.

II

Private federal securities fraud actions are based upon federal securities statutes and their implementing regulations. Section 10(b) of the Securities Exchange Act of 1934 forbids (1) the "use or employ[ment] … of any … deceptive device," (2) "in connection with the purchase or sale of any security," and (3) "in contravention of" Securities and Exchange Commission "rules and regulations." Commission Rule 10b-5 forbids, among other things, the making of any "untrue statement of a material fact" or the omission of any material fact "necessary in order to make the statements made … not misleading."

The courts have implied from these statutes and Rule a private damages action, which resembles, but is not identical to, common-law tort actions for deceit and misrepresentation. And Congress has imposed statutory requirements on that private action.

In cases involving publicly traded securities and purchases or sales in public securities markets, the action's basic elements include:

(1) *A material misrepresentation (or omission);*

(2) *Scienter, i.e.,* a wrongful state of mind;

(3) *A connection with the purchase or sale of a security;*

(4) *Reliance,* often referred to in cases involving public securities markets (fraud-on-the-market cases) as "transaction causation,"

(5) *Economic loss;* and

(6) *"Loss causation,"* *i.e.,* a causal connection between the material misrepresentation and the loss.

Dura argues that the complaint's allegations are inadequate in respect to these last two elements.

A

We begin with the Ninth Circuit's basic reason for finding the complaint adequate, namely, that at the end of the day plaintiffs need only "establish," *i.e.,* prove, that "the price *on the date of purchase* was inflated because of the misrepresentation." In our view, this statement of the law is wrong. Normally, in cases such as this one (*i.e.,* fraud-on-the-market cases), an inflated purchase price will not itself constitute or proximately cause the relevant economic loss.

For one thing, as a matter of pure logic, at the moment the transaction takes place, the plaintiff has suffered no loss; the inflated purchase payment is offset by ownership of a share that *at that instant* possesses equivalent value. Moreover, the logical link between the inflated share purchase price and any later economic loss is not invariably strong. Shares are normally purchased with an eye toward a later sale. But if, say, the purchaser sells the shares quickly before the relevant truth begins to leak out, the misrepresentation will not have led to any loss. If the purchaser sells later after the truth makes its way into the marketplace, an initially inflated purchase price *might* mean a later loss. But that is far from inevitably so. When the purchaser subsequently resells such shares, even at a lower price, that lower price may reflect, not the earlier misrepresentation, but changed economic circumstances, changed investor expectations, new industry-specific or firm-specific facts, conditions, or other events, which taken separately or together account for some or all of that lower price. (The same is true in respect to a claim that a share's higher price is lower than it would otherwise have been—a claim we do not consider here.) Other things being equal, the longer the time between purchase and sale, the more likely that this is so, *i.e.,* the more likely that other factors caused the loss.

Given the tangle of factors affecting price, the most logic alone permits us to say is that the higher purchase price will *sometimes* play a role in bringing about a future loss. It may prove to be a necessary condition of any such loss, and in that sense one might say that the inflated purchase price suggests that the misrepresentation (using language the Ninth Circuit used) "touches upon" a later economic loss. But, even if that is so, it is insufficient. To "touch upon" a loss is not to *cause* a loss, and it is the latter that the law requires.

For another thing, the Ninth Circuit's holding lacks support in precedent. Judicially implied private securities fraud actions resemble in many (but not all) respects common-law deceit and misrepresentation actions. The common law of deceit subjects a person who "fraudulently" makes a "misrepresentation" to liability "for pecuniary loss caused" to one who justifiably relies upon that misrepresentation. And the common law has long insisted that a plaintiff in such a case show not only that had he known the truth he would not have acted but also that he suffered actual economic loss.

Given the common-law roots of the securities fraud action (and the common-law requirement that a plaintiff show actual damages), it is not surprising that other Courts of Appeals have rejected the Ninth Circuit's "inflated purchase price" approach to proving causation and loss. Indeed, the Restatement of Torts, in setting forth the judicial consensus, says that a person who "misrepresents the financial condition of a corporation in order to sell its stock" becomes liable to a relying purchaser "for the loss" the purchaser sustains "when the facts ... become generally known" and "as a result" share value "depreciate[s]." Treatise writers, too, have emphasized the need to prove proximate causation.

We cannot reconcile the Ninth Circuit's "inflated purchase price" approach with these views of other courts. And the uniqueness of its perspective argues against the validity of its approach in a case like this one where we consider the contours of a judicially implied cause of action with roots in the common law.

Finally, the Ninth Circuit's approach overlooks an important securities law objective. The securities statutes seek to maintain public confidence in the marketplace. They do so by deterring fraud, in part, through the availability of private securities fraud actions. But the statutes make these latter actions available, not to provide investors with broad insurance against market losses, but to protect them against those economic losses that misrepresentations actually cause.

The statutory provision at issue here and the paragraphs that precede it emphasize this last mentioned objective. The statute [Private Securities Litigation Reform Act of 1995] insists that securities fraud complaints "specify" each misleading statement; that they set forth the facts "on which [a] belief" that a statement is misleading was "formed"; and that they "state with particularity facts giving rise to a strong inference that the defendant acted with the required state of mind. And the statute expressly imposes on plaintiffs "the burden of proving" that the defendant's misrepresentations "caused the loss for which the plaintiff seeks to recover."

The statute thereby makes clear Congress' intent to permit private securities fraud actions for recovery where, but only where, plaintiffs adequately allege and prove the traditional elements of causation and loss. By way of contrast, the Ninth Circuit's approach would allow recovery where a misrepresentation leads to an inflated purchase price but nonetheless does not proximately cause any economic loss. That is to say, it would permit recovery where these two traditional elements in fact are missing.

In sum, we find the Ninth Circuit's approach inconsistent with the law's requirement that a plaintiff prove that the defendant's misrepresentation (or other fraudulent conduct) proximately caused the plaintiff's economic loss. We need not, and do not, consider other proximate cause or loss-related questions.

B

Our holding about plaintiffs' need to *prove* proximate causation and economic loss leads us also to conclude that the plaintiffs' complaint here failed adequately to *allege* these requirements. We concede that the Federal Rules of Civil Procedure require only "a short and plain statement of the claim showing that the pleader is entitled to relief." And we assume, at least for argument's sake, that neither the Rules nor the securities statutes impose any special further requirement in respect to the pleading of proximate causation or economic loss. But, even so, the "short and plain statement" must provide the defendant with "fair notice of what the plaintiff's claim is and the grounds upon which it rests." The complaint before us fails this simple test.

As we have pointed out, the plaintiffs' lengthy complaint contains only one statement that we can fairly read as describing the loss caused by the defendants' "spray device" misrepresentations. That statement says that the plaintiffs "paid artificially inflated prices for Dura['s] securities" and suffered "damage[s]." The statement implies that the plaintiffs' loss consisted of the "artificially inflated" purchase "prices." The complaint's failure to claim that Dura's share price fell significantly after the truth became known suggests that the plaintiffs considered the allegation of purchase price inflation alone sufficient. The complaint contains nothing that suggests otherwise.

[H]owever, the "artificially inflated purchase price" is not itself a relevant economic loss. And the complaint nowhere else provides the defendants with notice of what the relevant economic loss might be or of what the causal connection might be between that loss and the misrepresentation concerning Dura's "spray device."

We concede that ordinary pleading rules are not meant to impose a great burden upon a plaintiff. But it should not prove burdensome for a plaintiff who has suffered an economic loss to provide a defendant with some indication of the loss and the causal connection that the plaintiff has in mind. At the same time, allowing a plaintiff to forgo giving any indication of the economic loss and proximate cause that the plaintiff has in mind would bring about harm of the very sort the statutes seek to avoid. It would permit a plaintiff "with a largely groundless claim to simply take up the time of a number of other people, with the right to do so representing an *in terrorem* increment of the settlement value, rather than a reasonably founded hope that the [discovery] process will reveal relevant evidence." Such a rule would tend to transform a private securities action into a partial downside insurance policy.

For these reasons, we find the plaintiffs' complaint legally insufficient. We reverse the judgment of the Ninth Circuit, and we remand the case for further proceedings consistent with this opinion.

Hypothetical Four

Success First has been sued by a group of purchasers of two Internet companies— Amy's Online and AppFirst—about which its research analysts issued research reports recommending that investors purchase their shares. Sean O'Connor, one of Success

First's top research analysts, issued favorable research reports about Amy's Online and AppFirst, even though he did not then believe that the companies were a good investment. Plaintiffs allege that Success First touted Sean to investors as an independent assessor of business prospects, but that he issued the falsely optimistic recommendations to cultivate Success First's investment banking clients. The plaintiffs' suit arose from an investigation of the Maryland Attorney General's office into investment recommendations and research issued by several broker-dealers operating in Maryland, including Success First.

A supporting affidavit produced by Maryland outlined a scheme by Success First's research unit to publish bogus analysis in an effort to generate investment banking business. The Maryland AG's papers cited dozens of internal communications that expressed bluntly negative views on Amy's Online and AppFirst stocks that Sean was recommending to the investing public. Sean issued more than 25 reports recommending the companies. Plaintiffs allege that they bought Amy's Online and AppFirst based on Sean's recommendations and that they lost millions when their true financial condition was disclosed. Specifically, plaintiffs allege that when they invested, they were relying on the integrity of the market (including the fraudulent recommendations and omissions made by Sean during the putative class period), that the shares plummeted, and that their investments became virtually worthless. However, there were no allegations that the market reacted negatively to a corrective disclosure regarding the falsity of buy and accumulate recommendations issued by Sean or that Sean misstated or omitted risks that led to the plaintiffs' losses. Success First has responded by making a motion to dismiss, asserting that plaintiffs have failed to plead loss causation. What is the likelihood of plaintiffs successfully establishing loss causation under § 10(b) and Rule 10b-5?

F. Damages

Section 10(b) and Rule 10b-5 do not state the measure of compensatory damages for private actions. Consequently, there is no single measure of damages for such claims brought against broker-dealers. Section 28(a) of the Exchange Act limits damages in private actions under § 10(b) and Rule 10b-5 to plaintiff's actual damages; however, the actual damages limitation has been interpreted broadly by the courts to mean out-of-pocket losses with a view to placing the plaintiff in the position she would have been in if the fraud had not taken place. In *Randall v. Loftsgaarden*, 478 U.S. 647, 663 (1986), the Supreme Court interpreted § 28(a) regarding the measure of damages under § 10(b) to allow plaintiffs to recover the defendant's profit if required to prevent unjust enrichment of the defendant along with rescission. In *Randall,* the Court stated that:

> In enacting § 28(a), Congress did not specify what was meant by "actual damages." It is appropriate, therefore, to look to "the state of the law at the time the legislation was enacted" for guidance in defining the scope of this limitation. When § 28(a) was enacted § 12(2) [of the Securities Act of 1933] stood as a conspicuous example of a rescissory remedy, and we have found that

Congress did not intend that a recovery in rescission under § 12(2) be reduced by tax benefits received. Accordingly, we think § 28(a) should not be read to compel a different result where rescissory damages are obtained under § 10(b).

Even apart from the analogy furnished by § 12(2), this Court has never interpreted § 28(a) as imposing a rigid requirement that every recovery on an express or implied right of action under the 1934 Act must be limited to the net economic harm suffered by the plaintiff. To be sure, this Court has noted that "Section 28(a) of the 1934 Act ... limits recovery in any private damages action brought under the 1934 Act to 'actual damages,'" and *Affiliated Ute Citizens* clearly interpreted § 28(a) as governing the measures of damages that are permissible under § 10(b). But the Court in *Affiliated Ute Citizens* also indicated that "where the defendant received more than the seller's actual loss ... damages are the amount of the defendant's profit." This alternative standard aims at preventing the unjust enrichment of a fraudulent buyer, and it clearly does more than simply make the plaintiff whole for the economic loss proximately caused by the buyer's fraud. Indeed, the accepted rationale underlying this alternative is simply that "[it] is more appropriate to give the defrauded party the benefit even of windfalls than to let the fraudulent party keep them."

Accordingly, courts have allowed various measures of damages depending on the particular facts and circumstances, including out-of-pocket, rescission, benefit-of-the-bargain, or restitution. In the remainder of this text, where appropriate, the measure of damages for particular types of fraudulent broker-dealer conduct will be identified in each chapter as applicable.

In addition, Section 21D(g) of the Exchange Act allows proportionate liability in private actions involving multiple broker-dealer defendants, i.e., the defendant is only liable for the percentage of the violative conduct that she committed. However, if the broker-dealer knowingly violated § 10(b) and Rule 10b-5, it may be potentially jointly and severally liable.

Notes and Questions

1. Is there a difference between an economic loss and loss causation for Justice Breyer? Why is not buying a stock at an inflated price considered an economic loss? Answer: Loss causation "is the causal link between the alleged misconduct and the economic harm ultimately suffered by the plaintiff." *Lentil v. Merrill Lynch & Co.*, 396 F.3d 161, 172 (2d Cir. 2005).

2. Although *Dura* requires pleading of loss causation, it provides minimal guidance about how to plead loss causation sufficiently. *Lentil v. Merrill Lynch & Co.*, 396 F.3d 161 (2d Cir. 2005) was decided three months before *Dura* and provides guidance for sufficiently pleading loss causation. Like *Dura*, investors alleged that they purchased at inflated prices based on material misrepresentations and omissions. In *Lentil*, non-customer investors of Merrill Lynch alleged that its analysts en-

couraged them to buy the securities of Merrill's investment banking clients by issuing analysts' reports that failed to disclose Merrill's true motivation for publishing fraudulent reports was to attract investment banking business. As a result of the fraudulent reports, the non-customer investors bought stocks touted in Merrill Lynch analysts' reports at inflated prices losing millions of dollars when prices plummeted. The court determined that plaintiffs failed to plead loss causation sufficiently. Specifically, the court stated that, "to establish loss causation 'a plaintiff must allege ... that the *subject* of the fraudulent statement or omission was the cause of the actual loss suffered.'" It is alleged that Merrill's "buy" and "accumulate" recommendations were false and misleading with respect to 24/7 Media and Interliant, and that those recommendations artificially inflated the value of 24/7 Media and Interliant stock. However, plaintiffs do not allege that the subject of those false recommendations (that investors should buy or accumulate 24/7 Media and Interliant stock), or any corrective disclosure regarding the falsity of those recommendations, is the cause of the *decline* in stock value that plaintiffs claim as their loss. Nor do plaintiffs allege that Merrill Lynch concealed or misstated any risks associated with an investment in 24/7 Media or Interliant, some of which presumably caused plaintiffs' loss. Plaintiffs therefore failed to allege loss causation.... Plaintiffs do allege that Merrill's "material misrepresentations and omissions induced a disparity between the transaction price and the true 'investment quality'" of 24/7 Media and Interliant securities; "that the market price of [the] securities was artificially inflated"; and that the securities were acquired "at artificially inflated prices and [the plaintiffs] were damaged thereby. Assuming (as we must) the truth of these allegations, they may establish transaction causation; but they do not provide the necessary causal link between Merrill's fraud and plaintiffs' losses." Does the Second Circuit's description of sufficient pleading for loss causation align with the standard for pleading loss causation in *Dura?* What is your understanding of how to sufficiently plead loss causation in a private cause of action under § 10(b) and Rule 10b-5?

Chapter 11

Broker-Dealer Conduct and the Antifraud Provisions

Regulatory Authority

Securities Exchange Act of 1934 Section 10(b)

Exchange Act Rules 10b-5, 15c1-7

FINRA Rules 2010, 2020, 2090, 2110, 2111, 2114, 2214, 4512(c), 6420

NASD Rule 2510

Motivating Hypothetical

It is time for Success First to conduct its annual compliance conference. This year's focus is specific broker-dealer conduct in relation to trading executed in the accounts of its customers, both retail and institutional. Topics at this year's compliance conference include suitability, churning, unauthorized trading, and market manipulation. Thus far, Success First does not have a disciplinary history and management and the board want it to remain this way. Accordingly, it is very important that registered persons obtain meaningful compliance training to avoid securities violations when interacting with customers. Specifically, Success First's registered representatives and other associated persons must have a clear understanding of the types of conduct that may violate federal rules and regulations and applicable FINRA rules. Carmen has appointed a committee to organize the program for the conference (the "Conference Committee"). The Conference Committee consists of Tatun Chen, chief operations officer; Malak Johnson, chief compliance officer; Josephine Wiseman, general counsel; and Naomi Watts, regional director for the southeast region. Each committee member is responsible for organizing a panel on topics to be presented at the conference. Each panel must have a moderator and at least two subject matter experts. Jane Wiseman's new staff attorney, Justin Ogilvy, has been charged with compiling lists of potential experts for each panel for all members of the Conference Committee. Josephine and Carmen have told Jane that they will be very disappointed if she fails to procure speakers from the Securities and Exchange Commission, FINRA, the Investment Company Institute, and the Municipal Securities Rulemaking Board. Justin, a recent law school graduate with a non-securities industry background, must research each of the potential conference topics in order to identify suitable participants for the panel. He begins his research by reading this chapter.

I. Introduction

We now turn to the use of the antifraud provisions of the federal securities laws by regulators and private plaintiffs to combat specific types of broker-dealer fraud. In this chapter we will focus on claims such as churning, unauthorized trading, suitability, and market manipulation. Since approximately 1987, such claims have been brought by private plaintiffs using arbitration because, when opening their brokerage accounts, they are required to agree to resolve disputes with broker-dealers using arbitration. Generally, this arbitration forum is administered by FINRA with SEC oversight.[1] This means that cases brought by individual customers in court concern pre-1987 broker-dealer fraudulent conduct. *See* Chapter 12, Securities Arbitration.

We begin this chapter with a discussion of when the broker-dealer has a fiduciary relationship with its customer. Discussion of the broker-dealer's fiduciary duty is appropriate before discussing claims for broker-dealer misconduct because, generally, such claims are alleged in conjunction with a claim for breach of fiduciary duty.

A. The Broker-Dealer and Fiduciary Duty

Generally, broker-dealers are not fiduciaries under the federal securities laws. The primary standard of conduct for broker-dealers when providing personalized investment advice about securities to retail investors has been characterized by the SEC as an obligation to deal fairly with customers and to observe high standards of commercial honor and just and equitable principles of trade. Contrary to public perception, this standard of conduct does not mean that the broker-dealer is a fiduciary whose duty is to serve the best interests of its customers, including an obligation not to subordinate customers' interests to its own. While investment advisers regulated under the Investment Advisers Act of 1940 ("Advisers Act") do have such a fiduciary duty to their customers, broker-dealers generally do not.[2] The broker-dealer's standard of conduct is markedly different from the fiduciary duty obligation of an investment adviser who is obligated to act in its customers' best interests without regard to its own financial or other interest when providing investment advice. Specifically, the Supreme Court has construed §§ 206(1) and (2) of the Advisers Act to mean that investment advisers have a fiduciary obligation to their customers. The standard of conduct required of an adviser as a fiduciary, which is applied to the entire adviser/customer relationship, is:

> the affirmative duty of utmost good faith, and full and fair disclosure of all material facts, as well as an affirmative obligation to "employ reasonable care to avoid misleading" their customers and prospective customers ...

---

1. *Shearson/American Express v. McMahon*, 482 US 220 (1987), discussed infra.

2. Section 202(c)(11) of the Advisers Act excludes broker-dealers: (1) whose performance of their investment advisory services is "solely incidental" to the conduct of their business as a broker-dealer; and (2) who receive no "special compensation" for their advisory services.

The adviser's fiduciary duty also includes the duty of loyalty and the duty of care. The duty of loyalty requires the adviser to place the customer's interests before its own. The duty of care requires the adviser to make a reasonable investigation to determine that it is not basing its recommendation on materially inaccurate or incomplete information.

Essentially, while applicable statutes and regulations uniformly impose a fiduciary duty on advisers, this is not the case for broker-dealers. In recognition of this distinction, the SEC was directed under Section 913 of Title IX of the Dodd-Frank Wall Street Reform and Consumer Protection Act ("Dodd-Frank Act") to conduct a study evaluating the standards of care of broker-dealers and advisers for providing personalized investment advice and recommendations about securities to retail customers.[3] The SEC's *Study of Investment Advisers and Broker-Dealers* (Jan. 2011) ("SEC Study") found that:

> [B]roker-dealers may have a fiduciary duty under certain circumstances. This duty may arise under state common law, which varies by state. Generally, broker-dealers that exercise discretion or control over customer assets, or have a relationship of trust and confidence with their customers, owe customers a fiduciary duty similar to that of investment advisers. Broker-dealers are also subject to a variety of requirements under the federal securities laws and SRO rules that enhance their business conduct obligations....

> *Business Conduct Obligations*

> Broker-dealers are subject to a comprehensive set of statutory, Commission and SRO requirements that are designed to promote business conduct that, among other things, protects investors from abusive practices, including practices that are not necessarily fraudulent. These business conduct obligations cannot be waived or contracted away by customers.

> *Duty of Fair Dealing*

> Broker-dealers are required to deal fairly with their customers. This duty is derived from the antifraud provisions of the federal securities laws. Under the so-called "shingle" theory, by virtue of engaging in the brokerage profession (e.g., hanging out the broker-dealer's business sign, or "shingle"), a broker-dealer makes an implicit representation to those persons with whom it transacts business that it will deal fairly with them, consistent with the standards of the profession. This essential representation implies certain duties and proscribes certain conduct, which has been articulated by the Commission and courts over time through interpretive statements and enforcement actions. Actions taken by the broker-dealer that are not fair to the

---

3. *Retail customer* is defined in Section 913(g) of the Dodd-Frank Act as "a natural person, or the legal representative of a natural person, who — (A) receives personalized investment advice about securities from a broker, dealer, or investment adviser, and (B) uses such advice primarily for personal, family or household purposes."

customer must be disclosed in order to make this implied representation of fairness not misleading.

Broker-dealers are also required under SRO rules to deal fairly with customers and to "observe high standards of commercial honor and just and equitable principles of trade." Among other things, this obligation includes having a reasonable basis for recommendations in light of a customer's financial situation to the extent known to the broker (suitability), engaging in fair and balanced communications with the public, providing timely and adequate confirmation of transactions, providing account statements, disclosing conflicts of interest, receiving fair compensation both in agency and principal transactions, and giving customers the opportunity for redress of disputes through arbitration.... SEC Study, at 51–52.

The SEC Study then recommended the following uniform fiduciary standard for both broker-dealers and advisers:

[T]he standard of conduct for all brokers, dealers, and investment advisers, when providing personalized investment advice about securities to retail customers (and such other customers as the Commission may by rule provide), shall be to act in the best interest of the customer without regard to the financial or other interest of the broker, dealer, or investment adviser providing the advice. SEC Study, at 109.[4]

The issue of whether a broker-dealer's standard of conduct in the broker-dealer/customer relationship includes a fiduciary duty that generally arises in the context of providing personalized investment advice about securities to retail customers. In many cases, it turns on whether the broker-dealer exercises discretionary authority over a customer's account. Generally, courts have concluded that the broker-dealer has a fiduciary duty if the customer account is discretionary, but not if the customer account is non-discretionary. The following case illustrates the prevailing view on whether the broker-dealer has a fiduciary duty to her customer when exercising discretionary authority over the customer's account.

Leib v. Merrill Lynch, Pierce, Fenner & Smith, Inc.

461 F. Supp. 951 (E.D. Mich. 1978)

I. INTRODUCTION

In August 1975 Sheldon Leib (Leib, also hereinafter designated as plaintiff) with his brother Joel Leib, as trustee, brought suit against Merrill Lynch, Pierce, Fenner & Smith, Inc. (Merrill Lynch) and John Kulhavi (Kulhavi), a stockbroker employed by Merrill Lynch, alleging as his first claim that these defendants "churned" his securities account. Plaintiff also submitted a second claim that Kulhavi had breached

---

4. The Study expressly states that "The Staff interprets the uniform fiduciary standard to include at a minimum, the duties of loyalty and care as interpreted and developed under Sections 206(1) and 206(2) of the Advisers Act." SEC study at 110–111.

his fiduciary duty by allowing Leib to pursue a course of heavy trading which could not possibly have resulted in a profit. Tied to this claim is plaintiff's contention that Kulhavi, as the broker in charge of the account, should have thoroughly explained to Leib the consequences of his pattern of trading, particularly with respect to the amount of commissions which would be generated as compared to the amount of profits which could be realized.

II. THEORIES OF THE PARTIES AND THE APPLICABLE LAW

Churning occurs "when a broker, exercising control over the volume and frequency of trading, abuses his customer's confidence for personal gain by initiating transactions that are excessive in view of the character of the account." *Carras v. Burns*, 516 F.2d 251, 258 (4th Cir. 1975). It is a deceptive device actionable under Section 10(b) of the Securities Exchange Act and Rule 10b-5 of the Securities and Exchange Commission. In order to evaluate plaintiff's second claim it is necessary to examine generally the duties owed by a stockbroker to his customer. Plaintiff argues that a broker has a fiduciary duty to his customer similar to that owed by an attorney to his client. Defendants contend that a stockbroker has a limited duty to serve his customer's financial interest within the framework of a single transaction only. Neither position is entirely accurate.

Defendants' limited definition of a broker's duty to his customer is correct so long as the customer has a non-discretionary account with his broker, i. e., an account in which the customer rather than the broker determines which purchases and sales to make. In a non-discretionary account each transaction is viewed singly. In such cases the broker is bound to act in the customer's interest when transacting business for the account; however, all duties to the customer cease when the transaction is closed. Duties associated with a non-discretionary account include: (1) the duty to recommend a stock only after studying it sufficiently to become informed as to its nature, price and financial prognosis; (2) the duty to carry out the customer's orders promptly in a manner best suited to serve the customer's interests; (3) the duty to inform the customer of the risks involved in purchasing or selling a particular security; (4) the duty to refrain from self-dealing or refusing to disclose any personal interest the broker may have in a particular recommended security; (5) the duty not to misrepresent any fact material to the transaction; and (6) the duty to transact business only after receiving prior authorization from the customer.

Of course the precise manner in which a broker performs these duties will depend to some degree upon the intelligence and personality of his customer. For example, where the customer is uneducated or generally unsophisticated with regard to financial matters, the broker will have to define the potential risks of a particular transaction carefully and cautiously. Conversely, where a customer fully understands the dynamics of the stock market or is personally familiar with a security, the broker's explanation of such risks may be merely perfunctory. In either case, however, the broker's responsibility to his customer ceases when the transaction is complete. A broker has no continuing duty to keep abreast of financial information which may affect his customer's portfolio or to inform his customer of developments which could influence his investments. Although a good broker may choose to perform these services for his customers, he is under no legal obligation to do so.

Remarkably absent from the above list is the duty, on the part of the broker, to engage in a particular course of trading. So long as a broker performs the transactional duties outlined above, he and his customer may embark upon a course of heavy trading in speculative stocks or in-out trading as well as upon a course of conservative investment in blue chip securities.

Unlike the broker who handles a non-discretionary account, the broker handling a discretionary account becomes the fiduciary of his customer in a broad sense. Such a broker, while not needing prior authorization for each transaction, must (1) manage the account in a manner directly comporting with the needs and objectives of the customer as stated in the authorization papers or as apparent from the customer's investment and trading history; (2) keep informed regarding the changes in the market which affect his customer's interest and act responsively to protect those interests; (3) keep his customer informed as to each completed transaction; and (4) explain forthrightly the practical impact and potential risks of the course of dealing in which the broker is engaged. *Stevens v. Abbott, Proctor and Paine*, 288 F. Supp. 836 (E.D.Va.1968).

Although no particular type of trading is required of brokers handling discretionary accounts, most concentrate on conservative investments with few trades usually in blue chip growth stocks. Where a broker engages in more active trading, particularly where such trading deviates from the customer's stated investment goals or is more risky than the average customer would prefer, he has an affirmative duty to explain the possible consequences of his actions to his customer. This explanation should include a discussion of the effect of active trading upon broker commissions and customer profits:

> The defendant, Winston's relationship with his uninformed customer was one of special trust and confidence, and the Court finds that he was because of this position, under a duty to frankly and forthrightly explain to plaintiff the nature of the commissions, concessions, losses and profits which were being generated in her account.

Stevens v. Abbott, Proctor and Paine, supra, at 846. As the court further stated in *Stevens*, the broker who acts in this capacity owes a special duty to his customer:

> In view of the Court's finding, it is apparent that a fiduciary relationship in law existed between the plaintiff and Winston which placed upon him the duty of acting in the highest good faith toward the plaintiff. *Stevens, supra* at 847.

Between the purely non-discretionary account and the purely discretionary account there is a hybrid-type account which plaintiff claims existed in this case. Such an account is one in which the broker has usurped actual control over a technically non-discretionary account. In such cases the courts have held that the broker owes his customer the same fiduciary duties as he would have had the account been discretionary from the moment of its creation.

In *Hecht v. Harris*, 430 F.2d 1202 (9th Cir. 1970), the plaintiff, a 77 year old widow, opened a non-discretionary account with a major brokerage firm. Consistent with the practice in such accounts plaintiff received confirmation slips of each transaction and monthly statements on the status of her account. In addition, she spoke personally with the defendant broker several times a week. Nonetheless, the court held that the broker was liable to plaintiff for churning her account on the ground that he had traded excessively without informing plaintiff of the potential hazards involved in such a course of trading. Since the plaintiff was informed, for the most part, of the individual transactions in her account, the court's holding assumed that the defendant owed plaintiff the additional fiduciary duty to explain the risks of pursuing a particular course of trading. That assumption derived from the court's finding that the broker had taken full control over the plaintiff's account and thus owed her those fiduciary duties normally associated with discretionary accounts.

In determining whether a broker has assumed control of a non-discretionary account the courts weigh several factors. First, the courts examine the age, education, intelligence and investment experience of the customer. Where the customer is particularly young, the courts are likely to find that the broker assumed control over the account. Second, if the broker is socially or personally involved with the customer, the courts are likely to conclude that the customer relinquished control because of the relationship of trust and confidence. Conversely, where the relationship between the broker and the customer is an arms-length business relationship, the courts are inclined to find that the customer retained control over the account. Third, if many of the transactions occurred without the customer's prior approval, the courts will often interpret this as a serious usurpation of control by the broker. Fourth, if the customer and the broker speak frequently with each other regarding the status of the account or the prudence of a particular transaction, the courts will usually find that the customer, by maintaining such active interest in the account, thereby maintained control over it.

III. FINDINGS OF FACT

Leib is now 34 years old. He attended college at Detroit Institute of Technology where he majored in applied science. After graduation from the Institute in 1964 Leib attended Walsh College. He received his accounting certificate from Walsh College in 1969. During his college career he took courses in economics and finance. He stated that the courses did include some limited instruction in securities and investment theory. Since 1969 Leib has held approximately eight different jobs, each involving accounting and bookkeeping and some additionally involving management and personnel supervision. He is now employed as an accountant and tax consultant with the firm of Samuel Tolchim.

Leib began trading in securities in 1966 when, at the recommendation of his uncle, he purchased 1200 shares of Frank's Nursery stock. That same year he purchased stock in at least five other small companies through the brokerage firm of Manley, Bennett, McDonald & Co. According to Leib, he simply informed the broker at Manley, Bennett, McDonald & Co. which stocks to purchase or sell and the broker executed his orders.

In the latter part of 1971 Leib was introduced to the defendant Kulhavi. Joel Leib, Sheldon's brother, an osteopathic surgeon, knew the Kulhavi family professionally and suggested to Leib that he should seek investment advice from Kulhavi. On December 8, 1971 Leib met with Kulhavi to discuss Leib's financial affairs, particularly as they related to a securities account. The parties discussed the advantages and disadvantages of trading on margin and, that same day, Leib opened a margin account with Merrill Lynch, depositing $ 30,000 which he had received as an inheritance. He stated in the authorization papers that his investment objectives were "growth" and "speculative."

Beginning almost immediately Leib, with the assistance of Kulhavi, embarked on a course of very active trading. Typically Kulhavi would suggest securities for purchase from the lists produced by the Merrill Lynch research department. The men would discuss the price of the suggested stock, the nature of the corporation involved, the type of product or service produced by the corporation and the prognosis of the stock in terms of long or short term profitability. Leib stated that Kulhavi answered all questions satisfactorily and never purchased or sold any stock without prior authorization.

Merrill Lynch sent Leib confirmation slips and monthly statements on the status of his account. Leib read these slips and statements and, by his own admission, understood their contents. He stated that if he did have a question regarding the information in these papers he asked Kulhavi, who provided an explanation for him.

Although Kulhavi and Leib disagree as to which of them initiated most of the phone calls, they do agree that they conferred with each other over the phone usually four or five times a day and occasionally six or seven times a day. Leib personally visited the Merrill Lynch office upon occasion where he spoke to Kulhavi regarding investments, read The Wall Street Journal or studied the ticker-tape. From December 1971 to approximately June 1972 the Leib account realized modest profits.

In May 1972 Leib accepted a position with the National Bank of Detroit. Since his duties included some work with securities he had to consider the bank's policy of disallowing any employee dealing with securities to have his own margin account in stocks. In June 1972 Leib transferred his account with Merrill Lynch to the name of his brother Joel, as trustee. All parties agreed that Leib would remain in full control of the account in the same manner as before the transfer. Joel Leib executed a power of attorney in his brother Sheldon for that purpose.

Trading in the account continued as it had before the transfer. However, at about this time the account began losing money. Additional sales had to be made to meet the more and more frequent margin calls since Leib steadfastly refused to invest more capital in the account to meet these calls. The relationship between Leib and Kulhavi deteriorated, Kulhavi complaining that Leib refused to take his advice and Leib complaining that Kulhavi's advice was unsound. Eventually the equity in the Leib account dwindled to virtually nothing. In April 1973 Leib directed Kulhavi to "sell him out." Within a few days the account was closed.

From December 1971 to April 1973 the life of his margin account Leib purchased $298,507.32 in securities; he paid $8,318.35 in broker commissions and $ 1,807.35

in interest charges. The account turned over 9.95 times. Turnover is defined as the ratio of total cost of the purchases made for the account during a given period of time to the amount invested.

According to plaintiff, this pattern of trading is, by definition, not profitable for the customer and benefits only the broker. Plaintiff claims that Kulhavi breached his fiduciary duty and churned the account by allowing Leib to pursue this unprofitable pattern of trading. Specifically, it is contended that Kulhavi breached his fiduciary duty (1) by not informing Leib that the course of trading was unprofitable and (2) by excessively trading in the account for the sole purpose of generating commissions for himself. For the reasons discussed ... above, if plaintiff is to prevail in his claim under any theory he must first prove that Kulhavi controlled the account.

IV. CONCLUSIONS OF LAW

The parties have stipulated that the Leib account was established as a non-discretionary account. I note from the papers that plaintiff makes no claim that Kulhavi violated any of the limited, transactional duties owed to him as a holder of a non-discretionary account. Furthermore, after considering all the evidence presented at trial I must conclude that plaintiff has not sustained his burden of proving that Kulhavi in fact usurped control of the account.

Leib is a man with professional experience in managing the financial affairs of others. He understood the dynamics of the stock market at the time he opened the account with Merrill Lynch and he appreciated the risks of trading on margin. From his college courses and from practical experience, he knew how to handle a securities account. When he dealt with the broker at Manley, Bennett, McDonald & Co., Leib retained full control over the account, relying upon the advice of friends or relatives in making purchases and sales. The relationship between Kulhavi and Leib was strictly professional. The frequent conversations between the two allowed Leib to keep tabs on the account on a daily basis often on an hourly basis. No transactions occurred without Leib's personal approval after he had discussed the matter thoroughly with Kulhavi. Leib also kept himself informed on each transaction after it had occurred. Upon receiving confirmation slips and monthly statements Leib read them and either understood their contents or asked his broker for an explanation.

The fact that virtually all of the stocks purchased by Leib were recommended by Kulhavi does not demonstrate that Kulhavi controlled the account. A customer normally depends upon his broker to supply information, advice and recommendations. In accepting these recommendations Leib acted independently and voluntarily. In every case the final decision to buy, sell, or hold was his alone.

Under the circumstances Kulhavi, as broker, owed Leib only those limited, transactional duties discussed in Part II. He was not obligated to inform Leib that his pattern of trading heavily, taking profits, and holding losses was almost too risky to be profitable. Nor was he obligated to point out the disparate amount paid in commissions as compared with the amount realized in profits. In addition Kulhavi had no duty to restrain Leib from trading heavily. Since Leib controlled the account, the pattern of trading, even if excessive, was Leib's sole responsibility. That this pattern generated substantial commissions for his broker is irrelevant under the circumstances of this case.

This analysis not only disposes of plaintiff's claim of breach of fiduciary duty, it also disposes of the traditional claim of churning. The law is clear that if a customer controls his own securities account he cannot prevail against his broker under a theory of churning, even where he can prove that the account suffered an excessive number of trades.

———

As illustrated in *Leib*, breach of fiduciary duty claims are rarely brought in isolation. As you read about broker-dealer fraud in the following sections, evaluate whether a claim for breach of fiduciary duty could also be established.

B. Churning

 Churning involves excessive trading in a customer's account in conflict with the customer's investment objectives. Churning is a scheme or artifice to defraud or deceptive device and therefore violates § 10(b) and Rule 10b-5. The elements of a churning claim under § 10(b) and Rule 10b-5 are: (1) trading that is excessive in light of the customer's investment objectives; (2) control over the account by the broker; and (3) scienter. The remaining elements for a § 10(b) and Rule 10b-5 cause of action — reliance and loss causation — are subsumed under elements (1) and (2). As you read the following case, consider the importance of determining the customer's investment objectives in successfully bringing a churning claim.

Mihara v. Dean Witter
619 F.2d 814 (9th Cir. 1980)

Opinion by: Campbell

* * *

On January 6, 1971, plaintiff Mihara opened a joint securities account with the Santa Monica office of Dean Witter. At that time Mihara was employed by the McDonnell-Douglas Corporation as a supervisory engineer. He was 38 years old and possessed a Bachelor of Science and Master's Degree in Engineering. He and his wife were the parents of two daughters. Mihara's assets at the time consisted of approximately $30,000 in savings, an employee's savings account at McDonnell-Douglas of approximately $16,000, an equity in his home for approximately fifteen to seventeen thousand dollars. He also held shares of McDonnell-Douglas stock obtained through an employee payroll deduction plan.

Prior to opening his account with Dean Witter, Mihara had invested in securities for approximately ten years. He had dealt with several other firms during that period, but apparently felt that his account had not received adequate attention, and was looking for a new investment firm. Mihara opened his account with Dean Witter in

January of 1971 by telephoning Stuart Cypherd, the office manager for Dean Witter's Santa Monica office, and asking to be assigned an account executive. Cypherd, in turn, instructed defendant Gracis to phone Mihara to set up an appointment.

The evidence as to the content of the initial meeting between Mihara and Gracis is conflicting. Mihara testified that as an engineer he lacked a finance and economics background and was looking for someone with expertise on which he could rely. He also stated that he was concerned about possible cutbacks at McDonnell-Douglas, noting that layoffs were common in that industry. He indicated that he was concerned about the education of his two daughters, and their financial security.

Gracis' testimony with regard to their initial meeting, and specifically relating to Mihara's investment objectives, differs substantially. Gracis testified that Mihara was not concerned about a possible layoff, that he was primarily interested in growth, and that he was knowledgeable about margin accounts and broker call rates.

Mihara invested $ 30,000 with Dean Witter. This money was to be invested according to Gracis' recommendations but subject to Mihara's approval.

The history of Mihara's investment account with Dean Witter & Company reflects speculative investments, numerous purchases and sales, and substantial reliance on the recommendations of Gracis. The initial recommendations of Gracis were that Mihara purchase shares of companies engaged in the double-knit fabric industry.... From 1971 to 1973, Mihara's account lost considerable sums of money. Since many of the purchases were on margin, Mihara would often have to come up with additional funds as the equity in his account declined. The final trading losses in the account totaled $46,464. This loss occurred during the period of January 1971 to May 1973.

Mihara first began to complain of the handling of his account when it showed a loss in April 1971. At that time he complained to Gracis because his account was losing money, then about $ 3,000. Throughout 1971, as Mihara's account lost money, he continued to complain to Gracis. In October of 1971, Mihara went to Mr. Cypherd, the office manager for the Santa Monica office of Dean Witter. Mihara complained to Cypherd about the handling of the account by Gracis. He did not, however, close out the account. As the value of Mihara's securities account continued to dwindle, he visited Cypherd on several occasions to complain further about Gracis. While Cypherd told Mihara he was "on top" of the account, the performance and handling of the account did not improve.

At about the same time that Mihara first contacted him, Cypherd was also made aware of substantial trading in the account by means of a Dean Witter Monthly Account Activity Analysis. This analysis was initiated by the Dean Witter computer whenever an account showed 15 or more trades in one month or commissions of $1,000 or more. Because Mihara's account reflected 16 trades for the month of April 1971, Cypherd was alerted to the problem at that time. In May of 1971, the Dean Witter computer generated another monthly account activity analysis as the result of 21 trades during that month in Mihara's account. Mihara's account in March of

1971 reflected 33 transactions, however, the computer did not generate an account analysis.

In November 1973, Mihara went to the San Francisco office of Dean Witter and complained to Paul Dubow, the National Compliance Director for Dean Witter, Inc. At that point Mihara's account had suffered considerable losses. Apparently not satisfied with the results of that meeting, Mihara filed this suit in April 1974.

* * *

Plaintiff's expert, Mr. White, a former attorney with the Securities & Exchange Commission, testified at trial that the pattern of trading in the Mihara account reflected a pattern of churning. Plaintiff's Exhibit 20, Chart G, introduced at trial, indicated the following holding periods for Mihara's securities. In 1971, 50% of the securities were held for 15 days or less, 61% for 30 days or less, and approximately 76% were held for 60 days or less. Through June of 1973, 81.6% of the securities in the Mihara account were held for a period of 180 days or less. White also relied on the "turnover rate" in Mihara's account in reaching his conclusion. The turnover rate for a given period is arrived at by dividing the total dollar amount of stock purchases for a given period by the average monthly capital investment in the account. Plaintiff's Exhibit No. 20, Chart C, indicates that between January 1971 and July 1973, Mihara's average monthly investment of $36,653 was turned over approximately 14 times. On an annualized basis, Mihara's average capital monthly investment in 1971 of approximately $40,000 was turned over 9.3 times. His average capital investment in 1972 was $39,800 and that was turned over approximately 3.36 times. His average monthly capital investment for the first half of 1973 was $23,588 and that was turned over approximately .288 times. White testified that a substantial turnover in the early stages of the account followed by a significant decline in the turnover rate was typical of a churned account.

White also testified that the holding periods for securities in Mihara's account reflected a pattern of churning. He noted that churned accounts usually reflect significant turnover in the early stages, that is, a very short holding period for the securities purchased, followed by longer holding periods in the later stages of the account. Thus, the typical churned account is churned in the early stages of the account generating large commissions at the outset, followed by less trading and longer holding periods in the latter stages of the account, after significant commissions have been generated. Mihara's account reflects precisely that pattern. The cumulative total of commissions earned by Gracis was $12,672, the majority of which came in the early stages of the account.

* * *

A stock broker at an investment firm Mihara had dealt with in the past testified that Mihara had been interested in growth stocks, had discussed margin accounts, though never initiated one, and had a "good knowledge" of the stock market.

* * *

The jury was then charged, returned for its deliberations, and returned a verdict for the plaintiff.

Appellants present numerous issues on appeal. The main points raised on appeal can be summarized as follows: Whether plaintiff established a prima facie case of a violation of Rule 10b-5 ... We affirm the judgment below in all respects.

When a securities broker engages in excessive trading in disregard of his customer's investment objectives for the purpose of generating commission business, the customer may hold the broker liable for churning in violation of Rule 10b-5. In order to establish a claim of churning, a plaintiff must show (1) that the trading in his account was excessive in light of his investment objectives; (2) that the broker in question exercised control over the trading in the account; and (3) that the broker acted with the intent to defraud or with the willful and reckless disregard for the interests of his client.

churning

Whether trading is excessive is a question which must be examined in light of the investment objectives of the customer. While there is no clear line of demarcation, courts and commentators have suggested that an annual turnover rate of six reflects excessive trading. [T]his Court affirmed a finding of churning where an account had been turned over 8 to 11.5 times during a six-year ten-month period. In that case, 45% of the securities were held for less than six months, 67% were held for less than nine months, and 82% were held for less than a year. Under this Court's holding in *Hecht*, the evidence in the present case clearly supports a finding of excessive trading.

With regard to the second prerequisite, we believe that Gracis exercised sufficient control over Mihara's account in the present case to support a finding of churning. The account need not be a discretionary account whereby the broker executes each trade without the consent of the client.... [T]he requisite degree of control is met when the client routinely follows the recommendations of the broker. The present case ... reflects a pattern of de facto control by the broker.

The third requisite element of a 10b-5 violation scienter has also been established. The manner in which Mihara's account was handled reflects, at best, a reckless disregard for the client's investment concerns, and, at worst, an outright scheme to defraud plaintiff. Perhaps in recognition of this, appellants have constructed a curious argument as to the scienter element. They suggest that plaintiff must establish an intent to defraud as to each trade executed by the broker. This assertion is entirely without merit. The churning of a client's account is, in itself, a scheme or artifice to defraud within the meaning of Rule 10b-5. With regard to the definition of scienter, this circuit has held that reckless conduct constitutes scienter within the meaning of *Ernst & Ernst v. Hochfelder*, 425 U.S. 185, 96 S. Ct. 1375, 47 L. Ed. 2d 668 (1976). The evidence in the present case reflects, at the very minimum, a reckless disregard for the client's stated interests.

––––––

1. *Excessive Trading*

Excessive trading in a customer's account is generally evaluated quantitatively and qualitatively. As noted in *Mihara,* qualitative factors include the determination of the customer's investment objectives, investment strategy, and aversion to risk. Quantitative factors include the annualized turnover ratio, the annualized cost-to-equity ratio (or breakeven), frequent in-and-out purchases and sales of securities that appear to conflict with the customer's investment objective. The annualized turnover ratio measures how often, on average, the securities in a customer's portfolio are traded in a year. Although there are several methods to calculate the annualized turnover ratio, the simplest method is to divide total security purchases by the average month-end equity balance, and then to annualize the turnover ratio by dividing it by the number of months in which the fraudulent conduct occurred. Annualized turnover rates of six percent or more are indicative of excessive trading. See Figure 11.1 below.

Figure 11.1. Annualized Turnover Ratio (ATR)

> Annualized Turnover Ratio = (Purchases/Average Equity) / (Number of Months Traded/12)
>
> Total purchases are determined from the customer's account statements. Most account statements show an entry that lists the total amount of money used during the month to buy securities. If the customer's account statements do not show a total, this information can be obtained from the activity section of the account statement by adding together the cost of each security position in the customer's account for the month. The average equity is computed by taking the month ending value of the customer's account on each monthly account statement, adding them together, and dividing by the number of months the questionable trading has occurred.

The annualized cost-to-equity ratio or breakeven percentage measures the rate of return an account must earn on an annual basis just to cover transaction costs. Again, although there are several methods of calculating the annualized cost-to-equity ratio, generally it is calculated by dividing the total costs of trading activity by the average equity of the account and annualized by dividing the result by the number of months in which the fraudulent conduct occurred. See Figure 11.2. Thus, the account will show a profit only if account returns exceed the annualized cost-to-equity ratio. An annualized cost-to-equity ratio in excess of 20 percent is indicative of excessive trading.

Figure 11.2. Annualized Cost-to-Equity Ratio

> (Commissions, margin interest, fees/Average Equity) / (Number of Months/12)
>
> The numerator should include the total costs of trading activity. The average equity is computed by taking the month ending value of the customer's account on each monthly account statement, adding them together, and dividing by the number of months the questionable trading has occurred.

Excessive trading is also prohibited by FINRA Rule 2111.05(c).[5] FINRA also uses both qualitative and quantitative factors to prove excessive trading. However, it dis-

---

5. FINRA Rule 2111 is a suitability rule. However, FINRA now describes excessive trading as quantitative suitability. Suitability and churning claims may overlap because in trading excessively

tinguishes excessive trading from churning. As you read the decision by FINRA's National Adjudicatory Council below, consider how and why FINRA distinguishes excessive trading from churning.

In the Matter of Department of Enforcement v. Alan Jay Davidofsky

Before the National Adjudicatory Council, FINRA

Complaint No. 2008015934801 (Apr. 26, 2013)

Decision

Alan Jay Davidofsky appeals a Hearing Panel decision issued on March 30, 2012. The Hearing Panel found that Davidofsky engaged in unauthorized trading, excessive trading, and churning in a customer's individual retirement account. The Hearing Panel barred Davidofsky for the unauthorized trading, imposed a separate bar for the excessive trading and churning, and ordered Davidofsky to pay a fine of $11,741.78 as disgorgement of the financial benefit from his misconduct. After an independent review of the record, we affirm the Hearing Panel's findings and sanctions.

I. Factual Background

A. Davidofsky

During the period relevant to the conduct in this case, December 2007 through October 2008, Davidofsky was associated with Oppenheimer & Co., Inc.

B. Davidofsky Joins Oppenheimer and Experiences Financial Difficulties

In November 2004, Davidofsky joined Oppenheimer as a general securities representative. When he joined the firm, he brought a book of business with him. In return, Oppenheimer gave Davidofsky an upfront signing bonus structured as a five-year forgivable loan. Under the terms of the loan agreement, Oppenheimer forgave a portion of the loan each month that he remained with the firm. If Davidofsky left Oppenheimer for any reason before the end of the five-year term, the firm required him to repay the balance of the loan.

Davidofsky did relatively well during his first two years at Oppenheimer. By 2006, however, he had lost two of his largest accounts and began to experience financial difficulties. Davidofsky's commissions declined and his financial difficulties continued throughout 2007 and 2008. In April 2008, Davidofsky contemplated filing for bankruptcy. Davidofsky's filing of bankruptcy, however, was contingent upon Oppenheimer's approval of the plan to restructure his debt. The firm agreed to approve the bankruptcy plan and continue Davidofsky's employment, on the condition that he maintain certain levels of commissions, continue his compliance with Oppenheimer's loan agreement, and did not attempt to discharge Oppenheimer's loan as part of the bankruptcy proceedings. In September 2008, Davidofsky filed for bankruptcy. The bankruptcy court discharged Davidofsky's debt in February 2009.

C. Davidofsky Manages JL's Traditional Individual Retirement Account

---

the broker-dealer may execute trades that are not suited to the investors' investment objective and risk tolerance.

In the midst of handling these personal financial matters, Davidofsky gained a new account at Oppenheimer, JL's traditional individual retirement account. Davidofsky began managing JL's individual retirement account in March 2007, after her former Oppenheimer representative, Charles Shalmi, could no longer handle the account.

1. JL's Background and Investment Experience

JL lives in Massachusetts. She is a college graduate with a degree in mass communications. JL develops and produces multimedia training and marketing materials for corporations. In 2003, she also began providing educational consulting services to her sister's company.

JL described her investment experience as limited. She testified that she started investing in the 1970s, with a small account at DWS Scudder. JL explained that she invested in growth, income, and mutual funds, which she characterized as "self-managed" investments. She also stated that she traded stocks infrequently, and that she had purchased "two stocks in [her entire] life."

JL's account information form at Oppenheimer identified her as 57 years old, single, with no dependents, and 10 years of investment experience. The form noted that JL had been self-employed for 10 years and earned an annual income of $50,000. The form stated that JL's total net worth was approximately $300,000, and that her liquid net worth, "exclusive of home, auto, etc.," was $10,000.

2. Davidofsky Revises the Trading Strategy for JL's Account

Prior to the period at issue in this case, there was minimal activity in JL's individual retirement account. The account maintained an average monthly balance of $127,000 and held positions in four closed-end mutual funds, three open-end mutual funds, and two corporate bonds. JL's account contained only one position in an individual stock. JL owned 114 shares of Delta Airlines common stock.

After Davidofsky gained responsibility for JL's account, he reviewed the account activity and spoke to Shalmi about JL. Davidofsky's review led him to conclude that JL's conservative investment objectives did not match the holdings in her account, and that JL "was completely wrong [about] her stated [investment] objectives."[6] Davidofsky communicated his findings to JL during their first conversation.

In line with these findings, Davidofsky began implementing a revised trading strategy for JL's individual retirement account. Under this revised strategy, Davidofsky tried to "take advantage of the turns in the market." Specifically, he looked for "brand name" companies that were currently trading at 25 to 40 percent below their highest per-share price. Davidofsky reasoned, "if [these stocks are] all being recommended at, say, $50.00 a share by all the analysts on Wall Street and at $30.00 a share the analysts are still recommending them, that's a bargain."

---

6. [6] When Davidofsky began managing JL's individual retirement account, JL's account information form at Oppenheimer reflected that JL's investment objectives were "current income (conservative)" and "capital appreciation (conservative)." At the hearing, JL testified that conservative current income and capital appreciation were her investment objectives throughout the time she had the individual retirement account at Oppenheimer.

Davidofsky also turned to preferred stocks to increase short-term returns. He noted that many preferred stocks, particularly those from financial and mortgage companies, presented opportunities for gains because they "were trading at extraordinary yields and discounts to their coupon." Davidofsky explained that if he "could buy a preferred stock at $20.00, on or around the time they are going to declare a dividend, which is every three months, [he had] the chance of collecting a dividend and holding onto the stock and selling it for capital appreciation." Davidofsky characterized this as a "win-win scenario."

Davidofsky testified that he told JL about his revised trading strategy, and that she said that "it was a little bit riskier than what she was used to, but she was not against the idea." JL, however, did not authorize Davidofsky to employ the revised, riskier strategy in her individual retirement account. Despite this fact, Davidofsky began implementing the revised trading strategy in JL's account in December 2007.

3. Davidofsky Implements the Revised Trading Strategy and Drastically Increases the Frequency of Trading in JL's Account

With the implementation of the revised trading strategy in December 2007, the frequency and tenor of Davidofsky's trading in JL's account also increased drastically. Between December 2007 and October 2008, Davidofsky liquidated JL's then-current holdings and effected 104 transactions in 38 different securities. He effected these trades on 61 different days during the relevant period and often made multiple trades in a single day. Davidofsky's purchases totaled approximately $760,000, and his total transactions amounted to more than $1.4 million.

Davidofsky's activity in JL's account also evidenced a strategy of "in-and-out trading."[7] For example, Davidofsky purchased and sold 4,350 shares of Evergreen Solar, Inc. in eight transactions between January and July 2008. Davidofsky also purchased and sold 3,050 shares of Agfeed Industries, Inc. in 10 transactions between April and September 2008. In several instances, Davidofsky purchased and sold securities in as few as two days and often held securities for less than a few weeks.[8]

4. JL's Investment Objectives Are Changed

As the frequency and tenor of the trading activity in JL's account continued to intensify, JL's account information form was amended to change her investment objectives. In June 2008, a sales assistant at Oppenheimer updated JL's account information form. The sales assistant changed JL's investment objectives to "current income (aggressive)" and "capital appreciation (aggressive)." The sales assistant also updated the form to acknowledge that JL had approved the use of "short-term trading" in her account. JL testified that she did not initiate or approve any of these changes....

---

7. [10] "In-and-out trading" is the sale of all or part of the securities in an account and reinvestment of the sales proceeds in other securities, followed by the sale of the newly acquired securities.

8. [11] For example, Davidofsky purchased 1,100 shares of Canadian Solar, Inc.; 3,500 shares of Pacific Ethanol, Inc.; and 750 shares of Lehman Brothers Holdings, Inc. on December 5, 2007; January 28, 2008; and August 13, 2008, respectively. Davidofsky sold the purchased shares of each company two days later.

Davidofsky was unable to recall what specifically prompted the changes to JL's account information form, but he explained how such changes usually occurred.

Saia (Davidofsky's Branch Manager] testified that JL's individual retirement account appeared in an account review exception report in June 2008.... Although it is unclear what caused JL's account to generate the exception report, Saia called JL when she received the exception report in June 2008. Saia reached JL, but JL said that she did not have time to talk and would return Saia's call at a later date. JL did not return Saia's call in June or July, and Saia tried to reach JL again in August 2008. This time, Saia left a voice message for JL. JL did not return Saia's call and did not approve the changes to her investment objectives.

JL reviewed her account statements after a steep market decline in September 2008.... JL discovered the activity in her account in October 2008, as she reviewed statements from the prior months. JL immediately emailed Davidofsky after she reviewed the statements and told him that she would call him later that day to discuss her findings. She also filed a complaint with Oppenheimer, which initiated an internal investigation and review of JL's account.

During the 10-month period that Davidofsky implemented his revised trading strategy, JL's individual retirement account lost approximately 90 percent of its value, which equated to an account balance decline of approximately $108,000. The annualized turnover ratio was 10.89, and the annualized cost-to-equity ratio was 44.86 percent. JL paid over $31,000 in commissions to Oppenheimer, of which $11,741.78 went directly to Davidofsky.[9]

* * *

Enforcement filed a three-cause complaint in February 2011. The first cause of action alleged that Davidofsky engaged in unauthorized trading, in violation of NASD Rule 2110 and NASD Interpretative Material ("IM") 2310-2. The second cause of action alleged that Davidofsky excessively traded JL's account, in violation of NASD Rules 2110, 2120, 2310, and IM-2310-2. The third cause of action alleged that Davidofsky churned JL's account, in violation of Section 10(b) of the Securities Exchange Act of 1934 ("Exchange Act"), Exchange Act Rule 10b-5, and NASD Rules 2110 and 2120.[10]

* * *

III. Discussion

* * *

B. Davidofsky Excessively Traded and Churned JL's Account

The Hearing Panel found that Davidofsky violated NASD Rules 2110, 2310, and NASD IM-2310-2 because he excessively traded JL's individual retirement account. In related findings, the Hearing Panel also concluded that the volume of Davidofsky's

---

9. [18] This amount represented 18 percent of Davidofsky's total commissions for 2008.

10. [21] The conduct rules that apply in this case are those that existed at the time of the conduct at issue.

trading in JL's account constituted churning, in violation of Section 10(b) of the Exchange Act, Exchange Act Rule 10b-5, and NASD Rules 2110 and 2120. We affirm the Hearing Panel's findings.

NASD Rule 2310(a) provides that "[i]n recommending to a customer the purchase, sale, or exchange of any security, a member shall have reasonable grounds for believing that the recommendation is suitable for such customer upon the basis of the facts, if any, disclosed by such customer as to his other security holdings and as to his financial situation and needs." Among the obligations under such suitability rules is "quantitative suitability," which focuses on "whether the number of transactions within a given timeframe is suitable in light of the customer's financial circumstances and investment objectives."

excessive trading

*

To demonstrate excessive trading, or quantitative unsuitability, requires proof of two elements. The first element is "broker control over the account in question." The second element is "excessive trading activity inconsistent with the customer's financial circumstances and investment objectives." Excessive trading is closely related to, but distinct from, churning. Churning exists where excessive trading involves fraud. Thus, to prove that Davidofsky's excessive trading amounts to churning, a third element, scienter, must be show. As explained below, the record amply shows that Davidofsky controlled JL's account, there was excessive trading activity inconsistent with JL's financial circumstances and investment objectives, and that Davidofsky excessively traded the accounts with scienter, and consequently, churned JL's account.

* * *

2. Excessive Activity

[W]e next turn to whether there was excessive trading activity inconsistent with JL's financial circumstances and investment objectives. The "assessment of the level of trading ... does not rest on any magical per annum percentage, however calculated." Nevertheless, "factors such as turnover rate, cost-to-equity ratio, and use of 'in-and-out' trading in an account may provide a basis for a finding of excessive trading." The record in this case demonstrates that JL sought to invest with a conservative amount of risk.... The tempo and quantity of Davidofsky's trading in JL's account was entirely inconsistent with JL's financial circumstances and investment objectives. Prior to Davidofsky's management of JL's individual retirement account, the account had minimal activity. When Davidofsky took over management of JL's account, however, the volume of trading in the account changed dramatically. Over a period of 10 months, Davidofsky effected 104 transactions in 38 different securities. He effected these trades on 61 different days during the relevant period, often made multiple trades in a single day, and engaged in in-and-out trading of numerous stocks.

Davidofsky's trading yielded an annualized turnover ratio of 10.89,[11] and an annualized cost-to-equity ratio of 44.86 percent,[12] both of which are substantially above

---

11. [29] "Turnover rates between three and five have triggered liability for excessive trading, and it has been generally recognized that an annual turnover rate of greater than six evidences excessive trading.

12. [30] A cost-to-equity ratio in excess of 20 percent indicates excessive trading.

the levels that have supported findings of excessive trading in other cases. The record demonstrates that Davidofsky excessively traded JL's account and violated NASD Rules 2110, 2310, and NASD IM-2310-2.[13]

<hr />

2. Control

The second element of churning requires the broker-dealer to exercise control over the customer's account. This control can be direct or indirect. Direct control is easily established if the broker-dealer exercises discretionary authority over the customer's account. This means that the broker-dealer is permitted to execute trades in the customer's account without first obtaining the customer's approval. However, the broker-dealer's discretion is circumscribed by the customer's investment objectives. Despite the fact that the broker-dealer has discretionary authority over the customer's account, it is not permitted to trade in conflict with the customer's stated investment objectives. Exchange Act Rule 15c1-7 defines trades in conflict with the customer's investment objectives and personal and financial circumstances as fraud. It also expressly prohibits excessive trading in discretionary accounts. In addition, the Rule states that failure to document trades in a discretionary account is fraud. The record must include the name of the customer; the name, amount, and price of the security; and the date and time of execution.

FINRA's Manual contains two rules that facilitate compliance with Exchange Act Rule 15c1-7. These rules are NASD Rule 2510 and NYSE Rule 408, which set forth the obligations of the broker-dealer and its associated persons regarding the exercise of discretionary authority over a customer's account. Both rules require that the grant of discretionary authority be in writing and that such accounts be approved by an appropriate supervisor. Also, both rules expressly obligate the broker-dealer to detect and prevent unauthorized and excessive trading in discretionary accounts. In addition, NYSE Rule 408 obligates the broker-dealer to comply with the same requirements when accepting an order for a customer's account from someone other than the customer.

The broker-dealer may exercise de facto control over the customer's account, even in the absence of the grant of discretionary authority. De facto control is established when the customer routinely follows the broker-dealer's advice because the customer is unable to evaluate the broker-dealer's recommendations and to exercise independent judgment. This determination is fact-intensive. Courts, the SEC, and FINRA have recognized de facto control over the customer's account based on several factors. In *M & B Contracting Corp. v. Dale*, 601 F. Supp. 1106, 1111 (E.D. Mich. 1984), *aff'd* 795 F.2d 531 (6th Cir. 1986), the court identified several factors that should be considered in determining the existence of de facto control: (1) the identity, age, education, intelli-

<hr />

13. [31] The Hearing Panel noted that Davidofsky's excessive trading also violated NASD Rule 2120 [renumbered as FINRA Rule 2020]. [FINRA Rule 2020] requires a showing of scienter, similar to Exchange Act Rule 10b-5. We do not affirm a violation of Rule [2020] because scienter is not necessary to establish an excessive trading violation.

gence, and investment and business experience of the customer; (2) the relationship between the customer and the broker-dealer, that is, whether it is an arms-length one or a particularly close relationship; (3) knowledge of the market and the account; (4) the regularity of discussions between the broker-dealer and the customer; (5) Whether the customer actually authorized each trade; and (6) who made the recommendations for the trades. In *Dale,* the Court determined that de facto control did not exist because the customer "was a sophisticated businessman and a CPA, and well acquainted with financial matters ... the relationship between M & B and Dale was one of strictly business.... Nor was there usurpation of control by Dale, since he always had M & B's prior approval. Finally, there was regular consultation between the parties as to the trades. At no time was a trade made without consultation." In *In re Sandra K. Simpson,* Exchange Act Rel. No. 45923 (2002), the SEC found de facto control exists when the a broker-dealer "controlled the account either because the customer relied on [the broker-dealer], or because the customer was incapable of controlling the account." In *Simpson,* the SEC stated that control "was shown by the many unauthorized transactions and the customers' general lack of investment knowledge and sophistication, which left control of the account in the hands of [the broker-dealer]." In *Department of Enforcement v. Medeck,* Complaint No. E9B2003033701, 2009 FINRA Discip. LEXIS 7, at *34, the NAC found that de facto control was not established based on several factors. "Customer ... has college degrees in mathematical statistics and production and operations management.... four years prior to opening his account ... he had traded technology and Internet stocks on margin in his self-directed online brokerage account ... and stated that he understood the risks and rewards of his margin trading ... he day traded stocks priced less than $5...." The customer also "had $100,000–149,999 annual income and $1,000,000–$2,499,999 total net worth." Most important, the NAC found that Medeck had rejected past recommendations from his broker-dealer.

3. Scienter

Scienter is required to establish a churning violation. However, courts have held that scienter required by § 10(b) and Rule 10b-5 is implicit in the nature of the broker-dealer's conduct, i.e., the volume of trading conducted in the customer's account in disregard of the customer's investment objectives. Because of the excessive trading in the customer's account in conflict with the customer's investment objectives and for the benefit of the broker-dealer, this conduct, in and of itself, constitutes scienter under a recklessness standard. In *Mihara* (discussed above), the court found that "[t]he manner in which Mihara's account was handled [ATR in excess of 6 and short holding periods] reflects, at best, a reckless disregard for the client's investment concerns, and at worst, an outright scheme to defraud ..." at 821. Accordingly, proof of elements one and two of a churning claim generally establishes the element of scienter. In *Arceneaux v. Merill Lynch Pierce, Fenner & Smith,* 767 F.2d 1498 (11th Cir. 1985), the court held that the velocity of trading in the customer's account (ATR of 8 and 25% of the original starting capital ended up in the hands of the broker-dealer) made no sense, other than to generate commissions and therefore established the element of scienter. *Arceneaux,* at 1502. As previously noted, proof of scienter is not required for excessive trading cases initiated by FINRA.

4. Damages

The types of compensatory damages available for churning cases include restitution, out-of-pocket (recovery of portfolio loss) and recovery of lost profits. These types of compensatory damages are also available in suitability cases excluding restitution. Traditionally, the measure of damages for churning claims is restitution. The broker-dealer is required to return commissions, margin, interest, fees, and capital gains and transfer taxes, i.e., costs resulting from the churning of the customer's account. Restitution presumes that all the trades during the period that the customer's account was churned constitutes one violation because it is difficult to identify particular trades that were excessive without examining all trading activity during the period in which the customer's account was churned. This measure of damages, however, assumes that the customer's account was only adversely affected by the expenses resulting from churning of the account. In reality, it is likely that while churning the customer's account, the broker-dealer executed trades that were unsuitable for the customer and generated portfolio losses. Accordingly, merely awarding commissions and account expenses is insufficient. As the court observed in *Miley v. Oppenheimer & Co.,* 637 F.2d 318, 326–328 (5th Cir. 1981):

> Once the gravamen of the churning complaint is clearly identified, the argument that awarding both excess commissions and excess portfolio decline constitutes double recovery appears to be without merit. The willful misconduct at the core of a churning complaint is the broker's excessive trading of an account in an effort to amass commissions. While excessive commissions represent the sole source of gain to the broker from his misconduct, there are in fact two distinct harms which may be proximately caused by the broker's churning of an account. It is necessary to remedy both harms in order to fully compensate the victimized investor.
>
> First, and perhaps foremost, the investor is harmed by having had to pay the excessive commissions to the broker the "skimmed milk" of the churning violation. The broker's wrongful collection of commissions generated by the intentional, excessive trading of the account constitutes a compensable violation of both the federal securities laws and the broker's common law fiduciary duty, regardless of whether the investor's portfolio increased or decreased in value as a result of such trading. Second, the investor is harmed by the decline in the value of his portfolio the "spilt milk" of the churning violation as a result of the broker's having intentionally and deceptively concluded transactions, aimed at generating fees, which were unsuitable for the investor. The intentional and deceptive mismanagement of a client's account, resulting in a decline in the value of that portfolio, constitutes a compensable violation of both the federal securities laws and the broker's common law fiduciary duty, regardless of the amount of the commissions paid to the broker. In

sum, once a jury finds that the broker has churned an investor's account, it may also find that the investor would have paid less commissions and that his portfolio would have had a greater value had the broker not committed the churning violation. See Nichols, *The Broker's Duty to His Customer Under Federal Fiduciary and Suitability Standards*, 26 Buff. L. Rev. 435, 445 (1977) ("Where there is excessive trading in an account ("churning"), the customer can be damaged in many ways. He must pay the brokerage commissions on both purchases and sales, he may miss dividends, incur unnecessary capital gain or ordinary income taxes depending on the holding period, and, most difficult to measure, he may lose the benefits that a well-managed portfolio in long-term holdings might have brought him."); Brodsky, *Measuring Damages in Churning and Suitability Cases*, 6 Sec. Reg. Law J. 157, 159–160 (1978) ("Most often, the customer complains that the broker churned unsuitable securities. Then, both causes of action are appropriate and both damage theories (excess commissions and excess decline in portfolio value) should be considered.")

* * *

Although not briefed by defendant Oppenheimer, it appears that the real problem with compensating the victimized investor for the decline in the value of his portfolio (as well as for the excess commissions) is not the fear of double recovery, but rather, the difficulty in accurately measuring the loss in portfolio value proximately caused by the excessive trading and unsuitable transactions. The task of fully compensating the investor without being unduly speculative at the expense of the broker-dealer has never been undertaken by this court, and has plagued and divided other courts which have faced the problem. See *McNeal v. Paine, Webber, Jackson & Curtis, Inc., supra,* 598 F.2d at 894 n. 14 (5th Cir. 1979). It is and has been clear that, in theory, the plaintiff is entitled to recover the difference between what he would have had if the account has been handled legitimately and what he in fact had at the time the violation ended with the transfer of the account to a new broker. However, the nature of the churning offense as well as the inherent uncertainties of the operation of the stock market make exact implementation of this elementary legal theory impossible.

* * *

[A] refusal by a court to estimate the amount of trading losses caused by the churning of an account could only yield a certain windfall for either the investor or the broker. However, the essence of the judicial power to set damages the source and maintenance of its legitimacy is not the power to choose between alternative windfalls, but is rather the duty to attempt to correct existing windfalls. Thus, a court in a churning case must attempt to approximate the trading losses sustained as a result of the broker's misconduct. *See Fey v. Walston & Co., Inc.,* 493 F.2d 1036, 1055 (7th Cir. 1974). ("It is now elementary that when precise damage measurements are precluded by wrongful acts, the wrongdoer cannot insist upon exact measurements and the precise tracing of causal lines to an impractical extent; fair approximations are in order."); Brodsky, *supra* at 158-159.

In order to approximate the trading losses caused by the broker's misconduct, it is necessary to estimate how the investor's portfolio would have fared in the absence of the such misconduct. The trial judge must be afforded significant discretion to choose the indicia by which such estimation is to be made, based primarily on the types of securities comprising the portfolio. However, in the absence of either a specialized portfolio or a showing by either party that a different method is more accurate, it seems that the technique discussed by Judge Oakes in *Rolf v. Blyth, Eastman, Dillon & Co.*, Inc., 570 F.2d 38, 49 (2d Cir.), cert. denied, 439 U.S. 1039, 99 S. Ct. 642, 58 L. Ed. 2d 698 (1978) and employed by Judge Mahon in this case is preferable. *See* Brodsky, *supra* at 157. ("Given the recognized difficulty in computing damages in these cases, that (the *Rolf*) formula is a logical approach toward compensating a customer for loss.") This mode of estimation utilizes the average percentage performance in the value of the Dow Jones Industrials or the Standard and Poor's Index during the relevant period as the indicia of how a given portfolio would have performed in the absence of the broker's misconduct.

In the case at bar, Judge Mahon instructed the jury to compute trading loss damages by finding:

> "by a preponderance of the evidence the difference between the amount of plaintiff's original investment and dividends therefrom less any withdrawals received by Mrs. Miley and less the ending value of her account with defendants. This amount is to then be reduced by the average percentage decline in value of the Dow Jones Industrials or the Standard and Poor's Index during the relevant period of time.

> Answer in dollars and cents, if any, or none."

In addition, as part of this same instruction Judge Mahon told the jury that they could award "only such damages as will reasonably compensate her for such injury and damage. You are not permitted to award speculative damages." We feel that this instruction was both correct and sufficient on the issue of trading losses caused by churning.

C. Unauthorized Trading

While SROs (e.g., FINRA) recognize unauthorized trading as a violation of their rules, it is not recognized as fraud under §10(b) and Rule 10b-5 by a majority of the federal courts without some showing of deception. While this is in keeping with the holding of *Santa Fe Industries,* the practical result is that a claim for unauthorized trading is rarely alleged on its own; generally, it is alleged with a claim of churning or suitability, both of which meet the deception and scienter requirements of §10(b) and 10b-5. Compare the two cases below. Both involved unauthorized trading, both were decided in the U.S. District Court for the Southern District of New York, but disagree as to whether unauthorized trading standing alone violates § 10(b) and Rule 10b-5. Moreover, unlike churning, the elements needed to establish an unauthorized trading violation under § 10(b) and Rule 10b-5 are anything but clear.

Pross v. Baird, Patrick & Co., Inc.

585 F. Supp. 1456 (S.D.N.Y. 1984)

CONNER, District Judge:

* * *

In his complaint, Pross states that he had a nondiscretionary account with Baird. He alleges that during November and December of 1982, Baird made trades for that account in the stock of Nitron, Inc. ("Nitron"), without his prior consent and, indeed, at times contrary to his specific instructions. Pross further alleges that in making the trades, Baird failed "to disclose any facts to [Pross] concerning the corporation whose shares were being traded on his behalf," including the fact that Baird was "making a market" in Nitron stock, and that Baird engaged in the transactions for its own benefit.

In order to state a cognizable claim for fraud under Rule 10b-5, a plaintiff must allege conduct by the defendant which can fairly be viewed as "manipulative or deceptive" within the meaning of § 10(b) of the Securities Exchange Act of 1934. Manipulation is "virtually a term of art when used in connection with the securities markets," and refers narrowly to practices, such as wash sales, matched sales, or rigged prices, which artificially affect market activity in order to mislead investors. However, in situations not involving a manipulative scheme, the conduct alleged as fraudulent must include deception, misrepresentation, or nondisclosure to violate § 10(b) or Rule 10b-5.

Baird's actions, which Pross has alleged to be fraudulent in the instant case, clearly involve no manipulative activity in the technical sense in which that term is used in the securities laws. Thus, Pross must point to some deceptive action, or material misrepresentation or nondisclosure by Baird in order to maintain his claim of a violation of Rule 10b-5. In his complaint and affidavits in opposition to the instant motion, the only material misstatement or omission Pross identifies is Baird's failure to disclose that it was "making a market" in the stock of Nitron at the time that stock was purchased for plaintiff's account. Although failure by a broker to disclose that it is "making a market" in a particular security is a material omission, which nondisclosure by itself establishes reliance, Baird has demonstrated, without contradiction by plaintiff, that it adequately disclosed its market-maker status.

In support of its motion, Baird has shown that immediately following each purchase of Nitron stock, and well prior to the settlement date for each transaction, it sent to Pross a confirmation slip that clearly stated "we make a mkt in this security." In addition, in Pross's monthly statements dated November 26, 1982 and December 31, 1982, Baird reiterated its disclosure that "we make a mkt in this security." Plaintiff has not disputed the evidence that Baird made these disclosures. Thus, under these circumstances, there exists no factual basis for concluding that Baird failed adequately to disclose to Pross that it was making a market in Nitron stock. So long as a broker adequately discloses its status to its customer, "it is not a fraudulent practice for a brokerage firm to act as a market-maker and to sell securities to its customers as a principal." *In re Scientific Control Corp. Sec. Lit.,* 71 F.R.D. 491, 508 (S.D.N.Y.1976). Accordingly, in light of Baird's disclosure of its status, there is no legal basis for Pross's charge that Baird acted improperly in purchasing Nitron securities for his account at a time when Baird was making a market in those shares.

Stripped of its one allegation of nondisclosure,[14] plaintiff's complaint is reduced to a claim that Baird made trades on his behalf which were contrary to his express instructions and in derogation of the parties' brokerage agreement. The only issue to be determined in the instant case is whether the transactions in Nitron stock were authorized. While the conduct in which Baird allegedly engaged was reprehensible, it does not involve the element of deception necessary to be violative of Rule 10b–5. At most, it provides the basis for a claim of breach of fiduciary duty or breach of contract, which, without more, cannot be converted into a fraud claim under §10(b) and Rule 10b-5.[15]

————

Cruse v. Equitable Securities of New York Inc.

678 F. Supp. 1023 (S.D.N.Y. 1987)

Lowe, District Judge.

The Complaint

William T. Cruse ("Cruse") commenced this action against Equitable Securities of New York, Inc. and Steven A. Fishman ("defendants") to seek the recovery of damages for alleged violation of the federal securities laws ... Defendants have moved for an Order dismissing the complaint pursuant to Rule 9(b) of the Federal Rules of Civil Procedure, for failure to allege fraud with the requisite particularity, and Rule 12(b)(6) of the Federal Rules of Civil Procedure for failure to state a claim upon which relief can be granted.

In essence, Cruse alleges that he told Fishman that because Cruse was dependent upon dividend income from his portfolio, no stock given as collateral for a proposed options trading strategy was to be liquidated under any circumstances. Cruse also claims that Fishman was fully aware of Cruse's conservative investment objective and lack of any experience in or understanding of options. Plaintiff further alleges that his account at Equitable Securities was a non-discretionary account. More specifically,

---

14. [3] If plaintiff was relying upon other misrepresentations or nondisclosures by defendant, he was required, in response to a motion for summary judgment, to come forward with enough proof of his allegations to create an issue for trial. Pross has failed to do so in response to the instant motion. His use of conclusory charges of fraud without any supporting factual allegations, no matter how frequently stated, does not meet this burden.

15. [4] Moreover, assuming the adequacy of Baird's disclosure of its status, the facts alleged by Pross fail to establish scienter, another essential element of a claim under §10(b) and Rule 10b-5.

he alleges that no one other than Cruse was ever authorized to purchase or sell securities for the account.

On September 30, 1985, Cruse claims that pursuant to Fishman's trading strategy, he deposited as collateral into the Equitable account ("the account") securities with a value of approximately $160,000. This collateral was comprised of 2,968 shares of Kerr McGee Corporation and 1,200 shares of Pepsico, Inc.

Plaintiff claims that from the date he deposited the aforementioned collateral in the account through mid-March 1986, Fishman engaged in unauthorized and unsuitable trading.

In regard to the period in question, October 1985 through March 1986, it is alleged that defendant Fishman's trading resulted in a net loss to plaintiff of over $260,000. This figure is alleged to include commissions of over $16,000. Cruse claims that this figure stems from a turnover ratio1 of 16, a rate Cruse alleges is excessive in light of his conservative investment objectives.

Defendants allege: ... (3) that plaintiff has not alleged any affirmative misrepresentations or deception in regard to his claim of unauthorized trading....

Background

Cruse alleges that defendant Fishman was at all relevant times an employee and registered representative of defendant Equitable Securities, and conducted business from Equitable Securities' office at 55 Waterside Plaza, New York, New York. Cruse further alleges that at commencement of the activities complained of, Fishman was 22 years old, and unknown to Cruse, he had been a registered representative for only 2 months.

Cruse claims to be an 82 year old successful business man whose sole investment experience prior to opening his securities account with defendant was the purchase of "blue-chip" stocks on a cash basis and the derivation of dividend income therefrom. Prior to the opening of an account with defendants, Cruse claims never to have traded or to have had an understanding of options.

Cruse claims to have first met Fishman in 1984 at social events sponsored by a common college fraternal organization. In September 1985, defendant Fishman is alleged to have told Cruse that despite his inexperience with options and conservative investment objectives, a substantial return could be made trading index options; that through index options trading, a 10–15% return above the dividends now received from Cruse's common stock portfolio could be reasonably expected; while Cruse would have to put up a portion of his common stock portfolio as collateral, such stock would never be liquidated; that no trade would be made without first consulting plaintiff Cruse; Fishman would at all times monitor trading to prevent losses; that the options strategy to be pursued was a conservative one with a limited risk of approximately 10% of the amount invested; that this trading strategy was one Fishman was using with success for his own immediate family; and finally, that although Cruse would be getting trading confirmations and monthly statements, they would be difficult to understand and that for this reason, Fishman would subsequently explain their meaning and impact to plaintiff Cruse.

Cruse claims that on the same day that he first transferred collateral into the account, Fishman engaged in an unauthorized and unsuitable transaction by selling 29 call options on Cruse's Kerr McGee stock and 12 call options on his Pepsico stock. Cruse claims that all of his Pepsico stock was eventually sold without his receipt of the benefits of such sale.

Plaintiff further claims that Fishman's assurance that he would monitor trading to prevent losses proved to be untrue as plaintiff lost $63,000 in November 1985, $117,000 in December 1985, $16,500 in January 1986, $45,000 in February 1986, and $22,000 in March 1986. Cruse claims that at no time during the period in question did Fishman advise him of the true extent of his losses, despite the fact that Fishman knew that Cruse did not understand the monthly account statements issued.

Cruse alleges that he received margin maintenance notices on his account prior to December 20, 1985, and that on each occasion Fishman told him that the notice had been sent in error. Cruse further claims that from late December 1985, through mid-March 1986, Fishman represented to Cruse that earlier, temporary losses were now profits, and that additional profits had been made, and that these profits should be reinvested. Because Cruse alleges that he could not understand the monthly account statements issued, he claims that he believed Fishman's assertions.

In mid-March 1986, plaintiff Cruse claims that he received approximately 17 trading confirmations for trades he had never authorized. Cruse claims he subsequently tried to contact Fishman and learned that he had left for vacation in Jamaica. Cruse alleges that he then had a meeting with the branch manager of defendant Equitable Securities, at which an officer of the company admitted to Cruse that Equitable had been concerned about plaintiff's account but had not contacted Cruse because defendant Fishman had told them that Cruse was a man of "vast wealth" and that his account represented his "risk portfolio."

As a result of the alleged meeting with officers of defendant Equitable Securities, Cruse claims that his account was transferred to Edward Swikart, III ("Swikart"), who is believed to be the branch manager of Equitable Securities. Cruse alleges that after Swikart performed his own analysis of the trading activity in Cruse's account, he offered to personally guarantee the return of all losses over an unspecified period of time, if Cruse agreed to liquidate securities being held as collateral and allowed Swikart to trade the account on a discretionary basis. Cruse claims that when this was rejected as being contrary to the rules of Fair Practice of the National Association of Securities Dealers, Inc. ("N.A.S.D."), Swikart offered a gift of restricted stock in an over-the-counter market company. Cruse alleges that this offer was also rejected.

Claim One: The Rule 10b-5 Allegations

Plaintiff Cruse first alleges violations of Section 10(b) of the Securities Exchange Act of 1934, and Rule 10b-5, promulgated thereunder. Cruse's securities claims are founded upon allegations of fraudulent misrepresentation, unauthorized trading, churning and unsuitable trading.

* * *

B. *Unauthorized Trading*

Plaintiff Cruse further alleges in Claim I of the Complaint that Fishman engaged in unauthorized trading by making purchases and sales of securities for the account without first obtaining Cruse's authority. Defendants urge dismissal of this claim contending that Cruse has not alleged any affirmative misrepresentations or deception and that unauthorized trades disclosed in regular account documentation cannot give rise to a 10b-5 claim, and finally, that Cruse has failed to allege reliance on defendant Fishman's conduct. For the reasons which follow, Cruse's allegation of unauthorized trading in violation of Rule 10b-5 survives defendants' Fed.R.Civ.P. 12(b)(6) motion, but is dismissed without prejudice to the filing of a motion for leave to amend pursuant to Fed.R.Civ.P. 9(b), if such motion is made within 20 days of the date of this opinion.

Defendants rely initially on the case of *Santa Fe Industries, Inc. v. Green,* 430 U.S. 462, 473, 97 S.Ct. 1292, 1300, 51 L.Ed.2d 480 (1977), for their argument that Cruse's claim of unauthorized trading must fall because Cruse fails to allege any affirmative misrepresentations or deception on the part of defendant Fishman. This assertion, however, appears to be founded upon too narrow a reading of the Supreme Court's decision of *Santa Fe.* The Court in *Santa Fe,* expressly permitted an action under Section 10(b) of the Exchange act and Rule 10b–5 based upon a material omission or nondisclosure. Plaintiff Cruse has alleged such material omission or nondisclosure by stating that the account was a non-discretionary one and that defendant Fishman traded securities for the account without first obtaining the requisite authority.

Defendants further argue that unauthorized trades disclosed in regular account documentation cannot give rise to a 10b-5 claim. For this proposition, defendants cite *Pross v. Baird Patrick & Co., Inc.,* 585 F.Supp. 1456 (1983–1984 Transfer Binder), Fed.Sec.L.Rep. (CCH) ¶ 99,668 (S.D.N.Y.1984) (Conner, J.). *Pross,* however, is in a significant respect inapposite to the instant situation. In *Pross,* the court dealt with the question of whether a broker had failed to disclose that he was making a market in a stock traded for plaintiff. The court held that the broker had not engaged in such material omission in violation of Rule 10b-5 as the broker's "market maker" status had indeed been disclosed prior to the settlement date for each transaction. No analogous disclosure is alleged in either the Complaint or Motion to dismiss at bar. Moreover, plaintiff in *Pross* merely complained that his broker had failed to disclose one selective piece of information, *i.e.* his "market maker" status. Plaintiff Cruse alleges to the contrary that defendant Fishman traded Cruse's account without any prior disclosure or authorization whatsoever. It must also be stressed that even if, *arguendo* defendants are correct in their assertion that a customer's receipt of regular account documentation cures a prior unauthorized trade, Cruse explicitly claims that Fishman himself thought that Cruse would have a difficult time deciphering account statements, and for this reason offered to explain their meaning to plaintiff.

Finally, defendants assert that Cruse's claim of unauthorized trading must be dismissed because of a failure to assert reliance on defendant's conduct. Defendants cite the recent decision of *Bischaff v. B.K. Scott,* No. 85–4677, slip op. at 14 (E.D.N.Y. August 29, 1986), which, in contrast to defendant's reliance argument, adheres to an established line of securities cases which has disposed of any requirement of proof of reliance as a prerequisite to recovery in a private action. Thus, as stated by Justice Blackman in *Affiliated UTE*:

> ... positive proof of reliance is not a prerequisite to recovery. All that is necessary is that the facts withheld be material in the sense that a reasonable investor might have considered them important in the making of this decision.... This obligation to disclose and this withholding of a material fact establish the requisite element of *causation in fact*. 406 U.S. at 153–54, 92 S.Ct. at 1472 (citations omitted) (emphasis added).

Plaintiff Cruse has fulfilled this requisite element of causation in fact by claiming explicitly in his complaint that due to Fishman's unauthorized trading, *inter alia*, plaintiff has suffered a net loss of over $260,000.

* * *

FINRA Rule 2010 has been used to establish a claim for unauthorized trading. While it does not expressly prohibit unauthorized trading, it does require broker-dealers and their associated persons to observe high standards of commercial honor and just and equitable principles of trade.

Notes and Questions

1. *Other FINRA Rules.* FINRA Rules 2020 and 2090 may also be helpful in establishing a claim of unauthorized trading. FINRA Rule 2020 prohibits broker-dealers from effecting any transaction in, or inducing the purchase or sale of, any security by means of any manipulative, deceptive, or other fraudulent device or contrivance. FINRA Rule 2090, among other things, requires the broker-dealer to understand the authority of each person acting on behalf of the customer.

2. *The Shingle Theory.* The Shingle Theory states that every broker-dealer makes an implied representation to its customers that it will deal fairly with its customers. This Theory has been used to successfully establish a claim for unauthorized trading by providing the element of deception required by § 10(b) and Rule 10b-5. For example, the broker-dealer's implied representation to its customers that it will deal fairly with them may contain a representation that the broker-dealer will only execute transactions authorized by its customer.

Hypothetical One

George and Dorothy Mae David (the "Davids") were elderly retired customers of Anne Simpson, a high-producing registered representative in Success First's Chicago branch office. The Davids have filed a written complaint against Anne Simpson in connection with transactions effected by Anne in their account at Success First. In their customer complaint filed with Success First, The Davids assert that they told

Anne that they wanted only low-risk investments. In November of this year, they gave Anne $5,000—including $3,000 cash that Anne accepted in violation of Success First's policy—to deposit in their account. Anne gave the Davids a receipt for $5,000 but deposited only $4,000 in the Davids' account. On another occasion, the Davids were due to receive a $500 check from their account. Anne did not send the check. When the Davids demanded an explanation from Anne, Anne paid them the $500 with two money orders, instead of a check drawn on their account.

The Davids never requested any specific transaction, and Anne never called to request trading authorization. During the 14 months following the opening of the Davids' account with Success First, Anne executed 19 transactions in the Davids's account, generating $2,823 in gross commissions. The annualized turnover rate was 5.04. The annualized break-even rate of return was 29.69 percent. Seventy percent of the securities in the Davids' account were held for 90 days or less. The Davids' account documents also showed that front-load mutual funds were purchased for the account but were held for only a few months, costing the Davids the sales charges paid to purchase the funds. The Davids never discussed the use of margin with Anne or authorized any margin trades. Nevertheless, there was a margin purchase of AT&T stock for $2,700 that cost the Davids $13 in margin interest.

The Davids' accountant told them that the trading in their account was excessive. They called Anne from their vacation home and demanded that the activity in their account stop. Anne assured them that she would "look into" the matter. The trading did not stop. When they returned to Chicago from their vacation, they met personally with Anne and told her to stop the activity in their account. Only then did the trading stop. Has Anne churned and executed unauthorized transactions in the Davids' account in violation of § 10(b) and Rule 10b-5? → Yes.

D. Suitability

The suitability doctrine prohibits broker-dealers from recommending securities and trading strategies that conflict with their customers' investment objectives. This means that a suitability claim requires a recommendation from the broker-dealer to the customer and ascertainment of the customer's investment objectives. Recommendations that conflict with a customer's investment objectives violate § 10(b) and Rule 10b-5 of the Exchange Act. This means that suitability claims may be initiated by regulators and private plaintiffs. However, since 1987, private causes of action for suitability claims, generally, are brought through arbitration. Since the Court held in *Shearson/American Express v. McMahon*, 482 U.S. 220 (1987), that pre-dispute arbitration agreements are an enforceable part of a brokerage contract, suitability claims are conducted mostly through FINRA's securities arbitration forum. *See* Chapter 12, Securities Arbitration. In addition, although we discuss suitability claims alone in this section, they are usually brought in concert with claims for churning, unauthorized trading, and breach of fiduciary duty.

While suitability claims in federal courts seem to be based on SRO and FINRA suitability rules, the circuits have failed to agree about the elements that must be proved in suitability cases. Compare the following cases. What are the elements of a suitability claim in each case and the legal theories used by the two circuits?

O'Connor v. R.F. Lafferty & Co., Inc.

965 F.2d 893 (10th Cir. 1992)

BRORBY, Circuit Judge.

Plaintiff appeals the district court's grant of summary judgment disposing of her federal and state securities law claims. She also appeals the district court's decision to submit her remaining state law tort claims to arbitration. We affirm in part, and reverse in part.

I. FACTS

In 1975, Carol M. O'Connor received a $200,000 property settlement from her divorce. She deposited this entire sum into an account with the investment firm of R.F. Lafferty & Company, Inc., to be handled by Roy Foulke. Ms. O'Connor's brother recommended Mr. Foulke who was a family friend and who had previously handled accounts for other members of Ms. O'Connor's family.

Ms. O'Connor gave Mr. Foulke and Lafferty complete discretion to handle her account. Mr. Foulke knew Ms. O'Connor was not an experienced investor. In fact, prior to her association with Lafferty she had only invested in a savings account. Her husband or her father had always handled her finances. Ms. O'Connor informed Mr. Foulke the money she deposited represented virtually all of her assets. Ms. O'Connor also instructed Mr. Foulke she would need to rely on the $700 income generated from her deposit and the $800 maintenance payments from her ex-husband to meet her monthly living expenses. Ms. O'Connor also expected her account to generate sufficient income to cover the taxes on her alimony and on the account, the fees of her accountant and the servicing fees for her account. Mr. Foulke knew Ms. O'Connor relied on him to make all decisions concerning her securities account. Consequently, Mr. Foulke traded on Ms. O'Connor's account and notified her of the trading activity by sending a trade ticket within thirty-six hours and again at the end of the month in her statement.

In 1985, because of the success in Ms. O'Connor's investment account, her husband was relieved of his alimony obligation. Understandably, this event changed the nature of her financial plan. From that point, Ms. O'Connor's account would have to generate $2,100 a month.

Ms. O'Connor first became concerned about the value of her account in February 1987. Ms. O'Connor contends that from 1982 through 1987 Mr. Foulke and Lafferty purchased several securities unsuitable for her investment objectives. Specifically, Ms. O'Connor objects to investments in oil and gas limited partnerships; units of stock and warrants in Patient Medical Systems Corporation; units of International Surgical and Pharmaceutical Corporation securities; units in Job Stores, Inc. securities;

units in R.T. Acquisition Corporation securities; and units of Kerkoff Industries, Inc. securities. Ms. O'Connor requested a judgment for actual damages of $329,000 plus a reasonable rate of return on amounts unsuitably invested that earned no income.

In 1988, Ms. O'Connor directed Mr. Foulke to stop all trading on her account. She brought suit against Mr. Foulke and against Lafferty for the acts of Mr. Foulke as a controlling person and under the doctrine of respondeat superior asserting seven claims: (1) violation of § 10(b) of the 1934 Securities Exchange Act and Rule 10b–5 promulgated thereunder; (2) breach of a fiduciary duty; ... (5) common law fraud; ... and (7) violations of Colo.Rev.Stat. §§ 11-51-123 and 11-51-125(2), (3) and (5).

The district court granted Defendants' motion for summary judgment as to count one and subsequently dismissed counts five and seven. The court submitted the remaining state law claims to arbitration. The court later adopted the arbitrator's award of $30,000 in favor of Ms. O'Connor.

Ms. O'Connor appeals all the district court's rulings. She asserts the district court erred in (1) granting summary judgment on her § 10(b) and Rule 10b-5 claim ...

II. ANALYSIS

A. Unsuitability

The district court granted Defendants' motion for summary judgment against Ms. O'Connor's § 10(b) and Rule 10b-5 claim. The court found the Defendants did not possess the requisite scienter or intent to defraud to sustain such a claim. The court also found that although the Defendants did invest in securities unsuitable for Ms. O'-Connor's investment objectives, Ms. O'Connor could not demonstrate her justifiable reliance on the purchases where she had information the securities may be unsuitable and acted recklessly by failing to investigate. The court found persuasive deposition testimony by Ms. O'Connor where she admitted Mr. Foulke did not intend to defraud or hurt her. She further testified he did not willfully withhold information or lie to her.

Ms. O'Connor asserts several errors by the district court. She claims the court did not understand the nature of the allegations; facts existed to establish the requisite scienter; the court erred by relying on Ms. O'Connor's non expert opinion testimony; and Ms. O'Connor's reliance was justified or in the alternative, reliance need not be shown.

* * *

Ms. O'Connor claims Defendants bought securities which were unsuitable for her investment needs. Federal courts recognize such a claim as a violation of § 10(b) and Rule 10b-5.... The unsuitability doctrine is premised on New York Stock Exchange Rule 405—Know Your Customer Rule and the National Association of Securities Dealers Rules of Fair Practice.[16] Unsuitability claims can be analyzed as omission cases or fraudulent practices cases.

---

16. [4] Article 3, § 2 of these Rules states:
    In recommending to a customer the purchase, sale or exchange of any security, a member
    shall have reasonable grounds for believing that the recommendation is suitable for such

Some courts examining a § 10(b), Rule 10b-5 unsuitability claim have analyzed it simply as a misrepresentation or failure to disclose a material fact. In such a case, the broker has omitted telling the investor the recommendation is unsuitable for the investor's interests. The court may then use traditional laws concerning omission to examine the claim.

Under a misrepresentation or omission theory, a plaintiff can establish § 10(b), Rule 10b-5 liability by showing that in connection with the purchase or sale of a security—the broker made an untrue statement of a material fact, or failed to state a material fact, that in so doing, the broker acted knowingly with intent to deceive or defraud, and that plaintiff relied on the misrepresentations, and sustained damages as a proximate result of the misrepresentations.

In contrast, Ms. O'Connor asserts an unsuitability claim based on fraud by conduct. She does not assert Mr. Foulke omitted to tell her the stocks he purchased were unsuitable for her investment needs. Rather, she claims that his purchase of the stocks for her account acted as fraud upon her.

Fraud by conduct is a violation of Rule 10b-5(a) and (c) and is analogous to a churning claim.... This circuit has also recognized a violation of the NYSE Know Your Customer rule and the NASD Suitability Rule can be used to determine whether an account had been churned.

[U]nsuitability concerns the quality of the purchased securities. Federal courts have used the NYSE and NASD rules to analyze both forms of broker misconduct. Thus, we will examine the elements of a churning claim to aid our analysis of unsuitability elements.

While the elements of a churning claim are well established, the elements of an unsuitability claim based on fraud are not.... Because an unsuitability claim is so similar to a churning claim, we are persuaded the established "churning" elements can aid in our determination of the appropriate elements for an unsuitability cause of action. Today we adopt three elements to establish unsuitability based on fraud by conduct: The plaintiff must prove (1) the broker recommended (or in the case of a discretionary account purchased) securities which are unsuitable in light of the investor's objectives; (2) the broker recommended or purchased the securities with an intent to defraud or with reckless disregard for the investor's interests; and (3) the broker exercised control over the investor's account.[17]

---

customer upon the basis of the facts, if any, disclosed by such customer as to his other securities holdings and as to his financial situation and need.

17. [6] In establishing these elements we incorporate the Second Circuit's test for unsuitability and add the element of control. The Second Circuit has developed elements for an unsuitability claim not based on misrepresentations or omissions. The plaintiff must merely prove a recommendation of unsuitable securities and scienter. *Lamula,* 583 F.2d at 600. Unsuitability can be found where the investor proves the broker knew or reasonably believed the recommended securities were unsuitable but recommended them anyway. We acknowledge the unsuitability cases do not always distinguish between fraud by conduct and fraud by misrepresentation or omission. In fact, the *Lamula* court uses omission language in its discussion of fraud by conduct. Essentially, the court

Whether the control element of a churning claim applies to its cousin the unsuitability claim has been an open question. We believe the control element is essential to satisfy the causation/reliance requirement of a § 10(b), Rule 10b-5 violation.

In this case, we conclude the scienter element is dispositive. Based on our review of the record we hold Ms. O'Connor has failed, as a matter of law, to establish the scienter requirement of an unsuitability claim and affirm the district court's summary judgment against Ms. O'Connor's § 10(b), Rule 10b-5 claim.

[I]n our test for unsuitability a plaintiff must show the broker purchased the securities with an intent to defraud or with reckless disregard for the investor's interests. Recklessness is defined as "conduct that is 'an extreme departure from the standards of ordinary care, and which presents a danger of misleading buyers or sellers that is either known to the defendant or is so obvious that the actor must have been aware of it.'"

Ms. O'Connor alleges facts exist sufficient to prove Defendants' scienter. She asserts this proof consists of evidence of self-dealing including an increase in fees, and misrepresentations and omissions[18] concerning (1) the commissions; (2) Mr. Foulke's lack of qualifications as an investment advisor; (3) the unsuitable nature of the purchased securities; (4) the depletion of principal due to monthly withdrawals; and (5) the promise that she would receive $20,000 a year in income from the oil and gas investment.

The parties do not dispute the basic facts of this case. Ms. O'Connor presented the fact that Mr. Foulke charged a one percent fee per year for financial services. In addition, he received a fifty percent commission split with Lafferty. However, the record reflects Ms. O'Connor was aware of the fees and commissions she paid to Mr. Foulke because they were reported in the monthly statements she received concerning her account.

Ms. O'Connor also presented deposition testimony that Lafferty was the underwriter for R.T. Corporation and Patient Medical Systems. Additional evidence established that Mr. Foulke was himself a director of Kerkoff. Yet, when deposed, Ms. O'Connor testified that she considered an investment less risky if Mr. Foulke were involved with the company. Furthermore, the prospectuses Ms. O'Connor received properly disclosed the fact Lafferty was the underwriter for several of the issues in which Mr. Foulke invested.

Next, Ms. O'Connor contends Mr. Foulke omitted to tell her he was not qualified as an investment advisor.... But Mr. Foulke's deposition also revealed he never held himself out to be an investment advisor.

To prove the unsuitable nature of securities purchased by Mr. Foulke, Ms. O'Connor presented evidence that her investment objectives were conservative. She then presented evidence tending to show the securities in which Mr. Foulke invested were risky. For example, Ms. O'Connor demonstrated that the prospectus for Patient Med-

---

examined the alleged omission as probative of the defendant's scienter. No separate fraud by omission claim existed.

18. [7] Ms. O'Connor does not allege a separate claim of fraud based on misrepresentation and omission. Instead, she claims the Defendants' misrepresentations and omissions evidence sufficient recklessness to sustain the scienter requirement for a § 10(b), Rule § 10b-5 claim.

ical Systems said it involved a high degree of risk and the investor should be prepared to lose her entire investment. However, in his deposition, Mr. Foulke testified he believed that Patient Medical Systems was only modestly risky and that risk was mitigated because Lafferty was the underwriter.

Ms. O'Connor testified in her deposition a geologist friend told her the oil and gas partnerships which Mr. Foulke purchased for her account were a bad investment and she should get out of them. But, Ms. O'Connor knew that Mr. Foulke had investigated the oil and gas operation before investing in it. In fact, he personally investigated all investment opportunities before he purchased any securities for Ms. O'Connor's account.

Furthermore, Mr. Foulke was able to give his reasons for purchasing each of the units of stock to which Ms. O'Connor objects. For example, Mr. Foulke testified the purchase of units in R.T. Acquisition Corporation was appropriate for Ms. O'Connor's account because he believed only low risk was involved because each shareholder would get back dollar for dollar invested with no dilution. He also felt the purchase of units in Kerkoff was appropriate based on the company's long-standing reputation and own[sic] his conversations with the owners of the company. He was also very impressed with the fact that the first day Kerkoff stock was listed it listed on the American Stock Exchange.

Additionally, Ms. O'Connor claimed Mr. Foulke omitted to tell her that her principal was being depleted by monthly withdrawals. She then presented Mr. Foulke's deposition testimony wherein Mr. Foulke stated he never expressly informed Ms. O'Connor that her monthly withdrawals were depleting her principal. Further testimony revealed that Mr. Foulke knew the $200,000 with which Ms. O'Connor opened her account comprised nearly all of her assets. Testimony also established Mr. Foulke knew Ms. O'Connor was unemployed, so if the account lost money she had no way to replace it other than through the account itself. Yet, Ms. O'Connor was notified of the activity in her account by trade tickets and monthly statements. These statements clearly reflect the fact the monthly withdrawals did deplete her principal.

We conclude the facts presented fail to rise to the level of recklessness necessary to sustain a section § 10(b), Rule 10b-5 claim. No indication appears in the record that Mr. Foulke intentionally or recklessly defrauded Ms. O'Connor. Instead, the record reflects Mr. Foulke successfully handled Ms. O'Connor's account for many years. Therefore, we affirm the district court's summary judgment order against Ms. O'Connor's § 10(b), Rule 10b-5 claim.

———

Brown v. E.F. Hutton Group, Inc.

991 F.2d 1020 (2d Cir. 1993)

Jacobs, Circuit Judge:

Plaintiffs-appellants appeal from so much of a judgment in the United States District Court for the Southern District of New York, John M. Walker, *Circuit Judge,* …

as (a) granted summary judgment to defendant E.F. Hutton Group, Inc. ("Hutton") on plaintiffs-appellants' claim that they were sold unsuitable securities in violation of Section 10(b) of the Securities Exchange Act of 1934.... We affirm.

BACKGROUND

Plaintiffs-appellants are approximately 400 presumably unsophisticated, income-oriented investors in a limited partnership called the Hutton/Indian Wells 1983 Energy Income Fund, Ltd. (the "Partnership"). According to the Partnership's October 14, 1983 prospectus (the "Prospectus"), it was organized to acquire properties upon which existing oil and gas wells are located and to provide regular cash distributions to investors from sales of oil and gas produced from those properties.

After their investments allegedly became worthless, the plaintiffs-appellants (the "Limited Partners") brought suit in the United States District Court for the Southern District of New York against Hutton, the Indian Wells Production Company and related entities (collectively, the "defendants"). In their amended complaint, the Limited Partners assert ... claims arising under § 10(b) ...

In response to the amended complaint, the defendants moved below (a) to dismiss the amended complaint for failure to state a claim and for failure to plead fraud with particularity, and (b) in the alternative for summary judgment. The district court granted summary judgment as to the first count, which alleges that defendant Hutton sold the Limited Partners unsuitable securities in violation of § 10(b).... This appeal followed the district court's denial of the Limited Partners' motion for reargument as to the first count.

The Limited Partners contend that this Court should reverse the grant of summary judgment as to the unsuitability claim (1) because the district court erroneously relied in part upon the supplement to the Prospectus (the "Supplement") which may not have been distributed to each of the Limited Partners prior to their investment in the Partnership; (2) because the promotional brochure used by Hutton to market the Partnership interests (the "Brochure") and the Prospectus did not expressly and directly contradict certain oral misrepresentations allegedly made by Hutton account executives; and (3) because the district court failed to consider all relevant factors to determine whether each of the Limited Partners justifiably relied on his or her broker's assurances.

A. Allegations in the Amended Complaint

The district court, for purposes of Hutton's summary judgment motion and without objection from Hutton, accepted as true the following allegations from the amended complaint: (a) that each of the more than 400 Limited Partners was unsophisticated; (b) that each Limited Partner told a Hutton account executive that his or her investment objectives included some combination of income, capital appreciation, tax benefits and savings; and (c) that the Hutton account executives gave oral assurance to each Limited Partner that the Partnership had either no risk or low risk. Hutton's motion did, however, contest the Limited Partners' allegations that they made their purchases in justifiable reliance on the brokers' oral representations and that the Brochure and Prospectus were materially false and misleading.

B. The Offering Materials

As the Limited Partners contend, the Brochure depicts the Partnership's financial outlook in bright terms. In this regard, the Brochure distinguishes the Partnership from prototypically risky oil and gas investments by emphasizing that the purchase of "only producing oil and gas properties" eliminates exploration risk. The Brochure's disclosure concerning other risks is by reference to the Prospectus. The jacket of the Brochure contains the following caution:

> The use of this material is authorized only when preceded or accompanied by a prospectus for Hutton Indian Wells 1983 Energy Income Fund, Ltd. Prospective investors are encouraged to read the prospectus, including the section entitled "Risk Factors."

Although the Brochure again and again references the risk disclosure sections in the Prospectus, nowhere does the Brochure quote or otherwise recite the cautionary statements in the Prospectus.[19]

After a review of the Brochure in its entirety there can be no doubt that it is a selling tool. In contrast, the Prospectus' disclosure of the Partnership's risks is thorough and materially complete, if not decidedly glum. The cover of the Prospectus warns that "[n]o person has been authorized to give any information or to make any representations, other than those contained in this prospectus, and if given or made, such information or representations must not be relied upon." The first page of the prospectus states:

THIS OFFERING INVOLVES CERTAIN RISKS

See "RISK FACTORS"

The "RISK FACTORS" section takes up roughly three single spaced pages. It is prominently featured immediately after the opening "SUMMARY OF OFFERING" section. The "RISK FACTORS" section states at the outset that "[t]here can be no assurance that properties selected will produce oil or gas in the quantities or at the cost anticipated, or that they will not cease producing entirely." It ends by disclosing the Limited Partners' potential obligations in the event the Partnership is "involuntarily liquidated because of insolvency." The "RISK FACTORS" section is divided by headings entitled "General Risks" and "Specific Risks", and by fourteen subheadings entitled "Risks Inherent in Oil and Gas Operations", "Competition and Markets", "Regulation", "Operating and Environmental Hazards", "General Partners' Limited Prior Activities", "Diversification", "Lack of Opportunity to Review Partnership Properties", "Conflicts of Interest", "Limitations on Cash Distributions", "Limited Transferability", "Limited Liquidity", "Loss of Limited Liability", "Distribution of Partnership Properties", and

---

19. [2] Hutton asserts that the Brochure refers the reader to the appropriate subsections of the Prospectus "for a more detailed explanation." Brief of Defendants-Appellees at 7. In fact, other than the cautionary paragraph on the jacket encouraging potential investors to read the Prospectus, the Brochure's references to the Prospectus could be read to suggest that the contents of the Brochure are borne out by the more detailed disclosures in the Prospectus.

"Partnership Liquidation". The "RISK FACTORS" section also directs the potential investor to numerous other sections of the Prospectus.

There is little in the Prospectus to tranquilize the investor:

* * *

Competition and Markets. The oil and gas industry is highly competitive. The Partnership will be involved in competition for desirable properties, and will be competing with many entities which possess financial resources and technical staffs significantly greater than those available to the Partnership.

* * *

General Partners' Limited Prior Activities. The General Partners were recently organized and have no operating history.... The success of the Partnership will be dependent upon the ability of the General Partners to identify and acquire Producing Properties. Since the General Partners have only limited experience in such activities, there can be no assurance that the Partnership will be able to acquire Producing Properties on a timely or profitable basis....

In addition, the Prospectus warns that the Limited Partners would "own no direct interest in any oil and gas properties or other assets owned by the Partnership"; that "[t]here will be no ready market" for the Partnership units; and that there is "no assurance that the Partnership will have the financial resources to honor its repurchase commitments."

* * *

II. § 10(B) UNSUITABILITY CLAIM

In granting Hutton's motion for summary judgment on the Limited Partners' § 10(b) unsuitability claim, the district court concluded that "the offering materials are not misleading as a matter of law, or, to the same effect, that plaintiffs' reliance on certain portions of the materials was not reasonable as a matter of law." The district court also concluded that the Limited Partners could not have reasonably relied on the alleged oral representations by Hutton account executives. Based on our review of the facts and the law, we believe the district court reached the proper result.

This Court recognized the viability of a § 10(b) unsuitability claim in *Clark v. John Lamula Investors, Inc.,* 583 F.2d 594, 600–01 (2d Cir. 1978). A plaintiff must prove (1) that the securities purchased were unsuited to the buyer's needs; (2) that the defendant knew or reasonably believed the securities were unsuited to the buyer's needs; (3) that the defendant recommended or purchased the unsuitable securities for the buyer anyway; (4) that, with scienter, the defendant made material misrepresentations (or, owing a duty to the buyer, failed to disclose material information) relating to the suitability of the securities; and (5) that the buyer justifiably relied to its detriment on the defendant's fraudulent conduct. Scienter may be inferred by finding that the defendant knew or reasonably believed that the securities were unsuited to the investor's needs, misrepresented or failed to disclose the unsuitability of the securities, and proceeded to recommend or purchase the securities anyway. A plaintiff's burden with respect to the reliance element of an unsuitability claim, as in other § 10(b) and Rule 10b-5 actions, may vary depending on whether the claim alleges fraudulent representations or fraudulent omissions.

Analytically, an unsuitability claim is a subset of the ordinary § 10(b) fraud claim in which a plaintiff must allege, *inter alia,* (1) material misstatements or omissions, (2) indicating an intent to deceive or defraud, (3) in connection with the purchase or sale of a security. For purposes of this summary judgment motion we accept as true (as did the district court) the Limited Partners' allegations that the Partnership investment was incompatible with their needs for income, capital appreciation and savings, and we consider the aspects of the investment relating to those needs to be material facts as a matter of law.

A. DISCLOSURE OF SUITABILITY

The first count of the amended complaint generally asserts that Hutton's account executives' oral recommendations of the Partnership as a low risk, conservative investment misled the Limited Partners into purchasing unsuitable securities. The Limited Partners acknowledge that Hutton sent the Brochure and Prospectus, and that they received those documents; they insist, however, that the Brochure and Prospectus (a) fail to state expressly that the Partnership is unsuited to an investor who seeks an opportunity for "no risk", "low risk" or "conservative" capital appreciation, income or savings, and (b) understate, obscure or elide discussion of the real risks of the investment.

We disagree.

We find that the Limited Partners' reliance on the oral statements presumptively made by Hutton as to the low risk, conservative character of the investment is not justified as a matter of law and that the alleged oral statements are contradicted by the offering materials sent to the Limited Partners. We find further that the information available to the Limited Partners about the suitability of their investments was materially complete and not misleading.

An investor may not justifiably rely on a misrepresentation if, through minimal diligence, the investor should have discovered the truth. Under this standard, § 10(b) liability will not be imposed when an investor's conduct rises to the level of recklessness. To determine whether an investor acted recklessly, and therefore without justifiable reliance, no single factor is dispositive, and all relevant factors must be considered and balanced. [W]e considered the plaintiff's sophistication and expertise in finance and in the subject matter of the securities transaction; the plaintiff's representation by counsel; the plaintiff's opportunity to detect the fraud; whether the fraud was concealed; and the nature of the fraud. This Court has never established a list of all relevant factors, although many courts have been guided by the following:

> (1) The sophistication and expertise of the plaintiff in financial and securities matters; (2) the existence of longstanding business or personal relationships; (3) access to the relevant information; (4) the existence of a

fiduciary relationship; (5) concealment of the fraud; (6) the opportunity to detect the fraud; (7) whether the plaintiff initiated the stock transaction or sought to expedite the transaction; and (8) the generality or specificity of the misrepresentations.

Although for present purposes we presume that the Limited Partners are unsophisticated investors and that the brokers initiated the transactions, the other relevant factors preclude a conclusion that the alleged reliance could have been justifiable. Initially, we note that none of the Limited Partners allege the existence of a fiduciary relationship or of a longstanding business or personal relationship with Hutton or its brokers. The dominant considerations here, however, are that the Hutton brokers forwarded the offering materials to the Limited Partners; that the offering materials detailed the investment characteristics bearing upon suitability; that they did so in comprehensive and understandable language; and that the offering materials thereby contradicted the brokers' alleged general assurances.

Specifically, with respect to the Partnership's risks, the Brochure directs the potential investor to the Prospectus, the single most important document and perhaps the primary resource an investor should consult in seeking that information.[20] The Prospectus in turn indicates that the Partnership could collapse altogether depending on a variety of factors and developments, none of which is dismissed as remote. The first paragraph of the Prospectus' "RISK FACTORS" section tells prospective investors that their profits depend on the Partnership's purchase of properties that-assuming they produced oil or gas in the quantity and at the cost anticipated in the first place-may cease production altogether; and that whatever oil or gas may be produced would be sold in a regulated market that fluctuates and had been recently sinking. These warnings are reinforced in the Prospectus by disclosures ... No reasonable investor reviewing the disclosure documents could fail to appreciate that the Partnership could result in a total loss.

The disclosure of risks adequately informed the Limited Partners that the investment was not suitable for the purpose of generating low risk capital appreciation or income, and the disclosure of the investment's limited transferability and liquidity adequately informed the Limited Partners that the investment was not a suitable savings vehicle. Thus, the information made available to the Limited Partners accurately reflected the suitability of the investment (or lack thereof) for the individual investors; the Limited Partners' asserted reliance on the brokers' alleged oral statements, without further inquiry, was therefore reckless and unjustifiable.... There is no requirement

---

20. [4] The Prospectus' express warning to potential investors that they not rely on information or representations obtained elsewhere further establishes its primacy as the source of risk disclosures. However, we agree with the Limited Partners that, despite this warning, information or representations outside of the Prospectus may be material and justify reliance. As stated by the Tenth Circuit in *Zobrist*, "we do not imply that the defendants can disclaim responsibility for their misrepresentations simply by disclosing the risks in the memorandum and therein warning investors not to rely on representations not contained within the memorandum."

that written offering materials counteract the enticements of salesmen by anticipating each sales pitch and rebutting it explicitly.

CONCLUSION

As a matter of law, the facts adduced by the Limited Partners cannot support a finding that the Limited Partners justifiably relied on the Hutton account executives' alleged assurances of suitability, or a finding that the Brochure and Prospectus contained material omissions or misrepresentations concerning the suitability of the investment. The Limited Partners, having thus failed to make a showing "sufficient to establish the existence of an element essential to that party's case, and on which that party will bear the burden of proof at trial," cannot maintain their unsuitability claim and Hutton is entitled to a judgment as a matter of law.

———

Unlike private plaintiffs, regulators such as the SEC have brought suitability claims against broker-dealers under §17(a) of the Securities Act in addition to §10(b) and Rule 10b-5 of the Exchange Act. The SEC may bring such claims in federal court or in an administrative proceeding. The following case involves an SEC administrative proceeding. As you read the case, consider the difference between an SEC administrative proceeding and a private cause of action when establishing the elements of a suitability claim. Are the required elements in a suitability claim the same or similar? Is the SEC more or less stringent in accepting facts needed to establish the elements of a suitability claim under the antifraud provisions?

In the Matter of Steven E. Muth and Richard J. Rouse

Exchange Act Rel. No. 52551
86 S.E.C. Docket 956 (Oct. 3, 2005)

* * *

II.

Background

Muth entered the brokerage industry in 1983. He was associated with Schneider as a salesperson from September 2000 until May 2001. Immediately prior to Schneider, Muth had been associated with Kirkpatrick, Pettis, Smith, and Polian, Inc. ("KPSP"), where he was the top salesperson.... In his sales activities, Muth focused on one or two issuers. Rouse [Muth's supervisor] testified that it was unusual for a salesperson to focus on only two securities. At both Schneider and KPSP, Muth urged customers to purchase on margin the stock of Bonso Electronics International, Inc. ("Bonso"), a manufacturer of electronic products, and of Creative Host Services, Inc. ("Creative Host"), an airline catering company. Bonso and Creative Host were high-risk stocks, suitable only for investors with the financial resources and risk tolerance for speculative investments. Bonso traded on the NASDAQ National Market. Its closing stock price ranged from $6.00 to $12.87 per share. After March 2001, it generally closed between $4.00 and $6.00 per share. Bonso's daily trading volume ranged from a low of 1,100 shares on November 17, 2000, to a high of 295,000 shares on April 5, 2001. Creative Host traded on the NASDAQ Small-Cap Market. Its closing stock price steadily declined from $8.75 per share on October 9, 2000, to $0.75 per share on April 12, 2001. Its daily trading volume ranged from a high of 381,400 shares on November 29, 2000, to a low of 200 shares on January 26, 2001.

During 2000, KPSP received at least four customer complaints about Muth, alleging unauthorized trading, failure to execute sell orders, and/or unsuitability for margin trading, all with respect to Creative Host transactions. KPSP prohibited margin purchases of Bonso and Creative Host. In May 2000, KPSP began an internal review of Muth's sales activities. KPSP terminated the review before its completion when Muth resigned in September 2000. . . .

At the time Muth was hired, Rouse knew that Muth wanted to engage in customer margin transactions in Bonso and Creative Host, that Muth had left KPSP because KPSP no longer permitted margin transactions in those securities, and that Muth had been a "big producer" at KPSP. Muth joined Schneider based on the Firm's agreement to permit him to engage in margin transactions in Bonso and Creative Host. . . . Rouse also knew that Muth had . . . customer complaints pending at KPSP for . . . unsuitable use of margin, and refusal to effect customer sell orders as to Bonso and/or Creative Host.

When Schneider sought approval to associate Muth, several state securities regulators required that Schneider undertake heightened supervision, granted only conditional registration, or, in one instance, requested that Schneider withdraw its request. The State of Colorado Division of Securities ("CDS") required Schneider to impose heightened supervisory procedures as a condition for registering Muth. Rouse was copied on the Schneider letter, dated October 2, 2000, memorializing those procedures. Schneider stated that Rouse would be Muth's "direct supervisor" and that Rouse, among other things, would hold quarterly reviews with Muth, review his initial transactions to determine suitability, conduct daily review of Muth's transactions, and review monthly a journal of telephone calls to Colorado customers that Muth was to keep.[21]

---

21. [9] The Schneider letter stated:
(1) Muth will act only as a Series 7 registered agent conducting the majority of his business in equity securities in states in which he is registered; (2) Muth's direct supervisor is Richard J. Rouse. Muth and his supervisor will hold quarterly reviews, which will consist of daily and monthly reviews of Muth's accounts with Colorado residents and a review for excessive activity. All new accounts with Colorado residents will be reviewed and approved by Muths supervisor to determine the suitability of the transaction prior to the execution of the initial transaction; (3) All of Muth's transactions will be reviewed on a daily basis by Rouse or his designee in his absence; (4) Muth and Rouse will meet monthly to discuss the transactions during the period. Muth will maintain a journal of all conversations that result in a transaction with Colorado residents, and this journal will be reviewed and initialed by Rouse on a monthly basis; and (5) Schneider will provide the CDS any written customer complaints on Muth within fifteen days of receipt.

On January 18, 2001, one of Muth's customers, Paul V. Lundy, sent a written complaint to the Commission, accompanied by a tape of Lundy's telephone conversation with Muth. On January 31, 2001, Commission staff notified Schneider about Lundy's complaint. Driver testified that Rouse also read the letter. At a meeting held on May 10, 2001, among Muth, Driver, and members of Schneider's board of directors, including Rouse, a copy of the tape was played. Following the meeting, Schneider suspended Muth for two weeks, "which eventually led to [Muth's] termination or his resignation from the firm."

III.

Steven E. Muth

* * *

C. *Unsuitable Trading. Poljanec.*

In 2000, Poljanec [Muth's customer] was seventy-five years old. Her only sources of income were Social Security and her husband's pension. On October 25, 2000, she transferred her account from KPSP to Schneider. She signed but did not fill out the requested information on the Schneider new account form. Neither Muth nor anyone else at Schneider ever discussed with her the financial and risk tolerance information that Schneider recorded on the form. The resulting new account form inflated her income and misstated her investment objectives and risk tolerance.[22]

Poljanec's investment goals were "very conservative."[23] Prior to transferring her account to Schneider, Poljanec was "very stressed out." She was caring for her husband and sister both of whom had been suffering from Alzheimer's disease.[24] When Poljanec transferred her account to Schneider in October 2000, "the bills were mounting up." As Muth knew, Poljanec's husband had entered a nursing home that cost at least $3,000 per month, so she "didn't want to take any risks." Poljanec depended on Muth because she did "not understand the stock market that well."

Cassidy. Muth was aware that Cassidy [Muth's customer] suffered from cardiac-related medical problems. Although Muth effected trades for Cassidy in December, Cassidy did not sign a blank Schneider new account form until January 31, 2001. He did not complete the information on the form. No one at Schneider, including Muth, asked him about his risk tolerance or about any other information on the form. Cassidy stated that the risk tolerance information entered on the form inflated his will-

---

22. [42] The new account form overstated her annual income by approximately 100% (it stated "$70,000+"), incorrectly set forth her investment objectives as including fifty percent speculation and thirty percent aggressive growth, and incorrectly set forth her risk tolerance as fifty percent maximum risk, thirty percent high risk, and twenty percent businessman's risk.

23. [43] Poljanec testified that her net worth was $300,000, which included her house, and that her liquid net worth was $40,000.

24. [44] In addition, in 1998, her daughter (Tena Saltzman) had brain surgery, and her grandson was attending Columbine High School at the time of the 1999 shooting tragedy.

ingness to accept risks.[25] Cassidy executed a margin agreement on January 18, 2001. The handwritten words, "Doesn't Qualify," appear at the top.

Nabozniak. Nabozniak [Muth's customer] "did not like high risk." Muth took over Nabozniak's account … and knew that Nabozniak had a medium risk tolerance.[26] Nabozniak understood that margin trading was risky and initially refused to trade on margin based on a previous bad experience with margin. However, Muth gained Nabozniak's trust and convinced Nabozniak that "you can't make money unless you go on margin."

When Nabozniak transferred his account to Schneider from KPSP in October 2000, he owned positions in Bonso and Creative Host, had a margin balance of more than $5,500, and his account had a total value of more than $28,000. While he received a new account form, Nabozniak did not complete the form or sign it. However, someone at Schneider completed the form despite the absence of Nabozniak's signature. Because of pressures at work, Nabozniak did not review the resulting account form or his account statements in detail. However, at the hearing, Nabozniak stated that the risk tolerance information was overstated.[27]

Lundy. Lundy [Muth's customer] was retired. He did not want to engage in margin transactions. When Lundy opened his account, he signed a blank new account form, but he did not sign a margin agreement. Lundy testified that the liquid net worth figure was somewhat overstated.[28] According to Driver's notes, at the May 10, 2001 meeting between Muth and the Schneider board to review Lundy's tape of his conversation with Muth, Muth admitted that the transaction was not suitable for Lundy.

* * *

A salesperson's recommendations "must be suitable for the client in light of the client's investment objectives, as determined by the client's financial situation and

---

25. [45] Because of his health problems, Cassidy did not want to invest in speculative securities. Cassidy testified that the risk tolerance breakdown of fifty percent businessman's risk, thirty percent high risk, and twenty percent maximum risk was "too high. I'm too old to get in that much risk." Cassidy's net worth was $535,000, and his annual income and liquid net worth were accurately described as $40–45,000 and $25,000, respectively.

26. [47] Nabozniak typically invested only "very small amounts of money" in speculative stocks, which he traded with Muth at previous firms.

27. [49] The form claimed that Nabozniak's risk tolerance was fifty percent maximum risk, thirty percent high risk, and twenty percent "businessman's risk." The record does not indicate whether Nabozniak's financial information (net worth—$500,000+, annual income—$80,000+, or liquid net worth—$50,000+) was accurate.

28. [50] Lundy's new account form stated that he had a $250,000 net worth; $50,000 in income, and $90,000 liquid net worth.

Muth notes that Lundy was a securities broker for approximately two years in the late 1950s. We do not believe that this fact, alone, makes the otherwise unsuitable transaction in 2000 in Lundy's account suitable.

needs." A salesperson's unsuitable recommendations violate the antifraud provisions of the securities laws if (i) the recommended securities were unsuited to the customer's needs; (ii) the salesperson knew that his recommendations were unsuitable or acted recklessly regarding their suitability in making them; and (iii) the salesperson made material misrepresentations or failed to disclose material information relating to the suitability of the securities, including the associated risks.

Muth admits that Bonso and Creative Host were highly speculative securities. He nonetheless urged his customers to purchase them, although these stocks were not consistent with the customers' investment needs. Poljanec, Cassidy, Lundy, and Nabozniak were each more than sixty years old, and only Nabozniak still was working. Poljanec, Cassidy, and Lundy had relatively modest financial profiles. Poljanec, Cassidy, and Nabozniak were unsophisticated. These customers wanted to pursue relatively conservative investment strategies. Poljanec told Muth that she needed money for her husband's medical treatment. Muth knew that Cassidy had serious cardiac disease. Nabozniak had only moderate risk tolerance and was hoping to retire. At his meeting with the Schneider board, Muth admitted that the transactions in Lundy's account were not suitable for Lundy.

Muth increased the risks to these customers by recommending that they purchase these speculative securities on margin. Poljanec and Lundy told Muth that they did not want the risk of margin or did not want to make additional purchases on margin. Muth misrepresented material facts to persuade his customers that there was no risk to purchasing on margin at Schneider, claiming that the price of the stock would rise substantially or that their accounts would not be subject to margin calls.

While Muth suggests that the customers' account documents demonstrate that they were suitable for purchasing these securities on margin, none of the customers completed the information reported in their account forms. Nabozniak did not even sign his account form. The information Schneider inserted subsequent to receiving customers' signatures inflated the customers' financial information and/or risk tolerance. Many of these customers did not understand the mechanics of margin. Some customers did not sign margin agreements until after margin purchases were made, and at least one customer never signed any margin agreement. Muth gave these customers a false sense of security by misleading them regarding the adverse impact of margin trading on their accounts.

Muth claims that the investments were suitable for these customers because they had previously purchased Creative Host and/or Bonso on margin. This fact did not give Muth a license to disregard his customers' current financial situation or investment objectives. Muth failed to fulfill his responsibility to ensure that his customers, on a current basis, fully understood the risks involved and were both able and willing to take those risks.

* * *

Accordingly, we find that Muth, by making material misstatements and omissions and engaging in unauthorized and unsuitable trades, willfully violated Securities Act Section 17(a), Exchange Act Section 10(b), and Exchange Act Rule 10b-5.

Notes and Questions

→ Yes

1. In *E.F. Hutton*, did the court basically allow broker-dealers to commit fraud? If plaintiff's version of the facts is taken as true, didn't the broker-dealer commit *→ Yes* fraud by making material misrepresentations? Is it equitable to allow broker-dealers to orally make statements that contradict the offering materials that the broker-dealers use to sell securities to investors and then blame the investors by *→ No* stating that their reliance was unreasonable? Did the Court rule this way because *→ Perhaps* this was a private cause of action, not a regulatory enforcement action? Shouldn't the burden be on the expert — the broker-dealer — to determine suitability for the customer of the securities that she is recommending? *→ Yes*

---

1. FINRA Rule 2111. Suitability

FINRA Rule 2111 requires the broker-dealer to have a clear understanding of both the security and investment strategy that it recommends to its customer.

> FINRA Rule 2111(a). A member or an associated person must have a reasonable basis to believe that a recommended transaction or investment strategy involving a security or securities is suitable for the customer, based on the information obtained through the reasonable diligence of the member or associated person to ascertain the customer's investment profile. A customer's investment profile includes, but is not limited to, the customer's age, other investments, financial situation and needs, tax status, investment objectives, investment experience, investment time horizon, liquidity needs, risk tolerance, and any other information the customer may disclose to the member or associated person in connection with such recommendation.

FINRA Rule 2111 is only triggered when the broker-dealer makes a recommendation and applies on a recommendation-by-recommendation basis. The term *recommendation* is not defined in the rule. According to FINRA, determining when a recommendation is made that causes the application of FINRA Rule 2111 is based on "a flexible facts and circumstances approach." In addition, the rule applies to both specific securities and investment strategies, as well as potential customers if the recommendation causes the customer to take action, e.g., purchase the recommended security or comply with the recommended investment strategy.

The term "investment strategy" is also not defined in the rule, but FINRA asserts that the term should be interpreted broadly. Moreover, FINRA states that FINRA Rule 2111 is triggered when the broker-dealer recommends a strategy regardless of whether the recommendation results in a transaction. FINRA Notice 11-02 states that "the rule recognizes that customers may rely on firms' and associated persons' investment expertise and knowledge, and it is thus appropriate to hold … [them] responsible for the recommendations … regardless of whether those recommendations result in transactions or generate transaction-based compensation." However, certain categories of investment education material are exempted under the rule, including general financial information about the basic concept of investing and descriptive information about an employer-sponsored retirement or benefit plan. This exemption also includes interactive investment materials that incorporate such educational material.

FINRA Rule 2111 does not require proof of scienter but enumerates three obligations of broker-dealers and their associated persons. The obligations are: (1) Reasonable basis suitability (know your security/investment strategy); (2) Customer-specific suitability; and (3) Quantitative suitability (churning). Reasonable basis suitability requires the broker-dealer to have an understanding of the potential risks and rewards of a security or strategy that it recommends to its customers. Failure to have such an understanding violates the rule. Specifically, reasonable-basis suitability requires the broker-dealer "to have a reasonable basis to believe, based on reasonable diligence, that the recommendation is suitable for at least *some* investors. Although the rule does not define reasonable diligence, it does identify factors that may be used in determining what constitutes reasonable diligence with respect to a particular security or investment strategy: (1) complexity; (2) risk; and (3) the broker-dealers or its associated person's familiarity with the security or investment strategy. Customer-specific suitability requires the broker-dealer to have a reasonable basis to believe that the recommendation is suitable for a particular customer based on that customer's investment profile. To ascertain the customer's investment profile, the rule requires the broker-dealer to obtain and analyze certain customer-specific factors. *See* Figure 11.3. However, if the broker-dealer determines that one or more of these factors are

---

Figure 11.3. Customer-Specific Factors

- Age
- Other Investments
- Financial Situation and Needs
- Tax Status
- Investment Objectives
- Investment Experience
- Investment Time Horizon
- Liquidity Needs
- Risk Tolerance
- Any Other Information the Customer May Disclose to the Broker-Dealer or Associated Person in Connection with such Recommendation

---

not relevant to the customer's investment profile, it must document this assessment with specificity. Customer-specific suitability also requires the broker-dealer to have a reasonable basis to believe that the customer has the financial ability to purchase the recommended security or to engage in the recommended investment strategy. Essentially, the broker-dealer is required to use reasonable diligence to acquire a thorough understanding of the customer's personal and financial circumstances in order to recommend a suitable security or investment strategy. The last obligation, quantitative suitability, prohibits excessive trading and expressly identifies the annual turnover ratio and cost-to-equity ratio as measurements to establish excessive trading by the broker-dealer in a customer's account. Excessive trading, along with churning, was examined in section II.A.1 of this chapter.

Michael Frederick Siegel

Exchange Act Rel. No. 58737

2008 SEC LEXIS 2459 (Oct. 6, 2008)

OPINION OF THE COMMISSION

REGISTERED SECURITIES ASSOCIATION—

REVIEW OF DISCIPLINARY PROCEEDINGS

I.

Michael Frederick Siegel, formerly a general securities representative associated with Rauscher Pierce Refsnes, Inc. ("Rauscher"), an NASD [nka FINRA] member firm, appeals from NASD disciplinary action.... NASD ... found that Siegel made unsuitable recommendations to two couples in violation of NASD Conduct Rules 2310 [now FINRA Rule 2111] and 2110 [now FINRA Rule 2010].... We base our findings on an independent review of the record.

II.

Siegel's Involvement with World Environmental Technologies, Inc.

Siegel has been registered as a general securities representative since 1981 and was associated with Rauscher from October 24, 1997 until June 16, 1999. At the beginning of 1997, Siegel met World Environmental Technologies, Inc. ("World ET") president, Jim Finkenkeller, and the chairman of World ET's board, Tom Denmark, to discuss a business opportunity. During several meetings with Finkenkeller and Denmark over the next three or four months, Siegel learned that World ET recently had been founded to offer antibacterial services to the poultry and swine industry and intended to acquire the rights to an odor-eradicating product called "Nok-Out."

Sometime in late 1997, Siegel agreed to become a director of World ET and to raise capital for the Nok-Out venture. He believed that, as a director, he would be well positioned to be selected for the company's potential initial public offering. In a letter dated October 22, 1997, Finkenkeller informed Siegel that World ET immediately required Siegel's fundraising efforts in connection with, among other things, fulfilling a "$200,000 commitment" and obtaining "operating capital" and that Siegel could show his "investors" a "small job" that World ET was to perform at the end of the month.

On November 24, 1997, Siegel requested in writing permission from Rauscher to serve as a director of World ET. Siegel represented that he was not recommending World ET securities to his customers. Rauscher granted Siegel permission to serve as a director but informed Siegel that he would "not be able to effect transactions in the securities of World [ET]...." At the hearing, Siegel testified that his supervisor, Scott Grandbouche, told him that it was highly unlikely that Rauscher would ever approve a Rauscher registered representative selling unregistered securities. Rauscher never approved Siegel's offer or sale of World ET securities.

On December 6, 1997, Finkenkeller sent Siegel a draft employment agreement that provided that Siegel would use his best efforts to obtain, by March 31, 1998, at least $15 million to fund World ET's "development and operations" in exchange for payments of cash and stock. Siegel signed the agreement in January 1998. In the executed agreement, Siegel substituted his home address for his office address for the purpose of receipt of all "notices, demands, and requests" under the agreement ("Notice Provision"). Grandbouche testified that all mail received through the firm was opened and reviewed by administrative personnel before being delivered to a registered representative. Siegel never informed Rauscher about his employment agreement with World ET....

Siegel's Dealings with the Downers

Huntington and Linda Downer had been investing with Siegel since 1993.[29] Siegel had discretion over their account. Over time, Siegel invested their funds in a combination of fixed-income products, mutual funds, and stock.[30] The Downers testified that they had invested mainly in certificates of deposit prior to investing with Siegel and "looked to him for financial guidance."

In early November 1997, Siegel visited the Downers' home to discuss their account, as he had done routinely since they began investing with him. During the visit, Siegel brought up World ET. He told the Downers that World ET was a new company and that he was going to invest in the company. Siegel also told the Downers that World ET planned on acquiring the rights to "Nok-Out." He said that he was very excited about the formula (which he described to them) and gave them a sample of "Nok-Out" to use on their cat's litter box. Based on Siegel's representation that he was investing in World ET, Huntington Downer asked Siegel to contact the company to inquire about any investment opportunities for the Downers. Following the visit, Siegel spoke with Finkenkeller or Denmark who informed him that the Downers could invest $300,000 in World IEQ Technologies, Inc. ("World IEQ"), purportedly a subsidiary of World ET. Siegel conveyed this information to the Downers who asked him to obtain the relevant paperwork on their behalf.

On November 24, 1997, Siegel visited the Downers a second time and brought with him several documents related to World IEQ. The World IEQ subscription agreement provided that the subscriber waived the right to receive a document "typically called a Prospectus or Private Placement Memorandum." It also provided that a subscriber's $300,300 investment would purchase a 120-day debenture for $300,000 plus 300,000 shares of World IEQ common stock for $300 at $0.001/share. The World IEQ questionnaire, in contrast, requested that the subscriber confirm the purchase of a 365-day debenture for $300,000 plus 300,000 shares of "Class Common Stock"

---

29. [5] Huntington Downer earned $150,000 annually as a legislator and focused on finance and budget issues. Downer previously had been a partner in a law firm. Linda Downer, his wife, had no separate income. The Downers had a net worth of approximately $1.5-2.0 million, excluding their home

30. [6] The Downers relied on the income generated from their investments and sought growth and income as their investment objective.

without specifying a price. The documents contained no information regarding an interest rate or repayment terms for the debenture.

Siegel testified that he did not review or analyze any of the documents. Without completing any blank sections or discussing the contents of the documents with Siegel, Huntington Downer signed and returned to Siegel the World IEQ subscription agreement and the World IEQ questionnaire. Huntington Downer testified that he often signed documents that Siegel provided without reviewing them or questioning Siegel.[31] Linda Downer gave Siegel a personal check made payable to World IEQ in the amount of $300,300. She testified that, "I know that sounds really strange to invest $300,000 [sic] in something that you know nothing about, but ... I trusted [Siegel] to do whatever." Siegel faxed the forms to World ET.

Shortly thereafter, the Downers decided to pay for the World IEQ investment by using funds from their Rauscher account instead of paying with the check that Linda Downer wrote and which was never negotiated. Siegel provided, and the Downers signed, a letter dated November 28, 1997 that authorized him to wire $300,300 from their Rauscher account to a World IEQ bank account in Texas. Rauscher effected the wire transfer on December 1, 1997.

Approximately one or two weeks later, Finkenkeller called Siegel and told him that the Downers could no longer invest in World IEQ and had the option of receiving a refund or investing in World ET. Siegel conveyed this information to the Downers. When Huntington Downer asked Siegel for advice on how to decide, Siegel stated that he "would rather be in the mother company if [he] had a choice." The Downers told Siegel that they opted to invest in World ET. Siegel was the Downers' only source of information regarding their decision to invest in World IEQ and World ET.

Siegel's Contacts with the Landrys

Dorothy and Barry Landry opened a Rauscher account with Siegel in November 1997 based on a referral by Huntington Downer. The Landrys vested Siegel with discretion over their account. The Landrys sought to increase the return on $1 million that they acquired from the recent sale of their healthcare business. Siegel told them that he subsequently might recommend that they invest in higher-risk, start-up companies.

Later that month, Siegel visited the Landrys' home to complete some follow-up paperwork regarding their new account and to discuss their portfolio. Siegel raised the topic of World ET, stating that he thought it was something in which they might be interested and that he wanted them "to take a look at" the company. Siegel told them that World ET was a new company that intended to introduce Nok-Out to the poultry and swine industry and that he and the Downers were investing "three times" the minimum investment amount in the company.

---

31. [7] For example, Huntington Downer testified, "Mr. Siegel was my friend. He would come to my house. He would give me recommendations. Whatever he said, whatever he put in front of me, I signed. I trusted him implicitly. I never once filled out any forms, to the best of my recollection. He filled out whatever and showed me where to sign, and I signed."

The Landrys testified that, while Siegel did not pressure them to invest, he did "promote the benefits of [Nok-Out]" and assure them that "this looked like a really good deal." For example, Dorothy Landry testified that Siegel told them that Nok-Out "looked like a product that … is going to be needed" and "is going to have lots of sales," that it "could be global," that "the opportunities existed to get in on the ground floor," and that "distribution is going to be coast-to-coast almost immediately because of the nature of the poultry and swine industries." Barry Landry testified that Siegel told them that he "knew of a company [i.e., World ET] that was on its ground floor getting started up and might be a nice place to invest some money," and that "it looked like a good idea." Dorothy Landry testified that Siegel told the couple that the minimum investment amount was $100,000 and that they could get their money back in as little as ninety days or perhaps one year.

Dorothy Landry asked Siegel to call World ET to determine whether any investment opportunity existed. Siegel said he would be "glad to" and called Denmark when he returned to his office. After speaking with Denmark, Siegel told the Landrys that they could invest in World ET.

On a subsequent visit a couple of weeks later, Siegel gave the Landrys a folder containing World ET documents and including Siegel's Rauscher business cards. Siegel testified that he did not review the documents or discuss them with the Landrys. A World ET subscription agreement provided that a subscriber could invest in a debenture at $100,000 per "unit" and would waive the right to receive a document "typically called a Prospectus or Private Placement Memorandum." A World ET strategic plan described World ET's first-year plan to provide odor- and bacteria-combating services to the swine industry, with a "[s]econdary focus" in the poultry industry. Siegel also gave the Landrys a World ET outline and a World ET "pro forma summary information" statement that contained conflicting repayment terms. None of the documents contained information about an interest rate or a maturity date for the debenture.

On Siegel's advice, the Landrys kept the documents to review for a couple of months before making a decision on whether to invest in World ET. Dorothy Landry testified that Siegel's planned investment in World ET led them to the conclusion that, "if [Siegel] was interested in it, consider it solid." The Landrys testified that learning from Siegel that the Downers had invested in World ET further validated their decision to invest.

On February 5, 1998, the Landrys faxed to Rauscher and Siegel a request to wire transfer $100,000 from their Rauscher account to their joint bank account with Hibernia National Bank, which Rauscher effected on that same day. On February 11, 1998, the Landrys gave the signed World ET subscription agreement and a $100,000 check made payable to World ET to Siegel, who sent them to World ET. World ET negotiated the check. Siegel was the Landrys' only source of information about World ET prior to making their investment decision.

World ET Goes Out of Business

Pursuant to an arbitration decision rendered on August 28, 2002, World ET lost the rights to Nok-Out because World ET defaulted on payments it owed to the company that had developed the product. On February 13, 2004, the Texas Secretary of State revoked World ET's corporate charter. The Downers and Landrys never received any payments of any kind on their World ET investments.

Siegel's Testimony at the Hearing

Siegel testified that he believed the Downers invested in World IEQ because he told them that he was going to invest in World ET. Siegel further testified that the World IEQ and World ET documents that he provided to the Downers and Landrys were deficient because they either lacked or contained conflicting or confusing information about details that private placement transaction documents typically specify, such as maturity dates, interest rates, and repayment terms.

Siegel conceded at the hearing that these documentary deficiencies rendered an investment in World IEQ and World ET unsuitable for the Downers, the Landrys, or any investor. For example, Siegel agreed with an NASD hearing panelist who commented at the hearing that, with respect to the World IEQ and World ET documents, "[t]his is one of the worst sets of offering documents I have ever seen in my life. I mean you can't tell what these people are investing in." Siegel also stated, "I didn't know how bad they were because I was trying to not sell away.... Had I looked over the documents, yes, I probably would have been discouraged with the company right then and there. I didn't look them over. I wish I had." Siegel did not claim at any time during the proceeding, and the record does not indicate, that his communications with Finkenkeller or Denmark or his position as a World ET director provided him any additional information about the potential risks and rewards associated specifically with a World ET investment.

* * *

Unsuitable Recommendations

Siegel Made Recommendations. NASD Conduct Rule 2310 requires that a transaction recommended by a registered representative to a customer be suitable. Whether the communication between a registered representative and a customer constitutes a recommendation is a "'facts and circumstances' inquiry to be conducted on a case-by-case basis." Such an inquiry "requires an analysis of the content, context, and presentation of the particular communication." NASD has stated that factors considered in conducting this inquiry include whether the communication "reasonably could be viewed as a 'call to action'" and "reasonably would influence an investor to trade a particular security or group of securities." For the reasons set forth below, we find that Siegel's communications with the Downers and the Landrys constitute recommendations.

The nature of the relationship between Siegel and his customers, their reliance on him, the nature of the specific conversations, and Siegel's initiation of the subject of World ET are the main factors supporting a finding that Siegel made recommendations. Siegel visited the Downers' home in November 1997 to discuss their portfolio. Siegel raised the topic of investing in World ET during that discussion. The Downers had never heard of World ET. Siegel was the Downers' sole source of information about the company. He told the Downers that he was very excited about Nok-Out.

Siegel also told the Downers that he was going to invest in the company. The Downers had sought Siegel's investment guidance for three years and routinely deferred to his decisions without question. Siegel admitted that he believed the couple invested in World ET because he told them that he planned on investing in the company. Siegel claims that his communications with the Downers were merely conversations about World ET, but we disagree.

Siegel made further inquiries, obtained and conveyed information, and facilitated execution of subscription documents and payment for the purchase of World IEQ shares. After Siegel informed the Downers that it was no longer possible to invest in World IEQ, he advised them to invest in World ET rather than receive a refund on their World IEQ investment, stating that he "would rather be in the mother company if [he] had a choice." Siegel admits that he could have refused Huntington Downer's request to obtain additional information about investing in World ET.

With respect to the Landrys, Siegel raised the topic of investing in World ET while reviewing their portfolio. He was the Landrys' sole source of information about the company prior to making their investment decision. Siegel told the Landrys that he and the Downers were investing "three times" the minimum investment amount in the company. The Landrys testified that the knowledge that Siegel and the Downers also were investing in World ET comforted them. He gave them glowing projections about its potential success. Siegel made encouraging statements about the investment and proceeded on behalf of the Landrys to make further inquiries, obtain and convey information, deliver documents, return executed originals, and facilitate payment to World ET.

We find that Siegel's conduct constitutes a recommendation because it was a "call to action" that reasonably influenced the Downers and the Landrys to invest in World ET. The Downers and the Landrys relied on Siegel for investment advice. Within the context of Siegel's visits to the Downers and the Landrys to provide such advice, he introduced them to World ET, made encouraging statements about investing in World ET, and facilitated his customers' overall investments.

Siegel's Arguments. Siegel contends that the NAC improperly found that he made a recommendation to the Downers "only by ignoring key evidence." In support of that argument, he claims that the Downers "were able to distinguish a recommendation — a 'call to action' — from the mere mention of a company in personal conversation" because they are "among the most sophisticated investors under the law" and thus able to "fend for themselves." However, while sophistication of the investor may be relevant, sophistication alone does not mean that a communication is not a recommendation. Siegel did not merely mention World ET to the Downers. He repeatedly provided the Downers with positive details about the company and associated investment opportunities during ongoing conversations that began in the context of his periodic review of their investments.... Siegel provided significant information and assistance to the Downers in making their investment in World ET while it was a nonpublic company, including encouraging them to invest in World ET after learning they could not invest in World IEQ.

Siegel's Recommendations Were Unsuitable. NASD Conduct Rule 2310 requires that, in recommending a transaction to a customer, a registered representative "shall have reasonable grounds for believing that the recommendation is suitable for such customer upon the basis of the facts, if any, disclosed by such customer as to his other security holdings and as to his financial situation and needs." The suitability rule thus requires that, before making a customer-specific suitability determination, a registered representative must first have an "adequate and reasonable basis" for believing that the recommendation could be suitable for at least some customers. The reasonableness of any recommendation is predicated on a registered representative's understanding of "the potential risks and rewards inherent in that recommendation." We have stated that "a broker may violate the suitability rule if he fails so fundamentally to comprehend the consequences of his own recommendation that such recommendation is unsuitable for any investor, regardless of the investor's wealth, willingness to bear risk, age, or other individual characteristics."

The record establishes, and Siegel does not dispute, that he had no basis, and certainly not a reasonable and adequate basis, for believing that his recommendations regarding an investment in World IEQ and World ET could be suitable for at least some customers. Siegel testified that he did not read any of the World IEQ and World ET documents that he provided to the Downers and the Landrys.

Even if Siegel had read them, he would not have had a reasonable basis for recommending World ET securities. Siegel admitted at the hearing that the World IEQ and World ET documents that he provided to the Downers and the Landrys were deficient: they either lacked or contained conflicting or confusing information about details that private placement transaction documents typically specify, such as maturity dates, interest rates, and repayment terms. Siegel agreed with a Panelist's comment at the hearing that the material provided to the Downers and the Landrys was "one of the worst sets of offering documents" he had ever seen and that "you can't tell what these people are investing in." During the exchange with the Panelist, Siegel further testified that, had he reviewed the documents, he "probably would have been discouraged with the company right then and there." Siegel also conceded at the hearing that the deficiencies in the documents rendered an investment in World IEQ and World ET unsuitable for the Downers, the Landrys, or any investor, particularly because there was no other information on which a prospective investor could rely to make an investment decision.[32]

The next case focuses on the broker-dealer's customer-specific suitability obligation. How does this obligation differ from the reasonable basis obligation of FINRA Rule 2111? ↘ *More focus on the "fit."*

---

32. [26] Because we have determined that Siegel did not have a reasonable basis for his recommendation of World ET, we do not address whether World ET was suitable for the Downers and the Landrys based upon their personal situations.

Dept. of Enforcement v. Wall Street Strategies, Inc.

Disc. Proceeding No. 2012033508702 (Sept. 15, 2015)

I. Introduction

In July 2012, RR, President of a FINRA member firm, received a letter, unsigned but with a signature block with "Karl L. Kittlaus" typed underneath and a letterhead reading "ALTERNATIVE INVESTMENTS COMPANY." The letter contained a pitch for "alternative investments" and invitation to attend "our next dinner meeting." Attached to the letter were two pages describing "Renewable Secured Debentures" issued by GWG Holdings, Inc.

Enforcement learned that Karl L. Kittlaus was registered with FINRA member firm Wall Street Strategies, Inc. ("WSSI" or the "Firm"). In the ensuing investigation, Enforcement concluded that Kittlaus was responsible for sending the letter to RR. Enforcement also learned that WSSI, through Garry Savage, the Firm's President, Chief Executive Officer, and Chief Compliance Officer, had recommended a high-risk alternative investment to a number of customers. The recommendations were for registered debt instruments called Renewable Secured Debentures issued by GWG Holdings, Inc. ("GWG"). GWG purchases life insurance policies on the secondary market at a discount, pays the policy premiums, and collects the face value of the policies upon the death of the insured persons, anticipating it will collect more than it spends to buy and maintain the policies....

II. The Complaint and Answers

The Complaint describes the GWG debentures as a "high-risk, illiquid, alternative investment." From January to November 2012, the relevant period, the Complaint alleges that WSSI through Savage recommended the GWG debentures to approximately 13 WSSI customers.... [N]one [of the customers] said that the investments were unsuitable. Nonetheless, the first cause of action charges that the recommendations Savage made to nine of the customers were unsuitable based on the customers' overall investment profiles, and violated NASD Rule 2310 and FINRA Rules 2111 and 2010.

* * *

In their Answers, Respondents generally deny the charges. In response to the first cause of action, WSSI and Savage assert that (i) Savage properly reviewed the risks disclosed in the GWG debentures prospectus with all customers, (ii) the customers understood the risks, and (iii) the recommendations were suitable for them....

III. Summary of Findings

The Hearing Panel concludes that Enforcement did not establish by a preponderance of the evidence that (i) Savage's recommendations were unsuitable for the nine customers ...

* * *

V. WSSI and the GWG Renewable Secured Debentures

A. Background

In early 2012, [Savage] was looking for income-producing investments with specific maturity dates that offered a better rate of return than was available from certificates of deposit. Sometime in January 2012, Savage saw information about GWG's renewable secured debentures offering, and he contacted a company field representative to ask for a due diligence package. Reviewing the package, Savage noted that GWG had a brief operating history and that the offering was a speculative, high-risk investment. Nonetheless, he went on to learn that GWG offered debentures with differing maturity dates and interest rates, which Savage thought would fit the needs of some clients. In addition, Savage had experience with life insurance and liked the fact that the GWG debentures are "backed by life insurance policies."

Savage's due diligence review included attending a two-day meeting at the company's headquarters in Minneapolis and meeting with a local GWG representative who came to Savage's office. Savage reviewed the company's SEC filings and proxy statements and spoke with GWG's president when he had questions about particular risks. Savage informed himself of the value of the life insurance policies GWG purchased and determined that the liquidation value of the policies was sufficient to repay investors if the company were to go out of business. He also reviewed a third-party valuation of the policies and familiarized himself with DZ Bank, which had extended a $100 million line of credit to GWG.

B. Underwriting

On March 5, 2012, Savage signed a participating dealer agreement with FINRA member firm Arque Capital, Ltd. ("Arque") qualifying WSSI to sell GWG Renewable Debentures. As a participating dealer, WSSI agreed to distribute only those sales materials that were authorized and provided by Arque and GWG.

GWG Holdings, Inc. is the issuer of the GWG Renewable Secured Debentures. GWG is publicly listed with the Securities and Exchange Commission ("SEC"); its SEC registration statement for the debentures became effective in January 2012, and since then it has filed periodic required financial statements with the SEC that are audited by an independent accounting firm. GWG purchases life insurance policies on the secondary market from seniors who no longer want or need them.

Arque is GWG's lead underwriter. One of Arque's responsibilities is to enlist broker-dealers to sell the debentures. GWG and Arque together assembled the due diligence package for the debentures. The package included the prospectus, GWG's audited financials for the prior three years, GWG's articles of incorporation and by-laws, the customer subscription agreement, outside counsel opinion letters, and the "Client Fact Sheet."

C. The Offering

The debentures marketed by WSSI in 2012 had maturity dates ranging from six months to seven years, with interest rates ranging from 4.75 to 9.5 percent per year for the longest maturities. GWG buys life insurance policies in the secondary market with the goal of earning returns from the policies greater than the costs required to buy, finance, and service the policies to maturity. As explained by a FINRA investigator,

> In general terms, they make money by selling the debentures and then the debentures assist in paying the premiums on the life insurance policies. And then when the people that hold the life insurance policies pass away, they'll make the value of the life insurance policy.

As described in the prospectus and summarized in a third-party due diligence report, GWG acquires life insurance policies through its wholly owned subsidiary, GWG Life Settlements, LLC, which purchases the policies. The majority of the policies are then held by GWG DLP Funding II, LLC, a direct subsidiary of GWG Life Settlements.

The first page of the prospectus issued in May 2012 contains a section titled "Suitability Standards." It explains that the debentures "are suitable only as a long-term investment for persons of adequate financial means who have no need for liquidity in this investment." It states that "it may be impossible" for an investor to resell the debentures and that to qualify to invest a prospective purchaser must have both a net worth of at least $70,000 and income of at least $70,000, or a net worth of at least $250,000, exclusive of home, furnishings, and automobiles. It warns that potential purchasers must be able to bear the risks, including lack of liquidity and loss of the entire investment. The prospectus contains a list of "Risks Relating to Forward-Looking Statements" that appear in the prospectus, followed by 14 pages enumerating in detail the risks associated with investing in the debentures.

* * *

VII. Enforcement Failed to Prove that Savage and WSSI Made Unsuitable Recommendations to Nine Customers

Enforcement alleges in the first cause of action that Savage, and the Firm through Savage, made unsuitable recommendations to nine customers by failing to take into account their financial situations and needs, including their investment objectives, investment experience and knowledge, risk tolerance, liquidity needs, age, liquid net worth, and annual income.

A. The Applicable Suitability Rules

Savage made the recommendations at issue in this case between January and November 2012. As noted above, NASD's suitability rule, NASD Rule 2310, was in effect until July 9, 2012; after that, it was replaced by FINRA Rule 2111. Although differing in language, both rules require that a broker's recommendation of an investment in securities must be suitable to the customer based on the customer's financial needs and circumstances. NASD Rule 2310(a) stated:

> In recommending to a customer the purchase, sale or exchange of any security, a member shall have *reasonable grounds* for believing that the recommendation is suitable for such customer upon the basis of the facts, if any, disclosed by such customer as to his other security holdings and as to his financial situation and needs. (Emphasis supplied.)

The more expansive but substantively similar language of FINRA Rule 2111(a) states:

> A member or an associated person must have a *reasonable basis* to believe that a recommended transaction or investment strategy involving a security or securities is suitable for the customer, based on the information obtained through the reasonable diligence of the member or associated person to ascertain the customer's investment profile. A customer's investment profile includes, but is not limited to, the customer's age, other investments, financial situation and needs, tax status, investment objectives, investment experience, investment time horizon, liquidity needs, risk tolerance, and any other information the customer may disclose to the member or associated person in connection with such recommendation. (Emphasis supplied.)

The use of the term "reasonable" in both rules is consistent with the long-established principle that implicit in the suitability rule is the "fundamental responsibility for fair dealing" inherent in all members' dealings with customers. Essentially, a recommendation must be "consistent with the customer's financial situation and needs," and the customer's best interests. Thus, a broker should make a recommendation only after considering information provided by the customer and making a "reasonable inquiry concerning the customer's investment objectives, financial situation, and needs" so that the recommendation is "not unsuitable for the customer." He must also "tailor his recommendations to the customer's financial profile and investment objectives."

Informing a customer of the risks inherent in an investment is essential, but risk disclosure alone is insufficient. A broker must make sure that a customer *understands* the risks involved in an investment, and must determine that the investment is suitable considering the customer's needs and circumstances. Furthermore, "[a] recommendation is not suitable merely because the customer acquiesces in the recommendation." Therefore, a broker must expend reasonable effort to learn a customer's "financial status, tax status, investment objectives, and any other information," such as a customer's age and investment experience, reasonably relevant to making a recommendation. When a broker fails to discuss the risks and speculative nature of a recommended investment, the customer's objectives, and the advantages and disadvantages of making an investment, and fails to make reasonable attempts to learn about the customer's financial status, tax status, and investment objectives, the broker fails to comply with fundamental suitability requirements.

A violation of the suitability rule is also a violation of FINRA Rule 2010 requiring adherence to high standards of commercial honor and just and equitable principles of trade.

* * *

1. Customers RB and PB

a. RB's Testimony

RB and PB opened accounts with WSSI in 2009, when RB was 70 and his wife was 67 years old. Their new account forms state that both are retired, but RB testified that he has practiced his profession for 40 years, and continues to operate his own small firm. When RB opened his account, he told Savage that he had 29 years of investment experience with stocks, bonds, mutual funds, and certificates of deposit. Nonetheless, he described his investment knowledge as "limited" on his account opening document because, he explained, "I don't know everything."

The couple estimated their net worth at $7.3 million, their liquid net worth at $3.1 million, and their total annual income at $149,000, although RB testified that in 2009 it was actually about $275,000. They estimated their risk tolerance at five on a scale of one to ten. On their account financial questionnaire, they described their financial goals and ranked asset protection, along with reducing taxes and increasing income, as highly important. Although their financial objectives in 2012 were not identical to their objectives in 2009, when they filled out the documents, RB testified that preservation of principal is always important to him.

After opening their WSSI account, RB and PB initially invested in fixed annuities, life insurance, and gas and oil. In 2012, they had profited from their investments, which affected their objectives. RB testified that he "was interested in making the money grow." Thus, although their investment objectives in 2009 were "Growth/with safety of principal," he testified that because they had made money from their investments, in 2012 they could make a case-by-case determination of whether or not safety of principal was the controlling objective for any particular investment. At that point, he was looking for an investment that would pay interest "similar to what bank CDs used to pay." This led him to become interested in GWG.

In the spring of 2012, when RB was 73 and PB was 70, Savage reviewed the GWG prospectus and discussed the risks with RB. RB testified that Savage pointed out the risks "time and time again." RB read the prospectus carefully and understood the risky nature of the investment. RB testified that he did not need the funds and could afford to lose what he invested in GWG.

In April 2012, RB and PB invested $75,000 in GWG renewable debentures for a six-month term at 4.75 percent interest; at the end of six months, they rolled the investment over for another six months. They received all of the interest payments and recouped their principal. RB believes that he should have continued to invest in GWG.

During the investigation of this case, FINRA staff contacted RB. RB told the staff that he and his wife had invested because they wanted to do so, and would not have invested if they could not afford to lose the entire $75,000. Long before the hearing, in March 2013, RB signed a letter that he assumed someone on Savage's staff had prepared. He testified that it states accurately that he understood the risks of investing in the GWG debentures and that the investment was suitable for him and his wife.

b. Savage's Testimony

Savage testified that he met with RB approximately once each quarter and "knew his entire financial position." Savage testified that he advised RB fully of the speculative nature and the risks of GWG. Based upon the couple's liquidity, assets, investment objectives and financial condition, Savage believed their investment in GWG was suitable.

c. Discussion

The Complaint alleges that Savage's recommendation to RB and PB was unsuitable because "their account documents listed their investment knowledge as limited, risk tolerance as moderate, and investment objectives as accumulation of retirement capital and preservation of principal." Enforcement notes that RB was 73 when he invested. Because his investment objectives were safety of principal and long-term growth, Enforcement argues that the couple sought a safe investment, like a bank CD. Enforcement notes that the GWG debentures "satisfied none of these" objectives and were "inconsistent with [RB's] objectives, investment experience, and risk tolerance."

RB, however, testified convincingly that he invested in the debentures because he wanted to do so; he would not have invested if he could not afford to lose the entire amount; and he was fully aware that he could lose the funds. He stated: "[I]f I have money that I'm going to invest and I know I can lose all of it and I can afford to lose all of it and I want to invest in it, that's what I do."

RB's high net worth, substantial liquid net worth, and significant income support RB's testimony that the couple could afford to lose the funds they invested in the debentures. Furthermore, although their account documents indicate that they had limited investment knowledge, RB had a 29-year history of investing in stocks, bonds, and mutual funds.

RB and PB were not unsophisticated investors who were steered into unduly speculative investments that were contrary to their objectives and interests. The evidence establishes that Savage reviewed the prospectus with them at length and disclosed the risks and speculative nature of the debentures; they understood the risks when they invested; and they made a reasoned decision that investing in the debentures was consistent with their investment objectives. Investing in GWG was what they wanted to do with a relatively small portion of their available capital.

For these reasons, the Hearing Panel finds that Enforcement failed to establish by a preponderance of the evidence that Savage's recommendation of GWG debentures to RB and PB was unsuitable. [The hearing panel went on to find that Enforcement failed to establish by a preponderance of the evidence that Savage's recommendations to all nine customers were suitable.]

———

FINRA Rule 2111(b) provides an exemption to customer-specific suitability for institutional customers[33] if certain conditions are met. The broker-dealer must doc-

---

33. FINRA Rule 4512(c) defines an institutional account as: (1) a bank, savings and loan association, insurance company or registered investment company; (2) an investment adviser registered either with the SEC under Section 203 of the Investment Advisers Act or with a state securities commission (or any agency or office performing like functions); or (3) any other person (whether a natural person, corporation, partnership, trust or otherwise) with total assets of at least $50 million.

ument that it has a reasonable basis to believe that the institutional customer is capable of evaluating investment risks independently. Also, the institutional customer must affirmatively indicate that it is exercising independent judgment in evaluating the broker-dealer's recommendations. The institutional customer may indicate that it is exercising independent judgment on a trade-by-trade basis, on an asset-class-by-asset-class basis, or with respect to all potential transactions for its account. This exemption only applies to the broker-dealer's customer-specific suitability obligation. The broker-dealer must continue to meet its reasonable-basis suitability and quantitative suitability obligations.

Notes and Questions

1. *FINRA Rule 2090. Know Your Customer.* The know-your-customer obligation requires the broker-dealer to use "reasonable diligence, in regard to the opening and maintenance of every account, to know (and retain) the essential facts concerning every customer and concerning the authority of each person acting on behalf of such customer." Supplementary Material .01 defines essential facts as those required to (a) effectively service the customer's account, (b) act in accordance with any special handling instructions for the account, (c) understand the authority of each person acting on behalf of the customer, and (d) comply with applicable laws, regulations, and rules. The know-your-customer obligation does not depend on whether the broker-dealer has made a recommendation and starts at the beginning of the broker-dealer's relationship with its customer.

2. *Investment Strategy and Asset Allocation Models.* Supplementary Material .03 under FINRA Rule 2111 exempts asset allocation models from the term investment strategy if they are "(i) based on generally accepted investment theory, (ii) accompanied by disclosures of all material facts and assumptions that may affect a reasonable investor's assessment of the asset allocation model or any report generated by such model, and (iii) in compliance with FINRA Rule 2214 (Requirements for the Use of Investment Analysis Tools) if the asset allocation model is an 'investment analysis tool' covered by Rule 2214."

3. *Customer's Best Interests.* In interpreting FINRA Rule 2111, many cases explicitly hold that a broker-dealer's recommendations must be consistent with its customers' best interests. FINRA Regulatory Notice 12-25 provides many examples of the type of conduct that violates the suitability rule because the broker-dealer has placed its interests ahead of its customers' interests, including: (1) recommending one product over another to receive larger commissions; (2) recommending the purchase of promissory notes to provide money to use in the broker-dealer's business; and (3) recommending margin trading so that the broker-dealer could purchase larger numbers of securities in order to increase its commissions.

4. *Implicit Recommendations.* FINRA Rule 2111 applies to implicit recommendations. An implicit recommendation occurs when a broker-dealer effects transactions on

a customer's behalf without telling the customer. This unauthorized trade is considered an implicit recommendation and violates FINRA Rule 2111. However, FINRA Rule 2111 does not apply to implicit recommendations to hold a security, e.g., when the broker-dealer remains silent with respect to security positions in a customer's account. Only explicit hold recommendations are covered by the rule. *See Paul C. Kettler*, 51 S.E.C. 30, 32 n.11 (1992).

5. *Recommendations to Customers in OTC Equity Securities.* FINRA Rule 2114 prohibits recommendations that a customer purchase or sell short any OTC equity security (defined in FINRA Rule 6420), unless the broker-dealer has reviewed the issuer's current financial statements and current material business information and determined from this information that the broker-dealer has a reasonable basis for making such a recommendation. Current financial statements must include a balance sheet and income statement. Current material business information must include "information that is ascertainable through the reasonable exercise of professional diligence and that a reasonable person would take into account in reaching an investment decision." The employee conducting the required review must be registered as a General Securities Principal or General Securities Sales Supervisor (or be subject to their supervision) and must have the skills, background, and knowledge to conduct the review. The reviews conducted under this rule must be documented and documentation must include the information reviewed, the date, and the name of the person performing the review. Institutional accounts [FINRA Rule 4512(c)] and certain other transactions are exempted from the requirements of this rule. *See* FINRA Rule 2114(e).

Hypothetical Two

Jeremy Berman has recently joined Success First as a registered representative at its headquarters in NYC. Berman has been in the securities business for some time and brought customers with him from his previous broker-dealer employer. One of these customers is Anita Jones. Ms. Jones opened her account with Berman when he worked for another broker-dealer. At the time that Ms. Jones opened her account with Berman at his previous employer, she was 47 years old with no dependents and had impaired vision. Ms. Jones attended high school for three years. A psychological evaluation performed subsequent to the opening of her account with Berman to assess her intellectual, academic, and emotional abilities revealed that she could read at the fourth-grade level and perform arithmetic at a beginning sixth-grade level. After Ms. Jones left school, she worked as a keypunch operator at several companies for nine years. However, she has not worked during the last five years. Ms. Jones has limited securities investment experience. Her father opened her account for her with Berman to provide income for Ms. Jones in the event of his death. Ms. Jones' father made all of the investment decisions in her account. Although Ms. Jones' father tried to teach her about the stock market, Ms. Jones had difficulty grasping the concepts. Ms. Jones' father died last year. After the death of Ms. Jones' father, Berman opened a margin account on her behalf. At the time, Ms. Jones reported annual income of approximately $30,000 and a net worth of $300,000. She derived her income from interest on bank accounts, an investment in a parking garage, and Social Security. Ms. Jones' new account form at Berman's previous employer reported her investment objective was long-term growth. When Berman arrived at Success First, the market value of Ms. Jones account was $208,495. After Berman's arrival at Success First, Berman opened a margin account and begin trading heavily in Ms. Jones' account during a period of 11 months. At Success First, Ms. Jones' investment objective on her new account form was changed to aggressive growth. Ms. Jones said that she had a hard time reading the new account form before she signed it. Ms. Jones also gave Mr. Berman discretionary authority over the trading in her account.

At Success First, Berman made 59 purchases and 80 sales, the majority of which involved repeated purchases and sales of the same securities. For example, on March 20 Berman sold 100 shares of Boeing stock in Ms. Jones' account and on March 30 he purchased 500 shares of Boeing stock. Two weeks later, Berman sold 500 shares of Boeing. He purchased another 500 shares of Boeing stock on May 7, which he sold on May 18. Berman also actively traded options in Ms. Jones' account, usually buying call options shortly before the expiration date. By the time Ms. Jones closed her account, it was worth only $594.63. Ms. Jones' account generated total gross commissions of $76,362.51, margin interest of $11,295.81, and a realized loss of $1,999,719.17. Are Berman's transactions in Ms. Jones' account suitable? Has Berman violated § 10(b) and Rule 10b-5 of the Exchange Act along with FINRA Rule 2111?

E. Market Manipulation

Market manipulation occurs when the price of a security is not determined by the natural interplay of supply and demand and violates the antifraud provisions of the federal securities acts. It is accomplished by injecting inaccurate information into the market or by creating a false impression of market activity through deceptive trading activities. Broker-dealers, as major market participants, have singular opportunities to engage in market manipulation by engaging in deceptive trading activities. The types of deceptive trading activities are myriad and limited only by the imagination of broker-dealers and their associated persons. Deceptive trading activities include wash sales, matched orders, pump-and-dump, and marking the close. *See* Figure 11.4 for a listing and description of common deceptive trading activities.

The following case discusses the elements required to establish a market manipulation claim based on a deceptive trading activity commonly known as a death spiral. As you read the case, consider how the court distinguishes between the legal practice of short selling and the short selling scheme used in the death spiral. The case also addresses special pleading requirements for market manipulation claims based on

Figure 11.4. Types of Deceptive Trading Activity

Deceptive Trading Activity	Description
Wash Sale	Transactions in a security that involve no change in the beneficial ownership of the security combined with a fraudulent intent. The same broker-dealer is on both sides of the trade by selling the security to one broker-dealer and buying back the same security from another broker-dealer. Effectively there is no change in beneficial ownership.
Matched Order	Broker-dealer trades in a security with a co-conspirator for the purpose of creating an appearance of trading activity or a change in the price of the security.
Boiler Rooms	Broker-dealer uses high pressure, fraudulent sales tactics to sell speculative securities (unknown, thinly traded, or nonexistent) to customers who are cold called. Often engaged in a Pump-and-Dump Scam.
Pump-and-Dump	Broker-dealer promotes a stock that it holds or owns to increase its price and then sells the stock once the price has risen based on its promotion. Stocks used tend to be highly illiquid and traded over-the-counter.
Spoofing	Broker-dealers place large orders for securities to make it appear that the price for the security is changing, then immediately cancel such orders and place opposite orders to take advantage of other traders in the market who believe that the orders are bona fide. Essentially, the broker-dealer places orders that it really does not intend to fill.
Marking the Close	Broker-dealer attempts to influence the closing price of a security by executing purchase or sale orders at or near the close of normal trading hours. This activity can artificially inflate or depress the closing price for a security.

deceptive trading activities. Why are these pleading requirements different from alleging material misrepresentations or omissions?

Sharette v. Credit Suisse Intern.

127 F.Supp.3d 60 (S.D.N.Y. 2015)

DECISION AND ORDER

Victor Marrero, District Judge.

Lead plaintiffs Willard A. Sharette, David Goldman, and Esta Goldman (collectively, "Plaintiffs"), three former shareholders of Energy Conversion Devices, Inc. ("ECD"), brought this suit on behalf of a putative class of "all other persons or entities who purchased or otherwise acquired common stock of [ECD] between June 18, 2008 and February 12, 2012 (the "Class Period")." They named defendants Credit Suisse International and Credit Suisse Securities (USA) LLC (collectively, the "Credit Suisse

Defendants") and asserted various claims pursuant to Section[] ... 10(b) of the Securities Exchange Act of 1934, (the "Exchange Act"), and Rule 10b–5 promulgated thereunder.

* * *

[T]he Credit Suisse Defendants ... filed a Motion to Dismiss the CACAC [Plaintiffs' complaint] pursuant to Federal Rule of Civil Procedure 12(b)(6) and that Motion is presently before the Court....

I. BACKGROUND

A. TWO OFFERINGS OF ECD STOCK

ECD was a manufacturer of solar power technology. Specifically, it manufactured photovoltaic solar laminates that generated renewable energy by converting sunlight into electricity. ECD's products were particularly suitable for rooftop application, and were manufactured using a proprietary process and technology developed by ECD through almost 30 years of research.

In 2008, to boost production as demand for its products grew, ECD needed to raise capital. To this end, ECD entered into a share lending agreement (the "Share Lending Agreement") with the Credit Suisse Defendants, who agreed to serve as the lead underwriters for two offerings of ECD stock that were made in tandem. The principal offering (the "Convertible Notes Offering") involved $316 million in notes convertible into ECD common stock (the "Convertible Notes") and the second securities offering (the "Common Stock Offering," collectively the "Offerings") involved 4,714,975 shares of ECD common stock ("ECD Stock"). Through the Common Stock Offering, ECD created a pool of 3,444,975 shares that were made available to the Credit Suisse Defendants to lend out pursuant to the Share Lending Agreement, while the remaining 1,270,000 shares were sold by the Credit Suisse Defendants directly to investors. In the Share Lending Agreement, the Credit Suisse Defendants agreed that the Credit Suisse Defendants would use the ECD stock

> solely for the purpose of directly or indirectly ... facilitating the sale and the hedging of the Convertible Notes by the holders thereof or, ... with the prior consent of the Lender, facilitating the sale and the hedging of any additional convertible securities the Lender may issue from time to time by the holders thereof.

As described in the Common Stock Prospectus,

> in advance of the [O]ffering[s], [the] Credit Suisse [Defendants] "solicited indications of interest, based on the purchase price negotiated with those potential purchasers, from convertible notes investors seeking to establish a hedge position" and "established a 'clearing price' for a number of borrowed shares at which both purchasers of our common stock were willing to purchase borrowed shares offered hereby and investors in our convertible notes were willing to establish hedge positions."

B. *SHORT SALES OF ECD STOCK SKYROCKET WHILE THE PRICE OF ECD STOCK PLUMMETS, SENDING ECD INTO BANKRUPTCY*

The Offerings occurred on June 18, 2008, and the Credit Suisse Defendants lent out for short sales almost all of the 3,444,975 shares ECD had provided, retaining less than 200,000 shares. At the time of the Offerings, the short interest in ECD stock was approximately 6.7 million shares, so the additional approximately 3.2 million shares shorted after the Offerings represented an increase of roughly 48 percent in short interest in ECD stock.

As the volume of short sales of ECD stock rose sharply, the price of ECD stock dramatically plunged, dropping from approximately $72 per share on June 18, 2008, to less than $1 per share in February 2012. In February 2012, ECD filed for bankruptcy protection, causing massive losses to investors.

C. *THE CREDIT SUISSE DEFENDANTS' ALLEGED MISREPRESENTATIONS AND MANIPULATIVE SCHEME*

Plaintiffs allege that the rampant shorting of ECD stock after the Offerings, followed by ECD's eventual bankruptcy, was all part of a scheme, orchestrated by the Credit Suisse Defendants, to allow "predatory hedge funds" to reap enormous profits while sending ECD stock into a downward spiral. According to the CACAC, the Share Lending Agreement and the Prospectuses misrepresented that the purpose of the Offerings and the related Share Lending Agreement was to promote the sale of the Convertible Notes by assisting investors in "hedging" their investment in these securities. The CACAC alleges, however, that the Credit Suisse Defendants intended all along to allow predatory hedge funds to place massive negative bets on ECD stock with very little risk, shorting huge amounts of ECD Stock, such that the short sales effectuated could not be considered part of the "legitimate hedging strategy" contemplated by the Share Lending Agreement and described in Prospectuses. Plaintiffs allege that the Credit Suisse Defendants were the "architect[s] of and key participant[s] in" this manipulative scheme.

1. *Convertible Notes, Short Sales, and "Hedging"*

A "convertible note" is a hybrid security with characteristics of both stocks and bonds. "Like bonds, convertible notes pay interest (in this case 3%) and have a maturity date (here, June 15, 2013)." However, "like stock, the price of convertible notes is more sensitive to the earnings prospects of the issuer than an ordinary bond because each note can be converted to equity." If the price of a company's stock rises enough, it becomes advantageous to an investor in convertible notes to convert its notes into stock at the maturity date. The interests of a company and a purchaser of its convertible notes are therefore aligned.

"Shorting" or "short selling" stock refers to a process whereby an investor borrows stock from a third party and makes a promise to return the stock to the lender at a later date. The investor then sells the stock, which puts downward pressure on the stock. If the stock price goes down, the investor eventually buys the stock back at the new, lower price and then returns the stock to the lender, having turned a profit. However, a short sale exposes the investor to potentially unlimited downside risk because there is theoretically no limit to how high the price of a shorted stock can rise, and the short seller is obligated to purchase the stock at the prevailing market price on the agreed date and return it to its lender regardless of whether the stock price drops, rises, or stays the same. Thus, short selling is essentially a bet *against* a company's stock; the more a stock price drops, the greater a short seller's profit, but the more a stock price rises, the greater a short seller's loss.

Given the properties of convertible notes and short sales, an investor is able to "hedge" against the risk of purchasing a company's convertible notes by coupling the purchase of such notes with short sales of the same company's common stock. When the two investments are made in tandem, if a company's stock prices do drop, causing investors in the company's convertible notes to lose money in the long term, those same investors are able to minimize or recover that loss in the short term when they buy back, at a reduced price, the common stock shares they have shorted.

Plaintiffs allege that "the term 'hedge' in the context of convertible notes specifically refers to a market neutral investment strategy." According to the CACAC, when "hedging," investors do not make "rampant short sales." Rather, they

> short only the number of shares necessary to protect against the downside risk to the notes created by swings in the equity price of the underlying stock, thereby creating a market neutral position. The appropriate number of shares necessary to do this is called the "hedge ratio."

In the case at hand, each individual Convertible Note had a face value of $1,000 and could be converted into 10.892 shares of ECD stock. This valuation meant that a purchaser of a Convertible Note effectively paid $91.80 per share of ECD stock. Since the price of ECD stock was approximately $72 at the time of the Offerings, the price of ECD stock would have had to rise significantly — to a value of at least greater than $91.80 — in order for a holder of a Convertible Note to have an incentive to convert the note to ECD stock. The CACAC posits that under conditions such as these, when the market price of the underlying stock is substantially below the conversion price, the hedge ratio is "less than 50 percent of the number of shares that a note can be converted into." Furthermore, the CACAC alleges that

> the hedge ratio declines as the price of underlying stock goes down because under these circumstances the convertible note behaves more like a bond and less like a stock. For this reason, an investor pursuing a strategy of hedging an investment in convertible notes will actually start buying the stock of a company when the price of the stock declines, taking downward pressure off the stock and creating buy-side demand that would support the price of the stock.

Thus, when an investor in convertible notes pursues a "legitimate hedging strategy" by engaging in short sales, even though short sales in isolation constitute a short term bet *against* a company,

> the interests of [the hedging] investor ... are [actually] aligned with those of the underlying company's shareholders because both are *'long'* on the

Company, that is, both are betting on the Company and hoping *for* its profitability.

In other words, the CACAC alleges, as part of a "hedge," an investor does not short sell in excess of the hedge ratio, attempting to drive down the price of a company's stock and make a profit through buying the stock back at a lower price. Instead, an investor pursuing a hedging strategy shorts only a limited amount of stock in accordance with the hedge ratio, offsetting the risk of investment in that company's convertible notes while maintaining its "long" investment in the company's success.

2. Short Sales with Almost No Risk; Misaligned Investor and Shareholder Interests

The CACAC asserts that two considerations traditionally limit investors' ability to make short sales. First, as discussed above, short sales have potentially unlimited downside risk because there are technically no bounds to how high the price of a stock can rise. Second, an investor must pay a fee to the lender in order to borrow the stock and short it, and "[t]his fee can be quite high, especially as interest in shorting a stock increases."

Plaintiffs allege that both of these risks were purposefully eliminated by Credit Suisse when it structured the Offerings. A short seller's potentially unlimited risk due to the possibility of rising stock prices was effectively removed by the conversion option embedded in the Convertible Notes, since investors could ultimately change their Convertible Notes into stock to cover losses incurred through short sales if the price of ECD stock rose. Since each Convertible Note could be converted into 10.8932 shares of ECD stock,

> a hedge fund could short up to this number of shares without running any risk that the price of ECD stock would go up and cause the hedge fund to lose money on its short position. This conversion right acted as an insurance policy on hedge funds' shorting.

Additionally, the borrowing costs traditionally associated with short sales were also all but eliminated, because the Share Lending Agreement provided that the Credit Suisse Defendants would lend ECD stock to investors to short for the nominal fee of only one cent. This fee was allegedly far below market rates, as — according to the CACAC —

> a short seller ordinarily may have to pay a significant percentage of the value of a stock that is difficult to borrow (such as one where the share price is declining as was the case with respect to ECD).... Thus, whereas it [typically] would have cost ... millions of dollars a year to borrow the roughly 3.4 million ECD shares loaned pursuant to the Share Lending Agreement, the [total] borrowing cost was just $34,000.

The CACAC alleges that this arrangement "created a perfect 'heads I win, tails you lose' investment vehicle [for the Credit Suisse Defendants] to sell to hedge funds." This result follows because, as the CACAC further alleges with the support of detailed calculations, pursuant to the structure of the Offerings "a hypothetical hedge fund that purchased a single Convertible Note and who sold short 10.8932 shares, the number of ECD shares that the Note could be converted into[,]" stood to earn more money the further ECD's stock declined, and actually lost money if the stock rose. In fact, Plaintiffs assert, if such a hedge fund shorted 10.8932 shares of ECD stock at the market price of $72 per share, and ECD's stock price then fell to only $0.02 per share, that hedge fund would make a profit of 519% on its initial investment, with almost all the profit coming from the short sales. In contrast, in the event that ECD's stock prices rose significantly to $150 per share, such a hedge fund would suffer a 19% decline in its investment.

Thus, the CACAC alleges, unlike with a traditional "hedge," in which the interests of shareholders and noteholders are *aligned,* here those interests were *opposed.* In fact, according to Plaintiffs, the potentially massive profits for a hypothetical hedge fund purchasing one Convertible Note and shorting 10.8932 shares would accrue even in the event of ECD's bankruptcy—which ultimately did occur—because

> ECD was a capital—intense Company whose assets allowed for a substantial recovery on the Convertible Notes in bankruptcy. Thus even if the bankruptcy only paid fifty cents on the dollar, an investor in the Note-short sale scheme would still double its money.

Furthermore, the relatively low risk to investors of a significant rise in ECD's stock price when shorting 10.8932 shares of ECD stock (only 19% loss if the stock rose to $150 per share) combined with the potential for massive gains if ECD's stock price plummeted (a generous 519% profit if the stock fell to $0.02 per share and a 100% profit even if ECD fell into bankruptcy), made the Offerings—and the prospect of shorting shares well in excess of the hedge ratio—even more attractive to investors and even more ripe for exploitation by the Credit Suisse Defendants and the "predatory hedge funds."

In contrast, the CACAC asserts that if investors had engaged in proper "hedging" of the convertible notes, the incentives would have been drastically different. According to Plaintiffs, who again support their allegations with a detailed set of calculations, a hypothetical hedge fund purchasing one Convertible Note and shorting 5.4466 shares would have a 99% return on its investment if the price of ECD stock plummeted to $0.02 per share and a 67% return on its investment if the price rose to $150. Additionally, such an investor would likely not profit, and could potentially even lose money, in the event ECD declared bankruptcy.

3. *Allegations Against the Credit Suisse Defendants*

Plaintiffs allege that the Credit Suisse Defendants, were the "architect [s] of and key participant[s] in" a scheme to manipulate the price of ECD stock to ECD's detriment. According to the CACAC, the Credit Suisse Defendants—although hired by ECD to advance ECD's interests as the underwriters of the Offerings—"carried out a plan which was intended to and did (a) deceive the investing public, including Plaintiffs and the Class; and (b) artificially drive down the price of ECD stock." The CACAC alleges that, while it was "predatory hedge funds" who actually conducted the massive short sales that decimated ECD's stock price, the Credit Suisse Defendants orchestrated the Offerings, as outlined above, for the very purpose of creating an investment vehicle that would allow those hedge funds to make a windfall while sending the price of ECD stock into a downward spiral.

According to the CACAC, the Credit Suisse Defendants—who solicited and negotiated with interested investors prior to the Offerings—"knew in advance of the Offerings how hedge funds planned to exploit the financing scheme to make large sales of ECD stock." They misled investors by representing in the Share Lending Agreement, to which they were parties, and in the Prospectuses, which they "prepared and/or substantially contributed to" that they would use borrowed ECD shares only to facilitate investors' hedging of their investments in ECD's convertible notes. Then, in their capacity as lead underwriter of the Offerings and contrary to the representations made in the Share Lending Agreement and the Prospectuses, the Credit Suisse Defendants facilitated the market manipulation and destruction of ECD's stock price by lending out far more shares of common stock for short sales than was actually necessary for investors to "hedge" their positions in ECD's convertible notes. The actions of the Credit Suisse Defendants, who were allegedly "on both sides of the [O]fferings, simultaneously selling the stock and Notes to investors while soliciting hedge funds to make giant bets against the stock," allowed hedge funds to make "huge, coordinated" short sales of ECD stock.

The price of ECD stock then "predictably" collapsed in response, sinking from approximately $72 per share on June 18, 2008 to less than $1 per share in February 2012. The "sharp decline" in the value of ECD stock hindered ECD's ability to secure further financing to run its business, and so "inhibited ECD's ability to continue operate." Ultimately, in February 2012—allegedly as a result of the Credit Suisse Defendants' market manipulation and misrepresentations—ECD filed for bankruptcy protection, causing ECD shareholders to suffer tremendous losses, even as the Credit Suisse Defendants' hedge fund clients reaped enormous rewards.

* * *

2. Market Manipulation

A claim of market manipulation under Section 10(b) and Rule 10b-5 "requires a plaintiff to allege (1) manipulative acts; (2) damage (3) caused by reliance on an assumption of an efficient market free of manipulation; (4) scienter; (5) in connection with the purchase or sale of securities; (6) furthered by the defendant's use of the mails or any facility of a national securities exchange." "In order for market activity to be manipulative, that conduct must involve misrepresentation or nondisclosure." However, allegations of misrepresentations or omissions alone cannot support a claim of market manipulation. Rather, there must be "wash sales, matched orders, rigged prices, or some other manipulative act intended to mislead investors by artificially affecting market activity." Essentially, a claim of market manipulation

> require[s] a showing that an alleged manipulator engaged in market activity aimed at deceiving investors as to how other market participants have valued a security.... The gravamen of manipulation is deception of investors into believing that prices at which they purchase and sell securities are determined by the natural interplay of supply and demand, not rigged by manipulators.

In order to satisfy the heightened pleading standards for fraud, a complaint alleging market manipulation must "plead with particularity the nature, purpose, and effect of the fraudulent conduct and the roles of the defendants."

A claim of manipulation, however, can involve facts solely within the defendant's knowledge; therefore, at the early stages of litigation, the plaintiff need not plead manipulation to the same degree of specificity as a plain misrepresentation claim.

Accordingly, a plaintiff has adequately pleaded market manipulation when

the complaint sets forth, to the extent possible, what manipulative acts were performed, which defendants performed them, when the manipulative acts were performed, and what effect the scheme had on the market for the securities at issue.

* * *

V. DISCUSSION

A. ACTS OF MARKET MANIPULATION

The Credit Suisse Defendants assert a two-pronged argument with regard to the Plaintiffs' claims of market manipulation under Section 10(b) and Rule 10b-5. First, the Credit Suisse Defendants posit that the CACAC fails to plead facts demonstrating the existence of any market manipulation of ECD stock. Second, the Credit Suisse Defendants argue that Plaintiffs have failed to allege facts supporting the inference that the Credit Suisse Defendants participated in any market manipulation of ECD stock, even if such manipulation did occur.

The Court finds that Plaintiffs have pleaded enough facts to support a reasonable inference that market manipulation of ECD stock occurred, and that the Credit Suisse Defendants participated in it.

1. *Manipulative Acts Under Section 10(b) and Rule 10b-5*

As discussed above ... a claim of market manipulation under Section 10(b) and Rule 10b-5 promulgated thereunder requires that a plaintiff plead "manipulative acts." The Credit Suisse Defendants argue that Plaintiffs have failed to allege such manipulative acts.

a. *ATSI* and *Cohen*

The Motion, relying heavily on *ATSI* and *Cohen,* claims that the CACAC fails to allege facts giving rise to an inference of manipulative activity. The Motion argues that in the case at hand—as in ATSI—Plaintiffs have based their allegations of market manipulation on "high-volume selling of ... stock with coinciding drops in the stock price" and "trading patterns," and that such allegations are merely "speculative inferences" and insufficient to state a claim. The Credit Suisse Defendants draw parallels between Plaintiffs in the instant action and the *ATSI* plaintiffs, who failed to "particularly allege what the defendants did—beyond simply mentioning common types of manipulative activity—or state how this affected the market in ATSI's stock." The

Credit Suisse Defendants further argue that, like the plaintiffs in *Cohen*, Plaintiffs "fail to allege even the most basic details of the ... purported illegal short selling," and that such groundless allegations are the type of claims prohibited by *Twombly*.

However, Plaintiffs are correct that the case at hand is clearly distinguishable from *ATSI* and *Cohen*. In *ATSI*, the plaintiffs alleged that the defendants had manipulated the price of ATSI stock by engaging in "death spiral financing," which was defined as making high-volume short sales and then converting convertible securities into common stock to cover their short positions. The *ATSI* plaintiffs attempted to support their allegations by claiming that the *ATSI* defendants had participated in such schemes in the past, as evidenced by "searches in the SEC's Edgar database[, which] reveal[ed] that of the 38 companies that reported the Levinson Defendants as investors, 30 experienced stock price declines indicative of a 'death spiral' financing scheme." The *ATSI* plaintiffs also did not allege any specific acts of short selling or other transactions, but rather argued that the occurrence of high-volume selling and a drop in ATSI stock prices indicated that short selling—as part of "death spiral financing"—had taken place. The ATSI plaintiffs then "narrow[ed] the list of potential culprits to the defendants because ATSI's major shareholders said that they were not selling stock, leaving only the defendants with large enough blocks of shares to trade at the observed volumes."

The *Cohen* plaintiffs' pleadings suffered from similar weaknesses. The plaintiffs in *Cohen* alleged that the defendants had engaged in "naked short selling," a practice that involves executing short sales of stock without first borrowing the stock or ensuring that the stock can be borrowed to settle the short sale. However, the *Cohen* plaintiffs could not point to any specific short sales made by any particular defendants, and in support of the occurrence of "naked short sales" only alleged that a particular seller was unable to deliver a security on a settlement date.

In contrast, in the case at hand, Plaintiffs have alleged how many shares were made available to the Credit Suisse Defendants through the Offerings and how many shares the Credit Suisse Defendants lent out for short sales, and these allegations are based on data rather than on circumstantial evidence. Plaintiffs have also alleged the number of ECD convertible notes sold, demonstrating that investors were shorting on average more than 10 shares of ECD common stock for each convertible note. The CACAC explains in some detail how the Credit Suisse Defendants allegedly structured the Offerings to allow for manipulation and how the price of ECD stock then plummeted as ECD's short volume steadily rose after the Offerings. Plaintiffs' allegations as to how the alleged manipulative scheme operated are therefore far less speculative than the allegations made by the plaintiffs in *ATSI* and *Cohen*.

b. "Something More"

The Motion further contends that Plaintiffs have merely alleged high-volume short selling, and that "courts have recognized that there is nothing 'manipulative' about short selling, even in large volumes." This argument mischaracterizes both ATSI and the CACAC. The ATSI court stated that short selling—even in high volumes—is not, *by itself,* manipulative ... To be actionable as a manipulative act, short selling must be willfully combined with something more to create a false impression of how market participants value a security. Similarly, purchasing a floorless convertible security is not, by itself or when coupled with short selling, inherently manipulative.

Consistent with *ATSI,* other courts in this district have found that open-market transactions that are not, in and of themselves, manipulative or illegal, may constitute manipulative activity within the meaning of Section 10(b) when coupled with manipulative intent.

In the case at hand, Plaintiffs have clearly alleged that short selling was "willfully combined with something more" as required by *ATSI* and Rule 10(b). Plaintiffs allege that the Credit Suisse Defendants were the "architect[s] and key participant[s] in [a] manipulative scheme." Plaintiffs further allege that the Credit Suisse Defendants orchestrated the Offerings for the purpose of allowing their hedge fund clients to make huge profits while sinking the price of ECD stock, hid this purpose from ECD and its investors, and then intentionally lent out far more shares of common stock for short sales than was necessary for investors to "hedge" their positions in ECD's convertible notes, facilitating the market manipulation—and depression—of ECD's stock price. Plaintiffs have therefore alleged not only high-volume short selling, but also a coordinated scheme engineered by the Credit Suisse Defendants to use short selling to manipulate the price of ECD stock, "creat[ing] a false impression of how market participants value a security."

It bears consideration that many of the allegations in the CACAC regarding how the alleged scheme actually operated—how, for example, the hedge funds worked together to engage in "coordinated" short sales—and from which manipulative intent can be inferred, do not contain extensive factual detail. Moreover, Plaintiffs' allegations of manipulation must meet the heightened pleading requirements of [FRCP] Rule 9(b)—Plaintiffs must "state with particularity the circumstances constituting fraud."

However, where factual detail is absent from the CACAC, it is important to note that a manipulation claim need not be pleaded to the same degree of specificity as a misrepresentation claim when relevant information is likely to be solely within the defendant's knowledge. Undoubtedly, the private communications between the Credit Suisse Defendants and their clients as they allegedly collaborated carry out an unlawful scheme to manipulate the price of ECD stock fall squarely in the purview of information that is likely to be in the exclusive control of the Credit Suisse Defendants and their clients, and that may be resolved only through discovery, making dismissal of the action inappropriate at this stage of the proceedings.

c. *"Legitimate" Hedging*

The Motion also criticizes the CACAC for "hing[ing] entirely on the fact that the volume of short sales after the Offerings exceeded what Plaintiffs' claim was 'necessary' for 'legitimate' hedging activity." The Motion points out that the CACAC cites only to a single source for its contention that the appropriate "hedge ratio" under circumstances such as those alleged in the case at hand would have been less than 50 percent of the number of shares the ECD convertible notes could be converted into, and the cited source is "a knowledge-based document prepared by an asset management firm located in Switzerland, and serving primarily clients in the German-speaking region of Europe. The Motion further avers that "[w]hy, or how, this European-based asset management firm serves as any authority whatsoever for what a 'legitimate hedging' strategy would be is a mystery—that is unexplained by Plaintiffs [sic] conclusory allegations on such."

It is true that many of Plaintiffs' allegations regarding manipulation are heavily dependent on what they claim the term "hedging" means in the finance world. Essentially, Plaintiffs argue that "hedging" is defined as a market neutral strategy, the employment of such—in the context of the facts at issue—would have resulted in investors shorting far fewer shares per convertible note than they ultimately did. Plaintiffs argue that the Credit Suisse Defendants covenanted and represented that they would use the ECD shares only to facilitate hedging, all the while intending to—and then actually—lending out far more stock for short sales to investors than would be required for hedging, allowing their investors to engage in massive short sales and manipulate the price of ECD stock. If the term "hedging" does not in fact refer to the specific, market neutral strategy alleged by Plaintiffs, and if the strategies employed by the Credit Suisse Defendants' hedge fund clients can appropriately be characterized as "hedging," then the Credit Suisse Defendants' "scheme" entailed little misrepresentation.

In questioning the definition of "hedging" and "hedge ratio" used in the CACAC, however, the Credit Suisse Defendants have merely raised a factual dispute inappropriate for resolution at the pleading stage, before the development of a fuller factual record of discovery, including the opinion of other experts whose testimony may shed better light on these complex economic and industry practice issues. Resolving a disagreement over the interpretation of terminology instrumental to the alleged manipulative scheme ... would require "assay[ing] the weight of the evidence," which is not permitted when adjudicating a motion to dismiss.

The Court therefore finds that the Plaintiffs have alleged enough facts to support a reasonable inference of the occurrence of manipulative acts of ECD stock within the meaning of Section 10(b) and Rule 10b-5 and have satisfied the heightened pleading standards of Rule 9(b).

2. The Credit Suisse Defendants' Participation in Manipulative Acts Under Section 10(b) and Rule 10b-5

The Motion next asserts that even if there was market manipulation of ECD's stock, the CACAC has not alleged facts supporting an inference that the Credit Suisse Defendants actually participated in such manipulation. The Motion points out that the CACAC does not state who actually engaged in the "manipulative" short sales; the "predatory hedge funds" are unnamed and unspecified. Furthermore, the Credit Suisse Defendants assert that Plaintiffs have not pleaded facts showing that Credit Suisse provided shares to any of the "predatory hedge funds" in particular. From the allegations in the CACAC, the Motion argues, "there is no basis to infer that Credit Suisse did anything other than what the Prospectuses said Credit Suisse would do. That can hardly be deemed 'manipulative' or 'deceptive' act in furtherance of some 'scheme' ..."

The Credit Suisse Defendants are correct that the CACAC does not specifically name any of the "predatory hedge funds" or provide evidence of the specific transactions in which the Credit Suisse Defendants allegedly lent shares to those predatory hedge funds in particular. However, Plaintiffs have alleged that Does 1 through 100, named as codefendants in this action with Credit Suisse, "are [the] hedge funds that engaged in [the] short selling alleged" in the Complaint. Plaintiffs have indicated that they are "unaware of the true names and capacities" of these defendants but "will seek leave to amend this Complaint when such names are ascertained."

Furthermore, the "predatory hedge funds" are not moving to dismiss the suit; the Credit Suisse Defendants are, and Plaintiffs have pleaded sufficient facts to show the Credit Suisse Defendants' participation in the alleged manipulative scheme. As discussed above ... Plaintiffs have alleged how many shares were made available to the Credit Suisse Defendants through the Offerings, how many shares the Credit Suisse Defendants lent out for short sales, and the number of convertible notes sold. Plaintiffs have also alleged that the Credit Suisse Defendants structured the Offerings expressly for the purpose of facilitating the market manipulation of the price of ECD stock and hid this purpose from ECD and its investors. Plaintiffs further allege that the Credit Suisse Defendants then loaned far more shares to investors than necessary for "legitimate hedging," allowing their hedge fund clients to engage in rampant, coordinated short sales of ECD stock, manipulating and depressing the price of ECD's stock.

Certainly, while providing a great deal of detail about the perverse incentives offered to investors through the Offerings and demonstrating how the structure of the Offerings "created a perfect 'heads I win, tails you lose' investment vehicle [for the Credit Suisse Defendants] to sell to hedge funds", the facts Plaintiffs allege in support of the inference that the Credit Suisse Defendants were the "architect[s]" of the scheme—that the Credit Suisse Defendants orchestrated the Offerings with the purpose of facilitating a manipulative scheme to decimate the price of ECD stock and then lent excessive numbers of shares to their investor clients in service of the scheme—are far more limited. The CACAC's main factual allegation in this regard is that the Credit Suisse Defendants "knew in advance of the Offerings how hedge funds planned to exploit the financing scheme to make large sales of ECD stock" because the Credit Suisse Defendants solicited indications of interest and established a clearing price with potential investors prior to the Offerings. Plaintiffs have not alleged specific conversations, names, or dates as to when or how exactly the scheme was engineered and carried out by Credit Suisse.

However, it is once again important to note that a manipulation claim need not be pleaded to the same degree of specificity as a misrepresentation claim when relevant information is likely to be solely within the defendant's knowledge. The private communications in which the Credit Suisse Defendants allegedly orchestrated a manipulative scheme and collaborated with their hedge funds clients to manipulate the price of ECD stock certainly constitute information likely to be in the exclusive control of the Credit Suisse Defendants at this stage of the proceedings.

Weighing all inferences in Plaintiffs' favor, as the Court is required to do in adjudicating a motion to dismiss, Plaintiffs have sufficiently pleaded that the Credit Suisse Defendants engaged in acts of market manipulation of ECD stock. Plaintiffs have pleaded with enough particularity, and "to the extent possible," the nature (large-scale coordinated short sales), purpose (to drive down the price of ECD stock), and effect of the fraudulent conduct (the depression of the price of ECD's stock price) and the roles of the defendants (the "architect[s]" of the scheme — the designer of the Offerings and, as underwriter of the Offerings, the lender of the shares to the investors who engaged in the short selling).

Accordingly, the Court finds that the CACAC has alleged enough facts to give rise to a reasonable inference that the Credit Suisse Defendants participated in the alleged acts of market manipulation of ECD stock, and has pleaded this element of market manipulation under Section 10(b) and Rule 10b-5 with enough particularity to satisfy the heightened pleading requirements of Rule 9(b).

* * *

C. SCIENTER

The Credit Suisse Defendants argue that Plaintiffs have failed to allege facts giving rise to a strong inference of scienter....

* * *

1. Motive and Opportunity

To demonstrate "motive and opportunity" to defraud, Plaintiffs must allege that the Credit Suisse Defendants benefited in some concrete and personal way from the purported fraud. Opportunity is generally assumed where the defendant is a corporation or corporate officer, such as the Credit Suisse Defendants. However, motive must be pleaded with particularity, and "[m]otives that are common to most corporate officers, such as the desire for the corporation to appear profitable and the desire to keep stock prices high to increase officer compensation, do not constitute 'motive'" for purposes of demonstrating scienter....

The CACAC alleges that the Credit Suisse Defendants "benefited in two ways from the scheme alleged herein." First, the Credit Suisse Defendants were "paid a share of the $8.25 million commission for underwriting the Convertible Note Offering." Second, the Credit Suisse Defendants were able to

> promote [themselves] to hedge funds by helping them gain exorbitant profits through the short selling scheme Credit Suisse operated. Investment banks, such as Credit Suisse, competed heavily for the approximately $4 billion in brokerage fees paid to investment banks by hedge funds by providing these funds with access to information and favorable investment options. The short selling scheme Credit Suisse devised was an attractive investment option that

allowed Credit Suisse to strengthen its brand name in the lucrative hedge fund brokerage fee market.

That the Credit Suisse Defendants received a "share" of the $8.25 million commission for underwriting the offerings does not by itself support a strong inference of scienter. The CACAC does not allege that any particular financial benefit was contingent upon the Credit Suisse Defendants allegedly carrying out their manipulative scheme. Rather, it alleges that the Credit Suisse Defendants received a "share" of the $8.25 million commission simply by playing the role of underwriter, regardless of the alleged scheme. This bare allegation therefore fails to show that the Credit Suisse Defendants "benefitted in some concrete and personal way from the purported fraud." Rather, the CACAC makes allegations that essentially "amount to no more than allegations of a general business motive to make a profit."

However, the allegation that the Credit Suisse Defendants employed the alleged scheme to "strengthen [their] brand name in the lucrative hedge fund brokerage fee market" in order to enhance their ability to compete for brokerage fees paid to investment banks by hedge funds is compelling. The Credit Suisse Defendants argue that "it is nonsensical that [the Credit Suisse Defendants] would devise a scheme to drive *down* the stock of an issuer in order to 'promote' [themselves] to hedge funds. Perhaps the Credit Suisse Defendants are not aware that it is not unusual for businesses engaged in stiff competition to engage in short term practices that may strike common sense as uneconomic, counter-intuitive, even irrational—loss leaders, for instance. At times, carried to excess, some such common commercial behavior crosses the line into illegality. Here, the clear implication of Plaintiffs' allegations is that the hedge fund market was highly lucrative, intensely competitive, and attractive to the Credit Suisse Defendants, while the business of young companies strapped for cash, such as ECD, was paltry and inessential in comparison.

It is not at all implausible that, in such circumstances, the business of companies such as ECD would seem relatively expendable to "global leader[s] in investment banking" such as the Credit Suisse Defendants. It is equally plausible that the Credit Suisse Defendants might have seen the intensely profitable business of hedge funds, on the other hand, as a golden goose, and might therefore have thought it worth taking a risk in order to obtain some of its hatch. Furthermore, it is not unreasonable to infer, as Plaintiffs' allegations suggest, that the fraud claimed, through which the Credit Suisse Defendants' hedge fund clients were allegedly able to reap massive profits with hardly any downside, could have been seen by the Credit Suisse Defendants as a promising way to ingratiate themselves with the hedge fund market, opening the door for more and more lucrative business from that market in the future—business that may been unattainable by them without the manipulation and deception Plaintiffs describe in the CACAC ...

However, the CACAC's allegations that the manipulation and deception alleged on the part of the Credit Suisse Defendants allowed them to "promote" themselves to hedge funds in order to better compete for the highly lucrative business of hedge funds is not generalized.... Fairly read, the CACAC strongly suggests that, through the fraud alleged therein, the Credit Suisse Defendants were able to improve their ability to access a specific and extremely profitable market, potentially worth billions of dollars.

* * *

While accepting all well-pleaded factual allegations in the CACAC as true and drawing all reasonable inferences in Plaintiffs' favor, as the Court is required to do when adjudicating a motion to dismiss, the Court finds that the factual allegations pleaded by Plaintiffs give rise to a strong inference of scienter as required by ... Plaintiffs' claims for relief—market manipulation under Section 10b and Rule 10b-5 ... and that Plaintiffs have pleaded scienter with the particularity required by the heightened pleading standards provided by Rule 9(b) and the PSLRA. While there may be opposing, nonculpable inferences that may be drawn from the facts pleaded, the Court finds that "a reasonable person would deem the inference of scienter cogent and at least as compelling as any opposing inference one could draw from the facts alleged."

D. LOSS CAUSATION

The Credit Suisse Defendants argue that Plaintiffs have failed to adequately allege loss causation with regard to their market manipulation and misrepresentation claims under Section 10(b) and Rule 10b-5. While the term "loss causation" is more frequently used with regard to claims of misstatements and omissions, all securities fraud claims made pursuant to the Exchange Act require plaintiffs to "adequately allege and prove the traditional elements of causation and loss." However, "[l]oss causation need not be pled with particularity. A short and plain statement in accordance with Rule 8 of the Federal Rules of Civil Procedure is sufficient."

1. Loss Causation with Regard to Market Manipulation

The Credit Suisse Defendants argue that Plaintiffs have failed to show loss causation with regard to their manipulation claims. The Motion argues that Plaintiffs have failed to link "any conduct *on the part of Credit Suisse*" to their damages, asserting that

> "[t]he [CACAC] alleges only that [the Credit Suisse Defendants] underwrote the Offerings ... and ... made certain shares available for short sales ... Absent allegations linking "fraudulent conduct" on the part of Credit Suisse to Plaintiffs' losses (as opposed to blaming Plaintiffs' losses on massive 'short selling' by unidentified traders) using shares that Plaintiffs have made no effort to link to [the] Credit Suisse Defendants, Plaintiffs have failed to allege loss causation."

The Court has already found that Plaintiffs have adequately alleged that the Credit Suisse Defendants participated in a manipulative scheme to depress the price of ECD stock, so Plaintiffs have adequately pleaded "fraudulent conduct" on the part of the Credit Suisse Defendants.

Plaintiffs have also clearly pleaded enough facts evidencing a link between the alleged manipulative scheme and their damages. Plaintiffs have shown in some detail exactly how the structure of the Offerings allowed investors to manipulate and depress the price of ECD stock, and have shown that following the Offerings, short sales of ECD stock skyrocketed while the price of ECD stock plummeted. While it is true, as the Credit Suisse Defendants point out, that ECD did not declare bankruptcy until more than four years after the Offerings, Plaintiffs have more than adequately pleaded facts giving rise to a plausible inference that the Offerings caused a depression in the price of ECD stock from which ECD never recovered. Plaintiffs have therefore "made allegations sufficient to support a reasonable inference that the [manipulative actions of the Credit Suisse Defendants] 'bear upon the loss suffered such that [Plaintiffs] would have been spared all or an ascertainable portion of that loss absent the fraud.'"

———

The following case, like *Sharette,* illustrates market manipulation by a broker-dealer engaged in deceptive trading activity. Unlike *Sharette,* this case is an SEC administrative proceeding. Compare the required elements in an SEC administrative proceeding regarding market manipulation by trading activity with the required elements in a private cause of action. Are they the same?

In the Matter of the Application of Kirlin Securities, Inc. Anthony Kirincic and Andrew Israel

Exchange Act Rel. 34-61135 (Dec. 10, 2009)

I.

Kirlin Securities, Inc., formerly a broker-dealer registered with FINRA ("Kirlin" or the "Firm"); Anthony Kirincic, Kirlin's co-chief executive officer; and Andrew Israel, Kirlin's head equity trader, appeal from FINRA disciplinary action. FINRA found that Kirlin, Kirincic, and Israel (together, "Applicants") manipulated the stock price of Kirlin's publicly-traded parent company, Kirlin Holding Corporation ("KILN"), and thereby violated Section 10(b) of the Securities Exchange Act of 1934, Rule 10b-5 thereunder, and NASD Conduct Rules 2120 and 2110.[34]

II.

* * *

A. Background

With David Lindner, Kirincic was co-CEO and co-founder of Kirlin. At the Firm, Kirincic's primary role "was to evaluate the [company's] financial matters, to deal with liquidity and to deal with the overall structure of our company...." Israel, who had joined the Firm in 1989, became Kirlin's head equity trader in January 2002. Only one other trader in the office traded in equity securities at the time; he served as Israel's assistant. When Kirincic wanted to place an order to buy or sell securities for

---

34. [4] NASD Rule 2120 (now FINRA Rule 2020) prohibits inducing the purchase or sale of a security by means of "any manipulative, deceptive or other fraudulent device or contrivance." NASD Rule 2110 (now FINRA Rule 2010) requires that members "observe high standards of commercial honor and just and equitable principles of trade." ...

his customers' accounts, he would generally call the trading desk and instruct Israel (or Israel's assistant) to enter the order. Israel testified that, when Kirincic called to place an order for his customer, Kirincic specified the price, number of shares, and how to route the order. Israel or his assistant would then write the order ticket and enter it as instructed. Israel testified that, although he was not always the one who received Kirincic's calls, he would nevertheless review all of the trading department's order tickets (including, presumably, Kirincic's) "to make sure there was nothing inappropriate" about them.

Kirlin was at all times relevant to this proceeding a wholly-owned subsidiary of KILN. KILN was incorporated in 1994 by Kirincic and Lindner, who both served as co-chief executive officers and members of the five-person board of directors. KILN has been publicly traded since its listing on the Nasdaq Small Cap Market in 1995. In 1999, the company achieved compliance with the standards set by Nasdaq's National Market ("NNM") and transferred its listing there. Kirincic testified that, "given the choice" between the two market levels, he "would prefer to be on the one that was more highly recognized by the market," and that KILN's move to NNM was "a positive development in the evolution of the company moving forward." A press release issued by the company in 1999 noted that "[t]he prestige and viability of the listing [on] the Nasdaq National Market would enhance the company's accessibility with both the institutional investment community and the financial media."

As Applicants acknowledged at the hearing, KILN was a thinly-traded stock: the average daily volume of KILN trading prior to the events at issue was generally less than 10,000 shares. Israel testified that there was "really no outside interest" in KILN shares beyond the interest Kirlin and its customers may have had. KILN's public float in the spring of 2002 was approximately 8.5 million shares held by 193 owners of record; Israel estimated that about eighty percent of the stock was held in accounts serviced by Kirlin. Kirincic himself owned twenty percent of KILN's stock.[35]

B. Nasdaq notifies KILN of possible delisting based on low stock price

Although KILN's stock had once traded at prices as high as $57 or $58 per share, the company reported substantial net losses in 2000 and 2001, and the price of KILN shares declined. By early 2002, KILN's closing bid price dropped below $1.00, the minimum price required to maintain listing on Nasdaq, and remained below that level for thirty consecutive trading days.

As a result, on February 20, 2002, Nasdaq notified KILN that its stock would be delisted from the exchange in accordance with Nasdaq Marketplace Rule 4450(e)(2) unless, within the next ninety calendar days, KILN's bid price closed at or above $1.00 for at least ten consecutive trading days. In its letter, Nasdaq noted that "[u]nder

---

35. [11] Lindner also owned 20% of KILN's stock. In 2006, Kirincic came to hold approximately 35% of the company's shares when he agreed to a reduction in salary in exchange for KILN shares. Israel testified that in 2002 his only KILN holdings were options on 10,000 shares that had not yet vested.

certain circumstances, to ensure the Company can sustain long-term compliance, Staff may require that the closing bid price equals $1.00 per share or greater for more than 10 consecutive trading days before determining that the Company complies." The letter also suggested that KILN consider transferring its securities to the Nasdaq Small Cap Market. The Small Cap Market also required listed companies to maintain a $1.00 minimum bid price but offered an extended period within which to regain compliance with that requirement.

C. Kirincic places trades in parents' accounts following delisting notice

Shortly after Nasdaq notified KILN that its low bid price threatened its listing status, Kirincic placed several trades in accounts held at Kirlin by his parents. Although Kirincic did not have formal discretionary authority over these accounts, he testified that he exercised time and price discretion in placing orders to effect his customers' trades "to get the best execution for my customer without impacting the market." On March 5, 2002, Kirincic placed an order with Israel to cross four sell orders (two from his parents' retirement accounts and two from the accounts of his parents-in-law) with a buy order for his parents' joint (non-retirement) account for 140,000 KILN shares at $.85 per share. During the hearing, Kirincic could not recall any details about these transactions or discussions with his parents regarding their reasons for these trades, other than that they served certain unspecified "tax planning" purposes. Despite these trades, KILN's bid price closed at $.80.

From March 7 through March 15, 2002, Kirincic placed several more orders to purchase KILN shares for his parents' joint account, purchasing a total of 10,981 shares in twelve transactions.[36] Kirincic testified that he had no understanding of his parents' strategy in KILN at the time and no recollection of how these orders were executed. Kirincic directed the trading desk to place these orders through the Firm's clearing broker, Bank of New York, which automatically routed the orders to Herzog Heine Geduld ("Herzog"), a market maker in KILN stock.[37] Despite this increase in activity, the price of KILN generally declined through these first two weeks of March, and after the Kirincics' purchases on Friday, March 15, KILN's inside bid price closed at $.64, the lowest closing price since KILN began trading on the NNM in 1999.

D. Kirincic changes his trading strategy, and KILN's price increases

The next trading day, Monday, March 18, Kirincic began placing orders to purchase substantial amounts of KILN stock for his sister, Susan Paduano, and would continue to do so through April 22 (the "Trading Period"). Kirincic, who testified that he exercised time and price discretion over Paduano's orders and also determined how to

---

36. [15] Kirincic's parents purchased 2,800 shares at $.75 on March 7; 500 shares at $.73 on March 8; 100 shares at $.73 on March 11; 581 shares at $.73 and 622 shares at $.71 on March 13; 1,378 shares at $.76 in two transactions on March 14; 2,000 shares at $.6499, 1,000 shares at $.65, and 2,000 shares in three transactions at $.64 on March 15. Kirincic's parents purchased no more KILN shares for this account at least through June 2002, but, as discussed later in this opinion, they sold a total of 385,498 KILN shares back to the company in April 2002.

37. [16] In addition to Herzog, five other firms made a market in KILN stock. Kirlin, however, was not a KILN market maker.

route them in the market, placed most of these orders not through Herzog but through BRUT, an electronic communications network ("ECN"), for execution. A significant feature of trading on ECNs, as Applicants' expert explained, is that, when a broker places an order with an ECN at a price above the highest, or "inside" bid, the ECN automatically displays that bid as its own, creating a new inside bid price that is displayed to the market. According to Applicants' expert, of the 65 orders Kirincic placed for Paduano on the BRUT ECN during the Trading Period, 41 of them were priced at or above the inside bid, and an additional 20 of them were priced at or above the inside ask; more than 93% of Kirincic's orders were therefore responsible for setting a new inside bid. Paduano's KILN purchases would total over $200,000 in a five-week period, account for 43% of the total trading volume in KILN, and increase the price of KILN over 57%.

In March 2002, Paduano was divorced, unemployed, caring for three children, and receiving as income only $3,600 per month in alimony. She nevertheless testified that she gave instructions to Kirincic to purchase shares in large dollar amounts, such as $25,000 or $50,000, depending on what she was "comfortable with" at the time. During the hearing, neither Paduano nor Kirincic could recall specific details about any of the orders she gave Kirincic. Although Paduano had not been an active purchaser of KILN shares in the four years preceding 2002 and had purchased none in January or February 2002, she testified that she wanted to acquire KILN stock because "it was [her] desire to always hold a large position in the company" that her ex-husband (formerly a partner of Kirincic and Lindner) and brother had built. The KILN shares were intended, she said, to be a "legacy for my children." Although each of Paduano's children had a custodial account at another financial institution, all the KILN purchases Paduano made in 2002 were bought through her own account at Kirlin. There is no evidence that Paduano transferred any of the acquired KILN shares to her children's accounts; in fact, as discussed later in this opinion, Paduano sold all the shares she acquired at the end of 2002.

Kirincic did not recall discussing with his sister the wisdom of acquiring substantial amounts of KILN, and Paduano testified that she did not consider news regarding KILN, or the delisting notice it received, when she decided to purchase shares of KILN. Paduano testified that she considered March 2002 to be a good time to acquire KILN because she "had a better cash flow" than in the past. Despite her professed improved cash flow, however, Paduano borrowed substantial amounts from her parents to help finance at least some of these purchases. For example, on April 16, Kirincic effected a transfer of $75,000 from one of his parents' accounts at Kirlin to Paduano's account by means of a letter of authorization to which Kirincic admittedly signed his parents' names. Although Kirincic claims he signed this document, and others discussed later, with his parents' authorization, nothing in the record evidences that authorization.

Kirincic placed his first order for Paduano's account at 9:33 a.m. on March 18, for 7,000 shares (with 500 shares displayed to the market and 6,500 kept "in reserve," i.e., hidden from the market until the displayed portion of the order was filled) at a limit price of $.68 via the BRUT ECN. Because this price was $.01 above the inside ask, Kirincic quickly received a partial fill of about 2,500 shares. An hour later, Kirincic directed that the order for the remaining shares be cancelled and replaced with an order for 4,400 shares (showing 500 with 3,900 in reserve) at $.74 (again, $.01 above the inside ask). Kirincic quickly received a partial fill on 1,500 shares, and the inside market for KILN moved to $.74–$.76. Less than an hour later, Kirincic directed the remaining order be cancelled. At 1:00 p.m., with the inside market at $.66–$.76, Kirincic placed another order for 10,000 shares (showing 1,000 with 9,000 in reserve) at $.76. He immediately received a partial fill of 3,000 shares, and the inside market moved to $.76–$.79. The remainder of this order was filled in increments throughout the afternoon and was completed just before 4:00 p.m. KILN's inside bid price closed at $.68, $.04 higher than the previous day's close.

This pattern of trading activity by Kirincic—*i.e.*, placing an order for several thousand shares (most held in reserve) on the BRUT ECN at a price well above the inside bid (and sometimes at or above the inside ask), receiving partial fills, and then shortly thereafter cancelling and resubmitting the order at a higher price—characterized his trading for Paduano throughout the Trading Period.23 Paduano ultimately purchased 224,653 KILN shares in approximately 115 transactions, including 65 orders placed on the BRUT ECN at prices that equaled or exceeded the existing bid and frequently even equaled or exceeded the existing ask, for a total price of $219,952 during the Trading Period. Applicants' expert calculated that the average time lapse between Kirincic's original orders and his subsequent increases in his bid price was just under ninety minutes. The average daily volume during the Trading Period tripled to 32,019 shares per day based almost exclusively on the activity in Paduano's account, compared to 9,904 shares per day from January 1 through March 15, 2002. As discussed below, KILN's closing bid price rose from $.68 on March 18 to as high as $1.15 on April 16, closing at $1.01 at the end of the Trading Period on April 22.

E. KILN's Board of Directors considers responses to the Nasdaq delisting letter

While Kirincic was beginning to place substantial orders to buy KILN shares for his sister's account at increasing prices, KILN's board of directors was considering its options for addressing its decreasing share price and the potential delisting notice from Nasdaq.... KILN's board authorized a stock repurchase program in which the company agreed to buy back up to $1 million of KILN stock. Kirincic and Lindner were given authority to act as brokers on behalf of KILN's account and were given an upper limit of about $1.30 on the price per share KILN would pay.

F. Kirincic's orders increase in size and KILN's closing bid price rises over $1.00

On April 1 and 2, 2002, KILN made two news announcements that, although positive, had no significant impact on the market. After the market closed on April 1, KILN announced its earnings for 2001 and reported that its net loss of $3.6 million for 2001 was significantly less than its reported net loss of $11 million for 2000. The inside bid for KILN nevertheless dropped $.04, to $.73, on the morning of April 2. Later that morning, KILN publicly announced the stock repurchase program that the board had previously authorized on March 27. Again, the market exhibited no significant response.

A few minutes after the announcement of the repurchase plan, Kirincic resumed purchasing shares for his sister, now in amounts substantially larger than before. Paduano testified, however, that she could not recall why the size of her orders increased in April. Paduano's account purchased a total of 12,500 shares through Herzog at prices beginning at $.9479 in the morning and ending at $.99 just before 3:00 p.m. At approximately 3:30 p.m., the inside bid had risen to $.97; Kirincic placed an order for 50,000 shares (showing 2,500 with 47,500 in reserve) at a price of $1.02 ($.02 above the inside ask price) and immediately began receiving fills on 24,800 shares. Three minutes later, at 3:39 p.m., the inside bid had moved to $1.01. Kirincic cancelled the order for the remaining shares and replaced it with an order for 25,000 shares (showing 2,500 and with 22,500 in reserve) at the inside ask price of $1.04. He received a fill on 400 shares before the market closed, still reflecting his outstanding order as the inside bid price. KILN's inside bid closed at $1.04, the first time it had reached the $1.00 mark in three months.

From April 3 through April 17, 2002, Kirincic continued placing orders of significant size for his sister's account at prices that generally increased from a low of $.95 on April 3 to a high of $1.15 on April 16. KILN's inside bid price closed above $1.00 on each of these ten trading days. Throughout the period, Kirincic placed a total of seventeen orders on BRUT ECN, and the purchases he made on behalf of his sister (totaling over 100,000 shares at over $112,000 total cost) accounted for the vast majority of trading volume in KILN. He placed three orders on April 3 for 10,000 shares and one for 25,000 shares on April 5, but the remaining orders were in much larger amounts — 50,000 and 75,000 shares. Consistent with his strategy earlier in the Trading Period, Kirincic generally placed an order at a price above the inside bid, received partial fills, and then replaced the order with one at a higher price.

Also during this period, on April 3, Kirincic placed an order for Paduano on Bank of New York's system, which was routed to Herzog, for 2,000 shares at $1.01. This order was placed just one minute after Kirincic placed an order for 50,000 shares at $1.02 on BRUT ECN. It was entered as "good til cancelled," which meant that the order remained active in the market without expiring until fully executed or cancelled. During the hearing, Kirincic testified that he had no "specific recollection" of why he placed this order while he was already placing large orders through BRUT ECN at higher prices, though he admittedly understood that the effect of doing so would create the appearance that there were two different purchasers of KILN in the market. Kirincic received a fill on 1,000 shares on April 4, but the balance of the order remained active in the market until it was filled thirteen trading days later, on April 22. Kirincic's good til cancelled order therefore set a floor of $1.01 on the inside

G. KILN regains compliance with Nasdaq listing requirements

On the morning of April 18, 2002, Nasdaq sent an e-mail to Kirincic noting that KILN's bid price had closed above $1.00 for twelve consecutive days. Nasdaq staff stated that, "[p]rovided the bid price does not close below $1.00 for the next two trading days, on Monday (4/22/02) Staff will issue a formal notice of compliance."

Kirincic placed a few more orders for his sister's account in April after receiving KILN's compliance notice, making purchases for her account totaling 6,200 shares at prices ranging from $1.041 to $1.1489 on April 18 and 22. During subsequent months, Kirincic continued to purchase shares of KILN for Paduano's account, but with less apparent urgency. During the five-week Trading Period, Paduano had purchased a total of 224,653 shares (for a total price of $219,952) on 19 out of 26 trading days;[38] she was therefore buying KILN shares on 73% of the days in the Trading Period with an average purchase of $8,641 per trading day. Following the end of the Trading Period through October 2002, Paduano's account purchased 303,285 KILN shares (for a total price of $228,419) on 59 out of 133 trading days; she was therefore buying KILN shares on only 44% of the remaining days in 2002 with an average purchase of $1,717 per trading day. The price of KILN shares declined along with the frequency of Paduano's purchases. According to data provided by Applicants, KILN's inside bid price closed at or above $1.00 on only four more days in April, two days in May, and one day in June 2002.

On July 30, 2002, KILN received notice from Nasdaq that the stock was again out of compliance with the minimum bid price rule and was given until October 28, 2002 to regain compliance. On August 14, 2002, KILN filed a Form 10-Q for the period ending June 30, 2002, in which it noted that it "will need to phase down to the Nasdaq SmallCap Market," which would extend the deadline for compliance with the $1.00 minimum bid price rule. On October 25, 2002, KILN submitted an application to transfer to Nasdaq's Small Cap Market, which was granted on November 21, 2002.

On December 24, 2002, Paduano sold back to KILN all of the shares she had bought that year: she sold 600,000 shares back to KILN at $.45 per share, for a total sale price of $270,000. When asked why she sold most of her KILN holdings in December, Paduano testified that she was "really extended out there," "was going on a very expensive trip to Europe," and was still waiting for her ex-husband to pay her the money she was owed. She felt she "had to put this dream of my legacy on the back burner...."

On January 6, 2003, KILN effected a one-for-eight reverse stock split, and the company's board of directors announced that it "hope[d] that a higher stock price with fewer shares outstanding will enable our Company to be better received by the marketplace in the future." KILN traded on the Small Cap Market until August 2008, when the company changed its name to Zen Holdings Corp., and is currently quoted in the Pink Sheets.

---

38. [38] Paduano was in the market, however, on 23 out of 26 days because her good til cancelled order with a KILN market maker was active from April 3 through April 22.

* * *

III.

A. Manipulation

Section 10(b) of the Exchange Act and Exchange Act Rule 10b-5, as well as NASD Rule 2120, make it unlawful for any person to use any manipulative or fraudulent device in connection with the purchase or sale of any security, which includes manipulative trading. We have characterized manipulation as "the creation of deceptive value or market activity for a security, accomplished by an intentional interference with the free forces of supply and demand." Manipulation of the market for securities is at the core of conduct that the securities laws were designed to prevent. Indeed, it "strikes at the heart of the pricing process on which all investors rely [and] attacks the very foundation and integrity of the free market system." We have explained in the past that, "[w]hen investors and prospective investors see activity, they are entitled to assume that it is real activity."

In determining whether a manipulation has occurred, the Commission generally looks to see whether the trading and surrounding circumstances suggest an effort to "interfere[] with the free forces of supply and demand." We have noted that "[p]roof of a manipulation almost always depends on inferences drawn from a mass of factual detail" including "patterns of behavior[] and ... trading data." We have also observed that manipulations often display several characteristics, including, among other things, a rapid surge in the price of a security, little investor interest in the security, the absence of any known prospects for the issuer or favorable developments affecting the issuer or its business, and market domination.

In order to establish that the manipulative conduct at issue constitutes a violation of Exchange Act Section 10(b) and Rule 10b-5 thereunder, as well as analogous NASD rules, we must also find that Applicants acted with scienter, defined as "a mental state embracing intent to deceive, manipulate, or defraud." A finding that Applicants acted recklessly can satisfy this requirement. Recklessness in this context has been defined as "an extreme departure from the standards of ordinary care, ... which presents a danger of misleading buyers or sellers that is either known to the defendant or is so obvious that the actor must have been aware of it."

The evidence demonstrates that Kirincic traded in KILN during the Trading Period, as assisted by Israel, for the purpose of increasing the inside bid price of KILN shares. Kirincic's trading in KILN on behalf of his family displays many of the common characteristics of a manipulative scheme. The price of KILN dramatically increased over the Trading Period, rising from $.68 on March 18 to $1.15 on April 16, closing at $1.01 on the last day of the Trading Period. This is an increase of up to 69% despite the lack of any public news that could explain the change and despite the lack of any significant outside interest in KILN stock. Moreover, the trading Kirincic brokered on behalf of his family accounted for the vast majority of volume in KILN shares during the Trading Period: Paduano's purchases (plus trading in KILN shares by other market participants that was necessary to fill her orders) represented 43% of all trading in KILN. The figure climbs to 79% when including KILN's repurchases from Kirincic's parents and cousin. We find KILN's dramatic movement in price, unexplained by other legitimate market forces and considered along with Kirlin's domination of the market for KILN, constitute compelling evidence that Kirincic manipulated the market for KILN.

The specific pattern of trading Kirincic used also strongly suggests fraud. Kirincic learned in late February 2002 that KILN faced delisting from the NNM. Shortly thereafter, in early March, he placed several trades for his parents with a KILN market maker that did not increase KILN's closing bid price. The day after KILN's bid price closed at a historic low despite his parents' purchases, Kirincic began placing orders for his sister's account using a different strategy—placing orders on an ECN at a price above the inside bid (often well above the inside bid), and cancelling and re-entering the order at increasingly higher prices even after his lower bids had generated market interest. On April 2, as KILN's bid price approached $1.00 for the first time in months, Kirincic began placing substantially larger orders for his sister—orders of a size that dwarfed the normal daily volume for the stock—while continuing to enter increasingly higher bids. According to Applicants' exhibits, Kirincic's orders set a new inside bid or equaled the inside bid more than 90% of the time during the Trading Period and were placed at or above the inside ask more than 30% of the time. This kind of price leadership, especially for the stock of a company dealing with substantial financial losses, declining stock prices, and potential delisting from the Nasdaq, is a "classic element []" of manipulation.

Kirincic's intent to move the price of KILN upward is further supported by the circumstances surrounding his purchases. KILN's board of directors, of which Kirincic was a member, consistently declared in its meeting minutes and public filings that it considered its listing on the NNM to be important, noting in a 10-K filing that delisting could "adversely affect" the company's liquidity and depress its stock price. Kirincic himself conceded that, "[g]iven the choice of being on either [National or Small Cap Market], I would prefer to be on one that was more highly recognized by the market." Moreover, even if the company would ultimately have to phase down to the Small Cap Market because it could not maintain the shareholder equity requirements of the National Market, KILN still needed to maintain a $1.00 minimum closing bid price to qualify for Nasdaq's Small Cap market. Kirincic was also a significant holder of KILN stock, and, although he himself never sold his holdings, Kirincic's parents and cousin sold substantial amounts of KILN stock back to the company in its repurchase program and received an inflated price for their shares....

Applicants argue that they did not engage in manipulation and that, rather, "[t]he trading pattern exhibited by Kirlin's purchases for the Paduano account is consistent with a prudent accumulation strategy designed to minimize the affect [sic] on KILN's market price and to acquire large amounts of stock at better prices." However, neither Kirincic nor Paduano could adequately or credibly explain the reasons for his trading on her behalf: the National Adjudicatory Council ("NAC") accepted the Hearing Panel's finding that "Kirincic's attempts to explain the trading in [Paduano's] account, his claim that [Paduano] directed and initiated the purchases in her account, and [Paduano's] explanation that the increased trading in her account was meant to leave a legacy of Kirlin Holding stock for her children were not credible." We, too, find no basis to disturb FINRA's rejection of Kirincic's and Paduano's explanation of the trading in her account.

Applicants further assert that "[t]he manner in which Mr. Kirincic placed orders through BRUT allowed him to obtain lower prices for Ms. Paduano. If the total size of the orders had been exposed, the market might have viewed that order differently and could have been more aggressive in its pricing. In this case, the orders entered by Mr. Kirincic did not drive the price up." However, the record evidence demonstrates otherwise. With Paduano as the only significant participant in the market during the Trading Period, excluding the other repurchase transactions by Kirincic's parents and cousin, and with no other market developments or news that had any apparent effect on the market for KILN, the price of KILN rose from a near historic low of $.68 to as high as $1.15. This price change occurred while Kirincic was placing orders for Paduano that habitually set new inside bid prices. Moreover, although Kirincic did not show the entire amount of his order when he placed orders on BRUT, his pricing strategy—entering orders well above the inside bid, receiving partial fills, and shortly thereafter re-entering the order at a higher price—is inconsistent with a strategy to obtain the best price for Paduano. Kirincic's willingness to bid increasingly higher prices without waiting long for the market to come to him suggests an urgency to his acquisition of stock that neither he nor his sister could explain. Moreover, Applicants fail to explain how Paduano's eventual liquidation in December 2002 of all the shares she acquired that year is consistent with her professed legitimate acquisition strategy.

Applicants also argue that "the trade data shows support for the market when Kirlin had no ECN orders pending as well as activity not involving the firm. This is further evidence that the price of KILN was set as a result of the independent judgments of the various market makers providing a market and liquidity in the security." Again, the record evidence demonstrates otherwise. As noted, transactions by Kirincic's family members accounted for 79% of the trading in KILN during the Trading Period. Although there were five days during the Trading Period when Kirincic did not place orders on BRUT while the bid price still remained over $1.00, the April 3 good-til-cancelled order for 2,000 shares at a limit price of $1.01 (which received a partial fill on April 4) was pending with Herzog and supported the price on all of those days. Moreover, after the Trading Period, when Kirincic was no longer making frequent purchases for Paduano, the price of KILN dropped dramatically and steadily declined. The record does not support Applicants' argument, therefore, that the market supported a price over $1.00 for KILN during the Trading Period without Kirincic's intervention.

Applicants argue that at least one district court has held that, in open market transactions in which "the beneficial ownership of the securities change and the volume of trading reflects actual market activity," the Commission "must prove that but for the manipulative intent, the defendant would not have conducted the transaction." Moreover, Applicants argue, "if a securities transaction was made 'for an investment purpose,' then 'there is no manipulation, even if an increase or domination in price was a foreseeable consequence of the investment.'" As discussed, the Hearing Panel that observed their demeanor did not credit the testimony of Kirincic and Paduano that Kirincic placed trades in Paduano's account "for an investment purpose," *i.e.*, as part of a legitimate strategy to acquire KILN shares as a legacy for Paduano's children, and we have acceded to that determination. In addition, Paduano's subsequent liquidation of KILN shares in December 2002 further contradicts her stated "investment purpose." Moreover, the Commission has consistently held that an applicant's scienter renders his interference with the market illegal, and this understanding of the antifraud provisions has been explicitly ratified by at least one reviewing court.

We conclude, therefore, that Kirincic manipulated the market for KILN and that Israel, who entered or reviewed all of Kirincic's orders excepting one week in April, was at least reckless in his participation in the scheme. Based on Kirincic's and Israel's conduct, Kirlin is also liable for the manipulation. We affirm FINRA's finding that Kirincic, Israel, and Kirlin thereby violated Exchange Act Section 10(b), Exchange Act Rule 10b-5, and NASD Rules 2120 and 2110.[39]

Notes and Questions

1. What must the defendant control to successfully manipulate the market in a particular security? How was this illustrated in *Kirlin*?

2. *FINRA Rule 2020. Use of Manipulative, Deceptive or Other Fraudulent Devices.* No member shall effect any transaction in, or induce the purchase or sale of, any security by means of any manipulative, deceptive or other fraudulent device or contrivance. If a broker-dealer violates FINRA Rule 2020, does it also violate FINRA Rule 2111?

3. *Market Manipulation and Profitability.* Most circuits hold that profit is not a necessary element in establishing a market manipulation claim. It is sufficient to show that the defendants purposely endeavored to raise or depress the price of the security. However, there are a few cases that hold that profit is an element of a market manipulation claim. *See Baum v. Phillips, Appel & Walden, Inc.*, 648 F. Supp. 1518 (S.D.N.Y. 1986); *United States v. Mulheren*, 938 F.2d 364 (2d. Cir. 1991); and *In re College Bound Consolidated Litigation*, Fed. Sec. L. Rep. (CCH) ¶ 98,310 (S.D.N.Y. 1994).

---

39. [81] It is well established that a violation of a Commission or NASD rule or regulation is inconsistent with just and equitable principles of trade, and is therefore also a violation of Rule 2110 [now FINRA Rule 2010]. *Frank Thomas Devine*, 55 S.E.C. 1180, 1192 n.30 (2002).

Hypothetical Three

Through a terminal at Success First's New York City headquarters, Krystal Owu, a trader, entered small buy or sell limit orders into Ajax, an electronic communications network, at a price better than the existing NBBO. When Krystal placed these orders, her price became the new NBBO. As soon as Krystal placed a single small limit order through Ajax, she directed her assistant to immediately enter a larger sell or buy order on the opposite side of the market into Success First's order and execution system. Market makers would automatically execute the order at the newly created NBBO price, a better price than would otherwise have been available in the market. The market maker's execution of the larger order entered by Krystal's assistant at the improved price would occur within seconds after Krystal entered her initial order into Ajax. As soon as the market maker executed the larger order at the improved price, Krystal canceled the small Ajax limit order. Because Krytal's transactions only took seconds, there were no other market changes that affected the NBBO. For example, on March 19 at 12:01:00 the NBBO for ANAD was $16 bid and $16.5 offer. At 12:02:57, Krystal sent a limit order to Ajax to buy 100 shares of ANAD at $16.4375, which changed the Ajax quote and the NBBO for ANAD to $16.4375 bid and $16.5 offer. Then, as directed by Krystal, her assistant sent an order through Success First's order and execution system to sell 2,000 shares of ANAD, which was executed by the market maker for $16.4375 at 12:03:01 and reported at 12:03:02. At 12:03:06, Krystal canceled the Ajax limit order, which resulted in the Ajax quote and the NBBO for ANAD returning to $16 bid and $16.5 offer. In eight transactions, Krystal altered the Ajax quote and NBBO by entering a sell order; in 12 transactions, she altered the market by entering a buy order. As a result of Krystal's transactions, she obtained advantageous price gains totaling approximately $5,675. Malak Johnson is currently reviewing Krystal's trading to determine whether Krystal has engaged in market manipulation in violation of § 10(b) and Rule 10b-5. Has she?

Chapter 12

Securities Arbitration

Regulatory Authority

Federal Arbitration Act 9 U.S.C. § 1, et seq.

Uniform Arbitration Act (1956, rev. 2000)

Uniform Mediation Act (2001, am. 2003)

FINRA Rules 10000 Series Uniform Practice Code; 12000 Series Code of Arbitration Procedure for Customer Disputes; 13000 Series Code of Arbitration Procedure for Industry Disputes; 14000 Series Code of Mediation Procedure

Other

ABA/AAA Code of Ethics for Arbitrators in Commercial Disputes

AAA Code of Arbitration for Securities Disputes

Motivating Hypothetical

Pram Poi, a registered representative, is a successful financial advisor in the Chicago, Illinois, office of Success First. Martha White, Poi's customer, recently filed an arbitration against the firm complaining of losses of $45,000 in her managed IRA account which she believes were caused by being placed in risky, illiquid, and unsuitable REIT's. Poi is concerned the customer complaint will be disclosed on BrokerCheck and intends to obtain an expungement of the complaint via the arbitration process. Poi is unsure of whether she will succeed in clearing her record because she is not a named party in the arbitration and the firm will likely settle with the customer.

In addition to the customer complaint, Poi, after receiving exceptional performance ratings for five years, recently received a below-average performance rating from Manj Kirb, a new supervisor. After speaking with White, Kirb requested that Poi resign immediately and withheld her year-end bonus despite Poi being one of Success First's best performing registered representatives in Chicago. Kirb stated that if Poi did not resign quietly then entries would be made on Poi's Form U5. Poi is fairly certain Kirb is retaliating because Poi refused to go out with Kirb. Poi voluntarily resigned but was surprised to receive a Form U5 stating that she was discharged and that she engaged in conduct inconsistent with firm policy.

Poi filed a discrimination claim in court against Success First and Kirb. Additionally, Poi has also filed an arbitration with FINRA against Success First alleging breach of her employment contract, to recover her annual bonus, and to obtain expungement of the comments on her Form U5. After receipt of the Form U5, FINRA requested that Success First and Poi submit statements explaining the circumstances of Poi's termination to determine if any violation of the federal securities laws or FINRA rules occurred. Success First's mandatory arbitration clause applies to customers and employees but not to statutory discrimination cases. Consider what steps each party should take to obtain their intended outcome.

I. Development of Arbitration in the United States

Arbitration is a form of final and binding alternative dispute resolution whereby a neutral third party resolves a dispute. Arbitration is a creature of contract, and parties enter into agreements either before or after the conflict arises. Arbitration in the United States developed in the eighteenth and nineteenth centuries along with the development of trade and trade associations. In 1768, the New York Chamber of Commerce initiated an arbitration system for its merchants to "settl[e] business disputes according to trade practices rather than legal principles." The problem with these private agreements to arbitrate was enforcement—either party could avoid the obligation to arbitrate. An arbitration agreement could neither be enforced by statute nor common law. American courts followed English contract law, finding that arbitration of disputes in lieu of a judicial forum was unenforceable and the courts continued to retain their jurisdiction.

New York, home to two arbitration proponents, would lead the way in the development and enforceability of arbitration agreements. Recognizing the limitations on the growth of arbitration, Julius Cohen, general counsel for the New York State Chamber of Commerce, and Charles Bernheimer, a merchant and chair of the Chamber's arbitration committee, became the architects of the Arbitration Law of New York.[1] Enacted in 1920, the Arbitration Law of New York became the first modern state statute declaring all arbitration agreements, including agreements to resolve future disputes, enforceable. Thus, arbitration became enforceable across all sectors in the state. However, citizens and merchants conducting business with those outside the state could not enforce the arbitration statute if the other state did not have a similar statute, nor could the arbitration statute be enforced in federal court under diversity jurisdiction because the federal court could not enforce a state arbitration statute. Cohen and Bernheimer set their sights upon the national stage with the intent to pass a federal law that would make arbitration agreements enforceable in federal courts.

---

1. Margaret L. Moses, *Statutory Misconstruction: How the Supreme Court Created a Federal Arbitration Law Never Enacted by Congress*, 34 Fla. St. U. L. Rev. 99, 101 (2006) citing to Ian R. Macneil, American Arbitration Law 28, 34–37 (1992).

A. The Federal Arbitration Act

Modeled on the New York statute, the Federal Arbitration Act ("FAA") provided for the enforcement of arbitration awards in federal court. In congressional hearings, Cohen presented the FAA as a procedural statute, which allows for enforcement of arbitration agreements voluntarily entered into by merchants who needed speedy resolution of disputes by experts. Congress, in enacting the FAA in 1925, intended to make arbitration agreements enforceable and irrevocable between businesses in the same manner as business contracts. Bernheimer, testifying before the Joint Hearings of the Senate and House Subcommittees in support of the FAA, stated that arbitration "preserves business friendships."[2] The FAA promoted arbitration by enforcing arbitration agreements as irrevocable, with limited exceptions, staying alternative proceedings in favor of arbitration, and limiting the grounds for vacating an arbitration award.[3] Under § 2 of the FAA, "an agreement in writing to submit to arbitration an existing controversy arising out of such a contract, transaction, or refusal, shall be valid, irrevocable, and enforceable" unless there exist grounds "at law or equity for the revocation of any contract." Thus, the arbitration agreement is presumed to be valid and enforceable unless a traditional contract defense (e.g., fraud, unconscionability, mistake, or duress) is available to the claimant, who bears the burden of demonstrating its invalidity. If any party fails to arbitrate pursuant to an agreement, the aggrieved party may petition any United States district court for an order directing that the matter proceed in arbitration. The FAA also provides for the enforcement of arbitration awards as well as the vacatur of the award under limited circumstances.

B. Enforceability of Mandatory Arbitration Agreements

Years after the establishment of the FAA, arbitration remained a device to be used between businesses rather than between businesses and individuals. When faced with arbitration agreements between businesses and individuals, the courts recognized and affirmed the individual's access to the courts in cases such as *Wilko v. Swan*. In *Wilko*, Joseph Wilko purchased 1,600 shares of the common stock of Air Associates, Inc. from Joseph Swan, a broker with Hayden, Stone & Co. Wilko alleged he purchased the shares relying on the broker's statements about a merger, notable parties who were purchasing the stock, and the expected increase in the value of the stock by $6.00 per share. Two weeks later, Wilko sold the stock for a loss.

Wilko filed a claim under § 12(a)(2) of the Securities Act of 1933 alleging misrepresentation and omission of material facts. The respondents moved to stay the trial pursuant to the FAA asserting that the terms and conditions of the margin agreement,

---

2. Arbitration of Interstate Commercial Disputes: Hearing on S. 1005 and H.R. 646 Before the J. Comm. of Subcomms. on the Judiciary, 68th Cong. 16, 7–8 (1924).

3. 9 U.S.C. §§ 2, 3 & 10 (2000).

which contained a mandatory alternative dispute resolution clause, required arbitration. The District Court denied the stay, finding the anti-waiver provision of § 14 of the Securities Act of 1933 evidenced a congressional intent to provide a court remedy.[4] Hayden, Stone & Co. appealed and the Second Circuit ruled that the FAA demonstrates a congressional policy to favor arbitration, and if Congress had intended to forbid arbitration for § 12(a)(2), such intent would have been expressed by Congress. Wilko appealed to the Supreme Court.

Wilko v. Swan

346 U.S. 427 (1953)

Mr. Justice Reed delivered the opinion of the Court.

This action by petitioner, a customer, against respondents, partners in a securities brokerage firm, was brought in the United States District Court for the Southern District of New York, to recover damages under § 12 (2) of the Securities Act of 1933.[5] The complaint alleged that on or about January 17, 1951, through the instrumentalities of interstate commerce, petitioner was induced by Hayden, Stone and Company to purchase 1,600 shares of the common stock of Air Associates, Incorporated, by false representations that pursuant to a merger contract with the Borg Warner Corporation, Air Associates' stock would be valued at $ 6.00 per share over the then current market price, and that financial interests were buying up the stock for the speculative profit. It was alleged that he was not told that Haven B. Page (also named as a defendant but not involved in this review), a director of, and counsel for, Air Associates was then selling his own Air Associates' stock, including some or all that petitioner purchased. Two weeks after the purchase, petitioner disposed of the stock at a loss. Claiming that the loss was due to the firm's misrepresentations and omission of information concerning Mr. Page, he sought damages.

---

4. Under § 14 of the Securities Act of 1933 any "condition, stipulation, or provision" waiving compliance with the Act is "void."

5. [1] 48 Stat. 74, *15 U. S. C. § 77a et seq.* § 12 (2), 48 Stat. 84, *15 U. S. C. § 77l* (2), provides:
   "Any person who— ...
   "(2) sells a security (whether or not exempted by the provisions of section 77c of this title, other than paragraph (2) of subsection (a) of said section 77c), by the use of any means or instruments of transportation or communication in interstate commerce or of the mails, by means of a prospectus or oral communication, which includes an untrue statement of a material fact or omits to state a material fact necessary in order to make the statements, in the light of the circumstances under which they were made, not misleading (the purchaser not knowing of such untruth or omission), and who shall not sustain the burden of proof that he did not know, and in the exercise of reasonable care could not have known, of such untruth or omission, shall be liable to the person purchasing such security from him, who may sue either at law or in equity in any court of competent jurisdiction, to recover the consideration paid for such security with interest thereon, less the amount of any income received thereon, upon the tender of such security, or for damages if he no longer owns the security."

Without answering the complaint, the respondent moved to stay the trial of the action pursuant to § 3 of the United States Arbitration Act[6] until an arbitration in accordance with the terms of identical margin agreements was had. An affidavit accompanied the motion stating that the parties' relationship was controlled by the terms of the agreements and that while the firm was willing to arbitrate petitioner had failed to seek or proceed with any arbitration of the controversy.

Finding that the margin agreements provide that arbitration should be the method of settling all future controversies, the District Court held that the agreement to arbitrate deprived petitioner of the advantageous court remedy afforded by the Securities Act, and denied the stay. A divided Court of Appeals concluded that the Act did not prohibit the agreement to refer future controversies to arbitration, and reversed.

The question is whether an agreement to arbitrate a future controversy is a "condition, stipulation, or provision binding any person acquiring any security to waive compliance with any provision" of the Securities Act which § 14[7] declares "void." We granted certiorari to review this important and novel federal question affecting both the Securities Act and the United States Arbitration Act.

As the margin agreement in the light of the complaint evidenced a transaction in interstate commerce, no issue arises as to the applicability of the provisions of the United States Arbitration Act to this suit, based upon the Securities Act.

Designed to protect investors, the [Securities] Act [of 1933] requires issuers, underwriters, and dealers to make full and fair disclosure of the character of securities sold in interstate and foreign commerce and to prevent fraud in their sale. To effectuate this policy, § 12 (2) created a special right to recover for misrepresentation which differs substantially from the common-law action in that the seller is made to assume the burden of proving lack of scienter. The Act's special right is enforceable in any court of competent jurisdiction — federal or state — and removal from a state court is prohibited.

The United States Arbitration Act establishes by statute the desirability of arbitration as an alternative to the complications of litigation. The reports of both Houses on that Act stress the need for avoiding the delay and expense of litigation, and practice

---

6. [3] *9 U. S. C. (Supp. V, 1952) § 1 et seq.* § 3 provides:
   "If any suit or proceeding be brought in any of the courts of the United States upon any issue referable to arbitration under an agreement in writing for such arbitration, the court in which such suit is pending, upon being satisfied that the issue involved in such suit or proceeding is referable to arbitration under such an agreement, shall on application of one of the parties stay the trial of the action until such arbitration has been had in accordance with the terms of the agreement, providing the applicant for the stay is not in default in proceeding with such arbitration."

7. [6] 48 Stat. 84, *15 U. S. C. § 77n.* § 14 provides:
   "Any condition, stipulation, or provision binding any person acquiring any security to waive compliance with any provision of this subchapter or of the rules and regulations of the Commission shall be void."

under its terms raises hope for its usefulness both in controversies based on statutes or on standards otherwise created. This hospitable attitude of legislatures and courts toward arbitration, however, does not solve our question as to the validity of petitioner's stipulation by the margin agreements, set out below, to submit to arbitration controversies that might arise from the transactions.[8]

Petitioner argues that § 14, note 6, shows that the purpose of Congress was to assure that sellers could not maneuver buyers into a position that might weaken their ability to recover under the Securities Act. He contends that arbitration lacks the certainty of a suit at law under the Act to enforce his rights. He reasons that the arbitration paragraph of the margin agreement is a stipulation that waives "compliance with" the provision of the Securities Act, set out in the margin, conferring jurisdiction of suits and special powers.

Respondent asserts that arbitration is merely a form of trial to be used in lieu of a trial at law, and therefore no conflict exists between the Securities Act and the United States Arbitration Act either in their language or in the congressional purposes in their enactment. Each may function within its own scope, the former to protect investors and the latter to simplify recovery for actionable violations of law by issuers or dealers in securities.

Respondent is in agreement with the Court of Appeals that the margin agreement arbitration paragraph, note 15, does not relieve the seller from either liability or burden of proof, note 1, imposed by the Securities Act. We agree that in so far as the award in arbitration may be affected by legal requirements, statutes or common law, rather than by considerations of fairness, the provisions of the Securities Act control. This is true even though this proposed agreement has no requirement that the arbitrators follow the law. This agreement of the parties as to the effect of the Securities Act includes also acceptance of the invalidity of the paragraph of the margin agreement that relieves the respondent sellers of liability for all "representation or advice by you or your employees or agents regarding the purchase or sale by me of any property...."

The words of § 14, note 6, void any "stipulation" waiving compliance with any "provision" of the Securities Act. This arrangement to arbitrate is a "stipulation," and we think the right to select the judicial forum is the kind of "provision" that cannot be waived under § 14 of the Securities Act. That conclusion is reached for the reasons set out above in the statement of petitioner's contention on this review. While a buyer and seller of securities, under some circumstances, may deal at arm's length on equal terms, it is clear that the Securities Act was drafted with an eye to the disadvantages under which buyers labor. Issuers of and dealers in securities have better opportunities to investigate and appraise the prospective earnings and business plans affecting se-

---

8. [15] "Any controversy arising between us under this contract shall be determined by arbitration pursuant to the Arbitration Law of the State of New York, and under the rules of either the Arbitration Committee of the Chamber of Commerce of the State of New York, or of the American Arbitration Association, or of the Arbitration Committee of the New York Stock Exchange or such other Exchange as may have jurisdiction over the matter in dispute, as I may elect. Any arbitration hereunder shall be before at least three arbitrators."

curities than buyers. It is therefore reasonable for Congress to put buyers of securities covered by that Act on a different basis from other purchasers.

When the security buyer, prior to any violation of the Securities Act, waives his right to sue in courts, he gives up more than would a participant in other business transactions. The security buyer has a wider choice of courts and venue. He thus surrenders one of the advantages the Act gives him and surrenders it at a time when he is less able to judge the weight of the handicap the Securities Act places upon his adversary.

Even though the provisions of the Securities Act, advantageous to the buyer, apply, their effectiveness in application is lessened in arbitration as compared to judicial proceedings. Determination of the quality of a commodity or the amount of money due under a contract is not the type of issue here involved. This case requires subjective findings on the purpose and knowledge of an alleged violator of the Act. They must be not only determined but applied by the arbitrators without judicial instruction on the law. As their award may be made without explanation of their reasons and without a complete record of their proceedings, the arbitrators' conception of the legal meaning of such statutory requirements as "burden of proof," "reasonable care" or "material fact," see note 1, cannot be examined. Power to vacate an award is limited. While it may be true, as the Court of Appeals thought, that a failure of the arbitrators to decide in accordance with the provisions of the Securities Act would "constitute grounds for vacating the award pursuant to *section 10* of the Federal Arbitration Act," that failure would need to be made clearly to appear. In unrestricted submissions, such as the present margin agreements envisage, the interpretations of the law by the arbitrators in contrast to manifest disregard are not subject, in the federal courts, to judicial review for error in interpretation. The United States Arbitration Act contains no provision for judicial determination of legal issues such as is found in the English law. As the protective provisions of the Securities Act require the exercise of judicial direction to fairly assure their effectiveness, it seems to us that Congress must have intended § 14, note 6, to apply to waiver of judicial trial and review.

By the terms of the agreement to arbitrate, petitioner is restricted in his choice of forum prior to the existence of a controversy. While the Securities Act does not require petitioner to sue, a waiver in advance of a controversy stands upon a different footing.

Two policies, not easily reconcilable, are involved in this case. Congress has afforded participants in transactions subject to its legislative power an opportunity generally to secure prompt, economical, and adequate solution of controversies through arbitration if the parties are willing to accept less certainty of legally correct adjustment. On the other hand, it has enacted the Securities Act to protect the rights of investors and has forbidden a waiver of any of those rights. Recognizing the advantages that prior agreements for arbitration may provide for the solution of commercial controversies, we decide that the intention of Congress concerning the sale of securities is better carried out by holding invalid such an agreement for arbitration of issues arising under the Act.

Notes and Questions

1. Why did the *Wilko* court decide that arbitration was inadequate to enforce statutory rights created under the Securities Act?

2. The respondent argued that arbitration is simply "a form of trial to be used in lieu of a trial at law ..." Do you agree that submitting a dispute to a court of law and an arbitration forum involve the same treatment of the claim? Outline the similarities and differences between the arbitration forum and a judicial forum.

3. Justice Frankfurter and Justice Minton dissented, arguing "We have not before us a case in which the record shows that the plaintiff in opening an account had no choice but to accept the arbitration stipulation, thereby making the stipulation an unconscionable and unenforceable provision in a business transaction." How do current agreements to arbitrate disputes between the customer and the broker-dealer compare to this view?

4. The SEC participated actively in all stages of the case and, as *amicus curiae* on behalf of Wilko, asserted that claims under the Securities Exchange Act of 1934 should not be arbitrable.

C. Toward a National Policy Favoring Arbitration

After the *Wilko* decision in 1953, the Court changed course and issued a series of opinions strongly favoring arbitration. The Court became less receptive to the concerns of unequal bargaining power between customers and broker-dealers and found the arbitration process to be adequate. The Court's belief that the arbitration forum was inferior to a judicial forum in the resolution of cases with public policy implications gave way to a policy favoring arbitration. The preference for arbitration arose in an environment in which courts facing backlogs in their dockets were considering alternatives to litigation.

Among the judiciary, there was increased discussion of using arbitration to settle disputes. In April 1976, Chief Justice of the Supreme Court Warren Burger delivered the keynote address at the "National Conference on the Causes of Popular Dissatisfaction with the Administration of Justice," titled *Agenda for 2000 A.D. — A Need for Systematic Anticipation*. Chief Justice Burger proposed the use of arbitration as an alternative to litigation and the overburdened federal dockets, stating "[a]s the work of the courts increases, delays and costs will rise and the well-developed forms of arbitration should have wider use." Additionally, he stated that "a reappraisal of the values of the arbitration process is in order, to determine whether ... arbitration can divert litigation to other channels."[9]

Around this time, several changes in the field of securities arbitration made the arbitration process more uniform. In June 1976, the SEC solicited comments on the

---

9. Warren E. Burger, Chief Justice, United States Supreme Court, Keynote Address at the National Conference on the Causes of Popular Dissatisfaction with the Administration of Justice, 70 F.R.D. 79, 94 (April 7–9, 1976).

development of uniform arbitration procedures for the resolution of small claims between brokerage firms and customers.[10] Several SROs suggested the creation of a task force to develop uniform arbitration procedures. In 1977, the Securities Industry Conference on Arbitration ("SICA") consisting of representatives from the 10 SROs, the public, and the securities industry was established.[11] SICA subsequently issued uniform procedures for the handling of small claims ($2,500 or less) and a Uniform Code of Arbitration setting forth procedures for all claims between customers and broker-dealers.[12] The SEC also tried to ensure that customers were informed of the predispute arbitration agreements they were signing. In 1979, the SEC warned broker-dealers that the use of mandatory arbitration clauses without adequate disclosure to the customer violates SROs' rules of fair dealing.[13]

The modern trend in favor of arbitration began in the early 1980s. In *Moses H. Cone Memorial Hospital v. Mercury Construction Corp.*, 460 U.S. 1, 24 (1983), the Court held that the FAA established a "liberal federal policy favoring arbitration." In 1985, in *Mitsubishi Motors Corp. v. Soler Chrysler-Plymouth, Inc.*, 473 U.S. 614 (1985), the Court held that the enforceability of an arbitration agreement is no less mandatory when based on statutory rights. According to the Court, "[b]y agreeing to arbitrate a statutory claim, a party does not forgo the substantive rights afforded by the statute; it only submits to their resolution in an arbitral, rather than a judicial, forum." This decision was followed in 1987 by *Shearson/American Express Inc. v. McMahon*, 482 U.S. 220, 231 (1987), where the Court criticized the *Wilko* court for its "mistrust of the arbitral process." In *McMahon*, the SEC's amicus brief, unlike the one it filed in *Wilko*, asserted that 1934 Act claims should be arbitrable and stressed its oversight of SRO arbitration forums.

Shearson/American Express Inc. v. McMahon

482 U.S. 220 (1987)

Justice O'CONNOR delivered the opinion of the Court.

This case presents ... questions regarding the enforceability of predispute arbitration agreements between brokerage firms and their customers. The first is whether a claim brought under § 10(b) of the Securities Exchange Act of 1934 (Exchange Act) must be sent to arbitration in accordance with the terms of an arbitration agreement.

---

10. Constantine N. Katsoris, *Securities Arbitration After McMahon*, 16 FORDHAM URB. L. J. 361, 362 (1987) (citing Sec. Exch. Act Release No. 12528 (June 9, 1976), *reprinted in* 9 SEC Docket 833-35 (Mar.–July 1976)) available at: http://ir.lawnet.fordham.edu/cgi/viewcontent.cgi?article=1322&context=ulj.

11. SEC. INDUS. CONFERENCE ON ARBITRATION, FOURTEENTH REPORT OF THE SECURITIES INDUSTRY CONFERENCE ON ARBITRATION SEPTEMBER 2009, 1 (2009) available at: http://www.finra.org/web/groups/arbitrationmediation/@arbmed/@arbtors/documents/arbmed/p120019.pdf.

12. SEC. INDUS. CONFERENCE ON ARBITRATION, FOURTEENTH REPORT OF THE SECURITIES INDUSTRY CONFERENCE ON ARBITRATION SEPTEMBER 2009, 1 (2009) available at: http://www.finra.org/web/groups/arbitrationmediation/@arbmed/@arbtors/documents/arbmed/p120019.pdf.

13. Sec. Exch. Act Release No. 15984 (July 2, 1979).

Between 1980 and 1982, respondents Eugene and Julia McMahon, individually and as trustees for various pension and profit-sharing plans, were customers of petitioner Shearson/American Express Inc. (Shearson), a brokerage firm registered with the Securities and Exchange Commission (SEC or Commission). Two customer agreements signed by Julia McMahon provided for arbitration of any controversy relating to the accounts the McMahons maintained with Shearson. The arbitration provision provided in relevant part as follows:

> "Unless unenforceable due to federal or state law, any controversy arising out of or relating to my accounts, to transactions with you for me or to this agreement or the breach thereof, shall be settled by arbitration in accordance with the rules, then in effect, of the National Association of Securities Dealers, Inc. or the Boards of Directors of the New York Stock Exchange, Inc. and/or the American Stock Exchange, Inc. as I may elect."

In October 1984, the McMahons filed an amended complaint against Shearson and petitioner Mary Ann McNulty, the registered representative who handled their accounts, in the United States District Court for the Southern District of New York. The complaint alleged that McNulty, with Shearson's knowledge, had violated § 10(b) of the Exchange Act and Rule 10b-5, by engaging in fraudulent, excessive trading on respondents' accounts and by making false statements and omitting material facts from the advice given to respondents.

Relying on the customer agreements, petitioners moved to compel arbitration of the McMahons' claims pursuant to § 3 of the Federal Arbitration Act. The District Court granted the motion in part. It then found that the McMahons' § 10(b) claims were arbitrable under the terms of the agreement, concluding that such a result followed from this Court's decision in *Dean Witter Reynolds Inc. v. Byrd*, and the "strong national policy favoring the enforcement of arbitration agreements."

The Court of Appeals ... reversed on the Exchange Act claims.

* * *

II

The [Federal Arbitration] Act was intended to "revers[e] centuries of judicial hostility to arbitration agreements," by "plac[ing] arbitration agreements 'upon the same footing as other contracts.'" The Arbitration Act accomplishes this purpose by providing that arbitration agreements "shall be valid, irrevocable, and enforceable, save upon such grounds as exist at law or in equity for the revocation of any contract." The Act also provides that a court must stay its proceedings if it is satisfied that an issue before it is arbitrable under the agreement; and it authorizes a federal district court to issue an order compelling arbitration if there has been a "failure, neglect, or refusal" to comply with the arbitration agreement.

The Arbitration Act thus establishes a "federal policy favoring arbitration," requiring that "we rigorously enforce agreements to arbitrate." This duty to enforce arbitration agreements is not diminished when a party bound by an agreement raises a claim founded on statutory rights. As we observed in *Mitsubishi Motors Corp. v. Soler*

Chrysler-Plymouth, Inc., "we are well past the time when judicial suspicion of the desirability of arbitration and of the competence of arbitral tribunals" should inhibit enforcement of the Act " 'in controversies based on statutes.' " Absent a well-founded claim that an arbitration agreement resulted from the sort of fraud or excessive economic power that "would provide grounds 'for the revocation of any contract,' " the Arbitration Act "provides no basis for disfavoring agreements to arbitrate statutory claims by skewing the otherwise hospitable inquiry into arbitrability."

The Arbitration Act, standing alone, therefore mandates enforcement of agreements to arbitrate statutory claims. Like any statutory directive, the Arbitration Act's mandate may be overridden by a contrary congressional command. The burden is on the party opposing arbitration, however, to show that Congress intended to preclude a waiver of judicial remedies for the statutory rights at issue. If Congress did intend to limit or prohibit waiver of a judicial forum for a particular claim, such an intent "will be deducible from [the statute's] text or legislative history," or from an inherent conflict between arbitration and the statute's underlying purposes.

III

When Congress enacted the Exchange Act in 1934, it did not specifically address the question of the arbitrability of § 10(b) claims. The McMahons contend, however, that congressional intent to require a judicial forum for the resolution of § 10(b) claims can be deduced from § 29(a) of the Exchange Act which declares void "any condition, stipulation, or provision binding any person to waive compliance with any provision of [the Act]."

First, we reject the McMahons' argument that § 29(a) forbids waiver of § 27 of the Exchange Act. Section 27 provides in relevant part:

"The district courts of the United States ... shall have exclusive jurisdiction of violations of this title or the rules and regulations thereunder, and of all suits in equity and actions at law brought to enforce any liability or duty created by this title or the rules and regulations thereunder."

The McMahons contend that an agreement to waive this jurisdictional provision is unenforceable because § 29(a) voids the waiver of "any provision" of the Exchange Act. The language of § 29(a), however, does not reach so far. What the antiwaiver provision of § 29(a) forbids is enforcement of agreements to waive "compliance" with the provisions of the statute. But § 27 itself does not impose any duty with which persons trading in securities must "comply." By its terms, § 29(a) only prohibits waiver of the substantive obligations imposed by the Exchange Act. Because § 27 does not impose any statutory duties, its waiver does not constitute a waiver of "compliance with any provision" of the Exchange Act under § 29(a).

We do not read *Wilko v. Swan* as compelling a different result. In *Wilko*, the Court held that a predispute agreement could not be enforced to compel arbitration of a claim arising under § 12(2) of the Securities Act. The basis for the ruling was § 14 of the Securities Act, which, like § 29(a) of the Exchange Act, declares void any stipulation "to waive compliance with any provision" of the statute. At the beginning of its analysis, the *Wilko* Court stated that the Securities Act's jurisdictional provision was "the kind of 'provision' that cannot be waived under § 14 of the Securities Act." This statement, however, can only be understood in the context of the Court's ensuing discussion explaining why arbitration was inadequate as a means of enforcing "the provisions of the Securities Act, advantageous to the buyer." The conclusion in *Wilko* was expressly based on the Court's belief that a judicial forum was needed to protect the substantive rights created by the Securities Act: "As the protective provisions of the Securities Act require the exercise of judicial direction to fairly assure their effectiveness, it seems to us that Congress must have intended § 14 ... to apply to waiver of judicial trial and review." *Wilko* must be understood, therefore, as holding that the plaintiff's waiver of the "right to select the judicial forum," was unenforceable only because arbitration was judged inadequate to enforce the statutory rights created by § 12(2).

Indeed, any different reading of *Wilko* would be inconsistent with this Court's decision in *Scherk v. Alberto-Culver Co.* In *Scherk*, the Court upheld enforcement of a predispute agreement to arbitrate Exchange Act claims by parties to an international contract. The *Scherk* Court assumed for purposes of its opinion that *Wilko* applied to the Exchange Act, but it determined that an international contract "involve[d] considerations and policies significantly different from those found controlling in *Wilko*." The Court reasoned that arbitration reduced the uncertainty of international contracts and obviated the danger that a dispute might be submitted to a hostile or unfamiliar forum. At the same time, the Court noted that the advantages of judicial resolution were diminished by the possibility that the opposing party would make "speedy resort to a foreign court." The decision in *Scherk* thus turned on the Court's judgment that under the circumstances of that case, arbitration was an adequate substitute for adjudication as a means of enforcing the parties' statutory rights. *Scherk* supports our understanding that *Wilko* must be read as barring waiver of a judicial forum only where arbitration is inadequate to protect the substantive rights at issue. At the same time, it confirms that where arbitration does provide an adequate means of enforcing the provisions of the Exchange Act, § 29(a) does not void a predispute waiver of § 27—*Scherk* upheld enforcement of just such a waiver.

The second argument offered by the McMahons is that the arbitration agreement effects an impermissible waiver of the substantive protections of the Exchange Act. Ordinarily, "by agreeing to arbitrate a statutory claim, a party does not forgo the substantive rights afforded by the statute; it only submits to their resolution in an arbitral, rather than a judicial, forum." *Mitsubishi Motors Corp. v. Soler-Chrysler-Plymouth, Inc.* The McMahons argue, however, that § 29(a) compels a different conclusion. Initially, they contend that predispute agreements are void under § 29(a) because they tend to result from broker over-reaching. They reason, as do some commentators, that *Wilko* is premised on the belief "that arbitration clauses in securities sales agreements generally are not freely negotiated." According to this view, *Wilko* barred enforcement of predispute agreements because of this frequent inequality of bargaining power, reasoning that Congress intended for § 14 generally to ensure that sellers did not "maneuver buyers into a position that might weaken their ability to recover under the Securities Act." The McMahons urge that we should interpret § 29(a) in the same fashion.

We decline to give *Wilko* a reading so far at odds with the plain language of § 14, or to adopt such an unlikely interpretation of § 29(a). The concern that § 29(a) is directed against is evident from the statute's plain language: it is a concern with whether an agreement "waive[s] compliance with [a] provision" of the Exchange Act. The voluntariness of the agreement is irrelevant to this inquiry: if a stipulation waives compliance with a statutory duty, it is void under § 29(a), whether voluntary or not. Thus, a customer cannot negotiate a reduction in commissions in exchange for a waiver of compliance with the requirements of the Exchange Act, even if the customer knowingly and voluntarily agreed to the bargain. Section 29(a) is concerned, not with whether brokers "maneuver[ed customers] into" an agreement, but with whether the agreement "weaken[s] their ability to recover under the [Exchange] Act." The former is grounds for revoking the contract under ordinary principles of contract law; the latter is grounds for voiding the agreement under § 29(a).

The other reason advanced by the McMahons for finding a waiver of their § 10(b) rights is that arbitration does "weaken their ability to recover under the [Exchange] Act." That is the heart of the Court's decision in *Wilko*, and respondents urge that we should follow its reasoning. *Wilko* listed several grounds why, in the Court's view, the "effectiveness [of the Act's provisions] in application is lessened in arbitration." First, the *Wilko* Court believed that arbitration proceedings were not suited to cases requiring "subjective findings on the purpose and knowledge of an alleged violator." *Wilko* also was concerned that arbitrators must make legal determinations "without judicial instruction on the law," and that an arbitration award "may be made without explanation of [the arbitrator's] reasons and without a complete record of their proceedings." Finally, *Wilko* noted that the "power to vacate an award is limited," and that "interpretations of the law by the arbitrators in contrast to manifest disregard are not subject, in the federal courts, to judicial review for error in interpretation." *Wilko* concluded that in view of these drawbacks to arbitration, § 12(2) claims "require[d] the exercise of judicial direction to fairly assure their effectiveness."

Instead, the reasons given in *Wilko* reflect a general suspicion of the desirability of arbitration and the competence of arbitral tribunals—most apply with no greater force to the arbitration of securities disputes than to the arbitration of legal disputes generally. It is difficult to reconcile *Wilko's* mistrust of the arbitral process with this Court's subsequent decisions involving the Arbitration Act.

Indeed, most of the reasons given in *Wilko* have been rejected subsequently by the Court as a basis for holding claims to be nonarbitrable. In *Mitsubishi*, for example, we recognized that arbitral tribunals are readily capable of handling the factual and legal complexities of antitrust claims, notwithstanding the absence of judicial instruction and supervision. Likewise, we have concluded that the streamlined procedures of arbitration do not entail any consequential restriction on substantive rights. Finally, we have indicated that there is no reason to assume at the outset that arbitrators will not follow the law; although judicial scrutiny of arbitration awards necessarily is limited, such review is sufficient to ensure that arbitrators comply with the requirements of the statute.

The suitability of arbitration as a means of enforcing Exchange Act rights is evident from our decision in *Scherk*. Although the holding in that case was limited to international agreements, the competence of arbitral tribunals to resolve § 10(b) claims is the same in both settings. Courts likewise have routinely enforced agreements to arbitrate § 10(b) claims where both parties are members of a securities exchange or the National Association of Securities Dealers (NASD), suggesting that arbitral tribunals are fully capable of handling such matters.

Thus, the mistrust of arbitration that formed the basis for the *Wilko* opinion in 1953 is difficult to square with the assessment of arbitration that has prevailed since that time. This is especially so in light of the intervening changes in the regulatory structure of the securities laws. Even if *Wilko*'s assumptions regarding arbitration were valid at the time *Wilko* was decided, most certainly they do not hold true today for arbitration procedures subject to the SEC's oversight authority.

In 1953, when *Wilko* was decided, the Commission had only limited authority over the rules governing self-regulatory organizations (SROs) — the national securities exchanges and registered securities associations — and this authority appears not to have included any authority at all over their arbitration rules. Since the 1975 amendments to § 19 of the Exchange Act, however, the Commission has had expansive power to ensure the adequacy of the arbitration procedures employed by the SROs. No proposed rule change may take effect unless the SEC finds that the proposed rule is consistent with the requirements of the Exchange Act, and the Commission has the power, on its own initiative, to "abrogate, add to, and delete from" any SRO rule if it finds such changes necessary or appropriate to further the objectives of the Act. In short, the Commission has broad authority to oversee and to regulate the rules adopted by the SROs relating to customer disputes, including the power to mandate the adoption of any rules it deems necessary to ensure that arbitration procedures adequately protect statutory rights.

In the exercise of its regulatory authority, the SEC has specifically approved the arbitration procedures of the New York Stock Exchange, the American Stock Exchange, and the NASD, the organizations mentioned in the arbitration agreement at issue in this case. We conclude that where, as in this case, the prescribed procedures are subject to the Commission's § 19 authority, an arbitration agreement does not effect a waiver of the protections of the Act.

We conclude, therefore, that Congress did not intend for § 29(a) to bar enforcement of all predispute arbitration agreements. In this case, where the SEC has sufficient statutory authority to ensure that arbitration is adequate to vindicate Exchange Act rights, enforcement does not effect a waiver of "compliance with any provision" of the Exchange Act under § 29(a). Accordingly, we hold the McMahons' agreements to arbitrate Exchange Act claims "enforce[able] ... in accord with the explicit provisions of the Arbitration Act."

Notes and Questions

1. While the decision in *McMahon* appears to be a sudden change in course from the Supreme Court's decision in *Wilko*, a review of cases prior to 1987 demonstrates a changing direction in the Court's view of the FAA. In a trilogy of cases in the 1980s, the Supreme Court signaled a new and expansive view of the FAA.

   a.*Moses H. Cone Memorial Hospital v. Mercury Construction Corp.*, 460 U.S. 1 (1983).

   While the issue in this case centered on a procedural question concerning the applicability of the abstention doctrine and not arbitration itself, the Court's expansive views of the FAA would have a lasting impact on future cases. Moses. H. Cone Hospital sought a declaratory judgment in a state court seeking a declaration that there was no right to arbitration after Mercury Construction sought damages for the hospital's delay during construction. Mercury in response filed a diversity-of-citizenship action in federal district court seeking an order compelling arbitration under the FAA. The District Court, under the abstention doctrine, declined to exercise jurisdiction and stayed the federal action pending resolution of the state claim because both concerned the arbitrability of the construction company's claims. The Court of Appeals for the Fourth Circuit disagreed and remanded the matter for arbitration. The Supreme Court affirmed the Fourth Circuit and announced the FAA was "a congressional declaration of a liberal federal policy favoring arbitration agreements, notwithstanding any state substantive or procedural policies to the contrary." The Court declared, the FAA created "a body of federal substantive law of arbitrability, applicable to any arbitration agreement within the coverage of the Act." The Court also noted "any doubts concerning the scope of arbitrable issues should be resolved in favor of arbitration, whether the problem at hand is the construction of the contract language itself or an allegation of waiver, delay, or a like defense to arbitrability." The question of whether the FAA was intended to preempt contrary state law would be decided the following year in *Southland Corp. v. Keating*.

   b. *Southland Corp. v. Keating*, 465 U.S. 1 (1984).

   Keating, on behalf of 800 franchisees of 7-Eleven, filed a class action against Southland Corp., owner and franchisor of 7-Eleven convenience stores, alleging fraud, breach of contract, breach of fiduciary duty and violation of the disclosure requirements of the California Franchise Investment Law. Keating moved for class certification and Southland moved to compel arbitration pursuant to the franchise agreement. The California Supreme Court held the California Franchise Investment Law required judicial consideration of claims brought under the statute and that it did not contravene the FAA. Southland appealed to the Supreme Court the question whether the California Franchise Investment Law could invalidate an arbitration agreement made pursuant to the FAA. The Supreme Court held the California Franchise Investment Law conflicted with the FAA and as such violated the Supremacy Clause. The Court, relying on *Moses H. Cone*, reiterated that the FAA created "a national policy favoring arbitration and withdrew the power of the states to require a judicial forum for the resolution of claims which the contracting parties agreed to resolve by arbitration." The dissenters, led by Justice O'Connor, disagreed with this conclusion, arguing that the legislative history of the FAA supports an interpretation of the FAA as a procedural rather than a substantive statute intended to apply only in the federal courts. After *Southland*, the Court would turn to considering public policy exceptions to the enforcement of arbitration agreements.

c.   *Mitsubishi Motors Corp. v. Soler Chrysler-Plymouth, Inc.*, 469 U.S. 916 (1985).

Mitsubishi, a Japanese automobile manufacturer, and Soler, a Puerto Rican corporation, entered into a Sales Procedure Agreement, which provided for the sale of Mitsubishi's vehicles to Soler. All disputes arising "out of or in relation to" the sales agreement were to be settled by arbitration in Japan according to the standards of the Japan Commercial Arbitration Association. After initial success in selling the vehicles, Soler was unable to meet the expected sales volume and its request to ship the vehicles to the continental United States and Latin America for sale was denied. Mitsubishi filed an action in District Court to obtain an order to compel arbitration pursuant to the sales agreement. Soler responded by alleging violations of the Sherman Antitrust Act for Mitsubishi's refusal to allow Soler to resell to buyers in North, Central, or South America and argued the arbitration of a statutory cause of action could not have been intended by the arbitration agreement. The Supreme Court granted *certiorari* to determine whether an agreement to arbitrate antitrust claims in an international transaction should be enforced by an American court. The Court relied on *Moses H. Cone* and the "liberal federal policy favoring arbitration agreements" to find for the enforcement of the arbitration agreement, explaining that the enforcement of an arbitration agreement is no different when claims arise based on statutory rights, thereby decimating the public policy exception to the enforcement of arbitration agreements. Evidencing how far the Court has shifted since *Wilko*, the Court proclaimed the public interest in the enforcement of antitrust laws and that the "remedial and deterrent function" intended by the public law can also be attained in an arbitral forum.

2. Three years after *McMahon*, the Court in *Rodriguez de Quijas v. Shearson/American Express Inc.*, 490 U.S. 477 (1989), overturned *Wilko* completely and held that claims under the 1933 Act do not require a judicial forum and thus should proceed in an arbitral forum if an arbitration agreement exists.

3. Review the BrokerCheck report for Mary Ann McNulty (CRD# 858949) using www.finra.org/brokercheck to determine how *McMahon* eventually settled.

4. Section 2 of the FAA, containing the "savings clause," provides that an arbitration agreement is "valid, irrevocable, and enforceable, save upon such grounds as exist at law or in equity for the revocation of any contract." In the current marketplace

where virtually every broker-dealer uses a mandatory predispute arbitration clause as a condition of account opening on a take-it-or-leave-it basis, why are unconscionability and other traditional common law contract defenses as arguments against predispute mandatory arbitration clauses unsuccessful?

5. When the Securities Industry Conference on Arbitration ("SICA") was first formed in 1977, there were 10 SROs with arbitration forums. According to SICA's 2009 14th report, case filings for 2008 showed that 99.9 percent of arbitrations take place in FINRA's arbitration forum. Do you anticipate any conflict of interest with FINRA administering arbitrations involving the securities industry? What may be the advantages and disadvantages of a FINRA-administered dispute resolution forum?

D. Finality of Arbitration Awards

The FAA applies to the vast majority of securities arbitrations because such activity generally involves interstate commerce. With the exception of the few circumstances allowing for modification, correction, or vacatur, the arbitration award is final. Under § 12 of the FAA, a party wishing to challenge an arbitration award must file a motion to vacate within three months after the award is filed or delivered. FAA § 10 provides for vacatur under four circumstances: "(1) where the award was procured by corruption, fraud or other undue means; (2) where there was evident partiality or corruption by any of the arbitrators; (3) where the arbitrators were guilty of misconduct in refusing to postpone the hearing, ... or in refusing to hear evidence pertinent and material to the controversy; or of any other misbehavior by which the rights of any party have been prejudiced; or (4) where the arbitrators exceeded their powers, or so imperfectly executed them that a mutual, final, and definite award upon the subject matter submitted was not made." If vacatur is not the proper remedy, then under § 11, within one year of the award, a party may petition a court for an order modifying or correcting an award to "effect the intent thereof and promote justice" (e.g., where the award contains a material miscalculation or a material mistake in the description of a person, place, or thing described in the award, a decision on matters not submitted to arbitration was made, or the award is defective in some way not impacting the merits of the claim).

II. FINRA's Arbitration Process

FINRA Dispute Resolution, Inc., formed in 2007 as a result of the consolidation of the NASD and NYSE dispute resolution functions, offers both arbitration and mediation to resolve disputes between and among member firms, associated persons, and customers.[14] FINRA operates the largest securities arbitration forum in the United

---

14. In 2000, the NASD created NASD Dispute Resolution, a subsidiary for mediation and arbitration functions. Effective July 30, 2007, the SEC approved the consolidation between NASD and the arbitration functions (in addition to member regulation and enforcement) of the NYSE finding "that NASD's proposal to consolidate the NASD and NYSE arbitration forums is consistent with the Act because it will maintain a fair arbitration forum available for all NYSE arbitration claims, while

States, handling approximately 90 percent of all securities-related arbitrations and mediations.[15] Since 1845, the NYSE has provided for arbitration to settle disputes between its members, and in 1869 expanded the arbitration program by providing for non-members to arbitrate with its members.[16] The NASD has offered voluntary arbitration between members and the public since 1968, and in 1972 made it mandatory for members to arbitrate disputes at the request of the customer.[17] Similar to other FINRA functions, oversight of the FINRA arbitration and mediation forums by the SEC is discharged through the approval of new and amended rules, routine inspections, and inquiries related to complaints received by the SEC.

To account for the diversity of the parties in the forum, FINRA maintains a Code of Arbitration Procedure for Customer Disputes ("Customer Code") and a Code of Arbitration for Industry Disputes ("Industry Code"). There is also a Code of Mediation Procedure ("Mediation Code"). Under the Customer Code, all arbitrations between a customer and an associated person or member broker-dealer must be arbitrated at the request of the customer or pursuant to a written agreement. Under the Industry Code, disputes arising from the business activities of a member broker-dealer and an associated person may be arbitrated between or among members, or associated persons. The FINRA forum may not be used to resolve claims after six years have passed from the event or occurrence giving rise to the claim. Only an arbitrator may decide whether a claim is ineligible pursuant to the six-year limitations period. The filing of an arbitration claim will toll the statute of limitations period should the parties wish to pursue the matter in court.

A. Initiating and Responding to Claims

To initiate arbitration, a claimant must file a statement of claim describing the details of the dispute and the type of relief requested, a submission agreement electing to submit the controversy for arbitration and agreeing to adhere to any award rendered in the matter, and must pay the applicable filing fees unless a fee waiver or deferral is obtained due to financial hardship. FINRA will serve the statement of claim on respondents identified in the statement of claim. Respondents must provide an answer within 45 days after receipt of the statement of claim. Depending on the amount of

---

continuing to maintain a fair forum for NASD claims and claims that it already administers on behalf of other SROs." *Order Approving Consolidation of NASD and NYSE Regulation, Inc.*, Exchange Act Release No. 34-56145, (July 26, 2007) available at: http://www.sec.gov/rules/sro/nasd/2007/34-56145.pdf.

15. FINRA, INC., FINRA DISPUTE RESOLUTION PARTY'S REFERENCE GUIDE SIMPLIFIED CASES, 4 (March 12, 2014), http://www.finra.org/web/groups/arbitrationmediation/@arbmed/@arbion/documents/arbmed/p011177.pdf.

16. NORMAN S. POSER, BROKER-DEALER LAW AND REGULATION 8-4 (rev. 2nd ed. Supp. 2005) (citing New York Stock Exchange Archives (1817–present)). *Id.* at 8-4.1 (citing Arbitration Committees 1845-1869, Inventory of Records of the New York Stock Exchange Board, 7 (on file with NYSE Archives)).

17. NORMAN S. POSER, BROKER-DEALER LAW AND REGULATION 8-5 (rev. 2nd ed. Supp. 2005) (citing Letter from Susie M. Dippel, Quality Assurance Analyst, NASD Regulation, Inc. Dispute Resolution, to author (June 3, 1996) (on file with author)).

the claim either one arbitrator or a panel of three arbitrators with a chairperson will be assigned to the arbitration. If the claim amount is $50,000 or less and is proceeding under the simplified arbitration procedures, the panel will be limited to one arbitrator, unless the parties agree otherwise in writing. For matters between $50,000 and $100,000 one arbitrator will also be assigned unless the parties agree in writing to have a panel of three arbitrators. For claims above $100,000, or if no money damages are requested, a panel of three arbitrators, of which one must be qualified to act as chair, will hear the matter unless the parties agree in writing to have one arbitrator.

B. Appointment, Disqualification, and Authority of Arbitrators

FINRA maintains a roster of non-public (industry), public, and chair-qualified arbitrators. A non-public arbitrator is an arbitrator who currently or within the past five years has worked in the securities industry, spent a substantial part of his or her career engaged in a securities business, or devoted 20 percent or more of his or her professional work serving clients in the securities industry. A public arbitrator is a person who is not engaged in a securities business, has not been engaged in a securities business for the past 20 years, derives no more than 10 percent of income from providing services to securities industry participants, and is not employed by, nor the spouse or immediate family member of an individual engaged in, the securities business. Chair-qualified arbitrators are experienced public and non-public arbitrators with additional arbitration training. Arbitrators have the authority to interpret FINRA's codes of arbitration procedures and those interpretations are final and binding on the parties. All rulings are made by the arbitrators unless the code or the pertinent law provides otherwise or the parties reach a mutual agreement.

Minimum requirements for inclusion on the current list of approximately 6,000 arbitrators include at least five years of paid professional or business experience, two years of college-level credits, and the completion of the basic arbitrator training program. FINRA arbitrators are not FINRA employees, rather they are independent contractors. After becoming a member of the roster, FINRA arbitrators are eligible to serve on any type of securities arbitration with the exception of employment discrimination cases. To be eligible for these cases, an arbitrator must have special qualifications, such as a law degree, a bar membership, substantial knowledge of employment law, 10 or more years of legal experience, and must not have represented primarily the views of employers or employees within the last five years.

FINRA's arbitrator selection process for specific claims commences with the Neutral List Selection System, a computer program that generates, on a random basis, a list of 10 available arbitrators for each available position, based on the hearing location. The selection list is then distributed to the parties along with an arbitrator disclosure report, which includes employment history, education, completed trainings, disclosure/conflict information, publicly available awards, current cases, and a biographical statement for each arbitrator. The parties may strike up to four arbitrators and rank the remaining six arbitrators for each arbitrator position that needs to be filled. For customer cases decided by one arbitrator, a list of 10 public arbitrators will be provided. For customer cases requiring a panel of three arbitrators, parties are provided with a list of 10 chair-qualified public arbitrators, 10 public arbitrators and 10 non-public arbitrators for cases in which the customer does not want a panel composed of all public arbitrators. A party may strike all the arbitrators on the non-public arbitrator list in order to obtain an all-public arbitration panel.

FINRA combines the rankings of the parties and appoints the highest ranked available arbitrator(s). If, after combining the strikes and the rankings, there remain an insufficient number of arbitrators to complete a panel, then FINRA will assign an arbitrator from a list of randomly available chair-qualified arbitrators using the Neutral List Selection System. Parties, after receiving disclosure information for this arbitrator, may challenge the arbitrator. The appointed arbitrators are notified of the identity of the parties and the nature of the dispute. Each arbitrator must make a reasonable effort to ascertain and disclose to FINRA any "interest, relationship or circumstance" that might preclude an "objective and impartial" decision.[18] Any disclosures made by the arbitrator must be provided to the parties.

For good cause, a party may request an arbitrator's recusal from the case. The arbitrator decides the recusal. Parties may also request FINRA to remove the arbitrator if it is "definite and capable of demonstration" that the arbitrator is "biased, lacks impartiality, or has a direct or indirect interest in the outcome of the arbitration."[19] A recusal and a removal may be requested at any time during the arbitration process; however, the standards that apply to a removal depend on the stage of the arbitration. Before the first hearing session has commenced, any close questions regarding the bias or conflict of the arbitrator will be resolved in favor of the customer. After the first hearing session has commenced, FINRA will remove the arbitrator only if the arbitrator failed to disclose any direct or indirect interest required to be disclosed under FINRA Rule 12405.

C. Pre-Hearing Procedures, Discovery, Hearings, and Awards

Where arbitrations involve a hearing, an initial telephonic pre-hearing conference is held to discuss preliminary matters such as discovery, motion deadlines, and subsequent hearing sessions. Discovery tends to be more streamlined in arbitration and FINRA's Document Production Lists describe documents that are presumptively discoverable in customer arbitrations as well as industry arbitrations. Parties may request additional information or documents by serving a written discovery request. Arbitrators may direct non-parties to produce documents by issuing an order or a subpoena. Where parties do not act in good faith, a motion requesting an order to compel

---

18. FINRA Rule 12405.
19. FINRA Rule 12410.

discovery may be filed with the arbitrators. Failure to cooperate in discovery (e.g., failure to produce or frivolous objections) may result in sanctions, including dismissal with prejudice. Motions may be made orally or in writing; if in writing, the motion need not take a particular form. Before parties make a motion, the parties are required to attempt to resolve the matter among themselves.

The hearing venue is determined based on whether the case is brought by a customer or an industry member. For customer cases, the hearing venue is a hearing location closest to the customer's residence at the time events in the dispute arose. For industry cases, the venue is the hearing location closest to where the associated person was employed at the time events in the dispute arose. During the hearing session, testimonial and documentary evidence may be introduced by the parties. Usually at the end of the hearing session, the record is considered complete and no additional submissions are allowed. Arbitration sessions are recorded with a digital tape recorder operated by the arbitrator. A party wishing to have a transcript must bear the cost of transcription services. The lack of a stenographer reduces the overall cost of the arbitration. However, it may also present an impediment to those parties wishing to file an appeal as procuring a transcript may be cost-prohibitive.

FINRA requests that arbitrators render a decision within 30 days of the closing of the record. The arbitrators complete and provide to FINRA the award information sheet which is drafted into a formal award by staff and then made available online to the public at FINRA Arbitration Awards Online after service to the parties. The award will contain basic information regarding the parties, the claim, and the outcome (i.e. names of the parties, their representatives, and the arbitrators; location, dates, and number of hearing sessions held; date the claims were submitted and award rendered; acknowledgement by the arbitrators that they have reviewed the submissions; summary of issues in controversy; any other issues resolved; damages and other relief requested and awarded and allocation of fees). Pursuant to FINRA Rule 12904(f) Awards, a rationale for the award "may" be provided. If jointly requested, 20 days prior to the first scheduled hearing date, arbitrators will provide an explained decision ("a fact based award stating the general reason(s) for the arbitrators' decision.") under Rule 12904(g). After the arbitration, a voluntary evaluation of arbitrators takes place by the parties and by fellow arbitrators. FINRA's arbitrator experience survey seeks input from arbitrators about their colleagues' "dedication, attentiveness and objectivity."[20] This feedback is used to assess the quality of the arbitrators and their continued membership on the arbitration roster.

Arbitration awards are not the common result for claims arbitrated in FINRA's forum. Most arbitration cases in the FINRA forum settle before arbitrators decide the case. In 2013 only 23 percent of cases were decided by arbitrators—of which five percent were decided after a review of the documents (simplified arbitrations) and

---

20. FINRA, Inc., Arbitrator Experience Survey, http://www.finra.org/arbitrationandmediation/arbitrators/caseguidanceresources/evaluations/.

18 percent after a hearing.[21] The remaining 77 percent were resolved by either direct settlement between the parties (52%), by using FINRA mediation (7%), were withdrawn (11%), or were resolved by other means such as a stipulated award or for other reasons such as forum denial, a deficient claim, or stay of arbitration by court action (7%).[22] All fees and assessments arising from the arbitration are due upon receipt of the award. All parties, including customers, must pay fees for using the forum unless the arbitrator reallocates the fees to the opposing party. All monetary awards must be paid within 30 days of receipt of the award unless a motion to vacate has been filed. Failure to pay an award or comply with an arbitration or mediation settlement agreement will result in the suspension or cancellation of membership of the broker-dealer or the registration of the associated person involved in the matter.

D. Special Procedures

FINRA offers a variety of special arbitration procedures. Special arbitration procedures include a simplified arbitration program for small cases with claims of $50,000 or less; a voluntary program for large cases with claims of at least $10 million; expungement procedures for disclosure information; and procedures for investment advisors and non-FINRA member firms.

1. Simplified Arbitration Procedures

To address the needs of investors with small claims, FINRA allows simplified arbitration procedures where the amount of damages alleged is $50,000 or less. These simplified arbitrations (also known as "paper" or "small claims" cases) have procedures designed to further the expedited and cost-efficient resolution of a dispute. Such procedural efficiencies include: a panel composed of a single arbitrator instead of three (unless the parties agree in writing), a decision based on the documents without a hearing (unless the customer requests a hearing), and less extensive discovery. Simplified arbitration procedures cannot be used in cases in which the pleadings allege damages greater than $50,000.

2. Voluntary Program for Large Cases

Where damages involve at least $10 million, a voluntary program for large cases allows the parties to customize FINRA arbitration procedures. For example, the parties may elect to change arbitration selection procedures, such as selecting a non-FINRA arbitrator, or requesting a list of arbitrators who meet specific criteria (e.g., attorney arbitrators, arbitrators with 15 years of experience, and arbitrators with

21. FINRA, Inc., Dispute Resolution Statistics, http://www.finra.org/ArbitrationAndMediation/FINRADisputeResolution/AdditionalResources/Statistics/ (accessed April 10, 2014).

22. FINRA, Inc., Dispute Resolution Statistics, http://www.finra.org/ArbitrationAndMediation/FINRADisputeResolution/AdditionalResources/Statistics/ (accessed April 10, 2014).

M.B.A.s). Parties may also customize discovery such that discovery is broader than allowed by the code (e.g., use of interrogatories and depositions).

3. Expungement

Arbitration procedures provide for the expungement of disclosures in Forms U4 and U5 retained in the Central Registration Depository (CRD) system—the registration system for the securities industry and its regulators maintained by FINRA. Information in the CRD system is disclosed to the public as permitted under FINRA Rule 8312 using FINRA's BrokerCheck service. In order to remove information from the CRD, and, depending on the information, also from BrokerCheck, an expungement order must be presented to FINRA's Registration and Disclosure Department. Expungement of customer dispute information and intra-industry disclosures are treated differently. Where an associated person wishes to expunge customer dispute information, FINRA Rule 2080 requires a court order either directing the expungement or confirming the award granting expungement. An arbitrator may only recommend expungement of customer dispute information after a telephonic or in-person hearing is held to determine if the claim or allegation is: (1) false, (2) clearly erroneous or factually impossible, or (3) the associated person was not involved in the alleged violation.[23] Unlike other arbitration awards, arbitrators are required to provide the grounds for the expungement pursuant to Rule 2080 as well as a written explanation of why expungement of the information was recommended. Afterward, the party must obtain court confirmation of the award where FINRA must be named as a party unless FINRA waives its right to be a party. Unlike the expungement of customer complaints, judicial intervention for intra-industry expungements is not necessary where an arbitration award recommends expungement of information disclosed by a member broker-dealer due to the defamatory nature of the disclosure. However, where an arbitrator grants an expungement request based on the misleading, inaccurate, or erroneous nature of the information, a court order confirming the award is necessary in intra-industry disputes.

4. Investment Advisers

FINRA accepts cases between investment advisers ("IA") and customers and their employees on a voluntary case-by-case basis. FINRA will accept cases between the IA and the customer if the customer submits a post-dispute agreement to participate, the member broker-dealer surcharge is paid by the IA or other parties, and the special submission agreement is signed by all the parties after the events giving rise to the arbitration arose. In the submission agreement, the parties acknowledge that FINRA does not have the authority to enforce the awards as there is no regulatory authority over the parties. The aggrieved party must seek judicial redress if the opposing party does not perform according to the award because FINRA cannot sanction a non-

---

23. FINRA Rule 2080.

member firm or non-registrant. Similar requirements exist for cases between IAs and their employees. The mediation process is also available for IA-related disputes on a voluntary basis.

E. FINRA's Mediation Process

FINRA instituted a voluntary and confidential mediation program in 1995.[24] A mediation is an informal dispute resolution mechanism by which a neutral third party guides parties toward a resolution that is acceptable to all parties. The mediator is jointly selected by the parties from a list supplied by FINRA or another source selected by the parties. In order to become a mediator, candidates must have applicable training and experience as a mediator and appropriate references supporting their application. To remain on FINRA's mediation roster, a mediator must pay an annual fee. Mediation commences when all parties voluntarily submit a mediation submission agreement. Mediation may be initiated prior to the filing of a formal claim in the arbitration forum or at any stage of the arbitration process. Pursuing mediation will not stay arbitration unless the parties agree to do so. Similar to the arbitration process, a party may be represented by an attorney or a non-attorney in the mediation process.

Once commenced, the mediation will either result in an impasse, parties do not come to an agreement, or a settlement, where parties agree to resolve their dispute. Mediators do not have the authority to decide the controversy between the parties.

The terms of the agreement, if one is reached, are incorporated into a settlement agreement. Parties may withdraw from mediation at any time prior to the execution of a written settlement agreement. The settlement agreement is binding and enforceable. FINRA will assist parties in enforcing written settlement agreements.[25] In 2013, of the 130 closed mediation cases, 76 percent resulted in settlements.[26]

Notes and Questions

1. According to statistics provided by FINRA to *The Chicago Tribune* in 2011, $51 million of the $481 million awarded to investors went unpaid (approximately 10%).[27] The article indicated that unrecovered claims in 2009 and 2010 were at four percent. Small firms with lower net capital requirements were the source of many of these unpaid awards. According to analysis by SNL Financial for the

---

24. FINRA, INC., FINRA DISPUTE RESOLUTION PARTY'S REFERENCE GUIDE SIMPLIFIED CASES, 4 (March 12, 2014), http://www.finra.org/web/groups/arbitrationmediation/@arbmed/@arbion/documents/arbmed/p011177.pdf.

25. FINRA, INC., *Settlement*, http://www.finra.org/ArbitrationAndMediation/Mediation/Process/Settlement/index.htm.

26. FINRA, Inc., *Dispute Resolution Statistics*, http://www.finra.org/ArbitrationAndMediation/FINRADisputeResolution/AdditionalResources/Statistics/ (accessed April 10, 2014).

27. Suzanne Barlyn, *Choices for Recouping Unpaid FINRA Awards Seen as Flawed*, Reuters, Oct. 24, 2013, http://www.reuters.com/article/2013/10/24/finra-arbitration-idUSL1N0IC22020131024.

WALL STREET JOURNAL, 940 broker-dealers had net capital of less than $50,000 as of July 1, 2013.[28] Several solutions have been proposed, such as requiring firms to carry errors and omissions (E&O) insurance that covers customer awards, increasing net capital requirements, developing a recovery fund for unpaid awards funded by an assessment on each broker-dealer, and expanding Securities Investor Protection Corporation (SIPC) coverage to include unpaid arbitration awards. What are the advantages and disadvantages of each proposed solution? Which proposal would best serve the needs of investors?

2. According to a study by the Public Investors Arbitration Bar Association (PIABA), a bar association for attorneys representing customers in the FINRA arbitration forum, between January 1, 2007, and May 17, 2009, expungement was granted in 89 percent of all cases resolved by "settlement or stipulated award," i.e., where the parties reach a settlement and request the arbitrator to incorporate their settlement into an award. Between May 18, 2009, and December 31, 2011, expungement was granted in 96.9 percent of cases where the dispute was resolved by settlement or stipulated award. After mid-May 2009, amendments to Forms U4 and U5 resulted in the addition of six new regulatory action disclosure questions. Even where there are stipulated awards, an arbitrator must still assess whether under FINRA Rule 2080 standards (i.e., claim or allegation is false, clearly erroneous or factually impossible, or the associated person was not involved in the alleged violation) the expungement should be recommended and the award confirmed by a court of law.

3. FINRA, in addition to expanding expungement-related trainings offered to its arbitrators, responded to the study by noting that the number of expungements executed by FINRA following a court order was less than five percent for the five-year study period or 833 executed expungement orders compared to 17,635 total customer disputes filed in the arbitration forum.

4. Review the PIABA study *Stockbroker Arbitration Slates Wiped Clean 9 out of 10 Times When "Expungement" Sought in Settled Cases*, and FINRA's *Statement on PIABA's Expungement Study*.

III. Special Issues in Securities Arbitration

A. FINRA Arbitration Forum Eligibility

The vast majority of securities arbitrations occur using FINRA's arbitral forum. The FINRA forum is used by exchanges such as BATS Exchange, Inc., BATS Y-Exchange, Inc., Direct Edge, International Securities Exchange (ISE), NASDAQ, NASDAQ OMX, New York Stock Exchange, NYSE Amex, NYSE Arca, and other regulatory

---

28. Jean Eaglesham & Rob Barry, *FINRA to Consider Requiring Brokerages to Carry Arbitration Insurance*, WALL STREET J., Oct. 4, 2013, http://online.wsj.com/news/articles/SB1000142405270230 4906704579115403444093932.

organizations such as the Municipal Securities Rulemaking Board (MSRB). In order to be eligible to use the FINRA forum, one of the parties must be an individual or entity registered with FINRA, and the claim must be filed within six years from the time the events giving rise to the dispute occurred.

FINRA Rule 12206 for customers and FINRA Rule 13206 for securities industry disputes allow a claim to be filed within six years of the "occurrence or event giving rise to the cause of action." This time limit of six years is separate and apart from the statute of limitations; a case may still be eligible under the FINRA arbitration codes upon case filing, but the opposing party may advance a statute of limitations defense where the period is much shorter than six years. Questions regarding the eligibility of claims are to be resolved by the arbitration panel. If a dismissal under FINRA Rules 12206 or 13206 is granted, the dismissal will be without prejudice, allowing parties to pursue their claims in court.

Often, customers of broker-dealers and associated persons have a predispute arbitration clause in their customer agreements and employment agreements, respectively. However, even if no written arbitration agreement exists, a "customer" may demand arbitration with a FINRA member or associated person under FINRA Rule 12200 as long as the "dispute arises in connection with the business activities" of the broker-dealer or the associated person. Courts have struggled with identifying who is a customer along with the business activities that are covered under the Customer Code. FINRA offers various definitions of a customer based on the specific context. Under the Customer Code and the Industry Code, FINRA defines *customer* by stating that "a customer shall not include a broker or dealer." Accordingly, courts have been forced to balance a strong federal policy in favor of arbitration with determining whether a customer relationship as contemplated by FINRA rules exists.

In *Fleet Boston v. Innovex*, the Eighth Circuit attempted to answer whether Innovex (formerly AdFlex) could compel a FINRA member broker-dealer, Fleet Boston, to arbitrate a dispute regarding a fee agreement. Neither Innovex nor AdFlex was a broker-dealer.

Fleet Boston Robertson Stephens, Inc. v. Innovex, Inc.

264 F.3d 770 (8th Cir. 2001)

I. BACKGROUND

Fleet Boston Robertson Stephens, Inc. (Robertson Stephens), a multi-service brokerage firm and member of the National Association of Securities Dealers (NASD), commenced the underlying breach of contract action against AdFlex in an attempt to collect over $800,000 in fees and expenses it claimed it was owed for providing financial advice and assistance to AdFlex in AdFlex's merger with Innovex. The contract between the parties did not call for Robertson Stephenson to act as a broker for AdFlex securities. AdFlex, which has since merged with Innovex, disputes that it owes these monies for a variety of reasons and filed a motion to stay litigation and compel arbitration under the Federal Arbitration Act, 9 U.S.C. §§ 1–14.

The essence of the dispute before this court is whether AdFlex was a customer of Robertson Stephens under the NASD Code. If the answer is yes, then, according to the NASD Code, Robertson Stephens has agreed to submit any claim by a customer to arbitration, thus, the motion to stay litigation and compel arbitration should be granted. If the answer is no, then there has been no agreement to submit to arbitration, and the litigation shall continue.

II. ANALYSIS

In deciding whether to stay litigation and compel arbitration under the Federal Arbitration Act, a court must first consider whether the parties have agreed to arbitrate the underlying dispute. Here, the parties agree that the contract in dispute does not contain any agreement to arbitrate. Rather, AdFlex points to provisions of the NASD Code in support of its claim that the court should compel arbitration.

As a member of the NASD, Robertson Stephens is bound to follow the rules and regulations of the NASD, including the NASD Code. That Code, in pertinent part, requires NASD members to arbitrate disputes if they "aris[e] out of or in connection with the business of any member" and are "between or among members or associated persons and public customers." The Code further provides that the matter shall be submitted to arbitration upon the demand of the customer.

The district court summed up the issues thus:

The parties here do not dispute that Robertson Stephens is an NASD member, that AdFlex is not an associate of Robertson Stephens, that the controversy arises in connection with the business of Robertson Stephens, that the contract does not contain an arbitration provision and that AdFlex has not waived any right to arbitration it may have had.

Thus, the only question is whether AdFlex is a "customer" of Robertson Stephens under the NASD Code. This question hinges upon whether the term "customer" applies only to those who received investment or brokerage services, or whether it also applies to those who received banking and financial advice, as AdFlex did in this case.

The NASD Arbitration Code does not define the term "customer." AdFlex points to the definition section of the NASD Manual which specifies, "The term 'customer' shall not include a broker or dealer." AdFlex argues that by negative inference this definition means a "customer" is everyone who is not a broker or dealer. We agree with the district court that this definition is too broad. We do not believe that the NASD Rules were meant to apply to every sort of financial service an NASD member might provide, regardless of how remote that service might be from the investing or brokerage activities, which the NASD oversees.

Although not entirely clear, or consistent, other NASD Rules support a general definition of "customer" as one who receives investment and brokerage services or otherwise deals more directly with securities than what occurred here. The district court relied on a provision in the NASD Rules of Conduct—which outline the standards of conduct expected of NASD members when dealing with customers—define a "customer" as "any person who, in the regular course of such member's business, has cash or securities in the possession of such member." NASD Rules of Conduct § 2270. Although that particular provision defines customer in one specific context, there are numerous other provisions in the NASD Rules of Conduct that support this definition of customer.[29]

Additionally, the NASD's Manual and Notices to Members states that the arbitration forum exists "[t]o assist in the resolution of monetary and business disputes between investors and their securities firms (as well as between member firms)." This further supports the proposition that "customer" in the NASD Code refers to one involved in a business relationship with an NASD member that is related directly to investment or brokerage services.

Although other cases interpreting the term "customer" have in some ways taken a broad view of the term, in all of these cases there existed some brokerage or investment relationship between the parties.[30] We decline to extend the definition where the business relationship did not include these activities.

In sum, while this is a close call, we do not believe the NASD Rules require a member to submit to arbitration in every dispute that involves its business activities with a non-member — as AdFlex's proposed definition of "customer" would require. We agree with the district court that "customer" does not include an entity such as AdFlex, which only received financial advice, without receiving investment or brokerage related services, from an NASD member. AdFlex correctly recognizes that, where the parties have agreed to arbitrate, there is a strong federal policy in favor of arbitration. However, this does not change the fact that one cannot be compelled to arbitrate her disputes unless she has agreed to do so. Robertson Stephens did not, by virtue of its membership in the NASD, agree to arbitrate this type of dispute over fees for giving financial advice apart from investment or brokerage services.

Accordingly, we affirm the denial of the motion to stay litigation and compel arbitration.

———

In *UBS Financial Services, Inc. v. Carilion Clinic,* the Fourth Circuit opted to use a plain English definition of *customer* as defined in MERRIAM-WEBSTER'S COLLEGIATE

---

29. [2] Apparently ignoring these provisions, AdFlex directs us to an isolated NASD Rule relating to membership and registration that defines a "customer" to include those receiving investment banking services. NASD Membership and Registration Rule § 1120(b)(1). This rule, which does not specifically deal with customer protection or relations, is insufficient to expand the definition of "customer" for purposes of the arbitration provision.

30. [3] AdFlex cites *Patten Securities Corporation* v. *Diamond Greyhound & Genetics, Inc.,* to support the proposition that a "customer" is not defined by an investor relationship with the NASD member. 819 F.2d 400, 406 (3d Cir. 1987). That case involved a claim by a securities issuer against an underwriter, who was an NASD member. Although the relationship between the two was not a broker/investor relationship, it still related directly to the issuance of securities, rather than banking advice, and is thus unavailing here.

DICTIONARY, a decision also followed by the Second Circuit in *UBS Financial Services, Inc. v. West Virginia University Hospitals, Inc.,* 660 F.3d 643 (2d Cir. 2011).

UBS Financial Services, Inc. v. Carilion Clinic

No. 12-2066 (4th Cir. Jan. 23, 2013)

Before NIEMEYER, KEENAN, and DIAZ, Circuit Judges.

OPINION

This case presents the question of whether UBS Financial Services, Inc. ("UBS") and Citigroup Global Markets, Inc. ("Citi") are required, as members of the Financial Industry Regulatory Authority, Inc. ("FINRA"), to arbitrate disputes arising out of the services they provided to Carilion Corporation in connection with its multi-million dollar bond issues. Carilion claimed that during the course of providing those services, UBS and Citi made numerous misrepresentations to it and breached numerous duties. To resolve its claims, Carilion initiated an arbitration proceeding against UBS and Citi under FINRA Rule 12200 (which requires FINRA members to arbitrate disputes with a customer at the customer's request).

We affirm. As explained herein, we conclude that Carilion, by purchasing UBS and Citi's services, was indeed a "customer" entitled to arbitration under FINRA Rule 12200....

I

Carilion is a not-for-profit healthcare organization that operates hospitals and clinics in Virginia. In 2005, it decided to issue municipal bonds to finance the renovation and expansion of one of its hospitals and to refinance existing debt. Carilion retained UBS and Citi to advise it on the structure of the bond issues and to assist it in implementing the financing plan.

In addition to providing Carilion with advice on the structure of the bond issues, Carilion claims that UBS and Citi also (1) served as underwriters for the auction-rate bonds, purchasing the bonds from Carilion and reselling them to investors; (2) served as lead broker-dealers for Carilion's auction-rate bond auctions; (3) sold to Carilion, through their affiliates, interest rate swaps that they had recommended to protect Carilion from fluctuations in the bonds' interest rates; (4) acted as Carilion's agents in dealing with the rating agencies; (5) conducted discussions with bond insurers on Carilion's behalf; and (6) provided monitoring and advisory services on the bonds and the swaps. For their services, UBS and Citi earned an underwriter's discount, part of which constituted a management fee for their assistance in structuring and managing the transaction, and annual broker-dealer fees of 25 basis points in exchange for managing the auction-rate bond auctions.

The parties documented their business arrangements in two types of contracts—broker-dealer agreements and underwriting agreements. The broker-dealer agreements, executed on December 1, 2005—two with UBS and two with Citi—provided that UBS and Citi would run the periodic auctions. The underwriting agreements, executed on December 13, 2005—one with UBS and one with Citi—provided that UBS and Citi would purchase the auction-rate bonds from Carilion and resell them to the public.

As Carilion alleges in its arbitration claim, in February 2008, the auction-rate bond market for Carilion's bonds collapsed when UBS and Citi stopped submitting support bids for the bonds at the auctions. Carilion's interest payments skyrocketed, and the swaps did not provide the designed protection. Consequently, Carilion was forced to refinance, losing millions of dollars in the process. Carilion claimed that UBS and Citi misled it on the true nature of the auction-rate bond market by failing to disclose that they had a practice of placing support bids to prevent failure at every auction for which they were the lead broker-dealer. Carilion claimed that UBS and Citi's conduct violated their fiduciary duty, amounted to fraud and negligent misrepresentation, violated the Securities Exchange Act of 1934, violated the Virginia Securities Act, and violated Municipal Securities Rulemaking Board ("MSRB") and FINRA duties. To resolve these claims, Carilion initiated the arbitration proceedings with FINRA on February 11, 2012, naming UBS and Citi as respondents.

II

UBS and Citi, as FINRA members, are generally required by the FINRA Rules to arbitrate disputes with customers when (1) arbitration is "requested" by the customer and (2) the dispute "arises in connection with the business activities of the member." FINRA Rule 12200.[31] Carilion, claiming to be a "customer" of UBS and Citi, requested arbitration of its claims that UBS and Citi breached duties in connection with services they provided to Carilion on its auction-rate bond issues. The parties agree that if Carilion was indeed a "customer" of UBS and Citi, UBS and Citi became contractually obligated to proceed with arbitration on Carilion's request.... But UBS and Citi claim that Carilion was not a "customer," as that term is used in the FINRA Rules, and that therefore they have no contractual obligation to arbitrate. They maintain that Carilion's claims did not "relate to a brokerage account or investment relationship with UBS or Citi" and that the term customer under the FINRA Rules is limited to persons who received investment or brokerage services, citing *Fleet Boston Robertson Stephens, Inc. v. Innovex, Inc.*, 264 F.3d 770 (8th Cir.2001) (holding that a party receiving banking and financial advice was not a "customer" under the National Association of Securities Dealers ("NASD") Rules and therefore could not invoke members' arbitration obligations).

---

31. [1] FINRA Rule 12200 provides:
   Parties must arbitrate a dispute under the Code if: Arbitration under the Code is either:
   (1) Required by a written agreement,
   or (2) Requested by the customer;
      The dispute is between a customer and a member or associated person of a member; and
      The dispute arises in connection with the business activities of the member or the associated person, except disputes involving the insurance business activities of a member that is also an insurance company.

Carilion argues that "customer," as used in the FINRA Rules, is a broad term that is not limited to only investors. It contends that the scope of FINRA's regulation is broader than just protecting investors and that courts have not so limited the term "customer" in construing the FINRA Rules. Relying on a dictionary definition, Carilion claims that a customer is anyone "who purchases some commodity or service."

The FINRA Rules do not define "customer." They do limit the term to exclude from its scope any "broker or dealer." FINRA Rule 12100(i). But as to non-brokers and non-dealers, the term is left undefined. Nonetheless, the FINRA Rules do give an informing context by providing that arbitrable disputes must arise in connection with the "business activities" of the FINRA member, thus suggesting that for a person to obtain arbitration, the person must be a customer with respect to a FINRA member's business activities. The FINRA Rules give further context by suggesting that the business activities of a FINRA member involve "investment banking or securities business." See FINRA Rule 12100(r).[32] Finally, the scope of FINRA's regulatory interest similarly indicates the scope of relevant business activities. FINRA's mission, among other things, is "[t]o promote through cooperative effort the investment banking and securities business, to standardize its principles and practices, to promote therein high standards of commercial honor, and to encourage and promote among members observance of federal and state securities laws;" "[t]o adopt, administer, and enforce rules of fair practice and rules to prevent fraudulent and manipulative acts in practices;" and "[t]o promote self-discipline among members, and to investigate and adjust grievances between the public and members and between members." Restated Certificate of Incorporation of Financial Industry Regulatory Authority, Inc. §3 (July 2, 2010) (emphasis added)....

But subject to the scope indicated by its context in the FINRA Rules, the term "customer" in Rule 12200 still retains its generally accepted meaning—"one that purchases a commodity or service." MERRIAM-WEBSTER'S COLLEGIATE DICTIONARY 308 (11th ed. 2007).

Coupling the contextual indicators from FINRA and the dictionary definition of "customer," we thus conclude that when FINRA uses "customer" in Rule 12200, it refers to one, not a broker or dealer, who purchases commodities or services from a FINRA member in the course of the member's business activities insofar as those activities are covered by FINRA's regulation, namely the activities of investment banking and the securities business. To construe "customer" in a manner that is consistent with the context of the FINRA Rules serves not only to provide customers of FINRA

---

32. [4] FINRA Rule 12100(r) provides: The term "person associated with a member" means: (1) A natural person who is registered or has applied for registration under the Rules of FINRA; or (2) A sole proprietor, partner, officer, director, or branch manager of a member, or other natural person occupying a similar status or performing similar functions, or a natural person engaged in the investment banking or securities business who is directly or indirectly controlling or controlled by a member, whether or not any such person is registered or exempt from registration with FINRA under the By-Laws or the Rules of FINRA.

members the opportunity to arbitrate disputes arising in connection with FINRA members' business activities, but also to fulfill FINRA's charter "to investigate and adjust grievances between the public and members."

Our definition is also fully supported by the decisions of other courts that have faced analogous questions of who is a "customer" within the meaning of FINRA Rule 12200.

In *West Virginia University Hospitals*, UBS sought to enjoin arbitration under the FINRA Rules, as it did here, contending that West Virginia University Hospitals was not a "customer." Just as here, UBS had provided services to West Virginia University Hospitals in connection with the Hospitals' issuance of auction-rate bonds. The court observed that UBS served West Virginia University Hospitals "as both the lead underwriter and the main broker-dealer responsible for facilitating the Dutch auctions in which [the Hospitals'] bonds were resold and their interest rates set." In concluding that West Virginia University Hospitals was a "customer" of UBS entitled to FINRA arbitration, the Second Circuit held that the term "customer" in FINRA Rule 12200 "includes at least a non-broker or non-dealer who purchases, or undertakes to purchase, a good or service from a FINRA member." Thus, because West Virginia University Hospitals "purchased a service, specifically auction services, from UBS," it was UBS's customer.

In reaching its conclusion, the court rejected the same arguments that UBS and Citi make here—that the term "customer" is restricted by FINRA's investor-protection mandate to those persons receiving investment or brokerage services. The court explained that while FINRA's mission does indeed include investor protection, its role and scope of authority is clearly broader:

> FINRA's purposes are not limited to investor protection. Rather, as previously noted, FINRA serves as the sole self-regulatory organization chartered under the Exchange Act and exercises comprehensive oversight of the securities industry. Among its stated purposes are to "encourage and promote among members observance of federal and state securities laws;" "[t]o investigate and adjust grievances between the public and members and between members;" and "[t]o adopt, administer, and enforce rules of fair practice." UBS does not explain why "customer" should be limited to investors in light of FINRA's purposes, its other broad definitions of "customer" applicable to other provisions, and the ordinary usage of the term.

W. Va. Univ. Hosps., 660 F.3d at 652 (citations omitted). We find the court's reasoning persuasive and equally applicable to the circumstances here.

UBS and Citi rely heavily on the Eighth Circuit's decision in Fleet Boston to support their more limited definition of "customer" as referring to investors. In Fleet Boston, the court construed language in the NASD Rules, a predecessor to the FINRA Rules, and rejected a claim that "customer" means broadly "everyone who is not a broker or dealer." The court explained, "We do not believe that the NASD Rules were meant to apply to every sort of financial service an NASD member might provide, regardless of how remote that service might be from the investing or brokerage activities, which the NASD oversees." It then found that the NASD Rules support a general definition of "customer" as "one who receives investment and brokerage services or otherwise deals more directly with securities than what occurred here." The court, however, did not explain its definition further by describing what relationship might deal "more directly with securities than what occurred here." For this reason and because the court was faced with a purported customer who had merely received financial advice, we cannot take its holding to limit the scope of "customer" to "one who receives investment and brokerage services," as UBS and Citi argue.

UBS and Citi also contend that finding Carilion to be a customer "creates an unnecessary conflict between FINRA and MSRB rules" because Carilion, as a new issuer of securities, would be a "customer" under the FINRA Rules but not under the MSRB Rules. The MSRB (Municipal Securities Rulemaking Board) is a self-regulatory organization that, similar to FINRA, regulates the municipal securities market.

MSRB Rule D-9 defines a customer as "any person other than a broker, dealer, or municipal securities dealer acting in its capacity as such or an issuer in transactions involving the sale by the issuer of a new issue of its securities." Thus, while Carilion is a customer under the FINRA Rules, as we hold, it might not be a customer under the MSRB Rules. But being subject to two different regulatory schemes, each of which defines customer differently, does not necessarily create any tension. To be sure, Carilion was a new issuer of municipal securities and therefore might not have been a customer under the MSRB Rules. But it also purchased underwriting and auction services from UBS and Citi and therefore was a customer of those entities for purposes of arbitrating disputes arising out of the business activities of those FINRA members. UBS and Citi have not demonstrated how these regulatory differences create irreconcilable conflicts.

UBS and Citi further contend that the broker-dealer agreements they entered into with Carilion used "customer" to refer to investors purchasing Carilion's bonds and thus indicate that Carilion is not a customer of UBS or Citi. The broker-dealer agreements, however, were written to serve the purposes of those agreements such that their labeling the purchasers of bond securities from Carilion as customers does not foreclose reaching the conclusion that Carilion itself was also a customer of UBS or Citi with respect to their services. Moreover, even though parties are free to exempt themselves from Rule 12200, their private agreements do not alter the definition of "customer" in the FINRA Rules.

Finally, UBS and Citi argue that our holding is inconsistent with FINRA's stated purpose of "protecting investors." As we have already pointed out, however, even though FINRA undertakes in its mission to protect investors, it also serves a broader purpose, that of serving as "the sole self-regulatory organization chartered under the Exchange Act to exercise comprehensive oversight of the securities industry." Its mission includes the specific purpose of promoting observance of federal and state securities laws and investigating and adjusting grievances between the public and FINRA members under those laws. FINRA Rule 12200 serves that mission.

In short, we conclude that "customer," as that term is used in the FINRA Rules, refers to one, not a broker or a dealer, who purchases commodities or services from a FINRA member in the course of the member's business activities insofar as those activities are regulated by FINRA — namely investment banking and securities business activities.

We have little difficulty concluding that Carilion is such a "customer." To finance the renovation and expansion of its hospital and refinance debt, Carilion issued over $308 million in bonds, some $234 million of which were auction-rate bonds. To assist it in structuring and underwriting the financing, Carilion retained UBS and Citi, entering into broker-dealer and underwriting agreements with them. Pursuant to these agreements, UBS and Citi advised Carilion on the structure of its financing; served as the underwriters for the auction-rate bonds, meaning that they purchased the bonds from Carilion and resold them to investors; served as the lead broker-dealers for Carilion's auction-rate bond auctions; sold to Carilion, through affiliates, interest rate swaps, which they recommended to protect the financing structure; acted as Carilion's agents in dealing with the rating agencies; conducted discussions with bond insurers on Carilion's behalf; and provided monitoring and advisory services on the bonds and the swaps. For their services, UBS and Citi earned an underwriter's discount, part of which constituted a management fee for their assistance in structuring and managing the transaction, and annual broker-dealer fees of 25 basis points in exchange for managing the auction-rate bond auctions.

Because Carilion, as a customer of UBS and Citi, has requested arbitration, UBS and Citi as FINRA members are obligated to participate in the arbitration pursuant to the FINRA Rules.

Notes and Questions

1. Compare and contrast the way in which the Fourth Circuit defines the term "customer" versus the definition relied on by *Fleet Boston Robertson Stephens, Inc. v. Innovex, Inc.* 264 F.3d 770 (8th Cir. 2001). Are the two definitions contradictory?

2. In the above case, assume that UBS Financial Services, Inc. and Citigroup Global Markets, Inc., submitted a Submission Agreement to commence the arbitration process such that they could file an answer and a motion to dismiss. Review the Respondent(s) Submission Agreement found on www.finra.org. What effect, if any, will the Submission Agreement have on the firms' motion to enjoin the arbitration?

Hypothetical One

Mary Joe Genovese, a public arbitrator at FINRA and a professor of economics at a small liberal arts college, decides that she would like to experience the exciting world of Wall Street. She decided an arbitration involving Morgan Stanley last month and thinks Morgan Stanley is a well-known firm that would be a great launching pad for her Wall Street career. She agrees that all information she has learned during the arbitration will remain confidential. (1) Is there any restriction that will prevent Genovese from obtaining a position with Morgan Stanley's brokerage division? What about a division of Morgan Stanley that is not regulated by FINRA? (2) What if Genovese waits a year and in the interim does not accept any cases involving Morgan Stanley? Review FINRA's Code of Arbitration Procedure and AAA/ABA Code of Ethics for Arbitrators.

B. Statutory Employment Arbitration

The arbitration of employment disputes in the securities industry commenced in 1986.[33] Where employment agreements lacked an arbitration clause, broker-dealers were able to utilize SRO rules and arbitration clauses in the Uniform Application for Securities Industry Registration or Transfer (Form U4), which required registrants to arbitrate. The FAA's exemption provision appeared to preclude employment-related arbitration, stating "nothing herein contained shall apply to contracts of employment of seamen, railroad employees, or any other class of workers engaged in foreign or interstate commerce."[34] In *Gilmer v. Interstate/Johnson Lane Corp.*, 500 U.S. 20 (1991), the Supreme Court was presented with the question of whether the FAA exempted workers engaged in intrastate commerce. Gilmer, a stockbroker terminated at age 62, brought a claim under the Age Discrimination in Employment Act of 1967 (ADEA). The firm, Interstate/Johnson Lane Corp., sought to compel arbitration by relying on the FAA and by arguing that, in Gilmer's Form U4 filed with the NYSE, he agreed to arbitrate matters arising between him and the firm according to the rules of the NYSE.

Gilmer v. Interstate/Johnson Lane Corp.
500 U.S. 20 (1991)

Justice WHITE delivered the opinion of the Court.

Gilmer concedes that nothing in the text of the ADEA or its legislative history explicitly precludes arbitration. He argues, however, that compulsory arbitration of ADEA claims pursuant to arbitration agreements would be inconsistent with the statutory framework and purposes of the ADEA. Like the Court of Appeals, we disagree.

A

Congress enacted the ADEA in 1967 "to promote employment of older persons based on their ability rather than age; to prohibit arbitrary age discrimination in em-

---

33. David B. Lipsky, Ronald L. Seeber & Ryan J. Lamare, *The Arbitration of Employment Disputes in the Securities Industry: A Study of Awards, 1986-2000*, 11 J. DISP. RESOL. 53, 54 (2010).

34. 9 U.S.C. § 1.

ployment; [and] to help employers and workers find ways of meeting problems arising from the impact of age on employment." ... As Gilmer contends, the ADEA is designed not only to address individual grievances, but also to further important social policies. We do not perceive any inherent inconsistency between those policies, however, and enforcing agreements to arbitrate age discrimination claims. It is true that arbitration focuses on specific disputes between the parties involved. The same can be said, however, of judicial resolution of claims. Both of these dispute resolution mechanisms nevertheless also can further broader social purposes.... "[S]o long as the prospective litigant effectively may vindicate [his or her] statutory cause of action in the arbitral forum, the statute will continue to serve both its remedial and deterrent function."

We also are unpersuaded by the argument that arbitration will undermine the role of the EEOC in enforcing the ADEA. An individual ADEA claimant subject to an arbitration agreement will still be free to file a charge with the EEOC, even though the claimant is not able to institute a private judicial action. In any event, the EEOC's role in combating age discrimination is not dependent on the filing of a charge; the agency may receive information concerning alleged violations of the ADEA "from any source," and it has independent authority to investigate age discrimination. Moreover, nothing in the ADEA indicates that Congress intended that the EEOC be involved in all employment disputes. Such disputes can be settled, for example, without any EEOC involvement. Finally, the mere involvement of an administrative agency in the enforcement of a statute is not sufficient to preclude arbitration. For example, the Securities Exchange Commission is heavily involved in the enforcement of the Securities Exchange Act of 1934 and the Securities Act of 1933, but we have held that claims under both of those statutes may be subject to compulsory arbitration. Gilmer also argues that compulsory arbitration is improper because it deprives claimants of the judicial forum provided for by the ADEA. Congress, however, did not explicitly preclude arbitration or other nonjudicial resolution of claims, even in its recent amendments to the ADEA. "[I]f Congress intended the substantive protection afforded [by the ADEA] to include protection against waiver of the right to a judicial forum, that intention will be deducible from text or legislative history." Moreover, Gilmer's argument ignores the ADEA's flexible approach to resolution of claims. The EEOC, for example, is directed to pursue "informal methods of conciliation, conference, and persuasion," which suggests that out-of-court dispute resolution, such as arbitration, is consistent with the statutory scheme established by Congress. In addition, arbitration is consistent with Congress' grant of concurrent jurisdiction over ADEA claims to state and federal courts (allowing suits to be brought "in any court of competent jurisdiction"), because arbitration agreements, "like the provision for concurrent jurisdiction, serve to advance the objective of allowing [claimants] a broader right to select the forum for resolving disputes, whether it be judicial or otherwise."

B

In arguing that arbitration is inconsistent with the ADEA, Gilmer also raises a host of challenges to the adequacy of arbitration procedures. Initially, we note that in our recent arbitration cases we have already rejected most of these arguments as insufficient to preclude arbitration of statutory claims. Such generalized attacks on arbitration "res[t] on suspicion of arbitration as a method of weakening the protections afforded in the substantive law to would-be complainants," and as such, they are "far out of step with our current strong endorsement of the federal statutes favoring this method of resolving disputes." Consequently, we address these arguments only briefly.

Gilmer first speculates that arbitration panels will be biased. However, "[w]e decline to indulge the presumption that the parties and arbitral body conducting a proceeding will be unable or unwilling to retain competent, conscientious and impartial arbitrators." In any event, we note that the NYSE arbitration rules, which are applicable to the dispute in this case, provide protections against biased panels. The rules require, for example, that the parties be informed of the employment histories of the arbitrators, and that they be allowed to make further inquiries into the arbitrators' backgrounds. In addition, each party is allowed one peremptory challenge and unlimited challenges for cause. Moreover, the arbitrators are required to disclose "any circumstances which might preclude [them] from rendering an objective and impartial determination." The FAA also protects against bias, by providing that courts may overturn arbitration decisions "[w]here there was evident partiality or corruption in the arbitrators." There has been no showing in this case that those provisions are inadequate to guard against potential bias.

Gilmer also complains that the discovery allowed in arbitration is more limited than in the federal courts, which he contends will make it difficult to prove discrimination. It is unlikely, however, that age discrimination claims require more extensive discovery than other claims that we have found to be arbitrable, such as RICO and antitrust claims. Moreover, there has been no showing in this case that the NYSE discovery provisions, which allow for document production, information requests, depositions, and subpoenas ... will prove insufficient to allow ADEA claimants such as Gilmer a fair opportunity to present their claims. Although those procedures might not be as extensive as in the federal courts, by agreeing to arbitrate, a party "trades the procedures and opportunity for review of the courtroom for the simplicity, informality, and expedition of arbitration." Indeed, an important counterweight to the reduced discovery in NYSE arbitration is that arbitrators are not bound by the rules of evidence. A further alleged deficiency of arbitration is that arbitrators often will not issue written opinions, resulting, Gilmer contends, in a lack of public knowledge of employers' discriminatory policies, an inability to obtain effective appellate review, and a stifling of the development of the law. The NYSE rules, however, do require that all arbitration awards be in writing, and that the awards contain the names of the parties, a summary of the issues in controversy, and a description of the award issued. In addition, the award decisions are made available to the public. Furthermore, judicial decisions addressing ADEA claims will continue to be issued because it is unlikely that all or even most ADEA claimants will be subject to arbitration agreements. Finally, Gilmer's concerns apply equally to settlements of ADEA claims, which, as noted above, are clearly allowed.

It is also argued that arbitration procedures cannot adequately further the purposes of the ADEA because they do not provide for broad equitable relief and class actions. As the court below noted, however, arbitrators do have the power to fashion equitable relief. Indeed, the NYSE rules applicable here do not restrict the types of relief an arbitrator may award, but merely refer to "damages and/or other relief." The NYSE rules also provide for collective proceedings. But "even if the arbitration could not go forward as a class action or class relief could not be granted by the arbitrator, the fact that the [ADEA] provides for the possibility of bringing a collective action does not mean that individual attempts at conciliation were intended to be barred." Finally, it should be remembered that arbitration agreements will not preclude the *EEOC* from bringing actions seeking class-wide and equitable relief.

C

An additional reason advanced by Gilmer for refusing to enforce arbitration agreements relating to ADEA claims is his contention that there often will be unequal bargaining power between employers and employees. Mere inequality in bargaining power, however, is not a sufficient reason to hold that arbitration agreements are never enforceable in the employment context. Relationships between securities dealers and investors, for example, may involve unequal bargaining power, but we nevertheless held in *Rodriguez de Quijas* and *McMahon* that agreements to arbitrate in that context are enforceable. As discussed above, the FAA's purpose was to place arbitration agreements on the same footing as other contracts. Thus, arbitration agreements are enforceable "save upon such grounds as exist at law or in equity for the revocation of any contract." "Of course, courts should remain attuned to well-supported claims that the agreement to arbitrate resulted from the sort of fraud or overwhelming economic power that would provide grounds 'for the revocation of any contract.'" There is no indication in this case, however, that Gilmer, an experienced businessman, was coerced or defrauded into agreeing to the arbitration clause in his registration application. As with the claimed procedural inadequacies discussed above, this claim of unequal bargaining power is best left for resolution in specific cases.

We conclude that Gilmer has not met his burden of showing that Congress, in enacting the ADEA, intended to preclude arbitration of claims under that Act. Accordingly, the judgment of the Court of Appeals is

Affirmed.

———

The question of whether the FAA exempted interstate employees under the exemption provision in § 1 would be answered in *Circuit City Stores v. Adams*, 532 U.S. 105 (2001). Saint Clair Adams was hired as a sales counselor for a Circuit City store in Santa Rosa, California. Adams signed an employment application that contained an arbitration clause requiring the arbitration of all claims regardless of whether it was based on federal, state, or local statutory or common law. Two years after being hired, Adams filed an employment discrimination lawsuit under California's Fair Employment and Housing Act, and other claims under California law.

Circuit City Stores v. Adams

532 U.S. 105 (2001)

Section 1 of the Federal Arbitration Act (FAA) excludes from the Act's coverage "contracts of employment of seamen, railroad employees, or any other class of workers engaged in foreign or interstate commerce." All but one of the Courts of Appeals which have addressed the issue interpret this provision as exempting contracts of employment of transportation workers, but not other employment contracts, from the FAA's coverage. A different interpretation has been adopted by the Court of Appeals for the Ninth Circuit, which construes the exemption so that all contracts of employment are beyond the FAA's reach, whether or not the worker is engaged in transportation. It applied that rule to the instant case. We now decide that the better interpretation is to construe the statute, as most of the Courts of Appeals have done, to confine the exemption to transportation workers.

This comprehensive exemption [by the Ninth Circuit] had been advocated by amici curiae in *Gilmer*, where we addressed the question whether a registered securities representative's employment discrimination claim under the Age Discrimination in Employment Act of 1967 could be submitted to arbitration pursuant to an agreement in his securities registration application. Concluding that the application was not a "contract of employment" at all, we found it unnecessary to reach the meaning of § 1.... So the issue reserved in *Gilmer* is presented here.

Respondent, at the outset, contends that we need not address the meaning of the § 1 exclusion provision to decide the case in his favor. In his view, an employment contract is not a "contract evidencing a transaction involving interstate commerce" at all, since the word "transaction" in § 2 extends only to commercial contracts. This line of reasoning proves too much, for it would make the § 1 exclusion provision superfluous. If all contracts of employment are beyond the scope of the Act under the § 2 coverage provision, the separate exemption for "contracts of employment of seamen, railroad employees, or any other class of workers engaged in ... interstate commerce" would be pointless.

Respondent, endorsing the reasoning of the Court of Appeals for the Ninth Circuit that the provision excludes all employment contracts, relies on the asserted breadth of the words "contracts of employment of ... any other class of workers engaged in ... commerce." Referring to our construction of § 2's coverage provision in *Allied-Bruce*— concluding that the words "involving commerce" evidence the congressional intent to regulate to the full extent of its commerce power—respondent contends § 1's interpretation should have a like reach, thus exempting all employment contracts. The two provisions, it is argued, are coterminous; under this view the "involving commerce" provision brings within the FAA's scope all contracts within the Congress' commerce power, and the "engaged in ... commerce" language in § 1 in turn exempts from the FAA all employment contracts falling within that authority.

This reading of § 1, however, runs into an immediate and, in our view, insurmountable textual obstacle. Unlike the "involving commerce" language in § 2, the words "any other class of workers engaged in … commerce" constitute a residual phrase, following, in the same sentence, explicit reference to "seamen" and "railroad employees." Construing the residual phrase to exclude all employment contracts fails to give independent effect to the statute's enumeration of the specific categories of workers which precedes it; there would be no need for Congress to use the phrases "seamen" and "railroad employees" if those same classes of workers were subsumed within the meaning of the "engaged in … commerce" residual clause. The wording of § 1 calls for the application of the maxim ejusdem generis, the statutory canon that "where general words follow specific words in a statutory enumeration, the general words are construed to embrace only objects similar in nature to those objects enumerated by the preceding specific words." Under this rule of construction the residual clause should be read to give effect to the terms "seamen" and "railroad employees," and should itself be controlled and defined by reference to the enumerated categories of workers which are recited just before it; the interpretation of the clause pressed by respondent fails to produce these results.

Canons of construction need not be conclusive and are often countered, of course, by some maxim pointing in a different direction. The application of the rule *ejusdem generis* in this case, however, is in full accord with other sound considerations bearing upon the proper interpretation of the clause. For even if the term "engaged in commerce" stood alone in § 1, we would not construe the provision to exclude all contracts of employment from the FAA. Congress uses different modifiers to the word "commerce" in the design and enactment of its statutes. The phrase "affecting commerce" indicates Congress' intent to regulate to the outer limits of its authority under the Commerce Clause. The "involving commerce" phrase, the operative words for the reach of the basic coverage provision in § 2, was at issue in *Allied-Bruce*. That particular phrase had not been interpreted before by this Court. Considering the usual meaning of the word "involving," and the pro-arbitration purposes of the FAA, *Allied-Bruce* held the "word 'involving,' like 'affecting,' signals an intent to exercise Congress' commerce power to the full." Unlike those phrases, however, the general words "in commerce" and the specific phrase "engaged in commerce" are understood to have a more limited reach. In *Allied-Bruce* itself the Court said the words "in commerce" are "often-found words of art" that we have not read as expressing congressional intent to regulate to the outer limits of authority under the Commerce Clause. It is argued that we should assess the meaning of the phrase "engaged in commerce" in a different manner here, because the FAA was enacted when congressional authority to regulate under the commerce power was to a large extent confined by our decisions. When the FAA was enacted in 1925, respondent reasons, the phrase "engaged in commerce" was not a term of art indicating a limited assertion of congressional jurisdiction; to the contrary, it is said, the formulation came close to expressing the outer limits of Congress' power as then understood. Were this mode of interpretation to prevail, we would take into account the scope of the Commerce Clause, as then elaborated by the Court, at the date of the FAA's enactment in order to interpret what the statute means now.

A variable standard for interpreting common, jurisdictional phrases would contradict our earlier cases and bring instability to statutory interpretation. The Court has declined in past cases to afford significance, in construing the meaning of the statutory jurisdictional provisions "in commerce" and "engaged in commerce," to the circumstance that the statute predated shifts in the Court's Commerce Clause cases.

The Court's reluctance to accept contentions that Congress used the words "in commerce" or "engaged in commerce" to regulate to the full extent of its commerce power rests on sound foundation, as it affords objective and consistent significance to the meaning of the words Congress uses when it defines the reach of a statute. To say that the statutory words "engaged in commerce" are subject to variable interpretations depending upon the date of adoption, even a date before the phrase became a term of art, ignores the reason why the formulation became a term of art in the first place: The plain meaning of the words "engaged in commerce" is narrower than the more open-ended formulations "affecting commerce" and "involving commerce." It would be unwieldy for Congress, for the Court, and for litigants to be required to deconstruct statutory Commerce Clause phrases depending upon the year of a particular statutory enactment.

In rejecting the contention that the meaning of the phrase "engaged in commerce" in § 1 of the FAA should be given a broader construction than justified by its evident language simply because it was enacted in 1925 rather than 1938, we do not mean to suggest that statutory jurisdictional formulations "necessarily have a uniform meaning whenever used by Congress." As the Court has noted: "The judicial task in marking out the extent to which Congress has exercised its constitutional power over commerce is not that of devising an abstract formula." We must, of course, construe the "engaged in commerce" language in the FAA with reference to the statutory context in which it is found and in a manner consistent with the FAA's purpose. These considerations, however, further compel that the § 1 exclusion provision be afforded a narrow construction. As discussed above, the location of the phrase "any other class of workers engaged in … commerce" in a residual provision, after specific categories of workers have been enumerated, undermines any attempt to give the provision a sweeping, open-ended construction. And the fact that the provision is contained in a statute that "seeks broadly to overcome judicial hostility to arbitration agreements," which the Court concluded in *Allied-Bruce* counseled in favor of an expansive reading of § 2, gives no reason to abandon the precise reading of a provision that exempts contracts from the FAA's coverage. In sum, the text of the FAA forecloses the construction of § 1 followed by the Court of Appeals in the case under review, a construction which would exclude all employment contracts from the FAA. While the historical arguments respecting Congress' understanding of its power in 1925 are not insubstantial, this fact alone does not give us basis to adopt, "by judicial decision rather than amendatory legislation," an expansive construction of the FAA's exclusion provision that goes beyond the meaning of the words Congress used. While it is of course possible to speculate that Congress might have chosen a different jurisdictional formulation had it known that the Court would soon embrace a less restrictive reading of the Commerce

Clause, the text of § 1 precludes interpreting the exclusion provision to defeat the language of § 2 as to all employment contracts. Section 1 exempts from the FAA only contracts of employment of transportation workers.

Nor can we accept respondent's argument that our holding attributes an irrational intent to Congress. "Under petitioner's reading of § 1," he contends, "those employment contracts most involving interstate commerce, and thus most assuredly within the Commerce Clause power in 1925 ... are excluded from [the] Act's coverage; while those employment contracts having a less direct and less certain connection to interstate commerce ... would come within the Act's affirmative coverage and would not be excluded."

We see no paradox in the congressional decision to exempt the workers over whom the commerce power was most apparent. To the contrary, it is a permissible inference that the employment contracts of the classes of workers in § 1 were excluded from the FAA precisely because of Congress' undoubted authority to govern the employment relationships at issue by the enactment of statutes specific to them. By the time the FAA was passed, Congress had already enacted federal legislation providing for the arbitration of disputes between seamen and their employers, see Shipping Commissioners Act of 1872, 17 Stat. 262. When the FAA was adopted, moreover, grievance procedures existed for railroad employees under federal law, see Transportation Act of 1920, §§ 300–316, 41 Stat. 456, and the passage of a more comprehensive statute providing for the mediation and arbitration of railroad labor disputes was imminent. It is reasonable to assume that Congress excluded "seamen" and "railroad employees" from the FAA for the simple reason that it did not wish to unsettle established or developing statutory dispute resolution schemes covering specific workers.

As for the residual exclusion of "any other class of workers engaged in foreign or interstate commerce," Congress' demonstrated concern with transportation workers and their necessary role in the free flow of goods explains the linkage to the two specific, enumerated types of workers identified in the preceding portion of the sentence. It would be rational for Congress to ensure that workers in general would be covered by the provisions of the FAA, while reserving for itself more specific legislation for those engaged in transportation. Indeed, such legislation was soon to follow, with the amendment of the Railway Labor Act in 1936 to include air carriers and their employees....

* * *

Furthermore, for parties to employment contracts not involving the specific exempted categories set forth in § 1, it is true here, just as it was for the parties to the contract at issue in *Allied-Bruce*, that there are real benefits to the enforcement of arbitration provisions. We have been clear in rejecting the supposition that the advantages of the arbitration process somehow disappear when transferred to the employment context. Arbitration agreements allow parties to avoid the costs of litigation, a benefit that may be of particular importance in employment litigation, which often involves smaller sums of money than disputes concerning commercial contracts. These litigation costs to parties (and the accompanying burden to the Courts) would be compounded by the difficult choice-of-law questions that are often presented in disputes arising from the employment relationship, and the necessity of bifurcation of proceedings in those cases where state law precludes arbitration of certain types of employment claims but not others. The considerable complexity and uncertainty that the construction of § 1 urged by respondent would introduce into the enforceability of arbitration agreements in employment contracts would call into doubt the efficacy of alternative dispute resolution procedures adopted by many of the Nation's employers, in the process undermining the FAA's pro-arbitration purposes and "breeding litigation from a statute that seeks to avoid it." The Court has been quite specific in holding that arbitration agreements can be enforced under the FAA without contravening the policies of congressional enactments giving employees specific protection against discrimination prohibited by federal law; as we noted in *Gilmer*, "by agreeing to arbitrate a statutory claim, a party does not forgo the substantive rights afforded by the statute; it only submits to their resolution in an arbitral, rather than a judicial, forum."

Notes and Questions

1. The Form U4 contains an arbitration provision in the acknowledgement and consent section where it states:

    > I agree to arbitrate any dispute, claim or controversy that may arise between me and my firm, or a customer, or any other person, that is required to be arbitrated under the rules, constitutions, or by-laws of the SROs indicated in Section 4 (SRO REGISTRATION) as may be amended from time to time and that any arbitration award rendered against me may be entered as a judgment in any court of competent jurisdiction.

    Despite the language in Form U4, since January 1, 2000, statutory claims of employment discrimination (e.g., age, gender, or race) under Rule 13201 of the FINRA Code of Arbitration for Industry Disputes may be arbitrated only if both parties agree, either before or after the dispute arises. Thus, a member firm must point to an agreement to arbitrate these specific claims other than the arbitration clause found in Form U4. Review the Industry Code, specifically Part VIII Simplified Arbitration; Default Proceedings; Statutory Employment Discrimination Claims; and Injunctive Relief, to learn more about FINRA's statutory employment arbitration process.

2. In a review of employment arbitrations in the FINRA forum between 1986 and 2008, researchers David B. Lipsky, Ronald L. Seeber, and J. Ryan Lamare found the following types of claims were made by employees: outstanding compensation (28%); defamation (27.4%); statutory discrimination (17.1%); wrongful termination (13.5%); and contract breach (8.4%). They also found that after FINRA instituted the requirement in 2000 that there be an agreement other than the

clause enumerated in the Form U4 to arbitrate statutory discrimination claims, there was a significant drop in statutory claims. From 1986 to 1999, the researchers found a total of 288 discrimination awards (averaging 22 awards per year).[35] From 2000–2008, there were only 50 discrimination awards (averaging six awards per year).[36]

Hypothetical Two

Success First has retained you in the matter involving Poi to determine: (1) if it is possible to pursue both of the employment matters together in arbitration or in court instead of having two parallel proceedings; (2) whether Success First should use the arbitration forum or the court forum; and (3) to identify strategies to manage any risks associated with a dual process, if two parallel cases must be pursued. What are your recommendations?

C. Class Action Waivers

Proponents argue class action lawsuits are particularly important for groups of investors because often the "stake of an individual plaintiff is small, but the wrong significant," making class actions the only viable action against irresponsible actions by businesses.[37] They argue that customers with smaller amounts at stake may have a difficult time vindicating their rights if not part of a class. Opponents find that individualized action against a large company is just as effective as a large action without the abuses prevalent in the class action procedure where companies often settle to avoid the expenses involved in defending themselves. In 2011, Charles Schwab & Company amended its customer agreement by requiring its customers to "waive any right to bring a class action, or any type of representative action" in a judicial forum. The amendment resulted in all customers being required to pursue claims on an individual basis using arbitration and negated a FINRA arbitrator's ability to consolidate individual claims in arbitration.

FINANCIAL INDUSTRY REGULATORY AUTHORITY
BEFORE THE BOARD OF GOVERNORS
Department of Enforcement v. Charles Schwab & Co., Inc.

Decision, Complaint No. 2011029760201
April 24, 2014

* * *

---

35. David B. Lipsky, Ronald L. Seeber & Ryan J. Lamare, *The Arbitration of Employment Disputes in the Securities Industry: A Study of Awards, 1986-2000*, 11 J. Disp. Resol. 53, 59 (2010).

36. *Id.*

37. Richard M. Alderman, *Predispute Mandatory Arbitration in Consumer Contracts: A Call for Reform*, 38 Houston L. Rev. 1237, 1259 (2001).

A. Enforcement's Allegations

On February 1, 2012, Enforcement filed a three-cause complaint against Schwab. The first cause of action alleged that Schwab, by placing the Waiver in its customer agreements and attempting to limit customers' ability to bring or participate in class actions when class actions are permitted under the FINRA Code of Arbitration Procedure for Customer Disputes ("Customer Code"), violated NASD Rule 3110(f)(4)(C), from October 2011 until December 4, 2011, and FINRA Rule 2268(d)(3), from December 5, 2011, to the present.[38] FINRA Rule 2268(d)(3) prohibits member firms from placing "any condition" in a predispute arbitration agreement that "limits the ability of a party to file any claim in court permitted to be filed in court under the rules of the forums in which a claim may be filed under the agreement." As a result of these rule violations, Enforcement also alleged that Schwab violated FINRA Rule 2010.

The second cause of action, which directly relates to the first, alleged that including the Waiver in Schwab's customer agreements also violated NASD Rule 3110(f)(4)(A), and FINRA Rules 2268(d)(1) and 2010. FINRA Rule 2268(d)(1) states that "[n]o predispute arbitration agreement shall include any condition that ... limits or contradicts the rules of any self regulatory organization." Enforcement alleged that the Waiver limits or contradicts Rule 12204(d) of the Customer Code. Rule 12204(d) provides:

A member or associated person may not enforce any arbitration agreement against a member of a certified or putative class action with respect to any claim that is the subject of the certified or putative class action until:

- The class certification is denied;

- The class is decertified;

- The member of the certified or putative class is excluded from the class by the court; or

- The member of the certified or putative class elects not to participate in the class or withdraws from the class according to conditions set by the court, if any.

The third cause of action alleged that Schwab violated NASD Rule 3110 CDfM, and FINRA Rules 2268(d)(1) and 2010, because the Waiver contradicts Rule 12312(b)[39]

---

38. [6] NASD Rule 3110(f)(4) was effective until December 4, 2011, and was superseded without change to its text by FINRA Rule 2268(d) on December 5, 2011, as part of the FINRA consolidated rulebook process. For ease of reference, this decision discusses the rule using its current numbering.

39. [7] Rule 12312(b) states:

After all responsive pleadings have been served, claims joined together under paragraph (a) of this rule may be separated into two or more arbitrations by the Director before a panel is appointed, or by the panel after the panel is appointed. A party whose claims were separated by the Director may make a motion to the panel in the lowest numbered case to reconsider the Director's decision.

Schwab represented to FINRA that, beginning in January 2013, the Firm removed from customer account agreements the Waiver provision that relates to the consolidation of claims and notified its customers of the amendment. Schwab, in May 2013, removed the Waiver in its entirety from customer account agreements, for disputes related to events on or after May 15, 2013.

of the Customer Code, which provides that arbitrators have the authority to consolidate claims.

B. Proceedings Before the Hearing Panel and the Hearing Panel's Finding

On August 28, 2012, the Hearing Officer issued an order informing the parties that the Hearing Panel had decided to dismiss causes one and two of Enforcement's complaint, but to find a violation under cause three....

The Hearing Panel's decision concentrated primarily on two issues: (1) whether Schwab's Waiver conflicts with FINRA rules, and (2), if so, whether the FAA preempts FINRA rules. The Hearing Panel found that both FINRA Rules 2268(d)(3) and (d)(1), acting in conjunction with Rule 12204 of the Customer Code, banned the use of class action waivers by FINRA members. The Hearing Panel next turned to the issue of whether the FAA preempts FINRA Rule 2268(d)(3) and Rule 12204 of the Customer Code. The Hearing Panel noted that §2 of the FAA, by its own terms, applies to any written agreement to arbitrate, observing also that Schwab, FINRA, and numerous courts have previously concurred that the FAA applies to FINRA arbitration rules and its members' arbitration agreements. This, according to the Hearing Panel, put the FAA in direct conflict with FINRA Rule 2268(d)(3) and Rule 12204 of the Customer Code because these rules place a substantial roadblock in the way of arbitration of claims.

The Hearing Panel determined that, under the holdings of the Supreme Court, the FAA's mandate that arbitration agreements be "valid, irrevocable, and enforceable" outweighs any countervailing rule or law (state, federal or regulatory) unless "overridden by a contrary congressional command," with the burden of proving such a command placed on the party opposing arbitration. The Hearing Panel determined that FINRA rules, promulgated pursuant to the SEC's delegation of authority, and approved by the SEC, are subject to the same limits. Finally, the Hearing Panel concluded that nothing in the securities laws exempted FINRA rules from the FAA's general applicability. The Hearing Panel noted that the Supreme Court repeatedly has relied on the FAA to enforce arbitration clauses in claims brought under federal securities statutes. Because the Hearing Panel found no clear expression of congressional intent to preserve judicial class actions as an option for customer claims where there is an agreement providing for arbitration of those claims, the Hearing Panel granted Schwab's motion for summary disposition on causes one and two concerning the Waiver's class-action provision.

With respect to the third cause of action, the Hearing Panel found that the FAA did not preclude enforcement of FINRA rules governing the powers of FINRA arbitrators and FINRA arbitration procedures.... The Hearing Panel found that the language in Schwab's Waiver prohibiting the consolidation of claims related primarily to the "governance of arbitration forums or arbitration procedures" and therefore improperly attempted to circumscribe the power of FINRA arbitrators....

II. Discussion

We affirm the Hearing Panel's findings that Schwab's Waiver violated NASD and FINRA rules, but reverse the finding that the FAA precludes FINRA from enforcing the rule violations in causes one and two. We affirm the findings in cause three in their entirety....

A. Causes One and Two

* * *

FINRA Rule 2268 sets forth the requirements for FINRA members when using predispute arbitration agreements for customer accounts. The rule governs both the allowable form and content of a predispute arbitration agreement with a customer.... Rule 2268(e) informs broker-dealers that if a customer files a complaint in court against the firm, and the complaint contains claims that are subject to arbitration pursuant to a predispute arbitration agreement, the firm may seek to compel arbitration of the arbitrable claims. If the member seeks to compel arbitration of such claims, the member must agree to arbitrate all of the claims contained in the complaint if the customer so requests. Rule 2268 also requires, in subsection (f), that all predispute arbitration agreements for customer accounts state that no person may bring a class action in arbitration, nor seek to enforce a predispute arbitration agreement against a person who has initiated a judicial class action or is a member of a putative class until class certification issues are decided.

Enforcement alleged that the class action prohibition contained within Schwab's Waiver violated FINRA Rules 2268(d)(1) and (d)(3). Subsection (d) prohibits members from incorporating four conditions in a predispute arbitration agreement, including a provision that limits or contradicts the rules of any self-regulatory organization and one that "limits the ability of a party to file any claim in court permitted to be filed in court under the rules of the forums in which a claim may be filed under the agreement." Enforcement argues that FINRA Rule 2268(d)(3)'s phrase "any claim" includes class actions and therefore Schwab's Waiver contravenes this prohibition.... because the rules of FINRA's arbitration forum, and specifically Rule 12204 of the Customer Code, reference class action claims in court, the waiver of any ability to file class action claims in court constitutes a prohibited limit on "any claim" within the meaning of FINRA Rule 2268 and contradicts Rule 12204 of the Customer Code.

Schwab argues that FINRA Rule 2268(d)(3) cannot be referring to class actions when the rule language uses the term "claim" because class actions are procedural mechanisms and not claims.... We therefore must determine how the rules of FINRA's arbitration forum treat class actions and whether class actions are included in "any claim" for purposes of FINRA Rule 2268.

b. "Class Action Claims" under Rule 12204 of the Customer Code

In determining the intent and meaning of a term used in FINRA rules, the words must be considered in their context and sections of the rule relating to the same subject are said to be *in pari materia*, as well as cognate rules, and must be considered in order to arrive at the true meaning and scope of the words.[40] We therefore look to

---

40. [10] Rules "in pari materia" (i.e., in relation to the same matter or subject) are those having a common purpose such that they should be "construed together" for the purpose of learning and

FINRA's Customer Code to harmonize sections covering the same subject matter (arbitrations involving customer disputes), in order to determine if the phrase "any claim" in FINRA Rule 2268, when interpreted together with FINRA arbitration rules, includes judicial class actions for customer disputes involving member firms.

Rule 12100(d) of the Customer Code defines a "claim" as "an allegation or request for relief." Rule 12204 of the Customer Code is titled "Class Action Claims" and specifically addresses the status of class action claims in FINRA arbitration. Rule 12204(a) states that "[c]lass action claims may not be arbitrated under the [Customer] Code," while subsection (d) forbids members and associated persons from enforcing arbitration agreements against members of certified or putative class actions, until the class certification is denied or the class is decertified, or the member is excluded or withdraws from the class.[41] A careful reading of the rule text reveals that Rule 12204 uses the phrase "class action claims" interchangeably with "a claim [that] is part of a class action" and "any claim that is the subject of the certified or putative class action." Rules 12204(a), (c), (d) of the Customer Code.

We also consider the presumption against surplusage to be important here. It is "a cardinal principle of statutory construction that we must give effect, if possible, to every clause and word of a statute." *Williams v. Taylor*, 529 U.S. 362, 404 (2000) (internal quotation omitted). Enforcement and Schwab present us with two competing interpretations. Only Enforcement's interpretation of Rule 12204 "avoids surplusage." See *Freeman v. Quicken Loans, Inc.*, 132 S. Ct. 2034, 2043 (2012). Were we to adopt Schwab's construction of the rules, we would render the adjective "class action" preceding "claims" in Rule 12204 not only insignificant but wholly superfluous. Under Schwab's rendition, FINRA's inclusion of the phrase "class action," in both the rule's title and substantive provisions, has no operative effect on the scope of the provision because class actions are not claims. We are reluctant "to treat statutory terms as surplusage" where, as here, the term occupies a pivotal place in the regulatory scheme related to arbitration of customer disputes and the availability of bringing class action claims in court. See *Babbitt v. Sweet Home Chapter of Cmtys. for a Great Or.*, 515 U.S. 687, 698 (1995). We determine that a securities-law claim brought as a class action therefore is a category of claim that was intended to be filed in court under FINRA

---

giving effect to the legislative intention. *See* BLACK'S LAW DICTIONARY 794. A primary rule of statutory construction is that when interpreting multiple statutes dealing with a related subject or object, the statutes are in pari materia and must be considered together. The proper comprehensive analysis thus reads the parts of a regulatory scheme together, bearing in mind the intent underlying the whole scheme.

41. [11] Schwab contends that the statement at the end of Rule 12204(d) of the Customer Code stating that "[t]his paragraph does not otherwise affect the enforceability of any rights under this Code or any other agreement" means that its Waiver is permissible under FINRA rules because the Waiver is "any other agreement." We reject this argument based on a plain reading of the rule language. Rule 12204(d) of the Customer Code expressly applies to "any arbitration agreement" with a customer. Thus, "any other agreement" means an agreement other than the predispute arbitration agreement with a customer. Schwab's Waiver is part of a predispute arbitration agreement with customers.

rules. Our determination is also supported by the rulemaking history discussed in detail below.

While the inclusion of Rule 12204(a) in the Customer Code squarely addresses that class actions may not proceed in FINRA's arbitration forum, the Customer Code on its face does not state directly that it preserves the right for customers to bring claims via judicial class actions. Rather, Rule 12204(d) of the Customer Code presupposes that judicial class actions are possible and then sets forth restrictions on enforcement of existing arbitration agreements with respect to any claim that is part of a putative or certified class action. Schwab argues that a customer can agree, through Schwab's Waiver, to relinquish participation in a class action, without Schwab violating FINRA rules. The timing of Schwab's Waiver, requiring customers to agree when they open an account, conflicts with FINRA rules. Rule 12204(d) of the Customer Code by its terms prevents a firm from enforcing a predispute arbitration agreement until a court disposes of the class action allegations or the customer opts out of the putative or certified class. Thus, none of the exceptions listed in subsection (d) apply until a customer is given the opportunity to participate in a class action. It therefore stands to reason that Rule 12204 of the Customer Code does not contemplate a prospective waiver of a customer's right to participate in a class action.

Schwab argues that several cases involving class-action waivers inserted in employment agreements between firms and employees direct the outcome here.... We disagree that these cases are controlling over disputes with customers. The cases upon which Schwab relies analyze Rule 13204 of the Industry Code. While Rule 13204(a)'s text is identical to Rule 12204 of the Customer Code, there are no restrictions upon firms regarding the content of predispute arbitration agreements with employees, unlike the strict parameters set forth by FINRA Rule 2268 for predispute arbitration agreements with customers. In comparison, FINRA Rule 2268 expressly prohibits provisions that contradict SRO rules or which limit the ability of customers to file the kind of claims that FINRA arbitration rules determine can be brought in court. This difference makes the employment agreement cases inapplicable to this dispute.

We also review the rulemaking history of FINRA Rule 2268 and Rule 12204 of the Customer Code to determine the intent of the drafters.... In the wake of the Supreme Court's decision in *Shearson/Am. Express Inc. v. McMahon*, 482 U.S. 220 (1987), which held that customers who enter into predispute arbitration agreements with brokerage firms can be compelled to arbitrate claims under the Exchange Act, the SEC approved the SROs' arbitration rules. The SEC found the new rules were "designed to prevent fraudulent and manipulative acts and practices, promote just and equitable principles of trade, provide for an equitable allocation of fees, and, in general, protect investors and the public interest," and that they were consistent with Exchange Act § 15A....

2. The Rulemaking History

a. FINRA Rule 2268

FINRA adopted the provisions now contained in Rule 2268 to address SEC concerns about the "fairness and efficiency of the arbitration process administered by the

SROs." ... The SEC made clear that "[a]greements cannot be used to curtail any rights that a party may otherwise have had in a judicial forum." ...

b. Rule 12204 of the Customer Code

FINRA proposed what is now Rule 12204 of the Customer Code to exclude class action matters from arbitration proceedings conducted by FINRA and to require that predispute arbitration agreements contain a notice that class action matters may not be arbitrated. FINRA stated in the July 1992 Proposal that the rule provisions were developed in response to former SEC Chairman David S. Ruder's suggestion that SROs "consider adopting procedures that would give investors access to the courts in appropriate cases, including class actions." ... FINRA stated "that it agrees that the bar on class actions in arbitration was designed to provide investors with access to the courts, which already have developed the procedures and the expertise for managing class actions." ... Moreover, ... "paragraph (d)(3) [now Rule 12204(d) of the Customer Code] clearly prohibits NASD members from enforcing existing arbitration contracts to defeat class certification or participation." The SEC in its approval order stated that "in all cases, class actions are better handled by the courts and that investors should have access to the courts to resolve class actions efficiently. "The SEC explained that "[w]ithout access to class actions in appropriate cases, both investors and broker-dealers have been put to the expense of wasteful, duplicative litigation.... The SEC ..."believes that investor access to the courts should be preserved for class actions ..."

3. Schwab's Waiver Violates FINRA Rules

After reviewing the rule language and rulemaking history, we determine that Rule 12204 of the Customer Code was intended to preserve investor access to the courts to bring or participate in judicial class actions, and that through its Waiver, Schwab violated FINRA Rules 2268(d)(1) and (d)(3), and Rule 12204 of the Customer Code.... FINRA crafted Rule 12204 of the Customer Code to prevent member firms from using an existing arbitration agreement as a weapon against customers "to defeat class certification or participation." Consistent with this purpose and in harmony with the prohibitions of Rule 12204(d) of the Customer Code, FINRA Rule 2268(f) requires firms to include a statement in customer predispute arbitration agreements that such agreements are not enforceable against a person who has initiated a judicial class action or is a member of a putative class until class certification issues are decided. Moreover, the SEC's directive in approving the rule echoed this sentiment: "investor access to the courts should be preserved for class actions." Schwab's Waiver eliminates access to the courts in violation of FINRA rules.

* * *

4. The Federal Arbitration Act

a. Applicability to FINRA Rules

As a threshold matter, Enforcement and several of its amici argue that the FAA does not apply to this case. They argue that the FAA has no effect on the application of FINRA rules governing predispute arbitration agreements because the rules are enforceable as a result of a private contract, Schwab's membership agreement with FINRA. We agree, but only to a point. Through Schwab's membership agreement, FINRA's arbitration rules apply to Schwab. *See, e.g., Anderson v. Beland*, 672 F.3d 113, 128 (2d Cir. 2011) (FINRA membership constitutes an agreement to adhere to FINRA's rules and regulations, including its Code and relevant arbitration provisions contained therein." (Internal quotation omitted)). The FAA, however, does apply to this case because it governs virtually every arbitration agreement arising out of a commercial transaction, and Schwab's customer transactions are no exception.

Federal circuit courts also have recognized that FINRA arbitration rules themselves constitute an "agreement in writing" under the FAA.... We accordingly determine that a necessary component of a comprehensive legal analysis in this case requires us to review how FINRA arbitration rules (promulgated pursuant to and acting in concert with the Exchange Act) interact with the requirements of the FAA and the FAA's presumption of arbitrability of Exchange Act claims.

b. The Federal Arbitration Act's Statutory Purpose

The Supreme Court has consistently recognized two key aspects of the FAA. The Court has explained that the "FAA's primary purpose [is to] ensur[e] that private agreements to arbitrate are enforced according to their terms." Second, the FAA establishes a federal policy favoring arbitration. "The Arbitration Act establishes that, as a matter of federal law, any doubts concerning the scope of arbitrable issues should be resolved in favor of arbitration, whether the problem at hand is the construction of the contract language itself or an allegation of waiver, delay, or a like defense to arbitrability."

C. The Federal Arbitration Act's Presumption in Favor of Arbitrability Yields to Federal Law that Limits Arbitration of Claims

Despite the "liberal federal policy favoring arbitration agreements," the FAA has limits. See *Howsam v. Dean Witter Reynolds, Inc.*, 537 U.S. 79, 83 (2002). "The FAA directs courts to place arbitration agreements on equal footing with other contracts." The savings language in §2 of the FAA explicitly directs adjudicators to do what other laws require. If a valid arbitration agreement exists, then an adjudicator must determine whether any external legal constraints preclude arbitration of the claims in question.

In *CompuCredit Corp. v. Greenwood*, the Supreme Court reaffirmed the principle that the mandate of the FAA is not absolute, explaining that it may be "overridden by a 'contrary congressional command.'" 132 S. Ct. 665, 669 (2012) (quoting *McMahon*, 482 U.S. at 226). In *McMahon*, the Court specified that congressional intent to overcome the FAA would be "deducible from [the statute's] text or legislative history, or from an inherent conflict between arbitration and the statute's underlying purpose."

d. The Exchange Act Contains Congress's Command that the SEC Can Approve FINRA's Rules that Govern Arbitration

Here, both the text of the Exchange Act and the rulemaking history of NASD's proposal to adopt what are currently FINRA Rule 2268 and Rule 12204 of the Customer Code demonstrate a statutorily authorized intent to overcome the FAA. Congress, through the Maloney Act amendments to the Exchange Act, gave registered securities associations, such as FINRA, front-line responsibility for regulating the brokerage industry. Specifically, Exchange Act § 15A empowers FINRA to regulate broker-dealers including how they resolve disputes with their customers, subject to SEC oversight. FINRA must file with the SEC a proposal to change one of its rules and the SEC must approve the rule for the proposal to become effective. In the past twenty years, the SEC approved dozens of FINRA's arbitration rules, including FINRA Rule 2268 and Rule 12204 of the Customer Code and their predecessor rules ...

Congress explicitly authorized the SEC to approve SRO proposed rule changes, including rule changes regarding arbitration, when the SEC finds that the rule change is consistent with the requirements of the Exchange Act. *McMahon*, 482 U.S. at 233; Exchange Act § 19(b)(2). In its opinion regarding arbitration of Exchange Act claims, the Supreme Court explained "the Commission has broad authority to oversee and to regulate the rules adopted by the SROs relating to customer disputes, including the power to mandate the adoption of any rules it deems necessary to ensure that arbitration procedures adequately protect statutory rights." ... Therefore, the Exchange Act gives the SEC the authority to approve FINRA rules that govern arbitration in FINRA's forum and that regulate the content of predispute arbitration agreements.

Turning to another indication of congressional intent, the FINRA rulemaking history here highlights that the rules would restrict a broker-dealers' ability to use an arbitration agreement to defeat judicial class actions.[42] As noted previously, the rulemaking history for Rule 12204 of the Customer Code is explicit that FINRA would prevent its members from eliminating judicial class actions through provisions in predispute arbitration agreements. FINRA stated that "paragraph (d)(3) [now Rule 12204(d) of the Customer Code] clearly prohibits NASD members from enforcing existing arbitration contracts to defeat class certification or participation. The SEC's approval order concluded by stating that it "believes that investor access to the courts should be preserved for class actions and that the rule change approved herein [now-current Rule 12204 of the Customer Code] provides a sound procedure for the management of class actions arising out of securities industry disputes between NASD members and their customers."

* * *

The Hearing Panel mistakenly required that Congress restrict arbitration agreements directly in a statute. A "congressional command," however, is not strictly confined to an arbitration restriction that is written into a statute. Congress can also pass a statute that grants authority to an agency to restrict predispute arbitration agreements.... The SEC is implementing Congress's plan by evaluating and approving SRO rule proposals that govern the conduct of the securities industry, including the rules that govern what FINRA firms can include in their predispute arbitration agreements with their customers.

---

42. [21] Within the context of an SRO rule proposal, we rely on the SRO rulemaking history, including SEC approval, as the appropriate analog to legislative history under *McMahon* and *Compu-Credit*.

* * *

In summary, we find FINRA rules that restrict Schwab's ability to use a class action waiver to defeat customers from bringing or participating in judicial class actions are valid and enforceable.

B. Cause Three

Enforcement alleged in cause three of its complaint, and the Hearing Panel found, that Schwab's Waiver violated NASD Rule 3110(f)(4)(A), and FINRA Rules 2268(d)(1) and 2010, because the Waiver's statement that "the arbitrator(s) shall have no authority to consolidate more than one parties' [sic] claims" contradicts Rule 12312 of the Customer Code. Schwab does not contest this finding of violation, and after our independent review, we affirm it.

1. The Rule Language

Rule 12312 of the Customer Code permits one or more parties to join multiple claims together in the same arbitration under certain circumstances. [43] The rule further provides that if the Director of Arbitration separates the claims prior to the appointment of an arbitration panel, the panel may subsequently reconsider the Director's decision. Rule 12312 by its terms provides arbitrators with the authority to consolidate the claims of multiple parties. Schwab is bound by Rule 12200 of the Customer Code to arbitrate according to the procedures set forth "under the Code." We concur with the Hearing Panel's finding that Schwab is prohibited from modifying the SEC-approved arbitration procedures provided in the FINRA Customer Code. Accordingly, this provision in the Waiver is a condition in a predispute arbitration agreement that contradicts a FINRA rule, in violation of FINRA Rules 2268(d)(1) and 2010.

Notes and Questions

1. After FINRA's Board of Governors issued the preceding decision, Schwab settled with FINRA by permanently removing the waiver from its customer contracts and paying a $500,000 fine. Is this decision a statement by FINRA to all of its member broker-dealers that it will not tolerate their attempts to make arbitration clauses unfair or a statement about FINRA's ability to enforce its own rules?

2. *FINRA Rule 2268(d) Requirements When Using Predispute Arbitration Agreements for Customer Accounts.* This rule prohibits certain conditions from being included in arbitration agreements, such as conditions that: "(1) limit or contradict the rules of any self-regulatory organization; (2) limit the ability of a party to file any claim in arbitration; (3) limit the ability of a party to file any claim in court permitted to be filed in court under the rules of the forums in which a claim may

---

43. [29] Those circumstances include claims containing common questions of law or fact; claims asserting rights to relief jointly and severally; or claims arising out of the same transactions or occurrences. Rule 12312 of the Customer Code.

be filed under the agreement; and (4) limit the ability of arbitrators to make any award."

3. Are there meaningful distinctions between class action arbitrations, which are prohibited by FINRA rules, and consolidation of claims (submission of multiple claims jointly by one or more parties), which are permitted under FINRA Rules? *See* FINRA Rules 12204 and 12312.

Hypothetical Three

Jane Summer, an investor in her 80s, was notified that she might be able to recover a sizeable portion ($750,000) of her losses for her suitability claim against her broker-dealer Diaz & Wang because she is eligible to join a class action law suit. Summer is afraid that the class action in court might take a long time. She would rather pursue an expedited arbitration in FINRA's arbitral forum. Will Summer be able to proceed against Diaz & Wang in FINRA's arbitral forum despite the fact that there is a class action lawsuit that she is eligible to join? Using the "Arbitration Fee Calculator" on FINRA's website, estimate the amount of fees that Summer must pay to pursue arbitration with FINRA.

D. Dodd-Frank and the Future of Mandatory Arbitration

Section 921 of the Dodd-Frank Wall Street Reform and Consumer Protection Act of 2010 ("Dodd Frank"), amended Section 15 of the Exchange Act and provided the SEC with the authority to "prohibit, or impose conditions or limitations on the use of, agreements that require customers or clients of any broker, dealer, or municipal securities dealer to arbitrate any future dispute between them arising under the Federal securities laws, the rules and regulations thereunder, or the rules of a self-regulatory organization if it finds that such prohibition, imposition of conditions, or limitations are in the public interest and for the protection of investors." The Department of the Treasury's legislative proposal for section 921, which was adopted in whole, reasoned "mandating a particular venue and up-front method of adjudicating disputes—and eliminating access to courts—may unjustifiably undermine investor interests."[44] The Committee on Banking, Housing, and Urban Affairs in recommending passage of Section 921 of Dodd Frank, asserted that mandatory predispute arbitration is "unfair to the investors."[45] After the enactment of Dodd Frank, the SEC commenced accepting

---

44. Press Release, U.S. Department of the Treasury, Fact Sheet: Administration's Regulatory Reform Agenda Moves Forward Legislation for Strengthening Investor Protection Delivered to Capitol Hill (July 10, 2009), http://www.treasury.gov/press-center/press-releases/Pages/tg205.aspx). Press Release, U.S. Department of the Treasury, Title IX—Additional Improvements to Financial Markets Regulation 6 (July 10, 2009), http://www.treasury.gov/press-center/press-releases/Documents/tg205071009.pdf.

45. CHRISTOPHER J. DODD, THE RESTORING AMERICAN FINANCIAL STABILITY ACT OF 2010, S. REP. No. 111-176, at 110 (2d Sess. 2010) available at: http://www.banking.senate.gov/public/_files/Comittee_Report_S_Rept_111_176.pdf.

and publishing comments received regarding Section 921; however, currently there is no specific rule proposal by the SEC and no further action has been taken under the authority granted under Section 921.

Similarly, in § 1028 of Dodd-Frank, the Consumer Financial Protection Bureau (Bureau) was empowered to conduct a study on the use of predispute mandatory arbitration clauses and "prohibit or impose conditions or limitations" if it is necessary for the protection of consumers. While the CFPB does not have the authority to regulate the securities industry, preliminary findings of their study of consumer contracts and consumer arbitrations administered by the American Arbitration Association found, among other things, that consumers do not file arbitration for small claims, with the average arbitration claim being $38,000, 90 percent of contracts reviewed by the Bureau prohibited class-action arbitrations, and consumers preferred class action instead of arbitration where class-action was available.[46]

---

46. CONSUMER FINANCIAL PROTECTION BUREAU, ARBITRATION STUDY PRELIMINARY RESULTS, (December 2013) available at: http://files.consumerfinance.gov/f/201312_cfpb_arbitration-study-preliminary-results.pdf.

Chapter 13

Market Structure Regulation

Regulatory Authority

Securities Exchange Act of 1934 Sections 11A, 15(b), 15(c)(3), 15A, 17(a), 17(b), 19(b), 21(a), 21C

Exchange Act Rules 10b-5, 10b-10,15c3-5, 15c2-11, Regulation NMS (Rules 600–613)

FINRA Rules 3310, 5250, 5310, 6200 series, 6240, 6300A, 6300B, 6432, 6433, 6434, 6437,6450, 6460, 6530, 6540, 6550, 6620, 7100 series, 7200A, 7200B, 7300 series

The discussion of market structure in this chapter focuses solely on equity securities from the perspective of a broker-dealer. The regulatory framework for other securities such as options (including equity-based options) or other derivatives is beyond the scope of this textbook.

Motivating Hypothetical

Carmen, Success First's CEO and director, has decided that Success First should grow significantly its business line of market making in equity securities. She understands that this is a difficult business but a very profitable one. As she is always telling Success First personnel and the board of directors, with great risk comes great reward. However, Josephine, Success First's general counsel, and two of the outside board members are concerned about the regulatory risks embodied in market making, and they are wondering whether the risks in growing Success First's market making business might outweigh the expected rewards. However, Carmen and the remaining board members believe that the time is right for increasing this business line. The board has formed a committee to explore the feasibility of increasing Success First's market making business in equity securities. The committee is co-chaired by Carmen and Josephine and is charged with evaluating the risks and expected rewards of Success First acting as a market maker: (1) exclusively in exchange-listed equity securities; (2) OTC equity securities; or (3) some combination of the two stocks. As you read the materials in this chapter, consider your recommendation to the board. Would you recommend that Success First increase its business line as a market maker in equity securities? If so, would you recommend that Success First act as a market maker in exchange-listed equity securities or OTC equity securities?

I. Introduction

Congress mandated the establishment of a national market system and a national clearance and settlement system in 1975 as part of the Securities Acts Amendments of 1975 (the "1975 Amendments"). According to Congress, a national market system was required to provide greater investor protection, increase investor confidence, and "to assure … a strong, effective and efficient capital raising and capital allocating system in the years ahead."[1] A national clearance and settlement system was needed because of the breakdown in the handling of paperwork associated with the clearance and settlement of securities transactions during the "paperwork crisis" in the late 1960s.[2] During the four years prior to the 1975 Amendments, both Congress and the Commission conducted several studies and held hearings on the operation and regulatory framework of the U.S. securities markets. Committees in both the House of Representatives and the Senate responsible for enacting legislation regulating U.S. securities markets made findings that substantiated the need for the establishment of a national market system and a national clearing and settlement system.[3] Specifically, the Banking, Housing, and Urban Affairs Committee of the Senate reported the following findings substantiating this need.

Senate Report No. 94-75, 94th Congress, 1st Session 1975
A. National Market System and Self-Regulatory Organizations

Fundamental changes have occurred over the past forty years in the manner in which securities are traded, the role played in the securities markets by institutional investors, the structure of the national and international economy, and the capabilities and availability of communications and data processing equipment. Yet, despite these changes, the Committee found that the organized securities markets continue to operate by and large as they did when the Securities Exchange Act of 1934 (the "Exchange Act") was adopted. Rather than responding to changing investor needs and striving for more efficient ways to perform their essential functions, the principal stock exchanges and the majority of established securities firms appear to have resisted industry modernization and to have been unable or unwilling to respond promptly and effectively to radically altered economic and technological conditions. As a result, the securities industry has caused misallocation of capital, widespread inefficiencies, and undesirable and potentially harmful fragmentation of trading markets.

The Securities Industry Study Report of the Subcommittee on Securities[4] identified a number of causes for the securities industry's languor in the face of great change and great opportunity: price fixing with respect to commission rates, artificial restrictions on market making activities, unjustified barriers to access to markets and

---

1. H.R. Conf. Rep. 94-229 (1975).

2. The establishment of a national clearing and settlement system is discussed in Section VI of this chapter.

3. *See also* H.R. Rep. 94-123, 94 Cong., 1st Sess. 1975.

4. (S. Doc. No. 93-13, 93d Cong., 1st Sess. 1973).

market makers, opposition to market integration from powerful vested interests, monopoly control of essential mechanisms for dissemination of market information, and the absence of effective control of market developments and operations by the Securities and Exchange Commission (the "SEC" or the "Commission"). Whatever the causes of past inaction, however, the Committee is convinced that unless the securities industry can develop a new sense of confidence and vigor and unless the SEC is granted broad and flexible authority to shape a new market system adequate to the needs of investors in this country and around the world, there is a very real danger that the future capital requirements of American business will not be met and that an independent securities industry, as it has come to be understood since 1933, will cease to exist.

Recently the SEC has taken action in several areas which the Committee believes will contribute to a more efficient and responsive securities industry and more orderly, liquid and fair securities markets. The development of uniform capital requirements, regulations concerning a composite tape for the reporting of all transactions in listed securities, a letter pursuant to Section 19(b) of the Exchange Act requesting exchanges to eliminate those rules, practices or policies which restrict the dissemination of quotations of specialists[5] on such exchanges, the adoption of Rule 19b-3 prohibiting exchanges from fixing rates of commission charged by their members effective May 1, 1975, and assistance in the establishment of a national clearing system are all necessary and forward-looking steps. In addition, progressive forces within the industry have begun to assert themselves, thus affirming the continuing vitality of self-regulation.

Nevertheless, it is clear to the Committee that new legislation is necessary in order to assure investors—both in this country and abroad—that our securities markets will remain vigorous and efficient in the years ahead. [The 1975 Amendments] would lay the foundation for a new and more competitive market system, vesting in the SEC power to eliminate all unnecessary or inappropriate burdens on competition while at the same time granting to that agency complete and effective powers to pursue the goal to centralized trading of securities in the interest of both efficiency and investor protection.

Because of the unique system of self-regulation in the securities industry, the principal markets for securities, i.e., the exchanges, are also the principal regulators of the activities of broker-dealers using those markets. Meaningful reform of this country's securities trading mechanisms will, therefore, be impossible unless there is also a reform of the method and manner by which the self-regulatory organizations operate and in the way that the SEC oversees the performance of their regulatory responsibilities.

Accordingly, [the 1975 Amendments] would significantly amend the provisions of the Exchange Act dealing with the powers of the self-regulatory organizations and the oversight authority of the SEC with respect to these organizations. The Committee believes that self-regulation should be preserved in the securities industry, but it also believes that the self-regulatory organizations must display a greater responsiveness

---

5. Specialists are now designated market makers. *See* Chapter 2, Section III.B of this textbook.

to their statutory obligations and to the need to coordinate their functions and activities. In the new regulatory environment created by this bill, self-regulation would be continued, but the SEC would be expected to play a much larger role than it has in the past to ensure that there is no gap between self-regulatory performance and regulatory need and, when appropriate, to provide leadership for the development of a more coherent and rational regulatory structure to correspond to and to police effectively the new national market system.

The securities markets of the United States are indispensable to the growth and health of this country's and the world's economy. In order to raise the enormous sums of investment capital that will be needed in the years ahead and to assure that that capital is properly allocated among competing uses, these markets must continue to operate fairly and efficiently. In the Committee's view, the increasing tempo and magnitude of the changes that are occurring in our domestic and international economy make it clear that the securities markets are due to be tested as never before. Unless these markets adapt and respond to the demands placed upon them, there is a danger that America will lose ground as an international financial center and that the economic, financial and commercial interests of the Nation will suffer.

The rapid attainment of a national market system ... is important ...

———

Sections II through VI of this chapter examine the development of the national market system and Section VII examines the importance and development of the national settlement and clearance system. The establishment of the national market system focused on linking fragmented (including geographically fragmented) market centers while the national settlement and clearance system focused on ensuring the capacity to handle the increasing volume of securities transactions in the U.S. securities markets.

II. The National Market System

Both Congress and the SEC determined that a national market system that linked a fragmented U.S. securities market was required to ensure U.S. predominance in the capital markets both domestically and internationally. Market fragmentation existed, primarily because the U.S. Securities markets were comprised of many geographically dispersed trading centers and the significant increase of institutional investors, charged with investing Americans' savings, trading large blocks of shares off the floors of exchanges. Geographic dispersion of market centers resulted in market fragmentation because the trading centers lacked a means to share information among themselves when trading in the same security simultaneously (multiply-traded securities). Off-exchange trading of large blocks of shares by institutional investors exacerbated market fragmentation because it prevented access to information by all investors about the best combination of price, overall liquidity, and transaction costs in U.S. securities markets. These two core issues—market fragmentation and institutionalization—lead to:

(i) the need to perfect existing mechanisms for the disclosure of information concerning all completed transactions, in multiply-traded securities; (ii) the absence of a comprehensive, composite quotation system displaying buy and sell interest in those securities from all markets (whether on an exchange or over-the-counter); (iii) the inadequacy of existing means available to brokers for routing orders to and among markets in pursuit of the most favorable execution opportunities; (iv) the lack of a mechanism to provide nationwide agency limit order protection, affording time and price priority to such orders regardless of geographical location; (v) impediments to effective market-maker competition for orders of relatively small size; and (vi) the need to integrate block transactions more effectively into the normal course of securities trading.[6]

Congress's and the SEC's solution was to establish a national market system that would "maximize the depth and liquidity of [U.S. securities markets], so that securities [could] be bought and sold at reasonably continuous and stable prices, and to insure that each investor [would] receive the best possible execution of his order, regardless of where it originates...,"[7] i.e., to link a fragmented market structure.

A. Linking a Fragmented Market Structure

Section 11A of the Securities Exchange Act of 1934 ("Section 11A"), enacted as part of the 1975 Amendments, authorized the Commission to facilitate the establishment of a national market system for securities. It was the intent of Congress that the national market system "evolve through the interplay of competitive forces."[8] by removing unnecessary regulatory restrictions, and that the SEC's facilitation would occur in instances when competition would not be sufficient. As originally enacted, Section 11A contained congressional findings, and the SEC was directed to facilitate the establishment of the national market system for U.S. securities in accordance with Congress' findings.

Sec. 11A. (a)(1) The Congress finds that—

(A) The securities markets are an important national asset, which must be preserved and strengthened.

(B) New data processing and communications techniques create the opportunity for more efficient and effective market operations.

(C) It is in the public interest and appropriate for the protection of investors and the maintenance of fair and orderly markets to assure—

   (i) economically efficient execution of securities transactions;

   (ii) fair competition among brokers and dealers, among exchange markets, and between exchange markets and markets other than exchange markets;

---

6. *Development of a National Market System*, Rel. No. 14416 (1978).
7. 37 F.R. 5286 (Mar. 14, 1972).
8. H.R. Conf. Rep. 94-229, at 92 (1975).

> (iii) the availability to brokers, dealers, and investors of information with respect to quotations for and transactions in securities;
>
> (iv) the practicability of brokers executing investors' orders in the best market; and
>
> (v) an opportunity, consistent with the provisions of clauses (i) and (iv) of this subparagraph, for investors' orders to be executed without the participation of a dealer.
>
> (D) The linking of all markets for qualified securities through communication and data processing facilities will foster efficiency, enhance competition, increase the information available to brokers, dealers, and investors, facilitate the offsetting of investors' orders, and contribute to best execution of such orders....

The SEC was given broad rulemaking authority to accomplish the goals and objectives enumerated by Congress in Section 11A for establishing a national market system in the U.S. securities markets. Congress believed that the SEC could use its rulemaking authority to eliminate anticompetitive practices and to facilitate more efficient and effective operation of U.S. securities markets using technology. In fact, linking the existing fragmented market centers in the U.S. securities markets using technology was a core objective of Congress' enactment of Section 11A of the Exchange Act, reflected by, among other powers, the express authority given to the SEC over securities information processors ("SIPs"), i.e., organizations engaged in the business of collecting, processing, or publishing information relating to quotations for, and transactions in, securities. Accordingly, the SEC focused its rulemaking efforts on developing a national securities market system by linking fragmented market centers using communication and data-processing facilities. Specifically, the SEC focused on facilitating consolidated disclosure of market data about the transactions in, and quotations for, equity securities listed on a national securities exchange. Next, the SEC focused its rulemaking on facilitating competition, efficiency, and fairness in the handling of customer orders in the various markets (the order handling rules), and public disclosure of statistical information about the execution quality of customer orders in the various market centers. As discussed below, the SEC adopted and amended many rules between the enactment of the 1975 Amendments and the adoption of Regulation National Market System ("Reg NMS") in June 2005, to implement Congress's goal of developing a national market system based on private competition with the intervention of the SEC as needed when private competition was insufficient.

1. Consolidated Disclosure of Market Data

Although Congress expressly authorized the SEC to facilitate the development of a national market system with the enactment of Section 11A in the 1975 Amendments, the SEC's efforts to integrate its fragmented markets through consolidation and disclosure of market data on a limited basis actually began in 1972 with the adoption of the Consolidation Transaction Plan (CTP) under Rule 17a-15 of the Exchange Act.

Rule 17a-15 required exchanges, the NASD (n/k/a FINRA),[9] and non-member broker-dealers to establish a plan to disseminate price and volume information about executed transactions in exchange-listed securities ("last sale reports"), and securities admitted to unlisted trading privileges on the exchanges, through vendors or securities information processors (SIPs). The CTP established the Consolidated Tape Association (CTA), an unincorporated association, to administer the joint procedures developed to distribute last sale reports to SIPs.

The CTA established the Consolidated Tape System (CTS) as the central consolidator of market data streams from the participants[10] in the CTA plan.[11] The CTS was organized into two different data streams—Network A and Network B. Network A provided last sale transaction data for securities listed on the NYSE. Network B provided last sale transaction data for securities listed on other exchanges, and for exchange-listed securities traded over-the-counter in the Third Market.[12] The CTS also hired the Securities Industry Automation Corporation (SIAC) as the initial processor of last sale prices for inclusion in the Consolidated Tape System. *See* Figure 13.1 for an example of information contained on the Consolidated Tape.

Figure 13.1. Consolidated Tape System

| MSFT | 5k@ | 61.25 | ▼ | 1.35 |
| Ticker Symbol | Shares Traded | Price Traded | Change Direction | Change Amount |

Ticker Symbol	The Unique Characters used to identify the company
Shares Traded	The share volume of the transaction. Abbreviations are K = 1,000; M = 1 million, B = 1 billion
Price Traded	The price per share for the security traded
Change Direction	Shows whether the stock is trading higher or lower than the previous day's closing price
Change Amount	The difference in price from the previous day's closing price

---

9. At this time, NASDAQ was owned and operated by the NASD k/n/a FINRA. See Chapter 1 for a discussion of NASDAQ's origins.

10. SROs registered with the SEC, such as NYSE and NASDAQ.

11. The CTA plan is filed with the SEC and amended from time to time with the approval of the SEC. *See* CTA Plan at https://www.ctaplan.com/documentation.

12. Currently, Network B provides last sale transaction data (price and volume) for securities listed on AMEX, BATS, BATS Y, BSE, CBOE, CHX, EDGA, EDGX, ISE, NSX, NYSE Arca, PHLX or any other exchange other than NASDAQ, but not also listed on NYSE.

After March 1973, exchanges, the NASD, and non-member broker-dealers could not release, on a continuing basis, last sale reports of transactions in listed securities (including UTP securities) without complying with the terms of the CTA.

a. Early SEC Rulemaking Under the 1975 Amendments

The first rule adopted by the SEC under Section 11A of the 1975 Amendments required the registration of SIPs such as SIAC. Prior to the 1975 Amendments, the SEC did not have the authority to regulate SIPs. It only had the authority to regulate the consolidation and disclosure of market data through the exchanges and the NASD, not the entities processing market data on behalf of the exchanges and the NASD for disclosure. With the adoption of Rule 11Ab2-1, the SEC directly regulated SIPs by requiring registration on Form SIP.[13]

Next, the SEC adopted Rule 11Ac1-1 in January 1978, which required the exchanges and the NASD to establish a system to automatically disseminate consolidated quotation data from all market centers in exchange-listed securities to SIPs. Exchanges and the NASD adopted the Consolidated Quotation plan ("CQ Plan") to establish the system to automatically disseminate consolidated quotation data (CQS). Like the CTS, the CQS was operated under the terms of the CQ Plan and consisted of two different data streams processed by SIAC.[14] The CQS is currently operating.[15] With systems established for disclosure of consolidated transaction and quotation data for exchange-listed securities, the SEC next turned its attention to consolidating market data for exchange-listed securities traded simultaneously on different exchanges, i.e., multiply-traded securities.

The SEC approved the Intermarket Trading System ("ITS") as a pilot program to consolidate market data disclosure for exchange-listed securities traded simultaneously on different exchanges in April 1978. The ITS was a communications network linking the AMEX, NYSE, BSE, PSE, and PHLX pursuant to the Intermarket Communications Linkage Plan ("ITS Plan") adopted and filed with the SEC by the participating exchanges. The ITS permitted members of these exchanges to send orders for the purchase and sale of certain multiply-traded securities to any participating exchange. In particular, the ITS provided facilities and procedures for: (1) displaying on the floors of participating exchanges of composite quotation information; (2) routing of commitments to trade and administrative messages between and among participants; and (3) participation in opening transactions of participating exchanges. Essentially, the ITS enabled members from each participating exchange to identify the best bid and offer available from any participant for a particular multiply-traded security. With the establishment of these linkages between market centers, the SEC next turned

---

13. At its initial adoption, only vendors that exclusively engaged in processing securities market data for disclosure were required to register.

14. Information about CTS and CQS, including its participants, is available at https://www.ctaplan.com/index.

15. Current information about the CTA and CQ plans is available at: https://www.ctaplan.com/CTA.

its attention to the manner and form of the collection, display, and dissemination of market data in the national market system.

The SEC adopted Rules 11Ac1-2 and 11Aa3-1 to establish uniform requirements for market data collection and dissemination by SIPs and exchanges and the NASD in February 1980. Rule 11Ac1-2 governed the manner in which SIPs displayed transaction, quotation, and market information for exchanged-listed securities (including UTP) traded on exchanges and over-the-counter. Among other requirements, Rule 11Ac1-2 obliged vendors to display such information in a non-discriminatory manner, e.g., SIPs could not display information received from one market center more favorably than another market center. Rule 11Aa3-1 governed the manner of collection, consolidation, and dissemination of transaction information by exchanges and the NASD and required exchange-listed securities traded on exchanges and over-the-counter to be subject to transaction reporting plans prescribing the manner and form of the collection, consolidation, and dissemination of transaction information.

The SEC next took steps to maximize competition between and among markets and market participants and further the efficiency and fairness of the U.S. securities markets by requiring exchanges to amend their rules regarding off-exchange trading restrictions. It did so by adopting Rule 19c-3 in June 1980, which eliminated off-exchange trading restrictions with respect to most newly listed securities, thereby permitting member firms of the NYSE and Amex to make markets over-the-counter in what was then a small number of NYSE and Amex-listed securities. Off-exchange trading restrictions had anticompetitive effects because they effectively confined trading in securities to the exchange on which they were listed. The SEC was concerned that off-exchange trading restrictions were continuously being extended to an ever-increasing number of securities that were previously traded exclusively in the over-the-counter market; when these securities became exchange-listed securities, the previous over-the-counter market was virtually extinguished. Also, the SEC stated that the presence of additional market makers in such securities might: (1) place competitive pressure on primary market specialists, potentially narrowing spreads in Rule 19c-3 securities; and (2) create incentives for markets to disseminate quotations of greater size, adding to the depth, liquidity, and continuity of the markets for such securities. In addition, during the hearings conducted in connection with the adoption of Rule 19c-3, the NASD announced plans to enhance its NASDAQ system to include a computer-assisted execution system ("CAES") that would enable participating broker-dealers to route their orders for listed securities through the system to obtain automatic executions against quotations of third-market makers. The NASD also contemplated an automated interface between the ITS and CAES to permit automated execution of commitments sent from participating exchanges and to permit market makers participating in the enhanced NASDAQ system to route commitments efficiently to exchange markets for execution.[16] Next, the SEC turned its attention to ensuring that investors had access

---

16. The ITS/CAES interface was finally implemented under an SEC order amending the ITS Plan in 1982. However, technological advances obviated the need for ITS in 2007.

to market data about all securities with significant trading volume in U.S. securities markets, whether or not they were listed on an exchange.

The SEC adopted Rule 11Aa2-1 in February 1981 to prescribe procedures for designating securities with significant trading volume in U.S. securities markets as national market system securities. The adoption of Rule 11Aa2-1 resulted in the designation of approximately 40 over-the-counter securities as national market system securities. Prior to February 1981, the SEC's rulemaking efforts focused on exchange-listed securities traded on exchanges and over-the-counter in the third market. The adoption of Rule 11Aa2-1 combined with the corresponding amendment of Rule 11Aa3-1 resulted in the dissemination and disclosure of transaction and quotation information of both exchange-listed securities and over-the-counter securities with significant trading volume in U.S. securities markets.

Next, the SEC determined the need for uniform procedures and policies for establishing and amending national market system plans. Rule 11Aa3-2, adopted in May 1981, provided procedures and policies for establishing and amending existing national market system plans such as the CTA and CQ Plans. In particular, Rule 11Aa3-2 specified procedures for filing and amending national market system plans (including amendments initiated by the SEC) and established certain minimum procedural and substantive requirements for national market system plans. Eight years after the adoption of Rule 11Aa3-2, the NASD, together with the AMEX, BSE, MSE, and Phlx, filed with the SEC a national market system plan to govern the collection, consolidation, and dissemination of quotation and transaction information for exchange and OTC national market system securities upon which unlisted trading privileges were granted ("OTC/UTP Plan").[17] The SEC's approval of this plan consolidated market data dissemination of exchange-listed securities with OTC/UTP national market system securities and was based, in part, on the previously discussed enhancements to the NASD's NASDAQ quotation system for the collection and dissemination of interdealer quotations, which dramatically increased the availability of OTC quotations, narrowed spreads, and increased investor interest in OTC securities. Basically, the NASDAQ quotation system's enhancements at that time altered the conditions in which OTC securities traded and made OTC trading of NASDAQ securities traded as UTP by an exchange more compatible with exchange trading. The Commission determined to condition its grant of UTP to NASDAQ national market system securities to an exchange if the exchange provided NASDAQ market makers access to the exchange market in such securities to the same extent that NASDAQ market makers provided access to their trading facilities.

In light of its significant progress in the construction of the infrastructure required to link fragmented market centers through rulemaking and through the adoption of

---

17. Unlisted trading privileges gave exchanges the right to trade a security not listed on the exchange. Unlisted trading privileges authorized trading even though the security was not listed on the exchange and were granted by the Securities and Exchange Commission. This is no longer the case in the current national market system. *See* UTP Plan at: http://www.utpplan.com/overview.

national market system plans between SROs to govern the operation of linkages and mandated disclosure of consolidated market data to investors, the SEC turned its attention to facilitating competition, efficiency, and fairness in the national market system between and among market participants and investors.

2. Facilitating Competition, Efficiency, and Fairness

SEC rulemaking intervention addressed fairness in the national market system by regulating the practice of payment for order flow, which had become widespread in the 1990s, engendering much debate and controversy. Payment for order flow is the practice of remunerating[18] broker-dealers in return for the routing of customer orders. Some exchanges or market-makers will pay broker-dealers for routing their customer orders to them for execution. Payment for order flow is one of the many ways that broker-dealers make money from executing customer trades. The SEC's primary concern with this practice is that payment for order flow may unfairly influence the routing of customer orders to the detriment of achieving best execution. In general, the broker-dealer has a duty to seek to execute a customer's order in the best available market. "[I]n its purest form, best execution can be thought of as executing a customer's order so that the customer's total cost or proceeds are the most favorable under the circumstances."[19] To facilitate best execution, the SEC adopted Rule 11Ac1-3 in November 1994. Rule 11Ac1-3 required broker-dealers to disclose whether they received payment for order flow; if they received payment for order flow, they were required to provide the customer with a detailed description of the type of payments received in their annual account statements[20] In addition, broker-dealers were required to give the customer information about the routing of unspecified orders[21] and whether those orders could be executed at prices better than the national best bid or offer (NBBO)[22] at the time the order was received. This requirement was designed to give the individual customer, at least annually, information about its broker-dealer's routing practices. For example, whether a broker-dealer routinely executed orders at the NBBO, when prices better than the NBBO were available. These disclosure obligations applied to NMS, NASDAQ, and OTCBB[23] securities.

---

18. Remuneration may be any monetary payment, service, property, or any other benefit that results in compensation or consideration to a broker-dealer in return for the routing of customer orders.

19. 59 FR 55006-01, fn. 27. See section V of this chapter for an examination of a broker-dealer's duty of best execution.

20. Simultaneously, the SEC amended Rule 10b-10 of the Exchange Act, requiring disclosure of payment for order flow on customer trade confirmations and advise that the customer could make a written request to find out the source and type of the payment as to a particular transaction.

21. Orders are unspecified if the customer has not specified a particular market center in which to execute her order.

22. The NBBO is the best (lowest) available ask price and the best (highest) available bid price to customers when they buy and sell securities.

23. The OTCBB is an interdealer quotation system used to display quotations in OTC equity securities. For more information about the OTCBB, see Section III.D. of this chapter discussing the OTCBB.

The SEC continued to address competition, efficiency, and fairness in the national market system by adopting the order handling rules (OHR), new Rule 11Ac1-4 and amended Rule 11Ac1-1, in September 1996. The SEC adopted the OHR because of its growing concerns about the handling of customer orders for securities in the national market system. Rule 11Ac1-4 and amended Rule 11Ac1-1 together were designed to enhance the quality of published quotations for securities and to promote competition and pricing efficiency. Rule 11Ac1-4, the SEC's Limit Order Display Rule, required OTC market makers and exchange broker-dealer exchange members to display the price and full size of customer limit orders when these orders represented buying and selling interest that was at a better price than a specialist's or OTC market maker's public quote displayed in the CQS. OTC market makers and specialists were also required to increase the size of the quote for a particular security to reflect a customer limit order of greater than de minimis size when the limit order was priced equal to the specialist's or OTC market maker's disseminated quote and that quote was equal to the NBBO. Rule 11Ac1-4 facilitated competition of customer orders directly with OTC market-makers and broker-dealer exchange members in the quote-setting process. Customers benefited from the publication of their limit orders that were better than the market makers' and specialists' quotes because display of customer limit orders provided improved pricing opportunities. Rule 11Ac1-1, the SEC's Quote Rule, was amended with two new significant provisions designed to ensure that more comprehensive quotation information was made available to the public. First, specialists and OTC market makers were required to make publicly available the price of any order they placed in an ECN if the ECN price was better than their public quotation. This provision was adopted with an alternative (ECN display alternative) that deemed OTC market makers and specialists in compliance with the Quote Rule if prices they entered into an ECN were publicly disseminated and the ECN provided access to other broker-dealers to trade at those prices. Without the ECN amendment, broker-dealers had previously been able to quote one price publicly to retail customers, while showing a better price privately to other investors and dealers on an ECN. The ECN display alternative allowed OTC market makers and specialists to comply directly with the ECN amendment by changing their public quote to reflect their ECN order, or by using an ECN that facilitated their compliance through dissemination of better prices available on the ECN to the public.[24] The second amendment of the Quote Rule expanded the categories of securities included in the national market system by requiring OTC market makers and specialists to publish quotes in any listed security if their volume in that security exceeded one percent of the aggregate volume during the most recent calendar quarter. Previously, the Quotation Rule only applied to certain listed securities. Essentially, the OHR required market-makers and specialists to provide their most competitive quotes—the lowest price at which the broker-dealer is willing to sell a security to a customer and the highest price that the broker-dealer is willing to pay a customer in order to buy the securities—to the public.

---

24. The ECN Display Alternative required the cooperation of the SROs in order to include the ECN prices in the public quotation system.

Moreover, the SEC believed that the OHR would lead to increased quote-based competition that would reduce the possibility of the anti-competitive trading behavior that occurred in the NASDAQ Stock Market noted in the following report issued by the SEC pursuant to Section 21(a) of the Exchange Act.

Report Pursuant to Section 21(a) of the Securities Exchange Act of 1934 Regarding the NASD and the NASDAQ Market

* * *

VI. PROBLEMS OF THE NASDAQ STOCK MARKET

A. Impediments to Price Competition

1. Importance of Competition

The Exchange Act contemplates that the U.S. securities markets shall be "free and open" with safeguards "to protect investors and the public interest." Vigorous price competition is a hallmark of a free and open market and is critically important to the efficient functioning and regulation of a dispersed dealer market. Because Nasdaq market makers trade securities which are otherwise fungible, price should be a principal means of competition in the Nasdaq market. Any significant hindrance to price competition impedes the free and open market prescribed by the Exchange Act. The investigation found that certain activities of Nasdaq market makers have both directly and indirectly impeded price competition in the Nasdaq market.

2. Price Quotations in Nasdaq

The Nasdaq market is a dealer market, in which a number of broker-dealers make markets in the same security. Making a market consists of standing ready to buy and sell a security at displayed prices. The market makers in Nasdaq quote two prices: a "bid" price, at which they are willing to buy the security, and an "ask" price, at which they are willing to sell the security. In so doing, they seek to profit by buying at lower prices and selling at higher prices. A market maker's bid price will always be lower than its ask price, and the difference between the two prices is called the "dealer spread."

Market makers play an important role in financial markets. Demand for market making services generally arises because buyers and sellers of securities do not arrive at the market at the same time or with the same quantities to trade. The market maker helps provide a solution to the uneven flow of supply and demand by standing ready to buy and sell. The market maker is thus said to provide immediacy to the market. In general, market makers seek to sell to buyers at prices higher than the prices at which they buy from sellers. The spread represents part of the market maker's potential compensation.

Market makers are on one or both sides of almost all trades on Nasdaq. Each issuer must have at least two market makers for its stock, but the average stock has eleven market makers. Some of the more actively traded stocks have fifty or more.... Often these market makers display different bid and ask prices. Their quotes are displayed on the Nasdaq market's electronic quotation system. The highest bid and the lowest ask prices are also separately displayed together, as the "inside quotes," and the difference between the two is called the "inside spread." Display of the inside quotes allows a viewer to observe immediately the best prices quoted on the Nasdaq market for both buying and selling a given security.

In general, different market makers will be quoting the inside bid and the inside ask prices. This is because, at any given point in time, some market makers will want to display an interest in buying a given security and will therefore quote high bid prices, while other market makers will want to display an interest in selling the security and will therefore quote lower ask prices.[25]

Most Nasdaq market making firms not only trade as principals with other broker-dealers in their market making activities, but also accept customer orders for Nasdaq securities. When executing a customer order, market makers are required to seek the most favorable terms for the customer under the circumstances. Historically it was generally accepted among market makers that this obligation was satisfied for a customer market order[26] when it was executed at the appropriate inside quote (i.e., customer orders to buy would be executed at the inside ask price, and customer orders to sell would be executed at the inside bid price). The size of the inside spread therefore usually has direct cost implications for investors in the market.[27] A customer who buys at the ask price would experience a loss equivalent to the inside spread if he or she were to liquidate the position immediately at the bid price. Over the life of the investment, the spread between the ask and the bid represents a transaction cost for the investor, in addition to any other fees (such as commissions or mark-ups) that may be incurred: the wider the inside spread, the higher the transaction cost.

It is also a general practice for a Nasdaq market maker receiving a retail customer order to execute the order itself rather than to send it to another market maker, even if that other market maker is quoting the best price (i.e., the best inside bid or offer) and the executing market maker is not. The executing market maker will provide the customer with the price displayed in the inside quotes, whether or not it is quoting

---

25. [30] For example, assume there are three market makers in a stock. Market maker A quotes $20 bid and $20 3/4 ask. Market maker B quotes $20 1/4 bid and $21 ask. Market maker C quotes $20 1/2 bid and $21 1/4 ask. Each market maker has a $3/4 dealer spread, but at different prices. The inside spread is only $1/4 wide, consisting of $20 1/2 bid (by market maker C) and $20 3/4 ask (by market maker A).

26. [31] A market order is an order in which the customer does not specify any particular price, but where the broker-dealer is to execute the order at the best price available under the circumstances.

27. [33] Large institutional customers and sophisticated individual customers often attempt to negotiate for prices better than the inside quotes. The inside quotes are often important to these negotiations, however, because they may serve as a benchmark from which the negotiations proceed. Many institutional customers have access to other avenues of price discovery, including proprietary trading systems and direct telephone contact with market makers. Customers with less market power (e.g., trades of 1,000 shares or less) do not have access to such systems, generally cannot negotiate, and usually must accept the prices displayed at the inside quotes.

those prices itself.[28] By executing customer orders in-house, market makers attempt to capture the inside spread, rather than allowing another market maker to benefit from the spread.[29] Thus, market makers have a significant interest in each other's quotes because those quotes directly affect their actual trading prices. This interdependency of prices strongly affects the conduct of market makers and provides a significant economic incentive for establishing and enforcing the pricing convention described below.

3. The Nasdaq Pricing Convention

The evidence gathered in the investigation indicates that Nasdaq market makers followed and in some cases overtly enforced a pricing convention that was used to determine the increments in which they would adjust their displayed quotes. This practice resulted in most stocks being quoted only in increments of $1/4. Market makers testified that under the convention, stocks in which dealers were quoting spreads of $3/4 or more were to be quoted in even-eighths (i.e., $1/4, $1/2, $3/4), thereby giving rise to a minimum inside spread of $1/4 ("even-eighth stocks"). Stocks with dealer spreads less than $3/4 could be quoted in both even and odd-eighths, thereby allowing a minimum inside spread of $1/8. The dealer spread was understood by market makers as indicating which of the two quotation increments applied to a particular security. The Nasdaq pricing convention was generally treated by market makers as a pricing "ethic," "tradition," or "professional norm" that other market makers were expected to follow, and was sometimes enforced through harassment, or threatened or actual refusals to deal. This pricing convention both directly and indirectly restricted the independent pricing decisions of individual market makers, and thereby negatively impacted price competition. Pricing and quoting decisions independently arrived at by individual market participants do not, in and of themselves, raise the same anticompetitive concerns.

* * *

This pricing convention was well understood and widely observed by traders throughout the Nasdaq market.[30] According to some market makers, the pricing con-

---

28. [34] This may reduce the incentive of market makers to try to attract order flow on the basis of incremental improvements in quotes.

29. [35] Many market makers pay non-market making brokerage firms to send customer orders to them for execution, a practice known as "payment for order flow." This purchased order flow is also executed at the inside quotes. For example, market maker, Firm A, may pay a non-market maker brokerage firm, Firm B, two cents per share for orders, with the understanding that Firm A will execute those orders at prices at least as good as the inside quotes regardless of whether Firm A is quoting at the inside. Firm A's profits for purchased orders will be the inside spread, less the two cents per share it pays Firm B for the orders.

30. [42] Quoting in violation of the pricing convention was pejoratively described by traders as making a "Chinese market." Industry-wide recognition of the pricing convention is reflected in the third quarter 1989 newsletter of a securities industry trade association, Securities Traders Association of New York, which stated that "it is clearly UNETHICAL to make a Chinese Market or to run ahead of an order." (Emphasis and capitalization in original.) Facts and circumstances evidencing the existence of the pricing convention and its enforcement also were known to the NASD by 1990.

vention was based on tradition and represented the" professional" way to quote in the Nasdaq market. Indeed, a number of traders testified that senior traders at their respective firms trained them to follow the pricing convention. Other traders have described the practice as an "ethic," a "custom," or a "tradition."

Market makers who enforced adherence to the convention did so in a number of ways. When certain market makers attempted to violate the convention by quoting in smaller increments (such as $1/8 when the majority of dealers were quoting with dealer spreads of greater than or equal to $3/4), they were subjected to harassing telephone calls. One trader explained that the reason he called another market maker who was quoting in a manner that violated the pricing convention was "[t]o get him to get his increments and his spreads to conform to what I thought was the right thing to do." There was widespread awareness among market makers of the harassing telephone calls. Traders from numerous market making firms, including traders who served on various NASD committees, testified to having received or made telephone calls complaining about or questioning quotations that violated the pricing convention. Traders testified that the telephone calls were effective in deterring market makers from entering quotes that were inconsistent with the pricing convention and narrowed spreads. In general, the mere threat of such harassment was sufficient to discourage market makers from violating the convention. In addition, market makers who broke the convention and reduced the spreads were at times subjected to refusals by other market makers to trade with them. Such conduct lends strong support to the conclusion that the pricing convention, ... was not the result of natural, competitive economic forces or structural aspects of the Nasdaq market.

* * *

Market makers' adherence to the pricing convention often increased the transaction costs paid by customers trading Nasdaq securities. Most customer orders, particularly smaller orders, are executed by market makers at the inside spread. Because market makers primarily moved their quotations in even-eighth increments for most domestic Nasdaq NMS stocks, the inside best bid and offer for these stocks almost always moved in even-eighth increments. This often resulted in wider inside spreads, which caused trades to be executed at prices that were less favorable for investors than if there had been no pricing convention. The practice also had an impact on the ability of some institutional investors to obtain favorable prices and may have placed them at a disadvantage in price negotiations.

* * *

4. The Nasdaq Size Convention

The investigation has also determined that many Nasdaq market makers have adhered to a convention under which they would not display a new inside quote unless they were willing to trade in an amount substantially greater than the minimum volume required by NASD rules (the "size convention").[31] The size convention

---

31. [57] NASD rules require market makers to be willing to trade at least 1,000 shares at their quoted prices for the more actively traded stocks and lesser amounts for other Nasdaq stocks. (citations

required the market maker to be willing to trade in the range of two to five times the minimum NASD volume requirement when creating a new inside quote. The effect of this convention was that market makers would narrow the inside spread on Nasdaq only if they were willing to trade at the substantially larger volume required by the convention. Thus, a market maker in a stock where the minimum NASD quotation amount is 1,000 shares who narrowed the spread from $1/2 to $1/4, or from $1/4 to $1/8, was expected to trade between 2,000 and 5,000 shares. Like the pricing convention, the size convention was in some instances overtly enforced by Nasdaq market makers through intimidation, harassment or other improper conduct.

The size convention had an anticompetitive effect. It inhibited price transparency by limiting quote changes to those circumstances where a Nasdaq market maker was willing to trade in substantially greater volume than the NASD prescribed minimum. This impaired price competition in the Nasdaq market, because improved quotations to reflect orders smaller than those required by the convention were deterred....

* * *

B. Coordination of Quotations, Trades, and Trade Reports

The investigation has determined that a number of Nasdaq market makers have coordinated quotations, trades, and trade reports with other Nasdaq market makers for the purpose of advancing or protecting the market makers' proprietary trading interests. By engaging in such conduct, these market makers may have acted contrary to the best interests of their customers and created a false or misleading appearance of trading activity in the Nasdaq market. *** Cooperating market makers acceded to these requests because of an expectation that the requesting market maker would reciprocate in the future. Such cooperative activity improperly influenced prices, often at the expense of investors, while creating an inaccurate picture of market conditions....

The investigation also revealed instances in which some Nasdaq market makers agreed to delay reporting trades they had done with each other. The report of a trade, particularly a large trade, can affect market price. Thus, the delay of a trade report can provide an information advantage to a market maker. The investigation found that cooperating market makers have agreed to withhold a trade report until one of them could inappropriately trade for the firm's own account in a market unaware of the unreported transaction. Certain Nasdaq market makers also asked other market makers to delay trade reports in order to prevent a customer from judging the quality of an order execution against substantially contemporaneous

---

omitted). The Commission recognizes that an independent decision to trade in greater size than the published quote is a service that a market maker may extend to its customers. However, to the extent that the size convention became the "professional norm" that all other market makers were expected to follow or was enforced as described above, this convention was anticompetitive and resulted in artificially wide spreads.

dealer-to-dealer transactions. If the dealer-to-dealer trades were reported on time, the customer might have been able to tell if its price was worse than other contemporaneous trades and then question whether it had received the best price available under the circumstances.

* * *

The above-described tendency of some Nasdaq market makers to protect each other without regard to the interests of their customers and other market participants underscores the need for significant market reform.

———

The SEC, in December 2000, adopted Rules 11Ac1-5 and 11Ac1-6 to improve public disclosure of order execution and routing practices of participants in the national market system.[32] Rule 11Ac1-5 required market centers[33] trading securities in the national market system to disclose to the public uniform statistical measures about execution quality in monthly electronic reports. The scope of the rule included any market or limit order received or executed by a market center during regular trading hours while an NBBO was being disseminated.[34] The information contained in the monthly reports was designed to facilitate evaluation of order execution quality by comparing execution prices with the consolidated BBO at the time of order receipt.[35] However, the preamble to Rule 11Ac1-5 cautioned investors that the statistical information provided in the reports was not a basis for successful customer litigation against a broker-dealer for failing to obtain best execution.

Rule 11Ac1-6 required all broker-dealers that routed customer orders in equity securities[36] to publicly disclose their routing practices for customer orders on a quarterly basis. Disclosure must include, among other information, the venues to which customer orders were routed for execution and the nature of the broker-dealer's relationship with identified venues, including the existence of any internalization or payment for order flow arrangements. Broker-dealers were also required to disclose

---

32. Both rules only applied to securities that were designated as national market system securities under Exchange Act Rule 11Aa2-1. In December 2000, this only included exchange-listed equities and equities designated as nations market system securities in the National Market tier of Nasdaq.

33. In December 2000, the term market center was, and continues to be, defined as any exchange market maker, OTC market maker, alternative trading system, national securities exchange, or national securities association.

34. Certain types of orders were specifically excluded including orders executed at a market opening or closing price, stop orders, short sales, and orders for other than regular settlement.

35. Much of the information required under Rule 11Ac1-5 is now required under Rule 605 of Regulation NMS. Disclosure requirements under Rule 605 and their usefulness in evaluating the quality of order execution are discussed in Section of this chapter.

36. Equity securities consisted of: (1) Equity securities listed on the NYSE, (2) Equity securities qualified for inclusion in Nasdaq, (3) Equity securities listed on the AMEX or any other national securities exchange. Although disclosures regarding options are also required, the regulation of options is beyond the scope of this textbook. The author has also excluded the consolidated quotation system for options, the Options Price Reporting Authority (OPRA), which was established to disseminate real-time quotations for options, and is operated pursuant to a national market system plan filed with the SEC.

directly to their customers, upon request, the venues to which their customers' individual orders were routed, including the time of any executed orders. Rule 11Ac1-6 was broader in scope than Rule 11Ac1-5 because it covered a wider range of securities; in addition to national market system securities, Rule 11Ac1-6 also applied to NASDAQ SmallCap equities.[37] However, Rule 11Ac1-6 disclosure requirements were confined to smaller customer orders (a market value of less than $200,000) because the SEC believed that a general overview of order routing practices was more useful for smaller orders that tended to be more homogeneous. In addition, unlike Rule 11Ac1-5, Rule 11Ac1-6 applied to all types of orders that were non-directed (i.e., customer orders that the customer did not instruct the broker-dealer to route to a particular venue for execution).

The SEC believed that the organization and content of the quarterly reports required under Rules 11Ac1-5 and 11Ac1-6 would alert customers to potential conflicts of interest that might influence the broker-dealer's order-routing practices to the detriment of obtaining best execution. In addition, Rule 11Ac1-5 also ensured that customers had ready access to routing information concerning their own individual orders.

With the adoption of the rules pursuant to Section 11A of the Exchange Act discussed above, the SEC had established a regulatory framework designed to address the fragmentation of U.S. securities markets, which adversely impacted market efficiency and best execution of customer orders. Last sale reporting, which enabled investors to determine the current market for a security, had been extended to OTC-traded securities. The Consolidated Quotation System ("CQS"), which allowed investors to view in a single source quotes disseminated from dispersed market centers, had been established. The Intermarket Trading System ("ITS"), which permitted investors' orders in certain exchange-listed securities to be routed to the market center displaying the best quotation, had greatly facilitated quote competition. Moreover, technological developments not envisioned 20 years ago had enabled market centers to handle volume levels many times greater than those that led to the "paperwork" crisis of the late 1960s and early 1970s.[38] Taken together, the basic regulatory infrastructure required to establish a national market system was constructed. The fragmented market centers were linked, allowing for competition among orders and market centers and investors' orders could be executed more rapidly at far lower cost.

B. The Adoption of Regulation National Market System

In June 2005, the SEC adopted Regulation NMS (Reg NMS), continuing its mandate of facilitating a national market system for equities in light of changing market conditions and the development of new data processing and communication technologies. Reg NMS reorganized the existing rules promulgated pursuant to Section 11A of the Exchange Act governing the national market system and added new pro-

---

37. Issuers with total equity value of less than $500 million.
38. See section VI of this chapter discussing the national clearance and settlement system.

visions using a new rule series numbered 600-612. Reg NMS rules consisted of national market system rules adopted prior to the adoption of Reg NMS, which were re-designated under the new rule series as Rules 600–609, in addition to three new rules—Rules 610 through 612. To place the adoption of Reg NMS in context, we will first discuss Rules 600-609, which superseded the national market system rules in existence pre-Reg NMS; some of the pre-Reg NMS rules were amended with the adoption of Reg NMS to further the consolidation, distribution, and display of market data in the national market system. Next, the impact of newly adopted Rules 610-612 will be analyzed. Finally, the SEC's amendment to the national market system plans updating the governance and allocation of revenue among plan participants will be reviewed.

1. Reg NMS Rules 600–609

Rule 600 of Reg NMS combined all the definitions scattered throughout the pre-Reg NMS rules into a single rule. An NMS security was now defined as any security for which transaction reports were collected, processed, and made available under a transaction reporting plan.[39] Rule 600 also contained a definition for an NMS stock, which meant any NMS security other than an option. A distinction between an NMS security and an NMS Stock was needed to differentiate rules that only applied to options. Rule 600 also added definitions required to implement newly adopted Rules 610–612.

Rule 601, formerly Rule 11Aa3-1, continued to govern the manner of collection, consolidation, and dissemination of transaction information by the exchanges and the NASD. Rule 601 required exchanges and the NASD to file a transaction reporting plan with the SEC for NMS stocks. Transaction reporting plans were required to identify NMS stocks subject to the plan, along with reporting requirements (in the form of transaction reports) for member broker-dealers executing transactions in NMS stocks. Transaction reporting plans also were required to specify the method of: collecting, processing, sequencing, and consolidating market data; consolidating transaction reports submitted by broker-dealers; and developing standards and procedures to ensure prompt and accurate reporting of transactions and prohibiting fraud and manipulation in transaction reports. Broker-dealers were prohibited from executing transactions in NMS stocks on the exchanges or in the OTC market unless subject to a transaction reporting plan. Finally, Rule 601 addressed a prior prohibition on retransmission by market data vendors of market data collected under transaction reporting plans. Specifically, the exchanges and the NASD could not preclude retransmission by market data vendors for display in moving tickers,[40] but they were allowed to impose reasonable and uniform charges for the distribution of such market data.

---

39. It also included a national market system plan for reporting transactions in listed options.

40. Moving ticker means any continuous real-time moving display of transaction reports or last sale data (other than a dynamic market monitoring device) provided on an interrogation or other display device.

Rule 602, former amended Rule 11Ac1-1,[41] and Rule 604, and former Rule 11Ac1-4, are the Order Handling Rules of Reg NMS. Rule 602, the Firm Quote Rule, required exchanges and the NASD during trading hours to provide market data vendors with the national best bid or offer ("NBBO") and aggregate quotation sizes for NMS securities[42] received from their member broker-dealers acting as both market makers and agents in NMS securities.[43] In addition, quotations were required to be firm. This meant that the member broker-dealer must execute any order to buy or sell, other than an odd-lot order, presented to it at a price that was at least as favorable as the bid price or offer price comprising its published bid or offer in an amount up to the published quotation size. Rule 602 contained two exceptions. A broker-dealer was not bound by its published quotation and corresponding size if, prior to the presentation of an order to buy or sell, it had transmitted to its exchange or association a revised quotation and corresponding size, or at the time of presentment it was in the process of effecting a transaction and revised its quotation and corresponding size immediately after completing the transaction. Otherwise, all quotations were final unless there were unusual trading activities or market conditions, or failures in the trading systems of the exchanges or the NASD. Rule 602 also prohibited exchanges, OTC market makers, and market data vendors from disseminating market data if a security was not subject to a transaction reporting plan or a national market system plan. In addition, market makers in NMS securities placing orders with ECNs were required to report such orders to their respective exchange or the NASD. They were also required to display the highest priced bid and the lowest priced offer placed with the ECN. This display requirement was met, however, if the ECN ensured that the highest priced bid and the lowest priced offer entered into its system by such market makers were transmitted to the respective exchange, NASD, or market data vendors for public dissemination. The ECN was also required to transmit its best bid and best offer for inclusion in the consolidated quote system or CQS data stream.[44]

Rule 604, the Limit Order Display Rule, was the second rule of the OHR and concerned the display of customer limit orders. The Limit Order Display Rule required an exchange member performing the activities of a specialist or an OTC market maker to display the full size of a customer limit order in each NMS stock that was priced

41. Rule 11Ac1-1 was significantly amended in September 1996.

42. The exchanges and FINRA are not subject to these requirements for bids and offers executed immediately after transmission by their member broker-dealers, if trading in the security has been halted or suspended, and for bids and offers transmitted prior to the opening of the trading day.

43. These member broker-dealers are designated responsible broker-dealers in Rule 600 (a)(65) of Regulation NMS. On the exchanges, designation as a responsible broker-dealer in an NMS security is subject to the exchanges' rules of priority and precedence, and if more than two broker-dealers are acting as an agent, only the last broker-dealer transmitting the bid or offer is considered the responsible broker-dealer. With respect to FINRA members, the responsible broker-dealer is the broker-dealer transmitting the bid or offer.

44. ATSs that display orders, provide the ability to effect transactions in orders, and are otherwise in compliance with Regulation ATS (§ 242.300-303) can also be relied on for compliance by market makers with the requirements of Rule 602.

better than their respective bids or offers. It also required the display of the full size of each customer limit order that was priced equal to the specialist's or OTC market maker's bid or offer, if the bid or order was at the NBBO and the customer limit order represented more than a de minimis change in size relative to the specialist's or OTC market maker's bid or order. Essentially, Rule 604 required the display of customer limit orders that were better priced and that were equal to the NBBO. Figure 13.2 contains an example of the operation of Rule 604 and exceptions to the display requirements contained in the rule.

Essentially, the purpose of the OHR was to ensure that the NBBO of NMS stocks was publicly available and accessible and that responsible broker-dealers must, with certain exceptions, execute orders in accordance with their published quotations.

Rule 603, former Rule 11Ac1-2, governed the distribution, consolidation, and display of quotations for, and transactions in, NMS stocks but was substantially rewritten when re-designated as Rule 603 to account for the impact of technology on the operation of the securities markets. Rule 603 focused on providing uniform standards for the distribution of the NBBO and consolidated last sale information in NMS stocks by requiring processors and broker-dealers (including ATSs and market makers) that were the exclusive source of such information to provide it to SIPs or market data vendors on terms that were fair and reasonable. In addition, any SRO or broker-dealer distributing such information to SIPs was required to do so on terms that were not unreasonably discriminatory. In addition, uniform distribution standards were established to ensure that distributors of quotation and transaction data did not make such information available to vendors on a more timely basis than to the network processors under transaction reporting plans approved by the SEC. However, distributors of market data were allowed to determine whether and on what terms they would provide any additional market information. For example, some market participants wanted the best bids and best offers of each SRO in addition to the NBBO, as well as more comprehensive depth-of-book information. With respect to consolidation of market data information, Rule 603 required the NBBO[45] and the most recent trade price for each individual NMS security be distributed to investors and other users by a single processor, no matter where such information was displayed in the NMS. Thus, all national market system plans required SROs to act jointly to disseminate consolidated information through a single processor. Rule 603 also substantially reduced the requirements for the display of consolidated information. The new consolidated display was limited to the prices, sizes, and market center identifications of the NBBO and consolidated last sale information.[46] Market data vendors

---

45. National best bid and national best offer means, with respect to quotations for an NMS security, the best bid and best offer for such security that are calculated and disseminated on a current and continuing basis by a plan processor pursuant to an effective national market system plan; Rule 600(b)(42).

46. Consolidated last sale information means the price, volume, and market identification of the most recent transaction report for a security that is disseminated pursuant to an effective national market system plan. Rule 600(b)(14).

Figure 13.2

Example 1. The BBO for XYAD is $15.00 bid for 500 shares and $15.05 offer for 300 shares.

XYAD	Bid	Ask	Size
BBO	15.00	15.05	5 x 3
MM 1	14.90	15.10	10 x 10
MM 2	15.00	15.20	5 x 5
MM 3	14.85	15.05	2 x 3

MM2, who is the best bid, receives a customer limit order to buy 200 shares of XYAD at $15.02. Because the customer limit order improves MM2's bid, MM2 is required to update its quote as follows:

XYAD	Bid	Ask	Size
BBO	15.02	15.05	2 x 3
MM 1	14.90	15.10	10 x 10
MM 2	15.02	15.20	2 x 5
MM 3	14.85	15.05	2 x 3

If MM2 instead received a customer limit order to buy 600 shares at $15.00, MM2 would have to update its quote to reflect the size of the customer limit order as follows:

XYAD	Bid	Ask	Size
BBO	15.00	15.05	15 x 3
MM 1	14.90	15.10	10 x 10
MM 2	15.00	15.20	11 x 5
MM 3	14.85	15.05	2 x 3

De minimis Exception

If the customer limit order is equal in price to the firm's displayed quote but is 10 percent or less than its displayed size, the firm does not have to update the size of its quote to reflect the customer limit order.

Orders that are not required to be displayed include:

- Odd lot orders
- All or none orders
- Block orders for at least 10,000 shares or $200,000 in market value
- Orders sent to a qualifying ECN
- Orders sent to another market maker that complies with the display rule
- Orders that the customer request not be displayed
- Orders that are immediately executable

could, but were not required, to provide information other than the NBBO and consolidated last sale; however, they could provide a montage of information (e.g., the BBOs of various market centers) if requested by investors and other data users for an additional charge. According to the SEC, the consolidated display requirement adopted under Rule 603 would allow "market forces, rather than regulatory requirements, to determine what, if any, additional quotations outside the NBBO [were] displayed to investors."[47] This amendment generated a new revenue stream for SROs and their members.

The content of Rules 605 through 609 remained essentially the same as their former pre-Reg NMS counterparts. Rule 605, former Rule 11Ac1-5, continued to require the public disclosure of uniform, statistical measures of order execution quality by market centers. Rule 606, formerly Rule 11Ac1-6, continued to require disclosure of market venues to which customer orders were routed and the relationship between the broker-dealer and the market venue (if any), including the existence of payment for order flow arrangements. Rule 607, formerly Rule 11Ac1-3, continued to require broker-dealers to provide to customers information regarding their payment for order flow practices when a new account is opened and in their annual customer accounts thereafter. Rule 608, formerly Rule 11Aa3-2, continued to specify procedures for filing and amending national market system plans (including transaction reporting plans), and Rule 609, formerly Rule 11Ab2-1, continued to require the registration of securities information processors or SIPs with the SEC.

2. Rule 611. Order Protection Rule

The Order Protection Rule ("OPR") was adopted to establish protection against trade-throughs for all NMS stocks.[48] A trade-through occurs when a stock is traded in more than one market and transactions occur in one market at a price that is inferior to a better price offered on another market. The market center with the inferior quotation was said to "trade through" the superior quotation in the second market center. Because NMS securities are traded across multiple market centers, the SEC was concerned that transactions in NMS securities could be executed in one market center at prices inferior to quotations available in another market center. From an investor's point of view, she would not want her broker to buy shares for $20 in one market when there is a seller of the same shares in another market willing to sell to the customer for $19.

The OPR required trading centers[49] to establish, maintain, and enforce written policies and procedures that were reasonably designed to prevent trade-throughs on

---

47. Reg NMS 2005 adopting release.

48. NMS stock was defined in Rule 600(b)(47) of Regulation NMS as adopted in 2005 as any NMS security other than an option. NMS security was defined in Rule 600(b)(46) as any security or class of securities for which transaction reports were collected, processed, and made available pursuant to an effective transaction reporting plan.

49. In 2005, trading centers included national securities exchanges, exchange specialists, ATSs, OTC market makers, and block positioners.

protected quotations. Protected quotations were bids and offers in NMS stocks that were displayed by an automated trading center, disseminated pursuant to an effective national market system plan, and the automated best bid or offer of an exchange, NASDAQ, or the NASD. Automated quotations were defined as quotations that were displayed and immediately accessible through automatic execution.[50] The OPR also contained a variety of exceptions to "make intermarket price protection as efficient and workable as possible." Two of these exceptions were notable. The first exception, an intermarket sweep order (ISO), allowed market participants to access multiple price levels simultaneously at different trading centers. Trading centers that received ISOs were allowed to execute such orders immediately without waiting for better-priced quotations in other markets to be updated. The ISO must be a limit order for an NMS stock designated to be executed exclusively at one market center even when other market centers were publishing better quotations; when sending an ISO, the broker-dealer must simultaneously send limit orders for the same NMS stock to all market centers to execute against the full displayed size of any protected quotations in the NMS stock. These additional limit orders must also be marked as ISOs. Essentially, an ISO is a limit order designated for automatic execution in a specific market center even when another market center is publishing a better quotation, as long as the trader submits concurrent orders to the other market. The second exception to the OPR was for trading centers experiencing, among other things, a material delay in providing a response to incoming orders and for flickering quotations[51] with prices that have been displayed for less than one second. According to the SEC, the purpose of both exceptions was to ensure that only those quotations that were truly automated and accessible were protected by the OPR.

3. Rule 610. Access to Quotations

Rule 610 provided new standards to govern access to quotations in NMS stocks to ensure that broker-dealers could access such quotations fairly and efficiently. It eliminated the requirement that a collective linkage facility such as the ITS must be used to access quotations and allowed the use of private linkages from a variety of providers.[52] At the time, private linkages were used successfully in the NASDAQ Stock Market that were much more useful and faster than the ITS. Rule 610 prohibited trading centers from imposing unfair discriminatory terms that would prevent access through their members, subscribers, or customers. In the absence of mandatory public linkages, the SEC wanted to prohibit unfair discrimination that would prevent non-members from piggybacking on the access of broker-dealer members. It also imposed a $0.003

---

50. In 2005, this would have excluded most of the quotations at the NYSE, which was primarily floor-based or non-automated. Shortly after the adoption of Regulation NMS, both the NYSE and NASDAQ bought companies engaged in computer-based-trading systems known as alternative trading systems.

51. A flickering quotation occurs when the price of a trading center's best displayed quotations change multiple times in a single second.

52. At that time access to ITS was free but its governance mechanism of majority approval prohibited changes needed to take advantage of constantly evolving technology.

per share limit on the fees that any trading center could charge for accessing the trading centers protected quotations as well as manual quotations at the best bid and offer.[53] Accordingly, the scope of the fee cap was limited to the price of the best bid and offer, whether automated or manual, of each exchange, The NASDAQ Market Center, and the ADF.[54] Essentially, the fee cap applied as long as the fees were based on the execution of an order against a protected quotation or a BBO quotation. The SEC asserted that Rule 610 was necessary to support the integrity of the OPR and stated that "[i]n the absence of a fee limitation, some 'outlier' trading centers might take advantage of the requirement to protect displayed quotations by charging exorbitant fees to those required to access the outlier's quotations." However, the Rule 610 fee limitation applied not only to protected quotations under the OPR, but to other quotations that were the best bid or best offer of an exchange, the NASDAQ Market Center, or the NASD's ADF. Finally, Rule 610 required the exchanges and the NASD to establish, maintain, and enforce written rules that required their members to reasonably avoid displaying quotations that locked or crossed protected quotations in NMS stock, or of displaying manual quotations that locked or crossed quotations in NMS stock. However, it allowed automated quotations to cross or lock manual quotations.

4. Rule 612. Minimum Pricing Increment (Sub-Penny Rule)

Rule 612 established a uniform quoting increment for NMS stock. Specifically, market participants were prohibited from accepting, ranking, or displaying orders, quotations, or indications of interest in a pricing increment smaller than a penny, unless the NMS stock was priced at less than $1.00. NMS stocks priced at less than $1.00 could be quoted in increments of $.0001. According to the SEC, the Sub-Penny rule was designed to address the practice of "stepping ahead" of displayed limit orders by trivial amounts, i.e., limiting the ability of a market participant to gain execution priority over a competing limit order by stepping ahead by an economically insignificant amount. The Sub-Penny Rule was quite comprehensive because it covered exchanges, the NASD, ATSs, SIPs, and broker-dealers. In addition, the SEC believed that Rule 612 would "further encourage the display of limit orders and improve the depth and liquidity of trading in NMS stocks." The SEC was also compelled to establish a minimum price variant for trading NMS stocks because some ECNs permitted their subscribers to quote in sub-pennies when trading in NASDAQ-listed securities, which resulted in NASDAQ being less competitive for its own listed securities with the ECNs.

5. Amendments to National Market System Plans

The SEC amended the national market system plans to address revenue allocation and governance. The SEC amended the allocation of revenue among SROs under the

---

53. If the protected quotation was less than $1.00, the fee limit was 0.3 percent of the quotation price per share. Rule 610's fee limitation also applied to BBOs of an SRO or NASDAQ. In addition, the unfair discrimination standard of Rule 610(a) only applied to access to quotations, not to the full array of services that markets generally provided only to their members.

54. The ADF is discussed in Section III.B. of this chapter.

national market system plans to eliminate certain distortive practices[55] and to allocate more revenue to those markets that contributed the most useful market data to investors. Also, revenue allocation for manual quotations was eliminated. The SEC amended the governance rules of the national market system plans ("the Governance Amendment") to increase transparency and to streamline administration and operations. Prior to the adoption of the Governance Amendment, only SROs were permitted to participate in management. Market participants complained of the non-responsiveness of plan participants and inefficiency of plan operations. The Governance Amendment addressed these issues by requiring the formation of a non-voting advisory committee whose composition included non-SRO participants with the express authority to participate in governance. Specifically, the Governance Amendment specified that the advisory committee must include at least one representative "from each of the following five categories: (1) A broker-dealer with a substantial retail investor customer base; (2) A broker-dealer with a substantial institutional investor customer base; (3) an ATS; (4) a data vendor; and (5) an investor." In addition, each of the SRO plan participants was allowed to select one additional member that was not employed by, or affiliated with, any SRO plan participant or its affiliates or facilities. The advisory committee was authorized to submit its views concerning the administration of the national market system plans and to receive any information distributed to the operating committees of the national market system plans. It was also authorized to attend all meetings of the operating committees unless a majority of the members voted to meet in executive session because they determined that an item of business required confidential treatment.

In summary, Regulation NMS organized the national market system rules enacted pursuant to § 11A of the Exchange Act under a single regulation. In doing so, it adopted three new rules (610, 611, 612) focused on the collection and dissemination of market data and renumbered existing national market system rules as Rules 600-612. Existing rules concerning market linkages and disclosure of execution quality and order routing remained. Reg NMS has remained substantially the same since its adoption as we will discover when discussing the current Reg NMS in section III of this chapter.

Notes and Questions

1. It is important to consider whether the regulatory framework adopted in Regulation NMS accomplished the goals for a national market system as envisioned by Congress with the adoption of Section 11A of the Exchange Act. According to the SEC, Regulation NMS was "[P]remised on promoting fair competition among individual markets, while at the same time assuring that all of these markets are linked

---

55. Distortive practices included wash sales and trade shredding. Wash sales occur when one sells or trades securities at a loss and within 30 days before or after the sale one buys or acquires substantially identical securities. Trade shredding is the splitting of large trades into a series of 100-share trades in order to receive a greater allocation of revenue.

together, through facilities and rules, in a unified system that promotes interaction among the orders of buyers and sellers in a particular NMS stock. The NMS thereby incorporates two distinct types of competition — competition among individual markets and competition among individual orders — that together contribute to efficient markets. Vigorous competition among markets promotes more efficient and innovative trading services, while integrated competition among orders promotes more efficient pricing of individual stocks for all types of orders, large and small. Together, they produce markets that offer the greatest benefits for investors and listed companies. Accordingly, the Commission's primary challenge in facilitating the establishment of an NMS has been to maintain an appropriate balance between these two vital forms of competition. It particularly has sought to avoid the extremes of: (1) Isolated markets that trade an NMS stock without regard to trading in other markets and thereby fragment the competition among buyers and sellers in that stock; and (2) a totally centralized system that loses the benefits of vigorous competition and innovation among individual markets. Achieving this objective and striking the proper balance clearly can be a difficult task. Since Congress mandated the establishment of an NMS in 1975, the Commission frequently has resisted suggestions that it adopt an approach focusing on a single form of competition that, while perhaps easier to administer, would forfeit the distinct, but equally vital, benefits associated with both competition among markets and competition among orders."[56] Identify and describe which Reg NMS rules facilitated the twin goals of competition among markets and competition among orders.

2. SEC Commissioners Cynthia A. Glassman and Paul S. Atkins were strongly opposed to the adoption of Regulation NMS. In particular, they were extremely opposed to the Order Protection Rule (Rule 611) because they believed that it "creat[ed] comparable barriers to off-board trading restrictions, which were among the barriers Congress sought to remove." Is this a meaningful comparison?

3. Other countries with significant equity trading typically have a single, overwhelmingly dominant public market. The U.S., in contrast, is fortunate to have equity markets that are characterized by vigorous competition among a variety of different types of markets, including (1) traditional exchanges with active trading floors; (2) purely electronic markets, which offer both standard limit orders and conditional orders that are designed to facilitate complex trading strategies; (3) market-making securities dealers, which offer both automated execution of smaller orders and the commitment of capital to facilitate the execution of larger, institutional orders (4) regional exchanges, many of which have adopted automated systems for executing smaller orders; and (5) automated matching systems that permit investors, particularly large institutions, to seek counter-parties to their trades anonymously and with minimal price impact. The U.S. equity markets currently are the largest and most liquid in the global securities market. Should other equity markets adopt our regulatory framework?

---

56. Adopting Release, Regulation NMS, 70 FR 3796-01, 37498-499 (Jun. 2005).

Hypothetical One

Josephine Wiseman, director and general counsel of Success First, has just finished reading a new book published by one of her favorite law school professors about the national market system mandated by Congress in the 1975 Amendments to the federal securities laws. It has reminded her of the importance of the national market system plans in understanding the infrastructure of the national market system in U.S. securities markets. She is considering whether obtaining a better understanding of the national market system plans that directly affect the operations of Success First would be a reliable indicator of future regulatory changes. After all, Success First trades in NMS stocks for its own account. She understands that federal securities laws are frequently changing in order to regulate effectively the dynamic, technology-driven U.S. securities markets. Based on her favorite law school professor's book, she believes that the national market system plan that might directly affect the operations of Success First is the CTA Plan. She has asked one of her staff (you) to locate this plan, summarize its purpose, and identify all plan participants. *See* the Consolidated Tape Association plan available at: https://www.ctaplan.com/index

III. Current Regulatory Framework of the National Market System

A. Regulation NMS Today

To date, the rules adopted under Reg NMS have remained substantially the same except for the adoption of Rule 613.[57] Its primary components continue to include consolidated market data, linkages between markets governed by national market system plans, and protection against trade-throughs. Consolidated market data continues to be comprised of real-time information on the best-priced quotations (including the NBBO) for, and real-time reports of trades as they are executed, in NMS securities throughout the trading day. The collection, dissemination, and consolidation of quotation and last sale information for equities remain governed by three national market system plans—CTA, CQ, and NASDAQ UTP. As discussed earlier in this chapter, Rule 603(b) of Reg NMS requires the exchanges and FINRA to act jointly under one or more national market system plans to disseminate consolidated market data information. The adoption of Reg NMS resulted in the elimination of the ITS in June 2007; its functions were replaced with private linkages (e.g., broker-dealer routing services). In summary, in compliance with Section 11A of the Exchange Act, the rules adopted under Reg NMS link dispersed market centers in order to facilitate fair and efficient trading markets, i.e., ready access for market participants and the

---

57. The text of Rules 600 through 612 have remained unchanged except for Rule 608, which now requires SROs to post national market system plans, amendments, and proposed amendments to a plan web site or to a web site designated by plan participants to provide public access.

public to comprehensive, accurate, and reliable information about the prices and volume for NMS securities throughout the trading day.

1. Rule 613. Consolidated Audit Trail

The SEC adopted Rule 613 of Reg NMS in August 2012 to require all SROs to develop a national market system plan to establish a central data repository to track trading in NMS securities from order inception through execution across all market centers in the national market system. Specifically, Rule 613, the Consolidated Audit Trail ("CAT"), required SROs to create and maintain a comprehensive audit trail in the U.S. securities markets that provides prompt and accurate recording about all orders in NMS securities as the orders are generated and then routed throughout the U.S. markets until execution, cancellation, or modification and to consolidate this information in a uniform electronic format made readily available to regulators. Although the SEC was aware previously of the need for CAT, the Flash Crash of 2010[58] was the catalyst for requiring the SROs to create, and be responsible for, a comprehensive audit trail across all market centers. Prior to the adoption of CAT, SROs used various forms of electronic audit trails to regulate the markets they were responsible for overseeing, but there was no uniformity in the various audit trail systems used among SROs (*See* Table 13.1 for a list of SRO audit trail systems). Matching data across the various audit trail systems is difficult, if not impossible in some cases, due to the disparate methods used to collect and store data. Disparate audit trail systems significantly hampered the SEC's investigation of the Flash Crash of 2010. The SEC faced significant challenges in obtaining, reconciling, and making effective use of the various audit trail systems, which hampered its ability to quickly reconstruct the trading that caused the Flash Crash of 2010.

The Flash Crash of 2010 occurred on May 6, 2010, and the SEC, in conjunction with the CFTC, was only able to issue a preliminary report on May 18, 2010. In the preliminary report, the regulators noted:

> It is important to emphasize that the review of the events of May 6 is in its preliminary stages and is ongoing. The reconstruction of even a few hours of trading during an extremely active trading day in markets as broad and complex as ours—involving thousands of products, millions of trades and hundreds of millions of data points—is an enormous undertaking. Although trading now occurs in microseconds, the framework and processes for creating, formatting, and collecting data across various types of market participants, products and trading venues is neither standardized nor fully automated. Once collected, this data must be carefully validated and analyzed. Such further data and analysis may substantially alter the preliminary findings presented in this report. The staffs of the Commissions therefore expect to supplement this report with further additional findings and analyses.[59]

---

58. See Chapter 14, section IV.B. for a discussion of the events that caused the flash crash of 2010.
59. SEC preliminary report on the Flash Crash.

Table 13.1. Available Order Audit Systems in 2010

Data Source	Description	Deficiencies Limiting Its Use for Regulators
The EBS System	Allows regulators to obtain the identity of broker-dealer customers who have executed trades; data obtained from individual clearing broker-dealers; provided upon request.	Only available data source; not generally useful for price or short sale manipulations analysis, order flow analysis, depth-of-book analysis, or large-scale market reconstructions in which timing of events is required. Does not contain information on orders or quotes, and consequently no routing, modification, or cancellation information. Only contains aggregate price execution information with respect to average-price accounts; does not include trade execution time.
Equity Cleared Reports	Data obtained from NSCC. Shows number of trades and daily volume in all equity securities in which transaction took place, sorted by clearing member. Generated on a daily basis but provided upon request.	Adequate for initial regulatory inquiries and used by the SEC to narrow down the clearing firms to contact concerning transactions in a specified security.
FINRA OATS	Contains order execution data for OTC equity securities, NASDAQ-listed securities, and all NMS stocks. Also contains data from broker-dealers that are both NYSE and FINRA members.*	Inconsistent accuracy, lack of timeliness, and incomplete data; for more comprehensive view of market activities, must obtain some data from non-FINRA members; orders generated by market-making activities of broker-dealers are excluded; excludes order activity that occurs on exchange or broker-dealers that are not FINRA or NASDAQ members; does not include exchange quotes, principal orders, or options data; cannot identify customers behind each trade so must contact individual broker-dealers.
NYSE OTS	Order tracking information collected using OATS beginning October 2011.	As of 2011, OTS is being phased out and replaced by OATS; see OATS for deficiencies
Consolidated Options Audit Trail System (COATS)	Data sourced from several options exchanges; contains orders, quotes (but only top of the market quotes for all market participants).	Each options exchange uses a different format and includes different supplemental data items in order audit trails submitted to COATS.

* This includes NYSE, NYSE AMEX, NYSE Arca

Notably, Rule 613 only directs the SROs to develop and submit a national market system plan that includes the data elements specified in the rule. The required data elements are categorized by reportable event. For example, a reportable event would be the original receipt or origination of an order; the corresponding data elements would include the customer identification, date, time, and material terms. According to the SEC, it will not make a determination of the nature and scope of the data elements included in the consolidated audit trail until after the SROs submit the required national market system plan, and the SEC and the public have had an opportunity to consider the proposed data elements.[60]

All data collected under the plan established pursuant to CAT must be stored in a central repository. The SEC, exchanges, and FINRA must have unlimited access to this central repository. The central repository must have the ability to run searches and generate reports; safeguard the security and confidentiality of all reported information; confirm the timeliness, accuracy, integrity, and completeness of reported data; and ensure the accuracy of the data consolidated by the plan processor and provided to the central repository. In addition, a maximum error rate must be specified for the central repository for reported data along with procedures for identifying, correcting, and reducing the maximum error rate. In addition, the central repository must have the ability to provide the NBBO for each NMS security, transaction reports under effective transaction reporting plans, and last sale reports under the Plan for Reporting Consolidated Options Last Sale Reports and Quotation information. Also, the SROs must establish an advisory committee to aid in the implementation, operation, and administration of the central repository.

The SROs submitted a plan under Rule 613 on September 30, 2014.[61] As of the date of publication, the SEC has not approved the plan and a plan processor has not been selected. The participating SROs have established a website,[62] which identifies, among other items, companies that have submitted bids to build the system needed to implement CAT. As of March 25, 2016, the short list included FINRA, SunGard Data Systems, Inc., and Thesys Technologies, LLC.

B. FINRA and the National Market System

FINRA is responsible for surveilling and examining compliance with Reg NMS for transactions effected in NMS stocks by its member broker-dealers in the OTC Market. Broker-dealer members must report transactions in NMS stocks executed in the OTC market directly to FINRA in accordance with applicable FINRA rules. Broker-dealer members report OTC transactions in NMS stocks using one of three trade reporting facilities — the Alternative Display Facility (ADF), the FINRA/NASDAQ Trade Reporting Facility (FINRA/NASDAQ TRF) and the FINRA/NYSE Trade Reporting Fa-

---

60. CAT adopting release, p. 55.

61. The SROs required two extensions to submit a plan under Rule 613(a) — December 6, 2013 and September 30, 2014.

62. The CAT website is located at http://catnmsplan.com/.

cility (FINRA/NYSE TRF). The ADF is an electronic system that collects and disseminates quotations and reports and compares trades in NMS stocks traded in the OTC market. It does not provide trade routing and execution services to participants. However, ADF trade reports are included in the consolidated data stream along with NASDAQ-listed securities. All member broker-dealers are eligible to participate in the ADF but must complete certain documentation and register as either an ADF Market Maker or an ADF ECN to gain access to the ADF. The ADF is governed under FINRA Rule Series 6200 and 7100. FINRA Rule Series 6200 includes prohibitions against entering locked or crossed quotations and prohibits the display of manual quotations. Quote requirements and obligations include a two-sided quote obligation, which must be firm, and compliance with pricing increments specified in Rule 612 of Reg NMS (the Sub-Penny Rule). FINRA Rule series 6200 also prescribes data elements that must be entered by participants along with time restrictions for reporting the data, and prohibits participants from preventing access to quotes from other participants and broker-dealers. In addition, ADF participants must report transactions within 10 seconds after execution during normal market hours. FINRA Rule Series 7100 includes ADF requirements for trade reporting participation, trade report input, trade report processing, obligations to honor trades, and audit trail requirements.

FINRA/NASDAQ TRF and FINRA/NYSE TRF are automated trade reporting and reconciliation services operated on technology platforms of NASDAQ and the NYSE. These trade reporting services electronically facilitate trade reporting, trade comparison, and clearing of trades for NMS stocks listed on NASDAQ and NYSE, respectively, that are traded in the OTC market. They are governed by FINRA Rule Series 6300A and 7200A and 6300B and 7200B respectively; these rules include requirements for report content, clearance and settlement, and transaction reporting in exchange-listed NMS stocks traded in the OTC market.

C. The Market Access Rule

On November 3, 2010, the SEC adopted the Market Access Rule, Rule 15c3-5 of the Exchange Act, which required broker-dealers providing customers with direct access to exchanges and ATSs to establish specific risk management controls and supervisory procedures when providing such access. Under direct market access arrangements (also called sponsored access arrangements) the broker-dealer allows its customer (an individual, institution, or another broker-dealer) to use its market participant identifier ("MPID") to trade electronically on the exchange or ATS. The broker-dealer's MPID is used to identify the broker-dealer when it trades on an exchange or ATS. Prior to the adoption of Rule 15c3-5, broker-dealers permitted some of their customers using the broker-dealers' MPID to enter orders electronically into an exchange or ATS without requiring such orders to flow through the broker-dealer's trading systems prior to reaching the exchange or ATS. This meant that the customer could trade on the exchange or ATS as though it were the broker-dealer, but the broker-dealer had no opportunity to ensure that such customers were complying with applicable regulatory requirements. Essentially, the customer could trade directly with the exchange or ATS using the broker-dealer's MPID without being monitored by the broker-dealer allowing use of its MPID; thus, the broker-dealer remained legally responsible for all trading activity conducted under its MPID with no mechanism to control such trading activities.[63] Direct access or sponsored arrangements were profitable to all parties involved—the broker-dealer, the customer, and the exchange or ATS. The broker-dealers, exchanges, and ATSs received greater volume and a wider variety of order flow under such arrangements. Specifically, broker-dealers could more readily take advantage of volume discounts offered by exchanges or ATSs by aggregating order flow from multiple market participants under one MPID in order to qualify for more favorable pricing tiers. The customer was able to trade more rapidly, preserve confidentiality of sophisticated, proprietary trading strategies, and reduce operational costs, commissions, and exchange fees.

The SEC asserted that the adoption of Rule 15c3-5 was required because direct access or sponsored access arrangements represented a particularly serious vulnerability of the U.S. securities markets. With the proliferation of electronic trading, such arrangements had increased substantially without a corresponding increase in appropriate risk controls to address financial and operating risks associated with the provision of market access to broker-dealer customers. The SEC asserted that risk management controls and supervisory procedures that were not applied on a pre-trade basis or that were not under the exclusive control of the broker-dealer, were inadequate to address the risks of market access arrangements, including potential systemic risk, in the national market system. Indeed, even some market participants asserted that such access arrangements proposed a systemic risk because, in some instances, non-regulated entities were allowed to trade directly on an exchange or ATS without broker-dealer intermediation. In fact, the SEC in its proposing release for Rule 15c3-5 noted that incidents involving algorithmic or other trading errors occurred with some regularity in connection with direct access or sponsored access arrangements.

Rule 15c3-5 was designed to provide a uniform standard to address the financial, regulatory, and operational risks of direct access or sponsored access arrangements, which applied to trading in all securities on an exchange or ATS. Broker-dealers allowing such arrangements must establish effective financial and regulatory risk management controls reasonably designed to limit financial exposure and to ensure compliance with applicable regulatory requirements. Specifically, broker-dealers must establish and maintain a system of risk management controls and supervisory procedures reasonably designed to manage the financial, regulatory, legal, and operational risks related to market access. In addition, Rule 15c3-5 expressly prohibits the practice of allowing customers using the broker-dealer's MPID to bypass the broker-dealer's

---

63. Some broker-dealers did require customer orders to flow through the broker-dealers' trading systems when using their MPIDs to conduct trading activity on an exchange or ATS.

trading system. In summary, Rule 15c3-5(a) requires a broker-dealer providing market access to customers—whether an individual, institution, or another broker-dealer— to: (1) maintain risk management controls and supervisory procedures, identifying specific minimum requirements; (2) maintain such controls and supervisory procedures under the direct and exclusive control of the broker-dealer providing market access; and (3) regularly review, at least annually, the effectiveness of the such risk management controls and supervisory procedures and adjust them if necessary. The broker-dealer's CEO must annually certify that the risk management controls and supervisory procedures comply with Rule 15c3-5.

Rule 15c3-5 requires broker-dealers and ATSs operated by broker-dealers[64] to maintain specific risk management controls and supervisory procedures in two basic categories: financial risk management and (2) regulatory risk management. The SEC cautions, however, that the standards enumerated in the rule are only uniform baseline standards that should be implemented; additional standards may be required based on the nature of the broker-dealer's business, its customer base, and other specific circumstances. Financial risk management controls and procedures must be reasonably designed to prevent the entry of orders that exceed appropriate preset credit or capital thresholds in the aggregate for each customer and, where appropriate, more finely tuned by sector, security, or otherwise, by rejecting orders exceeding the applicable credit or capital thresholds.[65] The SEC based aggregate customer credit limits on order entry instead of executed orders because the speed of U.S. securities markets results in rapid financial exposure. However, the broker-dealer may discount the credit or capital exposure assigned to outstanding customer orders to account for the likelihood of actual execution using reasonable risk management models. The broker-dealer must monitor the accuracy of its risk management models on an ongoing basis and must make appropriate adjustments as warranted. Financial risk management controls and procedures must also be designed to prevent the entry of erroneous orders, by rejecting orders that exceed appropriate process or size parameters and that indicate duplicative orders. Again, such controls and procedures must be applied on a pre-trade basis (before orders are routed to the exchange or ATS.

The Market Access rule also requires the implementation of regulatory risk management controls and supervisory procedures, which must be reasonably designed to ensure compliance with regulatory requirements. The term "regulatory requirements" is specifically defined in Rule 15c3-5 to mean all federal securities laws, rules,

---

64. Requiring ATSs to comply with Rule 15c3-5 was intended to ensure that non-broker-dealer ATS subscribers would also be subject to the risk management controls and supervisory procedures specified in Rule 15c3-5. According to the SEC, "similar ... risks are present when a non-broker-dealer subscriber directly accesses an ATS as when a broker-dealer accesses an exchange or ATS." Adopting release, p. 18.

65. This includes appropriate capital thresholds for proprietary trading by the broker-dealer's customers.

and regulations and rules of SROs applicable in connection with market access. Specifically, regulatory risk management controls and supervisory procedures must be automated and reasonably designed to:

a. Prevent the entry of orders unless there has been compliance with all regulatory requirements that must be satisfied on a pre-order entry basis;

b. Prevent the entry of orders for securities that the broker-dealer, customer, or other person, as applicable, is restricted from trading;

c. Restrict access to trading systems and technology that provide market access to persons and accounts pre-approved and authorized by the broker-dealer; and

d. Assure that appropriate surveillance personnel receive immediate post-trade execution reports that result from market access.

Rule 15c3-5 contains two limited exceptions. The first exception allows the broker dealer to allocate certain risk management controls and supervisory procedures to certain customers. The broker-dealer providing market access may allocate specific risk management controls and supervisory procedures to a customer who is another registered broker-dealer only if the registered broker-dealer customer has specific knowledge about the ultimate customer and its trading activity that the broker-dealer providing market access would not have. This allocation must be in a written contract that specifies the controls and supervisory procedures being allocated. Allocation, of course, does not relieve the allocating broker-dealer of its obligations under Rule 15c3-5. Accordingly, the broker-dealer providing market access must conduct thorough due diligence to establish a reasonable basis for its determination that the customer broker-dealer has the capability and the relationship to have better access to the ultimate customer. The second exception relieves compliance with Rule 15c3-5 for broker-dealers that provide outbound routing services to an exchange or ATS in order for those trading centers to meet the requirements of Rule 611 of Reg NMS, except with regard to the prevention of entering erroneous orders. Exchanges and ATSs generally comply with the prohibition on trade-throughs of protected quotations in NMS stocks under Rule 611, in part, by employing an affiliated or unaffiliated broker-dealer to route orders received by the exchange or ATS to other trading centers displaying protected quotations. Imposing Rule 15c3-5 requirements would be duplicative because such broker-dealers would only handle orders that have already been subjected to the broker-dealer risk management controls required under Rule 15c3-5 by the exchanges or ATSs.

The following cases illustrate the importance of the Market Access Rule in the technology-driven U.S. securities markets. *Wedbush* demonstrates the impact of failing to implement compliant risk management and supervisory controls when allowing a broker-dealer's customer unfettered access to trading venues. *Knight Capital* demonstrates the effect of non-compliance with the Market Access Rule when a broker-dealer's trading activities place its own capital at risk. In addition, both cases illustrate how violation of the Market Access Rule results in violations of other financial responsibility and Reg NMS rules.

In the Matter of Wedbush Securities Inc.

Securities and Exchange Commission,
Admin. Proc. File No. 3-15913 (Nov. 20, 2014).

I.

The Securities and Exchange Commission ("Commission") deems it appropriate and in the public interest to enter this Order Making Findings and Imposing Remedial Sanctions and a Cease-and-Desist Order Pursuant to Sections 15(b) and 21C of the Securities Exchange Act of 1934 ("Exchange Act") ...

II.

Respondent Wedbush has submitted an Offer of Settlement (the "Offer") that the Commission has determined to accept. Respondent admits the facts..., and consents to the entry of this Order Making Findings and Imposing Remedial Sanctions and a Cease-and-Desist Order Pursuant to Sections 15(b) and 21C of the Securities Exchange Act of 1934.... ("Order"), as set forth below.

III.

On the basis of this Order and Wedbush's Offer, the Commission finds that:

* * *

Respondents

5. Wedbush Securities Inc. is a California corporation with its headquarters in Los Angeles, California. The firm was founded in 1955 and registered with the NASD as a broker-dealer in 1955, with the Commission as a broker-dealer in 1966 and as an investment adviser in 1970. Wedbush is a wholly-owned subsidiary of Wedbush, Inc., a privately-held company. As of December 31, 2012, Wedbush had 79 branch offices and 844 employees. During the relevant period, Wedbush was consistently ranked as one of the five largest firms by trading volume on NASDAQ.

6. During the relevant period, Jeffrey Bell was Executive Vice President of the Correspondent Services Division of Wedbush, reporting to the firm's President, and was an associated person of Wedbush. Bell also was President of Lime Brokerage LLC ("Lime"), another wholly-owned subsidiary of Wedbush, Inc. Bell, age 40, is a resident of Austin, Texas, and holds Series 7 and 24 licenses.

7. Christina Fillhart is a Senior Vice President in the Correspondent Services Division of Wedbush and is an associated person of Wedbush. Fillhart reported to Bell until late 2012, when she began reporting to one of Wedbush's Co-Chief Compliance Officers. Fillhart, age 56, is a resident of Covina, California, and holds Series 7, 24, 27, 53, and 63 licenses.

The Market Access Rule

8. The Commission adopted the Market Access Rule in November 2010 to require that broker-dealers with market access "appropriately control the risks associated with market access, so as not to jeopardize their own financial condition, that of other market participants, the integrity of trading on the securities markets, and the stability

of the financial system." *Risk Management Controls for Brokers or Dealers with Market Access*, 75 Fed. Reg. 69792, 69792 (Nov. 15, 2010) (Final Rule Release).

9. Section (b) of the Market Access Rule requires a broker-dealer with market access, or that provides a customer or any other person with access to an exchange through the use of its market participant identifier ("MPID") or otherwise, to "establish, document, and maintain a system of risk management controls and supervisory procedures reasonably designed to manage the financial, regulatory, and other risks" of its market access business.

10. Section (c) of the Market Access Rule identifies specific required elements of a broker-dealer's system of risk management controls and supervisory procedures relating to market access. Subsection (c)(1) addresses financial controls and procedures and subsection (c)(2) addresses regulatory controls and procedures. Under subsection (c)(2), a broker-dealer must have controls and procedures that are reasonably designed to ensure compliance with all regulatory requirements, including controls to prevent the entry of orders that do not comply with all regulatory requirements that must be satisfied on a pre-order entry basis and controls to restrict access to trading systems and technology that provide market access to persons and accounts pre-approved and authorized by the broker-dealer with market access.

11. Section (d) of the Market Access Rule requires the risk management controls and supervisory procedures to be under the "direct and exclusive control" of the broker-dealer with market access. Subsection (d)(1) contains an exception to the direct and exclusive control requirement that applies when a broker-dealer with market access reasonably allocates, by written contract, after a thorough due diligence review, control over specific regulatory risk management controls and supervisory procedures to a broker-dealer customer who is registered with an exchange in the United States where the broker or dealer with market access has a reasonable basis for determining that such broker-dealer customer, based on its position in the transaction and relationship with an ultimate customer, has better access to the ultimate customer and its trading information such that it can more effectively implement the specified controls or procedures.

12. Section (e) of the Market Access Rule requires a broker-dealer with market access to establish, document, and maintain a system for regularly reviewing the effectiveness of its risk management controls and supervisory procedures relating to market access. Subsection (e)(1) requires the broker-dealer to conduct and document a review of its market access business at least annually in accordance with written procedures, and subsection (e)(2) requires the CEO to certify annually that the broker-dealer conducted the review and is in compliance with the Rule.

13. Wedbush's primary market access business is part of the Correspondent Services Division, which originally handled only traditional clearing operations for introducing broker-dealers, otherwise known as "correspondent" firms. Wedbush began providing "sponsored" market access to customer firms in 2004, which allowed customer firms and their traders to send orders that bypassed Wedbush's trading systems

and were routed directly to exchanges and other trading venues under a Wedbush MPID. Sponsored access customers were able to send orders that bypassed Wedbush's systems by using online trading platforms or software programs that the customer either owned directly or leased from a third-party platform provider, referred to as a service bureau.

Wedbush's Market Access Business

14. During the relevant period, Wedbush had about 50 sponsored access customers that generated average monthly trading volume of 10 billion shares. Several of Wedbush's sponsored access customer firms had hundreds or thousands of authorized traders each. Wedbush's correspondent services business was the most profitable operation of Wedbush, Inc. Bell and Fillhart each received bonus compensation based in part on the profitability of the Correspondent Services Division, which depended largely on the trading volumes of Wedbush's market access customers. During the relevant period, Bell received salary of $ 344,000 and bonus compensation of $ 310,000 and Fillhart received salary of $ 150,000 and bonus compensation of $ 105,000.

15. In June 2011, Wedbush acquired Lime Brokerage LLC, a provider of trading technology platforms. After Wedbush acquired Lime, about 20% of Wedbush's sponsored access customers began using the Lime platform. The other 80% continued to use sponsored access either through their own proprietary trading platform or through a third-party platform that the customer leased from a service bureau. As a result, during the relevant period, the vast majority of orders from Wedbush's sponsored access customers did not flow through Wedbush's own risk management systems.

16. Wedbush's primary risk management controls and supervisory procedures relating to market access were described in Chapter 31 of the firm's written supervisory procedures ("WSPs"), titled "Sponsored Access." On July 14, 2011, the day most provisions of the Market Access Rule took effect, Wedbush updated Chapter 31 to cite certain provisions of the Rule.

17. Bell and Fillhart, along with one other senior Wedbush employee in the Correspondent Services Division, had the primary responsibility for preparing and adopting Wedbush's controls and procedures relating to market access. Bell and Fillhart had authority to adopt and revise the firm's controls and procedures relating to market access, including the WSPs, without approval of Wedbush's President or Co-Chief Compliance Officers.

Wedbush Knew of Compliance Issues for Its Sponsored Access Trading

18. Prior to the effective date of Rule 15c3-5, Wedbush received a number of indications that its sponsored access trading business posed particular regulatory and compliance risks. In 2009 and 2010, just before the relevant period, two of Wedbush's sponsored access customer firms extended their market access to a Latvian trader who used that access to conduct profitable trading as part of a widespread account intrusion and market manipulation scheme. The Commission obtained a judgment by default against the Latvian trader in connection with the scheme after learning the trader's identity from Fillhart in 2011. *(citations omitted)*.

* * *

20. Wedbush was well aware of the requirements, objectives, and importance of Rule 15c3-5. During the public comment period for the then-proposed Rule 15c3-5, Bell submitted [a comment letter to the Commission on behalf of Wedbush on March 31, 2010. Bell also submitted a comment letter to the Commission on behalf of Wedbush on February 23, 2009 addressing a Nasdaq proposed rule change relating to sponsored market access, which was later approved by the Commission. Although proposing certain changes to the Nasdaq proposed rule, Bell and Wedbush stated in the 2009 comment letter that sponsoring non-broker-dealer customers "requires the highest level of due diligence, oversight and controls. In this case, the sponsoring member is also the broker-dealer of record and would be accountable for all the responsibilities as such." Despite this acknowledgement, one of Wedbush's largest sponsored access customers was not a broker-dealer registered in the United States, and Wedbush failed to engage in the "highest level of due diligence, oversight and controls."

21. On May 17, 2011, Commission staff from the Office of Compliance Inspections and Examinations ("OCIE") sent an Examination Deficiency Letter to Wedbush, which was addressed to Bell. That letter advised Wedbush that the staff had identified deficient Wedbush controls relating to short sales, in violation of Regulation SHO, due in part to an excessive reliance upon a non-broker-dealer sponsored access client to locate shares before placing a short sale order. The Deficiency Letter also identified problems with internal controls over a third-party order management system. The Letter also stated that Wedbush had failed to respond promptly to compliance issues.... This letter put Wedbush on notice that it was relying on inadequate regulatory controls that were outside of its direct and exclusive control.

22. On July 5, 2011, Wedbush representatives, including Bell and Fillhart, met with representatives of OCIE to discuss the impending effectiveness of the final Rule 15c3-5. During that meeting, the Commission's staff expressed concerns about Wedbush's largest sponsored non-broker-dealer client and the need to identify the ultimate traders. Wedbush's presentation to the staff cited the Market Access Rule requirements relating to allocating compliance responsibilities to sponsored access broker-dealer clients and maintaining "direct and exclusive control" of risk settings in trading platforms.

Market Access Through Third-Party Trading Platforms

23. Section (d) of the Market Access Rule requires Wedbush to maintain exclusive control over the risk settings in the trading platforms that its customers use to access the markets, including both Wedbush's own Lime platform and the non-Wedbush trading platforms that 80% of Wedbush's customers used. As described below, for many customers that used non-Wedbush trading platforms, Wedbush's control was not exclusive because it allowed customers to have access to determine and make changes to risk settings in the trading platforms.

24. Wedbush did not directly set or monitor regulatory risk settings in the third-party or client-proprietary trading platforms that 80% of Wedbush's customers used. Cus-

tomers had access to set and revise the risk settings, and could disable risk settings intended to prevent violations of specific regulatory requirements, such as illegal short sales, wash trades, and violations of Regulation NMS. In addition to Wedbush not having exclusive control over the settings, Wedbush's customers, rather than Wedbush, leased the trading platforms from third parties and Wedbush had no contractual relationship with the platform providers.

25. Wedbush employees in the Correspondent Services Division received access from platform providers to view risk settings and trading activity in the platforms, but Bell and Fillhart knew that Wedbush did not have exclusive control over the settings.

26. Shortly before most provisions of the Market Access Rule took effect, Wedbush obtained email statements from many of the trading platform providers that the risk management settings in the platforms were under the direct and exclusive control of Wedbush. In reality, Wedbush did not have exclusive control of the risk management settings because Wedbush continued allowing sponsored access customers to determine and make changes to the risk settings in the platforms, and Wedbush had no contractual relationship with the platform providers. These statements also were not part of any legally enforceable contract; Wedbush had no contractual relationship with the platform providers.

27. Wedbush's WSPs stated that each new sponsored access customer would perform an initial "risk demonstration" to show Wedbush the customer's trading platform settings for certain financial and regulatory risk controls. Wedbush had a checklist for the risk demonstration that included settings to prevent clearly erroneous trades, wash trades, illegal short sales, and, unless authorized by Wedbush, intermarket sweep orders ("ISOs"). That Wedbush needed the customer to show the settings to Wedbush demonstrates that Wedbush did not have "direct and exclusive control" over the risk settings in the platforms, as required by Rule 15c3-5(d).

28. In June 2012, platform providers, rather than sponsored access customers, provided Wedbush demonstrations of risk settings in their trading platforms. During a demonstration, the provider would submit test orders and confirm that certain risk settings were in place at the time of the demonstration.

29. Wedbush did not receive demonstrations of the actual risk settings in effect for particular sponsored access customers, and Wedbush did not have any physical ability to prevent customers from subsequently changing the settings shown during the platform provider's demonstration. Wedbush also did not maintain records of the risk settings in the platforms so that it could determine whether any settings had been changed without its consent.

30. Customers could, and sometimes did, change the risk settings without Wedbush's knowledge or consent. For example, as discussed below, Fillhart learned that on numerous occasions a risk setting to prevent illegal short sales failed to prevent violations of Regulation SHO because the wrong list of securities that were easy to borrow was loaded into the customer's third-party trading platform. Fillhart also learned that a customer repeatedly circumvented a risk setting that was designed to prevent the use

of ISOs. For other risk settings, such as controls to prevent wash trades, Wedbush often did not require customers or platform providers to activate the settings.

Attempts to Allocate Responsibility for Regulatory Controls and Procedures

31. The Final Rule Release for the Market Access Rule stated that Section 15c3-5(d) "is designed to eliminate the practice ... whereby the broker-dealer providing market access relies on its customer, a third-party service provider, or others, to establish and maintain the applicable risk controls." *(citations omitted)* The Final Rule Release further cautioned that "the Commission continues to be concerned about circumstances where broker-dealers providing market access simply rely on assurances from their customers that appropriate risk controls are in place.... Accordingly, the Commission emphasizes that in any permitted allocation arrangement, the broker-dealer providing market access may not merely rely on another broker-dealer's attestation that it has implemented appropriate controls or procedures." (citation omitted)

32. After the Market Access Rule took effect, Wedbush simply relied on attestations in the exact manner that the Final Rule Release said was improper. Wedbush attempted to assign to other broker-dealers the responsibility for regulatory risk management controls and supervisory procedures for many of its sponsored access customers. Wedbush employees documented purported agreements to assign responsibilities to other broker-dealers, but as described below, despite the plain language of Rule 15c3-5(d) and the staff's statements on July 5, 2011, Wedbush failed to conduct the required "thorough due diligence review" when purporting to allocate responsibility to another broker-dealer and continued to simply rely on the other broker-dealer's attestation that it had implemented appropriate controls and procedures.

33. For some customers, Wedbush entered into an allocation agreement with a registered introducing broker-dealer. For other customers, Wedbush entered into an allocation agreement directly with the sponsored access customer itself, if it was a registered broker-dealer trading its own capital on a proprietary basis. Some of these sponsored access customers used trading platforms that they themselves owned, either directly or through a corporate affiliate that they controlled. As a result, Wedbush often relied on a broker-dealer customer to monitor its own trading.

34. All of Wedbush's purported allocation agreements were based on the same form, which Bell approved. The agreements did not specify any particular controls or procedures that Wedbush purported to be allocating. Even though Wedbush, as the party with market access, purportedly was attempting to allocate responsibility for controls or procedures to another broker-dealer, the agreements mistakenly stated that the other broker-dealer, rather than Wedbush, had "allocatable regulatory responsibilities as defined within SEC Rule 15c3-5." As a result, it was not even clear from the documents themselves from and to which broker-dealer the controls or procedures purportedly were being allocated.

35. Bell knew or should have known that Wedbush did not conduct the required due diligence reviews of the other broker-dealers in connection with its attempts to allocate responsibilities for market access controls and procedures, and that Wedbush also

did not conduct later reviews to determine whether the other broker-dealers were adequately carrying out the responsibilities purportedly allocated. The agreements simply contained a statement by the introducing broker-dealer or registered customer firm that its regulatory risk management controls and supervisory procedures were reasonably designed to ensure compliance with all regulatory requirements.

36. Better access to the ultimate customer was discussed in the Final Rule Release as the reason why control over certain regulatory controls could be allocated after due diligence. Yet Wedbush did not have any policies or procedures for determining whether a broker-dealer to which it claimed to have assigned responsibilities had better access than Wedbush to ultimate customers such that the other broker-dealer could more effectively implement the risk management controls and supervisory procedures relating to market access.

Regulatory Requirements that Must Be Satisfied on a Pre-Order Entry Basis

37. Subsection (c)(2)(i) of the Market Access Rule required Wedbush to have risk management controls and supervisory procedures that were reasonably designed to prevent the entry of orders that do not comply with all regulatory requirements that must be satisfied on a pre-order entry basis. The Final Rule Release for the Market Access Rule specifically identified Regulations SHO and NMS as examples of regulatory requirements that must be satisfied on a pre-order entry basis, and with which a broker-dealer's controls and procedures must ensure compliance. As described below, Wedbush's risk management controls and supervisory procedures were not reasonably designed to satisfy these pre-trade regulatory requirements and, in fact, did not prevent Wedbush customers from entering numerous orders that violated Regulations SHO and NMS.

38. Wedbush was responsible for ensuring that all short-sale orders submitted by its sponsored access customers complied with Regulation SHO. Among other things, Regulation SHO required Wedbush, prior to accepting or effecting a short sale order, to borrow the security or enter into an agreement to borrow the security, or have reasonable grounds to believe that the security could be timely borrowed (generally known as the "locate" requirement). Absent countervailing factors, "easy-to-borrow" lists may provide "reasonable grounds" for a broker-dealer to believe that the security sold short is available for borrowing without directly contacting the source of the borrowed securities (known as "easy-to-borrow securities").... the Commission has stated that repeated failures to deliver in securities included on an "easy-to-borrow" list would indicate that the broker-dealer's reliance on such a list did not satisfy the "reasonable grounds" standard ...

39. Wedbush's WSPs stated that the firm sometimes relied on sponsored access customers to meet the short-sale requirements of Regulation SHO. Wedbush maintained a list of easy-to-borrow securities, but Wedbush relied on sponsored access customers or their platform providers to load that list into third-party trading platforms rather than taking direct steps to make sure that customers were using the correct list. Maintaining up-to-date lists in the trading platforms was a key step in the control process because the platforms relied on the lists to determine whether Regulation SHO had been satisfied before routing a short-sale order for execution.

40. Wedbush's procedures asserted that Wedbush allowed customers to submit short-sale orders for securities on the easy-to-borrow list and that it required customers to otherwise locate shares to borrow before submitting short-sale orders for securities not on the easy-to-borrow list. However, if a customer or platform provider failed to load the correct easy-to-borrow list, Wedbush had no controls or procedures to prevent the customer from submitting a short-sale order for a security that was not easy-to-borrow without first obtaining a locate.

41. On three occasions between July 2011 and November 2012, Fillhart learned that a customer or platform provider loaded the wrong easy-to-borrow list, ... Bell and Fillhart knew that similar incidents had occurred numerous times before July 2011, based on the May 2011 OCIE Deficiency Letter and face-to-face meetings that Bell and Fillhart attended with Commission staff. The incidents demonstrated that Wedbush did not have "direct and exclusive control" over these risk settings in the trading platforms as required by Rule 15c3-5(d) and did not have controls reasonably designed to ensure compliance with all regulatory requirements that must be satisfied on a pre-order entry basis.

42. Wedbush was responsible for ensuring that all orders marked as ISOs by its sponsored access customers complied with Regulation NMS, which requires the broker-dealer responsible for routing an ISO to route simultaneously additional orders, as necessary, to execute against the full size of all better-priced protected quotations. Sending the simultaneous orders to sweep the market of better-priced protected quotations is essential to ensuring that the ISO order type is not misused and that other market participants willing to trade at more favorable prices do not have their orders bypassed.

43. Wedbush's WSPs asserted that in order to comply with Regulation NMS, Wedbush did not permit a customer to use ISOs unless the customer swept the market of all better-priced protected quotations. However, Wedbush did not have any controls or procedures reasonably designed to ensure that its customers complied with this regulatory requirement.

44. As a result of Wedbush's lack of "direct and exclusive control" over risk settings designed to ensure ISO compliance, and its failure to have controls and procedures reasonably designed to ensure compliance with the ISO requirements of Regulation NMS, at least one Wedbush customer submitted ISOs without Wedbush's prior knowledge and without a broker-dealer acting to ensure compliance with the relevant regulatory requirements. In April 2011, Fillhart learned from an exchange that one of Wedbush's largest sponsored access customers was submitting ISOs even though Wedbush did not authorize the customer to submit ISOs and even though Wedbush had not allocated responsibility to another registered broker-dealer to ensure that ISOs submitted by the customer complied with Regulation NMS. Without Wedbush's knowledge, the customer and its third-party platform provider had enabled an order route that was configured to allow ISOs, even though the platform provider had previously informed Wedbush that the customer was not able to submit ISOs. This also demonstrated that it was unreasonable for Wedbush to rely on the written attestations that it received from the platform providers, as described above.

45. Because Wedbush had not authorized the customer to submit ISOs, Wedbush had not taken any steps to ensure that the ISOs complied with Regulation NMS. Fillhart instructed the platform provider to close the ISO route, but she did not directly close or disable the route and she knew that Wedbush did not have any controls or procedures to prevent a similar route from being enabled again in the future.

46. In November 2011, Fillhart learned that the same customer had again enabled an ISO route in its trading platform and submitted ISOs without Wedbush's knowledge. As in April 2011, Wedbush had not taken any steps to ensure that the ISOs complied with Regulation NMS because Wedbush had not authorized the customer to submit ISOs. These incidents demonstrate that Wedbush did not have "direct and exclusive control" over these risk settings as required by Rule 15c3-5(d), and did not have controls reasonably designed to ensure compliance with all regulatory requirements that must be satisfied on a pre-order entry basis.

Other Regulatory Requirements

47. Subsection (c)(2) of the Market Access Rule required Wedbush to have risk management controls and supervisory procedures that were reasonably designed to ensure compliance with all existing regulatory requirements. Wedbush did not have controls and procedures in connection with its market access business that were reasonably designed to ensure that Wedbush complied with all AML reporting and recordkeeping requirements applicable to Wedbush.

* * *

49. Wedbush's SRO, FINRA, requires its members to establish and implement policies and procedures that can be reasonably expected to detect and cause the reporting of suspicious transactions as required by the Bank Secrecy Act and Treasury regulations thereunder. See FINRA Rule 3310. As described below, on numerous instances Fillhart became aware of potential wash trading and other forms of potential manipulation, but she did not cause Wedbush to file reports regarding the suspicious activity, and Wedbush's policies and procedures did not cause Wedbush to detect suspicious activity and file such reports.

50. Wedbush's WSPs asserted that it did not permit its customers to execute wash and pre-arranged trades. Wedbush's WSPs defined "wash trades" as "transactions which result in no beneficial change of ownership" and defined a "pre-arranged trade" as "an offer to sell coupled with an offer to buy back at the same or at an advanced price, or the reverse."

51. In most of the trading platforms used by Wedbush sponsored access customers, individual traders were identified by a unique trader ID. While most traders received a single trader ID, on some occasions a single trader had multiple trader IDs. Wedbush did not have any controls or filters to prevent a single trader from trading with himself or herself in a customer firm's account, or to prevent two different traders from trading with each other in a customer firm's account.

52. Most trading platforms used by Wedbush's customers had risk settings to prevent potential wash trades, but Wedbush often did not require customers or platform

providers to activate the settings, and Wedbush had no controls or procedures to prevent customers or platform providers from deactivating the settings if they were activated. Some exchanges offered functionality to block wash trades, but Wedbush had no controls or procedures requiring customers to use this anti-wash trade functionality.

53. Wedbush personnel responsible for filing suspicious activity reports pursuant to the Bank Secrecy Act relied on Fillhart and other employees in the Correspondent Services Division, which Bell oversaw, to review trading activity by sponsored access customers to determine whether it was relevant to potential violations of securities laws or regulations. But Bell and Fillhart knew or should have known that Wedbush did not have policies or procedures describing how Correspondent Services employees were to review trading to determine whether it was suspicious and should be reported.

54. The WSPs stated that Wedbush would review reports of potential wash trades from vendors and exchanges, determine whether there were potential securities violations, and if so, obtain representations from sponsored access customers regarding their internal wash trade reviews and systems.

55. A Wedbush employee who reported to Fillhart received reports of potential wash or pre-arranged trades from exchanges on a daily basis during the relevant period. For most of the trades on the reports, which involved two trader IDs in a single customer account, Fillhart did not ask the Wedbush employee to follow up with the customer firm because Fillhart assumed the two traders were independent and did not consider the trading suspicious. No one from Wedbush ever attempted to contact traders to determine whether they were pre-arranging their trades.

56. For trades with a single trader ID on both sides, Fillhart relied on the customer firm to follow up with the trader. On many occasions, the customer simply responded that it was not wash trading or was an error. On some occasions, the customer did not respond at all. Fillhart generally did not ask the Wedbush employee to follow up with customers for further explanation and did not report the trading to the AML officer as suspicious.

57. In February and March 2012, Fillhart learned from exchanges that numerous traders in the account of one of Wedbush's largest sponsored access customers, which had recently become a customer of a Wedbush correspondent broker-dealer under common ownership with the customer, appeared to be engaged in wash or pre-arranged trading. The customer and correspondent broker-dealer had not enabled pre-trade controls in the trading platform used by the customer that would have prevented wash or pre-arranged trades, and Wedbush did not take steps to enable such controls. The customer and correspondent broker-dealer informed Wedbush that they would either enable the controls in the platform or send future orders through a route that blocked wash trades. Fillhart did not directly enable the risk controls and Wedbush did not take any steps to ensure that the customer or correspondent broker-dealer either enabled the controls or sent future orders through a route that blocked wash trades.

58. The correspondent broker-dealer informed Wedbush that it had disabled one of the traders involved in the incidents, but Wedbush did not directly disable any of the

traders. Wedbush had no controls or procedures for preventing traders who had been disabled by a customer or correspondent broker-dealer from obtaining a new trader ID through the same or a different Wedbush customer account.

59. On multiple occasions, Fillhart learned from exchanges that traders in the same customer account appeared to be engaged in potentially manipulative trading referred to as "layering," which involves submitting and cancelling large numbers of non-*bona fide* orders on one side of the market in order to obtain executions at more favorable prices for smaller *bona fide* orders on the other side (citations omitted).

60. As early as February 2011, Fillhart notified the customer of potential layering activity in its account and told the customer that layering "is a manipulative activity." Until at least September 2012, Fillhart continued receiving reports from exchanges of potential layering activity through the same customer account, but she did not cause Wedbush to develop or acquire any tools to detect or cause the reporting of potential layering activity and did not warn the customer's principals that the account would be disabled if the trading activity continued.

61. In late 2011, Bell and Fillhart met with another senior officer in the Correspondent Services Division to discuss the substantial compliance risks posed to Wedbush by sponsored access customers like the one that had been the subject of numerous reports of potential layering and wash trading and had been addressed in face-to-face meetings with Commission staff—the customer that had thousands of essentially anonymous foreign traders trading through a single Wedbush customer account. Bell, Fillhart, and the other officer decided not to terminate the customer's relationship with Wedbush, but agreed that Wedbush should not take on new market access customers with similar business models because of the compliance risks to Wedbush. In October 2012, Bell, Fillhart, and the other officer met again and decided to terminate Wedbush's relationship with the customer.

62. During the relevant period, Wedbush did not file any suspicious activity reports relating to potential layering and filed only two suspicious activity reports relating to potential wash or pre-arranged trading....

Authorization of Traders

63. Subsection (b) of the Market Access Rule requires a broker-dealer with market access, or that provides a customer or any other person with access to an exchange or ATS through the use of its MPID or otherwise, to "establish, document, and maintain a system of risk management controls and supervisory procedures reasonably designed to manage the financial, regulatory, and other risks" of its market access business. Subsection (c)(2)(iii) of the Market Access Rule required Wedbush to have risk management controls and supervisory procedures that were reasonably designed to restrict access to trading systems and technology that provide market access to persons and accounts pre-approved and authorized by Wedbush, the broker-dealer with market access. As described below, for many of its largest sponsored access customers, Wedbush only pre-approved and authorized the principals for the account and relied on its customer to pre-approve and authorize the thousands

of individual traders who received market access through the account without reasonably designed controls and supervisory procedures to restrict access to trading systems and technology that provide market access to persons and accounts pre-approved and authorized by the broker or dealer. Accordingly, Wedbush failed to have controls and procedures that complied with Subsection (c)(2)(iii) of the Market Access Rule. Wedbush also did not effectively allocate these obligations, to the extent permitted by Subsection (d)(1) of the Market Access Rule, to its registered broker-dealer customers.

64. Wedbush's WSPs asserted that sponsored access customers were required to provide authorized trader information to Wedbush "upon commencement of sponsored access and when a change occurs." The WSPs also asserted that Wedbush would verify authorized trader information annually. Wedbush did not have any controls or procedures requiring customers to obtain approval from Wedbush before authorizing new traders.

65. When Wedbush opened a sponsored access account, Wedbush employees obtained identifying information and performed background checks only on the principals of the entity opening the account, not on other individuals that the entity authorized to trade through the account.... Wedbush did not have any written policies or procedures for pre-approving or authorizing new traders for existing sponsored access accounts.

66. Some customer firms and platform providers used a one-page "AccountID creation form" that called for certain information about each authorized trader, but Wedbush did not require use of the form and Wedbush rarely obtained copies of the forms from customers....

67. For customer firms with hundreds or thousands of traders, Wedbush usually relied on the customer firm to maintain a list of authorized traders and their trader IDs. Beginning in September 2011, Wedbush employees who reported to Fillhart occasionally obtained lists of authorized traders from customer firms with large numbers of traders and ran searches by name to determine whether any traders were subject to sanctions or restrictions on business activity.... These searches were done after, not before, the customer firm extended market access to the traders....

68. For customer firms with hundreds or thousands of traders, neither Fillhart nor Bell asked Wedbush employees to take any steps to verify trader names or identities or to speak to any of the traders. Bell and Fillhart knew that Wedbush relied exclusively on the customer firms, some of which were not registered broker-dealers, to confirm trader identities and oversee their trading strategies. Fillhart herself had the experience of being unable to find a list of trader information for a particular Wedbush client. Because of these facts, particularly the component of Wedbush's business that provided sponsored access to hundreds or thousands of traders through Wedbush's customers, Wedbush's controls and procedures for the pre-approval and authorization of traders were not reasonable....

Review of Effectiveness of Market Access Controls and Procedures

69. Section (e) of the Market Access Rule required Wedbush to establish, document, and maintain a system for regularly reviewing the effectiveness of its risk management

controls and supervisory procedures relating to market access and to conduct a review of its market access business in accordance with written procedures at least annually. Wedbush did not have any written procedures for regularly reviewing the effectiveness of its market access controls and procedures, and Bell and Fillhart both acknowledged that they had primary responsibility for designing and implementing Wedbush's controls and procedures relating to its market access business ...

70. On Friday, March 23, 2012, in preparation for Wedbush's required certification of supervisory controls pursuant to SRO rules, one of Wedbush's Co-Chief Compliance Officers asked the two internal audit employees at Wedbush to review five areas of Wedbush's business, including one described as "High Frequency Trading." The memorandum containing this request did not mention the Market Access Rule, any other Commission rules, or sponsored access.

71. The internal audit employees prepared a written report dated Monday, March 26, 2012, describing their review, including one page relating to "High Frequency Trading/Exchange Traded Funds." The report did not mention the Market Access Rule, any other Commission rules, sponsored access, Wedbush's WSPs, or any specific risk management controls or supervisory procedures that Wedbush had adopted to comply with the Rule.

72. According to the report, the employees reviewed documents, observed procedures, and spoke with three employees in the Correspondent Services Division as part of the review. The report cited two specific step—reviewing the checklist for onboarding new customers and observing software applications used for monitoring customer buying power and trading activities. The report noted that the software applications included risk management settings, but did not state that any specific settings were reviewed or tested.

73. The report concluded that, based on the internal audit employees' review, management's controls in the "High Frequency Trading/Exchange Traded Funds" area were adequate and functioning as intended.

74. The Co-Chief Compliance Officer incorporated this section of the report verbatim in a report that he sent to Wedbush's President and the rest of Wedbush's management team and Board on March 30, 2012. Like the internal audit report, this report did not mention the Market Access Rule ... No other reviews of the market access business were conducted by Wedbush employees during the relevant period.

75. Based on the report, as well as conversations with and information previously provided by Bell and others, Wedbush's President signed a certification dated March 30, 2012, citing SRO rules and Rule 15c3-5 (the Market Access Rule), and stating that the firm's risk management controls and supervisory procedures in connection with market access complied with Rule 15c3-5.... [T]hat certification was inaccurate.

Violations

77. As discussed above, Wedbush willfully violated Section 15(c)(3) of the Exchange Act and Rule 15c3-5 thereunder because it did not maintain exclusive control over

risk management controls in sponsored access trading platforms; did not have a system of risk management controls and supervisory procedures that was reasonably designed to ensure compliance with all regulatory requirements, including those that must be satisfied on a pre-order entry basis; did not have controls and procedures reasonably designed to restrict access to market access trading systems to persons and accounts pre-approved and authorized by Wedbush; did not establish, document, and maintain a system for regularly reviewing the effectiveness of its risk management controls and supervisory procedures relating to market access; and did not conduct an adequate review of its market access controls and procedures during the relevant period.

* * *

81. Rule 611(c) of Regulation NMS requires the broker-dealer responsible for routing an ISO to take reasonable steps to establish that the order meets the requirements of Rule 600(b)(30), which requires the broker-dealer routing the ISO to sweep the market by routing simultaneously additional orders, as necessary, to execute against the full size of all better-priced protected quotations. As discussed above, Wedbush willfully violated Rule 611(c) of Regulation NMS because it allowed sponsored access customers to submit ISOs without Wedbush taking reasonable steps to ensure that it satisfied the requirements for sending ISOs.

Undertakings

Wedbush has undertaken to do the following:

82. Retain, at its own expense, one or more qualified independent consultants (the "Consultant") not unacceptable to the Commission staff to conduct a comprehensive review of Wedbush's current system of controls and procedures for compliance with all applicable regulatory requirements relating to its market access business, including but not limited to Exchange Act Rules 15c3-5 ... ; to assess Wedbush's corporate governance and culture of compliance with respect to its market access business; and to provide recommendations for improvements as may be needed....

IV.

In view of the foregoing, the Commission deems it appropriate in the public interest to impose the sanctions agreed to in Respondent Wedbush's Offer.

Accordingly, pursuant to Sections 15(b) and 21C of the Exchange Act ... it is hereby ORDERED that:

Respondent Wedbush cease and desist from committing or causing any violations and any future violations of Sections 15(c)(3) and 17(a) of the Exchange Act; Rules 15c3-5, ... and Rule 611(c) of Regulation NMS.

B. Respondent Wedbush is censured.

C. Respondent Wedbush shall, within ten (10) days of the entry of this Order, pay a civil money penalty in the amount of $ 2,447,043.38 to the Securities and Exchange Commission.

———

In the Matter of Knight Capital Americas LLC

Securities and Exchange Commission,
Admin. Proc. File No. 3-15570 (Oct. 16, 2013).

I.

The Securities and Exchange Commission (the "Commission") deems it appropriate and in the public interest that public administrative and cease-and-desist proceedings be, and hereby are, instituted pursuant to Sections 15(b) and 21C of the Securities Exchange Act of 1934 ("the Exchange Act") against Knight Capital Americas LLC ("Knight" or "Respondent").

II.

In anticipation of the institution of these proceedings, Respondent has submitted an Offer of Settlement (the "Offer"), which the Commission has determined to accept.... Respondent consents to the entry of this Order Instituting Administrative and Cease-and-Desist Proceedings, Pursuant to Sections 15(b) and 21C of the Securities Exchange Act of 1934, Making Findings, and Imposing Remedial Sanctions and a Cease-and-Desist Order ("Order"), as set forth below:

III.

On the basis of this Order and Respondent's Offer, the Commission finds that:

* * *

FACTS

A. Respondent

11. Knight Capital Americas LLC ("Knight") is a U.S.-based broker-dealer and a wholly-owned subsidiary of KCG Holdings, Inc. Knight was owned by Knight Capital Group, Inc. until July 1, 2013, when that entity and GETCO Holding Company, LLC combined to form KCG Holdings, Inc. Knight is registered with the Commission pursuant to Section 15 of the Exchange Act and is a Financial Industry Regulatory Authority ("FINRA") member. Knight has its principal business operations in Jersey City, New Jersey. Throughout 2011 and 2012, Knight's aggregate trading (both for itself and for its customers) generally represented approximately ten percent of all trading in listed U.S. equity securities. SMARS [Knight's automated routing system for equity orders] generally represented approximately one percent or more of all trading in listed U.S. equity securities. Knight's aggregate trading (both for itself and for its customers) generally represented approximately ten percent of all trading in listed U.S. equity securities. SMARS generally represented approximately one percent or more of all trading in listed U.S. equity securities.

B. August 1, 2012 and Related Events

Preparation for NYSE Retail Liquidity Program

12. To enable its customers' participation in the Retail Liquidity Program ("RLP") at the New York Stock Exchange,5 which was scheduled to commence on August 1, 2012, Knight made a number of changes to its systems and software code related to

its order handling processes. These changes included developing and deploying new software code in SMARS. SMARS is an automated, high speed, algorithmic router that sends orders into the market for execution. A core function of SMARS is to receive orders passed from other components of Knight's trading platform ("parent" orders) and then, as needed based on the available liquidity, send one or more representative (or "child") orders to external venues for execution.

13. Upon deployment, the new RLP code in SMARS was intended to replace unused code in the relevant portion of the order router. This unused code previously had been used for functionality called "Power Peg," which Knight had discontinued using many years earlier. Despite the lack of use, the Power Peg functionality remained present and callable at the time of the RLP deployment. The new RLP code also repurposed a flag that was formerly used to activate the Power Peg code. Knight intended to delete the Power Peg code so that when this flag was set to "yes," the new RLP functionality—rather than Power Peg—would be engaged.

14. When Knight used the Power Peg code previously, as child orders were executed, a cumulative quantity function counted the number of shares of the parent order that had been executed. This feature instructed the code to stop routing child orders after the parent order had been filled completely. In 2003, Knight ceased using the Power Peg functionality. In 2005, Knight moved the tracking of cumulative shares function in the Power Peg code to an earlier point in the SMARS code sequence. Knight did not retest the Power Peg code after moving the cumulative quantity function to determine whether Power Peg would still function correctly if called.

15. Beginning on July 27, 2012, Knight deployed the new RLP code in SMARS in stages by placing it on a limited number of servers in SMARS on successive days. During the deployment of the new code, however, one of Knight's technicians did not copy the new code to one of the eight SMARS computer servers. Knight did not have a second technician review this deployment and no one at Knight realized that the Power Peg code had not been removed from the eighth server, nor the new RLP code added. Knight had no written procedures that required such a review.

Events of August 1, 2012

16. On August 1, Knight received orders from broker-dealers whose customers were eligible to participate in the RLP. The seven servers that received the new code processed these orders correctly. However, orders sent with the repurposed flag to the eighth server triggered the defective Power Peg code still present on that server. As a result, this server began sending child orders to certain trading centers for execution. Because the cumulative quantity function had been moved, this server continuously sent child orders, in rapid sequence, for each incoming parent order without regard to the number of share executions Knight had already received from trading centers. Although one part of Knight's order handling system recognized that the parent orders had been filled, this information was not communicated to SMARS.

17. The consequences of the failures were substantial. For the 212 incoming parent orders that were processed by the defective Power Peg code, SMARS sent millions of

child orders, resulting in 4 million executions in 154 stocks for more than 397 million shares in approximately 45 minutes. Knight inadvertently assumed an approximately $3.5 billion net long position in 80 stocks and an approximately $3.15 billion net short position in 74 stocks. Ultimately, Knight realized a $460 million loss on these positions.

18. The millions of erroneous executions influenced share prices during the 45 minute period. For example, for 75 of the stocks, Knight's executions comprised more than 20 percent of the trading volume and contributed to price moves of greater than five percent. As to 37 of those stocks, the price moved by greater than ten percent, and Knight's executions constituted more than 50 percent of the trading volume. These share price movements affected other market participants, with some participants receiving less favorable prices than they would have in the absence of these executions and others receiving more favorable prices.

BNET Reject E-mail Messages

19. On August 1, Knight also received orders eligible for the RLP but that were designated for pre-market trading.[66] SMARS processed these orders and, beginning at approximately 8:01 a.m. ET, an internal system at Knight generated automated e-mail messages (called "BNET rejects") that referenced SMARS and identified an error described as "Power Peg disabled." Knight's system sent 97 of these e-mail messages to a group of Knight personnel before the 9:30 a.m. market open. Knight did not design these types of messages to be system alerts, and Knight personnel generally did not review them when they were received. However, these messages were sent in real time, were caused by the code deployment failure, and provided Knight with a potential opportunity to identify and fix the coding issue prior to the market open. These notifications were not acted upon before the market opened and were not used to diagnose the problem after the open.

C. Controls and Supervisory Procedures

SMARS

20. Knight had a number of controls in place *prior* to the point that orders reached SMARS. In particular, Knight's customer interface, internal order management system, and system for internally executing customer orders all contained controls concerning the prevention of the entry of erroneous orders.

21. However, Knight did not have adequate controls in SMARS to prevent the entry of erroneous orders. For example, Knight did not have sufficient controls to monitor the *output* from SMARS, such as a control to compare orders leaving SMARS with those that entered it. Knight also did not have procedures in place to halt SMARS's operations in response to its own aberrant activity. Knight had a control that capped the limit price on a parent order, and therefore related child orders, at 9.5 percent below the National Best Bid (for sell orders) or above the National Best Offer (for

---

66. [6] These orders were distinct from the 212 incoming parent orders that led to the executions described above.

buy orders) for the stock at the time that SMARS had received the parent order. However, this control would not prevent the entry of erroneous orders in circumstances in which the National Best Bid or Offer moved by less than 9.5 percent. Further, it did not apply to orders—such as the 212 orders described above—that Knight received before the market open and intended to send to participate in the opening auction at the primary listing exchange for the stock.

Capital Thresholds

22. Although Knight had position limits for some of its trading groups, these limits did not account for the firm's exposure from outstanding orders. Knight also did not have pre-set capital thresholds in the aggregate for the firm that were linked to automated controls that would prevent the entry of orders if the thresholds were exceeded.

23. For example, Knight had an account—designated the 33 Account—that temporarily held multiple types of positions, including positions resulting from executions that Knight received back from the markets that its systems could not match to the unfilled quantity of a parent order. Knight assigned a $2 million gross position limit to the 33 Account, but it did not link this account to any automated controls concerning Knight's overall financial exposure.

24. On the morning of August 1, the 33 Account began accumulating an unusually large position resulting from the millions of executions of the child orders that SMARS was sending to the market. Because Knight did not link the 33 Account to pre-set, firm-wide capital thresholds that would prevent the entry of orders, on an automated basis, that exceeded those thresholds, SMARS continued to send millions of child orders to the market despite the fact that the parent orders already had been completely filled. Moreover, because the 33 Account held positions from multiple sources, Knight personnel could not quickly determine the nature or source of the positions accumulating in the 33 Account on the morning of August 1.

25. Knight's primary risk monitoring tool, known as "PMON," is a post-execution position monitoring system. At the opening of the market, senior Knight personnel observed a large volume of positions accruing in the 33 Account. However, Knight did not link this tool to its entry of orders so that the entry of orders in the market would automatically stop when Knight exceeded pre-set capital thresholds or its gross position limits. PMON relied entirely on human monitoring and did not generate automated alerts regarding the firm's financial exposure. PMON also did not display the limits for the accounts or trading groups; the person viewing PMON had to know the applicable limits to recognize that a limit had been exceeded. PMON experienced delays during high volume events, such as the one experienced on August 1, resulting in reports that were inaccurate.

Code Development and Deployment

26. Knight did not have written code development and deployment procedures for SMARS (although other groups at Knight had written procedures), and Knight did not require a second technician to review code deployment in SMARS. Knight also

did not have a written protocol concerning the accessing of unused code on its production servers, such as a protocol requiring the testing of any such code after it had been accessed to ensure that the code still functioned properly.

Incident Response

27. On August 1, Knight did not have supervisory procedures concerning incident response. More specifically, Knight did not have supervisory procedures to guide its relevant personnel when significant issues developed. On August 1, Knight relied primarily on its technology team to attempt to identify and address the SMARS problem in a live trading environment. Knight's system continued to send millions of child orders while its personnel attempted to identify the source of the problem. In one of its attempts to address the problem, Knight uninstalled the new RLP code from the seven servers where it had been deployed correctly. This action worsened the problem, causing additional incoming parent orders to activate the Power Peg code that was present on those servers, similar to what had already occurred on the eighth server.

D. Compliance Reviews and Written Description of Controls

Initial Assessment of Compliance

28. Knight's assessment of its controls and procedures began prior to the July 14, 2011 compliance date. Knight's compliance department initiated the assessment, which involved discussions among staff of that department, as well as the pertinent business and technology units. The participants concluded that Knight's system of controls satisfied Rule 15c3-5. The assessment largely focused on compiling an inventory of Knight's existing controls and confirming that they functioned as intended. The assessment did not consider possible problems within SMARS or the consequences of potential malfunctions in SMARS. This assessment also did not consider PMON's inability to prevent the entry of orders that would exceed a capital threshold. Further, Knight did not document sufficiently the evaluation done of the controls so that subsequent reviewers could identify these gaps in the assessment.

Written Description

29. During the initial assessment, the compliance department prepared a document that listed Knight's systems and some of the controls. This document was incomplete and therefore did not satisfy the documentation requirements of Rule 15c3-5(b). In September 2011, nearly two months after the compliance date of Rule 15c3-5's provision requiring the written description of the risk management controls, the compliance department drafted a narrative intended to describe Knight's market access systems and controls. This document also was incomplete, and was inaccurate in some respects. For example, the narrative omitted Knight's proprietary Electronic Trading Group ("ETG"), which was a significant source of Knight's trading and order volumes. The compliance department and supervisory control group ("SCG"), working together with pertinent business and technology units, began to address the missing elements of the document in November 2011, which resulted in a revised draft in January 2012, nearly six months after the compliance date of Rule 15c3-5(b). Although this draft included aspects of ETG, it lacked the Lead Market Making ("LMM") desk

and other important systems. As of the CEO certification in March 2012, discussed below, Knight still was adding key systems and controls to the document. Prior to certification, the CEO was informed about the pending revisions. It was not until July 2012, nearly a year after the compliance date, that Knight added the LMM desk, which had experienced erroneous trade events over the previous months.

Written Supervisory Procedures

30. In August 2011, subsequent to the compliance date of Rule 15c3-5's provision requiring written supervisory procedures, Knight adopted written supervisory procedures ("WSPs") to guide regular reviews of its compliance with Rule 15c3-5. Knight's compliance department drafted the WSPs, which assigned various tasks to be performed by SCG staff in consultation with the pertinent business and technology units. Taken together, the WSPs had the goal of evaluating the reasonableness of Knight's market access controls and Knight's compliance with Rule 15c3-5 on an ongoing basis. Each WSP required a senior member of the pertinent business unit to approve the work of the SCG staff. Further, a separate compliance department procedure required a compliance analyst twice a year to review the work done under the WSPs.

31. Some of the WSPs were incomplete as written, and Knight personnel had conflicting views regarding what some of the WSPs required. For example, relevant Knight personnel differed on whether some WSPs required an evaluation of the controls or merely an identification that controls and procedures existed. In addition, the WSP that was supposed to require an evaluation of the reasonableness of Knight's controls only required a review of certain types of controls and did not require an evaluation of controls to reject orders that exceed pre-set capital thresholds in the aggregate for the firm or that indicate duplicative orders.

Post-Compliance Date Reviews

32. Knight conducted periodic reviews pursuant to the WSPs. As explained above, the WSPs assigned various tasks to be performed by SCG staff in consultation with the pertinent business and technology units, with a senior member of the pertinent business unit reviewing and approving that work. These reviews did not consider whether Knight needed controls to limit the risk that SMARS could malfunction, nor did these reviews consider whether Knight needed controls concerning code deployment or unused code residing on servers. Before undertaking any evaluation of Knight's controls, SCG, along with business and technology staff, had to spend significant time and effort identifying the missing content and correcting the inaccuracies in the written description.

33. Several previous events presented an opportunity for Knight to review the adequacy of its controls in their entirety. For example, in October 2011, Knight used test data to perform a weekend disaster recovery test. After the test concluded, Knight's LMM desk mistakenly continued to use the test data to generate automated quotes when trading began that Monday morning. Knight experienced a nearly $7.5 million loss as a result of this event. Knight responded to the event by limiting the operation of the system to market hours, changing the control so that this system would stop pro-

viding quotes after receiving an execution, and adding an item to a disaster recovery checklist that required a check of the test data. Knight did not broadly consider whether it had sufficient controls to prevent the entry of erroneous orders, regardless of the specific system that sent the orders or the particular reason for that system's error. Knight also did not have a mechanism to test whether their systems were relying on stale data.

E. CEO Certification

34. In March 2012, Knight's CEO signed a certification concerning Rule 15c3-5. The certification did not state that Knight's controls and procedures complied with the rule. Instead, the certification stated that Knight had in place "processes" to comply with the rule. This drafting error was not intentional, the CEO did not notice the error, and the CEO believed at the time that he was certifying that Knight's controls and procedures complied with the rule.[67]

F. Collateral Consequences

35. There were collateral consequences as a result of the August 1 event, including significant net capital problems. In addition, many of the millions of orders that SMARS sent on August 1 were short sale orders. Knight did not mark these orders as short sales, as required ... [and] did not obtain a "locate" in connection with Knight's unintended orders and did not document compliance with the requirement with respect to Knight's unintended orders.

VIOLATIONS

A. Market Access Rule: Section 15(c)(3) of the Exchange Act and Rule 15c35

36. Section 15(c)(3) of the Exchange Act, among other things, prohibits a broker or dealer from effecting any securities transaction in contravention of the rules and regulations the Commission prescribes as necessary or appropriate in the public interest, or for the protection of investors, to provide safeguards with respect to the financial responsibility and related practices of brokers or dealers. Knight violated this Section through its violations, described below, of a rule promulgated by the Commission thereunder.

37. Subsection (c)(1)(i) of Rule 15c3-5 requires that a broker or dealer's risk management controls and supervisory procedures shall be reasonably designed to prevent systematically the entry of orders that exceed appropriate pre-set credit or capital thresholds in the aggregate for each customer and the broker or dealer. Knight violated this requirement by failing to link pre-set capital thresholds to Knight's entry of orders so that Knight would stop sending orders when it breached such thresholds. Instead, Knight relied on tools, including PMON, that were not capable of pre-

---

67. [8] Before signing the certification, the CEO received a report concerning reviews that Knight personnel had performed pursuant to the WSPs. The report contained sub-certifications from eight senior Knight employees. Although the report contained a similar drafting error as the certification, all of the employees who signed the report to the CEO believed that Knight was in compliance with Rule 15c3-5.

venting the entry of orders whose execution would exceed a capital threshold and did not link the 33 Account to pre-set capital thresholds. These inadequacies contributed to Knight's failure to detect promptly the severity of, and to resolve quickly, the problems on August 1 or to mitigate the effects prior to the resolution of the software issue.

38. Subsection (c)(1)(ii) of Rule 15c3-5 requires that a broker or dealer's risk management controls and supervisory procedures be reasonably designed to prevent systematically the entry of erroneous orders that exceed appropriate price or size parameters on an order-by-order basis or over a short period of time, or that indicate duplicative orders. Knight violated this requirement by failing to have controls reasonably designed to prevent the entry of erroneous orders at a point immediately prior to the submission of orders to the market by SMARS, which had the core function of dividing parent orders into child orders and sending them to the market. The controls that Knight had in place were not reasonably designed to limit Knight's financial exposure arising from errors within SMARS, such as problems in the operation of the software that sent child orders to fill parent orders. As evidenced by the events of August 1, the absence of adequate controls at the point immediately prior to Knight's submission of orders to the market left Knight vulnerable to the financial and regulatory risks of Knight's erroneous entry of orders and had substantial consequences to both Knight and the market.

39. Subsection (b) of Rule 15c3-5 requires, among other things, that a broker or dealer preserve a copy of its supervisory procedures and a written description of its risk management controls as part of its books and records ... As highlighted in the Adopting Release, this document serves the purpose of assisting Commission and Self-Regulatory Organization staff during an examination of the broker or dealer for compliance with the rule. It also assists the broker or dealer in conducting the reviews and performing the certification required by the rule. Knight violated this requirement by failing to have an adequate written description of its risk management controls. Knight did attempt to create a narrative of its risk management controls after the compliance date of Rule 15c3-5, but this document remained incomplete and, in some instances, inaccurate through the summer of 2012. The insufficiencies in this document adversely affected the quality of the reviews Knight conducted of its risk controls after the compliance date of Rule 15c3-5. As described above, Knight's staff had to spend considerable time and effort identifying the missing content and correcting the inaccuracies in this document before they could evaluate Knight's controls.

40. Knight also violated the overarching requirement of subsection (b) of Rule 15c3-5 that brokers or dealers "shall establish, document, and maintain a system of risk management controls and supervisory procedures reasonably designed to manage the financial, regulatory, and other risks of" its market access. As explained above, Knight lacked adequate controls for its order router and failed to have an automated control to prevent the entry of orders that exceeded firm-wide pre-set capital thresholds. Knight also lacked reasonably designed controls and supervisory procedures to detect and prevent software malfunctions that can result from code development and deployment.

41. For example, a written procedure requiring a simple double-check of the deployment of the RLP code could have identified that a server had been missed and averted the events of August 1. Having a procedure that integrated the BNET Reject messages into Knight's monitoring of its systems likewise could have prevented the events of August 1. Further, in 2003, Knight elected to leave the Power Peg code on SMARS's production servers, and, in 2005, accessed this code to use the cumulative quantity functionality in another application without taking measures to safeguard against malfunctions or inadvertent activation. A written protocol requiring the retesting of the Power Peg code in 2005 could have identified that Knight had inadvertently disabled the cumulative quantity functionality in the Power Peg code. These shortcomings were made more consequential by the fact that Knight did not have controls in SMARS that were sufficient to address the risk posed by possible problems in the operation of the software as it sent child orders to fill a parent order.

42. Further, Knight did not have adequate controls and supervisory procedures to guide employees' response to incidents such as what occurred on August 1. In light of Knight's market access, Knight needed clear guidance for its technology personnel as to when to disconnect a malfunctioning system from the market.

43. Subsection (e) of Rule 15c3-5 requires that a broker or dealer establish, document, and maintain a system for regularly reviewing the effectiveness of the risk management controls and supervisory procedures required by Rule 15c3-5(b) and (c). Subsection (e)(1) of Rule 15c3-5 requires, among other things, that a broker or dealer review, no less frequently than annually, the business activity of the broker or dealer in connection with market access to assure the overall effectiveness of such risk management controls and supervisory procedures. Reasonably designed WSPs are an important component of the system required by the rule, because they help ensure that the broker or dealer fulfills its obligations to conduct a review of the overall effectiveness of its risk management controls and supervisory procedures.

44. Knight violated subsection (e) of Rule 15c3-5 because its system for regularly reviewing the effectiveness of its risk management controls was inadequate. For example, Knight's WSPs were incomplete as written and did not provide clear guidance as to what they required. Further, Knight's initial assessment of its market access controls did not sufficiently consider whether the controls were reasonably designed to manage Knight's market access risks or whether Knight needed additional controls. This review, and the post-compliance date reviews, failed to consider adequately the risks posed by possible malfunctions in SMARS, one of Knight's primary systems for accessing the markets, and failed to consider Knight's inability to prevent the entry of orders whose execution would exceed pre-set capital thresholds. These reviews also failed to assess adequately the consequences of Knight's reliance on PMON as a primary risk monitoring tool, such as the risks posed by the lack of automated alerts and PMON's inability to prevent the entry of orders that would exceed a capital threshold or position limit. Further, Knight's reviews did not adequately consider the root causes of previous incidents involving the entry of erroneous orders and the reasons why Knight's controls failed to limit the harm from those incidents. Knight

reacted to the events narrowly, limiting its responses to changes designed to prevent the exact problem at hand from recurring.

45. Subsection (e)(2) of Rule 15c3-5 requires that a broker or dealer's CEO (or equivalent officer) certify on an annual basis that the firm's risk management controls and supervisory procedures comply with paragraphs (b) and (c) of Rule 15c3-5. The certification signed by Knight's CEO did not state that Knight's controls and supervisory procedures complied with those provisions of the rule. Rather, it stated that Knight had in place "processes" to comply with the rule. Certifying to the existence of processes is not equivalent to certifying that controls and procedures are reasonably designed and comply with the rule. Accordingly, Knight violated subsection (e)(2) of Rule 15c3-5.

REMEDIAL EFFORTS

50. In determining to accept the Offer, the Commission considered remedial acts that Knight undertook and the cooperation that Knight afforded to the Commission staff following the August 1 event.

noindent:51. Respondent has undertaken to do the following:

A. Retain at its own expense one or more qualified independent consultants (the "Consultant") not unacceptable to the Commission staff to conduct a comprehensive review of Respondent's compliance with Exchange Act Rule 15c3-5 ...

IV.

In view of the foregoing, the Commission deems it necessary and appropriate in the public interest, and for the protection of investors, to impose the sanctions agreed to in Respondent's Offer.

Accordingly, pursuant to Sections 15(b) and 21C of the Exchange Act, it is hereby ORDERED that:

A. Respondent Knight cease and desist from committing or causing any violations and any future violations of Section 15(c)(3) of the Exchange Act and Rule 15c3-5 thereunder ...

B. Respondent Knight is censured.

C. Pursuant to Section 21B(a)(1) and (2) of the Exchange Act, Respondent Knight shall, within ten (10) days of the entry of this Order, pay a civil money penalty in the amount of $12,000,000 ($12 million) to the United States Treasury.

―――――

Notes and Questions

1. The 2010 Concept Release requested comment on whether the SEC should consider a trade-at rule that would prohibit any trading center from executing a trade at the price of the national best bid and offer unless the trading center was dis-

playing that price at the time it received the incoming contra-side order. Such a rule would eliminate dark pools. The 2010 Concept Release also discusses potential expansion of the trade-through rule to provide trade-through protection to the displayed "depth-of-book" quotations of a trading center, which could also have significant competitive impact.

2. In investigating the Flash Crash of 2010, the SEC and the CFTC engaged in market reconstruction. That is, their staff collected and processed detailed trade and order data from multiple and varied sources to recreate the sequence of events and market conditions leading up to the Flash Crash of 2010. As discussed in the text, there was a preliminary report issued on May 18, 2010. However, the final report was not issued until September 30, 2010. The final report can be accessed at: https://www.sec.gov/news/studies/2010/marketevents-report.pdf. Among the regulatory responses was CAT. What is the status of the establishment and operation of a consolidated audit trail? *See* the Consolidated Audit Trail web site at: http://catnmsplan.com/.

Hypothetical Two

Success First offers its institutional customers direct market access through an electronic trading desk that is part of its Institutional Equity Division ("SFET"). One of its long-standing customers is Rochdale LLP ("Rochdale"), a registered broker-dealer. When Rochdale became an SFET customer, Success First established an aggregate credit threshold for Rochdale of $200 million. It was Success First's general practice to set an initial aggregate credit threshold for SFET customers who were registered broker-dealers. Success First's written supervisory procedures did not contain guidelines, criteria, or other qualifications to use when establishing initial aggregate credit thresholds for its SFET customers. On October 25, 2015, Rochdale (through its registered representative) entered a series of buy orders in Rochdale's internal entry system totaling 1,625,000 shares of Apple, Inc., at a cost of $1 billion. Ultimately, approximately 860,200 of the Apple shares purchased by Rochdale were executed by SFET for an aggregate value of approximately $525 million, exceeding Rochdale's aggregate credit threshold of $200 million. To accommodate Rochdale's orders, SFET twice raised Rochdale's aggregate credit threshold—first from $200 million to $500 million and then from $500 million to $750 million. Personnel in the SFET increased Rochdale's aggregate credit threshold both times based on their determination that Rochdale's order flow would exceed its existing credit threshold of $200 million. Unbeknownst to SFET personnel, the Rochdale customer on whose behalf the Apple shares were purchased only authorized Rochdale's registered representative to purchase 1,625 Apple shares. Rochdale's order for 1,625,000 shares of Apple was part of a fraudulent scheme for the Rochdale registered representative to personally profit by sharing the anticipated proceeds with the Rochdale customer if Apple's stock price increased following the earnings announcement on October 25, 2015. When Apple's stock price began dropping later that day, and it became clear that the trades would not be profitable, the Rochdale registered representative falsely claimed that he had made a mistake. Rochdale promptly traded out of the position, but as a result of the decrease in stock price, Rochdale suffered a loss of approximately $5.3 million by the following day. Regulatory net capital requirements prohibited Rochdale from continuing to trade securities, and it ceased all business operations shortly thereafter. Has Success First violated the Market Access Rule (Rule 15c3-5)?

D. The Over-The-Counter Market

The over-the counter securities market (OTC market) encompasses all trading that does not occur on registered national exchanges. Specifically, securities traded in the OTC market include corporate stocks or equities (including exchange-listed securities), corporate and government bonds, debentures, and mutual funds. With respect to equity securities trading in the OTC market, there are two general categories—NMS stocks and non-NMS stocks (OTC equity securities).[68] This discussion focuses on equities that are OTC equity securities traded in the OTC market. The OTC market is characterized by networks of trading relationships centered on one or more broker-dealers acting as a dealer. Unlike an exchange, the OTC market is a decentralized marketplace in which geographically dispersed dealers are linked by telephones and computers. Dealers act as market makers by quoting prices at which they will sell or buy to other dealers and to their customers. Accordingly, prices of OTC equity securities traded in the OTC market are determined through competition among OTC market makers. Quotations (bid and ask prices) are conveyed using various manual and electronic devices including the telephone, mass e-mail messages, and instant messaging. Quotations for OTC equity securities are available on quotation systems such as the OTCBB and the OTC Markets. Trading in OTC equity securities is executed between the dealers either manually or through whatever private electronic linkages they share. Clearing and settlement are left to the buying and selling broker-dealers but FINRA Rule 6540, which applies to OTCBB, requires OTC market makers to clear and settle with a registered clearing agency using a continuous net settlement system, if eligible. Much of the trading in the OTC market for OTC equity securities is comprised of the securities of issuers who are thinly traded and capitalized.

FINRA is the only SRO with authority to regulate broker-dealer activity in OTC equity securities pursuant to Section 15A of the Exchange Act. The OTCBB and the OTC Markets operate interdealer quotation systems used by broker-dealers to display quotations in OTC equity securities. FINRA Rule 6620 series requires all broker-dealer members to report transactions in OTC equity securities to the OTC Reporting Facility.

---

68. FINRA Rule 6420(f) defines OTC equity security as any equity security that is not an NMS stock as that term is defined in Rule 600(b)(47) of SEC Regulation NMS; provided, however, that the term "OTC Equity Security" shall not include any Restricted Equity Security.

1. OTCBB

The OTCBB provides an electronic, real-time quotation medium that FINRA member broker-dealers can use to enter, update, and view quotations in OTC equity securities. Securities eligible to be quoted on the OTCBB are limited to reporting companies that must file current financial reports under either Sections 13 or 15(d) of the Exchange Act or, as appropriate, with their banking or insurance regulator. There are no listing requirements for issuers seeking to have their securities quoted on the OTCBB. Market makers make an independent decision as to whether to quote any particular issuer's security. In addition, pursuant to Rule 15c2-11 of the Exchange Act, OTC market makers are required to obtain and submit certain financial, operational, and identifying information about the issuers of OTCBB-eligible securities, including current financial statements, and must have a reasonable basis for believing that this information is accurate. An overview of FINRA rules for the OTCBB is provided in Table 13.2.

Table 13.2. OTCBB Quoting Rules

FINRA Rule	Requirement
6530	Eligibility— · Not listed on an exchange except for a regional stock exchange and does not qualify for dissemination of transaction reports via facilities of the Consolidated Tape; AND · Required to file reports under Sections 13 or 15(d) of the Exchange Act or is a security issued by a registered investment company; OR · Insurance company current in its filings with a state insurance regulator; OR · A bank or savings association not required to file with the SEC but current in required filings with applicable federal banking regulator
6540	Market Maker Requirements: · Participation is voluntary and includes ATSs or ECNs that are FINRA members; must meet financial/operational requirements for OTC market making; Must comply with, or be eligible for, an exception, from Rule 15c2-11 of the Exchange Act. *See* FINRA Rule 6432 for requirements demonstrating compliance with Rule 15c2-11. · Quotations for domestic equity securities must be firm up to minimum quotation size (FINRA Rule 6433) · Allowed to trade only OTCBB-eligible securities · Must clear and settle transactions in OTCBB-quoted securities with registered clearing agency using CNS system if OTCBB securities are eligible for clearing; ex-clearing allowed if both parties agree.
6550	Transaction Reporting · Broker-dealers must report transactions in OTCBB-eligible securities pursuant to FINRA Rule 6620 series. Among other requirements, last sale reports of transactions must be reported using FINRA's OTC Reporting Facility (ORF) within 10 seconds after execution

2. OTC Markets

OTC Markets is an ATS and an inter-dealer quotation system that displays quotes in OTC equity securities. In addition, all subscribers to the OTC Markets must be broker-dealers that are members of FINRA. Subscribers are permitted to quote any OTC equity security eligible for quoting, or for an applicable exemption, under Rule 15c2-11. Transactions occurring on OTC Markets are subject to the same transaction reporting rules as the OTCBB in addition to federal rules and regulations and FINRA rules.

OTC Markets provides, among other services, the ability to send and receive trade messages to negotiate trades and trade execution for subscribing broker-dealers. OTC Markets offers three tiers — OTCQX, OTCQB, and OTC Pink. The three tiers reflect information required by OTC Markets to quote on its respective tiers; however, OTC Markets has no regulatory authority under the federal securities laws to enforce its requests for information. See Table 13.3.

The following case demonstrates the operation of the regulatory framework for OTC equity securities.

General Bond Share Co. v. SEC
39 F.3d 1451 (10th Cir. 1994)

Brown, District Judge.

Petitioner General Bond & Share Company ("General Bond") seeks review of disciplinary action taken against it by the Securities and Exchange Commission (hereinafter "the Commission" or "SEC"). The Commission found that General Bond violated several Rules of Fair Practice of the National Association of Securities Dealers, Inc. ("NASD"), of which General Bond was a member. Specifically, the Commission determined that General Bond, through its president Samuel C. Pandolfo, acted improperly in accepting compensation from approximately forty-five issuers of securities in exchange for publicly listing General Bond as a wholesale dealer for the securities, that it failed to maintain current information in its files as required by Commission rules, and that it failed to respond fully to requests for information made by NASD in the course of its investigation of General Bond. General Bond now asks this court to vacate the sanctions imposed by SEC.

I.

Regulatory Background. The NASD is registered with SEC as a securities association pursuant to Section 15A of the Securities Exchange Act of 1934, 15 U.S.C. §78o-3. As such, the NASD is responsible for self-regulation of its members, subject to oversight by SEC. Id. NASD is required to adopt rules regulating the conduct of its members and to enforce those rules through disciplinary proceedings. Id. Under NASD procedures, the NASD Market Surveillance Committee ("MSC") brings disciplinary actions concerning member violations. Any final action taken by the MSC is subject to review by the NASD's National Business Conduct Committee ("NBCC"), which may affirm, reverse or modify the action taken by the MSC.

Disciplinary action taken by the NASD is subject to review by SEC. 15 U.S.C. §78s(d)(2). In such cases, SEC conducts a de novo review of the record and makes its own finding as to whether the conduct in question violated the NASD rule charged. 15 U.S.C. §78s(e)(1). See also Sorrell v. SEC, 679 F.2d 1323, 1326 n.2 (9th Cir. 1982).

Table 13.3. OTC Markets Group Marketplaces

Marketplace	Sponsorship/Quotes	Issuer type	Financial Information	Reporting Information
OTCQX U.S.*	Must have proprietary priced quotations published by a FINRA member and SEC-regulated broker-dealer on OTC Link; Minimum bid of $0.10 (for preceding 30 consecutive calendar days).	Shell companies and blank check companies are prohibited. Must not be subject to bankruptcy or reorganization proceedings. Must meet one of the exemptions from the definition of a penny stock under Rule 3a51-1 of the Exchange Act; at least 50 beneficial shareholders.	Two years of audited annual financial statements; total assets $2 million; total assets $2 million; Revenue of $2 million or net tangible assets of $1 million, or net income of $500,000, or market value of listed securities $5 million.	If SEC reporting company, must be current; Non-SEC reporting companies must be published in the S&P or Mergent Manual for Blue Sky compliance;** a Designated Advisor for Disclosure ("DAD") letter of introduction confirming public disclosure of adequate current information
OTCQB	Must have proprietary priced quotations published by an OTC Link market maker with closing bid price of at least $0.01 for each of the 30 calendar days immediately preceding application.	Early state and developing U.S. companies.* Must not be subject to bankruptcy or reorganization proceedings; organized and in good standing in each jurisdiction in which it does business; maintain an SEC registered transfer agent authorized to provide information to OTC Markets Group.	Financial statements prepared in accordance with GAAP with no adverse, disclaimed, or qualified opinion.	SEC or Bank reporting company current in reporting obligations. If non-reporting, must post OTC disclosure requirements on OTC Markets website. CEO or CFO certification of issuer exemption under Rule 12g3-2(b) of the Exchange Act.
OTC Pink (Formerly the Pink Sheets)	Must be sponsored by broker-dealer; no minimum bid.	All types of companies that are there by reasons of default, distress, or design; organized in tiers based on disclosure using the following categories—current information, limited information, no information.	Not required but encouraged.	Not required but encouraged.

* There are additional requirements for international companies and banks.

** Allows broker-dealers to recommend the security in up to 38 states.

The SEC may also modify or cancel the sanctions imposed if it finds them to be excessive or oppressive. 15 U.S.C. § 78s(e)(2).

A person aggrieved by a final order of SEC in such a case may obtain review of the order in the appropriate U.S. Court of Appeals. § 78y(a)(1). A court reviewing the order must uphold the factual findings of SEC if they are supported by substantial evidence. § 78y(a)(4).

II.

Facts. The following facts, which were adopted by SEC, are supported by substantial evidence in the record. General Bond, located in Denver, Colorado, has been an NASD member since 1961. At all times relevant to this case, General Bond was a one-man broker/dealer owned and operated by its president, Samuel C. Pandolfo. General Bond was a wholesale trader which dealt only with "Pink Sheet" securities. It had no retail customers.

The "Pink Sheets" are published on a daily basis by the National Quotation Bureau, Inc. They contain broker-dealer submitted "bid" and "ask" prices for, or indications of interest in, specified securities. During the periods December, 1988 to July, 1990 and November, 1990 to January, 1991, General Bond received a total of $ 25,750 from about forty-five issuers in return for General Bond entering its name in the pink sheets as a "market maker" for the securities. A "market maker" includes any dealer who, with respect to a security, holds himself out (by entering quotations in an inter-dealer communications system or otherwise) as being willing to buy and sell such security for his own account on a regular and continuous basis. General Bond normally charged a negotiable fee for an individual listing, ranging between $ 250 and $ 1,000. The amount negotiated depended, according to Mr. Pandolfo, upon "supply and demand."

General Bond commanded these fees for at least ten years; in 1989 and 1990 about 25% of the firm's revenues consisted of such issuer-paid compensation. Pandolfo testified that the firm could not have stayed in business during 1989 and 1990 without these payments. He acknowledged that General Bond did not list issues based on expectations or promises of order flow and that potential trading activity was unimportant to him. If trading interest surfaced, General Bond would continue the listing; if not, the listing would be pulled. Sixteen of the issues identified in the complaint were listed by General Bond for periods of less than thirty days.

The NASD contacted Mr. Pandolfo in September of 1990 concerning applications he had filed to have General Bond listed in the pink sheets as a market maker for two stocks. At that time, the NASD staff advised Pandolfo that NASD member firms were prohibited from accepting issuer-paid compensation for making a market in a security. NASD staff also furnished Pandolfo with a NASD Notice to Members, issued in February 1975, which set forth NASD's position on the matter of issuer-paid compensation. Thereafter, Pandolfo agreed to refund $ 500 he had received from an issuer and to accept no further issuer-paid compensation. Despite these representations, Pandolfo did not refund the money and General Bond continued its practice of accepting compensation for entering the pink sheets.

In mid-March 1991, NASD staff requested that Pandolfo furnish documentation concerning issuer-paid compensation the firm received between July, 1990 and the date of the request. Pandolfo furnished documentation for the period December, 1990 through March of 1991, but did not provide the pre-December 1990 documentation requested.

III.

The disciplinary action against General Bond was initiated by the filing of two separate complaints which were consolidated for purposes of the hearings before NASD and SEC. The first complaint alleged that General Bond violated Article III, Section 1 of the NASD Rules of Fair Practice, by accepting payments totaling $ 23,250 from issuers in return for listing itself as a market maker for the securities in the pink sheets during the period December, 1988 to July, 1990. Article III, Section 1 states: "A member, in the conduct of his business, shall observe high standards of commercial honor and just and equitable principles of trade." The complaint further alleged a violation of Section 15(c) of the 1934 Act and Rule 15c2-11 promulgated thereunder, which requires a broker-dealer who has submitted a quotation or an indication of interest in a security to maintain current information on the issuer. The second complaint alleged a violation of Article III, Section I by virtue of General Bond's receipt of $ 2,500 in return for listing itself as a market maker for securities between November, 1990 and January, 1991, and by virtue of the fact that Mr. Pandolfo was notified that NASD considered such payments improper and represented to NASD that he would cease accepting such compensation but continued to accept payments. The second complaint also alleged that General Bond failed to produce documents requested by NASD in the course of its investigation and that such failure was a violation of Article III, Section 1 and Article IV, Section 5 of the Rules of Fair Practice. Following a hearing and decision before the NASD Market Surveillance Committee, NASD's National Business Conduct Committee determined on appeal that General Bond had engaged in the conduct alleged and found such conduct to be violations of NASD Rules of Fair Practice. NASD imposed sanctions consisting of fines, costs, and expulsion from membership in the association.

General Bond then sought a hearing before SEC. After that hearing, the Commission determined that General Bond's practice of accepting compensation for listing General Bond in the pink sheets as a market maker violated Article III, Section 1 of NASD's Rules of Fair Practice. The Commission noted that the typical market maker is compensated by trading for its own account and that, in deciding whether to list a stock in the pink sheets, the typical market maker is concerned with factors that affect the stock's liquidity and the security's intrinsic value. In contrast, General Bond's primary motivation in listing stocks was the payment that it received to list the security.

According to the findings of the Commission, market participants view a pink sheet listing as an indicia of some measure of liquidity in the market and of the listing broker-dealer's interest in buying or selling the security. Market participants, the Commission found, had no way to know that General Bond was indifferent to the market factors likely to affect trading profits. The Commission concluded that General Bond's practice of accepting compensation "compromised the integrity of the market and misled market participants." The Commission further found that General Bond violated Article III, Section I by telling NASD that it would cease accepting issuer-paid compensation and then continuing to command such fees. The SEC adopted NASD's finding that Mr. Pandolfo "deceived the staff by claiming that he had ceased accepting such listing fees, while continuing business as usual." The Commission also held that General Bond violated Rule 15c2-11 by failing to maintain reasonably current information in its files on two issuers. Finally, SEC concluded that General Bond's failure to produce documents requested by NASD was not excusable and was a violation of the Rules of Fair Practice.

The SEC approved the sanctions levied by NASD with one exception. A majority of the Commission determined that an "additional remedial fine" of $ 14,250 imposed by NASD was not appropriate. Otherwise, the Commission upheld the NASD'S imposition of censure and expulsion from the association as well as a total fine of $ 45,750 for the violations committed by General Bond.

IV.

1. Article III. Section 1—Acceptance of Compensation by a Market Maker. We first examine two related arguments asserted by General Bond. These arguments concern the Commission's determination that General Bond violated Article III, Section 1 of NASD Rules of Fair Practice by accepting compensation for listing General Bond in the "Pink Sheets" as a market maker for the securities. The first argument asserts that Article III, Section 1 of NASD rules, standing alone, is unconstitutionally vague. The second argument pertains to whether NASD was required by statute to submit its "interpretation" that the acceptance of such compensation was a violation of Article III, Section 1, to SEC prior to enforcing it. As is set forth herein, we find General Bond's second argument to be persuasive. We need not decide, therefore, whether the NASD rule standing alone is unconstitutionally vague.

a. Vagueness. General Bond first argues that the provisions of the rule requiring members to "observe high standards of commercial honor and just and equitable principles of trade" failed to provide fair warning to General Bond that its acceptance of compensation from issuers of securities would be considered a violation of the rule. Citing Rose v. Locke, 423 U.S. 48, 50, 96 S. Ct. 243, 46 L. Ed. 2d 185 (1975) (The Due Process Clause of the Fifth Amendment requires that sufficient warning be given so that individuals may conduct themselves so as to avoid that which is forbidden.) In its response, SEC does not challenge the applicability of the Due Process Clause to the disciplinary proceeding below, nor does it dispute the assertion that due process requires that NASD rules give fair warning of what conduct is prohibited before NASD members may be disciplined for engaging in such conduct. See Handley Investment Co. v. S.E.C., 354 F.2d 64, 66 (10th Cir. 1965). Moreover, SEC's brief does not assert that the provisions of Article III, Section 1 standing alone were sufficient to give adequate notice. The SEC maintains, however, that the requirements of due process were satisfied because General Bond had specific notice that its conduct violated NASD rules. In support of this assertion, SEC cites two documents: a 1973 publicly available "No-Action Letter" and a 1975 NASD "Notice to Members." These two documents are described below.

In Monroe Securities, Inc., SEC No-Action Letter (Pub. Avail. June 4, 1973), SEC responded to a question from a broker as to whether he could charge an issuer a service charge for expenses incurred in entering quotations and making a market for the issuer's securities. The SEC's response included the following comments:

> It is generally understood that broker-dealers have wide freedom to commence or
>
> terminate making an over-the-counter market. The pricing of a stock or making of a market at any given time should involve a combination of factors, including the firm's current inventory position, its attitude toward the market, and any market being made in competition. In view of the common understanding of a market maker's role and economic motivations, an arrangement whereby a broker-dealer charges an issuer a fee for making a market in its stock may conflict with the antifraud provisions of the federal securities laws.
>
> * * * Your attention is also directed to Section 17(b) of the Securities Act which makes it unlawful for any person for consideration to be received from an issuer to publish, give publicity to or circulate, any notice, circular, advertisement, or communication which, though not an offering for sale, describes such security without fully disclosing the compensation arrangement with the issuer.

Id. After discussing other aspects of the broker's proposal to charge fees, SEC concluded: "In our view your proposal raises serious questions under the federal securities laws; any attempt to implement such a plan would appear to be inadvisable."

On February 20, 1975, NASD issued Notice to Members 75-16, which echoed the matters set forth in the 1973 SEC No-Action Letter. The Notice stated in part:

> Recently, questions have arisen with respect to the propriety of an issuer paying a member to make a market in its securities and whether it would be permissible under applicable securities laws for a member to charge an issuer for out of pocket expenses incurred in the course of making a market in an issuer's securities. An additional question concerns the acceptance by a member of unsolicited payments from an issuer in whose securities the member makes a market.
>
> In connection with the above, the Association wishes to advise members that ramifications of these and several other related questions are currently being reviewed. As part of this review, the Association staff has recently met with the Securities and Exchange Commission staff to discuss, in general terms, the applicability of the federal securities laws to these practices and whether there were areas where some measure of liberalization could be achieved. For the reasons discussed below, both members and issuers are cautioned that it appears such payments may be prohibited under existing laws and are advised to consult with their counsel prior to taking any action

in this regard. By way of background to the above, it is important to note that members generally have considerable latitude and freedom to make or terminate market making activities in over-the-counter securities. The decision to make a market in a given security and the question of "price" are generally dependent on a number of factors including, among others, supply and demand, the firm's attitude toward the market, its current inventory position and exposure to risk and competition. The additional factor of payments by an issuer to a market maker would probably be viewed as a conflict of interest since it would undoubtedly influence, to some degree, a firm's decision to make a market and thereafter, perhaps, the prices it would quote. Hence, what might appear to be independent trading activity may well be illusory. In view of these and other factors, any arrangement whereby a member charges an issuer a fee for making a market or accepts an unsolicited payment from an issuer whose securities the member makes a market in raises serious questions under the anti-fraud provisions of the federal securities laws. In addition, the payment by an issuer to a market maker to facilitate market making activities may also violate Section 5 of the Securities Act of 1933.

Members should also be aware that in addition to the above mentioned concerns, Section 17(b) of the Securities Act of 1933 explicitly makes it unlawful for any person receiving consideration, directly or indirectly from an issuer, to publish or circulate any material which describes such issuer's securities without fully disclosing the receipt of such consideration, whether past or prospective, and the amount thereof. In addition, such conduct may violate the provisions of Section 10(b) of the Securities Exchange Act of 1934 and Rule 10b-5 promulgated thereunder.

The SEC contends that these documents provided sufficient notice that the conduct engaged in by General Bond was a violation of NASD rules. Additionally, the SEC points out that prior to five of the transactions in question, NASD staff members informed General Bond orally and in writing of NASD's view that acceptance of compensation of General Bond was prohibited by NASD rules.

b. Invalid Rule Change. General Bond's second argument is that the finding that its acceptance of compensation violated Article III, Section 1, constituted a "rule change" which was required by statute to be submitted by NASD to the SEC for approval prior to taking effect. General Bond relies upon 15 U.S.C. §78s(b)(1), which provides:

Each self-regulatory organization shall file with the Commission, in accordance with such rules as the Commission may prescribe, copies of any proposed rule or any proposed change in, addition to, or deletion from the rules of such self-regulatory organization (hereinafter in this subsection collectively referred to as a "proposed rule change") accompanied by a concise general statement of the basis and purpose of such proposed rule change. The Commission shall, upon the filing of any proposed rule change, publish notice thereof together with the terms of substance of the proposed rule change or a description of the subjects and issues involved. The Commission shall give interested persons an opportunity to submit written data, views, and arguments concerning such proposed rule change. No proposed rule change shall take effect unless approved by the Commission or otherwise permitted in accordance with the provisions of this subsection.

Article III, Section 1 of NASD rules was submitted to and approved by SEC. It is undisputed, however, that NASD did not file Notice to Members 75-16 with SEC prior to the disciplinary action against General Bond, nor did NASD file any other document with SEC indicating that a market maker's acceptance of compensation in exchange for listing a security in the pink sheets was conduct prohibited by Article III, Section 1.

The SEC contends that NASD was not required to submit Notice to Members 75-16 to the Commission for approval as a proposed rule or a rule change. The SEC points out that the Notice was issued on February 20, 1975. At that time, the Maloney Act required self-regulatory organizations to file "any changes in or additions to the rules of the association" with the Commission, but the statute did not provide any guidance on what constituted a "rule change." Subsequently, SEC notes, the Securities Acts Amendments of 1975 defined the "rules of an association" to include the constitution, articles of incorporation, bylaws, and rules of an association, together with "such of the stated policies, practices, and interpretations of such ... association ... as the Commission, by rule, may determine to be necessary or appropriate in the public interest or for the protection of investors to be deemed to be rules of such ... association...." § 78c(a)(27) (emphasis added). After this amendment was added to the statute, SEC adopted Rule 19b-4, which provided that a stated policy, practice, or interpretation of a self-regulatory organization shall be deemed a rule change unless: 1) it is reasonably and fairly implied by an existing rule of the organization, or 2) it is concerned solely with administration of the organization and is not a stated policy, practice or interpretation with respect to the meaning or enforcement of an existing rule of the organization. The SEC concedes that NASD Notice to Members 75-16 (which SEC describes as a "statement of policy") would have to be submitted to the Commission for approval were it to be proposed today. But, SEC contends "nothing in the statute, which requires approval of proposed rules or rule changes, requires the submission of rules that were in existence prior to the adoption of the amendments."

c. Discussion. After carefully considering the arguments of both parties, we must agree with General Bond that NASD's interpretation of Article III, Section 1 concerning acceptance of compensation was a "rule change" and was required by statute to be submitted to SEC for approval prior to enforcement of that interpretation. Because no such interpretation was filed with SEC prior to the disciplinary proceeding below, we conclude that the enforcement of the rule against General Bond was contrary to 15 U.S.C. § 78s(b)(1) and is therefore invalid. ("No proposed rule change shall take effect unless approved by the Commission...."). We believe that such a view is the only result consistent with the statutory responsibility of SEC—both before and after the Securities Acts Amendments of 1975 — to oversee the rule-making activities of a registered national securities association.

We do not quarrel with SEC's assertion that nothing in the 1975 Securities Acts Amendments required submission to SEC of NASD rules "that were in existence prior to adoption of the amendments." Nor can it be denied that the 1975 Amendments, unlike former § 78o-3(j), specifically indicated that NASD interpretations and policy statements could be considered rules changes. From these facts, SEC apparently concludes that under the Maloney Act, as it existed prior to the Securities Acts Amendments of 1975, the issuance of an NASD interpretation or policy statement such as Notice to Members 75-16, although it established a new standard of conduct, was not considered a "rule change" and did not have to be submitted to SEC for approval. We disagree with this premise as applied in this case.

The Maloney Act of 1938 established extensive guidelines for the formation and oversight of "self-regulatory organizations" such as NASD. The Act supplemented SEC's regulation of over-the-counter markets by providing a system of cooperative self-regulation through voluntary associations of brokers and dealers. In order to become registered as a national securities association under the Maloney Act, an association such as NASD was required to adopt extensive rules to ensure that the purposes of the Act were carried out. See former 15 U.S.C. § 78o-3 (1970). Those rules had to include a provision stating that the association's members would be disciplined for any violation of its rules and had to provide for a fair and orderly procedure with respect to the disciplining of members. Id. § 78o-3(b)(10) & (11).

The Securities Exchange Commission was given extensive oversight responsibilities for such associations, including the responsibility of determining whether the association's rules as initially filed met the requirements of the Maloney Act. In order to become a registered association, the association had to file with SEC "copies of its constitution, charter, or articles of incorporation or association, with all amendments thereto, and of its existing bylaws, and of any rules or instruments corresponding to the foregoing, whatever the name, hereinafter in this chapter collectively referred to as the 'rules of the association.'" Id. § 78o-3(a)(2). Pursuant to former § 78o-3(j), any subsequent changes in or additions to the rules of the association were required to be filed with the Commission to become effective:

> (j) Filing changes or additions to association rules and current information.

> Every registered securities association shall file with the Commission in accordance with such rules and regulations as the Commission may prescribe as necessary or appropriate in the public interest or for the protection of investors, copies of any changes in or additions to the rules of the association, and such other information ... as the Commission may require....

The Maloney Act additionally authorized SEC to request changes in NASD rules and gave SEC authority to order such changes if such a request were not complied with. See former § 78o-3(k)(2). See also United States v. National Association of Securities Dealers, 422 U.S. 694, 733, 95 S. Ct. 2427, 45 L. Ed. 2d 486 (1975). If, as

SEC contends, NASD Notice to Members 75-16 established that acceptance of issuer-paid compensation by a market maker was a violation of Article III, Section 1, we find that such a determination was a "change in or addition to the rules" of NASD. Although SEC apparently had no regulations defining "rule change" at the time Notice to Members 75-16 was issued, the establishment of a new standard of conduct such as this must be considered a "rule change" under any common sense definition of that term. Cf. United States v. National Association of Securities Dealers, 422 U.S. 694, 733, 95 S. Ct. 2427, 45 L. Ed. 2d 486 (1975) ("We see no meaningful distinction between the [NASD's] rules and the manner in which it construes and implements them. Each is equally a subject of SEC oversight.") More specifically, we conclude that the establishment of such a new standard was within the definition of "rule change" contemplated by Congress when it enacted former § 78o-3(j). As such, the change had to be filed with SEC under the provisions of former § 78o-3(j) prior to becoming a valid rule of the association.

We note that SEC was faced with a somewhat similar issue in In the Matter of The Rules of the National Association of Securities Dealers, Inc., Securities Exchange Act Rel. No. 3623 (Nov. 25, 1944), 1944 SEC LEXIS 114. In that case, objections were filed with SEC concerning a policy issued by NASD Board of Governors. The policy concerned an interpretation of Article III, Section 1 relating to price spreads and commissions charged by NASD members. Members objecting to the Board's interpretation of the rule argued that it constituted a rule change that had to be submitted to SEC under § 78o-3(j). In its decision, SEC indicated that the resolution of this issue turned on whether the purported interpretation "'does no more than express what must be clearly implied in the rule itself,' or whether it has the effect of adding some duty or standard not otherwise contained in the rules." Because the interpretation of the rule in that case was simply an application of a standard of conduct already expressed in another NASD rule, the Commission found that the Board's interpretation of Article III, Section 1 did not establish a new standard. By contrast, in this case SEC has not cited any previously established NASD rule (aside from its reliance on Notice to Members 75-16) that prohibited acceptance of issuer-paid compensation by a market maker under circumstances similar to those presented. Nor can we conclude that this type of conduct was so inherently deceptive that a ban against it was "clearly implied" by a provision requiring members to observe "high standards of commercial honor and just and equitable principles of trade."…. When a prohibition sets a new standard of conduct for its members, however, the NASD is required by statute to submit such a change to SEC prior to enforcing it. In sum, we find that the enforcement of Article III, Section 1 against General Bond in this case for its acceptance of compensation represented a change in NASD rules that was invalid under 15 U.S.C. § 78s(b)(1).

Article III, Section 1—General Bond's Deceit of NASD Staff. The SEC also determined that General Bond violated Article III, Section 1 when it continued to accept issuer-paid compensation after informing NASD that it would cease this practice. The SEC found that Mr. Pandolfo "deceived the staff by claiming that he had ceased accepting such listing fees, while continuing business as usual." General Bond argues that under the circumstances it was not bound to cease accepting compensation because the NASD incorrectly determined that acceptance of payments was prohibited by NASD rules. This argument ignores the fact that Mr. Pandolfo's deception of NASD staff formed the basis of this portion of SEC's ruling. Although we have determined that NASD rules in effect at the time did not prohibit the acceptance of these payments, our ruling does not absolve General Bond of culpability for making misrepresentations to NASD.

Under Article IV, Section 5 of NASD Rules, General Bond had an obligation to provide the information sought by NASD. General Bond attempts to cast Mr. Pandolfo's conduct as the product of a good faith dispute concerning the scope of an NASD rule and intimates that Pandolfo may have decided to continue accepting payments on advice from counsel. It is clear to us from SEC's opinion, however, that the Commission determined that Mr. Pandolfo intentionally deceived NASD staff concerning his practice of accepting compensation. This determination is supported by substantial evidence in the record. Moreover, we find that any reasonable person would know that such intentional deception of NASD while it is engaged in an investigation violates the prohibition against conduct contrary to high standards of commercial honor and just and equitable principles of trade. Consequently, we do not disturb the Commission's ruling that General Bond's deception of NASD staff violated Article III, Section 1.

3. Rule 15c2-11 — Failure to Maintain Reasonably Current Financial Information. Rule 15c2-11 requires a broker-dealer submitting a quotation to maintain in its files certain information concerning the issuer that is "reasonably current" in relation to the day the quotation is submitted. The SEC found that General Bond violated Rule 15c2-11 by failing to maintain in its records reasonably current information with respect to two issuers. In so ruling, SEC stated that "the broker-dealer has the burden of production under the Rule because the broker-dealer is in a better position than NASD or other authority to know the condition of a company whose stock it intends to list, and to obtain the requisite up-to-date financial information about the issuer." The SEC concluded that General Bond failed to show that information in its files was reasonably current.

General Bond now contends that SEC's determination that it had the "burden of production" on this issue constituted informal rule making. As such, General Bond argues, the rule should not have been applied retroactively. We agree with SEC, however, that SEC's determination did not constitute rule making, but was an interpretation of the requirements implied in an existing rule. The SEC's opinion indicates that when information in the broker's file falls outside of the regulatory presumption of what is "reasonably current," the broker bears the burden of producing documentation showing that the information in its files is nevertheless reasonably current. Although Rule 15c2-11 says nothing explicit about the burden of production, we find that SEC's interpretation is fairly implied by the rule's express requirements, which place an affirmative duty on the broker to maintain reasonably current information. See 17 C.F.R. §240.15c2-11 ("It shall be unlawful for any broker or dealer to publish any quotation for a security or … to submit any quotation for publication … unless such broker or dealer has in its records the documents and information required by this paragraph….

* * *

5. Sanctions. General Bond's final argument is that the sanctions affirmed by SEC were excessive and constituted an abuse of discretion. General Bond contends that, because Mr. Pandolfo is now deceased, the sanctions imposed "impact no one except Mr. Pandolfo's estate and the heirs thereunder."

General Bond is the petitioner in this case, not Mr. Pandolfo or his heirs. Our review is limited to determining whether the Commission abused its discretion in connection with the sanctions imposed upon General Bond for its violations of NASD Rules.

As is evidenced by the opinion of the National Business Conduct Committee, the sanctions affirmed by SEC consisted of censure and an assessment of costs of $ 1,114, expulsion of General Bond from membership, a fine of $25,750 "representing the ill-gotten gains attributable to the listing fees charged by [General Bond]," and a fine of $20,000 "representing the monetary sanction attributable to [General Bond's] failures to respond."

With the exception of the fine of $25,750, we affirm the sanctions imposed by SEC….

The fine of $25,750 imposed below, which was said to represent General Bond's "ill-gotten gains," was based at least in part on General Bond's acceptance of compensation for listings in the pink sheets. Inasmuch as we have determined that Article III, Section 1 did not prohibit such conduct at the time General Bond engaged in it, we find it necessary to vacate that portion of the fine imposed. No sanction should be imposed for that alleged violation. The record does not disclose, however, whether this $25,750 was also based in part on any of the other violations committed by General Bond or whether the imposition of such a fine is necessary to adequately remedy these other violations. Accordingly, we remand the case to SEC for a reconsideration of whether this portion of the fine is appropriate.

The order of the Commission is affirmed in part and vacated in part. The case is remanded to SEC for reconsideration of a portion of the sanctions imposed upon Petitioner.

———

Notes and Questions

1. *FINRA Rule 5250. Payments for Market Making.* FINRA Rule 5250, which is the current codification of the policy/guidance that FINRA and the SEC relied on in *General Bond Share Co.*, prohibits broker-dealers from accepting any payment or other consideration from an issuer for publishing a quotation or acting as a market maker in the issuer's security. However, FINRA Rule 5250 does permit broker-dealers to accept payment for bona fide services, such as investment banking services and reimbursement for listing fees imposed by SROs and registration fees

imposed by the SEC or state regulatory authorities. How, if at all, is payment of these regulatory fees for bona fide services different from the prohibited payments to market makers discussed in *General Bond Share Co.*?

2. *Exchange Act Rule 15c2-11.* Rule 15c2-11 requires broker-dealers to obtain specified information from issuers to publish any quotation for a security or to submit a quotation for a security in any quotation medium. It also requires the broker-dealer to have a reasonable basis to believe that the information obtained from the issuer is accurate in all material respects and that the sources of such information are reliable. Securities Exchange Act Release No. 29094 (April 17, 1991) discusses procedures for gathering and reviewing the information required by Rule 15c2-11. Identify two types of information required under Rule 15c2-11 and the corresponding procedures for gathering and reviewing the information.

3. Effective in 2011, FINRA implemented new rules that extend certain Reg NMS protections to quoting and trading OTC equity securities. The new rules set forth permissible pricing increments for displaying quotations and accepting orders, required broker-dealers to avoid locking and crossing quotations within an inter-dealer quotation system; established a cap on access fees imposed against a broker-dealer's published quotations, and required OTC market makers (with certain exceptions) to display the full size of customer limit orders that improve the market maker's displayed quotation or that represent more than a de minimis change in the size of the market maker's quote if at the best bid or offer. *See* FINRA Rules 5310, 6240, 6434, 6437, 6450, 6460, and 6540.

4. OTC Reporting Facility. FINRA maintains the OTC Reporting Facility (ORF) for reporting trades in OTC Equity securities. Broker-dealers using ORF must comply with the Rule 6600 and 7300 Series.

Hypothetical Three

Sean O'Connor, a research analyst at Success First, and Naomi Watts, Success First's regional director for its southeast region, are meeting with Baltimore Apps, Inc. ("Baltimore Apps"), a Baltimore, Maryland, company. During the meeting, Justin McGibbon, Baltimore Apps' CEO, asks if Success First might have an interest in making a market in its equity securities in OTC markets. Baltimore Apps is an Internet company that develops and sells mobile software applications for smartphones and tablets. McGibbon tells Sean and Naomi that he understands that Success First will incur expenses for publishing a quotation and/or acting as a market maker for its securities. McGibbon is willing to pay Success First's out-of-pocket expenses for publishing a quotation and acting as a market maker in in Baltimore Apps' equity securities. McGibbon also tells Sean and Naomi that he would be willing to provide financial statements (a balance sheet and a profit and loss statement) for Baltimore Apps as they become available, but that the financial information is prepared internally by its in-house accountant; at this point, Baltimore Apps does not have sufficient capital to pay a certified independent accountant. Would Success First violate FINRA Rule 5250 and/or Exchange Act Rule 15c2-11 if it agrees to publish quotations in OTC markets and to act as a market maker for Baltimore Apps?

Chapter 14

Regulation of Trading Venues

Regulatory Authority

Securities Exchange Act of 1934 Sections 3(a)(1), 3(a)(23), 6, 10(b), 11(b), 11A(c)(1), 15, 17(a), 17A, 19, 21(a), 21B(a)(3), 21C

Exchange Act Rules 3a1-1, 3b-16, 6a-1–6a-3, 11b-1, 10b-5, 17a-3, 17a-4(b)(1), 17Ab2-1, 17Ad-22, Regulation ATS (Rules 300-303), Regulation SHO (Rules 200–204)

FINRA Rules 2010, 2121, 4311, 4560, 5210, 5310, 6350A, 6350B, 6420, 9216

Motivating Hypothetical

Success First's new trainee program is almost completed. Six months ago, Success First established a new trainee program to ensure loyalty and the depth of knowledge needed for the broker-dealer industry from Success First's perspective. Trainees successfully completing the program will be hired after a 14-month probationary program. John DoGoode, a 10-year registered representative working in compliance, has been assigned as a mentor to the trainees. The training program included a basic understanding of the financial responsibility and books and records requirements under federal securities laws and FINRA rules. Modules in the financial responsibility unit included net capital and the customer protection rule. The last unit of the training program consists of an introduction to trading venues used by Success First in its daily operations. The trainees are required to study the materials in this chapter in preparation for the comprehensive exam administered at the end of the training program.

I. Introduction

This chapter provides an overview of the regulatory framework governing the primary trading venues for equity securities in the U.S. securities markets. The rules governing national securities exchanges and alternative trading systems are examined, along with the broker-dealer's obligation of best execution when effecting transactions on exchanges and ATSs. Trading venues registered with the SEC as SROs play a special role in monitoring compliance with the federal securities laws by their member broker-dealers. They are also important participants in the SEC's efforts regarding market stability, quality, and fairness in the U.S. securities markets.

Although this chapter discusses the dominant national securities exchanges for trading equity securities in U.S. securities markets, there are approximately 22 national securities exchanges registered with the SEC providing trading facilities for various types of securities. The SEC exercises oversight of the national securities exchanges through its staff in the Division of Trading and Markets and maintains a list of currently registered national securities exchanges along with pending applications on its web site. It also lists exchanges that are no longer registered with the SEC.

II. Trading Venues

A. National Securities Exchanges

An exchange is defined in Section 3(a)(1) of the Exchange Act as any organization " … which constitutes, maintains, or provides a market place or facilities for bringing together purchasers and sellers of securities … and includes the marketplace and the market facilities maintained by such exchange." Rule 3b-16 of the Exchange Act further provides that an exchange must use established, non-discretionary methods under which orders between purchasers and sellers interact with each other and under which purchasers and sellers agree to the terms of a trade. For many years there was one dominant registered national securities exchange with respect to trading in equity securities — the New York Stock Exchange ("NYSE"). However, with registration of the NASDAQ Stock Market ("NASDAQ") in 2007, there are now two dominant registered national securities exchanges. Although much has changed in the governance and operation of registered national securities exchanges in U.S. securities markets, the NYSE and NASDAQ continue to garner the lion's share of the market for trading in equity securities.

Registered exchanges function as SROs and marketplace facilities in the national market system, with extensive regulatory power in U.S. securities markets. Congress adopted a regulatory framework making the exchanges directly responsible for enforcement of the federal securities laws and for establishing standards of professional conduct for their broker-dealer members and associated persons. The SEC, under Sections 6 and 19 of the Exchange Act, was given oversight responsibilities with respect to the operation of national securities exchanges in their capacity as SROs in the regulatory framework, to ensure the effectiveness of the system of self-regulation adopted by Congress. Section 6 of the Exchange Act provides for the registration of a national securities exchange with the SEC under specified terms and conditions and in accordance with the provisions of Section 19(a) of the Exchange Act. The exchange must file an application for registration on Form 1 with the SEC. The exchange must file Form 1 even if it is exempt from the registration requirements of Section 6 based on limited volume. The information contained in Form 1 provides the SEC with the information necessary to perform its oversight functions and to determine whether the exchange has the capacity to perform its regulatory responsibilities; the SEC also uses Form 1 to determine whether an exchange qualifies for an exemption from the registration requirements of Section 6. Rules 6a-1 through 6a-3, along with the instructions contained in Form 1, enumerate the type of information and frequency of submission required under Section 6. *See* Table 14.1 for a summary of statutes and rules governing the registration framework of registered national exchanges.

Table 14.1

Statute/Rule	Description
Section 6 of the Exchange Act [15 U.S.C. § 78f]	Registration with the SEC by filing an application. Establishes criteria for obtaining status as registered national securities exchange or SRO.
Rules 6a-1 through 6a-3 of the Exchange Act [17 C.F.R. § 240.6a-1–6a-3]	Designates required application form (Form 1) and provides instructions for completing the application form.
Section 19 of the Exchange Act [15 U.S.C. § 78s]	Procedures for granting/denying SRO status, SRO rulemaking process, and review of SRO final disciplinary actions.

Section 6 of the Exchange Act prohibits the SEC from conferring SRO status on an exchange unless it meets certain criteria focused on its organization, rulemaking authority, and policing of its broker-dealer members. The exchange must assure fair representation of its members in the selection of its directors and administration of its affairs and also must include directors representative of issuers and investors who are not associated with the exchange or a broker-dealer member. Its rules must be designed to prevent fraudulent and manipulative acts and practices, to promote just and equitable principles of trade, to remove any impediments to the national market system, and to protect investors and the public interest. The exchange must have a mechanism for allowing only registered broker-dealers to become members of the exchange; membership may be denied if the broker-dealer does not meet standards of financial responsibility or operational capacity and its associated persons do not meet standards of training, experience, and competence prescribed in the rules of the exchange. Notably, the exchange may bar any person from becoming associated with a member broker-dealer if they refuse to supply information and to permit examination of books and records to verify the accuracy of such information. The rules of the exchange must prescribe procedures and policies to appropriately discipline its members and their associated persons for violating the federal securities laws and may impose sanctions for such violations, including expulsion, suspension, or fines. However, Section 6 establishes specific criteria for any proceeding to determine whether a member should be disciplined, including requiring the exchange to bring specific charges and allow the member broker-dealer or its associated person an opportunity to defend against such charges. Overall, the exchange as an SRO must have the capacity to stand in the shoes of the SEC in interpreting securities laws for its members and in monitoring compliance with applicable securities laws and the exchange's own rules. The following administrative proceeding discusses the responsibilities conferred by SRO status as a registered national securities exchange, the importance of SRO status in facilitating a fair and efficient national market system, and the SEC's oversight role with respect to SROs.

Securities and Exchange Commission (S.E.C.)
In the Matter of New York Stock Exchange, Inc., Respondent
Administrative Proceeding File No. 3-11892 (Apr. 12, 2005)

I.

The Securities and Exchange Commission ("Commission") deems it necessary and appropriate in the public interest and for the protection of investors that public administrative proceedings be, and hereby are, instituted pursuant to Sections 19(h) and 21C of the Securities Exchange Act of 1934 ("Exchange Act") against the New York Stock Exchange, Inc. ("NYSE").

II.

In anticipation of the institution of these proceedings, the NYSE has submitted an Offer of Settlement (the "Offer") that the Commission has determined to accept....

III.

On the basis of this Order and the Offer submitted by the NYSE, the Commission finds that:

A. RESPONDENT

1. The NYSE is a New York not-for-profit corporation that is, and at all times relevant hereto was, registered with the Commission as a national securities exchange pursuant to Section 6 of the Exchange Act. The NYSE first registered as a national securities exchange with the Commission on October 1, 1934....

B. FACTS

Summary

* * *

2. This matter concerns the failure of the NYSE to properly detect, investigate, and discipline widespread unlawful proprietary trading by specialists on the floor of the NYSE. Section 19(g)(1) of the Exchange Act obligates the NYSE, as a self-regulatory organization ("SRO"), to comply, and enforce compliance by its members, with the Exchange Act, the rules and regulations thereunder, and the rules of the NYSE. In carrying out its duty to "enforce compliance," SROs must develop and maintain surveillance over its members, and "be vigilant in surveilling for, evaluating, and effectively addressing issues that could involve violations" of the securities laws. (citation omitted).

* * *

Overview of Specialists' Obligations

6. In the NYSE's continuous two-way agency auction market, specialist firms are responsible for the quality of the markets in the securities in which individual specialists are registered. A specialist is expected to maintain, insofar as reasonably practicable, a "fair" and "orderly" market. Specialists have two primary duties in maintaining a fair and orderly market: performing their "negative obligation" to execute customer orders at the most advantageous price with minimal dealer intervention, and fulfilling their "affirmative obligation" to offset imbalances in supply and demand. Specialists participate as both broker (or agent), absenting themselves from the market to pair executable customer orders against each other, and as dealer (or principal), trading for the specialists' dealer or proprietary accounts when needed to facilitate price continuity and fill customer orders when there are no available contra parties to those orders.

7. Whether acting as brokers or dealers, specialists are required to hold the public's interests above their own and, as such, are prohibited from trading for their dealers' accounts ahead of pre-existing customer buy or sell orders that are executable against each other. When matchable customer buy and sell orders arrive at specialists' trading posts—generally either through the NYSE's Super Designated Order Turnaround System ("DOT")[1] to an electronic display book (the "Display Book"),[2] or by floor brokers gathered in front of the specialists' trading posts—specialists are required to act as agent, and cross or pair off those orders and to abstain from participating as principal or dealer.

8. The specialists' obligations are embodied in the federal securities laws and NYSE rules, which prohibit trading ahead and interpositioning. Section 11(b) of the Exchange Act and Rule 11b-1 thereunder limit a specialist's dealer transactions to those "reasonably necessary to permit him to maintain a fair and orderly market."[3] NYSE Rule 92 provides that "no member or member organization shall cause the entry of an order to buy (sell) any Exchange-listed security for any account in which such member or member organization ... is directly or indirectly interested (a 'proprietary order'), if the person responsible for the entry of such order has knowledge of any particular unexecuted customer's order to buy (sell) such security which could be executed at the same price." NYSE Rule 104.10 states in relevant part: "No specialist

---

1. [2] The DOT system is the NYSE's primary order processing system, supporting equity trading on the trading floor and providing the NYSE with the current status of any equity order. Customers can transmit orders through NYSE member organizations electronically to the floor through the DOT system.

2. [3] The Display Book is an electronic workstation provided by the NYSE to the firm for use by its specialists at their post panels, operated by means of a customized keyboard containing function, letter, number, and arrow keys. The Display Book allows specialists to, among other things, receive and process orders, disseminate trade and quote information, report trade executions, research order and execution status, manage positions and view profit and loss in the dealer account.

3. [4] Where specialists effect trades for their accounts that are not "reasonably necessary to permit [such specialists] to maintain a fair and orderly market," they have violated Section 11(b) and Rule 11b-1 of the Exchange Act.

shall effect ... purchases or sales of any security in which such specialist is registered ... unless such dealings are reasonably necessary to permit such specialist to maintain a fair and orderly market."

The NYSE's Obligation to Regulate the Conduct of Specialists

9. Section 6(b) of the Exchange Act requires the NYSE, as a national securities exchange, to have the capacity to be able to carry out the purposes of the Exchange Act and to comply, and to enforce compliance by its members, with the rules and regulations of the Exchange Act and the NYSE's own rules. Rule 11b-1 under the Exchange Act sets forth the specific rules that a national securities exchange must have if it registers its members to act as specialists. Sections 19(g) and 19(h) of the Exchange Act further require the NYSE, as a self-regulatory organization, to comply with, and enforce the provisions of, the Exchange Act, the rules and regulations thereunder and its own rules. The NYSE has an affirmative obligation to be vigilant in surveilling for, evaluating, and effectively addressing activity that could involve violations of these provisions.

10. The NYSE's Regulatory Group has the responsibility to enforce compliance by its members with the Exchange Act, the rules and regulations thereunder, and the NYSE's own rules. During the relevant time period, the Regulatory Group was comprised of three divisions: (1) Market Surveillance; (2) Member Firm Regulation; and (3) the Enforcement Division. Market Surveillance had the principal responsibility to surveil and investigate specialists for trading violations. Specialist Surveillance, a unit of Member Trading II, a department of Market Surveillance, was primarily responsible for conducting surveillance of specialists' trading. Analysts within Specialist Surveillance reviewed "alerts" from automated surveillances and referred potential violations to Trading Investigations, which during the relevant time period was also organized within the Member Trading II department of Market Surveillance. Trading Investigations was responsible for conducting in-depth investigations of potential rule violations referred by, among others, Specialist Surveillance. Market Surveillance, based on the results of the investigation, could impose informal discipline, primarily letters of admonition or summary fines, but serious rule violations had to be referred to the NYSE's Enforcement Division with a recommendation for formal disciplinary action.

The NYSE's Failure to Enforce Statutes and Rules Governing Trading by Specialists

The Specialists' Unlawful Trading Ahead and Interpositioning

11. During the period January 1999 through 2003, various NYSE specialists repeatedly violated their duty to refrain from dealing for their own accounts while in possession of buy and sell customer orders executable against each other. They did this primarily in two ways: (i) by "interpositioning"—*i.e.*, effecting two improper proprietary trades close in time by filling *both* opposing orders from the proprietary account at prices that enable the specialist firm to profit from the spread between both prices; and (ii) by "trading ahead"—*i.e.* filling one executable order out of the firm's own account instead of matching it with another executable public order—and then by filling the second executable public order through an agency trade at a less advantageous price.

12. The unlawful proprietary trading by NYSE specialists was widespread and pervasive, involving all seven equity specialist firms operating on the NYSE. In March and July 2004, the Commission and the NYSE instituted settled administrative proceedings against all seven firms. The Commission and the NYSE found that, between 1999 and 2003, these specialist firms (i) willfully violated Section 11(b) of the Exchange Act and Rule 11b-1 thereunder; (ii) violated various NYSE rules, including NYSE Rules 92 and 104.10; and (iii) failed adequately to supervise certain specialists, who themselves engaged in fraud through proprietary trading in violation of Section 10(b) of the Exchange Act and Rule 10b-5 thereunder. The Commission and the NYSE further found that unlawful proprietary trading at the seven specialist firms caused in the aggregate more than $158 million in customer harm. Pursuant to the settlements between the specialist firms, the Commission and the NYSE, the specialist firms agreed to disgorge this amount and were penalized a total of $90 million.

The NYSE Failed to Adequately Surveil for Trading Ahead and Interpositioning Violations

13. From 1999 through almost all of 2002, the NYSE's surveillance systems failed to detect the vast majority of trading ahead and interpositioning by specialists. This failure was in part due to the NYSE's reliance on an automated surveillance system whose parameters and procedures were unnecessarily and unreasonably broad. The DOT Inferior Price Execution Surveillance ("DOT Surveillance") had been implemented by the NYSE in the late 1980s to detect trading ahead by specialists. When specialists engaged in trading that exceeded certain parameters of the DOT Surveillance, alerts were generated identifying potential trading ahead activity. The most significant parameters of the DOT Surveillance were the time and spread parameters.

14. Although every instance of trading ahead and interpositioning constitutes a violation, the DOT Surveillance only generated an alert if the specialist traded ahead of an agency DOT order that had been visible on the Display Book for a certain period of time. From 1999 through 2002, the time parameter was reduced from 90 seconds to 60 seconds, but was consistently set beyond a level that could be reasonably justified. As a result of using unnecessarily long time parameters, the DOT Surveillance failed to detect the vast majority of trading ahead and interpositioning violations.

15. Similarly, the DOT Surveillance only generated an alert if there was a certain price spread in the specialist's quote (bid and ask) at the time the specialist traded ahead of the customer agency order. Historically, the spread parameter was set at the minimum price variation for trades in a security. In the late 1990s, when the minimum trading increment was a 1/16th of a dollar ($.0625), the spread parameter was $.0625. However, the $.0625 spread parameter remained in place until June 2002, nearly one and a half years after decimalization of stock quotes, which reduced the minimum price variation to one cent. In June 2002, the NYSE lowered the spread parameter slightly to five cents. There is no reasonable justification for a spread parameter beyond the minimum price increment. Because the DOT Surveillance did not capture vio-

lations involving small monetary amounts, the specialists were able to trade in small increments and evade detection.

16. Over the years, the NYSE's internal audit group, Regulatory Quality Review ("RQR"), and others advised Market Surveillance on several occasions that the parameters of the DOT Surveillance were unnecessarily broad and recommended reducing the parameters. For example, in 1999 when the time parameter was 90 seconds, RQR issued a report that concluded: "Not to surveil specialists for 90 seconds increases the likelihood that a specialist taking advantage of his dealer and agency capacities for self-interest would remain undetected by Market Surveillance." Similarly, in 2001 and 2002, sample tests were performed by an employee in Market Surveillance's Automation Data Group using a narrower spread parameter, revealing a significant increase in the number of alerts generated. Despite repeated indications that the parameters were too broad, the NYSE made only incremental changes to the DOT Surveillance. The NYSE knew or should have known that these incremental changes were inadequate to gauge the full extent of the trading ahead activity.

17. In addition, the NYSE incorporated an unreasonably narrow review period for the DOT Surveillance. From at least 1996 until June 2002, Specialist Surveillance analysts generally reviewed alerts for each specialist firm for a single day chosen at random each month.[4] As early as 1996, RQR recommended expanding the review period to one week in order for analysts to better surveil for trading ahead. RQR proposed that the DOT Surveillance generate alerts for an entire week before the analyst selected which day to review. RQR observed that Specialist Surveillance had, on a number of occasions, failed to conduct any review for trading ahead and interpositioning because no alerts were generated for the single day that was randomly selected for review. Despite the fact that Market Surveillance agreed in 1996 to adopt this change, Market Surveillance did not implement a one-week review period until June 2002.

18. The NYSE did not establish an automated surveillance system specifically designed to detect interpositioning misconduct until late 2002. Although the DOT Surveillance was intended to capture trading ahead violations, the surveillance did not automatically detect interpositioning violations. Rather, Market Surveillance staff used a manual process of reviewing trade data for interpositioning. The NYSE knew that interpositioning was an egregious form of trading ahead and considered this type of conduct a serious regulatory concern. The 1998 and 1999 versions of the Specialist Surveillance procedures manual instructed Specialist Surveillance analysts to "be especially aware of situations where the specialist, after buying/selling the stock,

---

4. [6] Analysts were generally only required to review a maximum of three alerts for three different stocks. The three stocks were selected pursuant to a specified selection process. If any of these alerts for these three stocks were found to reflect potential violations, the review would be expanded to alerts in the same stock[s] generated for other days in the same week. In 1999, the procedure was changed to require an expanded review of alerts for the same post-panel generated for the rest of the week.

turns around and sells/buys stock against the system order at a profit." However, the 2000 version of the Specialist Surveillance procedures manual, drafted after the 1999 Order, de-emphasized the detection of interpositioning by merely instructing analysts to "also review[] inferior price execution situations for specialist arbitrage." Despite knowledge of interpositioning violations, the NYSE did not begin to develop a surveillance system specifically designed to capture interpositioning until mid-2002 and did not fully implement such a system until late 2002.

The NYSE Failed to Adequately Investigate Trading Ahead and Interpositioning Violations

19. Even though the surveillance parameters were unnecessarily broad, they still generated numerous alerts that put the NYSE on notice that trading ahead and interpositioning was widespread. From 1999 through 2002, the DOT Surveillance generated close to 4,000 alerts.[5] Nonetheless, because of inadequate sampling and selection procedures, the NYSE only reviewed a portion of the alerts generated, and because of inadequate referral procedures (requiring a pattern of likely violations), Specialist Surveillance only referred a smaller fraction of the alerts — approximately 200 — for further investigation. For example, in April 1999, hundreds of alerts were generated for two specialist firms. At one specialist firm, there were over 100 alerts, with 12 alerts in a single specialist's post and panel and multiple alerts in 19 different stocks. Also in April 1999, at another specialist firm, there were almost 200 alerts, including over 40 alerts in a single stock and 10 or more alerts in two other stocks. Yet, the surveillance analysts failed to refer any of these alerts for further investigation. When alerts were referred for further investigation, pursuant to Market Surveillance procedures, Specialist Surveillance only reviewed and referred a small portion of the total alerts generated. For example, at one specialist firm, there were at least 140 alerts in a seven month time period in 2000; yet, Specialist Surveillance referred only 28 of these alerts, failing to refer multiple alerts in several stocks.

20. Some of the failures by the NYSE's Specialist Surveillance unit included: (1) Specialist Surveillance regularly overlooked likely instances of trading ahead and interpositioning, even when the specialist firms under review had recently been informally disciplined; (2) due primarily to inadequate referral procedures, Specialist Surveillance failed to refer the full extent of trading ahead and interpositioning conduct to Trading Investigations; (3) despite procedures that called for regular and routine surveillance of specialist firms, Specialist Surveillance in at least two instances suspended DOT Surveillance reviews of specialist firms for a period of time after disciplinary action was imposed; and (4) although Rule 92 explicitly prohibits trading ahead conduct, Specialist Surveillance almost always referred likely trading ahead and interpositioning violations to Trading Investigations under Rule 104.10. Rule 92

---

5. [7] According to Specialist Surveillance management and analysts, approximately 75% of the alerts they reviewed were likely trading ahead violations.

violations (which generally require proof of intent) would generally have necessitated a referral to Enforcement for formal disciplinary action; by contrast, Rule 104.10 violations (which do not require proof of intent) could be sanctioned informally by Market Surveillance.

21. Trading Investigations failed to adequately investigate trading ahead and interpositioning misconduct. Trading Investigations had the responsibility to properly investigate trading ahead and interpositioning violations, which included determining (1) the extent of such conduct; (2) whether specialists were engaging in repeated instances of misconduct; (3) whether the misconduct was intentional; and (4) whether the conduct should be referred to the Enforcement Division with a recommendation for formal disciplinary action.

22. Trading Investigations, however, failed in these responsibilities in a number of ways. Investigators did not conduct a thorough investigation of the trading ahead and interpositioning instances that were referred to them. Trading Investigations merely confirmed the specific instances of trading ahead and interpositioning that Specialist Surveillance had referred and did not investigate whether the specialists or specialist firms involved had engaged in additional trading ahead or interpositioning. Investigators believed it was Specialist Surveillance that was responsible for determining the extent of the misconduct.[6] Furthermore, investigators did not examine or probe the specialists' intent. Other than soliciting an explanation from the firm, which always stated that the trading ahead was accidental, Trading Investigations did not undertake any effort to determine whether the trading ahead was in fact intentional. For example, in an investigation of 28 instances of trading ahead at one specialist firm in 2001, the firm responded in writing that most of the instances were "inadvertent clerical error." As a result, the investigators concluded that "the[se] occurrences appear to be more operational in nature." The investigators did not interview the specialist or his clerk, but simply relied on the firm's written response in determining to impose only informal discipline.[7] Finally, Trading Investigations usually did not expand its reviews of trading ahead to other time periods. In the limited instances

---

6. [9] Investigators often lacked basic knowledge of the DOT Surveillance and the selection procedures that Specialist Surveillance used for its referrals. Some investigators erroneously believed that Specialist Surveillance reviewed all alerts generated and referred all alerts that were not false positives. Investigators also did not know how the Display Book operated. This lack of knowledge significantly impaired the investigators' ability to fully investigate instances of trading ahead and interpositioning.

7. [10] Trading ahead and interpositioning require several deliberate steps executed on the Display Book by the specialist or his clerk that demonstrate a specialists' intent. The Display Book highlights in yellow marketable customer orders. To fill a customer order with a specialist's dealer trade, the specialist or his clerk must take the Display Book out of its "default mode" and input several other keyboard commands. Pairing off two customer orders requires only two keystrokes, whereas trading ahead and interpositioning conduct requires several extra keystrokes. The investigative files do not reflect any attempt to reconcile specialists' repeated claims that multiple instances of trading ahead and interpositioning were "inadvertent" with the fact that such conduct required the specialists to undertake several deliberate steps.

that Trading Investigations expanded its reviews, the expansion was cursory in nature and lacked adequate review.[8]

23. Moreover, Market Surveillance failed to pursue what it considered *de minimis* violations, *i.e.* violations that only caused a small amount of customer harm or only resulted in a small amount of specialist gain. For example, in September 1999, Member Firm Regulation referred a single instance of possible interpositioning to Trading Investigations, which did not review the conduct further because it concluded that the customer disadvantage resulting from this single trade ($37) was *de minimis*. In these types of situations, Market Surveillance wrongly assumed that specialists would not knowingly engage in unlawful conduct for a small amount of pecuniary gain. In fact, various specialists repeatedly engaged in small scale unlawful transactions that in the aggregate added up to tens of millions of dollars.

24. In addition to Specialist Surveillance and Trading Investigations, other units at the NYSE, specifically Member Firm Regulation, which conducts annual and "for cause" examinations of NYSE members, and the Trading Correspondence unit, which handles complaints from member firms and the public, also detected trading ahead conduct during the period 1999 through 2002. Member Firm Regulation referred several trading ahead violations it detected to Market Surveillance under Rule 92 and expected that Trading Investigations would conduct a full investigation of the violative conduct. Trading Investigations, however, during the relevant time period, failed to fully investigate the referred conduct and considered only whether the referred conduct violated Rule 104.10. For example, in August 2001, an examination of one specialist firm by Member Firm Regulation uncovered a significant amount of trading ahead by a single specialist: 94 instances of trading ahead in one stock on a single day, and 44 instances of trading ahead in another stock in a 1 1/2 hour period on that same day. Member Firm Regulation referred the conduct to Trading Investigations in November 2001; yet, Trading Investigations failed to take timely action to investigate this conduct. The Trading Correspondence unit also received customer complaints involving trading ahead misconduct, which in some cases involved significant monetary disadvantage to the customer. The Trading Correspondence unit generally took no disciplinary action so long as the specialist firm agreed to pay back the disadvantaged customer.

The NYSE Failed to Appropriately Discipline Trading Ahead and Interpositioning Violations

25. Trading Investigations failed to recommend appropriate discipline of specialists for trading ahead and interpositioning. Throughout the relevant time period, Trading

---

8. [11] For example, in an investigation of 7 instances of trading ahead and interpositioning at one specialist firm in 2002, Trading Investigations noted that in reaching its decision to impose informal discipline, it had conducted an "expanded" review comprised of additional trade dates during 5 different calendar months and determined that there were no additional violations. In fact, the expanded review yielded several additional trading ahead alerts in the stocks surveyed.

Investigations was the sole NYSE unit recommending discipline of specialists for trading ahead and interpositioning violations. The discipline almost always took the form of informal discipline consisting of admonition letters and summary fines.[9] Historically, the NYSE's Regulatory Group considered informal disciplinary actions as "warnings" to the specialists firms that further trading misconduct could lead to formal enforcement action. During the period 1999 to 2002, however, the informal disciplinary actions were not used to "warn" the firms that if they engaged in additional violations in the future, they would face formal regulatory action. Instead, repeat violations were generally addressed by additional informal action rather than a referral to Enforcement for formal disciplinary proceedings. With respect to trading ahead and interpositioning violations, the NYSE's Regulatory Group treated the informal disciplinary actions as similar in nature to "traffic tickets," which were not followed up with more formal regulatory action.

26. Trading Investigations also failed to consider whether the trading ahead and interpositioning instances it was investigating warranted a referral to the Enforcement Division for formal discipline under Rule 92. Instead, when Trading Investigations received a trading ahead referral, it treated the conduct as a minor technical violation of Rule 104.10. Even where the specialist firms engaged in recidivist conduct, the NYSE still failed to refer matters for formal disciplinary action.... from 1999 to December 2002, Trading Investigations did not refer any trading ahead or interpositioning violations to the Enforcement Division.

* * *

Actions Taken by the NYSE

28. In June 2002, after discovering significant interpositioning activity by a single specialist that had occurred as early as January 2000, the NYSE began developing a special study to assess the extent of interpositioning practices throughout the trading floor. The study, which culminated in a December 2002 report on interpositioning in all NYSE stocks for a three-month period, revealed widespread interpositioning conduct by various specialists, and prompted the NYSE to open a broader investigation into the unlawful trading. Since that time, the NYSE has undertaken various measures to address its regulatory failures in policing trading ahead and interpositioning, including changes to its surveillance system and implementation of computer software to better enable the NYSE to detect ongoing trading ahead and interpositioning. The NYSE and the Commission further investigated such violations and instituted formal disciplinary proceedings, which led to settled enforcement actions against all seven equity specialist firms.

29. The NYSE has recently made extensive changes to its governance and regulatory structure. These changes include: (1) amendments to the NYSE constitution that re-

---

9. [13] There were a total of 6 admonition letters and 24 summary fines for trading ahead and interpositioning misconduct from 1999 through December 2002. Summary fines typically ranged from $500 to $1,000 for trading ahead misconduct. The total of the 24 summary fines was approximately $17,500 ($2,500 in 1999, $3,000 in 2000, $500 in 2001, and $11,500 in 2002).

quire all directors to be independent from members, member organizations, listed companies and (except for the CEO) management, and give the independent directors sole authority over the NYSE's conduct of its regulatory functions; (2) the creation of the new position of Chief Regulatory Officer, which reports to the Board of Directors, rather than senior NYSE management; (3) the creation of a standing Board of Directors committee, the Regulatory Oversight Committee, with direct oversight of all budgetary, compensation and staffing decisions affecting the NYSE's regulatory function, including those affecting RQR; (4) the appointment of a new head of regulation as the Chief Regulatory Officer and new leadership in the NYSE's Divisions of Market Surveillance, Member Firm Regulation and Enforcement; (5) moving Trading Investigations from Market Surveillance to Enforcement, in order to foster more consistent determinations of whether formal or informal discipline is appropriate; (6) the creation of a new Specialist Surveillance unit to focus exclusively on the effectiveness of existing surveillances and the need for new or modified surveillances; (7) the creation of the Risk Assessment Unit, which analyzes trends and conducts risk assessment for the NYSE's Regulatory Group (now known as NYSE Regulation); (8) increases in staff and other resources available to the NYSE's regulatory units, including Market Surveillance; and (9) the retention by the Regulatory Oversight Committee of an independent consultant, who has reviewed the NYSE's oversight of specialist trading.

* * *

D. CONCLUSION

31. Section 19(g)(1) of the Exchange Act requires the NYSE, "absent reasonable justification or excuse," to enforce compliance by its members with provisions of the Exchange Act, the rules and regulations thereunder, and the NYSE's own rules.[10] The Commission has stated that "the obligation to enforce imposed by Section 19(g) on an exchange necessarily includes an obligation to monitor and maintain surveillance over its members." (citations omitted). Exchanges violate Section 19(g) when they fail "to be vigilant in surveilling for, evaluating, and effectively addressing issues that could involve violations of the securities laws." (citations omitted)

———

Registered national securities exchanges, such as the NYSE and NASDAQ, operate facilities for trading. Most trading facilities are electronic, although the NYSE maintains a physical floor. A security may not be traded on a national securities exchange unless it is listed on the exchange or has been extended unlisted trading privileges by the particular exchange. Each exchange has its own initial listing and maintenance

———

10. [14] An SRO is relieved of its obligation to enforce compliance only when there is "reasonable justification or excuse" to fail to detect and stop violative conduct. (citation omitted). There is no "reasonable justification or excuse" when an SRO knew, or, in view of all the facts and circumstances, should have known that its systems of reports, examinations and inspections were materially inadequate relative to the resources reasonably available to that SRO for detecting the misconduct (citation omitted).

criteria. These criteria include both quantitative and qualitative standards. For example, quantitative standards for initial listing for common equity securities on the NYSE include aggregate adjusted pre-tax income for the last three fiscal years of $10 million or more and a minimum share price of $4. Qualitative standards are extensive and include corporate governance requirements such as a board comprised of a majority of independent directors and an audit committee composed of independent directors who are financially literate, one of whom must have accounting or related financial management expertise. Maintenance listing requirements similarly include both quantitative and qualitative standards such as a minimum stock price of $1.00 and timely, adequate disclosures to shareholders and the investing public.

Notes and Questions

1. National securities exchanges, as SROs, stand in the shoes of the SEC in monitoring compliance with many federal securities laws. Accordingly, national securities exchanges are entitled to the same immunity enjoyed by the SEC when performing functions delegated by the SEC to the exchange. *D'Alessio v N.Y. Stock Exch., Inc.* (2001, CA2 N.Y.) 258 F.3d 93, CCH Fed Secur. L. Rep. P. 91523, *cert. den.* (2001) 534 U.S. 1066, 122 S. Ct. 666, 151 L. Ed. 2d 580 and (criticized in *Rubel v Pfizer Inc.* (2003, N.D. Ill.) 276 F. Supp. 2d 904).

2. The SEC's oversight authority includes more than assessing fines and penalties against national securities exchanges that fail to properly perform their delegated regulatory functions. The SEC also imposes undertakings, i.e., mandated changes to the operation and governance of the exchange. For example, in *In the Matter of New York Stock Exchange*, Admin. File No. 3-11892 (Apr. 12, 2005), reviewed above, the SEC required, among other undertakings, the NYSE to retain a third-party regulatory auditor to conduct a comprehensive regulatory audit of NYSE's surveillance, examination, investigation, and disciplinary programs applicable to specialists, member floor brokers, independent brokers, and registered market makers every two years for a total of four two-year periods. Is this an effective sanction?

Hypothetical One

Success First has been hired by Durham, Inc., an entertainment company that owns several television stations and cable television operations, to conduct an IPO of its equity securities. Katie Jerome, a registered representative working in Success First's investment banking division, is leading the team for Durham's IPO. At this point, Katie is considering conducting the IPO on NASDAQ. NASDAQ has several listing tiers and she is unsure of their initial listing requirements. Katie has asked Malak Johnson, Success First's chief compliance officer, if he would obtain this information to assist in her decision making. Malak has given this assignment to Ashly

Beaver, a compliance staff person. Malak has instructed Ashly to identify NASDAQ's listing tiers and their corresponding requirements for initial listing by close of business tomorrow. Identify NASDAQ's listing tiers and at least three qualitative and quantitative initial listing requirements for each of the identified tiers. Which tier has the most stringent initial listing requirements?

B. Alternative Trading Systems

Alternative trading systems ("ATSs"), operated by broker-dealers, are private trading systems that facilitate electronic trading. Like exchanges, ATSs bring together buyers and sellers of securities but, unlike exchanges, they do not engage in self-regulatory conduct, make markets, or provide a listing service for securities. In addition, ATSs have subscribers, not members. ATS subscribers are generally institutional investors, other broker-dealers, and market makers that trade directly with the ATS, *i.e.*, subscribers are willing to buy or sell securities by submitting bid or offer quotations, market orders, limit orders, or other priced orders. Electronic Communications Networks ("ECNs")[11] are a type of ATS. They are computerized trading facilities that match customer buy and sell orders. ECNs accept orders directly from their own subscribers in addition to customer orders routed from other broker-dealers. They post orders on their systems for subscribers to view and then automatically match orders for execution. ECNs facilitate compliance by broker-dealers acting as market makers with their obligations under the Quote Rule, Rule 611 of Reg NMS, by transmitting the top of their order book (best bid and best offer) to national securities exchanges or registered securities associations (FINRA).

Snapshot of ECN Book for DYUR

BUY ORDERS		SELL ORDERS	
SHARES	PRICE	SHARES	PRICE
1,000	18.83	3,800	18.90
1,000	18.80	1,000	18.90
500	18.75	1,000	18.90

The SEC adopted Regulation ATS in 1998 to integrate ATSs into the national market system. The adoption of Regulation ATS also required the SEC to adopt two additional rules under the Exchange Act—Rules 3b-16 and 3a1-1. Accordingly, the regulatory framework for ATSs adopted in 1998 consisted of Rules 300–303 of Regulation ATS

---

11. ECNs are defined in Rule 600(b)(23) of Reg NMS.

and Rules 3b-16 and 3a1-1 of the Exchange Act. Table 14.3 summarizes the overall regulatory framework for ATSs.

Table 14.2

Exchange Act Rules	Requirements	Regulation ATS	Requirements
3b-16	Further defines the term *exchange* in § 3(a)(1) of the Exchange Act for purpose of Regulation ATS.	Rule 300	Definitions
3a1-1	Exempts certain ATS if registered as a broker-dealer and comply with Regulation ATS.	Rule 301	Requires registration as an exchange or a broker-dealer; broker-dealer registration requires compliance with order display, fair access, and Rules 302 and 301.
		Rule 302	Recordkeeping Requirements
		Rule 303	Record preservation requirements

Rule 3b-16 was adopted to interpret key language in the statutory definition of *exchange* under § 3(a)(1) of the Exchange Act. The SEC required a more comprehensive interpretation of the term *exchange* in light of the development of ATSs, because advancing technology allowed market participants to use them as the functional equivalent of exchanges. Under Rule 3b-16, an *exchange* is defined as: "any organization, association, or group of persons that: (1) brings together the orders of multiple buyers and sellers; and (2) uses established, non-discretionary methods (whether by providing a trading facility or by setting rules) under which such orders interact with each other, and the buyers and sellers entering such orders agree to the terms of a trade." Rule 3b-16 explicitly excludes those systems that: (1) merely route orders to other facilities for execution; (2) are operated by a single registered market maker to display its own bids and offers and the limit orders of its customers, and to execute trades against such orders; and (3) allow persons to enter orders for execution against the bids and offers of a single dealer. Rule 3a1-1 exempts ATSs from the definition of exchange in Rule 3b-16, and therefore the requirement to register as an exchange, if they comply with Regulation ATS. Specifically, Rule 3a1-1 exempts from the definition of exchange any ATS that: (1) complies with Regulation ATS; (2) is not required to comply with Regulation ATS pursuant to Rule 301 of Regulation ATS; or (3) is operated by a national securities association. In addition, ATSs on which trading does not meet certain specified volume levels are also exempt from the definition of exchange. ATSs are exempt if during three of the preceding four calendar quarters they had: (1) less than 50 percent of the average daily dollar trading volume in any security and five percent or more of the average daily dollar trading volume in any class of securities[12] or (2) less than 40 percent of the average daily dollar trading volume in any class of securities. ATSs with less than five percent of the trading volume in all securities in which an ATS trades must: (1) file a notice of operation on Form ATS and quarterly reports using Form ATS-R; (2) maintain records, including an audit trail of transactions; and (3) refrain from using the words exchange, stock market, or similar terms in the ATS's name. However, despite these specified volume levels, the SEC retains the authority to require registration of an ATS as an exchange if it deems it necessary in the public interest or consistent with the protection of investors.

Regulation ATS permits ATSs to register with the SEC as national securities exchanges or as broker-dealers who comply with the additional requirements prescribed in Regulation ATS. If the ATS determines to register as a broker-dealer rather than a national securities exchange, Regulation ATS adds an additional layer of regulation. However, Rule 301 of Regulation ATS expressly excludes certain types of ATSs from the additional regulatory requirements in Rule 301(b), including those registered as an exchange under Section 6 of the Exchange Act, operated by a national securities association, or operated by broker-dealers whose securities activities are limited to trading U.S. government and related securities and commercial paper. Otherwise, if the ATS is not exempt nor chooses to register as an exchange, Rule 301 of Regulation ATS requires ATSs to register as a broker-dealer under Section 15 of the Exchange Act and to file an initial operation report on Form ATS 20 days prior to commencing operation and to report trading activity quarterly on Form ATS-R. Information requested on Form ATS includes a detailed description of how the ATS will operate, its prospective subscribers, the securities it intends to trade, and procedures for reviewing systems capacity, security, and contingency planning. The ATS must notify the SEC of any material changes in the information required in Form ATS; all information submitted on Form ATS is kept confidential because such information may be proprietary and disclosure might place the ATS in a disadvantageous competitive position.

Regulation ATS contains order display and execution access requirements to ensure that ATSs with significant trading activity in NMS stocks participate directly in the national market system's public quotation stream. Specifically, ATSs with five percent or more of the trading volume in any NMS stock must publicly disseminate their best priced orders by providing them to a national securities exchange or registered securities association. Only orders that are displayed to more than one ATS subscriber are required to be included in the public quotation stream. ATSs must also provide all registered broker-dealers with access to publicly displayed orders. In essence, this

---

12. Class of securities is defined in paragraph (b)(3) of Rule 3a1-1 and includes equity securities.

requirement ensures compliance with the Order Handling Rules of Reg NMS (Rules 602 and 604). Interestingly, the Order Handling Rules combined with advances in technology spurred the growth of ATSs as a significant component of the U.S. securities markets.

In the Matter of Brutt, LLC

Admin. Proc. File No. 3-11320 (Oct. 30, 2003)

I.

The Securities and Exchange Commission ("Commission" or "SEC") deems it appropriate and in the public interest that public administrative and cease-and-desist proceedings be, and hereby are, instituted pursuant to Sections 15(b) and 21C of the Securities Exchange Act of 1934 ("Exchange Act") against Brut, LLC ("Brut" or "Respondent").

II.

In anticipation of the institution of these proceedings, Respondent has submitted an Offer of Settlement (the "Offer"), which the Commission has determined to accept.... and without admitting or denying the findings herein..., Respondent consents to the entry of this Order ... as set forth below.

III.

On the basis of this Order and Respondent's Offer, the Commission finds that:

Respondent

1. Brut, LLC, a wholly-owned subsidiary of SunGard Data Systems, Inc., is a broker-dealer registered with the Commission pursuant to Section 15(b) of the Exchange Act, a registered alternative trading system, and a member of the NASD. Brut is headquartered in New York City. It operates The Brut ECN System, an electronic communications network ("ECN").

Background

2. In 1998, Brut created the Brut ECN System, which permits market makers that subscribe to Brut's services to display priced orders for Nasdaq and listed equity securities on Brut's ECN on an anonymous basis. Subscribers generally enter buy and sell orders through their computers. The ECN displays the symbol, price, time of entry and size of each order to all system subscribers. In addition, the ECN sends its best bid and offer on each security (sometimes in rounded form, as discussed below) to the public quotation system for display. The public quotation system is the structure through which the stock exchanges and NASD disseminate quotes through vendors to the public.

3. During the relevant time period, non-subscribers could execute orders against Brut's publicly displayed bids and offers through SelectNet, a Nasdaq-owned order-routing vehicle (SelectNet is no longer in use. The Nasdaq order-routing service is provided by a new system called "SuperMontage").

4. Some of Brut's subscribers are market makers. Under the Limit Order Display Rule (Exchange Act Rule 11Ac1-4(b)), market makers must display on the public quotation system the price of any customer limit order that is priced better than the market maker's own public quote. The market maker can satisfy this requirement, however, by delivering the limit order to an ECN for display, so long as the ECN complies with the ECN Display Alternative Rule (Exchange Act Rule 11Ac1-1(c)(5)(ii)).

5. When a subscribing market maker attempts to use Brut to fulfill its display obligations by entering a customer limit order into Brut's ECN system, and that order is better than Brut's current quote for that security, Brut is required to disseminate the market maker's quote to the public quotation system on behalf of the market maker. If the market maker's quote is at a non-standard price increment (one not approved by the primary market for the security) and the market maker uses Brut to fulfill its display responsibilities, Brut is permitted under the Commission's order handling rules to round the disseminated quote to the nearest quote increment allowed by the disseminating market. Buy orders are rounded down and sell orders rounded up. For example, during the relevant time period, which occurred prior to the implementation of decimalization, a Nasdaq stock could be quoted at increments of $1/16, such as $12 15/16. A priced order using smaller increments, such as $12 61/64, would be rounded down to $12 15/16 if a buy, and up to $13 if a sell.

6. When Brut rounded an order for display purposes, it was still required to execute the quoted order at the actual, non-rounded price. To return to the example of an order placed by a market maker at $12 61/64, which Brut rounded for display on the public quotation system to $12 15/16 when a buy, and $13 when a sell, Brut was required to execute the buy or the sell at the non-rounded price, $12 61/64, or it failed to comply with the conditions contained in the ECN Display Alternative Rule; in turn, the market maker violated the Limit Order Display Rule.

7. Brut's ECN system was originally programmed to execute rounded orders at the appropriate, non-rounded prices when the execution involved a transaction between two Brut subscribers. But when non-subscribers executed against rounded Brut orders through SelectNet, Brut's ECN system was originally programmed to execute the orders at rounded prices rather than the actual, non-rounded prices. To return to the example, Brut programmed its system to execute a market maker's $12 61/64 buy order at $12 61/64 if the seller was a Brut subscriber but at $12 15/16 if the seller was a non-subscriber, and a market maker's $12 61/64 sell order at $12 61/64 if the buyer was a Brut subscriber but at $13 if the buyer was a non-subscriber.

8. Rule 301(b) under Regulation ATS required Brut to file an initial operation report on Form ATS before beginning to operate as an alternative trading system. Brut filed its initial Form ATS on May 11, 1999. In this report, which required, among other things, that Brut describe its manner of operation, Brut stated, "top of the book orders [that is, the best bids and offers Brut has] can be accessed by non-subscribers," but failed to say that non-subscriber orders would be *executed* at inferior prices.

9. On February 12, 2001, in connection with an SEC examination, SEC staff discovered that Brut was incorrectly executing rounded SelectNet orders. Upon learning of this programming issue, Brut immediately reprogrammed its system to execute all rounded orders at their actual, non-rounded prices. Re-programming work was completed on March 5, 2001.

10. As a result of the way Brut's ECN system was misprogrammed, from May 1998 until March 5, 2001, Brut executed certain SelectNet orders at rounded prices.

Legal Analysis

11. Section 21C of the Exchange Act authorizes the Commission to enter a cease-and-desist order against any person (including a broker or dealer) who "causes" a violation of any provision of the Exchange Act or rule thereunder.

12. The order handling rules are designed to enhance the quality of published quotations for securities and promote competition and pricing efficiency in U.S. securities markets. (citations omitted). When Brut executed rounded orders at rounded prices, as described above, Brut caused its market maker subscribers to violate one of the order handling rules, the Limit Order Display Rule, Exchange Act Rule 11Ac1-4.

13. Section 11A(c)(1) of the Exchange Act prohibits a member of a self-regulatory organization, broker, or dealer from using the mails or any means or instrumentality of interstate commerce to effect any transaction in, or to induce or attempt to induce the purchase or sale of, any security in violation of any Commission rules or regulations as the Commission shall prescribe as necessary or appropriate to, among other things, assure the prompt, accurate, reliable, and fair processing and publication of information with respect to quotations and transactions in such securities. By causing its subscriber market makers to violate the Limit Order Display Rule, Brut also caused the market makers to violate Section 11A(c)(1) of the Exchange Act.

14. Section 15(b)(4)(A) of the Exchange Act authorizes the Commission to impose sanctions in an administrative proceeding on any broker or dealer if it finds, on the record after notice and opportunity for hearing, that such broker or dealer has, in any report required to be filed with the Commission, willfully made any statement which was at the time and in the light of the circumstances under which it was made false or misleading with respect to any material fact. Section 21B(a)(3) of the Exchange Act authorizes the Commission to impose civil penalties in such a proceeding.

15. Rule 301(b) under Regulation ATS requires alternative trading systems, such as Brut, to file an initial operation report on Form ATS at least twenty days prior to commencing operation as an alternative trading system. (citation omitted). Form ATS is a report required to be filed with the Commission within the meaning of Section 15(b)(4)(A). (citation omitted). The form requires alternative trading systems to provide information about their system, including a detailed description of how it will operate. One purpose of the filing is to alert the Commission before the system begins to operate to potential problems that might affect investors.... In light of that purpose, and in light of the circumstances under which a Form ATS is filed, the failure to disclose that a system will operate to cause violations of the securities laws

that impact the price at which certain investors' orders are executed, renders the filing misleading as to a material fact.

16. In filing its Form ATS, Brut willfully failed to disclose that its system would cause violations of the federal securities laws that would impact investors. Specifically, in contravention of the Limit Order Display Rule, the system would execute non-subscribers' orders against rounded quotes at rounded (not actual) prices, failing to pass on the better, actual prices to non-subscribers. Thus Brut willfully filed a Form ATS that was misleading as to a material fact. Sections 15(b)(4)(A) and 21B(a)(3) of the Exchange Act authorize the Commission to impose sanctions, including civil penalties, for Brut's filing of the materially misleading Form ATS.[13]

* * *

Accordingly, it is hereby ORDERED:

A. That Respondent Brut cease and desist from committing or causing any violations and any future violations of Section 11A(c)(1) of the Exchange Act and Rule 11Ac1-4 thereunder ...

———

Regulation ATS also requires the establishment of standards for access to ATS systems, which must be applied fairly to all prospective subscribers. Fair access standards are required under Rule 301(b)(3), if the ATS, during four of the preceding six months, accounts for five percent or more of the average daily volume in any NMS stock. The goal is to ensure fair access to the best prices in the U.S. securities markets.

In the Matter of INET ATS, Inc.

Admin. Proc. 3-12259 (Apr. 12, 2006)

I.

The Securities and Exchange Commission ("Commission" or "SEC") deems it appropriate and in the public interest that public administrative and cease-and-desist proceedings be, and hereby are, instituted pursuant to Sections 15(b) and 21C of the Securities Exchange Act of 1934 ("Exchange Act") against INET ATS, Inc. ("Respondent").

II.

In anticipation of the institution of these proceedings, Respondent has submitted an Offer of Settlement (the "Offer"), which the Commission has determined to accept.... Respondent consents to the entry of this Order ... as set forth below.

III.

On the basis of this Order and Respondent's Offer, the Commission finds that:

———

13. [1] "Willfully" as used in this Order means intentionally committing the act that constitutes the violation. *See* Wonsover v. SEC, 205 F.3d 408, 414 (D.C. Cir. 2000); Tager v. SEC, 344 F.2d 5, 8 (2d Cir. 1965). There is no requirement that the actor also be aware that he is violating one of the Rules or Acts.

1. INET ATS, Inc. ("INET"), a subsidiary of Instinet Group Incorporated ("Instinet Group") during the relevant period, is a Jersey City, NJ-based registered broker-dealer that operates an alternative trading system ("ATS") pursuant to Regulation ATS under the Exchange Act. INET was formed between December 2003 and February 2004, through the combination of two ATSs: (i) an ATS operated by Instinet Corporation ("Instinet's ATS"), a subsidiary of Instinet Group, and (ii) The Island ECN, Inc. ("Island"), another ATS purchased by Instinet Group on September 20, 2002. The combined ATS was then renamed INET. The conduct addressed in this order was committed by Instinet's ATS before it was merged with Island and renamed INET. An ATS is any organization, association, person, group of persons, or system: (a) that constitutes, maintains, or provides a market place or facilities for bringing together purchasers and sellers of securities or for otherwise performing with respect to securities the functions commonly performed by a stock exchange within the meaning of Exchange Act Rule 3b-16; and (b) that does not: (i) set rules governing the conduct of subscribers other than the conduct of such subscribers' trading on such organization, association, person, group of persons, or system; or (ii) discipline subscribers other than by exclusion from trading.

2. Rule 301(a) of Regulation ATS provides that an ATS must comply with Rule 301(b) of Regulation ATS, unless the ATS is registered as a national securities exchange or qualifies for another enumerated exclusion. During the relevant period, Instinet's ATS was not registered as a national securities exchange and did not qualify for an enumerated exclusion. Therefore, Instinet's ATS was required to comply with Rule 301(b) of Regulation ATS.

3. During the relevant period, Rule 301(b)(5) of Regulation ATS required an ATS that had 20 percent[14] or more of the average daily volume (the "fair access threshold") for any covered security[15] during four of the preceding six months to comply with "fair access" requirements including: (a) establishing written standards for granting access to trading on its system with respect to such security; and (b) not unreasonably prohibiting or limiting any person in respect to access to services offered by the ATS with respect to such security by applying such standards in an unfair or discriminatory manner (citations omitted). The fair access requirements apply on a security-by-security basis. Adopting Release, 68 SEC Docket at 2217 ("The twenty percent volume threshold will be applied on a security-by-security basis for equity securities. Accordingly, if an alternative trading system accounted for twenty percent or more of the share volume in any equity security, it must comply with fair access requirements in granting access to trading in that security."). A denial of access is reasonable if it is based on objective standards that are applied in a fair and non-discriminatory manner. A denial of access might be unreasonable if it were discriminatorily applied among similar subscribers. (citations omitted).

---

14. The 20 percent volume requirement has been reduced to 5% or more of the average daily volume of any NMS stock.

15. Currently, a covered security is an NMS stock as defined in Rule 600 of Reg NMS.

4. The fair access requirements of Regulation ATS were based on the principle that qualified market participants should have fair access to the nation's securities markets. (citations omitted). Fair treatment of potential and current subscribers by an ATS is particularly important when an ATS captures a large percentage of the trading volume in a security because viable alternatives to trading may be limited. (citation omitted). Direct participation in an ATS offers certain benefits with respect to which an ATS that crosses the fair access threshold for a covered security should not unfairly discriminate in granting access with respect to such security. (citations omitted). These benefits include the ability to view all orders (depth of book), not just the best bid or offer (top of book), which provides important information about the depth of interest in that security. (citation omitted).

5. Regulation ATS requires an ATS that crosses the fair access threshold in a covered security to report all grants, denials, and limitations of access (and the reasons, for each applicant, for granting, denying, or limiting access) with respect to such security on its quarterly Form ATS-R. (citations omitted).

6. Instinet's ATS crossed the fair access threshold every month between February 2002 and July 2003 (the "relevant period") with respect to between 12 and 105 covered securities in each month. Therefore, with respect to these securities during the relevant period, Instinet's ATS was subject to the fair access requirements of Regulation ATS as well as the requirement to report all grants, denials, and limitations of access (and the reasons, for each applicant, for granting, denying, or limiting access) with respect to such securities on its quarterly Form ATS-R.

7. During the relevant period, Instinet's ATS functioned as an agency broker and as an ATS. As an ATS, Instinet's ATS collected, prioritized, displayed, provided routing services and matched orders within its member network, and provided certain other services.

8. During the relevant period, Instinet's ATS had a member network composed of broker-dealer subscribers, who entered into contractual agreements to access the ATS for purposes of effecting transactions in securities or submitting, disseminating, or displaying orders on the ATS.

9. In early 2002, Instinet's ATS developed a data-only product called "BookStream" that allowed a subscriber the ability only to view orders contained in the ATS book without interacting with the order book, or submitting, disseminating or displaying orders on the ATS. BookStream featured the full "depth of book" data that allowed a subscriber the ability to view not only the best bids and offers, but all of the bids and offers on the ATS. BookStream was an important ATS feature because it enabled subscribers to view, on a real-time basis, market data regarding the depth of trading interest in covered securities.

10. During the relevant period, Instinet's ATS had written access standards that incorporated by reference subscriber agreements that contained a clause governing "redistribution" of services, which stated, in relevant part: "subscribers are prohibited from making Instinet services and data available, directly or indirectly, to third parties

(other than subscriber's properly authorized employees, affiliates, employees of affiliates) without the prior written approval of Instinet." This "redistribution" standard was not an objective standard applied in a fair and non- discriminatory manner because it did not specify the circumstances under which Instinet's ATS would authorize subscribers to provide or redistribute these services to customers.

11. After BookStream was implemented by Instinet's ATS, various broker-dealer subscribers requested to redistribute BookStream to their customers.

12. BookStream was an ATS function and a benefit to ATS membership to which an ATS could not unreasonably prohibit or limit access in an unfair or discriminatory manner with respect to those covered securities for which Instinet's ATS crossed the fair access threshold. (citation omitted)

13. During the relevant period, Instinet's ATS contractually granted permission to some subscribers to redistribute BookStream while other similarly situated subscribers were not permitted to redistribute BookStream. While such disparate treatment may be justified if it is based on objective standards that are applied in a fair and non-discriminatory manner (citations omitted) this was not the case here. Therefore, Instinet's ATS willfully violated Rule 301(b)(5)(ii)(B) of Regulation ATS under the Exchange Act.

14. During the relevant period, Instinet's ATS filed five Forms ATS-R with the Commission. These filings did not disclose all required grants, denials and limitations of access to BookStream.

15. By failing to disclose, with respect to covered securities in which Instinet's ATS exceeded the fair access threshold, all required grants, denials, or limitations of access on its Form ATS-R during the relevant period, Instinet's ATS willfully violated Rule 301(b)(5)(ii)(D) of Regulation ATS under the Exchange Act.

* * *

Accordingly, it is hereby ORDERED:

A. That Respondent be, and hereby is, censured;

B. That Respondent cease and desist from committing or causing any violations and any future violations of Rules 301(b)(5)(ii)(B) and 301(b)(5)(ii)(D) of Regulation ATS under the Exchange Act ...

———

1. Dark Pools

Dark pools are also ATSs, but they do not display quotations to the public. Accordingly, they are electronic trading facilities in which the bids and offers of their subscribers are not disseminated in the consolidated quotation data or public quotation stream of the national market system. Such quotations are, however, communicated only to a subset of market participants. According to the SEC, this means that dark pool subscribers "have access to information about a potential trade that other investors using the public quotations do not. As a result, dark pool participants are able to have their orders filled, while those on publicly displayed markets go unfilled, even though dark pools use the information from publicly displayed markets to price the dark pool transactions. When dark pools share information about their trading interest with other dark pools, they can function like private networks that exclude the public investor.... The practice could lead to a two-tiered market in which the public does not have fair access to information about the best available prices and sizes for a stock that is available to some market participants."[16] Dark pools were established, in part, to meet the demand from institutional investors seeking to buy or sell big blocks of shares without causing large price movements. However, dark pools raise market integrity issues, including a perceived decline in the transparency of the national market system. Moreover, investors may be less willing to display quotes if dark pools free ride off such quotes and privatize order flow. Because dark pools are ATSs, they are subject to the regulatory regime of Regulation ATS and Rules 3b-16 and 3a1-1 of the Exchange Act.

In the Matter of UBS Securities LLC

Admin. Proc. File No. 3-16338, Jan. 15, 2015)

I.

The Securities and Exchange Commission ("Commission") deems it appropriate and in the public interest that public administrative and cease-and-desist proceedings be, and hereby are, instituted pursuant to Section 8A of the Securities Act of 1933 ("Securities Act") and Sections 15(b) and 21C of the Securities Exchange Act of 1934 ("Exchange Act") against UBS Securities LLC ("UBS").

II.

In anticipation of the institution of these proceedings, UBS has submitted an Offer of Settlement ("Offer") which the Commission has determined to accept.... without admitting or denying the findings herein, ... UBS consents to the entry of this Order ... ("Order"), as set forth below.

III.

On the basis of this Order and UBS's Offer, the Commission finds that:

Summary

1. UBS is the owner and operator of UBS ATS, an alternative trading system ("ATS") commonly referred to as a "dark pool." UBS ATS is a private execution venue that accepts, matches, and executes orders to buy and sell securities that it receives from UBS clients and UBS ATS subscribers. Those clients and subscribers include many of the world's largest asset managers, broker-dealers, and institutional investors, who may place trades on behalf of all kinds of investors, including pension funds and individuals with retail brokerage accounts. Between May 2008 and August 2012, UBS

---

16. Securities and Exchange Commission Fact Sheet, *Strengthening the Regulation of Dark Pools,* Oct. 21, 2009, available at: https://www.sec.gov/news/press/2009/2009-223-fs.htm.

ATS was among the largest ATSs. As measured by dollar volume, it was the nation's largest equity ATS during the second quarter of 2014, having executed over $ 416 billion in equity securities transactions in that period. During the same quarter, UBS executed trades for nearly 10.7 billion shares on UBS ATS.

* * *

Respondent

10. UBS is a Delaware entity with principal executive offices in New York, New York. It is a broker-dealer registered with the Commission. Since 2008, it has operated UBS ATS, which operates pursuant to Regulation ATS.

Facts

Sub-Penny Orders

11. Rule 612 of Regulation NMS provides that "[n]o ... alternative trading system ... or broker or dealer shall display, rank, or accept from any person a bid or offer, an order, or any indication of interest in any NMS stock priced in an increment smaller than $ 0.01," unless the price of the quotation is less than $ 1.00, in which case the minimum increment is $ 0.0001. In adopting Rule 612, the Commission noted that "Rule 612 will deter the practice of stepping ahead of exposed trading interest by an economically insignificant amount." *(citations omitted)*.

12. During the relevant period, UBS ATS's Form ATS indicated that UBS ATS complied with Rule 612. UBS ATS's Form ATS reported that "[o]nly orders priced in penny increments will be accepted by the UBS ATS." In the same document, UBS indicated that "[t]he UBS ATS will screen for orders priced in increments other than pennies...."

13. Despite those representations and from at least May 2008 through March 2011, UBS accepted and ranked hundreds of millions of orders priced in sub-penny increments. Those sub-penny orders were generated in the following ways: (a) as a result of the [Primary Peg Plus] PPP order type, (b) as a result of the Whole Penny Offset order type, and (c) as a result of various technical or coding problems, at least one of which UBS did not remedy in a timely fashion.

14. Following the order type's internal approval at UBS, UBS ATS accepted and ranked PPP orders for execution from June 2010 through March 2011. Throughout that period, a large number of PPP orders were accepted and ranked by UBS ATS, resulting in executions on a daily basis.

15. The price of a PPP order was fixed to—or "pegged to"—the national best bid or the national best offer (prices that are referred to collectively as the "NBBO"[17]) *plus or minus* a subscriber-entered percentage of the "spread."[18] Therefore, PPP allowed

---

17. [6] Rule 600(b)(42) of Regulation ATS provides that, with respect to quotations for an NMS stock, the NBBO is typically the best (*i.e.*, highest) bid price and the best (*i.e.*, lowest) offer price for that stock "that are calculated and disseminated on a current and continuing basis by a plan processor pursuant to an effective national market system plan...."

18. [7] For the purpose of calculating the price of a PPP order, the "spread" was the difference between the national best bid for a stock and the national best offer for that stock. For example, if

a UBS ATS subscriber to place an order at numerous price points greater than the national best bid and less than the national best offer.

16. Because the second component of the formula determining the price of a PPP order—a subscriber-determined percentage of the spread—nearly always yielded a sub-penny amount, PPP orders were nearly always priced in illegal, sub-penny increments. (Even the UBS ATS user manual described PPP by using an example in which—when the national best bid ("NBB") was $ 50.00 and the national best offer ("NBO") was $ 50.02—PPP yielded an illegal, sub-penny price: "Example: NBBO 50.00 x 50.02—Primary peg BUY order, plus 10%—order is resident in the ATS at effective price 50.002.") UBS ATS accepted and ranked such sub-penny PPP orders, even though Rule 612 of Regulation NMS barred it from doing so and UBS ATS's Form ATS indicated it would not do so.

17. Generally, UBS ATS operated based upon principles of price-time priority. The best-priced marketable order for a security—*i.e.*, the highest bid or lowest offer—had priority in the dark pool's order queue and was executed before all others and if two bids or two offers shared the same price the first one received by the ATS had priority in the queue. Thus, UBS ATS would execute a marketable PPP order to buy at $ 50.002 per share before an order to buy the same security at $ 50.00 per share. As a result, the PPP order type facilitated the very result that Rule 612 was designed to prevent: it allowed one subscriber to gain execution priority over another in the order queue by offering to pay an economically insignificant sub-penny more per share. Further, because UBS ATS allowed its subscribers to place orders at prices that were unavailable at ATSs and exchanges that complied with Rule 612 of Regulation [NMS], UBS ATS obtained an unfair competitive advantage over those venues in its efforts to attract and execute orders from market participants.

18. When a resting PPP order executed in UBS ATS, the order that executed against it—such as one from a retail broker-dealer—received a slightly better execution price than if the trade had occurred at the bid or offer. Referred to as "price improvement," the magnitude of that improvement was dictated by the percent of spread component of the PPP order. (In the example above, a sell order pegged to the bid—$ 50.00 per share—could execute against the resting PPP buy order at $ 50.002, receiving price improvement of 10 percent of the spread or $ 0.002.) UBS employees understood that certain UBS ATS subscribers would want to use PPP to gain execution priority over orders in the queue that were simply pegged to the bid or the offer, in return for providing some price improvement.

19. When PPP was launched in June 2010, PPP orders could move ahead of orders pegged to the bid or the offer in the queue by providing only a minimal amount of price improvement, *i.e.*, one percent of the spread. Concerned that this increment was too small, UBS raised the minimum percent of spread for PPP orders to 10 percent on August 3, 2010, but did not amend UBS ATS's Form ATS to reflect that

---

the national best bid for a stock was $50.00 and the national best offer was $50.02, the spread was $0.02.

change. As a result of that change, a firm that engaged in high-frequency trading and market making ("Subscriber A") stopped using PPP.

20. UBS did not disclose the existence of PPP to all UBS ATS subscribers. Instead, more than three months before PPP's launch in June 2010, UBS employees began pitching PPP to some potential subscribers and to a subset of the ATS's existing subscribers. Recipients of that pitch received an updated version of the UBS ATS user manual — the "Rules of Engagement" — that provided the coding instructions a subscriber needed to place a PPP order.[19]

21. UBS employees believed the PPP order type would be particularly well-suited to the trading strategies of market makers and HFT firms, which typically traded at or near the best bid or offer. Accordingly, nearly all of the subscribers who received the pre-launch notice of PPP were market makers and/or HFT firms.

22. On at least one occasion, UBS employees discussed the possibility of disclosing PPP broadly or to all of the ATS's subscribers. In May 2010, approximately one month before PPP's June 2010 launch, a UBS employee responsible for communicating with potential and existing subscribers to UBS ATS emailed the principal for UBS ATS. Mentioning a firm that engaged in high-frequency trading and market making and that had recently been pitched PPP (an order type that UBS employees referred to as "percent of spread"), the employee wrote, "[l]everaging the % of spread may be a way to help get [Subscriber A] in the black and generate some added flow from other subscribers. We should explore the impact and make sure all of our ATS client[s] are aware of the new % of spread functionality as well. If we haven't already we should consider creating an ATS client distribution list for these types of announcements." The ATS principal responded, "I would like to not push % of spread to[o] hard to the full subscriber base, until we see the results with [Subscriber B and Subscriber A]," two firms that engaged in high-frequency trading and market making. The other employee responded, "yep, makes sense."

23. At the time the order type was launched, UBS did not disseminate a notice to all of the ATS's subscribers advising them of the PPP order type. Prior to July 2012, UBS had no policy or procedure requiring the Rules of Engagement to be sent to all subscribers every time it was amended. Typically, UBS sent an up-to-date version of the Rules of Engagement to new subscribers and to any existing subscriber that asked for them. (At that time, PPP was described on page 10 of the 17-page Rules of Engagement.) Even though they were UBS ATS subscribers in June 2010, several entities

---

19. [8] The instructions to Form ATS provide that an ATS must attach to its Form ATS "[a] copy of the alternative trading system's subscriber manual and any other materials provided to subscribers." The Rules of Engagement, a document provided to a number of UBS ATS subscribers, included information that subscribers needed to use the ATS and that was of the sort one would reasonably expect to find in a subscriber manual. Nevertheless, prior to December 2011, UBS ATS's Form ATS and amendments thereto reported that "UBS ATS does not have a subscriber manual" and did not attach a copy of the Rules of Engagement.

were emailed a PPP-referencing version of the Rules of Engagement months later, and well after the order type was launched.

24. In July 2010, a UBS employee emailed an employee of a potential subscriber to the UBS ATS, cutting-and-pasting into his email the lengthy coding instructions that a subscriber needed to place orders on UBS ATS. Before sending the email and for reasons that included a prior business dispute between UBS and the potential subscriber, the UBS employee intentionally removed the portion of those instructions that described PPP and that provided the instructions needed to enter PPP orders. While the entity subsequently traded on the ATS, UBS never provided it with notice of PPP.

25. In October 2010, the same employee was asked to review a draft PowerPoint marketing presentation that mentioned PPP ("New Order Types & Functionality: % of Spread") and the natural-only crossing restriction ("Intelligently leverage UBS ATS—> Non natural vs. Natural designation"). The employee removed both of those references from the presentation. In an email attaching his edits to the PowerPoint deck, the employee wrote to another UBS employee, "I took out references to our % of spread and non-natural vs natural as well because that stuff is very proprietary and changes. It's something we should talk to rather than put in the slide...."

26. In March 2011, UBS sent a spreadsheet containing certain trading information to a firm that engaged in high-frequency trading and market making ("Subscriber C") in an effort to encourage its expanded usage of PPP. For each of the thousands of orders Subscriber C had executed in UBS ATS on two prior trading days, the spreadsheet showed, without providing any customer-identifying information, whether the firm's order had executed against a retail order or a non-retail order. (Such information was not data that UBS typically disclosed to other UBS ATS subscribers and was not information that subscribers could readily ascertain through other means.) The UBS employee that proposed sending the spreadsheet to Subscriber C understood that Subscriber C wanted to use the spreadsheet's data to adjust its algorithmic trading strategies in ways that would increase the likelihood of its PPP orders executing against orders from retail broker-dealers.

27. On March 11, 2011, and after a Commission examination team had identified PPP and raised concerns that it might violate Rule 612 of Regulation NMS, UBS decommissioned the PPP order type. At that time, a number of the ATS's subscribers still had not received notice of PPP's existence: UBS never provided a PPP-referencing version of the Rules of Engagement to at least one entity that became a subscriber of UBS ATS after PPP's June 2010 launch and UBS never provided such notice to about eight of the approximately 35 entities that were already ATS subscribers in June 2010. Notice of the existence and selective disclosure of the PPP order type would have been important to subscribers.

Whole Penny Offset Orders

28. From 2008 until it was decommissioned in June 2010, a second order type— referred to in this Order as the Whole Penny Offset order type—permitted subscribers

in certain instances to place orders priced in sub-penny increments that were accepted and ranked by UBS ATS.

29. The Whole Penny Offset order type allowed subscribers to enter orders priced at the NBB, the NBO, or the midpoint of the NBBO (*i.e.*, the average of the national best bid and national best offer), *plus or minus* $0.01. The order type yielded orders priced in impermissible sub-penny increments whenever the price of the order was pegged to the midpoint and the spread between the national best bid and national best offer was an odd number of cents, e.g., if the national best bid and offer were $30.00 and $30.03, the midpoint would be $30.015 and orders plus and minus the one-cent offset would be illegally priced at $30.005 and $30.025 per share. Between January 2009 and June 2010, Whole Penny Offset orders resulted in executions for approximately 1.5 million shares of stock on UBS ATS.

Additional Orders Priced in Sub-Penny Increments

30. In addition to the violative orders placed as a result of the PPP and Whole Penny Offset order types, UBS accepted and ranked tens of millions of other orders priced above $1.00 in sub-penny increments. Those sub-penny orders resulted from at least two technical problems.

31. The first technical problem, which caused the overwhelming majority of the additional sub-penny orders, involved a coding error in UBS's smart order router, an application that utilized pre-programmed logic to route or direct orders to UBS ATS and to other venues for execution. When seeking to place an order in UBS ATS at the NBBO midpoint, UBS's smart order router would send an immediate-or-cancel limit order that was explicitly denominated at the price the router had calculated to be the midpoint of the NBBO, rather than sending an order with a price that was *pegged* to the midpoint of the NBBO.[20] To the extent those orders sent by the router to UBS ATS were sub-penny-priced, UBS ATS failed to identify and reject them and, instead, accepted them in violation of Rule 612 of Regulation NMS. After discovering this coding error in May 2010, UBS fixed it within a few weeks.

32. The second technical problem arose from defects in UBS's algorithmic trading platform — called PTSS — that generated sub-penny orders which, in some instances, were routed to third-party venues for execution and, in others, were routed to UBS ATS, which accepted and ranked them. PTSS's problems persisted as a result of numerous delays in the rollout of a replacement algo platform called Rainier.

33. In March 2010, after receiving an automated report indicating that UBS had routed over a thousand PTSS-generated sub-penny orders to third-party venues on

---

20. [9] While an ATS does not violate Rule 612 by accepting and ranking an order *pegged* to the midpoint of the NBBO (even if the midpoint is a sub-penny price), this limited exception does not permit an ATS to accept and rank an order that is explicitly denominated in a sub-penny price (even if that sub-penny price is equal to the midpoint of the NBBO). *See* Exchange Act Release No. 51808, at 231 ("Rule 612 will not prohibit a sub-penny execution resulting from a midpoint or volume-weighted algorithm or from price improvement, so long as the execution did not result from an impermissible sub-penny order or quotation.").

the prior trading day, a UBS compliance officer wrote, "[w]e need to have some system control in place to prevent sub penny pricing violations caused by bad market data feeds.... Please let me know what can be done to prevent recurrence of this issue going forward."

34. Aware that PTSS was the cause of the sub-penny orders, another UBS employee proposed awaiting the rollout of the replacement algo platform rather than immediately remedying the issue with PTSS. "We plan to decommission PTSS in two months," he wrote in an internal email. "Our new algo system Rainier doesn't have the issue. Since it happened rarely, we would like to make no change to PTSS, and let the migration take care of the issue."

35. Nearly four months later, on July 13, 2010, a UBS employee again reported in an internal email that UBS was routing PTSS-generated sub-penny orders to third-party venues for execution. The UBS ATS principal responded by explaining that the problem would be resolved by the upcoming migration from PTSS to Rainier. "If we confirm this pricing decision came from PTSS classic," he wrote, "can we not spend to[o] much time on research — we know classic has this issue, its being phased out, and we have dug through examples — to[o] many times already." On July 14, 2010, the UBS ATS principal and other UBS employees received a message reporting that UBS had routed over 17,000 additional PTSS-generated sub-penny orders to third-party venues on the prior trading day.... sub-penny orders continued to be generated by PTSS and accepted by UBS until at least September 2010.

* * *

Fair Access

49. Rule 301(b)(5) of Regulation ATS requires an ATS with at least five percent of the average daily volume for any covered security (the "fair access threshold") during four of the preceding six months to comply with "fair access" requirements. Under Rules 301(b)(5)(ii)(A), (B), and (D) of Regulation ATS, those requirements include: (a) establishing written standards for granting access to trading on its system, (b) not unreasonably prohibiting or limiting any person in respect to access to services offered by the ATS, and (c) reporting all grants, denials, and limitations of access (and the reasons for granting, denying, or limiting access) with respect to such security on its quarterly Form ATS-R. (citation omitted). For equity securities, the fair access requirements apply on a security-by-security basis. (citation omitted). A denial of access is reasonable if it is based on objective standards that are applied in a fair and non-discriminatory manner. *(citation omitted).*

50. In June 2011 and from August 2011 through November 2011, as a result of a lapse in monitoring, UBS ATS crossed the fair access threshold during four of the preceding six months with respect to as many as four covered securities. Therefore, with respect to those securities during that time period, UBS ATS was subject to the fair access requirements of Regulation ATS and was required, among other things, to report all of its grants, denials, and limitations of access (and, for each applicant, its reasons for granting, denying, or limiting access) on its quarterly Form ATS-R.

51. During that time period, UBS ATS did not have written standards for granting access to trading on its system, in particular, with respect to granting access to the natural-only crossing restriction, which was available only to orders generated by certain UBS algorithms.

52. Under Rule 301(b)(5)(ii)(B) of Regulation ATS and with respect to covered securities for which UBS ATS had crossed the fair access threshold for the requisite time period, the natural-only crossing restriction was an ATS function to which UBS could not unreasonably prohibit or limit access in an unfair or discriminatory manner. UBS's failure to permit UBS ATS subscribers access to this function was not based upon a fair and non-discriminatory application of objective standards and, therefore, did not comply with Rule 301(b)(5)(ii)(B).

53. UBS ATS filed three Forms ATS-R with the Commission concerning the periods in which it exceeded the fair access threshold for one or more covered securities in four of the six preceding months. With respect to those securities, in each of those Forms ATS-R, UBS ATS was required to disclose, but did not disclose, all required grants, denials, and limitations of access, including with respect to the natural-only crossing restriction.

Order Book Access

54. Rule 301(b)(10) of Regulation ATS provides that an ATS "shall establish adequate safeguards and procedures to protect subscribers' confidential trading information," including "[l]imiting access to the confidential trading information of subscribers to those employees of the alternative trading system who are operating the system or responsible for its compliance with these or any other applicable rules."

55. Prior to August 2012, 103 UBS employees (primarily IT personnel) who neither operated UBS ATS nor had responsibility for its compliance functions had full, live access to data concerning orders pending in UBS ATS, *i.e.*, the ATS's order book.

Record Preservation

56. Section 17(a) of the Exchange Act and Rule and 17a-4(b)(1) thereunder require broker-dealers to keep for prescribed periods and preserve a "memorandum of each brokerage order, and of any other instruction ... show[ing] the terms and conditions of the order...." Rules 301(b)(8) and 303 of Regulation ATS impose record preservation obligations on ATSs and require them to preserve records of "[t]he designation of [an] order as a market order, limit order, stop order, stop limit order, or other type of order."

57. For at least the periods August 2008 through March 2009 and August 2010 through November 2010, UBS failed to keep for prescribed periods and preserve records of certain order information for UBS ATS, including data indicating whether orders had utilized the natural-only crossing restriction.

Violations

58. As a result of the conduct described above, UBS willfully violated:

a. Section 17(a)(2) of the Securities Act, which prohibits, directly or indirectly, in the offer or sale of securities, obtaining money or property by means of any untrue statement of a material fact or any omission to state a material fact necessary in order to make the statements made, in light of the circumstances under which they were made, not misleading;

b. Section 17(a) of the Exchange Act and Rule 17a-4(b)(1) thereunder, which require brokers and dealers to keep for prescribed periods and preserve certain records;

c. Rule 301(b)(2) of Regulation ATS, which requires an ATS to file an initial operation report on Form ATS at least 20 days prior to commencing operation as an alternative trading system and to file an amendment on Form ATS at least 20 days prior to implementing a material change to the operation of the ATS, within 30 days after the end of a quarter when information contained in an initial operation report filed on Form ATS becomes inaccurate, and promptly upon discovering that an initial operation report filed on Form ATS or an amendment on Form ATS was inaccurate when filed;

d. Rule 301(b)(5)(ii)(A) of Regulation ATS, which requires an ATS that crosses the fair access threshold during four of the preceding six months in a covered security to establish written standards for granting access to trading on its system;

e. Rule 301(b)(5)(ii)(B) of Regulation ATS, which requires an ATS that crosses the fair access threshold during four of the preceding six months in a covered security to not unreasonably prohibit or limit any person in respect to access to services offered by the ATS with respect to such security by applying standards required by Rule 301(b)(5)(ii)(A) in an unfair or discriminatory manner;

f. Rule 301(b)(5)(ii)(D) of Regulation ATS, which requires an ATS that crosses the fair access threshold during four of the preceding six months in a covered security to report all grants, denials, and limitations of access (and the reasons, for each applicant, for granting, denying, or limiting access) with respect to such security on its quarterly Form ATS-R;

g. Rules 301(b)(8) and 303 of Regulation ATS, which require an ATS to preserve certain records;

h. Rule 301(b)(10) of Regulation ATS, which requires an ATS to establish adequate safeguards and procedures to protect subscribers' confidential trading information and to adopt and implement adequate oversight procedures to ensure that the safeguards and procedures for protecting subscribers' confidential trading information are followed; and

i. Rule 612 of Regulation NMS, which provides that "[n]o ... alternative trading system ... or broker or dealer shall display, rank, or accept from any person a bid or offer, an order, or an indication of interest in any NMS stock priced in an increment smaller than $ 0.01," unless the bid or offer, order, or indication of interest is priced less than $ 1.00 per share, in which case the minimum increment is $ 0.0001.

IV.

In view of the foregoing, the Commission deems it appropriate and in the public interest to impose the sanctions agreed to in Respondent UBS's Offer.

Accordingly, pursuant to Section 8A of the Securities Act and Sections 15(b) and 21C of the Exchange Act, it is hereby ORDERED that:

A. UBS cease and desist from committing or causing any violations and any future violations of Section 17(a)(2) of the Securities Act, Section 17(a) of the Exchange Act and Rule 17a-4(b)(1) thereunder, Rules 301(b)(2), 301(b)(5)(ii)(A), 301(b)(5)(ii)(B), 301(b)(5)(ii)(D), 301(b)(8), 301(b)(10) and 303 of Regulation ATS, and Rule 612 of Regulation NMS.

B. UBS is censured.

C. UBS shall, within ten days of the entry of this Order, pay a civil money penalty in the amount of $ 12,000,000.00, disgorgement of $ 2,240,702.50 and prejudgment interest of $ 235,686.14.

———

Notes and Questions

1. Rule 301(b)(7) of Regulation ATS requires an ATS to permit the examination and inspection of its premises, systems, and records, and to cooperate with the examination, inspection, or investigation of subscribers, whether such examination is being conducted by the SEC or by a self-regulatory organization of which such subscriber is a member. Rule 302 of Regulation ATS specifies the recordkeeping requirements for ATSs, which include daily summaries of trading in securities and time-sequenced records of order information.

2. Certain types of trading facilities are not subject to the fair access, display and order execution access, and system capacity requirements in Rule 301(b) of Regulation ATS. These trading facilities include facilities that: (1) match customer orders for a security with other customer orders; (2) such customer orders are not displayed to any person, other than employees of the ATS; and (3) such orders are executed at a price for such security disseminated by an effective transaction reporting plan, or derived from such prices.

Hypothetical Two

Success First operates a block-trading ATS, or dark pool, for large institutional investors. Success First launched its ATS as an institutional trading network for large institutional investors seeking to execute their trades in large quantities, with maximum anonymity and minimum information leakage. Over the last 12 months, Success First sought to expand its business and to find additional sources of liquidity for its ATS by offering its services to corporate issuers and control persons of corporate issuers, as well as to private equity and venture capital firms looking to execute large equity capital market transactions. This effort was undertaken, in part, through the use of confidential information about Success First's large institutional customers' intentions to buy or sell securities. Has Success First violated Regulation ATS by using its customers' confidential information? *See* Rule 301(b)(10) of Regulation ATS.

C. Broker-Dealer Internalization

Broker-dealer internalization involves the broker-dealer acting as the exclusive counterparty to its own customers' orders. The broker-dealer also acts as a dealer and trades against its customers' orders for its own account. Broker-dealer internalization allows the broker-dealer to make a profit while avoiding transaction fees levied by exchanges or ATSs. Moreover, other broker-dealers do not have the ability to compete for these trades, and orders executed in this manner do not interact with other orders because they are not exposed in the public market data. However, the general practice is for broker-dealers to obtain the best execution[21] for their clients, which generally means execution at the NBBO. Broker-dealers benefit from the practice of internalization to avoid fees, receive payment for order flow, and step in front of the displayed order queue.

The SEC, by rule, has determined that broker-dealer internalization systems are not exchanges or trading venues. Therefore quotations and orders in such systems are not displayed in the public market. Internal broker-dealer systems are defined in Rule 17a-3(a)(16)(ii)(A) as

> any facility, other than a national securities exchange, an exchange exempt from registration based on limited volume, or an alternative trading system as defined in Regulation ATS, ... that provides a mechanism, automated in full or in part, for collecting, receiving, disseminating, or displaying system orders and facilitating agreement to the basic terms of a purchase or sale of a security between a customer and the disseminating, or displaying system orders and facilitating agreement to the basic terms of a purchase or sale of a security between a customer and the sponsor, or between two customers of the sponsor, through use of the internal broker-dealer system or through the broker or dealer sponsor of such system.

17 CFR 240.17a-3(a)(16)(ii)(A).

In addition, Rule 3b-16 expressly excludes such broker-dealer internal systems from the definition of an exchange. The SEC asserts that broker-dealer internalization systems should be excluded because such systems are used to increase efficiency rather than to provide a non-discretionary trading system for customers. Specifically, executions on such systems never leave the office of the broker-dealer; the broker-dealer itself is the other side of the trade because it crosses its customer orders with either

---

21. See Section V of this chapter for a discussion of the broker-dealer's obligation to obtain best execution on behalf of its customers.

its other customers or with its own proprietary orders. Accordingly, systems that allow persons to enter orders for execution against the bids and offers of a single dealer, and systems that automate the activities of registered market makers are not subject to the regulatory framework governing exchanges and other public trading venues. However, FINRA has proposed amending its ATS rules to require reporting of transactions executed through a broker-dealer's internalization network.[22] Presumably collecting the data will allow regulators and others to assess the impact that internalization has on market quality, price discovery, and overall fairness of the U.S. securities markets.

Internalization is a contentious topic because the practice has inherent conflicts of interest. The broker-dealer has a fiduciary duty to obtain best execution, but acting as a dealer trading against its own customers, there is an incentive to execute customer orders at the most favorable price to the broker-dealer. This generally results in an execution of the customer's order at the NBBO that is publicly displayed. The publicly displayed NBBO may not be the best bid or offer available in the non-displayed order flow. In addition, research conducted about the impact of internalization has shown an adverse impact on the NBBO, i.e., internalization results in wider spreads, especially for less-liquid securities.

III. Best Execution

Broker-dealers have a duty to obtain the best execution for their customers' orders. Section 11A(a)(1)(C)(iv) of the Exchange Act states that one of the goals of the national market system is to ensure the practicability of brokers executing investors' orders in the best market. Despite this mandate, the SEC has determined not to adopt a rule prescribing best execution standards. Instead it has opted to provide guidance about the scope of a broker-dealer's best execution obligations in light of the evolving structure of the national market system.

> The duty of best execution requires a broker-dealer to seek the most favorable terms reasonably available under the circumstances for a customer's transaction. The scope of this duty of best execution must evolve as changes occur in the market that give rise to improved executions for customer orders, including opportunities to trade at more advantageous prices. As these changes occur, broker-dealers' procedures for seeking to obtain best execution for customer orders also must be modified to consider price opportunities that become "reasonably available."[23]

In the absence of an SEC rule, a broker-dealer's duty of best execution has evolved over the years in light of developments in market structure and advances in technology. The following case discusses this evolution from a focus merely on price to other relevant factors.

---

22. *See* FINRA Regulatory Notice 14-48.
23. Exchange Act Release No. 37619A (September 6, 1996) 61 FR 48290 (September 12, 1996).

Newton v. Merrill Lynch Pierce Fenner and Smith, Inc.

135 F.3d. 266 (Jan. 30, 1998)

Class action lawsuit was brought by customers of National Association of Securities Dealers Automated Quotation System (NASDAQ) broker-dealers, claiming that broker-dealers had engaged in securities fraud by executing customer orders at National Best Bid and Offer (NBBO) prices, even when those prices were not best available. The United States District Court For the District of New Jersey, … granted summary judgment for broker-dealers, and customers appealed. The en banc Court of Appeals, Stapleton, Circuit Judge, held that: (1) fact issues precluding summary judgment existed as to whether it was feasible for broker-dealers to execute trades through private on-line services when those prices were more favorable than NBBO; (2) fact issues existed as to broker-dealers' scienter; and (3) fact that trading at NBBO was universal practice did not preclude finding of securities fraud.

Reversed and remanded.

OPINION OF THE COURT

STAPLETON, Circuit Judge.

I.

Plaintiff-Appellants are investors who purchased and sold securities on the NASDAQ market, the major electronic market for "over-the-counter" securities, during the two year period from November 4, 1992 to November 4, 1994 ("the class period"). The defendants are NASDAQ market makers. NASDAQ is a self-regulating market owned by the National Association of Securities Dealers ("NASD"), subject to oversight by the Securities and Exchange Commission ("SEC").

An "over-the-counter" market like NASDAQ differs in important respects from the more familiar auction markets, like the New York and American Stock Exchanges. The NYSE and AMEX markets are distinguished by a physical exchange floor where buy and sell orders actually "meet," with prices set by the interaction of those orders under the supervision of a market "specialist." In a dealer market like NASDAQ, the market exists electronically, in the form of a communications system which constantly receives and reports the prices at which geographically dispersed market makers are willing to buy and sell different securities. These market makers compete with one another to buy and sell the same securities using the electronic system; NASDAQ is, then, an electronic inter-dealer quotation system.

In a dealer market, market makers create liquidity by being continuously willing to buy and sell the security in which they are making a market. In this way, an individual who wishes to buy or sell a security does not have to wait until someone is found who wishes to take the opposite side in the desired transaction. To account for the effort and risk required to maintain liquidity, market makers are allowed to set the prices at which they are prepared to buy and sell a particular security; the difference between the listed "ask" and "bid" prices is the "spread" that market makers capture as compensation.

The electronic quotation system ties together the numerous market makers for all over-the-counter securities available on NASDAQ. All NASDAQ market makers are required to input their bid and offer prices to the NASD computer, which collects the information and transmits, for each security, the highest bid price and lowest ask price currently available. These prices are called the "National Best Bid and Offer," or NBBO. The NASD computer, publicly available to all NASDAQ market makers, brokers and dealers, displays and continuously updates the NBBO for each offered security.

Plaintiffs allege that technological advances made it feasible during the class period for the defendant market makers to execute orders at prices quoted on private on-line services like SelectNet and Instinet and that those prices were frequently more favorable to their investor clients than the NBBO price. According to plaintiffs, the defendants regularly used these services and knew that prices better than NBBO were often available through them. Even though they knew that their investor clients expected them to secure the best reasonably available price, plaintiffs say, the defendants executed plaintiffs' orders at the NBBO price when they knew that price was inferior and when they, at the same time, were trading at the more favorable price for their own accounts. In this way, they were able to inflate their profit margins at the expense of their investor clients. This practice is alleged to violate section 10 of the Securities Act of 1934, 15 U.S.C. §78j, and Rule 10b-5 promulgated thereunder, 17 C.F.R. §240.10b-5.

The plaintiffs also charge defendants with two other violations of section 10 and Rule 10b-5. Market makers who simultaneously hold a market order for both sides of a transaction may obtain more favorable prices than the NBBO by "crossing" these in-house orders. Transactions handled in this way are executed within the spread, giving both the purchaser and seller a better price. Similarly, a customer order can be matched by a market maker with an in-house limit order on the other side of the transaction. Since a limit order specifies a particular price at which to execute a transaction, matching another customer order at that price may beat the currently displayed NBBO quote for that security. Plaintiffs allege that the failure of the defendants to execute orders of their clients in these ways when feasible constitutes a fraudulent practice because, by executing at the NBBO rather than matching customer orders, the defendants capture the full market "spread" as a fee for their services without incurring any actual risk in the transaction.

II.

The defendants filed a motion to dismiss for failure to state a claim upon which relief could be granted. At the direction of the district court, this motion was converted into a motion for summary judgment, which was ultimately granted. *See In re Merrill Lynch Securities Litigation,* 911 F.Supp. 754 (D.N.J.1995). The district court rested its decision on two principal grounds. First, the court determined that the defendants made no misrepresentation. Though recognizing that the defendants, by accepting plaintiffs' orders, impliedly represented that they intended to execute those orders in conformity with the "duty of best execution," the court considered the scope of this duty sufficiently ill-defined that execution at the NBBO could not, as a matter of law, be found inconsistent with the duty. The court concluded that in the face of uncertainty about the scope of defendants' duty of best execution, holding them liable would be "highly imprudent." 911 F.Supp. at 771. Second, the court held that, even if defendants made a material misrepresentation, they could not, as a matter of law, have acted with the requisite scienter.

To state a claim for securities fraud under §10 of the Securities Act of 1934 and Rule 10b-5, plaintiffs must demonstrate: (1) a misrepresentation or omission of a material fact in connection with the purchase or sale of a security; (2) scienter on the part of the defendant; (3) reliance on the misrepresentation; and (4) damage resulting from the misrepresentation. (Citation omitted). Because plaintiffs have demonstrated that a genuine issue of material fact exists as to the elements of their securities fraud claim, we will reverse the district court.

III.

The parties agree that a broker-dealer owes to the client a duty of best execution. They further agree that a broker-dealer, by accepting an order without price instructions, impliedly represents that the order will be executed in a manner consistent with the duty of best execution and that a broker-dealer who accepts such an order while intending to breach that duty makes a misrepresentation that is material to the purchase or sale. The parties differ, however, on whether a trier of fact could conclude from this record that the implied representation made by the defendants included a representation that they would not execute at the NBBO price when prices more favorable to the client were available from sources like SelectNet and Instinet.

As we explain hereafter, this difference can be resolved only by determining whether, during the class period or some portion thereof, it was feasible for the defendants to execute trades through SelectNet and Instinet when prices more favorable than the NBBO were being quoted there. This is a matter concerning which the record reflects a material dispute of fact. If such prices were reasonably available and the defendants, at the time of accepting plaintiffs' orders, intended to execute them solely by reference to the NBBO, they made a material misrepresentation in connection with the purchase or sale of the securities involved. If a finder of fact could infer, in addition, that the defendants' implied representation was knowingly false or made with reckless indifference, it would follow that summary judgment for the defendants was inappropriate.

The duty of best execution, which predates the federal securities laws, has its roots in the common law agency obligations of undivided loyalty and reasonable care that an agent owes to his principal.[24] Since it is understood by all that the client-principal

---

24. [1]*See, e.g., Hall v. Paine*, 224 Mass. 62, 112 N.E. 153, 158 (1916) ("broker's obligation to his principal requires him to secure the highest price obtainable"); RESTATEMENT OF AGENCY (SECOND) §424 (1958) (agent must "use reasonable care to obtain terms which best satisfy the manifested purposes of the principal"). *See also Opper v. Hancock Securities Corp.*, 250 F.Supp. 668, 676 (S.D.N.Y.) ("[T]he duties of a securities broker are, if anything, more stringent than those imposed by general agency law."), *aff'd*, 367 F.2d 157 (2d Cir. 1966). Moreover, as the district court correctly recognized, the best execution duty "does not dissolve when the broker/dealer acts in its capacity as a principal." 911 F.Supp. at 760. *Accord, E.F. Hutton & Co.*, Exchange Act Rel. No. 25887, 49 S.E.C. 829, 832 (1988)

seeks his own economic gain and the purpose of the agency is to help the client-principal achieve that objective, the broker-dealer, absent instructions to the contrary, is expected to use reasonable efforts to maximize the economic benefit to the client in each transaction.

The duty of best execution thus requires that a broker-dealer seek to obtain for its customer orders the most favorable terms reasonably available under the circumstances (citations omitted). That is, the duty of best execution requires the defendants to execute the plaintiffs' trades at the best reasonably available price.[25] While ascertaining what prices are reasonably available in any particular situation may require a factual inquiry into all of the surrounding circumstances, the existence of a broker-dealer's duty to execute at the best of those prices that are reasonably available is well-established and is not so vague as to be without ascertainable content in the context of a particular trade or trades.

As the SEC has recognized on a number of occasions, the scope of the duty of best execution has evolved over time with changes in technology and transformation of the structure of financial markets. For example, before the creation of NASDAQ, a broker in an over-the-counter market satisfied her duty of best execution by contacting at least three market makers prior to executing a client's order. (citation omitted). With the advent of NASDAQ and the NBBO computer system providing instant access to the best bid and offer available nationwide, the standard for satisfying the duty of best execution necessarily heightened. After the class period, the SEC issued rules that altered the definition of the NBBO to include consideration of many of the alternative sources of liquidity that plaintiffs claim should have been consulted during the class period, such as SelectNet and Instinet. *(citation omitted)*. Prospectively, at least, this heightened the standard still further.

Because the scope of the duty of best execution is constantly evolving and because the "reasonably available" component of the duty is fact dependent, broker-dealers have long been required to conform customer order practices with changes in technology and markets. For example, the NASD's Rules of Fair Practice, adopted in 1968, required brokers in the over-the-counter market to "use reasonable diligence to ascertain the best inter-dealer market for the subject security and buy or sell in

---

("A broker-dealer's determination to execute an order as principal or agent cannot be 'a means by which the broker may elect whether or not the law will impose fiduciary standards upon him in the actual circumstances of any given relationship or transaction.'") (citation omitted).

25. [2] Other terms in addition to price are also relevant to best execution. In determining how to execute a client's order, a broker-dealer must take into account order size, trading characteristics of the security, speed of execution, clearing costs, and the cost and difficulty of executing an order in a particular market (citation omitted). When the plaintiffs state that better "prices" were reasonably available from sources other than the NBBO, we understand that to mean that, given an evaluation of price as well as all of the other relevant terms, the trade would be better executed through a source of liquidity other than the NBBO (e.g., SelectNet, Instinet, in-house limit orders or market orders held by the defendants, or limit orders placed by the public in the Small Order Execution System). Similarly, for convenience, we use the phrases "best reasonably available price" and "best terms" interchangeably.

such market so that the resultant price to the customer is as favorable as possible under the prevailing market conditions." (citation omitted). Included in the factors used to satisfy the requirement of "reasonable diligence" are both "the number of primary markets checked," and the "location and accessibility to the customer's broker-dealer of primary markets and quotations sources." *Id.*

Almost a year before the end of the class period, the SEC staff issued a report entitled "Market 2000: An Examination of Current Equity Market Developments." This report notes that the SEC has consistently taken the position that the evolving nature of the markets requires a broker-dealer to "periodically assess the quality of competing markets to ensure that its order flow is directed to markets providing the most advantageous terms for the customer's order." (citation omitted). As the term "periodically assess" suggests and as the SEC confirms June in its amicus briefing before us, this segment of the report was not speaking to the issue of whether, during the class period, the duty of best execution included a requirement that broker-dealers engage in an order-by-order analysis of competing markets. It does, however, expressly recognize a duty on the part of broker-dealers to periodically examine their practices in light of market and technology changes and to modify those practices if necessary to enable their clients to obtain the best reasonably available prices.

The plaintiffs' orders did not specify the price at which they should be executed. It is a reasonable inference that plaintiffs, in placing their orders, sought their own economic advantage and that they would not have placed them without an understanding that the defendants would execute them in a manner that would maximize plaintiffs' economic benefit from the trade. Given the objective of the agency and the regulatory background we have reviewed, we conclude that a trier of fact could infer that the defendants' acceptance of the orders was reasonably understood as a representation that they would not be executed at the NBBO price when better prices were reasonably available elsewhere. Accordingly, we must examine the record evidence relevant to whether prices quoted on private on-line services like SelectNet and Instinet were reasonably available during the class period and whether those prices were more favorable than the NBBO when plaintiffs' orders were executed.

The evidence pointed to by plaintiffs indicates that (1) SelectNet and Instinet were in existence throughout the class period; (2) the quotations reported by these services reflected buyers and sellers ready to trade at the quoted prices; (3) the defendants themselves actively traded on SelectNet and Instinet during the class period; and (4) other respected members of the brokerage community, since before the class period, have regarded these services as providing reasonably available prices and have executed orders through them when the prices reported were more favorable to the client than the NBBO price. In addition, the plaintiffs have tendered expert testimony confirming the reasonable availability of execution sources other than the NBBO during the class period.

With respect to whether SelectNet and Instinet prices were more favorable at the time their orders were executed, plaintiffs point to an SEC study of prices during the three month period from April through June 1994. The SEC found that "approximately 85% of the bids and offers displayed by market makers in Instinet and 90% of the bids and offers displayed on SelectNet were at better prices than those posted publicly on NASDAQ." (citation omitted). Plaintiffs have also tendered evidence of a few trades executed for them by defendants at the NBBO where evidence of contemporaneous offers on Instinet and SelectNet indicate that lower prices were available....

To be sure, the defendants, with record support, insist that consulting other sources besides the NBBO would have added substantial expense and delay to the execution of plaintiffs' orders, more than offsetting any improvements that might have been available in terms of price.[26] This, however, does nothing more than create a material dispute of fact which we are not permitted to resolve in favor of the defendants at this juncture.

We believe the evidence is sufficient to allow a reasonable trier of fact to conclude that, by the time of the class period, both technology and over-the-counter markets had developed to a point where it was feasible to maximize the economic benefit to the client by taking advantage of better prices than the NBBO. Summary judgment for defendants on this element of plaintiffs' claim was therefore not appropriate.

As we have noted, recovery on a federal securities fraud claim requires a showing of scienter: a deliberate or reckless misrepresentation of a material fact. *See Ernst & Ernst v. Hochfelder,* 425 U.S. 185, 193, 96 S.Ct. 1375, 1380–81, 47 L.Ed.2d 668 (1976); *Eisenberg v. Gagnon,* 766 F.2d 770, 776 (3d Cir.1985). The alleged misrepresentation here is an implied representation made by the defendants when they agreed to execute the plaintiffs' orders that they intended to maximize the plaintiffs' economic gain in the transaction. Since the defendants knew of the plaintiffs' profit motivation, they must have understood, according to the plaintiffs, that plaintiffs would expect them to obtain a price more advantageous to the plaintiffs than the NBBO when one was readily available. If the defendants intended not to act in a manner consistent with this expectation when they accepted the orders and yet did not so advise plaintiffs,

---

26. [5] In particular, the defendants rely upon the existence during the class period of the Small Order Execution System ("SOES"). SOES is an electronic routing system that was created in 1984 to allow orders from small investors to be automatically executed at the NBBO. Defendants claim that since the NBBO was the exclusive source for trades executed through SOES, the duty of best execution was presumptively met for these trades. The evidence to which the defendants point supports their position that execution at the NBBO was a common practice in handling orders from small investors. It does not alone, however, require a finding that trades at better prices through SelectNet or Instinet were not reasonably available even for small orders or that a broker-dealer's duty of best execution was automatically discharged by executions through SOES. While size is undoubtedly a relevant factor in determining the scope of the duty of best execution, for summary judgment purposes we find the state of the record with respect to small orders no different than the record with respect to other orders. The affidavit of Richard Y. Roberts, who served as the chairman of the SEC throughout the class period, notes that, to his knowledge, the SEC did not take the position that execution through SOES automatically satisfied the duty of best execution, and indicates that, in his opinion, such a position would be contrary to several SEC releases. At any rate, not all of plaintiff's orders were executed through SOES.

plaintiffs insist that the defendants can be found to have made an implied representation that they knew to be false.

We believe that a reasonable trier of fact could find this chain of inferences persuasive based on a straight forward economic analysis of the plaintiffs' relationship
with the defendants. In addition, however, plaintiffs rely upon evidence showing that
respected members of the brokerage community recognized, even prior to the class
period, that trades were readily available from sources other than the NBBO and that
their clients expected them to take advantage of those sources whenever it would benefit the client. (citations omitted). Moreover, the plaintiffs have shown that an SEC
study found clear evidence of a two-tiered market during the class period, in which
NASDAQ market makers routinely traded at one price with retail clients like the
plaintiffs and at a better price for themselves through quotation services like SelectNet
and Instinet. *(citation omitted)*. They have further shown that the possibility that the
duty of best execution might require resort to sources other than the NBBO was being
actively debated during the class period and that that debate ultimately resulted,
shortly after the class period, in a regulation effectively requiring as much. *Id.*

* * *

Defendants have countered with affidavits of other respected members of the brokerage community stating that their practice during the class period was the same as
that of the defendants....

But the defendants, in elevating the practice of a segment of the industry to be
outcome determinative, lose sight of the fact that the basis for the duty of best execution is the mutual understanding that the client is engaging in the trade—and retaining the services of the broker as his agent—solely for the purpose of maximizing
his own economic benefit, and that the broker receives her compensation because
she assists the client in reaching that goal. Based on this mutual understanding and
the absence of any express limitations on the brokers' responsibility, a trier of fact
could find that the defendants, although intending to execute with sole reference to
the NBBO, understood that they were expected to utilize sources other than the NBBO
when a better price was readily available.[27]

In concluding as we do, we are not unmindful of the fact, deemed determinative
by the district court, that execution of customer orders at the NBBO was a practice
"widely, if not almost universally followed" in the securities industry during the class
period. (citation omitted). Under the district court's logic, a Section 10(b) defendant

---

27. [6] The forgoing analysis is generally applicable to plaintiffs' claim that it was reasonably
feasible for defendants to "cross" customer orders on opposing side of a transaction and match customer
orders with in-house limit orders. Plaintiffs' record support, including affidavits from respected members of the investment community, raises a disputed issue of material fact as to whether these practices
were reasonably feasible during the class period. If the defendants intended to execute plaintiffs' orders
at the NBBO despite the reasonable availability of these alternative pricing sources, and if the defendants
acted knowingly or with reckless indifference to the falsity of their material representations, then
plaintiffs have a securities fraud claim for these practices as well.

would be entitled to summary judgment even if it were her regular practice to knowingly violate the duty of best execution, so long as she could identify a sufficient number of other broker-dealers engaged in the same wrongful conduct to be able to argue in good faith that the underlying duty was "ambiguous." We cannot accept an analysis that would produce such a result.

Even a universal industry practice may still be fraudulent. *See Chasins v. Smith, Barney & Co.,* 438 F.2d 1167, 1171–72 (2d Cir.1970) (non-disclosure of widespread industry practice may still be non-disclosure of material fact); *Opper v. Hancock Securities Corp.,* 250 F.Supp. 668, 676 (S.D.N.Y.) (industry custom may be found fraudulent, especially on first occasion it is litigated) *aff'd,* 367 F.2d 157 (2d Cir.1966); *see also Vermilye & Co. v. Adams Express Co.,* 88 U.S. (21 Wall.) 138, 146, 22 L.Ed. 609 (1874). Indeed, the SEC recently completed an investigation in which it found that certain practices by NASDAQ market makers, not at issue here, were fraudulent even though they were widely followed within the industry. *(citation omitted).*

As defendants emphasize, the practice of exclusive reliance on the NBBO has never been held to be fraudulent by any court or regulator. On the other hand, there is no statute, rule, regulation, or interpretation, by the SEC or by a court, that authoritatively establishes that, for all trades, the NBBO exhausted the category of "reasonably available prices" during the class period. This absence of precedent did not, however, absolve the district court of the duty to resolve the plaintiffs' securities fraud claim once it was presented in this suit.

* * *

VI.

On the record before us, we believe a reasonable trier of fact could conclude that the defendants misrepresented that they would execute the plaintiffs' orders so as to maximize the plaintiffs' economic benefit, and that this misrepresentation was intentional or reckless because, at the time it was made, the defendants knew that they intended to execute the plaintiffs' orders at the NBBO price even if better prices were reasonably available. A reasonable trier of fact could thus find scienter with respect to a material misrepresentation, as well as the other elements essential to a Section 10(b) fraud claim. Accordingly, we will reverse the summary judgment entered by the district court and remand for further proceedings.

———

To date, the SEC has not adopted a rule to define best execution. Moreover, determining whether a broker-dealer has met its duty of best execution has become ever more complex in light of advances in technology, increased trading volume, and the proliferation of trading strategies and order types. Accordingly, the broker-dealer's duty of best execution is not merely about obtaining the best price, but includes the requirement that it seek to obtain for its customer orders the most favorable terms reasonably available under the circumstances. In addition, the broker-dealer is not required to meet its duty of best execution on an order-by-order analysis of competing market centers, but instead, must regularly and rigorously evaluate the quality of executions obtained for its customers' orders. The following case illustrates the complexity of determining whether a broker-dealer has met its duty of best execution; as discussed in the case, failure to meet the duty of best execution is considered a fraudulent practice in violation of, among others, Sections 15(c)(1)(A) and 10(b), and Rule 10b-5 of the Exchange Act.

SEC v. Pasternak

561 F.Supp.2d 459 (Dist. New Jersey 2008)

I. BACKGROUND

A. Procedural History

This case inquires into Knight's "market making" business and the actions of one of Knight's institutional sales traders, Joseph Leighton ("Joseph") — John's brother. In particular, the SEC focused its claims on forty-two trades executed by Joseph in 1999 and 2000 on behalf of "buy-side" institutional firms, such as mutual funds and investment advisors. All of the complained-of trades occurred in the NASDAQ Stock Market ("NASDAQ"). During the relevant time period, John, as head of Knight's institutional sales desk, supervised Joseph, while Pasternak held ultimate supervisory responsibilities as Knight's CEO and Chairperson of the Board of Directors.

* * *

The SEC submits that "Joseph Leighton failed to make full and appropriate disclosures and failed to provide best execution for orders placed by the institutional customers." During the trial, the SEC expressed that this pattern of fraud amounted to improper front-running; that is, Joseph, upon receipt of an institutional order, would take a position in the ordered security and delay the execution of the order to take advantage of fluctuating market conditions, thereby generating profits that the SEC deems improper.

The SEC further alleges that Defendants knew of, or were reckless in not knowing of, Joseph's fraud. The Commission claims Defendants participated in the perpetration of this fraud by misstating to Knight's customers and the public that Knight provided "best execution" and failing to disclose "the manner in which [Joseph] priced executions to customers." During the trial, the SEC explained that John and Pasternak owed an independent fiduciary obligation to disclose to Knight's institutional customers Joseph's profits, and the failure to so inform the customers breached their fiduciary duties. The SEC further argued that Pasternak made a false and misleading statement by signing Knight's 1999 and 2000 Form 10–Ks, which stated that Knight provided its customers with best execution....

* * *

II. STATUTORY AND REGULATORY BACKGROUND

The Court must consider this case against the backdrop of the complex and intricate statutory and regulatory body of law applicable to the securities industry. For that reason, the Court sets forth at the outset the relevant statutes and regulations. In addition, the Court details the rules and notices promulgated by the National Association of Securities Dealers, Inc. ("NASD") implicated by the SEC's allegations.[28]

A. Applicable Statutes under the Securities Act and the Exchange Act

The SEC's Amended Complaint seeks to impose primary and secondary liability for alleged violations of the following statutes and regulations: Section 17(a) of the Securities Act; Sections 10(b), 15(c)(1)(A), and 17(a) of the Exchange Act; and Rules 10b-5 and 17a-3. Those statutes and regulations fall into two categories: first, statutes and regulations prohibiting fraudulent conduct—Securities Act Section 17(a), Exchange Act Sections 10(b) and 15(c)(1)(A), and Rule 10b-5; and, second, the statute and regulation governing record-keeping by broker-dealer firms—Exchange Act Section 17(a) and Rule 17a-3.

* * *

B. Applicable NASD Regulations

The NASDAQ is a self-regulating market owned and regulated by the NASD. The SEC exercises oversight authority over the NASD. To regulate the market and its members, the NASD promulgates rules, policies, and guidelines. The present case necessarily implicates some of those rules and regulations in effect in 1999 and 2000. (citations omitted).

On all trading, the NASD requires "best execution." NASD Rule 2320.[29] Subsection (a) of Rule 2320 states:

> In any transaction for or with a customer or a customer of another broker-dealer, a member and person associated with a member shall use reasonable diligence to ascertain the best market for the subject security and buy or sell in such market so that the resultant price to the customer is as favorable as possible under prevailing market conditions. Among the factors that will be considered in determining whether a member has used "reasonable diligence" are:
>
> (1) the character of the market for the security, e.g., price, volatility, relative liquidity, and pressure on available communications;
>
> (2) the size and type of transaction;
>
> (3) the number of markets checked;
>
> (4) accessibility of the quotation; and
>
> (5) the terms and conditions of the order which result in the transaction, as communicated to the member and persons associated with the member.

---

28. [5] In July of 2007, the NASD was consolidated with the regulatory, enforcement, and arbitration bodies of the New York Stock Exchange to form the Financial Industry Regulatory Authority ("FINRA").

29. NASD Rule 2320 has been superseded by FINRA Rule 5310 but the provisions have remained the same.

NASD Rule 2320(a); Subsection (f) of that Rule further explains that the best execution obligation applies "where the member acts as agent for the account of his customer" and "where retail transactions are executed as principal and contemporaneously offset." NASD Rule 2320(f); However, "[s]uch obligations do not relate to the reasonableness of commission rates, markups or markdowns which are governed by Rule 2440 and IM–2440." NASD Rule 2320(f) ...

To further explain Rule 2320, the NASD issued Interpretive Memo ("IM") 2320, entitled "Interpretive Guidance with Respect to Best Execution Requirements." IM-2320. To also explain Rule 2320, the NASD issued Notice to Members ("NTM") 97-57 in 1997, providing guidance on SEC order handling rules, NASD limit order protection rules, and best execution responsibilities. (citations omitted) NTM 97-57 explains that "the application of best execution concepts necessarily involves a 'facts and circumstances' analysis[ ]" and that the best execution obligation "evolves as rules and systems change." (citations omitted) In addition, this NTM specifically discusses how a market maker meets the best execution requirement when handling a discretionary, not-held order. (citation omitted).

III. FINDINGS OF FACT

The Court notes that it rejects the proposed findings of fact submitted on numerous occasions by the SEC. Rather, the Court finds that a preponderance of the evidence submitted supports the facts proposed by Defendants.

A. Background of the NASDAQ Market in 1999–2000 and Formation of Knight Securities

The presently complained-of trades executed by Joseph occurred in the NASDAQ stock exchange, an over-the-counter securities market. The NASDAQ market operates through multiple market-making firms. Essentially, a market maker serves as a broker-dealer to execute sell and buy orders for traded stocks on behalf of its customers.

In so doing, the NASD requires market makers to buy or sell on behalf of a customer "at a price that is fair, taking into consideration all relevant circumstances[.]" NASD Rule 2440. Thus, a market maker must find the best price of a particular stock, whether the best priced stock is from the market making firm's own inventory of stock or from another source. The best price depends on whether the order is to buy or to sell: the best offer price is the cheapest price at which one could buy a stock, whereas the best bid price is the highest price at which one could sell a stock.[30] To find the best price, the market maker must consider the market conditions for the particular security, the expense of the transaction, and the market maker's entitlement to a profit. To ascertain if a price is "fair and reasonable," one must compare that price with other prices in the marketplace and conduct a trade-by-trade "facts and circumstances analysis[,]" ...

As part of their business, and to maintain an orderly market, these firms must necessarily commit their own capital, particularly in instances where the firm's in-

---

30. [8] These prices are reported as the national best bid and offer ("NBBO") prices.

ventory of stock provides the best offer or bid prices. As a result, market making firms compete against each other by publicizing quotes on a particular stock in their inventory to attract order flow and volume.

In carrying out its business, a market making firm handles different types of orders. One type is the "market order," which a market maker must execute "instantaneously against the best quoted market." The purpose of a market order is immediate best execution. Another type of order is the "limit order," where the customer specifically instructs the market maker to execute a trade when the stock reaches a particular price. The focus of a limit order is the price.

A market maker also executes "not-held orders." A customer placing a not-held order provides the market maker with the volume of a particular stock sought to be bought or sold and grants the market maker discretion as to price and time of execution of that trade, with the goal of achieving "best execution." On a not-held order, a market maker is not "held" to the immediacy and price requirements imposed in a market or limit order.

The NASD has defined a not-held, or "working," order as "an order voluntarily categorized by the customer as permitting the member to trade at any price without being required to execute the customer order." When handling such an order, a broker-dealer "must use its brokerage judgment in the execution of the order, and if such judgment is properly exercised, the broker is relieved of its normal responsibilities with respect to the time of execution and the price or prices of execution of such an order." Although the customer bestows discretion to the broker-dealer, a customer nevertheless monitors the transaction and modifies the parameters of the order as it deems necessary.

In the NASDAQ market, a trade in stock can be either on a principal or agency basis. The NASD defines a principal trade as "a trade in which the broker-dealer buys or sells for an account in which the broker-dealer has a beneficial ownership interest[,]" such as a proprietary account. In contrast, an agency trade is "a trade in which a broker-dealer ... acts as an independent intermediary for the account of its customer[ ]" and does not execute orders in a proprietary account). An agency trade is generally considered to be a riskless transaction for the broker-dealer.

A principal trade may also be riskless. The NASD defines a riskless principal trade as a trade "in which a broker-dealer, after having received an order to buy [or] sell a security, purchases [or] sells a security as princip[al] at the same price ... to satisfy that order." On a riskless principal trade, the broker-dealer charges its customer a disclosed mark-up, mark-down, or commission.

Most market makers executing institutional orders between the years 1999 to 2000, executed net trades, "accumulating shares at one price and executing to customers at a different price." The NASD defines a net trade as one in which "a market maker, at the request of a customer[,] while holding a customer order[ ] to buy [or] sell executes a buy [or] sell as princip[al] at one price from the street or another customer and then executes an offsetting sell [or] buy from the customer at a different price."

The market maker's profit is then the difference between the price of the market maker's transaction and the price of the transaction to the customer, or the "spread." Such profit on net trades, generally, are not separately disclosed to the customer. Furthermore, apart from the fair and reasonable price requirement, no NASD rule or regulation, or industry standard, sets a maximum limit on the profit or spread generated on a net order.

However, the NASD specifically requires traders to provide "best execution" on not-held orders. According to NASD Rule 2320, a broker-dealer must "use reasonable diligence to ascertain the best market for the subject security and buy or sell in such market so that the resultant price to the customer is as favorable as possible under prevailing market conditions." ... That Rule further sets forth various factors considered to determine whether "reasonable diligence" is met; those factors include: "the character of the market for the security" — such as, price, volatility, and liquidity; "the size and type of transaction;" "the number of markets checked;" the "accessibility of the quotation;" and "the terms and conditions of the order[.]" Thus, whether a broker-dealer provides best execution depends upon a plethora of factors, including, but not limited to: market conditions; the trade's impact on the market; the ultimate price paid or received; the availability of anonymity to the customer; and the trade's impact on the customer's overall portfolio.

In addition, Section II of NTM 97-57 explains that a market maker handling a not-held order "does not owe the same best execution obligations to [its customer] as it would if the order were a non-discretionary market or limit order." NTM 97-57 explains that the discretion granted in a not-held order "means that the firm may trade at the same price or at a better price than that received by the discretionary order[,]" provided the market maker seeks "to obtain the best fill considering all of the terms agreed to with the customer and the market conditions surrounding the order." To seek that "best fill," the customer and market maker could agree that the market maker may, "if necessary to fill the entire order at an acceptable price, trade ahead of the institutional customer's order."

Importantly, whether a market making firm meets the best execution requirement on a particular trade is based primarily on the customer's assessment of the firm's ability to follow instructions. A customer generally focuses on the ultimate price received for the trade, comparing that price with the volume-weighted average price, or "VWAP," to determine the quality of a trade. Essentially, the customer is in the best position to ascertain whether best execution is met, as the customer knows its instructions and specific trading strategy. As a result, unless the customer raises a concern about the execution of a trade, it would be difficult for a trader or supervisor to determine that the customer was not satisfied with an execution.

* * *

Knight's structure included an institutional sales desk composed of the sales traders and a market making desk composed of the market makers.

* * *

In March of 1998, Knight became a publicly-traded company by making an initial public offering ("IPO")…. As part of its obligations as a publicly-traded company, Knight, through its Directors, filed the SEC-required Form 10–K in 1999 and 2000. Those documents represented that Knight offered best execution to its customers.

* * *

B. Knight's Execution of Trades and Retail Order Flow

Considering the background of the NASDAQ market and the formation of Knight, the Court now turns to the methodology employed by Knight to execute institutional orders. Knight's business goal was to commit capital, creating a risk, and to effectively manage that risk to generate a profit. To further that goal, Knight handled both institutional orders and retail order flow, resulting in unique business practices. At issue in this case is Knight's handling of institutional orders. However, Knight's traders executed those institutional orders in tandem with the retail order flow; thus, it is pivotal in this case to understand how Knight handled both types of orders.

1. *Institutional Orders*

Between 1999 and 2000, Knight, on behalf of its institutional customers, primarily executed not-held orders, typically conducted on a "net basis[,]" … To generate institutional orders, Knight used the electronic medium, AutEx. Through AutEx, Knight sent electronic advertisements to the buy-side, indicating that Knight could provide a natural trade of a particular volume in a stock. Knight, as part of a mandatory protocol, required its traders to advertise over AutEx any order imbalance above 25,000 shares.

During the relevant time period, institutional orders streamed into Knight via an electronic message or the telephone. If the order came to Knight via telephone, then a sales trader, or his assistant, would complete an order ticket. An order ticket specified the date and time of receipt of the order, the stock symbol, the volume of shares, whether the order is held or not-held, and whether the order is a short or long sale.

Upon receipt of an order, a sales trader discussed the order with the customer to understand the customer's goals for that order. The customer would give the sales traders any particular instructions it had on the order, including how the trader should work the order, the price parameters, and size. Such instructions could include a request for the staggering of the trade; that is, the customer gave the sales trader its ultimate volume goal, but instructed the trader to initially execute only a portion thereof. On net trades, the customer and sales trader would negotiate the final price of the stock bought by or sold to the customer. Generally, order sizes ranged, during the 1999 to 2000 time period, from under one hundred shares to millions of shares.

After obtaining the instructions from the customer, the sales trader contacted the market maker who maintained an account, or "book," on the particular stock included in the order. The sales trader passed the order on to the market maker, who would relay to the trader any relevant market information. The sales trader then provided the customer with feedback and information obtained from the market maker, while the market maker began to execute the order, either buying or selling the stock.

As the market maker worked the institutional order, the sales trader monitored the market maker's activity through Knight's automated, computer-based trade and order management tool, the Brokerage Real Time Application Support System ("BRASS"). On BRASS, a sales trader can observe the market maker's position in the stock and attempt to sift out the position taken on behalf of the trader's institutional customer, rather than for another institutional order, retail order, or proprietary trading. If anything appeared on BRASS that the execution of the order might not be going well, the sales trader would call the customer to determine how the customer would like to react. In addition, throughout the entire transaction, the customer would closely monitor the marketplace in respect of the ordered trade, observing price and volume fluctuations. Based on the changes in the market, the customer may modify or cancel the order at any moment.

As part of working a not-held order, a market maker fulfilling that order may commit Knight's capital to facilitate that trade, resulting in a "risk trade." For example, a market maker may commit capital if the institutional order requires stock not readily available in the market. Although this practice is not required of a market making firm, it benefits customer relations. If he chooses to do so, a market maker may commit capital at any point in the working of the institutional order. In instances in which a market maker commits capital, a sales trader, as a matter of courtesy, not as a requirement, tells the customer that Knight committed capital on the particular trade. Other times, a customer may specifically request that Knight commit capital, such as where the customer sought an immediate print.

The final step in executing an institutional order is "the print" to NASDAQ "tape[,]" the Automated Confirmation Transaction ("ACT") Service — a consolidated record reflecting all transactions occurring in the NASDAQ market. The print is essentially a confirmation to the customer and a record to NASDAQ of the trade conducted on behalf of the institutional customer. The print to the customer indicates the volume of the stock traded and the final price at which the customer bought the stock or at which the customer sold Knight the stock.

* * *

Once a print was made, the customer would receive acknowledgment of the print from its electronic order management system or by a telephone call from the Knight sales trader working the order.

Importantly, a customer could provide specific instructions on when it wanted the transaction printed, and those instructions varied from customer to customer. Based on customer instructions, or in the sales trader's discretion in working the order, the complete execution of an institutional order could occur over a period of time and include multiple, piecemeal prints to the customer. If an order was for a large volume of shares or a highly-volatile stock, a sales trader or his assistant could print the transaction outside of the national best bid and offer price. In those instances, Knight's compliance department required the print to include an "ACT modifier," such as "SLD" or "PRP[,]" indicating that the print was out of time sequence.

At Knight, in addition to the NASD requirements of fair price and best execution, the sales traders had a performance commitment to satisfy their customers' expectations as to price. Because the institutional customer "focused on the price [it] receive[d] against [its] instructions[,]" the sales trader needed "to create an outcome that satisfie[d] the customer[.]" If the trader failed to create a satisfactory outcome, then Knight would "have to buy stock at inferior prices ... and essentially lose money." In such an instance, a sales trader would not discuss the issue with the customer, but, rather, would print the transaction to the customer at what the trader believed to be a fair price. Indeed, all not-held institutional orders required a performance commitment. At times, an institutional order could require both capital and performance commitments by Knight. In those instances, capital commitments could occur at any point in the execution of an order and would be in addition to the performance commitment that is always existent.

2. Retail Orders

In conjunction with institutional orders, Knight also handled retail orders. Those orders were both buy and sell orders; thereby, Knight accumulated positions in a security by executing those retail orders.

Knight automatically executed much of that retail order flow to provide its retail customers with liquidity not otherwise available. Essentially, Knight would provide automatic execution on a stock based on its liquidity and volatility up to a certain volume in a particular period of time. Knight labeled that threshold volume and period of time as a "firewall." Theoretically, once retail order executions reached that firewall, Knight's computer system prevented any further automatic execution of retail orders, which would then "go to a manual mode[.]" The manual mode ensured that Knight did not provide non-existent liquidity for a particular stock.

However, due to a computer or technical error in Knight's system, the manual mode did not initiate once the actual firewall was reached; rather, the manual mode initiated when Knight was in a net position of the firewall. In other words, the automatic executions would deplete Knight's inventory in a particular stock and continue thereafter until reaching the volume set in the firewall. Despite this issue, Knight's provision of automatic executions was pivotal to its unique business practice.

Because of that firewall issue, however, the automatic execution of retail orders could deplete an inventory acquired to fill an institutional order. As a result, Knight's market makers could protect positions built for an institutional order by moving those inventories to a "back book[.]" Typically, the back book was used by market makers as a principal account; that is, an account used to take positions for the firm, rather than on behalf of customers.

To distinguish itself from its competitors, Knight offered on its retail orders an "opening guarantee[,]" which was generally unprofitable to Knight, but provided

Knight with the opportunity to attract more volume to its business. Knight's opening guarantee assured customers that Knight would execute both buy and sell trades at the midpoint of the opening national best bid price and national best offer price. Essentially, the opening guarantee guaranteed customers execution of trades at the same price, irrespective of the timing in which the customer placed the order.

3. *Sales Credit Data*

Knight's trading data collected both retail order executions and institutional order executions. The recorded data reflects the position held by Knight in a particular security and does not differentiate between the types of orders executed.

Knight used this trading data to compensate its institutional sales traders. Knight remunerated its institutional sales traders a percentage of the profit or loss on a particular institutional trade. At the end of a trading day, each market maker would have a BRASS-generated profit and loss number, called "P & L[,]" attributed to all of the trades he executed that day. Generally, assistant traders would calculate manually, from the P & L number, a sales trader's "sales credit"—that is, the allocation of the overall P & L on a particular stock to an institutional order transacted by the sales trader.

Essentially, the calculation of a sales credit was "a negotiation of who would get what share of the profits for each day, based on what each party thought they contributed to that P & L[.]" This is because Knight's trade run data did not differentiate between trades executed for retail orders, institutional orders, and proprietary trading. Such an allocation necessarily required an analysis of multiple factors that interacted throughout the daily trading of the particular stock. Knight did not maintain any internal written guidelines as to how to allocate sales credit to a sales trader.

D. Joseph Leighton's Trading Practices

Having considered the background of Knight's trading practices and structure, the Court turns to the particular facts surrounding Joseph Leighton's trading practices.

* * *

On all of his trades, Joseph's institutional customers "quarterbacked" their orders, monitoring the market, providing specific instructions throughout the transaction, and, in some cases, "doling out" the order—that is, giving Joseph an order in increments.... Breaking up, or doling out, the orders left control over the trade in the hands of the institutional customer, rather than with Joseph.

Because the customers closely monitored the market after placing an order with Joseph, the customers continually communicated with Joseph throughout the execution of the order, and changed their instructions and strategies as the customer deemed appropriate in light of the market conditions.

Indeed, Joseph's customers found, at the time that they transacted business with Joseph, that Joseph provided them with the best prices and volume in light of their instructions and market conditions.... None of Joseph's customers ever lodged a complaint against him for his trading.

Between 1999 and 2000, Joseph generated one of the highest gross sales credits each month amongst Knight's sales traders.

* * *

[T]he pure essence of a not-held order is to allow a sales trader, such as Joseph, to monitor the market and various conditions and to exercise his discretion to determine when to print to the customer. In exercising that discretion, a sales trader is held to only two requirements: to use reasonable diligence to provide best execution and, if committing capital on the order, to execute at a fair price. As part of the best execution requirement, the NASD has expressed that a sales trader may, "if necessary to fill the entire order at an acceptable price, trade ahead of the institutional customer's order." Further, the discretion granted in a not-held order "means that the firm may trade at the same price or at a better price than that received by the discretionary order." A not-held working order, thus, necessarily requires the sales trader to manipulate the execution of the trades to arrive at best execution for the customer.

Furthermore, as explained by Cangiano,[31] best execution obligations could be divided into two categories: (1) "plain vanilla," or simple, best execution; and (2) sophisticated best execution. Plain vanilla best execution occurs where an order for a small amount of shares is executed immediately at the best available price, which must be inside the national best bid and offer price for that stock. This type of best execution applies to market or limit orders. In contrast, sophisticated best execution applies to not-held orders for high-volume, volatile stock. To satisfy the sophisticated best execution requirement, a sales trader must use his best efforts to fill the order at the best price in accordance with NASD Rule 2320. Joseph's trades fall in the category of sophisticated best execution.

Whether a sales trader uses reasonable diligence to provide best execution or executes a trade at a fair price requires a fact-sensitive inquiry. The Court must consider the type of security traded, including its price, volatility, and liquidity, the size of the transaction, the market conditions existent at the time of the transaction, the instructions given by the customer, and the prices offered by other market making firms. However, the SEC has not proffered sufficient evidence as to these factors, with the exception of possibly three trades: (1) a March 16, 2000 trade of ETEK shares on behalf of Putnam; (2) a May 24, 2000 trade of COST shares on behalf of Davis Selected; and (3) a June 30, 2000 trade of JNPR shares on behalf of Putnam....

In fact, the institutional customers never complained about the price paid or received for a trade executed through Joseph. Contemporaneous with Joseph's executions, the institutional customers had knowledge as to all of the various factors that contribute to the determination of whether a sales trader provided best execution; the customers knew: the market conditions for the particular stock; the type and volume of the order; their strategy goals for the trade; their instructions to Joseph; and

---

31. James Cangiano was the SEC's expert witness.

the prices offered, if any, by other market making firms via AutEx. Joseph's customers, thus, were in the best position to determine if Joseph provided best execution.

Furthermore, these trades did not occur in a vacuum. Rather, Joseph operated through the "next generation" market making firm, and at the intersection of extraordinary factors: unprecedented volatility; the internet bubble; and the "democratization" of individual investors. The Court then must consider Joseph's trading practices in light of the general market conditions in 1999 and 2000 and Knight's business model—in which high-volume retail order flow interacted with positions acquired to fill institutional orders, and which provided automatic executions and opening guarantees.

Indeed, market conditions dictated Knight's capital commitments and the manner in which it executed institutional orders. For example, Knight's retail order flow included buy and sell orders. If those orders depleted Knight's inventory of a particular stock, then Knight might have to commit its capital to acquire positions to fill an institutional order. The depletion of an inventory by retail order flow and automatic executions could also dictate the timing of executions to fill an institutional order; such an event is not within Joseph's abilities to manipulate. Significantly, any profit generated due to Knight's own capital commitments, where it places itself at risk, rightly belongs to Knight, not to its institutional customers.

* * *

V. CONCLUSION

After presiding over a fifteen-day trial, during which the Court heard the testimony of twenty-four witnesses and accepted into evidence 273 documents, the Court holds that the SEC failed to prove by a preponderance of the evidence that Defendants violated any provision of the Securities Act or the Exchange Act. Rather, the overwhelming evidence indicates that Defendants, Joseph Leighton, and Knight did nothing improper in executing the forty-two trades singled out by the SEC.

———

The SEC continues to rely on SRO rulemaking to codify a broker-dealer's duty of best execution. Specifically, FINRA adopted Rule 5310(a)(1) in May 2012 to prescribe standards for meeting the duty of best execution:

FINRA Rule 5310. Best Execution and Interpositions

(a)(1) In any transaction for or with a customer or a customer of another broker-dealer, a member shall use reasonable diligence to ascertain the best market for the subject security and buy or sell in such market so that the resultant price to the customer is as favorable as possible under prevailing market conditions. Among the factors that will be considered in determining whether a member has used "reasonable diligence" are:

(A) the character of the market for the security (e.g., price volatility, relative liquidity, and pressure on available communications);

(B) the size and type of transaction

(C) the number of markets checked

(D) accessibility of the quotation; and

(E) the terms and conditions of the order which result in the transaction, as communicated to the member and persons associated with the member.

Exercising reasonable diligence in ascertaining whether a broker-dealer has met its duty of best execution involves a facts and circumstances analysis. Actions in one set of circumstances may allow the firm to meet its duty of best execution, but those same actions in another set of circumstances may result in the broker-dealer not meeting its duty of best execution. FINRA stresses that the duty of best execution is evolving and that broker-dealers must be aware that technological developments and changes to market structure are significant factors in determining whether a broker-dealer has met its best execution obligation. Moreover, broker-dealers must modify their order execution procedures, in light of these factors, to consider price opportunities that become reasonably available. Thus, broker-dealers must periodically examine their practices to determine whether customers are receiving best execution. FINRA Rule 5310 expressly requires broker-dealers to periodically (at a minimum, on a quarterly basis) conduct regular and rigorous reviews of the quality of the executions of its customers' orders if an order-by-order review is not conducted. Periodic reviews must be conducted on a security-by-security basis (e.g., limit order, market order, and market on open order). In addition, executing customer orders at the NBBO does not automatically meet the broker-dealer's best execution obligation, but may be used as a factor in determining whether this obligation has been met. Where reliable, superior prices are readily accessible in market centers such as ECNs, the broker-dealer should consider such prices in making decisions regarding best execution, including routing. FINRA Rule 5310 requires the broker-dealer to consider the following factors in conducting its regular and rigorous review of execution quality: (1) price improvement opportunities (i.e., the difference between the execution price and the best quotes prevailing at the time the order is received by the market); (2) differences in price disimprovement (i.e., situations in which a customer receives a worse price at execution than the best quotes prevailing at the time the order is received by the market); (3) the likelihood of execution of limit orders; (4) the speed of execution; (5) the size of execution; (6) transaction costs; (7) customer needs and expectations; and (8) the existence of internalization or payment for order flow arrangements. Broker-dealers that route customer orders to other broker-dealers for execution and those that internalize customer order flow, must have procedures to ensure regular and rigorous reviews of the quality of execution of their customers' orders. If a broker-dealer determines that there is a material difference in the execution quality among markets trading a particular security, it must modify its order routing arrangements or justify why there was no modification. Moreover, the broker-dealer must compare, among other things, the quality of executions obtained using its current order routing and execution arrangements with competing markets. No broker-dealer can transfer its obligation of best execution even if it doesn't execute its customers' orders. In addition, FINRA Rule 5310 defines the term *market* broadly.

Best execution is construed broadly in order to illustrate that broker-dealers must consider an expansive scope of trading venues to meet their duty of best execution. Accordingly, the term *market* includes exchanges, broker-dealers, and emerging trading venues in order to satisfy the broker-dealer's best execution obligation.

FINRA Rule 5310 also contains a number of other significant provisions dealing with the duty of best execution. First, it prohibits interpositioning (i.e., the injection of a third party between the broker-dealer and the best market for a security) if it prevents the broker-dealer from meeting its best execution obligation. If interpositioning is required to obtain best execution, the broker-dealer has the burden of justifying its necessity. Second, it expressly states that inadequate staffing of the department assigned to execute customers' orders does not justify failure to meet the duty of best execution. Third, it imposes liability on an executing broker-dealer if it knows that an introducing broker-dealer has failed to meet its duty of best execution. Fourth, it expressly states that the duty of best execution applies whether the broker-dealer is acting in an agency or principal capacity. Fifth, the duty of best execution is distinguished from determining reasonableness of commission rates, markups, or markdowns.

Notes and Questions

1. Increasing advances in technology have made programing for order routing increasingly important in meeting the broker-dealer's best execution obligation. In addition, Rules 605 and 606 of Reg NMS have provided public information facilitating the ability of an investor to more readily discern whether a broker-dealer is meeting its legal obligation to obtain best execution.

2. To address the practices enumerated in *Newton v. Merrill Lynch Pierce Fenner and Smith, Inc.*, the SEC adopted Rules 602–604 of Regulation NMS (formerly Rules 11ac1-1- 4). These rules were previously discussed in Section II of this chapter. What do these rules require?

3. When working not-held orders, will the broker-dealer be held liable for failing to obtain best execution when an institutional customer complains?

Hypothetical Three

Lindner was founder and CEO of Kirlin Holding Corp. ("Kirlin Holding") a thinly traded issuer in the OTC equity market. Kirlin Holding owned Kirlin BD, a broker-dealer registered with the SEC. Lindner directed that Amber Israel (the head equity trader for Kirlin BD) offer, on behalf of Kirlin Holding and pursuant to an existing stock repurchase program, Success First $.80 per share for Linder's 114,000 shares of Kirlin Holding. Lindner arbitrarily selected the purchase price for Success First's shares. At the time Kirlin BD received Success First's request to sell, there was an open order to purchase 24,700 shares of Kirlin Holding at $1.10 per share, and the inside bid price at the time of Success First's sale was $1.04 on Brat ECN. Moreover, two hours prior to execution of Success First's sell order, there was a sale to of 243,000 shares by Lindner's parents of Kirlin Holding shares to Kirlin Holding at $1.05 per share (a premium to the inside bid at the time). Did Israel obtain best execution for Success First at $.80 per share?

IV. Market Stability, Quality, and Fairness

A. High-Frequency Trading

High-frequency trading is a subset of algorithmic trading characterized by the high speed used to detect and act on profitable trading opportunities in the U.S. securities market. Algorithmic trading is a computerized system of trading using advanced mathematical models to make decisions about the timing, price, and quantity of transactions in U.S. securities markets. While there is no clear definition of high-frequency trading, the SEC defines high-frequency trading as firms comprised of "professional traders acting in a proprietary capacity that engage in strategies that generate a large number of trades on a daily basis." It notes that high-frequency trading firms may be organized, among other ways, as broker-dealers[32] and has identified certain characteristics associated with high-frequency trading: "(1) the use of extraordinarily high-speed and sophisticated computer programs for generating, routing, and executing orders; (2) use of co-location services and individual data feeds offered by exchanges and others to minimize network and other types of latencies; (3) very short time-frames for establishing and liquidating positions; (4) the submission of numerous orders that are canceled shortly after submission; and (5) ending the trading day in as close to a flat position as possible (that is, not carrying significant, unhedged positions over-night)."

Computer programs employed by high-frequency trading firms deploy various strategies for generating, routing, and executing orders measured in microseconds. In its 2010 market structure concept release, the SEC identified several strategies used by high-frequency traders, including passive market making, arbitrage, and directional. The passive market making (the broker-dealer has no obligation to be the buyer of last resort) strategy involves the submission of bids and offers (quotes) for securities and profiting on the spread between the bid and the offer. High-frequency market makers submit and cancel a large number of quotes for each transaction in response to, among other things, other order submissions or cancellations in the marketplace. They may also use algorithms to earn liquidity rebates (sometimes referred to as maker fees) from trading venues based on the volume of quotes submitted providing

---

32. Institutional and retail investors may also engage in high-frequency trading through their broker-dealers.

liquidity to a particular trading venue. In general, an arbitrage strategy seeks to capture pricing inefficiencies between related products or markets. Specifically, it involves the simultaneous purchase and sale of similar or identical securities on different markets or in different forms. There are various types of arbitrage strategies. For example, if a security's price on the NYSE is trading out of sync with its corresponding futures contract on the CME, a trader would simultaneously sell short the most expensive of the two and buy the other to profit on the difference. Today, arbitrage strategies require rapid computer processing capability and the fastest possible link between trading venues and the high-frequency trading firm. Directional strategies are based on anticipation of an intra-day price movement in a security in a particular direction. Regulators have identified two types of directional strategies that are of concern—order anticipation strategies and momentum ignition strategies. High-frequency firms using order anticipation strategies seek to profit by trading before others trade; they make money when they correctly anticipate how other traders will affect prices. For example, if a large institutional trader is accumulating a large position in the shares of DEF and a high frequency trader ascertains this information by identifying a sequence of large buy orders over the space of several minutes, the high frequency trader would purchase DEF shares, driving the price up and increasing the price that the institutional trader must pay to buy DEF shares. Essentially, order anticipation strategies allow high frequency traders to prey on other traders. Momentum ignition strategies allow high frequency traders to ignite a rapid price movement (up or down) in a security by initiating a series of orders and trades. The following Acceptance Waiver and Consent issued by FINRA illustrates the execution of a fraudulent momentum ignition strategy.

Trillium Brokerage Services, LLC

AWC No. 20070076782-01 Aug. 5, 2010

Pursuant to FINRA Rule 9216 of FINRA's Code of Procedure, Trillium Brokerage Services, LLC f/k/a Trillium Trading LLC (the "firm" or "TRIL") ... submit[s] this Letter of Acceptance, Waiver, and Consent ("AWC") for the purpose of proposing a settlement of the alleged rule violations described below.

* * *

I.

ACCEPTANCE AND CONSENT

A.   TRIL, Balber, Gutbrod, Hochleuter, Jaffe, Hohnson, Plotkin, F. Raffaele, J. Raffaele, M. Raffaele, Sharon, and Yoon hereby accept and consent, without admitting or denying, ... to the entry of the following findings by FINRA:

BACKGROUND

Balber entered the securities industry in January 1995. During all times relevant to this AWC, Balber was registered as a general securities principal at TRIL.

* * *

SUMMARY

[T]he staff of FINRA's Department of Market Regulation (the "staff") reviewed TRIL's trading activity conducted through the NASDAQ Stock Market and the NYSE Arca Marketplace during the period November 1, 2006 through January 31, 2007 (the "review Period").

FACTS AND VIOLATIVE CONDUCT

TRIL's Trading Violations

1. During the review period, TRIL, by and through nine TRIL proprietary traders [the "Trillium Traders"] ... engaged in a repeated pattern of layering conduct to take advantage of trading, including algorithmic trading by other firms, when the Trillium Traders entered a buy (sell) limit order in a NASDAQ security through NASDAQ Single Book ("Single Book") primarily at a price that was either at the NASDAQ Best Bid (Offer) or that improved the NASDAQ Best Bid (Offer) ("NASDAQ BBO") in such a security (the "limit order"), and obtained a full or partial execution for that order through the entry of numerous layered, non-bona fide, market moving orders on the side of the market opposite the limit order, as described in greater detail below.

2. After entering a buy (sell) limit order into Single Book, a Trillium Trader repeatedly entered numerous layered, non-bona fide, market moving sell (buy) orders through Single Book on the opposite side of the market from the limit order at prices primarily outside the NASDAQ BBO (the "non-bona fide orders").

3. The Trillium Trader knowingly and intentionally entered these non-bona fide orders through Single Book to create the appearance of substantial pending sell (buy) orders in the security for the purpose of inducing the sale (purchase) of his limit order of such a security by others, and was successful in most instances in obtaining a full or partial execution of the limit order.

4. By knowingly and intentionally engaging in this course of conduct, the Trillium Trader bought (sold) shares of these securities at prices that were lower (higher) than he would otherwise have been able to buy (sell) shares of these securities but for his entry of the numerous non-bona fide sell (buy) orders into Single Book.

5. Within seconds after the Trillium Trader received the execution or partial execution of the buy (sell) limit order, he intentionally and knowingly canceled the non-bona fide orders that he had placed into Single Book. At the time that he placed the non-bona fide sell (buy) orders through Single Book, he anticipated that those orders would be cancelled prior to execution. In fact, he generally entered these orders at prices primarily outside of the NASDAQ BBO and thereby reduced the risk that these non-bona fide orders would be executed contrary to his intent.

6. Upon cancellation of the non-bona fide orders, the Trillium Trader typically repeated the above-described trading activity on the opposite side of the market, beginning with the entry of a sell (buy) limit order for the same security, followed by the placement of numerous non-bona fide buy (sell) orders for that security through

Single Book, the execution or partial execution of the sell (buy) limit order, and the cancellation of the numerous non-bona fide orders.

7. During the review period, TRIL, by and through the Trillium Traders, also entered orders and obtained executions in NASDAQ securities through the NYSE Arca Marketplace ("NYSE Arca") ... in that the Trillium Traders engaged in a repeated pattern of layering conduct to take advantage of trading, including algorithmic trading by other firms, when the Trillium Traders entered a buy (sell) limit order in a NASDAQ security through NYSE Arca at a price that was either at the NASDAQ BBO or that improved the NASDAQ BBO in such a security (the "limit order"), and obtained a full or partial execution of that order through the entry of numerous layered, non-bona fide, market moving orders on the side of the market opposite the limit order.

8. TRIL, by and through the Trillium Traders, bought and sold NASDAQ securities, ... in at least 46,152 instances, thereby securing total profits of approximately $575,765.17, of which the firm retained $173,357.49 ... As a result, TRIL, by and through the Trillium Traders, as described above, violated NASD Rules 2110, 2120, 3310, and IM-3310.

––––––

1. Co-Location and Trading Center Data Feeds

Co-location is the practice of placing the computers of HFT broker-dealers in the data centers next to the servers at trading centers. In essence, trading centers rent rack space to HFT broker-dealers to enable them to place their servers in close physical proximity to the matching engines of trading centers. HFT broker-dealers must engage in co-location in order to minimize latency, i.e., "the overall time it takes to receive signals from a trading venue, make trading decisions, and transmit the resulting order messages back to the trading venue. Most HFT broker-dealers rely on this direct data feed from trading centers instead of the consolidated data feed disseminated through SIPs.[33] Co-location is required by HFT broker-dealers because light and electrical signals travel at a finite speed of 186,000 miles per second in a vacuum and are even slower through fiber optic cables and other media. Consequently, locating the computers of HFT broker-dealers next to the servers of trading centers is needed to minimize latency by providing the fastest delivery of market data and transaction execution. Ever in search of faster speeds, HFTs are now using microwave and laser network technology for data transmission; microwaves travelling in air suffer a less than 1% speed reduction compared with 30% slower travel time of light travelling in a vacuum using conventional fiber optics.

The trading center's fee for providing co-location services to a broker-dealer is regulated by the SEC because it may provide a trading advantage to market participants

––––––––––––

33. Distribution of the consolidated data feed requires an extra step when compared to direct data feeds obtained through co-location. The SROs must transmit market data to plan processors (SIPs) and the SIPs must consolidate the information and distribute it to the public. Consequently, individual data fees from SROs and ECNs that include consolidated data feed information are distributed faster than the same market data in the consolidated data feeds.

with the financial wherewithal to purchase co-location services. Accordingly, exchanges that intend to offer co-location services must file proposed rule changes and receive approval in advance of offering such services. Moreover, the terms of co-location services must not be unfairly discriminatory, and fees must be equitably allocated and reasonable. Rules 601 and 603 of Reg NMS allow SROs to distribute their own market data in addition to Reg NMS requirements concerning the consolidated data feed. However, some complain that SROs have created systems and pricing tiers (including special order types) specifically for HFT firms as a means of competing for order flow.[34]

B. The Flash Crash of 2010 and Its Aftermath

On May 6, 2010, U.S. equity markets plummeted between 2:40 p.m. and 3:00 p.m. (the "2010 Flash Crash"). The following report issued jointly by the SEC and the Commodity Futures Trading Commission ("CFTC") describes both the cause and the events that led up to the 2010 Flash Crash.

THE MARKET EVENTS OF MAY 6, 2010

REPORT OF THE STAFFS OF THE CFTC AND SEC TO THE JOINT ADVISORY COMMITTEE ON EMERGING REGULATORY ISSUE

EXECUTIVE SUMMARY

On May 6, 2010, the prices of many U.S.-based equity products experienced an extraordinarily rapid decline and recovery. That afternoon, major equity indices in both the futures and securities markets, each already down over 4% from their prior-day close, suddenly plummeted a further 5-6% in a matter of minutes before rebounding almost as quickly.

Many of the almost 8,000 individual equity securities and exchange traded funds ("ETFs") traded that day suffered similar price declines and reversals within a short period of time, falling 5%, 10% or even 15% before recovering most, if not all, of their losses. However, some equities experienced even more severe price moves, both up and down. Over 20,000 trades across more than 300 securities were executed at prices more than 60% away from their values just moments before. Moreover, many of these trades were executed at prices of a penny or less, or as high as $100,000, before prices of those securities returned to their "pre-crash" levels.

By the end of the day, major futures and equities indices "recovered" to close at losses of about 3% from the prior day.

WHAT HAPPENED?

May 6 started as an unusually turbulent day for the markets. As discussed in more detail in the Preliminary Report, trading in the U.S. opened to unsettling political and economic news from overseas concerning the European debt crisis. As a result,

---

34. Facing increasing competition from new exchanges and ATSs, co-location, among other services, has been used by SROs such as exchanges to compete for order flow, which is essential in generating revenue for exchanges.

premiums rose for buying protection against default by the Greek government on their sovereign debt. At about 1 p.m., the Euro began a sharp decline against both the U.S Dollar and Japanese Yen.

Around 1:00 p.m., broadly negative market sentiment was already affecting an increase in the price volatility of some individual securities. At that time, the number of volatility pauses, also known as Liquidity Replenishment Points ("LRPs"), triggered on the New York Stock Exchange ("NYSE") in individual equities listed and traded on that exchange began to substantially increase above average levels.

By 2:30 p.m., the S&P 500 volatility index ("VIX") was up 22.5 percent from the opening level, yields of ten-year Treasuries fell as investors engaged in a "flight to quality," and selling pressure had pushed the Dow Jones Industrial Average ("DJIA") down about 2.5%.

Furthermore, buy-side liquidity[35] in the E-Mini S&P 500 futures contracts (the "E-Mini"), as well as the S&P 500 SPDR exchange traded fund ("SPY"), the two most active stock index instruments traded in electronic futures and equity markets, had fallen from the early-morning level of nearly $6 billion dollars to $2.65 billion (representing a 55% decline) for the E-Mini and from the early-morning level of about $275 million to $220 million (a 20% decline) for SPY. the Preliminary Report, trading in the U.S opened to unsettling political and economic news from overseas concerning the European debt crisis. As a result, premiums rose for buying protection against default by the Greek government on their sovereign debt. At about 1 p.m., the Euro began a sharp decline against both the U.S Dollar and Japanese Yen.

Around 1:00 p.m., broadly negative market sentiment was already affecting an increase in the price volatility of some individual securities. At that time, the number of volatility pauses, also known as Liquidity Replenishment Points ("LRPs"), triggered on the New York Stock Exchange ("NYSE") in individual equities listed and traded on that exchange began to substantially increase above average levels.

By 2:30 p.m., the S&P 500 volatility index ("VIX") was up 22.5 percent from the opening level, yields of ten-year Treasuries fell as investors engaged in a "flight to quality," and selling pressure had pushed the Dow Jones Industrial Average ("DJIA") down about 2.5%.

Furthermore, buy-side liquidity[36] in the E-Mini S&P 500 futures contracts (the "E-Mini"), as well as the S&P 500 SPDR exchange traded fund ("SPY"), the two most

---

35. [3] We use the term "liquidity" throughout this report generally to refer to buy-side and sell-side market depth, which is comprised of resting orders that market participants place to express their willingness to buy or sell at prices equal to, or outside of (either below or above), current market levels. Note that for SPY and other equity securities discussed in this report, unless otherwise stated, market depth calculations include only resting quotes within 500 basis points of the mid-quote. Additional liquidity would have been available beyond 500 basis points. See Section 1 for further details on how market depth and near-inside market depth are defined and calculated for the E-Mini, SPY, and other equity securities.

36. [5] We define fundamental sellers and fundamental buyers as market participants who are trading to accumulate or reduce a net long or short position. Reasons for fundamental buying and

active stock index instruments traded in electronic futures and equity markets, had fallen from the early-morning level of nearly $6 billion dollars to $2.65 billion (representing a 55% decline) for the E-Mini and from the early-morning level of about $275 million to $220 million (a 20% decline) for SPY.[37] Some individual stocks also suffered from a decline their liquidity.

At 2:32 p.m., against this backdrop of unusually high volatility and thinning liquidity, a large fundamental trader (a mutual fund complex) initiated a sell program to sell a total of 75,000 E-Mini contracts (valued at approximately $4.1 billion) as a hedge to an existing equity position.

Generally, a customer has a number of alternatives as to how to execute a large trade. First, a customer may choose to engage an intermediary, who would, in turn, execute a block trade or manage the position. Second, a customer may choose to manually enter orders into the market. Third, a customer can execute a trade via an automated execution algorithm, which can meet the customer's needs by taking price, time or volume into consideration. Effectively, a customer must make a choice as to how much human judgment is involved while executing a trade.

This large fundamental trader chose to execute this sell program via an automated execution algorithm ("Sell Algorithm") that was programmed to feed orders into the June 2010 E-Mini market to target an execution rate set to 9% of the trading volume calculated over the previous minute, but without regard to price or time.

The execution of this sell program resulted in the largest net change in daily position of any trader in the E-Mini since the beginning of the year (from January 1, 2010 through May 6, 2010). Only two single-day sell programs of equal or larger size — one of which was by the same large fundamental trader — were executed in the E-Mini in the 12 months prior to May 6. When executing the previous sell program, this large fundamental trader utilized a combination of manual trading entered over the course of a day and several automated execution algorithms which took into account price, time, and volume. On that occasion it took more than 5 hours for this large trader to execute the first 75,000 contracts of a large sell program.[38]

However, on May 6, when markets were already under stress, the Sell Algorithm chosen by the large trader to only target trading volume, and neither price nor time, executed the sell program extremely rapidly in just 20 minutes.[39]

This sell pressure was initially absorbed by:

- high frequency traders ("HFTs") and other intermediaries in the futures market;
- fundamental buyers in the futures market; and

---

selling include gaining long-term exposure to a market as well as hedging already-existing exposures in related markets.

37. [4] However, these erosions did not affect "near-inside" liquidity — resting orders within about 0.1% of the last transaction price or mid-market quote.

38. [6] Subsequently, the large fundamental trader closed, in a single day, this short position.

39. [7] At a later date, the large fundamental trader executed trades over the course of more than 6 hours to offset the net short position accumulated on May 6.

- cross-market arbitrageurs[40] who transferred this sell pressure to the equities markets by opportunistically buying E-Mini contracts and simultaneously selling products like SPY, or selling individual equities in the S&P 500 Index.

HFTs and intermediaries were the likely buyers of the initial batch of orders submitted by the Sell Algorithm, and, as a result, these buyers built up temporary long positions. Specifically, HFTs accumulated a net long position of about 3,300 contracts. However, between 2:41 p.m. and 2:44 p.m., HFTs aggressively sold about 2,000 E-Mini contracts in order to reduce their temporary long positions. At the same time, HFTs traded nearly 140,000 E-Mini contracts or over 33% of the total trading volume. This is consistent with the HFTs' typical practice of trading a very large number of contracts, but not accumulating an aggregate inventory beyond three to four thousand contracts in either direction.

The Sell Algorithm used by the large trader responded to the increased volume by increasing the rate at which it was feeding the orders into the market, even though orders that it already sent to the market were arguably not yet fully absorbed by fundamental buyers or cross-market arbitrageurs. In fact, especially in times of significant volatility, high trading volume is not necessarily a reliable indicator of market liquidity.

What happened next is best described in terms of two liquidity crises—one at the broad index level in the E-Mini, the other with respect to individual stocks.

LIQUIDITY CRISIS IN THE E-MINI

The combined selling pressure from the Sell Algorithm, HFTs and other traders drove the price of the E-Mini down approximately 3% in just four minutes from the beginning of 2:41 p.m. through the end of 2:44 p.m. During this same time cross-market arbitrageurs who did buy the E-Mini, simultaneously sold equivalent amounts in the equities markets, driving the price of SPY also down approximately 3%.

Still lacking sufficient demand from fundamental buyers or cross-market arbitrageurs, HFTs began to quickly buy and then resell contracts to each other—generating a "hot-potato" volume effect as the same positions were rapidly passed back and forth. Between 2:45:13 and 2:45:27, HFTs traded over 27,000 contracts, which accounted for about 49 percent of the total trading volume, while buying only about 200 additional contracts net.

At this time, buy-side market depth in the E-Mini fell to about $58 million, less than 1% of its depth from that morning's level. As liquidity vanished, the price of the E-Mini dropped by an additional 1.7% in just these 15 seconds, to reach its intraday low of 1056. This sudden decline in both price and liquidity may be symptomatic of the notion that prices were moving so fast, fundamental buyers and cross-market arbitrageurs were either unable or unwilling to supply enough buy-side liquidity.

---

40. [9] Cross-market arbitrageurs are opportunistic traders who capitalize on temporary, though often small, price differences between related products by purchasing the cheaper product and selling the more expensive product.

In the four-and-one-half minutes from 2:41 p.m. through 2:45:27 p.m., prices of the E-Mini had fallen by more than 5% and prices of SPY suffered a decline of over 6%. According to interviews with cross-market trading firms, at this time they were purchasing the E-Mini and selling either SPY, baskets of individual securities, or other index products.

By 2:45:28 there were less than 1,050 contracts of buy-side resting orders in the E-Mini, representing less than 1% of buy-side market depth observed at the beginning of the day. At the same time, buy-side resting orders in SPY fell to about 600,000 shares (equivalent to 1,200 E-Mini contracts) representing approximately 25% of its depth at the beginning of the day.

Between 2:32 p.m. and 2:45 p.m., as prices of the E-Mini rapidly declined, the Sell Algorithm sold about 35,000 E-Mini contracts (valued at approximately $1.9 billion) of the 75,000 intended. During the same time, all fundamental sellers combined sold more than 80,000 contracts net, while all fundamental buyers bought only about 50,000 contracts net, for a net fundamental imbalance of 30,000 contracts. This level of net selling by fundamental sellers is about 15 times larger compared to the same 13-minute interval during the previous three days, while this level of net buying by the fundamental buyers is about 10 times larger compared to the same time period during the previous three days.

At 2:45:28 p.m., trading on the E-Mini was paused for five seconds when the Chicago Mercantile Exchange ("CME") Stop Logic Functionality was triggered in order to prevent a cascade of further price declines. In that short period of time, sell-side pressure in the E-Mini was partly alleviated and buy-side interest increased. When trading resumed at 2:45:33 p.m., prices stabilized and shortly thereafter, the E-Mini began to recover, followed by the SPY.

The Sell Algorithm continued to execute the sell program until about 2:51 p.m. as the prices were rapidly rising in both the E-Mini and SPY.

LIQUIDITY CRISIS WITH RESPECT TO INDIVIDUAL STOCKS

The second liquidity crisis occurred in the equities markets at about 2:45 p.m. Based on interviews with a variety of large market participants, automated trading systems used by many liquidity providers temporarily paused in reaction to the sudden price declines observed during the first liquidity crisis. These built-in pauses are designed to prevent automated systems from trading when prices move beyond pre-defined thresholds in order to allow traders and risk managers to fully assess market conditions before trading is resumed.

After their trading systems were automatically paused, individual market participants had to assess the risks associated with continuing their trading. Participants reported that these assessments included the following factors: whether observed severe price moves could be an artifact of erroneous data; the impact of such moves on risk and position limits; impacts on intraday profit and loss ("P&L"); the potential for trades to be broken, leaving their firms inadvertently long or short on one side of the market; and the ability of their systems to handle the very high volume of trades and orders they were processing that day. In addition, a number of participants reported that because prices simultaneously fell across many types of securities, they feared the occurrence of a cataclysmic event of which they were not yet aware, and that their strategies were not designed to handle.[41]

Based on their respective individual risk assessments, some market makers and other liquidity providers widened their quote spreads, others reduced offered liquidity, and a significant number withdrew completely from the markets. Some fell back to manual trading but had to limit their focus to only a subset of securities as they were not able to keep up with the nearly ten-fold increase in volume that occurred as prices in many securities rapidly declined.

HFTs in the equity markets, who normally both provide and take liquidity as part of their strategies, traded proportionally more as volume increased, and overall were net sellers in the rapidly declining broad market along with most other participants. Some of these firms continued to trade as the broad indices began to recover and individual securities started to experience severe price dislocations, whereas others reduced or halted trading completely.

Many over-the-counter ("OTC") market makers who would otherwise internally execute as principal a significant fraction of the buy and sell orders they receive from retail customers (i.e., "internalizers") began routing most, if not all, of these orders directly to the public exchanges where they competed with other orders for immediately available, but dwindling liquidity.

Even though after 2:45 p.m. prices in the E-Mini and SPY were recovering from their severe declines, sell orders placed for some individual securities and ETFs (including many retail stop-loss orders, triggered by declines in prices of those securities) found reduced buying interest, which led to further price declines in those securities.

Between 2:40 p.m. and 3:00 p.m., approximately 2 billion shares traded with a total volume exceeding $56 billion. Over 98% of all shares were executed at prices within 10% of their 2:40 p.m. value. However, as liquidity completely evaporated in a number of individual securities and ETFs, participants instructed to sell (or buy) at the market found no immediately available buy interest (or sell interest) resulting in trades being executed at irrational prices as low as one penny or as high as $100,000. These trades occurred as a result of so-called stub quotes, which are quotes generated

---

41. [10] Some additional factors that may have played a role in the events of May 6 ... include: the use of LRPs by the NYSE, in which trading is effectively banded on the NYSE in NYSE-listed stocks exhibiting rapid price moves; declarations of self-help by The Nasdaq Stock Market, LLC ("Nasdaq") against NYSE Arca, Inc. ("NYSE Arca") under which Nasdaq temporarily stopped routing orders to NYSE Arca; and delays in NYSE quote and trade data disseminated over the Consolidated Quotation System ("CQS") and Consolidated Tape System ("CTS") data feeds. Our findings indicate that none of these factors played a dominant role on May 6, but nonetheless they are important considerations in forming a complete picture of, and response to, that afternoon.

by market makers in order to fulfill continuous two-sided quoting obligations even when a market maker has withdrawn from active trading.

The severe dislocations observed in many securities were fleeting. As market participants had time to react and verify the integrity of their data systems, buy-side and sell-side interest returned and an orderly price discovery process began to function. By approximately 3:00 p.m. most securities had reverted back to trading at prices reflecting true consensus values. Nevertheless, during the 20 minute period between 2:40 p.m. and 3:00 p.m., over 20,000 trades (many based on retail-customer orders) across more than 300 separate securities, including many ETFs, were executed at prices 60% or more away from their 2:40 p.m. prices. After the market closed, the exchanges and FINRA met and jointly agreed to cancel (or break) all such trades under their respective "clearly erroneous" trade rules.

———

The regulatory response to the 2010 Flash Crash included SEC approval of an NMS Plan to Address Extraordinary Market Volatility ("Plan"). Under the Plan, FINRA and the exchanges were required to adopt rules that provide for a market-wide limit up and limit down mechanism to prevent trades in NMS stocks at prices outside of specified price bands. They were also required to issue five-minute trading pauses if NMS stocks experienced certain volatility events. The trading pauses were designed to allow market participants time to consider available information and provide stabilizing liquidity if a large price move in an NMS stock did not appear warranted based on fundamental information.

Notes and Questions

1. A stub quote is an offer to buy or sell a stock at a price so far away from the prevailing market price that it is not intended to be executed, such as an order to buy at a penny or an offer to sell at $100,000. A market maker may enter stub quotes to nominally comply with its obligation to maintain a two-sided quotation at those times when it does not wish to actively provide liquidity. In November 2010, the SEC approved new rules adopted by the exchanges and FINRA that prohibited stub quotes by market makers. The new rules required market makers in exchange-listed equities to maintain continuous two-sided quotations during regular market hours that are within a certain percentage band of the NBBO. *See* Securities and Exchange Commission, Release No. 34-63255 (Nov. 5, 2010).

2. The SEC approved amendments to the exchanges and FINRA rules for clearly erroneous trades to provide for, among other things, uniform treatment of such trades in exchange-listed and OTC-traded equities. *See* Securities Exchange Act Release No. 62885 (September 10, 2010); 75 FR 56641 (September 16, 2010) (Order Approving SR-FINRA-2010-032). On September 10, 2010, the SEC also approved similar rule changes filed by several exchanges.

V. Clearing and Settlement

The national clearing and settlement system is an essential component of the national market system because parties to securities transactions must receive the results of such transactions—money and securities—in a timely fashion. As noted in Section I of this chapter, Congress mandated the establishment of a national clearance and settlement system in the 1975 amendments because of the Paperwork Crisis in the late 1960s. The clearing and settlement function involves the comparison, accounting for, and settlement of securities transactions effected by broker-dealers, among others, and is performed by clearing agencies registered with the SEC. See Table 14.3 for a description of clearing and settlement activities.

Table 14.3. Clearing and Settlement Activities

Activity	Description
Comparison	Comparison is the process by which previously executed trades are matched to ensure that both sides to a trade agree in advance of settlement. Comparison may be performed by broker-dealers before submission to a clearing agency or subsequently by the clearing agency.
Account for	Generates the money and securities settlement obligations of participants in clearing agencies. The accounting system generally used is the Continuous Net Settlement system, which generates a single, daily net buy or sell position for each securities issue in which a participant has compared trades scheduled to settle on the third day after trade date and nets accumulated settlement obligations in that issue. The CNS system is the contra side for each net settlement rather than the original parties to the trades, and therefore is responsible for delivery or receipt of securities and money.
Settlement	Obligations generated by the accounting function are satisfied through the settlement process by the delivery and receipt of funds and securities. Net securities movements are made at the affiliated securities depository.

Clearing agencies are regulated by the SEC under 17A of the Exchange Act. Section 3(a)(23) of the Exchange Act defines a clearing agency as:

[A]ny person who acts as an intermediary in making payments or deliveries or both in connection with transactions in securities or who provides facilities for comparison of data respecting the terms of settlement of securities transactions, to reduce the number of settlements of securities transactions, or for the allocation of securities settlement responsibilities. Such term also means any person, such as a securities depository, who (i) acts as a custodian of securities in connection with a system for the central handling of securities whereby all securities of a particular class or series of any issuer deposited within the system are treated as fungible and may be transferred, loaned, or pledged by bookkeeping entry without physical delivery of securities certificates, or (ii) otherwise permits or facilitates the settlement of securities transactions or the hypothecation or lending of securities without physical delivery of securities certificates.

Clearing agencies also function as SROs required to register with the SEC under Section 17A of the Exchange Act and Rule 17Ab2-1 thereunder unless they qualify for an exemption from registration.[42] They register with the SEC using Form CA-1 and must be: (1) organized to have the capacity to safeguard securities and funds in their custody or control or for which they are responsible; (2) have rules that assure the safeguarding of securities or funds that are in their custody or control or for which they are responsible; and (3) have rules that do not impose any schedule of prices, or fix rates or other fees, for services rendered by participants. Moreover, as SROs, clearing agencies have both the authority and the obligation, among other things, to deny participation to statutorily disqualified or incompetent applicants for membership, to discipline participants, and to provide participants with due process when they may be adversely affected by those decisions. The following case illustrates the contentious beginning of the national clearing and settlement system and the difficulty the SEC encountered in exercising its authority under Section 17A of the Exchange Act to facilitate the rapid establishment of a safe, efficient, and computerized national clearing system.

Bradford Nat. Clearing Corp. v. SEC
590 F.2d 1085 (1978)

McGowan, Circuit Judge.

These two unconsolidated direct review proceedings involve challenges by subsidiaries of Bradford National Clearing Corporation to successive orders of the Securities and Exchange Commission (SEC or the Commission). In No. 77-1199, petitioners ask this court to set aside the Commission's conditional approval of the application of intervenor National Securities Clearing Corporation (NSCC) for registration as a clearing agency pursuant to section 17A(b) of the Securities Exchange Act, 15 U.S.C. §78q-1(b). In re The Application of Nat'l Securities Clearing Corp. for Registration as a Clearing Agency (hereinafter Order I)(citations omitted). No. 77-1547 seeks reversal of a subsequent SEC order under section 19(b) of the Securities Exchange Act, 15 U.S.C. §78s(b), allowing NSCC to adopt two self-regulatory rules that are purportedly aimed at meeting the conditions set by the Commission in approving NSCC's registration as a clearing agency. In re Nat'l Securities Clearing Corp. (hereinafter Order II) (citation omitted).

In light of the significant overlap in the issues involved in the two petitions, we have decided to treat both in the same opinion. The order involved in No. 77-1199 is affirmed, except insofar as the Commission approved NSCC's use of "geographic price mutualization" and its mode of allocating its facilities management contract. As to those issues the case is remanded to the SEC for further consideration. The order under review in No. 77-1547 is affirmed.

* * *

---

42. Section 3(a)(23(B) expressly excludes certain types of entities including, but not limited to, any Federal Reserve bank, Federal home loan bank, or Federal land bank.

In the 1960's and early 1970's, however, more attention began to be paid to the possibility of changing the overall structure of the securities industry in order to make it more competitive, national, and efficient. Of particular relevance in this suit, the late 1960's saw the breakdown of the efficient functioning of brokers' "back offices" i.e., of the segment of the industry that effectuates trades after they are initially negotiated on an exchange or in the over-the-counter market.[43] As a result of this "paperwork crisis," many purchasers never actually received their stock certificates nor sellers their money. Moreover, a goodly number of brokers, faced with liability for these incomplete transactions, went bankrupt.

In response to these "operational breakdowns and economic distortions," Congress and the Commission undertook "the most searching reexamination of the competitive, statutory, and economic issues facing the securities markets, the securities industry, and … public investors, since the 1930's." The outgrowth of these investigations was the Securities Acts Amendments of 1975. With this legislation, the SEC's regulatory authority under the 1934 Act was expanded to enable it to effect major changes in the method of handling securities transactions.

Two such changes bear directly on the issues raised by the petitions. Most critically, in terms of these petitions, Congress recognized the need for a "(n)ational system for clearance and settlement of securities transactions," the objective of which is to interconnect all American clearing agencies and place them under uniform rules, so that together they can provide prompt, safe, and efficient clearance facilities that take

---

43. [2] When two brokers agree on the floor of an exchange, or over the counter (I. e., usually, over the telephone), to a buy-sell transaction for their clients, the actual transaction has only begun. Thereafter, several steps must be taken to complete the course of dealing. These steps are typically the responsibility of a clearing agency, one of which traditionally has been linked to each of the national and regional exchanges, and one of which has served the over-the-counter market. The clearing agency has three functions. First, the agency "compares" submissions of the seller's broker with those of the buyer's to make sure that there is a common understanding of the terms of the trade. Following this process, the resulting "compared trade" is "cleared." Most simply, this amounts to the clearing agency advising the selling and buying brokers, respectively, of their delivery and payment obligations. The system becomes far more complicated although, with the help of computers, also more efficient insofar as the clearing agency attempts, for a given period of time, to net all of a broker's transactions in each security as well as all of his monetary obligations. By this means, and by making all rights and duties run between the broker on either side of the transaction and the clearing agency, rather than between the brokers themselves, each broker is reduced to making or receiving one delivery for each security traded, and one cash payment, per day. In addition to reducing transactions costs, this latter method of clearing, referred to as "continuous netting," eases the risk to each broker and his client that the other party will become insolvent or otherwise fail to complete the transaction. The final, "settlement," stage in the process involves the delivery of securities certificates to the purchasing broker and the payment of money to the selling broker. Modernization of this task has led to storage of most stock certificates in a depository affiliated with the clearing agency. Thus, "delivery" amounts to a bookkeeping entry that removes the security from one account and places it in another. The breakdown in these processes during the late 1960s largely antedated, and supplied the impetus for, the modern computerization and netting trends. The breakdown was occasioned by the sharp increase in securities transactions during the period, which prevented many trades from being compared, cleared, and settled within the five-business-day period traditionally allotted for the process.

full advantage of modern data processing and communications technology. (citation omitted). The 1975 Amendments direct the Commission to "facilitate the establishment" of this national system … "having due regard for" … the "maintenance of fair competition among brokers and dealers, clearing agencies, and transfer agents."[44]

To carry out this broad directive, Congress gave the SEC authority to register clearing agencies that meet certain specified criteria, including an ability to clear and settle securities transactions promptly and accurately and an absence of rules that impose "any burden on competition not necessary or appropriate in furtherance of the purposes" of the 1934 Act. Without such registration, or an SEC exemption therefrom, it is illegal to operate such an agency.

That Congress conceived of the registration process as a means toward the end of a Commission-generated national clearing system is apparent from that process.[45] Rather than mandating an adjudicatory procedure, as might be expected of an administrative mechanism aimed at conferring a government license, Congress made the process distinctly legislative in nature. After the application is filed, the agency must publish it and receive public comments thereon. The Commission may then grant registration, or institute proceedings to determine whether the application should be denied. The quasi-legislative nature of registration decisions is further indicated by congressional references to the informal rulemaking provision in the Administrative Procedure Act and to the need to preserve the SEC's rulemaking authority in the clearing area, and by the fact that judicial review of the SEC's decision, while controlled by the "substantial evidence" rule in its factual aspects, is otherwise left

---

44. [3] Section 17A(a), 15 U.S. C. §78q-1(a), provides in relevant part:

(1) The Congress Finds that

(A) The prompt and accurate clearance and settlement of securities transactions including the transfer of record ownership and the safeguarding of securities and funds related thereto, are necessary for the protection of investors and persons facilitating transactions by and acting on behalf of investors.

(B) Inefficient procedures for clearance and settlement impose unnecessary costs on investors and persons facilitating transactions by and acting on behalf of investors

(C) New data processing and communications techniques create the opportunity for more efficient, effective, and safe procedures for clearance and settlement.

(D) The linking of all clearance and settlement facilities and the development of uniform standards and procedures for clearance and settlement will reduce unnecessary costs and increase the protection of investors and persons facilitating transactions by and acting on behalf of investors.

(2) The Commission is directed, therefore, having due regard for the public interest, the protection of investors, the safeguarding of securities and funds, and maintenance of fair competition among brokers and dealers, clearing agencies, and transfer agents, to use its authority under this chapter to facilitate the establishment of a national system for the prompt and accurate clearance and settlement of transactions in securities (other than exempted securities) in accordance with the findings and to carry out the objectives set forth in paragraph (1) of this subsection.…

45. [5] "… determinative impact on the development of a national system for clearance and settlement of transactions…," and it accordingly widened its inquiry (and the scope of public comment thereon) to include consideration of the consistency of registration with its duty to establish a national clearing system as envisioned by section 17A(a).…

unspecified, and, therefore, is apparently limited to review for arbitrariness, caprice, and abuse of discretion.

Congress further cemented the SEC's control over the shape of the clearing industry by requiring its approval of any new or modified rules adopted by a clearing agency. A similarly quasi-legislative procedure is established for the Commission's consideration of such rules, and its decision is judicially reviewable under the same provision governing review of its registration decisions.

The drafters of the 1975 Amendments assumed that the national market and national clearing systems would reinforce each other. (citation omitted). Together, they would allow an investor anywhere in the United States to initiate and then complete a securities transaction with the aid solely of a local broker of his choice, dealing on a regional exchange and clearing through a regional agency also of his choosing, and having available throughout the process the most complete and up-to-date national information possible. (citations omitted). Instead, it hoped that the impetus for both would come from the private sector and it provided the Commission with "intentionally broad" and "clear power" and "discretion" to shape the developing systems. As to both systems, the Commission's primary directive from Congress was to be "bold and effective" and to act quickly.

Despite their interdependence and their common subjection to broad SEC authority, the national market and clearing systems were not perceived by Congress as identical pillars supporting the legislators' conception of a modernized approach to securities marketing. Most importantly, Congress' directives to the Commission with respect to the two systems vary slightly but significantly. Although in facilitating the establishment of both systems, the SEC is required to adhere to "the findings and to carry out the objectives set forth" in the first subsection of each of the two relevant provisions, those findings and objectives are not entirely parallel. (citations omitted). Thus, while both lists of objectives include the full exploitation of technological advances in communication and data processing equipment, efficiency, and the linkage of all relevant facilities nationally, only the national market system objectives include the "enhance(ment)" of "fair competition among brokers and ... exchange markets ..." and only the national clearing system objectives include promptness and the development of uniform standards and procedures. (citations omitted).[46]

II

A.

At the time of the passage of the 1975 Amendments, a separate clearing agency owned by each of the national and regional stock exchanges, and one owned by the National Association of Securities Dealers (NASD) which operates the over-the-

---

46. [12] As summarized by the drafters, the goal of the national market system is the "centraliz(ation of) trading of securities in the interest of both efficiency and investor protection" and the "eliminat(ion of) all unnecessary or inappropriate burdens on competition," while the goal of the national clearing system is the "centraliz(ation of) every facet of the securities handling process" and "the prompt development" of an efficient "paper-handling" process.

counter (hereinafter "OTC") market performed all of the clearing services for transactions initiated on the exchange or in the market with which it was affiliated.[47] Recently, petitioner Bradford National Clearing Corp. (BNCC) has made inroads into the clearing industry by competitively bidding on and winning two facilities management contracts under which it operates the clearing agencies owned by the Pacific Stock Exchange one of the regional exchanges and by NASD.[48]

In the past, the rigid division of the clearing market along the lines of the various trading markets virtually precluded any competition between clearing agencies. This division stemmed in large part from rules promulgated by each of the exchanges and by NASD that required brokers trading in that market to utilize only the clearing agency affiliated therewith.

Even before the 1975 Amendments passed, Congress, representatives of various exchanges, NASD, and independent associations of brokers and dealers had begun exploring the possibility of dramatically centralizing the clearing facilities in this country. The initial efforts in this discretion began in earnest in the fall of 1973 and contemplated the merger of several existing clearing agencies, including those owned by NYSE, AMEX, NASD, and most of the regional exchanges. The impetus for merger came from the expectation that by the elimination of duplicative services and facilities the clearing industry would reduce costs and avoid a recurrence of the "paperwork crisis." The negotiators particularly those representing brokers and dealers apparently concentrated on finding a way to combine the three clearing agencies (NYSE's SCC, AMEX's ASECC, and NASD's NCC (hereinafter, "the New York clearing agencies"))

---

47. [13] The national exchanges are the New York Stock Exchange (NYSE) and the American Stock Exchange (AMEX), both of which are located in New York. Each owns its own clearing agency — the Stock Clearing Corp. (SCC) and the American Stock Exchange Clearing Corp. (ASECC), respectively although a separate company, Securities Industry Automation Corp. (SIAC), which is jointly owned by NYSE and AMEX, currently acts as facilities manager and data processor for both SCC and ASECC. Together, SCC and ASECC account for about 73% of the clearing and settling functions performed in this country. The major regional exchanges are the Boston Stock Exchange, which owns and operates the Boston Stock Exchange Clearing Corp., the Midwest Stock Exchange, which owns and operates the Midwest Clearing Corporation, the Pacific Stock Exchange, which owns the Pacific Clearing Corp. (operated by petitioner Bradford National Clearing Corp.), and the Philadelphia Stock Exchange, which owns and operates the Stock Clearing Corp. of Philadelphia. These exchanges and their clearing associates together handle about 15% of the securities transactions nationwide. The bulk of the remaining share of the securities market (about 12%) stems from the OTC trade under the auspices of the NASD and its subsidiary, the National Clearing Corp. (NCC). The rules "tying" exchanges and subsidiary clearing agencies were designed at least in part to serve goals other than market division and preservation of customer pools. See note 21 *infra*. Nonetheless, those rules also have these latter results. In addition, because most exchange-listed securities, including those on the NYSE and AMEX, may be traded on all of the regional exchanges and over the counter, these rules meant, for example, that a broker outside of New York could initiate NYSE and AMEX transactions locally, but still had to clear them through New York.

48. [14] Of particular note in the present context, BNCC underbid SIAC (the facilities manager/data processor owned jointly by NYSE and AMEX, See note 13 *supra*) for the facilities management contract with NASD's clearing agency, NCC.

then operating virtually identical facilities located within a few blocks of each other in downtown New York.[49]

Actually, NYSE and AMEX had already pioneered the merger approach by jointly establishing the Securities Industry Automation Corp. (SIAC), and by contracting with SIAC to operate the two clearing corporations (SCC and ASECC) affiliated with the two parent exchanges. Nevertheless, the NYSE-AMEX "merger" was not complete because SIAC continued to operate the two clearing corporations separately, and the exchanges continued to enforce their rules that tied each of their trading facilities to their clearing facilities. The 1973-74 merger negotiations seem to have contemplated an expansion of SIAC not only to take over the operation of all of the merged clearing agencies, but also to integrate them fully. Nonetheless, these negotiations proved unsuccessful and were discontinued in mid-1974. Soon after passage of the 1975 Amendments, NYSE, AMEX, NASD, and committees made up of their member-brokers renewed their efforts to negotiate a merger of the New York clearing agencies. These efforts came to fruition on July 15, 1975 when representatives of NYSE, AMEX, and NASD signed an agreement in principle to establish a jointly owned entity to which would be transferred the operations of the three New York clearing corporations. The agreement further provided for participant control of the new entity by way of a board of directors composed in the main of brokers and dealers,[50] although its structure and rules would be designed to "avoid any loss (of revenues) to the respective parent companies (NYSE, AMEX, NASD)."[51]

In addition, the agreement in principle specified that SIAC would act as facilities manager and processor for the new entity. The parties included this last provision in their agreement despite the fact that during these latest negotiations BNCC offered to bid competitively against SIAC for the management-processing contract with the new entity. The parties to the agreement informed BNCC that its offer was premature, because negotiations were still going on, and they refused to honor BNCC's request for information on which to base its bid. In the negotiators' eyes, however, the time for BNCC's proposal apparently never matured, as they accepted SIAC as the manager-processor without further exploration of BNCC's counter proposal.[52]

---

49. [15] Thus, when NCC merged with the other two New York clearing agencies it gave the new entity a capacity for dealing locally with brokers and dealers located outside of Manhattan.

50. [16] As eventually agreed to, users comprised 12 of the 16 members of the board of directors, with the other four seats taken by one representative each of NYSE, AMEX, and NASD, and one by the president of the entity. Nonetheless, the three parent organizations have a qualified veto power with respect to all rules of the entity save those imposed by law.

51. [17] In its final form, the merger agreement provided essentially that each of the three New York clearing agencies would receive one-third of the new entity's 30,000 outstanding shares of common stock in return for the transfer of their operating assets. In addition, the three parent organizations, NYSE, AMEX, and NASD, were to receive $.12 for each buy and sell of trades in equity securities executed on their respective markets. Total annual payments, however, were not to exceed $3 million to NYSE, $1 million to AMEX, and $550,000 to NASD.

52. [18] Under the merger plan finally settled upon, SIAC was given a five-year management contract, albeit one that could be terminated by the clearing entity at any time after two years upon

Final negotiations continued throughout 1975 and into 1976, leading in March of that year to the incorporation of the National Securities Clearing Corp. (NSCC), the entity into which the three New York clearing organizations were to be merged, and to the filing with the Commission of NSCC's application for registration as a clearing agency....

In summary, NSCC's application contemplated that the merger would be accomplished in two phases. During Phase I, projected to last approximately four months, NSCC, through SIAC, would operate the three merged New York clearing agencies as separate divisions, and the rules tying each of the two parent exchanges and NASD's over-the-counter market to one of those divisions would be retained.

In Phase II, NSCC would convert the three New York clearing operations into a single system capable of providing its participants with all of the services that previously were provided by at least one of the New York clearing agencies. At this point, of course, the rules tying trading markets to clearing agencies, if still intact, ... would become obsolete. Moreover, NSCC's plan called for its services to be made available not only to the current participants in the three New York clearing agencies, but also to certain other (financially responsible and otherwise qualified) entities.

Nonetheless, even during Phase II, NSCC proposed to restrict its "comparison" services, ... and thus the possibility of "one-shot" clearing and settlement, to (1) its participants located in New York who submit NYSE, AMEX, or OTC transactions for comparison, (2) its participants located outside of New York insofar as (a) they act through the regional network formerly operated by NCC, ... and (b) the transactions submitted for comparison occurred over the counter. Only later would it compare NYSE and AMEX transactions through its regional offices. Hence, its restrictions on comparison facilities even in Phase II assured that only NYSE, AMEX, and OTC traders in New York, OTC traders outside of New York, and eventually NYSE and AMEX traders outside of New York would have direct access to its one-shot comparison, clearing, and settlement services.[53] As in Phase I, a nonparticipant

---

payment of a specified termination fee. SIAC agreed not to charge the clearing entity more than cost for its services. That NYSE and AMEX own SIAC, are part owners of the clearing entity, and control two of the sixteen members of the board of directors of that entity, ... suggest that SIAC has significant leverage in retaining its contract.

53. [21]At this stage of technological development, comparison presents the greatest obstacle to the establishment of a simple and efficient national clearing system. Because comparison "interfaces" between clearing facilities are not yet feasible, it is impossible for the two brokers involved in a transaction to submit their trade data to different clearing facilities and to receive an immediate comparison. The rules linking exchanges to subsidiary clearing facilities alleviated this problem by providing a common facility at which the two parties to a transaction could compare their trade without agreeing in each instance on a mutually satisfactory comparison agency. NSCC's proposal also had to face this problem, and it did so by restricting its comparison services primarily to NYSE, AMEX, and OTC traders in New York, who are in a position to submit their data directly to NSCC's facility located in the City. Recently, however, NCC has developed a system of regional branch office comparison, whereby comparison data for OTC trades may be submitted to different facilities around the country and then transferred to a common locus for comparison. NSCC proposed to continue this service so that OTC traders outside of New York could compare their trades through the regional branch or

in NSCC, even if trading NYSE, AMEX, or OTC securities and even if trading with an NSCC participant, would not have access to NSCC's comparison facilities. Nor, of course, would any one participant or nonparticipant in NSCC have such access if the trade took place on a regional exchange.

In both phases, NSCC proposed to base its fees to participants on the total cost of providing its services.... The fees charged individual participants in a transaction, however, would not necessarily reflect the cost of that transaction. Instead, the merged entity would design its fee structure so that participants in New York and those outside of New York who utilized the regional network formerly operated by NCC, ... would pay the same clearing fees, even though, as was likely, at least in the early stages, the New York transactions cost less. This pricing scheme, "geographic price mutualization," was designed to allow greater "competition" between brokers in and outside of New York.[54]

As required by statute, the SEC made NSCC's proposal the subject of public notice, and received comments thereon from various parties.... It did so in recognition of the "likely ... determinative impact" this particular application would have on its accomplishment of its duty to facilitate the establishment of a national clearing system.

[O]n January 13, 1977, the Commission, in a lengthy order, granted NSCC registration with four conditions. Under Condition 1, NSCC must, before Phase II begins, establish "full interfaces" or "appropriate links" with several specified clearing agencies most particularly, those affiliated with the regional exchanges, including one operated by petitioner BNCC.[55] Other clearing agencies, including petitioners herein, have been offered the right to like interfaces as soon as they have the capability of offering minimally adequate clearing services.[56] NSCC must offer these interfaces without

---

branches nearest them. Furthermore, it proposed in the future to extend the service so that NYSE and AMEX traders could do the same. NCC's regional system also establishes the feasibility of linking all clearing agencies electronically, so that brokers can submit data to the clearing agency of their choice from whence the data can be transferred to a common site and compared. Moreover, the industry has also experimented with interfaces by which trades compared by one clearing agency may be transferred to another for clearing and settlement. Together, these innovations allow a broker to use only one clearing agency, wherever located, as his sole agent for comparing, clearing, and settling all trades on any exchange or market with any other broker. Nonetheless, until comparison interface technology is fully developed, that one agent may have to use another clearing agency to perform the comparison function.

54. [22] Geographic price mutualization achieves the objective of expanding the securities market into a geographically nationalized operation, rather than one dominated by New York. This objective is served by allowing brokers outside New York to "compete" more effectively with those inside New York....

55. [24] The Commission defined a "full interface" as "one through which any participant in either of the interfacing clearing corporations can move all its transactions in issues eligible for comparison, clearing and settlement at both clearing corporations."

56. [25] None of the petitioners herein has the ability independently to compare, clear, and settle securities transactions by way of continuous netting a prerequisite to the right to interface with NSCC.... In its briefs, BNCC has contended that it cannot fully develop a continuous netting capability until its client base expands. And that expansion, it further claims, has been prevented by the "tying" rules through which NYSE and AMEX have traditionally insisted that their traders use their subsidiary

any charges amounting to a fee for moving data through an interface. Consequently, all users of NSCC will help fund its establishment and maintenance of the interfaces.[57]

Condition 2 requires NSCC, before inaugurating Phase II, to provide at cost facilities to which other clearing agencies as well as its own branch offices may forward trade data for comparison. Together, Conditions 1 and 2 assure that any clearing agency in which a broker chooses to participate either (1) may clear and settle that broker's transaction after the parties to it have compared their trade themselves through NSCC, or (2) may itself submit the broker's data to NSCC for comparison, and then complete the clearing and settlement functions. In either case, the agency may represent any broker no matter what clearing agency serves the broker or the other side of the transaction, what kind of security is traded, and what market or exchange is involved.

Under Condition 3, NSCC must share with any competing clearing agency that comes forward the operation (and expenses) of the regional branches that NCC has operated in the past. By this mechanism, a regional clearing agency located in one city might find it easier to compete with NSCC in other cities as well.

Finally, Condition 4 attempts to fill the void created by NSCC's refusal to compare OTC trades between nonparticipants and between a participant and a nonparticipant. Under this requirement, NSCC (1) must, without charge, share its computer program technology with any clearing agency that proposes to compare OTC transactions between that agency's participants, and it (2) must convince some other clearing agency, or must itself offer, to compare OTC transactions between participants in different clearing agencies.

The upshot of the four conditions plus NSCC's proposal is that, for purposes of comparing NYSE and AMEX transactions, NSCC is essentially a public utility that is afforded a monopoly but must offer its services to all qualified customers (its own participants or other clearing agencies) at cost. NSCC (or some other clearing agency, if one comes forward) must also serve this utility function for purposes of making OTC comparisons for participants in different clearing agencies. By contrast, as to the remaining clearing functions, NSCC is perceived by the Commission as in competition with all other agencies offering like services. Given NSCC's geographic monopoly in New York as well as its established set of regional branches, however, the Commission realized that NSCC would be "likely to achieve a dominant position" as to All "securities processing" functions. Consequently, in order partially to blunt that competitive edge, the SEC insisted that NSCC allow full interfaces with other qualified clearing agencies

---

clearing operations. As promised, however, the Commission recently forced all of the exchanges and NASD to abandon the assailed "tying" rules, and BNCC presumably is or will soon be free to offer its services even to traders on the NYSE and AMEX, and thus to develop the capability of interfacing with NSCC ...

57. [26] In 1975, several members of the clearing industry, including SCC and some of the regional exchange affiliates, initiated a pilot interface program, called the Regional Interface Organization (RIO). Under this program, the clearing agency affiliated with the exchange in which a transaction is initiated compares the trade, but then routes the compared trade to any other participating clearing agency for clearing and settlement ...

so that they can clear and settle any of their customers' transactions even if an NSCC participant is on the other side of the trade. It also encouraged other agencies to expand their portion of the market at NSCC's expense by requiring the latter to share with them its computer program technology and its branch office facilities.

* * *

It also bears remembering that, despite the undoubted relevance of competitive concerns to the disposition of these petitions, these are not cases brought initially in the courts under the antitrust laws, but are administrative review petitions brought under the 1975 Amendments to the 1934 Act. Thus, the tendency in antitrust adjudication to view business relationships in the black and white terms of legality or illegality, based solely on their competitive or anticompetitive impact, has no place here.[58] Stated another way, we see no reason generally to treat competitive concerns as any more important or any less subject to judicial deference to administrative choices, than any other factor that is relevant to the legality of administrative action. (citations omitted).

* * *

Petitioners argue that the statute charges the SEC with enforcing the antitrust laws or at least with avoiding any unnecessary anticompetitive consequences. Their position thus approaches that taken by the Justice Department in the proceedings below that the Commission must achieve its objectives in the least anticompetitive manner possible. The statute, however, does not support such an interpretation. At most, it only requires the Commission to decide that any anticompetitive effects of its actions are "necessary or appropriate" to the achievement of its objectives. In fact, Congress responding to importunities by the Justice Department explicitly refused to include a "least anticompetitive" requirement in the 1975 legislation....

Instead, to the extent that the legislative history provides any guidance to the Commission in taking competitive concerns into consideration in its deliberations on the national clearing system, it merely requires the SEC to "balance" those concerns against all others that are relevant under the statute. Accordingly, only if some action's anticompetitive impact outweighs in importance the product of the 1975 Amendments' other objectives and the likelihood that the action will achieve those objectives, is the Commission prohibited from taking that action.

Accordingly, an independent review of the statute and legislative history bears out the Commission's view that it need do no more than "balance the maintenance of fair competition and a number of other equally important express purposes of the Act...."

1.

The Commission approved NSCC's registration with the recognition that doing so would largely determine the shape of the national clearing system. It assumed,

---

58. [31] Thus, these petitions do not raise the question of whether NSCC's actions would constitute a violation of the antitrust laws or whether those laws are implicitly repealed by the 1975 Amendments with respect to NSCC's clearing operations (citations omitted).

however and petitioners apparently do not disagree that, at the time, only two established plans existed that would allow such a system to be initiated with anything approaching the degree of dispatch desired by Congress. The first plan, of course, is NSCC's while the second, referred to as Model II, was developed by petitioners.

Model II contemplated that NASD's clearing agency NCC (operated under contract by petitioner BNCC) would remain independent of the other, merged New York clearing agencies (SCC and ASECC), and that, bolstered by its regional branch offices, it would attempt to compete therewith. Under this approach, petitioners argued, two national clearing agencies would exist, and would compete with each other (and with the regional clearing agencies) for clearing business both within and without New York.

Although based on their former volumes of trade, NCC would be likely to begin competing with a much smaller market share (12%) than the SCC-ASECC group (73%), … petitioners nonetheless contend that, under Model II, NCC would confront the other New York clearing operation with a geographically and quantitatively closer competitor than would any of the regional agencies that are NSCC's chief competition under its plan. The result, it is argued, would be a greater likelihood that competition would have the congressionally desired effect of keeping clearing prices down, and, in turn, would relieve the SEC of much of the regulatory burden of assuring that a giant and peerless clearing agency such as NSCC does not attain and exploit a monopoly position. Put in the statutory terms developed earlier, petitioners claim that Model II would not only reduce the anticompetitive effects below those characteristic of NSCC's plan, but would increase the effectiveness of the Commission and industry efforts to achieve the other goals of the Act because it would reduce regulatory costs.

Whether or not petitioners' analysis of the comparative costs and benefits of NSCC's plan and Model II is correct,[59] however, it cannot by itself convince us to overturn Order I. That is to say, even if the SEC could have struck a Better balance in favor of achieving the Act's goals and against anticompetitive impacts, its decision passes statutory muster so long as the former achievements by whatever margin outweigh the latter impacts. Stated differently, our task is not to decide whether the Commission made the "right" (or least anticompetitive) decision or the one that this court might have made were it charged with doing so but rather whether the Commission's decision falls within the boundaries of its broad authority. We think that, in its basic outlines, Order I meets this test.

On the benefits side of the scale, the SEC made several predictions about NSCC operations. As undisputed matters, the Commission noted that those operations seem capable of providing "a first … important step" toward achievement of a national clearing system itself a "prior or at least contemporaneous" prerequisite to the "early achievement of a national market system."

---

59. [35] In fact, the Commission's choice between the two plans seems reasonable. Thus, the NSCC plan had a considerably greater capacity for rapid development, having been in the planning stage for a year prior to SEC approval, and requiring fewer interfaces than Model II. …

* * *

Most important, the NSCC plan would allow brokers formerly forced to deal with several clearing agencies to deal with one, and to have only one daily settling position in each NYSE, AMEX, or OTC security, and one daily money settlement....

As a final important benefit of the NSCC plan, the Commission noted that it would significantly improve competition between brokers and dealers, particularly between those located inside and outside of New York. This improvement primarily would follow from the "expansion and upgrading of the existing NCC branch network" and also from the interface and comparison requirements in Condition 1 and 2 all of which would enhance the range and quality (and reduce the cost) of services that brokers outside of New York could offer their customers.

* * *

The Commission originally approved NSCC's adoption of "geographic price mutualization" (GPM), because it felt that that GPM would allow NSCC participants outside of New York to obtain the same services for the same price as participants in New York.... The upshot of the foregoing analysis is that Order I has apparently relied on two benefits of NSCC registration that cannot coexist: Either NSCC's plan and the four conditions will allow and even foster regional competition among clearing agencies, Or, through GPM, it will provide local brokers who participate in NSCC with a subsidy that allows them to operate at the same levels of cost and service as New York brokers. We have accordingly resolved to remand the GPM issue to the Commission for a better explanation, if one exists, of how GPM may be utilized without thwarting regional competition. Failing that, the Commission must either condition registration on NSCC's abandonment of GPM, or at least convincingly conclude that the loss of regional competition engendered by GPM will not upset the favorable balance of benefits and anticompetitive effects that it originally calculated on the assumption that such competition would exist.

* * *

In its application for registration, NSCC, a subsidiary of NYSE and AMEX as well as NASD, listed SIAC, itself a subsidiary of the two national exchanges, as its facilities manager and data processor. Earlier, NSCC's parent organizations had rejected petitioner BNCC's offer to bid against SIAC for that privilege. Petitioners, with the support of the Justice Department, argued before the Commission that NSCC should be forced to put the management-processing contract up for competitive bids.

The Commission chose not to force NSCC to open up the subject contract for competitive bidding, a decision we do not find inherently unsupportable. The issue is remanded, however, because of the SEC's reasoning for this particular decision that, so long as SIAC's ability to assure safe, accurate, and efficient clearing services is not in doubt, NSCC's choice of that facilities manager is not of statutory concern and is a matter for the exercise of NSCC's "business judgment." The result of such an analysis, of course, is to shield NSCC's choice of manager-processor from the 1975 Amendments' concern for competition.

Without the ability to scrutinize NSCC's choice of manager-processor in the full light of the Act's objectives and requirements, therefore, the Commission's "broad powers (to act in a) bold and effective manner to facilitate the rapid development of a nationwide system for processing securities transactions," would amount to nothing more than the ability to regulate "shell corporation(s)" while leaving the "extensive" operations that actually "accomplish clearance" beyond its reach.... [T]he Commission offered no reason, and we can think of none, that explains why NSCC's manager-processor decision must further two objectives of the Act (safety and efficiency) but not a third objective (competition).

The proper test, it seems to us, is whether any exercise of "business judgment" by a clearing agency may affect the realization of the national clearing system envisioned by Congress, i.e., one that is safe, efficient, and competitive.

By the Commission's own admission, a facilities manager and data processor is, in substance, the clearing agency. Consequently, if one such processor (SIAC) is offered an opportunity by a clearing agency "shell" that is not available to any other processor (whether it be BNCC or one controlled by the regional clearing agencies), the impact on competition and new entry in the industry and thus the nexus to statutory authority is manifest.... Accordingly, on remand the SEC should consider whether the SIAC contract has anticompetitive impacts, and, if so, whether they are justifiable in terms of the overall balance of benefits and anticompetitive impacts that it otherwise has calculated in a salutary manner.

The order at issue in No. 77-1199 is affirmed in all respects excepting its treatment of geographic price mutualization and the facilities management-data processing contract. The case is remanded for further exploration of whether these two aspects of NSCC's registration application are consistent with the 1975 Amendments' admonition that anticompetitive impacts not outweigh other regulatory benefits. The order at issue in No. 77-1547 is affirmed.

———

Currently, clearing agencies for equities are organized into two general categories based on the services provided to participants—Clearing Corporations and Depositories. Clearing corporations receive trade data from broker-dealers about their trades and compare, clear, and prepare instructions for automated settlement of trades. When performing these activities using a continuous net settlement system, they guarantee participant obligations and interpose themselves as the contraparty to both sides of any trade. Clearing corporations notify participants of their securities delivery and payment obligations on a daily basis. Depositories act as custodians of securities and maintain ownership records of the securities for participants. Securities certificates are held in bulk form[60] in vaults and ownership records are maintained on the books of the depositories. Essentially, depositories accept deposits of securities from bro-

---

60. This means that each participant with an interest in a particular securities issue has credited to its account a pro rata interest in the securities certificate held in custody in bulk form by the depository in its nominee name.

ker-dealers, credit those securities to the depositing participants' accounts, and in accordance with a participant's instructions, effect book-entry movements of securities. Depositories receive instructions for the movement of securities in their custody from both clearing corporations and participants or broker-dealers. Clearing corporations instruct depositories to make deliveries resulting from settlements and participants instruct depositories to move securities or money from one participant's account to another. There is only one registered depository and one registered clearing agency for equity securities. The registered depository, the Depository Trust Company (DTC), and the registered clearing agency for equity securities (the NSCC) are owned by the same parent company, the Depository Trust and Clearing Corporation (DTCC). As a depository, DTC immobilizes securities and makes book-entry changes to ownership of securities for NSCC's net settlements. NSCC provides clearing, settlement, risk management, central counterparty services, and a guarantee of completion for certain transactions for virtually all broker-dealer trades involving equities.

Most broker-dealers are not members of clearing agencies because of the qualifications required for membership. Only large clearing broker-dealers are able to meet membership requirements, which include substantial amounts of assets, liquidity, and net capital. Moreover, clearing broker-dealers must maintain the technology infrastructure and back-office personnel needed to communicate electronically with clearing agencies. Clearing broker-dealers also must have significant banking relationships in order to regularly move the money required to settle securities transactions. Consequently, broker-dealers that do not meet clearing agency membership requirements must enter into a clearing arrangement with clearing broker-dealers for the clearing and settlement of their transactions.

Non-clearing broker-dealers, known as correspondent or introducing broker-dealers, memorialize the outsourcing of their clearing and settlement functions to clearing broker-dealers in clearing agreements. Generally, there are two types of clearing arrangements — fully disclosed and omnibus. In a fully disclosed clearing agreement, the introducing broker-dealer introduces transactions to a clearing broker-dealer that is a member of the NSCC and DTC for clearance, settlement, and custody; the clearing arrangement is disclosed to the customers of the introducing broker-dealer. In an omnibus clearing agreement, the clearing broker-dealer carries in a single account the positions of introduced customer transactions of the introducing broker-dealer. The introducing broker-dealer remains legally responsible for custody, clearing, capital requirements, reserve deposits, and books and records, but the clearing broker-dealer contractually performs certain of these functions on behalf of the introducing broker-dealer.

FINRA Rule 4311 governs the terms of clearing agreements between its broker-dealer members and allows such agreements only between FINRA broker-dealer members. Both direct and indirect clearing agreements must be disclosed to the clearing broker-dealer that is a clearing agency participant; specifically, when an introducing broker-dealer acts as an intermediary for another introducing broker-dealer for the purpose of obtaining clearing services from the clearing broker-dealer, the intermediary broker-dealer must notify the clearing broker-dealer of the existence of such arrangements and identify the introducing broker-dealer, who does not have a direct relationship with the clearing broker-dealer. Each clearing agreement between the introducing broker-dealer, the introducing intermediary broker-dealer, and the clearing broker-dealer must bind each direct and indirect recipient of clearing services as a party. FINRA must approve any clearing agreement, and material changes to an existing clearing agreement, before it becomes effective. The clearing broker-dealer is also required to notify FINRA as early as possible, but not later than 10 business days, prior to providing clearing services to a new introducing broker-dealer; this notification allows FINRA to evaluate the impact of the new introducing broker-dealer on the clearing broker-dealer's financial and operational condition. Moreover, the clearing broker-dealer is required to conduct due diligence to assess the financial, operational, credit, and reputational risk of providing clearing services to a new introducing broker-dealer prior to entering into a clearing agreement.

Fully disclosed clearing agreements must allocate responsibilities between the introducing broker-dealer and the clearing broker-dealer. FINRA Rule 4311(c) contains a non-exclusive list of responsibilities that must be allocated between the introducing broker-dealer and the clearing broker-dealer. *See* Table 14.4.

Table 14.4. FINRA Rule 4311(c). Allocation of Responsibilities

Opening and approving accounts
Transmission of orders for execution
Extension of credit
Preparation and transmission of confirmations
Monitoring of accounts
Acceptance of orders
Execution of orders
Receipt and delivery of funds and securities
Maintenance of books and records

The clearing agreement must expressly allocate to the clearing broker-dealer the responsibility for safeguarding funds and securities pursuant to the Customer Protection Rule (Rule 15c3-3). The clearing broker-dealer is also responsible for preparing and transmitting customer account statements; this responsibility may be allocated to the introducing broker-dealer with the prior written approval of FINRA. Each customer of the introducing broker-dealer must be notified in writing when opening her account of the existence of the clearing agreement and the allocation of responsibilities. The customer must also be notified in writing of any change in parties to the agreement and any material change to the allocation of responsibilities. Customer notification is not required if customers' accounts are being transferred pursuant to ACATS using an authorized form or where notification is provided by an alternative method such as affirmative or negative response letters. Moreover, each clearing agreement must expressly state that the parties will supply to each other the necessary data in their possession for the proper performance and supervision of allocated responsibilities. The clearing agreement must expressly authorize the clearing broker-dealer to provide written customer complaints to both FINRA and the introducing broker-dealer; the clearing broker-dealer must furnish written notice to the complaining customer that its complaint has been received and forwarded to the introducing broker-dealer and to FINRA. Finally, with respect to intermediary clearing arrangements, the clearing broker-dealer must maintain customer and proprietary accounts of the introducing broker-dealer in a manner that allows FINRA to specifically identify the proprietary and customer accounts belonging to each introducing broker-dealer.

Notes and Questions

1. Pursuant to Section 21(a) of the Exchange Act, the SEC can invoke its enforcement powers to initiate and conduct investigations to determine violations of the federal securities laws that are specifically applicable to clearing agencies. This means that the SEC may institute civil actions seeking injunctive and other equitable remedies and/or administrative proceedings to impose sanctions against clearing agencies, including the suspension or revocation of its registration, and the imposition of limitations on its activities, functions, or operations.

2. Clearing agencies are broadly defined under the Exchange Act and undertake a variety of functions. One such function is to act as a central counterparty (CCP). A CCP is an entity that interposes itself between the counterparties to a trade. For example, when a securities transaction between two broker-dealers that are members of the CCP is executed and submitted for clearing, the CCP enters into two separate contracts with the two original broker-dealers; consequently, the original broker-dealers are no longer counterparties to each other but, instead, each acquires the CCP as its counterparty, and the CCP assumes the counterparty credit risk of each of the original counterparties that are members of the CCP.

3. "Title VIII of the Dodd-Frank Act, entitled the Payment, Clearing, and Settlement Supervision Act of 2010 ("Clearing Supervision Act"), establishes an enhanced supervisory and risk control system for systemically important clearing agencies ... In part, the Clearing Supervision Act provides that the Commission, considering relevant international standards and existing prudential requirements, may prescribe regulations that contain risk management standards for the operations related to payment, clearing, and settlement activities ("PCS Activities") of a Designated Clearing Entity.... In prescribing such standards, the Commission must consult the Board of Governors of the Federal Reserve System ("Federal Reserve" or "the Board") and the Financial Stability Oversight Council ("Council"). On July 11, 2011, the Council published a final rule concerning its authority to designate [Clearing Agencies] as systemically important, and on July 18, 2012, the Council designated The Depository Trust Company ("DTC"), ... National

Securities Clearing Corporation ("NSCC") . . . as systemically important." Clearing Agency Standards, Exchange Act Release No. 68080 (Oct. 22, 2012). In response to this designation, the SEC adopted two tiers of regulations under Rule 17Ad-22: (1) enhanced rules for covered clearing agencies under Rule 17Ad-22(e); and (2) the existing rules for all other registered clearing agencies under Rule 17Ad-22(d). The two tiers would provide flexibility for new entrants that might seek to operate as registered clearing agencies while applying enhanced requirements to those clearing agencies that raise systemic risk concerns due to, among other things, their size, systemic importance, global reach, or the risks inherent in the products they clear. Given the technological infrastructure and capital required to function as a registered clearing agency, is it likely that another clearing agency will be established for equity securities to compete with the NSCC?

4. *Regulation Short Sale (Reg SHO).* Short selling is now regulated under Rules 201–204 of Reg SHO (17 C.F.R. § 242.200 et al.). Rule 200 of Reg SHO defines a short sale as "the sale of a security which the seller does not own or any sale which is consummated by the delivery of a security borrowed by . . . the seller." Reg SHO, among other things, requires broker-dealers, prior to effecting short sales in all equity securities, to locate securities available for borrowing in order to be able to deliver securities on settlement date, unless the seller owns or is long in the security. Reg SHO also requires clearing broker-dealers to close out any fails positions of equity securities of certain reporting issuers that have a substantial number of fails to deliver by purchasing securities of like kind and quantity if such securities have been subject to fails to deliver for 13 consecutive days with certain exceptions. Rule 203(b)(3) of Reg SHO. FINRA Rule 4560 requires broker-dealers to maintain a record of total short positions in all customer and proprietary accounts in all equity securities (other than a restricted equity security as defined in FINRA Rule 6420) and to regularly report such information to FINRA. How do Reg SHO and FINRA Rule 4560 facilitate an efficient national clearing and settlement system, if at all?

5. FINRA requires its member broker-dealers to clear and settle transactions in designated securities through the facilities of a registered clearing agency that uses a continuous net settlement system. However, broker-dealers are permitted to settle ex-clearing (manually through the broker-dealer's Purchase and Sales department) if both parties to the transaction agree. *See* FINRA Rules 6350A and 6350B.

Index